WHO'S WHO
ON TELEVISION

WHO'S WHO
ON TELEVISION

Anthony Hayward

B■XTREE
in association with

First published in Great Britain in 1996 by Boxtree Limited
Text © Anthony Hayward 1996

The right of Anthony Hayward to be identified as Author of this Work has been asserted by him in accordance with the Copyright, Designs and Patents Act 1988.

1 2 3 4 5 6 7 8 9 10

Printed and bound in Great Britain by the Bath Press for
Boxtree Limited
Broadwall House
21 Broadwall
London SE1 9PL

A CIP catalogue entry for this book is available from the British Library

ISBN 0 7522 1067 X

Cover pictures © *TVTimes*

CONTENTS

FOREWORD

Welcome to a new edition of *Who's Who on Television*, completely revised and updated, and featuring more than 1,300 stars of the small screen. In the following pages, you will find details of the professional and personal lives of actors, actresses, presenters and entertainers seen on British television. Entries are listed alphabetically by surname (with those starting Mc and Mac beginning the 'M' section) and their screen credits, both in television and films, are intended to be as comprehensive as possible. In half-a-dozen cases, I have had to edit actors' film credits for space reasons, but I have indicated where this is so by pointing out that what follows is a selection, and I have endeavoured to add how many films they have made in total. Stars' television credits have not been edited and represent a lengthy and authoritative list of appearances by the biggest names in British TV. Where I know that programmes have been broadcast only in individual regions, I have noted this. Where space permits, I have indicated where stars have appeared in complete series and serials, and given the dates of these, as well as giving alternative titles of television programmes and films, normally starting with the title in the country of origin and following it with any others. Where there is not enough room and a British title is not the original, I have simply mentioned the British one because that is the one by which the production is known in this country. I have not been able to give complete listings of stage appearances, but wherever possible I have indicated major roles actors have played or major productions in which they have taken part. Likewise, I have indicated radio work, books and awards where space allows. This is all intended to represent as complete a profile as possible of each of the stars featured. A list of addresses of theatrical agents and television companies appears at the back of the book.

I would like to thank the stars and their agents, as well as a number of TV companies, the casting directory *Spotlight*, the actors' union Equity and the British Film Institute library, for the help they have extended to me during my research for this book. Finally, my thanks to Susanna Wadeson, Penny Simpson and Catherine Randall at Boxtree. Special thanks, as always, to Deborah.

Anthony Hayward

LIST OF ABBREVIATIONS

The following is a list of abbreviations used throughout this book:

ASM = assistant stage manager
b. = born
BAFTA = British Academy of Film and Television Arts
BFA = British Film Academy (forerunner to SFTA and BAFTA)
d. = daughter
dec = deceased
dis = marriage dissolved
m. = married
qv = included under separate entry
RSC = Royal Shakespeare Company
RTS = Royal Television Society
s. = son
SFTA = Society of Film and TV Arts (BAFTA's predecessor)
SWET = Society of West End Theatres
TRIC = Television and Radio Industries Association
TVM = TV movie

ABBOT, Russ

Russ Abbot. Comedian/Entertainer/Actor. b. Chester, 16 September 1947. Started career while at school, playing drums with pop groups. Turned professional and, in 1965, formed the Black Abbots, before going solo. West End plays include *Little Me* and *One for the Road*.
TV: *London Night Out; What's on Next?; Who Do You Do?; The Comedians; Bruce Forsyth's Big Night; Russ Abbot's Madhouse* (six series); *Des O'Connor Now; Live from Her Majesty's; Tarby and Friends; Wogan; The Bob Monkhouse Show; Live from the Palladium; The Russ Abbot Show* (BBC series); *The Russ Abbot Christmas Show; Russ Abbot; Stars in Their Eyes – Elvis Special* (presenter, 1993);Ted Fenwick in *September Song* (three series, 1993-5); *The Russ Abbot Show* (ITV, two series, 1994-5); *Live for Peace – A Royal Gala* (VE Day 1995); Ted Butler in *Married for Life* (series, 1996).
Records: Singles: *Atmosphere; All Night Holiday; Let's Go to the Disco.* Album: *I Love a Party.*
Awards: *TVTimes* Funniest Man on Television award (five times); British Comedy Awards Top Variety Act (1990). Address: c/o Mike Hughes Entertainments/Lake-Smith Griffin Associates. m. Tricia; 1 d. Erika, 3 s. Richard, Gary, Christopher.

Russ Abbot

ABDELA, Lesley

Lesley Julia Abdela. Presenter/Writer. b. London, 17 November 1945. MBE, 1990.
TV: *Head Over Heels; Great Expectations: Women with 'X' Appeal; Breaking Glass.* Guest appearances: *Question Time; Have I Got News for You; Newsnight.* Address: c/o Jacque Evans Management. m. 1972 (dis); 1 s. Nicholas (b. 1973). Partner: Tim Symonds. Hobbies: Travel, painting.

ACKLAND, Joss

Joss Ackland. Actor. b. Kensington, West London, 29 February 1928.
TV: *The Crezz; Enemy at the Door; A Nightingale Sang in Berkeley Square; Dangerous Davies – The Last Detective* (IVM); *Tinker, Tailor, Soldier, Spy; Constance Kent; Shadowlands; Queenie; First and Last; The Man Who Lived at the Ritz; The Intercom Conspiracy; Never the Sinner; Jekyll & Hyde* (TVM); *Ashenden; Agatha Christie's Miss Marple: They Do It with Mirrors; The Secret Life of Ian Fleming* (TVM); *John Le Carré's A Murder of Quality* (TVM); *Sherlock Holmes and the Incident at Victoria Falls* (TVM); Aristotle Onassis in *A Woman Named Jackie; Voices in the Garden* (TVM); *Mr Nobody's Eyes* (story-teller); *Julius Caesar* (Shakespeare: The Animated Tales); *Citizen Locke; Jacob* (TVM); *Citizen X* (TVM)
Films: *Seven Days to Noon; Ghost Ship; Next to No Time!; A Midsummer Night's Dream* (dubbed voice only); *The Bridge; In Search of the Castaways; Rasputin the Mad Monk; East West Island; Crescendo; The House That Dripped Blood; Villain; Mr Forbush and the Penguins; England Made Me; The Happiness Cage; Hitler: The Last Ten Days; Penny Gold; The Three Musketeers: The Queen's Diamonds; S*P*Y*S; The Black Windmill; The Little Prince; Royal Flash; Great Expectations; Operation Daybreak; One of Our Dinosaurs Is Missing; The Magic Dream; World within a Ring; Silver Bears; Watership Down; The Greek Tycoon; Who Is Killing the Great Chefs of Europe?* (UK title *Too Many Chefs*); *Cuba; The Love Tapes; Saint Jack; Rough Cut; The Apple* (UK title *Star Rock*); *Lady Jane; A Zed and Two Noughts; The Sicilian; White Mischief; To Kill a Priest; It Couldn't Happen Here; Lethal Weapon 2; The Hunt for Red October; To Forget Palermo; Tre Colonne in Cronaca; The Object of Beauty; The Princess and the Goblin; The Bridge; Bill and Ted's Bogus Journey; Once upon a Time; The Mighty Ducks* (UK title *Champions*); *Project Shadowchaser; Nowhere to Run; Raging Earth; Mad Dogs and Englishmen; Miracle on 34th Street; Giorgino; Occhiopinocchio; A Kid in King Arthur's Court.*
Books: *I Must Be in There Somewhere* (autobiography, 1990). Address: ICM. m. Rosemary Kircaldy; 5 d. Melanie, Antonia, Penelope, Samantha, Kirsty, 2 s. Paul (dec), Toby.

Lesley Abdela

Joss Ackland

ACTON, Dawn

Dawn Jean Acton. Actress. b. Ashton-under-Lyne, Lancashire, 15 March 1977. Trained at Oldham Theatre Workshop.
TV: Took over the role of Tracy Barlow in *Coronation Street* at the age of 11.
Address: c/o Granada Television. Lives in Oldham, Lancashire.

Dawn Acton

ADAMS, Tom

Tom Adams. Actor. b. London, 3 September 1938. Started career with the Unity Theatre, London.
TV: Villain in *Dixon of Dock Green* (début); *Emergency – Ward 10;* Major Sullivan in *Spy Trap* (two series); *Journey into Midnight* (TVM); Bernard in *Villains; Madigan: The Lisbon Beat* (TVM); Dr Wallman in *General Hospital* (two series); Daniel Fogarty in *The Onedin Line* (three series); Nick Lewis in *The Enigma Files* (two series); Ken Stevenson in *Strike It Rich* (two series); Mal Bates in *Emmerdale Farm;* John Ross in *Remington Steele;* Calico Jack in *Pyrates;* The Hard Man in *West Country Tales.*
Films: *The Great Escape; This Is My Street; The Peaches; Licensed to Kill;* Charles Vince in *Where the Bullets Fly; The Fighting Prince of Donegal; Somebody's Stolen Our Russian Spy; Fathom; Subterfuge; The House That Dripped Blood; The Red Baron; The Fast Kill; Duel of Love; Das ist dein Ende.* Address: c/o Langford Associates. Lives in Maidenhead, Berkshire. Single. Hobbies: Golf, cricket, sport.

Tom Adams

Jenny Agutter

Holly Aird

Suzy Aitchison

Maria Aitken

John Alderton

AGUTTER, Jenny

Jennifer Anne Agutter. Actress. b. Taunton, Somerset, 20 December 1952. Trained at Elmhurst Ballet School. Stage plays include *Breaking the Code* (Broadway) and *Love's Labour's Lost* (RSC).
TV: *Alexander Graham Bell; The Newcomers; The Railway Children; The Great Mr Dickens; The Wild Duck; The Cherry Orchard; The Snow Goose* (TVM); *The Ten Commandments; Omnibus: Shelley; A War of Children* (TVM); Louise de la Vallière in *The Man in the Iron Mask* (TVM); *A House in Regent Place; Kiss Me and Die; A Legacy; The Waiting Room; School Play; A Dream of Alice; Mayflower: The Pilgrims' Adventure* (TVM,); *Beulah Land; This Office Life; Love's Labour's Lost; Magnum; Silas Marner: The Weaver of Raveloe; The Two Ronnies; Magnum PI; The Twilight Zone; Murder, She Wrote; The Royal Knockout Tournament;* Lauren in *The Equalizer; The Outsiders* (TVM); *Dear Jane; Not a Penny More, Not a Penny Less; Dear John; TECX; Help Me Make It through the Night; Boon; The Good Guys;* Kryten's Creator in *Red Dwarf VI;* Jeanette Summers in *Love Hurts; Heartbeat; September;* Idina Hatton in *The Buccaneers* (series); *The All New Alexei Sayle Show 2* (series); *And the Beat Goes On* (series).
Films: *East of Sudan* (début, 1964, aged 11); *Ballerina; A Man Could Get Killed; The Gates of Paradise; Star!* (retitled *Those Were the Happy Times*); *I Start Counting; The Railway Children; Walkabout; Logan's Run; The Eagle Has Landed; Equus; Sois-belle et Tais-toi; China 9; Liberty 37/Gunfighters* (US title *Clayton and Catherine*); *Dominique; The Riddle of the Sands; Sweet William; Miss Right; The Survivor; Amy; An American Werewolf in London; Late Flowering Love; Secret Places; Dark Tower; King of the Wind; Child's Play II; Darkman; Freddie as F.R.O.7; Blue Juice.*
Books: *Snap.* **Awards:** TV: Emmy Best Supporting Actress award for *The Snow Goose* (1971). Films: BAFTA Best Supporting Actress award for *Equus* (1976). Address: c/o Marmont Management. Lives in South Kensington, London. m. Johan Tham; 1 s. Jonathan (b. 1990). Hobbies: Photography.

AIRD, Holly

Holly Aird. Actress. b. Aldershot, Hampshire, 18 May 1969. Trained at the Bush Davies Dance and Education School. Acted as a child.
TV: Young Miss Polly in *The History of Mr Polly* (aged 10); *The Flame Trees of Thika; The Tales of Beatrix Potter; The Muse Secrets; Spider's Webb; Seal Morning; TVTimes Star Family Challenge; Affairs of the Heart; Happy Valley; Inspector Morse;* Gina Hudd in *Agatha Christie's Miss Marple: They Do It with Mirrors;* Jace in *Hope It Rains;* Corporal/Sgt Nancy Thorpe/Garvey in *Soldier Soldier* (Series 1-3, 1991-3; Series 5, 1995); Karen Panter in *15: The Life and Death of Philip Knight* (drama-doc); Judy Simmons in *Kavanagh QC;* Dawn Boll in *Rules of Engagement* (pilot, 1995); Carla in *Dressing for Breakfast* (series, 1995); Sarah Ellis in *Circles of Deceit.* Address: c/o Hutton Management.

AITCHISON, Suzy

Susan Jane Aitchison. Actress. b. London, 4 June 1960. Daughter of actress June Whitfield (qv). Gained a BA in drama from Birmingham University.
TV: Susan in *Are You Being Served?;* Suzie in *Terry and June; Filthy Rich and Catflap; The Russ Abbot Show* (three series, 1986-9); *'Udds 'Arf 'Undred; Little and Large; Up to Something; Casualty;* Nurse in *Absolutely Fabulous;* Trudy Hackman in *The 10%ers* (series); *Goodnight Sweetheart; Mr Bean.*
Films: Lesley in *Bloody New Year;* Mary Delaney in *Handel – Honour, Profit & Pleasure.*
Address; c/o Scott Marshall. Lives in London. Single. Hobbies: Reading, gardening, tennis.

AITKEN, Maria

Maria Aitken. Actress. b. Dublin, 12 September 1945. Stage plays include *Travesties* (RSC).
TV: *Murder; The Gold Robbers; The Exiles; Manhunt; Counterstrike; Codename; Take Three Girls; The Regiment; The Three Marias; The Edwardians; Scotch on the Rocks; Moths; Quiet as a Nun; Company and Co; Private Lives* (own chat show); *Lizzie & Maria* (TVM); Colette Clayton in *The Good Guys;* Lady Flamborough in *Love on a Branch Line* (series, 1994).
Films: *Some Girls Do; Mary Queen of Scots; Half Moon Street; A Fish Called Wanda; The Fool.*
Address: c/o Michael Whitehall. m. 1st Richard Durden (dis), 2nd actor Nigel Davenport (qv); 1 s. Jack.

ALDERTON, John

John Alderton. Actor. b. Gainsborough, Lincolnshire, 27 November 1940.
TV: Dr Moon in *Emergency – Ward 10;* Bernard Hedges in *Please Sir!* (1968-71) and *The Fenn Street Gang;* George Bassett in *My Wife Next Door* (series, 1972); Thomas in *Upstairs, Downstairs;* Charles Danby in *No, Honestly* (series, 1974); *The Wodehouse Playhouse;* Mike Upchat in *The Upchat Line* (series, 1977); title role in *Thomas and Sarah;* Lyall Jarvis in *Father's Day* (two series, 1983-4); Jack Boult in *Forever Green* (three series); *Trading Places* (guest); *Fireman Sam* (narrator, series).
Films: Bernard Hedges in *Please Sir!; Zardoz; James Herriot in *It Shouldn't Happen to a Vet.*
Address: c/o James Sharkey Associates. Lives in Hampstead, North London. m. 1st actress Jill Browne (dis), 2nd actress Pauline Collins (qv); 1 d. Catherine, 2 s. Nicholas, Richard.

ALDRED, Sophie

Sophie Aldred. Actress/Presenter. b. Greenwich, London, 20 August 1962. Gained a BA (Hons) degree in drama from Manchester University. Trained as a soprano at the Northern College of Music.
TV: *Knock-Knock* (as 12 characters); *Knowhow; Playbus; Jackanory* (storyteller); *Noel's Christmas Presents; Corners;* Ace (Doctor's last assistant) in *Doctor Who* (1987-9); *Rainbow;* Maureen in *Melvin and Maureen's Music-a-Grams* (two series); Sophie Socket in *It's Droibee Time; Tiny and Crew, Words and Pictures;* Suzie in *EastEnders; Love Call Live* (co-presenter, Anglia Television only).
Book: *Ace — The Inside Story of the End of an Era* (Virgin, 1996).
Address: c/o John Grantham. Lives in south-east London. Partner: TV presenter Vince Henderson. Hobbies: Walking on the north Norfolk coast, sailing, football (Charlton Athletic supporter).

Sophie Aldred

ALEXANDER, Jean

Jean Alexander. Actress. b. Liverpool, 24 February 1926. Library assistant for five years, before joining the Adelphi Guild Theatre in Macclesfield and touring Lancashire, Cheshire and Staffordshire.
TV: *Deadline Midnight* (1961); *Television Club; Top Secret; Jacks and Knaves; Z Cars;* Hilda Ogden in *Coronation Street* (1964-87); *Boon;* Auntie Wainwright in *Last of the Summer Wine* (Christmas specials, plus four series,1992-5); *Woof!;* Marjory Hunt in *Cluedo* (series, 1993); Irene Patterson in *Harry.*
Films: Mrs Keeler (Christine Keeler's mother) in *Scandal.* **Books:** *The Other Side of the Street* (autobiography, 1989). **Awards:** Winner, RTS Best Performance award (1984-5); *TVTimes* Best Actress on TV award (1987). Address: c/o Joan Reddin. Lives in Southport. Single.

Jean Alexander

ALEXANDER, Maev

Maev Alexandra Reid McConnell. Actress. b. Glasgow, 3 February 1948. Trained at the Royal Scottish Academy of Music and Drama. Stage roles include Perdita in *The Winter's Tale* (RSC).
TV: *This Man Craig; The Revenue Men; The Borderers; A Leap in the Dark; The Standard; The Befrienders; The Main Chance; Take the Stage; Kids;* Janet Campbell in *The New Road* (series); Christine Russell in *Sutherland's Law* (Play for Today, plus Series 1 and 2); *Smeddum* (Play for Today); *The New Avengers; A Christmas Carol; Angels; Visitors; Hazell;* WPC Sandra Williams in *The Gentle Touch* (Series 2); Jen-Jen Quilley in *Holding the Fort* (three series); *Pictures; By the Sword Divided; Inspector Ghote Moves In; The Kit Curran Radio Show; That's Life!* (newsdesk presenter, 1985); *The Fools on the Hill; Scoop; Drummonds; EastEnders.* Address: c/o Nina Quick Associates. Lives in St Albans, Hertfordshire. m. 3 February 1981 writer-director Simon Dunmore; 1 d. Alix Joan (b. 10 Sep 1982). Pets: Two cats, Miss Brodie and Cleopatra. Hobbies: Running a small textile design company called Pure Fabrication.

Maev Alexander

ALEXANDER, Peter

Peter Alexander. Actor. b. Midsomer Norton, Somerset, 15 October 1952. Trained at the Guildford School of Acting. West End plays include *No Sex, Please — We're British* and *Beyond the Rainbow.*
TV: *Family Man; Chessgame; Winning Streak; Affairs of the Heart; Minder;* car salesman and Mr Wilson in *Coronation Street; Travelling Man; Eric Ackroyd Disasters; Chessgame; The Practice;* Phil Pearce in *Emmerdale Farm* (1986-9); *All Creatures Great and Small; Medics; Singles; Mission Top Secret;* Martin in *Tuesdays and Thursdays;* Special Branch Officer and Tom Ashby in *Brookside; Heartbeat; The Bill.*
Address: c/o McIntosh Rae Management. Lives in Yorkshire. m. former dancer and choreographer Penny Stevenson; 1 d. Emily, 1 s. Nicholas. Pets: Horses, cows, sheep. Hobbies: Golf, music, Italy.

Peter Alexander

ALEXANDER, Terence

Terence Alexander. Actor. b. London, 11 March 1923.
TV: *Codename; The Forsyte Saga; Run a Crooked Mile* (TVM); *The Unpleasantness at the Bellona Club; The Solarium; Flea in Her Ear; The Pallisers; Moody and Pegg; The Good Old Days;* Churchill and the Generals; *The Les Dawson Show; The Dick Emery Show; Devenish; Unity; Just Liz; Terry and June; Suntrap; The Fall and Rise of Reginald Perrin; Ike* (TVM); *The Jim Davidson Show; The Seven Dials Mystery;* Charlie Hungerford in *Bergerac; Crown Court, Strangers and Brothers;* Sir Donald Penrose in *Don't Wait Up;* Sir Greville in *The New Statesman* (series); *The Laughing Prisoner; The Detectives.*
Films: *Comin' thro' the Rye; The Elusive Pimpernel; The Woman with No Name; Death Is a Number; A Tale of Five Cities; The Gentle Gunman; Top Secret; The First Elizabeth; The Stately Home of Kent; Just a Drop; Glad Tidings; Park Plaza 605; The Runaway Bus; Dangerous Cargo; The Green Scarf; Hands of Destiny; Out of the Clouds; Portrait of Alison; Who Done It?; The Green Man; The One That Got Away; The Square Peg; Death Was a Passenger; Danger Within; Breakout; Don't Panic Chaps!; The Doctor's Dilemma; The Price of Silence; The League of Gentlemen; The Bulldog Breed; Carry On Regardless; Man at the Carlton Tower; The Gentle Terror; She Always Gets Their Man; On the Beat; The Fast Lady; The Mind Benders; The VIPs; Bitter Harvest; All in Good Time; The Intelligence Men; Judith; The Long Duel; The Spare Tyres; Only When I Larf; What's Good for the Goose; The Magic Christian; All the Way Up; Waterloo; Vault of Horror; The Day of the Jackal; The Internecine Project; The Boy Who Never Was.* Address: c/o Brunskill Management. m. 1st June, 2nd actress Jane Downs; 2 s. Nicholas, Marcus (both from 1st m.).

Terence Alexander

Colin Alldridge

Dave Allen

Keith Allen

Patrick Allen

Sheila Allen

ALLDRIDGE, Colin

Colin Alldridge. Actor/Singer. b. Bournemouth, Dorset, 19 June 1965. Trained at The Drama Centre.
TV: *Press Gang*; PC Phil Young in *The Bill* (1989-91); Joe Simpson in *Dead Men's Tales: Hanging by a Thread*.
Address: c/o Spotlight. Lives in London. Single. Hobbies: Dancing, rock-climbing, scuba-diving, breathing, keeping fit, water-skiing.

ALLEN, Dave

David Tynan O'Mahony. Comedian. b. Tallaght, County Dublin, 6 July 1936. Nephew of poet Katharine Tynan. Worked as a journalist on the *Irish Independent* and *Drogheda Times*, then as a Redcoat at Butlin's in Skegness, before turning professional.
TV: *Tonight with Dave Allen; The Val Doonican Show* (resident comedian); *The London Palladium Show* (compère); *The Dave Allen Show; Dave Allen* (series, 1993, and Christmas special, 1994).
Address: c/o The Richard Stone Partnership. Lives in Kensington, West London. m. actress Judith Stott.

ALLEN, Keith

Keith Allen. Actor. b. c. 1953.
TV: *The Crying Game* (The Comic Strip Presents...); *Making Out;* Jim Ryman in *Between the Lines;* John Peter Barrie in *Inspector Morse: The Day of the Devil;* Bonehead in *Detectives on the Edge of a Nervous Breakdown,* Dr Genghis in *Gregory — Diary of a Nutcase* and *Gino: Full Story and Pics* (all The Comic Strip Presents...); *4 Goes to Glastonbury; Blow Your Mind: One More Thing; French and Saunders in... Space Virgins from Planet Sex;* Jeff Wagland in *Faith* (series, 1994); *Time Out With: Keith Allen* (Carlton only); Jonas Chuzzlewit in *Martin Chuzzlewit* (series, 1994); *The Mind Field* (co-presenter, series); Dave Exec in *Preston Front;* Quentin in *Class Act.*
Films: *Chicago Joe and the Showgirl; Rebecca's Daughters;* Pepi in *Carry On Columbus; Beyond Bedlam.* Address: c/o Lou Coulson.

ALLEN, Patrick

Patrick Allen. Actor. b. Malawi, 17 March 1927. Came to Britain as a child.
TV: *The Survivors;* title role in *Crane; Brett; Van Der Valk; Life and Soul; Thriller; Sutherland's Law; Dangerous Knowledge; Churchill's People; The Light of Experience; Travel by Dark; Jane Eyre; The Lover;* Gradgrind in *Hard Times;* Prestongrange in *Kidnapped;* Auchinleck in *Churchill and the Generals; Space 1999; Doctors and Nurses; Hamlet; The Trial of Lady Chatterley; A Spy at Evening; The Brack Report; Agatha Christie's Murder is Easy* (TVM); *The Dick Emery Show; Tugs* (voice only); *The Winds of War* (mini-series); *East Lynne; The Black Adder; Pericles; Bergerac; The Last Viceroy; Time for Murder; The Return of Sherlock Holmes: The Empty House; Love after Lunch; Roman Holiday* (TVM); *Sarah* (mini-series); *Fergie & Andrew: Behind the Palace Doors* (TVM); Walter Street in *Body & Soul* (series); announcer in *Vic Reeves Big Night Out* and *The Smell of Reeves and Mortimer.* Plus many voice-overs.
Films: *World for Ransom; Dial M for Murder; Cross Channel; King's Rhapsody; Dead on Time; Confession; Wicked as They Come; High Tide at Noon; The Long Haul; Accused; The Man Who Wouldn't Talk; High Hell; Tread Softly, Stranger; Dunkirk; I Was Monty's Double; Jet Storm; Never Take Sweets from a Stranger; The Sinister Man; The Traitors; Captain Clegg; Flight from Singapore; The Night of the Generals; The Life and Times of John Huston Esquire; Night of the Big Heat; Cream's Last Concert; Carry On Doctor; The Body Stealers; When Dinosaurs Ruled the Earth; Puppet on a Chain; The World at Their Feet; Erotic Fantasies; The Sword and the Geisha; Winter with Dracula; Diamonds on Wheels; Way Out East; Persecution; The Wilby Conspiracy; The Domino Principle* (UK title *The Domino Killings*); *The Battle of Billy's Pond; The Wild Geese; Caligula; The Sea Wolves; Who Dares Wins.*
Address: c/o ICM. m. 1956 actress Sarah Lawson; 2 s. Stephen, Stuart.

ALLEN, Sheila

Sheila Marion Essex Allen. Actress. b. Chard, Somerset, 22 October 1932. Trained at RADA (1949-51) and gained a diploma in theatre history from the University of London. RSC productions (1962-78) include *Romeo and Juliet, Macbeth* and *Cymbeline.*
TV: George Eliot (title role) in *A Portrait of Marion Evans; The Regiment; Danger Man; The Four Just Men;* Number Fourteen in *The Prisoner;* Jocasta in *Oedipus;* Cassie in *A Bouquet of Barbed Wire* and *Another Bouquet; Shoulder to Shoulder; Shroud for a Nightingale;* Fiona in *The Life and Loves of a She-Devil; The Hedgehog Wedding; Agatha Christie's Poirot; Stolen; Act of Will* (mini-series); *Casualty;* Rhiannon Weaver in *The Old Devils* (mini-series, 1992); *Fire in the Dark; Antonia and Jane* (ScreenPlay); Rebecca West/Dilys Powell in *The Trial of Lady Chatterley;* Sheila in *Dangerfield; The Ring.*
Films: *The Prince and the Pauper; The ABC Murders;* Mrs Marchant in *Pascali's Island;* Olga in *Shining Through.* Address: c/o Mayer & Eden. Lives in London. m. David H Jones (sep); 2 s. Joseph, Jesse. Pets: One dog, one cat. Hobbies: Reading, films, music, art galleries, swimming.

ALTMAN, John

John Altman. Actor. b. Reading, Berkshire, 2 March 1952. Became a professional actor after graduating in photography. Trained at York Academy of Speech and Drama.
TV: *The Scarlet Pimpernel; Further Adventures of Lucky Jim; Life after Death* (Play for Today); *Take Two; Going to Work; Attachments; Minder; Bouncing Back;* Nick Cotton in *EastEnders* (on and off, 1985-); *Gentlemen & Players; The Paradise Club; Up Yer News; Scrag Tag and Toddles; Jack and the Beanstalk; The Ghosts of Oxford Street; TV Squash;* Supt Jellings in *Seekers* (mini-series); *Blackhearts in Battersea; The Famous Five; Cold Lazarus.*
Films: *The First Great Train Robbery;* John in *Quadrophenia;* George Harrison in *Birth of The Beatles; An American Werewolf in London; Return of the Jedi; Memoirs of a Survivor;* Steve in *Remembrance; The Higher Mortals; To Die For.* Address: c/o Roger Carey Associates. Lives in London. m. Brigitte; 1 d. Rosanna. Hobbies: Music, photography, writing, swimming.

John Altman

AMORY, Peter

Peter Amory. Actor. b. 2 November. Trained at RADA (Tree Prize winner).
TV: *Boon; Running Wild* (two series); *Casualty; Chelworth; Inspector Morse; Gentlemen and Players; The Chief;* Chris Tate in *Emmerdale* (1989-). Address: c/o David Daly Associates/Emmerdale Production Centre. m. 1994 actress Claire King (qv); 1 s. Thomas (from previous relationship with Sarah).

ANDERSON, Clive

Clive Anderson. Presenter. b. Stanmore, Middlesex, 1953. Former president of Cambridge University's Footlights club, writing and performing in revues, while studying law at Selwyn College (1972-5).
TV: *Not the Nine O'Clock News* (writer); *Alas Smith and Jones* (writer); *Whose Line Is It Anyway?* (host, 1988-); *Clive Anderson Talks Back* (series, 1989-); *Wogan* (guest host); *Evening Standard Film Awards* (twice); *1991 BAFTA Craft Awards; Points of View; Just for Laughs: Goodbye Piccadilly, Did You See...?* (guest host); *The Channel Four Debate; Notes & Queries with Clive Anderson* (two series, 1992-3); *Every Picture Tells a Story; Great Railway Journeys of the World: Hong Kong to Ulaanbaatar (1994); Clive, Our Man in... (1995); Clive Anderson — Our Man in...* (series, 1996).
Videos: *Stick It Out* (Right Said Fred video, 1993). **Awards:** British Comedy Awards as Comedy Presenter of the Year (1991) and Channel Four Presenter (1992). Address: c/o London Management. Lives in North London. m. doctor Jane; 2 d. Isabella, Flora, 1 s. Edmund.

Peter Amory

ANDERSON, Jean

Jean Anderson. Actress. b. Eastbourne, East Sussex, 12 December 1907. Trained at RADA.
TV: *Maigret; Dr Finlay's Casebook;* Mother in *The Railway Children* (two series); *Run a Crooked Mile* (TVM); *Paul Temple; Kate; Jackanory; Bachelor Father; Fathers and Sons;* Mary Hammond in *The Brothers* (1972-6); *This Is Your Life; Little Women; Scoop;* Joss Holbrook in *Tenko* (1981-2, 1984); *Paris; Agatha Christie's Miss Marple; The Good Doctor Bodkin Adams; Campion; Circles of Deceit; Back Home; Survival of the Fittest; Casualty; The House of Eliott; Keeping Up Appearances;* Catherine Cookson's *The Black Velvet Gown; The Good Guys; Heartbeat;* Lady Hinksey in *Inspector Morse: Twilight of the Gods; G.B.H.; Trainer; The Bogie Man* (TVM); Queen Mother in *The Whipping Boy* (TVM); *Rab C Nesbitt;* Lady Fermoy in *Diana: Her True Story; Moonacre; Second Thoughts; Doctor Finlay .*
Films: *The Mark of Cain; The Romantic Age; Elizabeth of Ladymead; The Franchise Affair; Out of True; Life in Her Hands; White Corridors; The Brave Don't Cry; Street Corner; The Kidnappers; The Dark Stairway* (short); *Lease of Life; Secret Tent; A Town Like Alice; Heart of a Child; Robbery under Arms; Lucky Jim; The Barretts of Wimpole Street; Solomon and Sheba; SOS Pacific; Spare the Rod; The Inspector; The Waltz of the Toreadors; The Silent Playground; The Three Lives of Thomasina; Half a Sixpence; Country Dance; The Night Digger; The Lady Vanishes; Madame Sousatzka; Leon the Pig Farmer.* Address: c/o The Brunskill Management. Lives in West London. m. theatre director Peter Powell (dec); 1 d. theatrical agent Aude Powell. Hobbies: Walking, gardening, horse racing.

Clive Anderson

ANDRÉ, Annette

Annette Andreallo. Actress. b. Sydney, Australia, 24 June 1939. Danced with the Australian Ballet Company. An actress since living in Britain from 1962.
TV: *Maigret; Sergeant Cork; The Saint* (six episodes); Watchmaker's Daughter in *The Prisoner; The Avengers; The Baron;* Jeannie Hopkirk in *Randall & Hopkirk (Deceased)* (series, 1969-70); *Man at the Top; The Persuaders!; The Brothers; The Mill on the Floss; Return of the Saint; Mickey Dunne; The Little White God; Taurus Rising; The Guns of Will Sonnet;* Jessica in *The Merchant of Venice;* Isabela in *Wuthering Heights; Cop Shop;* Camellia Wells in *Prisoner: Cell Block H;* Sarah Alexander in *Crossroads.*
Films: *This is My Street; Panic Button; Up Jumped a Swagman;* Philia in *A Funny Thing Happened on the Way to the Forum; He Who Rides a Tiger; Mister Ten Per Cent.* Address: c/o A.I.M. Lives in London and Los Angeles. m. producer-writer Arthur Weingarten; 1 d. Anouska. Pets: Five cats, one dog. Hobbies: Active supporter of the Born Free Foundation for Wildlife Welfare.

Jean Anderson

Annette André

ANDREWS, Anthony

Anthony Andrews

Anthony Andrews. b. Hampstead, North London, 12 January 1948. Son of a BBC musical arranger.
TV: *A Beast with Two Backs; Romeo and Juliet; Alma Mater; The Mating Machine; Dixon of Dock Green; Doomwatch; Woodstock; A Day Out; The Judge's Wife; Follyfoot; QB VII; A War of Children; Fortunes of Nigel;* Lord Silverbridge in *The Pallisers; The Duchess of Duke Street; David Copperfield; Upstairs, Downstairs; London Assurance; French without Tears; The Country Wife; A Superstition; Much Ado about Nothing;* Brian Ash in *Danger UXB; Romeo and Juliet;* Sebastian Flyte in *Brideshead Revisited; Mistress of Paradise; Love Boat; The Black Bayu; La Ronde; Ivanhoe; The Scarlet Pimpernel; Z for Zachariah; Sparkling Cyanide; Suspicion; A.D.;* Duke of Windsor in *The Woman He Loved; Bluegrass; Columbo Goes to the Guillotine; The Strange Case of Dr Jekyll and Mr Hyde; Hands of a Murderer; The War Lord; Danielle Steel's Jewels; The Ruth Rendell Mystery Movie: Heartstones.*
Films: *Take Me High; Percy's Progress; Operation Daybreak; Les Adolescentes; Under the Volcano; The Holcroft Covenant; The Second Victory; The Lighthorsemen; Hanna's War; Innocent Heroes; Lost in Siberia.* **Awards:** BAFTA Best Actor Award for *Brideshead Revisited* (1981). Address: c/o Peters Fraser & Dunlop. m. former actress Georgina Simpson; 2 d. Jessica, Amy-Samantha, 1 s. Joshua.

ANGELIS, Michael

Michael Angelis

Michael Angelis. Actor. Trained at the Royal Scottish Academy of Music and Drama.
TV: *The Liver Birds* (series); *Rock Follies; Pride of Our Alley; World's End; Wood and Walters Review; Bergerac; Minder; The Professionals; Reilly — Ace of Spies; The Black Stuff* (Play for Today); *Boys from the Blackstuff; The Marksman; Bread; The Russ Abbot Show; G.B.H.; Wail of the Banshee;* DI Bill Kendrick in *Between the Lines; Boon; Lovejoy; Casualty;* Arnie in *September Song* (three series, 1993-5); Harold Craven in *Luv* (two series, 1993-4); Roy in *Against All Odds* (series, 1994); *Snatched.*
Films: *George and Mildred; Birth of the Beatles; A Nightingale Sang; No Surrender.*
Address: c/o London Management. Lives in London and Cheshire. m. actress Helen Worth (qv).

ANGELIS, Paul

Paul Angelis

Paul Angelis. Actor.
TV: *Z Cars* (150 episodes); *The Liver Birds; Porridge; Softly Softly; The Adventures of Black Beauty; Under the Age; Armchair Theatre: A Dog's Ransom; Kidnapped; Man about the House; George and Mildred; Robin's Nest; Thriller; Conan Doyle; Public Eye; Callan; Armchair Theatre; Dick Turpin; The Gentle Touch; Juliet Bravo* (three roles in three series); *Tucker's Luck; QED; Father's Day* (two series, 1983-4); *Hungry Times; Bulman; Crown Court; Brookside; The Brothers McGregor; Truckers* (series); *The Saint* (1989); *Moon and Son; The Bill; The Bullion Boys;* Brian Bowes in *Coronation Street; The Knock.*
Films: *Yellow Submarine; Inadmissible Evidence; Otley; The Battle of Britain; The Garnett Saga; Force 10 from Navarone; Hussey; For Your Eyes Only; Runners.* Address: c/o Burdett-Couts Associates.

ANHOLT, Tony

Tony Anholt

Anthony Anholt. Actor. b. Singapore, 19 January 1941. Trained at the Royal Court.
TV: *Angels; Alice; Court Martial; The Fell Sergeant;* Orlando Vigaretti in *A Family at War; The Mind of Mr J G Reeder; Jason King; Kate; The Strauss Family;* Paul Buchet in *The Protectors; Napoleon and Love; Crown Court; The Sweeney;* Tony Verdeschi in *Space: 1999* (Series 2); David Law in *Coronation Street; Wilde Alliance; The Copyist; Citizen Smith; Season; Terry and June; Kelly Monteith; Marked Personal; Midsummer Nightmare;* Nick Steven in *Triangle; Seasons;* Leipidus in *The Last Days of Pompeii; Minder; Juliet Bravo; Bulman;* Charles Frere in *Howards' Way* (six series, 1985-90); Abdul in *Only Fools and Horses; At Any Time;* Brent in *Singles;* John Stonehouse in *The Stonehouse Affair* (Crime Story).
Films: *Fear Is the Key; The Late Nancy Irving.*
Address: c/o Roger Carey Associates. Lives in London. m. 1st Sheila (dis), 2nd 1 July 1995 actress Tracey Childs (qv); 1 s. actor Christien. Hobbies: Travelling, reading, walking, swimming.

ANNIS, Francesca

Francesca Annis

Francesca Annis. Actress. b. London, 14 May 1944. Trained at the Corona Stage Academy.
TV: *The Human Jungle; Heritage; Danger Man; Dr Finlay's Casebook; Great Expectations; View from the Bridge; The Family Is a Vicious Circle; A Pin to See the Peepshow; Madame Bovary;* Lillie Langtry in *Lillie; Why Didn't They Ask Evans?; Coming Out of the Ice* (TVM); *The Secret Adversary; Partners in Crime; Inside Story; Onassis; Parnell and the Englishwoman* (mini-series); *The Gravy Train Goes East; Absolute Hell* (Performance); *Between the Lines; Haunting Harmony;Headhunters; Dalziel and Pascoe.*
Films: *The Cat Gang; His and Hers; The Young Jacobites; No Kidding; Cleopatra; West 11; The Eyes of Annie Jones; Crooks in Cloisters; Saturday Night Out; Murder Most Foul; Flipper and the Pirates; The Pleasure Girls; Run with the Wind; The Walking Stick; The Sky Pirates; Macbeth; Penny Gold; Short Cut to Haifa; Stronger than the Sun; Krull; Dune; Coming Out of the Ice; The Golden River; Under the Cherry Moon; Romeo-Juliet* (voice only). **Awards:** TVTimes Best Actress on TV award for *Lillie* (1978-9). Address: c/o ICM. 1 d. Charlotte (from relationship with photographer Patrick Wiseman).

ANTHONY, Lysette

Lysette Anthony. Actress. b. London, 1963. Past member of the National Youth Theatre.

TV: *Ivanhoe; Oliver Twist; Princess Daisy; Dombey and Son; Beauty and the Beast; Jemima Shore Investigates; Night Train to Murder; Auf Wiedersehen Pet; Lovejoy;* Angie in *Three Up, Two Down* (series, 1985-9); *The House on Kirov Street; The Bretts; Look Good, Feel Fantastic; Cosmopolitan; Home to Roost; The Emperor's New Clothes; The Lady and the Highwayman; Jack the Ripper; A Ghost in Monte Carlo; Through the Looking Glass; Campion; Dark Shadows; Cluedo* (series, 1992).

Films: *Krull; Tug of Love; A Drop in the Ocean; The Emperor's New Clothes; In Search of Eileen; The Impostor of Baker Street; Without a Clue; 29 Days in February; The Pleasure Principle; Switch; Husbands and Wives.* Address: c/o William Morris Agency (UK and US). Lives in Los Angeles. m. 1991 Dutch artist Luc Leestemaker (dis).

Lysette Anthony

ARCHER, Karen

Karen Archer. Actress. b. Lancashire, 26 July.

TV: *Keats; Jury; The Cleopatras; Father's Day; Rockliffe's Babies; Juliet Bravo; The Secret Garden; EastEnders; Hannay; The Ruth Rendell Mysteries: No Crying He Makes; The Bill; On the Line; Chancer;* Asst Chief Con Anne Stewart in *The Chief; Casualty; The Ruth Rendell Mysteries: The Strawberry Tree.*

Films: Gilda in *The Mouse and the Woman; Giro City; Forever Young.* Address: c/o Crouch Associates. Lives in Sussex and London. m. 1st Bill Rook (dis 1975), 2nd actor David Collings; 1 s. Sam, 1 d. Eliza (twins, b. 1987). Pets: A dog and a cat. Hobbies: Charity work, current affairs and the arts.

Karen Archer

ARDEN, Mark

Mark Arden. Actor. Stage plays include *Rosencrantz and Guildenstern Are Dead* (Piccadilly Theatre).

TV: *Romeo and Juliet; The Young Ones* (two series); *Carrott's Lib; Big Deal; Happy Families; The Black Adder;* The Comic Strip Presents...; *Little Armadillos; Money Talks; Checkpoint Chiswick; Inner City Fairy Tales; Girls on Top; This Is David Lander;* Fireman 'Vaseline' in *London's Burning* (Series 1 and 2); *Spitting Image;* Detective Dingwall in *Lazarus and Dingwall; Bottom; The Bill; Berlin Break; If You See God, Tell Him; All Quiet on the Preston Front; A Skirt through History: A Reputation; Downwardly Mobile; Pirates and Treasure Islands; Space Vets* (series); *The Woman in Grey* (In Suspicious Circumstances); *Harry Enfield and Chums; Here Comes the Mirror Man* (Chiller); *The Bill; Men of the World.*

Films: George in *Bearskin;* Alan in *Trying to Connect You;* Dean in *My Friend Hellman;* Mark in *Carry On Columbus.* Address: c/o Mayer & Eden.

Mark Arden

ARIS, Ben

Benjamin Patrick Aris. Actor. b. World's End, Chelsea, London, 16 March 1937.

TV: *Muffin the Mule* (1949); *Variety Parade; Secombe Here; Cool for Cats; The World Our Stage; The Nina and Frederick Show; Laudes Evangelii; David and the Donkey; Gazette; 3 to 1 On (Dee Time); How Late It Is; Mad Jack; The Silver Sword; Jamie; Owen MD; The Dirtiest Soldier in the World; Some Mothers Do 'Ave 'Em; Doctor Who; World in Action; Husband to Mrs Fitzherbert; Sam and the River; Crown Court; Village Hall; Wodehouse Playhouse; Get Some In; Hazell; Target; The Famous Five; Clouds of Glory; The After Dinner Joke; Fearless Frank; Spy John Vassalll; Masterspy; The Assassination Run; Hazell; Dr Jekyll and Mr Hyde; To the Manor Born; The Treachery Game; Jackanory Playhouse; The Bagthorpe Saga; Target; Cribb; Christmas Spirits; Astronauts; Bergerac; Newsnight* (drama-documentary); *The Falkland Factor; Where Were You...; By the Sword Divided; Video Stars* (Play for Today); Julian Dalrymple-Sykes in *Hi-de-Hi!; Shine on Harvey Moon; Chance in a Million; Paradise Postponed; All In Good Faith; Star Quality; Call Me Mister; Slinger's Day; Hold the Dream; Executive Stress; The Kenny Everett Show;* The Comic Strip Presents...; *First of the Summer Wine; Young Charlie Chaplin; Agatha Christie's Poirot; Mr Majeika; You Rang, M'Lord?; Boon; No Job for a Lady; Hope It Rains; Further Up Pompeii; The Good Guys; In Suspicious Circumstances; Families; The Bill; Me You and Him; Eldorado; The Good Guys; Food and Farming; September Song; The Last Englishman* (Heroes & Villains).

Films: (Selection from 33): *Tom Brown's Schooldays; How I Won the War; The Charge of the Light Brigade; If...; Hamlet; O Lucky Man; The Three Musketeers; Tommy; The Fool.* Address: c/o Barry Brown & Partner. Lives in London. m. 3 July 1966 ballet dancer Yemaiel Oved; 1 d. Rachel (b. 1967), 1 s. actor Jonathan (b. 1970). Pets: A cat. Hobbies: Ornithology, music, 'pleasures of the table'.

Ben Aris

ARMITAGE, Peter

Peter Armitage. Actor.

TV: *White Goods; How We Used to Live;* Bill Webster in *Coronation Street* (1984-5, 1995-); *The Bill; Shadow Juries; Plaza Patrol; In Suspicious Circumstances; The Laughter of God; The Sharp End; Woof!; Lovejoy; Chimera; Cannon & Ball Playhouse; Parnell and the Englishwoman; Jack the Ripper* (mini-series); *Rockliffe's Babies;* Norman Burns in *G.B.H.;* Len Veitch in *The Advocates;* Jim Butler in *Sam Saturday* (series); Fred Huggett in *Heartbeat; Mr Wroe's Virgins; Medics; The Bill; Harry; Casualty;* Rob Clulow in *Peak Practice; Chandler & Co; The Vet.* Address: c/o Stephen Hatton Management.

Peter Armitage

Alun Armstrong

ARMSTRONG, Alun

Alun Armstrong. Actor. b. Annfield Plain, 17 July 1946. Plays include *Les Misérables* (Palace Theatre).
TV: *Whatever Happened to the Likely Lads?; A Sharp Intake of Breath;* Spraggon in *Porridge; Measure for Measure; Our Day Out; All Day on the Sands; The Stars Look Down; One in a Thousand; Days of Hope; Shooting the Chandelier; Only Make Believe; Get Lost; Nicholas Nickleby; Sharing Time; The Book Tower; Bulman; Joe Lives* (one-man show); *The Caucasian Chalk Circle; No 27; This Is David Lander; A Night on the Tyne; Breaking Rank; Sticky Wickets; Murder in Eden; Stanley and the Women;* Supt Holdsby in *Inspector Morse: Happy Families;* Roy Grade in *Goodbye Cruel World* (mini-series); Uncle Teddy in *The Life and Times of Henry Pratt;* Gerald Faulkner in *Goggle Eyes* (mini-series); *My Little Eye* (Short and Curlies); Mickey in *Sorry about Last Night;* Austin Donohue in *Our Friends in the North* (serial).
Films: *The Duellists; A Bridge Too Far; Get Carter; The Fourteen; The French Lieutenant's Woman; Krull; Number One; The House; Billy the Kid and the Green Baize Vampire; White Roses; White Hunter, Black Heart; The Child Eater; American Friends; The Widow Maker; London Kills Me; Split Second; Blue Ice; Patriot Games.* Address: c/o Markham & Froggatt.

Fiona Armstrong

ARMSTRONG, Fiona

Fiona Armstrong. Newscaster. b. Preston, Lancashire, 28 November 1956. Studied German at London University. Worked as a reporter with Radio 210, in Reading, before moving to television.
TV: BBC North West (reporter); Border TV (reporter and presenter); ITN (reporter and presenter); *GMTV* (presenter, 1993); *Fantastic Facts!* (roving reporter, series, 1993); *Screaming Reels; Up Front* (series, Meridian and Channel Television only); *This Christmas Eve;* TV Interviewer in *Annie's Bar; A Bit on the Side* (*This Morning*, 1996). Address: c/o Knight Ayton Management. m. Rodney Potts.

Pamela Armstrong

ARMSTRONG, Pamela

Pamela Armstrong. Presenter. b. North Borneo, 25 August 1951. Educated in Sarawak, Indonesia and Britain. Trained in media and communications at Central London Polytechnic. Subsequently broadcast as a presenter for Capital Radio, in London, before moving to television.
TV: *London Today; Well Being* (two series); ITN newscaster, including *News at Ten; Pamela Armstrong; Breakfast Time; Daytime Live;* BBC World Service Television.
Radio: *London Today* (presenter, daily news and current affairs programme, Capital Radio); *Operation Drake* (Capital Radio, reporting on the expedition retracing the round-the-world voyage, sailing in a square-rigged brigantine from Panama to Papua New Guinea).
Address: c/o 5 Shaftesbury Villas, Allen Street, London W8 6UZ. Lives in Gloucestershire.

Debbie Arnold

ARNOLD, Debbie

Debbie Arnold. Actress. b. Sunderland, 14 June. Daughter of impressionist-comedian-actor Eddie Arnold and theatrical agent Mary Arnold; granddaughter of Polish comedian Arnold Griminger. Theatre includes *The Sleeping Prince* (with Omar Sharif) and *Women behind Bars* (both West End).
TV: *Rockliffe's Babies; Once in a Lifetime; Agatha Christie's Miss Marple: The Body in the Library; The Funny Side* (series); *Bootle Saddles* (series); *Terry and June; Oliver Twist* (TVM); *C.A.T.S. Eyes; Four in a Million; The Two Ronnies; Minder; The Laughter Show; Don't Wait Up; The Bill; Ticket to Ride* (US series); *Coronation Street; Up the Elephant and Round the Castle; The Citadel; Minder on the Orient Express* (TVM); Debbie Wilson in *Emmerdale;* Sylvia in *All Creatures Great and Small; Radio Rue; The Good Sex Guide;* April Branning in *EastEnders* (1996); Janice in *Hollyoaks.*
Films: *Valentino; Even Break.* Address: c/o Sharon Hamper Management. Lives in Thames Ditton, Surrey. m. 1st actor John Challis (dis), 2nd actor David Janson; 2 d. Ciara Judith, Talia (both from 2nd m.). Pets: One dog (Legie), two cats. Hobbies: Sleeping and reading.

Sean Arnold

ARNOLD, Sean

Sean Arnold. Actor. b. Wickwar, Gloucestershire, 30 January 1941. Trained at the Guildhall School of Music and Drama (1962-5). Stage plays include *Queen's Highland Servant* (Savoy Theatre) and *The Doctor's Dilemma* (Comedy Theatre).
TV: *Crime Buster; Hunter's Walk; Love Story; Boy Meets Girl; Mr Wodehouse; Out of the Unknown; Colditz; Pistol Shot; The Caesars; Wilde Alliance; Public Eye; The Death of Adolf Hitler; Haunters of the Deep; Remembrance* (TVM); *Knockback; Carrie's War; The Practice; Holocaust;* Chief Insp Barney Crozier in *Bergerac* (nine series, 1981-91); Headmaster in *Grange Hill; Time of My Life; Shoestring; Great Expectations* (US series); Mr Hart in *The Bill; The Trial of Lord Lucan; The Crusades; BUGS* (Series 2).
Films: *Quiller Memorandum; Dominique; North Sea Hijack; Speaking of the Devil.*
Address: c/o Scott Marshall. Lives in Jersey, Channel Islands.

ASH, Leslie

Leslie Ash. Actress. Sister of former Hot Gossip dancer Debbie Ash. TV début in a Fairy Liquid commercial in 1964, aged four. Began career as a model, before turning to acting. Appeared in pop promotional videos, including Dire Straits' *Tunnel of Love*. Stage plays include *Paris Match* (Garrick Theatre).

TV: *The Gentle Touch; Cupid Darts; Good Night and God Bless; Worlds End; Seconds Out; Shelley; La Ronde; Holding the Fort; Outside Edge; The Balance of Nature;* Nancy Gray in *The Happy Apple* (series, 1983); *The Two Ronnies; Four Track Live; The Tube* (co-presenter, series); *Murder — Ultimate Grounds for Divorce;* Fred in *C.A.T.S. Eyes* (series, 1985-7); *Sporting Chance; The Marksman* (mini-series); *Home to Roost; Natural Causes; The Bill; Give Us a Clue* (guest panellist); Deborah in *Men Behaving Badly* (four series, 1991-5); Dickon in *Haggard; Perfect Scoundrels;* Val in *Love Hurts;* dancer Jo in *Stay Lucky; Going for a Song* (team captain, antiques panel game, series, 1995).

Films: *Rosie Dixon Night Nurse; Quadrophenia;* Sharon in *The Nutcracker; Curse of the Pink Panther; Shadey.* Address: c/o Sharon Hamper Management. Lives in South London. m. footballer Lee Chapman; 2 s. Joe, Max.

Leslie Ash

ASHBOURNE, Jayne

Jayne Mary Ashbourne. Actress. b. Manchester, 10 February 1969. Great-granddaughter of one of the original Black and White Minstrels; sister of actress Lorraine Ashbourne. Ballet dancer until the age of 16. Trained at the Drama Studio. Stage roles include Eliza Doolittle in *Pygmalion* (Birmingham Rep).

TV: Miss Skipdale Breweries in *Emmerdale* (1991); *A Time to Dance* (mini-series); *The Young Indiana Jones Chronicles; My Father's House; The Inspector Alleyn Mysteries;* Angela Pearson in *The Bill;* Carmen in *The Riff Raff Element* (two series, 1993-4); Marie in *Peak Practice;* Lisa in *Money for Nothing* (Screen One); Mary in *Casualty;* Sue in *Blood and Peaches* (mini-series); Ellie Nugent in *Sharpe's Gold;* Little Orphan Annie in *Sir Daddy;* Sarah Madson in *Madson* (series, 1996). Address: c/o ICM. Single. Lives in London. Pets: A cat called Tom. Hobbies: Watching films, walking, reading.

Jayne Ashbourne

ASHER, Jane

Jane Asher. Actress. b. London, 5 April 1946. Started acting, aged five, in the film *Mandy*. Stage plays include *Peter Pan* (Scala Theatre), *Romeo and Juliet* (New York), *Look Back in Anger* (Royal Court and Criterion Theatres), *The Philanthropist* (Mayfair Theatre and Broadway), *Whose Life Is It Anyway?* (Queen's Theatre), *Blithe Spirit* (Vaudeville Theatre), *Henceforward* (Vaudeville Theatre) and *The School for Scandal* (National Theatre). Owns and runs Jane Asher Party Cakes.

TV: *The Mill on the Floss; Love Story; Brideshead Revisited; Love Is Old, Love Is New; A Voyage Round My Father; East Lynne; Bright Smiler; The Mistress; Wish Me Luck* (three series); *Still Life; Eats for Treats; French and Saunders;* Lydie Howling in *Murder Most Horrid; Health UK* (series); *Herbal Lore* (*This Morning*); Anna in *Closing Numbers* (TVM); *The Evening Standard British Film Awards* (presenter, 1995); Felicity Troy in *The Choir* (series); *The 12 Days of Christmas* and *Family Favourites* (both series in *Nine O'Clock Live,* as presenter).

Films: *Mandy; Third Party Risk; Dance Little Lady; Adventure in the Hopfields; The Quatermass Experiment; Charley Moon; The Greengage Summer; The Prince and the Pauper; Girl in the Headlines; The Masque of the Red Death; Alfie; The Winter's Tale; The Buttercup Chain; Deep End; Henry VIII and His Six Wives; Careless Love* (short); *Hands Up!; Runners; Success Is the Best Revenge; Dreamchild; Paris by Night.* **Books:** *Jane Asher's Party Cakes; Jane Asher's Fancy Dress; Silent Nights for You and Your Baby; Jane Asher's Quick Party Cakes; The Moppy Stories; Easy Entertaining; Keep Your Baby Safe; Children's Parties; Calendar of Cakes; Eats for Treats.*

Address: c/o Chatto and Linnit. Lives in London. m. artist Gerald Scarfe; 1 d. Katie, 2 s. Alexander, Rory. Pets: One dog, two cats, one hamster, three fish. Hobbies: Reading, cooking, skiing.

Jane Asher

ASHLEY, Caroline

Caroline Smith. Actress. b. Coatbridge, Lanarkshire, 4 March 1958. Trained at the Queen Margaret College Drama School, then taught drama, before acting professionally. Gained her Equity actors' union card by doing a six-week tour singing in miners' clubs.

TV: Fiona Ryder (née Cunningham) in *Take the High Road* (1980-92).
Address: c/o Equity. Lives in London. m. 1993 actor Alan Hunter (qv); 1 s. Jack Liem.

Caroline Ashley

ASHTON, John

John Groves. Actor. b. London, 29 November 1950. Trained at the Bristol Old Vic Theatre School. Stage plays include *Jesus Christ Superstar* (Palace Theatre) and *Force and Hypocrisy* (Young Vic).

TV: *The Demolition Man;* Niko Tinbergen in *The Discovery of Animal Behaviour* (drama-documentary); *Out of Court; Crimewatch; Grange Hill;* Det Insp Balfour in *Brookside;* Chief Supt Don Henderson in *Waterfront Beat* (two series, 1990-91); three roles in *The Bill;* Det Sgt Ken Beever in *Michael Winner's True Crimes: The Prints on the Coffee Cup;* Graham Ridley in *Love Hurts;* Mr Robinson in *London's Burning;* Mr Hodge in *Shine on Harvey Moon;* Mr Corby in *EastEnders* (two episodes, 1995).

Films: *Possessions.*
Address: c/o Sandra Griffin Management. Lives in London. m. actress Serretta Wilson; 1 s. Chaden.

John Ashton

ASHTON, Marcia

Marcia Ashton. Actress. b. Sheffield, South Yorkshire. Trained at RADA.
TV: Lily in *Compact* (serial); *On the Buses; Father Dear Father; Upstairs, Downstairs; The Interior Decorator; The Sauna; Francis Durbridge Thriller; The Brothers; The Misfit; In Sickness and in Health; Pulaski; Mathspy; The Bill; Rumpole of the Bailey; Collision Course; Bernard and the Genie;* Jean Crosbie in *Brookside.* Address: c/o Shane Collins Associates. m. Gerald Lee; 1 s. Edward, 1 d. Annabel. Pets: A cat called CK. Hobbies: Gardening, working, travel.

Marcia Ashton

ASHWORTH, Dicken

Terence Dicken Ashworth. Actor. b. Todmorden, West Yorkshire, 18 July 1946. A teacher of drama and English for four years, before becoming a professional actor.
TV: *Doctor Who; Blake's 7; Minder; Juliet Bravo; The Gentle Touch; C.A.T.S. Eyes; Flying Lady; The Chinese Detective; Return to Treasure Island;* Alan Partridge in *Brookside; Scab; Making Out; Better Days; The Two of Us; Gentlemen and Players; Strangers in a Dark Night; Nanny;* Mr Bigsbury in *We Are Seven; King of the Wind* (TVM); *The Bill;* Jeff Horten in *Coronation Street* (1992, 1993); George Drummond in *Inspector Morse;* Jeremy in *B&B;* Boris in *Keeping Up Appearances;* Nelson in *The Riff Raff Element* (two series, 1993-4); Bill Francis in *Heartbeat; Casualty;* Derek in *The Detectives.*
Films: *Tess; Krull; Chariots of Fire; Force 10 from Navarone; The Biggest Bank Robbery.* Address: c/o Howes and Prior. Lives in London. m. set and costume designer Jane Ripley; 1 d. Tamasin Cathy. Pets: Two cats, Trouble and Biscuit. Hobbies: VW camper vans, gardening, bowling, cricket, cooking, eating.

Dicken Ashworth

ASPEL, Michael

Michael Terence Aspel. Presenter. b. London, 12 January 1933. Began career as an actor with BBC radio (1954-7), before becoming a BBC TV announcer (1957-60) and newsreader (1960-68).
TV: *Miss World; Crackerjack; Ask Aspel; Give Us a Clue; The Six O'Clock Show* (LWT); *Child's Play; Aspel & Company* (10 series); *This Is Your Life* (ITV 1988-94, BBC series 1995-); *BAFTA Awards; Trouble with the Fifties; The British Academy Awards; The Trouble with the Sixties; Wish You Were Here…?* (guest presenter); *Strange… but True?; The World's Greatest Commercials; In the Hot Seat – 25 Years of Classic Conversation; Caught on Camera; The Trouble with the Seventies; VE Day Celebrations* (1995); *DesRes; Lights Camera Action! A Century of the Cinema* (series, 1996).
Address: c/o Bagenal Harvey Organisation. Lives in Surrey. m. 1st Dian (dis), 2nd Ann (dis), 3rd actress Elizabeth Power (sep); 2 s. Gregory (dec), Richard (both from 1st m.), twins Edward and Jane (both from 2nd m.), 2 s. Patrick, Daniel (both from 3rd m.). Hobbies: Writing, swimming, boating, films, learning golf, various charities.

Michael Aspel

ATKINS, Eileen

Eileen Atkins. Actress. b. Clapton, East London, 16 June 1934. CBE, 1990. Trained at Guildhall School of Music and Drama. Stage plays include *As You Like It* and *Passion Play* (both RSC).
TV: *Hilda Lessways; The Duchess of Malfi; The Lady's Not for Burning; An Age of Kings; Electra; The Letter Double Bill; The Heiress; Three Sisters; Olive; A Midsummer Night's Dream; The Lady from the Sea; Omnibus: The Jean Rhys Women; She Fell Among Thieves; Sons and Lovers; Smiley's People; Oliver Twist* (TVM); *Titus Andronicus; Eden's End; Nellie's Version; Breaking Up; The Vision; The Burston Rebellion; A Room of One's Own; Roman Holiday* (TVM); *A Hazard of Hearts* (TVM); *Shades of Darkness; The Madonna of Medjugorje* (narrator); *The Lost Language of Cranes* (TVM); *The Maitlands* (Performance); *Cold Comfort Farm.* As creator (with Jean Marsh): *Upstairs, Downstairs; The House of Eliott.*
Films: *The Devil within Her; Equus; The Dresser; "Let Him Have It".* Address: c/o Jonathan Altaras Associates. m. 1st actor Julian Glover (qv) (dis 1988), 2nd TV producer Bill Shepherd.

Eileen Atkins

ATKINSON, Rowan

Rowan Sebastian Atkinson. Actor. b. Newcastle upon Tyne, 6 January 1955. Gained degrees from Newcastle and Oxford Universities with the aim of becoming an electrical engineer.
TV: *The Innes Book of Records; The Lena Zavaroni Show; The Peter Cook Show; Canned Laughter; Not the Nine O'Clock News* (also co-writer, four series, 1979-82); title role in *The Black Adder* (also co-writer, series, 1983); Edmund Blackadder in *Blackadder II* (series, 1986); *Comic Relief;* E Blackadder Esq in *Blackadder the Third* (series, 1987); *Just for Laughs II;* Ebenezer Blackadder in *Blackadder's Christmas Carol* (1988); *The Appointments of Dennis Jennings;* Captain Blackadder in *Blackadder Goes Forth* (series, 1989); title role in *Mr Bean* (also co-writer); The Boss in *Bernard and the Genie;* HBO Comedy Hour; Rowan Atkinson on Location in Boston; *Full Throttle; Funny Business* (presenter and co-deviser); *Mr Bean on Blind Date* (*Total Relief: A Night of Comic Relief,* 1993); Sir Henry 'Tim' Birkin in *Full Throttle* (Heroes & Villains); *Torvill and Bean* (*Comic Relief,* 1995); *Live for Peace – A Royal Gala* (VE Day, 1995); Insp Raymond Fowler in *The Thin Blue Line* (series, 1995, Christmas special 1995).
Films: *The Secret Policeman's Ball* (also co-writer); *The Secret Policeman's Other Ball;* Small-Fawcett in *Never Say Never Again;* Ron Anderson in *The Tall Guy; The Appointments of Dennis Jennings*

Rowan Atkinson

(short); Mr Stringer in *The Witches; Camden Town Boy; Hot Shots! Part Deux; Four Weddings and a Funeral;* voice of Zazu in *The Lion King.*
Awards: TV: BAFTA Best Light Entertainment Performance award for *Blackadder Goes Forth* (1989). Address: c/o PBJ Management. Lives in Oxfordshire. m. 1990 make-up artist Sunetra Sastry; 1 s.

ATTENBOROUGH, David
David Attenborough. Broadcaster/Director/Writer. b. London, 8 May 1926. Knighted, 1985. Worked for education book publishers, before joining the BBC as a trainee producer (1952).
TV: *Zoo Quest;* controller of BBC2 (1965-8); director of BBC TV programmes (1969-72); *The Tribal Eye; Wildlife on One; Eastward with Attenborough; Life on Earth; The Living Planet; Wildlife 100; Born to Be Wild* (Birthnight); *Writers' Houses; Summer Wildlife; Life in the Freezer* (series); *Arena Radio Night; Rainbow Safari; An Evening in with David Attenborough* (celebrating BBC2's 30th anniversary, 1994); *Wildlife on Two; Twentieth Century Fox* (narrator); *The Swarm; The Private Life of Plants* (series, 1995); *Watch Out; The Natural World* (narrator, series, 1996).

David Attenborough

Awards: SFTA Special Award (1961), RTS Silver Medal (1966), SFTA Desmond Davis Award (1970). Address: c/o BBC Bristol. Lives in Richmond-upon-Thames. m. Jane; 1 d. Susan, 1 s. Robert.

AUBREY, James
James Aubrey Tregidgo. Actor. b. British zone of occupation, Klagenfurt, Austria, 28 August 1947. Acted as a child. Trained at The Drama Centre (1967-70).
TV: *All Who Sail In Her;* Gavin in *A Bouquet of Barbed Wire* and *Another Bouquet;* Tom in *The Glass Menagerie; Danton's Death; St Joan; A Variety of Passion; Infidelities; The Cleopatras; Tales of the Unexpected; Run Rabbit Run; Return of The Saint; The Sweeney; Minder; The Last Place on Earth; The Possessed; Figure in a Landscape; Lytton's Diary; Lovejoy; Voice from the Gallows; Great Writers: William Golding; Great Writers: James Joyce; Thin Air; The Mountain and the Molehill* (Screen Two); *The Final Frame* (TVM); *Rockliffe's Folly; Mission Eureka; Rites of Passage;* Steve in *The Men's Room; TECX; Selling Hitler; A Fatal Inversion; Inspector Morse: Absolute Conviction; Casualty;* Steve in *The Men's Room* (series); *Full Stretch* (series); *Harry; The Choir;* Mr Stewart in *Brookside; The Bill.*

James Aubrey

Films: *Lord of the Flies; Home before Midnight; Terror; Galileo; The Hunger; Forever Young; The Great Rock and Roll Swindle; The American Way; Cry Freedom; Buddy's Song; A Demon in My View.* Address: c/o Conway, van Gelder, Robinson. Lives in London. m. (dis). Hobbies: Marine archaeology.

AYRES, Rosalind
Rosalind Ayres. Actress. b. Birmingham, 7 December 1946.
TV: *Nearest and Dearest; Coronation Street; The Lovers; Home and Away* (Granada Television series); *Suspicion; General Hospital; Country Matters; Play for Today; 30-Minute Theatre; Shoulder to Shoulder; Within These Walls; Affairs of the Heart; Father Brown; Holding On; The House of Bernarda Alba; Hindle Wakes; Public Eye; Warship; Two's Company; Charades; The Limbo Connection; The Dick Emery Show; Rings on Their Fingers; Penmarric; The Gentle Touch; Agony; Psy-warriors; Only When I Laugh; The Bounder; Father's Day; The Weather in the Streets; The Gay Lord Quex; Women of Durham; Nurses Do; Juliet Bravo; Who Dares Wins; New World; The Cat Brought It In;* Gladys Herbert in *Mistress of Suspense;* Sarah Clements in *Casualty;* Mary MacFell in *Catherine Cookson's The Cinder Path* (mini-series).

Rosalind Ayres

Films: *The Lovers;* Jeanette in *That'll Be the Day; Little Malcolm; Stardust;* Isobella in *The Slipper and the Rose; Cry Wolf.* Address: c/o Lou Coulson. Lives in London. m. actor Martin Jarvis (qv).

AZIZ, Lisa
Lisa Soraya Aziz. Television news and business presenter. b. Totnes, South Devon, 19 June 1962.
TV: BBC Television West (1984-5); HTV West news reporter/presenter (1985-8); TV-am reporter (1988-91), presenter of *TV-am Reports* (1988-9), daily newscaster (1989-91) and features reporter (1989-91); BBC World Service Television News freelance presenter, newsreader and interviewer, including *BBC World Business* (1993); *Sky News* freelance presenter (1993); *Business Daily* (Dubai Television, 1994-); *Financial Times Business Tonight* (NBC Superchannel, 1995-).

Lisa Aziz

Address: c/o Jane Hughes Management. Lives in Fulham, London. m. 1990 Frank L Ter Voorde; 1 d. Leah Soraya Ter Voorde. Hobbies: Cinema, gym, travel, reading.

BADAWI, Zeinab
Zeinab Badawi. Dual nationality: Sudanese and British. Gained BA (Hons) in PPE from St Hilda's College, Oxford, and MA in history of the Middle East from London University.
TV: Yorkshire Television (1982-6), working on *Calendar* (presenter-journalist, regional news magazine), *7 Days* (researcher), *A Question of Economics* (presenter-researcher-reporter) and *Politics of Food* (associate producer); *Brass Tacks* (reporter); ITN (1988-), presenting night-time news summaries, *ITN Morning News, Channel Four News* and *House To House* (Channel Four parliamentary programme); *Out of Africa* (series, 1993); *Sunday Live* (1995). Address: c/o ITN. Lives in London. m.

Zeinab Badawi

BADEL, Sarah

Sarah Badel. Actress. b. London, 30 March 1943.
TV: *The Visitors; Now Lies She There; Between the Wars; The Pallisers; Cold Comfort Farm; She; King Lear; Three Sisters; The Prime Minister's Daughter; Seven Faces of Woman; The Taming of the Shrew; Dear Brutus; Bavarian Night; Out of Order; Affairs of the Heart; The Irish RM; A Perfect Spy; The Cloning of Joanna May* (mini-series); Celia Cooke in *Casualty;* Avice in *Cadfael;* Mrs Hubbard in *Agatha Christie's Poirot: Hickory Dickory Dock;* Lady Julia Fish in *P G Wodehouse's Heavy Weather; The Vet.*
Films: *The Shooting Party; Not Without My Daughter.* Address: c/o Peters Fraser & Dunlop.

Sarah Badel

BADEN-SEMPER, Nina

Nina Baden-Semper. Actress.
TV: *Armchair Theatre; Callan; Thick as Thieves; Machinegunner;* Barbie Reynolds in *Love Thy Neighbour* (five series, 1972-6); *This Is Your Life* (subject); *Comedy Hour; The Story of Caedman; Five to Eleven; Take Three Girls; Love Story; The Doctors; Private Eye; George and Mildred; The Corridor People; Mystery and Imagination; The Bill; Children's Ward; Little Napoleons; It's a Girl.*
Films: *Kongi's Harvest; The Hand of Night; The Love Bug; Love Thy Neighbour.*
Awards: TV: Variety Club Joint ITV Personality of the Year award; Pye Television Outstanding Female Personality of the Year award.
Address: c/o Collis Management. m. 1973 Rev Murray Grant; 1 d. Caroline, 1 s. Joseph.

Nina Baden-Semper

BADLAND, Annette

Annette Badland. Actress. RSC productions include *Romeo and Juliet* and *Love's Labour's Lost.*
TV: *The Naked Civil Servant; Partisans; Flat Bust; Bognor; Shoestring; Pictures; Bergerac; Nanny; Minder; Great Expectations; Last Song; Lace; Lace 2; Newstime; Young Persons' Guide to Going Backwards in the World; The Young Visiters* (TVM); *Last Day of Summer;* Sister Mercy in *Sacred Hearts; Agatha Christie's Miss Marple; The Old Men at the Zoo; Trouble and Strife; A Little Princess; In No Time; You Must Be the Husband; PM Course; Hale & Pace; The Kitchen Child; Chinese Whispers; A Bit of Fry and Laurie; Happy Families; All Creatures Great and Small; The Pied Piper;* Willow in *Making Out; You and Me; The Bill* (two roles); *The Mushroom Picker; Goggle-Eyes; The Life and Times of Henry McGovern; Casualty;* Dawn in *2point4 Children* (series, 1993); *Smoke Screen; Nil by Mouth; The Prisoner* (BBC); *Mike and Angelo; Roughnecks; Jackanory; Love Hurts; Frank Stubbs; Jackanory: Dimanche Diller* (storyteller); *The Bill; English File: Love and War; Black Hearts in Battersea; Caught in the Act; Outside Edge.*
Films: Griselda Fishfinger in *Jabberwocky;* Stella in *Knights and Emeralds; The Anchoress; Syrop; Bedlam; Angels & Insects; The Grotesque; Hollow Reed.* Address: c/o Scott Marshall.

Annette Badland

BAILEY, Robin

Robin Bailey. Actor. b. Hucknall, Nottinghamshire, 5 October 1919.
TV: *The $64,000 Question* (compère); *Oliver Latimer's Husband; Seven Deadly Sins; The Power Game; Public Eye; Person to Person; Split Level; The Newcomers; The Troubleshooters; The Discharge of Trooper Lusby; Armchair Theatre; Brett Owen, M.D.; Solidarity; General Hospital; Murder Must Advertise; Vienna 1900; Justice;* Chamberlain in *The Gathering Storm; Upstairs, Downstairs; North and South; A Legacy; The Wild Duck; Brett; Crown Court; I Didn't Know You Cared; The Pallisers; The Couch; The Way of the World; Punch Revue; Took & Co; For Services Rendered; The Good Companions; Bognor; Cupid's Darts; If You Go Down in the Woods Today; Sorry, I'm a Stranger Here Myself; Jane; Tales from a Long Room; Walk with Destiny; Potter; Sharing Time; Bleak House;* Charters in *Charters and Caldicott; On Stage; Looks Familiar; Drummonds; Mozart; Return to the Broads;* Judge Mr Justice Gerald Graves in *Rumpole of the Bailey; A Kind of Living; A Gentleman's Club; Number 27; Tinniswood Country; The Good Guys; Tales from Hollywood* (Performance); *Kavanagh QC; Bed* (Performance); *Dalziel and Pascoe.*
Films: *Commuter Husbands; Catch Us if You Can; The Eliminator; Blind Terror; Nightmare Rally; School for Secrets; Private Angelo; Portrait of Claire; Glory at Sea; His Excellency; Folly to Be Wise; Sailor of the King* (also titled *Single-Handed* and *Able Seaman Brown*); *For Better or Worse* (also titled *Cocktails in the Kitchen*); *Just My Luck; Another Time, Another Place; The Diplomatic Corpse; Hell Drivers; The Mouse on the Moon; Having a Wild Weekend; The Spy with a Cold Nose; The Whisperers; You Only Live Twice; Danger Route; See No Evil; The Four Feathers* (TVM only in US); *Screamtime; Jane and the Lost City.* Address: c/o Michael Whitehall. m. Patricia Weekes; 3 s. Nicholas, Simon, Justin.

Robin Bailey

BAIRSTOW, Amanda

Amanda Bairstow. Actress. b. Bingley, West Yorkshire, 12 November 1960. Trained at the Italia Conti Stage Academy.
TV: *Lytton's Diary;* Susan Denton in *Coronation Street; Juliet Bravo; Cockles; Tears before Bedtime; Only Children* (Play for Today); *Salad Days; The Bill;* Shop Assistant in *Mulberry;* Sheila Simmonds in *3-7-11.* Address: c/o Sharon Hamper Management. Lives in North London. m. theatre producer Brian Hewitt-Jones; 1 s. Tom Hewitt-Jones. Pets: A dog called George.

Amanda Bairstow

BAKER, Cheryl

Rita Maria Crudgington. Presenter/Singer. b. Bethnal Green, East London, 8 March 1955. Previously a singer with the groups CoCo and Bucks Fizz (1981 Eurovision Song Contest winners).
TV: *How Dare You; The Six o'Clock Show* (LWT); *Game for a Laugh; Surprise, Surprise; The Saturday Picture Show; Record Breakers; The Funny Side; Eggs 'n' Baker* (series, 1989-93); *My Secret Desire; The Survival Guide to Food* (series); *Superdogs;* resident cook in *Good Morning... with Anne & Nick; Walking the Dog; The 11th Hour; Sick as a Parrot.* Address: c/o Razzamatazz Management. Lives in Eltham, South London. m. bass guitarist Steve Stroud. Pets: A dog called Malcolm. Hobbies: Cooking.

Cheryl Baker

BAKER, Colin

Colin Baker. Actor/Writer/Songwriter. b. London, 8 June 1943. Trained at LAMDA (1967-9).
TV: *Roads to Freedom;* Paul Merroney in *The Brothers; Cousin Bette; Hamlet; The Silver Sword; The Edwardians; A Fall of Eagles;* Prince Anatol in *War and Peace; Harriet's Back in Town; For Maddie with Love; Blake's 7; Cuckoo; Swallows and Amazons Forever; Dangerous Davies – The Last Detective* (TVM); title role in *Doctor Who* (sixth Doctor, 1984-6, eight stories, 31 episodes); *Casualty; The Young Indiana Jones Chronicles; Doctor Who: Dimensions in Time (Children in Need,* 1993); *Harry's Mad.*
Films: *A Clockwork Orange; No Longer Alone;* The Stranger in *The Airzone Solution, The Zero Imperative* and *The Eye of the Beholder.* **Books:** *The Age of Chaos* (full-length graphic novel, published by Marvel Comics, 1994). Address: c/o Barry Burnett Organisation. Lives in High Wycombe, Buckinghamshire. m. 1st actress Liza Goddard (dis), 2nd actress Marion Wyatt; 1 s. Jack (dec), 4 d. Lucy, Bindy (Belinda), Lally, Rosie. Pets: Three dogs, six cats, two horses. Hobbies: 'See children and pets!'

Colin Baker

BAKER, Danny

Danny Baker. Presenter. b. Deptford, South London, 22 June 1957. Rock journalist before entering TV.
TV: *20th Century Box; The Six o'Clock Show* (LWT); *Danny Baker on...; 6 o'Clock Live* (LWT); *Win, Lose or Draw* (host); *Live; Work Is a Four-Letter Word; Video View; TV Hell – Hello & Goodbye; TV Heroes* (series); Chat Show Host in *Frank Stubbs Promotes; Danny Baker After All* (host, series, 1993); *Bygones* (host, quiz show series, 1994); *Pets Win Prizes* (host, Series 1 only, 1994); *The Danny Baker Show* (series, 1994-5). Address: c/o Noel Gay Artists. m. Wendy; 1 d. Bonnie, 1 s. Sonny.

Danny Baker

BAKER, George

George Baker. Actor/Writer/Director. b. British Embassy, Varna, Bulgaria, 1 April 1931.
TV: *Fan Show; Ron Raudell Show; Guinea Pig; Death of a Salesman; The Last Troubadour; The Square Ring; Nick of the River; Mary Stuart; Probation Officer; Far Away Music; It Happened Like This; Boule de Suif; Maigret; Zero One; Rupert of Hentzau; Miss Memory; Any Other Business; The Navigators; Common Ground; Alice; The Queen and Jackson; The Big Man Coughed and Died; Up and Down; Call My Bluff; The Baron; St Patrick; Love Life; Seven Deadly Virtues; The Prisoner; The Sex Games; Z Cars; Paul Temple; Candida;* Bowler in *The Fenn Street Gang* and *Bowler; The Man Outside; The Persuaders!; The Main Chance; Ministry of Fear; Voyage in the Dark; Dial M for Murder; Zodiac; The Survivors; Medea;* Mr Lewis in *Some Mothers Do 'Ave 'Em;* Tiberius in *I Claudius; Print Out;* Insp Roderick Alleyn in *Died in the Wool/Opening Night/Vintage Murder/Colour Scheme* (New Zealand TVMs); *The Biggest Bank Robbery* (TVM); *Goodbye Darling; Minder; Triangle; The Chinese Detective; Secret Adversary; Hart to Hart; Goodbye, Mr Chips; Dead Head; The Bird Fancier; Marjorie and Men; The Canterville Ghost; Time after Time; A Woman of Substance; If Tomorrow Comes; Coast to Coast* (TVM); *Room at the Bottom; Robin of Sherwood; Miss Marple at Bertram's Hotel; The Charmer; Verdi – Wolf to the Slaughter; Bergerac;* Det Chief Insp Wexford in *The Ruth Rendell Mysteries* (21 stories 1987-92, 1996); Godfrey Eagan in *No Job for a Lady; Little Lord Fauntleroy.*
Films: *The Intruder; The Dam Busters; The Ship That Died of Shame; The Woman for Joe; The Feminine Touch; The Extra Day; A Hill in Korea; These Dangerous Years; No Time for Tears; The Moonraker; Tread Softly, Stranger; Lancelot and Guinevere; The Finest Hours; The Curse of the Fly; Mister Ten Per Cent; Goodbye, Mr Chips; Justine; On Her Majesty's Secret Service; The Executioner; A Warm December; The Rape; The Laughing Girl Murder; The Firefighters; Three for All; The Twelve Tasks of Asterix; Intimate Games; The Spy Who Loved Me; The Thirty Nine Steps; A Nightingale Sang in Berkeley Square; North Sea Hijack; Hopscotch; Out of Order; For Queen and Country.* Address: c/o CDA. m. 1st costume designer Julia Squires (dec), 2nd actress Sally Home (dec 1992); 3rd actress Louie Ramsay (qv); 5 d. Charlie, Ellie (twins), writer Candida, chef Tessa (all from 1st m.), Sarah (from 2nd m.).

George Baker

BAKER, Richard

Richard Douglas James Baker. Presenter. b. Willesden, North London, 15 June 1925. OBE, 1979.
TV: BBC newsreader (1954-82); *Omnibus; The Proms; Last Night of the Proms; New Year's Day Concert from Vienna; Face the Music* (panellist); *Mary, Mungo and Midge* (narrator); *New Year's Day Concert; Royal British Legion Festival of Remembrance.* Address: c/o Bagenal Harvey Organisation. Lives in Radlett, Hertfordshire. m. Margaret; 2 s. Andrew, James. Hobbies: Music, theatre, the sea.

Richard Baker

BAKER, Tom

Tom Baker

Tom Baker. Actor. b. Liverpool. Stage plays include *Educating Rita* (RSC national tour).
TV: Title role in *Doctor Who* (1974-81, 41 stories, 172 episodes); *The Hound of the Baskervilles; Robin Hood; The Life and Loves of a She-Devil; Selling Hitler;* Sir Lionel Sweeting in *The Law Lord* (TVM); Professor Geoffrey Hoyt in *Medics* (Series 2-5, 1992-5); Professor Plum in *Cluedo* (1992); *Tales of Aesop* (narrator); *Doctor Who: Dimensions in Time* (Children in Need, 1993); *Wall to Wall* (narrator, series, 1994).
Films: Rasputin in *Nicholas and Alexandra;* Sea Captain in *Frankenstein: The True Story; The Canterbury Tales; Luther; Vault of Horror; The Mutations; Sinbad's Golden Voyage.*
Address: c/o Annette Stone Associates. Lives in Kent. m. 1st Anna Wheatcroft (dis), 2nd actress Lalla Ward (dis), 3rd TV director Sue Jerrard; 2 s. Daniel (b. 1960), Piers (b. 1962) (both from 1st m.).

BALDWIN, Peter

Peter Baldwin

Peter Baldwin. Actor. b. Chesterfield, Derbyshire, 1933. Trained at Bristol Old Vic Theatre.
TV: *Bergerac; Agatha Christie's Miss Marple; Seven Deadly Sins;* Derek Wilton in *Coronation Street* (on and off 1976-87, regular 1988-); *Royal Variety Performance* (with *Coronation Street* cast).
Address: c/o Christina Shepherd/Granada Television. Lives in North London and Manchester. m. actress Sarah Long (dec); 1 d. Julia, 1 s. Matthew. Hobbies: Collecting toy theatres.

BALL, Bobby

Bobby Ball

Robert Harper. Comedian/Entertainer. b. Oldham, Lancashire, 28 January 1944. Half of the comedy duo Cannon & Ball, originally welders in an Oldham engineering factory who sang semi-professionally by night as the Shirrell Brothers, then the Harper Brothers, before changing their name to Cannon & Ball for the TV talent show *Opportunity Knocks* (1968), but came last.
TV: *Opportunity Knocks; The Wheeltappers' and Shunters' Social Club; Bruce Forsyth's Big Night; Royal Variety Performances; This Is Your Life* (subjects); *The Cannon & Ball Show* (1979-88); *Cannon & Ball's Casino* (hosts, quiz show); *Plaza Patrol* (situation comedy); *Cannon & Ball Playhouse.*
Films: *The Boys in Blue.*
Records: Single: *Don't Forget My Christmas Present* (1992).
Address: c/o International Artistes, Albert House, Albert Street, Chadderton, Oldham. Lives in Rochdale. m. 2nd Yvonne; 2 s. Robert, Darren, 1 d. Joanne. Hobbies: Reading the Bible and being with family, writing books and poems, music – especially rock 'n' roll – fishing.

BALL, Johnny

Johnny Ball

Johnny Ball. Presenter/Writer. b. Bristol, 23 May 1938. Worked for DeHavilland Aircraft, served in the RAF (1957-9), where he began writing comedy, then was a Butlin's Redcoat and a drummer in Liverpool (1960-2). Switched to stand-up comedy (1963) and appeared in Northern clubs and in cabaret. TV since 1966.
TV: *Late Date with Johnny Ball; Play School* (1967-83); *Play Away* (writer only); *Star Turn; Great Egg Race; Snooker Taylor Made; Secret's Out* (two series); *Don't Ask Me* (writer, three series); *Fun and Games; Star Turn* (writer, five series); *Battle of the Sexes* (writer); *Crackerjack* (writer); *The Hot Shoe Show* (writer); *Cabbages and Kings* (two series); *Think of a Number* (six series); *Think Again* (five series); *Think It – Do It* (two series); *Think Backwards; Think This Way; Philomena; Knowhow; EXPO; Sixth Sense* (two series); *Johnny Ball Reveals All* (five series); *Small Business Bookkeeping* (Open University); *Help Your Child with Maths; Away with Numbers.*
Videos: *You Are What You Eat.*
Awards: ITVA Craft Award for Best Presenter (1986).
Address: c/o The Living History of Science, Highfield, Beaconsfield Road, Farnham Common, South Buckinghamshire SL2 2JD. m. Dianne; 1 d. TV presenter Zoë, 2 s. Nicholas, Daniel. Pets: Two budgerigars. Hobbies: Recreational maths, snooker, chess, cricket.

BANKS, David

David Banks

David Banks. Actor/Writer/Director. b. Hull, East Yorkshire, 24 September 1951. Gained a BA (Hons) in drama from Manchester University. Trained at Bristol Old Vic Theatre School.
TV: Dave in *The Cuckoo Waltz;* Cowley's Aide in *The Professionals;* Leslie in *Keep It in the Family;* Cyberleader in *Doctor Who* and *The Five Doctors;* Dennis O'Donovan in *Man of Letters* (Play for Today); Gavin the photographer in *EastEnders;* DI Graveney in *The Bill;* Graeme Curtis in *Brookside* (1991-2); Ray in *A Time to Dance* (mini-series); Derek Wakeley in *Rough Justice;* axe murderer Dennis Smalley in *Going Under.*
Films: *Talking to John* (director); *The Last Interview;* Slavedriver in *Hawk the Slayer.*
Books: *Doctor Who – Cybermen* (1988); *Good Digs Guide* (co-writer, 1989); *Iceberg* (novel, 1993). Address: c/o Shane Collins Associates. Lives in Islington, North London. Partner: Maureen Purkis. Hobbies: Apple Mac computer, films, literature, t'ai chi.

BANKS, Jeff

Jeffrey Tatham-Banks. Presenter/Fashion designer. GFCSD Doctor of Arts; BA (Hons) Newcastle.
TV: *Pebble Mill at One; The Clothes Show; The British Fashion Awards; Children in Need Clothes Show; Clothes Show Classics; The British Fashion Awards; Children in Need Clothes Show* (1992); *The Clothes Show – New York.* **Awards:** Designer of the Year (twice); Retailer of the Year (1984); Chead Medal winner. Address: c/o BBC TV. Lives in London. m. 1968 singer Sandie Shaw (dis), m. Sue Mann; 3 d. Grace, Coco, India. Pets: Basset-hound called Bisto. Hobbies: Cycling.

Jeff Banks

BANKS, Morwenna

Morwenna Tamsin Banks. Writer/Performer. b. Flushing, Cornwall, 20 September. Gained a BA (Hons) in English from Cambridge University; took part in Cambridge Footlights revues. West End plays include *An Evening with Gary Lineker* (Duchess Theatre).
TV: *The Lenny Henry Show; Saturday Live; The Alexei Sayle Show; Only Joking* (producer, documentary); *Signals* (presenter, arts series); *Absolutely* (writer and performer, four series); *A Season of Heavenly Gifts.* **Books:** *The Joke's on Us.* Address: c/o ICM/Curtis Brown. Lives in Greenwich, south-east London. Single. Pets: Fish and a monkey.

Morwenna Banks

BANNEN, Ian

Ian Bannen. Actor. b. Coatbridge, Lanarkshire, 29 June 1928.
TV: *Jesus of Nazareth;* Jim Prideaux in *Tinker, Tailor, Soldier, Spy; Dr Jekyll and Mr Hyde* (TVM); *The Hard Word; Hart to Hart; Tickets for the Titanic; Bookie; On the Orient North; The Fifteen Streets; The Lady and the Highwayman* (TVM); *The Paris Deception; Uncle Vanya* (TVM); *Murder in Eden; The Common Pursuit; Ashenden; Arise and Go Now;* Otto Rosen in *Perry Mason: The Case of the Desperate Deception* (TVM); David Lloyd George in *The Treaty* (mini-series); Dr Cameron in *Doctor Finlay* (four series 1993-6); *Measure for Measure* (Performance); *The Politician's Wife* (mini-series).
Films: *Private's Progress; The Long Arm; Yangtse Incident; Miracle in Soho; The Birthday Present; A Tale of Two Cities; She Didn't Say No!; Behind the Mask; Carlton-Browne of the FO; On Friday at 11; A French Mistress; Suspect; Macbeth; Station Six – Sahara; Psyche 59; Mister Moses; The Hill; Rotten to the Core; The Flight of the Phoenix; Penelope; Sailor from Gibraltar; Too Late the Hero; Lock Up Your Daughters!; Jane Eyre; The Deserter; Fright; Doomwatch; The Offence; The Mackintosh Man; From Beyond the Grave; Il Viaggio; Identikit, Bite the Bullet, Sweeney!, The Inglorious Bastards; Ring of Darkness; The Watcher in the Woods; Eye of the Needle; Night Crossing; Gandhi; The Prodigal; Gorky Park; Defence of the Realm; Lamb; Hope and Glory; The Courier; The Match; Ghost Dad; George's Island; The Gambler; Witch Story; The Big Man; Speaking of the Devil; Damage; A Pin for the Butterfly.* Address: c/o London Management. Lives in London and Arizona. m. Marilyn.

Ian Bannen

BARBER, Frances

Frances Barber. Actress. b. Wolverhampton, Staffordshire, 13 May 1958.
TV: *Visitors; Tales of the Unexpected; Home Sweet Home; A Flame to the Phoenix; Those Glory, Glory Days* (TVM); *Reilly – Ace of Spies; Hard Feelings* (Play for Today); *Clem; Twelfth Night; Duck; Annie Besant* (drama-documentary); *Behaving Badly* (series); *The Grasscutter; This Is David Lander; Inspector Morse: The Death of the Self; The Nightmare Years* (mini-series); *The Storyteller: Greek Myths; Do Not Disturb* (Screen Two); *The Orchid House* (mini-series); *Hancock* (Screen One); *A Statement of Affairs* (mini-series); *The Leaving of Liverpool* (mini-series); *Blow Your Mind: Ulysses* (reading a monologue); *Return to Blood River* (Screen Two); *Continental Drift; In the Cold Light of Day* (Screen Two); *The Inspector Alleyn Mysteries: Scales of Justice; Chef!; Dirty Old Town* (Rik Mayall Presents); *Scarborough Ahoy!; Rules of Engagement* (pilot); *Aristophanes – The Gods Are Laughing; It Might Be You.*
Films: *The Missionary; Acceptable Levels; White City; A Zed and Two Noughts; The Soul of the Machine; Castaway;* Leonie Orton in *Prick Up Your Ears;* Rosie in *Sammy and Rosie Get Laid;* Megan in *We Think the World of You; Chambre à Part* (Separate Rooms); *Young Soul Rebels* (BFI production); *Secret Friends; The Lake; Where the Wolves Howl, Soft Top, Hard Shoulder, The Fish Tail* (BFI production); *Three Steps to Heaven* (BFI production). Address: c/o James Sharkey Associates.

Frances Barber

BARDON, John

John M Jones. Actor. b. London, 25 August 1939. Originally trained as an industrial designer.
TV: *Seconds Out;* Ron Armitage in *Hi-de-Hi!; Campion; After Henry; Birds of a Feather;* Professor Otto in *The Return of the Antelope; The Paradise Club; Frontiers;* Stan Gale in *Giving Tongue;* Jack Morris in *Casualty; Spatz;* Mr Blanchfield in *The Darling Buds of May; Mrs Shaw's Missing Millions;* Robbo in *The Bill;* Walter Gimbert in *Lovejoy; Rumpole of the Bailey;* Mr Jarvis in *Johnny Jarvis* (series); Sam Carver in *Love Hurts* (series); Bernie Sweet in *Get Back* (two series); *Goodnight Sweetheart; The Detectives.*
Films: *The Keeper; S*P*Y*S; 84 Charing Cross Road; Ordeal by Innocence; Fords on Water; Clockwise; Seasick; Gulliver's Travels; Death Fish II.* Address: c/o Barry Brown & Partner. Lives in West London. Single. Hobbies: Golf, water-colour painting.

John Bardon

Judith Barker

BARKER, Judith

Judith Barker. Actress. Stage plays include *Last Tango in Whitby* (national tour) and *Total Eclipse* (Lyric Theatre, Hammersmith).

TV: Janet Barlow in *Coronation Street* (eight years); Pauline Kent in *The Practice* (three series); Eileen Salter in *Brookside; How We Used to Live; All for Love;* Margie in *G.B.H.;* Shirley James in *Coasting;* Motorway Supervisor in *September Song;* Ticket Lady in *Dancing Queen* (Rik Mayall Presents); Mrs Corrie in *Harry;* Mrs Roberts in *Between the Lines;* Mrs Tate in *Ain't Misbehavin'* (series, 1994); Audrey Manners in *Brookside* (1994-5); Tessa Shaw in *Medics*.
Films: *Distant Voices, Still Lives.*
Address: c/o Billy Marsh Associates.

Peter Barkworth

BARKWORTH, Peter

Peter Barkworth. Actor. b. Margate, Kent, 14 January 1929. Trained at RADA. West End plays include *Roar Like a Dove, Crown Matrimonial, Donkey's Years, Can You Hear Me at the Back?* and *A Coat of Varnish.* Directed a national tour of *Sisterly Feelings.*
TV: *The Power Game; Manhunt; End of Story; A Roof Over Our Mouths; Tarnish on a Golden Boy; The Company Man; Office Party; Asquith in Orbit; Rasputin; The Passenger; The Rivals of Sherlock Holmes; Dear Octopus; The Millionairess; Return Flight; Colditz; Who Sank the Lusitania?; Crown Matrimonial; Intent to Murder; Good Girl; Melissa; The Apple Cart; An Accident of Class and Sex; The Saturday Party; The Little Minister; The Five Pound Orange; Omnibus: Thomas Mann; The Country Party; Professional Foul; Secret Army; The Ragazza; Telford's Change; The Morecambe and Wise Christmas Show; Winston Churchill — The Wilderness Years; Tales of the Unexpected; The Secret Adversary; Reith; The Price; Late Starter; The Gospel According to St Matthew; The London Embassy; The Return of Sherlock Holmes;* Frank Milner in *Heartbeat.*
Films: *Tiara Tahiti; A Touch of Larceny; No Love for Johnnie;* Berkeley in *Where Eagles Dare; Mr Smith; Escape from the Dark;* Pilot in *International Velvet; Champions.*
Books: *About Acting; First Houses; More about Acting.*
Address: c/o Jonathan Altaras Associates. Lives in Hampstead, North London. Single.

Thelma Barlow

BARLOW, Thelma

Thelma Barlow. Actress. b. Middlesbrough, 19 June 1937. Worked for seven years as a secretary in Huddersfield and took speech and drama evening classes, appearing in amateur productions, before turning professional when she joined Joan Littlewood's Theatre Workshop, in East London.
TV: Classical serials such as *Vanity Fair; A Classic Christmas Ghost Story;* Mavis Riley/Wilton in *Coronation Street* (1972-); Royal Variety Performance (with *Coronation Street* cast, 1989).
Books: *Organic Gardening with Love* (1992).
Address: c/o Granada Television. Lives in North Yorkshire and Manchester. m. designer Graham Barlow (dis); 2 s. Clive, theatre director James. Hobbies: Cookery, organic gardening, yoga.

Carol Barnes

BARNES, Carol

Carol Lesley Barnes. Newscaster. b. Norwich, Norfolk, 13 September 1944. Gained BA in French and Spanish at Sheffield University and a post-graduate teaching diploma. Worked as a public relations officer at the Royal Court Theatre, London, managing editor of *Time Out* magazine and was a founder member of LBC (London independent news and information radio station), working as a reporter and newscaster with IRN, before moving to BBC Radio 4, then into television with ITN in 1975.
TV: ITN reporter (1975-9); ITN newscaster from 1979; *News at Ten* (1986-9); *The Sharp End; The Channel Four Daily* presenter (1989-91); *News at 5.40* presenter (1991-2); *Diana: Progress of a Princess;* regular presenter of *ITN Lunchtime News, ITN Early Evening News* and ITN weekend programmes (1992-); *After 5 with Carol Barnes* (Carlton only, guest presenter, 1995).
Radio: *World at One* (BBC Radio 4).
Awards: TRIC Newscaster of the Year (1994). Address: c/o ITN. Lives in Brighton, East Sussex. m. TV news cameraman Nigel Thomson; 1 d. Clare Barnes (from previous relationship with journalist Denis McShane), 1 s. James. (from m.). Pets: A cat. Hobbies: Golf.

Dominique Barnes

BARNES, Dominique

Dominique Barnes. Actress. b. Barnet, Hertfordshire, 21 June 1966. Trained at the Arts Educational Trust as a child.
TV: *Father's Day* (two series, from the age of 16); *Return to Waterloo; Demons; Lytton's Diary; Queen of Hearts; Gems; Watching* (BBC play); *Brat Farrar; Jessie's Place; Hannay; All Creatures Great and Small; Rockliffe's Babies; Maigret; Bergerac; William Tell* (US title *Crossbow*); *The Bill; Casualty; Young, Gifted and Broke;* Sophie in *A Touch of Frost.*
Films: *Lubo's World; Bert Rigby, You're a Fool.*
Address: c/o Spotlight. Lives in Enfield, Middlesex. Single.

BARON, Lynda

Lynda Baron. Actress. b. Manchester, 24 March. Trained in ballet at the Royal Academy of Dancing. **TV:** *Play of the Month; Don't Forget to Write; Heartlands; Grundy; Z Cars; KYTV; Doctor Who* (two roles); Nurse Gladys Emmanuel in *Open All Hours; Playhouse; Minder; The Cannon & Ball Show;* Lily-Bless-Her in *Last of the Summer Wine; Kelly; Plaza Patrol;* Auntie Pat in *The Upper Hand* (series). **Films:** *Trauma;* Louise in *Hot Millions;* Long Liz in *Hands of the Ripper.* Address: c/o Peter Charlesworth. m. John M Lee; 1 d. Sarah, 1 s. Morgan.

Lynda Baron

BARRACLOUGH, Roy

Roy Barraclough. Actor. b. Preston, Lancashire, 12 July 1935. Worked as a draughtsman for 12 years, acting in amateur productions in his spare time. Became entertainments manager at a holiday camp, also playing the piano and telling jokes, before turning professional as an actor. **TV:** *Castlehaven; Don't Touch Him, He Might Resent It; Nearest and Dearest; Never Mind the Quality, Feel the Width; Love Thy Neighbour; Pardon My Genie; Sez Les* (half of fictional gossips Cissie and Ada, with Les Dawson); *Les Dawson on Christmas* (1980); *Foxy Lady;* Butterfly Collector in *The Return of the Antelope; Lost Empires; T-Bag Strikes Again;* five speaking roles in *Coronation Street,* including Alec Gilroy (on and off 1972-5, regular 1986-92, 1995, 1996); *Royal Variety Performance* (with *Coronation Street* cast, 1989); *The Krypton Factor* (series, 1993); Joe Wilson in *Peak Practice;* Leslie Flitcroft in *Mother's Ruin* (series, 1994); Walter Aurifaber in *Cadfael; Les Dawson: The Entertainer* (presenter). **Films:** *The Slipper and the Rose; Car Trouble.* **Radio:** *Death of an Ugly Sister* (BBC Radio 4, 1994); *Kelly's Eye* (Thirty Minute Theatre, BBC Radio 4, 1995). Address: c/o PBR Management. Lives in Stalybridge, Cheshire. Single. Pets: Terrier called Whisky. Hobbies: Good food, cooking.

Roy Barraclough

BARRIE, Amanda

Shirley Ann Broadbent. Actress. b. Ashton-under-Lyne, Lancashire, 14 September 1939. Started dancing and singing in public at the age of three in her grandfather's theatre in Ashton-under-Lyne, and later trained in ballet. Aged 14, became a chorus girl in London, making her début in *Babes in the Wood* at the Finsbury Park Empire. Has danced on stage with Lionel Blair and Danny La Rue. **TV:** Dancer, then actress, in Morecambe and Wise's first series, *Running Wild;* hostess in quiz show *Double Your Money;* receptionist Sandra Prentiss in *The Bulldog Breed* (series); appeared in Jimmy Tarbuck's first TV series, *The Jimmy Tarbuck Show,* Hermia in *A Midsummer Night's Dream, Struggles, Horizontal Hold* (Playhouse); *Are You Being Served?; Spooner's Patch; Sanctuary; L for Lester;* Alma Sedgwick/Baldwin in *Coronation Street* (1981 and 1989-). **Films:** Rona in *Doctor in Distress;* Glamcab driver in *Carry On Cabby;* Cleopatra in *Carry On Cleo; I Gotta Horse; One of Our Dinosaurs Is Missing.* Address: Peter Charlsworth. Lives in Covent Garden, London. m. actor and theatre director Robin Hunter (sep). Hobbies: Watching horse racing.

Amanda Barrie

BARRON, James

James Nicholas Richard Barron. Actor/Singer. b. London, 24 December 1964. Son of actor Keith Barron (qv) and stage designer Mary Pickard. Member of the National Youth Theatre, before training at The Drama Centre. West End musicals include *Leonardo* and *Les Misérables.* **TV:** *West Country Tales* (two episodes while still at school); *Three Up, Two Down; Laura and Disorder; The Return of Shelley; On Her Majesty's National Service* (pilot); *The Endless Game* (pilot); *Home to Roost; 'Allo, 'Allo.* **Records:** Album: *A Portrait of Love* (with Simon Burke, 1994). Address: c/o The Narrow Road Company. Lives in Thames Ditton, Surrey. m. actress Shona Lindsay (qv) (dis). Pets: Beagle called Barney. Hobbies: Theatre visits, travelling (especially to Australia), singing, flying.

James Barron

BARRON, John

John Barron. Actor. b. Marylebone, London, 24 December 1920. Trained at RADA. TV since 1948. **TV:** *Mountain Air* (début, 1948); *Emergency — Ward 10; Girl in a Black Bikini; The Beverly Hillbillies; The Saint; Department S; Softly Softly; Doomwatch;* The Dean in *All Gas and Gaiters; Ace of Wands; The Mind of Mr J G Reeder; Timeslip; The Pathfinders; Spyder's Web; The Rivals of Sherlock Holmes; The Protectors; Crown Court; Potsdam; The Late Wife; The Fosters;* CJ in *The Fall and Rise of Reginald Perrin; Victorian Scandals; The Foundation; Wodehouse Playhouse; Potter; The Taming of the Shrew; Bernie; Spooner's Patch; Shelley; The Glums; The Wizard of Crumm; The Gentle Touch; Cowboys; Yes Minister; Othello; To the Manor Born; Whoops Apocalypse!; To Catch a King* (TVM); *Let's Parlez Français; No Place Like Home; Kelly Monteith; Me & My Girl; Terry and June; Thirteen at Dinner* (TVM); *Duty Free; Don't Wait Up; Brush Strokes; In Sickness and in Health* (series); *The Chamber* (pilot). **Films:** *Italian Secret Service; The Last Days of Hitler; The Great Question.* Address: c/o Green and Underwood. Lives in West Sussex. m. 1st actress Joan Peart (dec), 2nd Helen Christie (dec). Hobbies: 'Wine collection and consumption.'

John Barron

BARRON, Keith

Keith Barron

Keith Barron. Actor. b. Mexborough, South Yorkshire, 8 August 1934.
TV: *The Odd Man; The New Adventures of Lucky Jim; My Good Woman; A Family at War; Let's Get Away from It All; Stand Up Nigel Barton; Vote Vote Vote for Nigel Barton; Telford's Change; Watching Me, Watching You; West Country Tales; Duty Free* (three series, 1984-6)*; Leaving; Room at the Bottom;* Tom in *Take Me Home* (mini-series, 1989)*; 1996;* title role in *Haggard* (two series, 1991-2)*; Plaza Patrol;* Guy Lofthouse in *The Good Guys* (two series, 1992-3)*; Ticket to Write* (*This Morning*); Bob Ferguson in *Sherlock Holmes: The Last Vampyre; Under the Hammer; The Lifeboat;* Bill Chivers in *All Night Long* (series, 1994); Masters in *The Ruth Rendell Mysteries: A Case of Coincidence* (mini-series, 1996).
Films: Dr Haynes in *Nothing but the Night.* Address: c/o Michael Whitehall. Lives in Hampton Court and Cornwall. m. stage designer Mary Pickard; 1 s. actor James (qv).

BARRY, David

David Barry

Meurig Wyn Jones. Actor/Writer. b. Bangor, Gwynedd, 30 April 1943. Trained at the Corona Academy.
TV: Frankie Abbott in *Please Sir!* (1968-70) and *The Fenn Street Gang* (three series, 1971-3)*; Owain Glyndwr; Never the Twain; Brookside;* Hillyer in *A Mind to Kill.* As writer: *Keep It in the Family.*
Films: Frankie Abbott in *Please Sir!;* Elvis in *George and Mildred.*
Address: c/o Pelham Associates. Lives in Tunbridge Wells, Kent. m. 1st Zelie (dis 1977), 2nd Pat Donoghue (actress Pat Carlile); 1 d. Emma, 1 s. Morgan (both from 2nd m.). Pets: Two cats, one hamster. Hobbies: Reading.

BARRYMORE, Michael

Michael Barrrymore

Michael Parker. Entertainer. b. Bermondsey, South London, 4 May 1952. Worked as a hairdresser, with clients including Shirley Bassey and Lulu, before entering showbusiness.
TV: Warm-up man for *Are You Being Served?, Little and Large* and *The Marti Caine Show; The Royal Variety Performance; 40 Years On; Barrymore Special; Michael Barrymore's Saturday Night Out; Strike It Rich* (two pilots for *Strike It Lucky*)*; Strike It Lucky* (game show, host)*; Live from Her Majesty's; Get Set, Go; Russ Abbot's Madhouse; Barrymore* (five series, 1992-6)*; Strike It Lucky Special* (Christmas, 1993)*; Shut That Door* (presenter, 1995)*; Live for Peace – A Royal Gala* (VE Day 1995)*; Barrymore – The Best Bits* (three compilations, 1995)*; Michael Barrymore's 'My Kind of People'* (series, 1995).
Radio: *Barrymore Plus.*
Address: c/o Norman Murray and Anne Chudleigh. m. Cheryl St Clair.

BASTEDO, Alexandra

Alexandra Bastedo

Alexandra Lendon Bastedo. Actress/Presenter/Writer. b. Hove, Sussex, 9 March 1946. A descendant of Richard Wagner on her mother's side of the family. Discovered by Columbia Pictures aged 16.
TV: *House of Pride; The Horseman;* Sharron Macready in *The Champions* (series, 1969-71)*; Department S; Codename* (series)*; The Headwaiter; Scobie Man; The Aphrodite Inheritance; Aren't We All; Draw!* (TVM)*; Boon;* Penny Caspar in *Absolutely Fabulous; Europe on the Brink.*
Films: *Casino Royale; The Ghoul; Find the Lady; Hushabye.* Address: c/o CAM. Lives in Chichester, West Sussex. m. theatre director Patrick Garland. Pets: 167 animals. Hobbies: Reading, walking.

BATE, Anthony

Anthony Bate. Actor. b. Stourbridge, Worcestershire.
TV: *Grady; Ivanhoe; Julius Caesar; Les Misérables; The Idiot;* title role in *Horizon: T H Huxley; Out of the Unknown: The Last Witness; Fathers and Sons; Second Time Around; Some Distant Shadow; Oedipus Rex; Ego Hugo; Hail Caesar;* Dave in *Up the Junction; Helen – A Woman of Today; Intimate Strangers; Shades of Greene: Chagrin in Two Parts; During Barty's Party; Double Echo; Nobody's Conscience; Jubilee; Philby, Burgess and Maclean; Live at Stake: Dutch Train Hijack; Treasure Island; The Seagull; Crown Court; The Saint; The Avengers; Wilde Alliance; Englishman's Castle; Tinker, Tailor, Soldier, Spy; Crime and Punishment; Dalhousie's Luck; Network; 'Tis Pity She's a Whore; Leap in the Dark; Square Mile of Murder; Psy-Warriors; Fanny by Gaslight; Smiley's People; Golda; Shackleton; Grand Duo; Kisch-Kisch; Nellie's Version; Maybury; War and Remembrance; A Visit from Outer Space; Call Me Mister; Reykjavik – The Weekend That Changed the World; Game, Set & Match; Last Bus to Woodstock; Countdown to War; Agatha Christie's Poirot; Inspector Morse; Medics; Prime Suspect: Inner Circles.*
Films: *Bismark;* Trevor Graham in *Stop-Over Forever;* Dr Borden in *Ghost Story; Destination Treason; Davey Jones' Locker; Act of Murder; Give My Regards to Broad Street; Our Exploits at West Pole;* Kowal in *Eminent Domain.* Address: c/o London Management. Lives in London. m. Diana; 2 s. Gavin, Mark.

BATTLEY, David

David Battley. Actor.
TV: *BBC-3; Second City Reports; Alice in Wonderland; One Man, One Boat, One Girl; A Man in the Zoo; Moll Fanders; Rutland Weekend Television* (1975-6); Bill in *The Good Life* (Christmas special,

Anthony Bate

1977); Took & Co; Much Ado about Nothing; Supergran; The Climber (series); Comrade Dad (series); Relative Strangers (two series, 1985-7); Dramarama; The Beiderbecke Affair; Little and Large; One Foot in the Grave; Gordon the Gopher; The Paul Merton Show; The Darling Buds of May; The Bill; Minder; The 10%ers; Lovejoy; All Quiet on the Preston Front; As Time Goes By; Mr Bean; Sharpe.
Films: The Bells of Hell Go Tingalingaling; Hotel Paradiso; That's Your Funeral; Quilp; The London Connection; SOS Titanic; Krull. Address: c/o Scott Marshall.

David Battley

BAXTER, Lynsey
Lynsey Baxter. Actress. Stage plays include As You Like It and The Devil's Disciple (both RSC).
TV: The Prime of Miss Jean Brodie; The Devil's Crown; Knifedge; Accidental Death; To the Lighthouse; Partners in Crime; The Gentle Touch; Horizon; Real Life; Succubus; Bust; Hedgehog Wedding; Starlings; Punishment Without Crime; After the War; Saracen; Goldeneye; Act of Will (mini-series); Chancer; Seduction – Ultimate Object of Desire; But Beautiful; Snakes and Ladders; The Grass Arena; Remember; Zorro; Bella in Clarissa; Natural Lies; Boon; Clea in The Mushroom Picker; The Darling Buds of May; Broken Lives; The Trial of Lord Lucan; The Night Show (Without Walls); BUGS; Pie in the Sky.
Films: Ernestina Freeman in The French Lieutenant's Woman; Real Life; The Girl in a Swing; The Pleasure Principle; The Moment; The Return of I Spy; Le Blanc avec Lunettes; The Cold Light of Day; Madalena in The Grass Arena. Address: c/o ICM.

Lynsey Baxter

BAXTER, Sally
Sally Baxter. Actress. Trained at the Bristol Old Vic Theatre School.
TV: Lisa O'Shea in Albion Market (1985-6); French Fields; Que Sera; Rainy Day Woman; Home Is the Sailor; Out on the Floor; Beau Geste; On the Line; Maggie Daniels in Anna Lee (series); Cadfael. Address: c/o Stephen Hatton. Lives in West London. m. 1981 actor Philip Jackson (qv); 1 s. George, 1 d. Amy.

BAYLDON, Geoffrey
Geoffrey Bayldon. Actor. b. Leeds, 7 January 1924. Trained at the Old Vic Theatre School.
TV: Z Cars; Danton; Black Beauty; An Age of Kings; The Massingham Affair; The Victorians; Nicholas Nickleby; Under Western Eyes; Platonov; The Wood Demon; title role in Catweazle; The Avengers; The Saint; Devenish; Alice through the Looking Glass; Abide with Me; QB VII (TVM); Edward the Seventh; Tales of the Unexpected; The Trial of Lady Chatterley; Just Desserts; The Venlo Incident; The Crowman in Worzel Gummidge; All Creatures Great and Small; Bergerac; Worzel Gummidge Down Under; Juliet Bravo; Hallelujah; There Comes a Time; This Office Life; Doctor Who; Ganglion in Blott on the Landscape (series); All Passion Spent; Star Cops; Cause Célèbre; The Return of Sherlock Holmes; The Storyteller; Pisces Connection; The Tenth Man (TVM); The Chronicles of Narnia; Little Pig Robinson; Casualty; Campion; Soldier Soldier; Last of the Summer Wine; Pie in the Sky; Wycliffe.
Films: The Beggar's Opera; The Stranger Left No Card; Three Cases of Murder; A Night to Remember; Dracula; The Camp on Blood Island; The Two-Headed Spy; Whirlpool; Idle on Parade; Yesterday's Enemy; The Rough and the Smooth; Libel; Suspect; The Day They Robbed the Bank of England; Cone of Silence; Greyfriars Bobby; Bomb in the High Street; The Webster Boy; The Prince and the Pauper; The Amorous Prawn; The Longest Day; Jigsaw; 55 Days at Peking; Becket; A Jolly Bad Fellow; King Rat; Dead Man's Chest; Life at the Top; Where the Spies Are; Sky West and Crooked; To Sir, with Love; Assignment K; Two a Penny; Casino Royale; A Dandy in Aspic; Inspector Clouseau; The Bush Baby; Otley; Frankenstein Must Be Destroyed; The Raging Moon; Fade Out; Say Hello to Yesterday; Scrooge; The House That Dripped Blood; The Magnificent Seven Deadly Sins; Asylum; Au Pair Girls; Tales from the Crypt; Gawain and the Green Knight; Steptoe and Son Ride Again; The Slipper and the Rose; The Pink Panther Strikes Again; Charleston; Porridge; Bullshot; Madame Sousatzka; The Necessary Love. Address: c/o Joy Jameson. Lives in Barnes, south-west London. Hobbies: 'Watching the garden grow!'

Sally Baxter

Geoffrey Bayldon

BEACH, Ann
Ann Beach. Actress/Singer. b. Wolverhampton, Staffordshire, 7 June 1938. Trained at RADA.
TV: James and the Giant Peach; The Rag Trade; Steptoe and Son; This Year's Model; Brecht on Brecht; Fred Bassett (voice-over); Jackanory (storyteller); Rainbow (storyteller); Nanny; Pilgrim's Way; Only When I Laugh; Tandoori Nights; The History of Mr Polly; Timothy's Salad Days; Diary of a Nobody; The Vanishing Army; A Bit of a Lift; Rising Damp; The Winslow Boy; Cranford; A Bouquet of Barbed Wire; The Widowing of Mrs Holroyd; The Great Glass Hive; The Government Inspector; Special Duties; Service Not Included; Villa Maroc; Rasputin; Blodwen, Home from Rachel's Marriage; That Uncertain Feeling; Sonia Barratt in Fresh Fields; Brookside; French Fields; A Question of Attribution (TVM); Land of Hope and Gloria; Selected Exits; Gwyn Thomas; The Lifeboat; The Bill; Two Golden Balls; Stick with Me, Kid.
Films: Polly Garter in Under Milk Wood; Hotel Paradiso; On the Fiddle; City of the Dead; Never Mind the Quality, Feel the Width; Mrs Sowerberry in Oliver Twist; King Ralph. Address: c/o Barry Brown & Partner. Lives in North London. m. TV producer-director Francis Coleman; 2 d. actresses Charlotte Coleman (qv) and Lisa Coleman (qv). Pets: One dog, two cats. Hobbies: Music, painting, travel, camcorder.

Ann Beach

Stephanie Beacham

BEACHAM, Stephanie

Stephanie Beacham. Actress. b. Casablanca, 28 February 1949. Trained at RADA.
TV: Mary, Queen of Scots, in *The Queen's Traitor* (début, 1967); *The Saint; Love Story; Armchair Theatre; Public Eye; Callan; Jason King; Sentimental Education; Tales of Piccadilly; UFO; Marked Personal; Jane Eyre; Napoleon and Love; Prometheus; Hadleigh; Forget-Me-Not; The Old and the Young; Singular Life of Albert Nobbs; An Audience Called Edouard; Tenko; Sorrell & Son;* title role in *Connie* (series); Sable Colby in *The Colbys* and *Dynasty; Lucky Chances* (mini-series); *The Lilac Bus; Napoleon and Josephine;* Mrs Elizabeth Peacock in *Cluedo;* Sabina Quarles in *Danielle Steel's Secrets* (TVM); Molly Carter in *Jilly Cooper's Riders* (mini-series); *Foreign Affair;* Dr Kristin Westphalen in *seaQuest DSV* (series); *No Bananas.*
Films: *The Games; Tam Lin* (UK title *The Devil's Widow*); *The Nightcomers; Dracula AD1972; The Aries Computer; Blue Movie Blackmail; And Now the Screaming Starts; Schizo; Mafia Junction; House of Mortal Sin; Inseminoid; The Wolves of Willoughby Chase; Troop Beverly Hills; Harry and Harriet.*
Address: c/o Peters Fraser & Dunlop. Lives in Malibu, California. m. actor John McEnery (qv) (dis); 2 d. Phoebe, Chloe. Partner: Cameraman Steve Silver.

Jeremy Beadle

BEADLE, Jeremy

Jeremy James Anthony Gibson Beadle. Presenter/Writer. b. Hackney, East London, 12 April 1948. Has been a ringmaster for Gerry Cottle's Circus.
TV: *Deceivers; Eureka; Fun Factory; Definition; Game for a Laugh; Beadle's About* (series, 1986-); *People Do the Funniest Things; Chain Letters; Born Lucky; Beadle's Box of Tricks; You've Been Framed!* (series, 1990-); *You've Been Framed! Late!; Beadle's About Compilation; It's Beadle; Beadle's Daredevils; The Inside Track... on Parenting; Beadle's Hot Shots* (one-off and series); *You've Been Framed! Special; Christmas You've Been Framed!; You've Been Framed! Christmas Special.* As writer: *Lucky Numbers; You Must Be Joking; Under Manning; April Fool; Ultra Quiz.* As producer: *Pop the Question.*
Books: *Today's the Day; Outlawed Inventions* (with Chris Winn); *Book of Lists* (contributor).
Address: c/o MPC Entertainment. Lives in London. m. Susan; 1 s. Leo, 3 d. Clare, Cassandra, Bonnie. Pets: A cat.

Oliver Beamish

BEAMISH, Oliver

Oliver Beamish. Actor. Trained at the Manchester Polytechnic School of Theatre. Stage plays include *Fuente Ovejuna, Ghetto* (both National Theatre) and *Blood Brothers* (Lyric Theatre).
TV: *Brookside; Agatha Christie's Poirot; The Darling Buds of May;* Richard Willmore in *Coronation Street;* Hedges in *Stay Lucky.*
Radio: *The Jew of Malta* (BBC Radio 3); *Fair-Play* (BBC Radio 4).
Address: c/o John Markham Associates.

Sean Bean

BEAN, Sean

Sean Bean. Actor. b. Sheffield, South Yorkshire, 17 April 1958. Trained at RADA. RSC stage roles include Starveling in *A Midsummer Night's Dream*, Spencer in *The Fair Maid of the West* and Romeo in *Romeo and Juliet.*
TV: *The True Bride; Samson and Delilah; The Fifteen Streets; Small Zones; My Kingdom for a Horse; In the Border Country* (4-Play); *The Loser; Wedded; Tell Me That You Love Me; Prince;* Lovelace in *Clarissa* (series); Alex Bailey in *Inspector Morse: Absolute Conviction;* Micky McAvoy in *Fool's Gold* (TVM); Oliver Mellors in *Lady Chatterley* (series, 1993); Richard Sharpe in *Sharpe's Rifles, Sharpe's Eagle, Sharpe's Company, Sharpe's Enemy, Sharpe's Honour, Sharpe's Gold, Sharpe's Battle, Sharpe's Sword, Sharpe's Regiment, Sharpe's Siege* and *Sharpe's Mission;* Paul in *A Woman's Guide to Adultery* (mini-series); *The Contenders* (narrator); *Jacob* (The Bible); The Earl of Fenton in *Scarlett* (mini-series).
Films: *Winter Flight; War Requiem; Windprints;* Brendan in *Stormy Monday;* Tadgh McCabe in *The Field;* Carver Doone in *Lorna Doone;* Renuncio in *Caravaggio;* Sean Miller in *Patriot Games; Shopping; Black Beauty; GoldenEye; When Saturday Comes.*
Address: c/o ICM. Lives in North London. m. actress Melanie Hill (qv); 2 d. Lorna, Molly.

Maureen Beattie

BEATTIE, Maureen

Maureen Beattie. Actress. b. Bundorran, Co Donegal, Ireland. Trained at the Royal Scottish Academy of Music and Drama. Started with four years at Dundee Rep and the Royal Lyceum Theatre, Edinburgh, where she played Rosalind in *As You Like It*, Pegeen Mike in *Playboy of the Western World*, Titania in *A Midsummer Night's Dream*, Varya in *The Cherry Orchard* and Anitra in *Peer Gynt.*
TV: *The Lost Tribe; The Daftie; The Donegals; The People versus Scott; City Lights; The Long Roads; The Campbells; Taggart;* Staff Nurse Sandra Nicholl in *Casualty* (29 episodes); defence barrister Gemma Marshall in *The Chief;* Vanda in *All Night Long* (series); Kathleen Leigh in *The Bill;* Beattie in *Ruffian Hearts* (Love Bites).
Address: c/o Peter Browne Management. Lives in London. Single. Hobbies: Reading, writing, cooking, cake decorating, flamenco dancing.

BEAVIS, Ivan

Ivan Beavis. Actor. b. Liverpool, 22 April 1926. After three years in Fleet Air Arm (1943-6), joined Price Waterhouse accountants' Manchester office, then became company accountant for Industrial Models, Manchester. While convalescing from TB, started amateur dramatics, finishing with Little Theatre Guilds Unnamed Society, Manchester, before turning professional. RSC roles include Leonato in *Much Ado about Nothing*, Agamemnon in *Troilus and Cressida*, Lovewit in *The Alchemist* and Montague in *Romeo and Juliet*.

TV: *Skyport; Knight Errant; Biggles; The Army Game; Famous Trials;* Harry Hewitt in *Coronation Street; Z Cars; Crown Court; Special Branch; The Liver Birds; No Honestly; The Onedin Line; The Enigma Files; Jury; Juliet Bravo; Charters and Caldicott; Shine on Harvey Moon; Truckers; The Return of the Antelope;* Ben Leverett in *Paradise Postponed; The Bill; Casualty.*

Address: c/o Michael Ladkin Personal Management. Lives in Northampton. m. 27 October 1956 teacher Kathleen Atkins (sep); 1 d. Hilary, 1 s. Michael. Hobbies: Crosswords, reading.

Ivan Beavis

BECK, Robert

Robert Beck. Actor. b. Chiswick, West London, 1 August 1970. Gained a BA (Hons) in theatre arts from the University of Surrey. Trained at the Arts Educational School. Voted Sexiest English Star by *Playgirl* readers (1993) and Best Looking Man on Television by *TVTimes* readers (1994). Stage roles include Alan Strang in *Equus* (Theatre Museum, London), Dromio of Ephesus in *The Comedy of Errors*, Paul Morel in *Sons and Lovers* (both national tours), Romeo in *Romeo and Juliet* (Citizens' Theatre, Glasgow) and Algernon in *The Importance of Being Earnest* (Leatherhead).

TV: Harris in *Three Men in Another Boat;* Peter Harrison in *Brookside* (1992-3); Dan in *The Upper Hand* (series, 1995); *Surprise, Surprise.*

Films: Nathan in *Pressing Engagement.*

Radio: Graham in *Are You from the Bugle?* (BBC Radio 4). Address: c/o Langford Associates. Lives in London. Single. Hobbies: Sport (football, hockey, tennis), watching films.

Robert Beck

BECKINSALE, Kate

Kate Beckinsale. Actress. Daughter of actor Richard Beckinsale and actress Judy Loe (qv). Stage roles include Nina in *The Seagull* (national tour)

TV: *One Against the Wind; Rachel's Dream; Devices and Desires;* Thea Hahn in *Anna Lee — Headcase* (pilot, 1993); Flora Poste in *Cold Comfort Farm.*

Films: Hero in *Much Ado about Nothing; The Prince of Jutland; Uncovered; Marie Louise; Haunted.* Address: c/o ICM.

Kate Beckinsale

BEENY, Christopher

Christopher Beeny. Actor. b. London, 7 July 1941. Danced with the Ballet Rambert at the age of six. Trained at the Arts Educational School and RADA. Stage plays include *Run for Your Wife, Bedroom Farce, Move Over, Mrs Markham, Boeing, Boeing, One of Our Howls Is Missing, Local Affairs, How the Other Half Loves, The Long, the Short and the Tall, Stop the World I Want to Get Off* and *Present Laughter* (all national tours).

TV: Lennie Grove in *The Grove Family* (1954-7, from the age of 12); *Dixon of Dock Green; Emergency — Ward 10; The Plane Makers; Armchair Theatre; Z Cars; Softly Softly;* Edward in *Upstairs, Downstairs* (1971-5); *The Rivals of Sherlock Holmes; Whodunnit?; Play of the Week;* Geoffrey in *Miss Jones and Son* (two series, 1977-8); Tony in *The Rag Trade* (two series, 1977-8); Grandad, Billy in *In Loving Memory* (six series, 1979-86); *Play Away.*

Films: *The Kidnappers; The Long Memory; Trouble in Store; Child's Play; Doctor in Distress.* Address: c/o Paul du Fer Associates. Lives in Hastings, East Sussex. m. 1st (dis), 2nd singer Diana Kirkwood; 1 d. Joanne, 2 s. Richard (both from 1st m.), James (from 2nd m.).

Christopher Beeny

BELL, Ann

Ann Bell. Actress. b. Wallasey, Cheshire, 29 April 1940. Trained at RADA. Stage plays include *Say Who You Are* (Broadway).

TV: *The Midnight Family; The Saint; Callan; Mr Rose; Public Eye; Frontier; Danger Man; The Baron; Melanie; Jane Eyre; Company of Five; Uncle Vanya; The Lost Boys; Very Like a Whale; Three Sisters; Ghost Sonata; Macbeth; The Way of the World; War and Peace; For Whom the Bell Tolls;* Marion Jefferson in *Tenko;* Anitra Cyon in *Spectre* (TVM); *Resurrection; An Unofficial Rose;* Helen Stubbs in *Tumbledown* (TVM); *Christabel; Double First; Inspector Morse;* Emma in *Medics;* Lillian in *Casualty;* Gracie Ellis in *Head over Heels* (series, 1993); Lady Astwell in *Agatha Christie's Poirot;* Eve Lambert in *Anna Lee;* Marjorie Maitland in *Doctor Finlay.*

Films: Sue Chambers in *Stop-Over Forever;* Sally in *The Witches; Fahrenheit 451; To Sir, with Love; The Reckoning; The Statue; Champions.*

Address: c/o Julian Belfrage Associates. m. actor Robert Lang (qv); 1 d. Rebecca, 1 s. John.

Ann Bell

BELL, Tom

Tom Bell

Tom Bell. Actor. b. Liverpool, 1932. Trained at Bradford Civic Theatre School.
TV: *A Night Out; Cul de Sac; No Trams to Lime Street; Angels Are So Few; Be Lucky; The Virginian; The Frighteners; Hedda Gabler; Straight on Till Morning; The Samaritan; A Man without Friends; Sea Song; Death of an Informer; Horizon: Carl Jung; Play for Britain: The Proofing Season; Pope Pius XII; Caversbridge; Holocaust; Out; Blue Peter: Duke of Wellington; Hester for Example; The South Bank Show: Roald Dahl; Words of Love; Love Story: Sweet Nothings; Sons and Lovers; King's Royal; Reilly — Ace of Spies; Desert of Lies; Summer Lightning; Hard Travelling; The Detective; Unfinished Business; Hidden Talents; The Rainbow; Red King, White Knight; Chancer; Hope It Rains;* DS Bill Otley in *Prime Suspect* and *Prime Suspect 3; Angels* (single drama); *Seconds Out; Spender; Catherine Cookson's The Cinder Path; Possession; The Young Indiana Jones Chronicles; The Great Kandinsky; No Bananas.*
Films: *The Criminal; Echo of Barbara; Payroll; The Kitchen; HMS Defiant; A Prize of Arms; The L-Shaped Room; Ballad in Blue; He Who Rides a Tiger; Sands of Beersheba; In Enemy Country; The Long Day's Dying; Lock Up Your Daughters!; The Violent Enemy; All the Right Noises; Quest for Love; The Spy's Wife* (short); *Straight on Till Morning; Royal Flash; The Sailor's Return; Stronger than the Sun; The Innocent; The Magic Toyshop; Wish You Were Here; Resurrected; The Krays; Dark River.*
Address: c/o Christina Shepherd. m. Lois Dane (dis); 1 s. Aran.

BELLAMY, David

David Bellamy

David Bellamy. Botanist/Writer/Broadcaster. b. London, 18 January 1933.
TV: *Life in Our Sea; Bellamy on Botany; Bellamy's Britain; Animal Game; What on Earth Are We Doing?; Bellamy's Europe; Don't Ask Me; It's Life; It's More Life; Botanic Man; Looks Natural; Bellamy on Heathland; Up a Gum Tree; Backyard Safari; Discovery; The End of the Rainbow Show; Turning the Tide; Bellamy's Bird's Eye View; Bellamy's Hidden Country; Moa's Ark; Bellamy Rides Again; The Four Great Seasons; Colour TV; Wish You Were Here...?; Blooming Bellamy* (series, 1993); *3-D Nature Trail* (*Children in Need*, 1993); *Kingdoms in Conflict; Will's World* (Bard on the Box); *Bodycounts.*
Awards: TV: BAFTA Richard Dimbleby Award (1978). Address: c/o Jonathan Clowes. m. marine biologist Rosemary; 3 d. Henrietta, Brighid, Iseabal, 2 s. Rufus, Eoghain.

BELLINGHAM, Lynda

Lynda Bellingham

Lynda Bellingham. Actress. b. Montreal, Canada, 31 May 1948. Moved to Britain as a child. Trained at the Central School of Speech and Drama (1966-9).
TV: *Cottage to Let; Yes Honestly; Second Opinion; Don't Forget to Write;* Nurse Hilda Price in *General Hospital; Angels; The Sweeney; Z Cars;* WPC Purvis in *The Fuzz; The Pink Medicine Show; Hazell;* Gwen in *Funny Man; Mackenzie; Doctor Who;* Helen Herriot in *All Creatures Great and Small;* Faith Grayshot in *Second Thoughts* (four series); *Harum Scarum* (storyteller); *The Inside Track... on Parenting;* Mrs Lupin in *Martin Chuzzlewit;* Faith in *Faith in the Future.* TV commercials: Mum in the Oxo campaign.
Films: *Sweeney!;* Valerie in *Stand Up Virgin Soldiers; Waterloo Bridge; Handicap; Heavy Metal.*
Address: c/o Saraband Associates. m. restaurateur Nunzio Peluso; 2 s. Michael, Robbie (Robert). Pets: A collie called Star. Hobbies: Cinema, reading — 'If I ever have the time.'

BELLMAN, Gina

Gina Bellman

Gina Bellman. Actress. b. Auckland, New Zealand, 10 July 1966. Gained a theatre studies A-level.
TV: *Mussolini* (mini-series); *Sitting Targets; First Love* (play for Anglia TV's arts series *Folio*); *The Storyteller; Only Fools and Horses;* title role in *Blackeyes* (series, 1989); *Horse Opera.*
Films: *King David; Secret Friends;* Lisa in *Leon the Pig Farmer.* Address: c/o ICM.

BENJAMIN, Christopher

Christopher Benjamin

Christopher Benjamin. Actor. b. Trowbridge, Wiltshire, 27 December 1934. Trained at RADA.
TV: *The Prisoner; The Avengers; Churchill's People; Private Affairs; The Forsyte Saga; A Spy at Evening; Poldark; Doctor Who* (two series); *The Executioner; Dick Turpin; Chintz; Shoestring; Minder; A Brush with Mr Potter; Thérèse Racquin; Donkey's Years; Shine on Harvey Moon; We the Accused; It Takes a Worried Man; Holding the Fort; Nicholas Nickleby; Blott on the Landscape; Black Silk; The Caucasian Chalk Circle; Dempsey and Makepeace; The Return of Sherlock Holmes; Boon; The Diary of Anne Frank; The Refuge; The Index Has Gone Fishing; The Miser; Where There's a Will; Yes, Prime Minister; Birmingham Six Appeal; King and Castle; Charlie the Kid; Gentlemen's Club; Anything More Would Be Greedy; Saracen; Campion; Haggard; Brass; Thatcher: The Final Days; Rumpole of the Bailey; Maigret; A Likely Lad; Inspector Morse: Cherubim and Seraphim; London's Burning; Very Like a Whale; Nelly Melba; The Strauss Dynasty;* Anthony Gullmington in *Catherine Cookson's The Black Velvet Gown; Casualty; The Tomorrow People; Lovejoy; Double Dealer;* Sir William Lucas in *Pride and Prejudice.*
Films: *Brief Encounter; Hawk the Slayer; The Plague Dogs* (voice of Rowf).
Address: c/o Scott Marshall. Lives in Hampstead, North London. m. 1980 Anna Fox; 2 d. Kate, Emilia, 1 s. Sebastian. Pets: A mongrel called Poppy. Hobbies: Watching cricket and motor-racing.

BENJAMIN, Floella

Floella Benjamin. Actress/Presenter/Producer/Writer. b. Trinidad, 23 September.
TV: *Within These Walls; Crown Court; Doctor on the Go; Send in the Girls; Anansi; Angels;* Karen in *Mixed Blessings; Kids; Waterloo Sunset; The Ladies; Hole in Babylon; The Gentle Touch; Maybury; Bergerac; Strangers.* As presenter: *Play School; What's Inside; Fast Forward; Play Away; Switch on to English; How Dare You!; About Books; Lay on Five; Flo's Frolics SS (Breakfast Time); Daytime Live; A Houseful of Plants; Tree House; The Lord Mayor's Show; Playabout; Wish You Were Here...?; Hullaballoo.*
Films: *Black Joy.* Address: c/o Benjamin-Taylor Associates, 73 Palace Road, London SW2 3LB. Lives in South London. m. Keith Taylor; 1 s. Aston, 1 d. Alvina. Hobbies: Golf, keeping her children happy and 'bringing some happiness to those with sad lives'.

Floella Benjamin

BENNETT, Alan

Alan Bennett. Writer/Actor. b. Leeds, 9 May 1934.
TV: As writer: *On the Margin; An Evening With; A Day Out; Sunset across the Bay; A Little Outing; A Visit from Miss Prothero; Me, I'm Afraid of Virginia Woolf; Doris and Doreen; The Old Crowd; Afternoon Off; One Fine Day; All Day on the Sands; Our Winnie; A Woman of No Importance; Rolling Home; Marks; Say Something Happened; An Englishman Abroad; The Insurance Man; Talking Heads; 102 Boulevard Haussman; A Question of Attribution.* As actor: *Beyond the Fringe; My Father Knew Lloyd George; Sunday Night; Plato — The Drinking Party;* Augustus Hare in *Famous Gossips; Streets Ahead; On the Margin; The Alan Bennett Series; Alice in Wonderland; A Day Out;* Denis Midgley in *Intensive Care* (also writer); *The Merry Wives of Windsor;* Housemaster in *Breaking Up;* Lord Pinkrose in *Fortunes of War; Talking Heads;* Hugh Trevor-Roper in *Selling Hitler.* As presenter: *Portrait or Bust; Canvas: Alan Bennett Revisits Leeds City Art Gallery; Looks Like a Chair, Actually It's a Lavatory; Poetry in Motion.* Voice only: *Wind in the Willows* (1992); *The Long Summer* (series); *The Story Store* (series); *The Abbey with Alan Bennett* (series); *The Wind in the Willows* (1995).
Films: As writer: *Parson's Pleasure; A Private Function; Prick Up Your Ears; A Handful of Dust.* As actor: *Pleasure at Her Majesty's* (documentary); *The Secret Policeman's Other Ball;* Neville's Doctor in *Long Shot;* voice of Mock Turtle in *Dreamchild;* the Bishop in *Little Dorrit.* Address: c/o Chatto and Linnit.

Alan Bennett

BENNETT, Hywel

Hywel Bennett. Actor/Director. b. Garnant, South Wales, 8 April 1944. Brother of actor Alun Lewis (qv). After a brief spell as a school teacher, won a scholarship to train at RADA.
TV: *Unman, Wittering and Zigo; A Month in the Country; The Idiot; Romeo and Juliet; Redcap; Where the Buffalo Roam; Death of a Teddy Bear; The Sweeney; Pennies from Heaven; Strangers; Malice Aforethought; Tinker, Tailor, Soldier, Spy; Artemis 81; Coming Out; Shelley* (1979-82, 1990-92); *The Return of Shelley* (1988); *The Critic; The Consultant; Absent Friends; The Secret Agent; Frankie and Johnnie; The Twilight Zone; Checkpoint Chiswick; Age Unknown; Virtual Murder; Trust Me; A Mind to Kill* (pilot); *Casualty; Frank Stubbs Promotes; Murder Most Horrid II; Survival Special* (narrator); *Karaoke; Frontiers.*
Films: *The Family Way; Twisted Nerve; The Virgin Soldiers; The Buttercup Chain; Loot; Percy; Endless Night; It's a Two-Feet-Six-Inches-Above-the-Ground World; Alice's Adventures in Wonderland* (voice only); *Murder Elite; War Zone;* Purvis in *The Other Side of Paradise; Deadly Advice.*
Address: c/o James Sharkey Associates. m. TV presenter Cathy McGowan (dis); 1 d. Emma.

Hywel Bennett

BENNETT, Rosalind

Rosalind Sophia Bennett. Actress. b. Rochdale, Lancashire, 13 May 1966. Trained at The Drama Centre.
TV: *Heart of the Country;* Tina Wagstaff in *Coronation Street;* Rose in *Campaign; The Fear; The Facts of Life;* Pauline Wilson in *The Manageress;* Niza in *Incident in Judea; Agatha Christie's Poirot;* Penny in *Shrinks;* Carmen in *Growing Rich* (series); Genevieve in *Covington Cross;* Sue in *A Statement of Affairs.*
Films: *American Roulette;* Lyn in *Vroom;* Bonnie in *Dealers;* Elisabeth in *Smack and Thistle;* Kate in *The Grass Arena; Halcyon Days;* Eleanor in *Restoration.* Address: c/o ICM. Lives in North London. Partner: Actor Linus Roache (qv). Pets: Two cats called Shakti and Henry. Hobbies: Travel, philosophy.

Rosalind Bennett

BENNETT, Tracie

Tracey Anne Bennett. Actress. b. Leigh, Lancashire, 17 June 1961. Trained at the Italia Conti Academy.
TV: *Going Out;* Sharon Gaskell in *Coronation Street; The Rector of Stiffkey; Shame; Knock-Knock; Relative Strangers;* Patsy in *Boon; Black Silk;* Cheryl in *Unnatural Causes; The Refuge;* Angie in *The Ritz;* Connie Fazackerley in *The Bretts; Alas Smith and Jones;* Miss Wilson in *Brush Strokes;* Norma in *Making Out* (three series); Monica in *Made in Heaven; The Ruth Rendell Mysteries: The Best Man to Die;* Nikki in *Rich Tea & Sympathy;* Tracy in *Joking Apart;* Mrs Howell in *All Creatures Great and Small;* Michelle in *The Upper Hand;* Stella in *The Gingerbread Girl; The Bill; Casualty;* Liz in *Next of Kin.*
Films: Tina in *Knights and Emeralds;* Ana in *Deep Red Instant Love;* Millandra in *Shirley Valentine.*
Awards: Theatre: Laurence Olivier Award as Best Supporting Actess for *She Loves Me* (1995). Address: c/o Annette Stone Associates. Lives in London. Single. Hobbies: Qualified scuba-diver, pianist.

Tracie Bennett

Timothy Bentinck

BENTINCK, Timothy

Timothy Charles Robert Noel Bentinck. Actor. b. Tasmania, 1 June 1953. Gained a BA (Hons) in history of art from the University of East Anglia. Trained at Bristol Old Vic Theatre School.

TV: Wing Cmdr John Raikes in *Strike Force;* Captain Johnson in *Smuggler;* Meech in *Tales of the Unexpected: The Stinker;* Tom Lacey in *By the Sword Divided* (20-part serial); Garth Stanford in *Griffins* (pilot); Keen in *Boon;* Baines in *Tigers of Kumaon;* Montague in *Melba* (Australian series); Mr Viren in *The Four Minute Mile* (speaking four lines of fluent Finnish); George in *Three Up, Two Down; A Tale of Two Cities* (voice-over only); *Easy Money* (composer of theme tune and incidental music only); Nigel Barrington in *Square Deal* (two series); Steve Nicholson in *Made in Heaven* (four-part series); *White House Farm Murders;* Tony Trew in *Side by Side;* Captain Murray in *Sharpe's Rifles;* Greg Mitchell in *Grange Hill;* Raikes in *Strike Force;* Phillip Drake in *Faith in the Future;* Gosling in *Kavanagh QC.*

Films: Harris in *North Sea Hijack;* Pirate in *Pirates of Penzance;* Lieutenant Flynn in *Winter Flight;* Pieter in *Success Is the Best Revenge;* Richard in *Year of the Comet.* **Radio:** David Archer in *The Archers* (1982-). **Awards:** Carleton Hobbs (BBC Drama Schools) Radio Prize (1978).

Address: c/o JM Associates. Lives in London. m. Judith Ann Emerson; 2 s. William Jack Henry, Jasper James Mellowes. Hobbies: Songwriting, inventing, computers, house renovation, writing.

Nick Berry

BERRY, Nick

Nick Berry. Actor. b. Woodford Green, Essex, 16 April 1963. Trained at the Sylvia Young Theatre School from the age of eight. Stage plays include *Oliver!* (West End) and *Why Me?* (Strand Theatre).

TV: *Dramarama: Rip It Up* and *The Purple People Eater; The Gentle Touch; Box of Delights; Cover Her Face; The Audition;* Simon 'Wicksy' Wicks in *EastEnders* (1985-90); Jac in *The Grove Family* (The Lime Grove Story); *Cluedo;* PC Nick Rowan in *Heartbeat* (six series, 1992-7); Rick Caulker in *Paparazzo* (pilot, 1995); *Respect.*

Films: *Party Party; Forever Young; Leave It to You, OK?; Tank Malling.*

Records: Singles: *Every Loser Wins* (No 1, 1986); *Heartbeat.* Address: c/o Conway, van Gelder, Robinson. Lives in Epping, Essex. m. actress Rachel Robertson; 1 s. Louis Valentine (b. 2 Apr 1995).

Suzanne Bertish

BERTISH, Suzanne

Suzanne Bertish. Actress. b. London, 7 August 1953. Half-American, half-English. Acted in RSC productions of *Nicholas Nickleby* (London and Broadway), *Othello, The Three Sisters, Twelfth Night* and *Pericles,* and in *Les Liaisons Dangereuses* and *Taking Sides* (both West End) and *Salome* (Broadway).

TV: *The Limbo Connection; Are You Watching the Mummy?; Wings of a Dove; The Three Sisters; The South Bank Show: The RSC on Tour; The Making of Nicholas Nickleby; The Life and Times of Nicholas Nickleby; To the Lighthouse; Freud; The Comedy of Errors; Rainy Day Women; Shine on Harvey Moon; Maybury; Creditors; The Lenny Henry Show; Ladies in Charge; A Day in Summer; The Katie Koerstner Story; Inspector Morse;* Margaret Harris in *15: The Life and Death of Philip Knight* (drama-doc); Rosa Klein in *Wall of Silence* (Screen One); Mirav Levison in *Love Hurts* (series, 1994); *Mr Bean; The Theosophists;* Gina in *Absolutely Fabulous; Space Precinct; The Ruby Wax Show* (director only).

Films: *Hanover Street; The Hunger; Hearts of Fire; Venice/Venice; Crimetime.* Address: c/o Kerry Gardner Management. Lives in London and New York. Single. Pets: One cat. Hobbies: Tennis.

Gillian Bevan

BEVAN, Gillian

Gillian Bevan. Actress. b. Stockport, Cheshire, 13 February. Attended Manchester Youth Theatre; trained at the Central School of Speech and Drama. Stage roles include Dorothy in *The Wizard of Oz* and Celia in *As You Like It* for the RSC and Young Phyllis in *Follies* (Shaftesbury Theatre).

TV: Lorraine in *Never the Twain;* Beryl Wainwright in *Sharon and Elsie;* Cissie Mapes in *Lost Empires; Act of Will* (mini-series); Miranda in *Shelley; No Job for a Lady; Screaming; Pie in the Sky;* Sharon in *Coppers* (Screen One); Dr Lin Pascoe in *Ghostwatch; Number Six* (Chiller); Det Supt Rose Penfold in *The Chief* (Series 5, 1995); *The Bill;* Suzanne Michaelson in *A Touch of Frost; Peak Practice.*

Radio: *Fifteen Love* (co-writer, BBC Radio 5 drama series); *No Rights — Only Wrongs* (co-writer and producer, BBC Radio 4). **Records:** *Follies; Wizard of Oz* (both original cast recordings).

Address: c/o ICM. Lives in London. m. Stephen Bailie; 1 s. Jack George. Pets: Soft-coated wheaten terrier called Dingle. Hobbies: Gardening.

Rodney Bewes

BEWES, Rodney

Rodney Bewes. Actor/Writer. b. Bingley, West Yorkshire, 27 November 1938. Trained at RADA.

TV: *The Likely Lads; Dear Mother... Love Albert* (also producer and co-writer); *Whatever Happened to the Likely Lads?; Love Story; Z Cars; Albert; Jonah and the Whale; Just Liz; Camera Club; She Stoops to Conquer; 'Tis Pity She's a Whore; My Friend Dennis* (also writer); Norman Ellerson in *Spender.*

Films: *Billy Liar; Decline and Fall; Spring and Port Wine; Dance to Your Daddy; The Likely Lads; The Spaceman and King Arthur; Saint Jack; Wildcats of St Trinian's; The Gothic Chimney.* Address: c/o Michelle Braidman Associates. m. Daphne Black; 1 d. Daisy, 3 s. Joe, Tom, Billy (triplets).

BHATTACHARJEE, Paul

Paul Bhattacharjee. Actor. Stage plays include *Murmuring Judges* (National Theatre), *Blood Wedding* (as Bridegroom, Royal Court) and *Indian Ink* (Aldwych Theatre).
TV: *A Summer's Day Dream; Sister Wife; Clubland; Black and Blue; Northern Crescent;* Jaz in *Albion Market;* Prince Javad in *Saracen;* Steve in *Here Is the News;* Reg Ferney in *Bergerac;* Said Farrukh in *Shalom Salaam;* Quereshi in *Lovebirds;* Valet in *Maigret; Maganlal;* Ranjit in *Johnny Jarvis;* Jag in *Chilli in Your Eyes;* Old Man in *Ancestral Voices;* General Dyer in *Inkalaab* (Open University); Ramiz Akhtar and Rajpal in *The Bill; Harum Scarum* (storyteller); Devinder in *Two Oranges and a Mango* (Stages).
Films: Amir in *Wild West.* Address: c/o ICM.

Paul Bhattacharjee

BIGGINS, Christopher

Christopher Biggins. Actor/Director. b. Oldham, Lancashire, 16 December 1948. Trained at Bristol Old Vic Theatre School.
TV: *Paul Temple; The Likely Lads;* Lukewarm in *Porridge; Man of Straw; Upstairs, Downstairs;* Student in *Some Mothers Do 'Ave 'Em; Kidnapped; The Brontë Connection; Dancing Princess; Jackanory; Rentaghost; Watch This Space; Brendan Chase; Shoestring;* Nero in *I Claudius,* Rev Ossie Whitworth in *Poldark; On Safari* (co-presenter); *Surprise, Surprise* (co-presenter); *Wife of the Week;* Reverend Green in *Cluedo.*
Films: *Eskimo Nell; Applause; The Rocky Horror Picture Show; The Tempest; Masada.*
Address: c/o ICM.

Christopher Biggins

BILLINGTON, Michael

Michael Billington. Actor/Writer/Teacher. b. Blackburn, Lancashire. Trained in repertory theatre and at the RSC in Stratford-upon-Avon, beginning in *Incident at Vichy* (Phoenix Theatre, 1966). A freelance teacher of method acting at the Lee Strasberg Studio, London, since 1991.
TV: Goalkeeper Neil Murray in *United!* (1966); Col Paul Foster in *UFO;* Daniel Fogarty in *The Onedin Line;* Alphons Berg in *War and Peace;* Czar Nicholas II in *Edward the Seventh;* Mr Fainall in *The Way of the World;* Freddie Hepton in *Hadleigh;* John Coogan in *The Professionals;* Col Sgt Jackson in *Spearhead;* Kenyon Jones in *Sister Dora;* Ben Adams in *Thundercloud; Hart to Hart;* Dardinay in *The Quest; Magnum PI;* Ventidius in *Antony and Cleopatra;* Philip Marlowe PI; *Gavilan; Fantasy Island; The Greatest American Hero; Today's FBI;* Tom Gibbons in *The Collectors* (series); Oscar in *Maigret; Stick with Me, Kid.*
Films: Sergei in *The Spy Who Loved Me;* Peter Hubbard in *KGB — The Secret War.* As writer: *Silver Dream Racer.* Address: c/o The Brunskill Management. Lives in London and Los Angeles. m. dancer Katherine; 1 s. child actor Michael Jr. Hobbies: Sports.

Michael Billington

BIRD, John

John Bird. Actor/Director/Writer. b. Nottingham, 22 November 1936. Acted in and directed plays at Cambridge University. Worked as assistant to the director, and later associate artistic director, at the Royal Court. West End plays include *Habeas Corpus.*
TV: *Not So Much a Programme, More a Way of Life; BBC3; Last Laugh; The Late Show; My Father Knew Lloyd George; A Series of Birds; With Bird Will Travel; John Bird/John Wells; Blue Remembered Hills; Shades of Greene; Timon of Athens; King Lear; The Falklands Factor; Marmalade Atkins; Blue Money; Oxbridge Blues; Travelling Man; A Very Peculiar Practice; Joint Account; Bejewelled;* Douglas Bromley in *El C.I.D.* (two series, 1990, 1992); John Reid in *After the Dance* (Performance); *The Motor Show* (guest reporter); Professor Plum in *Cluedo* (series, 1993); Bryan Brynford-Jones in *To Play the King* (mini-series); *Rory Bremner... Who Else?* (four series, 1993-6); *Rory Bremner's Christmas Turkey* (1994); Lewis Atterbury in *One Foot in the Grave; The Long Johns* (two series, 1995-6); *Our Hands in Your Safe* (also writer); *The Chamber* (also writer, pilot); *Rory Bremner, Apparently* (1995).
Films: *Take a Girl Like You; The Seven Per Cent Solution; Yellow Pages;* Herbert Greenslade in *30 Is a Dangerous Age, Cynthia.* Address: c/o Chatto and Linnit. Lives in Surrey. m. pianist Libby Clandon

John Bird

BIRDSALL, Jesse

Jesse Birdsall. Actor. b. Highbury, North London, 13 February 1963. Trained at the Anna Scher Theatre School. Started acting at the age of 12. RSC productions include *The Merry Wives of Windsor* and *Days of the Commune.*
TV: *A Sudden Wrench; Remembrance; Jangles; Walter* (TVM); *Who'll Be Mother?; Tales out of School;* Pete in *Annika; Minder; We'll Support You Evermore; Honeymoon; Elvis;* Marty in *The Fear; Soldier Soldier;* Julian in *Rides;* Nick in *Bunch of Five* (series, 1992); Marcus Tandy in *Eldorado* (1992-3); Mike in *Casualty; Sean's Show;* record company boss William Gilmore in *Anna Lee;* Des Carter in *Kavanagh QC;* Beckett in *BUGS* (two series, 1995-6); Dennis Worsley in *Thief Takers.*
Films: *Quadrophenia; Bloody Kids;* Peasy in *Revolution; The Ballad of Kid Divine; Shadey;* Dave in *Wish You Were Here; Getting It Right.* Address: c/o Conway, van Gelder, Robinson.

Jesse Birdsall

Cilla Black

BLACK, Cilla

Priscilla White. Presenter. b. Liverpool, 27 May 1943. A pop singer before becoming a TV presenter.
TV: *Cilla; Cilla's World of Comedy* (situation comedy); *Surprise, Surprise* (series, 1984-); *Blind Date* (11 series, 1985-96); *Cilla's Goodbye to the Eighties; Blind Date Wedding of the Year; The Best of Blind Date; Cilla's Celebration* (special, marking her 30 years in showbusiness, 1993); *Best of Blind Date; Blind Date: The Wedding and the Best of the Rest* (1994); *Blind Date — The 10th Aniversary Show* (1994); *Cilla's World* (1995).
Films: *Ferry Cross the Mersey; Work Is a Four-Letter Word.*
Books: *Step Inside* (1985); *Through the Years — My Life in Pictures* (1993).
Awards: *TVTimes* Favourite Female Personality on TV award (three consecutive years).
Address: c/o Hindworth Management. m. manager Bobby Willis; 3 s. Robert, Benjamin, Jack.

BLACKMAN, Honor

Honor Blackman

Honor Blackman. Actress. b. London, 22 August 1925. West End plays include *The Sound of Music.*
TV: *The Four Just Men; Probation Officer; Man of Honour; Ghost Squad; Top Secret;* Cathy Gale in *The Avengers* (1962-4); *The Explorer; Visit from a Stranger; Out Damned Spot; The Movie Quiz; Wind of Change; Robin's Nest; Never the Twain; The Secret Adversary* (TVM); *Lace* (mini-series); *The First Modern Olympics* (mini-series); *Minder on the Orient Express* (TVM); *Doctor Who; William Tell* (US title *Crossbow*); *Voice of the Heart* (mini-series); Laura West in *The Upper Hand* (six series, 1990-5).
Films: *Daughter of Darkness; Fame Is the Spur; Quartet; A Boy, a Girl and a Bike; Conspirator; Diamond City; So Long at the Fair; Green Grow the Rushes; Come Die My Love; The Rainbow Jacket; The Yellow Robe; The Delavine Affair; Diplomatic Passport; The Glass Tomb; Breakaway; Suspended Alibi; You Pay Your Money; Account Rendered; Danger List* (short); *A Night to Remember; The Square Peg; A Matter of Who; Serena; A Sense of Belonging; Jason and the Argonauts;* Pussy Galore in *Goldfinger; Life at the Top; The Secret of My Success; Moment to Moment; A Twist of Sand; Shalako; The Struggle for Rome; Twinky; The Struggle for Rome II; The Virgin and the Gypsy; The Last Grenade; Fright; Something Big; To the Devil a Daughter; Summer Rain; Age of Innocence; The Cat and the Canary.*
Address: c/o Michael Ladkin Personal Management. m. Maurice Kaufmann; 1 d. Lottie, 1 s. Barnaby.

BLAIR, David

David Blair

David Blair. Actor. b. Surrey, 19 April 1973. Trained at the Guildhall School of Music and Drama.
TV: Simon in *The Bill;* Stuart in *Island* (series, 1995).
Address: c/o Dennis Lyne Agency. Single. Hobbies: Collecting Asterix books.

BLAIR, Isla

Isla Blair-Hill. Actress. b. South India, 29 September 1944. Trained at RADA. West End plays include *Popkiss, A Funny Thing Happened on the Way to the Forum* and *Henry IV.*
TV: Sarah in *The Liars;* Daphne in *Present Laughter; The Dickie Henderson Show; The Avengers; The Saint; Department S;* Linda in *The Doctors; Jason King; The Three Princes;* Female Alien in *Space 1999; The Crezz;* title role in *Jean Brodie* (Open University); Caroline in *A Legacy; Quiller;* Lady Caroline in *When the Boat Comes In; Blake's 7; Celebration; Wilde Alliance; Forgotten Love; Songs; Only When I Laugh;* Alexa in *Love Story: Alexa; An Englishman's Castle;* Flora in *The History Man;* Laura in *The Bounder* (two series); Jenny in *The Beggar's Opera; Doctor Who; Storybook International* (narrator); *Crown Court; Six Centuries of Verse;* Elizabeth in *Off Peak; Poppyland; Taggart; The Tennis Court; C.A.T.S. Eyes; King and Castle; Boogie Outlaws; Bookie;* Mrs Hawkins in *Treasure Island* (TVM); Ruth in *Mother Love; Haggard;* Katherine Dunbar in *The Advocates* (two series); Caroline in *Boon;* Maggie in *The Good Guys;* Jenny Wilson in *Inspector Morse: Cherubim and Seraphim;* Caroline Lime in *The Darling Buds of May;* Janet Wendell in *Medics;* Lavinia Martin in *Taggart: Hellfire;* Stroma Kennedy in *Doctor Finlay;* Claire Carlsen in *The Final Cut* (mini-series); Rosalie Martin in *A Touch of Frost.*

Isla Blair

Films: *Flea in Her Ear; Battle of Britain;* Lucy Paxton in *Taste the Blood of Dracula;* The Baroness in *Valmont; Indiana Jones and the Last Crusade; Real Life; The Tennis Court;* Mother Agatha in *The Monk.*
Address: c/o ICM. Lives in London. m. 1988 actor Julian Glover (qv); 1 s. Jamie. Pets: Two cats.

BLAKE, Christopher

Christopher Blake. Actor. b. London, 23 August 1949. Trained at the Central School of Speech and Drama (John Gielgud Prize winner).
TV: *Anne of Avonlea; Death or Glory Boy; Prometheus; Warship; Crown Court; Second City Firsts; Love for Lydia; The Lost Boys; The Mill on the Floss; Mixed Blessings; Alexa;* Dr Robert Price in *That's My Boy; Love's Labour's Lost; To Be the Best;* Tim Derby in *Brookside;* Chris Longford in *So Haunt Me; Casualty;* Colin Bannister in *The Bill;* Chris in *Down to Earth* (series, 1995).
Films: *No Turning Back; The Trials of Brother Webster; Aces High; Hennessy.*
Address: c/o Ken McReddie. Lives in West Sussex. m. Wendy (dis 1992); 2 d. Charlotte, Louise, 1 s. Sean (from marriage). Partner: Heather Wright. Hobbies: Music, football, cricket, golf.

Christopher Blake

BLAKE, Susie

Susie Blake. Actress. b. Highgate, North London. Stage productions include *Godspell* (national tour), *The Bed before Yesterday* (Lyric Theatre), *Tonight at 8.30* (Apollo Theatre), *Snoopy* (Duchess Theatre), *Under Their Hats* (Vienna English Theatre) and *Exclusive Yarns* (West End).

TV: *Zodiac; Love School; Ghost Sonata; Comet among the Stars; Born and Bred; A Dog's Ransom; Russ Abbot's Madhouse; The Russ Abbot Christmas Show; How to Present a Case – Alice in Wonderland and Self; The Stanley Baxter Show; Noel Gay's Music; 6 for Gold, King's Road; Victoria Wood – As Seen on TV; The Laughter Show; Russ Abbot Bonanza; Paradise Postponed; Thank You Miss Jones; Barrymore Plus; The Jim Davidson Show; Star Terk II;* Jackie in *Singles* (four series); *Alcoholics; The Gang Show; Blore, MP; Victoria Wood: Mens Sana in Thingummy Doodah* and *We'd Quite Like to Apologise;* Mrs Jerebohm in *The Darling Buds of May;* Fay Morgan in *The Wail of the Banshee;* Susan Hopkins in *A Year in Provence;* Mrs Inglid in *One Foot in the Grave* (Series 1); *Victoria Wood's All Day Breakfast; Paradise Road* (presenter); *Mud* (two series, 1994-5); *Return to Blood River* (ScreenPlay); Libby Hughes in *Wake Up with...* (pilot); *Fierce Creatures; Eleven Men against Eleven;* Louise in *April Fool's Day.*

Films: *Prick Up Your Ears.*

Address: c/o James Sharkey Associates. Lives in Surrey. m. actor Martin Potter; 1 s. Ben.

Susie Blake

BLAKISTON, Caroline

Caroline Blakiston. Actress. b. London, 13 February 1933. Trained at RADA.

TV: *The Avengers; Emergency – Ward 10; The Saint; The Forsyte Saga; The Caesars; Wives and Daughters; Saturday, Sunday, Monday; Kids; Raffles; The Racing Game; The Prince Regent; The Mallens; Crown Court; Private Schultz;* Mme Thenardier in *Les Misérables* (TVM); *Shoestring; Nanny;* Lady Patience Hardacre in *Brass* (two series, 1983, 1990); *Charters and Caldicott; Mr Palfrey of Westminster; Agatha Christie's Miss Marple; The Refuge;* Scarlett in *Rides* (two series, 1992-3); Adele in *Mulberry;* Natasha Lee in *Harry; The Memoirs of Sherlock Holmes;* Margaret in *As Time Goes By.*

Films: *The Idol; The Magic Christian; Sunday, Bloody Sunday; Yanks; Return of the Jedi; The Fourth Protocol.* Address: c/o Chatto and Linnit. m. actor Russell Hunter (qv) (dis); 1 s. Adam, 1 d. Charlotte.

Caroline Blakiston

BLANCH, Dennis

Dennis Blanch. Actor. b. Barnet, Hertfordshire, 4 February 1947. Trained at Mountview Theatre School.

TV: *Sunday Night Theatre; Fraud Squad; Thriller; Van Der Valk; Villains; New Scotland Yard; The Sweeney; Dad's Army; No Honestly; Warship; General Hospital; The Fenn Street Gang;* Det Con Willis in *The XYY Man* and *Strangers; Sherlock Holmes; The Naked Civil Servant; Upstairs; Downstairs; Bulman; Give Us a Break; Grange Hill;* Derek Warner in *Emmerdale Farm; One by One;* Jim Latimer in *Emmerdale;* Pallister in *Demob* (series, 1993); Tom Gordon in *Heartbeat; Chandler & Co; The Bill.*

Films: *The Spy Who Loved Me; Permission to Kill; The Eagle Has Landed; International Velvet.*

Address: c/o John Markham Associates. m. Carol Wilks; 1 s. David.

Dennis Blanch

BLEASDALE, Alan

Alan Bleasdale. Writer. b. Liverpool, 1946. Worked as a schoolteacher becoming a full-time writer. West End stage plays include *Are You Lonesome Tonight?* and *Having a Ball.*

TV: *Early to Bed; Television Club; Watch Words; Scully's New Year's Eve; The Black Stuff* (Play for Today); *The Muscle Market* (Play for Today), *Boys from the Blackstuff* (series, 1983), *Scully; The Monocled Mutineer* (series, 1986); *G.B.H.* (series, 1991); *Julie Walters & Friends; Alan Bleasdale Presents* (producer, series, 1994); *Jake's Progress* (serial, 1995).

Films: *No Surrender* (winner, Critics' Award, Toronto Film Festival, 1984).

Books: *Scully; Who's Been Sleeping in My Bed?; Boys from the Blackstuff; No Surrender; The Monocled Mutineer.* **Awards:** TV: BAFTA, Pye Television and Broadcasting Press Guild Television awards for *Boys from the Blackstuff* (1983).

Address: c/o Lemon Unna & Durbridge. Lives in Liverpool. m. Julie; 2 s. Tim, Jamie, 1 d. Tamana.

Alan Bleasdale

BLEASDALE, Ian

Ian Bleasdale. Actor. b. Lancashire. Worked as a teacher before entering acting at the Everyman Theatre, Liverpool. Stage plays include *September in the Rain* (national tour).

TV: *Emmerdale Farm;* photographer in *Coronation Street; All Creatures Great and Small; A Sense of Guilt; Hard Cases; Andy Capp; The Adventures of Sherlock Holmes; Flying Lady; The Beiderbecke Affair;* Simon Dannerflower in *Boon;* Stan McHugh in *Brookside; First of the Summer Wine; The Ruth Rendell Mysteries: No Crying He Makes;* Joe Reilly in *Take the High Road; Brick Is Beautiful; No Job for a Lady;* Ron in *Making News* (series); Daz in *Soldier Soldier;* Josh in *Casualty* (series, 1990–); *The World of Eddie Weary; The Brittas Empire; Stay Lucky;* Roy Beamish in *The Bill;* Chief Insp Frost in *Drop the Dead Donkey; To Be the Best* (mini-series); Jimmy in *Mission Top Secret;* Gordon Briggs in *Heartbeat.*

Films: *Last Bus to Woodstock.*

Address: c/o Barry Brown & Partner. Lives in Haworth, West Yorkshire.

Ian Bleasdale

Brian Blessed

BLESSED, Brian
Brian Blessed. Actor. b. Mexborough, South Yorkshire, 9 October 1936. Worked as a steeplejack, plasterer and undertaker's assistant on leaving school. Trained at the Bristol Old Vic Theatre School.
TV: PC Fancy Smith in *Z Cars; Double Agent; The Wine of India; The Avengers; Jackanory; Public Eye; Love Story; Doctor Who; Arthur of the Britons; Lorna and Ted; The Recruiting Officer; Boy Dominic; The Three Musketeers; Twenty Years After; Hadleigh; The Half Gods; Space 1999; Justice; Brahms; Cold Comfort Farm; Georges Sand; Churchill's People; Blake's 7; I Claudius; The Aphrodite Inheritance; The Little World of Don Camillo; My Family and Other Animals; Omnibus; The Secret Agent; St Vitus Dance; Tales of the Unexpected; The Sweeney; The Hound of the Baskervilles; The Master of Ballantrae; The Last Days of Pompeii; William the Conqueror; Return to Treasure Island; War and Remembrance; Minder; The Black Adder; Boon; The Joy of Bach; The Young Person's Guide to the Orchestra; MacGyver — The Lost Treasure of Atlantis; Lovejoy; Galahad of Everest; Gorillas in the Midst of Man.*
Films: (Selection from 15): *Henry VIII and His Six Wives; Flash Gordon; Henry V; Robin Hood: Prince of Thieves; Much Ado about Nothing.* Address: c/o A.I.M. Lives in Bagshot, Surrey. m. 1st actress Anne Bomann (dis), 2nd actress Hildegard Neil; 2 d. Catherine (from 1st m.), Rosalind (from 2nd m.).

Brenda Blethyn

BLETHYN, Brenda
Brenda Anne Bottle. Actress. b. Ramsgate, Kent, 20 February 1946. Trained at Guildford School of Acting.
TV: *King Lear; Singles Weekend; The Storyteller; Tales of the Unexpected; Death of an Expert Witness; The Double Dealer; Bedroom Farce; The Shaw; Henry VI; Sheppey; Yes Minister; Claws; Floating Off; That Uncertain Feeling; The Imitation Game; Grown Ups; Chance in a Million; Alas Smith and Jones; Rumpole of the Bailey;* Erica Parsons in *The Labours of Erica; The Richest Woman in the World; Maigret; The Bullion Boys; The Buddah of Suburbia; All Good Things;* Miriam Dervish in *Outside Edge.*
Films: *The Witches; A River Runs Through It; Untitled '95.* Address: c/o ICM. Lives in Honor Oak, London. m. (dis). Partner: Michael Mayhew. Pets: Cats. Hobbies: Cycling, swimming, crosswords.

Claire Bloom

BLOOM, Claire
Patricia Claire Blume. Actress. b. London, 15 February 1931.
TV: *Cyrano de Bergerac; Caesar and Cleopatra; Romeo and Juliet; First Love; Victoria Regina; Misalliance; Beauty and the Beast; Person to Person; Checkmate; Anna Karenina; Wuthering Heights; Camera Three: Claire Bloom Reads Poetry; A Time to Love; Soldier in Love; Ivanov; An Imaginative Woman; The Legacy; Wessex Tales; In Praise of Love; Ann and Debbie; Orson Welles' Great Mysteries: Ice Storm; A Legacy; Love for Lydia; The World of Emily Dickinson; The Oresteia; Henry VIII;* Edith Galt Wilson in *Backstairs at the White House; Hamlet;* Lady Marchmain in *Brideshead Revisited; Misunderstood Monsters* (voice only); *Separate Tables; Cymbeline; Ellis Island; The Ghost Writer; The Life and Death of King John; Promises to Keep; Anna Karenina; Shadowlands; Florence Nightingale; Liberty; Hold the Dream; Anastasia: The Mystery of Anna; Queenie; Intimate Contact; Beryl Markham: A Shadow on the Sun; Oedipus the King; The Lady and the Highwayman; Time and the Conways; Women Writers; The Belle of Amherst; Vivien Leigh: Scarlett and Beyond; The Princess and the Goblin* (voice only); *The Camomile Lawn; Agatha Christie's Miss Marple: The Mirror Crack'd; It's Nothing Personal; A Village Affair.*
Films: (Selection from 33): *The Blind Goddess* (début, 1948); *Limelight; Richard III; Ballet Girl; Alexander the Great; The Brothers Karamazov; Look Back in Anger; The Spy Who Came in from the Cold; A Doll's House; Clash of the Titans; Sammy and Rosie Get Laid; Crimes and Misdemeanors.*
Address: c/o Conway, van Gelder, Robinson. m. 1st 1959 actor Rod Steiger (dis 1969), 2nd 1969 director Hillard Elkins, (dis 1972), 3rd 1990 author Philip Roth; 1 d. Ann-Justine Steiger (from 1st m.).

John Bluthal

BLUTHAL, John
John Bluthal. b. Poland, 12 August 1939.
TV: *It's a Square World* (series); Emmanuel 'Manny' Cohen in *Never Mind the Quality, Feel the Width* (Armchair Theatre 1967, series 1968-71); *City '68: The Visitors;* Spike Milligan's *Q* series; *There's a Lot of It About; Home Sweet Home; Gaslight Music Hall; Reilly — Ace of Spies; The Life and Loves of a She-Devil; Casualty; Birds of a Feather; A View from the Bridge; Design for Living; Minder; Bergerac; Rumpole of the Bailey; Freddie and Max; One Foot in the Grave; Taggart: Ring of Deceit; Inspector Morse: Twilight of the Gods; A Pinch of Snuff;* Frank Pickle in *The Vicar of Dibley* (series); *Lovejoy* .
Films: *A Hard Day's Night; Help!;* Angry Father in *The Knack… and how to get it; A Funny Thing Happened on the Way to the Forum; A Talent for Loving; Casino Royale; Never Mind the Quality, Feel the Width; The Great Magonogal; Stan and George's New Life; Death Duties; The Return of the Pink Panther; Superman III; Teeny Weenies.* Address: c/o Ken McReddie. Lives in London. m. Judyth (sep); 2 d. Nava, Lisa. Hobbies: Tennis, golf, chess.

Ross Boatman

BOATMAN, Ross
Ross Boatman. Actor. Trained at RADA (1984-6).
TV: *The Finding; All in Good Faith; Dramarama; Death of a Son;* Kevin Medhurst in *London's Burning.*

Films: *Oil and Water* (student film); *Maurice; The Storyteller.*
Address: c/o Marina Martin Associates. m. 1995 waitress Sophie.

BOHT, Jean
Jean Dance. Actress. b. Bebington, Cheshire, 6 March 1936. Trained at Liverpool Playhouse.
TV: *Sons and Lovers; Some Mothers Do 'Ave 'Em; The Sweeney; Where Adam Stood; Cranford; Arthur's Hallowed Ground; Spyship; Last of the Summer Wine; Funnyman; Boys from the Blackstuff; Scully; Juliet Bravo; I Woke Up One Morning;* Nellie Boswell in *Bread; A Perfect Spy; Agatha Christie's Miss Marple; Bergerac; The Cloning of Joanna May; Pass the Story;* Josephine in *Brighton Belles.*
Films: *Rapunzel Let Down Your Hair* (BFI); *Meddle Not with Change;* Mrs Taswell in *The Girl in a Swing;* Aunt Nell in *Distant Voices, Still Lives.* Address: c/o Peters Fraser & Dunlop. m. 1st William P Boht (dis 1970), 2nd 1970 composer Carl Davis; 2 d. Hannah Louise, Jessie Jo (both from 1st m.).

Jean Boht

BOLAM, James
James Bolam. Actor. b. Sunderland, 16 June 1938. Trained at the Central School of Speech and Drama. Stage plays include *The Kitchen, In Celebration, The Knack, A Midsummer Night's Dream, The Happy Haven, The Veterans, Treats* (all Royal Court), *The White Liars, Who Killed Agatha Christie?, Arms and the Man, Run for Your Wife, Jeffrey Bernard is Unwell* (all West End), *How's the World Treating You?* (New York) and *Wild Oats* (National Theatre).
TV: *Love on the Dole; Take Three Girls; The Rivals of Sherlock Holmes; Somerset Maugham;* Terry Collier in *The Likely Lads* (three series, 1964-6); *The Protectors;* Terry Collier in *Whatever Happened to the Likely Lads?* (two series, 1973-4, and 1974 Christmas special); *Macbeth; The Philanthropist;* Jack Ford in *When the Boat Comes In* (four series, 1976-7, 1981), *The Maze, The Limbo Connection* (Armchair Thriller); *As You Like It;* Figgis in *Only When I Laugh* (three series, 1979-81); *Shades of Darkness;* Trevor Chaplain in *The Beiderbecke Affair, The Beiderbecke Tapes* and *The Beiderbecke Connection;* Nesbitt Gunn in *Room at the Bottom* (two series, 1986, 1988); Father Matthew in *Father Matthew's Daughter* (series, 1987); title role in *Andy Capp* (series, 1988); *Executive Stress; Sticky Wickets;* Bill in *Second Thoughts* (five series, 1991-4); *First Take* (Anglia TV only); *Eleven Men against Eleven.*
Films: *The Kitchen; A Kind of Loving; The Loneliness of the Long Distance Runner; Half a Sixpence; O Lucky Man!; Straight on Till Morning; Crucible of Terror; Otley; Murder Most Foul; In Celebration; The Likely Lads; The Great Question; Clockwork Mice.*
Address: c/o ICM. Partner: Actress Susan Jameson (qv); 1 d. Lucy.

James Bolam

BOLAND, Eamon
Eamon Denis Boland. Actor. b. Manchester, 15 July 1947. Trained at Bristol Old Vic Theatre School.
TV: *A Raging Calm; Fox; Winter Sunlight; Spearhead;* Phil in *Fox;* Ken in *To Have and to Hold; Crossfire;* Dave Ashton in *Fell Tiger;* Clive in *Singles* (three series); *Coronation Street; The Beiderbecke Connection; Missing Persons; Hot Dog Wars; Frontiers; This Is David Lander;* DCI Jim Gray in *The Chief; Casualty; Hope It Rains;* Gerry Hollis in *Kinsey* (series); *Boon; The Bill; Stay Lucky; Between the Lines;* Arthur Bryant in *Law and Disorder* (series, 1994); Inspector Rossiter in *Peak Practice; Woof!; Fair Game; Massage* (Ghosts); *Harry; Pie in the Sky; The Affair* (Screen One); *The Vet;* Ralph in *Bare Necessities;* Mr Lister in *Hetty Wainthropp Investigates;* Graham Keegan in *Annie's Bar* (serial, 1996).
Films: *Business as Usual; Red Tuesday.* Address: c/o Barry Brown & Partner. Lives in Lavenham, Suffolk. 1 d. Annie Eves-Boland. Hobbies: Climbing, guitar.

Eamon Boland

BOND, Denis
Denis Bond. Actor/Writer. b. London 22 November 1952. Trained at Rose Bruford College.
TV: As actor: Ron in *Beryl's Lot* (two series); *The Cuckoo Calls; A Day on the Sands; The Knowledge; The Professionals; Don't Forget to Write;* Mervyn in *No Appointment Necessary* (series); *The Legend of Robin Hood; Jubilee;* Corporal Higgins in *It Ain't Half Hot Mum* (series); *Rings on Their Fingers;* Kelly Monteith; *Oh Happy Band; The Kenny Everett Show* (series); *The Chinese Detective; Juliet Bravo;* Mike in *Keeping Up Appearances; The Bill* (two roles). As writer: *Pipkin's; Rainbow.*
Films: Ted in *Follow Me;* Potts in *A Bridge too Far.*
Address: c/o Langford Associates. Lives in Kent. Single. Hobbies. Teaching Spanish.

Denis Bond

BOND, Philip
Philip Bond. Actor. b. Burton-on-Trent, Staffordshire.
TV: *The Onedin Line; The Barrier; Justice; Dial M for Murder; Warship; The Main Chance; Z Cars; General Hospital; Snacker; Sister Dora; Children of the New Forest; Crown Court; An Englishman's Castle; Kids; The Sandbaggers; Hedda Gabler; Shoestring; Home Is the Sailor; Cold Warrior; Travellers by Night; Only Fools and Horses; Hilary; Bergerac; The Oldest Goose in the Business; Bowen; 63 Highmere Park; Forever Green;* Duncan Strong in *Lovejoy.*
Films: *I Want What I Want; Sleep Well, My Love.* Address: c/o JGM.

Philip Bond

BOORMAN, Imogen

Imogen May Pratt Boorman. Actress. b. Pembury, Kent, 13 May 1971. Stage roles include Sally in *Map of the Heart* (Globe Theatre).

TV: Fiona Vichott in *The Tripods;* Hayley Forbes-Clinton in *Alive and Kicking* (TVM); *Lovejoy;* Fernanda in *Frost in May;* Veronica Williams in *The Ruth Rendell Mysteries;* Jenny in *The Good Guys;* Vanessa Morgan in *Coronation Street;* Clothilde in *May to December; Get Back;* Nikki Wyatt in *Casualty* (series, 1992-3); Hannah Preston in *Westbeach* (series, 1993); Lady Davina in *Limestreet.*

Films: Lorina Liddell in *DreamChild;* Tiffany in *Hellraiser 2.*

Radio: Margaret in *Sense and Sensibility* (BBC Radio 4).

Address: c/o Conway, van Gelder, Robinson. Lives in London. Partner: Jason Bristow.

Imogen Boorman

BOOTH, Connie

Connie Booth. Actress/Writer. Stage plays include *Design for Living, Company, The Glass Menagerie, Little Lies* (all West End), *Edmond (Mamet)* (Royal Court) and *Enemy of the People* (Young Vic).

TV: *Monty Python's Flying Circus;* Polly in *Fawlty Towers* (also co-writer); *The Deadly Game; Crown Court; Redundant or The Wife's Revenge; Spaghetti Two Step; Worzel Gummidge; Why Didn't They Ask Evans?; The Unmade Bed; The Glittering Prizes; Readings from Dorothy Parker; Hello Comrades; The Story of Ruth; The Hound of the Baskervilles; Past Caring; Rocket to the Moon; Voice from the Gallows; The Return of Sherlock Holmes; Floodtide; Every Breath You Take; The Ronnie Corbett Show; The World of Eddie Weary; The Greater Good;* Pat Harbinson in *Faith* (series, 1994); Miss March in *The Buccaneers* (series, 1995).

Films: *Little Lord Fauntleroy; Romance with a Double Bass; The Revolutionaries; And Now for Something Completely Different; 84 Charing Cross Road; The Return of Sherlock Holmes;* Marge in *Hawks; High Spirits;* Caroline Hartley in *American Friends;* Yvonne Chadwick in *Leon the Pig Farmer.*

Address: c/o Kate Feast Management. m. actor-writer John Cleese (qv) (dis).

Connie Booth

BOULTER, Russell

Russell Boulter. Actor. b. Liverpool, 7 April 1963. Grandson of Thirties trapeze artist Reg Boulter. Trained at LAMDA (1981-4). Acted on stage with the RSC (1985-6) in *As You Like It, The Merry Wives of Windsor, Othello, Troilus and Cressida* and *Mephisto,* plus Mickey in *Blood Brothers* (Albery Theatre).

TV: Rob Day in *Dream Kitchen;* Kevin Phillips in *Brookside* (four episodes); Chris Cameron in *Watching; Scene* (HTV); PC Alfreds in *Between the Lines;* PC Trevor Gail in *The Bill;* Roger McGarry in *The Darling Buds of May: Cast Not Your Pearls Before Swine;* Eliot Cornes in *The Life and Times of Howard McGovern;* Victor Craven in *Luv* (series, 1993); Inspector Crossley in *Heartbeat;* Freddy Bywaters in *One Little Hour* (In Suspicious Circumstances); *Watching Flocks;* DC/DS John Boulton in *The Bill;* John the Baptist in *Christmas Is Coming;* Nigel in *The Upper Hand;* Terry Martin in *Casualty.*

Radio: Mike Brennan in *Citizens.* Address: c/o Stephen Hatton Managment. Lives in London. m. Hobbies: Playing guitar, water-skiing, gardening.

Russell Boulter

BOVELL, Brian

Brian Bovell. Actor. b. London, 26 October 1959. Acted with the Royal Court Youth Theatre Group.

TV: *Best of British; The Gentle Touch; Strangers; Bulman; The Hard Word; Driving Ambition; Miracles Take Longer; Casualty; Prospects;* David Baron in *Between the Lines;* Christopher McFarlane-Grey in *Michael Winner's True Crimes;* Terry Bamtema in *A Touch of Frost: Stranger in the House;* PC Charlie Webb in *The Chief* (series, 1995); Don Walsh in *Class Act;* Tim in *Lord of Misrule* (Screen One).

Films: *Babylon; Burning an Illusion; Up High; Real Life; Playing Away.*

Address: c/o Hope & Lyne.

Brian Bovell

BOWE, John

John Wilson. Actor. b. Greasby, Wirral, Cheshire, 1 February 1950. Trained at Bristol Old Vic Theatre School. RSC productions include *The Wizard of Oz, The Taming of the Shrew, The Body, King Lear, Arden of Faversham, Thirteenth Night, As You Like It, Richard II, Hamlet, The White Guard, Captain Swing, Antony and Cleopatra* and *The Merchant of Venice.*

TV: *Warship* (series); *Remington Steele; Cyrano de Bergerac; Clem; C.A.T.S. Eyes; Hard Cases; Gran Jones; After the War; The One Game; The Bill;* Lester Woodseaves in *Precious Bane; Testimony of a Child;* Leonard Ansen in *Capital City;* George Marlow in *Prime Suspect* (mini-series, 1991); Larry Richards in *Families; Boon;* Voroshilov in *Stalin;* Robert Firman in *Trainer* (Series 2, 1992); Daniel Stern in *Body & Soul; The New Statesman;* Capt Maurice Withers in *The Inspector Alleyn Mysteries;* Bill Brodie in *Lovejoy;* DCI Reynolds in *Wall of Silence* (Screen One); Jack Booker in *Class Act* (two series, 1994-5); *The Soldier;* Lt Col Ian Jennings in *Soldier Soldier* (series, 1994); *Poldark* (series, 1996).

Films: *Resurrection;* Col Feyador in *The Living Daylights.* Address: c/o Conway, van Gelder, Robinson. Lives in Oxfordshire. m. 1st (dis), 2nd Diane (dis); 1 s. Joseph Wilson (from 1st m.). Partner: Actress Emma Harbour. Pets: Two cats, Sasher and Lucy. Hobbies: Cinema.

John Bowe

BOWEN, Jim

Jim Bowen. Comedian/Presenter. b. Heswall, Cheshire, 20 August 1937. Originally a dustbinman, labourer, driver and teacher; a deputy head in Morecambe, Lancashire, when he decided to become a comic. Turned professional, working in clubs and cabaret, after appearing on TV in *The Comedians*.
TV: *The Comedians* (début, 1973); *Muck and Brass* (acting début); *Bullseye* (host, game show, 1981-); *El C.I.D.* (acting himself, 1992); Library Attendant in *Last of the Summer Wine*; *The Comedians Christmas Cracker* (1993); *The Big Country Quest* (team captain, series, 1994).
Books: *From a Bundle of Rags* (autobiography, 1994). Address: c/o George Bartram Associates. Lives in Carnforth, Lancashire. m. Phyllis; 1 d. Susan, 1 s. Peter. Hobbies: horse-riding, boating, tennis.

Jim Bowen

BOWLER, Norman

Norman Clifford Bowler. Actor. b. London, 1 August 1932. Spent two years travelling around the world as a deckboy on an oil tanker, before becoming an actor. Trained at the City Literary Institute. Stage plays include *The Caretaker* (New York), *Death Trap* (New Zealand) and *Educating Rita* (national tour).
TV: *Harpers West One*; *Deadline Midnight*; *The Ratcatchers*; *Letters from the Dead*; Det Chief Insp Harry Hawkins in *Softly Softly* and *Softly Softly: Task Force* (1966-76); *Cousin Kit*; *Love Story*; *The Avengers*; *Mogul*; *Gideon's Way*; *The Joel Brandt Story*; *The Unusual Miss Mulberry*; *Soldier from the Wars Returning*; *Masterspy*; *Whodunnit*; *Jesus of Nazareth*; David Martin in *Park Ranger*; *It Figures*; *Maggie's Moor*; *The Square Leopard*; *A Little Silver Trumpet*; *Escape to the West*; *Into the Labyrinth*; *The Amazing Avon*; *The Winds of War*; *The Forgotten Story*; *Jamaica Inn*; *The Magic Carpet*; *Robin of Sherwood*; *Mountain Men*; *The Good Doctor*; Sam Benson in *Crossroads* (1986-7); *Casualty*; *Exeter Fire*; *The Adventures of Sherlock Holmes*; Frank Tate in *Emmerdale* (1989-); *Some Other Spring*.
Films: *Passion of Christ*; *The Grass Is Greener*; *Tom Thumb*; *Naval Patrol*; *Submarine X-1*; *Shameless*; *Von Ryan's Express*; *Julius Caesar*; *Renegade*; *The Island of Adventure*.
Address: c/o Rebecca Blond Associates/Emmerdale Production Centre. Lives in Bristol and Leeds. m. 1st (dis), 2nd Berjouhi (dis), 3rd Diane; 2 d. Caroline (from 1st m.), Tamara (from 2nd m.), 2 s. Joshua (from 1st m.), Simon (from 3rd m.). Pets: One cat. Hobbies: Walking, travelling, sailing.

Norman Bowler

BOWLES, Peter

Peter Bowles. Actor. b. London, 16 October 1936. Trained at RADA.
TV: *The Avengers* (as five different villains); *A Magnum for Schneider* (Armchair Theatre); *The Saint*; *The Prisoner*; *Isadora*; *A Thinking Man as Hero*; *Shelley*; *Wittgenstein Brett*; *Napoleon and Love*; *Good Girl*; *Space 1999*; *The Survivors*; *Churchill's People*; *Only on Sunday*; *The Crezz*; *I Claudius*; *Flint*; *Prizewinners*; Mr Justice (Guthrie) Featherstone in *Rumpole of the Bailey* (1978-); Richard De Vere in *To the Manor Born*; Archie Glover in *Only When I Laugh* (three series, 1979-80); *Vice Versa*; *The Bounder* (1982-3); Resident Magistrate in *The Irish RM* (two series); Neville Lytton in *Lytton's Diary* (also creator); *Executive Stress*; *Shadow on the Sun* (mini-series); Guy Buchanan in *Perfect Scoundrels* (also co-creator, with Bryan Murray, two series, 1991-2); George Grant in *Running Late* (Screen One).
Films: *Blow Up*; *Charge of the Light Brigade*; *Laughter in the Dark*; *Eyewitness*; *A Day in the Death of Joe Egg*; *The Offence*; *For the Love of Benji*; *The Disappearance*; *Try This for Size*.
Address: c/o London Management. m. actress Susan Bennett; 1 d. Sasha, 2 s. Guy, Adam.

Peter Bowles

BOWN, Paul

Paul Bown. Actor. b. Fenton, Staffordshire, 11 October 1957. Gained a fine arts degree and learned drama at art college.
TV: *Staying Put* (Play for Today); *Coast to Coast* (TVM); *Upline*; Malcolm in *Watching* (six series); *Reasonable Force*; *Mr Bean*; *Time Riders*; Stranger in *Last of the Summer Wine*; Vladimir Ivanov in *Heartbeat*; *The Good Sex Guide*.
Films: Julian Topc in *Morons from Outer Space*; *The Assam Garden*; *Underworld*. Address: c/o The Brunskill Management. Lives in London. m. Tracy (sep); 1 s. Alfie. Partner: Actress Lesley Dunlop (qv).

Paul Bown

BOYD, Roy

Roy Boyd. Actor. b. Croydon, Surrey, 18 August 1938. Trained at the Webber Douglas Academy. West End plays include *Treasure Island*, *Krapp's Last Tape*, *Miss Julie* and *Little Eyolf*.
TV: *Goodbye Darling*; *Colditz*; *Secret Army*; *Blake's 7*; *The Professionals*; *Minder*; *House of Men*; *Survivors*; *Treasure Island*; *The Devil's Crown*; *Pennies from Heaven*; Mr Casey in *Coronation Street*; Capt Enemy of the People; Dryden Hogben in *Emmerdale Farm*; Eddie Lee in *Crossroads*; *The Froth Arm*; *Scarf Jack*; *Dempsey and Makepeace*; Fen in *Knights of God*; *Chocky's Challenge*; *EastEnders*; *The Bill*; Gregorio in *William Tell* (US title *Crossbow*); *Duel for Love*; *The Silver Chair*; *Agatha Christie's Poirot*; Joseph Laslo in *Heartbeat*; Marner in *Natural Lies* (mini-series); *Casualty*; Tilden in *Covington Cross*.
Films: *Sitting Target*; *A Nightingale Sang in Berkeley Square*; *A Bridge Too Far*; *Tuxedo Warrior*; *Black Arrow*; *Biggles*; *Dangerous Love*; *A Hazard of Hearts*. Address: c/o Peter Browne Management. Lives in Kingston-upon-Thames, Surrey. m. Zohra; 2 s. Jonathan, Jack, 1 d. Lila. Hobbies: 'My children.'

Roy Boyd

BOYLE, Tommy

Tommy Boyd

Tommy Boyle. Actor. b. Manchester, 3 May 1948. Worked in the docks, on a building site, then joined the merchant navy, before acting in amateur theatre.
TV: *Fallen Hero; Over There: The Racing Game; The Professionals; Came the Rapper; From the Roots; The New Avengers; Summer Season; Benny Lynch; Beneath the News; The Wackers; Crown Court; Poor Girl; Raging Calm; Z Cars* (as four different villains, then a detective inspector); *A Woman Sobbing; Mrs Podmore's Car; Home and Away* (Granada TV production); *Follyfoot; Slattery's Mounted Foot; Coronation Street* (as Frank Bradley, 1970, Phil Jennings, 1990-91); *Juliet Bravo;* Raymond in *Brookside; Strangers; Bulman; Travelling Man; All at No 20; The Bill; Brick Is Beautiful; Starlings; Hard Cases; Zatchi & Zatchi; William Tell* (US title *Crossbow*); *World in Action; Watching; Coasting; Waterfront Beat;* Stephen Kendrick in *House of Cards; Taggart: Instrument of Justice; Harry;* Kenny Maguire in *Brookside.*
Films: *Chariots of Fire.* Address: c/o Roger Carey Associates. Lives in London. Hobbies: Golf.

BRABIN, Tracy

Tracy Brabin

Tracy Brabin. Actress. b. Batley, West Yorkshire. Gained a drama degree from Loughborough University.
TV: Camille in *Red Dwarf; Corners* (presenter); *But First This* (presenter); Doreen in *Hale & Pace;* Mary Mary in *Mother Goose;* Princess Balroubadour in *Aladdin;* Young Flo in *Diamonds in Brown Paper;* Sandra in *A Bit of a Do* (two series, 1989); Fran in *El C.I.D.;* Duchess of York in *The Royal Romance of Charles and Diana;* Terry in *In the Dark* (pilot); Ginny in *Outside Edge* (three series, 1994-6, Christmas special, 1995); Lou Clarke in *Peak Practice;* Tricia Armstrong in *Coronation Street.*
Address: c/o Felix De Wolfe. Lives in North London. Partner: Actor Richard Platt; 1 d. Lois.

BRACKNELL, Leah

Leah Bracknell

Leah Bracknell. Actress. b. London, 12 July 1964. Daughter of assistant film director David Bracknell. Trained at the Webber Douglas Academy (1984-7).
TV: *Dealers; The Cannon & Ball Show; The Bill; Wogan;* Zoe Tate in *Emmerdale* (1989-).
Films: *The Chiffy Kids* (Children's Film & Television Foundation serial, four episodes); *Savage Island.* Address: c/o Spotlight/Emmerdale Production Centre. 1 d. Lily. Hobbies: Reading, embroidery, travelling, eating.

BRADY, Joseph

Joseph Brady

Joseph Brady. Actor. b. Glasgow. Played small parts at the Glasgow Citizens' Theatre before training at the Glasgow College of Dramatic Art and then returning to the Citizens' Theatre. Stage plays include *1984, Golden Boy* and *Murders* (all National Theatre), and *The Seagull* (West End).
TV: PC Jock Weir in *Z Cars* (series, 1962-8); *King of the River; All in Good Faith; The Borderers* (series); *The Boy Who Wanted Peace; Stories of Orkney; View from Daniel Pike; Justice; Sutherland's Law; Class of His Own; The Main Chance; Willie Rough; Angels; Who'll Take the Low Road; The Assailants; The Prime of Miss Jean Brodie; The Famous Five; Send in the Girls; 1999; Kidnapped; Airport Chaplain;* McBlane in *The Fall and Rise of Reginald Perrin; Print Out; Time to Think; Ladykillers; If You Go Down in the Woods Today* (TVM); *House with Green Shutters; Brideshead Revisited; Scene; Song and Dance Man; Ill Fares the Land; Secret Adversary; Old Master; It Could Happen to Anybody; Marjorie and Men; Highway; Attachments; Holy City; Dramarama; Casualty* (two roles) *Take the High Road; Votes for Them; Boon; Taggart; The Ship; Tell-Tale Hearts; Dead on Arrival;* Alan Shaw and Ricky Phelan in *The Bill;* Tom's Father in *Nervous Energy* (Screen Two).
Films: *Cause for Alarm; Cry Wolf; The Fourth Protocol.* Address: c/o Bryan Drew.

BRADY, Moya

Moya Brady

Moya Brady. Actress. b. Blackpool, Lancashire. Trained at the Arts Educational School. Began her career in cabaret. Stage roles include Hedgehog in *The Magic Olympical Games Show* (National Theatre).
TV: Clare in *Road;* Ariadne ('Klepto') in *Making Out* (three series); Dinah in *Mr Wroe's Virgins* (miniseries); *Sin Bin* (Screen Two); Stacey McNally in *The Bill.*
Films: *Little Dorrit; Vroom; Life Is Sweet.* Address: c/o London Management.

BRAGG, Melvyn

Melvyn Bragg. Presenter/Editor/Writer. b. Carlisle, Cumbria, 6 October 1939. Graduated from Oxford University with an MA in modern history. Joined the BBC as a trainee (1961). BBC producer (1961-7), writer and broadcaster (1967-78), LWT head of arts (1982-90), controller of arts (1990-); Border TV deputy chairman (1985-90), chairman (1990-). Co-writer of West End musical *The Hired Man.*
TV: *Monitor* (producer); *New Release; Writers' World; Take It or Leave It* (all as editor); *In the Picture* (presenter); *Second House* (presenter-producer, 1973-7); *Read All About It* (presenter-producer, 1976-7); *The South Bank Show* and *South Bank Show Specials* (presenter-editor, 1978-); *The Literary Island; Land of the Lakes; Maria Callas: An Operatic Biography* (editor); *Richard Burton: In from the Cold; Paris Live! The French Revolution Bicentennial* (1989); *The Andrew Lloyd Webber Story; Francis*

Bacon; Seamus Heaney; *A Time to Dance* (dramatisation of own novel, mini-series); *The Late Show* (regular presenter, BBC2, 1993-4); *Without Walls: Après le Déluge; The South Bank Show Special* (on Cliff Richard, Christmas special, 1993); *The Classical Music Awards* (presenter, 1994); *Then and Now* (series, BBC2, 1994); *Without Walls Special* (interviewing Dennis Potter, 1994).
Films: *Isadora* (co-writer); *Play Dirty* (co-writer); *The Music Lovers* (writer); *Jesus Christ Superstar* (co-writer); *Clouds of Glory* (co-writer, with Ken Russell); *The Tall Guy* (appearance); *Marathon: The Flames of Peace* (writer, official feature film of the Barcelona Olympics).
Awards: TV: BAFTA Richard Dimbleby Award (1986). Address: c/o LWT. Lives in Hampstead, North London. m. 1st 1961 Marie-Elisabeth Roche (dec 1971), 2nd 1974 TV producer Catherine (Cate) Mary Haste; 2 d. Marie Elsa (from 1st m.), Alice, 1 s. Tom (both from 2nd m.).

Melvyn Bragg

BRAID, Hilda
Hilda Braid. Actress. b. Northfleet, Kent, 3 March 1930. Won a scholarship to train at RADA (Lord Lurean Award winner). RSC productions include *Richard II, King John* and *I Was Shakespeare's Double.*
TV: The Snob Wife in *The Gorge;* Louisa Chick in *Dombey and Son;* Nurse Page in *On Giant's Shoulders;* Polly in *Dick Turpin;* Florence (Mum) in *Citizen Smith* (series, 1976-8); Mrs Davies in *L for Lester;* Mrs Bright in *The Bright Side;* Tabitha in *The Two Ronnies;* Mrs Bowen in *Paying Guests;* Aunt Lily in *The Cannon & Ball Show;* Mrs Adler in *The Bill;* Vera in *Campaign;* Maria in *Hard Cases;* Renee Roper in *Campion;* Dee Dee in *Keeping It Clean;* Miss McQuigan in *Press Gang;* Grandmother in *Fantasy of Light;* Lady Fred in *You Rang, M'Lord?;* Mrs Skimpson in *One Foot in the Grave;* Mrs Larwood in *Anglo-Saxon Attitudes;* Mrs Dawson in *Don't Tell Father;* Mrs Rothschild in *Robert and Les;* Enid in *The 10%ers* (series, 1994); *Moving Story;* Hurst Minnie in *Stick with Me, Kid; CITV Birthday Bonanza* (1995).
Films: *A.D.; Wildcats of St Trinian's;* Fizziwig Guest in *Scrooge; For the Love of Ada.* Address: c/o Ken McReddie. Lives in London. m. 1954 actor Brian Badcoe (dec 1992); 1 d. Penny Ann Badcoe, 1 s. Robin John Braid Badcoe. Pets: Russian blue cat called Lennie. Hobbies: Gardening, travel.

Hilda Braid

BRAILEY, Gil
Gil Brailey. Actress. b. Liverpool. Trained at the Central School of Speech and Drama.
TV: *Harry's Game* (mini-series and edited TVM); *Hold the Back Page; Home Video; Checkpoint Chiswick; Hard Cases; Casualty; Think About Science; Stay Lucky; The Adventures of Billy Webb* (two series); June Manston in *Heartbeat; The Bill; Men of the World; Taggart: Prayer for the Dead.*
Films: *Yanks; The Samaritans.* Address: c/o Tim Scott Personal Management.

BRAKE, Patricia
Patricia Ann Brake. Actress. b. Bath, Avon, 25 June 1942. Trained at Bristol Old Vic Theatre School.
TV: *Home Tonight; Z Cars;* Sarah Foster in *Emmerdale Farm; Fat; The Bouncing Boy;* Julie Renfield in *The Ugliest Girl in Town* (series, 1972-3); *Forget Me Not;* Vicki in *Second Time Around* (two series, 1974-5); Ingrid in *Porridge* and *Going Straight;* Madeleine Bray in *Nicholas Nickleby; A Sharp Intake of Breath;* Eth in *The Glums* (*Bruce Forsyth's Big Night* and series); Millie Mason in *The Good Companions; Escape to the West; The Morecambe and Wise Show* (two series); *Speak for Yourself* (20 episodes, adult education series); Anne in *Madge; The Two Ronnies* (series, in Charlie Farley-Piggy Malone serial); *Trelawny of the Wells; Brigadista;* Cherry in *Troubles and Strife* (two series, 1985-7); Doll in *Mann's Best Friends; Me & My Girl;* Trixie in *The Refuge; The Kept Man* (pilot); *Campion; The Bill; 2point4 Children;* Gwen Lockhead in *Eldorado* (serial, 1992-3); Peg in *The Upper Hand* (series, 1995); *Casualty; A Seat on the Board.* Address: c/o Scott Marshall. m. actor Robert McBain (dis); 1 d. Hannah, 2 s. Jonathan, Angus (step-s.). Pets: Two cats. Hobbies: Doing up junk, gardening.

Gil Brailey

Patricia Brake

BRANAGH, Kenneth
Kenneth Branagh. Actor/Director. b. Belfast, 10 December 1960. Trained at RADA. With RSC for two years before founding the Renaissance Theatre Company (1987). Also a director of Renaissance Films.
TV: Jack in *The Boy in the Bush;* Billy (trilogy); *Maybury;* Charles Tansley in *To the Lighthouse; Coming Through; Ghosts; The Lady's Not for Burning;* Guy Pringle in *Fortunes of War* (series, 1987); Adult Gordon Evans in *Strange Interlude; Thompson; Look Back in Anger* (Thames Television only); *Tales of Gold* (narrator, series, 1992); *Chasing the Light* (behind-the-scenes look at making the film *Much Ado about Nothing*); *The BAFTA Production Awards* (host, 1994); *Omnibus: Gielgud – Scenes from Nine Decades* (narrator); *De Niro Meets Frankenstein; Anne Frank Remembered* (narrator); *Cinema Europe: The Other Hollywood* (narrator, series); Donal Davoren in *The Shadow of a Gunman* (Performance).
Films: Rick in *High Season;* Charles Moon in *A Month in the Country; Another Country;* title role in *Henry V* (also director, producer and screenplay writer); Mike Church/Roman Strauss in *Dead Again* (also director); *Peter's Friends* (also director); *Swan Song* (director, short); Benedick in *Much Ado about Nothing* (also director); *Mary Shelley's Frankenstein* (also director); *In the Bleak Midwinter* (writer and director only); *Othello.* **Books:** *Beginning* (autobiography). Address: c/o Marmont Management. Lives in Surrey. m. 1989 actress Emma Thompson (qv) (sep 1995).

Kenneth Branagh

BREMNER, Rory

Rory Keith Ogilvy Bremner. Satirical impressionist/Writer. b. Edinburgh, 6 April 1961. Acted in revue and cabaret while studying French and German at King's College, London, from where he gained a BA (Hons).
TV: *It'll Be Alright on the Night* (co-presenter); *Spitting Image; Now Something Else; Rory Bremner* (series, 1986-92); *Rory Bremner and the Morning After the Year Before; Winchester* (documentary, Meridian only); *Without Walls: J'Accuse — Dame Edna Everage* (presenter); *Breakfast with Frost;* cricketer Kevin Beeseley in *You Me and It* (first straight acting role, mini-series, 1993); *Rory Bremner ... Who Else?* (four series, 1993-6); *Rory Bremner's Christmas* (1993); *The Best of Rory Bremner... Who Else?; Rory Bremner's Christmas Turkey* (1994); *The Late Show* (talking about the sculpture of Scottish artist Ronald Rae); *Bremner Bulletins; Rory Bremner, Apparently; Scott of the Arms Antics.*
Radio: *Week Ending* (BBC Radio 4); *News Revue* (LBC). **Videos:** *The Best of Rory Bremner* (1989); *The Morning After the Year Before* (1993); *Rory Bremner — Creased Up* (1995).
Records: *19* (Top 20 hit single, 1985). **Awards:** Montreux Festival Press Prize (1987); British Comedy Awards Top Male Performer (1992, 1995); BAFTA Best Light Entertainment award (1994); RTS Best Light Entertainment award (1994). Address: c/o The Richard Stone Partnership. Lives in Hampshire. m. artist Susan. Hobbies: Travel, cricket, opera.

Rory Bremner

BRENHER, Matthew

Matthew Alexander Benham. Actor. b. Hammersmith, West London, 26 February 1961. Trained at Mountview Theatre School.
TV: Assassin in *Bodyguards* (pilot); Clive in *Smokey Joe's* (pilot); Gangster in *In on the Racquet, Out on the Street.*
Films: Peter in *The Search for Roger Chatto.* Address: c/o Sue Hammer Personal Management. Lives in London. Single. Hobbies: Physical culture, reading, chess, backgammon, cards.

Matthew Brenher

BRIERLEY, Roger

Roger Brierley. Actor.
TV: *When We Are Married; The Franchise Affair; A Kind of Living;* Rev Phelps in *East of Ipswich* (TVM); Drathro in *Doctor Who; Children of Dynmouth;The Bill; A Very British Coup; She-Wolf of London;* Sir Roger in *Bottom; Rumpole of the Bailey; Foreign Affairs; Lovejoy;* Disraeli in *A Business Affair;* Montague in *House of Eliott;* Sir Roderick Glossop in *Jeeves and Wooster* (two series); *Pat and Margaret;* Dr Fenton in *Seaforth;* MP for Lincoln in *The Buccaneers;* Prof Brize Watney in *Surgical Spirit;* Richard Pearson in *The Politician's Wife; The Victoria Wood Show; Chef!;* Steve Nicklin in *Expert Witness.*
Films: *The Adventures of Barry Mackenzie; Young Sherlock Holmes; Superman II; The Wicked Lady; Killing Dad; A Fish Called Wanda; Beaumarchais.* Address: c/o Barry Brown & Partner.

Roger Brierley

BRIERS, Richard

Richard Briers. Actor. b. Merton, Surrey, 14 January 1934. Trained at RADA.
TV: *Brothers in Law; Marriage Lines;* Ben Travers farces; *Tall Stories; The Norman Conquests;* Tom Good in *The Good Life* (1975-8); *The Good Neighbours* (US); *The Other One; Goodbye Mr Kent; PQ17; Ever Decreasing Circles* (four series, 1984-7); *The Aerodrome; All in Good Faith; Twelfth Night; Mr Bean; Living Dangerously* (narrator, series, 1992); *The Church Mice and the Ring* (Jackanory, storyteller); Godfrey Spry in *If You See God, Tell Him* (series, 1993); Raymond Doncaster in *Lovejoy; Playing the Dane* (Bard on the Box); *Mole's Christmas* (voice only, Christmas Day,1994); Tony in *Down to Earth* (series, 1995); *Oliver 2* (Comic Relief); The Hon Galahad Threepwood in *P G Wodehouse's Heavy Weather, The Adventures of Mole* (voice only); *Classical Music Animations* (narrator).
Films: *Fathom; All the Way Up;* Gannet in *Rentadick;* Ted Washbrook in *A Chorus of Disapproval; Henry V; Peter's Friends;* Leonato in *Much Ado about Nothing; Swan Song* (short); *Mary Shelley's Frankenstein;* Old Arthur/George in *Skallagrigg;* Claudius in *In the Bleak Midwinter.*
Address c/o Hamilton Asper Management. m. actress Ann Davies (qv); 2 d. Katy, actress Lucy.

Richard Briers

BRIGGS, Johnny

Johnny Briggs. Actor. b. Battersea, South London, 5 September 1935. Won a scholarship to train at the Italia Conti Stage Academy from the age of 12 (1947-53).
TV: *The Younger Generation; The Plane Makers; The Saint;* DS Russell in *No Hiding Place; Department S; Private Eye; Softly Softly; Z Cars; Devil's Disciple; The Man with the Power; Do Me No Favours; Mogul; The Avengers; The Persuaders; Love Thy Neighbour; My Wife Next Door; Thick as Thieves; No Honestly; Yus My Dear;* Clifford Leyton in *Crossroads;* Mike Baldwin in *Coronation Street* (1976-).
Films: *Hye and Cry Quartet; Cosh Boy* (US title *The Slasher); Doctor in the House; Second Fiddle; The Diplomatic Corpse; Doctor in Love; Carry On Regardless; The Bulldog Breed; Light Up the Sky; The Wind of Change; Sink the Bismarck!; The Wild and the Willing; HMS Defiant; Doctor in Distress; The Leather Boys; A Stitch in Time; The Devil-Ship Pirates; 633 Squadron; The Intelligence Men; Information Received; Rosie; Carry On up the Khyber; The Last Escape; Bachelor of Arts* (short); *Perfect Friday;*

Johnny Briggs

Quest for Love; Au Pair Girls; Bless This House; Love Thy Neighbour; No Honestly; Mission to Monte Carlo; The Best Pair of Legs in the Business; Naughty Wives; Secrets of a Door-to-Door Salesman; Man about the House; Bedtime with Rosie; Carry On Behind; The Office Party; Carry On England.
Awards: Pye Television Award joint winner, with William Roache (qv) and Anne Kirkbride (qv), for *Coronation Street* (1983). Address: Marina Martin Associates/Granada Television. Lives in Stourbridge, Worcestershire, and Salford Quays. m. 1st Carole (dis), 2nd Christine; 1 s. Mark, 1 d. Karen (from 1st m.), 2 d. Jennifer, Stephanie, 2 s. Michael, Anthony (from 2nd m.).

Kellie Bright

BRIGHT, Kellie
Kellie Bright. Actress. b. 1 July 1976. Trained at the Sylvia Young Theatre School. Stage roles include Young Cosette in *Les Misérables* (Palace Theatre) and Munchkin in *The Wizard of Oz* (RSC, Barbican).
TV: Sally Simpkins in *T-Bag and the Revenge of the Tea Set, T-Bag and the Pearls of Wisdom* and *T-Bag's Christmas Carol;* Daphne Grove in *The Grove Family* (The Lime Grove Story); *Family Fortunes;* Nettles in *Maid Marian and Her Merry Men; Jim'll Fix It; Gimme 5;* Joanna Burrows in *The Upper Hand* (series). Address: c/o Sylvia Young Management. Single.

BRITTON, Tony
Tony Britton. Actor. b. Birmingham, 9 June 1924. Joined an amateur dramatics group while working in an estate agent's and an aircraft factory at Weston-super-Mare, then turned professional.
TV: *Horizontal Hold* (Playhouse); *Romeo and Juliet; Six Proud Walkers; Melissa; Father Dear Father; The Nearly Man; The Dame of Sark; Buffet; Robin's Nest* (four series, 1977-81); *Strangers and Brothers;* Dr Toby Latimer in *Don't Wait Up* (series, 1983-90); Vivian Bancroft in *Don't Tell Father* (series).
Films: *Dr Syn, Alias the Scarecrow; There's a Girl in My Soup; Forbush and the Penguins; Sunday, Bloody Sunday; The Day of the Jackal; Nightwatch.* Address: c/o Chatto and Linnit. m. 1st Ruth (dis), 2nd Danish sculptress Eve Birkefeldt (sep); 2 d. Cherry, TV presenter Fern (from 1st m.), 1 s. Jasper.

Tony Britton

BROOKE, Judy
Judith Sarah Brooke. Actress. b. Leeds, 21 February 1970. Began professional career while at school and trained in violin, piano and singing. Professional début aged 14 in *Our Day Out* (Leeds Playhouse).
TV: Yvonne in *The Beiderbecke Tapes* and *The Beiderbecke Connection; Living with AIDS;* Sharell in *How to Be Cool;* optician's receptionist Anita (1989) and Paula Maxwell (1992, 1994) in *Coronation Street;* Susie Thornton in *All Creatures Great and Small* (two episodes); Aileen in *Goodbye and I Hope We Meet Again* (4-Play); Rita Hebdon in *The World of Eddie Weary;* Jackie in *Coasting;* Paula Barker in *Emmerdale;* child-abuse victim in a *World in Action* reconstruction; Bev in *Children's Ward;* Anne in *A Time to Dance* (mini-series); Belinda in *Harry; Solutions* (voice-over); Julie Colman in *Medics* (Series 4, 1994); Rebecca Dawson in *Peak Practice;* Diana Byrne/Angela Sykes in *Wycliffe;* Julie Stanton in *Heartbeat.* Address: c/o Barbara Pemberton Associates. Lives in Leeds. Single. Pets: Two dogs, Ben and Molly. Hobbies: Walking the dogs, working out at the gym, decorating new home – 'not gardening!'

Judy Brooke

BROOKE-TAYLOR, Tim
Timothy Julian Brooke-Taylor. Actor/Writer. b. Buxton, Derbyshire, 17 July 1940. Hon LLD, St Andrews University. Began career in the Cambridge Footlights revue while at university. West End stage plays include *The Unvarnished Truth, Run for Your Wife* and *The Philanthropist.*
TV: *The Ed Sullivan Show; The Tonight Show; At Last the 1948 Show; Marty; Broaden Your Mind; On the Braden Beat; His and Hers; The Rough with the Smooth; The Goodies* (series, 1970-81); *Hello Cheeky; Shades of Greene; Does the Team Think?; Me & My Girl; You Must Be the Husband;* Trevor in *The Upper Hand; Bananaman* (voice only).
Films: *Twelve Plus One; The Statue; Willy Wonka and the Chocolate Factory.*
Radio: *I'm Sorry I'll Read That Again; I'm Sorry I Haven't a Clue; Hello Cheeky; Does the Team Think?; Loose Ends; The Fame Game; Hoax.*
Books: *Rule Britannia; Tim Brooke-Taylor's Golf Bag; Tim Brooke-Taylor's Cricket Box.* Address: c/o Jill Foster. Lives in Berkshire. m. 1968 Christine Wheadon; 2 s. Ben, Edward. Pets: A cat called Muriel. Hobbies: Golf, travel.

Tim Brooke-Taylor

BROOKS, Nikki
Nicola Ashton. Actress/Singer. b. Nottingham, 29 June 1968. Trained at the Kaleidoscope Theatre Company, Julie Beech Stage School, Nottinghamshire, Morrison's School of Dance, and Hoofers Jazz Centre. Early stage experience as principal dancer in *The Leslie Crowther Show.*
TV: *Make Believe; The Secret Diary of Adrian Mole Aged 13¾; The Kid; The Marlows; The Fear;* Rosie Harding in *Crossroads; Inspector Morse; The Bill;* Hilandra in *Jupiter Moon* (BSB); *EastEnders.*
Films: *Crosta Run; Bloody New Year.*
Records: Single: *Cheers to the Two of You.* Address: c/o CCA Management. Lives in Hampstead, North London. Single. Hobbies: Cinema, theatre, reading, travelling, exercise.

Nikki Brooks

Ray Brooks

BROOKS, Ray

Ray Brooks. Actor. b. Brighton, East Sussex, 20 April 1939. Became an ASM in repertory theatre at the age of 16. West End plays include *Snap*, *Absent Friends* and *And a Nightingale*.
TV: *Cathy Come Home; Gideon's Way; Taxi; Raging Moon; The Office Party* (Armchair Theatre); *The Cherry Orchard; Softly Softly; The Expert; Doomwatch; Wittgenstein II* (Black and Blue); *Brotherly Love; Couples; Two People; A Touch of the Tiny Hacketts* (Aspects of Love); *That Woman Is Wrecking Our Marriage; Death of an Expert Witness; An Office Romance; Pennywise; Rumpole of the Bailey;* Robby Box in *Big Deal* (two series, 1984-5); Max Wild in *Running Wild* (two series, 1987, 1989); title role in *The World of Eddie Weary; Cine Memo* (narrator); *Woof!; Jackanory;* Tom Hollingsworth in *Growing Pains* (two series, 1992-3); *Rupert* (voice only); *King Rollo* (voice only); *Scrimpers* (presenter, series).
Films: *HMS Defiant; Play It Cool; Some People; The Knack... and how to get it; Daleks — Invasion Earth 2150 AD; The Last Grenade; Assassin; Alice's Adventures in Wonderland; Tiffany Jones*.
Records: Album: *Lend Me Some of Your Time* (singing his own compositions).
Address: c/o Marmont Management. m. doctor's receptionist Sadie; 1 d. Emma, 2 s. William, Tom.

Paul Broughton

BROUGHTON, Paul

Paul John Broughton. Actor. b. Liverpool, 21 January 1957. Worked in various jobs, from bingo-caller to golf caddy, before training as a mature student at Sandown College of Performing Arts, Liverpool.
TV: Pete in *Needle; The Bill; Between the Lines; Terraces; Minder;* Dave Elliott in *Peak Practice; Casualty;* Eddie Banks in *Brookside* (1994-6); Baron's Steward in *Cadfael*.
Radio: *The British Bulldog*.
Address: c/o Scott Marshall. Lives in Liverpool m. 1975 Sandra; 1 s. Paul, 2 d. Collette, Kate. Pets: A cockateel called Billy and a cat called Tilly Mint. Hobbies: Golf, nightclubs, football.

Duggie Brown

BROWN, Duggie

Duggie Brown. Actor/Comedian. b. Rotherham, South Yorkshire, 7 August 1940. Brother of actress Lynne Perrie (née Jean Dudley, qv). Played guitar with The Four Imps pop group for 12 years, before turning professional as a comedian, then actor.
TV: *6.5 Special; The Good Old Days; The Comedians; The Wheeltappers and Shunters Social Club; Slattery's Mounted Foot; Leeds United;* Eric in *Say Goodnight to Grandma; Days of Hope;* Pit Manager in *The Price of Coal; The House That Jack Built; Bring on the Girls;* Harvey Hall in *Take My Wife; Crown Court; The Combination;* Phil Strong in *The Enigma Files; The Cuckoo Waltz* (acting himself); *My Brother's Keeper;* Ernest Garstang in *The Glamour Girls;* Billy Clough in *The Hard Word;* Hugh in *Combination* (Play for Today); Mr Tansy and Brian Appleby in *All Creatures Great and Small* (two roles); *The Bill; Minder;* Boat Owner in *Stay Lucky;* Wilfred in *Heartbeat; Rik Mayall Presents; The Comedians Christmas Cracker;* Ray Piper in *Brookside;* Joe Badger in *The Final Cut* (mini-series); *Ellington*.
Films: Tom the Milkman in *Kes;* Duggie the Hairdresser in *For the Love of Ada*.
Address: c/o ATS Casting. Lives near Doncaster, South Yorkshire. m. Jackie Ann; 1 d. Jacqueline.

June Brown

BROWN, June

June Brown. Actress. b. Creeting St Mary, nr Needham Market, Suffolk, 16 February 1927. Served with the Wrens after the Second World War until 1949, working as a cinema operator showing films to servicemen. Trained at the Old Vic Theatre School. Stage plays include *Macbeth*, *Hamlet* and *Twelfth Night* (all RSC).
TV: *Dixon of Dock Green; Coronation Street; The Sweeney; Oranges and Lemons; Home and Away* (Granada Television series); *Churchill's People; South Riding; The Prince and the Pauper; Angels; The Duchess of Duke Street; Couples; Shining Pyramid; A Christmas Carol; Shadows; The Ladies; The Hunchback of Notre Dame* (TVM); *Letters Home; Now and Then; Young at Heart; The Bill; Minder; Lace; Relative Strangers;* Dot Cotton in *EastEnders* (1985-93); *Doctor Who; Bed* (Performance, 1995).
Films: *The Fourteen; Sherlock Holmes; Nijinski.* Address: c/o Saraband Associates. Lives in Croydon, Surrey m. 1st actor John Garley (dec), 2nd actor Robert Arnold; 5 children, plus Chloe (dec).

Susan Brown

BROWN, Susan

Susan Elisabeth Brown. Actress. b. Bristol, 6 May 1946. Trained at the Rose Bruford College of Speech and Drama. Stage plays include *Road, Shirley, Downfall, Gibraltar Strait* (all Royal Court), plus RSC productions of *Easter* (as Mrs Hoyst), *Romeo and Juliet* (as Nurse) and *Richard III* (as Queen Elizabeth.)
TV: *Within These Walls; The Kids from 47A; Fanny by Gaslight* (series); *The Hanged Man* (series); *The Duchess of Duke Street;* Connie Clayton in *Coronation Street;* Helen in *Road,* Ruby in *Andy Capp;* Tracy in *Loving Hazel;* Avril in *Making Out* (series); *Murder Weekend;* Mrs Elliott in *The Chain; This Is David Lander, The Bill* (several roles); *The Paradise Club; The Sharp End;* Linda in *Prime Suspect;* Maria in *Nona* (Performance); Bill in *Absolute Hell* (Performance); Mrs Tribbly in *Prince* (TVM); *Children's Ward;* Mary Cox in *The Bill;* Julie Russell in *Casualty;* Brenda Harrison in *The Ruth Rendell Mysteries: Kissing the Gunner's Daughter;* Barbara in *Stay Lucky;* Janie Pickett in *The Bill;* Mrs Dimmock in *Love-*

joy; Cilla in *September Song* (series); Betsy Heppelwhite in *A Pinch of Snuff* (mini-series); Jackie in *EastEnders;* Maggie Belcher in *The Riff Raff Element* (series); Stella Boxley in *A Touch of Frost.*
Films: *The Year of the Bodyguard;* Mrs Evans in *Hope and Glory.*
Address: c/o Barry Brown & Partner. Lives in London. Partner: Toby Whale. Pets: A cat called Lucy.
Hobbies: Cooking, travel, spending time at her house in France.

BROWNE, Eithne

Eithne Browne. Actress. b. Huyton, Liverpool, 25 November 1954. Stage plays include *Blood Brothers* (Lyric Theatre, understudying Barbara Dickson and stepping in to play the role of Mrs Johnstone in the West End for more than 50 shows) and *Stags and Hens* (as Maureen, Young Vic Theatre).
TV: *Albion Market;* Mrs McClusky in *The Practice; The Marksman;* Chrissy Rogers in *Brookside.*
Films: Trisha Lane in *Business as Usual.* Address: c/o LWA. 1 s. Neil.

Eithne Browne

BROWNING, Michael

Michael Browning. Actor. b. Ongar, Essex, 15 May 1930. Trained at RADA. Stage plays include *The Visit* (Royalty Theatre) and *Lysistrata* (Duke of York's Theatre).
TV: Buster in *Harriet's Back in Town;* Harrison in *Airline;* Dr Banks in *Take Three Women;* Counsel for the Defence in *Minder;* Mathews in *The Bill;* Fawcett in *Emmerdale Farm;* Henry Carter in *Crossroads;* Dr Haydock in *Agatha Christie's Miss Marple: Murder at the Vicarage;* George Newton in *Coronation Street;* Sir John Ross Gifford in *Take the High Road* (1987-90); Tom Fisher in *Trainer;* Philip Stone in *The Bill.*
Films: Jenkins in *The Four Feathers;* Philip in *Night without Pity.*
Address: c/o Vernon Conway. Lives in London. Single. Hobbies: Travel, photography, sports.

Michael Browning

BRUNSON, Michael

Michael Brunson. Journalist. b. Norwich, Norfolk, 12 August 1940. After studying at Queen's College, Oxford, spent a year teaching in Sierra Leone with the British Voluntary Service Overseas, then joined the BBC in 1964, working both with the overseas service and BBC radio, before switching to TV. Has reported the General Elections of 1979, 1983, 1987 and 1992.
TV: *24 Hours* (two years); ITN reporter (1968-72), Washington correspondent (1972-7, including Watergate and the 1976 presidential election campaign), European correspondent (1978-80), diplomatic editor (1980-6), political editor (1986-). Address: c/o ITN. m. Susan; 2 s. Jonathan, Robin.

Michael Brunson

BRYAN, Dora

Dora Broadbent. Actress. b. Southport, Lancashire, 7 February 1923. Stage début as a child in pantomime (1935).
TV: *Both Ends Meet; Triangle; Foxy Lady; Dora; Rookery Nook;* Hester Blewett in *Casualty;* Mum in *On the Up;* Molly Bramley in *Frank Stubbs Promotes; Blow Your Mind: Wise Children;* Jane Thompson in *Heartbeat;* Kitty Flitcroft in *Mother's Ruin* (series, 1994); Simone in *Boon;* Maureen Stevens in *Moving Story; Bed* (Performance).
Films: *Odd Man Out; The Fallen Idol; No Room at the Inn; Now Barabbas Was a Robber...; Adam and Evelyne* (US title *Adam and Evalyn*); *Once upon a Dream; The Perfect Woman; The Interrupted Journey; Traveller's Joy; The Blue Lamp; The Cure for Love; No Trace; Something in the City; Files from Scotland Yard; The Quiet Woman; Circle of Danger; Scarlet Thread; No Highway* (US title *No Highway in the Sky*); *High Treason; Lady Godiva Rides Again; Whispering Smith Hits London* (US title *Whispering Smith versus Scotland Yard*); *13 East Street; Gift Horse* (US title *Glory at Sea*); *Time Gentlemen Please!; Mother Riley Meets the Vampire* (US title *Vampire over London*); *Made in Heaven; The Ringer; Miss Robin Hood; Women of Twilight* (US title *Twilight Women*); *Street Corner* (US title *Both Sides of the Law*); *The Fake; The Intruder; You Know What Sailors Are; Fast and Loose; The Crowded Day; Harmony Lane* (short); *Mad about Men; As Long as They're Happy; See How They Run; You Lucky People; Cockleshell Heroes; The Green Man; Child in the House; The Man Who Wouldn't Talk; Hello London!; Carry On Sergeant; Operation Bullshine; Desert Mice; Follow That Horse!; The Night We Got the Bird; A Taste of Honey; The Great St Trinian's Train Robbery; The Sandwich Man; Two a Penny; Hands of the Ripper; Up the Front; Screamtime* (video release only); *Apartment Zero.*
Books: *According to Dora.* **Awards:** Films: BFA Award for *A Taste of Honey.* Address: c/o James Sharkey Associates. m. William Lawton; 1 d. Georgina, 2 adopted s. Daniel, William.

Dora Bryan

BUCHANAN, Neil

Neil Buchanan. Presenter/Writer. b. Liverpool, 11 October 1961. Previously a musician and songwriter with the heavy-metal group Marseille.
TV: *Number 73; Motormouth; Motormouth 2; Art Attack* (also co-deviser, series); *Finders Keepers* (series); *Animal Crazy* (series); *Back with the Goggles; Simply the Best Awards* (host); *Disney Club.*
Records: Albums: *Marseille; Red, White and Slightly Blue* (both with group Marseille).
Address: c/o Severn Management Services. m. Niki Woodcock; 1 d. Molly.

Neil Buchanan

BUFFERY, Kate

Katharine Buffery. Actress. b. Cambridge, 23 July 1957. Sister of theatre director Bill Buffery. Trained at RADA. Acted on stage with the RSC in *As You Like It, The Winter's Tale, Golden Girls, The Party* and *Love's Labour's Lost*, and with the National Theatre in *Pravda, Hamlet* and *Wreck'd Eggs*.
TV: Charlotte in *Call Me Mister; Come Back; Love after Lunch; The Miser; Wish Me Luck* (three series); *Strife; The Ruth Rendell Mysteries: A Taste of Death;* Winifred Inger in *The Rainbow; Frankenstein's Baby; Perseus and the Gorgon;* Stella in *The Orchid House* (mini-series); *Boon; Sam Saturday;* Florrie Donnelly in *The Man Who Cried* (mini-series, 1993); *Agatha Christie's Poirot; Medics;* Madeleine Anderson in *Faith in the Future* (series, 1995); Kate Moore in *Circles of Deceit; The Ruth Rendell Mysteries*.
Films: *Dark River; The Long Way Home; Swing Kids; Halcyon Days.* Address: c/o ICM. Lives in Tufnell Park, North London. m. Roger Michell; 1 s. Harry. Hobbies: Painting, music.

Kate Buffery

BULLMORE, Amelia

Amelia Mary Bullmore. Actress. b. London, 31 January 1964. Gained a drama degree from Manchester University (1983-6).Stage plays include *Inadmissible Evidence* (National Theatre).
TV: *The Other Side of Midnight* (with the Red Stockings Theatre Company); Steph Barnes in *Coronation Street* (1990-1, 1992, 1995); Beth in *Stuck on You* (Comedy Playhouse, 1993); Catriona Bilborough in *Cracker* (Series 1 only, 1993); Ros in *Faith* (series, 1994); Caroline Poole in *Frontiers*.
Films: *The Wide Sargasso Sea.* Address: c/o Barbara Pemberton Associates. Lives in London. m. Paul Higgins. Hobbies: Cooking, running.

Amelia Bullmore

BULLOCH, Jeremy

Jeremy Andrew Bulloch. Actor. b. Market Harborough, Leicestershire, 16 February 1945. Trained at the Corona Stage Academy (1957-63). Acted as a child. Son Robbie played his son on TV in *Robin of Sherwood*. Eldest son Christian appeared on TV when younger. West End plays include *I Love You Mrs Patterson, Every Other Evening, What Every Woman Knows* and *Dangerous Obsession*.
TV: *Doctor Who; Billy Bunter; The Chequered Flag;* Philip Cooper in *The Newcomers* (three years); Paul Schroeder in *Jenny's War; The Master of Ballantrae; The Treasure Seekers; Chocky;* Hotspur in *Richard II; The Professionals; George and Mildred;* Rob Illingworth in *Agony; The Captain's Table;* Brother Gabriel in *All in Good Faith;* Edward of Wickham in *Robin of Sherwood; Kiss Me Goodnight; Boon;* George in *After Henry; Casualty;* Television Director Paul in *Singles; The Bill;* Harry Enfield's Dad in *Harry Enfield's Television Programme;* Barry Higgs in *Sloggers* (two series, 1994-5); *Faith;* Pearson in *Do the Right Thing;* Scott in *The Scott Inquiry;* Jack Bertrand in *The Chief;* Jacklin in *Dangerfield*.
Films: *Spare the Rod; A French Mistress; Las Leandras; The Devil's Agent; Play It Cool; Summer Holiday; Hoffman; The Virgin and the Gypsy; Mary, Queen of Scots; O Lucky Man!; Escape from the Dark;* Smithers (Q's assistant) in *The Spy Who Loved Me* and *Octopussy; The Lady Vanishes;* Boba Fett in *Star Wars, The Empire Strikes Back* and *Return of the Jedi;* Smithers in *For Your Eyes Only; Swing Kids.* Address: c/o Barry Brown & Partner. Lives in Tooting, South London. m. 1st 1965 Sandra (dis), 2nd 1970 Maureen; 3 s. Christian (from 1st m.), Jamie, actor Robbie (both from 2nd m.). Pets: A cat called Percy. Hobbies: Cricket, golf, gardening.

Jeremy Bulloch

BURDEN, Suzanne

Suzanne Burden. Actress. b. Yorkshire. Trained at RADA (Bronze Medal winner). Stage plays include *Piano, The Shaughraun, The Voysey Inheritance, Hedda Gabler, The White Chameleon, The Recruiting Officer* (all National Theatre), *Les Liaisons Dangereuses* and *The Winter's Tale* (both RSC).
TV: *'Tis Pity She's a Whore; Secret Orchards; The Cherry Orchard; Troilus and Cressida; An Office Romance; Sharma and Beyond; Love in a Cold Climate; Bleak House; Hard Travelling; The Rivals; Campion; Agatha Christie's Poirot;* Nicola in *A Small Dance* (TVM); Caitlin Carpenter in *Boon;* Sandra Radley in *Soldier Soldier;* Barbara Henderson in *You Me and It* (mini-series); Jo Austin in *Between the Lines;* Sister Ambrose in *A Mind to Murder;* Jennifer Holt in *The Vet* (two series, 1995-6).
Films: *Strapless; Very Like a Whale; The Devotee; Gertler.* Address: c/o ICM. Lives in London. m. carpenter Ken Franklin.

Suzanne Burden

BURDIS, Ray

Raymond John Burdis. Actor. b. London, 23 August 1958. Trained at the Anna Scher Theatre School.
TV: *Mary's Wife; Ain't Many Angels; Alice; Seconds Out; Triangle; Diamonds; Going Out; Scene: It's Different for Boys; Scum; Now and Then* (two series); *The Baker Street Boys; The Gentle Touch; The Professionals; Minder; I Thought You'd Gone; Walrus: What's It Gonna Be?; West; Dream Stuffing; The Kit Curran Radio Show; C.A.T.S. Eyes; Harem; Three Up, Two Down; The Lenny Henry Show; Ties of Blood: Invitation to a Party; Everyman: John Lennon; God's Chosen Car Park; Murder at the Farm.*
Films: *Junket 89* (professional début, 1970); *Scum; Trouble with 2B; Music Machine; Richard's Things; Gandhi.* As producer (with own company Fugitive Films): *The Reflecting Skin; The Krays.* Address: c/o Anna Scher Theatre Management. Lives in Islington, North London. m. Jacqui; 1 d. Sky.

Ray Burdis

BURGESS, John

John Burgess. Actor. Trained at RADA.
TV: *The Greeks; Together* (serial); *Murphy's Mob; Coriolanus; Love's Labour's Lost; To Have and to Hold; From the Top; The Bill; First Among Equals; Big Deal; Up Line; A Guilty Thing Surprised; Christabel; Laura and Disorder;* Mr Ludlow in *East Enders; Wiesenthal; Master of Innocents; Hale and Pace; Campion;* Dr Crocker in *The Ruth Rendell Mysteries; Medicine Through Time; Casualty; Chancer; Grange Hill; The Green Man; Agatha Christie's Poirot; Lovejoy; Josie; Sam Saturday; The House of Elliot;* David Crosbie in *Brookside.*
Films: *Give My Regards to Broad Street; Sakharov; Rosencantz and Guildenstern are Dead.*
Address: c/o David Daly Associates.

John Burgess

BURKE, Diane

Diane Burke. Actress. b. Liverpool, 17 July 1976.
TV: Took over the role of Katie Rogers in *Brookside* (1988-).
Address: c/o Mersey Television. Lives in Huyton, Liverpool. Single.

BURKE, Kathy

Kathy Burke. Actress. b. 13 June 1964. Trained at the Anna Scher Theatre School.
TV: *Educating Marmalade; The Falklands Factor; The Nation's Health; Love Kills; Eat the Rich; A Visitor from Outer Space; The Brief; Johnny Jarvis; No Problem; Round and Round; Bleak House; Past Caring; The History Trail: Plague and Fire; A Very Peculiar Practice; The Best Years of Your Life; Call Me Mister; Ladies in Charge; This Year's Model; French and Saunders; Go with Scrote; South Atlantic Raiders;* Iina Bishop in *The Last Resort* and *One Hour with Jonathan Ross; Work Experience; Set of Six; Amongst Barbarians;* Magda in *Absolutely Fabulous* (three series, 1992-5); Waynetta in *Harry Enfield's Television Programme;* Lorraine in *Casualty;* Helen in *Murder Most Horrid;* Mona Lisa in *A Word in Your Era;* Martha in *Mr Wroe's Virgins* (mini-series); *Jealousy* (The Comic Strip Presents…); *Late Licence* (presenter); *Sin Bin* (Screen Two); Sharon in *Common as Muck;* Perry, Waynetta Slob and others in *Harry Enfield and Chums* (series); *Jackanory: The Twits* (storyteller); *Oliver 2* (Comic Relief, 1995); *Life's a Bitch; Happy Days; After Miss Julie* (Performance).
Films: *Sacred Hearts; Funseekers; Sid and Nancy; Scrubbers.*
Address: c/o Stephen Hatton Mangement.

Diane Burke

BURNS, Gordon

Gordon Burns. Presenter. b. Belfast, 10 June 1942. Worked as a journalist on the *East Antrim Times, Belfast Telegraph* and BBC radio's sport department in London, before moving into television. During his career, he has interviewed seven Prime Ministers, including Edward Heath, Harold Wilson, Jim Callaghan and Margaret Thatcher. Runs a business called The Conference Factor, which introduces team-building, motivational and competitive elements to company conferences.
TV: Ulster Television (sports editor, then presenter of *UTV Reports*); *The Gordon Burns Hour* (Ulster Television); *Granada Reports* (co-presenter); *The Kick Off Match* (producer); *World in Action* (reporter); *Reports Politics* (presenter and producer, Granada TV); ITV commentator on live political party conference coverage from Blackpool for 10 years; *The Granada 500; The Krypton Factor* (host, 1977-); *Irish Angle* (two years); *A Way of Life; Password* (host, two years); *Surprise, Surprise* (presenter of Searchline feature for five years); *Situations Vacant* (BBC Northern Ireland); *Serve You Right; Future Perfect* (Meridian); *A Word in Your Ear* (host and co-deviser, quiz show, Tyne Tees Television two series, then BBC series); *Time Off* (series, Meridian only); *Treasure Trail* (host, quiz show, Meridian only); *Relatively Speaking* (host, series, 1996). **Radio:** *Sports Report; Sports Parade; Today;* BBC World Service; BBC Radio 2 show, filling in for Jimmy Young. Address: c/o Dave Warwick. Lives in Hale, Cheshire. m. Sheelagh; 1 s. TV researcher Tristun, 1 d. Anna.

Kathy Burke

BURRELL, Sheila

Sheila Burrell. Actress. b. Blackheath, south-east London, 9 May 1922. Trained at the Webber Douglas Academy. Stage plays include *Dark of the Moon, A Severed Head, West of Suez, Strange Interlude, Nuna* (all West End), *Richard II, King John* (both RSC), *The School for Scandal* (National Theatre at the Old Vic), *Salonika* (Royal Court), *Great Expectations, Marya* (both Old Vic) and *Absolute Hell* (National Theatre).
TV: *The Six Wives of Henry VIII; The Feathered Serpent; Love Lies Bleeding; Anna Karenina; Frost in May; The Tribute; Radio Pictures; Lizzie's Pictures; Gaudy Night; The Trial of Klaus Barbie; Brush Strokes; The Intercom Conspiracy; Devices and Desires; The Darling Buds of May* (two series); *The Young Indiana Jones Chronicles;* Aunt Ada Doom in *Cold Comfort Farm.*
Films: *Afraid of the Dark;* Mrs Eshton in *Jane Eyre;* Grandma Oliver in *Woodlanders.*
Address: c/o Barry Burnett Organisation. Lives in London. m. 1st actor Laurence Payne (dis 1953), 2nd David Sim; 2 s. Julius, Matthew, 1 d. Kate (all from 2nd m.).

Gordon Burns

Sheila Burrell

Malandra Burrows

BURROWS, Malandra

Malandra Elizabeth Newman. Actress. b. Woolton, Liverpool, 4 November 1966. Started dance classes at the age of two. Learned to play the violin and sang with her brother and sister, with her father accompanying them on piano. At the age of six, sang and danced regularly in the children's television talent show *Junior Showtime* and, three years later, became the youngest winner of *New Faces*. Trained at the Mabel Fletcher Drama College, Liverpool. Stage productions include *Dracula*, *Frankenstein*, *Snow White* and *Cinderella*.
TV: *Junior Showtime* (aged six); *New Faces* (winner, aged nine); *The Practice*; *Fell Tiger*; Sue and Lisa in *Brookside*; Kathy Bates/Merrick/Tate in *Emmerdale* (1985-).
Records: Single: *Just This Side of Love* (1990).
Address: c/o Emmerdale Production Centre. Lives near Leeds. Partner: Graphic designer Jonathan Armstead. Hobbies: Horse-riding, travel.

Amanda Burton

BURTON, Amanda

Amanda Burton. Actress. b. Londonderry, 10 October 1956. Moved to Manchester at the age of 18 and trained at Manchester Polytechnic's School of Theatre.
TV: *The Mersey Pirate*; Frank Best's daughter in *My Father's House*; *Thomas De Quincey*; *The Effective Manager* (Open University); Heather Haversham in *Brookside*; Margaret Daly in *Boon*; *Summer School*; *Inspector Morse*; *A Casualty of War*; *Van Der Valk*; *Stay Lucky*; *Lovejoy*; *Private Practice* (pilot); Prosecuting Counsel in *Minder*; Dr Beth Glover in *Peak Practice* (three series, 1993-5); Dr Samantha Ryan in *Silent Witness* (series, 1996).
Address: c/o ICM. Lives in London. m. 1st (dis), 2nd photographer Sven Arnstein; 2 d. Phoebe, Brid. Hobbies: Horse-riding, collecting watches.

Tyler Butterworth

BUTTERWORTH, Tyler

Tyler Butterworth. Actor. b. Redhill, Surrey, 6 February 1959. Son of actor Peter Butterworth and actress-comedienne Janet Brown. Trained at the Webber Douglas Academy.
TV: Proteus in *The Two Gentlemen of Verona*; *Ties of Blood*; *Casualty*; *Bergerac*; *Murder of a Moderate Man*; Nick in *What the Butler Saw*; *Boon*; *Singles*; *Home to Roost*; Angelo in *Mike & Angelo*; *Iphigenia at Aulis*; Reverend Candy in *The Darling Buds of May* (Series 2, 1992); Mike in *Birds of a Feather*; Eddie in *The Gingerbread Girl* (series, 1993); Rawle in *Minder*; Symonds in *The Bill*.
Films: *Consuming Passions*.
Address: c/o The Richard Stone Partnership. Lives in London. Hobbies: Walking, drawing.

Judy Buxton

BUXTON, Judy

Judy Buxton. Actress. Trained at the Rose Bruford College of Speech and Drama. West End plays include *Ghost Train*, *Baggage*, *A Murder Is Announced* (all Vaudeville Theatre), *La Ronde* (Aldwych Theatre), *The School for Scandal* (Theatre Royal, Haymarket), *Last of the Red Hot Lovers* (also Far East tour) and *Run for Your Wife* (Whitehall Theatre and Far and Middle East tour). Plus RSC productions of *Romeo and Juliet* (as Juliet), *The Merchant of Venice* (as Jessica), *The Swandown Gloves* (as Principal Boy) (all Shakespeare Memorial Theatre, Stratford-upon-Avon, and Aldwych Theatre), *The Greeks* (as Iphigenia) and *La Ronde* (as Sweet Girl) (both Aldwych Theatre only).
TV: *Dixon of Dock Green*; Nurse Shaw in *General Hospital* (83 episodes, 1972-9); *The Mike and Bernie Show*; *A Little Bit of Wisdom*; *Hunter's Walk*; *Justice*; *The Des O'Connor Show*; *Public Eye*; *A Woman's Place*; *In This House of Brede* (TVM); *Angels*; *Headmaster*; *Get Some In*; *Rising Damp*; *Wilde Alliance*; *Wodehouse Playhouse: A Certain Smile*; *I've Got a Great Idea*; *The Diary of a Nobody*; *The Harry Worth Show*; *Blake's 7*; *Quiz Kids*; *Chalk and Cheese*; *Masterspy*; Margo in *Storyboard Secrets*; Susan Protheroe in *By the Sword Divided* (two series); Joanna in *Chance in a Million*; Christine Hamer in *Bergerac*; Deborah Wyler in *Lovejoy*; Ruth Carpenter in *On the Up* (three series, 1990-2).
Films: *Medieval Society* (Gateway Educational Films); *I Don't Want to Be Born*; *The Bawdy Adventures of Tom Jones*; *Aces High*; *The Likely Lads*; *The Big Sleep*; *Sweeney!*; *Farewell My Problem*.
Address: c/o Christina Shepherd. Partner: Actor James Kerry.

Michelle Byatt

BYATT, Michelle

Michelle Marie Byatt. Actress. b. Liverpool, 3 November 1970. Sister of actress Sharon and actor Paul (qv) Byatt. Trained at the Merseyside Dance and Drama Centre and the London Studio Centre. Stage plays include *All Flesh Is Grass*, *Yer Dancing?*, *Innocent Mistress*, *Katie Krackernuts*, *The Pied Piper of Hamelin* and *Oliver!*
TV: Nikki White in *Brookside*; *Watching*; *World in Action* (scene reconstructing classroom violence); *Fun Factory*; *Coasting*; Karen in *Backup*. TV commercials: Allied Carpets; Clearasil.
Films: Jude in *Business as Usual*.
Address: c/o Nigel Martin-Smith Personal Management. Lives in Liverpool. Single. Hobbies: Keep-fit, going out, meeting people, reading.

BYATT, Paul
Paul Byatt. Actor. b. Liverpool, 22 December 1971. Brother of actresses Michelle (qv) and Sharon Byatt. Trained at Liverpool Playhouse Youth Theatre.
TV: Mike Dixon in *Brookside* (1990-); *Big Chance.* Address: c/o Chiltern Casting/Mersey Television.

Paul Byatt

BYRNE, Patsy
Patricia Anne Thirza Byrne. Actress. b. Ashford, Kent, 13 July 1933. Gained a diploma in theatre arts from the Rose Bruford College of Speech and Drama; taught speech and drama. Stage plays include *The Caucasian Chalk Circle, The Cherry Orchard* and *As You Like It* (all RSC).
TV: *Androcles and the Lion;* Dimyastra in *The Cherry Orchard;* Audrey in *As You Like It; Z Cars* (two roles); *The Cellar and the Almond Tree; Doomwatch; Hunter's Walk; Hazell; All Creatures Great and Small; Platonov; I Claudius; Just William;* Nurse in *Romeo and Juliet; Eleanor Marx Trilogy; My Son, My Son; The Devil's Crown;* Mrs Nubbles in *The Old Curiosity Shop; Help!* (four series); *The Little Silver Trumpet; Together; Worlds Beyond; Educating Marmalade; Tales of the Unexpected; Miracles Take Longer; Danger! Marmalade at Work; Bleak House;* Nursie in *Blackadder II; Hotel du Lac; The Dorothy L Sayers Mysteries: Strong Prison;* Mrs Stoneway in *Watching* (seven series, 1987-93); *A Taste for Death; Inspector Morse;* Nursie in *Blackadder's Christmas Carol; The Silver Chair* (series); *Talking About Science* (two series); *Playdays; Adam Bede; In Sickness and in Health;* Peggy in *2point4 Children; Early Travellers in North America* (documentary series); Maid Marian's Mother in *Maid Marian and Her Merry Men;* Mrs Mitchell in *The Inspector Alleyn Mysteries; Hard Times; Casualty; Delta Waves.*
Films: *The Ruling Class; Till Death Us Do Part; The Class of Miss McMichael; Britannia Hospital; Return of the Soldier; Mr Love; Stealing Heaven; Hannah's War; The Higher Mortals.*
Address: c/o Crouch Associates. Lives in London. m. Patrick John Seccombe; 6 step-children. Hobbies: Reading, travelling, gardening.

Patsy Byrne

BYRNE, Peter
Peter James Byrne. Actor/Director. b. London, 29 January 1928. Trained at the Italia Conti Stage Academy. West End plays include *The Blue Lamp, Caste, Boeing-Boeing, There's a Girl in My Soup, Deadly Nightcap, The Business of Murder* and *September Tide.*
TV: David Mason in *The Pattern of Marriage* (début, 1953); *The New Canadians;* Lt Bover in *Mutiny at Spithead;* PC, then Det Sgt, Andy Crawford in *Dixon of Dock Green* (series, 1955-75); *Three Live Wires; For the Love of Mike;* Justin in *Blake's 7; The Cinderella Gang;* Uncle Arthur in *Bluebirds* (series); Derek in *Bread* (1988-91).
Films: *The Case of the Second Shot; The Large Rope; Reach for the Sky; Raising the Wind; Carry On Cabby.* Address: c/o Michael Ladkin Personal Management. Lives in London. m.1st (dis), 2nd Renée Helen. Hobbies: Swimming, astronomy, golf.

Peter Byrne

BYRON, Kathleen
Kathleen Byron. Actress. b. London, 11 January 1923. Trained at the Old Vic Theatre School. Wartime work as censor for the Ministry of Information.
TV: *Emergency – Ward 10; The Avengers; Who Is Sylvia?; Countercrime; That Woman Is Wrecking Our Marriage; Emmerdale Farm; The Golden Bowl; Portrait of a Lady; Moonstone; Heidi; Tales of the Supernatural; The Professionals; Minder; General Hospital; Hedda Gabler; Together; Unity; Nancy Astor; Angels; From a Far Country: Pope John Paul II* (TVM); *Dearly Beloved; Gentlemen and Players; Casualty; Portrait of a Marriage; The Bill;* Agnes Burley in *Moon and Son;* Mrs Marker in *The Memoirs of Sherlock Holmes.*
Films: *The Young Mr Pitt; The Silver Fleet; A Matter of Life and Death* (US title *Stairway to Heaven*); *Black Narcissus; The Small Back Room; Madness of the Heart; The Reluctant Widow; Prelude to Fame; Tom Brown's Schooldays; Scarlet Thread; Life in Her Hands; Hell Is Sold Out; Four Days; The House in the Square* (US title *I'll Never Forget You*); *My Death Is a Mockery; The Gambler and the Lady; Young Bess; Star of My Night; The Night of the Full Moon; Profile; Secret Venturo; Handcuffs London; Hand in Hand; Night of the Eagle* (US title *Burn Witch Burn*); *Hammerhead; Wolfshead; The Legend of Robin Hood; Private Road; Twins of Evil; Nothing but the Night; Craze; The Abdication; One of Our Dinosaurs Is Missing; The Elephant Man.*
Address: c/o L'Epine Smith & Carney Associates. m. writer Alaric Jacob; 1 d. Harriet, 1 s. Jasper.

Kathleen Byron

CAESAR, Johnny
John Michael Caesar. Actor. b. South Shields, 30 October 1936. Worked as an engineer in Tyneside shipyards before turning professional as a guitarist in pop groups, then as an actor and stand-up comic.
TV: *The Stars Look Down; Coronation Street; Crown Court; The Practice; Truckers;* Bill Middleton in *Emmerdale; Stay Lucky; Catherine Cookson's The Gambling Man;* Eric Burdon in *Our Friends in the North.*
Records: Composer of *Come Home, Rhondda Boy,* recorded by Tom Jones (1981).
Address: c/o ATS Casting. m. Dianne; 1 s. James. Hobbies: DIY, metal-detecting.

Johnny Caesar

Michael Caine

CAINE, Michael

Maurice Joseph Micklewhite. Actor. b. Bermondsey, South London, 14 March 1933.

TV: *Z Cars; The Compartment; The Playmates; Hobson's Choice; Funny Noises with Their Mouths; The Way with Reggie; Luck of the Draw; Hamlet; The Other Man; Jack the Ripper* (mini-series); *Jekyll & Hyde* (TVM); *Hollywood Legends* (subject); *Live for Peace — A Royal Gala* (VE Day, 1995).

Films: *A Hill in Korea; How to Murder a Rich Uncle; The Key; Carve Her Name with Pride; The Two-Headed Spy; Blind Spot; Danger Within; Passport to Shame; Foxhole in Cairo; The Bulldog Breed; The Day the Earth Caught Fire; Solo for Sparrow; The Wrong Arm of the Law; Zulu; The Ipcress File; Gambit; Alfie; The Wrong Box; Funeral in Berlin; Hurry Sundown; Billion Dollar Brain; Woman Times Seven; Tonite Let's All Make Love in London; Deadfall; Play Dirty; The Magus; The Italian Job; Battle of Britain; Too Late the Hero; The Last Valley; Simon, Simon* (short); *Get Carter; Zee and Co; Kidnapped; Pulp; Sleuth; The Marseille Contract; The Black Windmill; The Wilby Conspiracy; The Man Who Would Be King; The Romantic Englishwoman; Peeper; Harry and Walter Go to New York; The Eagle Has Landed; A Bridge Too Far; Silver Bears; The Swarm; California Suite; Ashanti; Beyond the Poseidon Adventure; The Island; Dressed to Kill; The Hand; Escape to Victory; Deathtrap; The Jigsaw Man; Educating Rita; Beyond the Limit* (UK title *The Honorary Consul*); *Blame It on Rio; Water; The Holcroft Covenant; Sweet Liberty; Half Moon Street; The Whistle Blower; Mona Lisa; Hannah and Her Sisters; Surrender; The Fourth Protocol; Hero* (narrator only); *Jaws — The Revenge; John Huston; Without a Clue; Dirty Rotten Scoundrels; A Shock to the System; Bullseye!; Mr Destiny; Noises Off; Blue Ice.*

Books: *Not Many People Know That; Not Many People Know This Either; Not Many People Know This Is 1988; Not Many People Know This about the Movies.* Address: c/o ICM. m. 1st actress Patricia Haines, 2nd Shakira; 2 d. Dominique (from 1st m.), Natasha.

Beverley Callard

CALLARD, Beverley

Beverley Callard. Actress. b. Leeds. Previously acted under the name Beverley Sowden.

TV: *The Book Tower;* Angie Richards in *Emmerdale Farm; Dear Ladies; Hell's Bells; The Practice; Will You Love Me Tomorrow* (TVM); *Coronation Street* (June Dewhurst 1984, Liz McDonald 1989-). Address: c/o Spotlight/Granada Television. m. 1st (dis), 2nd Steve;1 d. actress Rebecca (qv) (from 1st m.), 1 s. Joshua.

Rebecca Callard

CALLARD, Rebecca

Rebecca Sowden. Actress. Daughter of actress Beverley Callard (qv). Previously acted under the name Rebecca Sowden.

TV: *The Book Tower;* Bev in *How We Used to Live;* Becky in *Emmerdale Farm;* Gwen in *Private: Keep Out!;* title role in *Marianne's Dreams;* Lucy in *Scab; All Creatures Great and Small;* Sukie in *My Brother Jonathan* (series); *Will You Love Me Tomorrow* (TVM); Frances in *The Cottingly Fairies;* Fiona in *Children's Ward* (series); Maggie in *Act of Will;* Arrietty in *The Borrowers* (two series); Vicki in *September Song;* Jazz Elliott in *Peak Practice;* Lucy Cornwell in *Bonjour la Classe* (series); *Casualty; Band of Gold.*

Films: Emma in *The Wolves of Willoughby Chase.*

Address: c/o Barbara Pemberton Associates. Lives in North London. Single.

Simon Callow

CALLOW, Simon

Simon Callow. Actor/Director/Writer. b. London, 15 June 1949. Graduated from Queens College, Belfast. Trained at The Drama Centre.

TV: *Wings of Song; Instant Enlightenment inc VAT; Man of Destiny; La Ronda; All the World's a Stage; The Dybbuk;* Tom Chance in *Chance in a Million* (four series); title role in *Handel;* Hugo in *Dead Head;* Mr Micawber in *David Copperfield; Cariani and the Courtesan;* Charles Laughton (documentary); *Old Flames; Honour; Profit and Pleasure; Revolutionary; Witness;* Inspector Lestrade in *The Crucifer of Blood* (TVM); John Mortimer in *The Trials of Oz* (Performance); Vicar Ronnie in *Femme Fatale* (Screen Two); Edward Feathers in *Little Napoleons* (series, 1994); *Oscar and Me* (Wilde Night, presenter).

Films: Emanuel Schikaneder in *Amadeus; The Good Father;* Rev Beebee in *A Room with a View;* Mr Ducie in *Maurice; Manifesto; Mr & Mrs Bridge; Postcards from the Edge; Soft Top, Hard Shoulder;* Gareth in *Four Weddings and a Funeral;* Jefferson in *Paris; Victory; Le Passager Clandestin; Ace Ventura: When Nature Calls;* Charles II in *England, My England.* As director: *At Freddy's; Ballad of the Sad Café.*

Books: *Being an Actor; The Infernal Machine; Jacques and His Master; A Difficult Actor — Charles Laughton; Shooting the Actor; Acting in Restoration Comedy; Orson Welles: The Road to Xanadu.* Address: c/o Marina Martin Associates.

Jennifer Calvert

CALVERT, Jennifer

Jennifer Calvert. Actress. b. Ontario, Canada, 7 December 1963. Settled in Britain in 1984. Trained at RADA (Bronze Medal and Sherek Memorial Prize winner). Stage plays include *The Philanthropist* (national tour and West End).

TV: Cheryl Boyanowsky in *Brookside; Go Getters;* Karen Hansson in *Spatz* (two series); Delphine in

Come Home Charlie and Face Them; Nurse in *Jack the Ripper* (mini-series, 1989); Ellen in *This Boy's Story* (TVM); Michelle in *Westbeach;* Frances Katz in *The Magician;* Mrs Gurney in *The House of Eliott;* Susannah Barton in *The Knock* (two series, 1994, 1996).
Films: Gloria in *An Uncertain Thing;* Mandy Candy in *The Candy Show* (both National Film and Television School). Address: c/o David Daly Associates. Lives in London. m. Matthew.

CAMPBELL, Colin

Colin Campbell. Actor. b. Twickenham, Middlesex, 17 January 1937. Actor from the age of 11 who went on to play character parts in television, films and theatre. Performed in the RSC UK and US tours of *Nicholas Nickleby* (1985-6).
TV: David Ashton in *A Family at War* (53 episodes); barrister Simon in *Rough Justice;* Batman Jones in *The Adventures of Sherlock Holmes;* Straker in *Playthings;* Sgt Willoughby in *The Ruth Rendell Mysteries; The Bill;* Gerry in *Minder.*

Colin Campbell

Films: Reggie in *The Leather Boys; The High Bright Sun* (US title *McGuire, Go Home!;* video title *A Date with Death); Saturday Night Out;* Alf in *Bloody Kids;* Butterfly Man in *My Beautiful Laundrette;* Norman in *Nuns on the Run.* Address: c/o MGA. Lives in London. m. (dis); 2 s. Ian, Robert, 1 d. Denise. Partner: 'Danish lady friend.'

CAMPBELL, Gavin

Gavin Campbell. Actor/Presenter. b. Letchworth, Hertfordshire, 17 March 1946. Trained at the Central School of Speech and Drama. Worked with Joan Littlewood's Theatre Workshop. Stage plays include UK première of *When One Is Somebody* and a season with the RSC. Became an announcer and newsreader for BBC radio, before switching to producing until joining the long-running consumer series *That's Life!* as a reporter-presenter.

Gavin Campbell

TV: As actor: *Softly Softly; Play for Tomorrow; Department S; Vendetta; Armchair Theatre; Travel by Dark;* Aline Bauch in *Maigret.* As presenter: *That's Life!* (1982-94); *Nationwide* (reporter, 1982-4)); *South-East at Six* (reporter, BBC South East, 1982-4)); *The Gift of Life; Children of Courage; Breakfast Time* (reporter, 1983-6); *London Plus* (reporter-newsreader, BBC South East, 1985-7); *Drugwatch; Trouble in Mind; Fire Special; Children of Courage and Achievement; Crisis in Africa* (1992); *If the Worst Happens* (presenter, series, 1993); *That's Life! Summer Special* (1993); *Africa in Crisis* (1993); *Africa on a Knife Edge* (1994); *BBC Breakfast News* (reporter, 1994); *Children in Need* (presenter, 1994); *The Travel Show* (guest reporter, 1994); *Champion Children* (two series, 1995-6).
Radio: BBC Radio drama (as actor); BBC Radio 4 announcer; BBC Radio 2 newsreader and producer; *You and Yours; The Food Programme; Newsstand* (voice-over and producer).
Books: *A Family at Law* (co-writer, with Douglas Stewart).
Address: c/o The Jules Bennett Agency. m. Liz Hendry; 3 d. Holly, Hannah. Hobbies: Scuba-diving, mountaineering, golf, tennis, cricket, music, travel.

CAMPBELL, Joanne

Joanne Campbell. Actress. b. Northampton, 8 February 1964. Stage appearances at the Theatre Royal, Stratford East, and the Belgrade Theatre, Coventry.

Joanne Campbell

TV: *Parents and Teenagers* (Open University); *Night Kids; Copperfield Comedy and Co; All Electric Amusement Arcade; Dramarama; Me & My Girl; Home James!; Chalkface;* Bev in *Us Girls* (series, 1992); Jancis in *Birds of a Feather;* Kate in *The Bill* (1994).
Address: c/o London Management. Hobbies: Horse-riding, playing tennis, dancing, swimming.

CAMPBELL, Nicky

Nicky Campbell. Presenter. b. Edinburgh, 10 April 1961. Gained a degree in history from Aberdeen University. Disc jockey and jingles writer for Northsound Radio, Aberdeen, before moving to Capital Radio in London, then joining Radio 1 in 1987.

Nicky Campbell

TV: *Top of the Pops; Video Juke Box; Spitting Image* (scriptwriter); *Wheel of Fortune; The New Year Show; Student Choice 92; Student Choice 93; The Big Race* (series, 1994); *TalkAbout* (series, 1995); *Ride On* (series, 1995-6).
Address: c/o Scottish Television. Lives in London. m. 1988 Linda.

CAMPI, Marji

Marji Campi. Actress. Stage plays include *Rialto Prom, Go West Young Woman, The Wedding Ring, Double Double, They Made Their Excuses and Left, Back-Street Romeo, Marriage, Relative Strangers, Soaplights* and *All in Good Time.*
TV: *Wear a Very Big Hat; Pioneers of Social Change; Woyzeck; Within These Walls; What Now?; The Man from the Pru;* Dulcie Froggatt in *Coronation Street;* Betty Hunt in *Brookside;* Joyce Watson in *Surgical Spirit* (seven series, 1989-95).
Address: c/o Carole James Management. Lives in London.

Marji Campi

CANNON, Tommy

Tommy Cannon

Thomas Derbyshire. Comedian/Entertainer. b. Oldham, Lancashire, 27 June 1938. Half of the comedy duo Cannon & Ball.
TV: *Opportunity Knocks; The Wheeltappers' and Shunters' Social Club; Bruce Forsyth's Big Night; Royal Variety Performances; This Is Your Life* (subjects); *The Cannon & Ball Show* (1979-88); *Cannon & Ball's Casino* (hosts, quiz show); *Plaza Patrol* (situation comedy); *Cannon & Ball Playhouse*.
Films: *The Boys in Blue.*
Records: Single: *Don't Forget My Christmas Present* (1992). Address: c/o George Bartram Associates/International Artistes, Albert House, Albert Street, Chadderton, Oldham. Lives in York. m. Margaret (sep); 2 d. Janet, Julie . Partner: Hazel 1 d. Kelly-Anne. Hobbies: Horse-riding, golf, keep-fit.

CAPRON, Brian

Brian Capron

Brian Capron. Actor. b. Woodbridge, Suffolk, 11 February 1949. Trained at LAMDA.
TV: *Murray; A Place to Hide;* Donald Worthington in *Coronation Street; Love Letters on Blue Paper; Carry On Laughing; Around the Corner;* Steven Waldorf; *Smiffs;* Sergeant Godley in *Jack the Ripper; The Gentle Touch; Angles – Babes in the Wood;* Jack in *Beryl's Lot; The Sweeney; Way up to Heaven; Clubs; Henry Intervening;* Mr Hopwood in *Grange Hill;* Napoleon in *Nelson; Just Liz; The Squad; Enemies of the State; Bergerac;* Stanley Baxter's Christmas Hamper; *Up the Elephant and Round the Castle;* Murray McCoy in *Full House; Never Say Die; The Bill* (two roles); *Casualty; Action Stations; Never Come Back; Uncle Jack; Moon and Son; Growing Pains; Birds of a Feather; The Bill; What You Looking At?* (series, 1993); Louis Calvino in *Class Act* (series, 1994); Rex Hall in *Crocodile Shoes* (series, 1994).
Films: Sid in *The Chiffy Kids* (serial). Address: c/o Markham & Froggatt. Lives in Brighton, East Sussex. m. actress Janette Legge; 2 d. Lucy Jane, Ellen Louise.

CARBY, Fanny

Fanny Carby

Fanny Carby. Actress. b. Sutton Coldfield, Warwickshire, 2 February. Trained at Joan Littlewood's Theatre Workshop, where she was an original member of the company.
TV: *Not So Much a Programme, More a Way of Life; Mitch; The Likely Lads; Love Story; The History of Mr Polly; The Good Companions; Forgive Our Foolish Ways; Crossroads; Nearest and Dearest;* Gladys in *On the Buses; Both Ends Meet; Who's Your Father?;* three *Q* series with Spike Milligan; *Angels; Private Schultz; The Cost of Loving; Cockles; Juliet Bravo; Room at the Bottom;* Alice in *Drummonds;* Mrs Crupp in *David Copperfield;* Nurse Randau in *The Good Dr Bodkin Adams; In Sickness and in Health; The Little Match Girl;* Amy Burton in *Coronation Street; Indiscreet* (TVM); *William Tell* (US title *Crossbow*); *The House Plant; Only Fools and Horses; Middlemarch; The Bill; Goodnight Sweetheart.*
Films: *The Family Way; How I Won the War; Oh! What a Lovely War; I Start Counting; A Day in the Death of Joe Egg; The Elephant Man; Loophole; The Doctor and the Devils; The Nightingale Saga; Queenie; Indiscreet; Bert Rigby, You're a Fool.*
Address: c/o Barry Burnett Organisation. m. (dis). Pets: A black cat. Hobbies: Gardening, antiques.

CARMICHAEL, Ian

Ian Carmichael

Ian Carmichael. b. Hull, East Yorkshire, 18 June 1920. Trained at RADA.
TV: *The Importance of Being Earnest; Simon and Laura; 90 Years On;* Bertie Wooster in *The World of Wooster* (series, 1966-8); *Mr Pastry's Progress* (director only); *It's a Small World* (director only); *We Beg to Differ* (director only); *Last of the Big Spenders; The Noël Coward Review; Frost on Sunday; Odd Man In; The Morecambe and Wise Show; Funny You Should Ask; Once Upon a Time;* Peter Lamb in *Bachelor Father* (three series); Jimmy Nicholson in *Alma Mater* (Play for Today); *Father Dear Father,* title role in *Lord Peter Wimsey: Clouds of Witness, Lord Peter Wimsey: The Unpleasantness at the Belona Club, Lord Peter Wimsey: Murder Must Advertise, Lord Peter Wimsey: The Nine Tailors* and *Lord Peter Wimsey: Five Red Herrings; Just Nimmo; Survival* (narrator); *Song by Song; All for Love: Down at the Hydro;* Bellenger in *A Day in Summer;* White in *Obituaries;* Sir James Menzies in *Strathblair* (two series, 1992-3); *Under the Hammer;* Patrick McCormick in *The Great Kandinsky;* Oswald in *Bramwell.*
Films: *Bond Street; Trottie True; Dear Mr Prohack; Time Gentlemen Please!; Ghost Ship; Miss Robin Hood; Meet Mr Lucifer; The Colditz Story; Betrayed; Storm over the Nile; Private's Progress; Brothers in Law; The Big Money; Lucky Jim; Happy Is the Bride!; Left, Right and Centre; I'm All Right, Jack; School for Scoundrels; Light Up the Sky; Double Bunk; The Amorous Prawn; Heavens Above!; Hide and Seek; The Case of the 44s; Smashing Time; The Magnificent Seven Deadly Sins; From Beyond the Grave; The Lady Vanishes; Diamond Skulls.* **Books:** *Will the Real Ian Carmichael...* (autobiography, 1979). Address: c/o London Management. m. Sheila Pyman Maclean (dec 1983); 2 d. Lee, Sally.

CARPENTER, Harry

Harry Carpenter

Harry Carpenter. Sports commentator. b. London, 17 October 1925. Boxing correspondent of the *Daily Express* before entering TV full-time in 1962.
TV: Commentator on boxing world heavyweight title fights and every Olympic Games since 1956;

presenter of BBC Wimbledon lawn tennis coverage, Open golf championships and Oxford-Cambridge boat race; *40 Years of Sports Review* (presenter, 1994).
Books: Author of three books on boxing. **Awards:** American Sportscasters' Association International Award, 1989. Address: c/o BBC TV Sport. m. Phyllis; 1 s. Clive.

CARR, Jack
Jack Carr. Actor. b. Kirkby Cane, Norfolk, 21 November 1944.
TV: *Death of an Expert Witness; Bleak House;* Tom Merrick in *Emmerdale Farm;* Tony Cunliffe in *Coronation Street; Private Practice* (pilot); *Snakes and Ladders; Tales of Sherwood Forest; Truckers; Making Out; Chancer; The Chief;* Atherton in *Medics; The Bill* (two roles); *Never the Twain; Stay Lucky; East-Enders; Covington Cross;* Moran in *Love and Reason;* Riper in *Catherine Cookson's The Dwelling Place;* Harry Taylor in *Casualty;* Norman Spears in *Out of the Blue; Heartbeat;* PC Hanley in *Dangerfield.*
Films: *Business as Usual; Suspect; A Soldier's Wife.* Address: c/o Barry Brown & Partner. Lives in London. m. 1st (dis), 2nd (dis). Partner: Petronella Wolfes. Hobbies: 'Wolf shooting.'

Jack Carr

CARROTT, Jasper
Robert Davies. Comedian. b. Birmingham, 14 March 1945. Worked as a market trader, driver, sales rep and lampshade maker before setting up a variety agency. Started his own career in 1969 as a compère in clubs, including his own, The Boggery. Became an all-round entertainer in clubs.
TV: *The Golden Game; Folk Club; An Audience with Jasper Carrott; Half Hour with Jasper Carrott; The Unrecorded Jasper Carrott; Carrott Del Sol; Carrott's Lib; Carrott Confidential; Canned Carrott; Specially Selected Canned Carrott* (compilation); *Carrott's Commercial Breakdown; Carrott's Commercial Breakdown 2; 24 Carrott Gold* (concert from the Shakespeare Memorial Theatre, Stratford-upon-Avon); *More Specially Selected Canned Carrott* (compilation); *One Jasper Carrott* (concert); *The Best of Carrott Confidential;* Bob Louis in *The Detectives* (four series, 1993-6); *Carrott's Commercial Breakdown 3; Canned Carrott — The Juicy Bits* (highlights from Series 2 of *Canned Carrott*); *Carrott-U-Like; Canned Carrott — More Juicy Bits* (more highlights from Series 2 of *Canned Carrott*).
Films: *Jane and the Lost City.* **Records:** Single: *Funky Moped/Magic Roundabout* (No 5, 1975). Albums: *Rabbits On and On* (No 10, 1975); *Carrott In Notts* (No 56, 1976); *The Best of Jasper Carrott* (No 38, 1978); *The Unrecorded Jasper Carrott* (No 19, 1979); *Beat the Carrott* (No 13, 1981); *Carrott's Lib* (No 80, 1982); *The Stun (Carrott Tells All)* (No 57, 1983); *Cosmic Carrott* (No 66, 1987). Address: c/o BBC TV. m. Hazel; 3 d. Lucy, Jennifer, Hannah, 1 s. Jake.

Jasper Carrott

CARTERET, Anna
Anna Wilkinson. Actress. b. Bangalore, India, 11 December 1942. Stage plays include *A Piece of My Mind* (Apollo Theatre) and *Tea at the Ritz* (Young Vic and National Theatres).
TV: *A Young Lady from London; The Ordeal of Richard Feveril; The Hon Bird; Mickey Dunne; The Reluctant Debutante; Riviera Police; The Saint; Constance; She Stoops to Conquer; The Pigeon Fancier* (Play for Today); *The Merchant of Venice; The Pallisers; Glittering Prizes; Fathers and Families; Mother Song; Send In the Girls; The Man Who Liked Elephants; Crown Court; Little Mrs Perkins; None of Your Business; Change Partners; Being Normal;* Inspector Kate Longton in *Juliet Bravo; In the Pink; Make It Work; Raving Beauties; Everyone's a Winner; Heat of the Day; The Shell Seekers; Time to Talk; 01- for London; Cluedo; Women in Aids; Ashenden;* Anna in *The Memoirs of Sherlock Holmes; Eskimo Day.*
Films: *Light up the Sky; Dateline Diamonds; The Plank.*
Address: c/o Peters Fraser & Dunlop. m. director Christopher Morahan; 2 d. Rebecca, Hattie.

Anna Carteret

CARTY, Todd
Todd Carty. Actor. b. Ireland, 1963. Started appearing in TV commercials at the age of four.
TV: *Z Cars; Our Mutual Friend; Drummer; Headmaster; Focus on Britain; The Idle Bunch; We're Happy* (RTE, Ireland); Tucker in *Grange Hill;* title role in *Tucker's Luck; Aladdin; Scene in New York* (narrator); *The Jungle Creatures* (narrator); *Counter Intelligence;* Mark Fowler in *EastEnders* (1990-).
Films: *Professor Popper's Problems; Please Sir!; The Gang's OK; The Magic Trip; Krull; What's in It for You; A Question of Balance; Serve Them Right; The Candy Show.*
Address: c/o John Redway and Associates/DDC Elstree Centre.

Todd Carty

CASHMAN, Michael
Michael Cashman. Actor/Writer. b. London, 17 December 1950. Began acting at the age of 12.
TV: *Season's Greetings; Angels; The Sandbaggers; Waste; The World of J B Priestley; Doctor Who; The Life of Shakespeare; Nobody's Perfect; The Gentle Touch; The Brief; A Cut in the Rates; Seven Deadly Virtues; Game for a Laugh; Bird of Prey; Dempsey and Makepeace; The Winning Streak;* Colin Russell in *EastEnders* (1986-8); Malcolm Paynter in *Casualty.*
Films: *The Virgin Soldiers; Zee & Co; Unman, Wittering and Zigo.*
Books: *Bloody Soap* (novel). Address: c/o Peters Fraser & Dunlop. Lives in East London.

Michael Cashman

John Castle

Mark Caven

Jonathan Cecil

Tom Chadbon

Cy Chadwick

CASTLE, John

John Castle. Actor. b. Croydon, Surrey, 14 January 1940.
TV: *Dead of Night; Pearcross Girls; Harlequinade; Town without Pity; Fight against Slavery; Ben Hall; I Claudius; The Prime of Miss Jean Brodie; The Three Hostages; Eagle's Wing; Lost Empires;* Tony Doyle in *Inspector Morse; The Crucifer of Blood* (TVM); Inspector Dermot Craddock in *Agatha Christie's Miss Marple: A Murder Is Announced;* Havisham in *Little Lord Fauntleroy* (series, 1995); *Pie in the Sky.*
Films: *The Lion in Winter; The Promise; Antony and Cleopatra; Man of La Mancha; Sarah; Eliza Fraser; Night Shift; Second Star to the Right.* Address: c/o Markham & Froggatt.

CAVEN, Mark

Mark Caven. Actor/Writer. b. London, Ontario, Canada, 23 April 1958. Began acting at the age of seven. Trained at LAMDA (1976-8). Co-founder of La Bonne Crêpe Café Theatre (1979).
TV: *Data Run* (TV-am, two years); *Follow the Star, Alas Smith and Jones* (Series 1, 1983); Anthony in *Executive Stress* (three series, 1986-8); The Texan in *Salvation Guaranteed;* Lee in *Nobody's Scared;* Dickey in *The Crying Game* (The Comic Strip Presents…); John Jacoby in *Virtual Murder* (TVM); Edward in *The Red Nose of Courage;* Bob in *The Upper Hand;* The Husband in *Who Dealt?;* Ed in *Detectives on the Verge of a Nervous Breakdown* (The Comic Strip Presents…); Jed in *Gregory – Diary of a Nutcase* (The Comic Strip Presents…); *Space Virgins from Planet Sex* (The Comic Strip Presents…); Tony in *Susan; The Glam Metal Detectives* (also co-writer, series, 1995); *The Motherless; Hale & Pace.*
Films: *A Brief Walk* (BFI); *The American Way;* Father Kelly in *Superman IV; The Pope Must Die* (US title *The Pope Must Diet*); Sam in *Dead Lucky;* Tom in *Who Dealt?* **Records:** *Everybody Up* (Top 30 single). Address: c/o Elaine Murphy Associates. Lives in London. Single. Hobbies: 'Helping to run the La Bonne Crêpe Café Theatre, entertaining the London Fringe for the past 17 years.'

CECIL, Jonathan

Jonathan Hugh Cecil. Actor/Writer. b. London, 22 February 1939. Grandson of drama critic Sir Desmond MacCarthy. Graduated in French from New College, Oxford. Trained at LAMDA.
TV: *Maggie* (début, 1964); *French Cricket; The Ordeal of Richard Feveril; Marriage Lines; The Fall of a Sparrow; Not So Much a Programme, More a Way of Life; Hudd; Major Barbara; The Whitehall Worrier* (series); *Eugénie Grandet; Sorry I'm Single;* Comedy Playhouse productions (including Pongo in *Uncle Fred Flits By*); *The Old Campaigner* (series); *Doctor in the House; The Culture Vultures* (series); Ben Travers Farces; *Vile Bodies;* Dominic in *It's Awfully Bad for Your Eyes, Darling* (series); *The Goodies; The Dick Emery Show; Katherine Mansfield; Jackanory; Dad's Army; Alice through the Looking Glass;* title role in *Romany Jones* (series); *The Rough and the Smooth; Are You Being Served?;* Holofernes in *Love's Labour's Lost; The Venetian Twins; Whodunnit; Spy Dukes of Piccadilly; Oh Happy Band* (series); *The Taming of the Shrew; It Ain't Half Hot Mum; Thank You;* Bertie Wooster in *P G Wodehouse; Gulliver in Lilliput; Farmer's Arms; The Lady Is a Tramp; The House; What the Censor Saw; The Puppet Man* (series); White Rabbit in *Alice in Wonderland; Thirteen at Dinner* (TVM); *Dead Man's Folly* (TVM); Hastings in *Murder in Three Acts* (also titled *Three Act Tragedy*) (TVM); *The Hospice; Hot Paint; The Sign of Command* (Italian mini-series); *F.L.I.P.; Beethoven Is Not Dead; The Rector's Wife; Murder Most Horrid; Late Flowering Lust;* Rawlings in *Just William; The Entertainers.*
Films: *The Yellow Rolls Royce; The Great St Trinian's Train Robbery; Otley; Catch Me a Spy; Up the Front; Barry Lyndon; Joseph Andrews; Rising Damp; History of the World Part 1; E La Nave Va; The Second Victory; Little Dorrit; The Fool; As You Like It.* Address: c/o Kate Feast Management. Lives in London. m. 1976 actress-singer Anna Sharkey. Pets: One dog, four cats. Hobbies: Reading, music.

CHADBON, Tom

Tom Chadbon. Actor. b. Luton, Bedfordshire, 27 February 1946. Trained at RADA.
TV: *The Brack Report; British Comedy Classics; Strangers and Brothers; Shine on Harvey Moon; Mitch; The Late Nancy Irving; Love Song; Bulman; Paradise Postponed; Floodtide; Crossfire; Doctor Who; Hard Cases; Wish Me Luck; Chancer; Devices and Desires; Sherlock Holmes and the Leading Lady* (mini-series); *The Bill; Thatcher: The Final Days;* Newspaper Editor in *Between the Lines;* Inspector Hawkins in *The Memoirs of Sherlock Holmes;* Patrick Hargreave in *Peak Practice;* Lenny Monk (Senior Crown Prosecutor) in *Crown Prosecutor* (series, 1995); Wyman in *BUGS;* Piers in *The Ruth Rendell Mysteries: The Strawberry Tree* (mini-series, 1995); PC Coleman in *Silent Witness.*
Films: *Tess; The Last of Linda Cleer; Dance with a Stranger; A Day in Summer.*
Address: c/o Peters Fraser & Dunlop. m. Jane; 2 s. Dominic, Nicholas, 2 d. Amelia, Felicity.

CHADWICK, Cy

Cy Chadwick. Actor. b. Leeds, 2 June 1969.
TV: *The Book Tower* (aged 13); *How We Used to Live* (aged 15); *On the Boat* (English-language series for German TV); Nick Bates in *Emmerdale* (1985-). Plus voice-overs for radio commercials.
Address: c/o Emmerdale Production Centre. Lives in Leeds. Single. Hobbies: Photography, pop music.

CHALMERS, Judith

Judith Chalmers. Presenter. b. Manchester, 10 October 1936. OBE, 1994.
TV: BBC TV announcer; *Come Dancing; Afternoon Plus; Wish You Were Here…?* (1973-); *This Is Your Life* (subject); *The Home Service* (also deviser); *Hot Property; Miss World; Miss United Kingdom;* royal film premières; The Derby; Royal Ascot; *VE Day Celebrations* (1995).
Radio: *Children's Hour* (aged 13); *Woman's Hour* (BBC Radio 4); *The Judith Chalmers Show* (BBC Radio 2). **Books:** *Wish You Were Here…? Judith Chalmers' 50 Best Holidays.*
Address: c/o IMG. m. sports commentator Neil Durden-Smith; 1 d. Emma, 1 s. Mark.

Judith Chalmers

CHATER, Geoffrey

Geoffrey Michael Chater Robinson. Actor. b. Barnet, Hertfordshire, 23 March 1921. Son of actress Gwendolyn Gwynne. Started career as an ASM in Windsor (1946).
TV: *Paris 1900; Orson Welles' Great Mysteries;* Colonel Pierce in *Dad's Army;* Bishop in *Callan; Special Branch; Gentle Rebellion; Fall of Eagles; General Hospital; Sprout; Father Brown; Ferryman's Rest; The Dick Emery Show; The Main Chance; Charles Bravo; Euthanasia; Village Hall; Thriller; Hogg's Back; Hadleigh; Moll Flanders; Hess; The Cedar Tree; Prince Regent; Rings on Their Fingers; Penmarric; The Network; Imitation Game; The Specialist; Brideshead Revisited; Agony; Othello; The Wilderness Years; Tales of the Unexpected; Father Charlie; Troilus and Cressida; Shelley; The Further Adventures of Lucky Jim; Harry's Game; The Fourth Man; Shackleton; A Married Man; The Cleopatras; Nanny; Aerodrome; Strangers and Brothers; Foxy Lady; Mapp and Lucia* (series); *Hotel du Lac* (TVM); Minister in *Blott on the Landscape; Blunt; Double Helix; Northanger Abbey; Saracen; The Secret Life of Ian Fleming* (TVM); *Bergerac; The New Statesman* (1990-3); *The Darling Buds of May; One Foot in the Grave; Rumpole of the Bailey; The Rector's Wife;* Mr Wilkinson in *The House of Eliott; Pie in the Sky; The Detectives.*
Films: *Dr Jekyll and Mr Hyde; Barry Lyndon; Gandhi; Riviera; Bethune; Anything More Would Be Greedy.* Address: c/o Bernard Hunter Associates. Lives in London. m. 1949 Jennifer R F Hill; 2 s. Simon Chater Robinson, impresario-writer-composer-director Piers Chater Robinson, 1 d. Annabel Chater Davies. Pets: Tortoises. Hobbies: Golf, swimming.

Geoffrey Chater

CHEGWIN, Keith

Keith Chegwin. Presenter/Actor. b. Bootle, Liverpool, 17 January 1957. Sang in Northern working-men's clubs with a family trio from the age of 11. Later sang with the pop group Kenny. Attended a London stage school for six years. Gained a degree in English literature from Oxford University.
TV: *Junior Showtime; Swop Shop; Saturday Superstore; Cheggers Plays Pop; The Wackers; Cheggers' Action Reports; Chegwin Checks It Out; The Ronnie Barker Show; The Liver Birds; The Chester Mystery Plays; Wackers; My Old Man; Black Beauty; Armchair Theatre; Village Hall; Star Turn; All Star Record Breakers; Sky Star Search; Go Getters; The Big Breakfast.*
Films: *Macbeth; Egghead's Robot; Elspeth's Double; Robin Hood Junior.* Address: c/o Dave Winslett Entertainments. Lives near Newbury, Berkshire. m. TV presenter Maggie Philbin (dis 1993); 1 d. Rose. Partner: Maria. Hobbies: Horse-riding, playing the piano, reading, writing.

Keith Chegwin

CHERITON, Shirley

Shirley Cheriton. Actress. b. London, 28 June 1955. Trained at the Italia Conti Academy.
TV: *Crown Court; Within These Walls; The Cuckoo Waltz; Z Cars; Bless This House; General Hospital; Angels; Hazell; Secombe with Music; The Final Frontier;* Debbie Wilkins in *EastEnders; Three Up, Two Down;* Miss Prescott in *Grace and Favour* (series). Address: c/o St James's Management. m. Howard Spinks (dis); 2 s. Mark, Adam. Hobbies: Swimming, keep-fit.

Shirley Cheriton

CHILD, Jeremy

Jeremy Child. Actor. b. Woking, Surrey, 20 September 1944. Trained at the Bristol Old Vic Theatre School. TV since 1965.
TV: *Take Three Girls; Coronation Street; Father Dear Father; The Glittering Prizes; Wings; Robin's Nest; Winston Churchill — The Wilderness Years; Backs to the Land; Cork and Bottle; The Upchat Line; The Sweeney; Anna Karenina; Edward and Mrs Simpson; 'Tis Pity She's a Whore; When the Boat Comes In; Play of the Month; Play for Tomorrow; Bird of Prey; Sapphire and Steel; Vice Versa; The Happy Apple; Minder; Bergerac; The Jewel in the Crown; Oxbridge Blues; Late Starter; Fairly Secret Army; Hart to Hart; First among Equals; Game, Set & Match; Lovejoy; Perfect Scoundrels;* Worth in *Fool's Gold* (TVM); Keith Koster in *Demob;* Roddy Metcalfe in *Headhunters* (mini-series, 1994); Sir Augustus in *Sharpe's Enemy;* Dimmock in *Frank Stubbs.*
Films: *Privilege; The Peace Game; The Breaking of Bumbo; Oh! What a Lovely War; Play Dirty; Young Winston; Emily; The Stud; Quadrophenia; Sir Henry at Rawlinson's End; Chanel Solitaire; Give My Regards to Broad Street; High Road to China; Taffin; A Fish Called Wanda.* Address: c/o Representation Joyce Edwards. m. 1st actress Deborah Grant (qv) (dis), 2nd Jan Todd (dis), 3rd Libby Morgan; 3 d. Melissa, Lenora, Eliza, 1 s. Alexander. Hobbies: Cooking, gardening, flying, laughing.

Jeremy Child

CHILDS, Tracey

Tracey Childs

Tracey Joanne Childs. Actress. b. Chiswick, West London, 30 May 1963. Trained at Elmhurst Ballet School and the Guildhall School of Music and Drama. Acted on TV from the age of 11.

TV: Jennifer in *Upstairs, Downstairs* (début, aged 11); Victoria in *Prometheus;* Princess in *The Snow Queen; Jackanory Playhouse;* Rose in *The Prime of Miss Jean Brodie* (series, 1978); Fan in *A Christmas Carol;* Marguerite in *The Devil's Crown;* Mary Harris in *The Amazing Affair of Adelaide Harris;* Henrietta in *Happy Autumn Fields;* Kate in *Strangers;* Lady Emily in *Landseer;* Bet McCellar in *Flesh and Blood;* Johanna in *Baal;* Marianne Dashwood in *Sense and Sensibility* (serial);Angie/Sheena in *Shades;* Alison Barnett in *Bergerac;* Jilly in *A Married Man;* Georgiana Read in *Jane Eyre;* Professor Vania in *Captain Zep;* Pamela in *A Talent for Murder;* Louise in *Morgan's Boy; Aladdin and the Forty Thieves;* Camilla in *Lobo's World; The Victoria Wood Show; Deceptions* (mini-series); Sophie Flemyng in *Cold Warrior;* Lynne Howard in *Howards' Way* (two series, 1985-6); Lucy in *Dempsey and Makepeace;* Jessica in *Gems;* Penelope in *The Shell Seekers;* Claire in *Runaway Bay; If You See God, Tell Him; The Bill.*
Films: Suzanne in *The Scarlet Pimpernel; My School Project; Richard's Things.*
Address: c/o Evans and Reiss. m. 1 July 1995 actor Tony Anholt (qv). Hobbies: Walking in the Himalayas, continuing to dance — especially tap — and eating out.

CHITTELL, Christopher

Christopher Chittell

Christopher John Chittell. Actor. b. Aldershot, Hampshire, 19 May 1948.
TV: *Freewheelers; The Tomorrow People; Tucker's Luck;* Eric Pollard in *Emmerdale* (1986-).
Films: *To Sir with Love; The Charge of the Light Brigade; Golden Rendezvous; Erotic Fantasies; Zulu Dawn.* Address: c/o David Daly Associates/Emmerdale Production Centre. Lives in Nottinghamshire. m. 1979 Caroline Hunt; 1 s. Benjamin, 1 d. Rebecca. Hobbies: Playing rugby and cricket, skin diving.

CHRISTIAN, Terry

Terry Christian

Terry Christian. Presenter. b. Manchester. Radio disc-jockey-turned-television presenter.
TV: *Devil's Advocate* (talking about his experiences of leaving school and being unemployed); *The Word* (five series, 1988-94); *Coca-Cola Hit Mix* (Sky One); *Capital City* (1995); *Best of the Word* (1994); *Big City* (series, Carlton only, 1995).
Address: c/o Neil Reading Publicity, 35 Soho Square, London W1V 5DG, tel 0171-287 7711.

CHRISTIE, Julie

Julie Christie

Julie Frances Christie. Actress. b. Chukua, Assam, India, 14 April 1941. Educated in Britain and France. Trained at the Central School of Speech and Drama. Stage plays include *The Comedy of Errors* (as Luciana, RSC), *Uncle Vanya* (as Yelena, New York) and *Old Times* (West End, 1995).
TV: *A for Andromeda* (début, series, 1961); Judith, Simon Templar's niece, in *The Saint* (one episode, 1963); Anne Shank and Sybil Railton-Bell in *Separate Tables; Mary, Mary* (mini-series); *Taking on the Bomb* (documentary); *Aspel & Company* (guest, 1988); Charlotte Deutz in *Sins of the Fathers* (also titled *Fathers and Sons*) (German mini-series); Barbara Barlow in *Dadah Is Death* (also titled *A Long Way Home, A Long Way from Home* and *Deadly Decision*) (mini-series); *Karaoke.*
Films: *Crooks Anonymous; The Fast Lady; Billy Liar; Young Cassidy; Darling;* Lara in *Doctor Zhivago; Fahrenheit 451; Far from the Madding Crowd; Tonite Let's All Make Love in London; Petulia; In Search of Gregory; The Go-Between; McCabe and Mrs Miller; Don't Look Now; Shampoo; Nashville; Demon Seed; Heaven Can Wait; Memoirs of a Survivor; Les Quarantièmes Rugissants* (*The Roaring Forties*); *The Animals Film* (narrator, documentary); *The Return of the Soldier; Heat and Dust; The Gold Diggers; Power; Miss Mary; La Mémoir Tatouée* (US title *Secret Obsession*); *The Control Room;* Mrs Quinton in *Fools of Fortune; The Railway Station Man.* Plus: Presented a film on Cambodia for Oxfam (1988).
Awards: Films: Best Actress Oscar, BFA Best Actress award and New York Film Critics' Award for *Darling* (1965); Donatello Award for *Doctor Zhivago* (1965).
Address: c/o ICM. Lives in Wales. Partner: Journalist Duncan Campbell.

CHURCH, Suzanne

Suzanne Church

Suzanne Church. Actress. b. High Wycombe, Buckinghamshire, 9 October 1951. Emigrated to Australia aged 19 and gained her first TV experience there. Returned to London in 1979. Stage plays include *House Guest* (Savoy Theatre) and *Dangerous Corner* (Ambassadors Theatre).
TV: *The Alvin Purple; Number 96* (three years); *Chopper Squad; Migrant* (all in Australia); Sharon Barrie in *Me & My Girl;* Dian Harrington in *No Place Like Home;* Julia in *Dempsey and Makepeace;* WPC Hartley in *Crossroads;* Estate Agent in *Big Deal;* PA in *Home James!;* Valerie Silverman in *Call Me Mister;* Dr Hunter in *Full House;* Miss Foster in *Slinger's Day;* Ethne Le Strange in *Rude Health;* Louise Jordan in *C.A.T.S. Eyes;* Miss Trench in *Press Gang;* Isabel in *The Upper Hand;* Customer In *Never the Twain;* Annie Lucas in *Surgical Spirit;* Susan in *London's Burning; Dead Men's Tales.*
Address: c/o RKM. Lives in London. m. Dr John Porter; 1 s. William. Pets: Two West Highland terriers. Hobbies: Reading, gardening, antique fairs, saving trees.

CLARKE, Jacqueline

Jacqueline Clarke. Actress. b. Slough, Buckinghamshire, 13 February 1942. Mother was a concert pianist who trained at the Royal Academy of Music. Trained at RADA (1959-61).
TV: *The Adventures of Don Quick; Dave Allen at Large* (character lady, 1972-82); *Thirty Minutes Worth; The Brighton Bell; Scott on...; The Basil Brush Show; Battle of the Sexes; The Mike Yarwood Show; Rings on Their Fingers; Partners;* Sheila Barnes in *A Sharp Intake of Breath* (series); *The Critic; It's Different for Boys; The Young Ones; Only When I Laugh; The Kenny Everett Show; Chish 'n' Fips; Slinger's Day; Little and Large; Maxwell's House; Crackerjack; The Bill;* Nurse in *Surgical Spirit.* Voice-overs: *The Dreamstone; Molly's Gang.*
Radio: *Our Les; Yarwood Weekly; Listen – Mike Yarwood; Castle's on the Air; Thirty Minutes Worth.* Address: c/o Barry Burnett Organisation. Lives in Gloucestershire. m. 1st actor Peter Cartwright (dis), 2nd actor Barrie Gosney; 1 d. Kate (Catherine-Anne) (from 1st m.). Hobbies: Painting, gardening.

Jacqueline Clarke

CLARKE, Margi

Margi Clarke. Actress/Presenter. b. Liverpool. Sister of TV and film writer-director Frank Clarke and actress Angela Clarke.
TV: Granada Television presenter; Queenie in *Making Out* (three series); *The Good Sex Guide* (presenter, two series, 1993-4); *The V Word* (1993); *Holiday* (guest presenter, series, 1993-4); *The Good Book Guide* (series); *Swank* (presenter, series, 1994); Connie in *Soul Survivors* (mini-series, 1995); *The Good Sex Guide Abroad* (series, 1995).
Films: Teresa in *Letter to Brezhnev; I Hired a Contract Killer; Loser Takes All; Blonde Fist.* Address: c/o Lou Coulson. Lives in Liverpool. m. (dis); 1 s. Lawrence, 1 d. Rowan Bud. Partner: Artist Jamie Reid.

Margi Clarke

CLARKE, Warren

Warren Clarke. Actor. b. Oldham, Lancashire. West End stage plays include *I, Claudius* and *Murderer.*
TV: *Our Mutual Friend; Softly Softly; Crown Court; The Sweeney; The Way of the World; Jennie, Lady Randolph Churchill; Heartland; Sound of Guns; The Hunchback of Notre Dame; The Onedin Line; The Tempest; Hallelujah Mary Plum; Psy-warriors; Jail Diary of Albie Sachs; Shelley; Never Speak Ill of the Dead; The Thirteenth Reunion; Wolcott; The Home Front; Two Weeks in Winter; The Battle of Waterloo; From a Far Country: Pope John Paul II* (TVM); *Reilly – Ace of Spies; The Jewel in the Crown; The Case of the Frightened Lady; Big Deal; The Greenhill Pals; SS – Becker; The Flying Devils* (Danish TV); *The Russian Soldier; Anything Legal Considered; Bergerac; The Yob; The Black Adder; Wish Me Luck; Cop Out;* Josiah Hardwood in *Blackadder the Third;* Alan Sefton in *Ice Dance; The Manageress* (two series); *Nice Work; Hands of a Murderer; All Creatures Great and Small; Stay Lucky; The Roughest Way; Sleepers;* Larry Patterson in *Gone to the Dogs* (series, 1991); *Boon;* Brian Nunn in *Lovejoy;* Charlie in *Angels* (1992); Chief Insp Heat in *The Secret Agent* (mini-series); Winston Plant in *Gone to Seed* (series, 1992); voice of Toby in *Conjugal Rites* (Series 1, 1993); Kenny Dawes in *All in the Game* (series, 1993); *Return to Blood River* (Screen Two); *I.D.;* Max Kelvin in *The House of Windsor* (series, 1994); Bamber in *Moving Story* (two series, 1994-5); Det Supt Andrew Dalziel in *Dalziel and Pascoe* (series, 1996).
Films: *A Clockwork Orange; The Virgin Soldiers; Antony and Cleopatra; O Lucky Man!; Dirty Money; Housework; The Antagonists; Enigma;* Pavel Upenskoy in *Firefox; The Cold Room.*
Address: c/o ICM. Lives in Buckinghamshire. m. 2nd Michele.

Warren Clarke

CLARKSON, Jeremy

Jeremy Charles Robert Clarkson. Presenter. b. Doncaster, South Yorkshire, 11 April 1960. Trained as a journalist on the *Rotherham Advertiser* before moving to London to start The Motoring Press Agency in 1984. Wrote as a columnist for *Performance Car* magazine (1986-93) and joined *Top Gear* on TV
TV: *Top Gear* (series, 1989-); *The London Motor Show; Clarkson's Star Cars* (series, 1993); *Jeremy Clarkson's Motorworld* (two series, 1995-6); *Pebble Mill* (presenting The Indies, 1995).
Books: *Clarkson on Cars* (1996); *Motorworld.* Address: c/o BBC Pebble Mill, Birmingham B6 7QQ. Lives in Oxfordshire. m. Frances Catherine; 1 d. Emily Harriet, 1 s. Finlow. Hobbies: 'Smoking.'

Jeremy Clarkson

CLAY, Nicholas

Nicholas Clay. Actor. b. London, 18 September 1946. Trained at RADA.
TV: *Will Shakespeare;* Sir Hugo in *The Hound of the Baskervilles* (TVM); *The Adventures of Sherlock Holmes; The Three Musketeers; In a Glass Darkly; Love Story; The Picture of Dorian Gray; Berlin Break; Virtual Murder; Gentlemen and Players; Poor Little Rich Girl; The Unknown Soldier; Saturday Sunday Monday; Russian Night;* Squadron Leader Cunningham in *Shine on Harvey Moon* (series, 1995).
Films: Mellors in *Lady Chatterley's Lover;* Lionel in *Lionheart; Sleeping Beauty;* Patrick Redfern in *Evil under the Sun;* Lancelot in *Excalibur;* Cesare Augustus in *Martyrdom of St Sebastian;* title rôle in *Alexander the Great;* title rôle in *Tristan and Iseult; Zulu Dawn; The Darwin Adventure; The Night Digger.* Address: c/o Peters Fraser & Dunlop. Lives in London. m. actress Lorna Heilbron; 2 d. Ella, Madge. Pets: A cat called Tybalt. Hobbies: Work.

Nicholas Clay

Edward Clayton

CLAYTON, Edward

Edward Clayton. Actor/Singer. b. Shelfield, Staffordshire, 9 October 1940.

TV: Stan Harvey in *Crossroads; Tucker's Luck; Ladies in Charge; Reflections of Evil; Boy with the Transistor Radio; Travelling Light;* Inspector Austin in *Juliet Bravo; Whoops Apocalypse!;* Brian in *Eh Brian, It's a Whopper;* Robson in *First among Equals;* Desk Sergeant in *Rockliffe's Babies; A Sort of Innocence; The Bell Run; The Contract;* Arthur Parkinson in *Brookside;* Tom Casey in *Coronation Street; The Bill; First and Last; The Ruth Rendell Mysteries: The Best Man to Die; This Is David Harper;* Chief Supt King in *The Chief; Agatha Christie's Poirot;* Chief Constable in *G.B.H.;* Barman in *Perfect Scoundrels; Underbelly; Peak Practice;* Mr Stubbs in *Wild Oats* (Comedy Playhouse); DI Jeff Harrison in *Resnick: Rough Treatment* (mini-series): *Blue Heaven;* Police Officer in *Bad Girl;* Councillor Higgett in *B&B; Kinsey;* Mr Bradley in *Love Hurts;* Jack Siddons in *Heartbeat;* DI Jenkins in *Calling the Shots* (mini-series).
Films: Tommy Mossop in *Wilt;* Tory Chairman in *Paris by Night;* Punter in *Prostitutes.*
Address: c/o Sandra Griffin Management. m. Caroline; 3 d. Ella, Joby, Rosalie.

Peter Cleall

CLEALL, Peter

Peter Cleall. Actor. b. London, 16 March 1944. Trained at East 15 Acting School.

TV: Eric Duffy in *Please Sir!* (1968-70) and *The Fenn Street Gang* (three series, 1971-3); *A Tale of Two Cities; The Lady Is a Tramp; Paul Hogan in Britain;* Stephen Crane in *Dempsey and Makepeace;* Arthur in *Big Deal; The Bill* (three roles); *A Bit of Fry and Laurie;* Malcolm in *EastEnders;* Percy Foreman in *London's Burning;* Roy in *Growing Pains* (series, 1993); Steve Lewis in *Casualty;* Wally Knowles in *Minder;* Stuart Best in *The Bill;* Mr Trap in *The Brittas Empire;* Head Teacher in *Silent Witness.*
Films: Jean in *Theatre of Death;* Duffy in *Please Sir!;* Edgar in *Seeing God;* Mr Ross in *The Bull.*
Address: c/o Pelham Associates. Lives in Brighton, East Sussex. m. 1st (dis), 2nd actress Dione Inman; 4 s. Miles, Damian (both from 1st m.), Dan, Spencer (both from 2nd m.).

John Cleese

CLEESE, John

John Cleese. Actor/Writer. b. Weston-super-Mare, Somerset, 27 October 1939. Started career in the Cambridge Footlights revue while at university.

TV: *The Frost Report; The Frost Programme; At Last the 1948 Show; Monty Python's Flying Circus;* Basil Fawlty in *Fawlty Towers* (co-writer, with Connie Booth); *The Strange Case of the End of Civilization as We Know It* (TVM); *The Taming of the Shrew* (TVM); *The South Bank Show* (subject); *Cheers; Prisoners of Conscience* (presenter); Harold Kingsby in *Look at the State We're In!: Secrecy; Look at the State We're In!: The Status Quo; Fierce and Gentle Creatures* (presenter).
Films: *Interlude; The Bliss of Mrs Blossom; The Best House in London; The Magic Christian; The Rise and Rise of Michael Rimmer; The Statue; And Now for Something Completely Different; It's a Two-Feet-Six-Inches-Above-the-Ground World; Romance with a Double Bass; Monty Python and the Holy Grail; Pleasure at Her Majesty's; Monty Python's Life of Brian* (also co-director); *Away from It All* (narrator only, short); *The Secret Policeman's Ball; The Great Muppet Caper; Time Bandits; Monty Python Live at the Hollywood Bowl; The Secret Policeman's Other Ball; Privates on Parade; Monty Python's Meaning of Life; Yellowbeard; Silverado; Clockwise; The Secret Policeman's Third Ball; A Fish Called Wanda; The Big Picture; Erik the Viking; Bullseye!; An American Tail 2; Fievel Goes West* (voice only).
Books: *Families and How to Survive Them* (with Robin Skynner).
Awards: *TVTimes* Funniest Man on TV award (1978-9). Address: c/o David Wilkinson. m. 1st actress Connie Booth (qv) (dis), 2nd film director Barbara Trentham (dis); 2 d. Cynthia, Camilla.

John Clive

CLIVE, John

Clive John Hambley. Actor/Writer. b. London, 6 January 1938. Began acting as a child.

TV: *Wear a Very Big Hat* (début); Professor Sommerby in *Robert's Robots* (series); *Perils of Pendragon; How Green Was My Valley; Great Expectations* (TVM); *No Longer Alone; The Government Inspector; The Sweeney; Rising Damp; The Dick Emery Show; Leave It to Charlie; Tropic; The History of Mr Polly; The Nesbitts Are Coming; Some of Our Airmen Are No Longer Missing* (associate producer, documentary); *A Dream of Alice; Lady Windermere's Fan; One Way Out; Bye Bye Baby* (TVM). As writer: *Barricade; The Vicar of Mountvernon; Broken Wings; Shutdown.*
Films: *Yellow Submarine* (voice of John Lennon); *Smashing Time; The Italian Job; A Clockwork Orange; Carry On Abroad; Tiffany Jones; Revenge of the Pink Panther.*
Books: *KG200; The Last Liberator; ARK; Barossa; Broken Wings; The Lion's Cage* (all novels).
Address: c/o CCA Management. Lives in Richmond-upon-Thames, Surrey m. Carole Ann White (dis); 1 d. Hannah, 1 s. Alexander. Partner: Canadian actress Bryony Elliott. Hobbies: Walking.

Martin Clunes

CLUNES, Martin

Martin Clunes. Actor. Son of classical actor Alec Clunes; actor Jeremy Brett was his mother's cousin. Stage plays include *The Henrys* (English Shakespeare Company), *The Admirable Crichton* (Theatre Royal, Haymarket), *Much Ado About Nothing* and *Julius Caesar* (both Open Air Theatre, Regent's

Park). Directed *The Loneliness of a Long Distance Runner* (Grove Theatre and tour).
TV: *Doctor Who* (TV début, four episodes); *Jury; The White Guard; No Place Like Home; All at No 20; Suspicion; Hannay; Boon; Never Come Back; Rides; Harry Enfield's Television Programme;* James Balcombe in *Inspector Morse: Happy Families;* Paul in *The Upper Hand; Gone to the Dogs; Jeeves and Wooster; About Face;* Gary in *Men Behaving Badly* (four series, 1992-5); *The Good Sex Guide* (Series 1, 1993); Sir Anthony Drury in *Lovejoy;* Dr Chambourcy in *Bonjour la Classe;* Donald in *Dancing Queen* (Rik Mayall Presents); Dick Dobson in *Demob* (series, 1993); Estate Agent in *If You See God, Tell Him; Awayday;* Dan in *An Evening with Gary Lineker* (TVM); *Harry Enfield and Chums* (series, 1994); Ray Knight in *Toby* (Chiller); Earl of Pangbourne in *Moving Story; Over Here; Lord of Misrule* (Screen One).
Films: Brock in *The Russia House; Swing Kids;* Martin in *Carry On Columbus; The Ballad of Kid Divine; Staggered* (also director).
Address: c/o ICM. m. actress Lucy Aston (sep 1993).

Norman Coburn

COBURN, Norman
Norman Coburn. Actor. b. Sydney, Australia, 6 March 1937. Started acting at the age of 14, working in radio and theatre in Sydney. Acted in the UK from the late Fifties until returning to Australia in 1981, appearing in repertory theatre and in television programmes, including a regular role in *No Hiding Place*. Has acted in Home and Away since it began in 1988. Daughter Nana appeared with him in it as rebellious pupil Vicki Baxter for a time.
TV: *Monitor; Compact; No Hiding Place; Dixon of Dock Green; The Professionals; Coronation Street* (all while in Britain); *Step in the Right Direction; Coral Island; The Young Doctors; A Country Practice; 1915; Peach's Gold; Waterloo Station; Special Squad; Possession; Rafferty's Rules; Losing; Land of Hope; Five Mile Creek;* Donald Fisher in *Home and Away* (1988-).
Films: *Circle of Deception; Oscar Wilde; Valiant Soldier.*
Address: c/o Australian Creative Management/Channel 7. m. (dis); 1 s. Troyt, 1 d. actress Nana.

Nicholas Cochrane

COCHRANE, Nicholas
Nicholas Marc Cochrane. Actor. b. Cheadle, Cheshire, 16 December 1973. Discovered by Granada Television while still at school.
TV: Andy McDonald in *Coronation Street* (1989-).
Address: c/o Granada Television. Lives in Cheadle. Single. Pets: Cross-terrier called Jackson. Hobbies: Sport, driving.

COCKERELL, Toby
Toby Johnathan Cockerell. Actor. b. London, 17 October 1976. Trained at the Anna Scher Theatre School from the age of eight. Stage roles include Falstaff's Page in *Henry IV* (RSC).
TV: Lee in *Streetwise* (series); *House of Eliott; The Bill;* Scott Windsor in *Emmerdale* (1993-).
Radio: *Not Just Anybody — Family.*
Address: c/o Anna Scher Theatre Management. Lives in London. Single. Pets: A dog called Cleo. Hobbies: Motorbike trials riding, snowboarding.

Toby Cockerell

COCKROFT, Peter
Peter Edward Cockroft. Weather presenter. b. Catterick, North Yorkshire, 13 April 1957. Studied at the Meteorological Office and joined the BBC in 1991.
TV: Weather presenter on BBC1, BBC2 and BBC World Service Television.
Radio: BBC national and local radio.
Address: c/o BBC Weather Centre. Lives in Oxfordshire. m. publisher Ann Arscott; 1 d. Rose Hannah. Hobbies: Sailing, cycling, walking.

COIA, Paul
Paul Coia. Presenter. b. Glasgow, 19 June 1957. Joined Radio Clyde, Glasgow, as a presenter on leaving university, before entering television. Was the first voice heard on Channel Four when he became one of the new channel's announcers (1982).
TV: Announcer for Scottish Television, then Channel Four; *Preview* (Channel Four); *Pebble Mill at One* (three years); *The 6.55 Show; Tricks of the Trade; The Spirit of Christmas; Doomsday Detectives; Railwatch; A Song for Europe; Holiday '87; Song for Europe; ITV Telethon* (Scottish host 1988, 1990); *The Birthday Show; Radio Industries Awards; The Paul Coia Show; European Special Olympics; Children in Need; Pick of the Week; Zig Zag; Catchword; Press Your Luck* (game show, HTV West only); *The Garden Party; Spotlight* (Sky Movies); Andy the tour guide in *Rab C Nesbitt;* Policeman in *Taggart; ITV Telethon '92; Win, Lose or Draw; Newshound; Quiz Call.*
Address: c/o Sara Cameron Management. Lives in Wimbledon, South London. m. 1992 TV presenter Debbie Greenwood (qv); 1 d. Annalie (b. 1994). Pets: Six cats. Hobbies: Music, writing, keeping fit, cats, kitten.

Peter Cockroft

Paul Coia

George Cole

Graham Cole

Julie Dawn Cole

Stephanie Cole

Charlotte Coleman

COLE, George

George Cole. Actor. b. Tooting, South London, 22 April 1925.

TV: *The Informer; Blackmail;* Comedy Playhouse; *Vendetta; A Man of Our Times; The Sex Game; Out of the Unknown; Thirty-Minute Theatre; Half-Hour Story; Murder; Root of All Evil; The Gold Robbers; The Comic; The Right Prospectus; Menace; A Room in Town; UFO; The Ten Commandments; Madigan: The London Beat; Six Faces of a Man; Away from It All; Dial M for Murder; Village Hall; Affair of the Heart; The Sweeney; Quiller; Lloyd George Knew My Father; The Good Humoured Man; Don't Forget to Write; Losing Her;* Mr Downs in *The Good Life; The Voyage of Charles Darwin; Return of The Saint; Getting in on Concorde;* Arthur Daley in *Minder* (1979-94); *The Bounder;* Sir Giles Lynchwood in *Blott on the Landscape* (series, 1985); *Heggerty, Haggerty; Comrade Dad; Minder on the Orient Express; A Day to Remember; Natural Causes; Life after Life; Single Voices;* Henry Root in *Root into Europe* (series, 1992); Paul Berman in *Fine Things* (mini-series); Peter Banks in *My Good Friend* (series, 1995).

Films: *Cottage to Let; Those Kids from Town; Fiddling Fuel* (short); *The Demi-Paradise; Henry V; Journey Together; My Brother's Keeper; Quartet; The Spider and the Fly; Morning Departure; Gone to Earth; Flesh and Blood; Laughter in Paradise; Scrooge; Lady Godiva Rides Again; The Happy Family; Who Goes There!; Top Secret; Folly to Be Wise; Will Any Gentleman?; The Intruder; Our Girl Friday; The Clue of the Missing Ape; An Inspector Calls; Happy Ever After; The Belles of St Trinian's; A Prize of Gold; Where There's a Will; The Constant Husband; The Adventures of Quentin Durward; It's a Wonderful Life; The Green Man; The Weapon; Blue Murder at St Trinian's; Too Many Crooks; Don't Panic Chaps!; The Bridal Path; The Pure Hell of St Trinian's; The Anatomist; Dr Syn Alias the Scarecrow; Cleopatra; One Way Pendulum; The Legend of Young Dick Turpin; The Great St Trinian's Train Robbery; The Green Shoes* (short); *The Vampire Lovers; Fright; Take Me High; The Blue Bird; Perishing Solicitors* (short). Address: c/o Joy Jameson. m. 1st 1954 Eileen Moore (dis), 2nd former actress Penny Morrell; 1 d. Harriet, 1 s. Crispin (both from 1st m.), 1 d. Tara , 1 s. Toby (both from 2nd m.)

COLE, Graham

Graham Coleman Smith. Actor. b. Willesden, North London, 16 March 1952.

TV: *Kelly Monteith; The Kenny Everett Show; Doctor Who;* PC Tony Stamp in *The Bill* (1987-); *The Children's Royal Variety Performance 1994.*
Address: c/o Evans and Reiss. Lives in Bromley, Kent. m. Cherry Anne; 1 s. Matthew, 1 d. Laura.

COLE, Julie Dawn

Julie Dawn Cole. Actress. b. Guildford, Surrey, 26 October 1957. Trained at Barbara Speake Stage School.

TV: Jo Longhurst in *Angels;* Rowella in *Poldark; The Many Wives of Patrick; Rings on Their Fingers;* Lucy in *The Mill on the Floss; Tales of the Unexpected; Terry and June; Kelly Monteith; Tandoori Nights; Bergerac; Casualty; Up the Elephant and round the Castle; Galloping Galaxies; Wysiwyg;* Geraldine in *EastEnders;* Lyn in *The Upper Hand; Moon and Son;* Judy Hollingsworth in *Married for Life* (series, 1996).

Films: *Willy Wonka and the Chocolate Factory; That Lucky Touch; Camille.* Address: c/o Hobson's Personal Management. Lives in Hampton Court, Surrey. m. 1st Peter Mellor (dis), 2nd Nick Wilton; 1 d. Holly India, 1 s. Barnaby (both from 2nd m.). Pets: Shambles, a standard Schnauzer. Hobbies: Running.

COLE, Stephanie

Stephanie Cole. Actress. b. Solihull, Warwickshire, 5 October 1941. Trained at Bristol Old Vic.

TV: Mrs Featherstone in *Open All Hours* (series); Sarah Mincing in *Return of the Antelope* (three series); *Going Gently; Amy;* Dr Beatrice Mason in *Tenko* (series, 1981-4) and *Tenko Reunion* (1985); Betty Sillitoe in *A Bit of a Do* (two series); *Talking Heads: Soldiering On; Tears in the Rain;* Diana Trent in *Waiting for God* (five series, 1990-4); *About Face; Agatha Christie's Poirot; Memento Mori; The Good Sex Guide; The Family Show; In the Cold Light of Day; The Enemy Within: Stephanie Cole on Phobias.*
Address: c/o Michael Ladkin Personal Management. Lives in London. m. 1973 writer and fight director Henry Marshall (dis 1989); 1 d. Emma. Pets: Cats. Hobbies: Reading, walking, books, music.

COLEMAN, Charlotte

Charlotte Ninon Coleman. Actress. b. London, 3 April 1968. Daughter of actress Ann Beach (qv) and producer-director Francis Coleman; sister of actress Lisa Coleman (qv). Trained at Anna Scher Theatre School.

TV: Emma in *Two People;* Sue in *Worzel Gummidge* (four series, from age of 10); Mohican Girl in *The Two of Us; Educating Marmalade; Danger: Marmalade at Work; Marmalade Atkins in Space;* Seamstress in *The Insurance Man;* Helen in *Inappropriate Behaviour;* Kim in *Campaign;* Irene Blakely in *A View of Harry Clark; The Dark Angel; Blackeyes;* Jess in *Oranges Are Not the Only Fruit* (mini-series, 1990); Freddie in *Freddie and Max;* Roz in *Sweet Nothing; Jackanory: Night Birds on Nantucket* (storyteller); Jessica in *Inspector Morse: Happy Families;* Sharon Palmer in *The Bill;* Sheila in *Olly's Prison* (mini-series); Mary in *The Vacillations of Poppy Carew; Mrs Hartley and the Growth Centre* (Screen Two); Cathy in *Oliver's Travels* (series, 1995); *Giving Tongue* (Screen Two).

Films: *The Bearskin; Map of the Human Heart;* Cindy in *The Footing;* Scarlett in *Four Weddings and* a Funeral; Alice in *Different for Girls; The Young Poisoner's Handbook*. **Awards:** TV: RTS Best Performance Award for a Scripted Fictional Performance for *Oranges Are Not the Only Fruit* (1991). Address: c/o Peters Fraser & Dunlop. Lives in North London. Single. Hobbies: Collages, art, sculpture.

COLEMAN, David

David Coleman. Sports commentator. b. Alderley Edge, Cheshire, 26 April 1926. Previously a newspaper journalist, including job as editor of the *Cheshire County Express*, and radio reporter/commentator.
TV: *Match of the Day; Grandstand; Sportsnight with Coleman; A Question of Sport* (host, 1979-); football World Cups; Olympic Games; *London's Marathon; A Question of Sport: The First 25 Years* (1995). Address: c/o Bagenal Harvey Organisation. m. Barbara; 3 d. Anne, Mandy, Samantha, 3 s. David, Dean (twins), Michael.

David Coleman

COLEMAN, Lisa

Lisa Coleman. Actress. b. London, 10 July 1970. Daughter of actress Ann Beach (qv) and producer-director Francis Coleman; sister of actress Charlotte Coleman (qv).
TV: *Doctors and Nurses; A Walk in the Forest; Elizabeth Alone; Travellers by Night; London's Burning; EastEnders; Redemption; Fatal Inversion; Seven Deadly Sins: Sloth; The Bill;* Joanna in *Absolutely Fabulous; Scene: Thin Ice; The Chief;* Elisa in *Scarlet & Black* (mini-series, 1993); *French and Saunders;* Philippa in *Press Gang; Scene: Sabs;* Staff Nurse Jude Kocarnik in *Casualty* (two series, 1994-6).
Films: *Loophole.* Address: c/o Sandra Boyce Management. Lives in London. Single.

Lisa Coleman

COLL, Christopher

Christopher Coll. Actor.
TV: *To Encourage the Others; The Flaxton Boys; Follyfoot; The Gentle Assassin; Death of an Informer; Victorian Scandals; The Cuckoo Waltz; Suez; Jack Be Nimble; The Fatal Spring; The Naked Civil Servant;* Group Capt Price in *Skylark;* Morley in *Minder;* Adams in *Sink or Swim;* Mr Parkinson in *Billy's Blues;* Watts in *After the Party;* Det Chief Insp Forrest in *Strangers;* Dad in *Mighty Mum and the Petnappers;* Tom in *Slinger's Day;* Victor Pendlebury in *Coronation Street;* Mr Redfers in *The Bill.*
Films: *Harry II; Whoops Apocalypse; Goody Two Shoes; The Jigsaw Man.* Address: c/o Hilda Physick.

Christopher Coll

COLLINS, Forbes

David Collins Actor/Director. b. London, 29 July 1941. Trained at the Mountview Theatre School.
TV: Zacky Martin in *Poldark;* Jonas in *Jesus of Nazareth;* Bosun Gridley in *Return to Treasure Island; Tales of the Unexpected; Doctor Who; Lovejoy; EastEnders; Coronation Street;* King John in *Maid Marian and Her Merry Men;* Brisco in *The Bill.* TV commercials: Attila the Hun for Bristol Cream Sherry.
Films: *Tess; Biggles; Time Bandits; Gulag.* Address: c/o Artist Management Group. Lives in North London. m. Nola Victoria Temple (dis); 1 d. Sasha Victoria. Hobbies: Sailing.

Forbes Collins

COLLINS, Joan

Joan Henrietta Collins. Actress. b. London, 23 May 1933. Trained at RADA. Daughter of theatrical agent Joe Collins; sister of novelist Jackie Collins.
TV: *Batman; Star Trek; The Virginian; The Man from U.N.C.L.E.; Drive Hard, Drive Fast; The Persuaders; Fallen Angels; Mission: Impossible; Baretta; Ellery Queen; Space 1999; Fantastic Journey; Tales of the Unexpected; Police Woman; The Man Who Came to Dinner; Fallen Angels; The Adventures of Tom Jones; Switch; Starsky and Hutch; Fantasy Island; Orson Welles' Great Mysteries; A Girl Can't Always Have Everything; The Wild Women of Chastity Gulch; Paper Dolls;* Alexis Colby Carrington in *Dynasty* (1981-9); *Fairie Tale Theater: Hansel and Gretel; The Making of a Male Model; The Cartier Affair; Her Life as a Man; Sins* (also producer); *Monte Carlo* (also producer); *Fame, Fortune and Romance; Dynasty: The Reunion; Roseanne; Mama's Back!; Joan Collins' Secrets* and *Health and Vitality* (both *This Morning*).
Films: *Lady Godiva Rides Again; The Woman's Angle; Judgment Deferred; I Believe in You; Decameron Nights; Cosh Boy; Turn the Key Softly; The Square Ring; Our Girl Friday; The Good Die Young; Land of the Pharaohs; The Virgin Queen; The Girl in the Red Velvet Swing; The Opposite Sex; Sea Wife; Island in the Sun; The Wayward Bus; Stopover Tokyo; The Bravados; Rally 'Round the Flag, Boys!; Seven Thieves; Esther and the King; The Road to Hong Kong; La Congiuntura; Warning Shot; Subterfuge; Can Hieronymous Merkin Ever Forget Mercy Humppe and Find True Happiness?; If It's Tuesday, This Must Be Belgium; Breve Amore; Three in the Cellar; The Executioner; Quest for Love; Revenge; The Aquarian; Fear in the Night; Tales from the Crypt; Tales that Witness Madness; Dark Places; Call of the Wolf; The Referee; Alfie Darling; The Bawdy Adventures of Tom Jones; I Don't Want to Be Born; The Great Adventure; Empire of the Ants; The Stud; The Big Sleep; The Day of the Fox; Zero to Sixty; The Bitch; Sunburn; Game for Vultures; Growing Pains; Homework; Nutcracker; In the Bleak Midwinter.* Address: c/o Peter Charlesworth. m. 1st actor Maxwell Reed (dis), 2nd 1963 actor Anthony Newley (dis 1971), 3rd 1972 producer Ron Kass (dis), 4th 1985 Peter Holm (dis); 1 d. Tara Cynara, 1 s. Sacha (Alexander Anthony) (both from 2nd m.), 1 d. Katyana (from 3rd m.).

Joan Collins

John D Collins

Lewis Collins

Matthew Collins

Michelle Collins

Pauline Collins

COLLINS, John D

John Christopher Dixon. Actor. b. London, 2 December 1942. Educated at Harrow School. Trained at RADA after winning Ivor Novello and Robert Donat scholarships. Ran his own theatre at Frinton-on-Sea (1963-4). Worked for 10 years with Spike Milligan as assistant director and actor.
TV: *Q* (Spike Milligan series); *A Family at War; Get Some In; Some Mothers Do 'Ave 'Em; Hammer House of Horror; Only Fools and Horses; Yes Minister; Hi-de-Hi!; Chance in a Million; Rude Health;* Fairfax in *'Allo, 'Allo* (series); Jerry in *You Rang, M'Lord?* (series); *On the Up;* Inspector in *The Brittas Empire; The Real McCoy;* David Cornish in *Peak Practice;* Man in *Oh Doctor Beeching!* (pilot); *Harry's Mad.* Address: c/o McIntosh Rae Management. m. Caryll Lesley Newnham; 1 d. Philippa, 1 s. Christopher. Pets: Two cats, one dog. Hobbies: Computers.

COLLINS, Lewis

Lewis Collins. Actor. b. Birkenhead, Cheshire, 27 May 1946. Worked as a hairdresser and played in pop groups before turning to acting. Trained at LAMDA.
TV: *Warship; The New Avengers;* Gavin Rumsey in *The Cuckoo Waltz* (three series, 1975-7); Bodie in *The Professionals* (1977-83); *Must Wear Tights; A Night on the Town; The Man Who Knew Too Little* (Alfred Hitchcock Presents); Sgt George Godfrey in *Jack the Ripper* (mini-series, 1988); Lord Drayton in *A Ghost in Monte Carlo* (TVM); Colonel Mustard in *Cluedo* (series, 1992).
Films: Capt Peter Skellern in *Who Dares Wins; Codename Wild Geese; Commando Leopard;* Alexander Prescott in *Carly's Webb.* Address: c/o Spotlight. m. schoolteacher Michelle Larrett; 1 s. Oliver.

COLLINS, Matthew

Matthew Collins. Presenter. b. London, 13 December 1960. Gained a BA (Hons) in French from Manchester University. Became independent traveller for *The Travel Show* after answering an advertisement for a student hitchhiker. Freelanced as a writer and TV presenter while working as a waiter and bicycle delivery boy, then did a post-graduate journalism course at University College, Cardiff.
TV: *The Travel Show* (special assignments and independent traveller, series, 1984-94); *Wogan* (outside broadcast reporter, 1987); *Paperchase* (host, quiz show series, 1990); *Daytime UK* (outside broadcast reporter, 1991); *Travel Show Extra; The Travel Show Guides* (series); *Children in Need* (1993); *Good Morning... with Anne & Nick* (travel expert, 1994-5); *This Morning* (travel expert, 1995-).
Films: Hitch-hiker/Leon's Conscience in *Leon the Pig Farmer* (also an investor in the film).
Radio: Talk Radio UK (travel expert, 1995-). **Books:** Author of Andalusia section in *Footloose Guide to Spain; Matthew's Travels – 10 Years of Trips for The Travel Show.* Address: c/o Arlington Enterprises. Lives in London. Partner: Khelga Ivanova; 2 s. Charles Patrick Rudolph, Nicolai Alexander. Pets: Goldfish, talking budgie called Doodie. Hobbies: Horse-riding, photography.

COLLINS, Michelle

Michelle Collins. Actress. b. Hackney, East London, 28 May 1963. Former singer with Mari Wilson and the Wilsations and backing singer, under the name Candide, with The Marionettes. Studied drama and theatre arts at Kingsway Princeton College. Stage plays include *Anybody for Murder* (national tour).
TV: *The David Essex Show; The Video Entertainers; Riverside;* Helen in *Morgan's Boy;* Jackie in *Marjorie and Men* (series); nurse Carol in *Albion Market* (eight episodes); Pru Murphy in *Gems* (serial); Sarah in *Bergerac; Good Neighbours; Going to Work;* Sophie in *Running Wild* (two series); Daisy in *Lucky Sunil; The Manageress;* Cindy Beale in *EastEnders; The Word* (co-presenter).
Films: Emma in *Empire State; Hidden City;* Jackie in *Personal Services.*
Records: Solo singles: *Get Ready; Ain't No Right or Wrong Way.* Plus singles with Mari Wilson and the Wilsations and with The Marionettes. Address: c/o ICM. Lives in London. Single.

COLLINS, Pauline

Pauline Collins. Actress. b. Exmouth, Devon, 3 September 1940. Granddaughter of opera singer Elaine Reid; great-niece of the poet Callanan. Trained at the Central School of Speech and Drama. West End stage plays include *A Woman in Mind, Shirley Valentine* (title role, also on Broadway) and *Shades.*
TV: *Emergency – Ward 10;* Dawn in *The Liver Birds* (Comedy Playhouse and Series 1, 1969); *Country Matters;* Sarah in *Upstairs, Downstairs;* Clara Danby in *No Honestly* (series, 1974); Sarah in *Thomas and Sarah; Wodehouse Playhouse; Tales of the Unexpected;* Sylvia in *Knockback; Tropical Moon over Dorking;* Maggie Hewson in *The Black Tower;* Harriet Boult in *Forever Green* (three series); *Flowers of the Forest;* Oliver 2 (*Comic Relief,* 1995).
Films: Pat Lord in *Secrets of a Windmill Girl;* title role in *Shirley Valentine;* Sister Joan in *City of Joy;* Elsa Tabouri in *My Mother's Courage.* **Books:** *Letter to Louise* (1992).
Awards: BAFTA: Best Film Actress award for *Shirley Valentine.* Theatre: Olivier Best Actress award, Drama Desk Award, Outer Critics' Circle Award and Tony award for *Shirley Valentine* (1988).
Address: c/o James Sharkey Associates. Lives in London. m. actor John Alderton (qv); 2 d. Louise (from a previous relationship, given up for adoption), Catherine, 2 s. Nicholas, Richard (all from m.).

COLOMBO, Tattiana

Tattiana Colombo. Actress. b. Amersham, Buckinghamshire, 26 November. Trained at the Vittorio Gassman Film School, Florence, Italy.
Television: Caroline in *Call Me Mister;* Emma Harness in *Howards' Way;* Donna Meliflua in *The Pyrates;* Isabel in *Talking in Whispers;* Leni in *Ten Great Writers: Franz Kafka — The Trial;* Roz in *Me & My Girl;* Françoise in *Capital City;* Miss Calais in *French Fields* (first and second series); Luciana Fontana in *The Manageress;* Marie-Louise in *After Henry;* Caroline and Hermione in *I Love Keith Allen;* Maria in *Clubland* (Screen Two); Piera Conti in *Inspector Morse: The Death of the Self* (1992).
Films: Valentina in *La Luna.* **Videos:** Promotional music videos with FM, The Scorpions, The Firm, Aerosmith and Robert Plant. Address: c/o Clive Corner Associates. Lives in London. Single.

Tattiana Colombo

COLTRANE, Robbie

Anthony McMillan. Actor. b. Rutherglen, Glasgow, 1950. Educated at a public school in Perthshire. Became a stand-up comedian and spent a while in America in the late Seventies.
TV: *Alfresco; A Kick up the Eighties; Five Go Mad in Dorset* (The Comic Strip Presents...); *The Beat Generation; War; Summer School; Five Go Mad on Mescalin* (The Comic Strip Presents...); *Susie; Gino — Full Story and Pics* (The Comic Strip Presents...); *The Bullshitters; Laugh, I Nearly Paid My Licence Fee; Girls on Top; Saturday Night Live;* Dr Johnson in *Blackadder the Third;* Danny McGlone in *Tutti Frutti* (series, 1987); *Midnight Breaks; Thompson; GLC* (The Comic Strip Presents...); *South Atlantic Raiders* (The Comic Strip Presents...); *The Robbie Coltrane Show; The Robbie Coltrane Special; Mistero Buffo;* Liam Kane in *Alive and Kicking* (TVM); *Open to Question* (subject); *The Bogie Man* (comedy-drama); Fitz in *Cracker* (three series, 1993-5) and *Cracker — The Movie* (edited repeat); Voice of the Old Man in *The Legend of Lochnagar* (animated); *Coltrane in a Cadillac* (presenter, series, 1993); Arnold Silverstein in *Demonella* (The Comic Strip Presents...); *Jealousy* (The Comic Strip Presents...); Dr Johnson in *Boswell and Johnson's Tour of the Western Isles* (ScreenPlay); *French and Saunders in... Space Virgins from Planet Sex; Michelle's Story* (presenter, Comic Relief special, 1995).
Films: *Balham — Gateway to the South* (short); *Flash Gordon; Subway Riders; The Ghost Dance; Scrubbers; Krull; Chinese Boxes; Loose Connections; Revolution; National Lampoon's European Vacation; Defence of the Realm; Caravaggio; The Supergrass; Absolute Beginners; Mona Lisa; The Secret Policeman's Third Ball; Eat the Rich; The Fruit Machine; The Strike; Midnight Breaks; Bert Rigby, You're a Fool; Slipstream; Danny the Champion of the World* (TVM only in US); *Lenny Live and Unleashed; Let It Ride; Henry V; Nuns on the Run; Perfectly Normal; The Pope Must Die* (US title *The Pope Must Diet*); *Triple Bogey on a Par 5 Hole; GoldenEye.* **Awards:** TV: BAFTA Best Actor award for *Cracker.*
Address: c/o CDA. Lives near Loch Lomond. Partner: Sculptor Rhona Gemmill; 1 s. Spencer.

Robbie Coltrane

COMAN, Gilly

Gilly Coman. Actress. Stage plays include *Stags and Hens* (Young Vic Theatre).
TV: Linda in *Emmerdale Farm;* Dixie's Clerk in *Boys from the Blackstuff;* Irene Kilbride in *Gathering Seed;* Marie in *Scully;* Aveline in *Bread;* Denise in *Brookside;* Holly Trevors in *Inspector Morse: The Day of the Devil;* Linda McNeill in *Against All Odds* (series, 1994).
Address: c/o Kate Feast Management.

Gilly Coman

CONLEY, Brian

Brian Conley. Comedian/Actor. b. Paddington, London, 7 August 1961. Trained as a child at the Barbara Speake Stage School and appeared in television commercials, left school at 16, lied about his age and landed a job as a Bluecoat at Pontin's in Devon, where he joined comedy showgroup Tomfoolery and spent the next few years touring Britain in cabaret. Went solo with a summer season in Jersey and made his TV début in 1982. Starred as Bill Snibson in the West End musical *Me and My Girl* (1991-2).
TV: *Make Us Laugh* (Tyne Tees Television); *Knees Up; Saturday Royal;* TV warm-up comedian; *Summertime Special; And There's More...; Wednesday at Eight; Live from Her Majesty's; Live from the Piccadilly; Live from the Palladium; Five Alive* (pilot and series); *This Way Up* (two series); *The Brian Conley Show* (four series, 1990-1, 1994-5); Kenny Conway in *Conley: Outside Chance* (1993) and *Time after Time* (two series, 1994-5); *The Royal Variety Performance* (1994, 1995).
Address: c/o LWT. Lives in Rickmansworth, Hertfordshire. Partner: Anne-Marie Aindow.

Brian Conley

CONNERY, Jason

Jason Connery. Actor. b. London, 11 January 1963. Son of actor Sean Connery and actress Diane Cilento.
TV: *The First Modern Olympics; Doctor Who;* title role in *Robin of Sherwood* (second and third series); *Serenade for Dead Lovers; The Train; The Secret Life of Ian Fleming* (TVM); *The Other Side of Paradise.*
Films: Mackinnon in *The Lords of Discipline;* Nemo (Teenager) in *Dream One;* John Kirkland in *The Boy Who Had Everything* (with his mother playing Mother).
Address: c/o Joy Jameson (UK)/STE Representation (US).

Jason Connery

Billy Connolly

CONNOLLY, Billy

Billy Connolly. Comedian. b. Glasgow, 24 November 1942. Apprentice shipyard welder, Territorial Army paratrooper, oil rig welder in Biafra and busker, before becoming a member of the Humblebums folk duo (with Gerry Rafferty), then a stand-up comedian. Stage roles include Beefy in *The Beastly Beatitudes of Balthazar B* (Duke of York's Theatre).

TV: *The Elephant's Graveyard* (Play for Today); *An Audience with Billy Connolly; The Kenny Everett Video Show; The Kenny Everett Television Show; Not the Nine O'Clock News; Minder;* The Comic Strip Presents…; *Blue Money* (TVM); *The British Academy Awards* (presenter, twice); *Whoopi Goldberg and Billy Connolly in Performance* (US, 1990); Billy MacGregor in *Head of the Class* (US series, 1990-2); *Billy Connolly: Pale Blue Scottish Person* (US, 1991); Billy MacGregor in *Billy* (US sitcom, pilot and series, 1992); *The South Bank Show* (subject, 1992); JoJo Donnelly in *Down among the Big Boys* (Screen One); *The Bigger Picture* (presenter, series on Scottish art, 1994); *Face to Face with Billy Connolly* (interviewee); *Billy Connolly's World Tour of Scotland* (series, 1994); *Billy Connolly's Return to Nose and Beak* (Comic Relief special, presenter, 1995); *Billy Connolly: A Scot in the Arctic.*

Films: *Big Banana Feet; The Secret Policeman's Ball; Dreaming; The Big Man; The Supergrass;* Hawkeye McGillicuddy in *Bullshot;* Delgado in *Water;* Blakey in *Absolution;* Frankie in *Crossing the Line; The Secret Policeman's Other Ball.* Address: c/o John Reid Enterprises. m. 1st (dis), 2nd 1990 actress Pamela Stephenson; 3 d. Daisy, Amy, Scarlett Amy, plus two children from first marriage.

Tom Conti

CONTI, Tom

Tom Conti. Actor. b. Paisley, Strathclyde, 22 November 1941. Stage plays include *Whose Life Is It Anyway* (West End and Broadway).

TV: *Adam Smith; Madame Bovary; The Glittering Prizes; The Norman Conquests; Treats; Blade on the Feather* (TVM); *Nazi Hunter: The Search for Klaus Barbie* (TVM); *The Quick and the Dead* (TVM); *Roman Holiday* (TVM); *Fatal Judgment* (TVM); *Voices Within: The Lives of Truddi Chaw; Spooks;* Lucas Frye in *The Old Boy Network* (series); *Holy Spirits* (presenter); *QED: I'm Not Stupid* (narrator, 1995).

Films: *Flame; Galileo; Eclipse; Full Circle; The Duellists; The Wall; Reuben, Reuben; Merry Christmas, Mr Lawrence; American Dreamer; Saving Grace; Miracles; Io e D'Annunzio; Heavenly Pursuits; Beyond Therapy; Two Brothers, Running; That Summer of White Roses;* Costas Caldes in *Shirley Valentine; Shattered; The Siege of Venice.* Address: c/o Chatto and Linnit. m. Kara Wilson; 1 d. Nina.

David Conville

CONVILLE, David

David Conville. Actor/Playwright. b. Kashmir, 4 June 1929. OBE. Trained at RADA.

TV: *A Little Big Business* (series); *A Pyre for Private James* (Play for Today); Minister of Defence in *Yes, Prime Minister; Bergerac; Deadline* (TVM); *Tumbledown* (TVM); George Hope-Wynne in *Surgical Spirit* (seven series, 1989-95); *Hannay; Unnatural Causes; Speaking of Mandarin; Stay Lucky.*

Films: *Dunkirk; The Evils of Frankenstein; Curse of the Werewolf; Clockwise; The Fourth Protocol; Sarah.* Address: c/o Bernard Hunter Associates. Lives in London. m. 1970 actress Philippa Gail; 1 d. Clare, 1 s. Leo. Pets: Two Jack Russell terriers. Hobbies: Real tennis, walking, battlefields.

Nick Conway

CONWAY, Nick

Nick Conway. Actor. b. Shrewsbury, 25 December 1962. Former member of Manchester Youth Theatre.

TV: *Keep on Running; Thank You Mrs Clinkscales;* Billy Boswell in *Bread; Bluebell; Starting Out; Sea View; Juliet Bravo; Going to Work; Miracles Take Longer; The Brief; The Practice.*

Address: c/o The Narrow Road Company.

CONWELL, Nula

Nula Conwell. Actress. b. London, 24 May 1959. Trained at the Anna Scher Theatre School

TV: *Magpie; Sykes; Dinner at the Sporting Club; Out; Vanishing Army;* Julie in *Telford's Change; Only a Game; The Police; If Only; Going Out; Shoestring; A Silly Little Habit* (Playhouse); *Stars of the Roller State Disco; Roll Over Beethoven; C.A.T.S. Eyes;* Maureen in *Only Fools and Horses; The Laughter Show; Home Cooking; You in Mind;* WDC Viv Martella in *Woodentop* (pilot, 1983) and *The Bill* (1984-93).

Films: *Fords on Water; Red Saturday; The Elephant Man.* Address: c/o Scott Marshall. Lives in North London. m. Martin Fredrick; 1 s. Elliott. Hobbies: Keeping fit, walking, cooking, making gifts.

Nula Conwell

COOK, Sue

Susan Thomas. Presenter. b. Ruislip, Middlesex, 30 March 1949. Gained a BA (Hons) in psychology.

TV: *Nationwide* (reporter, then presenter, 1979-83); *Breakfast Time; Out of Court; Crimewatch UK* (1984-95); *The Life and Loves of a She-Devil* (acting herself, 1986); *Children in Need; Childwatch; Daytime Live; Call My Bluff; Having a Baby; Omnibus at the Proms; The Children's Royal Variety Performance; Crimewatch File; Holiday* (reporter); *Crime Limited* (series); *Children in Need… The Countdown Begins!; Children in Need – Pause for Pudsey* (series, 1993); *Into the Night with Pudsey Bear* (Children in Need, 1993); *G.O.S.H. – Great Ormond Street Hospital; Sunday Matters* (two series,

1994-6); *Christmas Matters*. Address: c/o Curtis Brown. Lives in North London. m. 1st 1971 Brian C Cook (dis 1976), 2nd 1981 classical guitarist John Williams (dis 1987), partner William Macqueen (TV producer Billy Macqueen); 1 s. Charlie (from 2nd m.), 1 d. Megan (from current relationship with Billy Macqueen). Pets: One dog, one cat, three hamsters, one goldfish. Hobbies: Singing, tennis.

Sue Cook

COOMBS, Pat
Patricia Doreen Coombs. Actress. b. Camberwell, South London, 27 August 1926. Trained at LAMDA.
TV: Lana Butt in *Beggar My Neighbour* (Comedy Playhouse, 1966, three series, 1967-8); Violet Robinson in *Lollipop Loves Mr Mole* (series, 1971) and *Lollipop* (series, 1972); *The Dick Emery Show; Marty;* Dorothy Blake in *Don't Drink the Water!* (two series); Cissie Lupin in *You're Only Young Twice* (four series, 1977-81); *This Is Your Life* (subject); Lanky Pat in *The Lady Is a Tramp* (two series); *Till Death Us Do Part;* Mrs Carey in *In Sickness and in Health* (series); *Ragdolly Anna; And There's More; Mr Majeika;* Brown Owl Marge Green in *EastEnders; Roy's Raiders; An Actor's Life for Me; Noel's House Party;* Gloria in *Birds of a Feather;* Doris in *Boon;* Pru in *Noel 's House Party* .
Films: *Ooh... You Are Awful; Adolf Hitler — My Part in His Downfall.*
Address: c/o Barry Burnett Organisation. Lives in Harrow-on-the-Hill, Middlesex. Single. Pets: Two cats, Rudy and Nola. Hobbies: 'Work! And I love a pen in my hand.'

Pat Coombs

COPLEY, Paul
Paul Mackriell Copley. Actor/Writer. b. Denby Dale, West Yorkshire, 25 November 1944.
TV: *A Christmas Carol; Dear Harriet; Secret Army; Strangers; Glad Day; The Turkey Who Lives on the Hill; Days of Hope; Trinity Tales; Anthem — Story of an Escape, Chester Mystery Plays; Treasure Island; Some Enchanted Evening; Destiny; Travellers; After Julius* (mini-series); *Cries from a Watchtower; Happy; Mucking Out; Stepping Stones; Death of a Princess; God's Story* (narrator); *A Brush with Mr Porter on the Road to Eldorado; A Room for the Winter; PQ17;* Jesus in *All the World's a Stage; Minder; Turning Year Tales; West End Tales; Tenko; Big Deal; Juliet Bravo; Jackanory* (storyteller); *The Gathering Seed; The Bright Side* (series); *The Bird Fancier; Dangerous Journey* (narrator); *Silas Marner: The Weaver of Raveloe; Thunder Rock; Oedipus at Colonus; The Mistress* (series); *Our Geoff; Zig-Zag: The Vikings; Gruey* (series); *Young Charlie Chaplin; Gruey Twoey; Testimony of a Child; Daytime Live; War and Remembrance; View from the Woodpile* (voice-over); *Landmarks: Christopher Columbus; The Paradise Club; Grange Hill; The Bill; Scene: Collision Course; Trainer; Stay Lucky; Dispatches: The Arthur Legend* (voice-over); *The Seven Deadly Sins: Gluttony; Heartbeat; Rides; Wall to Wall: Dark Horses* (narrator); *Harry* (series, 1993); *Cracker* (three series, 1993-5); *A Pinch of Snuff* (mini-series); *Roughnecks* (series, 1994); *Scene: No Charge; Sloggers; Peak Practice; The All New Alexei Sayle Show; Casualty.*
Films: Bakey in *Alfie Darling;* Private Wicks in *A Bridge Too Far; Zulu Dawn; Doll's Eye; Ends and Means; Fish 'n' Ships* (narrator); *How's Business?;* Harry Smith in *The Remains of the Day;* Mr Willis in *Jude the Obscure.* Address: c/o Kate Feast Management. Lives in south-west London. m. 1972 actress Natasha Pyne. Pets: Frogs. Hobbies: Swimming, motorcycling, travel, photography.

Paul Copley

COPLEY, Peter
Peter Copley. Actor. b. Bushey, Hertfordshire, 20 May 1915. Trained at the Old Vic Theatre School.
TV: *The Gold Robbers; Hadleigh; Big Brother; The Forsyte Saga; The Regiment; Manhunt; Father Brown; Survivors; Sutherland's Law; Bill Brand; Bless This House; The Foundation; Churchill and the Generals; The Gentle Touch; United Kingdom; Bless Me, Father; Rabbit Pie Day; Tales of the Unexpected; German Spies; Witness for the Prosecution* (TVM); *Strangers and Brothers; Géricault;* Caesar in *Androcles and the Lion; The Prisoner of Zenda; Agatha Christie's Miss Marple; Hot Metal; The Trial of Klaus Barbie; Never Say Die; One Foot in the Grave; Future Worlds: Borderland; Agatha Christie's Poirot; Josie; Moon and Son; Casualty* (two roles); *The Ruth Rendell Mysteries: An Unwanted Woman; Zig-Zag: The Saxons; Lovejoy;* Vicar in *Grange Hill;* Abbot Heribert in *Cadfael* (series, 1994); *The Bill.*
Films: Selection (from 48): *Tell Me If It Hurts* (début, short, 1934); *Farewell Again; Golden Salamander; The Elusive Pimpernel; The Fighting Pimpernel; Follow That Horse!; Help!; The Knack... and how to get it; The Jokers; Quatermass and the Pit; The Shoes of the Fisherman; Mosquito Squadron; Frankenstein Must Be Destroyed; All at Sea;* Walk a Crooked Path; Jane Eyre; That's Your Funeral; Gawain and the Green Knight; Hennessey; Shout at the Devil; The Black Panther; Little Lord Fauntleroy; Empire of the Sun; Second Best; All or Nothing at All.* Address: c/o St James's Management. Lives in Bristol. m. 1st actress Pamela Brown (dis), 2nd actress Ninka Dolega (dis), 3rd writer Margaret Tabor; 1 d. Fanny, 1 step-d. Emma, 1 step-s. Gideon. Pets: Tortoises. Hobbies: Art history.

Peter Copley

CORBETT, Matthew
Matthew Corbett. Entertainer. b. Yorkshire, 28 March 1948. Son of Harry Corbett, creator of Sooty. Trained as an actor at the Central School of Speech and Drama.
TV: *Magpie; Rainbow; Matt and Gerry Ltd; The Sooty Show; Sooty's World; Sooty & Co.* Address: c/o Vincent Shaw Associates. Lives in Camberley, Surrey. Sallie; 1 d. Tamsin, 2 s. Benjamin, Joe,

Matthew Corbett

Ronnie Corbett

CORBETT, Ronnie

Ronnie Corbett. Actor/Comedian. b. Edinburgh, 4 December 1930.
TV: *Crackerjack; The Dickie Henderson Show; Let Yourself Go; Art of Living; The Frost Report; No, That's Me Over Here* (two series, 1968, 1970); *Frost on Sunday; The Corbett Follies; The Two Ronnies; Sorry!; Bruce and Ronnie; Small Talk* (host, panel show, two series, 1994-5); *The Royal Variety Performance* (1994); Arthur Askey in *Call Up the Stars* (VE Day concert, 1995); *The Entertainers.*
Films: *Casino Royale; Some Will, Some Won't; The Rise and Rise of Michael Rimmer; No Sex Please — We're British.* Address: c/o International Artistes. m. Anne Hart; 2 d. Emma, Sophie.

CORNWELL, Judy

Judy Valerie Cornwell. Actress/Author. b. London, 22 February 1942. Granddaughter of music-hall star 'Smiling Sarah' Bonner. Trained as a dancer and singer, and was a student dancing teacher.
TV: Runaway schoolgirl in *Dixon of Dock Green* (début, 1957); *Emergency — Ward 10; War of the Worlds; The Dickie Henderson Show; The Younger Generation; Paris 1900; All the World's a Stage;* Beattie in *Roots;* Miss Smith in *Call Me Daddy; Poor Cherry, The Memorandum; No Decision; Infidelity Took Place; The Rise and Fall of Kelvin Walker; The Anniversary; The Relatively Speaking; Cork Moustache; The Chinese Prime Minister; Night of the Tanks;* Miss Pegg in *Moody and Pegg* (series); Rosie in *Cakes and Ale; Man of Straw; Ruffian on the Stair;* Gay Spanker in *London Assurance; Cranford; The Bonus; The Dick Emery Show;* Touch of the Tiny Hacketts; Bessie in *The Mill on the Floss;* Miss Trant in *The Good Companions; A Little Rococo;* Dorothea Grimm in *Omnibus: The Brothers Grimm; A Case of Spirits; Jane Eyre; There Comes a Time; Play Acting; The Guest;* Miss Brock in *Good Behaviour, December Rose; Paying Guests; Bergerac; Rumpole of the Bailey; Farrington of the FO; Strong Poison; Doctor Who; Boon;* Daisy in *Keeping Up Appearances* (five series, 1990-5, plus Christmas Special, 1994); Aunt Peggy in *Nice Town* (mini-series, 1992); *Van Der Valk; Agatha Christie's Miss Marple: The Mirror Crack'd; Under the Hammer;* Mrs Musgrove in *Jane Austen's Persuasion* (Screen Two, 1995).
Films: *Two for the Road; The Chequered Flag; Paddy; Every Home Should Have One* (US title *Think Dirty); Wuthering Heights; The Devil's Lieutenant; Asking for Trouble; Santa Claus; Cry Freedom.*
Books: *Cow and Cow Parsley; Fishcakes at the Ritz; The Seventh Sunrise* (all novels).
Awards: TV: Emmy Award for *Call Me Daddy.* Address: c/o Ken McReddie. Lives in Sussex. m. 1960 BBC arts correspondent John Parry; 1 s. Edward (b. 1965). Hobbies: Travel.

Judy Cornwell

COSSINS, James

James Cossins. Actor. b. Beckenham, Kent, 4 December 1933. Trained at RADA (Silver Medal winner).
TV: *Mad Jack; A Day Out; Dombey and Son; The Pickwick Papers;* Watson in *Some Mothers Do 'Ave 'Em;* Judge in *Citizen Smith;* Mr Walt in *Fawlty Towers; Marjorie and Men; S.W.A.L.K.; Rude Health; Agatha Christie's Miss Marple: At Bertram's Hotel; Bergerac; Chelworth;* Justin Bryce in *Unnatural Causes;* Meredith Bland in *Under the Hammer.*
Films: *How I Won the War; The Anniversary; A Dandy in Aspic; Scrooge; Privilege; The Lost Continent; Melody; Wuthering Heights; Otley; Villain; Young Winston; Hitler: The Last Ten Days; The Man with the Golden Gun; The Great Train Robbery; Sphinx; The Confessions of Felix Krull; Gandhi; The Masks of Death; A Fish Called Wanda; Grand Larceny.*
Address: c/o Julian Belfrage Associates. Lives near Farnham, Surrey.

James Cossins

COSTIGAN, George

George Costigan. Actor. West End plays include *John Paul George Ringo... and Bert* and *Blood Brothers.*
TV: Philip the Bastard in *King John;* Tom Hannaway in *Fame Is the Spur; The Barchester Chronicles; The Sailor's Return; Red Monarch; Bloody Kids;* Arnie in *Connie* (series); Schasser in *Chimera;* Nolan O'Shaughnessy in *Under the Skin; Slip Up; The Adventures of Sherlock Holmes; London's Burning;* Johnnie Wiltshire in *Rockliffe's Babies;* Ben in *The Beiderbecke Connection;* Ollie Sutton in *Bergerac;* Billy in *Minder;* Ron Garrett in *Inspector Morse; Monster Maker,* Pete Rokeby in *So Haunt Me* (three series, 1992-4); Justin Bryce in *Unnatural Causes;* Sean in *Safe* (ScreenPlay); Vincent in *The Riff Raff Element* (series, 1993); *Sin Bin* (Screen Two); Det Insp Manciple in *The Ruth Rendell Mysteries: Master of the Moor;* Robin Cheeseman in *P D James' A Mind to Murder;* Michael Duggan in *Kavanagh QC; Coogan's Run* (series, 1995); George Dartnell in *Madson.*
Films: Bob in *Rita, Sue and Bob Too;* Dougie in *Shirley Valentine;* Stephen Marsh in *The Hawk.*
Address: c/o Jonathan Altaras Associates. Lives in France. m. actress Julia North.

George Costigan

COTTERILL, Chrissie

Anna Marie Christine Cotterill. Actress. b. Mile End, East London, 19 July 1955. Trained at the East 15 Acting School.
TV: *The Crezz; Fox; The Professionals;* Daphne in *Separate Tables;* Lindsay; Cynthia in *Crossroads; The Lady; Shades of Darkness; A Terrible Coldness; The Charmer; Bust; Boon; Valentine Park;* Wendy in *Minder;* Mona in *Prospects; The Bill* (four roles); June Smith in *EastEnders;* Debbie in *May to December*

Chrissie Cotterill

(six series, 1989-94); Roz Timson in *Rumpole of the Bailey;* Annie in *Love Hurts;* Trish in *Birds of a Feather;* Shirley in *Too Late to Talk to Billy;* Babs in *Rides;* Jo Brand through the Cakehole; Linda Bowman in *Expert Witness;* Di Smart in *A Terrible Coldness — Graham Young* (Crime Story).
Films: Belle in *Billy the Kid and the Green Baize Vampire;* Judy in *Yanks;* Jane in *Adventures of Caleb Williams;* Annette in *Scrubbers; Smoke.* **Awards:** Theatre: New York Critics' Circle Best Actress award for *Scrubbers.* Address: c/o Langford Associates. Lives in London. m. 1st lighting designer Edward Heron (dis), 2nd rock guitarist Robert Mooney; 1 d. Katie Cotterill (from 1st m.), 1 s. Jodie Mooney. Pets: A dog called Flash. Hobbies: Horse-riding, swimming.

COTTON, Oliver

Oliver Cotton

Oliver Charles Cotton. Actor. b. London, 20 June 1944. Trained at The Drama Centre.
TV: Cesare Borgia in *The Borgias; The Peasant Revolt; Rhodes; Sharpe's Battle; The Year of the French; Sovereign's Company; Ross; Robin of Sherwood; Lovejoy; Return to Treasure Island; Thank You Miss Jones; C.A.T.S. Eyes; David Copperfield; The Party; The Bretts; Hannay; Room at the Bottom; Hiding Out; Redemption;* Max in *The Camomile Lawn* (mini-series, 1992); Alan Cromer in *Westbeach* (series, 1993); *Fireworks;* Paul Collier in *Harry;* Loup in *Sharpe's Battle.* As writer: *The Intruder.*
Films: *Here We Go Round the Mulberry Bush; The Day Christ Died; Oliver Twist; Firefox; Eleni; The Sicilian; Hiding Out; Christopher Columbus: The Discovery; Son of the Pink Panther; The Innocent Sleep.* Address: c/o Jonathan Altaras Associates. Lives in London. m. 2nd Irene; 2 d. Abigail (from 1st m.), Sophie (from 2nd m.). Hobbies: Classical guitar, writing.

COUNSELL, Elizabeth

Elizabeth Counsell

Elizabeth Counsell. Actress. b. Windsor, Berkshire, 7 June 1942. Parents, John Counsell and Mary Kerridge, ran the Theatre Royal, Windsor.
TV: *The Top Secret Life of Edgar Briggs; Song by Song by Hart; Partners; Executive Stress; Brush Strokes;* Jackie Spicer in *Nelson's Column* (two series, 1994-5).
Address: c/o ICM. m. actor David Simeon; 1 s. Leo.

COURTENAY, Margaret

Margaret Courtenay

Margaret Carolyn Courtenay-Short. Actress. b. Cardiff, 14 November 1923. Trained at LAMDA. Stage plays include *Ring round the Moon* (West End), *Alfie* (West End and Broadway).
TV: *The Expert; Z Cars; Billy Liar; It Ain't Half Hot Mum; The Squirrels; The Howerd Confessions; London Belongs to Me; Best of Friends; The Upchat Line; A Sharp Intake of Breath; Mind Your Language; Out; Fearless Frank; Rings on Their Fingers; The Old Curiosity Shop; Goodbye Darling; Good Companions; Only When I Laugh; Winston Churchill — The Wilderness Years; Kelly Monteith; Shelley; Tom, Dick and Harriet; The Morecambe and Wise Show;* Nurse Clinch in *The Fasting Girl;* Lady Devereaux in *Never the Twain* (two series); *Fresh Fields; Moving House; The Stanley Baxter Show;* Lady Naboth in *Paradise Postponed; The Two Mrs Grenvilles* (mini-series); *Executive Stress; The Two of Us; Don't Wait Up; Dandy Dick;* Miss Pinkerton in *Vanity Fair;* Lady Sharpcott in *The House of Windsor* (series, 1994).
Films: *Isadora; Hot Millions; Under Milk Wood; Royal Flash; Sarah; Oh Heavenly Dog; The Mirror Crack'd;* Sonia in *Duet for One.*
Address: c/o Barry Burnett Organisation. Lives in London. m. Ivan G T Pinfield (dis 1969); 1 s. Julian Courtenay. Hobbies: Painting, gardening.

COURTENAY, Tom

Tom Courtenay

Tom Courtenay. Actor. b. Hull, East Yorkshire, 25 February 1937. Trained at RADA (1960-1).
TV: *Private Potter* (début, 1961); *The Lads; Ghosts; I Heard the Owl Call My Name* (TVM); *Jesus of Nazareth; Absent Friends; Chekhov in Yalta.*
Films: *The Loneliness of the Long Distance Runner; Private Potter; Billy Liar!; King and Country; Operation Crossbow* (US title *The Great Spy Mission*); *King Rat; Doctor Zhivago; The Night of the Generals; The Day the Fish Came Out; A Dandy in Aspic; Otley; Catch Me a Spy; One Day in the Life of Ivan Denisovitch; Today Mexico — Tomorrow the World* (short); *The Dresser; Happy New Year; Leonard Part VI; The Last Butterfly; "Let Him Have It".* Address: c/o Michael Whitehall

COWPER, Nicola

Nicola Cowper

Nicola Cowper. Actress. b. Chelsea, London, 21 December 1967. Sister of actress twins Gerry and Jackie Cowper. Modelled and appeared in TV commercials until age of nine. Trained at Corona Academy.
TV: *Break in the Sun* (aged 12); *Minder; Home Video; The Burston Rebellion; S.W.A.L.K.;* Heather Golding in *The Practice; Night Voices;* Gina in *Streetwise;* Inspector Morse; George in *Rides* (two series, 1992-3); Carl/Carol in *Casualty;* Sarah in *Crimewatch File;* Lisa in *Tears before Bedtime; The Bill.*
Films: Angie in *Winter Flight;* Lucy in *DreamChild; Underworld; Lionheart; Journey to the Centre I; Journey to the Centre II.*
Address: c/o Noel Gay Artists. Lives in Twickenham, Middlesex. Single.

Brian Cox

COX, Brian

Brian Cox. Actor. Trained at LAMDA. b. Dundee, 1 June 1946.

TV: *The Master of Ballantrae; The Changeling; Shades of Greene; Targets; The Devil's Crown; The Silent Scream; A Cotswold Death; King Lear, Churchill's People; Dalhouse's Luck; Bothwell; Thérèse Raquin; The House on the Hill; Minder; Crown Court; Florence Nightingale; Pope John Paul II; Jemima Shore Investigates; Bach; The Fourth Floor; Home Cooking; Shoot for the Sun; Shadow on the Sun; Rat in the Skull; Alas Smith and Jones; Murder by Moonlight; Perfect Scoundrels; Red Fox* (mini-series); Owen in *The Lost Language of Cranes;* Carl May in *The Cloning of Joanna May* (mini-series); *Van Der Valk;* Archdeacon Edward Hoyland in *The Big Battalions* (series); Producer in *Six Characters in Search of an Author* (Performance); *Sean's Show;* Michael Steppings in *Inspector Morse: Deadly Slumber;* Hogan in *Sharpe's Rifles* and *Sharpe's Eagle; Pigboy; The Cutter* (Short and Curlier); Picasso in *Yo Picasso;* title role in *Grushko* (mini-series); Charlie King in *The Negotiator; Survival Special* (narrator).

Films: Dr Hannibal Lecktor in *Manhunter; Secret Weapon; Hidden Agenda; Iron Will; Prince of Jutland; Grushko; Braveheart; Rob Roy.* Address: c/o Conway, van Gelder, Robinson. m. actress Caroline Burt (dis); 1 s. actor Alan, 1 d. Margaret. Partner: Actress Siri O'Neal (qv). Lives in North London.

Andy Craig

CRAIG, Andy

Andrew Timm Craig. Presenter/Journalist. b. Cumbria, 5 December 1954. Gained an honours degree in agriculture at Newcastle upon Tyne University.

TV: *Northern Life* (Tyne Tees Television); *Central News* (Central Television); *Good Morning Britain; Central Weekend Live; The Home Service; Hot Property; The Time The Place; Head to Head* (TVS); *Searchline Special; This Morning; Sporting Triangles* (host); *Daytime Live; Late and Live* (Tyne Tees Television); *One False Move* (BSB Galaxy); *Brain Waves; That's History; A Family Fortune* (*This Morning*); *Going, Going, Gone* (host, game show, series, 1995). As producer: *Everyone's Problem; First AIDS; Coconuts* (cartoon series); *Late and Live.* Address: c/o Orbi-Tel, 3 The Coppice, Seer Green, Beaconsfield, Buckinghamshire HP9 2SH, tel (01494) 677054. Lives in Nottingham. Single.

Wendy Craig

CRAIG, Wendy

Wendy Craig. Actress. b. Sacriston, Co Durham, 20 June 1934. Trained at Central School of Speech and Drama.

TV: *Candida; Wings of a Dove; Not in Front of the Children; And Mother Makes Three; And Mother Makes Five;* Ria Parkinson in *Butterflies* (1978-82); *Nanny; Laura and Disorder;* Valerie in *Without Walls: For Love or Money;* Annie in *Brighton Belles* (pilot, 1993, and series, 1993-4); *Celebration Concert: It's a Lovely Day Tomorrow* (guest narrator, VE 50, 1995).

Films: *Room at the Top; The Mind Benders; The Servant; The Nanny; Just Like a Woman; I'll Never Forget What's 'is Name; Joseph Andrews.* **Awards:** BAFTA TV Drama Actress of the Year award (1968). Address: c/o Richard Hatton. m. musician/writer Jack Bentley; 2 s. Alaster, Ross.

Andy Crane

CRANE, Andy

Andy Crane. Presenter. b. Morecambe, Lancashire, 24 February 1964. Former radio presenter.

TV: Children's BBC; *Motormouth* (series); *What's Up Doc?* (series); *Bad Influence!* (four series, 1992-5); *Sixth Sense* (series, 1993); *Sunday Live* (VE Day special, 1995); *Take Two* (series, 1995-6).

Radio: Piccadilly Radio; Capital Radio; *History Lost and Found* (BBC Schools).

Address: c/o PVA Management. 1 d. Eleanor.

Kenneth Cranham

CRANHAM, Kenneth

Kenneth Cranham. Actor. b. Dunfermline, 12 December 1944. Trained at RADA.

TV: Hippy in *Coronation Street; Sling Your Hook; Canterbury Tales; The Sound of Guns; The Chauffeur and the Lady; The Sin Bin; Donkey's Years; Butterflies Don't Count; La Ronde; The Caretaker; The Merchant of Venice; 'Tis Pity She's a Whore; Danger UXB; The Bell; Cribb; Thérèse Raquin;* title role in *Shine on Harvey Moon* (1982-5); *The Dumb Waiter; The Birthday Party; Brideshead Revisited;* Lenin in *Reilly — Ace of Spies; Lady Windermere's Fan; A Sort of Innocence; Agatha Christie's Dead Man's Folly; The Party; Normal Services; Inspector Morse; The Black and Blue Lamp; The Contractor; Boon; Master of the Marionettes; Frederick Forsyth Presents: Just Another Secret; Rules of Engagement;* Pastor Finch in *Oranges are Not the Only Fruit;* Mercer in *El C.I.D.* (two series); *TECX; Chimera; Van Der Valk; Casualty; Bergerac; Dunrulin; The Young Indiana Jones Chronicles; Murder Most Horrid; A Little Bit of Lippy; Between the Lines; Minder; Lovejoy; Royal Celebration; The Vision Thing; Requiem Apache* (Alan Bleasdale Presents).

Films: *Making Waves; Oliver!; Otley; All the Way Up; Fragment of Fear; Brother Sun, Sister Moon; Robin and Marian; Joseph Andrews; Heart of the High Country; The Clot; Stealing Heaven; Chocolat; Under Suspicion; Hellbound: Hellraiser II;* Sebastian in *Prospero's Books; Monkey Boy.*

Address: c/o Markham & Froggatt. Lives in North London. m. 1st actress Diana Quick (dis), 2nd actress Fiona Victory; 1 d. Nancy (from relationship with actress Charlotte Cornwell, between two m's).

CRAVEN, John

John Craven. Presenter. b. Leeds, 16 August. Newspaper journalist in Yorkshire before entering radio.
TV: *Sunday Break* (aged 16); *Look North; Points West; Search; Newsround* (presenter, 1972-9, then editor); *Multi-Coloured Swop Shop; Saturday Superstore; Breakthrough; Story behind the Story; Country File; CountryFile on Sunday* (new title from 1994); *Animal Sanctuary* (1994, 1995).
Address: c/o Noel Gay Artists. m. Marilyn; 2 d. Emma, Victoria.

John Craven

CRAWFORD, Michael

Michael Patrick Smith. Actor/Singer. b. Salisbury, Wiltshire, 19 January 1942. Began acting as a child. West End productions include *Billy, Barnum* and *The Phantom of the Opera* (also Broadway and LA).
TV: *Billy Bunter; Probation Officer; Emergency — Ward 10; The Chequered Flag; The Guinea Pig; Police Surgeon; The Siege of Kilfaddy; The Seekers;* John Drake in *Sir Francis Drake* (series); *Destiny; Still Life* (Canada); Byron in *Not So Much a Programme, More a Way of Life; The Move after Checkmate; The Three Barrelled Shotgun; Home Sweet Honeycomb; The Policeman and the Cook;* Frank Spencer in *Some Mothers Do 'Ave 'Em* (1973-8); *To Be Perfectly Frank* (documentary); *Sorry...: Private View/Audience;* Dave Finn in *Chalk and Cheese* (series); *Weekend Special: Tribute to Michael Crawford; The South Bank Show* (subject); *Barnum; Save the Children with Michael Crawford.*
Films: *Soapbox Derby; Blow Your Own Trumpet; Two Living, One Dead; The War Lover; Two Left Feet; The Knack... and how to get it; A Funny Thing Happened on the Way to the Forum; The Jokers; How I Won the War; Hello, Dolly!; The Games; Hello-Goodbye; Alice's Adventures in Wonderland; Condorman; Once Upon a Forest* (voice only). Address: c/o ICM. Lives in Bedfordshire and London. m. 1965 former actress-dancer Gabrielle Lewis (dis 1975); 3 d. Angelique (b. 1965, from previous relationship with Patricia Mansell), Emma (b. 1966), Lucy (b. 1967) (both from m.).

Michael Crawford

CRIBBINS, Bernard

Bernard Cribbins. Actor. b. Oldham, Lancashire, 29 December 1928. Joined Oldham Rep as ASM at 14.
TV: *Judgement Day; Cribbins* (series); Comedy Playhouse; *Val Doonican; Get the Drift; Children Singing; Jackanory; Patrick, Dear Patrick; The Good Old Days; The Wombles* (narrator, series); Feydeau Farces; *Junkin; We Want to Sing;* Mr Hutchinson in *Fawlty Towers; Space 1999; Dangerous Davies — The Last Detective* (TVM); *Star Turn;* Cuffy in *Shillingbury Tales* (series) and *Cuffy* (series); *Langley Bottom;* Ron Archer in *High and Dry* (series); *When We Are Married; Tonight at 8.30: Hands across the Sea; The Children's Royal Variety Performance 1992.*
Films: *Yangtse Incident; Davy; Dunkirk; Make Mine a Million; Tommy the Toreador; Two Way Stretch; Visa to Canton; The World of Suzie Wong; The Girl on the Boat; Nothing Barred; The Best of Enemies; The Wrong Arm of the Law; The Mouse on the Moon; Crooks in Cloisters; Carry On Jack; Carry On Spying; Allez France; A Home of Your Own; She; You Must Be Joking!; Cup Fever; The Sandwich Man; Daleks — Invasion Earth 2150 AD; Casino Royale ; A Ghost of a Chance; Don't Raise the Bridge, Lower the River; The Undertakers* (short); Mr Perks in *The Railway Children; Frenzy; Night Ferry; The Water Babies; The Adventures of Picasso; Carry On Columbus.* **Records:** Singles: *Hole in the Ground* (No 9, 1962); *Right Said Fred* (No 10, 1962); *Gossip Calypso* (No 25, 1962). Album: *The Snowman* (narrator) (No 54, 1984). Address: c/o James Sharkey Associates. Lives in Weybridge, Surrey. m. Gillian McBarnet. Pets: Jack Russell called Rosie. Hobbies: Fishing, shooting, golf.

Bernard Cribbins

CROFT, Jaq

Jacqueline Mycroft. Actress. b. Paris, 4 April 1968. Trained at the Drama Studio.
TV: Elizabeth Lester in *The Bill;* Monique in *Stick with Me, Kid;* Riana in *The Terminal Game;* Felicia in *Class Act;* Anna in *Making Waves;* Betty in *Inspector Shaikh.*
Films: Judy Holloway in *Rio;* Juliette in *The Reluctant Stranger.*
Address: c/o Langford Associates. Lives in Surrey. m. rock musician Conal Cunningham; 1 s. Jamie.

Jaq Croft

CROPPER, Anna

Anna Cropper. Actress. b. Brierfield, Lancashire, 13 May 1938. Trained at the Central School of Speech and Drama.
TV: Joan Akers in *Coronation Street; The Insect Play; The Rivals; Angel Pavement; Imperial Palace; Père Goriot; In Two Minds; Robin Redbreast; The Lost Boys; The Crucible; The Jewel in the Crown; Agatha Christie's Miss Marple: Nemesis; Van Gogh; The Ruth Rendell Mysteries: A New Lease of Death; Memento Mori;* Gwen Cellan-Davies in *The Old Devils; Early Travellers in North America; Agatha Christie's Poirot; The Marshal* (pilot); The Hon Violet Duffy in *The Inspector Alleyn Mysteries; Harry; Heartbeat; If You See God, Tell Him; Jealousy* (Capital Lives, Carlton only); Mrs Morrey in *Midnight Movie;* Margaret Castle in *Castles* (series, 1995); *Prisoners in Time* (Everyman special); *The Affair.*
Films: *All Neat in Black Stockings;* Ruth Carter in *Cromwell; The Shooting Party; Nanou.*
Address: c/o Kate Feast Management. Lives in West London. m. actor William Roache (qv) (dis 1974); 1 s. actor Linus Roache (qv), 1 d. Vanya Roache. Pets: Dog.

Anna Cropper

Annette Crosbie

CROSBIE, Annette

Annette Crosbie. Actress. b. Gorebridge, nr Edinburgh, 12 February 1934. Trained at Bristol Old Vic Theatre School.

TV: *Concussion; A Splinter of Ice;* Catherine of Aragon in *The Six Wives of Henry VIII; Separate Tables; Katharine Mansfield; The Boy Dave;* Queen Victoria in *Edward the Seventh; Lillie; Jessie; Family Dance; Northern Lights; The Disappearance of Harry; Off Peak; Paradise Postponed; Beyond the Pale; Game, Set & Match;* Liz in *Take Me Home* (mini-series); Margaret Meldrew in *One Foot in the Grave* (five series, 1990-5, plus Christmas Special, 1994); Penelope Stirling in *Heartbeat;* Irene Bell in *The Ruth Rendell Mysteries: The Speaker of Mandarin;* Janet MacPherson in *Doctor Finlay* (four series 1993-6); *One Foot in the Algarve (One Foot in the Grave* Christmas special, 1993); Tom's Mother in *Nervous Energy* (Screen Two); *One Foot in the Grave Christmas Special* (1995); *Rory Bremner, Apparently.*
Films: *The Public Eye;* Fairy Godmother in *The Slipper and the Rose; Leon the Pig Farmer.*
Address: c/o Julian Belfrage Associates. m. Michael Griffith; 1 s. Owen, 1 d. Selina.

Sara Crowe

CROWE, Sara

Sara Crowe. Actress. Has performed in street shows in Covent Garden and at the Hippodrome and Comedy Store, London, and Danceteria, New York, as well as touring the UK as support to Rory Bremner. Stage plays include *Henceforth* (Vaudeville Theatre), *Private Lives* (Aldwych Theatre), *Twelfth Night* (Playhouse Theatre), *A Woman of No Importance* (RSC) and *Hay Fever* (Theatre of Comedy).

TV: *Rory Bremner* (three series); Fanny in *Haggard; Alas Smith and Jones; Freddy and Max; Boogie Outlaws; Roy's Raiders;* Christine Draper in *The Good Guys; Harry Enfield's Television Programme; Carrott-U-Like;* Max in *Sometime, Never* (Comedy First). TV commercials: Philadelphia cheese.
Films: Fatima in *Carry On Columbus;* Fiona in *Four Weddings and a Funeral.*
Awards: Theatre: Critics' Circle Most Promising Newcomer, Variety Club Stage Actress of the Year and Laurence Olivier Supporting Actress awards, all for *Private Lives.*
Address: c/o London Management. Lives in London.

Nicky Croydon

CROYDON, Nicky

Nicky Croydon. Actress. Stage musicals include *Leave Him to Heaven* (West End), *A Chorus Line* (Theatre Royal, Drury Lane), *Songbook* (Globe Theatre), *I'm Getting My Act Together* (Apollo Theatre), *Snoopy* (Duchess Theatre) and *Figaro* (Ambassadors Theatre).

TV: *Rights and Responsibilities* (serial); *Wainwright's Law; Dear Heart;* Jane in *The Gentle Touch; Russ Abbot's Madhouse;* Emily in *The Ballad of Johnny Vanguard; And There's More; Jimmy Cricket Special;* Jean in *A Sometime Thing; Victoria Wood – As Seen on TV; Middle of the Road Show;* Bobby Davro series and Christmas special; *Omnibus: The Voice of the City – Irving Berlin;* Jean in *Brush Strokes* (series, 1986-91); Lorraine in *Say Hello to the Real Doctor Snide;* Karen Church and Rosemary Cox in *The Bill* (two roles); Claire Wilson in *Casualty.*
Films: Singing Maid in *Lady Jane.* Address: c/o Mayer & Eden.

Barry Cryer

CRYER, Barry

Barry Charles Cryer. Presenter/Comedian/Writer. b. Leeds, 23 March 1935. TV and radio writer and performer since 1957.

TV: *The Good Old Days; Jokers Wild* (chairman, five years); *Hello Cheeky* (also writer); *What's On Next?* (also writer); *The Steam Video Company* (also writer); *All Star Secrets* (performer); *I've Got a Secret; Cross Wits; Music Match;* writer for Bob Hope, George Burns, David Frost (*The Frost Report, Frost over England, The Frost Programme, Frost on Sunday*), Jack Benny, Phil Silvers, Phyllis Diller, Richard Pryor, Tommy Cooper, Stanley Baxter, Dick Emery, Dave Allen, Frankie Howerd, Les Dawson, The Two Ronnies, Mike Yarwood, Morecambe and Wise, Bruce Forsyth (*The Generation Game*), Kenny Everett (*The Kenny Everett Video Show, The Kenny Everett Show*), Les Dawson, Billy Connolly, *The Russ Abbot Show,* Bobby Davro, Jasper Carrott, Les Dennis, Rory Bremner and Clive Anderson; *Assaulted Nuts* (co-writer); Det Sammy Simpson in *The Detectives* (acting role); *That's Life!; The Stand Up Show* (pilot, 1994, and two series, both 1995); *Famous Faces, Favourite Places; Cryer's Crackers* (host, comedy quiz, series, 1996).
Radio: *I'm Sorry I Haven't a Clue* (1972-); *Hello Cheeky* (also writer).
Address: c/o Roger Hancock. Lives in Hatch End, Middlesex. m. singer Terry Donovan; 3 s. Anthony, David, Robert, 1 d. Jacqueline. Pets: three dogs, four cats. Hobbies: 'Macramé, cartophily.'

Frances Cuka

CUKA, Frances

Frances Cuka. Actress. b. London, 21 August 1936. Trained at Guildhall School of Music and Drama. Starred as Jo in the original West End and Broadway productions of *A Taste of Honey.*

TV: *The Old Wives' Tale; Days in the Trees; Day of the Tortoise; Retreat; Point of Departure; Sense and Sensibility; Miss Nightingale; Within These Walls; Boy Dominic; One Day at a Time; Crown Court* (two roles); *Tea on St Pancras Station; The Beggar's Opera; Member of the Wedding; Girl Talk; Charlie*

Boy; Love Story; Henry IV, Part 2; Mary Lancaster in Crossroads; Maigret; Lois Knox in The Ruth Rendell Mysteries: The Speaker of Mandarin; Sister Angelica in Minder.
Films: Henry VIII and His Six Wives; Scrooge; Watcher in the Woods.
Address: c/o Lou Coulson. Lives in North London.

CULBERTSON, Rod

Rod Culbertson. Actor. b. Sunderland. Father was in the Five Smith Brothers variety singing act. Trained at the Central School of Speech and Drama (1968-71). Stage plays include The Bundle and Factory Birds (both RSC), Strippers (Phoenix Theatre) and Play Strindberg (Mermaid Theatre).
TV: Village Hall; The Balcony; Hughie Fenwick in The Stars Look Down; The Sweeney; A Horseman Riding By; Bottles (Play for Today); After Julius; The Professionals; The World Cup — A Captain's Tale; Jamie Running; Probation Officer in Brookside; Courtney in William Tell (US title Crossbow); Kevin Redmond in Taggart; Dave Wilkes in Bust; No Further Cause for Concern (Screen Two); The Bill; Albert and the Lion; Bergerac; Casualty; Gas and Candles; Denny in Spender; An Actor's Life for Me; EastEnders; Alan Webb and Mickey Hagan in The Bill.
Films: Spy Story; Porridge; SOS Titanic; Paul McCartney in The Birth of the Beatles.
Address: c/o A.D.A. Enterprises. Lives in Thames Ditton, Surrey. m. (dis); 1 d.

Rod Culbertson

CULVER, Michael

Michael John Edward Culver. Actor. b. Hampstead, North London, 16 June 1938. Son of actor Roland Culver. Trained at LAMDA. West End stage appearances include Howards End and The Severed Head.
TV: Villains; Maclean in Philby, Burgess and Maclean; A Fine Romance; Limbo Connection; Reunion; Secret Army; Fanny by Gaslight; Diamonds; Squadron; Chessgame; The Adventures of Black Beauty; Mrs Silly; Agatha Christie's Miss Marple: The Moving Finger; A Breath of Fresh Air; Game, Set & Match; Hannay; The Creeper; Countdown to War; Boon; The Return of Sherlock Holmes: The Musgrave Ritual; Justice Game; Underhill in The Green Man (mini-series); Hugo Wittersham in The Piglet Files (two series, 1990-1); The Darling Buds of May; For the Greater Good; Shrinks; Losing Track; Timewatch of R.B.; Lovejoy; Ralph Saroyan in The House of Eliott (Series 2, 1992); Mr Gervaise in Losing Track (Screen One); Inspector Morse: The Day of the Devil; Prior Robert in Cadfael (series, 1994, plus Christmas special, 1995); Half the Picture (Screen Two).
Films: Goodbye, Mr Chips; The Empire Strikes Back; Crossplot; Conduct Unbecoming; The Bunker; A Passage to India. Address: c/o JM Associates. m. Lucinda Curtis (sep 1986); 2 s. Roderic John, Justin Elliot. Hobbies: Golf, reading.

Michael Culver

CUNLIFFE, Jane

Jane Louise Cunliffe. Actress. b. Oldham, Lancashire, 1 June 1962. Studied drama at Manchester Polytechnic. Stage plays include Shut Your Eyes and Think of England (Vienna English Theatre).
TV: Student in Albion Market; Susan in Bulman; The Practice; Reporter in Strike It Rich; Carol Longthorn in Emmerdale Farm (eight episodes, 1985); Laura Gordon-Davies (née Wright) in Brookside (1987); Lavinia and Sandra in Hale and Pace; Francesca Hamilton in Hollywood Sports (12 episodes); Det Sgt Eileen Scarrett in Shoot to Kill; Penelope Athelstone in Trouble in Mind; Annie in She-Wolf of London; voice of Catherine Kovalic in Chateauvallon (20 episodes dubbed for UK from French production); Jayne Palmer in Boon; Sue Fairbrother in Conjugal Rights; Susan and Lisa Hooper in The Bill.
Address: c/o Crawfords. Lives in North London. m. (sep); 1 s. Sam. Hobbies: Retail therapy.

Jane Cunliffe

CUNNINGHAM, Emma

Emma Cunningham. Actress. b. Lee Green, south-east London, 2 April 1968. Trained at LAMDA. Founder member of the Arts Threshold theatre company.
TV: Omnibus; Acting; Inspector Morse; Van Der Valk; Gloria (Ray Daley's photographer girlfriend) in Minder (two series); Dr Gail Benson in Medics (five series). TV commercials: Kenco coffee.
Address: c/o Scott Marshall. Lives in south-west London. Single. Hobbies: Skiing, water-skiing, swimming, sculpting, interior design/decoration.

Emma Cunningham

CURRAM, Roland

Roland Curram. Actor. Trained at RADA. Stage plays include Little Murders (RSC, Aldwych Theatre).
TV: Nana; A Bouquet of Barbed Wire; The Crezz; Some Mothers Do 'Ave 'Em; Dr Jekyll and Mr Hyde; Artemis '81; Birds of Prey; C.A.T.S. Eyes; Tandoori Nights; The Bretts; Grandfather in Till We Meet Again (mini-series); Harold Perkins in Big Jim and the Figaro Club (series); Freddy and Max; Maurice Gautier in Moon and Son; Don't Tell Father; Freddie in Eldorado (serial, 1992-3); Doctor Finlay.
Films: Top of the Form; Doctor in the House; Dunkirk; The Admirable Crichton; The Silent Play ground; Darling; Ooh... You Are Awful (US title Get Charlie Tully); Peeping Tom; The Queen's Guards; Decline and Fall; I'll Never Forget What's 'is Name; Madame Sousatzka.
Address: c/o London Management. Lives in Chiswick, West London. m. (dis); 2 children

Roland Curram

Mark Curry

CURRY, Mark

Mark Curry. Actor/Presenter. b. Stafford, 27 August 1961.
TV: As presenter: *Junior Showtime* (presenter-singer, 1969-74, from the age of seven); *Stars on Sunday* (singer, 1974-5); *Calendar Kids* (Yorkshire Television only, 1974-5); *Stop-Watch; Get Set for Summer; The Saturday Picture Show; Treasure Houses; Make 'Em Laugh; Screen Test; All Star Record Breakers; Blue Peter* (1986-90); *Children's Royal Variety Performance* (1987, 1988, 1989); *Children in Need; Queen Mother's Royal Birthday Gala* (1990); *Careering Ahead* (reporter and voice-over); *English Time* (actor-presenter); *Record Breakers.* As actor: *Sounding Brass* (six episodes); *Bread; London's Burning; Close to Home.* As commentator: *Careering Ahead;* WTA Tour tennis; angling (Channel Four, Chrysalis Sport, Wire TV); team tennis; Wimbledon tennis (Channel One cable TV, 1995); *Sportsbank.*
Films: Producer in *Bugsy Malone.*
Awards: TV and Radio Industries Club award and Sony award for his show *On Your Marks* (BBC Radio 5). Address: c/o Paul du Fer Associates. Lives in London. Single. Hobbies: Tennis.

Niamh Cusack

CUSACK, Niamh

Niamh Cusack. Actress. b. Dublin. Daughter of actor Cyril Cusack; sister of actresses Sinead, Catherine and Sorcha Cusack. Began professional career as a flautist freelancing with the RTE symphony and concert orchestra. Trained at the Guildhall School of Music and Drama. RSC productions (1985-7) include *Mary after the Queen, Othello, Romeo and Juliet* and *The Art of Success.*
TV: Denise in *Lucky Sunil;* Clara in *Shadow on the Sun* (TVM); Louise in *Till We Meet Again;* Melanie in *Chalkface;* Bobby in *Jeeves and Wooster;* Dr Kate Rowan in *Heartbeat* (five series, 1992-5); Mary in *Angels* (single drama); Beatrix Potter (narrator) in *Beatrix Potter: The World of Peter Rabbit and Friends.*
Films: Clara in *Paris by Night;* Josephine in *Fools of Fortune;* Ruth in *A Marriage of Inconvenience;* Brigid in *The Playboys.* Address: c/o Peters Fraser & Dunlop. m. musician Roland Saggs (dis). Partner: Actor Barry Lynch (known as Finbar Lynch in Ireland).

Iain Cuthbertson

CUTHBERTSON, Iain

Iain Cuthbertson. Actor. b. Glasgow, 4 January 1930. Gained an MA (Hons) in languages from Aberdeen University. Radio actor, then BBC radio journalist in Glasgow, before becoming an actor.
TV: *The Borderers; Diamond Crack Diamond;* Charlie Endell in *Budgie; The Onedin Line; Tom Brown's Schooldays; Scotch on the Rocks; Black Beauty;* title role in *Sutherland's Law; Children of the Stones; The Ghosts of Motley Hall; Ripping Yarns; Caledonian Cascade; Danger UXB; Dick Francis; The Voyage of Darwin; Doctor Who; The Standard; The Casting of the Runes;* title role in *Charles Endell Esquire; We the Accused; Happy Warrior; House with Green Shutters; Vice Versa; The Assam Garden; Supergran; A Perfect Spy; First among Equals; Smart Money; Heaven and Earth; Return of the Antelope; Bulman; The Life of Thomas Mann; A Venus De Milo Instead; Twist in the Tale; Minder; Rab C Nesbitt; Inspector Morse;* Lord Chancellor in *The Guilty* (mini-series, 1992); Gervase Chevenix in *Agatha Christie's Poirot;* Malcolm Standish in *Headhunters* (mini-series); *Moonacre* (serial); Davidson in *Oliver's Travels.*
Films: *The Railway Children; Up the Chastity Belt;* Dr Louis Leakey in *Gorillas in the Mist.*
Awards: TV: ITV Personality of the Year (1973). Address: c/o Janet Welch Personal Management. m. actress Anne Kirsten (dis). Partner: Mary Smith. Hobbies: Sailing, history, literature.

Timothy Dalton

DALTON, Timothy

Timothy Dalton. Actor. b. Colwyn Bay, Clwyd, 21 March 1944. Trained at RADA.
TV: *Centennial; Charlie's Angels; The Flame Is Love* (TVM); Mr Rochester in *Jane Eyre; The Master of Ballantrae* (TVM); Perry Kilcullen in *Mistral's Daughter* (mini-series); *Florence Nightingale* (TVM); *Sins* (mini-series); *Tales from the Crypt;* Philip Von Joel/Eddie Myers in *Framed* (mini-series); *In the Wild: Wolves with Timothy Dalton* (presenter); *Red Eagle* (mini-series); Rhett Butler in *Scarlett* (mini-series).
Films: *The Lion in Winter; Cromwell; Wuthering Heights; The Voyeur; Mary, Queen of Scots; Lady Caroline Lamb; Permission to Kill; The Man Who Knew Love; Sextette; Agatha; Flash Gordon; Chanel Solitaire; The Doctor and the Devils; Brenda Starr;* James Bond in *The Living Daylights* and *Licence to Kill; Hawks; The King's Whore; The Rocketeer; Naked in New York.* Address: c/o James Sharkey Associates.

Charles Dance

DANCE, Charles

Charles Dance. Actor. b. Rednal, Worcestershire, 10 October 1946.
TV: *Dreams of Loving;* Parker in *The Professionals;* Teddy in *Raffles;* O'Brien in *Father Brown;* Duke of Clarence in *Edward the Seventh;* Charleston in *Thunder Rock;* James Latimer in *This Lightning Always Strikes Twice; Little Eyolf; Frost in May; Rainy Day Woman; Tales of the Unexpected; Very Like a Whale;* Edward Hartford Jones in *Nancy Astor;* Alan in *The Last Day; The Fatal Spring;* Guy Perron in *The Jewel in the Crown; The Secret Servant; The McGuffin; Out on a Limb; Out of the Shadows; First Born* (mini-series, 1988); Ian Fleming in *Goldeneye;* Erik in *The Phantom of the Opera.*
Films: *The Spy Who Loved Me; For Your Eyes Only; Plenty; The Golden Child; Good Morning Babylon; White Mischief; Hidden City; A Cry in the Dark; Pascali's Island; Rikki and Pete; Secret Places of the*

Heart; China Moon; Alien³. **Awards:** BAFTA Best Actor award for *The Jewel in the Crown* (1984). Address: c/o ICM. m. 1970 artist Joanna Haythorn; 1 s. Oliver, 1 d. Rebecca.

Jill Dando

DANDO, Jill
Jill Dando. Presenter. b. Weston-super-Mare, Somerset, 9 November 1961.
TV: BBC South West (1987-8); *Six O'Clock News; BBC Breakfast News; Safari UK; Holiday* (presenter, 1992-); *BAFTA Awards* (1993); *Songs of Praise; Holiday Outings* (presenter, 1993, 1994); *The Family Show; Summer Holiday* (presenter, two series, 1994-5); *Beat Retreat — The Embarkation* and *The Drumhead Service — Departure* and *Flotilla Review* (both D-Day Remembered, presenter, 1994); *Hearts of Gold* (1995); *Buckingham Palace: The Day Peace Broke Out* and *Memories and Celebration* (both as commentator, VE Day, 1995); *Crimewatch UK* (presenter, 1995-). Address: c/o Speakeasy, 90 St Mary's Road, Market Harborough, Leicestershire. Lives in London. Single. Hobbies: Antiques, walking.

DANIELS, Paul
Newton Edward Daniels. Magician/Presenter. b. South Bank, Middlesbrough, 6 April 1938. Member of the Magic Circle. Worked as a local government clerk and internal auditor, then ran a mobile grocery business and shop, before becoming a professional entertainer in 1969.
TV: *Opportunity Knocks; Be My Guest; The Wheeltappers and Shunters Social Club; The Paul Daniels Show; Fall in the Stars; The Blackpool Bonanza; Wizbit; The Paul Daniels Magic Show; The Paul Daniels Easter Magic Show; Odd One Out* (host, game show); *Every Second Counts* (host, game show, nine series); *Wipeout* (host, game show, three series, 1994-6); *Secrets* (1994); *Paul Daniels' Secrets* (series, 1995-6).
Awards: Hollywood Academy of Magical Arts Magician of the Year award; Golden Rose of Montreux award for *The Paul Daniels Easter Magic Show* (1985).
Address: c/o Mervyn O'Horan Personal Management. Lives in Middlesex. m. 1st 1960 (dis 1975), 2nd 1988 assistant Debbie McGee; 3 s. Paul Newton (b. 1960), entertainer Martin (b. 1963), Gary (b. 1969) (all from 1st m.). Hobbies: 'Magic, photography, magic, computers, magic, golf...'

Paul Daniels

DANIELS, Phil
Phil Daniels. Actor. b. London, 25 October 1958.
TV: *Raven; Hanging Around; Jubilee; An Hour in the Life of...; Scum; The Country Wife; The Flockton Flyer; Four Idle Hands; A Midsummer Night's Dream; Nelson; Meantimes; Come to Mecca; The Pickwick Papers; Will You Love Me Tomorrow* (TVM); Boyd in *Lovejoy;* Miles in *The Big One* (Rik Mayall Presents); *The World of Lee Evans;* Vince in *N7* (Comic Asides); *After Miss Julie* (Performance); Melvin in *One Foot in the Grave Christmas Special* (1995).
Films: *Breaking Glass; Quadrophenia;* Richards in *Scum; Zulu Dawn; The Class of Miss MacMichael;* Bela in *The Bride; Billy the Kid and the Green Baize Vampire.*
Address: c/o Conway, van Gelder, Robinson.

Phil Daniels

DANVERS, Ivor
Ivor Danvers. Actor. b. Westcliff-on-Sea, Essex. Son of actor-director Charles Danvers. Trained at the Italia Conti Stage Academy and the Central School of Speech and Drama. West End productions include *Journey's End, The Mousetrap, The Norman Conquests, A Touch of Danger* and *Me and My Girl.*
TV: *Minder; Tenko; Terry and June; No Place Like Home; The World Walk; Dramarama: The World Walk; We're Going to Be All Right;* Gerald Urquhart in *Howards' Way* (six series); Richard's Boss in *Keeping Up Appearances;* Michael in *Brookside.* Address: c/o Felix De Wolfe. Lives in London. m. Henrietta; 1 d. actress-singer Lindsey, 1 s. musician Tom. Pets: One cat. Hobbies: Golf, chess, bridge.

Ivor Danvers

DAVENPORT, Claire
Claire Bernice Davenport. Actress. b. Sale, Cheshire, 23 April 1936. Trained at RADA.
TV: *Z Cars; Pollyanna; Song of Songs; On the Buses; Sez Les; Love Thy Neighbour; Churchill's People; George and Mildred; The Losers; Our Little Town; The Bruce Forsyth Show; Fawlty Towers; The Dick Emery Show* (as his wife, 1977-81); *Not the Nine o'Clock News; The Nesbitts; Metal Mickey; Just Good Friends; Sink or Swim; All for Love; The Frankie Howerd Show; 3-2-1; No Country for Old Men;* Teresa in *Freud;* Dorothy in *By the Sword Divided* (two series); *Minder;* Hilda in *Remington Steele; Alice in Wonderland ; Let There Be Love; The Hulk; Them and Us; Jack the Ripper; Emu's World; In Sickness and in Health; The Pink Windmill Show; Valentine Park; A Ticket to Ride; Shoulder to Shoulder; Roger McGough Poems; The Mushroom Picker; Reeves and Mortimer; Space Vets; Stick with Me, Kid.*
Films: *Otley; Some Will, Some Won't; Crossplot; Up Jumped a Swagman; Twinky; The Lecture; Ladies Who Do; Our Own and Private Place; On the Buses; The Best Pair of Legs in the Business; Adventures of a Plumber's Mate; Malachi Cove; The Tempest; Birth of the Beatles; Elephant Man; Carry On Emmannuelle; Trail of the Pink Panther; Return of the Jedi; War Requiem; Jubilee; Going Camping.*
Address: c/o MGA. Lives in Holland Park, West London. Single.

Claire Davenport

Nigel Davenport

Bernard Davey

Joanna David

Jim Davidson

Linda Davidson

DAVENPORT, Nigel

Nigel Davenport. Actor. b. Shelford, Cambridge, 23 May 1928. Former disc jockey.

TV: Breakdown; A Subject for Scandal and Concern; Point of Return; I Don't Like You; The Wrong Way Back; A Choice of Weapons; Until You Are Dead; Return to the Regiment; Double Stakes; To Bury Caesar; Gioconda Smile; Travelling Man; Guilty Party; Madame Bovary; The Picture of Dorian Gray; South Riding; The Applecart; Oil Strike North; Cry of the Innocent; Romance; The Prince Regent; Much Ado about Nothing; The Ordeal of Dr Mudd; Masada; A Midsummer Night's Dream; Don't Rock the Boat; Bird of Prey; A Christmas Carol; The Good Dr Bodkin Adams; The Biko Inquest; Sir Edward Frere in Howards' Way; James Brant in Trainer; The Detectives; Keeping up Appearances; The Cutter; The Upper Hand.

Films: Look Back in Anger; Desert Mice; Peeping Tom; The Entertainer; Lunch Hour; In the Cool of the Day; Operation Snatch; Return to Sender; Ladies Who Do; The Verdict; The Third Secret; A High Wind in Jamaica; Where the Spies Are; Sands of the Kalahari; Life at the Top; A Man for All Seasons; Sebastian; Red and Blue; The Strange Affair; Play Dirty; Sinful Davey; The Virgin Soldiers; The Mind of Mr Soames; The Royal Hunt of the Sun; No Blade of Grass; The Last Valley; Villain; Mary, Queen of Scots; L'Attentat (UK title Plot); Living Free; Charley One-Eye; Dracula; Phase IV; La Regenta; Stand Up Virgin Soldiers; The Island of Dr Moreau; Zulu Dawn; The London Connection (US title The Omega Connection); Lord Birkenhead in Chariots of Fire; Nighthawks; The Upper Crust; Greystoke: The Legend of Tarzan Lord of the Apes; Caravaggio; Without a Clue. Address: c/o Green and Underwood. m. 1st Helena (dis), 2nd actress Maria Aitken; 1 d. Laura, 2 s. Hugo (from 1st m.), Jack.

DAVEY, Bernard

Bernard Davey. Weather presenter. b. Belfast, 29 March 1943. Joined Meteorological Office on leaving school in 1962.

TV: BBC TV weather forecaster. Address: c/o BBC TV. m. Teresa; 1 s. Cormac, 2 d. Mica, Shauna.

DAVID, Joanna

Joanne Elizabeth Hacking. Actress. b. Lancaster, 17 January 1947. Trained at Elmhurst Ballet School and the Webber Douglas Academy. West End plays include Breaking the Code and The Cherry Orchard.

TV: John Brown's Body; When Johnny Comes Marching Home; Sense and Sensibility; Alice Monroe in The Last of the Mohicans; Sonia in War and Peace; Colditz; The Edwardians; Zodiac; Jenny; Rainbow; Ballet Shoes; Jane Austen; Omnibus; Softly Softly; The Duchess of Duke Street; Within These Walls; Just William; Two's Company; Affront; The Dancing Princess; Lillie; Mrs De Winter in Rebecca; Dominion Status; Mary Eleanor Pearcey in Ladykillers; Dear Brutus; The South Bank Show: No Need to Lie; Charlotte and Jane; Ann in Fame Is the Spur; Love Story; Jackanory; Agatha Christie; The Red Signal; Lady Maid's Bell; Brass; Rumpole of the Bailey (two roles); Anna Karenina; Time for Murder; Tender Is the Night; Comrades; Murder at Lynch Cross; Paying Guests; First among Equals; Queen Victoria in Treasure Houses; Agatha Christie's Miss Marple: The 4.50 from Paddington; Thompson; Hannay; Unexplained Laughter; Difficult People; Children of the North; Maigret; Secret Friends; Susan Fallon in Inspector Morse: Dead on Time; Mirabelle Jones in Rumpole of the Bailey; Tessa Townley in The Good Guys; Miss Jimson in The Darling Buds of May: The Happiest Days of Your Life; Susan Cushing in The Memoirs of Sherlock Holmes; Mrs Gardiner in Pride and Prejudice ; Prue Hastings in A Touch of Frost.

Films: The Smashing Bird I Used to Know; All Neat in Black Stockings; One Plus One; The Mind of Mr Soames; Comrades.

Address: c/o Michael Whitehall. Partner: Actor Edward Fox; 1 d. Emilia Fox, 1 s. Freddie Fox.

DAVIDSON, Jim

Jim Davidson. Actor/Comedian/Entertainer. b. Blackheath, South London, 13 December 1953.

TV: Gang Show; New Faces; What's on Next?; Night Out; Tiswas; Make 'Em Laugh; The Jim Davidson Show; Jim Davidson Special; Jim Davidson's Falklands Special; This Is Your Life (subject, 1984); Up the Elephant and Round the Castle; Home James! (both sitcoms); Jim Davidson in Germany; Jim Davidson's Comedy Package; Wednesday at Eight; ITV Telethon; Stand Up Jim Davidson; Big Break (host, game show, 1991-); Big Break Christmas Celebrity Special; Jim's Treasure Island; Big Break in Wonderland; Jack Warner in Call Up the Stars (VE Day concert, 1995); Big Break: Stars of the Future; Big Break Trick Shot Special (series); Jim Davidson's Generation Game (series, 1995-6); Big Break Christmas Show.

Films: A Zed and Two Noughts. **Books:** Too Risky; Jim Davidson Gets Hooked; Too Frisky; True Brit – A Comic's Guide to All Those Funny People Over There; The Full Monty (autobiography, 1994). Address: c/o International Artistes/Lake-Smith Griffin Associates. m. 1st Susan (dis), 2nd Julie (dis), 3rd TV presenter Alison Holloway (dis), 4th Tracie Hilton; 1 d. Sarah (from 1st m.), 2 s. Cameron (from 2nd m.), Charlie (from 4th m.). Hobbies: Fishing, football.

DAVIDSON, Linda

Lynda Davidson. Actress. b. Toronto, Canada, 18 June 1964. Mother a dancer with the Ballet Rambert. Brought up on Merseyside. Trained at the Italia Conti Stage Academy. Early theatre appearances included cabaret with Freddie Starr. Subsequent productions include *The Rocky Horror Show* (West End)

TV: *Bulman; Who Dares Wins;* Mary Smith in *EastEnders; 40 Minutes: Street Girls* (narrator, documentary on prostitution); *A-Z of Beliefs; Casualty;* Anita Pilsworth in *First of the Summer Wine* (two series); *The Full Wax* (two series); Kitty in *House of Eliott* (Series 2, 1992); *The Bill; Maria's Child* (Screen Two); Sarah Wallace in *The Bill* (1993).

Address: c/o JM Associates. Lives in Enfield, Middlesex. Single. Pets: Cats called Rosie, Pudding and Cous-Cous. Hobbies: Dance, theatre, cooking, walking, motorbikes.

Ross Davidson

DAVIDSON, Ross

Ross Davidson. Actor. b. Airdrie, 25 August 1949. PE teacher and international water-polo player before becoming a professional actor. Stage plays include *Guys and Dolls* (National Theatre).

TV: *The Stanley Baxter Show; Marco Baccer; Songs of Britain; Thingumyjig;* Andy O'Brien in *EastEnders; Rivals; Monkey Walk; POB* (guest presenter); *Daytime Live* (presenter); *Run the Gauntlet* (presenter); Supt Brand in *Taggart: Instrument of Justice;* Peter Odell in *High Road.*

Films: *The Pirates of Penzance; Monty Python's The Meaning of Life; Paracelsus.*

Address: c/o Mike Fisher Management. Lives in Barnes, south-west London. Single.

DAVIES, Ann

Ann Cuerton Davies. Actress. b. London, 25 November 1934. Trained at Liverpool Playhouse.

TV: Lucille in *Probation Officer;* Jean in *Doctor Who;* Ettie in *Within These Walls;* Matty in *Poldark;* Marjorie in *Equal Terms;* Mrs Halstead in *The Nation's Health;* Mrs Copley in *Happy;* ATS Lady in *A Voyage round My Father,* Mildred in *Widows,* Mrs Bates in *Shine on Harvey Moon;* Bridget in *Paradise Postponed;* Ethel in *All in Good Faith;* Mrs Ripper in *Ever Decreasing Circles;* Iris Davies in *The Specials;* Gwen in *After Henry; The Bill* (two roles); *Keeping Up Appearances;* Dorothy Clarke in *The Sculptress.*

Films: Geraldine Malik in *Love Is Not Enough;* Brenda in *Peter's Friends;* Mrs Branch in *In the Bleak Midwinter.* **Books:** *A Taste of the Good Life* (co-author, with Richard Briers, 1995).

Address: c/o Langford Associates. Lives in London. m. actor Richard Briers (qv); 2 d. Kate, actress Lucy Briers. Pets: Mongrel called Fred. Hobbies: Exercise class, swimming.

Ann Davies

DAVIES, Deddie

Deddie Davies. Actress. Bridgend, 2 March 1938. Trained at RADA.

TV: *The Forsyte Saga; Vanity Fair; Clochemerle; Pin to See the Peep Show; Jennie, Lady Randolph Churchill; Some Mothers Do 'Ave 'Em; Upstairs, Downstairs; Just William; The Rag Trade; The Mayor of Casterbridge; You're Only Young Twice; The Gentle Touch; Father Charlie; A J Wentworth BA; Partners in Crime; Murder at the Vicarage; Grange Hill; Metal Mickey; The Pickwick Papers, Solo, That's My Boy; Titus Andronicus; Chance in a Million; The Canterville Ghost; C.A.T.S. Eyes; My Husband and I; Trouble in Mind;* Miss Morgan in *Just a Gigolo;* Auntie Dot in *Conley: Outside Chance* (1993) and *Time after Time* (two series, 1994-5); Sister Sheila in *Waiting for God.*

Films: *The Railway Children; The Amazing Mr Blunden.*

Address: c/o Amor Reeves Management. m. actor Paddy Ward.

Deddie Davies

DAVIES, Diana

Diana Patricia Holme. Actress. b. Manchester, 20 July 1936. Daughter of a big-band musician. Trained as a model and at an actors' workshop in Manchester. Started her career as an extra for Granada Television. Stage plays include *Rose* (West End).

TV: Doris Jackson in *A Family at War; The Liver Birds;* Norma Ford in *Coronation Street* (1972-3); *Send in the Girls; Juliet Bravo; Enemy at the Door; Ready When You Are Mr McGill; Sheikh of Pickersgill; Shoestring; Brother to the Ox; Willie's Last Stand; How We Used to Live; Dog Food Dan;* Mrs Lipton in *Johnny Jarvis* (series); Letty Brewer, then Mrs (Caroline) Bates (1981-) in *Emmerdale; All Creatures Great and Small; Medics; Josie Smith; Celebration: Lights of Manchester; Stepping Stones* (presenter, children's series); *A Touch of Frost.* TV commercials: Mum in Lyons cakes ads. Address: c/o ATS Casting. Lives in Manchester. m. Peter Davies (dis); 1 s. Stephen. Hobbies: Bridge, crosswords, food.

Diana Davies

DAVIES, Emma

Emma Kate Davies. Actress. b. London, 7 March 1970. Daughter of actor Geoffrey Davies. Acting since the age of seven. Stage plays include national tours of *Little Women* and *While the Sun Shines.*

TV: *Double Trouble* (Swedish series); *The Tempest; The Book Tower; The Bill;* Joe in *Boon; Home James!; Never the Twain; Spatz; Bergerac; Freddie and Max;* Melissa in *Family Pride;* Juliet Bannerman in *Families;* Susan in *Law and Disorder* (series, 1994); *Queen of the East* (Heroes & Villains); *Harry Enfield and Chums;* Sarah Francis in *Crown Prosecutor* (series, 1995); Clarinda Bellow in *Just William.*

Films: *Full Circle; Mr Kitano Animal Puppets; Runners; Monty Python's The Meaning of Life.*

Address: c/o Barry Burnett Organisation. Lives in London. m. Ross Allan. Pets: A spaniel called Barty. Hobbies: Photography, riding.

Emma Davies

DAVIES, Freddie

Frederick Davies. Actor. b. Brixton, South London, 21 July 1937. Known for many years as Freddie 'Mr Parrot Face' Davies. Brought up in Lancashire. Started as a Redcoat at Butlin's in 1958, working as a bingo-caller in Skegness alongside Dave Allen. Turned professional as a comedian in 1964. Appeared in cabaret in clubs, major theatres, summer shows and pantomime. Turned to acting in 1990.

TV: *Opportunity Knocks* (TV début); *Sunday Night at the London Palladium;* title role in *The Small World of Samuel Tweet* (two series); caretaker Dennis in *Mickey Love* (Rik Mayall Presents); Arcade Owner in *Heartbeat;* Heron Man in *All Quiet on the Preston Front* (series, 1994); *Mangetout* (10 x 10); *Last of the Summer Wine;* Heron Man in *Preston Front;* Harry Miller in *Medics;* Owen Lovett in *Band of Gold; Elidor;* Jeweller in *Catherine Cookson's The Tide of Life* (mini-series, 1996); *Casualty.*
Films: *Number One; Treacle; Funny Bones.*

Freddie Davies

Address: c/o Minstrel Entertainments, 46-7 Chancery Lane, London WC2A 1BA. Lives in Yorkshire. m. 1st 1961 Jacqueline Clarke (dis 1995), 2nd Vanessa; 1 step-d. Jennifer, 1 s. Kent (both from 1st m.). Pets: A King Charles dog called Poppy, two cats called Sam and Rosie.

DAVIES, Geoffrey

Geoffrey Davies. Actor. b. Leeds, 15 December 1941. Commercial artist, then ASM with the White Rose Players at Harrogate Rep, before training at RADA. Stage plays include *Ghost Train* (Old Vic).
TV: *Kindly Leave the Raj;* Dick Stuart-Clark in *Doctor in the House* (two series, 1969-70), *Doctor at Large* (series, 1971), *Doctor in Charge* (series, 1972-3), *Doctor at Sea* (series, 1974), *Doctor on the Go* (series, 1975-7), *Doctor Down Under* (series in Australia, 1980) and *Doctor at the Top* (series, 1991); *The Other 'Arf;* Roger Dubree in *Bergerac;* Lord Wishbury in *The Bretts;* Dexter Rook in *The Labours of Erica* (two series, 1989-90); Mr Morgan in *Woof!;* Myles Barton QC in *Families;* Harold Chase QC in *Law and Disorder; Stick with Me, Kid.*

Geoffrey Davies

Films: *Oh! What a Lovely War* (acting début); *The Gap; Doctor in Trouble; Tales from the Crypt; Vault of Horror.* Address: c/o Barry Burnett Organisation. Lives in London. m. Ann; 1 d. actress Emma Davies. Pets: Two King Charles cavaliers. Hobbies: Cooking, reading, walking, tennis, gardening.

DAVIES, Martyn

Martyn Paul Davies. Weather presenter. b. Bloxwich, Staffordshire, 14 January 1956. Weather forecaster with the Meteorological Office for 12 years before entering television. Consultant meteorologist on various science-based and environmental programmes.
TV: *Central News* (Central Television,1983-4); *South Today* (BBC South, 1984-9); *ITV National Weather* (1989-); *Coast to Coast* (TVS); *LWT Weather* (LWT, 1990-1).
Address: c/o International Weather Productions. Lives in Hampshire. m. Margaret Wilden; 1 s. Nathan, 1 d. Jordan. Hobbies: Cooking, cars, squash.

Martyn Davies

DAVIES, Paul

Paul Davies. Journalist. OBE, 1993 (for his reporting from war zones). Started career in 1969 on the Southport *Visitor* group of newspapers; news editor, *Bootle Times* (1973-4); Radio City (Liverpool) reporter, sports reporter and assistant news editor (1974-8); IRN (Independent Radio News) reporter (1978-81); TVS reporter (1981-3); ITN reporter (1983-).
TV: *Coast to Coast* (TVS); ITN reporter covering Northern Ireland, the 1984 miners' strike and the bombing of the Grand Hotel, in Brighton, plus the Soviet withdrawal from Afghanistan, the Czechoslovak and Romanian revolutions (becoming first British TV reporter in Bucharest), the Gulf War and the war in Bosnia; ITN foreign news correspondent (1996-). **Awards:** RTS Television Journalist of the Year (1990) for work in Afghanistan, Czechoslovakia and, in particular, Romania. Address: c/o ITN.

DAVIES, Windsor

Windsor Davies. Actor. b. Canning Town, London, 28 August 1930. Returned to family's native Wales at the age of 10. Worked as a miner, factory worker and schoolteacher before taking a three-week drama course at Richmond College of Further Education and becoming a professional actor at age of 31.

Paul Davies

TV: *A Little Bit of Wisdom; Billy Liar; Shadow of the Tower; The View from Daniel Pike; The Perils of Pendragon; The Donati Conspiracy; Pathfinders; Grand Slam; Love Story; New Scotland Yard; Callan; The Main Chance; Crown Court; Thriller; Sam; The Heavy Mob;* Battery Sergeant Major Williams in *It Ain't Half Hot Mum* (series, 1974-81); Oliver Smallbridge in *Never the Twain* (11 series, 1981-91); *Sporting Chance; Old Scores; The New Statesman; Sean's Show; The Children's Royal Variety Performance 1994; Paris.*
Films: *The Family Way; Department K; Crimine; Hammerhead; Frankenstein Must Be Destroyed; Endless Battles; Adolf Hitler — My Part in His Downfall; Soft Beds, Hard Battles; Not Now, Comrade; Quilp; Carry On Behind; Carry On England.* **Records:** Singles (with Don Estelle): *Whispering Grass* (No 1, 1975); *Paper Doll* (No 41, 1975). Address: c/o Peter Prichard. Lives in Surrey. m. Eluned (Lyn); 4 d. Jane, Sarah, Nancy, Beth, 1 s. Daniel. Hobbies: Rugby, football, reading.

Windsor Davies

DAVISON, Peter

Peter Davison. Actor. b. London, 13 April 1951. Trained at the Central School of Speech and Drama.
TV: Stepan in *Black Beauty; The Tomorrow People; Love for Lydia; Print-Out; Once upon a Time;* Tristan Farnham in *All Creatures Great and Small; Holding the Fort; Sink or Swim; The Hitch-Hiker's Guide to the Galaxy;* title role in *Doctor Who* (1982-4, 20 stories, 69 episodes); *Anna of the Five Towns;* Dr Stephen Daker in *A Very Peculiar Practice; Agatha Christie's Miss Marple; Campion; A Very Polish Practice* (Screen One); Bob Stacey in *Kinsey* (series, 1992); *Fiddlers Three; The Real Thief* (storyteller); Jim in *Harnessing Peacocks; Doctor Who: Dimensions in Time* (Children in Need, 1993); Clive Quigley in *Ain't Misbehavin'* (two series, 1994-5); *A Man You Don't Meet Every Day* (Without Walls special); *Heavenly Bodies* (presenter, series, 1995); *The Adventures of Mole* (voice only). Wrote TV theme music for *Mixed Blessings* (series). Writes songs and made his singing début on *Pebble Mill at One.*
Address: c/o Conway, van Gelder, Robinson. Lives near Henley-on-Thames, Oxfordshire, and Los Angeles. m. actress Sandra Dickinson (qv) (dis 1995); 1 d. Georgia Elizabeth

Peter Davison

DAVRO, Bobby

Robert Christopher Nankeville. Comedian/Impressionist. b. Ashford, Middlesex, 13 September 1959. Started in amateur music-hall, talent contests and workingmen's clubs before entertaining in pubs and clubs, then entering radio and TV. Stage shows include *Bobby Davro's All Laughter Spectacular.*
TV: *Up for the Cup; Starburst; Crackerjack; Live from Her Majesty's; Go for It; Night of 100 Stars; Copycats; The Bobby Davro TV Annual; Bobby Davro on the Box; Bobby Davro's TV Weekly; Davro's Sketch Pad; Davro; Bobby Davro — Public Enemy Number 1* (series, 1992); *Long-Distance Karaoke* (Children In Need, 1992); *The Children's Royal Variety Performance 1993; Bobby Davro: Rock with Laughter* (series, 1993); *Wish You Were Here…?* (guest reporter, 1994); *Run the Risk* (host, children's game show, series, 1996). Address: c/o Nick Thomas Enterprises. Lives in Staines, Middlesex. m. 1994 Trudi Jameson; 1 d. Raine (b. 1995). Hobbies: Snooker, golf, fishing.

Bobby Davro

DAWN, Elizabeth

Sylvia Butterfield. Actress. b. Leeds, 8 November 1939. Worked as a machinist in a clothing factory, in Woolworths, a shoe shop, and as a cinema usherette, singing in clubs by night. Spotted by film director Alan Parker who cast her as a sympathetic mother in a TV commercial. Five years later, he cast her in another commercial, Larry Grayson saw her and cast her as his neighbour Dot in his TV show.
TV: Dot in *Larry Grayson Special; Z Cars; Sam; Country Matters; Raging Calm; Mr Ellis versus the People; The Greenhill Pals; Speech Day; Daft as a Brush; All Day on the Sands; Sunset across the Bay; Kisses at Fifty; Leeds United; Crown Court;* Vera Duckworth in *Coronation Street* (on and off 1976-83, regular 1983-); *Royal Variety Performance* (with *Coronation Street* cast, 1989); *One Foot in the Past* (1995, repeated 1996 as *One Foot in the Past: A Rover Returns*).
Films: *Who'd Be a Vet?*
Records: *I'll Be with You Soon* (single, with William Tarmey (qv), 1989).
Books: *Vera Duckworth — My Story* (autobiography, 1993). Address: c/o Granada Television. Lives in Salford, Lancashire. m. 1st (dis), 2nd Donald Ibbetson; 3 d. Dawn, Ann-Marie, Julie, 1 s. Graham.

Elizabeth Dawn

DAWSON, Anna

Anna Dawson. Actress. b. Bolton, Lancashire, 27 July 1937. Trained at Elmhurst Ballet School and the Central School of Speech and Drama. Appeared in farce with Brian Rix's Whitehall Theatre company.
TV: *Dixon of Dock Green; The Benny Hill Show; The Morecambe and Wise Show; Life Begins at Forty; 3-2-1;* Violet in *Keeping Up Appearances.*
Address: c/o Harbour & Coffey. m. Black and White Minstrel John Boulter. Hobbies: Cooking, gardening, the Loch Ness monster.

Anna Dawson

DE LA TOUR, Frances

Frances de la Tour. Actress. b. Bovingdon, Hertfordshire, 30 July 1944. Trained at The Drama Centre.
TV: *All Good Men; Housewives' Choice; Crime of Passion; Play for Today;* Miss Jones in *Rising Damp* (four series, 1974-8); *A Cottage to Let; Flickers; Clam; A Kind of Loving; Skirmishes;* Millie Renfrew in *Ellis Island* (mini-series); Miss Bellaver in *Agatha Christie's Murder with Mirrors* (TVM); *Duet for One* (TVM); *A Kind of Living* (two series, 1988); Mrs DeVere in *Strike It Rich;* Beatrice in *Bejewelled;* Shirley Silver in *Every Silver Lining* (series, 1993); *Stay Lucky;* Dr Helga Feuchtwanger in *Genghis Cohn* (Screen Two); Rosemary in *Downwardly Mobile* (series, 1994); *Playing the Dane* (Bard on the Box).
Films: *The Buttercup Chain; Every Home Should Have One; Brotherly Love; Our Miss Fred; To the Devil a Daughter; Wombling Free; Rising Damp; Time Bandits; Loser Takes All.*
Awards: Films: *Evening Standard* Best Actress award, 1980, for *Rising Damp.* Theatre: SWET, *Evening Standard* and Critics' Award as Best Actress for *Duet for One* (1981); SWET Best Actress award for *A Moon for the Misbegotten* (1983).
Address: c/o Kate Feast Management. m. playwright Tom Kempinski; 1 d. Tamasin, 1 s. Josh.

Frances de la Tour

Brian Deacon

DEACON, Brian

Brian Deacon. Actor. b. Oxford, 13 February 1949. Trained at the Webber Douglas
TV: *First Sight; The Guardians; Public Eye; Love and Mr Lewisham; Thirty Minute Theatre; What Shall We Do Next?; Full House; Public House; Sunday Night Theatre; Churchill's People; Good Girl; The Feathered Serpent; Ghosts; The Emigrants; Border Music; Lillie; Watching Me, Watching You; Inappropriate Behaviour; Henry VI, Parts 1, 2 and 3; Richard III; Bleak House; Separate Tables; Mr Palfrey of Westminster, Mr Wakefield's Crusade* (series); Hon Neil Kincaid in *Emmerdale* (1992-3); Bryan in *BUGS.*
Films: *The Triple Echo; Il Bacio; Vampyres; A Zed and Two Noughts; Jesus.*
Address: c/o Kate Feast Management. m. actress Rula Lenska (dis); 1 d. Lara.

DEACON, Eric

Eric Deacon

Eric Deacon. Actor. b. Oxford, 25 May 1950. Trained at the Webber Douglas Academy.
TV: *A Photograph; Postcards from Southsea; The Survivors; Penmarric* (series); *Minder; Secret Army; Spearhead* (two series); *No Place Like Home; Dark Secret; Contract; King's Royal* (two series); *Jackanory; Flashpoint; Only Children; Tess of the d'Urbervilles; The Caretaker; Operation Julie* (TVM); *Doctor Who; Dempsey and Makepeace; C.A.T.S. Eyes; London's Burning* (series); *Hard Cases* (series); *Casualty; Maigret;* DC Dennis Hardwick in *Lovejoy* (semi-regular); *Medics; The Bill;* Dr Gordon in *Prime Suspect 3* (mini-series); Les in *A Crowd in the Countryside; A Statement of Affairs* (writer, mini-series); *Wycliffe.*
Films: *A Nous Le Petit Anglais (Those Little English Girls); One of the Lads; It Could Happen to You; Bitter; Yesterday's Hero; A Zed and Two Noughts; Coming of Age.*
Address: c/o Burdett-Coutts Associates. m. Laraine Joy; 2 s. Sam, Max.

DEAN, Bill

Bill Dean

Bill Dean. Actor. b. Liverpool, 3 September 1921. Worked in local government before becoming a stand-up comedian in Lancashire pubs and clubs. Plays include *Comedians* (national tour and Old Vic).
TV: *Bank Holiday;* Charlie in *The Wackers* (series, 1975); Jack in *Oh No It's Selwyn Froggitt* (three series, 1976-7); Abraham Scarsdale in *Emmerdale Farm; Good Companions; When the Boat Comes In; Time out of Mind; A Turn for the Worst; Lovers of the Lake;* Harry Cross in *Brookside* (1983-90); *The Young Indiana Jones Chronicles;* Priest in *Clarissa; Skallagrigg* (ScreenPlay); *Heartbeat; 3-7-11* (series).
Films: *Kes;* Father in *Family Life;* Night Club Proprietor in *Gumshoe; Night Watch; Scum;* Workman in *Rising Damp; "Let Him Have It"; Priest.*
Videos: Appeared in promotional videos for Liverpool rock group The Farm.
Address: c/o Crouch Associates. m. (dec); 2 s. Peter, David, 1 d. Diane.

DEAN, Letitia

Letitia Dean

Letitia Dean. Actress. b. Wild Hill, nr Potters Bar, Hertfordshire, 14 November 1967. Started acting as a child. Trained at the Sylvia Young Theatre School. Played Pepper in *Annie* (aged 12, Victoria Palace).
TV: *Love Story* (BBC); *Tales out of School;* Lucinda in *Grange Hill;* Elaine Thornton in *Timmy and Vicky;* Dawn in *Brookside;* Lucy in *Relative Strangers;* drug addict in *The Bill;* Sharon Watts/Mitchell in *EastEnders* (1985-95); *The V Word;* Hannah in *Casualty.*
Films: *England, My England.* Address: c/o Gordon Priestley, 29a Riding House Street, London W1P 7PG. Lives in London and Lincolnshire. Single.

DEAN, Peter

Peter Dean. Actor. b. Hoxton, East London, 2 May 1939. Formerly a market trader, spotted by actress Prunella Scales, who suggested he go to drama school. Trained at Mountview Theatre School.
TV: Jack Lynn in *Law and Order; Target; Shoestring; Minder; To Turn a Blind Eye; First Love; Shine on Harvey Moon; The Chinese Detective; The Zoo;* Fangio Bateman in *Coronation Street; Give Us a Break; One Man's Bent; Acceptable Levels; Big Deal;* Sgt Wilding in *Woodentop* (Storyboard, *The Bill* pilot, 1983) and *The Bill* (1984); Pete Beale in *EastEnders* (1985-93).
Films: *Murder by Decree; Sweet William; The Great Rock and Roll Swindle; Sherlock Holmes; The Fiendish Plot of Dr Fu Manchu.*
Address: c/o Howes and Prior. m. 1st (dis), 2nd Jean; 1 d. Leah (from 1st m.).

DEAYTON, Angus

Peter Dean

Angus Deayton. Actor/Writer/Presenter. b. 6 January 1956. Graduated from Oxford University.
TV: *Friday Night Saturday Morning; '91 Take Two; Tiswas; Rebellious Jukebox* (also writer); *Saturday Stayback* (script editor); *Who Dares Wins; Karen Kay Show* (writer); *Aspel & Co* (writer); Lawyer in *Chelmsford 123; Alexei Sayle's Stuff* (three series); Mike Channel in *KYTV* (also co-writer, three series, 1990-3); *Mr Bean;* Patrick in *One Foot in the Grave;* Quint in *Doctor at the Top; Have I Got News for You* (host, 11 series, 1990-6); *Have I Got News for You — Election Special; TV Hell* (presenter); *Comic Relief's Red Nose Alert; Bore of the Year Awards* (presenter and co-writer); *Total Relief: A Night of Comic Relief* (presenter and participant in *Have I Got Sports News for You*, 1993); Paul Foot in *Bad*

Company (drama-doc); Bank Manager in *If You See God, Tell Him;* Dexter in *Two Golden Balls* (Screen One); *Oliver 2* (Comic Relief, 1995); *Doing Rude Things* (presenter); *In Search of Happiness* (presenter, series, 1995); *One Foot in the Grave Christmas Special* (1995); *The End of the Year Show with Angus Deayton* (1995-6); *The BAFTA Awards* (presenter, 1996); *Lord of Misrule* (Screen One).
Films: *The Tall Guy.* Address: c/o TalkBack.

Angus Deayton

DELANY, Pauline
Pauline Cathleen Delany. Actress. b. Dublin, 8 June. Trained at Brendan Smith Academy of Acting, Dublin.
TV: *Public Eye; The Dead; The Achurch Letters; Crime of Passion; The Seagull; Playboy of the Western World; The Expert; The Avengers; Z Cars; Softly Softly; Hammer House of Horror; Fallen Hero; Mixed Blessings; Maybury; Touch of Evil; Shoestring; Dangerous Davies — The Last Detective; The Mourning Thief; Late Starter; Bergerac; Rumpole of the Bailey; Beckett at 80; Bluebirds; The Bill; Casualty; Moving Story.*
Films: *The Very Edge; The Quare Fellow; Young Cassidy; Nothing but the Best; Percy; The Love Ban; Brannigan; Rooney; Trenchcoat; Good Girls.* Address: c/o David Daly Associates. Lives in London. m. writer Gerald Simpson; 1 d. Sarah. Pets: A cat, Ella. Hobbies: Music, reading, theatre, gardening, cooking.

Pauline Delany

DENCH, Judi
Judith Olivia Dench. Actress. b. York, 9 December 1934. OBE; DBE; 1988. Trained at the Central School of Speech and Drama. Old Vic company member (1957-61) and many RSC appearances.
TV: *Hilda Lessways; An Age of Kings; Village Wooing; Major Barbara; Pink String and Sealing Wax; On Giant's Shoulders; Langrishe; Go Down; The Teachers; Z Cars; Love Story; The Funambulists; Jackanory; Neighbours; Parade's End; Marching Song; On Approval; Days to Come; Emilie; Macbeth; Langrishe Go Down; Make and Break; Talking to a Stranger; The Morecambe and Wise Show; Love in a Cold Climate; Going Gently; The Cherry Orchard; Laura in A Fine Romance; Saigon — Year of the Cat; The Browning Version; Mr and Mrs Edgehill; Ghosts; Behaving Badly; Can You Hear Me Thinking; Birthday; Absolute Hell* (Performance); *All Our Children* (narrator); Jean Pargetter in *As Time Goes By* (five series, 1992-6); *The Comedy of Errors; Torch; Look Back in Anger* (director); *Middlemarch; The South Bank Show* (subject).
Films: *The Third Secret; Four in the Morning; A Study in Terror; He Who Rides a Tiger;* Titania in *A Midsummer Night's Dream; Luther; Dead Cert; Nela* (voice only); *Wetherby; The Angelic Conversation* (voice only); *A Room with a View; 84 Charing Cross Road; A Handful of Dust; Henry V.*
Books: *Judi Dench: A Great Deal of Laughter* (autobiography). **Awards:** TV: BAFTA Best Actress awards for *Talking to a Stranger* (1967) and *Going Gently* and *The Cherry Orchard* (both 1981); BAFTA Best Light Entertainment Performance for *A Fine Romance* (1981, 1984). Address: c/o Julian Belfrage Associates. m. 1971 actor Michael Williams; 1 d. Tara Cressida Frances (actress Finty Williams).

Judi Dench

DENISON, Michael
John Michael Terence Wellesley Denison. Actor. b. Doncaster, South Yorkshire, 1 November 1915. CBE, 1983. Trained at the Webber Douglas Academy (1937-8). More than 50 West End plays.
TV: *Marco Millions* (début, 1939); *The Will; Milestones; The Second Man; What's My Line?; Waiting for Gillian; Olympia; Rain on the Just; Who Goes Home; Festival Fever; The Sun Divorce;* title role in *Boyd QC* (six series, 1956-65); *Inside Chance; The Frankie Howerd Show; Late Extra; The Importance of Being Earnest; Dear Octopus; Joan Sutherland* (compère); *Funeral Games; Unexpectedly Vacant; The Twelve Pound Look; The Provincial Lady; This Is Your Life* (subject, 1977); *Crown Court* (twice); *The Generation Game; Private Schultz; Bedroom Farce;* Captain Percival in *Blood Money; Good Behaviour; Rumpole of the Bailey; The Agatha Christie Hour: Red Signal; The Critic; The Week of the Scorpion; See How They Run; Cold Warrior;* Admiral Redfern in *Howards' Way* (on and off, 1985-90); *An Invitation to Remember; Celebration Concert: It's a Lovely Day Tomorrow* (guest narrator, VE 50, 1995).
Films: *Inspector Hornleigh on Holiday; Tilly of Bloomsbury; Hungry Hill; My Brother Jonathan; The Blind Goddess; The Glass Mountain; Landfall; The Franchise Affair; The Magic Box; Angels One Five; The Importance of Being Earnest; Tall Headlines; There Was a Young Lady; Contraband Spain; The Truth about Women; Faces in the Dark; The Friendly Inn* (narrator); *The Rocking Horse Winner; Shadowlands.*
Books: *Overtures and Beginners* (autobiography, 1973); *Double Act* (autobiography (1985).
Address: c/o Barry Burnett Organisation. Lives in Amersham, Buckinghamshire. m. 1939 actress Dulcie Gray (qv). Pets: Dog. Hobbies: Golf, gardening, watching cricket.

Michael Denison

DENNIS, Les
Leslie Heseltine. Impressionist. b. Liverpool, 12 October 1954. Began career aged 14 in clubs.
TV: *New Faces* (TV début, winner of the talent show); *Who Do You Do?; The Comedians; Seaside Special; Live from Her Majesty's; Tarby and Friends; Russ Abbot's Madhouse; The Laughter Show* (three series, with comedy partner Dustin Gee, until his death in 1986); *Royal Variety Performance* (with Dustin Gee, 1984); *The Les Dennis Laughter Show; Family Fortunes* (host, 1987-); *The Russ Abbot Show; Russ Abbot* (series, 1992); *The Comedians Christmas Cracker* (1993). Address: c/o Lake-Smith Griffin Associates. m. Lynne (dis); 1 s. Philip. Partner: Actress Amanda Holden.

Les Dennis

Eileen Derbyshire

DERBYSHIRE, Eileen

Eileen Derbyshire. Actress. b. Urmston, Manchester, 6 October 1931. Took a teaching degree in speech and drama, trained at the Northern School of Music (now the Royal Northern College) and taught speech and drama before becoming assistant stage manager with Chorlton Rep, then acting with the Century Theatre mobile company for two years. Many radio plays from the age of 17.

TV: Emily Nugent/Bishop in *Coronation Street* (from Episode 15, January 1961); *Royal Variety Performance* (with *Coronation Street* cast, 1989). Address: c/o Granada Television. Lives in Cheshire. m. Thomas Holt; 1 s. Oliver. Hobbies: Reading literature, listening to opera, going to concerts, travelling.

DEU, Amerjit

Amerjit Singh. Actor. b. Banvalipur, Punjab, India, 3 September 1960. Trained at the Webber Douglas Academy. Stage roles include Tybalt in *Romeo and Juliet* (Albany Empire).

TV: *Umbrella; Never the Twain;* Dr Singh in *EastEnders* (1988); *Shadow of the Noose;* Sanjay in *Starting Out; Playbus; The Cloning of Joanna May; Mysteries of the Dark Jungle;* Ranjit in *Eldorado* (1993); *Jackanory;* Sanjeev Shavi in *The Bill; Crime Monthly;* Newsagent in *Jake's Progress; Conflict; Udam Singh;* Zafar Hussain in *The Bill;* Amil Chandani in *A Touch of Frost.* Documentaries: *Sight Savers; Slaves of the River; Life and Death of a Dynasty.*

Films: *Appeal; Playing for an Elephant;* Mr Shah in *Terminal Eye;* Rajam Prasad in *Caught; Deceivers.*

Address: c/o Scott Marshall. Lives in Chiswick, West London. Hobbies: Most sport, swimming, diving, travel, cinema.

Amerjit Deu

DEVANEY, Sue

Sue Devaney. Actress/Singer. b. Ashton-under-Lyne, Lancashire, 2 July 1967. Trained at Oldham Theatre Workshop. Stage roles include Ruby Birtle in *When We Are Married* (Whitehall Theatre), Gaoler's Daughter in *The Wind in the Willows* (National Theatre) and Karen in *Land of the Living* (Royal Court Upstairs). Half of funk duo Dunky Dobbers with actress Michelle Holmes (qv).

TV: Usherette in *Mating Call; Rainbow;* Mildred Bailey in *In Loving Memory;* Debbie Webster in *Coronation Street;* Rita Briggs in *Jonny Briggs;* Amanda in *Exclusive Yarns;* Janice in *The Index Has Gone Fishing;* Ruby in *When We Are Married;* Sandra in *Flying Lady;* Mad Bastard in *The Real Eddy English;* Betsy in *About Face: Mrs Worthington's Daughter;* Betty Bouncer in *Haggard;* Jo in *Spatz;* Zoe in *Gordon the Gopher; But First This* (presenter); *Paramount City* (presenter); Ruth Harcourt in *The Bill;* Jennifer Galvin in *Heartbeat; Metroland* (presenter, documentary about Soho, Carlton only, 1993); Trendy Wendy in *Model Millie;* Madonna/Abba/Linda McCartney in *Fan TC;* paramedic Liz Harker in *Casualty* (two series,1994-6).

Address: c/o Marmont Management. Lives in South London. Single.

Sue Devaney

DIAMOND, Anne

Anne Diamond. Presenter. b. Birmingham, 8 September 1954. Joined the *Bridgwater Mercury* as arts and music correspondent (1975-7) and Bournemouth *Evening Echo* (1977-9), before moving to TV.

TV: *ATV Today* and *Central News;* (1979-82); *Nationwide* (1982-3); BBC lunchtime newsreader (1982-3); *Good Morning Britain* and *Anne Diamond on Sunday* (TV-am, 1983-92); *TV Weekly* (series); *The Time The Place; This Morning; Six o'Clock Live* (all as guest presenter); *Good Morning... with Anne & Nick* (four series, 1992-6); *The Good Morning Advent Calendar with Anne & Nick; A Summer Good Morning* (series, 1993 *Good Morning* highlights).

Address: c/o The Roseman Organisation. Lives in Leamington Spa, Warwickshire. m. TV executive Mike Hollingsworth; 4 s. Oliver, Jamie, Sebastian (dec), Jake.

Anne Diamond

DIBLEY, Janet

Janet Dibley. Actress. b. Doncaster, South Yorkshire, 13 December 1958. Trained at the Rose Bruford College of Speech and Drama. National Theatre productions include *Carousel, Twelfth Night* and *Figaro.*

TV: *A Brother's Tale; Foxy Lady; Lytton's Diary; The Two of Us;* Linda in *The Gingerbread Girl* (series, 1993). Address: c/o Macfarlane Chard Associates.

DICKINSON, Sandra

Sandra Searles. Actress. Acts under the name Sandra Searles Dickinson in the US. b. Washington DC, USA, 20 October. Studied at the University of Wisconsin and Boston University. Trained at the Central School of Speech and Drama. First found success in TV commercials. Stage roles include Marilyn Monroe in *Legend,* Miss Lowell in *Light Up the Sky* (Globe Theatre), Jane in *Out of Order* (Shaftesbury Theatre) and Jane in *It Runs in the Family* (Playhouse Theatre).

TV: *The Tomorrow People; What's on Next?; Cover; The Hitch-Hiker's Guide to the Galaxy; Triangle; What Mad Pursuit; The Two Ronnies; The Tom O'Connor Show; The Des O'Connor Show; The Clairvoyant; Marlowe – Private Eye; Eisenhower and Lutz; Morning Glory; Real Life; Tales from the Crypt:The*

Janet Dibley

Reluctant Vampire; Tina in *2point4 Children; Present Spirits; Stick with Me, Kid; Clety Piod (Magpies' House)* (Welsh Fourth Channel TV film).
Films: *Point Blank; The Lonely Lady; The Final Programme; The Hunger; Superman III; Supergirl; Present Spirits; Balto* (three voices). Address: c/o William Morris Agency (UK)/The Artists Agency (US). m. actor Peter Davison (qv) (dis 1995); 1 d. Georgia Elizabeth. Pets: Three dogs, three cats, two rabbits, one fish. Hobbies: Mainly animal husbandry.

Sandra Dickinson

DICKSON, Barbara
Barbara Ruth Dickson. Actress/Singer. b. Dunfermline, Fife, 27 September 1947. Started as a singer on the folk circuit but found fame with her performances of Beatles songs in the West End musical *John Paul George Ringo… and Bert,* following it with hit singles and albums, before making her acting début in the lead role of the musical *Blood Brothers* (Lyric Theatre).
TV: Anita Braithwaite in *Band of Gold* (two series, 1995-6); Marie McDonald in *Taggart: Legends.*
Records: Singles (hits): *Answer Me* (No 9, 1976); *Another Suitcase in Another Hall* (No 18, 1977); *Caravan Song* (No 41, 1980); *January February* (No 11, 1980); *In the Night* (No 48, 1980); *I Know Him So Well* (duet with Elaine Paige, No 1, 1985). Many albums.
Awards: Theatre: SWET Best Actress in a Musical award for *Blood Brothers* (1983). Address: c/o Theobald Dickson Productions Ltd, The Coach House, Swinhope Hall, Swinhope, Lincolnshire LN3 6HT. Lives in Lincolnshire. m. Oliver Cookson; 3 s. Colm Alistair, Gabriel Rory, Archie Frederick.

Barbara Dickson

DIMBLEBY, David
David Dimbley. Presenter. b. London, 28 October 1938. Son of broadcaster Richard Dimbleby, brother of presenter Jonathan Dimbleby (qv). Chairman of the *Richmond & Twickenham Times.*
TV: BBC Bristol reporter (1961); *Panorama* (1967-) *24 Hours; People and Power; Yesterday's Men; Reporter at Large; Dimbleby Talk-In; Nationwide; The White Tribe of Africa* (winner, Royal Television Society Supreme Documentary award, 1979); *This Week, Next Week* (1984-6); *An Ocean Apart; Panorama Leaders; The Cenotaph; The Richard Dimbleby Lecture* (1992); *Neil Kinnock: The Lost Leader; Question Time* (1994-); *South Africa Votes* (1994); *Good Morning South Africa* (swearing-in of President Mandela, 1994); *Europe Decides* (1994); plus BBC General Election, by-election, local election and Budget coverage. Address: c/o BBC TV News & Current Affairs. m. cookery writer Josceline (sep); 2 d. Liza, Kate, 1 s. Henry.

David Dimbleby

DIMBLEBY, Jonathan
Jonathan Dimbleby. Presenter. b. Aylesbury, Buckinghamshire, 31 July 1944. Son of broadcaster Richard Dimbleby, brother of presenter David Dimbleby (qv).Intended to become a farmer and worked on the royal farm at Windsor, where he trained as a showjumper. Switched to journalism, joining the London *Evening Standard,* then moving to BBC Bristol.
TV: BBC Bristol reporter (1969-70); *This Week* (1972-9); *TV Eye; Jonathan Dimbleby in South America; Jonathan Dimbleby in Evidence; The Police; The Bomb; The Eagle and the Bear; The Cold War Game; The American Dream; Four Years On – The Bomb; First Tuesday* (presenter and associate editor); *Jonathan Dimbleby on Sunday* (presenter and editor); *This Week; Witness* (series editor); *On the Record; Election Call* (1992); *The Brain Game* (host and deviser, quiz show series, 1992); *Charles: The Private Man, The Public Role* (writer-presenter, 1994); *The War Machine Debate* (The War Machine, 1994); *Richard Dimbleby at Belsen* (presenter, 1995); *Jonathan Dimbleby* (1995-); *World in Action* (interviewing Gerry Adams after renewed IRA bombing, 1996); *The Scott Report – A Jonathan Dimbleby Special* (1996).
Radio: BBC Bristol reporter; *The World at One; Any Questions.*
Books: *Richard Dimbleby; The Palestinians.* **Awards:** BAFTA Richard Dimbleby Award. Address: c/o LWT. m. journalist-author Bel Mooney; 1 d. Kitty, 1 s. Daniel.

Jonathan Dimbleby

DINENAGE, Fred
Frederick Dinenage. Presenter. b. Birmingham, 8 June 1942. Worked as a journalist with the Birmingham *Evening Mail* and Brighton *Evening Argus* before moving into television in 1964.
TV: *Three Go Round; Day by Day; Afloat; Weekend; Miss Southern TV* (all Southern TV); *Calendar Sport; Sunday Sport; World of Sport; Bank Holiday Sport; Gambit* (host, quiz show); *How?; Miss Great Britain; Southsport* (Southern TV); *Pro-Celebrity Snooker; Pro-Celebrity Darts; Miss Anglia TV; Reflections; Cuckoo in the Nest; All Kinds of Everything; Showjumping;* Munich Olympics 1972; Moscow Olympics 1980; TVS 1982-92, presenting *Friday Sports Show, Sunday Sports Show* and *Coast to Coast; Tell the Truth; Vintage Quiz; Starkids; How 2* (six series, 1990-5); Meridian Broadcasting (1993-), presenting *Meridian Tonight, Southern Gold* and *D-Day Remembered.*
Books: *Our Story* (with Ronnie and Reggie Kray); *My Story* (Ronnie Kray). Address: c/o Severn Management Services/Meridian Broadcasting. Lives in Hampshire. m. Beverley; 2 d. Caroline, Sarah, 1 s. Christopher (Sarah's twin). Pets: Horses and greyhounds. Hobbies: Work, reading, swimming.

Fred Dinenage

Reece Dinsdale

DINSDALE, Reece

Reece Dinsdale. Actor. b. Normanton, West Yorkshire, 6 August 1959. Trained at the Guildhall School of Music and Drama. Stage plays include *Beethoven's Tenth* (Vaudeville Theatre).

TV: *Knife Edge; Out on the Floor; Glamour Night; Robin of Sherwood; Partners in Crime; Threads; Bergerac; Minder; Coppers; The Storyteller; Fear Not;* Martin in *Take Me Home* (mini-series); *The Attractions; The Secret Adversary; Home to Roost;* Roderick in *Haggard* (two series, 1990-2); Grand Duke Peter in *Young Catherine* (mini-series); Tarquin Woods in *Full Stretch* (series, 1993); Chief Insp Sharpe in *Lovejoy;* Dr Clive Sussman in *Bliss* (pilot, 1995); DI Charlie Scott in *Thief Takers* (series, 1996).

Films: Mal Stanton in *Winter Flight;* PC Penny in *A Private Function; I.D.*

Awards: Geneva Film Festival International Press Award as Best Actor for *I.D.* (1995).

Address: c/o William Morris Agency (UK). Lives in London.

DOBIE, Alan

Alan Dobie

Alan Dobie. Actor. b. Wombwell, South Yorkshire, 2 June 1932. Trained at Barnsley School of Art and Old Vic Theatre School. Début at the Old Vic as Paris's Page in *Romeo and Juliet* (1952).

TV: *The Planemakers; Dance of Death; The Corsican Brothers; The Siege of Manchester; Why Aren't You Famous?; Conquest; Resurrection; Danton; Diamond Crack Diamond; The Troubleshooters; War and Peace; The Defector; For Services to Myself; Double Dare; Our Young Mr Wignall; A Collier's Friday Night; Eleanor Marks; Hard Times; The Dick Emery Show; Zedicular; Waxwork;* title role in *Sergeant Cribb; Nanny; Death of Ivan Ilyich; Wobble to Death; The Detective Wore Silk Drawers; Madhatter's Holiday; Invitation to a Dynamite Party; Abra Cadaver; Hedda Gabler; Kessler; Gerican H; Master of the Game; House on Kirov Street; The Disputation; The Hospice.*

Films: *Seven Keys; The Comedy Man; Charge of the Light Brigade; The Chairman; Dr Syn – Alias the Scarecrow; White Bird; Long Day's Dying; Alfred the Great; Madame Sin; No Turning Back; White Mischief.* Address: c/o Vernon Conway. m. 1st actress Rachel Roberts (dis), 2nd singer Maureen Scott; 2 d. Millie, Natasha, 1 s. Casey.

DOBSON, Anita

Anita Dobson

Anita Dobson. Actress. b. Stepney, East London, 29 April 1949. Trained at the Webber Douglas Academy. West End stage plays include *Leave Him to Heaven, Budgie, Kvetch* and *Eurovision.*

TV: *What's Your Poison?;* Roxanne in *Leave Him to Heaven; Play Away* (presenter, two series); *Nanny; Take the Stage; Partners in Crime; Up the Elephant and round the Castle* (first series); Angie Watts in *EastEnders* (1985-8); Cath in *Split Ends* (series, 1989); Roxanne in *The World of Eddie Weary;* Marianne in *The Fireboy;* Captain Tau in *Red Dwarf VI;* Cath in *Rab C Nesbitt;* Mrs Fuller in *Woof!;* Sean's Show; Gertie in *Smokescreen* (series, 1994); Bertha Birthcanal in *It's a Girl;* Suzi Rudkin in *I'll Be Watching You* (Ghosts); *Go Back Out the Way You Came;* Miriam Lampter in *Dangerfield.*

Films: *The Euphoric Scale;* Brenda in *Need;* Blind Concierge in *Seaview Knights;* Judith in *Bedlam.*

Records: Singles: *Anyone Can Fall in Love* (No 4, 1986, Silver Disc); *Talking of Love* (No 43, 1987). Albums: *Talking of Love; On My Own.* **Books:** *My East End.*

Awards: Pye Television Personality of the Year award for *EastEnders* (1986); *TVTimes* Best Actress on TV award (joint winner) for *EastEnders.* Address: c/o CAM. Lives in London. Partner: Musician Brian May. Pets: Cat named Brandy. Hobbies: Reading, antique jewellery.

DOBSON, Wayne

Wayne Dobson

Wayne Dobson. Magician. b. Leicester. Became the youngest member of the Magic Circle at the age of 16. Worked as a laboratory technician before turning professional as a magician, aged 21.

TV: *Royal Variety Performance* (1989); *Wayne Dobson – A Kind of Magic* (three series, 1990-2); *The Children's Royal Variety Performance 1994; Wayne Dobson Close-Up* (1995).

Address: c/o Lake-Smith Griffin Associates.

DODD, Ken

Ken Dodd

Kenneth Arthur Dodd. Comedian. b. Knotty Ash, Liverpool, 8 November 1927. OBE, 1982. Self-taught entertainer and creator of the Diddymen. Performed as an amateur in concert halls, billed as Professor Yaffle Chuckabutty – Operatic Tenor and Sausage Knotter. Professional début at the Nottingham Empire (1954). Played Malvolio in *Twelfth Night* at the Royal Court, Liverpool. In the *Guinness Book of Records* for telling 1,500 jokes non-stop in three and a half hours.

TV: *The Ken Dodd Show; Doddy's Music Box; The Good Old Days; Super Trouper; Funny You Should Say That; Look Who's Talking; Ken Dodd's World of Laughter; Stars on Sunday; Ken Dodd's Showbiz; Ken Dodd at the London Palladium; This Is Your Life Special* (subject, 1990); *An Audience with Ken Dodd; Face to Face: Ken Dodd* (interviewee, 1995).

Records: Singles: *Love Is Like a Violin* (No 8, 1960); *Happiness* (No 31, 1964); *Tears* (No 1, 1965); *The River (Le Colline Sono in Fioro)*(No 3, 1965); *Promises* (No 6, 1966); plus 14 other chart entries. Albums: *Tears of Happiness* (No 6, 1965); *Hits for Now and Always* (No 14, 1966); *For*

Someone Special (No 40, 1967); *20 Golden Greats of Ken Dodd* (No 8, 1980).
Address: c/o George Bartram Associates. Lives in Knotty Ash, Liverpool. Partner: former Bluebell dancer Anne Jones. Pets: Poodle called Doodle. Hobbies: Reading, relaxing.

DONOHOE, Amanda

Amanda Donohoe. Actress. b. c. 1965. Trained at the Central School of Speech and Drama.
TV: *Star Quality; An Affair in Mind* (TVM); Gloria Kent in *Game, Set & Match; Laughter of God;* Cara Jean 'CJ' Lamb in *LA Law* (1990-2); *LA Law 100th Episode Special* (1991); Jane Clement in *Married to Murder;* Diana Cadell in *Shame; It's Nothing Personal* (also co-executive producer); Siobhan in *Briefest Encounter* (Rik Mayall Presents); Jo in *A Woman's Guide to Adultery* (mini-series, 1993); *The Substitute;* Carmela Vezza in *Murder Most Horrid II; The BAFTA Production Awards* (host, 1994); *Frasier; Dangerous Dreams* (The Hidden Room); Diana Cadell in *Shame II: The Secret;* Lara in *Deep Secrets.*
Films: *Foreign Body; Castaway; The Lair of the White Worm; The Rainbow; Tank Malling; Dark Obsession; Diamond Skulls; Paper Mask; The Madness of King George.* **Awards:** TV: Golden Globe Best Actress in a Series, Mini-Series or Telefilm, for *LA Law* (1992). Address: c/o Markham & Froggatt.

Amanda Donohoe

DORE, Edna

Edna Doré. Actress. Trained at drama school attached to the Croydon Repertory Company.
TV: *Play School* (writer and storyteller); *The Brothers; The Liver Birds; Doctor in the House; Doctor at Large; Open All Hours; Terry Scott; Roger Doesn't Live Here Anymore; Under the Skin; Reservation;* Edna in *Tenko; The Puppet Man; The Mysteries; The Bill; King of the Ghetto; Lizzie's Pictures; Casualty; Christabel; Hard Cases; Streets Apart;* Mo Butcher in *EastEnders* (1989-90); *Gas and Candles,* Mrs Salad in *Anglo-Saxon Attitudes;* Rose in *Trust Me* (Screen One); Grace Taplow in *Love Hurts* (series, 1993); Iris Cromer in *Westbeach* (series); *Food File* (report on eating healthily in later years); *My Little Eye* (Short and Curlies); Dorothy in *Moving Story; Possession* (Capital Lives, Carlton only); *No Bananas.*
Films: *High Hopes.* Address: c/o CDA. Lives in Barnes, south-west London. m. theatre director and former actor Alexander Doré; 1 s. Mike.

Edna Doré

DOTRICE, Michele

Michele Dotrice. Actress. b. Cleethorpes, Lincolnshire, 27 September 1948. Daughter of actor Roy Dotrice (qv); sister of actresses Karen and Yvette Dotrice. Spent childhood in Guernsey, where father ran a repertory company. Trained at the Corona Stage Academy. Performed with the RSC (1964-6).
TV: *Emma's Time; A Kind of Bonus; A Month in the Country;* Betty Spencer in *Some Mothers Do 'Ave 'Em* (three series, 1973-8); *The Three Sisters; The Sextet; On the Eve of Publication;* Catherine Winslow in *The Winslow Boy;* Lady Percy in *Henry IV, Pts 1 and 2; Chintz* (series); Vanessa Daniels in *The Equalizer; Boon;* Lady Cora Peters in *Bramwell* (series, 1995).
Films: *The Witches; And Soon the Darkness; The Devil's Touch; Not Now Comrade.* Address: c/o Eric Glass. Lives in Cornwall. m. actor Edward Woodward (qv); 1 d. Emily Beth.

Michele Dotrice

DOTRICE, Roy

Roy Louis Dotrice. Actor. b. Guernsey, Channel Islands, 26 May 1925. Taken prisoner by the Germans during the Second World War while serving as an air gunner in the RAF. Acted Caliban, Julius Caesar, Hotspur, Firs, Puntila and Edward IV with the RSC (1957-65), appeared in more than 30 West End and six Broadway productions, and performed three one-man shows.
TV: *Dear Liar; Brief Lives; The Caretaker; Imperial Palace; Misleading Cases; Clochemerle; Dickens of London; Stargazy on Zummerdown; Remington Steele; Hart to Hart; Family Reunion; Magnum PI; Fairie Tale Theatre; Tales from Darkside; The A-Team; The Wizard; Shaka Zulu; Young Harry Houdini* (TVM); *Beauty and the Beast; Tales of Gold Monkey; For the Greater Good; Going to Extremes; Wings.*
Films: *The Heroes of Telemark; A Twist of Sand; Lock Up Your Daughters; Buttercup Chain; Tomorrow; One of Those Things; Nicholas and Alexandra;* Leopold Mozart in *Amadeus; The Corsican Brothers; The Eliminators; Lamia; L-Dopa; The Lady Forgets; The Cutting Edge; Lounge People; The Scarlet Letter.*
Awards: TV: Emmy Award for *The Caretaker* (1966). Address: c/o Bernard Hunter Associates. m. Kay Newman; 3 d. actresses Michele (qv), Karen and Yvette Dotrice. Hobbies: Fishing, riding, golf.

Roy Dotrice

DOUGLAS, Angela

Angela Douglas. Actress. b. Gerrards Cross, Buckinghamshire, 29 October
TV: *The Hard Knock; A Smashing Day; Wuthering Heights; Rosemary; The Dragon's Opponent; The Gentle Touch; Misterioso; Sharing; Time; Oil Strike North;* Marjorie in *Strathblair; Casualty; Cardiac Arrest.*
Films: *Feet of Clay; Cleopatra; Some People; It's All Happening; The Comedy Man; John Goldfarb, Please Come Home;* Annie Oakley in *Carry On Cowboy;* Dan Dann in *Carry On Screaming; Carry On Follow That Camel; Digby — The Biggest Dog in the World.* **Books:** *Swings and Roundabouts; Angela Douglas's Present Affairs* (both autobiographies). Address: c/o Joan Brown Associates. Lives in London. m. actor Kenneth More (dec). Partner: Theatre director Bill Bryden. Hobbies: Design, music, cooking.

Angela Douglas

Kate Dove

DOVE, Kate

Kate Dove. Actress. b. Portsmouth, Hampshire, 8 March 1947. Trained at the Philippa Fawcett College of Education, London, and the Triangle Theatre Workshop, New York, while living in Manhattan for four years. Directed stage productions of *Hedda Gabler* and *Educating Rita*, and British Council tours. Wrote children's shows *Colours*, *Gawain and the Green Knight* and *Hiawatha* for Cleveland Theatre Company.
TV: Ageing Deputy Head in *The Book Tower*; American Supervisor in *Wipeout*; Gross American Tourist in *Jackson Pace*; Elizabeth Feldmann/Pollard in *Emmerdale*.
Address: c/o Paul du Fer Associates. Lives in York. m. director Alasdair Ramsay; 1 s. Michael Hales. Hobbies: Reading, swimming.

Jo Dow

DOW, Jo

Jonathan Bell Dow. Actor. b. Redditch, Worcestershire, 25 March 1965. Trained at the Guildhall School of Music and Drama. Previously acted as Jonathan Dow.
TV: Pilot 'Nim' Renoy in *Piece of Cake*; Young Medic in *London's Burning*; Student in *After the War*; Tim in *No Job for a Lady*; PC Barry Stringer in *The Bill*; Dr James Mortimer in *Cardiac Arrest* (three series, 1994-6); Martin Beckham in *Peak Practice*.
Address: c/o Walmsley Home Associates. Lives in London. Partner: Actress Anna Healy. Pets: A spider. Hobbies: Theatre, art, cinema, swimming.

Freda Dowie

DOWIE, Freda

Freda Dowie. Actress. b. Carlisle, Cumbria. Trained at the Central School of Speech and Drama. An original member of Peter Brook's Theatre of Cruelty and a member of the RSC's experimental season at the Arts Theatre. Many stage roles in Greek tragedies, including Iphigenia, Cassandra, Medea and Antigone, plus title role in *Electra*, Dorine in *Tartuffe*, Queen Victoria in *Brunel*, Queen Isabella in *I Learned in Ipswich How to Poison Flowers* and Emily Dickinson in *The Belle of Amherst* (one-woman show).
TV: *Dr Finlay's Casebook; Within These Walls; Crown Court; Upstairs, Downstairs; Angels; North and South; Cranford; War and Peace; I Claudius; Lillie; The Old Curiosity Shop; The Stone Dance; The Poisoning of Charles Bravo; Lovejoy; Alice in Wonderland; Cover Her Face; The Pickwick Papers; Zig-Zag: The Normans; The Brontës; Cider with Rosie; Death of Socrates; Sophia and Constance; The Adventures of Sherlock Holmes; Agatha Christie's Poirot; Goldeneye*; Mrs Green in *Oranges Are Not the Only Fruit* (mini-series, 1990); *Kinsey*; Maureen Spencer in *Thacker; Stay Lucky*; Muriel Gerard in *Heartbeat*; Eileen Wolley in *Boon*; Jane Waule in *Middlemarch*; Lady Peggy Hudson in *The Lady's Man – Archibald Hall* (Crime Story); Mrs Kimball in *Moving Story*; Dulcie in *Common as Muck* (series, 1994); Florrie Hutchinson in *Our Friends in the North* (serial, 1996); Mistress Keyse in *In Suspicious Circumstances*.
Films: *The Omen; Murder by Decree; Scandalous; Distant Voices, Still Lives; The Monk; A Life in Death* (Royal College of Art); *The Black Crow; Butterfly Kiss*.
Address: c/o Roxane Vacca Management. Lives in Suffolk. m. translator, art critic and painter David Thompson. Pets: A saluki dog. Hobbies: Piano, meditation, homoeopathy.

Susannah Doyle

DOYLE, Susannah

Susannah Doyle. Actress. b. Kingston-upon-Thames, Surrey, 5 July 1966. Daughter of actor Tony Doyle; niece of actor Nicholas Courtney. Trained at LAMDA (graduated 1987). Stage plays include *The Good Doctor, Looking at You (Revived) Again, A View from the Bridge, Man and Superman* and *Oedipus Flabbergasted* (as Antigone).
TV: *The Bill; Hang-Gliding*; Melinda in *Work* (4-Play); Joy in *Drop the Dead Donkey* (Series 2, 3 and 4, 1991-4); Maggie Lemass in *The Young Indiana Jones Chronicles*; Marguerite in *Maigret*; Susie in *Minder*; Juliet in *Dirtysomething* (Screen Firsts); Louise Everett in *Soldier Soldier* (series, 1994).
Films: Lisa Lovell in *Hero Hungry*; *Breakfast*; Jackie in *Scandal*.
Address: c/o Roxane Vacca Management. Lives in London. Single.

Gabrielle Drake

DRAKE, Gabrielle

Gabrielle Drake. Actress. b. Lahore, Pakistan. Worked as an au pair in Paris before training at RADA. Stage plays include *Tea Party, Noises Off, Jeeves* and *Court in the Act*.
TV: Jill Hammond in *The Brothers*; *Kelly Monteith*; Nicola Freeman in *Crossroads* (1985-7); *The Importance of Being Earnest; Number 10; Wellington*; Diana Hardy in *Medics* (series, 1995).
Films: Julia in *There's a Girl in My Soup; Au Pair Girls*.
Address: c/o International Artistes. m. artist Louis de Wet.

DRINKEL, Keith

Keith Anthony Drinkel. Actor. b. York, 14 November 1944. Father a former club comedian, mother a former dancer. Trained in drama at Birmingham University. Stage roles include Duncan McFee in *Double Double* (Fortune Theatre) and Sir Percival Browne in *The Boy Friend* (Players' Theatre).
TV: Philip Ashton in *A Family at War* (22 episodes, 1970); The Dauphin in *Henry V*; Sim Hoskins in

Tales of the Unexpected; Mark Gaskell in Agatha Christie's Miss Marple: The Body in the Library; Ernest Beevers in Time and the Conways; Mr Jones in Grange Hill; Chief Supt Wade in The Bill; John Major in Thatcher: The Final Days; Inspector Easton in Casualty; Julian in Love and Reason; The Gas Man in Bookmark: The Most Beautiful Dress in the World. Address: c/o McIntosh Rae Management. Lives in London. Single. Hobbies: Working out, cinema, theatre, listening to classical music, reading.

DRINKWATER, Carol
Carol Drinkwater. Actress. b. London, 22 April 1948. Trained at The Drama Centre. Stage plays include Black Ball Game (Lyric Theatre).
TV: Public Eye; Bill Brand; Softly Softly; The Sweeney; Raffles; Sam (third series); A Bouquet of Barbed Wire; Another Bouquet; Helen Herriot in All Creatures Great and Small; Ladykillers; Tales of the Unexpected; Take the Stage; Chocky; The Haunted School; Captain James Cook. As writer: Molly (children's serial, 1995).
Films: A Clockwork Orange; The Dawn Breakers; Mondo Candido; Queen Kong; Joseph Andrews; The Shout. **Awards:** Variety Club BBC TV Personality of the Year, joint winner, for All Creatures Great and Small (1979).
Address: c/o London Management. Hobbies: Scuba-diving, writing, maps and atlases, travel, music.

Keith Drinkel

DRIVER, Betty
Betty Driver. Actress. b. Leicester, 20 May 1920. Grew up in Manchester. Joined the Terence Byron Repertory Company in Longsight, Manchester, aged nine. Professional début in Burnley, aged ten, and performed for many years as an actress and singer. Stage shows include Mixed Bathing (revue on tour), Mr Tower of London (national tour), The Lovebirds, Pillar to Post and What a Racket. Spotted by film producer Basil Dean in Jimmy Hunter's Brighton Follies and cast in early Ealing comedies. Sang on radio with bandleader Henry Hall for seven years (1941-8). Also performed with the troops entertainment organisation ENSA during the Second World War.
TV: Love on the Dole; Pardon the Expression (series); Betty Turpin in Coronation Street (1969-); This Is Your Life (subject); Royal Variety Performance (with Coronation Street cast, 1989).
Films: Boots! Boots! (not seen in final edited version); Penny Paradise; Let's Be Famous; Facing the Music. **Radio:** Henry Hall's Guest Night; A Date with Betty (own show). **Records:** The Sailor with the Navy Blue Eyes; MacNamara's Band; Pick the Petals of a Daisy; September in the Rain. Address: c/o Granada Television. Lives near Altrincham, Cheshire. m. singer Wally Petersen (dis). Pets: Two boxer dogs, Totti and Polly, and one cat, Abby. Hobbies: Collecting antiques and paintings.

Carol Drinkwater

DU SAUTOY, Carmen
Carmen du Sautoy. Actress. b. London, 26 February 1952. Many RSC stage productions, including Troilus and Cressida, The Way of the World and Love's Labour's Lost.
TV: The Citadel; The Brothers (series); The Barretts of Wimpole Street; Chessgame; Praying Mantis (TVM); The Sweet Scent of Death; Strangers and Brothers; The South Bank Show; The Young Wife in La Ronde; Astronauts (series); Punch Review; Poor Little Rich Girl (mini-series); Julie Blane in Lost Empires; Marie Changal in Bergerac; Nicole in The Intercom Conspiracy; Agatha Christie's Poirot; Eve in Perfect Scoundrels; Jack the Ripper (mini-series); Mamselle in Orchid House; The Stone Age (pilot); Boon; Marie-Helen in Anglo-Saxon Attitudes; Irene in BUGS; Marjorie in Paparazzo (pilot, 1995).
Films: The Man with the Golden Gun; title role in Dracula's Daughter; Our Miss Fred; Bert Rigby, You're a Fool. Address: c/o ICM . Lives in London. m. Charles Savage. Pets: Cats. Hobbies: Reading, writing, tennis, walking, golf.

Betty Driver

DUCE, Sharon
Sharon Duce. Actress. b. Sheffield, South Yorkshire, 16 January 1950. Stage plays include When I Was a Girl I Used to Scream and Shout (Whitehall Theatre).
TV: Bank Holiday; The Moonlighter; Bermondsey (30 Minute Theatre); Away from It All; New Scotland Yard; Crime of Passion; Helen – A Woman of Today; Villains; Z Cars; Two Men from Derby; Housewife's Choice; The House That Jack Built; Bill Brand; Crown Court (two roles); The Foundation; Dominic Ayres (pilot); Send in the Girls; Abel's Will; Renoir; Funny Man; The Professionals; Braces High; Days at the Beach; Sheila Maddocks in Coming Home (series, 1981); Minder; Tales of the Unexpected; In Loving Memory; The Hard Word (series); The Winter Break; The Bounder; Strange but True; Jan Oliver in Big Deal (two series, 1984-5); Boon; Seeing Stars; Crime Squad; Casualty; Emily Jessop in First Born (mini-series, 1988); Time on Your Hands; Doctor Who; Singles; The Bill; Shooting Stars (TVM); Misterioso; Pat Hollingsworth in Growing Pains (two series, 1992-3); Maggie Fell in Natural Lies (mini-series, 1992); Trafford Tanzi; 99-1; The Tomorrow People; Anita in Into the Fire (mini-series, 1996).
Films: Knots; Carol in Buddy's Song. **Radio:** Pat Hollingsworth in Growing Pains (two series, 1989-90). Address: c/o Marmont Management. m. TV documentary-maker David Munro (dis); 1 s. William (from subsequent relationship with actor Dominic Guard).

Carmen Du Sautoy

Sharon Duce

DUFF, Blythe

Blythe Duff. Actress. East Kilbride, 25 November 1962. Acted in community theatre and with the Scottish Youth Theatre. Stage roles include Shirley Kaplan in *Street Scene* (Scottish Opera/English National Opera, 1989) and Rhona Clay in *Swing Hammer Swing* (Citizens' Theatre, Glasgow, 1995).
TV: DC Jackie Reid in *Taggart* (series, 1990-) and *Taggart – The Movie.*
Radio: Irene in *Blending In* (BBC Radio 3); Katerina in *The Lady Macbeth of Mtsensk* (BBC Radio 4). **Records:** Shirley Kaplan in *Street Scene* (Decca Records, 1989).
Address: c/o The Brunskill Management. Lives in Glasgow. Single. Hobbies: Antiques.

Blythe Duff

DUFFETT, Nicola

Nicola Duffett. Actress. b. Portsmouth, Hampshire. Trained at the Arts Educational School.
TV: *You the City; Perfect Scoundrels;* Ruth Hadley in *Shadow of the Noose;* Ruby Kumara in *Jupiter Moon* (BSB); *The Bill;* Elvira Barney in *Laugh Baby Laugh* (In Suspicious Circumstances); Charlotte in *Maigret;* Debbie Tyler/Bates in *EastEnders;* Mavis Thompson in *Hot Dog Wars* (Crime Story).
Films: Jackie Bast in *Howards End.* Address: Conway, van Gelder, Robinson. Lives in London. m. 1st theatrical agent Andy Easton (dis), 2nd 1994 actor Ian Henderson (qv); 1 d. Jessica (from 1st m.). Pets: A rabbit (Roger) and a diamond dove (Sylvie). Hobbies: Theatre, cinema, books.

Nicola Duffett

DUNCAN, Lindsay

Lindsay Duncan. Actress. b. Edinburgh, 7 November 1950. Stage plays include *Top Girls* (Royal Court and Broadway), *Les Liaisons Dangereuses, Troilus and Cressida* and *The Merry Wives of Windsor* (all RSC).
TV: *Reilly – Ace of Spies;* Pamela in *The Kit Curran Radio Show; Muck and Brass; The Winkler; New Girl in Town;* Laura Pellin in *TECX;* Karen Miller in *Rainy Day Women;* Gutrune Day in *These Foolish Things; Colin's Sandwich;* Dana in *Deadhead; On Approval; Grown Ups; One Upmanship;* Barbara Douglas in *G.B.H.* (series); Helen Lithgow in *Traffik* (series, 1989); Eirwen in *The Childeater; Redemption;* Annie Mayle in *A Year in Provence* (series, 1993); Anna Bouverie in *The Rector's Wife* (serial, 1994); *Jake's Progress* (serial, 1995); Lady Walton in *Just William* (serial, 1995).
Films: *Prick Up Your Ears;* Lily Sacher in *For a Night of Love;* Mrs Nankervis in *Samson and Delilah;* Sally in *Loose Connections;* Dolphin Blue in *The Reflecting Skin;* Dr Agatha Webb in *Body Parts;* Medea in *The Greek Myths.*
Awards: TV: FIPA D'Or award at Cannes Film Festival for *Traffik* (1989).
Address: c/o Ken McReddie. m. actor Hilton McCrae; one child.

Lindsay Duncan

DUNCAN, Peter

Peter Duncan. Actor/Presenter. b. London, 3 May 1954. Son of Alan Gale, who produced pantomimes, and a singer-actress. Daredevil action-man on *Blue Peter* who sailed a Chinese junk up the Thames, cleaned the face of Big Ben and fought a Sumo wrestler. Stage plays include *Treasure Island* (as Jim Hawkins, Mermaid Theatre), *Barnum* (title role, Shepherd's Bush) and *Me and My Girl.*
TV: *Oranges and Lemons; Dragon's Opponent; John Halifax; Crown Court; Sam; Play for Today; Space 1999; Survivors; The Flockton Flyer; Robin Hood; Fathers and Families; King Cinder; General Hospital; Renoir – My Father; Warship; All Creatures Great and Small; Fallen Hero; Family Affair; Sons and Lovers; Blue Peter* (presenter, 1980-4, 1985-6); *Duncan Dares; Teenage Health Freak; The Big Race.*
Films: *Stardust; Mr Quilp; The Lifetaker; Flash Gordon.*
Address: c/o Saraband Associates. Lives in Wandsworth, South London. m. trainee midwife Annie; 3 d. Lucy, Katie, Georgia, 1 s. Arthur. Pets: A cat called Star. Hobbies: Theatrical producer.

Peter Duncan

DUNLOP, Joe

Joseph Johnston Strain Dunlop. Actor/Writer. b. Galston, Strathclyde, 16 February 1942. Grandfather played music for silent films. Trained at the Royal Scottish Academy of Music and Drama. Stage plays include *Ivanov, The Devil's Disciple* (both RSC) and *Wild Oats* (Piccadilly Theatre).
TV: Mr Conway in *Some Mothers Do 'Ave 'Em; Danger UXB; The Upchat Connection; Chalk and Cheese; Accident; Secret Army; Chance in a Million; The Incredible Mr Tanner; The Week of the Scorpion; Blacksilk; What if It's Raining;* Jeremy in *Don't Wait Up* (four series); Mr Coulter in *Brookside* (two episodes); George Hay in *Taggart;* Walsh in *Advocates;* Jack in *Take the High Road* (eight episodes); Insp Joe Beattie in *Dancing with Death* (In Suspicious Circumstances); *Keeping Up Appearances.*
Films: *Callan; Some Kind of Hero; A Man Called Intrepid; The Stranger; Terror; The Whistle Blower.*
Address: c/o RKM. Lives in North London. m. Janet; 1 d. Kirsty, 1 s. Christopher.

Joe Dunlop

DUNLOP, Lesley

Lesley Dunlop. Actress. b. Newcastle-upon-Tyne, 10 March 1956. Stage plays include *Other Worlds* (Royal Court) and *Playing with Trains* (RSC).
TV: *A Drive in the Country; Walk with Destiny; South Riding; The Gathering Storm; The White Ele-*

phant; *The Rose Garden; Penmarric; Black Beauty; Our Mutual Friend; Play for Love; Mates; The Red Shift; The Deadly Game; Waters of the Moon; Season's Greetings; Smuggler; Angels* (first series); *The Little Princess; Stanley;* Susie Q in *Doctor Who; Thirteen at Dinner* (TVM); Sara in *Capstick's Law;* Zoe in *May to December* (series); Ellie Freeman in *Rich Deceiver* (mini-series, 1995); Marion Wallace in *Silent Witness.*

Films: *A Little Night Music; Tess; The Elephant Man; Trick of the Light; The Monster Club.*

Address: c/o Annette Stone Associates. m. actor Christopher Guard (qv) (sep); 2 d. Daisy, Rosie. Partner: Actor Paul Bown (qv).

Lesley Dunlop

DUTTINE, John
John Duttine. Actor. b. Barnsley, South Yorkshire, 15 March 1949. Trained at The Drama Centre.

TV: *Armchair Theatre; A Pin to See the Peepshow; Z-Cars; Holding On; Warship; Softly Softly; Lord Peter Wimsey; Rooms; Coronation Street; Churchill's People; Spend, Spend, Spend; Jesus of Nazareth; Beryl's Lot; Angels; Law Centre; Saturday, Sunday, Monday; The Devil's Crown; People Like Us; Wuthering Heights; Strangers; The Mallens; To Serve Them All My Days; Psy-Warriors; The Day of the Triffids* (serial); *The Outsider; Tales of the Unexpected; Family Man; Shades of Darkness; The Intercessor; Love and Marriage; The Groundling and the Kite; Hamlet; A Woman of Substance* (mini-series); *A Still, Small Shout; Lame Ducks; Long Live the King; Unnatural Causes; Lost Property; Master of the Marionettes; A Killing on the Exchange; Imaginary Friends;* John Creevey in *The Ruth Rendell Mysteries: Talking to Strange Men;* Paul Melthorn in *Heartbeat;* Nikolai Herzen in *Love Hurts;* Alec Howard in *Casualty;* Dave Drysdale in *Ain't Misbehavin'* (two series, 1994-5); Kavanagh in *The Bill;* Det Insp Eric Temple in *Out of the Blue* (series, 1995); Robert Stirling QC in *Taggart. Devil's Advocate.*

Films: Rod in *Who Dares Wins; The Hawk.*

Awards: TV: *TVTimes* Best Actor award for *To Serve Them All My Days* (1980).

Address: c/o A.I.M. 1 s. Oscar (from past relationship with Carolyn Hutchinson). Hobbies: Making wine/beer and drinking it, gardening, walking.

John Duttine

EAGLES, Leon
Leon Eagles. Actor. b. Cardiff, 6 April 1932. Trained at RADA.

TV: *The Onedin Line;* Jensen in *The Jensen Code; Love for Lydia;* Kowajinski in *Dog's Ransom; The Famous Five; Secret Army; The Danedyke Mystery; Love in a Cold Climate; The Squad; Invasion; We'll Meet Again; Gulliver's Travels; Bergerac; The Fourth Arm; Operation Julie; C.A.T.S. Eyes; Chocky; David Copperfield; The Bill; Heading Home;* Dr Leon Hull in *Drummonds;* CPS Barrister in *The Bill.*

Films: Matthews in *Puppet on a Chain;* Martin Hack in *Frenzy;* Jack in *Performance.*

Address: c/o Spotlight. Lives in London. m. Mary Preston (dec 1994); 1 d. Zillah. Hobbies: Music, food, cricket.

Leon Eagles

EARL, Vince
Vince Earl. Actor. b. Birkenhead, Cheshire, 11 June 1944. Singer with the Vince Earl Talismen and the Vince Earl Attraction before turning professional as a comedian and actor.

TV: *New Faces; The Comedians; The Video Entertainers; Starburst; The Jimmy Cricket Special; Boys from the Blackstuff;* Ron Dixon in *Brookside* (1990-).

Films: *No Surrender.* Address: c/o Mersey Television. Lives in Birkenhead, Cheshire. m. 1st (dis), 2nd Irene; 2 s. Vince (from 1st m.), Stephen, 2 d. Nikki (Nicole), Kimberley.

Vince Earl

EDMONDS, Noel
Noel Edmonds. Presenter. b. London, 22 December 1948. Joined Radio Luxembourg as a disc-jockey in 1968 while still a student teacher, instead of taking up a place at Surrey University. Moved to BBC Radio 1 in 1969 and a year later took over Kenny Everett's daily slot, before becoming presenter of the breakfast show. Subsequently moved into television. Starred in the stage show *Captain Beaky's Musical Christmas.*

TV: *Top of the Pops; Z-Shed; Multi-Coloured Swop Shop; Come Dancing; Top Gear; Taking the Strain; Lucky Numbers; Juke Box Jury* (host); *The Late, Late Breakfast Show; Time of Your Life; Christmas with Noel; Telly Addicts; Whatever Next; The Saturday Roadshow; Foul Ups, Bleeps and Blunders* (US); *Noel's House Party; Noel's Christmas House Party* (1992); *The Detectives* (acting himself, 1993); *Children in Need; 3-D Week – Doctor Who: Dimensions in Time* (Children in Need, 1993): *Noel's Christmas Presents; The Children's Royal Variety Performance 1994; The Best of Noel's House Party* (1994); *Ten Years of Telly Addicts* (1994); *The National Lottery Live* (first episode, 1994); *Telly Addicts Christmas Special* (1994, 1995); *Noel's New Year's Eve House Party* (1994); *Champion Telly Addicts* (series, 1995); *The Gotcha Hall of Fame; Noel's Christmas Past* (highlights from *Noel's Christmas Presents,* 1995); *The Gotcha Hall of Fame* (1995); *Noel's Telly Years* (series, 1996); *Noel's NTV Stars.* **Awards:** *TVTimes* Favourite Male TV Personality award (1989).

Address: c/o BBC TV. Lives in Devon. m. 1st Gill (dis), 2nd Helen; 3 d. Lorna, Charlotte, Olivia.

Noel Edmonds

Adrian Edmondson

EDMONDSON, Adrian

Adrian Edmondson. Actor/Comedian.
TV: *The Young Ones; Mister Jolly Lives Next Door* (The Comic Strip Presents…); *More Bad News* (The Comic Strip Presents…); *The Yob* (The Comic Strip Presents…); *Girls on Top; Saturday Night Live; Honest, Decent and True; Happy Families; Hardwicke House; Filthy Rich and Catflap; French and Saunders;* Billy in *GLC* (The Comic Strip Presents…); Fan in *Oxford* (The Comic Strip Presents…); Baron Von Richroven in *Blackadder Goes Forth;* Eddie Hitler in *Bottom* (three series, 1991-2, 1995); Hamish in *Absolutely Fabulous; Harvey Angell* (storyteller); Gregory Dawson in *Gregory – Diary of a Nutcase* (The Comic Strip Presents…); *French and Saunders in… Space Virgins from Planet Sex;* Gordon Spry in *If You See God, Tell Him* (series, 1993); Dominic Jones in *Anna Lee.*
Films: *The Supergrass; The Strike; The Pope Must Die.* Address: c/o Jonathan Altaras Associates. m. actress-comedienne Jennifer Saunders (qv); 3 d. Ella, Beattie, Freya.

Glynn Edwards

EDWARDS, Glynn

Glynn Edwards. Actor. b. Malaya, 2 February 1931. Trained at Joan Littlewood's Theatre Workshop and the Central School of Speech and Drama. Studied agriculture and managed a sugar plantation in Trinidad before turning to acting.
TV: *The Newcomers; Spindo; The Main Chance; Man about the House; Dixon of Dock Green; The Paper Lads; Target; Rising Damp; The Fall and Rise of Reginald Perrin; The History of Mr Polly; You're Only Young Twice; Shadow of Gunman; The Lucky Feller; The Dick Emery Show; The Les Dawson Show; Crown Court; The Harry Worth Show; Madame Bovary; Softly Softly; Steptoe and Son;* Mr Lewis in *Some Mothers Do 'Ave 'Em; Sweet Sixteen;* Dave in *Minder* (series, 1979-4) *and Minder on the Orient Express.*
Films: *The Heart Within; Tunes of Glory; A Prize of Arms; Sparrows Can't Sing; The Hi-Jackers; Smokescreen; Zulu; The Ipcress File; Robbery; The Blood Beast Terror; The Bofors Gun; Get Carter!; Fragment of Fear; Burke and Hare; Under Milk Wood; All Coppers Are…; Shaft in Africa; A Place to Die; 11 Harrowhouse; The Stick-Up; The Playbirds; Confessions from the David Galaxy Affair; Rising Damp; Red Monarch; Champions; Out of Order.* Address: c/o Representation Joyce Edwards. m. 1st actress Yootha Joyce (dis), 2nd Christine Pilgrim (dis), 3rd Valerie; 1 s. Tom (from 2nd m.).

Peter Egan

EGAN, Peter

Peter Joseph Egan. Actor. b. London, 28 September 1946. Trained at RADA (1964-6). Stage plays include *The Two Gentlemen of Verona, Hamlet, Richard II* and *Barbarians* (all RSC), *Journey's End, What Every Woman Knows, Rolls Hyphen Royce, You Never Can Tell* and *Arms and the Man* (all West End).
TV: Seth in *Cold Comfort Farm* (début, 1967); Hog in *Big Breadwinner Hog;* The Earl of Southampton in *Elizabeth R; Mother Love; The Inheritors; The Organisation;* Millais in *The Love School; The Deep Blue Sea;* Oscar Wilde in *Lillie;* George VI in *Prince Regent;* Fothergill in *Reilly – Ace of Spies; The Dark Side of the Sun; The Kitchen; Dear Brutus; Tales of the Unexpected; Thriller; The Greeks; Murder Mysteries; Arms and the Man; A Woman of Substance* (mini-series); *Ever Decreasing Circles* (four series, 1984-7); Henry Simcox in *Paradise Postponed;* Pym in *A Perfect Spy; Joint Account* (two series 1988-90, 1989 special); *A Day in Summer; The Price of the Bride;* Rev Henry Archery in *The Ruth Rendell Mysteries: A New Lease of Death; MacGyver;* Simon Duval in *The Chief;* Dr Harry Blunden in *The Ruth Rendell Mysteries: Vanity Dies Hard* (mini-series, 1995); Richard Cramer in *The Man Who Didn't Believe in Ghosts* (Chiller); Edward Gwithian in *The Peacock Spring* (mini-series, 1996). **Films:** *The Hireling; Hennessy;* Meres in *Callan;* Duke of Sutherland in *Chariots of Fire; One Brief Summer.*
Awards: TV: *TVTimes* Best Actor on TV award for *Paradise Postponed* (1986). Films: BAFTA Most Promising Newcomer award for *The Hireling* (1973). Theatre: *Manchester Evening News* Best Actor award for *Astrov* (1992). Address: c/o James Sharkey Associates. m. Myra Frances; 1 d. Rebecca. Pets: Two dogs. Hobbies: Travel, poker, swimming.

Jennifer Ehle

EHLE, Jennifer

Jennifer Ehle. Daughter of novelist John Ehle and actress Rosemary Harris. Trained at the Central School of Speech and Drama. Stage plays include *Breaking the Code* (national tour), *Tartuffe* (Playhouse, directed by Peter Hall) and RSC productions of *The Relapse, The Painter of Dishonour* and *Richard III.*
TV: Calypso in *The Camomile Lawn* (mini-series, 1992); *The Young Indiana Jones Chronicles;* Tamsin in *Micky Love* (Rik Mayall Presents); Phyllis Maitland in *The Maitlands* (Performance); *Self Catering* (Alan Bleasdale Presents); Emma in *Pleasure* (Alan Bleasdale Presents); Penny McAllister in *Beyond Reason;* Elizabeth Bennet in *Pride and Prejudice* (serial, 1995).
Films: Cynthia Lennon in *Backbeat.* Address: c/o ICM.

Michael Elder

ELDER, Michael

Michael Elder. Actor. b. London, 30 April 1931. Trained at RADA. Stage shows include *Whalers* (one-man show, 1986 Edinburgh Festival, winner of a Fringe First award).
TV: *Sam; Edward the Seventh; Weir of Hermiston; Five Red Herrings; The Prime of Miss Jean Brodie;*

Dr Wallace in *Take the High Road/High Road* (1980- , also writer and script editor). As writer: *The Walls of Jericho; King's Royal; Murder Not Proven*.
Address: c/o Young Casting Agency/Scottish Television. m. actress Sheila Donald; 2 s. David, Simon.

ELES, Sandor

Sandor Elès. Actor. b. Hungary, 15 June 1936. Trained at student theatre in Hungary and the Bristol Old Vic Theatre School. Stage plays include *Whodunnit* (national tour), *Watch on the Rhine* (National Theatre), *A Patriot for Me* (Royal Court), *Fallen Angels* (national tour) and Georg Solti's *Duke Blue Beard's Castle* (narrator, Barbican, London, Salle Pleyel, Paris and Théâtre de L'Opéra, Lille).

TV: *Bartok;* Bugatti in *Isadora;* David Mitzmann in *The Wyngate Trilogy; Colette; Conrad; The Jean Rhys Woman; Fall of Eagles;* Count Lissagary in *Karl Mark Trilogy;* Emile in *Vienna 1900; Timeslip;* Philippe in *The Foundation; The Executioner; Timeslip;* Col Grigor KGB in *The Assassination Run* and *The Treachery Game;* Agatha Christie's *The Seven Dials Mystery;* Paul Ross in *Crossroads* (1982-8); *Aubrey;* Hansl in *The Endless Game* (pilot); Ramon in *Down to Earth* (series, 1995).

Films: *The Naked Edge; The Rebel; French Dressing; San Ferry Anne; The Magnificent Two;* Hans in *The Evil of Frankenstein; And Soon the Darkness; Countess Dracula; Fun and Games; The Kremlin Letter; Scorpio; Young Toscanini*.
Address: c/o Paul du Fer Associates. Lives in London. Single.

Sandor Elès

ELLIOTT, Su

Susan Elliott. Actress. b. Newcastle upon Tyne, 18 December 1950. Trained at the Guildhall School of Music and Drama. Stage plays include *Adrian Mole* and *Can't Pay, Won't Pay* (both West End).

TV: June Fish in *Home Sweet Home* (Play for Today); Mrs Bingham in *Henry's Leg;* Marjorie Osborne in *Auf Wiedersehen Pet* (two series); *Tales Out of School; When the Boat Comes In; Minder; Travelling Man; Thinkabout Science; Hi-de-Hi!;* Doreen Slater in in *The Secret Diary of Adrian Mole, Aged 13¾* and *The Growing Pains of Adrian Mole; Do It; Close to Home;* Delilah in *The Worst Witch;* Zoë in *Chains of Love; The Paradise Club; I Love Keith Allen; Sauna You Than Me; Dear Rosie;* Agatha Christie's *Poirot;* Mum in *Heaven;* Julie Dewhurst in *Coronation Street; Casualty;* Mrs Hart in *Inspector Morse: Deadly Slumber;* Ellen Stevens in *The Bill;* Mum Goggle in *Simply the Best;* Maureen Cromer in *King Leek;* Maggie Gibson in *This Life*.

Films: *Girl on a Swing; Robin Hood; Where the Wolves Howl; Giorgino*.
Address: c/o Barry Brown & Partner. Lives in London.

Su Elliott

ELLIS, James

James Ellis. Actor.

TV: *Escape;* Bert Lynch in *Z-Cars* (1962-78); *One by One;* Sarge in *Nightingales;* Charley Adamson in *So You Think You've Got Troubles;* Michael in *In Sickness and in Health* (final series, 1992); Joe Deegan in *Perfect Scoundrels;* Niall Sheehan in *Lovejoy;* Customs Officer in *The Detectives;* Walter in *Common as Muck;* Ned in *Oliver's Travels;* The Landlord in *The Shadow of a Gunman* (Performance); *The Nation's Favourite Poems* (reader); *Everybody's Gone* (Northern Lights).

Films: *My Left Foot;* Father Ellerton in *Priest.* Address: c/o Peter Charlesworth.

James Ellis

ELLIS, Janet

Janet Michell Ellis. Actress/Presenter. b. Kent, 16 September 1955. Educated at seven schools, including three overseas, because her father was an officer in the Royal Engineers. Trained at the Central School of Speech and Drama. Stage plays include *The Misanthrope* (Roundhouse).

TV: As actress: *Jackanory Playhouse: Princess Griselda; Doctor Who; The Deceivers; April Fool; The Sweeney; Knock-Knock; ATV Playhouse.* As presenter: *Jigsaw* (four series); *Blue Peter* (1983-7); *Open Air; Top Gear; The Motor Show; Parenting; The Motor Show.* Guest appearances: *Blankety Blank; Give Us a Clue; Cool Cube; Now Listen.* TV commercials: Daz.

Radio: *Janet's Bottom* (presenter, GLR, London).
Address: c/o Noel Gay Artists. Lives in London. m. 1st TV director Robin Bextor (dis), 2nd John Leach; 2 d. Sophie (from 1st m.), Martha, 1 s. Jack. Hobbies: Shopping, writing.

Janet Ellis

ELLIS, Peter

Peter Ellis. Actor. b. Bristol, 30 May 1936. Trained at Central School of Speech and Drama. Spent three years with the Old Vic Company, three years with the RSC and worked with the Chichester Festival Company, Theatre Workshop and the Belt and Braces Company.

TV: *The Outsider; How We Used to Live; In Two Minds; Edward and Mrs Simpson; Coronation Street; The Victoria Wood Show; First among Equals; Knock Back; Lytton's Diary;* Chief Supt Brownlow in *The Bill*.

Films: *An American Werewolf in London; Agatha; Remembrance.* Address: c/o Lou Coulson. Lives in Bristol. m. (dis); 3 s. Christopher, Hugh, Charles. Hobbies: Gliding, walking, sailing.

Peter Ellis

ELLISON, Christopher

Christopher Ellison. Actor. b. London, 16 December 1946. Trained as a graphic designer, worked as a mini-cab driver and served in the merchant navy before training as an actor at Studio '68.

TV: *The Professionals; Dempsey and Makepeace; The Gentle Touch; Strangers; Brand; Three Up, Two Down;* DI Frank Burnside in *The Bill* (1988-93); Lomax in *The Detectives;* Voice of Toby in *Conjugal Rights* (Series 2); *Two Golden Balls* (Screen One); title role in *Ellington* (pilot, 1994, series, 1996).

Films: George in *Buster.* Address: c/o ICM. Lives in Hove, East Sussex. m. actress Anita Joannou; 1 s. Louis, 1 d. Francesca. Hobbies: Painting and illustrating, boats.

Christopher Ellison

ELLWOOD, Fionnuala

Fionnuala Rachel Ellwood. Actress. b. Dublin, 3 July 1964. Trained at the Rose Bruford College.

TV: *Scruples* (improvised sketches); Amanda Thompson in *Families* (pilot); *World in Action* (voice-over); Lynn Whiteley in *Emmerdale; Seeking Susan;* Angie in *Thanks for Having Her;* forensic scientist Marion in *Prime Suspect* (mini-series, 1991); Julia Watson in *The Bill.*

Radio: *Billy Liar* (BBC Radio 5). Address: c/o Sharon Hamper Management. Lives in South London. Single. Hobbies: Cookery, reading, embroidery, DIY, scuba-diving.

Fionnuala Ellwood

ELPHICK, Michael

Michael John Elphick. Actor. b. Chichester, West Sussex, 19 September 1946. Previously worked as an electrician at Chichester Theatre. Trained at the Central School of Speech and Drama.

TV: *Parkin's Patch; Road to Freedom; The Cherry Orchard; The Little Farm; Norma; Holding Forth; The Nearly Man* (series); *Holding On; The Sweeney; The Professionals; Hazell; Crown Court;* Val Parnell in *The One and Only Phyllis Dixey* (TVM, also titled *Peek-a-Boo); The Knowledge; Blue Remembered Hills* (Play for Today); *Masada* (mini-series); *This Year, Next Year; Wobble to Death;* title role in *Private Schultz* (series, 1981); *Bloomfield; Smiley's People;* Mellors in *Lady Chatterley's Lover; Chish 'n' Fips; Andy Robson; All the World's a Stage; Chains; Pocketful of Dreams; Don't Write to Mother; Supergran; Hamp; CQ; Much Ado about Nothing; Oxbridge Blues; Jenny's War; Pull the Other One; Late Starter; Bird Fancier; Arthur's Hallowed Ground* (TVM, cinema film in US); Sam Tyler in *Three Up, Two Down* (four series, 1985-9); Ken Boon in *Boon* (eight series 1986-92, final episode 1995); *The Absolute Beginner's Guide to Cookery* (co-presenter); *Stanley and the Women;* Harry Salter in *Harry* (two series, 1993, 1995); Billy Bones in *Ken Russell's Treasure Island* (1995); *Modern Times: Streetwise* (narrator).

Films: *Fräulein Doktor; Where's Jack?; Hamlet; Eyewitness; The Buttercup Chain; Cry of the Banshee; Blind Terror; O Lucky Man!; Footsteps; Stardust; Star Wars; The Odd Job; The Great Train Robbery; Black Island; Quadrophenia;* Night Porter in *The Elephant Man; The Antagonists; Privates on Parade;* Chief of Police in *Curse of the Pink Panther; Memed My Hawk;* Pasha Pavlovich in *Gorky Park; Krull; Oxford Blues; Forbrydelsens Element (The Element of Crime); Ordeal by Innocence; Arthur's Hallowed Ground; Hitler's SS: Portrait in Evil; The Supergrass; Valhalla* (voice only); *Pirates; Little Dorrit; Withnail & I; I Bought a Vampire Motorcycle; Buddy's Song; The Krays; "Let Him Have It"; The Ballad of Kid Divine.* Address: c/o ICM. Lives in Portugal. Partner: Julia; 1 d. Kate.

Michael Elphick

ELTON, Ben

Benjamin Charles Elton. Comedian/Writer. b. Catford, south-east London, 3 May 1959. Studied drama at Manchester University. Has written for Rowan Atkinson, Rik Mayall, Lenny Henry, French and Saunders, and Adrian Edmondson. Writer of *Gasping* and *Silly Cow* (both Theatre Royal, Haymarket).

TV: *Alfresco; The Young Ones* (co-writer, with Rik Mayall and Lise Meyer, BAFTA Best Comedy award 1984); *Happy Families* (writer); *Filthy Rich and Catflap* (writer); *Blackadder II* (co-writer, with Richard Curtis); *Saturday Live* (host); *Blackadder the Third* (co-writer, with Richard Curtis); *Blackadder Goes Forth* (co-writer, with Richard Curtis); *South of Watford* (presenter and co-writer); *Friday Night Live; Wogan with Ben Elton* (guest presenter); *Just for Laughs Special* (host); *The Ben Elton Show* (series); *Friday Night Live — Lives Again! (Total Relief: A Night of Comic Relief,* 1993); writer Colin 'CD' Dobson in *Stark* (also writer, mini-series, 1993); *Ben Elton — The Man from Auntie* (series, 1994); *Morecambe and Wise — Bring Me Sunshine* (host, series, 1994); *Harry Enfield and Chums; The Thin Blue Line* (writer only, series, 1995); *The Nose at Ten: The Best of Comic Relief* (presenter, 1996).

Films: *The Secret Policeman's Third Ball;* Verges in *Much Ado about Nothing.*

Videos: *The Very Best of Ben Elton Live; A Farties Guide to the Man from Auntie.*

Records: Albums: *Motormouth; Motovation.* **Books:** *Bachelor Boys (Young Ones* book); *Stark* (novel, 1989); *Silly Cow* (1993). Published plays: *Gasping* (1991); *Silly Cow* (1993). Address: c/o McIntyre Management. Lives in London. m. 1994 saxophonist Sophie Gare.

Ben Elton

EMBERG, Bella

Bella Emberg. Actress/Comedienne. b. Brighton, East Sussex, 16 September 1937. Stooged for Benny Hill, Frankie Howerd, Stanley Baxter and Les Dawson.

TV: *Take Three Girls; Softly Softly; Testament of Youth; And Mother Makes Three; Man about the*

Bella Emberg

House; Robin's Nest; Pennies from Heaven; Russ Abbot's Madhouse; Les Dawson on Christmas (Christmas special, 1980); The Russ Abbot Show; Les Dennis's Laughter Show; The Russ Abbot Christmas Show; Russ Abbot (series).
Films: History of the World Part I. Address: c/o Mike Hughes Entertainments/Lake-Smith Griffin Associates. Hobbies: Opera, driving, old films, reading biographies.

EMERICK, Louis
Louis Emerick Grant. Actor. b. Liverpool, 10 June 1953.
TV: Happy Families; The Practice; Albion Market; Home to Roost; Celebration; Floodtide; There Was an Old Woman; A View of Harry Clarke; Last of the Summer Wine; Coronation Street; Children's Ward; Ball-Trap on the Côte Sauvage; Mick Johnson in Brookside (1989-).
Films: The Fruit Machine. Address: c/o Barbara Pemberton Associates/Mersey Television. Lives in Manchester. m. Maureen; 2 d. Valerie, Zoe, 1 s. Louis. Pets: A cat called Tinker and two dogs called Jodie and Griffin. Hobbies: Sports, cinema, theatre.

Louis Emerick

ENFIELD, Harry
Harry Enfield. Comedian/Writer. b. Sussex, 30 May 1961. Formed a double-act, The Adventures of Dusty and Dick, with friend Brian Elsley while studying at York University, from which he gained a degree in politics. Famous for his comic creations Stavros, Loadsamoney, Buggerallmoney, You Don't Wanna Do It Like That, Smashie and Nicey, Tim Nice-but-Dim, The Slobs and The Scousers.
TV: Spitting Image (scriptwriter and voice impersonator from 1985); French and Saunders; Don't Miss Wax; The Tube; Filthy Rich and Catflap; The Lenny Henry Show, Girls on Top, Frocks on the Box; Comic Relief; Friday Night Live; Saturday Night Live; Norbert Smith — A Life (also co-writer, with Geoffrey Perkins, winner of the Silver Rose of Montreux, a Banff Gold Rockie and the International Emmy Award for Popular Arts Programme); Harry Enfield's Television Programme (two series, plus Christmas special); Gone to the Dogs (series); Dermot in Men Behaving Badly (Series 1 only, 1992); Harry Enfield's Guide to the Opera (series, 1993); Billy the Fish (voice only, cartoon); Total Relief: A Night of Comic Relief (presenter, 1993); Smashie and Nicey and Friday Night Live — Lives Again! (both in Total Relief: A Night of Comic Relief, 1993); Smashie and Nicey's Top of the Pops Party; Smashie and Nicey — The End of an Era; Harry Enfield and Chums (series, 1994); Harry Enfield and His Charidy] (Comic Relief, 1995); Robb Wilton in Call Up the Stars (VE Day concert, 1995).
Address: c/o PBJ Management. Lives in North London. Single.

Harry Enfield

ESHLEY, Norman
Norman Eshley. Actor. b. Bristol, 30 May 1945. Started working life in a bank but left to train at the Bristol Old Vic Theatre School. Stage plays include and The Rover (as Don Pedro, RSC).
TV: Randall & Hopkirk (Deceased); Parkin's Patch; Bouncing Boy; Vienna 1900; The Onedin Line; The Skin Game; Windgate; Warship (three series); The Duchess of Duke Street; I Claudius; Supernatural; Secret Army; Justice; Thriller; The Strength of Gemini; Man about the House; And Mother Makes Five; Return of The Saint; The Sweeney; Jeffrey Fourmile in George and Mildred (four series, 1976-9); Late Expectations; Maybury; The Professionals; The Outsider; The Black Tower; Alun Jones in Brookside; Executive Stress; William Tell; After Henry; The Ruth Rendell Mysteries: Achilles Heel; Commander Gunner in Taggart: Death Comes Softly; Baron Huon in Cadfael (series, 1994); Roy Morris in All Night Long.
Films: The Immortal Story; Blind Terror; House of Mortal Sin (US title The Confessional); The Disappearance; Yanks. Address: c/o Sandra Griffin Management. m. 1st actress-singer Millicent Martin (dis), 2nd Lynette Braid. Hobbies: Football, cricket, horse-racing, sailing.

Norman Eshley

EVANS, Chris
Chris Evans. Presenter. Began his career sorting Timmy Mallett's fan mail at Piccadilly Radio (Manchester), worked with Emma Freud and wrote scripts for Jonathan Ross.
TV: The Power Station (satellite channel); The Big Breakfast (1992-4); Don't Forget Your Toothbrush (series, 1994); Don't Forget Your Toothbrush II (series, 1994-5); Just for Laughs (Montreux Comedy Festival, 1994); Chris Evans — Don't Forget Your Nose (Comic Relief, 1995); Live for Peace — A Royal Gala (VE Day 1995); TFI Friday (series, 1996). **Radio:** Round at Chris's (Saturday-morning show, BBC GLR, London, 1989-93); Too Much Gravy (Sunday Show, BBC Radio 1, 1992); breakfast show, BBC Radio 1. Address: c/o Freud Communications.

Chris Evans

EVANS, Nicky
Nicky Evans. Actor. b. 20 April 1979.
TV: David in All Creatures Great and Small; Corrigan and Womack; Christmas Helpline (Yorkshire Television); Boy Scout in Stay Lucky; Graham Thompson in Heartbeat; BMX Boy 1 in Harry; Toddy in Criminal (Screen Two); Roy Glover in Emmerdale (1994-).
Address: c/o ATS Casting/Yorkshire Television.

Nicky Evans

Serena Evans

EVANS, Serena

Serena Evans. Actress. Trained at the Central School of Speech and Drama (1981-4).
TV: *Susie* (The Comic Strip Presents...); *Bad News Tour* (The Comic Strip Presents...); *Private Enterprise* (The Comic Strip Presents...); *Consuela* (The Comic Strip Presents...); *Hale & Pace; Mr Majeika; Never Come Back;* Sarah Chapman in *The Piglet Files* (two series, 1990-1); *Came Out, It Rained, Went Back in Again* (ScreenPlay Firsts); Caroline Finch in *The House of Windsor* (series); Sgt Patricia Dawkins in *The Thin Blue Line* (series, 1995, plus Christmas special, 1995); Ms Forelle in *Pie in the Sky; The Brit Awards 1996* (presenter). Address: c/o Rebecca Blond Associates.

EVE, Trevor

Trevor Eve. Actor. b. Birmingham, 1 July 1951. Trained at RADA.
TV: *The Portrait; Hindle Wakes; London Belongs to Me;* Eddie Shoestring in *Shoestring* (two series, 1979-80); *Jamaica Inn; A Brother's Tale; Lace* (mini-series); *The Corsican Brothers; Shadow Chasers; A Wreath of Roses; Flipside; Shadow on the Sun;* Felix Cramer in A Sense of Guilt (series, 1990); *Parnell and the Englishwoman;* Torvald Helmer in *A Doll's House* (Performance); *The President's Child;* Malcolm Iverson in *Murder in Mind* (Screen One); *Black Easter;* Duncan Matlock in *The Politician's Wife* (mini-series, 1995); Alex Fischer in *Black Easter* (Screen Two); Julian Fontaine in *Murder, She Wrote.*
Films: *Trilogy; Dracula; Scandal; The Knight's Tale; Aspen Extreme; Psychotherapy.*
Awards: Theatre: SWET Best Actor and Laurence Olivier Best Actor awards for *Children of a Lesser God* (1981). Address: c/o Julian Belfrage Associates. m. actress Sharon Maughan (qv); 1 d. Alice, 2 s. Jack, George. Pets: Horses. Hobbies: Polo, tennis, golf, skiing.

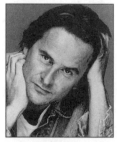

Trevor Eve

EWING, Barbara

Barbara Ewing. Actress. Trained at RADA (Bancroft Gold Medal winner).
TV: *Country Matters;* Dora in *Sam* (series); *Hard Times; The Sweeney; Steven* (Play for Today); *The Picture Show; Clouds of Glory; Boon;* Agnes Fairchild in *Brass; Comrade Dad* (series); *The Bill; Alas Smith and Jones; Rachel* (series); *Watch with Mother* (Play for Today); Chrissie Mills in *Freddie Mills* (In Suspicious Circumstances); Mrs Tandy in *The Bill;* Sarah Fenwick in *September Song;* Mrs Ashforth in *Boon; Casualty;* Iris Cressley in *The Bill;* Sheila in *Lovejoy;* Nina Hanley in *The Bill;* Selina in *Harry;* Mrs Keegan in *Number Six* (Chiller); Cassie Westbury in *The Vet.*
Films: *Torture Garden;* Zena in *Dracula Has Risen from the Grave; The Reckoning; Eye of the Needle; When the Whales Came.* Address: c/o Scott Marshall.

Barbara Ewing

EYTLE, Tommy

Tommy Eytle. Actor. b. Guyana. Arrived in UK on Festival of Britain Day, 1951, working first as a surveyor and draughtsman, then as a bandleader in London hotels.
TV: *Body Contact; Radical Indies* (Play for Today); *Johnny Jarvis; The Kenny Everett Television Show; Kelly Monteith; Rumpole of the Bailey; Act of Will; There's Something Wrong in Paradise; London's Burning; The Bill; Snakes and Ladders;* Jack in *Never Say Die; Words and Pictures;* Jules Tavernier in *EastEnders* (1990-).
Films: *The Tommy Steele Story; Day of the Fox; Elsa the Lioness; The Hi-jackers; Man Friday; Beyond the Sunrise; Blue Smoke, Red Mountains.* Address: c/o Crouch Associates/BBC Elstree Centre.

Tommy Eytle

FAITH, Adam

Terence Nelhams. Actor/Singer. b. Acton, West London, 23 June 1940. Joined Rank Studios aged 15 as a messenger boy, then worked in Pinewood Studios' cutting room and as an assistant editor at Beaconsfield Studios while singing in the skiffle group Working Men. Took up acting in 1966.
TV: *Oh Boy!; Drumbeat; Boy Meets Girls; The Adam Faith Show; (Cat) In the Night* (Play of the Week, TV acting début);title role in *Budgie; Video Video* (presenter); *Just Another Little Blues Song; Minder on the Orient Express* (TVM); Gordon Shade in *Shady Tales* (series); Frank Carver in *Love Hurts* (three series, 1992-4); *Freddie Starr; The Travel Show* (guest reporter, 1994); *Joint Ventures* (presenter, talking on the business potential of cannabis, Pot Night, C4 1995); *The Enemy Within* (talking about post-traumatic stress after a 1985 car crash, 1995).
Films: *Beat Girl* (US title *Wild for Kicks*); *Never Let Go; What a Whopper!; What a Carve-Up!* (US title *Home Sweet Homicide); Mix Me a Person; Stardust; Yesterday's Hero; Foxes; McVicar.*
Records: Singles: *What Do You Want* (No 1, 1959); *Poor Me* (No 1, 1960); plus 22 other chart singles. Albums: *Beat Girl* (film soundtrack, No 11, 1961); plus four other chart albums.
Address: c/o ICM. Lives in Wimbledon, South London. m. 1967 dancer Jackie Irving; 1 d. Katya.

Adam Faith

FANCY, Brett

Mark Brett Fancy. Actor. b. Portsmouth, Hampshire, 4 January 1964. Trained at the Guildhall School of Music and Drama (Gold Medal winner).
TV: Steve Hood in *Rockliffe's Babies;* Sean Hooper in *Square Deal; Treasure Island;* The Leveller in

Brighton Boy; The Bill; EastEnders; The Frontier (He-Play); Hex in BUGS; The Leveller in Resort to Murder (series); Steve in Paparazzo (pilot); Rob in The Vet. Address: c/o Jonathan Altaras Associates. Lives in London. Single. Hobbies: Art, sculpting, keeping fit, travel, kite flying, scuba-diving, jet-skiing.

Brett Fancy

FARLEIGH, Lynn

Lynn Farleigh. Actress. b. Bristol, 3 May 1942. Trained at Guildhall School of Music and Drama.

TV: Z Cars (20 episodes); All's Well That Ends Well; Hallelujah Handshake; Eyeless in Gaza; The Guardians; New Scotland Yard; Public Eye; The Strauss Family; Bill Brand; Scenes from Family Life; Fall of Angels; Steptoe and Son; Cakes and Ale; Cottage to Let; The Velvet Glove; Murder Most English; Scorpion Tales; The Three Kisses; Harry; The Person Responsible; Fall of Eagles (series); Bill Brand (series); Edith Cavell; Out; Sweet Nothings (series); A Walk in the Forest; Spooner's Patch; Antony and Cleopatra; Fothergill; Clare; The Hard Word (series); Waving to a Train; Let's Run Away to Africa; Coming Through; Fighting Back; God's Closer Car Park; Lost Belongings (series); The Border; Face of the Earth; Wish Me Luck (Series 2); Tales from Hollywood; Heartbeat; Boon; The Ruth Rendell Mysteries: The Mouse in the Corner; Finney; Christine Henshaw in Castles (series); Mrs Phillips in Pride and Prejudice.

Films: Three into Two Won't Go; Voices; Watership Down; The Word. Address: c/o Conway, van Gelder, Robinson. Lives in London. m. 1st actor Michael Jayston (qv) (dis), 2nd actor David Yip (qv); 2 s. Joe, Matthew (from 1st m.). Pets: Two half-Burmese cats. Hobbies: Gardening, swimming, walking.

Lynn Farleigh

FARMER, Mark

Mark Farmer. Actor. b. London, 22 May 1962. Trained at the Anna Scher Theatre School.

TV: How Green Was My Valley; The World about Us; The Squad; Omnibus: Heinrich Boll; Scene: On Your Bike; Fancy Wanders; Grange Hill; You Must Believe; Triangle; Metal Mickey; Union Castle; Radio; Partners in Crime; Jury: David; Educating Marmalade; Jack and His Computer; Let There Be Love; Shine on Harvey Moon; Johnny Jarvis; Relative Strangers; Minder; On Her Majesty's National Service; Glorious Day.

Films: Memoirs of a Survivor; Mr Corbett's Ghost. Address: c/o Anna Scher Theatre Management.

Mark Farmer

FARRINGTON, Ken

Kenneth William Farrington. Actor. b. Dulwich, South London, 18 April 1936. Trained at RADA.

TV: Where the Party Ended; The Splendid Spur; An Age of Kings (series); Billy Walker in Coronation Street (on and off, 1961-79, 1984); Bookstand: The Loneliness of the Long Distance Runner; This Happy Breed; Undercover Cat; The Avengers; Moonstrike; The Odd Man; Man of the World; The White Hot Coal; Nice Break for the Boys; The Villains; Love Story; It's a Woman's World; Love o' Women; Kipling; Redcap; Armchair Theatre: The Last Reunion; The Joe Baker Show; Z Cars; Softly Softly (two roles); The Whole Truth; The Revenue Men; The Troubleshooters; The Gamblers; The Expert; Detective; The Saint; Sanctuary; The Expert; The Borderers; Parkin's Patch; Play for Today; The Prime Minister's Daughter; Crime Buster; Boy Meets Girl; The Tomorrow People; Crown Court; General Hospital; Major Frances in Danger UXB; Tycoon; New Girl in Town; The Union; Whistling Wally; Juliet Bravo; A Married Man; A Killing on the Exchange; Valentine Park; Hannay; Minder; The Chief; All Creatures Great and Small; Trainer (Series 1); Boon; Grange Hill; Heartbeat; The Bill; Casualty; Space Precinct.

Films: One Way Pendulum; Beauty Jungle; The Knack... and how to get it; Submarine XI; Deep Waters; Walter Regen in Lime Street; Father in Party, Party.

Address: c/o Scott Marshall. Lives in Surrey. m. actress Patricia Heneghan (dis); 2 s. James, Mark, 2 d. Tessa (Theresa) (all from m.), Sally Ann. Hobbies: Photography, tennis, gardening.

Ken Farrington

FAULKNER, James

James Faulkner. Actor. b. Hampstead, North London, 18 July 1948.

TV: The View from Daniel Pike; Softly Softly; Miss Nightingale; Bentley Drummel in Great Expectations (TVM); Chips with Everything; Herod in I Claudius (series); Hazell (series); The Martian Chronicles; The Sound of Guns; Tales of the Unexpected; The Professionals; The Acts of Peter and Paul; Muck and Brass (series); Minder; Alas Smith and Jones; Strangers and Brothers (series); Lace II; Mr Paltrey of Westminster; The Bill; Deceptions (mini-series); Minder on the Orient Express (TVM); Simon Kerslake in First among Equals (series); Crazy like a Fox; The Contract; Radical Chambers; The Bourne Identity; Agatha Christie's Poirot; Bergerac; The Return of Sherlock Holmes; The Yellow Wallpaper; Just Another Secret; The Shadow Trader (series, New Zealand); Napoleon (series, France); Alex Mair in Devices and Desires (series); Inspector Morse; Lovejoy; Covington Cross (pilot); The Blackheath Poisonings (mini-series); Rudy Lorimer in Demob (series); Class Act; Guinevere; Highlander; Wycliffe; QC in The Trial of Lord Lucan; Hamish Macbeth; McKenna; Giles Cotham in Chandler & Co; Strike Force; A Touch of Frost.

Films: The Great Waltz; The Abdication; Conduct Unbecoming; The Whispering Death; One Take Two (also co-producer); Zulu Dawn; Nulpunkt; The Priest of Love; Eureka; Runners; Real Life; Icarus (National Film School); Catherine; The Maid; Genghis Khan; Carry On Columbus; $E=MC^2$; Det Crowley in Crimetime; Justice in Mind (London International Film School). Address: c/o Hutton Management. Lives in Hampstead, North London. m. Kate; 2 s. Guy, Leo. Pets: Belgium shepherd dog called Hercule.

James Faulkner

Jean Fergusson

Pam Ferris

Douglas Fielding

Felicity Finch

Steven Finch

FERGUSSON, Jean

Jean Mitchell Fergusson. Actress. b. Wakefield, West Yorkshire, 30 December 1944. Her mother played piano in a dance band. Moved to Wales aged 12 and trained at Cardiff College of Music and Drama. Stage tours include *A Bedfull of Foreigners* and *She Knows You Know*, her one-woman show about the life of actress-comedienne Hylda Baker.

TV: Caroline Herbert in *Crossroads* (1973); Mrs Tremayne in *All Creatures Great and Small*; Joyce Tibbs in *The Practice*; Marina in *Last of the Summer Wine* (series, 1983-); Mrs Minton in *A Woman of Substance* (mini-series); Helen Ashcroft in *Coronation Street* (1987); Mildred in *Lipstick on Your Collar*. Address: c/o Scott Marshall. Lives in London. Pets: One cat. Hobbies: Writing, horse-riding, reading.

FERRIS, Pam

Pamela Elizabeth Ferris. Actress. b. Germany. Stage plays include *Devil's Gateway, Lucky Chance, The Grace of Mary Traverse, Apples, The Queen and I, Road* (all Royal Court) and *Roots* (National Theatre).

TV: *Miss Julie* (New Zealand); Nesta in *Connie* (series); *The Bill; Casualty; Lizzie's Pictures; Ladies in Charge; Hardwicke House; Sense of Guilt; Oranges Are Not the Only Fruit;* Ma Larkin in *The Darling Buds of May* (three series 1991-3, plus 1992 Christmas special); Mrs White in *Cluedo;* Mad Marion in *Mr Wakefield's Crusade* (series); Mrs Bryant in *Roots* (Performance); *Sisters; The Blues; The Spheres; All Change;* Matron in *Once in a Lifetime* (Comedy Playhouse); Mrs Dollop in *Middlemarch* (series, 1994); Eleanor in *The Rector's Wife* (series, 1994); voice of Aunt Pettitoes in *Beatrix Potter: The World of Peter Rabbit and Friends — The Tale of Pigling Bland (1994);* Alice Hartley in *Mrs Hartley and the Growth Centre* (Screen Two, 1995).

Films: *Winnie; The House; Meantime.*
Address: c/o Hamilton Asper Management. Lives in Essex. m. actor Roger Frost.

FIELDING, Douglas

Brian Douglas Fielding. Actor. b. London, 6 June 1946. Former member of the National Youth Theatre. Trained at LAMDA. Plays include *The Importance of Being Earnest, St Joan* (both National Theatre), *The Business of Murder* (West End) and *A Christmas Carol* (as Ebenezer Scrooge, Mermaid Theatre).

TV: Alex Quilley in *Z Cars* (1968-78); *Callan; Tales of Mystery and Imagination; Softly Softly; Angels; Blake's 7; Juliet Bravo; Tom Grattan's War;* Roy Quick in *EastEnders* (1985-6); *The Knock; The Bill; Grange Hill.*

Films: *The Battle of Britain; The Day the Fish Came Out; What a Difference a Day Makes; The Darkening.* Address: c/o The Narrow Road Company. Lives in London. m. 1st Marilyn Adams (dis), 2nd Elizabeth Revill, partner actress Sarah-Jane Vant; 2 d. Nicola Jane, Sereina Marea (both from 1st m.), 2 s. Benjamin Douglas (from 2nd m.), Frederick (from relationship with partner Sarah-Jane Vant). Pets: Tropical fish. Hobbies: Music, drama, cooking, sport, Tottenham Hotspur FC.

FINCH, Felicity

Felicity Finch. Actress. b. Teesside, 14 March. Trained at The Drama Centre. Stage roles include Sarah in *Trelawny of the Wells* and Jessica in *The Merchant of Venice* (both Old Vic and tour of Europe).

TV: Margaret Pope in *Thomas and Sarah;* Nurse Young in *Little Miss Perkins;* Violet in *Love, Lust and Loneliness;* Joyce Mickle in *Eve Strikes Back;* Connie in *No Place Like Home;* Jeannie Harris in *Angels;* Rosa in *Bleak House;* Julia in *The Piglet Files;* Louise Hammond in *The Bill;* Lady Lucan in *Murder in Belgravia: The Lucan Affair;* Sally Wyatt in *The Sculptress* (serial).

Radio: *Danton's Death; Soft; The Stigma;* Ruth Archer in *The Archers* (1987-).
Address: c/o Langford Associates. Lives in London. Single. Hobbies: Dance, circus skills.

FINCH, Steven

Steven Charles Finch. Actor. b. Maidstone, Kent, 28 December 1961. Previously acted under the name Steven Pinner. Trained at the Guildhall School of Music and Drama, then The Theatre, Chipping Norton. Acted in the RSC's 1985 season in Stratford-upon-Avon.

TV: *The Life and Times of John Wycliffe; The Eye of the Yemanger;* Jonathan Gordon-Davies in *Brookside;* John Rae in *Tales of the Unexpected;* Robert Ayres in *Worlds Beyond;* Jeffrey Letwin in *The Bill;* Giles Mawhinney in *Agent 2;* Stuart Kydd in *Crown Prosecutor;* Tony in *What Next?;* Agent Z & the Penguin from Mars (children's series, 1996). TV commercials: Timotei, One-Cal; Yoplait.

Films: David Sterling in *Link;* Steve Boyd in *Life at the End of the Line.*
Radio: *Joy Ride; The Men's Group.* Address: c/o Langford Associates. m. actress Pam Bennett; 1 d. Emily. Pets: A toad. Hobbies: Odd jobs, music, running.

FINLAY, Frank

Frank Finlay. Actor. b. Farnworth, Lancashire, 6 August 1926. CBE, 1984. Won Sir James Knott Scholarship to train at RADA. Many classical theatre roles with RSC and National Theatre Company.

TV: Brutus in *Julius Caesar;* Jean Valjean in *Les Misérables; This Happy Breed;* Andrew Firth in *The Lie;*

title role in *The Death of Adolf Hitler*; Sancho Panza in *Don Quixote*; Voltaire in *Candide*; Shylock in *The Merchant of Venice*; Peter Manson in *A Bouquet of Barbed Wire* and *Another Bouquet*; Frank Doel in *84 Charing Cross Road*; Peppino in *Saturday, Sunday, Monday*; Prof Van Helsing in *Count Dracula* (mini-series); *The Last Campaign*; Napoleon in *Betzi*; Bridie in *Dear Brutus*; *Tales of the Unexpected*; *1001 Nights*; Mona in *Aspects of Love*; *A Christmas Carol* (TVM); *Arch of Triumph* (TVM); title role in *Casanova* (series); *In the Secret State*; *Mountain of Diamonds*; Justice Peter Mahon in *Erebus: The Aftermath* (mini-series); *King of the Wind* (TVM); Sir Arthur Conan Doyle in *Encounters: The Other Side*; Pavel Rhele in *Exchange of Fire* (mini-series); Professor Coram in *The Memoirs of Sherlock Holmes*; Harold Plumb in *Lovejoy*; Howard Franklin in *Heartbeat*; Prof Etherege in *P D James' A Mind to Murder*.

Films: *The Loneliness of the Long Distance Runner*; *The Longest Day*; *Life for Ruth*; *Private Potter*; *Doctor in Distress*; *The Informers*; *The Comedy Man*; *Hot Enough for June*; *The Wild Affair*; *A Study in Terror*; *Othello*; *The Sandwich Man*; *The Jokers*; *The Deadly Bees*; *I'll Never Forget What's 'is Name*; *The Spare Tyres*; *Robbery*; *The Molly Maguires*; *The Shoes of the Fisherman*; *Inspector Clouseau*; *Twisted Nerve*; *Cromwell*; *The Body* (narrator); *Assault*; *Gumshoe*; *Danny Jones*; *Sitting Target*; *Neither the Sea nor the Sand*; *Shaft in Africa*; *The Three Musketeers*; *The Four Musketeers: The Revenge of Milady*; *The Wild Geese*; *The Thief of Baghdad*; *Murder by Decree*; *Enigma*; *The Return of the Soldier*; *The Ploughman's Lunch*; *Sakharov*; *1919*; *The Key*; *Space Vampires* (retitled *LifeForce*); *The Return of the Musketeers*; *Othulhu*; *Sparrow*.

Address: c/o Ken McReddie. Lives in London. m. former actress and journalist Doreen Shepherd; 2 s. actor Stephen, actor Daniel, 1 d. actress Cathy.

Frank Finlay

FINNERAN, Siobhan

Siobhan Finneran. Actress. Trained at Grange Arts. Has also performed as a stand-up comic.

TV: Carol in *The Cannon & Ball Show*; *Pack of Lies*; Josie Phillips in *Coronation Street*; Molly in *Josie*; Tina in *Sharpend*; Milly in *Motormouth*; The Woman in *Mr Wroe's Virgins*; *The Russ Abbot Show* (two series); Janet in *Heartbeat*; Caroline Royal in *Peak Practice*; *Jackanory* (improvised storytelling); Lena in *Resort to Murder* (series, 1995); *Jackanory* (storyteller); *New Voices* (Yorkshire Television only).

Films: Rita in *Rita, Sue and Bob Too*.

Radio: *Sins of the Mother*; *Tony Hawkes Comedy Show*. Address: c/o Shane Collins Associates.

Siobhan Finneran

FINNIGAN, Judy

Judy Finnigan. Presenter. b. Manchester, 16 May 1948.

TV: Granada Television researcher; Anglia Television news reporter; Granada Television news reporter and presenter; *Reports Action*; *Flying Start*; *Scramble*; *Chalkface*; *ITV Telethon*; *This Morning* (co-presenter, with husband Richard Madeley); *Classic Coronation Street* (1992-); *The Judy Finnigan Debate* (two series, 1993-4); *Champion Children Awards* (1995); *Get a Life!* (health series, 1995); *Champion Children Awards* (1996). Address: c/o Granada Television. m. 1st (dis), 2nd co-presenter Richard Madeley (qv); 3 s. Tom, Dan (twins from 1st m.), Jack, 1 d. Chloe.

Judy Finnigan

FIRTH, Colin

Colin Firth. Actor. b. Grayshott, Hampshire, 10 September 1960. Trained at The Drama Centre. Stage plays include *Another Country* (as Guy Bennett), *The Lonely Road* (Old Vic) and *The Caretaker* (Comedy Theatre).

TV: Armand Duval in *Camille* (TVM); *Dutch Girls*; Colin as an adult in *The Secret Garden* (TVM); Richard Herncastle in *Lost Empires*; Rene Wilcox in *Tales from the Hollywood Hills*; Lt Robert Lawrence in *Tumbledown* (TVM); *Milos Forman: Portrait*; John McCarthy in *Hostages* (drama-documentary, 1992); *Out of the Blue*; Stephen Whalby in *The Ruth Rendell Mysteries: Master of the Moor*; Freddie Page in *The Deep Blue Sea* (Performance); Mr Darcy in *Pride and Prejudice* (serial, 1995); *The Widowing of Mrs Holroyd* (Performance).

Films: Tommy Judd in *Another Country*; Young Alexander in *1919*; Tom Birkin in *A Month in the Country*; *Apartment Zero*; Vicomte DeValmont in *Valmont*; Smith in *Wings of Fame*; Joe in *Femme Fatale*; Richard Courtois in *The Hour of the Pig*. **Awards:** RTS Best Actor award for *Tumbledown*. Address: c/o ICM. m. actess Meg Tilly (sep); 1 s. William.

Colin Firth

FIRTH, David

David Firth Coleman. b. Bedford, 15 March 1945. Actor. Stage plays include *As You Like It*, *Much Ado about Nothing*, *The Revenger's Tragedy* (all RSC US and Europe tour), *Romeo and Juliet*, *Saturday, Sunday, Monday*, *Did You Know Marilyn Monroe?*, *The Importance*, *The Phantom of the Opera* and *The Hunting of the Snark* (all West End).

TV: *Dancing in the Dark*; *Terra Firma*; *Love for Lydia*; *Wings*; *Raffles*; *Saint Joan*; *Nanny's Boy*; *Sorry I'm a Stranger Here Myself*; *Troilus and Cressida*; *The Further Adventures of Lucky Jim*; *Yes Minister*; *Drummonds*; *Stay Lucky*; Lord Horbury in *Agatha Christie's Poirot*.

Address: c/o Conway, van Gelder, Robinson. Lives in Twickenham, Middlesex.

David Firth

FIRTH, Peter

Peter Firth

Peter Firth. Actor. b. Bradford, West Yorkshire, 27 October 1953. Started acting as a child. Stage plays include *Equus, Romeo and Juliet, Spring Awakening* (all National Theatre) and *Amadeus* (as Mozart, Broadway).

TV: *The Double Deckers; The Flaxton Boys; Castlehaven; Home and Away* (Granada Television series); *The Sullens Sisters; Country Matters; The Simple Life; The Magistrate; The Protectors; Black Beauty; Arthur; Her Majesty's Pleasure; The Ballad of Ben Bagot; The Picture of Dorian Gray; Lady of the Camellias; The Flipside of Dominick Hyde; Another Flip for Dominick; The Aerodrome* (TVM); *Blood Royal; Northanger Abbey* (TVM); *The Way, the Truth, the Video; Murder In Eden; Children Crossing; The Laughter of God;* Geiger in *The Incident* (TVM); *Prisoner of Honour* (TVM); Peter Wainwright in *Anna Lee;* Dr James Radcliffe in *Heartbeat* (Series 4, 1994); Peter Dennigan in *Resort to Murder* (series, 1995); Major Ben Collins in *Soldier Soldier;* Ray Anderson in *Faith in the Future* (series, 1995); Brian Roberts in *Band of Gold* (series, 1996); *And the Beat Goes On.*

Films: *Diamonds on Wheels; Brother Sun, Sister Moon; Daniel and Maria; Aces High; Joseph Andrews; Equus; Tess; When You Comin' Back, Red Ryder?; White Elephant; The Flight of the Spruce Goose;* Peter in *Letter to Brezhnev; Space Vampires* (retitled *LifeForce*); *A State of Emergency; Born of Fire; Prisoner of Rio; Trouble in Paradise; The Tree of Hands; Burndown; The Hunt for Red October; The Pleasure Principle.* Address: c/o Markham & Froggatt.

FISH, Michael

Michael Fish

Michael John Fish. Weather presenter. b. Eastbourne, East Sussex, 27 April 1944. Fellow of Royal Meteorological Society. Joined the Meteorological Office in 1962, worked at Gatwick Airport, Bracknell and Birmingham, then in 1967, after taking a degree course at City University, London, moved to London Weather Centre. Radio broadcaster since 1971, BBC TV weatherman since 1974. Longest-serving weather presenter on British television. Has trained TV weather forecasters in several African countries.

TV: BBC TV weather forecasts (1974-); *The Sky at Night.*

Address: c/o BBC TV Weather Centre. m. Susan Page; 2 d. Alison Elizabeth, Nicola Katherine. Pets: Two cats, Penty and Mira. Hobbies: Travel, after-dinner speaking.

FISHER, Doug

Doug Fisher

Doug Fisher. Actor. Stage plays include *Alfie* (national tour), *The Ratepayers' Iolanthe* (Phoenix Theatre), *Sloane Ranger Revue* (Duchess Theatre), *Othello* (Arts Theatre) and *Jeffrey Bernard Is Unwell* (national tour). Directed *Boeing–Boeing* (Australia and Jersey), *Darling, Mr London* (New Zealand and three summer seasons), *Lying Low* (King's Head) and *Absurd Person Singular* (Edinburgh).

TV: *Helen – A Woman of Today; Man about the House* (three series); *Feet First; The Man Who Almost Knew Eamonn Andrews; Keeping in Touch; Yes Minister; Singer's Night; Ellis Island; Sorry; Home to Roost; All in Good Faith; Streets Apart; Maggie; Haggard; Prime Suspect; Singles; The Upper Hand;* Mellor in *The Bill* (1992); Solicitor in *Fool's Gold* (TVM, 1992); *The Detectives;* Jim in *London's Burning* (series, 1993); Mr Barnet in *Pie in the Sky; Shine on Harvey Moon;* John Fry in *The Bil.*

Films: *Man about the House;* Sammy in *The Stud; Tess; The Bitch.*

Address: c/o The Narrow Road Company.

FISHER, Gregor

Gregor Fisher

Gregor Fisher. Actor. Stage plays include *The Homecoming, As You Like It, A Midsummer Night's Dream, A Funny Thing Happened on the Way to the Forum, The Cherry Orchard* and *One, Two, Three.*

TV: *Just a Boy's Game; End of the Line; Naked Video* (four series); *City Lights; Rab C Nesbitt's Christmas Show; Scotch and Wry Hogmanay Show; Foxy Lady; Boon; Box 13; Blood Red Roses; Stan's First Night; The Bill; One for the Money; Rab C Nesbitt* (five series, 1989-94 and 1996, plus Christmas special, 1994); title role in *The Tales of Para Handy* (two series, 1994-5); *Naked Video 33⅓* (highlights from *Naked Video*); title role in *The Baldy Man* (series, 1995).

Films: *'1984'; Another Time, Another Place;* Bill in *The Girl in the Picture* (1985); *White Mischief; To Kill a Priest; Sherlock and Me; Silent Mouse* (Edinburgh Film & Video production).

Awards: Theatre: Toronto Festival Best Actor award for *One, Two, Three.*

Address: c/o William Morris Agency (UK). m. actress Vicki Burton.

FISHER, Jeannie

Jeannie Fisher

Jeannie Fisher. Actress. b. Glasgow, 18 February 1947. Trained at the Royal Scottish Academy of Music and Drama. Began career as an understudy at the Royal Court Theatre, London. Stage plays include *The Double Dealer, The Three Musketeers, Slag, Yarsdale* (world première, 1985 Edinburgh Festival), *Macbeth* (Indian tour), *Whose Life Is It Anyway?* and *Blithe Spirit.*

TV: *The Canterbury Tales; The Silver Sword; Adam Smith; Arthur of the Britons;* Morag Stewart in *Take the High Road.* Address: c/o Pat Lovett Agency. Lives in London and Edinburgh. Single. Hobbies: reading, going to the cinema and theatre.

FITZALAN, Marsha

Marsha Fitzalan. Actress. b. Bonn, West Germany, 10 March. Daughter of the Duke of Norfolk. Trained at the Webber Douglas Academy. Stage plays include *84 Charing Cross Road*.
TV: *Pride and Prejudice; Shelley; The Duchess of Duke Street; Armchair Thriller; Something in Disguise; The Professionals; Diamonds; Upstairs, Downstairs; Dick Barton; Angels; Pygmalion; By the Sword Divided; The Comedy of Errors; Three Up, Two Down; Nancy Astor; The Wife's Revenge; Paradise Postponed; Brush Strokes; Inside Story; Hedgehog Wedding;* Sarah B'Stard in *The New Statesman* (four series, 1987-92); *Soft Soap; Goldeneye* (TVM); Anita in *Rides;* Camilla Mounsey in *Under the Hammer* (series, 1994); Valerie Marchant-Hayne in *White Goods*.
Films: *International Velvet; Anna Karenina; A Handful of Dust.* Address: c/o Jonathan Altaras Associates. m. actor Patrick Ryecart; 2 d. Mariella, Jemima, 1 s. Frederick.

Marsha Fitzalan

FITZGERALD, Kate

Kate Fitzgerald. Actress. b. Anfield, Liverpool. Sister of actress Angela Walsh. Trained at The Drama Centre and began career at the Unity Theatre, Liverpool, then the Everyman Theatre, Liverpool. Stage productions include Willy Russell's *Stags and Hens* (Liverpool Playhouse and Old Vic), *Educating Rita* (title role, RSC national tour), *Blood Brothers* (Liverpool Playhouse and Lyric Theatre) and *Shirley Valentine* (title role, national tour and West End), plus *Dancing at Lughnasa* (national tour and Garrick Theatre). Other RSC appearances include *Children of the Sun, Men's Beano, Captain Swing, Wild Oats* and *Once in a Lifetime*. Has worked with the Women's Theatre Group.
TV: *The Daughters of Albion;* Doreen Corkhill in *Brookside* (1985-7, 1989); June Williamson in *Casualty;* Rita Carrard and Tricia James in *The Bill*.
Films: *Call Collect.* Address: c/o Saraband Associates.

Kate Fitzgerald

FITZ-SIMONS, Lesley

Lesley Fitz-Simons. Actress. b. Glasgow, 23 September 1961. Voice and movement lessons from Jeanne Gourlay. Stage plays include *The Merchant of Venice* and *The Kitchen*.
TV: BBC Schools; *The Standard; The Camerons; The Prime of Miss Jean Brodie; Playfair; Mendelssohn in Scotland; Annals of the Parish;* Ophelia in *Hamlet; Square Mile of Murder; House on the Hill;* Alison Houghton in *The Walls of Jericho; The Spaver Connection; Skin Deep; Funny You Should Say That;* Sheila Ramsay (née Lamont) in *Take the High Road* (1983-), *The Odd Job Man* (Play for Today).
Address: Young Casting Agency/Scottish Television. m. 1989 building company sales director Peter McIntyre (dis). Partner: Calum Thomson; 1 d. Marnie (b. Dec 1995). Pets: Two dogs called Raffles and Honey, three cats, two budgerigars and goldfish. Hobbies: 'Damon Hill fan (Formula 1).'

Lesley Fitz-Simons

FLEESHMAN, David

David Fleeshman. Actor. b. Glasgow, 11 July 1952. Educated in Birmingham. Professional début at Birmingham Rep (1973). More than 200 stage plays all over the UK. Roles include Malvolio in *Twelfth Night,* Demetrius and Bottom in *A Midsummer Night's Dream,* Rosencrantz in *Rosencrantz and Guildenstern Are Dead,* Mr Dean in the original production of Alan Bleasdale's *No More Sitting on the Old School Bench* and Eddie/Dr Scott in *The Rocky Horror Show*.
TV: Estate agent Peter Haines in *Coronation Street;* Barry Hill in *Emmerdale Farm; Dear Enemy; The Practice; The Outsider;* Derek in *Boys from the Blackstuff;* Det Sgt Jones in *Edge of Darkness;* Joseph Chamberlain in *Victorian Values;* Shimon in *Bulman;* Logan in *One by One;* Frank Taylor in *Truckers;* The Innkeeper in *Soldier and Death;* Enoch Taylor in *The Luddites;* Det Insp Grucock in *Blind Justice;* Gordon Knight in *After the War;* George's Dad in *Children's Ward;* Stanton in *Capstick's Law;* Serge Olsen in *The Ruth Rendell Mysteries* (re-edited as *The Ruth Rendell Mystery Movie);* Sgt Purkiss in *A Bit of a Do;* Charlie Aindow in *Emmerdale* (47 episodes); David Hurst in *Brookside;* Gus in *Medics;* Michael Sterne in *Sam Saturday* (series, 1992); Alexander Houghton in *How We Used to Live;* Lasky in *Heartbeat;* Hotel Manager in *Band of Gold;* Coroner in *In Suspicious Circumstances;* Immigration Officer in *Missing Persons;* Prison Officer Stone in *The Bill;* Soumies in *EastEnders* (six episodes, 1995); Mr Faber in *Heartbeat;* Immigration Officer in *Hetty Wainthropp Investigates*.
Films: *The Wall; The Nature of the Beast.*
Address: c/o RKM. Lives in Cheshire. m. 1978 actress Sue Jenkins (qv); 2 d. Emily, Rosie, 1 s. Richard. Pets: Two cats (Max and Lucy), one rabbit. Hobbies: 'Eating, sleeping and walking.'

David Fleeshman

FLEMYNG, Jason

Jason Flemyng. Actor. Trained at LAMDA. RSC productions include *All's Well That Ends Well, Barbarians, Moscow Gold, As You Like It* and *Coriolanus*.
TV: *For the Greater Good; Rich Tea & Sympathy;* Colin in *A Question of Attribution* (TVM); *Witchcraft; Bye Bye Baby; The Young Indiana Jones Chronicles; The Good Guys;* Danny in *Lovejoy;* Dr Neil in *Doctor Finlay* (two series 1993-4).
Films: *Diamond Swords; The Jungle Book.* Address: c/o Conway, van Gelder, Robinson.

Jason Flemyng

FLETCHER, Alexandra
Alexandra Fletcher. Actress.
TV: *Why Don't You...?; Cool Cube* (BSB); Jacqui Dixon in *Brookside* (1990-).
Address c/o Mersey Television.

Alexandra Fletcher

FLETCHER, Dexter
Dexter Fletcher. Actor. b. North London, 31 January 1966. Son of film and TV set designer Steve Fletcher and theatrical agent Wendy Fletcher; brother of actors Steve Fletcher and Graham Fletcher-Cook.
TV: Gavroche in *Les Misérables* (TVM); *Pig Ignorance; Didn't You Kill My Brother?; Across the Lake; Boon; Working Week; Down and Out; Out of the Blue;* Spike in *Press Gang* (five series); Shaun Leary in *The Bill; Murder Most Horrid; A Future in Fish* (4-Play); *The Big One; Soldier Soldier; Dread Poets Society; Seven Deadly Sins: Sloth & Lust; The Tempest; English File: Text in Time; Gamesmaster* (presenter, series); *Prince Cinders* (voice only); *Aristophanes – The Gods Are Laughing; Speakeasy AIDS Special.*
Films: *Bugsy Malone; 4D Kids; The Long Good Friday; The Elephant Man; The Bounty; Wings of Death;* Ned the Man in *Revolution;* Young Caravaggio in *Caravaggio; Lionheart; Gothic;* Tom in *The Raggedy Rawney; When the Whales Came;* Charles Highway in *The Rachel Papers; The Mad Monkey;* Angelo in *All Out.*
Address: c/o ICM. Lives in Maida Vale, London. Pets: Two cats called Vahagh and Indra.

Dexter Fletcher

FLETCHER, Freddie
Freddie Fletcher. Actor. b. Yorkshire. Former amateur boxer.
TV: *Queenie's Castle; Another Sunday and Sweet FA;The XYY Man; Clouds of Glory: Wordsworth; Bulman; The Wild West Show; Red Shift;* Gypsy in *The Old Firm;* Kenny in *Floodtide;* Mr Derek in *All Creatures Great and Small;* Crandon in *How We Used to Live;* Mr Smithson in *Children's Ward* (two series); poacher Vic in *G.B.H.;* Sam Carver in *Heartbeat;* George Milton in *Peak Practice;* Arnie Franks in *The Governor;* Mr Thompson in *Some Kind of Life.* Commercials: BP; Tetley's bitter.
Films: Jud in *Kes;* Wireless Operator in *Juggernaut;* Ronnie Boyd in *Fox;* Ned in *Nature of the Beast;* Mr Redway in *Brothers in Trouble.* Address: c/o ATS Casting.

Freddie Fletcher

FLOYD, Keith
Keith Floyd. Presenter/Cook. b. Reading, Berkshire, 28 December 1943. On leaving Wellington School, he became a journalist but subsequently joined the Army and rose to 2nd Lieutenant in the Royal Tank Regiment. Later jobs as a dishwasher and vegetable peeler led him to become a restaurateur. By 1971, he owned three restaurants in Bristol, but became disillusioned, bought a yacht and spent two years in Spain and Portugal. He then failed as a wine merchant and antiques dealer in France, so opened a restaurant near Avignon. He has since retired from the restaurant business to concentrate on broadcasting and writing.
TV: *Floyd on Food; Floyd on Fish; Floyd on France; Floyd on Spain* (series, 1992); *Far Flung Floyd* (series, 1993); *Floyd on Italy* (series, 1994); *A Feast of Floyd* (series, 1994); *The Egg – A Wildlife Guide; A Tale from the Riverbank* (subject, documentary); *Floyd on Africa* (series, 1996).
Books: *Floyd's Food; Floyd on France; Floyd on Fish; Floyd Britain and Ireland; Floyd in the Soup; Floyd American Pie; Floyd on Oz; Floyd on Spain; Floyd on Fire; A Feast of Floyd; Far Flung Floyd; Floyd on Hangovers; Floyd on Italy.* Address: c/o PO Box 4, Dartmouth, Devon TQ6 OYD. Lives in Ireland. m. 1st (dis), 2nd (dis), 3rd (dis); 1 s. Patrick, 1 d. Poppy. Pets: Dogs, cats, pigs, turkeys, doves.

Keith Floyd

FLYNN, Barbara
Barbara J McMurray. Actress. b. Hastings, East Sussex, 5 August 1948. Trained at the Guildhall School of Music and Drama (Gold Medal winner, as Barbara McMurray). Stage roles include Pip in *A Murder Has Been Announced,* Jane in *Two and Two Make Sex* (Cambridge Theatre), Epifania Ognisanti di Parega in *The Millionairess* (Greenwich Theatre), Sylvia Craven in *The Philanderer,* Gloria in *Early Days,* Helen Schwartz in *Tales from Hollywood* and title role in *Antigone* (all National Theatre).
TV: *Keep It in the Family; Second Chance; A Flight Fund; Murder Most English; Standing in for Henry; Bagthorpes;* Freda Ashton in *A Family at War; Afternoon Dancing; Love on a Gunboat; Maybury; No Visible Scar* (the story of Dr Sheila Cassidy); *The Last Song; The Further Adventures of Lucky Jim; Where Angels Fear,* Mary Bold in *Barchester Chronicles;* The Milkwoman in *Open All Hours;* Jill Swinburne in *The Beiderbecke Affair, The Beiderbecke Tapes* and *The Beiderbecke Connection;* Dr Rose Marie in *A Very Peculiar Practice* (series); Sheila Green in *Boon;* Belinda Bunker in *Season's Greetings* (Christmas special); Monica Height in *Inspector Morse: The Silent World of Nicholas Quinn;* Jane in *Benefactors;* Eleanor Goodchild in *The Justice Game* (Series 2); Madame Maigret in *Maigret* (second series, 1993, taking over the role from Ciaran Madden); Judith Fitzgerald in *Cracker* (three series, 1993-5); Dee Tate in *Chandler & Co* (Series 1 only, 1994).
Films: *Britannia Hospital.*
Address: c/o Markham & Froggatt. m. Jeremy Taylor. Hobbies: Cooking, writing, gardening.

Barbara Flynn

FORBES, Emma

Emma Forbes. Presenter. b. 14 May. Daughter of actor-director Bryan Forbes and actress Nanette Newman (qv). Has worked as a model, editor of PR trade magazine *The Diary*, a freelance stylist and fashion journalist. First TV presenting a regular cookery spot with Phillip Schofield on *Going Live!*

TV: *Hearts of Gold; Follow the Star; Press Gang; Home Show* (pilot); *Focus on Britain* (US satellite series); *World Television* (pilot, US satellite channel); *Body Talk* (Lifestyle channel); *Going Live!; Live & Kicking; Speakeasy* (series); *Follow the Star* (Christmas Day special from Queen Charlotte's Hospital, London, 1992); *Star Pets* (series, 1993); *Live & Kicking on Christmas Day* (special, 1993); *Talking Telephone Numbers* (three series, 1994-6); *It's My Life* (series, 1994); *Children in Need – The Countdown Continues* (1994); *What's My Line?* (host, game show series, Meridian and Channel Television only, 1994); *Children in Need – Lighting the Torch Paper* (1994); *Children in Need* (reporter, 1994); *Speakeasy AIDS Special; Antiques Roadshow – The Next Generation* (special for children, 1995); *Zoo Watch Live* (series, 1995). **Books:** *Entertaining; The Emma Forbes Going Live! Cookbook.* Address: c/o Noel Gay Artists. Lives in South Kensington, London. m. banker Graham. Hobbies: Cinema.

Emma Forbes

FORBES, Miranda

Maddalena Stephnie Weet. Actress. b. London, 11 August 1946. Trained at Bush Davies Theatrical School and LAMDA. Stage plays include *Jane Eyre, Patrick Pearce Motel* (both West End).

TV: *Felix Dexter on TV; Faith in the Future; Within These Walls* (five series); *Minder; Bergerac; Shine on Harvey Moon; Yes, Prime Minister; Hard Cases; London's Burning; Room at the Bottom; Gentlemen & Players; May to December; Castle of Adventure;* Lady in Queue in *As Time Goes By;* Mary in *A Small Dance* (TVM); Mrs Turton in *Agatha Christie's Poirot; Hancock; Casualty;* Miss Greve in *The Last Romantics; Ashenden; The Bill* (two roles); *Lovejoy; Sam Saturday;* Nanny in *Waiting for God; Absolutely Fabulous;* Mrs Drabble in *The Brittas Empire;* Rose Herbert in *Circles of Deceit.*

Films: *Back Home; Bejewelled; All Men Are Mortal; Jane Eyre.* Address: c/o The Narrow Road Company. Lives in the Cotswolds. Single. Pets: A cat called Willy. Hobbies: Gardening, travel.

Miranda Forbes

FORBES, Natalie

Natalie Forbes. Actress. b. Doncaster, South Yorkshire, 1 November.

TV: *The Other 'Arf; Nanny; Kelly Monteith; The Incredible Mr Tanner; Blood Money; The Gentle Touch; A Ferry Ride Away; Out on the Floor; Full House; Shadow of the Noose; Live and Kicking;* Laura Haylock in *Surgical Spirit* (series, 1994); Jean Selby in *Heartbeat.*

Films: *Loss Adjuster; Napoleon and Josephine.*

Address: c/o Susan Angel Associates. Hobbies: Reading, gardening, music, football.

Natalie Forbes

FORD, Anna

Anna Ford. Newscaster. b. Tewkesbury, Gloucestershire, 2 October 1943. Brought up in Cumbria, read social anthropology at Manchester Univesity, then took a post-graduate diploma in adult education there, before becoming an Open University staff tutor in Belfast. Moved into television in 1974.

TV: *Reports Action* (reporter/researcher); *Man Alive; Tomorrow's World;* ITN newscaster, 1978-81 (primarily on *News at Ten*); founder-member of TV-am (presenter of *Good Morning Britain*); *The Six o'Clock News* (BBC newsreader); *Breakfast with Frost* (stand-in presenter, 1993); *The Evening Standard British Film Awards 1993* (1994).

Awards: *TVTimes* Most Popular Female TV Personality (1978). Address: c/o JGPM. m. 1st Dr Alan Bittles (dis), 2nd cartoonist and *Tatler* editor Mark Boxer (dec); 2 d. Claire, Kate (both from 2nd m.).

Anna Ford

FORGEHAM, John

John Forgeham. Actor. RSC productions include *Henry IV, Henry V, Henry VIII* and *The Hollow Crown.*

TV: *Spy Catcher; 13 Against Fate; Mystery and Imagination; No Hiding Place; Z Cars; The Avengers; The Brothers; Father Brown; Armchair Theatre; Play of the Month; Seven Deadly Sins; The Idiot; The Likely Lads; Churchill's People, The Expert, Man in Room 17, Jim Baines in Crossroads; Logger; The Sweeney; Why Aren't You Famous?; The Hitch-Hiker; The Professionals; Minder; Number on End; Shoestring; The Incredible Mr Tanner, Crown Court; A Gift of Tongues; Knife Edge; Strangers; Juliet Bravo; Beau Geste;* Al in *L for Lester* (series); *Jury; Identikill; Give Us a Break; Hell's Bells; Letty; C.A.T.S. Eyes; Lovejoy; Prospects; The Military Wing; Duty Free; Boon; Divided We Stand; Big Deal; Bulman; Casualty, Y.E.S.; Final Run; Pulaski; Ernie's Incredible Hallucinations; Bergerac; London's Burning; Journey's End; Precious Bane; Storyboard: Snakes and Ladders; Nice Work;* Ronnie in *Not a Penny More, Not a Penny Less; This Is David Lander, The Laughter of God; Literary Islands* (voice-over); *T-Bag; Prime Suspect;* Frankie in *Making Out* (three series); DCI John Shefford in *Prime Suspect* (mini-series); *Birds of a Feather; Heartbeat; The Bill; Growing Pains;* Freddie Matthews in *All in the Game* (series); *Pie in the Sky; Blue Heaven* (series); *Staggered; Crocodile Shoes; Bare Necessities.*

Films: *Beckett; Spy Story; Star Wars; Pope Paul II; The Italian Job; The Partner; Ivanhoe; Sakharov; Sheena – Queen of the Jungle; The Inquiry; King of the Wind.* Address: c/o Peters Fraser & Dunlop.

John Forgeham

FORRESTER, Philippa

Philippa Forrester. Presenter. b. Winchester, Hampshire. Read English at Birmingham University.
TV: Children's BBC; ...*But First This*; *Edd the Duck's Megastar Trek* (1992); *Disney Club* (series, 1994-5); *Nine o'Clock Live* (1995); *Tomorrow's World* (series, 1995-).
Address: c/o Michael Ladkin Personal Management. Lives in Ealing, West London.

Philippa Forrester

FORSYTH, Brigit

Brigit Forsyth. Actress. b. Edinburgh, 28 July. Trained at RADA.
TV: *The Sinners*; *Adam Smith*; title role in *Holly*; Thelma Ferris in *The Likely Lads* and *Whatever Happened to the Likely Lads?*; *Graham's Gang*; *I Told You So, Didn't I*; *The Visit*; *The Master of Ballantrae*; *My World*; *Jackanory*; Henry (Playhouse); *Glamour Girls*; *Holding the Fort*; *Tom, Dick and Harriet*; *Bizarre and Rummage* (Play for Today); *Sharon and Elsie*; *The Practice*; *Agatha Christie's Poirot*; *Running Wild*; *Stanley's Vision*; *Boon*; *Nice Town* (mini-series, 1992); *Wycliffe*; *Waiting* (Comedy First); *Dangerfield*.
Films: *The Wrong Side of the Blanket*; *The Roadbuilder*; *The Likely Lads*; *The Crystal Stone*.
Address: c/o Barry Burnett Organisation. m. TV director Brian Mills; 1 d. Zoe, 1 s. Ben.

Brigit Forsyth

FORSYTH, Bruce

Bruce Forsyth Johnson. Entertainer/Presenter. b. Edmonton, North London, 22 February 1928.
TV: *Music Hall*; *Sunday Night at the London Palladium* (compère); *The Bruce Forsyth Show*; *The Canterville Ghost*; *The Mating Game*; *The Generation Game* (1971-7); *Bring on the Girls*; *The Muppet Show*; *Bruce and More Girls*; *The Entertainers*; *Bruce Forsyth's Big Night* (1978); *Play Your Cards Right*; *Hollywood or Bust*; *Slinger's Day* (sitcom); *Sammy and Bruce*; *You Bet!*; *Bruce and Ronnie*; *Takeover Bid*; *Bruce Forsyth's Generation Game* (1990-4); *Bruce's Guest Night* (1992-3); *Bruce Forsyth's Christmas Generation Game*; *Bruce Forsyth – 50 Years in Showbusiness*; *Bruce Forsyth's Play Your Cards Right*; *Wish You Were Here...?* (guest reporter); *Bruce's Price Is Right* (1995-6).
Films: *Star!*; *Can Hieronymous Merkin Ever Forget Mercy Humppe and Find True Happiness?*; *Bedknobs and Broomsticks*; *The Magnificent Seven Deadly Sins*. Address: c/o Billy Marsh Associates. Lives in Surrey. m. 1st Penny Calvert (dis), 2nd 1973 Anthea Redfern (dis), 3rd former Miss World Wilnelia Merced; 5 d. Deborah, Julie, Laura (from 1st m.), Charlotte, Louisa (from 2nd m.), 1 s. Jonathan.

Bruce Forsyth

FORTUNE, John

John Fortune. Actor/Writer. Directed, wrote for and performed in the Cambridge Footlights revue while at Cambridge University. Co-founder of Peter Cook's Establishment Club, writing and performing sketches with Eleanor Bron and John Bird, and touring the US with the group. Stage plays include *One Way Pendulum* (Toronto and Old Vic), *The Black Prince* (Aldwych Theatre).
TV: *Not So Much a Programme, More a Way of Life*; *BBC3*; *The Late Show* (all as writer and performer); *Birds and Well Anyway*; *On the Margin*; *Where Was Spring*; *The End of the Pier Show*; *In the Looking Glass*; *Roger Doesn't Live Here Anymore* (writer); *Round and Round* (writer); *First among Equals*; *Campaign*; *Dramarama*; *Haggard*; *The Good Guys* (also writer of four episodes); *Rory Bremner* (also co-writer); *Don't Leave Me This Way* (TVM); *Rory Bremner... Who Else?* (four series, 1993-6); *The Lenny Henry Christmas Special*; *Rory Bremner's Christmas Turkey*; *A Very Open Prison* (Screen Two); *The Long Johns*; *Our Hands in Your Safe* (also writer); *Rory Bremner, Apparently*.
Books: *A Melon for Ecstasy* (novel, with John Wells). Address: c/o Richard Stone Partnership.

John Fortune

FOSTER, Barry

Barry Foster. Actor. b. Beeston, Nottinghamshire, 21 August. Previously a plastics chemist. Trained at the Central School of Speech and Drama.
TV: *Hamlet*; *Ghosts*; *Jack's Horrible Luck*; *Where the Difference Begins*; *Dan Dan the Charity Man*; *Mogul*; *The Soldier's Tale*; *A Taste of Honey*; title role in *Van Der Valk*; *Divorce His/Hers*; *Fall of Eagles*; *Old Times*; *Under Western Eyes*; *Wingate*; *The Three Hostages* (TVM); *A Family Affair*; *Random Moments in a May Garden*; *Rabbit-Pie Day*; *Smiley's People*; *A Woman Called Golda*; *How Many Miles to Babylon*; *Death of an Expert Witness*; *Woyzeck*; *After Pilkington*; *Hotel du Lac* (TVM); *Born in the Gardens*; *Inspector Morse*; *A Curious Suicide*; *The Free Frenchman*.
Films: *The Battle of the River Plate*; *The Baby and the Battleship*; *High Flight*; *Yangtse Incident*; *Sea Fury*; *Sea of Sand*; *Dunkirk*; *Yesterday's Enemy*; *Playback*; *King and Country*; *The Family Way*; *Robbery*; *Inspector Clousea*; *Twisted Nerve*; *The Guru*; *Battle of Britain*; *Ryan's Daughter*; *Frenzy*; *A Quiet Day in Belfast*; *Der Letzte Schrei*; *Sweeney!*; *The Wild Geese*; *Danger on Dartmoor*; *The Bomber*; *Heat and Dust*; *To Catch a King*; *The Whistle Blower*; *Three Kinds of Heat*; *Maurice*; *King of the Wind*; *Impromptu*. Address: c/o Ken McReddie. Lives in Sussex. m. singer Judith Shergold; 2 d. actress Joanna, Miranda, 1 s. Jason.

Barry Foster

FOWLDS, Derek

Derek Fowlds. Actor. b. Balham, South London, 2 September 1937. Trained at RADA.
TV: *The Basil Brush Show*; *Armchair 30: Captain Video's Story*; *Edward the Seventh*; *Last of the Best*

Men; Captive Audience; The Doll; After That This; Miss Jones and Son; Clayhanger; Robin's Nest; Sergeant Cribb; Strangers; Triangle; My Son, My Son; Bernard in Yes Minister and Yes, Prime Minister; Rings on Their Fingers; Intensive Care; Affairs of the Heart; Rules of Enjoyment; Chancer; The Engagement; Die Kinder; Boon; Van Der Valk; Perfect Scoundrels; The Darling Buds of May; Sgt Blaketon in Heartbeat (six series); John Gutteridge in Firm Friends; This Is Your Life (subject); The Detectives.
Films: The Smashing Bird I Used to Know; Hotel Paradiso; Tower of Evil; Mistress Pamela; The 'Copter Kids. Address: c/o CDA. m. (dis); 2 s. James, Jeremy.

Derek Fowlds

FOWLER, Harry
Henry James Fowler. Actor/Writer. b. Lambeth Walk, London, 10 December 1926. MBE, 1970.
TV: Get This; Harry's Kingdom; Stalingrad; I Remember the Battle; Gideon's Way; That's for Me; Flogger Hoskins in The Army Game; Our Man at St Mark's; Dixon of Dock Green; Dr Finlay's Casebook; I Was There; Cruft's Dog Show; The Londoners; Jackanory; Movie Quiz; Going a Bundle (presenter); Get This (presenter); Ask a Silly Answer; London Scene; The Flockton Flyer; Sun Trap; The Little World of Don Camillo; World's End; Minder; Dead Ernest; The Morecambe and Wise Show; Gossip; Entertainment Express; Dramarama; Me and the Girls; Scarecrow & Mrs King; Fresh Fields; Supergran; A Roller Next Year; Body Contact; Davro's Sketch Pad; In Sickness and in Health; Big Deal; All in Good Faith; The Bill; Casualty; EastEnders; The Young Indiana Jones Chronicles; Love Hurts; Southside Party.

Harry Fowler

Films: Selection (from 82): Salute John Citizen (début, 1942); Those Kids from Town; Hue and Cry; A Piece of Cake; Landfall; For Them That Trespass; Now Barabbas Was a Robber...; Trio; Once a Sinner; Angels One Five; The Paper Chase; The Last Page; Height of Ambition; The Pickwick Papers; Shedding the Load; Top of the Form; A Sweeping Statement; A Day to Remember; Don't Blame the Stork!; Conflict of Wings; Up to His Neck; Stock Car; The Blue Peter; Fire Maiden from Outer Space; Behind the Headlines; Home and Away; Town on Trial!; The Supreme Secret; West of Suez; Booby Trap; Lucky Jim; The Birthday Present; Soapbox Derby; I Was Monty's Double; Diplomatic Corpse; Idle on Parade; The Heart of a Man; The Dawn Killer; Don't Panic Chaps!; Lawrence of Arabia; The Golliwog; Flight from Singapore; Crooks Anonymous; Tomorrow at Ten; The Longest Day; Just for Fun; Clash by Night; Ladies Who Do; 70 Deadly Pills; Life at the Top; Joey Boy; The Nanny; Doctor in Clover; Secrets of a Windmill Girl; Two by Two; Start the Revolution without Me; GREAT: Isambard Kingdom Brunel (voice only); The Prince and the Pauper; High Rise Donkey; Sir Henry at Rawlinson End; George and Mildred; Fanny Hill; Chicago Joe and the Showgirl. Address: c/o Kenneth Earle Personal Management. Lives in London. m. 1st 1951 actress Joan Dowling (dec 1954), 2nd Catherine. Hobbies: Collecting postcards of the Brandenburg Gate, Berlin.

FOX, James
William Fox. Actor. b. London, 19 May 1939. Son of theatrical agent Robin Fox and actress Angela Worthington; brother of actor Edward and producer Robert. Started acting as a child and used real name until his early twenties. Trained at the Central School of Speech and Drama.
TV: The Door; Espionage; Love Is Old, Love Is New; Nancy Astor; Country; The Road to 1984; Comrades; New World; Shadow on the Sun; Farewell to the King; Sun Child; These Foolish Things; She's Been Away; Slowly Slowly in the Wind; Never Come Back; A Perfect Hero; Hostage; A Question of Attribution (TVM); Headhunters; Catherine Cookson's The Dwelling Place (mini-series); Fall from Grace; The Choir; Gulliver's Travels (mini-series).

James Fox

Films: The Miniver Story; The Magnet; One Wild Oat; The Lavender Hill Mob; Timbuktu; The Queen's Guards; The Secret Partner; She Always Gets Their Man; What Every Woman Wants; The Loneliness of the Long Distance Runner (all as William Fox); Tamahine; The Servant; Those Magnificent Men in Their Flying Machines; The Chase; King Rat; Arabella; Thoroughly Modern Millie; Duffy; Isadora; Performance; No Longer Alone; Runners; Greystoke: The Legend of Tarzan Lord of the Apes; A Passage to India; Pavlova; Absolute Beginners; The Whistle Blower; High Season; Comrades; Finding Maubee; White Mischief; The Mighty Quinn; Afraid of the Dark; The Russia House; Patriot Games; No Place to Hide; As You Like It; The Remains of the Day; Heart of Darkness; Doomsday Gun. Address: c/o Michael Whitehall. m. 1973 Mary Elizabeth Piper; 4 s. Thomas (b. 1975), Robin (b. 1976), Laurence (b. 1978), Jack (b. 1985), 1 d. Lydia (b. 1979). Partner: Actress Joanna David (qv); 1 d. actress Emilia, 1 s. Freddie.

FOY, Julie
Julie Foy. Actress. b. Bolton, Lancashire, 5 May 1970. Trained at the College of Performing Arts, Salford.
TV: Jossy's Giants (two series); Dramarama: Forever Young; Gina Seddon in Coronation Street (1988); Deirdre in How to Be Cool; Dawn and the Candidate (4-Play); Press Gang; Missing Persons.
Films: Nurse in Strapless. Address: c/o PBR Management. Lives in London. Single.

Julie Foy

FRANCES, Paula
Paula Frances Muldoon. Actress. b. Liverpool, 7 September 1969. Trained at the Merseyside Dance and Drama Centre; took a theatre arts course at the Liverpool Theatre School.
TV: Diana Spence in Brookside (1990-3). Address: c/o Felix De Wolfe. Lives in Liverpool. Single.

Paula Frances

FRANCIS, Clive

Clive Francis

Clive Francis. Actor. b. London, 1946. Son of actor Raymond Francis.
TV: *David Copperfield; Poldark; Entertaining Mr Sloane; Masada; Bulman; The Rear Column; The Critic; The Far Pavilions; Dorothy L Sayers; As You Like It; Sherlock Holmes; Amy; Oedipus at Colonus; The Bretts; Quartermain's Terms; May to December; Yes, Prime Minister; Old Flames;* Drummond in *The Piglet Files* (two series, 1990-1); *Anna Lee;* Dominic in *The 10%ers; Sharpe's Company; The Plant.*
Films: *Inspector Clouseau; Villain; The Man Who Had Power over Women; A Clockwork Orange; Girl Stroke Boy.*
Address: c/o Ken McReddie.

FRANCIS, Jan

Jan Francis

Jan Francis. Actress. b. London, 5 August 1951. Trained as a dancer and performed with the Royal Ballet before becoming an actress.
TV: *Hawkeye the Pathfinder; Anne of Green Gables; Lonely Man's Lover; Sutherland's Law; Village Hall; Looking for Clancy; The Launderette; Love's Labour's Lost; Rooms; London Assurance; The Duchess of Duke Street; Raffles; Premier; Secret Army; The Party of the First Part; The Racing Game; Ripping Yarns; Target; Casting the Runes; Play for Love; The Good Companions; Tales of the Unexpected; A Chance to Sit Down; Jackanory; The Corvini Inheritance;* Penny Warrender in *Just Good Friends* (three series); Sally Hardcastle in *Stay Lucky* (three series, plus one episode in Series 4); Maggie Perowne in *Under the Hammer* (series); *The Ghostbusters of East Finchley* (series); *Turning Points* (interviewee).
Films: *Dracula; Champions.*
Address: c/o Julian Belfrage Associates. m. Martin C Thurley.

FRANKAU, Nicholas

Nicholas Frankau

Nicholas Frankau. Actor. b. Stockport, Cheshire, 16 July 1954. Trained at Webber Douglas Academy.
TV: Flight Officer Carstairs in *'Allo, 'Allo; The Last Term* (Play for Today); *I Remember Nelson; C.A.T.S. Eyes; Paradise Postponed.*
Films: *Plenty; Gunbus.*
Address: c/o Representation Joyce Edwards.

FRANKLIN, Gretchen

Gretchen Franklin

Gretchen Gordon Franklin. Actress. b. Covent Garden, London, 7 July 1911. Dancing and singing lessons as a child. Entered showbusiness as a chorus-girl in a Bournemouth pantomime.
TV: Else Garnett in *Till Death Us Do Part* (Comedy Playhouse, 1965); *Crossroads; The Ken Dodd Show; Crackerjack; I Didn't Know You Cared; Churchill's People; George and Mildred; Nicholas Nickleby;* Mrs Welch in *Some Mothers Do 'Ave 'Em; Lively Arts; Hazell; The Sweeney; The One and Only Phyllis Dixey; Rising Damp; Jackanory; Danger UXB; General Hospital; The Other One; Quatermass; Jekyll and Hyde; Fox; Potter; The Harry Worth Show; The Dick Emery Show; You're Only Young Twice; The Other 'Arf; Kelly Monteith; Dead Earnest; Hallelujah; Maybury; Blackadder; In Loving Memory; Return to Waterloo; Victoria Wood;* Ethel Skinner in *EastEnders* (1985-).
Films: *The Three Musketeers; Ragtime; The Night Visitor.*
Address: c/o Barry Burnett Organisation. Lives in Barnes, London. m. writer John Caswell Garth (dec). Pets: Dog. Hobbies: Needlework, gardening.

FRANKLYN, Sabina

Sabina Franklyn

Sabina Franklyn. Actress. b. London, 15 September. Daughter of actor William Franklyn (qv) and actress Margot Johns; granddaughter of actor Leo Franklyn. Stage plays include *Duty Free* (West End).
TV: *Pride and Prejudice; Fawlty Towers; Kelly Monteith; Strangers; Dave Allen Special; When the Boat Comes In; The Mike Yarwood Show; The Jim Davidson Show; Terry and June; Byron; Happy Ever After; Return of The Saint; Blake's 7; A Personal Tour; Keep It in the Family; Moving Finger; Full House* (three series); *Agatha Christie's Miss Marple: The Moving Finger; The Worst Witch; All Creatures Great and Small; Anne of Avonlea; Boon;* Zoe Trubshaw in *The Upper Hand* (series); *Covington Cross.*
Address: c/o CCA Management. Lives in East Sheen, south-west London. m. actor John Challis (dis).

FRANKLYN, William

William Franklyn. Actor/Director. b. Kensington, West London, 22 September 1926. Grandson of Arthur Rigby Sr; son of Leo Franklyn; nephew of Arthur Rigby Jr (all actors).
TV: *Mid Level* (first ITV play, 1955); *Douglas Fairbanks Junior Presents; The Count of Monte Cristo; The Adventures of the Scarlet Pimpernel; Charlie Chan; Dick and the Duchess; International Detective; Interpol Calling; Maigret; The Avengers; The Adventures of Sir Lancelot;* Peter Dallas in *Top Secret* (series, 1961); *The Saracens; The Baron; The Troubleshooters; Public Eye; No Wreath for the General; No Cloak, No Dagger; Curtain of Fear; Paradise Island; What's on Next?; Masterspy; The Steam Video Company; The Purple Twilight; G.B.H.; Moon and Son; The Upper Hand;* Lord Mountbatten in *Diana:*

Her True Story; The Young Indiana Jones Chronicles; Lovejoy. TV commercials: Schweppes.
Films: Secret People; Time Is My Enemy; The Love Match; Out of the Clouds; Above Us the Waves; Quatermass II; That Woman Opposite; The Flesh Is Weak; The Snorkel; Danger Within; The Big Day; Fury at Smuggler's Bay; Pit of Darkness; The Intelligence Men; The Legend of Young Dick Turpin; Cul-de-Sac; Ooh... You Are Awful; Torrence in The Satanic Rites of Dracula; This Made News (narrator); Nutcracker; Splitting Heirs. Address: c/o Hobson's Personal Management. Lives in London. m. 1st actress Margot Johns (dis), 2nd actress Susanna Carroll; 3 d. actress Sabina (qv) (from 1st m.), Francesca, Melissa. Pets: A schnauzer bitch. Hobbies: Cricket, squash, tennis, every aspect of Italy.

William Franklyn

FRANKS, Philip
Philip Franks. Actor. Former member of Oxford University Dramatic Society.
TV: To Serve Them All My Days; Love Is Old, Love Is New; Bleak House; The Murderers among Us; Shadow of the Noose; The Green Man; Charley in The Darling Buds of May (three series, 1991-3, plus Christmas special, 1992); Pardon My Spanish (presenter, This Morning, 1993); Poet in Absolutely Fabulous; The Done Thing (This Morning, series on etiquette, 1994, 1995); Tom Pinch in Martin Chuzzlewit (series, 1994); Giles Dutton in Pie in the Sky; Pardon My French (This Morning, two series, 1995-6); Calvin in Moniker (Wales Playhouse). Address: c/o The Richard Stone Partnership.

FRASER, Liz
Elizabeth Winch. Actress. b. London, 14 August 1935. Trained at the London School of Dramatic Art. Originally acted under her real name, then as Elizabeth Fraser, before switching to Liz Fraser.
TV: Sixpenny Corner (serial, 1955); Hancock's Half Hour; The Benny Hill Show; Matron in Whack-O!; Citizen James; Sight Unseen; Rumpole of the Bailey; The Rockers; Robin's Nest; The Professionals; Shroud for a Nightingale; Fairly Secret Army (two series); Hardwicke House; Agatha Christie's Miss Marple: Nemesis; Rude Health; Eskimos Do It; Capstick's Law; The Lady and the Highwayman (TVM); Streetwise; Birds of a Feather; Delilah in Minder; Edith in Demob (series, 1993); The Bill.

Philip Franks

Films: Touch and Go; The Smallest Show on Earth; Not Wanted on Voyage; Davy; Wonderful Things!; Top Floor Girl; I'm All Right, Jack; The Night We Dropped a Clanger; Desert Mice; Two Way Stretch; Doctor in Love; The Night We Got the Bird; The Pure Hell of St Trinian's; The Bulldog Breed; The Rebel; Fury at Smuggler's Bay; Double Bunk; Carry On Regardless; Watch It Sailor!; Raising the Wind; A Pair of Briefs; The Painted Smile; Carry On Cruising; The Amorous Prawn; Live Now — Pay Later; Carry On Cabby; Every Day's a Holiday; The Americanization of Emily; The Family Way; Up the Junction; Dad's Army; Hide and Seek; Three for All; Carry On Behind; Adventures of a Taxi Driver; Confessions of a Driving Instructor; Under the Doctor; Adventures of a Private Eye; Confessions from a Holiday Camp; Rosie Dixon Night Nurse; The Great Rock 'n' Roll Swindle; Chicago Joe and the Showgirl. Address: c/o Sara Cameron Management. Lives in London. m. director Bill Hitchcock (dec). Pets: Bassett hound. Hobbies: Bridge, antiques.

Liz Fraser

FRASER, Ronald
Ronald Gordon Fraser. Actor. b. Ashton-under-Lyne, Lancashire, 11 April 1930. Trained at RADA.
TV: The Lonesome Road; Sealed with a Loving Kiss; Stray Cats and Empty Bottles; John Bull's Other Island; The Walls Come Tumbling Down; Sword of Honour; The Corn Is Green; Ghosts; Omnibus: Max Beerbohm; The Misfit; Conceptions of Murder; A Man in a Zoo; Mr Big; The Bass Player and the Blonde; Pennies from Heaven; Brideshead Revisited; Do You Come Here Often?; Fortunes of War; The Practice; Life without George; In the Secret State; Pygmalion; Minder; City Lights; Omnibus: Oblomov; Obituaries; Lovejoy; Boon; Taggart: Violent Delights; The Blackheath Poisonings; Virtual Murder (TVM); The Young Indiana Jones Chronicles; Class Act; P G Wodehouse's Heavy Weather; The Vet; Moll Flanders.
Films: Selection (from 45): Black Ice (début, 1957); The Sundowners; The Punch and Judy Man; The VIPs; Girl in the Headlines; Crooks in Cloisters; The Killing of Sister George; The Bed Sitting Room; The Rise and Rise of Michael Rimmer; The Magnificent Seven Deadly Sins; Rentadick; Ooh... You Are Awful; Swallows and Amazons; Percy's Progress; Come Play with Me; The Wild Geese; Trail of the Pink Panther; Tangier; Curse of the Pink Panther; Absolute Beginners; Scandal; "Let Him Have It"; The Mystery of Edwin Drood. Address: c/o Rebecca Blond Associates. Lives in London. m. former actress Elizabeth Howe (dis); 2 d. Fiona Julie, Alison Sara. Hobbies: Golf, cricket, reading, cinema-going.

Ronald Fraser

FRASER, Shelagh
Shelagh Mary Fraser. Actress/Writer. b. Surrey, 25 November. Sister of Royal Ballet soloist Moyra Fraser.
TV: Emergency — Ward 10; Jean Ashton in A Family at War; House of Character; A Game Like... Only a Game; The Last Train through Harecastle Tunnel; The Professionals; The Girl; The Common; Frankie and Johnnie; The Old Men at the Zoo; Absolute Hell (Performance).
Films: Mrs Alison in Nothing but the Night; Mrs Banks in Persecution; The History of Mr Polly; Raising a Riot; Till Death Us Do Part; Two Gentlemen Sharing; The Staircase; Alive O; Aunt Bern in Star Wars; Hope and Glory; La Bas; Work Experience; Merrie Hill Millionaires (short). Address: c/o Ken McReddie. Lives in London. m. film writer-director Anthony Squire (dis). Pets: A corgi dog.

Shelagh Fraser

Alison Frazer

FRAZER, Alison

Alison Frazer-Skemp. Actress/Director/Producer/Presenter. b. London, 21 May 1947. Daughter of actress-turned-theatrical agent Norma Skemp. Trained at Elmhurst Ballet School and the Guildhall School of Music and Drama. West End stage plays include *The High Bid* and *Emil and the Detectives*.
TV: *Z Cars; Emergency — Ward 10; Blue Peter;* Helen in *Gentleman Jim; Dixon of Dock Green; The Sword and the Switchblade;* Mary Tudor in *The Six Wives of Henry VIII;* Princess Lisa Bolonskya in *War and Peace;* Nancy in *Oliver Twist;* Jane in *Deadly Confusions;* Beryl in *The Man Who Won the Pools;* regular presenter for BHHTV (Los Angeles); Susan Norrington in *Our Tune.*
Films: *Follow That Horse;* The Bride in *The Assassin;* Peg Farnham in *Three Bites of the Apple;* Sue in *Murder One, Murder Two;* Jane in *Bert Rigby, You're a Fool.* Address: c/o Frazer-Skemp Management. Lives in London. m. 1st David Peter Dixon (dis), 2nd Graham Eric Mitchell (dis); 2 d. Lavinia Claire Mitchell, Kristina Rosalind Mitchell (both from 2nd m.). Hobbies: Interior design and most sports.

Jane Freeman

FREEMAN, Jane

Jane Freeman. Actress.
TV: *Diary of a Young Man; Crossroads; The Fishing Party; Within These Walls; Maybury; Ghost in the Water;* Magaera in *Androcles and the Lion; Letty;* Mrs Kimble in *Silas Marner: The Weaver of Raveloe;* Helen in *A Taste of Honey;* Hannah; Mother in *Zigger Zagger;* Mother in *Lynsey;* Tully Applebottom in *Blackadder; The Hard Word;* Ivy in *Last of the Summer Wine.*
Films: *Who Dares Wins; Scrubbers; The Swimming Pool.* Address: c/o Saraband Associates.

Paul Freeman

FREEMAN, Paul

Paul Freeman. Actor. b. Barnet, Hertfordshire, 18 January 1943. Trained at the New College of Speech and Drama. Stage plays with the National Theatre, RSC and Royal Court.
TV: *Winston Churchill — The Wilderness Years; Death of a Princess; Falcon Crest; Sins* (mini-series); *Yesterday's Dreams; Cagney and Lacey; Sakharov; Willie's Last Stand; The Index Has Gone Fishing; The Paris Paradox;* Karl Myerhoff in *Perry Mason: The Case of the Desperate Deception* (TVM); Michael Tromp in *Van Der Valk;* Edward Cameron in *Boon;* Freddie Reid in *Full Stretch;* Sir Patrick Hastings in *Laugh Baby Laugh* (In Suspicious Circumstances); Nicholas Shaw in *Between the Lines;* Bosenka in *Grushko* (mini-series, 1994); Frederick Selous in *The Young Indiana Jones Chronicles;* Tom Makepeace in *The Final Cut* (mini-series, 1995).
Films: *The Dogs of War; The Long Good Friday; Who Dares Wins; Raiders of the Lost Ark; The Sender; Prisoner of Rio; Without a Clue; New Wine; Flight to Berlin; Shanghai Surprise; The Ronald Biggs Story; Sherlock and Me; The Last Island; Eminent Domain; A World Apart; Just like a Woman.* Address: c/o Ken McReddie. m. Maggie Scott; 1 d. Lucy.

Penelope Freeman

FREEMAN, Penelope

Penelope Freeman. Actress. b. Birmingham. Trained at LAMDA.
TV: Clare in *Sorrell and Son;* Nurse in *A Pattern for Life;* Hotel Receptionist in *Wild Things;* Betty in *Luv* (two series, 1993-4).
Films: *Chariots of Fire.*
Radio: Mrs Milvey in *Our Mutual Friend;* Trish in *Clagthorpe Viva.* Address: c/o Spotlight.

FRENCH, Dawn

Dawn French. Actress/Comedienne. Trained at the Central School of Speech and Drama, where she met Jennifer Saunders, with whom she teamed up after a brief spell as a teacher. Stage plays include *When I Was a Girl I Used to Scream and Shout* (Whitehall Theatre), *An Evening with French and Saunders* (national tour), *The Secret Policeman's Biggest Ball* and *Silly Cow.*
TV: *Five Go Mad in Dorset; Five Go Mad on Mescalin; Slags; Summer School; Private Enterprise; Consuela; Mr Jolly Lives Next Door; Bad News Tour; South Atlantic Raiders; GLC; Oxford; Spaghetti Hoops; Le Kiss* (all The Comic Strip Presents...); *Girls on Top* (series); *Happy Families; French and Saunders* (three series, 1987-8, 1992, 1995); *The Storyteller: Sapsorrow; Swank* (presenter); *Scoff* (presenter); Sally Fairfax in *Murder Most Horrid* (three series); *Jackanory* (storyteller); Kathy in *Absolutely Fabulous; Dreams; Daisy Pig* (storyteller); *French & Saunders & Prince & Barry White (Total Relief: A Night of Comic Relief,* 1993); *Ruby's Hit and Run;* Elaine Dobbs in *Tender Loving Care* (Screen One, 1993); *The Legends of Treasure Island* (voice only); *French and Saunders in... Space Virgins from Planet Sex; The South Bank Show* (her 'personal celebration of Big Women', 1994); *Dusty* (sketches with Jennifer Saunders, 1994); Rev Geraldine Granger in *The Vicar of Dibley* (series, 1994, plus Easter special, 1996); *French and Saunders Christmas Special* (1994); *French & Saunders Go to the Movies* (highlights from *French and Saunders,* 1995); Mrs Duvet in *Look at the State We're In: Secrecy.*
Films: *The Supergrass; The Strike.* **Books:** *A Feast of French & Saunders.*
Address: c/o Peters Fraser & Dunlop. m. comedian-actor Lenny Henry (qv); 1 adopted d. Billie.

Dawn French

FREUD, Emma

Emma Freud. Presenter. b. London, 25 January 1962. Daughter of MP Clement Freud.
TV: *Roundabout; The Six o'Clock Show* (LWT); *Pillowtalk* (Night Network); *Plunder* (series); *The Media Show* (series); *Drop the Dead Donkey* (acting herself); *The Pulse* (series); *Making Advances* (series); *The Great Pyramid: Gateway to the Stars* ; *Edinburgh Nights.* Address: c/o Noel Gay Artists.

Emma Freud

FRICKER, Brenda

Brenda Fricker. Actress. b. Dublin, Ireland, 17 February 1945.
TV: *Z Cars; The Gathering Seed; Quatermass; Telford's Change; Give Us a Break; Stephen D; The Man Outside; Mein Kampf; Juliet Bravo; The Sinners; Coronation Street; Eh Brian, It's a Whopper; The Practice; Helen — A Woman of Today; The Avenue; To Have and to Hold; The Picnic; The Ballroom of Romance;* Megan Roach in *Casualty* (five series, 1986-90); *Your Man from the Six Counties; Just Like Eddie; Licking Hitler;* Sister Agnes in *Brides of Christ; Utz; Lethal Innocence;* Stella Hazard in *Seekers;* Eliza Graham Bell in *The Sound and the Silence* (series); *A Woman of Independent Means; Journey.*
Films: *Of Human Bondage; Sinful Davey; The Woman Who Married Clark Gable; Bloody Kids; The Quatermass Conclusion; Our Exploits at West Polcy; My Left Foot; The Field; Lethal Innocence; Hook; Home Alone 2: Lost in New York; Deadly Advice; So I Married an Axe Murderer; Angels in the Outfield; A Man of No Importance; Out of Ireland* (voice only); *Moll Flanders;* Rose in *Swann; A Time to Kill.*
Awards: Best Supporting Actress Oscar for *My Left Foot.* Address: c/o Mayer & Eden. m. director Barry Davis (dec 1990). Partner: Joe. Pets: Two dogs. Hobbies: Pool, drinking Guinness.

Brenda Fricker

FRIEL, Anna

Anna Louise Friel. Actress. b. Rochdale, Lancashire, 12 July 1976. Trained at Oldham Theatre Workshop.
TV: *8.15 from Manchester; G.B.H.; Coronation Street; Emmerdale;* Holly Jarrett in *Medics;* Beth Jordache in *Brookside* (1992-5) and *Brookside Special: The Jordache Story* (1994); *Four Kisses and a Funeral; Punt and Dennis; Reeves and Mortimer; Cadfael; A Midsummer Night's Dream; Tales from the Crypt.*
Films: *You Drive Me* (short); *The Tribe.* Address: c/o Conway, van Gelder, Robinson. Lives in Rochdale and London. Single. Pets: Two cats, one blue Persian, one blue/cream British.

Anna Friel

FROST, David

David Paradine Frost. Presenter. b. Tenterden, Kent, 7 April 1939. OBE, 1970, knighted, 1993.
TV: *This Week; Let's Twist on the Riviera; That Was the Week That Was* (UK and USA); *A Degree of Frost; Not So Much a Programme, More a Way of Life; The Frost Report; The Frost Programme; Frost over America; We British; The Wilson Interviews; Frost over England; At Last the 1948 Show* (producer); *No, That's Me over Here* (producer); *David Frost's Night Out in London; David Frost Presents; Frost on Saturday; Frost on Sunday; David Frost Presents the Guinness Book of Records; A Degree of Frost; Frost over Australia; Frost over New Zealand; The Beatles — Once Upon a Time; 40 Years of Television; The Nixon Interviews; The Ordeal of Patty Hearst* (producer, TVM); *The Remarkable Mrs Sanger* (producer, TVM); *Elvis — He Touched Their Lives; The Shah Speaks; David Frost's Global Village; The Begin Interview; David Frost Presents the International Guinness Book of Records; Frost over Canada; The Falklands; Where Will It End?; The End of the Year Show; Through the Keyhole;* founder-member of TV-am (presenter of *Good Morning Britain* and *David Frost on Sunday*); *The Next President; The Spectacular World of Guinness Records; Talking with Frost* (US); *Breakfast with Frost* (1993-); *The Frost Programme* (Carlton Television, 1993-); *TV Violence — Will It Change Your Life?; George Michael: A Television Interview with David Frost; Good Fortune, Beyond Belief* (two episodes); *Through the Keyhole Classic Quiz; Thatcher: The Path to Power — and Beyond; The Man Who Broke the Bank.*
Films: *The VIPs; Four Days in November.* As producer: *The Rise and Rise of Michael Rimmer; Futtocks End; Charley One-Eye; Leadbelly; The Slipper and the Rose; James A Michener's Dynasty; The Ordeal of Patty Hearst; Remarkable Mrs Sanger.* Address: c/o David Paradine Productions, 115/123 Bayham Street, Greenland Place, London NW1. m. 1st 1981 actress Lynne Frederick (dis 1982), 2nd 1983 Lady Carina Mary Anne Gabrielle Fitzalan-Howard (daughter of 17th Duke of Norfolk); 3 s. Miles Paradine (b. 1984), Wilfred Paradine (b. 1985), George Paradine (b. 1987) (all from 2nd m.).

David Frost

FROSTRUP, Mariella

Mariella Frostrup. Presenter. b. Oslo, Norway, 12 November 1962. Brought up in Ireland.
TV: *Big World; At the Pictures; Video View* (also co-writer and researcher); *Relationships* (Anglia Television only, 1991-2); *Four Seasons* and *Nigel Plays Brunch* (specials on Nigel Kennedy); *Passengers; Notes & Queries... with Clive Anderson; Newman and Baddiel in Pieces; First Reaction — Sex in the Movies; The Little Picture Show; The Flintstones — Royal Première; Disney's The Lion King Film Première; Look Who's Talking with Mariella Frostrup* (Carlton only); *The ITV Movie Awards; One for the Road; 007... The Return; The Evening Standard British Film Awards* (1996); *Going for a Song* (team leader). Address: c/o ICM. Lives in Notting Hill, West London. m. TV presenter Richard Jobson (dis). Pets: A cocker spaniel, Dalglish. Hobbies: Scuba-diving, theatre, trekking, reading, cooking.

Mariella Frostrup

Stephen Fry

Fiona Fullerton

Jenny Funnell

Michael Gambon

Graeme Garden

FRY, Stephen

Stephen Fry. Actor/Comedian/Writer. b. Hampstead, North London, 24 August 1957. Member of Cambridge Footlights revue before turning professional. Wrote the West End musical *Me and My Girl*.
TV: *Alfresco; The Young Ones; Alas Smith and Jones; Filthy Rich and Catflap; Blackadder II; The Crystal Cube; The Tube; Saturday Live; Whose Line Is It Anyway?;* Duke of Wellington in *Blackadder the Third;* General Sir Anthony Cecil Hogmanay Melchett in *Blackadder Goes Forth* (series); *A Bit of Fry & Laurie; Grand Master Clash;* Jeeves in *Jeeves and Wooster* (three series, 1990, 1992-3); *Old Flames; This Is David Lander* (series, 1988); *Hysteria III* (host); *Mister Roadrunner* (narrator); *The Laughing Prisoner;* Wing Commander James Forrester in *Stalag Luft; Fry and Laurie Host a Christmas Night with the Stars* (1994); Mybug in *Cold Comfort Farm; Oliver 2 (Comic Relief,* 1995); Brig Blaster Sump in *The Thin Blue Line.*
Films: *The Good Father; A Handful of Dust; A Fish Called Wanda; The Secret Policeman's Other Ball; The Secret Policeman's Third Ball; Peter's Friends; I.Q.*
Radio: *Loose Ends; Delve Special.* Address: c/o Hamilton Asper Management. Lives in London.

FULLERTON, Fiona

Fiona Elizabeth Fullerton. Actress. b. Kaduna, Nigeria, 10 October 1956.
TV: *A Friend Indeed; Angels; Gaugin — The Savage; Lev Tolstoy; A Question of Faith; Strange but True; Hold the Dream; The Charmer;* Lady Isabel in *A Hazard of Hearts* (TVM); *Hemingway; A Taste for Death; Goldeneye; Shaka Zulu;* Lady Violet in *A Ghost in Monte Carlo* (TVM); *To Be the Best* (miniseries); *The Bogie Man.*
Films: *Run Wild, Run Free* (aged 11); *Nicholas and Alexandra; Alice's Adventures in Wonderland; The Human Factor; A View to a Kill; A Ghost in Monte Carlo; A Girl Called Harry.*
Address: c/o London Management. m. 1st 10 July 1976 actor Simon MacCorkindale (dis Sep 1983).

FUNNELL, Jenny

Jenny Victoria Funnell. Actress. b. Nairobi, Kenya, 20 May 1963. Trained at Webber Douglas Academy.
TV: Dilys Parry in *Brookside;* Lucy in *Bergerac;* Eileen in *Norbert Smith — A Life;* Janet in *David Copperfield;* Nurse Doyle in *Boon;* Nurse Andrews in *Peril at End House; Who Dares Wins; The Russ Abbot Show;* Michelle in *Drop the Dead Donkey;* Sandy in *As Time Goes By* (four series).
Radio: Many BBC single plays and series. **Awards:** Radio: Carleton Hobbs Radio Award winner.
Address: c/o Barry Brown & Partner. Lives in London. Single. Pets: Two cats called Robbie and Nell. Hobbies: Water-colour paintings, playing piano, swimming, cycling.

GAMBON, Michael

Michael Gambon. Actor. b. Dublin, Ireland, 19 October 1940. CBE, 1990. Stage plays include *King Lear, Antony and Cleopatra* (both RSC), *Otherwise Engaged, The Norman Conquests, Just between Ourselves, Alice's Boys, Old Times* and *Uncle Vanya* (all West End).
TV: *The Challengers; The Borderers; Eyeless in Gaza; The Other One; La Ronde; The Breadwinner; The Seagull; Ghosts; Oscar Wilde; The Holy Experiment; Absurd Person Singular;* Philip Marlow in *The Singing Detective; The Heat of the Day; The Storyteller; Minder;* Chief Inspector Maigret in *Maigret* (two series, 1992-3); Archie Rice in *The Entertainer* (Performance); *Mama's Back!;* Peter J Moreton in *Faith* (series, 1994); *Nautilus* (narrator, documentary series); *The Wind in the Willows* (voice only, 1995); Expert Witness (presenter, series, 1996).
Films: *The Beast Must Die; Turtle Diary; Paris by Night; Missing Link; A Dry White Season; The Rachel Papers; The Cook The Thief His Wife & Her Lover; Mobsters; The Innocent Sleep.* **Awards:** BAFTA Best TV Actor award for *The Singing Detective.* Address: c/o Conway, van Gelder, Robinson.

GARDEN, Graeme

David Graeme Garden. Actor/Writer/Director. b. Aberdeen, Grampian, 18 February 1943. Member of Cambridge Footlights revue while at university. Qualified in medicine at King's College, London. Stage plays include *The Unvarnished Truth* (Phoenix Theatre) and *Cloud Nine* (Royal Court Theatre).
TV: *Twice a Fortnight; Doctor in the House* and *Doctor at Large* (co-writer, with Bill Oddie); *Orson's Bag* (actor and writer); *Broaden Your Mind* (actor); *The Goodies* (actor and co-writer, seven BBC series); *The Goodies and the Beanstalk* (special); *The Goodies Rule: O.K.* (special); *The Goodies* (ITV series, 1981); *Charlie's Climbing Tree; Astronauts* (co-writer, with Bill Oddie); *Tell the Truth* (host, three series); *A Sense of the Past* (presenter, two series); *Bodymatters* (presenter, three series); *The Whole Hog* (writer); 'Mount Olympus' sequences for *Smith and Jones* (writer); *Bananaman* (voice only); *Surgical Spirit* (writer only, series, 1994).
Radio: *I'm Sorry I'll Read That Again* (co-writer, with Bill Oddie); *I'm Sorry I Haven't a Clue* (co-writer, with Bill Oddie, and panellist).
Records: Singles (with The Goodies): *The In Betweenies/Father Christmas Do Not Touch Me* (No 7, 1974, Silver Disc); *Funky Gibbon/Sick Man Blues* (No 4, 1975); *Black Pudding Bertha* (No 19,

1975); *Nappy Love/Wild Thing* (No 21, 1975); *Make a Daft Noise for Christmas* (No 20, 1975).
Books: *The Goodies Files; The Goodies Book of Criminal Records; The Goodies Disaster Movie; The Seventh Man* (novel); *Graeme Garden's Compendium of Very Silly Games; The Skylighters* (children's book, 1988) Address: c/o Roger Hancock. Lives in Oxfordshire. m. 1st Liz (dis), 2nd Emma Williams; 1 d. Sally (from 1st m.), 2 s. John (from 1st m.), Tom (from 2nd m.). Hobbies: TV, reading, fishing.

GARNER, Nadine
Nadine Garner. Actress.
TV: *Prisoner* (UK title *Prisoner: Cell Block H*); Jean in *My Brother Tom; The Factory;* Debbie in *Prime Time; A Country Practice;* Tamara Henderson in *The Henderson Kids* (aged 13); Judy in *The Flying Doctors; All the Way; Shadows of the Heart; All Together Now;* Arlene in *Boys from the Bush* (series); *Cluedo; Phoenix II; Under the Skin; Secrets; The Feds;* Gloria O'Grady in *Class Act* (two series); *GP.*
Films: *The Still Point; Bushfire Moon;* title role in *Mull; Speed; Metal Skin.* Address: c/o ICM.

Nadine Garner

GARWOOD, Patricia
Patricia Garwood. Actress. b. Paignton, Devon, 28 January 1941. Trained at the Arts Educational School and RADA. Member of MENSA.
TV: Beverly in *The Aweful Mr Goodall; Jennie; Nightingale's Boys; Public Eye;* Susannah in *Poor Baby;* Beth in *An Accident of Class and Sex;* Nurse in *Clayhanger;* Karen in *Packman's Barn;* Jean in *Within These Walls;* Pauline in *Crown Court;* Chief Wren Collins in *Warship;* Ann in *General Hospital;* Mrs Southey in *Clouds of Glory;* Dilys in *Accident* (series); Rachel in *Sister Dora* (series); Mrs Busby in *Danger UXB;* Eileen in *Some of My Best Friends;* Olive in *The Gentle Touch;* Leela in *The Garland;* Pearson in *Blunt Instrument;* Beryl in *No Place Like Home* (six series); Pat Brack in *The Brack Report* (series); Freda in *The Case of the Discontented Soldier;* Mrs Small in *Space Station Milton Keynes;* Josie in *A Walk under Ladders;* Lydia in *Lytton's Diary;* Mrs Whitney in *The Adventures of Sherlock Holmes;* Wendy in *C.A.T.S. Eyes; Love and Marriage;* Jenetta Cairnes in *The Inspector Alleyn Mysteries;* Mrs Martin in *Bad Voodoo.*
Films: *The Lavender Hill Mob* (aged nine). **Radio:** Clare in *The Ugly Man;* Lena in *Exchange.*
Address: c/o William Morris Agency (UK). m. 1960 playwright Jeremy Paul; 4 d. Amanda, Tara, Sasha, Sophie. Pets: A golden retriever, two cats. Hobbies: 'Playing with my grandchildren.'

Patricia Garwood

GASCOIGNE, Bamber
Bamber Gascoigne. Presenter. b. London, 24 January 1935. Scholarship to Yale School of Drama and later drama critic of *The Spectator* and *The Observer.*
TV: *University Challenge* (quizmaster, 1962-87); *The Christians; Victorian Values; Man and Music; The Great Moghuls; Connoisseur* (quizmaster, 1988); *Brother Felix and the Virgin Saint; A Meditation.*
Books: *World Theatre; The Great Moghuls; Treasures and Dynasties of China; Murgatreud's Empire; The Heyday; The Christians; Quest for the Golden Hare; How to Identify Prints.*
Address: c/o Curtis Brown. Lives in Richmond-upon-Thames, Surrey. m. Christina Ditchburn.

Bamber Gascoigne

GASCOINE, Jill
Jill Gascoine. Actress. b. Lambeth, South London, 11 April 1937. Trained at the Italia Conti Stage Academy. West End plays include *42nd Street.*
TV: *Dr Finlay's Casebook; Rooms; Plays for Britain; General Hospital; The Norman Wisdom Show; Three Kisses; Balzac; Z Cars; Six Days of Justice; Dixon of Dock Green; Within These Walls; Holding On; Raffles; The Trigger; General Hospital; Justice; Peter Pan; Beryl's Lot; Softly, Softly; Oranges and Lemons; The Onedin Line; Rooms; The Gentle Touch; C.A.T.S. Eyes; Taggart; King of the Wind* (TVM); *El C.I.D.;* Vivien Empson in *Trust Me* (Screen One); Jane Antrobus in *Taggart: Evil Eye.*
Films: *The Pure Hell of St Trinian's, Confessions of a Pop Performer.* **Awards:** *TVTimes* Best Actress on TV award (1984). Address: c/o CDA. m. 2nd actor Alfred Molina; 2 s. Sean, Adam.

Jill Gascoine

GAUNT, William
William Gaunt. Actor. b. Pudsey, West Yorkshire, 3 April 1937. Child actor with Otley Little Theatre. Trained at RADA. Then worked in the Dallas Theater Center, before returning to act in repertory theatre in the UK. West End stage plays include *Boys in the Band, The Flip Side, When Did You Last See Your Trousers?, Run for Your Wife.* Artistic director of the Liverpool Playhouse (1979-81).
TV: *54 Minute Theatre; Waiting for Wanda; Climate of Fear; Probation Officer; Harper's West One; Sergeant Cork; Softly, Softly; The Champions; Holly; The Saint; Cottage to Let; Nobody's House; The Foundation; Crown Court; Love and Marriage; No Place Like Home;* Edward Capstick in *Capstick's Law; Gentlemen's Club; Claire; Jury; Lucifer; The Good Sex Guide;* Andrew Prentice in *Next of Kin* (two series, 1995-6, Christmas special 1995).
Films: *The Revolutionary.* Address: c/o London Management. m. actress Carolyn Lyster; 1 d. Tilly (Matilda), 1s. Albie (Albert). Hobbies: Fell walking, gardening.

William Gaunt

Liz Gebhardt

GEBHARDT, Liz

Elisabeth Ann Gebhardt. Actress. b. Liverpool, 12 April 1945. Trained at Guildhall School of Music and Drama. Stage plays include *Swaggerer*, *The Curse of the Egyptian Mummy* and *The Mona Lisa Mystery* (all Open Air Theatre, Regent's Park).

TV: Maureen in *Please Sir!* and *The Fenn Street Gang*; *The Naked Civil Servant*; Fiona in *Bulman*; Patient in *Don't Wait Up*; Annette in *Trouble and Strife* (two series, 1985-6); Headmistress in *Grange Hill* (1986-7); Mother in *Dramarama*; Violet and Eva in *Words at Play* (series); Mrs Booth in *The Bill*; Mrs Rogers in *Brookside* (1989); Mrs Evans in *The Bill*; Mother in *Kids' Court*; Mrs Green in *Keeping Up Appearances*; Mrs Cook in *The Bill*; Frances Kelly in *Love Hurts*; Mrs Martin in *The Bill*.

Radio: Midge in *Time and the Conways*; *Midnite at the Starlite*; Rose in *Brighton Rock*; *Solidarity*; Patricia Hyde in *Crisis* (BBC World Service series, 1993-4).

Address: c/o McIntosh Rae Management. Lives in Southfields, South London. m. 1968 theatre director-actor Ian Talbot; 1 s. Joe. Pets: A Burmese cat, a dog, fish, frogs. Hobbies: Gardening, bird-watching, walking.

Robbie Gee

GEE, Robbie

Robert Grant. Actor. b. Greenwich, London, 24 March 1970. Stage plays include *Macbeth* and *Black Poppies* (both National Theatre), *A Clockwork Orange* (RSC), *Royal Borough* (Royal Court), *Job Rocking* (Dutch tour), *Dog* (Shaw Theatre), *Side Pockets*, *Black Poppies*, *The Posse* (all Theatre Royal, Stratford East), *Tony* (Sass Theatre) and *The Serpent* (Royal Court Upstairs).

TV: *Pie in the Sky*; *Midnight Breaks*; Snowy in *The Firm*; Tony Morris in *The Manageress* (two series); Lee in *Desmond's* (six series, 1989-94); *The Real McCoy* (four series); *Saracen*; *The Bill*; *Black Poppies*; *Underbelly*; *In Sickness and in Health*; Cameron in *Blisters*; Jon in *Anna Lee*; *Carnival '95* (Notting Hill Carnival, 1995); DC Macnab in *Pie in the Sky*.

Address: c/o Roxane Vacca Management. Lives in London. Single. Hobbies: Football.

Lisa Geoghan

GEOGHAN, Lisa

Lisa Geoghan. Actress. Trained at the Anna Scher Theatre School. Acted with the Old Vic Youth Theatre (1978-80). Other stage plays include *Widow's Weeds* (national tour).

TV: *Tucker's Luck*; *Big Deal*; *Honeymoon* (Play for Today); *Fox*; *The Squad*; *The Birth of a Nation*; *Disciplinary Tales*; *Court Report* (pilot); *All Packed Out*; *Going to Work*; *Grange Hill*; *Secret Orchard*; *Rockliffe's Follies*; Louise in *Desmond's*; *Saracen*; Beverley Tomlin in *The Bill* (1991); WPC Polly Page in *The Bill* (1992-).

Films: *The Wall*. Address: c/o Sharon Hamper Management.

Tom Georgeson

GEORGESON, Tom

Thomas Georgeson. Educated in Liverpool, Wales and Spain. Actor. b. Liverpool, 8 August 1941.

TV: *All's Well That Ends Well*; *Z Cars*; *Shabby Tiger*; *Doctor Who*; *Death or Glory*; *Rocky O'Rourke*; *Village Hall*; *Lizzie Dripping*; *Rooms*; *Coronation Street*; *Headmaster*; *Parole*; *Crown Court*; Stuart in *The Proofing Session*; Mr Greengross in *The Peppermint Pig*; The Journalist in *The After Dinner Joke*; Dixie Dean in *The Black Stuff* (Play for Today) and *Boys from the Blackstuff* (series); Malcolm in *Going Back*; Sutcliffe in *Turtle's Progress*; Mick Thomas in *Goodbye Darling*; Dad in *Boy with a Transistor Radio*; Alec Pickford in *Maybury*; Capt Moore in *When the Boat Comes In*; John Holden in *Juliet Bravo*; Isiah in *Scully*; Lashly in *The Last Place on Earth*; Jack Cade in *Dempsey and Makepeace*; David Morgan in *Strike It Rich*; Stanley in *Hidden Talents*; Conrad in *Les Girls*; Eddie in *The Manageress* (two series); Guthrie in *Island Gardens*; Milan and Derek in *The Bill*; Moore in *The Man from the Pru*; Punch in *Stay Lucky*; Blaney in *Devices and Desires*; Lou Barnes in *G.B.H.*; Insp Harry Naylor in *Between the Lines* (three series, 1992-4); Grice in *Resnick: Rough Treatment* (mini-series, 1993); Myles in *Dear Life*; *Bramwell*.

Films: *Kim*; *No Surrender*; George in *A Fish Called Wanda*. Address: c/o Hope & Lyne. Lives in Middlesex. m. actress-ballet dancer Primrose Elizabeth (née Sally Newby); 1 d. Rosalind, 1 s. Richard Hunter. Pets: A border collie called Jack. Hobbies: Snooker, backpacking.

Louise Germaine

GERMAINE, Louise

Louise Germaine. Actress.

TV: Sylvia Berry in *Lipstick on Your Collar* (series, 1993); Janice in *Frank Stubbs Promotes* (two episodes, 1993); Kate Hargreaves in *The House of Windsor* (series, 1994); Sally Clayton in *Sharpe's Company*; Amber Boyce/Mandy Mason in *Midnight Movie* (Screen Two).

Address: c/o William Morris Agency (UK).

GIBSON, Richard

Richard Gibson. Actor. b. Kampala, Uganda, 1 January 1954. Trained at the Central School of Speech and Drama. Stage plays include *'Allo, 'Allo* (Prince of Wales Theatre and London Palladium).

TV: *Tom Brown's Schooldays*; *The Children of the New Forest*; *Secret Diaries*; *Hadleigh*; *Wainwright's*

Law; Poldark; Penmarric; Prospects; The Key to Rebecca; Park Ranger; My Father's House; Four on Four; The Gate of Eden; Coral Island; Herr Flick in *'Allo, 'Allo* (series); Ben in *The Upper Hand.*
Films: *England Made Me; The Go-Between.* Address c/o Noel Gay Artists.

Richard Gibson

GIELGUD, John
Arthur John Gielgud. Actor/Director. b. London, 14 April 1904. Great-nephew of actress Dame Ellen Terry. Knighted, 1953; Companion of Honour, 1977. Trained at Lady Benson's School and RADA.
TV: *A Day by the Sea* (début, 1959); *To Chekhov with Love; Conversation at Night; Good King Charles' Golden Days; Saint Joan; Hassan, No Man's Land; The Cherry Orchard; Ivanov; The Mayfly and the Frog; Deliver Us from Evil; Probe* (TVM); *QB VII* (TVM); *Edward VII; Tales of the Unexpected;* Marius's Father in *Les Misérables* (TVM); *Why Didn't They Ask Evans?; English Gardens; Brideshead Revisited; The Hunchback of Notre Dame* (TVM); *Wagner* (TVM); *The Scarlet and the Black* (TVM); *Parson's Pleasure; Inside the Third Reich; Vatican Pimpernel; The Far Pavilions; Camille* (TVM); *The Master of Ballantrae* (TVM); *Frankenstein; Camille; Romance on the Orient Express* (TVM); *Time after Time* (TVM); *War and Remembrance; Quartermaine's Terms* (TVM); *A Man for All Seasons* (TVM); *Getting It Right; Summer's Lease; Inspector Morse: Twilight of the Gods; Lovejoy; Dance for the Camera; The Inspector Alleyn Mysteries: Hand in Glove; Under the Hammer; Omnibus: Gielgud — Scenes from Nine Decades* (subject); *Summer's Day Dream* (Performance); *Scarlett* (mini-series); *Gulliver's Travels* (mini-series).
Films: *Who Is the Man; The Clue of the New Pin; Insult; The Good Companions; The Secret Agent; Full Fathom Five* (voice only, short); *Hamlet; The Prime Minister; An Airman's Letter to His Mother* (voice only, short); *Unfinished Journey* (narrator only, short); *A Diary for Timothy; Julius Caesar; Romeo and Juliet; Richard III; Around the World in 80 Days; The Barretts of Wimpole Street; Saint Joan; The Immortal Land* (narrator only); *To Die in Madrid* (narrator only); *Hamlet; Becket; The Loved One; Chimes at Midnight* (US title *Falstaff*); *Sebastian; October Revolution* (narrator only); *Assignment to Kill; The Shoes of the Fisherman; The Charge of the Light Brigade; Oh! What a Lovely War; Eagle in a Cage; Frankenstein: The True Story* (TVM only in US); *Luther; 11 Harrowhouse; Gold; Murder on the Orient Express; Galileo; Aces High; Joseph Andrews; A Portrait of the Artist as a Young Man; Providence; Caligula; Sherlock Holmes: Murder by Decree* (UK title *Murder by Decree*); *Omar Mukhtar: Lion of the Desert; The Human Factor; Dyrygent* (also titled *The Conductor*); *Sphinx; Priest of Love; Arthur; Chariots of Fire; The Elephant Man; Gandhi; The Wicked Lady; Invitation to the Wedding; Scandalous!; The Shooting Party; Plenty; Leave All Fair; The Whistle Blower; Bluebeard, Bluebeard; Appointment with Death; Arthur 2: On the Rocks; Getting It Right; Strike It Rich; Daddy Nostalgie* (UK title *These Foolish Things*); *Prospero's Books; Shining Through; Swan Song* (short). **Books:** *Early Stages* (autobiography); *Stage Directions; Distinguished Company; An Actor and His Time.* Address: c/o ICM.

John Gielgud

GILBRIDE, Jacqueline
Jacqueline Gilbrook. Actress. b. Glasgow. Previously acted under her real name of Jacqueline Gilbrook. Trained at the Welsh College of Music and Drama.
TV: *Quartet; The Dark Room; The Justice Game* (mini-series); *Changing Steps; Brag;* Susan Duncan/Ross in *High Road.* Plus TV commercials. Address: c/o Ruth Tarko Agency. m.; 1 d.

Jacqueline Gilbride

GILES, Annabel
Annabel Claire Giles. Presenter/Actress. b. Griffithstown, Gwent, 20 May 1959. Temporary secretary for advertising agencies (1977-82), then became a model (1982-6), before entering TV (1986).
TV: *Razzmatazz; Going Live!; Night Network; The Showbiz Show; Jameson Tonight* (Sky TV); *Help Squad; Posh Frocks and New Trousers* (two series); *Head over Heels; Telethon '90; Blind Date; TV Weekly; 60something; This Morning; Home Stately Home; Come on Down and Out; Boredom Busters; Confidential; The Done Thing* (presenter, series on etiquette, *This Morning*, 1993-5); *Hit the Road* (team leader, game show, series, 1994); *Monkhouse's Memory Masters* (co-presenter, quiz show, series 1995). Acting roles: *The New Look* (film short); Grania Pringle in *Jilly Cooper's Riders* (mini-series); *The Krypton Factor.* Address: c/o Noel Gay Artists. Lives in London. m. rock musician Midge Ure (dis); 1 d. Molly. Pets: A goldfish called Daisy. Hobbies: 'Child rearing.'

Annabel Giles

GILES, Bill
William George Giles. Weather presenter. b. Dittisham, nr Dartmouth, South Devon, 18 November 1939. OBE, 1995 (New Year Honours List). FR Met S. Joined the Meteorological Office in Exeter in 1957 after leaving Bristol College of Science and Technology. Observer with the RAF in Germany (1961-3), lecturer at the Met Office's training college (1968-70) and moved to the London Weather Centre in 1972. Head of the BBC Weather Centre since 1983.
TV: BBC TV weather forecaster since 1975; *The Val Doonican Show.*
Books: *The Weather Story* (1990). Address: c/o BBC TV. Lives in Oxfordshire. m. 1st 1961 Eileen Myrtle Lake (dis 1992), 2nd 1993 Maureen Patricia Stafford; 1 s. Philip John (b. 1969), 1 d. Helen Mary (b. 1971) (both from 1st m.). Pets: Two dogs called Penny and Lucky. Hobbies: Gardening, golf.

Bill Giles

Robert Gillespie

GILLESPIE, Robert

Robert James Gillespie. Actor/Director/Writer. b. Lille, France, 9 November 1933. Mother Hungarian, father Canadian of Scottish descent. Spent early years in Nantes, France, until parents fled the Nazis when he was six and moved to Manchester. Trained at RADA after acting semi-professionally at the Library Theatre, Manchester. Directed *Fearless Frank* (Broadway).

TV: *That Was the Week That Was* (Writers' Guild Award of Merit, 1963); *The Black Brigand; Miss Em; Hotel Paradiso; The Queen and the Rebels; Maigret; Kipling; Crane; Danger Island; The Gamblers; Romeo and Juliet; The Drinking Party; Lord Peter Wimsey; Hugh and I; Mr Digby, Darling; New Scotland Yard; The Adventurers; Whatever Happened to the Likely Lads?; Freewheelers; Sadie, It's Cold Outside;* Mr Carter in *The Good Life; Couples; Rising Damp; Warship; Rosie; Robin's Nest; It Ain't Half Hot Mum; George and Mildred; Angels; Butterflies; The Fall and Rise of Reginald Perrin; Agony; Mary's Wife; Secret Army; Keep It in the Family* (five series); *I Woke Up One Morning; The Sweeney; The New Avengers; Van Der Valk; The Professionals; Return of The Saint; Sherlock Holmes; Blind Justice; Starting Out; Inmates; Heil Honey I'm Home;* Gilbert Herring in *Bonjour la Classe* (series, 1993).

Films: *A Severed Head; The Magnificent Seven Deadly Sins; The National Health; The Thirty-Nine Steps; At the Earth's Core; The Prisoner of Zenda.*
Address: c/o William Morris Agency (UK). Lives in London. Single. Hobbies: Reading, travelling.

Jeremy Gittins

GITTINS, Jeremy

Phillip Jeremy Gittins. Actor. b. Manchester, 30 January 1956. Trained at Guildhall School of Music and Drama. Stage productions include *King Lear* (Old Vic) and *The Rocky Horror Show* (Comedy Theatre).

TV: *Tenko; Doctor Who; The Kenny Everett Show; Andy Capp; The Kit Curran Radio Show; Tales of the Unexpected; Radio Pictures; All in Good Faith; Fresh Fields; Wink Three Times; Terry and June; Matlock — The Billionaire* (mini-series); *Masters of the Game* (mini-series); *Boon;* Pte Tipplewick in *Blackadder Goes Forth; Wish You Were Here...?* (guest presenter, with wife Sara Hollamby, for seven years); *Lazarus and Dingwall;* Vicar in *Keeping Up Appearances* (four series and Christmas specials); *Casualty;* Mike in *Stuck on You* (Comedy Playhouse, 1993); Dr Anderson in *The Upper Hand* (1995).

Films: *Blue Leader Missing; The Bitch;* John in *Anno Domini.*
Address: c/o Barry Burnett Organisation. Lives in Kingston-upon-Thames, Surrey. m. TV presenter Sara Hollamby; 1 d. Hayley, 1 s. Felix. Hobbies: Cooking, playing the piano, golf, squash.

Gabrielle Glaister

GLAISTER, Gabrielle

Gabrielle Glaister. Actress. b. Moreton-in-Marsh, Gloucestershire. Studied English and drama at Chichester College. Former member of the National Youth Theatre.

TV: *The Ben Elton Show; The Franchise Affair; Casualty; Grange Hill; Rockliffe's Babies;* 'Bob' in *Blackadder II* and *Blackadder the Third;* Driver Parkhurst in *Blackadder Goes Forth; Happy Families; Jury; Jane Eyre; Have a Heart; Play Away; Houseparty; All at No 20; Wish Me Luck; London's Burning; Mitch; The Man from Auntie;* Patricia Farnham in *Brookside* (1990-).

Films: *The Class of Miss MacMichael.* Address: c/o LWA/Mersey Television. Lives in London.

Iain Glen

GLEN, Iain

Iain Glen. Actor. b. Edinburgh, 24 June 1961. Trained at RADA (Bancroft Gold Medal winner).

TV: *Blood Hunt;* 'Sailor' in *Will You Love Me Tomorrow* (TVM); *The Picnic;* Carl Galton in *The Fear;* Tim Page in *Frankie's House* (mini-series, 1992); Commander Powell in *Black and Blue* (Screen One).

Films: Wallace in *Paris by Night;* John Hanning Speke in *Mountains of the Moon;* Larry Winters in *Silent Scream;* Brendan in *Gorillas in the Mist;* Willie Quinton in *Fools of Fortune; Rosencrantz and Guildenstern Are Dead.*
Address: c/o ICM. Partner: Actress Susannah Harker (qv); 1 s. Finlay (b. 1995).

Brian Glover

GLOVER, Brian

Brian Glover. Actor. b. Sheffield, South Yorkshire, 2 April 1934. Teacher and professional wrestler before becoming an actor. Plays include *Much Ado about Nothing* and *The Passion* (both National Theatre).

TV: *The Fishing Party; Rank and File; The Frighteners; A Day Out; Speech Day; The Regiment;* Heslop in *Porridge; Initiation; You'll Never Walk Alone; Dixon of Dock Green; Waiting at the Field Gate; The Wild Bunch; The Secret Army; Return of The Saint; Sounding Brass; Minder; Friday Night, Saturday Morning; Foxy Lady; Red Monarch* (TVM); *Educating Marmalade Atkins; The McGuffin* (TVM); *Campion;* Mr Rottweiler in *Bottom;* Selwyn Price in *Anna Lee: Headcase* (pilot, 1993) and *Anna Lee* (series, 1994); Johnny Pecs in *Rumble* (series, 1995). TV commercials: Tetley Tea Folk (voice-over).

Films: *Kes; O Lucky Man!; Mister Quilp; Brannigan; Trial by Combat; Sweeney!; Jabberwocky; Joseph Andrews; The First Great Train Robbery; Absolution; An American Werewolf in London; Britannia Hospital; The Company of Wolves; Ordeal by Innocence; Laughterhouse* (retitled *Singleton's Pluck*); *To Kill a Priest; Alien³; Leon the Pig Farmer; Kafka; Prince of Jutland.*
Address: c/o Felix De Wolfe. m. (dis); 1 d. Maxine, 1 s. Gus. Hobbies: Auctions.

GLOVER, Julian

Julian Wyatt Glover. Actor. b. St John's Wood, London, 27 March 1935. Trained at RADA.

TV: *An Age of Kings; Dubcek* in *Invasion* (drama-documentary); *Henry VIII; Henry V; The Diary of Albie Sachs; Journals of Bridget; Hitler; Guerre en Pays Neutre* (France); *Story of Jacob and Joseph* (TVM); *QB VII* (TVM); *Nancy Astor; Ivanhoe* (TVM); *QED; Six Centuries of Verse; Dombey and Son; Shakespeare Workshop: King Lear; Crown Court; By the Sword Divided; Mr Palfrey of Westminster; Cover Her Face; Travelling Man; Magnum; Remington Steel; Kim* (TVM); *OSS* (TVM); *Ladies in Charge; Only Yesterday; Mandela* (TVM); *Wish Me Luck; Never the Sinner; Bergerac; Casualty; TECX;* Sir Sebastian Pilgrim in *Rumpole of the Bailey; The Darling Buds of May; The Inspector Alleyn Mysteries; Money for Nothing* (Screen One); *Lovejoy;* Supt Drummond in *Taggart: Black Orchid;* Andrew Blake in *The Chief* (series, 1995); Jim in *Degrees of Error* (series, 1995); *Cadfael; In Hitler's Shadow.*

Films: *Tom Jones; The Girl with Green Eyes; I Was Happy Here; The Alphabet Murders; Theatre of Death; Quatermass and the Pit* (US title *Five Million Years to Earth); The Magus; The Adding Machine; Alfred the Great; The Last Grenade; Wuthering Heights; The Rise and Rise of Michael Rimmer; Nicholas and Alexandra; Antony and Cleopatra; Hitler: The Last Ten Days; Luther; The Internecine Project; Dead Cert; Quiller; Mirror of Deception; The Brute; Gulliver's Travels; The Empire Strikes Back; For Your Eyes Only; Back; Guerre en Pays Neutre; Heat and Dust; Tusks; 92 Grosvenor Street; Cry Freedom; The Fourth Protocol; Hearts of Fire; Treasure Island; Indiana Jones and the Last Crusade; King Ralph; The Chance; In the Mouth of Madness; Never the Sinner; Warburg — Man of Influence; Power and Conflict.*

Awards: Theatre: Laurence Olivier Award as Best Supporting Actor for title role in *Henry IV* (1993). Address: c/o Conway, van Gelder, Robinson. m. 1st actress Eileen Atkins (qv) (dis 1988), 2nd 1988 actress Isla Blair (qv); 1 s. actor Jamie (from 2nd m.). Pets: Two cats. Hobbies: Carpentry, gardening.

Julian Glover

GODDARD, Liza

Liza Goddard. Actress. b. Smethwick, West Midlands, 20 January 1950. Trained at the Arts Educational School. Emigrated to Australia in 1965 and made her TV acting début on TV in *Point of Departure,* followed by the series *Skippy,* before returning to Britain four years later.

TV: *Point of Departure; Clancy* in *Skippy; Victoria* in *Take Three Girls; The Befrienders; Lady Windermere's Fan; Holding On; Yes Honestly; The Brothers; The Upchat Line; Queen of a Distant Country; Whodunnit?; Wodehouse Playhouse; Murder at the Wedding; The Plank; Pig in the Middle; Watch This Space; Brendon's Chase; Wagner* (TVM); *Roll Over Beethoven; Doctor Who, Give Us a Clue; Bergerac; Tales of the Unexpected; Just His Luck;* Mrs Jessop in *Woof!; That's Love; Menopause (This Morning,* 1992); *Ticket to Write (This Morning,* 1993).

Films: *Ooh… You Are Awful* (US title *Get Charlie Tully); Shostakovich.*
Address: c/o Barry Burnett Organisation. Lives in Surrey. m. 1st actor Colin Baker (dis), 2nd singer Alvin Stardust (dis), 3rd David; 1 s. Thom (from 1st m.), 1 d. Sophie (from 2nd m.).

Liza Goddard

GODWIN, Christopher

Christopher Godwin. Actor. b. Loughborough, Leicestershire, 5 August 1943.

TV: *Don't Be Silly; Nice Work; Holding the Fort; Astronauts; The Other 'Arf; Nearly a Happy Ending; A Foggy Outlook; Return to Waterloo; Roll Over Beethoven; Return to Treasure Island; Ffizz; My Family and Other Animals; To Have and to Hold; Roger Doesn't Live Here Any More; Boon; Nice Work; Snakes and Ladders; The Chronicles of Narnia; Lovejoy; The Plant;* Mr Armitage in *Crown Prosecutor.*

Films: *Porridge; Charlie Muffin; A Handful of Dust.* Address: c/o ICM. m. Christine; 2 s. Ben, Tom.

Christopher Godwin

GONET, Stella

Stella Gonet. Actress. Seventh of 12 children born to parents who eloped to Buenos Aires before settling in Greenock, Scotland, to raise them. Trained at the Royal Scottish Academy of Music and Drama. Stage plays include *Trafford Tanzi* (Mermaid Theatre) and *Cyrano de Bergerac* (Haymarket Theatre).

TV: Ellie in *To Have and to Hold;* Mairi in *The Shuter Falls;* Dr Claire Wainwright in *Casualty; Down Where the Buffalo Goes; The Dill; Heading Home; Marigold* in *The Common Pursuit;* Alex in *The Advocates;* Beatrice Eliott in *The House of Eliott* (three series, 1992-4); Zena Ordzhonikidze in *Stalin* (TVM); Beatrice Eliott in *French and Saunders;* Kate Armstrong in *Trip Trap* (Screen One).

Films: *For Queen and Country.* Address: c/o Markham & Froggatt. Partner: Actor Nicholas Farrell.

Stella Gonet

GOODALL, Caroline

Caroline Goodall. Actress. b. London, 13 November 1959. Former member of the National Youth Theatre. Studied drama and English at Bristol University. Plays include *Susan's Breasts* (Royal Court), *True Dare Kiss, Command or Promise* (both National Theatre), *Richard III, Misalliance, Heresies* (all RSC).

TV: *The Moon Stallion; Gems; Remington Steele; Tales of the Unexpected; After the War;* Helen in *Ring of Scorpio* (mini-series); Mandy in *Royal Celebration* (Screen One); Rosalind Lee in *The Sculptress* (serial, 1996).

Films: *Every Time We Say Goodbye; Hook; White Squall.* Address: c/o Jonathan Altaras Associates.

Caroline Goodall

GOODMAN, Elinor

Elinor Goodman. Journalist. Began journalism career on the advertising industry's trade magazine *Campaign* 1970. Moved to the City office of the *Daily Telegraph* the following year, reporting on all aspects of media and marketing, and in 1972 joined the *Financial Times*, first as consumer affairs correspondent, then as political correspondent. Joined ITN as political editor of Channel Four News in 1982.
TV: *Channel Four News* (political editor, 1982-). Address: c/o ITN. m.

Elinor Goodman

GOODWIN, Harold

Harold Goodwin. Actor. b. Wombwell, South Yorkshire, 22 October 1917. Trained at RADA.
TV: *United!; Rogue's Rock; Love Story; The Adventures of Black Beauty; Oh No It's Selwyn Froggitt; Captain Varley Goes Home; The Onedin Line; The Dick Emery Show; The Crucible; A Brush with Mr Porter; On the Road; Eldorado; The Kamikaze Ground Staff Reunion Dinner; That's My Boy; A Voyage round My Father; Angels; Juliet Bravo; The Gentle Touch; Shoreline; Minder; Bulman; It's Never Too Late; Casualty; Our Geoff; All Creatures Great and Small; Brush Strokes; Woof!; The Paradise Club; Coronation Street.*
Films: *The Ware Case; Dance Hall; The Happiest Days of Your Life; The Magnet; Appointment with Venus; The Man in the White Suit; Green Grow the Rushes; Judgment Deferred; Angels One Five; The Last Page; The Card; The Cruel Sea; Grand National Night; The Case of Gracie Budd; The Million Pound Note; The Harassed Hero; One Good Turn; The Gay Dog; The Dam Busters; A Kid for Two Farthings; The Ship That Died of Shame; You Lucky People; The Ladykillers; Josephine and Men; Now and Forever; Charley M Zarak; The Last Man to Hang?; Three Men in a Boat; Barnacle Bill; The Prince and the Showgirl; The Bridge on the River Kwai; Seawife; Girls at Sea; The Square Peg; Law and Disorder; Sea of Sand; The Mummy; The Bandit of Zhobe; The Ugly Duckling; Wrong Number; Sink the Bismarck!; Spartacus; Operation Cupid; The Bulldog Breed; The Terror of the Tongs; Nearly a Nasty Accident; On the Fiddle; The Square Mile Murder; Never Back Losers; The Traitors; Hair of the Dog; Number Six; Phantom of the Opera; The Longest Day; Crooks Anonymous; The Fast Lady; The Hi-Jackers; The Comedy Man; Curse of the Mummy's Tomb; All in Good Time; Monster of Terror; Don't Raise the Bridge, Lower the River; Frankenstein Must Be Destroyed; Some Will, Some Won't; Hoverbus; All Creatures Great and Small; The Chiffy Kids* (serial); *Jabberwocky; Spirits.* Address: c/o Hilda Physick Agency. m. Beatrice.

Harold Goodwin

GOODWIN, Trudie

Trudie Goodwin. Actress. b. London, 13 November 1951. First professional work with the Theatre Centre, London, acting on two tours and directing another.
TV: *Fox; The Gentle Touch; The Law Machine; Play for Today; Woodentop* (pilot programme for *The Bill*); WPC June Ackland in *The Bill* (1984-). Address: c/o Ellison Combe Associates. Lives in South London. m. actor Kit Jackson; 2 d. Jessica, Eleanor. Hobbies: Painting, gardening.

Trudie Goodwin

GOODYEAR, Julie

Julie Kemp. Actress. b. Bury, Lancashire, 29 March 1942. Trained as a shorthand typist, did office work, sold washing machines and did modelling work before gaining repertory theatre experience in Oldham, starting as an ASM at the Coliseum theatre, then becoming an actress.
TV: *Pardon the Expression; Scene at 6.30;* Bet Lynch/Gilroy in *Coronation Street* (1966, 1970-95); *The Dustbinmen; City '68; The War of Darkie Pilbeam; Nearest and Dearest; A Family at War; This Is Your Life* (subject); *How to Be Cool* (acting herself); *Royal Variety Performance* (with *Coronation Street* cast, 1989). Address: c/o Equity. m. 1st Ray Sutcliffe (dis), 2nd Tony Rudman (annulled), 3rd Richard Skrob (dis); 1 s. Gary (from 1st m.).

Julie Goodyear

GORDON, Hannah

Hannah Campbell Grant Gordon. Actress. b. Edinburgh, 9 April 1941. DLitt, University of Glasgow. Gained Certificate in Dramatic Studies from University of Glasgow, diploma in speech and drama from Glasgow College of Music and Dramatic Art (James Bridie Gold Medal winner, 1962).
TV: *Johnson over Jordan* (1965); *Great Expectations; David Copperfield; Middlemarch; Love Story; The Ratcatchers; Hadleigh; Dr Finlay's Casebook; The Exiles; Abelard and Héloïse; Scobie in September;* Celia in *Three Stories of Orkney; When the Bough Breaks; Brett; The Persuaders; The Protectors; Dear Octopus; Allergy; My Wife Next Door* (series, 1972); Lady Virginia Bellamy (née Hamilton) in *Upstairs, Downstairs* (series, 1976); Maggie in *What Every Woman Knows; Play of the Month: Waste; Telford's Change* (series, 1979); *Miss Morrison's Ghosts; The Morecambe and Wise Show; Goodbye, Mr Kent; The Gay Lord Quex; Good Behaviour; Hammer House of Horror; Gardener's Calendar* (presenter, series); *The Day after the Fair;* Mrs Durrell in *My Family and Other Animals; Joint Account* (two series 1988-90, 1989 special); Dr Janet Napier in *Taggart: Fatal Inheritance* (1993); *Celebration Concert: It's a Lovely Day Tomorrow* (guest narrator, VE 50, 1995).
Films: *Spring and Port Wine; Alfie Darling;* voice of Hyzenthlay in *Watership Down; The Big Sleep;* Mrs Treves in *The Elephant Man.* **Books:** *Woman at the Wheel.* Address: c/o Hutton Management. m. 1970 film lighting cameraman Norman Warwick; 1 s. Ben. Hobbies: Gardening, walking, cookery.

Hannah Gordon

GORDON, Serena

Serena Gordon. Actress. b. London, 3 September 1963.

TV: Phyllida in *Tumbledown* (TVM); Annabel in *Shell Seekers*; Gwen in *Act of Will* (mini-series); Prunella Rumsey in *Queenie*; Annie Rose in *After the War*; Jane in *Till We Meet Again*; Lucy Manette in *A Tale of Two Cities* (mini-series); Tricia Mabbott in *Kinsey* (two series); *Sherlock Holmes*; Janey Henderson in *Jilly Cooper's Riders* (mini-series, 1993); *Awayday*; *Blue Heaven*; Sophie in *Dancing Queen* (Rik Mayall Presents); Caroline Finch in *The House of Windsor* (series, 1994); Serena Wise in *99-1*; Louise Knight in *Toby* (Chiller).

Films: Gladys Olcott in *Maurice*; *GoldenEye*. Address: c/o ICM.

Serena Gordon

GOUGH, Michael

Michael Gough. Actor. b. Malaya, 23 November 1916.

TV: *Suez*; *Smiley's People*; *In Search of the Nile*; *Vincent the Dutchman* (presenter, documentary); *Shoulder to Shoulder*; *Fall of Eagles*; *George Sand*; *Shades of Greene*; *The Rivals of Sherlock Holmes*; *To the Lighthouse*; *The Citadel*; *Heartbreak Hotel*; *Unfinished Business*; *A Killing on the Exchange*; *Inspector Morse*; *Cariani and the Courtesan*; *After the War*; *The Case of the Late Pig*; *Campion*; *The Mountain and the Molehill*; *Blackeyes*; *Boon*; *Children of the North*; *The Good Guys*; *A Village Affair*.

Films: *Blanche Fury*; *Anna Karenina*; *The Man in the White Suit*; *Robin Hood*; *The Sword and the Rose*; *Rob Roy*; *The Horse's Mouth*; *Mr Topaz*; *Dracula*; *They Came from Beyond Space*; *Circus of Blood*; *Un Soir un Train*; *The Playroom*; *Women in Love*; *Velvet House*; *Julius Caesar*; *Trog*; *The Go-Between*; *Henry VIII and His Six Wives*; *Horror Hospital*; *The Savage Messiah*; *Legend of Hell House*; *Justices*; *The Boys From Brazil*; *Memed*; *The Dresser*; *Top Secret!*; *Oxford Blues*; *A Christmas Carol*; Lord Delamere in *Out of Africa*; *Caravaggio*; *Maschenka*; *The Fourth Protocol*; *The Serpent and the Rainbow*; *Strapless*; *The Shell Seekers*; Alfred in *Batman* and *Batman Returns*; *Wittgenstein*. Address: c/o Peters Fraser & Dunlop. m. 1st Diana Graves (dis), 2nd Anne Leon (dis), 3rd Anneka Wills.

Michael Gough

GOUGH, Sandra

Sandra Gough. Actress. On radio from the age of 12 in *Children's Hour*.

TV: Irma Barlow (née Ogden) in *Coronation Street* (seven years); *Bingo*; *Foxy Lady*; *Travelling Man*; *Call Earnshaw*; *Time of Your Life*; *Hideaway*; Mrs Hilton in *Welcome to the Times*; Sylviane in *How to Be Cool*; Housing Officer in *A View of Harry Clark*; Mrs Bell in *All Creatures Great and Small*; Sheri in *Hollywood Sports*; Mrs Brickton in *Dawn and the Candidate* (4-Play); Mrs Goodrun in *Medics*; Doreen in *Emmerdale Farm*; Vox Pop in *I Like Bananas*; Rita Mullins in *A Little Bit of Lippy* (ScreenPlay); Mrs Calf (Mum) in *Video Diaries: Paul Calf*; Nellie Dingle in *Emmerdale* (1994-5); Mrs Calf (Mum) in *Three Fights, Two Weddings and a Funeral*; Woman Talking to Beck in *Cracker*; *Coogan's Run* (series, 1995).

Films: Actress in *The Dresser*, *The Rise and Rise of Roy 'Chubby' Brown*. Address: c/o ATS Casting.

Sandra Gough

GRACE, Nickolas

Nickolas Andrew Halliwell Grace. Actor. b. West Kirby, Liverpool, 21 November 1949. Great-grandfather Thomas Hughes built the first cinemas in Liverpool and ran the Empress and Lyceum circuits. Trained at the Central School of Speech and Drama. Acted with the RSC during two two-year stints, played the title role in *Richard II* at the Young Vic, and on Broadway in *The Mikado* and *HMS Pinafore*.

TV: *The Love School*; *The Anarchist*; *The Comedy of Errors*; *The Pink Medicine Show*; Anthony Blanche in *Brideshead Revisited*; *Bergerac*; *Morte D'Arthur*; Sheriff of Nottingham in *Robin of Sherwood*; *The Master of Ballantrae*; *Huis Clos*; *Lace*; *The Last Place on Earth*; *Candide*; *Max Headroom*; Nelson in *Napoleon and Josephine* (mini-series); Hitler in *Unreported Incident*; *The Man in the Brown Suit*; *Pursuit*; *Birds of a Feather*; *Cluedo*; *The Adventures of Sherlock Holmes*; *The Green Man* (mini-series); Mozart in *J'Accuse Mozart*; *Absolutely Fabulous*; *Lovejoy*; *Moon and Son*; *Hands across the Sea* (Tonight at 8.30); *Sherlock Holmes: Master Blackmailer*, *The Inspector Alleyn Mysteries*; *Smith and Jones*; Noel Coward in *Without Walls: For One Night Only*; *The Chief*; *Sharpe's Honour*; *Inside Victor Lewis-Smith*; *Space Police*; *The Young Indiana Jones Chronicles*; *DUGS*; Geoffrey Boozu Pill in *The Final Cut* (mini-series).

Films: *Europe after the Rain*; *Sleepwalker*; *Heat and Dust*; *Lorca — Death of a Poet*; *Dream Demon*; *Salome's Last Dance*; *Just Ask for Diamond*; *Tom and Viv*; *Two Deaths*; *Solomon and Sheba*. Address: c/o Christina Shepherd. Lives in London. Single. Hobbies: Travel, languages, running, riding, swimming.

Nickolas Grace

GRANT, Deborah

Deborah Grant. Actress. b. London, 22 February 1947. Trained at the Joyce Butler School of Dancing and Central School of Speech and Drama.

TV: *A Bouquet of Barbed Wire*; *Outside Edge*; *Mr Palfrey of Westminster*; *Victoria Wood — As Seen on TV*; *Bergerac*; *Bulman*; *Room at the Bottom*; *Pulaski*; Leonora Campbell in *Bread*; Jane in *Victoria Wood: Staying In*; Sarah Preston in *Westbeach* (series, 1993); Stella in *Pat and Margaret* (Screen One); Sheila Cody in *Crown Prosecutor* (series, 1995). Address: c/o Michelle Braidman Associates. m.1st actor Jeremy Child (dis), 2nd actor Gregory Floy; 2 d. Melissa, Miranda.

Deborah Grant

GRANT, Russell

Russell Grant

Russell John D'Ammerall Grant. Astrologer/Presenter. b. Hillingdon, Middlesex, 5 February 1952. Trained at the Daphne Davey School of Dance and Drama and LAMDA (Bronze Medal winner). Life member of the Astrologers' Guild of Great Britain.

TV: *Good Morning Britain* (TV-am); *People Today; After Nine* (TV-am); *The Zodiac Game; Star Choice; Six O'Clock Show; Russell's Horoscope Show; BBC Breakfast Time; A Question of Stars; Breakfast Time* (US); *Future Worlds* (*This Morning*); *Believe It or Not* (*This Morning*); *Russell Grant's All Star Show.*
Books: *Your Sun Signs; Your Year Ahead TVTimes Special; Your Love Signs; Dream Dictionary; Astro-Tarot; The Real Counties of Britain.* Address: c/o PO Box 5757, Lytham St Annes, Lancashire FY8 2TE. Lives in Middlesex. Single. Pets: Chocolate labrador called Owen and a 'mixed-up' mongrel called Dolly. Hobbies: Middlesex memorabilia, Middlesex sports.

GRANTHAM, Leslie

Leslie Grantham

Leslie Grantham. Actor. b. Camberwell, London, 30 April 1947. Trained at Webber Douglas Academy.
TV: *The Jewel in the Crown; Knock Back; Jake's End; Goodnight and God Bless; Doctor Who; Thought You'd Gone; Bulman;* Den Watts in *EastEnders* (1985-9); *Winners and Losers* (series); *Alas Smith and Jones; The Paradise Club* (two series, 1989-90); Bob Grove in *The Grove Family* (The Lime Grove Story); *The Good Guys;* psychiatrist Terence in *Gummed Labels; Library of Romance* (*Good Morning... with Anne & Nick*) (storyteller); *The Inside Track... on Parenting;* Roland in *Wild Oats* (Comedy Playhouse); Danny Kane in *The Detectives;* Colonel Mustard in *Cluedo* (series); *The Children's Royal Variety Performance 1993;* DI Mick Raynor in *99-1* (two series, 1994-5); *The Good Sex Guide; Delta Wave.*
Films: *Morons from Outer Space.*
Address: c/o Michael Whitehall. Lives in London. m. actress Jane Laurie; 1 s. Michael.

GRAVESON, Jan Kelly

Jan Kelly Graveon

Janice Graveson. Actress. b. Co Durham. Father a singer in North East clubs. Trained in dance from age of seven. Stage roles include Linda in *Blood Brothers* (Albery and Phoenix Theatres, Liverpool Playhouse, Toronto and Broadway). British tap-dancing champion for two consecutive years.
TV: *Joe Lives; Auf Wiedersehen Pet;* Rosalyn Greenwood in *Coronation Street;* Kathleen Tanner in *White Peak Farm* (series); Sharon in *Women in Tropical Places;* Li and Cindy Walker (two roles) in *Casualty;* Disa O'Brien in *EastEnders* (48 episodes, 1990-1); Angela in *Spender;* Betty Watford in *Catherine Cookson's The Glass Virgin* (mini-series, 1995); WPC Jane Brent in *A Touch of Frost.*
Awards: Theatre: Tony award nomination for performance in *Blood Brothers* (Broadway, 1993-4). Address: c/o Sharon Hamper Management. Lives in East London. Single. Pets: 'None, but I adore animals!' Hobbies: Designing and making greetings cards, singing, walking.

GRAY, Dulcie

Dulcie Gray

Dulcie Winifred Catherine Bailey. Actress/Writer. b. Kuala Lumpur, Malaysia, 20 November 1920. CBE, 1983. Trained at the Webber Douglas Academy. Forty-six West End plays.
TV: *The Will* (1949); *Crime Passionelle; Milestones; Art and Opportunity; A Fish in the Family; Olympia; September Revue; The Sun Divorce; Lesson in Love; The Happy McBains; The Governess; Boyd QC; The Importance of Being Earnest; Winter Cruise; The Letter; Village Wooing* (Australia); *Virtue; Beautiful for Ever; Unexpectedly Vacant; This Is Your Life* (subject, 1973, and joint subject with Michael Denison, 1995); *The Voysey Inheritance; Life after Death; Agatha Christie; Rumpole of the Bailey; The Thirties; Cold Warrior;* Kate Harvey in *Howards' Way* (six series, 1985-90); *An Invitation to Remember* (twice); *Three Up, Two Down; What's My Line?; Edward Eago Programme; The Clothes Show, Songs of Praise; Celebration Concert: It's a Lovely Day Tomorrow* (guest narrator, VE 50, 1995).
Films: *Banana Ridge; Victory Wedding* (short); *2,000 Women; Madonna of the Seven Moons; A Place of One's Own; They Were Sisters; Wanted for Murder; The Years Between; A Man about the House; Mine Own Executioner; My Brother Jonathan; The Glass Mountain; The Franchise Affair; Angels One Five; There Was a Young Lady; A Man Could Get Killed; The Black Crow.*
Radio: *Frontline Family* (serial, 1941-2). Address: c/o Barry Burnett Organisation. Lives in Amersham, Buckinghamshire. m. 1939 actor Michael Denison (qv). Pets: A tricolour Pembrokeshire corgi called Brett. Hobbies: British butterfly conservation.

GRAY, Muriel

Muriel Gray

Muriel Gray. Presenter. b. Glasgow, 30 August 1958. Trained as an illustrator at Glasgow School of Art.
TV: *The Tube; The Works; Casebook Scotland; Acropolis Now; The Hogmanay Show; Bliss; The Media Show; Frocks on the Box; Walkie Talkie; Art Is Dead... Long Live TV!; The Munro Show* (Discovery channel); *The Snow Show* (series, 1993); *Off the Wall* (series, 1993); *Without Walls: Carnography; BBC Design Awards* (1994); *Just for Laughs* (1990 Montreal Comedy Festival); *Ride On* (three series, 1994-6); *Under Exposed* (series, 1996). Address: c/o Gallus Benom Productions, Greenside House, 25 Greenside Place, Edinburgh EH1 3AA, tel 0131-556 2429. Hobbies: Hill climbing, drinking beer.

GREENACRE, Jill

Jill Elizabeth Greenacre. Actress. b. Norfolk, 3 June 1965. Gained a BA (Hons) in English and drama. Trained at the Drama Studio.
TV: Helga Mueller in *Andy Robson* (series); *Meditation* (co-presenter); Rosie in *Dramarama;* Kate Rogers in *The Bill;* Susan in *Brookside; The Main Event; Library of Romance;* Frances in *A Touch of Love;* Pat in *Sharon and Elsie;* Alice Russell in *Crime Limited;* Paula in *Moonlight and Roses;* Linda in *The Brittas Empire* (six series, 1991-6, plus Christmas special 1994). Address: c/o Langford Associates. Lives in London. Single. Partner: Actor Peter Clifford. Hobbies: Horse-riding, walking, yoga, meditation.

Jill Greenacre

GREENE, Harry

Harry Greene. Presenter/Actor. Trained in architecture and became a theatre designer before training with Joan Littlewood's Theatre Workshop for three years, where he was designer and stage director (1952-4). Appeared in British television's first soap opera, *Round at the Redways,* in 1955 and presented his first DIY series in 1957. Many TV commercials. Writer of more than 20 DIY books. Designer to the stars of *Coronation Street, The Bill, London's Burning, EastEnders* and *Emmerdale.*
TV: As actor: *Round at the Redways; The Adventures of Robin Hood; The Planemakers; The Three Musketeers; Richard the Lionheart.* As presenter: *Dream Home* (TV-am DIY series), *On the House; DIY Disaster; DIY Challenge; Housestyle; Bazaar; This Morning; DIY Garden; Summer Scene;* QVC satellite channel's DIY demonstrator since October 1993, including the weekly *DIY with Harry Greene.*
Address: c/o Michael Ladkin Personal Management. Lives in London. m. actress Marjie Lawrence; 2 d. TV presenter Sarah (qv), TV weather presenter Laura (qv), 1 s. Grundy Television assistant producer Robin. Hobbies: Swimming, cartooning, spoon-playing, walking, reading, camcorder.

Harry Greene

GREENE, Laura

Laura Beatrice Una Greene. Weather presenter. b. London, 16 February 1972. Daughter of presenter-actor Harry Greene (qv) and actress Marjie Lawrence; sister of TV presenter Sarah Greene (qv). Gained a geography degree from University College, London, then took the Met Office Training College presenters' course (1994). Since entering TV, started an MSc in environmental science at Birkbeck College.
TV: Appearances on *Blue Peter, Saturday Superstore* and *Going Live* (1980-88); *Carlton/LWT Weather* (1994); *ITV National Weather* (1995-). Address: c/o Jonathan Altaras Associates. Single. Hobbies: Travel, dance, skiing, good food and wine, keeping fit (including running and gym).

Laura Greene

GREENE, Sarah

Sarah Greene. Presenter/Actress. b. London, 24 October. Daughter of presenter-actor Harry Greene (qv) and actress Marjie Lawrence; sister of weather presenter Laura Greene (qv). Started career as a child in films and commercials. Gained a drama degree from Hull University. Worked in theatre in Birmingham and Manchester, before entering TV drama.
TV: Sandra in *The Swish of the Curtain* (serial); *Together* (serial); *Blue Peter* (1980-3); *Eureka; Saturday Superstore* (four series, 1983-7); *BBC Breakfast Time; Going Live!* (six series, 1987-93); *French and Saunders; The Longest Running Show on Earth; Dream Home; Emergency 999; The Domesday Book; Friday People; Début; Airport Watch; Bodycare; London Plus* (BBC South East); *Joy to the World; The British Fashion Awards* (1989); *Posh Frocks and New Trousers* (two series); *Life on One; Hospital Watch; Take Two* (two series, 1992-3); Reporter in *Ghostwatch* (drama); *Disneytime; Gone Live!; BAFTA Craft Awards* (1993); *The Red Nose Awards* (presenter, 1993); *All About Us* (series, 1993); *Happy Families* (presenter, game show series, 1993); *Young Musician of the Year; The Exchange Preview* (1995); *Pebble Mill* (presenting The Indies, 1995); *The Exchange* (series, 1995); *Good Morning Summer* (series, 1995); *Pebble Mill* (series, 1995-6).
Radio: *Radio Club; Woman's Hour.* **Books:** *The Multi-Racial Make-Up Book* (with Vicky Licorish, 1987); *We Can Say No!* (with David Pithers, 1988). **Awards:** SOS Best Woman on Television award (three years running). Address: c/o Michael Ladkin Personal Management. m. TV presenter Mike Smith. Hobbies: Addicted to radio, movies, friends, gardening, travel, reading, swimming, tennis.

Sarah Greene

GREENWOOD, Debbie

Debra Greenwood. Presenter. b. Liverpool, 16 September 1959. Gained a BA (Hons) in French and German. Won the 1984 Miss Great Britain beauty contest, held at the Waldorf Hotel, London, and broadcast by the BBC, before becoming a presenter with Granada Television.
TV: *Granada Reports; Weekend; Scramble* (all Granada Television, 1984-5); *Breakfast Time* (1985-6); *Lifeline; First Class* (1986-8); *Tricks of the Trade; The Tom O'Connor Road Show* (reporter, 1987); *International Eisteddfod; Children in Need; The Garden Party* (1988-91); *Streetwise* (*The Channel Four Daily,* 1989-90); *You Can Do It* (BSB); *Pick of the Week; TV Weekly* (reporter, 1992-). As actress: *Cinderella; Pulaski; Hold the Back Page; Hello Mum.*
Radio: *The Debbie Greenwood Show* (BBC Radio 2). Address: c/o Sara Cameron Management. Lives in London. m. TV and radio presenter Paul Coia; 1 d. Annalie (b. 1994). Hobbies: Tennis, writing, eating.

Debbie Greenwood

Richard Greenwood

Simon Gregson

Sheila Grier

Richard Griffiths

Sara Griffiths

GREENWOOD, Richard

Richard Peirse-Duncomb. Actor. b. South Wales. After studying at Trinity College, Glenalmond, spent a year at St Andrews University, where he took part in amateur dramatics. Trained at the Royal Scottish Academy of Music and Drama. Stage plays include *Witches of Traquair* (national tour).

TV: *The Campbells; The Houseman's Tale;* Eric Ross-Gifford in *Take the High Road* (1987-); *Taggart.*
Address: c/o Pat Lovett Agency. Lives in Glasgow. m. 1990 actress Gillian McNeill. Hobbies: Fishing, playing board games, golf, doing crossword puzzles.

GREGSON, Simon

Simon Alan Gregory. Actor. b. Wythenshawe, Manchester, 2 October 1974. Discovered by Granada Television while still at school. Originally acted under his real name but changed his stage name to Simon Gregson in 1991 when he became a full Equity actors' union member because there was already an actor called Simon Gregory.

TV: Steve McDonald in *Coronation Street* (1989-).
Address: c/o Langford Associates/Granada Television. Lives in Cheadle, Cheshire. Single. Hobbies: Motorcycles.

GRIER, Sheila

Sheila Grier. actress. b. Glasgow, 11 February 1959. Trained at the Royal Scottish Academy of Music and Drama.

TV: Miss Richardson in *Take the High Road* (1983); *The Odd Job Man; The End of the Line; Scotch and Wry; The Untied Shoelaces Show* (presenter); Sandra Maghie in *Brookside* (1984-6); *Bookie; Shadow on the Earth; Taggart; Making Out; Emmerdale.*
Address: c/o Felix De Wolfe. Hobbies: Designer knitwear business, dancing, swimming.

GRIFFITHS, Richard

Richard Griffiths. Actor. b. Cleveland, 31 July 1947. Stage plays include *The White Guard, Once in a Lifetime, Henry VIII, Volpone, Red Star* (all RSC), *Verdi's Messiah* (Old Vic), *Rules of the Game* and *Galileo* (both Almeida Theatre).

TV: *Nobody's Perfect* (series); *Amnesty; The Cleopatras; Bergerac; Bird of Prey* (series); *Whoops Apocalypse!; The World Cup – A Captain's Tale; The Merry Wives of Windsor; Anything Legal Considered; Ffizz* (series); *The Marksman; A Kind of Living* (series); *A Wanted Man; Goldeneye; Perfect Scoundrels; The Good Guys; El C.I.D.;* Porter in *Mr Wakefield's Crusade* (series); Humphrey Appleton in *Inspector Morse: The Day of the Devil; Pie in the Sky* (two series); *Breed of Heroes.*

Films: *Superman II; Chariots of Fire; Britannia Hospital; Gandhi; Ragtime; Shanghai Surprise; The French Lieutenant's Woman;* Captain Billings in *Greystoke: The Legend of Tarzan Lord of the Apes;* Anton in *Gorky Park; A Private Function; Withnail & I; King Ralph; The Naked Gun 2½: The Smell of Fear; Blame It on the Bellboy; Funny Bones.*
Address: c/o Michael Whitehall.

GRIFFITHS, Sara

Sara Griffiths. Actress. b. Sheffield, South Yorkshire. Brought up in Lancashire. Trained at Elmhurst School of Theatre Arts (1979-85) and took drama course with Andrew Neil and Graham Mitchell (1984-5). Stage roles include Edith in *Edith Grant* (Chichester Festival), Miranda in *The Tempest* (Pendley Shakespeare Festival) and Julia in *The Two Gentlemen of Verona* (Theatre Museum).

TV: Polly in *Late Expectations; Doctor Who;* Liz in *Gentlemen and Players* (two series); Clare in *Emmerdale Farm; Sisters* (pilot); *The Chief* (two series); *Kangaroo Valley* (pilot); *Van Der Valk; Rich Tea & Sympathy;* Penelope in *The Ruth Rendell Mysteries: Talking to Strange Men;* Helen Bradbury in *Number Six* (Chiller); Anita Castle in *Castles* (series, 1995).
Address: c/o Ken McReddie.

GROUT, James

James Grout. Actor. b. London, 22 October 1927. Trained at RADA. TV since 1949. Stage plays include *The Mousetrap* (West End), *Twelfth Night* (Old Vic), *Half a Sixpence* (West End and Broadway), *Lloyd George Knew My Father* (Savoy Theatre), *13 Rue de l'Amour* (Phoenix Theatre), *A Murder Is Announced* (Vaudeville Theatre), *Make and Break, The Way of the World, Man and Superman, Sweet Bird of Youth* (all Theatre Royal, Haymarket), *Quartermaine's Terms* (Queen's Theatre), *When We Are Married* (Whitehall Theatre) and *Johnny on a Spot* (National Theatre).

TV: *The First Lady* (series); *Diary of a Nobody; Born and Bred;* Granville Bennett in *All Creatures Great and Small; Z Cars; Sister Dora; The Marriage Counsellor; Hymn for Jim; Jenny Can't Work Any Faster; Microbes and Men; Juliet Bravo; Honky Tonk Heroes; Man and Superman; The Falklands Factor; Agatha Christie Hour; A Fine Romance; Reith; Stan's Last Game; The Bounder; Cockles; Box of Delights; Rachel and the Roarettes; Occupation Democrat; The Beiderbecke Affair;* Geoffrey Winfield in *Yes Minister; No*

Place Like Home; Murder of a Moderate Man; Bust; Ever Decreasing Circles; A Very Peculiar Practice; Chief Inspector Strange in *Inspector Morse; Vote for Them; After the War; Saracen; Northern Lights; Mother Love; Late Expectations; Singles; Stay Lucky; Roy's Raiders; Titmuss Regained;* Mr Justice Oliphant in *Rumpole of the Bailey;* George in *Shelley* (series); *About Face; Mr Wakefield's Crusade;* Peter Thomas in *The Old Devils* (mini-series, 1992); voices of Sir William Catesby and the Bishop of Ely in *Richard III* (Shakespeare the Animated Tales); *Henry IV, Parts 1 and 2;* Douglas in *Down to Earth.* Address: c/o Crouch Associates. m. Noreen Jean.

James Grout

GUARD, Christopher

Christopher Guard. Actor. b. London, 5 December 1953. Comes from a theatrical family; brother of actor Dominic Guard; cousin of actress Pippa Guard (qv). Stage plays include *Filumena* (West End).

TV: Title role in *David Copperfield; Tom Brown's Schooldays; Vienna 1900; Wilfred and Eileen; My Cousin Rachel; Les Misérables* (TVM); *A Woman of Substance; Return to Treasure Island; Blackeyes; The Memoirs of Sherlock Holmes; The Lifeboat; Lovejoy; Jackanory: Treasure Island* (storyteller).

Films: *A Little Night Music; Memoirs of a Survivor; Loophole; Lord of the Rings.*

Address: c/o ICM. Lives in London. m. actress Lesley Dunlop (sep); 2 d. Daisy, Rosie. Hobbies: Watching Fulham FC, playing football, arranging and performing songs.

Christopher Guard

GUARD, Pippa

Philippa Guard. Actress. b. Edinburgh, 13 October 1952. Cousin of actors Christopher (qv) and Dominic Guard. Educated in Canada. Trained at RADA (Ronson, Kendall and Pole Prizes winner).

TV: Maggie Tulliver in *The Mill on the Floss* (début, 1978); Barbara in *The Mallens;* Miranda in *The Tempest; All's Well That Ends Well;* Ava in *The Flipside of Dominic Hyde;* Maria Martin in *Murder in the Red Barn; Jackanory* (storyteller); Hermia in *A Midsummer Night's Dream; Another Flip for Dominic; To the Lighthouse; The Country Diary of an Edwardian Lady; Dramarama: A Couple of Charlies; The Life and Loves of a She-Devil; Boon; Campion; Casualty* (two roles); *Saracen; Bergerac; Close to Home; Agatha Christie's Poirot; The Upper Hand;* Rosemary in *The Old Devils* (mini-series); Phoenix in *The Riff Raff Element* (two series); *All or Nothing at All* (mini-series); India Wilkes in *Scarlett* (mini-series); *Space Precinct; Circle of Deceit;* Christina Rossetti in *The Late Show; Daisies in December; The Vet.*

Films: Cornelia in *An Unsuitable Job for a Woman.*

Address: c/o The Richard Stone Partnership. Lives in Kent. m. director Steve Goldie (dis); 1 d. Sama (from m.). Partner: Albert. Pets: A cat called Tom. Hobbies: Reading, gardening, painting.

Pippa Guard

GUBBA, Tony

David Anthony Gubba. Sports commentator. b. Manchester, 23 September 1943. National newspaper reporter before joining the BBC as a correspondent in North West. Switched to sports department 1972.

TV: *Grandstand; Sportsnight; Match of the Day;* soccer World Cups; summer and winter Olympic Games; has commentated on hockey, bobsleigh, cycling, rowing and ice skating; currently football commentator and reporter, and commentator on squash and table tennis.

Address: c/o BBC TV Sport. Lives in Maidenhead, Berkshire. m. 1969 (dis 1982); 2 d. Claire Louise (b. 1970), Elizabeth Mary (Libby) (b. 1972). Pets: Goldfish. Hobbies: Salmon fishing, golf.

Tony Gubba

GUINNESS, Alec

Alec Guinness de Cuffe. Actor. b. London, 2 April 1914. CBE, 1955; knighted, 1959; Companion of Honour, 1994. Advertising copy writer (1933 4). Trained at the Fay Compton School of Dramatic Art.

TV: *The Wicked Scheme of Jebel Jacks; The Ed Sullivan Show; The Actor;* Malvolio in *Twelfth Night; Solo; Conversation at Night; Caesar and Cleopatra; Gift of Friendship;* George Smiley in *Tinker, Tailor, Soldier, Spy* and *Smiley's People; Lovesick; Edwin;* Father Quixote in *Monsignor Quixote; Tales from Hollywood* (Performance); *A Foreign Field; QED: Plastic Fantastic* (narrator); James in *Eskimo Day.*

Films: *Evensong; Great Expectations; Oliver Twist; Kind Hearts and Coronets; A Run for Your Money; Last Holiday; The Mudlark; The Lavender Hill Mob; The Man in the White Suit; The Card; The Captain's Paradise; Malta Story; Father Brown; The Stratford Adventure; To Paris with Love; The Prisoner; Rowlandson's England* (narrator); *The Ladykillers; The Swan; Bridge on the River Kwai; Barnacle Bill; The Horse's Mouth; The Scapegoat; Our Man in Havana; Tunes of Glory; A Majority of One; HMS Defiant; Lawrence of Arabia; The Fall of the Roman Empire; Situation Hopeless… but not serious; Doctor Zhivago; Hotel Paradiso; The Quiller Memorandum; The Comedians; Cromwell; Scrooge; Brother Sun, Sister Moon; Hitler: The Last Ten Days; Murder by Death; Star Wars; The Empire Strikes Back; Raise the Titanic!; Little Lord Fauntleroy; Lovesick; Return of the Jedi; A Passage to India; Little Dorrit; A Handful of Dust; Prospero's Books; Kafka.* **Books:** *Blessings in Disguise* (autobiography, 1985).

Awards: TV: BAFTA Best Actor on TV award twice, for *Tinker, Tailor, Soldier, Spy* (1979) and *Smiley's People* (1982). Films: Best Actor Oscar and BAFTA award for *Bridge on the River Kwai* (1959); Special Oscar for services to films (1980).

Address: c/o London Management. m. 20 June 1938 actress Merula Salaman; 1 s. actor Matthew.

Alec Guinness

Peter Gunn

GUNN, Peter

Peter Stuart Gunn. Actor. b. St Anne's-on-Sea, Lancashire, 13 February 1963. Trained at RADA (1983-5, Fabia Drake Prize for Comedy winner, 1985).

TV: *Harry Enfield's Television Programme;* Ned Kellett in *Flying Lady;* Eddie Cleary in *The Paradise Club;* Malcolm in *Casualty;* Devlin in *Love Hurts;* Sgt Oliphant in *The Inspector Alleyn Mysteries;* Paul Shaw in *The Bill;* Clive in *Minder;* Pyke in *Pie in the Sky;* Rawlings Assistant in *Just William;* Private Clayton in *Sharpe's Company; The Russ Abbot Show;* Simon Thorpe in *Heartburn Hotel.*

Films: Frankie in *Treacle;* Bonner in *Resurrection;* Nicky in *Funny Bones;* Terry in *Blue Juice;* Tommy in *A Pint o' Bitter;* The Scientist in *Soup;* Simmo in *Brassed Off;* Fabian in *Twelfth Night.*

Radio: Member of the BBC Radio repertory company (1991-2).

Address: c/o Barry Brown & Partner. Lives in Walthamstow, London. Hobbies: 'Kites, cooking, cars, clothes, cycling – anything that begins with a C.'

Gwyneth Guthrie

GUTHRIE, Gwyneth

Gwyneth Guthrie. Actress. b. Ayr, 28 April 1936. Took to the stage at the age of four and, eight years later, made her professional début on radio in *Scottish Children's* Hour with 'Auntie Kathleen' Garscadden. She also acted in various radio plays before leaving school, enrolling at Skerry's Secretarial College, in Glasgow, and working in an office. She left to train at the Royal Scottish Academy of Music and Drama, where she won the James Bridie Silver Medal. Stage plays include *For Love or Money* (Scottish tour).

TV: *Sutherland's Law; Hill o' the Red Fox; Degree of Uncertainty; The Lost Tribe; The Reunion; The Prime of Miss Jean Brodie; Something's Got to Give;* Mrs (Mary) Mack and Florence Crossan in *Take the High Road/High Road* (1982-); *Now You See It;* Mary Cuthbertson in *Doctor Finlay.*

Films: *Privilege; Years Ahead.*

Radio: *Scottish Children's Hour; Book at Bedtime* (storyteller); title role in *Mary Queen of Scots.*

Address: c/o Ruth Tarko Agency. Lives in Darvel, Ayrshire. m. John Borland; 3 d. Karen, Debbie, Olwen.

Lucy Gutteridge

GUTTERIDGE, Lucy

Lucy Gutteridge. Actress. b. London, 28 November 1956. Trained at the Central School of Speech and Drama. Stage plays include *Nicholas Nickleby* (RSC, London and Broadway), *A King of Alaska* (Los Angeles) and *King Arthur* (opera, Buxton Theatre Festival).

TV: *The Hitchhiker; The Devil's Crown; The Marrying Kind; End of Season; Betzy; Renoir My Father; Tales of the Unexpected; Sweet Wine of Youth; Love in a Cold Climate; The Seven Dials Mystery; Nicholas Nickleby;* Belle in *A Christmas Carol* (TVM); *Hitler's SS: Portrait of Evil* (TVM); *The Trouble with Spies* (TVM); *Edge of the Wind; Till We Meet Again; The Woman He Loved* (mini-series).

Films: *The Greek Tycoon; Little Gloria; Merlin and the Sword; Elephant's Child; Top Secret!; Fire In Eden.* Address: c/o Spotlight. m. actor Andrew Hawkins (dis); 1 d. Isabella.

Reg Gutteridge

GUTTERIDGE, Reg

Reg Gutteridge. Commentator. b. Islington, North London, 29 March 1924. OBE, 1995. Father Dick and Uncle Jack were boxing instructors. Won several amateur titles but lost a leg during the Second World War Normandy campaign and turned to journalism. Joined London *Evening News* in 1938 and later became its boxing correspondent, staying for 41 years.

TV: TV boxing commentator; commentary on six Olympic Games and greyhound racing; Home Box Office and ABC TV in US; *10 Million* (co-presenter, consumer series); *Punch Drunk* (voice only, series, 1993); *Saint & Greavsie's World of Sport* (Carlton only, series, 1995).

Books: *Let's Be Honest* (Jimmy Greaves biography); *Boxing – The Great Ones; The Big Punchers.*

Awards: TRIC Sports Presenter of the Year award (1991). Address: c/o Bagenal Harvey Organisation. Lives in Barnet, Hertfordshire. m. Constance; 2 d. Sammi, Sally. Pets: Cats. Hobbies: Golf, theatre.

Claire Hackett

HACKETT, Claire

Claire Hackett. Actress. Trained at RADA. Stage rôles include Viola in *Twelfth Night*, Stella in *A Streetcar Named Desire*, Perdita in *The Winter's Tale* and Ophelia in *Hamlet.*

TV: *William Tell* (US title *Crossbow*); *Dawn and the Candidate* (4-Play); Annie in *Growing Rich* (series); Linda Uphill in *A Touch of Frost* (series); Tilly in *Gallowglass* (mini-series); Lindsey Hewitt in *The Bill;* Heather McKinnon in *Medics; Terraces; Men of the Month* (Screen Two); Deborah Wiley in *Cracker;* Donna in *Into the Fire* (mini-series).

Films: *Itch; A Nasty Story; Women at War*, Linda in *Dancin' thru the Dark.*

Address: c/o Annette Stone Associates.

HADDINGTON, Ellie

Ellie Haddington. Actress. b. Aberdeen, 17 February 1955. Trained at the Bristol Old Vic Theatre School (1975-7). Stage plays include *Richard III* and *Mother Courage* (both RSC), *The Sea* (National Theatre),

Educating Rita (title rôle, Octagon Theatre, Bolton) and *Female Parts* (one-woman show, Manchester).
TV: Billy Walker's girlfriend (1984) and Josie Clark (1994-) in *Coronation Street; Muck and Brass; Unnatural Causes; Loving Hazel; The Lorelei; Ball on the Slates;* Katherine Geach in *Wycliffe;* Mrs Barnes in *Cracker: The Big Crunch; In Suspicious Circumstances;* Diane in *Kavanagh QC.*
Radio: Many plays and *Morning Story.*
Awards: Theatre: *Manchester Evening News* Best Actress award.
Address: c/o Scott Marshall. Lives in London. Hobbies: 'Watching the garden grow.'

Ellie Haddington

HADDY, Anne
Anne Haddy. Actress. b. Quorn, South Australia, 5 October 1927. Her art teacher at Adelaide High School was Keith Michell, who became a famed actor. Stage plays include *Hostile Witness, The Far Country, The Love, The Workout, The Entertainer, Hay Fever, The Glass Menagerie, Misalliance, Twelfth Night, Cannonade of Bells, Say Who You Are, The Old Bachelor, Fallen Angel, Out of Crocodile, Richard III, Gaslight, Arms and the Man, Tchin-Tchin, The Restoration of Arnold Middleton, Oh, Killara, The Two of Us, 'Tis Pity She's a Whore, Down Under, Brass Hat, In Praise of Love, The Plough and the Stars, Double Edge, Father's Day, Bodies, Pillars of Society* and *Born Yesterday.*

Ellie Haddington

TV: *Hunter; Homicide; Division 4; Matlock; Play School; Dynasty; Over There; Lade and the Law; Crisis; The Evil Touch; Boney and the Bikeman; Behind the Legend; Boney and the Burial Tree; Seven Little Australians; Three Men of the City; Ben Hall; Boos and Cheers; Case for the Defence; Certain Women; Hunted; Chopper Squad; No Room to Move; Glenview High; A Place In the World;* Alice Hemmings in *Prisoner* (UK title *Prisoner: Cell Block H);* Toni Lee in *Skyways; A Family Affair;* Aggie Topp in *A Town Like Alice;* Louise Francis in *Cop Shop; Punishment; The Restless Years; 1915;* Rosie Palmer in *Sons and Daughters;* Helen Daniels in *Neighbours* (1985-); Mrs Spencer Grant in *The Private War of Lucinda Smith* (mini-series).
Films: Dr Kirk in *The Fourth Wish; The Alternative; Newsfront; Fighting Back.*
Address: c/o International Casting Service & Associates. Lives in Melbourne. m. 1st Max Dimmitt, 2nd actor James Condon; 1 d. Jane, 1 s. Tony (from 1st m.).

Anne Haddy

HAILES, Gary
Gary Hailes. Actor. b. North London, 4 November 1965. Trained at the Anna Scher Theatre School. Stage shows include *Doctor on the Boil, Aladdin, Jack and the Beanstalk, Gollocks, A Bedfull of Foreigners* and *Strip Poker.*
TV: *Pinocchio; Nobody's Hero; Grange Hill; Contact; Stars of the Rollerskate Disco; Woodentop* (pilot for *The Bill,* 1983); *Born and Bred; Sorry; The Other One; Nobody's Hero; Murder with Mirrors* (TVM); Barry Clark in *EastEnders.*
Films: *S.O.S. Titanic; Revolution.*
Radio: *The Amazing Mr Jupiter* (BBC Radio 4); *The Scrap Iron* (BBC Radio 5); writer of additional material for *The News Huddlines* (BBC Radio 4).
Address: c/o Spotlight. Lives in North London. Partner: Presenter Samantha Jones. Pets: Yorkshire terrier called Benji. Hobbies: Weight training, Batman (comics, movies memorabilia), rock 'n' roll.

Gary Hailes

HAINSWORTH, Richard
Richard Hainsworth. actor. Trained at the Guildford School of Acting (winner, Best Musical Actor, 1982). Stage productions include *Godspell* (Bloomsbury Theatre), *High Society* (Victoria Palace) and *Bring Me Smiles* (New End Theatre).
TV: John in *To Have and to Hold;* Doc and Bodyguard in *Red Dwarf;* Ricky Hayward in *Crimewatch UK;* Dick, Dog Handler in *The Bill;* Alec Henderson in *The Upper Hand* (series); Paul Fitzroy 'Bulldog' Drummond in *Jupiter Moon* (BSB); Pete the Pizza Man in *Grange Hill;* Don Dixon in *Casualty.*
Address: c/o Spotlight.

Richard Hainsworth

HALE, Gareth
Gareth Hale. Comedian. b. London, 15 January 1953. Student PT teacher before joining Fundation, also forming a double-act with fellow-member Norman Pace and performing on the fringe cabaret circuit before gaining their own radio and TV series. Stage shows include Hale & Pace UK tours.
TV: *Pushing Up Daisies; Coming Next; The Young Ones; Live from the Palladium; Saturday Live* (host); *Just for Laughs; The Saturday Gang; The Management* (sitcom); *Royal Variety Performance* (1987); *Hale & Pace* (1988- , Golden Rose of Montreux and the Press Jury Prize winner, 1989); *Doctor Who; Trading Places* (guest); *Hale & Pace – The Business;* Chief Supt Andy Dalziel in *A Pinch of Snuff* (mini-series, 1994); *Hale & Pace – The Tasty Morsels* (compilation series, 1995); *The Royal Variety Performance* (1995).
Videos: *Hale & Pace Live in Concert.*
Books: *Falsies; The Hale & Pace Book of Writes and Rons* (both with Norman Pace).
Address: c/o International Artistes. m. Deborah; 2 d. Sian, Cara.

Gareth Hale

Stuart Hall

HALL, Stuart

Stuart Hall. Presenter. b. Ashton-under-Lyne, Lancashire, 25 December 1929. Gained an MA (Hons) from Manchester University and, after National Service, joined the family business as director of catering. Played professional football for Crystal Palace (1953). Also raced cars at Oulton Park and Silverstone. Entered broadcasting when he complained about the commentaries and the BBC invited him to join their commentating team on *Sports Report* (1959), at the same time becoming a general reprter for *Radio Newsreel.* Succeeded David Vinc as presenter of *It's a Knockout* on TV in 1972.
TV: *Look North* and *North West Tonight* (presenter, BBC North West regional news magazine, 1965-90); *Nationwide North West; It's a Knockout* (1972-82); *Jeux Sans Frontières* (1972-82); *It's a Royal Knockout* (presenter and co-producer, 1987); *Travellers Check* (Granada only); *Stuart Hall's Christmas in Bosnia* (presenter-producer); *Stuart Hall Remembers Flanders* (presenter-producer); *Chefs Sans Frontières* (presenter-producer, Granada only); Time of Your Life Presenter in *Micky Love* (Rik Mayall Presents); *Quiz Night* (presenter).
Radio: *Sports Report; Radio Newsreel; Sports Reports* (BBC World Service).
Books: *Stuart Hall's Look North Cook Book.*
Address: c/o Jane Hughes Management. m. 1960 Francesca; 1 d. actress Francesca, 1 s. lawyer Daniel. Pets: A cocker spaniel called Gus. Hobbies: Collecting antique clocks, antiques, motor cars.

John Hallam

HALLAM, John

John Hallam. Actor. b. Lisburn, 28 October 1941. Trained at RADA. Stage plays include National Theatre and RSC productions.
TV: Johnny Cracken in *Randall & Hopkirk (Deceased); Devil's Crown; The Regiment; Wings; Arnhem; The Story of an Escape; Cicero; The Pallisers; The Mallens; A.D.* (mini-series); Barnsey (prisoner) in *EastEnders;* Cedric Crackenthorpe in *Miss Marple: The 4.50 from Paddington;* Matthew in *Rides;* Roderick Frew in *Lovejoy;* Gorgiano in *The Memoirs of Sherlock Holmes;* Mark Wise in *99-1* (series, 1995).
Films: *Hennessy; Love and Bullitts; Murphy's War; The Last Valley; Villain; Antony and Cleopatra; Burden of Proof; Nicholas and Alexandra; Flash Gordon; Dragon Slayer; Under Capricorn; Lifeforce; King David; Santa Claus.* Address: c/o ICM.

Steve Halliwell

HALLIWELL, Steve

Stephen Harold Halliwell. Actor/Writer. b. Bury, Lancashire, 19 March 1954. Apprentice engineer, gardener, cotton mill and paper mill worker, before training at Mountview Theatre School. Founder member of Interchange Theatre, Bury (actor, director and writer, 1981-4). Stage plays include *The Only Way Out* (Royal Court), *All My Joy* (writer, M6 Theatre Company North West tour), *A Midsummer Night's Dream, Wuthering Heights, Spring and Port Wine* and *Love on the Dole* (all Oldham Coliseum).
TV: *Pickersgill People; Donovan Dugdale;* PC Goole in *All Creatures Great and Small* (two Christmas specials); Stephen in *Brookside;* Peter Bishop in *The Practice* (two series); *Threads; First and Last* (Screen Two); Brian in *Merrihill Millionaires* (Screen Two); Clem in *Children of Winter;* Bob Cairns in *Coronation Street;* Chief Fire Officer in *Cracker;* Inspector Newall in *Just Us;* Inspector Halliwell in *That Nice Mrs Merton; Fair Game* (Screen Two); Terry Lucas in *Medics;* Zak Dingle in *Emmerdale* (1994-).
Films: Russian Courier in *The Fourth Protocol.*
Address: c/o Barbara Pemberton Associates. Lives in Burnley, Lancashire. m. 1st Susan Woods (dis), 2nd artist Valerie; 1 d. Charlotte Jane (from 2nd m.), 2 step-s. John James, Nicholas William (from 2nd m.). Pets: A cat called Leo. Hobbies: Pubs, rhythm and blues, reading, walking, cooking, philosophy, pub quizzes.

James Hamill

HAMILL, James

James Hamill. Actor. b. Los Angeles, 11 August 1958. Trained at Circle in the Square, New York, and the Central School of Speech and Drama, London. Stage plays include *Peer Gynt, Golden Boy, Sexual Perversity in Chicago, Death of a Salesman, A Midsummer Night's Dream, The Odd Couple: Female Version* (as Jesus) and *All My Sons.*
TV: Jeff Conroy in *Knots Landing;* Philip in *The Making of a Male Model* (TVM); The Dungeonmaster in *Knightmare;* Dan Jorgenson in *Dead Men's Tales;* Customs Officer in *A View from the Bridge;* I C Charisma in *Pigsty;* Brewster Hawkes in *Timebusters;* Weasel in *Hangar 17* (two series); Farrell in *Strange but True.* TV commercials: M&Ms (US); Galak chocolate (Holland); Heidelberg (Denmark).
Films: Sean David in *Search and Recover;* Rick Driver in *Murder on the Moon.* Address: c/o Langford Associates. Lives in London. m. Ute; 1 d. Julia (b. 1995). Hobbies: Bee-keeping, snorkelling.

Suzanna Hamilton

HAMILTON, Suzanna

Suzanna Hamilton. Actress. b. 1960. Joined the Anna Scher Theatre School and made her professional début at the age of 13 in the film *Swallows and Amazons,* followed by *Wild Cats of St Trinian's.* Trained at the Central School of Speech and Drama.
TV: *Wish Me Luck; Streetwise; Murder East, Murder West; The Ruth Rendell Mysteries: A New Lease*

of Death; Boon; The House of Bernarda Alba; Mrs Cryer in Inspector Morse: Absolute Conviction; Karen Goodliffe in Casualty (series, 1993-4); Gaye Fraser in The Bill; Joanna Sparks in McCallum (pilot).
Films: Swallows and Amazons; Wild Cats of St Trinian's; Izz in Tess; Brimstone and Treacle; Julia in '1984'; Karen Creasy in Wetherby; Felicity in Out of Africa; Veronica Puddephat in A Masculine Ending. Address: c/o Julian Belfrage Associates.

Susan Hampshire

HAMPSHIRE, Susan
Susan Hampshire. Actress. b. London, 12 May 1938.
TV: What Katy Did; A for Andromeda; Fleur in The Forsyte Saga (series); Vanity Fair; An Ideal Husband; The First Churchills; The Lady Is a Liar; The Improbable Mr Clayville; Dr Jekyll and Mr Hyde (TVM); The Pallisers; Barchester Chronicles; Dick Turpin (TVM); Leaving; Going to Pot; Natasha Bancroft in Don't Tell Father (series, 1992); My Garden and My Secret Garden II (both This Morning).
Films: The Woman in the Hall; Expresso Bongo; Upstairs and Downstairs; Idle on Parade (US title Idol on Parade); During One Night; The Long Shadow; Night Must Fall; The Three Lives of Thomasina; Wonderful Life (US title Swingers' Paradise); Paris in August; The Fighting Prince of Donegal; The Trygon Factor; The Violent Enemy; Monte Carlo or Bust! (US title Those Daring Young Men in Their Jaunty Jalopies); David Copperfield (TVM only in US); Time for Loving; Baffled!; Malpertuis (UK title The Legend of Doom House); Living Free; Roses Rouges et Piments Verts (US title The Lonely Woman); Neither the Sea nor the Sand; Bang!
Books: Susan's Story; The Maternal Instinct; Lucy Jane on Television; Trouble Free Gardening; Every Letter Counts.
Address: c/o Chatto and Linnit. m. 1st Eddie Kulukundis, 2nd French director Pierre Granier-Deferre (dis); 1 s. Christopher, 1 d. Victoria (dec) (both from 1st m.). Hobbies: Gardening, writing.

Meryl Hampton

HAMPTON, Meryl
Meryl Hampton. Actress. b. Chester, 26 August 1952. Trained at Guildhall School of Music and Drama.
TV: Softly Softly; Knock for Knock; Letty; The GPs; Death of the Heart; Crossroads; Brookside; First and Last; Listen to Me; Harry Enfield's Television Programme; Mrs Francis in The Ruth Rendell Mysteries: An Unwanted Woman; Margy Robinson in The Bill; Anna Becket in Casualty; Marie McKenner in Peak Practice; Gloria Burton in The Bill. Address: c/o Sue Hammer Personal Management.

HANCOCK, Sheila
Sheila Hancock. Actress. b. Blackgang, Isle of Wight, 22 February 1933. Trained at RADA. Stage plays include The Anniversary (West End) and Entertaining Mr Sloane (Broadway).
TV: The Rag Trade; Entertaining Mr Sloane; The Bed Sit Girl; Horizontal Hold (Playhouse); Thelma Teesdale in Mr Digby Darling (two series, 1969); Horizontal Hold; The Mating Machine; Now Take My Wife; But Seriously – It's Sheila Hancock; God Our Help; Obsessions (narrator); Mag Plant in Gone to Seed (series, 1992); Snapshots (subject); Frances in Brighton Belles (pilot, 1993, and series, 1993-4); Dowager Duchess in The Buccaneers (series, 1995); Sarah Ryan in Dangerous Lady (series, 1995).
Films: Light Up the Sky; The Girl on the Boat; Night Must Fall; Doctor in Love; Carry On Cleo; Mrs Gamble in The Moon Spinners; The Anniversary; The Lion, the Witch and the Wardrobe (voice only); Take a Girl like You; Mrs Rothery in Buster; Regina in Hawks; Vera in 3 Men and a Little Lady.
Books: Ramblings of an Actress.
Address: c/o London Management. m. 1st actor Alec Ross (dec), 2nd actor John Thaw; 2 d. actress Melanie Thaw (from 1st m.), Joanne, 1 step-d. actress Abigail Thaw (both from 2nd m.).

Sheila Hancock

HANN, Judith
Judith Hann. Presenter. b. Littleover, Derbyshire, 8 September 1942. Gained a BSc in zoology at Durham University, then trained as a journalist with Westminster Press.
TV: Tomorrow's World; Tomorrow's World in Berlin; Watchdog Healthcheck (two series, 1995-6).
Books: But What about the Children?; Family Scientist; The Perfect Baby?; Judith Hann's Total Health Plan; The Food of Love; How Science Works.
Awards: Twice winner of the Glaxo Award for science writers. Address: c/o Dave Winslett Entertainments/BBC. m. John Exelby; 2 s. Daniel, Jake. Hobbies: Walking, reading, food.

Judith Hann

HANRAHAN, Will
William Hanrahan. Presenter. b. Liverpool, 5 March 1959.
TV: Watchdog (1989-91); Family Matters (1989-91); On the Line (1990); Good Morning... with Anne & Nick (consumer spot, 1991-5); Verdict; The Good Food Show (series, 1995); Good Morning Summer (series, 1995).
Radio: BBC Radio 5 Live and London News Radio presenter (both 1995-).
Awards: Radio: Local Radio Personality of the Year (1985).
Address: c/o The Roseman Organisation. Lives in the Cotswolds. m. Hobbies: Sport.

Will Hanrahan

HARDCASTLE, Diana

Diana Hardcastle

Diana Hardcastle. Actress. Gained a degree in English from Bristol University. Trained at the Central School of Speech and Drama. Stage plays include *The Winter's Tale, The Two Gentlemen of Verona, Les Liaisons Dangereuses* (all RSC).

TV: *East Lynne; Reilly — Ace of Spies; Charlie; The House; Love Song; Frankie and Johnnie;* Louise in *First among Equals;* Edwina in *The Fortunes of War,* Patsy Redfern in *That's Love* (four series, 1988-92); Vikki Brown in *Punchdrunk* (pilot 1992, series 1993); Kate Newsome in *Boon;* Claire Millinder in *Resnick: Rough Treatment* (mini-series, 1993); Rona Birch in *Catherine Cookson's The Tide of Life* (mini-series, 1996). Address: c/o The Richard Stone Partnership. Partner: Actor Tom Wilkinson.

HARDIE, Kate

Kate Hardie

Kate Oddie. Actress. Daughter of actor-writer Bill Oddie (qv).

TV: Donna in *A Small Dance* (TVM); Tessa in *The Men's Room;* Decima Pomero in *The Inspector Alleyn Mysteries; Safe* (ScreenPlay); Vicky Gallant in *Smokescreen* (series, 1994); Sue Stephens in *Open Fire* (drama-documentary); Susan Christie in *Beyond Reason.*

Films: *Runners; Mona Lisa; The Krays; Under the Sun.* Address: c/o Jonathan Altaras Associates.

HARDIMAN, Terrence

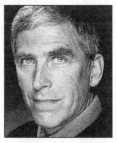

Kate Hardie

Terrence Hardiman. Actor. b. London, 6 April 1937. Many RSC productions on stage.

TV: Ronnie Corbett pilot; *Colditz;* Lysenko in *The Lysenko Affair; The Sinking of HMS Victoria;* rSoftly Softly; Crown Court; Ladykillers; Garden of Inheritance; God's Outlaw; Crawley in *Rebecca; Diary of a Nobody; Skorpion;* Reinhardt in *Secret Army; The Oresteia; My Father's House; All in Good Faith; Fresh Fields; Late Starter; Ladies in Charge; Bergerac; Home to Roost; The Bretts; The Charmer; Hannay; Inspector Morse; Wish Me Luck; This Is David Lander; Minder; Underbelly; Moon and Son; Agatha Christie's Poirot; Berlin Break; Agatha Christie's Miss Marple; Surgical Spirit; The Brittas Empire; Casualty; Keeping Up Appearances;* Michael Winner's *True Crimes;* Commander Chiswick in *Prime Suspect 3; Cadfael; Goodnight Sweetheart; The Ruth Rendell Mysteries: The Strawberry Tree; The Demon Headmaster; Independent Man;* Military Officer in *Circles of Deceit.*
Address: c/o Scott Marshall. Lives in London. m. actress Rowena Cooper.

HARDING, John

Terrence Hardiman

John Harding. Actor/Writer. b. Ruislip, Middlesex, 20 June 1948. Trained at Manchester University's drama department (1966-9) and gained a BA (Hons).

TV: *For Sylvia* (also co-writer, with John Burrows); *Edward the Seventh; Do You Dig It?; Three Men in a Boat; My Brother's Keeper; Bognor;* Dorimant in *The Man of Mode; The Double Dealer;* Paul in *Babytalk; Reluctant Chickens; Doodlebug* in *Sweet Echo; Swallows and Amazons for Ever; Goodbye Mr Chips;* Bernard in *The Young Visiters;* Luis in *C.A.T.S. Eyes;* Governor's Aid in *Mr & Mrs Edgehill; Unnatural Causes;* Hitchcock in *Scoop; Boon; Gentlemen and Players; Campion; Agatha Christie's Poirot;* Dave Smith in *Brookside; On the Up; Trauma* (also writer); *The Mixer; The Darling Buds of May;* DI Dunford in *Birds of a Feather;* Sam Martin in *Brookside* (1994); Charles in *The Man Who Didn't Believe in Ghosts* (Chiller); *Faith; Daisies in December; Faith in the Future; Rumble.*
Films: *Give My Regards to Broad Street; Little Dorrit; The Fool.* Address: c/o Scott Marshall.

HARDY, Robert

John Harding

Robert Hardy. Actor. b. Cheltenham, Gloucestershire, 29 October 1925. CBE.

TV: *David Copperfield; Mogul; The Troubleshooters; An Age of Kings; Spread of the Eagle; Daniel Deronda;* Robert Dudley in *Elizabeth R; Manhunt; Edward the Seventh; Walk with Destiny; Churchill's People;* Mussolini in *Caesar and Claretta; The Picardy Affair* (writer-presenter); *The History of the Longbow* (writer-presenter); *Heritage* (presenter); *Upstairs, Downstairs; The Duchess of Duke Street; Victorian Scandals; The Secret Agent; Bill Brand; The Peterloo Massacre* (presenter); *Supernatural; Warriors Return; Horses in Our Blood* (writer and presenter); Siegfried Farnon in *All Creatures Great and Small* (series, 1978-90); *Between the Covers; Twelfth Night; Speed King; Fothergill;* title role in *Winston Churchill — The Wilderness Years; The Cleopatras; Gordon of Khartoum* (writer-presenter); *The Far Pavilions; Jenny's War; Northanger Abbey; Shades of Darkness; Death of the Heart; Paying Guests; Hot Metal; The Woman He Loved* (mini-series); *Sherlock Holmes: Master Blackmailer;* Winston Churchill in *Bomber Harris* (drama-documentary); Andrew Baydon in *Inspector Morse: Twilight of the Gods;* Arthur Brooke in *Middlemarch* (series, 1994); Sir Herbert Hamilton in *Bramwell* (series, 1995); *Look at the State We're In!; Legal System; Gulliver's Travels* (mini-series).
Films: *Demons of the Mind; The Spy Who Came in from the Cold; How I Won the War; Ten Rillington Place; Yellow Dog; Frog; Dark Places; Young Winston; Le Silencieux; Gawain and the Green Knight; La Gifle; Robin Hood; The Shooting Party; Paris by Night; Sense and Sensibility.*
Books: *Longbow: A Social and Military History.* Address: c/o Chatto and Linnit. m. 1st (dis), 2nd actress Sally Pearson (actress Sally Cooper) (dis); 2 d. actress Emma, Justine, 1 s. Paul.

Robert Hardy

HARGREAVES, David

David Hargreaves. Actor. b. New Mills, Derbyshire, 1940. Worked as a schoolteacher before taking a teaching course at the Central School of Speech and Drama. Stage plays include *A View from the Bridge* (Young Vic), plus RSC (1963-5) and National Theatre Company (1965-7).
TV: *The XYY Man; Armchair Thriller; Strangers; Stronger than the Sun* (Play for Today); *The House of Carridus; Sally Ann; A Leap in the Dark; The Professionals; Minor Complications; Together; Juliet Bravo; Sorry, I'm a Stranger Here Myself; Science Workshop* (presenter); *Play School* (presenter); *Forever Young; Shades of Darkness; A Brother's Tale; Mistress Masham's Repose; Bulman; The Seagreen Man; Shine on Harvey Moon;* Derek Owen in *Albion Market;* Tom Houghton in *1914 All Out; Closing Ranks; Truckers; The Place of Safety; Erasmus Microman; No Further Cause for Concern;* Colin in *Making Out; Hard Cases; Saracen; She's Been Away; All Creatures Great and Small; Agatha Christie's Poirot; Madly in Love;* Arthur Scargill in *The Miners' Strike; TECX; The Conversion of St Paul; Kingdom Come; Keeper; Woof!; Josie; Bergerac; Thatcher: The Final Days;* Charlie Denby in *Heartbeat;* Bill in *Casualty;* Alan Slater in *The Bill;* Supt Harper in *The Inspector Alleyn Mysteries;* Mr Waters in *Harry;* Dr Philip Day in *Fighting for Gemma* (drama-documentary); Rev Neil Winters in *Peak Practice;* Jack Brigson in *The Bill;* Dennis Martin in *Casualty;* Mr Feast in *The Ruth Rendell Mysteries: Vanity Dies Hard* (mini-series, 1995); Picture Editor in *Hetty Wainthropp Investigates.*
Address: c/o The Richard Stone Partnership. m. actress Chloe Ashcroft.

David Hargreaves

HARGREAVES, Johanna

Johanna Louise Hargreaves. Actress/Presenter. b. Libya, 18 June 1963. Daughter of Allan Hargreaves, a former Thames Television reporter and head of talks at Capital Radio. Gained an A-level in theatre studies. Trained at the Anna Scher Theatre School.
TV: *Johnny Jarvis* (series); *Round and Round; Let There Be Love; Saturday Action; S.W.A.L.K.; Radio Phoenix; The Black Report; The Quiet Days of Mrs Stafford; Two People; Tenko; The Glory Boys; Late Starter* (series); Hilda in *Shine on Harvey Moon;* Jane in *The Lenny Henry Show;* Sandra Blair in *Take the High Road;* Henrietta in *The Little Princess;* Karen in *Dramarama: Direct Action;* Marilyn in *Slinger's Day;* Gale in *Casualty; Filthy Rich and Catflap; Red Dwarf;* Michelle in *Hard Cases;* Mrs Higgins in *The Bill;* June Marks in *Bergerac; Behind the Screen;* Debbie in *Casualty; Stay Lucky;* Linda Jordan in *Between the Lines.*
Films: *A Hazard of Hearts.* Address: c/o Evans and Reiss. Lives in London. Single.

Johanna Hargreaves

HARKER, Caroline

Caroline Harker. Actress. b. 21 March 1966. Daughter of actor Richard Owens and actress Polly Adams; sister of actress Susannah (qv). Trained at the Central School of Speech and Drama (1986-9).
TV: *Chancer; Casualty;* Laura in *Growing Rich* (series, 1992); WPC Hazel Wallace in *A Touch of Frost* (four series, 1992, 1994, 1995, 1996); Tory Lovell in *Jilly Cooper's Riders* (mini-series, 1993); *Covington Cross;* Celia Brooke in *Middlemarch* (series, 1994); Hon Lucy Courtney in *Honey for Tea* (series, 1994). Address: c/o Peters Fraser & Dunlop

Caroline Harker

HARKER, Susannah

Susannah Harker. Actress. b. London, 26 April 1965. Daughter of actor Richard Owens and actress Polly Adams; sister of actress Caroline (qv). Stage plays include *Racing Demon* (National Theatre) and *The Importance of Being Earnest* (Aldwych Theatre).
TV: *The Lady's not for Burning;* Angela in *Troubles;* Linda in *The Fear* (series); *Till We Meet Again; Chancer* (series); Mattie Storin in *House of Cards* (mini-series, 1990) and *To Play the King* (in flashback, mini-series, 1993); Irene St Claire in *The Crucifer of Blood* (TVM); Dinah Morris in *Adam Bede;* Adelaide Savage in *The Memoirs of Sherlock Holmes;* Holly Moreton in *Faith* (series, 1994); Jane Bennet in *Pride and Prejudice* (serial, 1995).
Films: *Burke and Wills; Wetherby; White Mischief; A Dry White Season.*
Address: c/o Peters Fraser & Dunlop. Partner: Actor Iain Glen (qv), 1 s. Finlay (b. 1995).

Susannah Harker

HARPER, Kate

Kate Harper. Actress. Trained at the University of California (Best Actress Award winner). US and UK Equity actors' union member.
TV: *Oppenheimer; Dylan; Diamonds; Water Lillies* (Play for Today); *Bright Eyes* (Play for Today); *Tales of the Unexpected; Shades of Darkness; Have a Nice Death; Lace* (mini-series); *Master of the Game* (mini-series); *Hold the Dream* (mini-series); *Tender Is the Night; Bergerac;* Felicity Grenville in *The Two Mrs Grenvilles; Hedgehog Wedding;* Paula Wilson in *Pulaski* (series); *Perfect Scoundrels; Spatz; The Upper Hand; She-Wolf of London; Agatha Christie's Poirot;* Patti Wilcox in *Inspector Morse: The Death of the Self;* Mrs Leroy in *Frank Stubbs Promotes;* Iona Datch in *Space Precinct.*
Films: *Little Lord Fauntleroy; Reds; Invitation to the Wedding; Murder Story; Batman; Dinosaurs; Night Watch; Passion of Darkly Noon; Surviving Picasso.* Address: c/o Burdett-Coutts Associates.

Kate Harper

HARRIES, Davyd

Davyd Harries

David Harries. Actor. b. Porthcawl, 31 January 1937. Won a scholarship to train at RADA. RSC stage productions include *Henry V, The Thwarting of Baron Bolligrew* and *The Investigation*.
TV: *Big Breadwinner Hog; Cousin Bette; Dombey and Son; The Dumb Waiter; Tom Brown's School-days;* Sgt Ridgeway in *Hunter's Walk* (three series, 1973-6); *Warship; Churchill's People; Anna Karenina; Accident; The Racing Game; Doctor Who; Goodbye Darling; Coming Out; Secret Army; John Brown's Body; Swish of the Curtain; Suez; Fatal Spring; Astercote; Dark Secret; Strangers; You're Only Young Twice; Angels; Ennals Point; Imaginary Friends; The Citadel; S.W.A.L.K.; In Loving Memory; That's My Boy; There Comes a Time; On Young Shoulders; Travelling Man; Crimewatch UK; Oliver Twist; Jackanory Playhouse; That Uncertain Feeling; Strife; Hannay; My Husband and I; Bergerac; The Bill; Making News; Merlin; Watt on Earth; Casualty* (two roles); *The Knock; Broke; Care; You Me and It; Science Fiction: Hair Soup;* Mr Jackson in *Anna Lee;* Presiding Judge in *Cadfael;* Sam Lester in *The Chief* (series, 1995); CIB Supt Halliwell in *The Bill*.
Films: *Zeppelin;* PC Atilla Rees in *Under Milk Wood;* Silver Bear-Berlin in *Overlord;* Thomas in *A.D.; Secret Friends; Beautiful Thing; Hair Soup*. Address: c/o CDA. Lives in Wiltshire. m. TV writer Pam Valentine; 2 s. Pets: A dog called Woof. Hobbies: Sailing.

HARRIS, Rolf

Rolf Harris

Rolf Harris. Presenter/Cartoonist/Singer. b. Perth, Australia, 30 March 1930. OBE. Won an Australian radio talent competition in 1949, then moved to the UK as an art student in 1952.
TV: *Showcase; It's a Great Life; Rolf's Walkabout; Hey Presto; It's Rolf; The Rolf Harris Show; Rolf on Saturday, OK?; Cartoon Time; Rolf's Cartoon Club; TV Heroes* (subject, 1993); *The Children's Royal Variety Performance 1993; Animal Hospital Live* (series); *Animal Hospital Christmas; Animal Hospital Week* (series); *Cat Crazy* (series); *Zoo Watch Live* (series); *Animal Hospital* (series); *Animal Hospital Down Under – A Christmas Special* (1995); *Animal Hospital Heroes* (series).
Films: Jake the Peg in *The Little Convict*. **Records:** *Tie Me Kangaroo Down Sport* (No 9, 1960); *Sun Arise* (No 3, 1962); *Johnny Day* (No 44, 1963); *Bluer than Blue* (No 30, 1969); *Two Little Boys* (No 1, 1969). Address: c/o Billy Marsh Associates. Lives in South London. m. sculptress Alwena Hughes; 1 d. Bindi. Hobbies: Painting, making jewellery, collecting rocks, woodwork, photography.

HARRISON, Carol

Carol Harrison

Carol Harrison. Actress/Writer. Stage plays include *Death of a Salesman* (National Theatre).
TV: *Softly Softly: Task Force* (TV début, 1976); *Jessie's Place; EastEnders; A Sort of Innocence; To Have and to Hold; Black Silk; Reservations; Now and Then; Danton's Death; Daylight Robbery; Leaving Home; Bergerac; Broke; The Secret; Gems* (writer of three episodes); Gloria in *Brush Strokes* (six series, 1986-91); Dorothy in *London's Burning* (two series); *The Bill* (writer of two episodes); *Casualty; Perfect Scoundrels; The Chief;* Loretta Sweet in *Get Back* (two series, 1992-3); Sally West in *The Bill;* Susan Hutton in *Kavanagh QC;* Lou Pownall in *The Bill*.
Films: *Quadrophenia; The Elephant Man; Loose Connections; Tank Malling*. Address: c/o CAM. Partner: Actor Jamie Foreman; 1 s. Alfie.

HARRISON, Louise

Louise Harrison

Louise Anna Imogen Harrison. Actress. b. Manchester, 26 November 1962. Trained at the Welsh College of Music and Drama.
TV: Suzanne in *A Very Peculiar Practice;* Ann in *Gentlemen and Players; The River;* Dawn Prescott in *Coronation Street* (1989-90); Lisa Barras in *The Sharp End* (series, 1990); WPC Donna Harris in *The Bill* (1991-).
Films: *The Contractor; Coma; Macheath* (all London Film School productions). Address: c/o Stephen Hatton Management. Lives in North London. Single. Hobbies: Cinema and theatre-going, travelling.

HART, Tony

Tony Hart

Norman Antony Hart. Presenter/TV Artist. b. Maidstone, Kent, 15 October 1925. Trained as a graphic designer at Maidstone College of Art (1947-50), became a display designer in Peter Robinson's Display Studio and had associations with the Walt Disney organisation in the UK.
TV: *Saturday Special; Playbox; In Town Tonight; Ask Your Dad; Disney Wonderland; Stories in Pictures;* unseen operator of Quackers in *Time for Tich, Tich Puzzle* and *Tich and Quackers; Vision On* (1964-76); *Take Hart* (1977-84); *Silent Perspective* (US); *Hartbeat* (1984-93).
Books: *Fun with Drawing; Fun with Art; Fun with Design; Fun with Picture Projects; Fun with Historical Projects; The Young Letterer; The Corporate Computer* (words by Norman Sanders); *Make It with Hart; Take Hart* project packs; *The Art Factory; Paint and Draw with Tony Hart*. Address: c/o Roc Renals, 10 Heatherway, Edgcumbe Park, Crowthorne, Berkshire RG11 6HG, tel/fax (0344) 773638. Lives in Shamley Green, Surrey. m. Jean; 1 d. Carolyn. Pets: Only the wild birds he feeds in his garden. Hobbies: Garden stonework, long walks, collecting attractive natural objects, chopping logs.

HARTMAN, Kim

Kim Hartman. Actress. b. London, 11 January 1955. ASM at the Belgrade Theatre, Coventry, for a year before training at the Webber Douglas Academy. Stage productions include *'Allo, 'Allo* (Prince of Wales Theatre and London Palladium), *Move Over, Mrs Markham* (Far and Middle East tours).

TV: *The Pedlar* (Play for Today); *Kelly Monteith; 'Allo, 'Allo.* Address: c/o Lou Coulson. m. John Nolan; 1 s. Tom, 1 d. Miranda. Hobbies: Antiques, painting, gardening.

Kim Hartman

HARVEY, Jan

Jan Harvey. Actress. b. Penzance, Cornwall, 1 June 1947.

TV: *Edward the Seventh; Sam; Bill Brand; A Family Affair; The Sweeney; Van Der Valk; Life and Death of Penelope; Song for Europe; Second Chance; A Different Drummer; The Forgotten Voyage; The Old Men at the Zoo;* Susan Harvey in *Fell Tiger; Five to Eleven;* Jan Howard in *Howards' Way* (six series, 1985-90); Friday Rees in *Inspector Morse: Greeks Bearing Gifts;* Mrs Marsh in *Woof!;* Claire in *Casualty; Mark My Words* (interviewing World Scrabble Champion Mark Nyman); Yvonne Newbiggin in *A Touch of Frost.* Address: c/o The Brunskill Management. m. 1st producer Kerry Lee Crabbe (dis), 2nd actor Alan David (dis).

Jan Harvey

HAVERS, Nigel

Nigel Havers. Actor. b. London, 6 November 1949. Son of the late former Attorney-General Sir Michael Havers. Trained at the Arts Educational School. Left acting for a while to work in the wine trade, then became a researcher on Jimmy Young's BBC Radio 2 show, before television success.

TV: *Richard II; Comet among the Stars;* title role in *Nicholas Nickleby; A Raging Calm; Upstairs, Downstairs; The Glittering Prizes; Pennies from Heaven; A Horseman Riding By; An Englishman's Castle; Coming Out; Goodbye Darling; Unity; Winston Churchill — The Wilderness Years; Nancy Astor; After the Party;* Dr Tom Latimer in *Don't Wait Up* (series); *Strangers and Brothers; Star,* title role in *The Charmer* (series); *Hold the Dream; A Perfect Hero; Polly* (TVM); Guy MacFadyean in *The Good Guys* (series); Harvey Stafford in *Murder Most Horrid.*

Films: George Martin in *Birth of the Beatles;* Lord Andrew Lindsay in *Chariots of Fire;* Bob Jones in *The Whistle Blower; Burke and Wills;* Dr Rawlins in *Empire of the Sun; A Passage to India; Farewell to the King; Naked under Capricorn; The Private War of Lucinda Smith; Sleepers.*

Radio: Billy Owen in *The Dales* (two years); *The Jimmy Young Show* (chief researcher). Address: c/o Michael Whitehall. m. 1st Carolyn (dis), 2nd Polly; 1 d. Kate (Katharine, from 1st m.).

Nigel Havers

HAWKINS, Carol

Carol Anne Hawkins. Actress. b. Barnet, Hertfordshire, 31 January 1949. Trained at the Corona Stage Academy. West End plays include *See How They Run, Run for Your Wife* and *Wife Begins at Forty.*

TV: Sharon Eversleigh in *Please Sir!* and *The Fenn Street Gang; The Two Ronnies; Mr Big; Porridge; Blake's 7; The Dick Emery Show; Leap in the Dark; Rings on Their Fingers;* Susi Powell in *Together* (24 episodes); *Bloomfield; Kelly Monteith; See How They Run; C.A.T.S. Eyes; That's My Boy; Happy Families; God's Chosen Car Park; Relative Strangers; My Husband and I; All at No 20; Don't Wait Up; About Face;* Madge in *El C.I.D.; The Bill* (two roles); Doreen in *Leaves on the Line;* Charmian in *Rides* (Series 2, 1993); Jane in *The Little Alan Show;* Mrs Sleepwalker in *All Night Long; Gail's World; Hollyoaks.*

Films: *Zeta One; When Dinosaurs Ruled the Earth;* Sharon Eversleigh in *Please Sir!;* Kate Baines in *Bless This House; Carry On Behind; Carry On Abroad; Percy's Progress;* Barbara Wilcox in *Not Now, Comrade.* Address: c/o McIntosh Rae Management. Lives in West Sussex. m. 1st (dis), 2nd Martyn Padbury. Pets: A dog called Trot. Hobbies: Painting, gardening.

Carol Hawkins

HAWTHORNE, Nigel

Nigel Barnard Hawthorne. Actor. b. Coventry, 5 April 1929. CBE. TV since 1956.

TV: *Marie Curie; Holocaust* (mini-series); *Edward and Mrs Simpson; Destiny; The Knowledge; Jessie; The Schoolmistress; Rod of Iron; The Sailor's Return* (TVM), *A Tale of Two Cities* (TVM), *The Tempest;* Sir Humphrey Appleby in *Yes Minister* and *Yes, Prime Minister; The World Cup — A Captain's Tale; The Hunchback of Notre Dame* (TVM); *A Woman Called Golda* (TVM); *The Critic; Pope John Paul II* (TVM); *The House; Barchester Chronicles; Jenny's War; Mapp and Lucia; Tartuffe; The Miser; The Shawl; King of the Wind* (TVM); *Relatively Speaking; Flea Bites* (TVM); *The Trials of Oz* (Performance); *Late Flowering Lust* (also deviser, 1994).

Films: *Young Winston; S*P*Y*S; The Hiding Place; Sweeney 2; Watership Down* (voice only); *History of the World Part I; Memoirs of a Survivor; Firefox; Gandhi; The Plague Dogs* (voice only); *The Black Cauldron* (voice only); *DreamChild; The Chain; Turtle Diary; Rarg* (voice-over, short); *En Handfull Tid (A Handful of Time); Demolition Man; Relatively Speaking; Freddie as F.R.O.7* (voice only); George III in *The Madness of King George; Richard III; Twelfth Night; Actor Inside.*

Awards: TV: Four BAFTA awards (twice for *Yes Minister,* twice for *Yes, Prime Minister*). Address: c/o Ken McReddie. Hobbies: Drawing, gardening, swimming.

Nigel Hawthorne

HAYCOCKS, Paddy

Paddy Haycocks

Patrick Haycocks. Presenter/Producer/Director. b. Portsmouth, Hampshire, 9 April 1950.
TV: *Streetwise* (*The Channel Four Daily*); *As It Happens; This Way Out; South Today* (BBC South); *Southern Eye; The Travel Show* (presenter/reporter, 1992-); *The Travel Show Guides;* anchorman for Channel One (cable channel). As producer/director: *Six o'Clock Show* (LWT); *South of Watford* (LWT); *The Good Life Guide* (LWT); *Concrete and Clay* (LWT); *How Do They Do That?*
Address: c/o Severn Management Services. Lives in Wokingham, Berkshire. m. 1976 Anne; 1 s. Timothy, 1 d. Elizabeth. Pets: A guinea pig. Hobbies: Crosswords, reading, theatre, wine, people-watching.

HAYDEN, Linda

Linda Hayden

Linda Mary Higginson. Actress. b. Stanmore, Middlesex, 19 January 1953. Trained at the Aida Foster Theatre School from the age of 11 and appeared in many TV comedy series over the next four years.
TV: *Village Hall; Heydays Hotel; Crown Court; Mackenzie; The Professionals; Robin's Nest; Galton & Simpson Half Hour; The Dick Emery Show; Give Us a Clue; Star Games; Let There Be Love; The Shillingbury Tales; Cuffy; Hart to Hart; Little and Large; Minder on the Orient Express* (TVM); Sonia in *Just Good Friends; The Upper Hand; Shelley.*
Films: *The Lion in Winter; Baby Love; Taste the Blood of Dracula; Satan's Skin; Something to Hide; Barcelona Kill; Night Watch; Vampira; Madhouse; Confessions of a Window Cleaner; Exposé; Confessions from a Holiday Camp; Let's Get Laid!; The Boys from Brazil.* Address; c/o Michael Ladkin. Lives in London. m. theatre impresario Paul Elliott; 1 d. Laura Jane, 1 s. Haydn Lewis. Hobbies: 'Children.'

HAYES, Melvyn

Melvyn Hayes

Melvyn Hayes. Actor. b. London, 11 January 1935. Performed with Terry's Juveniles troupe as a child.
TV: Serials and series: *Quatermass II; Whack-O!; Shadow Squad; Skyport; Oliver Twist; The Sunday Break* (two series); *Billy Bunter; The Unloved; The Silver Sword; The Cheaters; Probation Officer; Dixon of Dock Green; The Seven Faces of Jim; Rex Milligan; Jo's Boys; Beyond Belief; Sir Yellow; Our Mutual Friend; The Human Jungle; The Double Deckers* (series, also dialogue coach, writer of episodes and co-writer of title song); *Potter's Picture Palace* (two series); *Father Dear Father; Cosmo and Thingy; Home Sweet Home; State of the Union; Roy Kinnear; Black Beauty; The Chase;* Bombardier 'Gloria' Beaumont in *It Ain't Half Hot Mum* (series); *Stanley and Livingstone; Taxi.* Plays and TVMs: *The Unloved; Tearaway; The Dark Is Light Enough; The Common Man; Extra Item; The Wharf Road Mob; No Man's Land; The Snare of the Fowler; The Running Tide; The Ruffians; The Telescope; Spring and Port Wine* (*In the West End Tonight*); *The Lady from Maxims; The Magic Idol; Song of the March Hare; No Friendly Star; The Zany Adventures of Robin Hood; King of the Wind.* Light entertainment incl. *Sky Star Search* (judge). Voice-overs: Skeleton in *SuperTed;* Frizz in *The Dreamstone; Little Dracula; Alfred J Kwak.*
Films: *Face the Music; The Case of Soho Red; The Rainbow Jacket; Adventure in the Hopfields; The Blue Peter; The Man Who Loved Redheads; Stars in Their Eyes; Fun at St Fanny's; The Good Companions; The Curse of Frankenstein; Woman in a Dressing Gown; Violent Playground; Operation Amsterdam; No Trees in the Street; The Flesh and the Fiends; The Silent Invasion; Bottoms Up; The Young Ones; Summer Holiday;* Jerry in *Wonderful Life; Crooks in Cloisters; A Walk with Love and Death; The Magnificent Six and a Half; The Magnificent Seven Deadly Sins; Go for a Take; Love Thy Neighbour; Man about the House; Carry On England; Bachelor of Arts; What's Up Superdoc;* Goober in *Santa Claus.* Address: c/o Howes and Prior. Lives in Gloucestershire. m. 1st (dis), 2nd actress Wendy Padbury (dis); 4 d. Sacha, Talla, Joanna, Charlotte, 1 s. Damian. Pets: German shepherd dog.

HAYES, Patricia

Patricia Hayes

Patricia Hayes. Actress. b. London, 22 December 1911. Trained at RADA (Gold Medal winner).
TV: *The Benny Hill Show;* title role in *Edna, the Inebriate Woman; Last of the Baskets; The Trouble with You, Lilian; On the Move; The Portland Millions; Till Death Us Do Part; London Belongs to Me; The Corn is Green* (TVM); *The Tea Ladies; Spooner's Patch; Pat and Dandy; The Lady Is a Tramp; Cymbeline; Winter Sunlight; The Old Boy; Marjorie and Men; Mr Pye; Mrs Capper's Birthday;* Min in *In Sickness and in Health; Our Lady Blue; Casualty; The House of Bernarda Alba; Six Characters in Search of an Author;* Mrs Monro in *The Clothes in the Wardrobe; Return of the Native;* Ethel in *Lord of Misrule* (Screen One).
Films: *Broken Blossoms; Went the Day Well?; When We Are Married; The Dummy Talks; Candles at Nine; Hotel Reserve; Great Day; Nicholas Nickleby; To the Public Danger; Skimpy in the Navy; Poet's Pub; The Love Match; Cloak without Dagger; The Deep Blue Sea; The Battle of the Sexes; Kill or Cure; Reach for Glory; Heavens Above!; Saturday Night Out; The Bargee; The Sicilians; A Hard Day's Night; Help!; A Ghost of a Chance; The Terrornauts; Can Hieronymous Merkin Ever Forget Mercy Humppe and Find True Happiness?; Goodbye, Mr Chips; Carry On Again, Doctor; Fragment of Fear; Raising the Roof; Love Thy Neighbour; Blue Movie Blackmail; The Best of Benny Hill; Film* (short); *Danger on Dartmoor; The Neverending Story; Little Dorrit; Willow; A Fish Called Wanda; War Requiem; The Last Island; The Fool; Blue Ice; Crime and Punishment; The Steal.* Address: c/o Hazel de Leon. m. actor Valentine Brooke (dis); 2 d. Teresa, Gemma, 1 s. actor Richard O'Callaghan.

Tony Haygarth

HAYGARTH, Tony

Anthony Haygarth. Actor. b. Liverpool, 4 February 1945. Formerly a psychiatric nurse.

TV: *Last of the Summer Wine; Warrior Queen; Holocaust; The Beaux' Stratagem; I Claudius; Rosie; Z Cars; Shoestring; Kinvig; The Borgias; Dead Ernest; The Further Adventures of Lucky Jim; The Black Stuff* (Play for Today); *Two Gentlemen of Verona; The Caucasian Chalk Circle; The Insurance Man; The December Rose; Farrington of the FO; Hardwicke House; Making Out;* Frank in *El C.I.D.* (two series, 1990, 1992); Colin Keogh in *Between the Lines;* Mildeye in *The Borrowers* (two series, 1992-3); DS Gilmore in *A Touch of Frost;* Mitch Maddox in *All Quiet on the Preston Front* (series, 1994); Bill Wilson in *Pie in the Sky* (series, 1994); Pot au Feu in *Sharpe's Enemy;* Frank Thorp in *Casualty;* Patrick Hutton in *Kavanagh QC;* Cedric Mays in *The Last Englishman* (Heroes & Villains); Fr Benedict Spode in *Prophecy* (Chiller); Frank Harrison in *Bramwell;* Roy Johnson in *Our Friends in the North.*

Films: *Percy; Let's Get Laid; Dracula; Dick Turpin; SOS Titanic; The Human Factor; Caleb Williams; Britt; Ivanhoe; McVicar; A Private Function; Clockwise.* Address: c/o Conway, van Gelder, Robinson.

Philip Hayton

HAYTON, Philip

Philip John Hayton. News presenter. b. Keighley, West Yorkshire, 2 November 1947. Pirate disc-jockey before entering broadcasting with BBC Radio Leeds as a reporter-presenter (1968-71).

TV: *Look North* (reporter-presenter, BBC North, 1971-4); BBC TV news reporter (1974-80), Southern Africa correspondent (1980-3) and presenter of *One o'Clock News, Six o'Clock News, Nine o'Clock News* and *Breakfast News* (1984-93); *North West Tonight* and *Close Up North* presenter (BBC North, 1993-4); *The Great British Quiz* (quizmaster, two series, 1994-5); BBC World Service Television news presenter (1995). Address: c/o The Roseman Organisation. m. 1972 Thelma, 1 s. James, 1 d. Julia. Hobbies: Sailing, cycling, theatre, music.

Mike Hayward

HAYWARD, Mike

Mike Hayward. Actor.

TV: *Coronation Street; The Real Eddy English;* Alun Morgan in *Take the High Road/High Road* (1990-); Ian Gillespie in *The Bill.*

Address: c/o Harbour & Coffey/Scottish Television. Lives in Wales. m. with children.

HAZELDINE, James

James Hazeldine. Actor. b. Lancashire. Stage plays include *Troilus and Cressida, Love Girl and the Innocent, Timon of Athens, The Fool* (all RSC), *Kick for Touch, Small Change, Long Time Gone* (all National Theatre) and *Strange Interlude* (West End and Broadway).

TV: *Agatha Christie's Miss Marple: Murder at the Vicarage; Truckers; Streets Apart; Young, Gifted and Broke* (series); *Close Relations;* Mike 'Bayleaf' Wilson in *London's Burning* (eight series, 1988-95, also directed some episodes); *Pirate Prince; My Friend Walter;* Digby Tuckerman in *Inspector Morse: Greeks Bearing Gifts;* Brian Macklin in *A Small Dance* (IVM); Det Sgt Corrigan in *Boon; The Fireboy;* Reg Manston in *Heartbeat.*

Address: c/o Conway, van Gelder, Robinson. m. former actress Rebecca Moore; 1 s. Sam, 1 d. Chloe.

James Hazeldine

HAZLEGROVE, Jane

Susan Jane Hazlegrove. Actress. b. Manchester, 17 July 1968.

TV: *Picture Friend; Lovebirds; Threads; Travelling Man;* Sue Clayton in *Coronation Street;* Debbie Taylor in *Albion Market; Who's Our Little Jenny Lind?; The Book Tower; How We Used to Live;* WPC Madeline Forest in *Waterfront Beat* (two series); *Made in Heaven;* Rosie in *Making Out* (second and third series); Alison Gibson in *Shooting Stars* (TVM); Lisa Shepherd in *Families;* Maggie in *Heartbeat;* Maureen Shelby in *A Touch of Frost;* Yvonne in *Lovejoy;* Sandy in *Just a Gigolo;* Joanne Walsh in *Growing Pains* (series, 1993); Lisa Powell in *The Bill;* Marion in *Heartbeat;* DC Turner in *Band of Gold.*

Films: *The Whipping Boy; Heidi.*

Address: c/o Barry Brown & Partner.

Jane Hazlegrove

HEALY, Dorian

Dorian Healy. Actor. b. London. Stage plays include *Oi for England* (Royal Court) and *I'm Not Rappaport* (Apollo Theatre).

TV: *A Christmas Carol; Just the Job; Johnny Jarvis; No Place like Home; The Mistress; The Monocled Mutineer; Boxing for Boys; Journey's End; On Her Majesty's National Service; South of the Border;* Jimmy Destry in *Capital City; Witchcraft; Underbelly;* PC Geoff Richards in *Between the Lines;* Anthony Chapell in *Agatha Christie's Poirot;* Steve in *A Statement of Affairs* (mini-series, 1993); Captain/Acting Major Kieran Voce in *Soldier Soldier* (Series 3-4); Bernard in *Casualty;* Jim Piggot in *Class Act;* Tom Slater in *No Bananas.*

Films: *For Queen and Country; Young Soul Rebels; The Score.*

Address: c/o ICM.

Dorian Healy

HEALY, Tim

Tim Healy

Tim Healy. Actor. b. Newcastle upon Tyne, 29 January 1952. A paratrooper before becoming an actor.
TV: *Coronation Street; The World Cup – A Captain's Tale; Emmerdale Farm; When the Boat Comes In; Crown Court; Minder; Dennis in Auf Wiedersehen Pet; Boon; A Kind of Living; A Perfect Spy; Tickle on the Tum; Flea Bites* (TVM)*; Casualty; B&B;* Reg in *Boys from the Bush* (series, 1992)*; Cut and Run* (Comedy Playhouse)*; Stay Lucky; Cracker; Crime Limited Special: Hostage;* Ronny Goodall in *The Detective; The 10%ers; Frank Stubbs;* Foxy in *Common as Muck* (series, 1994)*; Heartbeat; Harry.*
Films: *Bird on a Wire.* Address: c/o ICM. Lives in London. m. actress Denise Welch; 1 s. Matthew.

HEDLEY, Jack

Jack Hedley

Jack Hawkins. Actor. b. London, 1930.
TV: *No Fixed Abode; The Small Back Room; Mine Own Executioner; The Big Client; The Lean Years; No Tram to Lime Street; Decision at Nine; The Outstation; Lucky Strike; Bed of Roses; Web of Deceit; The Darkness Outside; The Protest; The World of Tim Frazer* (serial)*; The Missing Links; You Can't Win 'Em All; A Little Winter Love; Voice in the Sky; Girl on the Cliff; Ask Any Neighbour; Life for a Life; Who Steals My Name; The End of the Game; Curtain Fall; No Trams to Ethiopia; Killer's Odds; Kate* (two series)*;* Lieut Col Preston in *Colditz* (two series)*; The Break; Cat on a Hot Tin Roof; Hindle Wakes; Who Pays the Ferryman?* (series)*; Brief Encounter* (TVM)*; Sophia Loren – Her Own Story* (TVM)*; Orient Express 'Jane'; Go an Extra Mile; The Heart of the Matter; One by One; Remington Steele;* Henry in *Only Fools and Horses* (Christmas special, 1986)*; Hard Cases;* Bobby Davro show; Charles Latimer in *A Quiet Conspiracy; Gentlemen and Players; 'Allo, 'Allo;* Judge in *Trainer; Mr Don and Mr George.*
Films: *The Pack; Behind the Mask; Room at the Top; Left, Right and Centre; Make Mine Mink; Cone of Silence* (US title *Trouble in the Sky*)*; Never Back Losers; In the French Style; The Longest Day; Lawrence of Arabia; Nine Hours to Rama; The Very Edge; The Scarlet Blade; Witchcraft; Of Human Bondage; Witch and Warlock; The Secret of Blood Island; How I Won the War; The Anniversary; Goodbye, Mr Chips; The Devil's Advocate; For Your Eyes Only; The Ripper; Three Kinds of Heat; Educational History of the World; The Plot to Kill Hitler; Kurtulus.* Address: c/o Sharon Hamper Management.

HEILBRON, Vivien

Vivien Heilbron

Vivien Sarah Frances Heilbron. Actress. b. Glasgow, 18 May 1944. Sister of actress Lorna Heilbron. Trained at LAMDA. Stage roles include Naomi in *A Heritage and Its History* (Phoenix Theatre).
TV: *Sunset Song; Cloud Howe, Grey Granite; The Unpleasantness at the Bellona Club; Kippers and White Wine* (*Love Story*)*; This Happy Breed;* Det Sgt Louise Colbert in *Target* (series, 1977-8)*; District Nurse Kay Grant in *Take the High Road; The New Statesman; Street Apart; EastEnders;* Helen Wills in *Brookside* (1992)*; Taggart: Gingerbread; The House of Eliott; In Suspicious Circumstances.*
Films: Catriona in *Kidnapped.* Address: c/o The Richard Stone Partnership. Lives in London. Partner: Actor David Rintoul (qv). Pets: Two cats. Hobbies: Music, travel, gardening.

HEINEY, Paul

Paul Heiney

Paul Heiney. Presenter. b. Sheffield, South Yorkshire, 20 April 1949.
TV: *That's Life!* (three series, 1979-81)*; Junior That's Life!; The Big Time* (two episodes)*; In at the Deep End* (three series)*; The Travel Show; What on Earth Is Going On?; Trading Places* (two series)*; Skill Shop* (series)*; Food and Drink* (1991-2)*; This Sunday* (presenter, 1993-).
Films: *Water.* **Books:** Two books, on yachting and horses (co-written with wife Libby Purves). Address: c/o JGPM. Lives in Suffolk. m. broadcaster/writer Libby Purves; 1 s. Nicholas, 1 d. Rose.

HENDERSON, Don

Don Henderson

Don Henderson. Actor/Writer/Producer/Director. b. London, 10 November 1932.
TV: *The Protectors; Warship* (three series)*; Poldark; New Scotland Yard; Softly Softly; Dixon of Dock Green; The XYY Man; Van Der Valk; Crossroads; One Day at a Time* (Play for Today)*; Crown Court; A.I.M. Strangers* (two series)*; Dead Reckoning; Dick Turpin; The Onedin Line; Mavis* (Play for Today)*; Goodbye Darling; The Baker Street Boys; Me and My Town; Jemima Shore Investigates; Bottle Boys; The Captive Clairvoyant; Squaring the Circle* (TVM)*; Annika; Bulman* (two series)*; Dead Head; Knights of God; Henry's Leg; The Adventures of Polly Flint; Doctor Who; Hot Metal; Jumping the Queue; Making Out; Minder; Dempsey and Makepeace; Last of the Summer Wine; Maigret; Spelling It Out; The Paradise Club* (two series)*; The Absolute Beginner's Guide to Cookery* (co-presenter)*; Boon; Merlin of the Crystal Cave; Moon and Son; Black and Blue; 2point4 Children; Look at It This Way; The New Statesman; Cracker; The Bill; The Detectives; Pat and Margaret; Tomorrow Calling; Harry; Medics; Casualty; The Ruth Rendell Mysteries: A Case of Coincidence* (mini-series, 1996).
Films: *A Midsummer Night's Dream; Callan; Sweeney!; The Big Sleep; The Island; Brazil; Billy the Kid and the Green Baize Vampire; The Adventures of Baron Munchausen; Murder Elite; Tank Malling; Outlaws; The BFG* (voice only)*; Carry On Columbus; White Angel ; The Trial.* Address: c/o A.I.M. m. 1st Hilary (dec 1977), 2nd 1979 actress Shirley Stelfox (qv); 1 d. Louise, 1 s. Ian (from 1st m.), 1 step-d. Helena.

HENDERSON, Ian

Ian Henderson. Actor. b. Edinburgh, 27 August 1968. Trained at Welsh College of Music and Drama.
TV: Billy in *Michael Winner's True Crimes*; *Playdays*; Callum in *Second Thoughts* (five series, 1991-4).
Films: Field in *The Dollar Bottom* (winner of Best Short Film Oscar). Address: c/o Sharon Hamper Management. Lives in London. m. 1994 actress Nicola Duffett (qv); 1 step-d. Jessica. Hobbies: Rugby.

Ian Henderson

HENRY, Lenny

Lenny Henry. Comedian/Actor. b. Dudley, Worcestershire, 29 August 1958.
TV: *New Faces* (winner, aged 16, 1975); *The Black and White Minstrel Show*; *The Fosters*; *Tiswas*; *OTT*; *Three of a Kind*; *Saturday Live*; *The Royal Variety Performance*; *Lenny Henry Tonite*; *The Lenny Henry Show*; *Coast to Coast* (TVM); *The Suicide Club*; *Just Like That!*; *Oxford* (The Comic Strip Presents...); *Bernard and the Genie*; *Alive and Kicking* (TVM); *The Real McCoy*; *Lenny Go Home*; *The South Bank Show: Lenny Henry Hunts the Funk* (subject); *Lenny Henry in Dreams*; Gareth Blackstock in *Chef!* (two series, 1993-4, plus Christmas special, 1993); *Comic Relief's Red Nose Alert*; *Total Relief: A Night of Comic Relief* (presenter, plus participant in *French & Saunders & Prince & Barry White*, 1993); *The Red Nose Awards* (presenter, 1993); *The Godsend* (Funky Black Shorts, also writer-director, 1994); *The South Bank Show: Darker than Me* (own report on African-American comedy, 1994); Charlie Collins in *White Goods*; *The Lenny Henry Christmas Show* (1994, 1995); *Prince Cinders* (voice only, 1995); *Lenny Henry Presents 'Belfast Live'* (*Comic Relief*, 1995); *French and Saunders*.
Films: *The Millionaires Club*; *Lenny Henry Live and Unleashed*; *The Secret Policeman's Third Ball*; *Double Take*; *Lenny Go Home*; *True Identity*. Address: c/o James Sharkey Associates/Robert Luff (manager). m. comedienne actress Dawn French (qv); 1 adopted d. Billie.

Lenny Henry

HENSON, Nicky

Nicholas Victor Leslie. Actor. b. London, 12 May 1945. Son of comedian Leslie Henson. Trained at RADA. Recorded his first single in 1961 and had a contract writing songs for The Shadows and Cliff Richard.
TV: *Prometheus*; *Arthur*; *The Keith Michell Show*; *Shirley's World*; *Life of Balzac*; *Seagull Island*; *A Midsummer Night's Dream*; *Chains*; *Anyone for Denis?*; *Happy Apple*; *Driving Ambition*; *Absurd Person Singular*; *Fawlty Towers*; *Tropical Moon over Dorking*; *Season's Greetings*; *Love after Lunch*; *Thin Air*; *Star Trap* (TVM,); *Inspector Morse*; *Boon*; *After Henry*; *The Upper Hand*; *The Green Man* (mini-series); *Lovejoy*; *Celebration '91* (presenter); *The Bill*; Chief Insp Charlie McGregor in *Between the Lines*; Martin Bowen in *Micky Love* (Rik Mayall Presents); *Fallen Sons*; *Sitting Pretty*; *Health and Efficiency*; *Class Act*; *The Healer*; Greg Scarry in *All Quiet on the Preston Front* (series, 1994) and *Preston Front* (series, 1995); Dr Ralph Rabryte in *The Healer* (mini-series); title role in *Shine on Harvey Moon* (series, 1995); Harrington Smithfield in *Pie in the Sky*; Henri de Venca in *Coronation Street*.
Films: *Father Came Too*; *Doctor in Clover*; *Here We Go Round the Mulberry Bush*; *Witchfinder-General*; *Mosquito Squadron*; *Crooks and Coronets*; *There's a Girl in My Soup*; *All Coppers Are...*; *The Love Ban*; *Psychomania*; *Penny Gold*; *Vampira*; *Bedtime with Rosie*; *The Bawdy Adventures of Tom Jones*; *No 1 of the Secret Service*. Address: c/o Richard Stone Partnership. m. 1st 1969 actress Una Stubbs (dis 1975), 2nd Marguerite Porter; 3 s. Christian, Joe (both from 1st m.), Keaton (from 2nd m.).

Nicky Henson

HERBERT, Philip

Philip Herbert. Actor/Comedy fire-eater/Improviser. b. London, 28 January 1957. Trained at East 15 Acting School (1975-8) and spent two years with the Royal Court Youth Theatre.
TV: Randolph the Remarkable in *The Tube*; *Saturday Live*; *Daytime Live*; *Short Change*; *The Pickwick Papers*; *My Family and Other Animals*; *Confidential*; *Fortune Numbers*; *The Bill*; *Mr Majeika*; *Bodger and Badger*; Hugh Jelly in *Sticky Moments* (two series); *Laughlines*; *I Love Keith Allen*; *Comic Relief '91*; *100%*; *Give Up* (presenter, Japanese-Fujian gameshow); *The Tub Club* (Fujian TV); *Hysteria III*; *Amnesty International Benefit Concert*; *Terry and Julian*; *Brace Yourself Sydney*; *Fireworks*; Randolph the Remarkable in *The Happening* and *Up the Junction*; *The Good Sex Guide* (Series 2).
Films: *Funny Hill*; *Victor/Victoria*; *Return of the Jedi*; *Christmas Present*; *Little Shop of Horrors*; *Larry On Columbus*. Address: c/o Elaine Murphy Associates. Lives in Highbury, North London. Single.

Philip Herbert

HEYWOOD, Jean

Jean Murray. Actress. b. Blyth, Northumberland, 15 July 1921. Librarian until married in 1945. Joined Castle Theatre, Farnham, 1963, as acting wardrobe mistress and then actress.
TV: Bella Seaton in *When the Boat Comes In* (1975-7); Miss Kay in *Our Day Out*; *Boys from the Blackstuff*; Dolly McGregor in *The Brothers McGregor*; *Cover Her Face*; *Missing Persons*; Mrs Alton (housekeeper) in *All Creatures Great and Small*; *A Very Peculiar Practice*; *Casualty*; *The Specials*; Sarah Ellis in *Spender*; *Shelley*; Aunt Dahlia in *Jeeves and Wooster*; *KYTV*; *The Bill*; Doreen in *White Goods*; *Side by Side*; Edna Sturgess in *Peak Practice*; *Men of the World*; *Heartbeat*; *Trip Trap* (Screen One).
Address: c/o Barry Burnett Organisation. Lives in Camberley, Surrey. m. 1945 Dr Roland B Heywood; 1 s. Bryon, 1 d. Carolyn (danced with the Young Generation and Second Generation).

Jean Heywood

HICKSON, Joan

Joan Hickson

Joan Hickson. Actress. b. Kingsthorpe, Northampton, 5 August 1906. Stage début in *His Wife's Children* (1927). West End début in *The Tragic Muse* a year later. Film début 1933.

TV: *Our Man at St Mark's; Bachelor Father; Nanny; Good Girl; Great Expectations; Poor Little Rich Girls; Time for Murder;* title role in *Agatha Christie's Miss Marple* (12 stories, 1984-92).

Films: *Trouble in Store; Widows Might; The Man Who Could Work Miracles; Love from a Stranger; The Lilac Domino; Second Thoughts; Don't Take It to Heart; The Trojan Brothers; I See a Dark Stranger; This Was a Woman; The Guinea Pig; Celia; Seven Days to Noon; The Magnet; High Treason; Hell Is Sold Out; Hunted; Haunt for a Gentleman; Tall Headlines; Hindle Wakes; Come Back Peter; The Card; Rough Shoot; Curtain Up; Deadly Nightshade; The Million Pound Note; Doctor in the House; The House across the Lake; Mad about Men; What Every Woman Wants; To Dorothy a Son; Dance Little Lady; The Crowded Day; As Long as They're Happy; Doctor at Sea; Value for Money; The Woman for Joe; Simon and Laura; A Time to Kill; Lost; Jumping for Joy; The Man Who Never Was; The Extra Day; Port of Escape; The Last Man to Hang?; Child in the House; Carry On Admiral; No Time for Tears; Happy Is the Bride!; Barnacle Bill; Law and Disorder; Upstairs and Downstairs; Please Turn Over; The 39 Steps; Carry On Constable; No Kidding; His and Hers; Carry On Regardless; Raising the Wind; In the Doghouse; Murder She Said; Nurse on Wheels; Heavens Above!; The Secret of My Success; Mrs Brown, You've Got a Lovely Daughter; Carry On Loving; Friends; A Day in the Death of Joe Egg; Theatre of Blood; Carry On Girls; Confessions of a Window Cleaner; One of Our Dinosaurs Is Missing; Yanks; The Wicked Lady; Mrs Trellis* in *Clockwise; King of the Wind; Century.* Address: c/o Plunket Greene. m. Dr Eric N Butler.

HIGGINSON, Huw

Huw Higginson

Huw Higginson. Actor. b. Hillingdon, Middlesex, 21 February 1964.

TV: *Big Deal; How We Used to Live; Floodtide; Defrosting the Fridge; Reaching Agreement;* PC George Garfield in *The Bill* (1989-).

Address: c/o Evans and Reiss. Lives in Teddington, Middlesex. Partner: Geraldine; 1 step-d. Charlotte. Hobbies: Golf, cricket, snooker, pool, travel.

HIGHMORE, Edward

Edward Highmore

Edward Thomas Highmore. Actor, b. Kingston-upon-Thames, Surrey, 3 April 1961. Studied at agricultural college to be a tree surgeon but failed to make the grade, decided to be an actor and trained at the Guildford School of Acting.

TV: Malkon in *Doctor Who;* Boll in *Tripods;* Ernie in *Lame Ducks* (two series); Leo Howard in *Howards' Way* (six series, 1985-90); Doctor in *The Detectives* (1996).

Address: c/o William Morris Agency (UK). Lives in London. Partner: Theatrical agent Sue Latimer.

HILL, Bernard

Bernard Hill

Bernard Hill. Actor. b. Manchester, 17 December 1944.

TV: Yosser Hughes in *The Black Stuff* (Play for Today) and *Boys from the Blackstuff* (series); *New World; The Burston Rebellion;* Lech Walesa in *Squaring the Circle* (TVM); Martin Allport in *The Law Lord* (TVM); Erwin Van Haarlem in *A Question of Identity* (Crime Story); Uncle Fred in *Lipstick on Your Collar* (series, 1993); Mike in *Olly's Prison* (mini-series, 1993); DS Gavin Douglas in *TellTale* (mini-series, 1993); Chief Constable Harmsworth in *Between the Lines; The Giant Nativity Festivity;* Captain Larry in *Dirtysomething* (Screen Firsts); Len Tollit in *Once upon a Time in the North* (series, 1994); Joe in *Speaking in Tongues* (Stages); Frank Nickle in *Catherine Cookson's The Gambling Man* (mini-series, 1995).

Films: *Restless Natives; The Chain; No Surrender;* Cole in *The Bounty; Bellman and True;* Henry Madgett in *Drowning by Numbers;* Joe in *Shirley Valentine; Mountains of the Moon;* John in *Skallagrigg;* Flint in *Madagascar Skin.* Address: c/o Conway, van Gelder, Robinson.

HILL, Melanie

Melanie Hill

Melanie Hill. Actress. Trained at RADA (winner, Vanbrugh Award). Stage plays include *Women Beware Women* (Royal Court), *Under Milk Wood* and *Bread* (stage version of the television comedy series).

TV: Hazel in *Auf Wiedersehen Pet; Juliet Bravo; A Night on the Tyne; Boon;* Aveline in *Bread;* Sue Styles in *Spender;* Lynda Chambers in *The Bill;* Janice Hutchins in *Casualty;* Sister Pamela Lockley in *Cardiac Arrest* (series, 1994); Emma Shepperd in *Crocodile Shoes* (series, 1994); Lena in *Finney* (series, 1994); Angie Norman in *Circles of Deceit.*

Films: *The Hawk; When Saturday Comes.*

Address: c/o Markham & Froggatt. Lives in North London. m. actor Sean Bean (qv); 2 d. Lorna, Molly.

HILL, Rose

Rose Hill. Actress/Singer. b. London, 5 June 1914. Won a scholarship to train at the Guildhall School of Music and Drama. Began her career as an opera singer, making her début at Glyndebourne and joining the Sadler's Wells Opera company. Stage productions include *Four to the Bar* (Criterion Theatre),

The Diary of a Nobody (Arts Theatre), *The Old Ones, Objections to Sex and Violence, Endgame, Foot-falls* (all Royal Court), *Separate Tables* (Apollo Theatre), *The Three Sisters* (as Anfisa, RSC), *Nicholas Nickleby* (four roles, RSC, London and Broadway) and *On the Razzle* (National Theatre).
TV: *Dixon of Dock Green;* Fay Bridge in *Thingumybob* (series, 1968); *The Barber of Stamford Hill; Take a Sapphire; The Wild Geese; Benbow Was His Name; The Three Sisters; Waterloo Sunset; Wayne and Albert;* Annie Benge in *Born and Bred* (two series, 1978, 1980); *Strangers; On the Razzle; The Cabbage Patch; Hallelujah; Caring;* Fanny (Madame Blanc/Leclerc) in *'Allo, 'Allo* (1984-92); *Island Gardens; Press Gang; Murder East, Murder West;* Mrs Temple in *The Bill;* Mrs Ryder in *A Touch of Frost: Widows and Orphans.*
Films: *Wildcats of St Trinian's; Heavens Above!; For the Love of Ada; Every Home Should Have One; Footsteps.* Address: c/o The Richard Stone Partnership. Lives in Rickmansworth, Hertfordshire. m. John St Leger Davis (dec); 1 s. John. Hobbies: Gardening, cooking, driving, visiting the theatre.

Rose Hill

HILLIER, Kate
Kate Hill. Actress. b. Maidenhead, Berkshire, 23 May 1970. Trained at the East 15 Acting School.
TV: *A Box Full of Stories;* Abita in *Walk with a Stranger;* Diana Collins in *Inspector Morse;* Zoë in *Second Thoughts;* Polly in *The Upper Hand;* Trudy Wright in *Lovejoy;* WPC Dodds in *Love Hurts;* Karen Dunsford in *Eve Strikes Back;* Jan Curtis in *Emergency;* WDS Rhode in *Crime Monthly;* Judi Simpson in *Strange but True;* Maggie in *Blood Bonds;* Laura Hunter in *Don't Look Back;* Staff Nurse Frazer in *The Bill.* Address: c/o Langford Associates. Lives in London. Single. Hobbies: Volleyball, tennis.

Kate Hillier

HINCHLEY, Pippa
Philippa Lucy Hinchley. Actress. b. London, 7 April 1966. Studied with Stanley Morris as a teenager before landing a role in *Z for Zachariah* (BBC 2, 1984) at the age of 17. Stage roles include Isabella in *Measure for Measure* (Thorndike Theatre), Julie in *Journeyman Jack* (Liverpool Playhouse), Elma in *Bus Stop* (West End) and Kitty in *Thark* (Watermill Theatre).
TV: Ann Burden in *Z for Zachariah;* Sarah Griffiths in *Morgan's Boy;* Anna in *East of Ipswich* (TVM); title role in *Janna Where Are You?;* Joyce in *And a Nightingale Sang;* Denise in *The Bill;* Phyllida Lee in *The Inspector Alleyn Mysteries: Artists in Crime;* Julie in *Tell Me That You Love Me;* Shaz in *Hangar 17;* Duchess of York in *Fergie & Andrew — Behind the Palace Doors* (TVM); Elaine Fenwick in *Coronation Street* (1993-4); *No Limit* (writer only, comedy sketches, Sky One, 1994); Bobbie in *Eskimo Day.*
Films: Barbara Baxter in *Secret Places;* Marlene in *Dead Man's Folly;* Valerie in *The Dressmaker; London Kills Me; Crimetime.* Address: c/o William Morris Agency (UK). Lives in London. Single. Hobbies: British motorcycles, sailing, flying, studying for MPhil in philosophy.

Pippa Hinchley

HINDLE, Madge
Madge Railton. Actress. b. Blackburn, Lancashire, 19 May 1938. Spent her early days in amateur theatre. Stage plays include *Whodunnit* and *Elsie and Norm's Macbeth* (both national tours).
TV: *On the Margin* (début); *Z Cars; Here's Harry; Miss A and Miss M;* Lily in *Nearest and Dearest* (series, 1968-72); Betty in *Mr Ellis versus the People;* Miss Prothero in *Sunset across the Bay;* Maggie in *Jack Point;* Valerie in *Vinegar Trip;* Joyce Webster in *Said the Preacher;* School Teacher in *Death of a Rebel; The Cuckoo Waltz; Get Some In;* Renee Roberts (née Bradshaw) in *Coronation Street* (1976-80); *The Dick Emery Show;* Governor's Secretary in *Porridge;* Mrs Jardine in *Open All Hours;* Bet Howell in *Mr and Mrs Edgehill* (Play for Today); Rose in *Intensive Care* (Play for Today); *The Two Ronnies* ('Picnic by the Sea' sketch); *The Bright Side* (series); *The Cannon & Ball Show;* Mrs Shurer in *Lost Empires;* Rose Hackling in *Stan's Last Game* (Play for Today); *Tickle on the Tum* (storyteller); Mrs Birtles in *Capstick's Law;* Marian Gaunt in *Thank You for Having Her;* Aunt Annie in *First of the Summer Wine;* Winnie in *My Friend Walter;* Elaine Dodswell in *The Rector's Wife* (series, 1994); Mrs Pain in *The Dwelling Place;* Lady in Hotel in *Pat and Margaret;* Doreen in *Barbara* (Comedy First, 1995); Mrs Heron Man in *Preston Front.*
Films: *Nearest and Dearest.* **Radio:** Vera Garside in *A Proper Charlie* (series, 1985).
Address: c/o Sandra Griffin Management. Lives in London and the Yorkshire Dales. m. solicitor Michael Hindle; 2 d. TV presenter Charlotte, barrister Frances.

Madge Hindle

HINES, Frazer
Frazer Hines. Actor. b. Horsforth, West Yorkshire, 22 September 1944. Trained at the Marjorie Newbury School of Dancing, Harrogate (aged eight), and the Corona Academy (aged ten).
TV: Jan in *The Silver Sword; Queen's Champion; Compact; Z Cars;* Jamie in *Doctor Who; Smuggler's Cove; No Man's Land; Coronation Street; The Villains; Samson and Delilah; Seasons;* Joe Sugden in *Emmerdale* (1972-94); *Duty Free; Country Challenge* (presenter).
Films: *X the Unknown; The Weapon; Peril for the Guy; Salvage Gang; A King in New York; The Last Valley; Zeppelin.* Address: c/o Peter Charlesworth. Lives in Yorkshire. m. 1st actress Gemma Craven (dis), 2nd Olympic world champion water-skier Liz Hobbs. Hobbies: Horse-riding.

Frazer Hines

HINSLIFF, Geoff

Geoffrey Hinsliff. Actor. b. Leeds. Trained at RADA. Many West End and Royal Court stage plays.
TV: *Z Cars; Softly Softly; Striker; Accident;* George Fairchild in *Brass* (first series); Don Brennan in *Coronation Street* (1988-) (previously appeared in the serial in two other roles).
Films: *A Bridge Too Far; O Lucky Man!* Address: c/o Spotlight/Granada Television. Lives in Manchester and near Matlock, Derbyshire. m. Judith; 2 d. Gabrielle, Sophie. Hobbies: Golf, sailing.

Geoff Hinsliff

HIRD, Thora

Thora Hird. Actress. b. Morecambe, Lancashire, 28 May 1913. OBE; Dame, 1993.
TV: *Meet the Wife; The First Lady; Ours Is a Nice House; Flesh and Blood; The Hard Case; Albert Hope; The Bed; She Stoops to Conquer; Your Songs of Praise Choice; Thomas and Sarah; Me, I'm Afraid of Virginia Woolf; Afternoon Off; Intensive Care; In Loving Memory* (five series); *Hallelujah; Praise Be!;* Edie in *Last of the Summer Wine; Uncle of the Bride* (TVM); *The Tailor of Gloucester;* Talking Heads: *A Cream Cracker under the Settee; The Good Guys; A Day in the Life...* (subject); *Memento Mori* (TVM); *Goggle Eyes; Thora on the Straight and Narrow* (series); *The Royal Television Society Hall of Fame; Wide Eyed and Legless; Pat and Margaret; The South Bank Show* (subject); *Heartbeat.*
Films: *Spellbound; The Big Blockade; The Black Sheep of Whitehall; Next of Kin; Went the Day Well?; The Foreman Went to France; 2,000 Women; The Courtneys of Curzon Street; My Brother Jonathan; Corridor of Mirrors; The Weaker Sex; The Blind Goddess; Portrait from Life; Once a Jolly Swagman; A Boy, a Girl and a Bike; Fools Rush In; Madness of the Heart; Maytime in Mayfair; Boys in Brown; Conspirator; The Cure for Love; The Magnet; Once a Sinner; The Galloping Major; The Frightened Man; Emergency Call; Time Gentlemen Please!; The Last Hours; The Great Game; Background; Turn the Key Softly; The Long Memory; Personal Affair; Street Corner; A Day to Remember; Don't Blame the Stork!; For Better, for Worse; The Crowded Day; One Good Turn; The Love Match; The Quatermass Experiment; Tiger by the Tail; Lost; Women without Men; Sailor Beware!; Home and Away; The Good Companions; These Dangerous Years; A Clean Sweep; Further up the Creek; The Entertainer; Over the Odds; A Kind of Loving; Term of Trial; Bitter Harvest; Rattle of a Simple Man; Some Will, Some Won't; The Nightcomers; Consuming Passions; The Wedding Gift* (US cinema version of TVM *Wide Eyed and Legless*).
Awards: BAFTA Best TV Actress award for *Talking Heads: A Cream Cracker under the Settee.*
Address: c/o Felix De Wolfe. m. James Scott; 1 d. actress Janette Scott.

Thora Hird

HODGE, Patricia

Patricia Hodge. Actress. b. Cleethorpes, Lincolnshire, 29 September 1946. Brought up in Grimsby. Trained as a teacher and taught for a year before going to LAMDA (Eveline Evans Award winner).
TV: *Menace; The Girls of Slender Means; Night of the Father; Great Big Groovy Horse; The Naked Civil Servant; Softly Softly; Jackanory Playhouse; Act of Rape; Crimewriters; Target;* Phyllida Erskine-Brown in *Rumpole of the Bailey; The One and Only Phyllis Dixey; Edward and Mrs Simpson; Disraeli; The Professionals; Holding the Fort* (three series); *The Other 'Arf; Rumpole's Return; Nanny;* title role in *Jemima Shore Investigates; Rumpole and the Female Species; Hayfever; The Death of the Heart; Robin of Sherwood; OSS* (TVM); *The Adventures of Sherlock Holmes; Time for Murder; Hotel du Lac* (TVM); Mary Fisher in *The Lives and Loves of a She-Devil* (series); *Exclusive Yarns; Let's Face the Music of...; Inspector Morse; Heat of the Day; The Shell Seekers; The Secret Life of Ian Fleming* (TVM); Moira in *Victoria Wood: Staying In; Rich Tea & Sympathy;* title role in *The Cloning of Joanna May; The Full Wax.*
Films: *The Disappearance; Rosie Dixon Night Nurse; The Waterloo Bridge Handicap; The Elephant Man; Heavy Metal;* Emma in *Betrayal; Sunset; Thieves in the Night; Just Ask for Diamond.*
Address: c/o ICM. Lives in London. m. musician Peter Owen; 2 s. Alexander Richard Charles, Edward Frederick James. Hobbies: Decorating, sewing, painting, music.

Patricia Hodge

HOLDERNESS, Sue

Sue Holderness. Actress. b. Hampstead, North London, 28 May 1949. Trained at the Central School of Speech and Drama. Stage roles include Myra Hindley in *Our Kid* (one-woman show).
TV: *Tightrope; Fly into Danger; Bless This House; Lollipop Loves Mr Mole; Harriet's Back in Town; Four Idle Hands; Canned Laughter; The Sandbaggers; End of Part One; The New Avengers; The Cleopatras; It Takes a Worried Man; Minder; The Brief;* Marlene in *Only Fools and Horses; Dear John; Lime Street; Long Live the King; Young, Gifted and Broke; Sob Sisters; You Me and It; Heartbeat; Revelations.*
Films: *That'll Be the Day; It Could Happen to You.* Address: c/o Barry Burnett Organisation. Lives in Windsor, Berkshire. m. Mark Piper (managing director, Theatre Royal, Windsor); 1 d. Harriet (b. 1985), 1 s. Frederick (b. 1987). Hobbies: Dancing, horse-riding, theatre.

Sue Holderness

HOLLAND, Jeffrey

Jeffrey Holland. Actor. b. West Midlands, 17 July 1946.
TV: *Russ Abbot's Madhouse;* Spike Dixon in *Hi-de-Hi!* (series); James Twelvetrees in *You Rang, M'Lord?* (series); Cecil Parkin in *Oh Doctor Beeching!* (pilot). Address: c/o London Management.

Jeffrey Holland

HOLLAND, Jools

Julian Holland. Presenter/Musician. Member of the pop group Squeeze (1974-80 and 1985-90).
TV: *Alas Smith and Jones; The Tube; Mister Roadrunner; Juke Box Jury* (host); *Later* (*The Late Show*); *The Happening; Later…with Jools Holland* (1992-); *The Jools Holland Big Band Inside; The Laughing Prisoner; Viva Cabaret!; Jools' Gems; Late Licence; Later with Jools Holland's New Year's Eve Hootenanny; Later with Jools Holland and Johnny Cash; Jools Goes to Portmeirion; Perpetual Motion; The Second Annual Jools' Hootenanny; Jools at the Ritz; The Legend of the Tube; Best of The Tube; The Beatles Anthology* (interviewer); *Third Annual Jools Hootenanny; Later Presents Paul Weller in Concert.* Address: c/o BBC TV. Lives in Greenwich, South London. Partner: Artist Christabel Durham; 1 s. George, 2 d. Rosie (both from a previous relationship), Mabel (with partner).

Jools Holland

HOLLINGBERY, Vilma

Vilma Jean Hollingbery. Actress/Writer. b. Walthamstow, East London, 21 July 1932. Trained at the Guildhall School of Music and Drama.
TV: *Timmy and Vicky; The Management; Abracadigance* (pilot); *The River; The Bill* (four roles); *Maigret; Children's Ward,* Esme Sutherland in *Waiting for God;* Crime Story; *Casualty;* Kitty in *Sitting Pretty* (two series); *A Touch of Frost; Do Your Own Thing; Time after Time.* As writer: *Far from the Madding Crowd; Great Expectations; A Christmas Carol* (all adaptations); *Is This the Day* (winner, Central Television Eileen Anderson Best Play award, 1990, co-written with husband, Michael Napier-Brown).
Films: *The Thin Line; Young Poisoner's Handbook.* Address: c/o McIntosh Rae Management. Lives in London and Northamptonshire. m. 1st 1954 Raymond Sleap (dis 1958), 2nd 1961 theatre director Michael Napier-Brown; 1 d. actress Kate Napier-Brown. Hobbies. Cartooning.

Vilma Hollingbery

HOLLOWAY, Julian

Julian Robert Stanley Holloway. Actor. b. Watlington, Oxfordshire, 24 June 1944. Son of entertainer Stanley Holloway. Trained at RADA. Stage roles include Alfred P Doolittle in *My Fair Lady* (Broadway).
TV: *Our Man Higgins; Rebecca; Helen — A Woman of Today;* Algy in *The Importance of Being Earnest; Snooker; Conjugal Rights; Elizabeth R; An Adventure in Bed; The New Avengers; The Sweeney; Rebecca; Minder; The Scarlet and the Black; Ellis Island; If Tomorrow Comes; My Darling Clementine; The Endless Game; Doctor Who; Michelangelo; The Chief; Rumpole of the Bailey; Casualty; The Vet.*
Films: *Hostile Witness; Rough Cut;* ten *Carry On* films; *Loophole* (co-producer); *The Spy's Wife* (co-writer and co-producer); *The Chairman's Wife* (co-writer and co-producer); *The Brute* (associate producer). Address: c/o Barry Burnett Organisation. Lives in London and Los Angeles. m. 1st actress Zena Walker (dis), 2nd 1991 actress Debbie Wheeler; 1 d. Sophie Dahl Holloway (from relationship with author Tessa Dahl); 1 step-d. Kate Gregory, 1 step-s. Joel Gregory (from 2nd m.).

Julian Holloway

HOLM, Ian

Ian Holm Cuthbert. Actor. b. Toodmayes, Essex, 12 September 1931. Trained at RADA.
TV: *Frankenstein; Edward the Confessor; Omri's Burning; End of the Line; Dostoyefsky; Funny; The Frighteners; The Dick Van Dyke Show; The Man from Heaven; Conjugal Rights; Oedipus; Napoleon and Love; Jubilee: Ramsey; Night School; Flayed; Mirage; Murder by the Book; Jesus of Nazareth; The Man in the Iron Mask* (TVM); *The Thief of Baghdad; Les Misérables* (TVM); *Holocaust, SOS Titanic; The Lost Boys* (TVM); *The Misanthrope; The Bell; The Browning Version; Murder by the Book; We, the Accused; The Bell; Strike; Inside the Third Reich; Arena: Bette Davis — The Benevolent Volcano; Mr and Mrs Edgehill; Game, Set & Match; The Tailor of Gloucester; Stalin* (narrator); *Mistress of Suspense; Uncle Vanya* (TVM); *Survival Special: Giant Otter* (narrator); *The Borrowers; The Last Romantics.*
Films: *Girls at Sea; The Fixer; The Bofors Gun; A Midsummer Night's Dream; Oh! What a Lovely War; A Severed Head; Nicholas and Alexandra; Mary, Queen of Scots; Young Winston; The Homecoming; Juggernaut; Robin and Marian; Shout at the Devil; March or Die; The Thief of Baghdad; Alien; SOS Titanic; All Quiet on the Western Front; Chariots of Fire; Time Bandits; Return of the Soldier; Greystoke: The Legend of Tarzan Lord of the Apes; Brazil; Laughterhouse* (retitled *Singleton's Pluck*); *Dance with a Stranger; Wetherby; Dreamchild; Another Woman; Henry V; Hamlet; Kafka; Blue Ice; The Last Romantics; The Hour of the Pig.* Address: c/o Julian Belfrage Associates. m. 1st 1955 Lynn Mary Shaw (dis 1965), 2nd 1982 Sophie Baker; 1 s., 3 d. (from 1st m.), 1 s. (from 2nd m.).

Ian Holm

HOLMES, Eamonn

Eamonn Holmes. Presenter. b. Belfast, 3 December 1959.
TV: *Good Evening Ulster* (Ulster TV); *Open Air; Holiday; Breakfast News* (sports reporter); BBC Sport darts, tennis and snooker coverage (presenter, 1990-2); *Pick of the Week; Pot Black Timeframe; Holiday Outings; Sunday Best* (GMTV, 1993); *GMTV* (1993-); *The Mystery & Magic Show; TV Weekly; Brookside* (acting himself); *Oddballs; The National Television Awards — The Viewers' Choice; How Do They Do That?* (two series); *The Coronation Street Party; Back to the Present.* Address: c/o Simpson Fox Associates. Lives in Belfast. m. Gabrielle; 2 s. Declan, Niall, 1 d. Rebecca.

Eamonn Holmes

Michelle Holmes

HOLMES, Michelle

Corinne Michelle Cunliffe. Actress. b. Rochdale, Lancashire, 1 January 1967. Trained at Oldham Theatre Workshop. Formed the funk group Dunky Dobbers with actress Sue Devaney (qv).

TV: *Juliet Bravo;* Mill Girl in *In Loving Memory;* Susan Turner in *The Practice;* Susan in *Divided We Stand;* Jenny in *Damon & Debbie* (mini-series); Tina Fowler in *Coronation Street* (1989-90); Maggie Coles in *Firm Friends* (two series, 1992, 1994); Annie in *Mr Wroe's Virgins;* Lindsay in *Emmerdale* (four episodes, 1993); Yvonne Sparrow in *Goodnight Sweetheart* (three series, 1993, 1995, 1996, plus Christmas special, 1995); Marie in *Common as Muck* (series, 1994); Britt Woods in *Emmerdale* (1995).

Films: Sue in *Rita, Sue and Bob Too; Once upon a Time.*

Address: c/o Roxane Vacca Management. Lives in Saddleworth, West Yorkshire. Single. Pets: A cat called Puddy Tat. Hobbies: Travelling, singing, interior design.

Bob Holness

HOLNESS, Bob

Robert Wentworth John Holness. Presenter. b. Vryheid, Natal, South Africa, 12 November. Brought up in Ashford, Kent. Became an actor and radio presenter in South Africa when his parents emigrated.

TV: *Take a Letter* (host, gameshow, 1961); *World in Action; Breakthrough* (narrator); *Horizon; Time Out; Out of School; Transworld Top Team; Science Session; Today* (Thames Television); *Junior Criss Cross Quiz; What the Papers Say; Today; Blockbusters* (quizmaster, 1982-); *The Geeks* (one episode of children's series, 1995); *Raise the Roof* (host, game show, series, 1995). **Awards:** Radio: Variety Club Joint Independent Radio Personality of the Year (1980 and 1985). Address: c/o Spotlight. Lives in Middlesex. m. Mary Rose Clifford; 2 d. Carol (singer Nancy Nova), Rosalind (sang with pop group Toto Coelo), 1 s. Jonathan. Pets: Garden birds. Hobbies: Gardening, music, walking.

Judy Holt

HOLT, Judy

Judy Holt. Actress. Trained at Manchester Polytechnic's School of Theatre.

TV: *Dads;* Mrs Grice in *Coronation Street;* Nurse/Sister Mitchell in *Children's Ward;* Nurse in *Old Flames;* Liz in *The Contract;* Mandy in *The Practice;* Susan in *The Road to 1984;* Anna in *My Father's House;* WPC Lunn in *Emmerdale* (1995).

Radio: *A Red Car in the Fountain.* Address: c/o Green and Underwood.

HOPE, Richard

Richard John Hope Walker. Actor. b. Thrapston, nr Kettering, Northamptonshire, 11 October 1953. Gained a BA (Hons) in law. Former member of the National Youth Theatre. Stage plays include *The Park* (RSC) and *1001 Nights with Le Grand Magic Circus* (Shaftesbury Theatre).

TV: *By Common Consent* (Play for Today); *Saturday, Sunday, Monday* (Laurence Olivier Presents...); *Secret Army; People Like Us; Crown Court; Margie and Me; Heartland;* Lt Hooper in *Brideshead Revisited; Wayne and Albert; Simulated Exercise;* title role in *Wuffer* (series); *December Flower;* Alan in *The Clinger;* Salto in *Bellman and True; Burning Ambition; A Piece of Cake* (series); *Dogplant; Casualty of War* (Frederick Forsyth Presents); *Happy Families* (two series); *Victoria Wood Playhouse; Children Crossing; Antonia and Jane* (Screen Two); *Itch; The Bill;* Sgt Keogh in *Boon;* Mortimer Tundish in *The Riff Raff Element* (two series, 1993-4); Stuart Freeman in *Tears before Bedtime* (series, 1995); Roy Shearer in *Peak Practice;* Richard in *Band of Gold* (Series 1, 1995); Colin English in *The Vet.*

Films: *Bloody Kids; Breaking Glass; The French Lieutenant's Woman; Scandalous;* Hubert in *Laughterhouse* (retitled *Singleton's Pluck*); *See You at Wembley, Frankie Walsh* (short); Salto in *Bellman and True;* Squire Wyman in *Feast of July.* Address: c/o Sally Hope Associates. Lives in London. m.; 1 s., 1 d. Pets: Two cats called Rhino and Phobos. Hobbies: DIY, rolling down hills, cycling.

Richard Hope

Anthony Hopkins

HOPKINS, Anthony

Philip Anthony Hopkins. Actor. b. Port Talbot, West Glamorgan, 31 December 1937. CBE, 1987; knighted, 1993. Trained at the Welsh College of Music and Drama (1956-7) and RADA (1961-3, Silver Medal winner). Plays include *Equus* (Broadway) and *Antony and Cleopatra* (National Theatre).

TV: *A Flea in Her Ear; A Walk through the Forest; A Heritage and Its History; A Company of Five; The Three Sisters; The Peasants' Revolt;* title role in *Danton;* title role in *Dickens; Hearts and Flowers; Uncle Vanya; The Poet Game; Decision to Burn;* Pierre in *War and Peace; Cuculus Canorus;* title role in *Lloyd George; QB VIII* (TVM); *Find Me; A Childhood Friend; Possessions; All Creatures Great and Small* (US); *The Arcata Promise; Dark Victory* (TVM); *The Lindbergh Kidnapping Case* (TVM); *Victory at Entebbe* (US); title role in *Kean; Mayflower: The Pilgrims' Adventure* (TVM); Hitler in *The Bunker* (TVM); *Peter and Paul* (TVM); title role in *Othello; Little Eyolf; The Hunchback of Notre Dame* (TVM); *A Married Man; Corridors of Power: Strangers and Brothers; Arch of Triumph* (TVM); *Hollywood Wives; Io e il Duce* (*Mussolini and I*) (mini-series and TVM); *Guilty Conscience* (TVM); *The Good Father* (TVM); Guy Burgess in *Blunt* (TVM); Donald Campbell in *Across the Lake* (TVM); *The Tenth Man* (TVM); *Heartland; Face of the Earth* (TVM); Magwitch in *Great Expectations* (TVM); *To Be the Best* (mini-series); *The*

South Bank Show (subject); *Hunters in the Wild* (narrator); *In the Wild: Lions with Anthony Hopkins* (presenter); The Priest in *The Trial* (Screen Two); *Selected Exits; Face to Face: Anthony Hopkins*.
Films: *The White Bus; The Lion in Winter; Hamlet; The Looking Glass War; When Eight Bells Toll; Young Winston; A Doll's House; Juggernaut; The Girl from Petrovka; All Creatures Great and Small; Victory at Entebbe* (TVM only in US)*; Audrey Rose; A Bridge Too Far; International Velvet; Magic; A Change of Seasons; The Elephant Man; The Bounty; 84 Charing Cross Road; Mickey; The Dawning; A Chorus of Disapproval; The Desperate Hours; The Silence of the Lambs; One Man's War; Spotswood; Howards End; Free Jack; Bram Stoker's Dracula; Chaplin; The Trial; The Innocent; The Remains of the Day; Shadowlands; Legends of the Fall; The Road to Wellville; August* (also director)*; Nixon.*
Awards: More than 30 include Oscar as Best Actor for *The Silence of the Lambs* (1992). Address: c/o ICM. m. 1st 1967 Petronella Barker (dis 1972), 2nd 13 January 1973 Jennifer Lynton; 1 d. Abigail (b. 1968, from 1st m.). Pets: One cat. Hobbies: Reading, playing piano, watching old films.

Clive Hornby

HORNBY, Clive
Clive Hornby. Actor. b. Liverpool, 20 October 1944. Trained as an accountant, played drums for The Dennisons pop group, then worked backstage at the Liverpool Playhouse. Trained at LAMDA.
TV: *Get Some In; Space 1999; Life at Stake; Minder*, Jack Sugden in *Emmerdale* (1980-).
Films: *No Longer Alone; Yanks.* **Radio:** *The War behind the Wire.* Address: c/o Vernon Conway/Emmerdale Production Centre. m. 1st (dis), 2nd actress Helen Weir; 1 s. Thomas, 1 step-s. Daniel.

HORROCKS, Jane
Jane Horrocks. Actress. b. Rossendale Valley, Lancashire, 18 January 1964. Trained at RADA (Bronze Medal winner). Plays include *The Rise and Fall of Little Voice* (National Theatre and Aldwych Theatre).
TV: *Welcome to The Times; Leaving Home;* Louise in *Road; The Storyteller; Heartland; Boon; La Nonna; The Ruth Rendell Mysteries: No Crying He Makes;* Christine Bracken in *The Fifteen Streets; Alive and Kicking;* Beatie Bryant in *Roots* (Performance); *Red Dwarf;* Bubble in *Absolutely Fabulous* (three series, 1992, 1994, 1995); *Bad Girl; Came Out, It Rained, Went Back in Again;* Deborah Hayes in *Suffer the Little Children* (Stages); Sally Bowles in *Cabaret* (Carlton only); *Self Catering* (Alan Bleasdale Presents); *The Travel Show* (guest reporter); Doll Tearsheet in *King Henry IV* (Performance).
Films: *The Dressmaker;* Patten the Maid in *The Wolves of Willoughby Chase;* Miss Irvine in *Witches; Getting It Right;* Nicola in *Life is Sweet;* Faith in *Memphis Belle, Deadly Advice, Second Best;* Alison in *Some Kind of Life.* Address: c/o Peters Fraser & Dunlop. Lives in Islington, North London.

Jane Horrocks

HORSFALL, Bernard
Bernard Horsfall. Actor. b. Bishops Stortford, Hertfordshire. Brought up in Sussex.
TV: *Dancers in Mourning; Death of a Ghost; Family Solicitor; Suspicion; Beasts; General Hospital; Big Boy Now; This Year, Next Year; Enemy at the Door; Our Little Town; Minder; Badger by Owl-light; The Lady Killers; When the Boat Comes In;* Taron in *Doctor Who; Strangers and Brothers; Goodbye Days; A Distant Scream; Grand Duo; The Hound of the Baskervilles; Casualty; Chelworth; The Bill; For the Greater Good; Agatha Christie's Poirot; The Advocates; Thatcher: The Final Days; Virtual Murder* (TVM); Lord Thornhill in *The Advocates* (series, 1992); Peter Dobson in *Nice Town* (mini-series, 1992); Chief Constable Gordon in *Between the Lines;* Sir William Pitt in *Queen of the East* (Heroes & Villains).
Films: *Shout at the Devil; Gold; On Her Majesty's Secret Service; Gandhi; Brass Target; Inside the Third Reich.* Address: c/o Michael Ladkin. m. Jane; 2 d. Hannah, Rebecca, 1 s. Christian.

Bernard Horsfall

HOW, Jane
Jane How. Actress. b. London, 21 December. Trained at the Webber Douglas Academy (winner, Rodney Millington Award). Stage plays include *Easy Virtue* (Garrick Theatre), *Don't Dress for Dinner* (Apollo).
TV: *Kate;* Rebec in *Doctor Who: The Little Princess; General Hospital; Ten from the Twenties; The Return of A J Raffles; Warriors Return; Shuttlecock; The Killers; Don't Forget to Write; The Foundation; Cribb; The Spoils of War; Take Three Women; The Citadel; Seaview; Kelly Monteith; Don't Wait Up; A.D.;* Jan Hammond in *EastEnders* (1986); *War and Remembrance; Matlock; Made in Heaven;* Helen Latimer in *Don't Wait Up* (series); *Charles and Diana; Anglo-Saxon Attitudes* (series); *Lovejoy; Class Act*
Films: *Gare au Male; Lent Rancunes.* Address: c/o James Sharkey Associates. m. actor Mark Burns (dis); 1 s. Jack. Pets: A cat called Teela. Hobbies: Gardening, interior design.

Jane How

HOWARD, Madeleine
Madeleine Howard. Actress. b. London, 15 March 1951. Trained at Guildhall School of Music and Drama (Comedy Prize winner). Stage roles include Olivia and Viola in *Twelfth Night.*
TV: Tricia Pope in *Gems; Howards' Way; The Bill* (two roles); *Strike It Rich; The Collectors;* Sarah Sugden (née Connolly) in *Emmerdale* (1988-94). Plus TV commercials.
Films: *Daylight Robbery.*
Address: c/o Felix De Wolfe. Lives in Richmond-upon-Thames, Surrey. Single. Hobbies: Reading.

Madeleine Howard

HOWELLS, Cliff

Cliff Howells. Actor. Trained drama and English teacher. Stage plays include *A Midsummer Night's Dream* (New Shakespeare Company, Open Air Theatre, Regent's Park).
TV: George Jackson in *Brookside; The Miners' Strike;* Customer in *Jobwatch;* Paul Stoker in *Reaching Agreement* (adult education); Plumber in *Emmerdale Farm; Sob Sisters;* George Leamington in *Dramarama: Snakes and Loofahs;* Crowder in *Sherlock Holmes: The Boscombe Valley Mystery;* Radio Presenter in *A Very British Coup;* Terry Seymour in *Coronation Street* (five episodes); Joseph Cartwright in *G.B.H.;* Hilary McCormack in *A Little Bit of Lippy* (ScreenPlay); Scase in *London's Burning;* Mike Venner in *The Bill.* Address: c/o Barbara Pemberton Associates. Lives in Manchester.

Cliff Howells

HOWMAN, Karl

Karl Howman. Actor. b. London. West End stage productions include *Me and My Girl.*
TV: Jakey Smith in *Get Some In* (Series 3, 1978); *The Prodigal Daughter; Shades of Greene; The Sweeney; Balcombe Street Siege; Hazell; People like Us; Fox; The Flipside of Dominic Hyde; The Professionals; Minder; Shelley; A Fine Romance; Oscar; Dempsey and Makepeace; Black Silk; Juliet Bravo; Ties of Blood; Upline; Boon;* Jacko in *Brush Strokes* (series); *Saracen;* title role in *Mulberry* (two series, 1992-3); Wayne Todd in *Bad Boys* (pilot).
Films: *That'll Be the Day; Stardust; Frankenstein; SOS Titanic; Babylon; The Long Good Friday; Party Party.* Address: c/o Noel Gay Artists. Lives in Kent. m. Clare; 2 d. Chloe, Katy-Jo.

Karl Howman

HUDD, Roy

Roy Hudd. Comedian/Actor. b. Croydon, Surrey, 16 May 1936. Stage productions include *The Giveaway, Danny at the Palace* (both West End), *Rosencrantz and Guildenstern Are Dead* (Young Vic). Also played Fagin in a revival of *Oliver!* and Bud Flanagan in *Underneath the Arches* (also co-writer).
TV: *Bid for Fame; Tell It to the Marines; Not So Much a Programme, More a Way of Life; Hudd; The Maladjusted Busker* (winner Press Prize, Montreux Festival, 1966); *The Illustrated Weekly Hudd; The Roy Hudd Show;* Dan Leno in *Omnibus: Dan Leno His Book* (also researcher and co-producer); *Comedy Tonight; Up Sunday; Hold the Front Page; Show of the Week; Poor Christmas; The 607080 Show; Movie Memories; The Puppet Man; Halls of Fame; Hometown; Hazard a Guess; Chaplin the Kid;* Harold Atterbow in *Lipstick on Your Collar* (series, 1993); *Blow Your Mind: Wise Children;* Sergei Prokofiev in *Peter and the Wolf;* John Gedgrave in *The Memoirs of Sherlock Holmes;* John Parry in *Common as Muck* (series, 1994); Beach in *P G Wodehouse's Heavy Weather;* Ben Baglin in *Karaoke* (series, 1996).
Films: *Blood Beast Terror; Up Pompeii; The Seven Magnificent Deadly Sins; Up the Chastity Belt; The Alf Garnett Saga; An Acre of Seats in a Garden of Dreams; What'll You Have?; Up Marketing.*
Radio: *Workers' Playtime; The News Huddlines; Huddwinks.*
Books: *Roy Hudd's Book of Music-Hall Variety and Showbiz Anecdotes* (1993). Address: c/o Aza Artistes. Lives in Oxfordshire. m. 1st Ann (dis), 2nd Deborah; 1 s. Max (from 1st m.).

Roy Hudd

HUDSON, Robert

Mark Robert Hudson. Actor. b. Sheffield, South Yorkshire, 24 February 1960. Trained at the Central School of Speech and Drama.
TV: Reg in *Fresh Fields;* Pete Ryan in *Dempsey and Makepeace;* PC 'Yorkie' Smith in *The Bill* (1984-9); Don in *Saracen;* Patrick in *Surgical Spirit;* Roberts in *Sloggers;* Ted Morgan in *Dalziel and Pascoe;* Harper in *999;* Gordon in *Sylvia's Wedding.* TV commercials: Shredded Wheat; AA; Asda. Address: c/o Langford Associates. Lives in London. Single. Hobbies: Football, drawing.

Robert Hudson

HUGHES, Geoffrey

Geoffrey Hughes. Actor. b. Liverpool, 2 February 1944. Began acting at Newcastle University and gained early stage experience with Stoke-on-Trent rep. Stage plays include *Maggie May, Say Goodnight to Grandma, Run for Your Wife* and *Dead of the Night.*
TV: *The Likely Lads; Z Cars; Curry and Chips; Hoggs Back; The Mind of Mr J G Reeder; Shadows of Fear; The Pigeon Fancier* (Play for Today); *An Arrow for Little Audrey;* Bridge Corporal in *Dad's Army; No Honestly; Don't Drink the Water,* Eddie Yeats in *Coronation Street* (1975-83); *Mr Big; The Bright Side; Doctor Who; The Flying Lady;* Det Sgt Bailey in *The Man from the Pru;* Dilk in *Making Out; Needle* (TVM); *Coasting;* Onslow in *Keeping Up Appearances* (five series, 1990-5, plus Christmas special, 1994); *You Rang, M'Lord?; I Lovett;* Trinculo in *The Tempest;* Squire Clodpole in *Good Friday;* Kenny Coates in *Spender;* Tim Watkins in *Boon;* eccentric restaurateur Ray in *The Upper Hand;* Dooley in *The Smiths* (Comedy First).
Films: Voice of Paul McCartney in *Yellow Submarine; The Virgin Soldiers; Carry On at Your Convenience;* Larry in *Adolf Hitler — My Part in His Downfall; The Man from the Pru; The Bofors Gun; Till Death Us Do Part; The Man Who Had Power Over Women; Revenge.*
Radio: Uncle Charlie in *Pigeon Summer.* Address: c/o The Richard Stone Partnership. Lives in Northamptonshire. m. Susan. Pets: Dogs, hens, goat. Hobbies: Sailing, golf, cricket.

Geoffrey Hughes

HUGHES, Nerys

Nerys Hughes. Actress/Presenter. b. Rhyl, Dyfed, 8 November 1941. Trained at the Rose Bruford College of Speech and Drama. Performed with RSC and English Stage Company at the Royal Court. Stage plays include *Two into One* (Canada and Shaftesbury Theatre), *Wild Duck* (Lyric Theatre, Hammersmith), *Under Milk Wood* and concerts with the London Mozart Players.
TV: *Flying Swan; Z Cars; The Likely Lads;* Welsh-language plays for BBC Wales; *Diary of a Young Man* (series); Sandra in *The Liver Birds* (series, 1969-78, 1996); *High Summer Seasons; How Green Was My Valley* (series); *Doctor Who; Third Time Lucky* (series); Nerissa in *The Merchant of Venice; Alphabet Zoo* (co-presenter, two years); *Play Away; Rainbow; Jackanory;* Megan in *The District Nurse* (two series, 1984, 1987); *Bazaar* (presenter, three years); *Survival of the Fittest; Bathing Elizabeth;* Diana in *Gallowglass; Molly; Capital Woman* (co-presenter, series, Carlton only, 1995).
Films: *Second Best.*
Books: *Let's Have a Story; Favourite Cat Stories.*
Address: c/o Barry Burnett Organisation. Lives in South London. m. Film cameraman and documentary director Patrick Turley; 1 s. Benjamin, 1 d. Mari-Claire. Pets: Two cats. Hobbies: Gardening.

Nerys Hughes

HUGHES, Nicola

Nicola Hughes. Actress. Trained at the LEGAT School of Professional Ballet. Stage productions include *Faust* (as a dancer with Bel Canto Opera) and *Crazy for You* (as Margie, Prince Edward Theatre).
TV: *Stars in Their Eyes; The Shoe That Fits* (S4C, Welsh Fourth Channel); *Ipso Facto; Heartburn Hotel.*
Address: c/o The Narrow Road Company.

Nicola Hughes

HUGHES, Sean

John Patrick. Comedian/Writer/Actor. b. London. Stage shows include *A One Night Stand with Sean Hughes* (Duke of York's Theatre and Los Angeles), *Sean Hughes Live* (Just for Laughs Festival, Montreal, 1991), *Sean Hughes Live* and *Sean's Tour* (both national tours).
TV: *Friday Night Live; Tonight with Jonathan Ross; London Underground; In the City; Comic Relief Special; Aah Sean; Sean's Show* (sitcom, two series); *Sean's Shorts* (comedy-documentary series, 1993); *Jackanory: Flour Babies* (storyteller); *Life's a Bitch; Patrick's Day* (writer only, series); *Dead End* (writer only, pilot).
Films: *The Commitments; Susan.* **Records:** *Bubonique – 20 Golden Showers.*
Books: *Sean's Book.* Address: c/o Richard Bucknall Management. Single. Pets: A dog called Bill.

Sean Hughes

HULLEY, Annie

Clara Anne Hulley. Actress. b. Yorkshire, 23 October 1955. Trained at Bristol Old Vic Theatre School. Stage plays include *The London Cuckolds* (Royal Court).
TV: *Crown Court;* Karen Moore in *Emmerdale Farm; L S Lowry; Spend Spend Spend; Teach Yourself Gibbberish; We the Accused; Strangers; Kinvig; Mitch; Fame Is the Spur;* Brelca in *Return of the Antelope; Campion; Watchdog;* Carol in *Between the Lines;* Jan Carrington in *Casualty;* Stella in *The Specials;* Sandra in *Sleepers;* Eunice in *A Brother's Tale;* Joanne Gallego in *Eldorado;* Di Higgs in *Sloggers* (two series, 1994-5); Julie Paley in *The Bill;* Myra in *September Song* (two series, 1994-5); Deirdre Burkill in *A Pinch of Snuff* (mini-series, 1994); Dolores in *Ain't Misbehavin';* Julie Cook in *The Bill;* Maureen Bradley in *Chandler & Co.*
Address: c/o Barry Brown & Partner. Lives in London. m. 1987 producer-director Chris Clough; 1 s. Jack, 1 d. Lizzie. Pets: A dog called Bobbie. Hobbies: Writing.

Annie Hulley

HUMPHRIES, Barry

Barry Humphries. Actor/Comedian. b. Melbourne, Australia, 17 February 1934. Creator of Dame Edna Everage and Sir Les Patterson. Early stage experience at Union Theatre, Melbourne, and Phillip Street Theatre. West End one-man shows include *A Nice Night's Entertainment, Excuse I, Just a Show, A Load of Olde Stuffe, At Least You Can Say You've Seen It, Housewife Superstar, A Night with Dame Edna, Last Night of the Poms, An Evening's Intercourse with the Widely Liked Barry Humphries* and *Back with a Vengeance.*
TV: *The Barry Humphries Scandals* (début, 1968); *An Audience with Dame Edna; The Dame Edna Experience; The South Bank Show* (subject); *Single Voices: Sandy Come Home;* Rupert Murdoch in *Selling Hitler; Dame Edna's Neighbourhood Watch* (two series, 1992-3); *Canvas: A Conder Fan* (presenter); *Dame Edna in Hollywood; A Night on Mount Edna; Dame Edna's Hollywood; The Dame Edna Christmas Experience!* (1995).
Films: *The Adventures of Barry McKenzie; Barry McKenzie Holds His Own; Side by Side;* Rev Mr Strachey in *The Getting of Wisdom; Shock Treatment.*
Awards: Variety Club Showbusiness Personality of the Year (1987).
Address: c/o Kate Feast Management. m. 1st dancer Rosalind Hollindrake (dis), 2nd (dis), 3rd Dianne Millstead; 2 d. actress Tessa, Emily, 2 s. Oscar, Rupert.

Barry Humphries

Gayle Hunnicutt

HUNNICUTT, Gayle

Virginia Gayle Hunnicutt. Actress. b. Fort Worth, Texas, USA, 6 February 1943. Trained at UCLA (University of California, Los Angeles) Film and Theatre School.

TV: *The Smugglers* (TVM); *Man and Boy; The Golden Bowl; The Ripening Seed;* Czarina Alexandra in *Fall of Eagles* (series); *Affairs of the Heart; Switch; Humbolt's Gift; The Ambassadors; Return of The Saint; The Martian Chronicles* (TVM); *A Man Called Intrepid* (TVM); *The Million Dollar Face* (TVM); *Fantomas; Kiss of Gold* (TVM); *The Love Boat; Tales of the Unexpected: The Luncheon; The Ladykillers: The Darlingest Boys; Philip Marlowe, Private Eye; Taxi; Fantasy Island; The Quest; Return of the Man from UNCLE* (TVM); *Savage in the Orient; Dylan Thomas; The First Modern Olympics; The Adventures of Sherlock Holmes; Privilege; A Woman of Substance; Strong Medicine; Lime Street; Dream West* (miniseries); *Dallas* (17 episodes); *The Saint; Voices in the Garden.*

Films: *The Wild Angels; P.J.* (UK title *New Face in Hell*); *Marlowe; Eye of the Cat; Freelance; Fragment of Fear; The Love Machine; Today Mexico – Tomorrow the World* (short); *Scorpio; Running Scared; The Legend of Hell House; Nuits Rouges/L'homme sans visage* (UK title *Shadowman*); *Voices; The Sellout; The Spiral Staircase; Blazing Magnum* (US title *Strange Shadows in an Empty Room*); *Tony Saitta/Tough Tony; Die Rebellen/One Take Two; Once in Paris; Target; Dream Lover; Turnaround; Hard to Be a God; Silence like Glass.* Address: c/o William Morris Agency (UK). Lives in London. m. 1st 1968 actor-director David Hemmings (dis 1974), 2nd Simon Jenkins; 2 s. Nolan (from 1st m.), Edward (from 2nd m.). Pets: A Norfolk terrier called Woodstock. Hobbies: Travel, reading.

Gloria Hunniford

HUNNIFORD, Gloria

Gloria Hunniford. Presenter. b. Portadown, Co Armagh, 10 April 1940. Started singing at the age of nine and starred on ITV, BBC and RTE in Ireland, as well as making records.

TV: *Good Evening Ulster* (Ulster TV, 1979-82); *Songs of Praise; Big Band Specials; Gloria Plus* (Ulster TV); *The Six o'Clock Show* (LWT); *The Val Doonican Show; Sunday Sunday; That's Showbusiness; Gloria Live; Wogan* (guest presenter) *Cashwise; Gloria* (series); *Family Affairs* (co-host with daughter Caron Keating, two series, 1992-4); *Holiday; Children in Need; Eurovision Song Contest Previews; Sunday* (two series, 1994, 1996); *Pebble Mill* (series 1994-5); *Good Fortune* (series, 1994); *Christmas Good Fortune* (1994); *Sunday Live* (series, 1995); *Pebble Mill Special* (interview with Doris Day, 1996); *The Ladies of the House* (series, 1996).

Radio: Own show in Canada (1959); *Up Country* (BBC Northern Ireland); *A Taste of Hunni; A Taste of Hunni – Irish Style* (BBC World Service); *Gloria Hunniford* (BBC World Service); *Gloria Hunniford* (BBC Radio 2). **Books:** *Gloria Hunniford's Family Cookbook* (1995). Address: c/o Simpson Fox Associates. Lives in Kent. m. Don Keating; 1 d. TV presenter Caron Keating (qv), 2 s. Paul, Michael.

Gareth Hunt

HUNT, Gareth

Gareth Hunt. Actor. b. London, 7 February 1943. Trained at the Webber Douglas Academy.

TV: *Worlds on War; Bless This House; The Hangman; The Organisation; Doctor Who;* Frederick the footman in *Upstairs, Downstairs;* Mike Gambit in *The New Avengers;* Thomas Warner in *The Love School;* Gerry in *That Beryl Marston...; Shaping Up* (pilot); *A Hazard of Hearts* (TVM); Dulton in *A Ghost in Monte Carlo* (TVM); Bill Cunningham in *A Castle of Adventure* (series); *Minder; An Actor's Life for Me;* Vince Tulley in *Side by Side* (two series, 1992-3); *The Detectives.* TV commercial: Nescafé.

Films: *Licensed to Love and Kill; The World Is Full of Married Men; The House on Garibaldi Street; And the Walls Came Tumbling Down; Gabrielle and the Doodlemen; Bloodbath at the House of Death; It Couldn't Happen Here;* Ian Hubbard in *A Chorus of Disapproval; Dangerous Love.*
Address: c/o ICM. m. 1st Carol (dis), 2nd Anette; 2 s. Gareth (from 1st m.), Oliver-Leigh.

Alan Hunter

HUNTER, Alan

Alan John Moore. Actor. b. Liverpool, 24 October 1952. Trained at Central School of Speech and Drama.

TV: *Crown Court; Strangers; John Vassal; Print Out; The Spoils of War; Squadron; Bergerac; Minder; Dempsey and Makepeace; Truckers; Hannay; The Bill; Snakes and Ladders;* Greg Ryder in *Take the High Road; London's Burning; A Touch of Frost;* Supt Johnson in *Dangerous Lady* (series, 1995); *Dangerfield; The Bill.* Address: c/o Roxane Vacca Management. Lives in London. m. 1st (dis), 2nd 1993 actress Caroline Ashley (qv); 1 s. Jack Liem (from 2nd m.) Hobbies: Sailing, diving, photography.

Russell Hunter

HUNTER, Russell

Russell Hunter. Actor. b. Glasgow, 18 February 1926.

TV: Lonely in *Callan; Ace of Wands; Mackenzie; The Standard; Five Red Herrings; Mind Your Language; Dickens of London; Rule Britannia;* Harry in *The Gaffer; Play for Tomorrow; The Dunroamin Uprising; Doctor Who; Casualty; Lovejoy; Taggart;* Dosser in *Rab C Nesbitt;* Sam McBride in *The Negotiator;* DS Prentice in *A Touch of Frost;* Spanner in *The Detectives.*

Films: *The Gorbals Story; Callan.* Address: c/o Marjorie Abel. m. actress Marjorie Thomson (dis), actress Caroline Blakiston (qv) (dis), Una McLean; 1 s. Adam, 1 d. Charlotte.

HUNTER ASHTON, Al

Al Hunter. Actor/scriptwriter. b. Liverpool. Writes under real name of Al Hunter; previously acted as Al Ashton (now Al Hunter Ashton). Trained at Manchester Polytechnic's School of Theatre and Television, and performed as a comedian in clubs and on the cabaret circuit.

TV: Mike Hathaway in *Angels; Juliet Bravo; You Don't Have to Walk to Fly; Lytton's Diary; C.A.T.S. Eyes;* Colin Duma in *Brookside; Lost Empires; Constant Hot Water; The Lenny Henry Show;* Ray Grice in *Crossroads; Rockliffe's Babies; The Bretts; Casualty; Surgical Spirit; Hard Cases; Flying High; Minder; Watching;* DC Dowsett in *Bergerac; Inspector Morse; The Endless Game* (pilot); *Alive and Kicking* (Screen One); *Just; Devices and Desires; She-Wolf of London; Birds of a Feather; Bread; Harry Enfield's Television Programme;* Inspector Brunskill in *The Guilty* (mini-series); Denis Capper in *Kinsey; Chef!; Femme Fatale* (Screen Two); *Marshal and the Madwoman* (TVM); *White Goods;* Barnstable in *The Bullion Boys* (Screen One); *Conley: Outside Chance;* Don Mellis in *The Chief; The Brittas Empire; Teaching Matthew;* Mr Baron; Colin Long in *Emmerdale;* Mr Eaton in *Time after Time;* Wart in *Rumble* (series, 1995); Pit Bull in *London's Burning;* Albert in *The Radio Ham* (Paul Merton in Galton & Siimpson's...); *Expert Witness.* As writer: *The Firm* (winner, Best TV Film, Czech Film Festival 1989, and Prix Europa 1990); *EastEnders; Casualty; The Bill; Emmerdale; Streetwise* (two series, also storyline writer); *Alive and Kicking* (Screen One); *Teaching Matthew* (BBC Schools); *White Goods; Hoops; Rumble* (Series 1, also storyline writer); *Muscle; Alison* (BBC Schools); *Raw Talent.*
Films: *Remembrance; Arthur's Hallowed Ground; A Fish Called Wanda; Widow-Maker; Wapping.*
Radio: Les Stafford in *The Archers.* Address: c/o The Narrow Road Company. Lives in West London. m. 1983 Sue; 1 d. Dale. Hobbies: 'Sex, bitching, eating — but not necessarily in that order.'

Al Hunter Ashton

HURLEY, Elizabeth

Elizabeth Hurley. Actress/Model.
TV: Title role in *Christabel* (mini-series, 1988); *The Orchid House; Act of Will; The Resurrector; Rumpole of the Bailey; Inspector Morse;* Candida Ashton in *The Good Guys; The Young Indiana Jones Chronicles; Sharpe's Enemy; Cry of the City.*
Films: *Aria: Rowing in the Wind; The Skipper; The Long Winter of 39; Passenger 57; Bedlam; Mad Dogs and Englishmen; The Spear.* Address: c/o ICM. Single.

Elizabeth Hurley

HURST, Samantha Jane

Samantha Jane Hurst. Actress. b. Stockton-on-Tees, 13 October 1976. Took private drama lessons for 10 years before taking exams with the Guildhall School of Music and Drama.
TV: Holly in *Father Matthew's Daughter;* Sorrel Starkey in *Celebration: Tony Warren* (Granada Television only, dramatised scenes from his novel *The Lights of Manchester*); salon receptionist in *Ain't Misbehavin';* Rosie in *Harry;* Dolores Sharp in *Emmerdale.*
Address: c/o ATS Casting. Lives in South Humberside. Single. Pets: Three German shepherd dogs, a hamster and a venus flytrap. Hobbies: Singing, swimming, painting, candle-making.

Samantha Jane Hurst

HUTCHINGS, Geoffrey

Geoffrey Hutchings. Actor. b. Dorchester, Dorset, 8 June 1939. Trained at RADA.
TV: D H Lawrence in *Death of My Mother* (Monitor, TV début, 1964); *The Squirrels; Clayhanger; Raffles; Strangers; Juliet Bravo; Widows; Made in Britain; Charlie; Lytton's Diary; Home James!; The Bill; Hot Metal; Saracens; Bergerac; The Gravy Train; Brass; Traitors;* Rochefort in *Pirate Prince;* Carwyn Phillips in *Filipina Dreamgirls* (TVM); PO Swift in *Bye Bye Baby;* Sgt Lucas in *Maigret* (two series, 1992-3); *Perfect Scoundrels; Minder;* Barton in *The Bullion Boys* (Screen One); *The Bill;* Ralph Tomkins in *A Year in Provence; Casualty;* John Edwards in *Our Friends in the North* (serial, 1996).
Films: *Clockwise; On the Black Hill; Wish You Were Here; Ari; Henry V; White Hunter, Black Heart.*
Radio: Bill Robertson (the vet) in *The Archers.* **Awards:** Theatre: SWET Best Comedy Performance award for *Poppy* (1982). Address: c/o Barry Burnett Organisation. Lives in Gloucestershire. m.; 1 s. Nathan, 2 d. Octavia, Holly. Pets: 'A cat, dogs, rats.' Hobbies: Golf.

Geoffrey Hutchings

HUTCHISON, Ken

Ken Hutchison. Actor. Stage plays include *The Ruling Class* (West End).
TV: *Dixon of Dock Green; Z-Cars; Softly Softly; The Persuaders; The Protectors; The Sweeney; Shoestring; Hazell; Targets; Space 1999; Bulman; Minder; The Borderers; Sutherland's Law;* Matt Harvey in *The Onedin Line; The Wild West Show;* Heathcliff in *Wuthering Heights; Hideaway;* Inspector Murphy in *Murphy's Mob; Loneliness of a Long Distance Piano Player; Just Another Saturday; Just a Boy's Game; The Red Shift; A Gift from Nessus; Jemima Shore Investigates;* Allan in *One of the Boys;* Hamacka in *All Quiet on the Western Front* (mini-series); *Masada* (mini-series); *The Bill* (two roles); George Donaldson in *Taggart: Death Benefits;* Ellis in *99-1;* Ron Jesson in *Milner; Casualty; Hamish Macbeth; The Chief.*
Films: *Julius Caesar; Straw Dogs; Wrath of God; Sweeney II; The First World Cup; Gandhi; Ball on the Slates; LadyHawke; Blonde Fist; From the Island/As an Eilean.* Address: c/o Michael Ladkin.

Ken Hutchison

Alan Igbon

Jon Iles

Celia Imrie

Seeta Indrani

John Inman

IGBON, Alan

Alan Igbon. Actor. b. Manchester, 29 May. Studied drama at The Actors Forum, London.

TV: Mike in *The Daughters of Albion;* Loggo in *The Black Stuff* (Play for Today) and *Boys from the Blackstuff* (series); Boswell in *Me, I'm Afraid of Virginia Woolf;* Rakim in *The Professionals;* Steve in *Mixed Blessings;* Danny in *Angels;* Gene in *Brookside;* Darren in *Life Begins at Forty;* David in *The Recording Studio;* Ola in *Nightingale's Boys;* Isaiah in *No Problem;* Sheldon in *The Front Line;* Teddy in *G.B.H.* (series); Dennis in *Moving Story* (series 1994-5); Colin West in *The Bill.*

Films: *Women in Tropical Places;* Tommy in *One-Armed Bandits;* Jesus in *Water;* William in *Babylon;* Meakin in *Scum;* Steve in *Bloody Kids.* Address: c/o Chuck Julian Associates. Lives in Manchester. m.

ILES, Jon

Jon Iles. Actor. b. Ripon, North Yorkshire, 17 May 1954. Trained at the Rose Bruford College of Speech and Drama. Stage plays include *Jungle Book* and *Dial M for Murder* (both West End).

TV: *To the Manor Born; Happy Endings;* medieval knight in *The Dick Emery Show; Bognor; Crown Court; C.A.T.S. Eyes; Supergran; Never the Twain; Fresh Fields;* DC Mike Dashwood in *The Bill* (1984-92); *3-7-11; Law and Order.*

Films: *Those Glory, Glory Days.* Address: c/o Hilary Gagan Associates. Lives in South London. Single. Pets: A retired greyhound called Maggie. Hobbies: weight training.

IMRIE, Celia

Celia Imrie. b. Guildford, Surrey, 15 July 1952. Stage plays include *The Last Waltz, Particular Friendships, School for Wives, The Philanthropist, Yerma* and an RSC world tour.

TV: *Upstairs, Downstairs; Cloud Howe; To the Manor Born; Bergerac; The Nightmare Man; Shoestring; Victoria Wood — As Seen on TV; Victoria Wood;* Miss Jewsbury in *Oranges Are Not the Only Fruit* (mini-series, 1990); *The World of Eddie Weary; The New Statesman;* Corinne Perigo in *The Darling Buds of May; Stay Lucky; Van Der Valk;* Harum Scarum (storyteller); *Victoria Wood's All Day Breakfast;* Joanna in *The Riff Raff Element* (two series, 1993-4); *A Question of Guilt; The Brown Man; Boswell and Johnson's Tour of the Western Isles* (ScreenPlay); Vera in *A Dark-Adapted Eye* (mini-series, 1994); *Pat and Margaret* (Screen One); *A Very Open Prison* (Screen Two); Claudia Bing in *Absolutely Fabulous;* part of Rob Wilton's Company in *Call Up the Stars* (VE Day concert, 1995); Bella Darcy in *Class Act; Return of the Native* (Screen Two); *Black Hearts in Battersea* (series, 1996).

Films: *The Wicked Lady; Assassin; The House of Whipcord; Highlander; Death on the Nile.* Address: c/o CDA.

INDRANI, Seeta

Seeta Indrani. Actress. b. Brixton, South London. Stage productions include *Cats* (as Cassandra, original West End Cast), *Orpheo ed Euridice* (Glyndebourne Opera), *Peter Pan* and *Poppy* (both RSC).

TV: *Timon of Athens; The Cleopatras; Omnibus; Here and Now; Rub a Dub Tub;* Christine in *Options;* Katrina in *Tripods;* Belinda in *Dido and Aeneas;* Haji in *C.A.T.S. Eyes;* Dr Nasir in *Dempsey and Makepeace;* Sita Sharma in *Albion Market;* Apala in *Damon & Debbie;* Mrs Chastri in *Hunting the Squirrel; Into Music* (presenter); Sam in *Mathspy; Storytime* (presenter); Marjorie in *Spatz;* WPC Norika Datta in *The Bill;* Cristina Ramirez in *Maria's Child* (Screen Two).

Films: *The Nutcracker;* Carmen in *Gunbus.* **Radio:** *Where Are You, Juliet?;* Anita Sharma in *Citizens.* Address: c/o Mayer & Eden. Lives in North London. Hobbies: Tending window-boxes.

INMAN, John

Frederick John Inman. Actor/Entertainer. b. Preston, Lancashire, 28 June 1935.

TV: Mr Humphries in *Are You Being Served?* (1973-84); *This Is Your Life* (subject); *Odd Man Out; Take a Letter Mr Jones; The Good Old Days;* Mr Humphries in *Grace and Favour* (two series, 1992-3, US title *Are You Being Served, Again?*); Frank Randle in *Call Up the Stars* (VE Day concert, 1995).

Films: Mr Humphries in *Are You Being Served?*

Awards: TV: Variety Club BBC TV Personality of the Year award (1976); *TVTimes* Funniest Man on Television award (1976). Address: c/o W&J Theatrical Enterprises, 51a Oakwood Road, London NW11 6RJ, tel 0181-458 1608. Lives in London. Single. Hobbies: 'Work.'

IRVING, Jayne

Jayne Irving. Presenter. b. Sheffield, South Yorkshire, 30 August 1956. Trained as a reporter on the *Doncaster Evening Post* (1977-80), before moving into radio, then television.

TV: *Thames News* reporter (1982); TV-am West Country correspondent, newscaster on the David Frost and Michael Parkinson shows and presenter of *Good Morning Britain* (1983-5) and *After Nine* (1985-9); *Open Air* (1986-90); *Garden Party* (series, 1990); *Sex, Lies and Love* (BSB series); *Late and Live* (series, Tyne Tees only); *Central Weekend* (series); *Help!* (Anglia Television only, series); *Patient Power* (*This Morning*); *Mental Health* (*This Morning*); *Love Call* (Anglia Television only, series);

Anglia Live (Anglia Television only, series); *On the Road* (Westcountry Television only, series); chief presenter with UK Living, including *Living Magazine*. Drama appearances: *American Roulette* (as TV Presenter); *Maxwell House* (as herself); *Doctors on Top* (as herself); *The New Statesman* (as herself).
Films: *American Roulette*. Address: c/o Jane Hughes Management/Downes Presenters Agency. Lives in London. m. TV director David Stewart. Hobbies: Horse-riding, swimming, working out, cinema, theatre, literature, psychology, New Age medicine.

Jayne Irving

IVORY, William
William Ivory. Actor/Writer.
TV: Oggie in *Vacant Possessions*; Ephraem Wharmby in *Strike Pay*; The Stranger in *Punishment without Crime*; Steve in *Ice Dance*; Ramsden in *Capstick's Law*; Evans in *Confessional*; Jed in *Emmerdale Farm*; Eddie Ramsden in *Coronation Street*; *How We Used to Live*; Harold Peart in *All Creatures Great and Small*; Ted in *Deptford Graffiti*; DC Mark Divine in *Resnick* (two series); Greg in *Chef!* (series, 1993); Patrick Dunphy in *3-7-11*; Thad in *Berlin Breaks*; Ashton in *Merrihill Millionaires*; Andrew Jackson in *Between the Lines* (Series 2); Vinny in *Common as Muck* (also writer, series, 1994); Chris in *Sardines* (Comedy First); *The All-New Alexei Sayle Show*. Address: c/o Roxane Vacca Management.

JACKSON, Philip
Philip Jackson. Actor. b. Retford, Nottinghamshire, 18 June 1948. Gained a BA in drama from Bristol University. Stage plays include *The Passion* (National Theatre) and *A Midsummer Night's Dream* (RSC).
TV: *The Pigeon Fancier* (début, 1971); *Blooming Youth*; Gordon in *Last of the Summer Wine*; *Pennies from Heaven*; *Pickersgill People*; *Afternoon Off*; *Sounding Brass*; *Pasmore*; *Pocketful of Dreams*; *Farmers Arms*; *Robin of Sherwood* (three series, 1984-6); *On the Palm*; *Lizzie's Pictures*; *Our Geoff*; *The Dark Room*; Inspector/Chief Inspector Japp in *Agatha Christie's Poirot*; *Murder Most Horrid*; *The Wimbledon Poisoner*; Stan Eastwood in *15: The Life and Death of Philip Knight*; Clem in *Downwardly Mobile* (series); *Boom Boom!* (Lloyds Bank Film Challenge); *Black Hearts in Battersea*; *Hamish Macbeth*.
Films: Greaves in *Scum*; Alan in *Give My Regards to Broad Street*; *Doctor and the Devils*; Thatcher in *The Fourth Protocol*; *High Hopes*; *Bad Behaviour*; Man in *Woe to the Hunter*; Jim in *Brassed Off*.
Address: c/o Markham & Froggatt. Lives in West London. m. 1981 actress Sally Baxter (qv); 1 s. George, 1 d. Amy. Pets: Two cats called Molly and Maisie. Hobbies: Tennis, football, books, guitar.

William Ivory

JAEGER, Frederick
Frederick Jaeger. Actor/Director/Producer. b. Berlin, Germany, 9 May 1928. Moved to Britain in 1939. Trained at the Guildhall School of Music and Drama (1946-8).
TV: *The Grove Family* (1955); *The Inside Man*; *The Pretenders*; *Special Branch*; *Warship*; *Z-Cars*; *Department S*; *Ryan International*; *Little Women*; *Man at the Top*; *The Persuaders*; *Paul Temple*; *Doctor Who*; *Dixon of Dock Green*; *Jason King*; *Me Mammy*; *The Sweeney*; *Hadleigh*; *The Main Chance*; *The Protectors*; *Oneupmanship*; *Nuts*; *The Dick Emery Show*; *Shelley*; *Home Movies*; *Doombolt Chase*; *The New Avengers*; *The Professionals*; *Some Mothers Do 'Ave 'Em*; *The Omega Factor*; *The Fall and Rise of Reginald Perrin*; *The Potsdam Quartet*; *Minder*; *Churchill*; *QED*; *The Onedin Line*; *Kelly Monteith*; *Take the High Road*; *The Jim Davidson Show*; *Shoestring*; *Yes Minister*; *St Ursula's in Danger* (serial); *I Woke Up One Morning* (two series); *Agatha Christie's Miss Marple: The Body in the Library*; *New World*; *Small World*; *Echoes*; *Mathspy*; *The Nightmare Years*; *Selling Hitler*; *Love Hurts*; *Moon and Son*; *Keeping Up Appearances*; *God on the Rocks* (TVM); *Cold Comfort Farm*; *Walking the Whale*.
Films: *The Black Tents*; *The War Lover*; *The Iron Petticoat*; *Song of Norway*; *Ice Cold in Alex*; *Farewell Performance*; *The One That Got Away*; *Scorpio*; *One of Those Things*; *The Situation*; *The Seven-Per-Cent Solution*; *The Voyage*; *Nijinsky*; *Indiana Jones and the Last Crusade*. Address: c/o Joan Gray Personal Management. Lives in Richmond-upon-Thames, Surrey. m. 1st painter Hazel Penwarden (dis); 2nd Elizabeth; 2 step-d. Caroline, Sarah. Pets: Two dogs. Hobbies: Squash, gardening.

Philip Jackson

Frederick Jaeger

JAMES, Clive
Clive Vivian Leopold James. Presenter. b. Sydney, Australia, 7 October 1939. After Sydney University, studied at Pembroke College, Cambridge, and was president of the Footlights revue. As a lyricist, he made albums with singer Pete Atkin. Television critic of *The Observer* (1972-82).
TV: *Cinema*; *Up Sunday*; *So It Goes*; *A Question of Sex*; *Saturday Night People*; *Clive James on TV*; *The Late Clive James*; *The Late Show with Clive James*; *Saturday Night Clive*; *The Talk Show with Clive James*; *Clive James — Fame in the Twentieth Century*; *Review of the Year*; *Clive James — Postcard from Paris*; *Clive James' Postcard from Sydney*; *Clive James on 1992*; *Clive James — Fame in the Twentieth Century* (series, 1993); *Clive James — Postcard from Cairo*; *Clive James — Postcard from Los Angeles*; *Mama's Back!*; *Clive James on 1993*; *Clive James' Postcard from New York*; *Sunday Night Clive* (series, 1994); *Clive James on 1994*; *Clive James' Postcard from Bombay*; *Clive James' Postcard from Berlin*; *The Clive James Show* (ITV, two series, 1995-6); *Clive James in... Buenos Aires*; *Clive James Goes Country*; *The Clive James Grand Prix Show*. Address: c/o Peters Fraser & Dunlop.

Clive James

Geraldine James

JAMES, Geraldine

Geraldine James. Actress. b. Maidenhead, Berkshire, 6 July 1950. Trained at The Drama Centre. Stage plays include *Passion of Dracula, When I Was a Girl I Used to Scream and Shout, Cymbeline, The Merchant of Venice* (West End and Broadway).

TV: *The Sweeney; Crown Court; Dummy; I Remember Nelson; The History Man; Chains;* Sarah Layton in *The Jewel in the Crown; Time and the Conways;* Lady Maud in *Blott on the Landscape* (series, 1985); *Echoes;* 'Ex' (TVM); Helen Field in *Inspector Morse: Who Killed Harry Field?;* Mrs Dewey in *Losing Track* (Screen One); Mrs Linde in *A Doll's House* (Performance); *In Suspicious Circumstances;* Dr Mercedes Honeysett in *The Healer* (mini-series, 1994); Sarah Williams in *Doggin' Around* (Screen One); Eleanor Harker QC in *Kavanagh QC;* Rose Garrity in *Band of Gold* (two series, 1995-6); *Over Here.*

Films: *Sweet William; Night Cruiser; Gandhi; The Wolves of Willoughby Chase; The Tall Guy; She's Been Away; If Looks Could Kill; The Bridge.* **Awards:** TV: Critics' Award as Best Actress for *Dummy* (1978). Films: Joint winner, Venice Film Festival Volpi Cup for Best Actress, for *She's Been Away.*
Address: c/o Julian Belfrage Associates. m. Joseph Blatchley; 1 d. Eleanor. Hobbies: Piano, gardening.

JAMES, Godfrey

Godfrey James. Actor. b. London, 16 April 1931. Stage plays include *King* (Piccadilly Theatre).

TV: *Dark Side of the Sun; Hart to Hart; Gwen John; Fanny by Gaslight; Bloomfield; Hawkmore;* Mr Bumble in *Oliver Twist* (series); *The Tripods; Minder; King Arthur; Camille; Mussolini: The Decline and Fall of Il Duce* (TVM); *Dempsey and Makepeace; Cold Warrior; Bulman; William Tell* (US title *Crossbow*); *Yes;* Harry Mowlem in *Emmerdale Farm; The Battle of Waterloo; Journey into the Shadows; Truckers; Return of the Antelope; Dickens; Shadow of the Noose; Prisoners of Childhood; Wish Me Luck* (series); *The Bill; The Labours of Erika; Agatha Christie's Poirot; About Face; Crime Monthly; El C.I.D.; Maigret; The Good Guys;* Vic in *The Darling Buds of May: Cast Not Your Pearls before Swine;* Kenneth Payne in *Just a Gigolo* (series, 1993); *Criss Cross;* Mr Ellis in *The Bill; Highlander; The Teenie Weenies; Stick with Me, Kid.*

Films: *The Shade of the Sandcastle; Warburg; Women Are Weak; Princess.*
Address: c/o Scott Marshall.

Godfrey James

JAMES, Raji

Raji James. Actor. b. London, 24 February 1970. Trained at the Welsh College of Music and Drama. Stage plays include *Backstroke in a Crowded Pool* (National Theatre).

TV: Frankie in *Chandler & Co;* Barney in *Crocodile Shoes;* Junior in *Harry;* Ravi in *Do the Right Thing; A Box Full of Stories;* Daniels in *Stick with Me, Kid;* Andy Hill in *The Bill;* Rick in *Call Red.*
Address: c/o Langford Associates. Lives in London. m. actress Cheryl Innes; 1 s. Shannon.

Raji James

JAMESON, Louise

Louise Marion Jameson. Actress. b. Wanstead, East London, 20 April 1951. Trained at RADA. Acted in RSC productions of *Romeo and Juliet, Love's Labour's Lost, The Taming of the Shrew, King Lear, King John, Summer Folk, The Marquis of Keith, Passion Play, Twelfth Night* (as Viola), *Barbarians* and *The Park* (as Titania).

TV: *Cider with Rosie; Tom Brown's Schooldays; The Game* (Play for Today); *Z-Cars;* Sharon in *Emmerdale Farm; Boy Dominic;* Leela in *Doctor Who* (series); *The Omega Factor;* Blanche in *Tenko* (series); *The Gentle Touch; The Secret Diary of Adrian Mole Aged 13¾;* Susan in *Bergerac; The Growing Pains of Adrian Mole; Casualty; The Bill;* Janet in *Rides* (two series, 1992-3); *My Friend Walter; The Tempest; Stick with Me, Kid* (series); *Molly; Degas & Pissarro; The Terror Game;* Tilly Rawle in *Wycliffe.*
Address: c/o Conway, van Gelder, Robinson. Lives in Kent. m. 1990 artist Martin Bedford; 2 s. Harry, Thomas. Pets: One cat, one dog. Hobbies: Taking workshops for teenagers.

Louise Jameson

JAMESON, Susan

Susan Jameson. Actress/Writer. b. Barnt Green, Worcestershire, 13 August 1944. Trained at the Birmingham School of Speech Training and Dramatic Art. Has read many stories on audio tape.

TV: *Z-Cars;* Myra Booth (née Dickenson) in *Coronation Street* (1963-8); Kate in *Take Three Girls* (Series 1, 1969); Jessie Seaton in *When the Boat Comes In* (four series, 1976-81); *To Serve Them All My Days;* Kate in *Take Three Women* (series, 1982); *The Dave Allen Show; Hi-de-Hi!; Home to Roost; Boon; All in Good Faith; Bad Boyes; Who Sir, Me Sir?; The Secret World of Polly Flint; Woof!; The Count of Solar; Archer's Goon;* Mrs Coombs in *The Gingerbread Girl;* Jennifer Bradshaw in *Heartbeat; Catherine;* Kathleen Ferguson in *Band of Gold;* Mrs Loam in *Catherine Cookson's The Girl* (mini-series, 1996); Controller in *Circles of Deceit.*

Films: *I, Monster; Last of the Long-Haired Boys; All Creatures Great and Small; International Velvet.*
Address: c/o Barry Burnett Organisation. Lives in Sussex. Partner: Actor James Bolam (qv); 1 d. Lucy. Pets: Three cats, two dogs, two ponies. Hobbies: 'National Hunt racing, swimming, gardening, travel, reading and dossing.'

Susan Jameson

JAMIESON, Charles

Charles Reginald Wingate Jamieson. Actor. b. Rutherglen, Strathclyde, 12 March 1952. Studied at Glasgow School of Art and Theatre and art at Texas Christian University, Fort Worth, Texas.

TV: Celtic Chieftain in *Around Scotland; The New Road; Daniel Pyke; Chick Murray Show;* Goalkeeper in *Bonny;* Shea in *The Omega Factor;* Sergeant in *Blake's 7;* Duel with an Teallach (narrator); Charlie in *Goodnight and Godbless;* Ruari Galbraith in *Take the High Road;* Jimmy McDonald in *Fast Religion;* Jamieson Fildes in *The Brief;* George in *Unhappily Ever After; Marooned;* Sir Galahad in *Wheels; Livewire* (Wire TV); Bank Manager in *Bad Boys.* Plus voice-overs for BSB music channel trailers.

Films: Jimmy McDonald in *Fast Religion* (Royal College of Art); narrator of *Early Cinema, Parts I* and *II* (BFI production); George in *Unhappily Ever After;* Businessman in *Marooned.*

Address: c/o Joan Gray Personal Management (England). Lives in Dunlop, Ayrshire. m. 1984 Sally Anne Muir. Hobbies: Painting, gardening.

Charles Jamieson

JAMIESON, Kathy

Kathy Jamieson. Actress.

TV: Policewoman in *Brookside;* Sandra Arden in *Coronation Street;* Eileen's Mum in *Josie Smith;* Mrs Whiteley in *Children's Ward;* Joanna in *Dramarama: Badger,* Maggie Selby in *How We Used to Live;* Jo in *Cracker;* Karen Davies in *Medics;* April in *Who's Our Little Jenny Lind?;* Wendy Spencer in *Love and Reason;* Margaret Adlington in *Emmerdale* (1995); Sophie Jackson in *Heartbeat.*

Films: *Business as Usual.*

Radio: Susie in *Healthy Pursuits;* Barbara in *The Garden.*

Address: c/o Barbara Pemberton Associates. Lives near Burnley, Lancashire. m. actor John McArdle; 1 d. Katie, 1 s. Justin.

Kathy Jamieson

JANSON, David

David Janson. Actor. b. London, 30 March 1950. Trained at the Phildene Stage School from the age of nine. Stage plays include *A Midsummer Night's Dream* (RSC), *Oliver!, Hanky Park, Roll on Four o'Clock, She Was Only an Admiral's Daughter, Out of the Crocodile, My Giddy Aunt, Season's Greeting, Taking Steps, The Rivals, Don't Start without Me* and *Run for Your Wife.*

TV: *The Newcomers;* Ken 'Puffhouse' Richardson in *Get Some In* (series, 1975-8); *Grundy; Don't Rock the Boat; Brush Strokes,* Herr Flick in *'Allo, 'Allo* (final series, 1992); Postman in *Keeping Up Appearances* (series, 1992, 1993, 1995); Terry in *The Upper Hand* (1993).

Films: *A Hard Day's Night.*

Address: c/o A.I.M. m. actress Debbie Arnold (qv); 1 d. Ciara.

David Janson

JANUS, Samantha

Samantha Janus. Actress. Also known as Sam Janus. Trained at LAMDA. Sang in the 1991 Eurovision Song Contest and came 10th with Britain's entry, *A Message to Your Heart.*

TV: *Spatz; Grange Hill; The Bill; Jekyll & Hyde* (TVM); *El C.I.D.; EastEnders; Ladies in Charge; A Murder of Quality* (TVM); Hedda in *Demob* (series, 1993); Sharon in *Mama's Back;* Charmaine in *Health and Efficiency;* Marian in *Minder;* Nicola in *Pie in the Sky* (Series 2-3, 1995-6); Mandy in *Game On* (series, 1995); Zoe Gail in *Call Up the Stars* (VE Day concert, 1995).

Address: c/o Thelma Wade.

Samantha Janus

JARVIS, Martin

Martin Jarvis. Actor. b. Cheltenham, Gloucestershire, 4 August 1941. Trained at RADA (Silver Medal and Vanbrugh Award winner). Stage plays include *The Rivals* (London and Broadway).

TV: *The Forsyte Saga;* title role in *Nicholas Nickleby; The Way of All Flesh; Ross; Little Women; Black Olives; The Moonstone; Crimes of Passion; The Samaritan; After Liverpool; The Rivals of Sherlock Holmes; Doctor Who; The Pallisers; David Copperfield; Goodbye, Mr Chips; Softly Softly; Zigger Zagger; She, Initiative Test; Within These Walls, The Bluzhig Cut Murder; I Remember...; Charades; True Patriot; Ike* (mini-series, re-edited as TVM *Ike: The War Years); Rings on Their Fingers; Enemy at the Door; The Business of Murder; The Otterbury Incident; The Big One; Mr Palfrey of Westminster; Who Dares Wins; Let's Parlez Franglais; Just William's Christmas; Horizon* (narrator); *Survival* (narrator); *Juliet Bravo; The Black Tower; Make and Break; Rumpole of the Bailey; Chelworth; Des Res; The Life Revolution* (narrator); *Comic Relief; Coast to Coast* (TVM); *The South Bank Show;* Randall Rees in *Inspector Morse;* Maurice Howling in *Murder Most Horrid;* Charles Longmuir in *The Good Guys; The Language of Birds* (narrator); Malcolm Ashforth in *Boon;* Bartholomew Clements in *Casualty; Library of Romance* (*Good Morning with Anne & Nick,* storyteller); *Survival* (narrator); Monsieur De Renal in *Scarlet & Black* (mini-series, 1993); Harvey Wade in *A Touch of Frost; Jackanory: Fantastic Mr Fox* (storyteller).

Films: *The Last Escape; Taste the Blood of Dracula; The Bunker;* Inspector Jack Mitchell in *Buster; Deadly Advice.*

Address: c/o ICM. m. actress Rosalind Ayres (qv); 2 s. Toby, Oliver.

Martin Jarvis

JASON, David

David John White. Actor. b. Edmonton, London, 2 February 1940. OBE. Brother of actor Arthur White. Acted in amateur theatre while working as an electrician, then turned professional as an actor.

TV: *Crossroads*; Captain Fantastic in *Do Not Adjust Your Set*; Abel (the magician's assistant) in *Randall & Hopkirk (Deceased)*; Dithers in *Hark at Barker*; *Six Dates with Barker*; *Doctor in the House*; *Doctor at Large*; *Doctor at Sea*; *The Top Secret Life of Edgar Briggs*; *Mr Stabbs*; Shorty Mestead in *Lucky Feller* (series); Blanco in *Porridge*; Granville in *Open All Hours* (four series, 1976-85); Peter Barnes in *A Sharp Intake of Breath* (three series, 1978-81); Derek 'Del Boy' Trotter in *Only Fools and Horses* (1981-); Skullion in *Porterhouse Blue* (series, 1987); Ted Simcock in *A Bit of a Do* (two series, 1989); *Jackanory*; *Single Voices: The Chemist*; George in *Amongst Barbarians*; Pop Larkin in *The Darling Buds of May* (three series 1991-3, plus Christmas special 1992); Det Insp Jack Frost in *A Touch of Frost* (four series, 1992-6); Billy Mac in *The Bullion Boyss* (Screen One). Voiceovers include *Dangermouse*, *Count Duckula* and *The Wind in the Willows*.

Films: *Under Milk Wood*; *Royal Flash*; *The Water Babies*; Odd Job Man in *The Odd Job*; *The B.F.G.* (voice only); Toad in *The Wind in the Willows*.

Awards: TV: BAFTA Best Actor award (1988). Address: c/o The Richard Stone Partnership.

David Jason

JAYSTON, Michael

Michael James. Actor. b. Nottingham, 29 October 1935. Trained at Guildhall School of Music and Drama.

TV: *The Power Game*; *Mad Jack*; *Charles Dickens*; *Beethoven*; *Mr Rolls and Mr Royce*; *Jane Eyre*; *The Merchant of Venice*; *Quiller*; *King Lear*; *Doctor Who*; *She Fell Among Thieves*; *The Last Romantic*; *Gossip from the Forest*; *Tinker, Tailor, Soldier, Spy*; *A Bit of a Do*; Colonel Mike Mustard in *Cluedo*; Supt Masters in *The Good Guys*; *Casualty*; Ernest Bristow in *The Darling Buds of May* (series, 1993); *Jackanory: Ice Palace* (storyteller); Bob Willis in *Outside Edge* (Series 2-3, 1995-6, plus Christmas special 1995); Chauncey in *99-1*; Yachtsman in *The Radio Ham* (Paul Merton in Galton & Simpson's...).

Films: *Cromwell*; *Nicholas and Alexandra*; *The Homecoming*; *The Internecine Project*; *Follow Me*; *Bequest to the Nation*; *Tales That Witness Madness*; *Craze*. Address: c/o Michael Whitehall. m. 1st actress Lynn Farleigh (qv) (dis), 2nd Heather Mary Sneddon (dis), 3rd Elizabeth Smithson.

Michael Jayston

JEAVONS, Colin

Colin Jeavons. Actor. b. Newport, Gwent, 20 October 1929. Trained at the Old Vic Theatre School.

TV: *The New Adventures of Lucky Jim*; *Scott on...*; Mr Shadrack in *Billy Liar*; *The Fuzz*; *Kinvig*; *Shoestring*; *Great Expectations*; *Jackanory*; *Ladykillers*; *The Hitch-Hiker's Guide to the Galaxy*; *Doctor Who*; *Dear Heart*; *Travelling Man*; *Reilly — Ace of Spies*; *Atlantis*; *Travellers by Night*; *The Adventures of Sherlock Holmes*; *Charters and Caldicott*; *Fairly Secret Army*; *Sea of Faith*; *Bleak House*; *Squaring the Circle* (TVM); *Hitler's SS*; *Paradise Postponed*; *Prospects*; *Brat Farrar*; *Big Deal*; *The Return of Sherlock Holmes*; *Call Me Mister*; *Blackeyes*; *The House of Eliott*; Tim Stamper in *House of Cards* and *To Play the King*; Makepeace in *The Blackheath Poisonings*; Bernard in *Lovejoy*; Lockwood in *Minder*.

Films: *Caleb Williams*; *The French Lieutenant's Woman*; *Absolute Beginners*; *Secret Friends*. Address: c/o Jonathan Altaras Associates. m. Rosie; 2 s. Saul, Barney.

Colin Jeavons

JEFFREY, Peter

Peter Jeffrey. Actor. b. Bristol, 18 April 1929. Acted in RSC and National Theatre productions.

TV: *The Planemakers*; *Triangle*; *Villette*; *The Atom Spies*; *Rifleman*; *For Services Rendered*; *Minder*; *All's Well That Ends Well*; *Boys and Girls Come Out to Play*; *Cakes and Ale*; *The Common*; *Destiny*; *London Belongs to Me*; Mr Wainwright in *Porridge*; *Mr and Ms Bureaucrat*; *The Old Crowd*; *One by One*; *The Jewel in the Crown*; *Elizabeth R*; *By the Sword Divided*; *Nanny*; *Quartermaine's Terms*; *Doctor Who*; Eric in *Yes Minister*; *Chelworth*; *The Nightmare Years*; *Lipstick on Your Collar* (series); *A Question of Guilt*; Nicholas Bulstrode in *Middlemarch* (series); *Down to Earth*; *A Village Affair*; *Twelve Angry Men* (Paul Merton in Galton & Simpson's...); Sir Colin Blamire in *Our Friends in the North*.

Films: *Becket*; *The Fixer*; *If...*; *Ring of Bright Water*; *Anne of the Thousand Days*; *The Horsemen*; *The Odessa File*; *The Return of the Pink Panther*; *Midnight Express*; *Britannia Hospital*; *The Adventures of Baron Munchausen*. Address: c/o London Management.

Peter Jeffrey

JEFFRIES, Lionel

Lionel Jeffries. Actor/Director. b. London, 10 June 1926. Trained at RADA (Kendal Award for Best Actor).

TV: *Facts of Life*; *A Quick Double*; *Room at the Bottom*; *Cream in My Coffee*; Major Langton in *Shillingbury Tales* (series, 1981); title role in *Father Charlie* (series, 1982); Thomas Maddison in *Tom, Dick and Harriet* (two series, 1982-3); *Letting the Birds Go Free* (All for Love); *First and Last*; *Ending Up*; *Inspector Morse*; *Jekyll & Hyde* (TVM); *The Wild Duck*; *Boon*; Grandpa Rudge in *Rich Tea & Sympathy* (series, 1991); *The Mixer*; Bill Tongue in *Casualty*; Bernie Koppel in *Look at It This Way* (mini-series); *An Invitation to Remember* (subject); Grandad in *Woof!* (series); *Bed* (Performance).

Films: *Stage Fright*; *Will Any Gentleman...?*; *The Colditz Story*; *The Black Rider*; *Windfall*; *No Smok-*

Lionel Jeffries

ing; *The Quatermass Experiment; All for Mary; Jumping for Joy; Eyewitness; Bhowani Junction; Lust for Life; The Baby and the Battleship; Up in the World; The High Terrace; The Man in the Sky; The Vicious Circle; Hour of Decision; Doctor at Large; Barnacle Bill; Blue Murder at St Trinian's; Law and Disorder; Dunkirk; Orders to Kill; Up the Creek; The Revenge of Frankenstein; Girls at Sea; The Nun's Story; Behind the Mask; Nowhere to Go; Life Is a Circus; Further Up the Creek; Idle on Parade; Please Turn Over; Bobbikins; Two Way Stretch; The Trials of Oscar Wilde; Jazzboat; Let's Get Married; Tarzan the Magnificent; The Hellions; Fanny; Operation Snatch; Mrs Gibbons' Boys; Kill or Cure; The Notorious Landlady; The Wrong Arm of the Law; Call Me Bwana; The Scarlet Blade; The Long Ships; First Men in the Moon; The Truth about Spring; Murder Ahoy; You Must Be Joking!; The Secret of My Success; Drop Dead, Darling; Oh Dad, Poor Dad, Mama's Hung You in the Closet and I'm Feeling So Sad; The Spy with a Cold Nose; Jules Verne's Rocket to the Moon; Camelot; Chitty Chitty Bang Bang; Twinky; Twelve Plus One; Eyewitness; Whoever Slew Auntie Roo?; Royal Flash; What Changed Charley Farthing; Wombling Free* (voice only); *The Water Babies* (voice only); *The Prisoner of Zenda; Ménage à Trois; A Chorus of Disapproval; Danny, the Champion of the World* (TVM only in US). As director: *The Railway Children* (also writer); *The Amazing Mr Blunden* (also writer); *Baxter!; Wombling Free; The Water Babies.* Address: c/o ICM. m. Eileen; 2 d. Martha, Elizabeth, 1 s. Timothy.

Sue Jenkins

JENKINS, Sue

Susan Elizabeth Jenkins. Actress. b. Liverpool, 31 July. Trained at the Elliott-Clarke Theatre School, Liverpool. Stage roles include Doreen in *Having a Ball* (specially written for her by Alan Bleasdale).
TV: *Z-Cars* (as a child); *Wood and Walters;* Charlotte Holroyd in *How We Used to Live;* Janey in *The Beiderbecke Affair,* Gloria Todd in *Coronation Street;* Julie Ryan in *Coasting;* Jackie Corkhill in *Brookside* (1991-); Mollie Mozelle in *Our Dearest Dear* (In Suspicious Circumstances). Address: c/o Scott Marshall. Lives in Cheshire. m. actor David Fleeshman (qv); 2 d. Emily Victoria, Rosie Annabelle, 1 s. Richard Jonathan. Pets: Two cats, Whisky and Charlie. Hobbies: Water-skiing, reading, writing, swimming.

Dominic Jephcott

JEPHCOTT, Dominic

Dominic Jephcott. Actor. b. Coventry, Warwickshire, 28 July 1957. Trained at RADA.
TV: *Enemy at the Door; The Scarlet Pimpernel* (TVM); *Napoleon and Josephine; The Aerodrome; The Jewel in the Crown; Oliver Twist; The Beiderbecke Affair; Hold the Dream; Paradise Postponed; Claws; Rumpole of the Bailey; Ticket to Ride; The Return of Sherlock Holmes; The Leading Lady; The Bill; Casualty; Stay Lucky,* Peter Davis in *Lovejoy,* George Compton in *A Touch of Frost, And the Beat Goes On;* Di Sam Fallowfield in *Dalziel and Pascoe.*
Films: *All Quiet on the Western Front; An American Dream.* Address: c/o Markham & Froggatt.

JERONIMO, Tonicha

Tonicha Elizabeth Lawrence Jeronimo. Actress. b. Jersey, Channel Islands, 4 November 1977. Trained in theatre from the age of two and for three years at Scala performing arts school.
TV: Linda Glover in *Emmerdale.* Address: c/o Jean Clarke Management. Lives in West Yorkshire. Partner: Actor Stuart Wade. Pets: A dog. Hobbies: Swimming, horse-riding, pistol shooting, all sports.

Tonicha Jeronimo

JERRICHO, Paul

Paul Jerricho. Actor/Director. b. Llandudno, Gwynedd, 18 November 1948. Trained at The Drama Centre.
TV: *Enemy at the Door; The Secret Army; Hay Fever; QED; Armchair Thriller* (six episodes); *Ladykillers;* Conrad Lorenz in *Animal Behaviour;* the Castellan in *Doctor Who* and *The Five Doctors; The Biko Inquest;* Charles Woodhouse in *Triangle;* Danny Moorcock in *Emmerdale Farm* (six episodes); Mr Hicks in *Grange Hill; Knights of God; Medicine through Time;* Robert Hastings in *Howards' Way; The Bill;* Rodney in *Love Hurts; Press Gang; Luv; For Valour; Hale & Pace; London Bridge.*
Films: *Force 10 from Navarone; The Empire Strikes Back; The Thirty-Nine Steps; Cry Freedom;* Ortutay in *Forced March;* MI5 Officer in *L'Accompagnatrice.* Address: c/o McIntosh Rae Management. Lives in London. Partner: Actress Helena Little; 1 s. Jack. Pets: A dog called Brando. Hobbies: Cricket.

Paul Jerricho

JEWEL, Jimmy

James Arthur Thomas Marsh. Actor. b. Sheffield, South Yorkshire, 4 December 1909. On stage from age of 10 and formed comedy duo with cousin Ben Warriss (1934-66). Straight actor since 1967.
TV: *The Jewel and Warriss Show; Re-Turn It Up; Sunday Night at the London Palladium; It's a Living; The Ed Sullivan Show* (all with Ben Warriss); Eli Pledge in *Nearest and Dearest; Thicker than Water;* Tommy Butler in *Spring and Autumn; Worzel Gummidge; Funny Man; Spanner in the Works; Oldest Goose in the Business; Arthur's Hallowed Ground; Hideaway* (TVM); *Missing Persons; One Foot in the Grave;* Sid Towers in *Casualty;* Simba Cochrane in *Look at It This Way* (mini-series); Boswell in *Lovejoy.*
Films: *Rhythm Serenade; What a Carry On!; Let's Have a Murder* (all with Ben Warriss); *The Man Who Had Power over Women; Nearest and Dearest; Rocinante; The Krays; American Friends.* Address: c/o Howes and Prior. Lives in West London. m. Belle Bluett (dec); 1 s. Kelly, 1 adopted d. Piper.

Jimmy Jewel

Milton Johns

Stratford Johns

Sue Johnston

Catherine Zeta Jones

Freddie Jones

JOHNS, Milton

Milton Johns. Actor. b. Bristol, 13 May 1938.
TV: *Poldark; Doctor Who* (three roles); *Some Mothers Do 'Ave 'Em; The Good Life; Whiphand; The Intruder; The Limbo Line; A Horseman Riding By; Spearhead* (four series); *Yes Minister; Butterflies; Bread and Blood; Oppenheimer; The Citadel; Campion; Home to Roost; Solo; Tishoo; Foxy Lady; Io e Il Duce* (TVM); *Murphy's Mob* (three series); *Fresh Fields; Dempsey and Makepeace; The Pickwick Papers; Hell's Bells; War and Remembrance; Remington Steele; Precious Bane; Trainer; El C.I.D.; Boon;* Brendan Scott in *Coronation Street; Roy's Raiders; Stanley's Dragon; Class Act; Down to Earth.*
Films: Vadar's Aide in *The Empire Strikes Back; The Wall.* Address: c/o Hilda Physick Agency.

JOHNS, Stratford

Stratford Johns. Actor. b. South Africa.
TV: Charlie Barlow in *Z-Cars, Softly Softly, Softly Softly: Task Force* and *Barlow at Large; An Extra Bunch of Daffodils; I Claudius; Doctor Who; Salome's Last Dance; A Small Mourning; Itch; Perfect Scoundrels; The Secret Agent; The Life and Times of Henry Pratt; The Good Guys; Scarlet & Black; Minder.*
Films: *Burnt Evidence; Hands of Destiny; The Ladykillers; The Night My Number Came Up; The Dark Avenger; The Ship That Died of Shame; Who Done It?; Eyewitness; The Long Arm; Tiger in the Smoke; Across the Bridge; The One That Got Away; Law and Disorder; No Trees in the Street; Indiscreet; Violent Playground; A Night to Remember; The Professionals; Hand in Hand; The Naked Edge; The Valiant; The Young Ones; Two-Letter Alibi; The Great St Trinian's Train Robbery; Jules Verne's Rocket to the Moon; The Plank; Cromwell; George and Mildred; The Fiendish Plot of Dr Fu Manchu; Dance with a Stranger; Wild Geese II; Hitler's SS: Portrait in Evil; Car Trouble; Foreign Body; Salome's Last Dance; The Lair of the White Worm; The Fool; A Demon in My View; Splitting Heirs.* Address: c/o Michael Whitehall.

JOHNSTON, Sue

Sue Johnston. Actress. b. Warrington, Cheshire, 7 December 1943. Trained at Webber Douglas Academy.
TV: Mrs Chadwick in *Coronation Street;* Sheila Grant/Corkhill in *Brookside* (1982-90); Mum in *The Grove Family* (The Lime Grove Story); Barbara Grade in *Goodbye Cruel World* (mini-series); Edith Rosse in *In Suspicious Circumstances: Maundy Money;* Ruth Parry in *Medics* (Series 2-5, 1992-5); Mrs Bailey in *Inspector Morse: Absolute Conviction;* Phyllis Bowman in *A Touch of Frost;* Grace Robbins in *Full Stretch* (series, 1993); Terese Craven in *Luv* (two series, 1993-4); *Summer Holiday* (guest reporter); Lyn in *Into the Fire* (mini-series, 1996).
Books: *Hold on to the Messy Times* (autobiography). Address: c/o Ken McReddie. Lives in Warrington, Cheshire. m. (dis); 1 s. Joel. Hobbies: Cooking, walking, reading and music.

JONES, Catherine Zeta

Catherine Zeta Jones. Actress. b. Swansea, West Glamorgan.
TV: Mariette Larkin in *The Darling Buds of May* (three series, 1991-3, plus Christmas special, 1992); *Out of the Blue;* Victoria Chapman in *Catherine Cookson's The Cinder Path* (mini-series, 1994); Mia in *The Young Indiana Jones Chronicles;* Eustacia Vye in *Return of the Native* (Screen Two).
Films: Title role in *Scheherazade; Christopher Columbus: The Discovery; Splitting Heirs.* Address: c/o ICM. Lives in Swansea and London. Single.

JONES, Freddie

Frederick Charles Jones. Actor. b. Stoke-on-Trent, Staffordshire, 12 September 1927. Laboratory assistant until winning a scholarship to the Rose Bruford College of Speech and Drama.
TV: *Sword of Honour; Nana; Treasure Island; Cold Comfort Farm; Uncle Vanya; The Caesars; Germinal; Sweeney Todd;* Sir George Uproar in *The Ghosts of Motley Hall; Kremlin Farewell; Mashenka; Shoot the Revolution; Pennies from Heaven; Sorry...* (Play for Today); *In Loving Memory; Fall of Angles; Through the Looking Glass; Joe's Ark; Omnibus: John Clare; Secret Orchards; Tiny Revolutions; The Last Evensong; The Secret Diary of Adrian Mole; Silas Marner: The Weaver of Raveloe;* Dr Emlyn Isaacs in *The District Nurse* (Series 2, 1987); *Lost in London; Ghost; Vanity Fair; The Return of Sherlock Holmes; Country Girl; Room at the Bottom; How to Be Cool; SON Sisters* (pilot); *Boon; The Kremlin Farewell; The Paper Man; Hale & Pace; TECX; Inspector Morse: Who Killed Harry Field; Permanent Red; Nana; Germinal; Sherlock Holmes: The Last Vampyre; Adam Bede; Christopher Columbus — The Great Adventure; Woof!; Hotel Room; The Young Indiana Jones Chronicles; Mr Wroe's Virgins; Heartbeat; Lovejoy; A Pinch of Snuff; Just William; Cold Comfort Farm; It Might Be You ; No Bananas.*
Films: *Marat/Sade; Deadfall; The Bliss of Mrs Blossom; Far from the Madding Crowd; Accident; Juggernaut; Zulu Dawn; Otley; Goodbye Gemini; Frankenstein Must Be Destroyed; The Man Who Haunted Himself; The Satanic Rites of Dracula; All Creatures Great and Small; The Elephant Man; Young Sherlock Holmes; Firefox; E La Nave Va (And the Ship Sailed); Krull; Dune; Firestarter; Spooks; Erik the Viking; Wild at Heart; Consuming Passions; The Last Butterfly; The Mystery of Edwin Drood; The Great Powys; NeverEnding Story III.* Address: c/o James Sharkey Associates. m. actress Jennifer Elizabeth

Heslewood; 3 s. actors Toby Edward (b. 7 Sep 1966), Rupert Frederick (b. 6 July 1968), Caspar Boyd (b. 16 Nov 1971). Pets: 'Three cats and a wife.' Hobbies: Cooking, gardening, golf.

JONES, Gareth

Gareth Jones. Presenter. b. Wales, 5 July 1961.

TV: Music Box cable TV; *Get Fresh* (co-host, three series); Children's ITV; *Your Number's Up* (HTV game show); *APB*; MTV Europe satellite TV (presenter-producer); *Kellyvision*; *Pssst... The Really Useful Guide to Alcohol* (series); *How 2* (six series, 1990-5); *Mwy Na Phapur Newydd* (acting début, Welsh Fourth Channel); presenter-producer of *The TCC Club* and *TCC on the Road* (both The Children's Channel); *An Afternoon on the Moon; Gaz Top Non Stop; It's Not Just Saturday* (presenter, series, 1996); *The Big Bang* (series, 1996). Address: c/o Sara Cameron Management. Lives in London. Single.

Gareth Jones

JONES, Ken

Kenneth Jones. Actor/Writer. b. Liverpool, 20 February 1930. Trained at RADA.

TV: *Z-Cars* (first episode); *United!; The Planemakers; Hunter's Walk; All Day on the Sands; The Big Flame; Go for Gold; The Golden Vision; The End of Arthur's Marriage; The Liver Birds; Jesus of Nazareth; Germinal; Her Majesty's Pleasure; The Last of the Baskets; The Wackers; Emmerdale Farm; Coronation Street; The Squirrels; First Class Friend; Dead Earnest;* Ives in *Porridge; Seconds Out; Valentine Park; Boon;* Uncle Bernard in *Watching* (series); *Germinal; Murder Most Horrid;* Owen Jones in *Goodnight Sweetheart;* King Harold in *The Detectives;* Edward Fellows in *Peak Practice.* As writer-director: *Gulpin.*
Films: *The File of the Golden Goose; The Human Factor; SWALK; Sherlock Holmes; Yanks; No Surrender; Judo tho Obscure.* Address: c/o William Morris Agency (UK). Lives in London. m. actress writer Sheila Fay. Hobbies: Stonewalling.

Ken Jones

JONES, Peter

Peter Jones. Actor/Writer. b. Wem, Shropshire, 12 June 1920. Has acted in 30 West End plays.

TV: Mr Fenner in *The Rag Trade; Long Live the King; From a Bird's Eye View; Beggar My Neighbour* (first series); title role in *Mr Digby Darling* (three series); *But Seriously – It's Sheila Hancock; Comedy Playhouse* (also writer); *Wodehouse Playhouse; Here's Harry; Love Thy Neighbour; The Goodies; Mr Big* (also co-writer, two series); *I Thought You'd Gone* (also co-writer, series); *Children of Dynmouth; One-upmanship* (three series); Prime Minister Kevin Pork in *Whoops Apocalypse!, C.A.T.S. Eyes, The Agatha Christie Hour; Singles Weekend; Rumpole of the Bailey; The Mixer; As the World Turns* (US soap); *Tender Loving Care* (Screen One); *The Lifeboat; Minder; The Upper Hand; Waiting* (Comedy First).
Films: *Fanny by Gaslight; Dead of Night; I See a Dark Stranger; Chance of a Lifetime; The Franchise Affair; Home to Danger; The Magic Box; The Browning Version; Miss Robin Hood; Time Gentlemen Please!; 24 Hours of a Woman's Life; Angels One Five; Elstree Story; The Yellow Balloon; The Long Memory; Albert RN; Always a Bride; Innocents in Paris; The Good Beginning ; A Day to Remember; The Red Dress; For Better, for Worse; John and Julie; Private's Progress; Charley Moon; Blue Murder at St Trinian's; Danger Within; Operation Bullshine; Never Let Go; The Bulldog Breed; School for Scoundrels; Nearly a Nasty Accident; Romanoff and Juliet; A Stitch in Time; Father Came Too; Press for Time; Just Like a Woman; Smashing Time; Hot Millions; Carry On Doctor; The Return of the Pink Panther; Carry On England; Marcia* (short). Address: c/o Salopian Plays, 32 Acacia Road, London NW8 6AS. m. US actress-writer Jeri Sauvinet; 1 d. actress Selena Carey-Jones, 2 s. TV and radio producer Bill Dare (William Dare Jones), Charles Daniel. Hobbies: Making plans.

Peter Jones

JONES, Simon

Simon Jones. Actor. b. Charlton Park, nr Malmesbury, Wiltshire, 27 July 1950.

TV: *Rock Follies; Victorian Scandals; Fothergill; The Kindness of Mrs Radcliffe; No Visible Scar; Muck and Brass;* Bridey in *Brideshead Revisited* (series); Arthur Dent in *The Hitch-Hiker's Guide to the Galaxy* (series); *Crown Court; Giro City* (TVM); *Hurt to Hurt; The News Is the News; The Price;* Sir Walter Raleigh in *Blackadder II; Claws* (TVM); *Newhart; Murder, She Wrote; Taminger's; Shrinks* (series); *Loving.*
Films: *Sir Henry at Rawlinson End; Reds; Monty Python's The Meaning of Life; Privates on Parade; Club Paradise; Brazil; Green Card; American Friends; For Better or Worse; Miracle on 34th Street* Address: c/o ICM. Lives in New York and London. m. Nancy Lewis; 1 s. Timothy Leveret Lewis Jones.

Simon Jones

JOSEPH, Lesley

Lesley Joseph. Actress. Trained at LAMDA. West End plays include *Godspell* and *Exclusive Yarns.*

TV: *My Country 'Tis of Thee* (début); *And Mother Makes Five; Sadie, It's Cold Outside; Horizon* (drama-doc); *The Ballad of Johnny Vanguard; No 10; The Knowledge; Roots* (ITV series); *Broken Homes; Les Girls; Minder; Exclusive Yarns; A Sleeping Life; P's and Q's* (team captain); Dorian in *Birds of a Feather* (six series, 1989-94); *Through the Lace Curtains* (*Good Morning... with Anne & Nick*); *Edd the Duck's Megastar Treck; Jacks and the Beanstalk; Easy Money* (presenter, series, 1993); Ma Pecs in *Rumble* (series, 1995). Address: c/o Silvester Management. 1 s. Andrew, 1 d. Elizabeth.

Lesley Joseph

JOSEPH, Michelle

Michelle Joseph

Michelle Joseph. Actress. Trained at the Rose Bruford College of Speech and Drama.
TV: Trish in *The Bill;* Nurse in *As Time Goes By;* Diane in *Without Walls;* Della in *EastEnders;* Bryony Oxford in *Thief Takers* (series, 1996).
Radio: Nurse/Nina in *Opening Up* (BBC Radio). Address: c/o CAM.

JOYCE, Paddy

Paddy Joyce. Actor.
TV: *Cathy Come Home; The Saint; Please Sir!; The Fenn Street Gang; Coronation Street; Crown Court; Huggy Bear; The Enigma Files; Marya; Pennies from Heaven; The Onedin Line; Churchill's People; The Big Flame; Profile of a Gentleman; King of the Dumpers; The Lump; Softly Softly; The Ghost Sonata* (Open University); *Z-Cars; Dixon of Dock Green; Six Days of Justice; Mother Ireland; Consternation; The Walkers; The Les Dawson Show; The Dick Emery Show; Two's Company; Metal Mickey; Bowler; The Rolf Harris Show; Into the Labyrinth; Jamaica Inn; The Melting Pot; Rosie; Terry and June; The Falklands Factor; Knock Back; All the Fun of the Fair; Turtle's Progress; Charlie; Auf Wiedersehen Pet; Attachments; Minder; Prospects; Educating Marmalade; The Bill* (two roles); *The Growing Pains of Adrian Mole; Frankenstein; S.O.S. Titanic; The Mannions of America; Lloyd's of London; Little and Large; The Charmer; Campion; Grass Arena; May to December;* Miles in *Lovejoy; Gone to the Dogs; EastEnders; You Rang, M'Lord?;* Spivey in *Ghosts: I'll Be Watching You;* Angus Moss in *The Bill.*
Films: *Poor Cow; Britannia Hospital; Red Monarch; The Chain; Lamb; The Lonely Passion of Judith Hearne; Spirit; Cresta Run.* Address: c/o Susan Angel Associates.

Paddy Joyce

JUNKIN, John

John Junkin. Actor/Writer. b. Ealing, West London, 29 January 1930. Began writing in 1956 after tracking down Spike Milligan in his office and persuading him to read a script. Joined Joan Littlewood's Theatre Workshop to train as an actor in 1960.
TV: *Z-Cars; Sam and Janet; Junkin* (four series); *Hello Cheeky; Marty; Looking for Clancy; Out; The Ravelled Thread; Till Death Us Do Part; Dick Turpin; Penmarric; All for Love; Blott on the Landscape; 25 Years of Ronnie Scott's; Ask No Questions* (presenter); *Langley Bottom* (co-writer); *Mike Yarwood in Persons* (script editor); *All Creatures Great and Small; Shelley;* Chief Insp Holroyd in *Inspector Morse: Cherubim and Seraphim;* Mal in *Harry;* Steven in *Law and Disorder* (series, 1994); *Mr Bean;* Mr Pritchard in *The Bill.* As programme associate/consultant: *Body Matters; Bob Says Opportunity Knocks; Bob's Full House; The $64,000 Question; Bob's Your Uncle.*
Films: *Sparrows Can't Sing; The Wrong Arm of the Law; The Break; Vengeance* (US title *The Brain*); *The Primitives; Hot Enough for June* (Agent 8¾); *A Hard Day's Night; The Pumpkin Eater; The Wrong Box; The Sandwich Man; Kaleidoscope; The Plank; How I Won the War; Simon, Simon* (short); *Confessions of a Driving Instructor; Confessions from a Holiday Camp; Marcia* (short); *Wombling Free; Rosie Dixon Night Nurse; Brass Target; That Summer!; Licensed to Love and Kill; A Handful of Dust; Chicago Joe and the Showgirl.* Address: c/o Elaine Murphy Associates. Lives in Buckinghamshire. m. Jennifer Claybourn (sep); 1 d. Annabel. Hobbies: Crosswords, reading, friends.

John Junkin

KANE, John

John Kane. Actor/Writer. b. Dundee, Tay, 27 October 1945. Trained at Glasgow College of Dramatic Art.
TV: As actor: *Softly Softly; Doctor Who; Doctor on the Go; Cymbeline; Love's Labour's Lost; The Seagull; Paradise Postponed.* As writer: *Scott on...; Son of the Bride; Black Beauty; The Vamp; The Feathered Serpent; Four Idle Hands; Cloppa Castle; A Little Touch of Wisdom; Smuggler; Dick Turpin; Funny Ha-Ha; Terry and June; Happy Ever After; Never the Twain; Me & My Girl; All in Good Faith; The Return of Sherlock Holmes;* John Bavistock in *The Chief;* Colin Smallwood in *Pie in the Sky .*
Address: c/o ICM. m. Alison; 2 d. Alice, Susanna, 1 s. Simon.

John Kane

KANSKA, Joanna

Joanna Kanska. Actress.
TV: *Rumpole of the Bailey;* Grete Grotowska in *A Very Peculiar Practice* (Series, 2, 1988); Sirka in *Capital City* (two series, 1989-90); *A Slight Hitch; Sleepers; The New Statesman;* Maria in *B&B;* Grete Grotowska in *A Very Polish Practice* (Screen One); Marisha Vosnensky in *Love Hurts* (Series 2, 1993); Anna Tabor in *Lovejoy; The Ruth Rendell Mysteries: Vanity Dies Hard* (mini-series, 1995); Magda Ostrowska in *Madson* (series, 1996).
Films: Tamara in *The Tall Guy.* Address: c/o ICM.

KAPLAN, Juliette

Marlene Juliette Kaplan. Actress. b. Bournemouth, Dorset, 2 October 1939. Trained at the Hampshire School of Drama. Stage plays include *Who Killed Agatha Christie?* (Ambassadors Theatre).
TV: Pearl in *Last of the Summer Wine* (11 series); Mrs Graham in *The Curse of King Tut;* Rachael in

Joanna Kanska

His Name Was John; Mother in *Ad Infinitum*; Miss Fish in *The Cash Trial Scandal*.
Address: c/o Langford Associates. Lives in London. m. Harold Samuel Hoser (dis); 1 s. Mark, 2 d. Perrina, Tania. Hobbies: 'Rifle shooting, bridge, sex!'

Juliette Kaplan

KAY, Bernard

Bernard Kay. Actor. b. Bolton, Lancashire, 23 February 1938. Trained at the Old Vic Theatre School. Plays include *Henry IV*, *Julius Caesar* (both RSC) and *The Portage to San Christobel of A.H* (Mermaid Theatre).
TV: *Venturers; Clayhanger; The Main Chance; The Sweeney; Softly Softly; The Prince and the Pauper; Space 1999; Doctor Who;* Robert Sharp and Metcalfe in *Emmerdale Farm;* Harry Maguire in *Crossroads; Warship; Colditz; Rosie; Sutherland's Law; Target; Survivors; The Idiot; Cellar and the Almond Tree; Two's Company; The Enigma Files; The Professionals; Fair Stood the Wind for France; Police Cadet; Scarf Jack; Tales of the Unexpected; The Gentle Touch; Juliet Bravo; Two Weeks in Winter; The Last Days of Pompeii; Sakharov; The Bill; The Fourth Floor; Rockliffe's Babies; The Most Dangerous Man in the World; A Very British Coup; Capstick's Law;* Inspector Rodier in *Hannay;* Air Marshal Thornby in *Bomber Harris; London's Burning; Colin's Sandwich;* Zafati in *Mithaelangelo;* Stalin in *Kremlin Farewell;* Richard Naismith in *Century Falls; A Ghost in Monte Carlo* (TVM).Police Officer Cronin in *Minder;* Cyril in *Coronation Street.*
Films: *Spy Story; Dr Zhivago; Darling Lili; Lady Caroline Lamb; Trog; Sweeney!; The Hunting Party; Voyage of the Damned; Hiding Place; The Sewers of Gold; The Nativity; Dinner Date; Fortunate Pilgrim.*
Address: c/o Marina Martin Associates.

Bernard Kay

KAY, Charles

Charles Piff. Actor. b. Coventry, Warwickshire, 31 August 1930. Trained at RADA (Bancroft Gold Medal winner). TV since 1958. Stage plays include *Wars of the Roses, Pentecost, Life's a Dream, Waste* (all RSC), *As You Like It, Edward II, The National Health, Danton's Death, The Miser, The Madness of King George* (all National Theatre at the Old Vic), *The Homecoming* (Garrick Theatre), *The Millionairess* (Haymarket Theatre), *Anyone for Denis?* (Whitehall Theatre), *The Scarlet Pimpernel* (Her Majesty's Theatre), *The Woman in Black* (Strand, Playhouse and Fortune Theatres) and *Pentecost* (Young Vic).
TV: *The Victorians* (series, 1963); *Prisoner's Plea* (Detective); *The Wars of the Roses; The Duchess of Malfi; The Merchant of Venice; Sister Alice; Microbes and Men; Miss Nightingale;* Tsar Nicholas in *Fall of Eagles; Jenny; The Prodigal Daughter; Loyalties; I Claudius; Countess Ilona; Target; The Devil's Crown; Minor Complications; Ladykillers; The Borgias; To the Manor Born; To Serve Them All My Days; A Visitor for Mr Hugh Peters; My Cousin Rachel; The White Guard; By the Sword Divided; Bergerac; The Citadel;* Philip, King of France, in *King John; Minder; Edge of Darkness; Time for Murder; West of Paradise; The London Embassy;* Dobson in *Fortunes of War; Menace Unseen; Rumpole of the Bailey; A Quiet Conspiracy; Bomber Harris; A Question of Commitment* (Storyboard); *The Casebook of Sherlock Holmes; Fiddlers Three;* Monsieur Mollet in *The Darling Buds of May; The Bill;* Columbo Dimitri in *The Inspector Alleyn Mysteries: Death in a White Tie; Heart of Darkness;* Humphrey in *Brighton Belles;* Judge Wallace in *Law and Disorder* (series, 1994).
Films: *Hennessey; Nijinsky; Amadeus;* Canterbury in *Henry V.* Address: c/o Marmont Management.

Charles Kay

KAYE, Gorden

Gorden Kaye. Actor. b. Huddersfield, West Yorkshire, 7 April 1941. Stage plays include *As You Like It* (National Theatre) and *'Allo, 'Allo* (Prince of Wales Theatre, London Palladium and national tour).
TV: Bernard Butler in *Coronation Street; It Ain't Half Hot Mum, Are You Being Served?; The Growing Pains of PC Penrose; Shoestring; Oh Happy Band; The Foundation; All Creatures Great and Small; The Strange Affair of Adelaide Harris; God's Wonderful Railway; The Party's Over; Born and Bred; Fame Is the Spur; Codename Icarus; Rainy Day Women; Mansfield Park; King John; Much Ado about Nothing; In the Secret State;* René Artois in *'Allo, 'Allo* (pilot, 1982, and nine series, 1984-92); Maynard Lavery in *Last of the Summer Wine; The Children's Royal Variety Performance 1993;* Nickson in *The Bullion Boys* (Screen One); *The Best of 'Allo 'Allo* (presenter, 1994).
Films: *Escape from the Dark* (also titled *The Littlest Horse Thieves*); *Jabberwocky; The Waterloo Bridge Handicap; Porridge; Brazil.* Address: c/o Markham & Froggatt.

Gorden Kaye

KEARNEY, Gillian

Gillian Louise Kearney. Actress. b. Liverpool, 9 May 1972. Began acting with the Liverpool Playhouse Youth Theatre. After five years of acting in television and film, trained at the Rose Bruford College of Speech and Drama (1992-5).
TV: Debbie McGrath in *Brookside* and spin-off *Damon & Debbie* (mini-series, 1987); Cassy in *The Final Frame* (TVM); Helen in *Waterfront Beat;* Mandy in *Casualty;* Jenny in *Men of the World;* Emily Kennedy in *Catherine Cookson's The Tide of Life* (mini-series, 1996).
Films: Young Shirley in *Shirley Valentine.* Address: c/o Janet Welch Personal Management. Lives in North London. Single. Hobbies: Reading, dancing, swimming.

Gillian Kearney

Caron Keating

KEATING, Caron

Caron Louisa Keating. Presenter. b. Fulham, West London, 5 October 1962. Daughter of presenter Gloria Hunniford (qv). Moved to Northern Ireland a couple of months after her birth. Gained a BA (Hons) in English and drama from Bristol University. During her teens landed several radio and TV commercials, and presented religious and youth programmes on television in Northern Ireland.

TV: *Green Rock; The Visit; Channel One* (all BBC Northern Ireland); *Blue Peter* (1986-90); *4th Dimension; Wide Angle; Summer Scene* (series, 1992); *Olympics; Family Affairs* (two series, 1992-3, 1993-4); *Jurassic Park: The Royal Film Première* (presenter); *Royal Film Performance* (presenter, 1993); *Schofield's Quest;* entertainment correspondent for *London Tonight* (Carlton and LWT only, 1993-4); *After 5 with Caron Keating* (Carlton and LWT only, 1994-); *Caron Keating's After 5 Christmas Special* (Carlton only, 1994); *Routes and Rhythms* (series, 1995); *Schofield's Quest (1995); Royal Film Première: French Kiss* (1995). Address: c/o James Grant Management. Lives in London. m. Russ Lindsay: 1 s. Charlie. Pets: A dog called Bailey. Hobbies: Fishing.

Anna Keaveney

KEAVENEY, Anna

Anna Keaveney. Actress. b. Runcorn, Cheshire, 5 October 1949. Trained at Studio '68.

TV: *Within These Walls; Enemy at the Door; Widows;* Maise in *Divided We Stand* (series); Marie Jackson in *Brookside;* June in *Security* (Channel Four film); Christine in *Widows;* Brenda Lynch in *Stay Lucky;* Audrey Pollard in *Needle;* Liverpool Lil in *Grass Arena;* April Brooks in *Emmerdale;* Marcia Hornsby in *The New Statesman;* Marjorie in *Casualty;* Denise in *Sin Bin;* Denise in *The Bill;* Green Candidate in *Birds of a Feather;* Marjorie in *Casualty;* Nina Case in *The Bill;* Cath Dawson in *Peak Practice;* Wendy Francis in *Here Comes the Mirror Man* (Chiller).

Films: Katie Arnold in *Young Americans;* Jeannette in *Shirley Valentine.*

Address: c/o Stephen Hatton Management. Lives in North London. Single. Pets: A cat called Rosie.

Diane Keen

KEEN, Diane

Diane Keen. Actress. b. London, 29 July 1946. Brought up in Kenya; returned to Britain aged 19.

TV: Sandra Gould in *Crossroads; Fall of Eagles; Softly Softly; Public Eye; The Legend of Robin Hood; The Sweeney; The Feathered Serpent; Country Matters; Crown Court;* Fliss in *The Cuckoo Waltz; The Sandbaggers; Rings on Their Fingers; The Shillingbury Blowers; The Shillingbury Tales; The Reunion; The Morecambe and Wise Show; Bruce Meets the Girls; Foxy Lady; Oxbridge Blues; Killer Waiting; Sleeps Six; You Must Be the Husband; Jekyll & Hyde; Three Go Round;* Jenny Burden in *The Ruth Rendell Mysteries; Key for Two;* Stella in *Brighton Belles;* Ann Eaton in *The White House Farm Murders* (Crime Story); Connie French in *September Song* (series, 1994); Janet Hurst in *The Bill;* Mary in *The Detectives;* Jenny Burden in *The Ruth Rendell Mysteries: Simisola* (mini-series). TV commercials: Nescafé.

Films: Claire in *Here We Go round the Mulberry Bush.*

Address: c/o Andrew Manson Personal Management. m. Neil Zeiger; 1 d. Melissa.

Penelope Keith

KEITH, Penelope

Penelope Keith. Actress. b. Sutton, Surrey, 2 April 1940. Trained at the Webber Douglas Academy.

TV: *The Army Game; Hadleigh; Six Shades of Black; Kate; The Pallisers; Two's Company; Jackanory; Saving It for Alvie; Private Lives;* Margo Leadbeatter in *The Good Life* (series, 1975-8); *Private Lives; The Norman Conquests; The Morecambe and Wise Christmas Show; Much Ado about Nothing; Donkey's Years; On Approval;* Audrey fforbes-Hamilton in *To the Manor Born* (three series, 1979-81); *Spider's Web; Waters of the Moon; Sweet Sixteen; Capability Brown; Moving; Executive Stress;* Jean Price in *No Job for a Lady* (three series, 1990-2); *What's My Line?* (presenter); Phillippa Troy in *Law and Disorder* (series, 1994); Maggie Prentice in *Next of Kin* (two series, 1995-6, plus Christmas special, 1995).

Films: *Rentadick; Take a Girl like You; Every Home Should Have One; Penny Gold;* Rennie in *Ghost Story; The Hound of the Baskervilles; Priest of Love.*

Awards: TV: *TVTimes* awards (1976, 1977, 1978, 1979, 1980); BAFTA Best Light Entertainment Performance award (1977); BAFTA Best TV Actress award (1978, 1979); Variety Club BBC TV Personality award (1979). Address: c/o London Management. m. Rodney Timson; 1 adopted s.

Sheila Keith

KEITH, Sheila

Sheila Keith. Actress. b. London, 9 June 1920. Trained at the Webber Douglas Academy. Stage plays include *Present Laughter* (Queen's Theatre), *Mame* (Theatre Royal, Drury Lane), *Banana Ridge* (Savoy Theatre), *Deathtrap* (Garrick Theatre), *Anyone for Denis?* (Whitehall Theatre), *Italian Straw Hat* (Shaftesbury Theatre), *Shape of the Table* (National Theatre) and *When She Danced* (Globe Theatre).

TV: *Crane; Public Eye; Crime Buster; George and the Dragon; Love Story; Present Laughter; Dr Finlay's Casebook; Crossroads; Mrs Thursday; Nicholas Nickleby; The Regiment; The Flaxton Boys; The Pallisers; David Copperfield; Moody and Pegg; Ballet Shoes; Within These Walls; The Liver Birds; The Dolls; Ronnie Barker Playhouse; The Kindness of Mrs Ratcliffe; Me Mammy; Hearts and Flowers* (Play for Today); *Kate; It's Murder — but Is It Art?; The Moonstone; Z Cars; Unpleasantness at the Bellona Club; Spring*

and Autumn; Father Brown; Angels; Mother; Nobody's Conscience; The Cedar Tree; Jubilee; Sea Walls; Roof over My Head; Working Arrangements; Heartland; Some Mothers Do 'Ave 'Em; The Racing Game; Escape; Rings on Their Fingers; Hell's Bells; Dear Ladies; Mog; Swing, Swing Together; Agony; Bless Me, Father; Antonia White Quartet; The Other 'Arf; Drummonds; Never the Twain; All in Good Faith; Fresh Fields; Lovejoy; Ticket to Ride; After Henry; Tell Tale Hearts; Sophia and Constance; The Paradise Club; Rex's Patient in Health and Efficiency; Lady Oppenheim in Love Hurts; The Brittas Empire; Auntie Ella in Hamish Macbeth; Mrs Renfrew in Doctor Finlay.
Films: Ooh... You Are Awful (US title Get Charlie Tully); House of Whipcord; Frightmare; The Confessional; The Comeback; House of the Long Shadows; Clockwise; Venus Peter; Wild Flowers.
Address: c/o Evans and Reiss. Lives in London. Single; 1 s. Hobbies: Reading biographies.

KELLY, Chris

Chris Kelly

Chris Kelly. Presenter/Writer/Producer. b. Cuddington, Cheshire, 24 April 1940. Studied at Clare College, Cambridge, where he was drama critic of Varsity, the university newspaper. Taught French and Spanish for almost two years before joining Anglia Television as an announcer and newsreader (1963), subsequently joining Granada Television as a producer before going freelance.
TV: Anglia Television announcer and newsreader; Granada Television producer; Sixth Form Challenge (quizmaster); Zoo Time; Anything You Can Do; Clapperboard (series); Friday Live; World in Action (narrator); Wish You Were Here...? (series); The Royal Film Performance; Folio; Fit for Living; The Royal Academy Summer Exhibition; I've Got a Secret; Never Too Early, Never Too Late; Friday Live; Cinema Scrapbook; Food and Drink; Zero Option (writer); The Telebook (writer); Soldier Soldier (producer, Series 1 and 2); The Forests of Gondwana; Food & Drink's Choice Cuts; The Food and Drink Christmas Quiz; Grass Roots Tiger (narrator); Kavanagh QC (producer, two series, 1995-6). Address: c/o Barry Burnett Organisation. m. Vivien; 1 d. Rebecca, 1 s. Nicholas. Hobbies: Reading, cooking, collecting.

David Kelly

KELLY, David

David Kelly. Actor. b. Dublin, Ireland, 11 July 1929. Studied at the National College of Art, Dublin. Trained at the Abbey Theatre School, Dublin.
TV: Cowboys; The Gentle Touch; Strumpet City; Whoops Apocalypse!; Robin's Nest; Oh! Brother; Fawlty Towers; Slinger's Day; 2point4 Children.
Films: Two by Forsythe; Ann Devlin; Pirates; The Red Monarch; The Jigsaw Man; Grandpa Ward in Into the West. Address: c/o Joan Brown Associates. m. actress Laurie Morton; 1 d. Miriam, 1 s. David. Hobbies: Painting landscapes.

KELLY, Elizabeth

Elizabeth Hutton Kelly. Actress. b. Newcastle upon Tyne, 29 May 1921. Trained at the Pentland-Robson Dramatic School. Stage plays include Elegies (Criterion Theatre).
TV: Betty in The Way of the World; Hilda in Home; Dividends; When the Boat Comes In; Coronation Street; Miracles Take Longer; Mrs Holroyd in How We Used to Live; Mrs Thomas in The Gemini Factor; Mrs O'Brady in Strange Interlude (TVM); The Bill; Resnick; Boon; Nellie Ellis in EastEnders.
Films: Without a Clue. Address: c/o Scott Marshall. Lives in Scarborough, North Yorkshire. m. (dec); 1 s., 1 d. Hobbies: Crosswords, gardening.

Elizabeth Kelly

KELLY, Henry

Henry Kelly. Presenter. b. Dublin, Ireland, 17 April 1946. Gained a BA (Hons) in English language and literature from University College, Dublin. Newspaper reporter for eight years on the Irish Times, where he reported on the early days of the present troubles and travelled the world before joining BBC Radio 4 (1976), then entering television.
TV: Game for a Laugh (three series); TV-am; Monkey Business; Scene '85, '86, '87, '88; Extra Time; Going for Gold; An Actor's Life for Me (acting himself); Big Decision.
Radio: The World Tonight; Profile; Woman's Hour; Midweek.
Books: How Stormont Fell. Address: c/o Downes Presenters Agency. m. Marjorie; 1 d. Siobhan.

Henry Kelly

KELLY, Lorraine

Lorraine Kelly. Presenter. b. Glasgow, 30 November 1959. Journalist with Scottish and Universal Newspapers before joining BBC Scotland as a researcher (1983) and moving into television with TV-am a year later.
TV: TV-am Scotland correspondent, then presenter of the Sunday show and Good Morning Britain (TV-am, 1984-92); GMTV (1993-), including Top of the Morning and Nine o'Clock Live); Brookside (acting herself, 1994); Hogmanay Live (New Year's Day, 1996).
Awards: TRIC Diamond Jubilee Award for New Talent of the Year (1991).
Address: c/o GMTV. m. freelance cameraman Stephen Smith; 1 d. Rosie. Pets: A cat called Jimmy. Hobbies: Gardening, cooking, hill-walking, watching Dundee United FC.

Lorraine Kelly

Matthew Kelly

KELLY, Matthew

Matthew Kelly. Actor/Presenter. b. Urmston, Manchester, 9 May 1950. Brother Ian works in film production at Pinewood Studios. After work with the Welsh National Theatre, took a teacher-training course in speech, drama and English at the Manchester Polytechnic School of Theatre. Spent 10 years in variety, repertory theatre and the West End. Played Stanley in *Funny Peculiar* (Liverpool and West End).
TV: *The Bonus; Pickersgill People* (Play for Today); *The Rather Reassuring Programme; Funny Man; The Critic;* Fitz in *Holding the Fort* (three series); *Game for a Laugh* (co-presenter, three series); *Madabout* (two series); *Quandaries; Relative Strangers* (two series); *The Sensible Show; Adventure of a Lifetime* (two series); *Kelly's Eye* (presenter); *You Bet!* (five series); *Krankies Television; Trading Places* (guest); *The Children's Royal Variety Performance 1992; Boon; Stars in Their Eyes; EuroDisney; BAFTA Craft Awards* (presenter, 1993); *Stars in Their Eyes New Year's Special* (1994); *Star in Their Eyes Special; Stars in Their Eyes — Live Final; Stars in Their Eyes Winners' Special; Eureka!* (series, 1995, four compilations, 1996); *Stars in Their Eyes: Christmas Special* (1995); Policeman in *Last of the Summer Wine* (Christmas special, 1995).
Films: *Gabrielle and the Doodleman.* Address: c/o Stella Richards Management. m. Sarah; 1 d. Ruth, 1 s. Matthew. Hobbies: Travelling, swimming, dancing, talking, laughing.

Nikki Kelly

KELLY, Nikki

Nicola Caroline Kelly. Actress/Presenter. b. Leamington Spa, Warwickshire, 23 November 1951. Daughter of Jill Forbes-Robertson, who was niece of actor Johnston Forbes-Robertson, who was knighted for his Hamlet and opened RADA with George Bernard Shaw. Trained at Rose Bruford College.
TV: *Dixon of Dock Green; The Russell Harty Show; The Ken Dodd Show; Life Begins at Forty; The Sweeney; Life of Shakespeare; Man Alive; Kelly Monteith; The Lenny Henry Show;* Sylvia in *Hi-de-Hi!* (eight series); *The Word;* Jackie in *The Upper Hand; The Docket Box.*
Address: c/o Collis Management. Lives in London. Single. Hobbies: Tennis, riding, sailing, scuba-diving.

Sam Kelly

KELLY, Sam

Sam Kelly. Actor. b. Manchester, 19 December 1943. Trained at LAMDA (1964-7).
TV: *Emergency — Ward 10* (1967); *The Liver Birds;* Bunny Warren in *Porridge; The Dave Allen Show* (one series); *The Dawson Watch; The Dick Emery Show; Who's Who; Grown Ups; Days at the Beach; Boys from the Blackstuff; Scully;* Bob Challis in *Coronation Street;* Mr Snagsby in *Bleak House;* Norman in *Now and Then* (two series); *Jenny's War; Victoria Wood — As Seen on TV; Heart of the Country; Chester Mystery Plays; Christabel;* Dr Hans Geering in *'Allo, 'Allo* (three series); *Will You Love Me Tomorrow* (TVM); *The Insurance Man;* Grunge in *Haggard* (two series, 1991-2); Sam in *On the Up* (three series, 1990-2); *Making Out;* Edward Castle in *The Bill;* George in *Blue Ice;* Adolf Hitler in *Stalag Luft;* Mr Mould in *Martin Chuzzlewit; Barbara* (Comedy First); Ron Griffiths in *Eleven Men against Eleven;* Tom Bryant in *The Bill;* Scully in *A Touch of Frost; Twelve Angry Men, Impasse, Don't Dilly Dally on the Way* and *The Lift* (all Paul Merton in Galton & Simpson's. . .); Sgt Globe in *Days at the Beach.*
Films: *Carry On Dick; Carry On Behind; Blue Ice.* **Radio:** *Listen with Mother* (presenter).
Address: c/o The Richard Stone Partnership. Lives in south-west London. Single.

Jeremy Kemp

KEMP, Jeremy

Edmund Jeremy James Walker. Actor. b. near Chesterfield, Derbyshire, 3 February 1935. National Service with the Gordon Highlanders. Trained at the Central School of Speech and Drama (1955-8).
TV: PC Bob Steele in *Z-Cars* (Series 1, 1962-3); *The Rainmaker; The Lovers of Florence; The Last Reunion; Colditz; Brassneck; The Bedmakers; The Rhinemann Exchange; Keefer* (TVM); *Lisa; Goodbye; School Play; The Winter's Tale; Henry VIII; St Joan; Evita; Unity; Phantom of the Opera* (TVM); *King Lear; The Contract; The Winds of War; Sadat* (mini-series); *George Washington* (mini-series); *Feet Foremost; The Speckled Band; Peter the Great* (mini-series); *War and Remembrance; Slip-Up; Duel of Hearts* (TVM); *Reasonable Force* (TVM); *Star Trek: The Next Generation; Summer's Lease; The Magician.*
Films: *Cleopatra; Dr Terror's House of Horrors; Face of a Stranger; Operation Crossbow; Cast a Giant Shadow; The Blue Max; A Twist of Sand; Assignment K; The Strange Affair; The Games; Darling Lili; Eyewitness; Pope Joan; The Belstone Fox; The Blockhouse; The Seven-Per-Cent Solution; East of Elephant Rock; Queen of Diamonds; The Thoroughbreds* (retitled *Treasure Seekers*); *A Bridge Too Far; Leopard in the Snow; The Prisoner of Zenda; Caravans; The Return of the Soldier; Uncommon Valor; Top Secret!; When the Whales Came; Prisoner of Honor; Four Weddings and a Funeral.*
Address: c/o Marina Martin Associates. Lives in London. Single. Hobbies: Rough games and travel.

Ross Kemp

KEMP, Ross

Ross Kemp. Actor. b. 1 July 1964. Trained at the Webber Douglas Academy.
TV: *Playing Away; Claws;* Graham Lodsworth (Dolly Skilbeck's illegitimate son) in *Emmerdale Farm* (1985); *The Money Men;* DI Monk in *Birds of a Feather* (Series 1, 1989); *London's Burning; The Chief;* Grant Mitchell in *EastEnders* (1990-). Address: c/o Jonathan Altaras Associates.

KENDAL, Felicity

Felicity Kendal. Actress. b. Olton, Warwickshire, 25 September 1946. Daughter of actor Geoffrey Kendal and actress Laura Kendal, who were travelling actors in a Shakespearean company and featured in James Ivory's film *Shakespeare Wallah*. They took her to India at the age of three months and she made her stage début, aged nine months, in *A Midsummer Night's Dream*. Returned to UK at the age of 19 to live with her aunt in Birmingham. Stage plays include *Kean, The Norman Conquests, Clouds, Amadeus, On the Razzle, The Second Mrs Tanqueray, Othello* (all National Theatre), *Made in Bangkok, Haggard, Much Ado about Nothing, Ivanov, The Real Thing* and *Jumpers*. Son Charlie made his stage début, agd six weeks, in *Dolly* and has appeared with her ever since.

TV: *The Mayfly and the Frog* (début); *Crime of Passion; The Woodlanders* (serial); *The Dolly Dialogues; Love Story; Edward VII; Home and Beauty; Cuckoo; Twelfth Night;* Barbara Good in *The Good Life; Solo; The Mistress;* Helena Cuthbertson in *The Camomile Lawn* (mini-series, 1992); Nancy Belasco in *Honey for Tea* (series, 1994); *French and Saunders*.

Films: *Shakespeare Wallah; The Seven-Per-Cent Solution; Valentino.*

Awards: Theatre: London *Evening Standard* Best Actress award for *Ivanov* (1989).

Address: c/o Chatto and Linnit. m. 1st actor Drewe Henley (dis), 2nd Michael Rudman; 2 s. actor Charlie (from 1st m.), Jacob.

Felicity Kendal

KENNEDY, Cheryl

Cheryl Kennedy. Actress. b. Enfield, Middlesex, 29 April 1947. Trained at the Corona Stage Academy. Stage plays include *Half a Sixpence, The Boy Friend, 1776, Time and Time Again, Absent Friends, Flowers for Algernon, My Fair Lady* (US), *Time and the Conways* (Old Vic) and *What a Way to Run a Revolution* (Young Vic).

TV: *The Cliff Richard Show; The Mike Yarwood Show; That's Life; Omnibus; Play for Today; Play of the Month; The Sweeney; Target; The Professionals; Brookside.*

Films: Jo Mason in *Ooh... You Are Awful* (US title *Get Charlie Tully*).

Address: c/o Larry Dalzell Associates. m. (dis); 2 d. Clarissa, Samantha. Hobbies: Stamp collecting, swimming.

Cheryl Kennedy

KENNEDY, Kevin

Kevin Patrick Kennedy. Actor. b. Manchester, 4 September 1961. Member of the Manchester Youth Theatre from the age of 13. Trained at Manchester Polytechnic School of Theatre. Stage plays include *Ducking Out* (Greenwich Theatre and West End) and *No Sex, Please — We're British* (as Runnicles, national tour and West End). Plays guitar with several country & western groups in the Manchester area and composes music. Has performed in Nashville and with his own group, The Bunch of Thieves, at the Reading Festival and the National Exhibition Centre, Birmingham.

TV: 'Team helper' in *Cheggers Plays Pop; Dear Ladies; The Last Company Car; Keep on Running;* Curly (Norman) Watts in *Coronation Street* (1982-); *Royal Variety Performance* (with *Coronation Street* cast, 1989).

Radio: *The Old Man Sleeps Alone; Metamorphosised Arkwright.*

Address: c/o Saraband Associates/Granada Television. Lives in Didsbury, Manchester. m. 1st 1987 Dawn (dis), 2nd 1996 Clare Johnson; 1 s. Ryan (from 1st m.). Hobbies: Playing guitar, cinema, socialising, eating out, football, playing golf.

Kevin Kennedy

KENNEDY, Sarah

Sarah Kennedy. Presenter. b. Wallington, Surrey, 8 July 1950. Worked in radio in Singapore and Germany before joining BBC radio in London, then moving into television.

TV: Southern Television (1978-81), including *Royle Progress; Animal Roadshow; Chipperfield Safari; Game for a Laugh* (three series); *60 Minutes; Daytime; Busman's Holiday* (host); *Animal Country* (series).

Radio: *String Sound; Colour Supplement.* **Books:** *Terrible Pets* (1996, No 1 best-seller).

Address: c/o Severn Management Services. Hobbies: Running, swimming, weeding, tennis.

Sarah Kennedy

KENNEDY, Tamara B

Tamara Brooks Kennedy. Actress. b. Edinburgh, 23 May 1962. While at school in Edinburgh, was awarded honours in the LAMDA Gold Medal Examination for Drama, then attended the National Youth Theatre in London, before gaining an MA in English and drama from Glasgow University.

TV: Eurydice and reader in *Orpheus through the Ages* (winner at 1984 Cannes Film Festival); Joanna Ross-Gifford (née Simpson) in *Take the High Road* (1986-); Psychologist in *Rab C Nesbitt*.

Films: *RA: The Path of the Sun God* (narrator). **Radio:** Secretary in *Curlew in Autumn;* Daughter in *Accidental Conversation;* Daughter in *Putting It Right;* Sarah in *Clocking Out;* Zhenya in *Blockada; Storyline: A Dill Pickle* (narrator, BBC Radio Scotland). Address: c/o Young Casting Agency. Lives in Glasgow. m. Robin Barbour; 1 d. Rosa Louise Mae (b. 1993). Hobbies: Swimming, writing, drawing.

Tamara B Kennedy

Jill Kerman

KERMAN, Jill

Jill Kerman. Actress. b. Mill Hill, North London, 4 July 1946. Trained at RADA (Comedy Award, Grace and Movement Award and Diction Award winner). Made her stage début as Isobel in *Period of Adjustment* at the Belgrade Theatre, Coventry, and followed it with repertory work in Bromley and an appearance at the Royal Court. Stage plays include *Spring and Port Wine* (West End).

TV: Carol Eccles in *Thicker than Water* (series, 1969); Penny Wheeler in *Please Sir!* (semi-regular, two series, 1970-1); *Bangelstein's Boys; Judge Dee; Crown Court; Strangers;* Jill Elston in *Now and Then* (two series, 1983-4); *The Other One; Cosmo and Thingy; The Cuckoo Waltz; Softly Softly; Rep;* Nancy in *Oliver; Fairly Secret Army;* Maggie Dunlop/Redman in *Coronation Street* (semi-regular). Address: c/o Essanay. Lives in Essex m. 1968 heating engineer Nicholas Dance; 1 d. Kira. Hobbies: Sailing, drawing, writing.

Noreen Kershaw

KERSHAW, Noreen

Noreen Ann Kershaw. Actress/Director. b. Bury, Lancashire, 16 October 1950. Trained at the Manchester Polytechnic School of Theatre. Stage plays include *Shirley Valentine* (title role, original production, Everyman Theatre, Liverpool). Also director of many stage productions.

TV: *Voice; That's the Way; And There's More; The Year of the Bodyguard; Not for Women Only; Boys from the Blackstuff; In the Secret State;* Lynne Harrison in *Albion Market; On the Market; Coronation Street; Yesterday's Girl;* Kathy Roach in *Brookside;* Mrs Wilson in *Watching; Needle; The Grass Arena; The Young Indiana Jones Chronicles;* Mrs Mac in *The Bullion Boys;* Joan Crawford in *Self Catering* (Alan Bleasdale Presents); Mrs Wildman in *Mother's Ruin;* Aunty Dia in *Blood on the Dole;* Steph in *Casualty; Travelog;* Noreen in *Jake's Progress;* Joan Fairbright in *Agony Again.* As director: *Grimm* (New Voices, Granada Television); *Coronation Street* (1996).

Films: *Hidden City.* Address: c/o Ken McReddie. Lives in Manchester. m. theatre director-painter Peter Oyston. Pets: Two dogs called Flo and Annie. Hobbies: 'Gardening, dreaming!'

John Kettley

KETTLEY, John

John Graham Kettley. Weather presenter. b. Halifax, West Yorkshire, 11 July 1952. Gained a BSc (Hons) in applied physics from Lanchester Polytechnic, Coventry, and joined the Meteorological Office in 1970, working with the meteorological research flight based in Farnborough, then in the fluid dynamics department at its Bracknell headquarters. Worked at the Nottingham Weather Centre (1980-5) as a TV weatherman for BBC and ITV, before joining the BBC's forecasting team in London. The pop group Tribe of Toffs released the record *John Kettley Is a Weatherman* in 1988.

TV: BBC TV weather presenter (1985-); *The Travel Show* (resident weather expert for three years); *The Travel Show Guides.* Guest appearances: *Blankety Blank; Telly Addicts.*

Radio: BBC weather presenter (1986-). Address: c/o PVA Management/BBC Weather Centre. Lives in Hitchin, Hertfordshire. m. children's books illustrator and designer Lynn Nicola Grundy; 2 s. Charles William (b. 1992), George Kit (b. 1994). Pets: Two cats. Hobbies: Cricket, horse-racing, photography, fell-walking, gardening, cycling, brewing.

Richard Keys

KEYS, Richard

Richard Keys. Presenter. b. Coventry, Warwickshire, 23 April 1957. Journalist on the Wolverhampton *Express & Star* and with Hayter's News and Sports Agency in Fleet Street, before spending six years in radio with Radio City, Liverpool, and Piccadilly Radio, Manchester, then moving into television. Switched from sports reporting on TV-am to presenting the flagship breakfast programme *Good Morning Britain,* before leaving to become chief sports presenter for the satellite channel BSB, then Sky Sports.

TV: TV-am sports reporter, then presenter of *Good Morning Britain, After Nine, Saturday Sport* and *The Morning Programme; The Motor Show; Tour de France; Worldwide Soccer,* chief sports presenter on BSB, then Sky Sports.

Radio: Radio City (Liverpool) news journalist and sports reporter; Piccadilly Radio (Manchester) deputy newsroom editor and sports editor. Address: c/o Pro-Active Sports Management, 17 Manchester Road, Wilmslow, Cheshire SK9 1BQ, tel (01625) 536411. Lives in Berkshire. m. Julia; 1 d. Jemma, 1 s. Joshua. Pets: 'A dog, a cat and loads of fish.' Hobbies: 'Working for Sky TV.'

Melanie Kilburn

KILBURN, Melanie

Melanie Kilburn. Actress. b. Bradford, West Yorkshire, 16 March 1956. Trained at the Guildhall School of Music and Drama (1975-8). Stage roles include Bianca in *Othello* (Young Vic) and Lois in *Straight and Narrow* (Wyndham's and Aldwych Theatre).

TV: Maureen in *The Last Company Car; Frankie and Johnnie; Juliet Bravo;* Hilda in *1914 All Out;* Mum in *Ernie's Incredible Illucinations;* Jill in *Making Out* (three series, 1989-91); prostitute Angela in *Chancer* (two episodes); Mrs Hebden in *The World of Eddie Weary; Hale & Pace* (two episodes); Carol in *Soldier Soldier* (Series 1, 1990); Rosie Tinniswood in *Heartbeat* (1993); Barbara Bibby in *The Lifeboat* (series, 1994); Charlotte in *Moving Story* (two series, 1994-5); Trudie in *Against All Odds;*

Edwina Sprott in *The Wimbledon Poisoner* (mini-series, 1994); Catherine in *Do the Right Thing; Jo Brand thru' the Cakehole;* Irene Brodie in *Peak Practice;* Jackie Whittaker in *The Ruth Rendell Mysteries: Vanity Dies Hard* (mini-series, 1995); Carol in *Casualty;* Carol in *April Fool's Day.*
Films: Eloise in *The Little Drummer Girl;* Kate in *Vroom.* Address: c/o The Richard Stone Partnership. Lives in London. Single. Hobbies: Reading, scuba-diving, tennis, keeping fit.

KILROY-SILK, Robert

Robert Kilroy-Silk. Presenter/Writer/Producer. b. Birmingham, 19 May 1942. Gained a BSc (Econ) from the London School of Economics. Worked as a lecturer at the University of Liverpool (1966-74) and was a Labour MP (1974-86) before entering television.
TV: *Day to Day; Kilroy!* (1986-); *Here to Stay; Behind the Headlines; Hearts of Gold; Birds of a Feather* (acting himself); *Family Watch; Tender Loving Care* (Screen One, acting himself); *Kilroy Down Under* (1994); *Kids' Kilroy* (series, 1994). Address: c/o Kilroy Television Company, Teddington Studios, Broom Road, Teddington, Middlesex TW11 9NT. Lives in Buckinghamshire. m. Jan; 1 s. Dominic, 1 d. Natasha. Pets: Dogs, cats, geese, hens. Hobbies: Gardening.

Robert Kilroy-Silk

KING, Claire

Claire King. Actress. b. Yorkshire, 10 January 1963. Trained at the Actors' Institute. Singer in groups Fidea and To Be Continued, managed other groups and formed record label Visual Records (1986-8).
TV: *Alas Smith and Jones; Robbie Coltrane; Hale & Pace;* Punk and Hooker in *Watch with Mother;* Model in *Hot Metal;* Model in *Starting Out;* Doctor's Receptionist in *The Bill; Shout* (presenter, US pop show); Kim Tate (née Barker) in *Emmerdale* (1989-).
Films: Groupie in *Heart of Fire;* Yuppie in *Eat the Rich;* Prostitute Jenny in *The Cold Light of Day.*
Videos: Pop promotional videos: Zodiac Mindwarp and The Love Reaction; Elvis Costello; LA Mix. Address: c/o David Daly Associates/Emmerdale Production Centre. Lives in Harrogate, North Yorkshire. m. 1994 actor Peter Amory (qv). Pets: A horse called Digger. Hobbies: Horse-riding, horse-racing, swimming, watching films.

Claire King

KING, Ross

Derek Ross King. Presenter. b. Glasgow, 21 February 1964. Became a hospital DJ aged 15, then Britain's youngest daytime presenter on Radio Clyde, Glasgow.
TV: *CTV1* (BBC Scotland); *Children in Need* (BBC Scotland); *Young Krypton* (two series); *Quiz Night* (three series); *My Secret Desire* (Granada Television); *Auto TX* (Night Network); *Run the Gauntlet; Pick of the Week; Who's Into* (Yorkshire Television); *Living It Up* (Yorkshire Television); *The Calendar Fashion Show* (Yorkshire Television); *ITV Telethon; Pebble Mill; 8.15 from Manchester* (two series); *Holiday '92; The Ross King Show* (two series); *Holiday; King of the Road* (two series, 1993); *The Wetter, the Better!* (host, game show); *Ross King* (series); *Hot Chefs* (series); *Pop Goes Summer* (series, 1993); *King of the Road Revisited* (compilation series, 1993); *Newshound* (presenter, series, 1993); *Pebble Mill* (1993-); *Pebble Mill – Summer in the City.*
Films: *Comfort and Joy.* **Radio:** *The Ross King Show* (Radio Clyde, Glasgow); *Take 5; Get Set Go; Barcelona Olympics; Fantasy Football; Sportsbeat* (all BBC Radio 5); *The Eurochart Show* (Independent Local Radio network); *The Ross King Show* (Capital FM, London).
Awards: Sony Award as Local Radio DJ of the Year. Address: c/o Razzamatazz Management. Lives in London and Stratford-upon-Avon. Single. Hobbies: Tennis, football, golf, collecting theatre memorabilia.

Ross King

KINGSTON, Mark

Mark Kingston. Actor. b. London, 18 April 1934. Trained at LAMDA. Stage plays include *Caesar and Cleopatra* (Old Vic) and Old Vic tours of Russia, Poland, Australia and New Zealand
TV: *United!; Beryl's Lot; Time of My Life; Driving Ambition; Shine on Harvey Moon;* Geoff in *No Job for a Lady* (three series, 1990-2); *About Face;* Lord Finisterre in *Old Boy Network;* Andrew Marsh in *Agatha Christie's Poirot;* Don in *Birds of a Feather;* Leonard Duglass in *The House of Eliott;* Lord MacKenzie in *Doctor Finlay;* Charlie in *Sitting Pretty;* Edward Avery in *Casualty;* Lenny Trainer in *Harry; The Bill;* Gerald Stiles in *Crown Prosecutor; Peak Practice.* Address: c/o CDA. m. Marigold Sharman.

Mark Kingston

KIRKBRIDE, Anne

Anne Kirkbride. Actress. b. Oldham, Lancashire, 21 June 1954. Daughter of cartoonist Jack Kirkbride. Joined the Saddleworth Junior Players aged 11 and Oldham Rep on leaving school, as ASM, then actress. Stage-managed a charity performance of *Snow White.*
TV: *Another Sunday and Sweet FA* (Jack Rosenthal play); Deirdre Hunt/Langton/Barlow in *Coronation Street* (1972-); *Royal Variety Performance* (with *Coronation Street* cast, 1989).
Awards: Joint winner, with William Roache (qv) and Johnny Briggs (qv), Pye Television Award for *Coronation Street* (1983). Address: c/o Granada Television. Lives in Didsbury, Manchester. m. 1992 actor David Beckett. Hobbies: Photography, gardening, reading, swimming, walking.

Anne Kirkbride

KIRWAN, Dervla

Dervla Kirwan

Dervla Kirwan. Actress. b. Dublin. Stage roles include Rosa in *Hush* (Royal Court) and Armandine in *An Absolute Turkey* (national tour and West End).
TV: *In the Border Country* (4-Play); Bernadette Kennedy in *A Time to Dance* (mini-series, 1992); Eileen in *The Wexford Trilogy: Poor Beast in the Rain;* Linda in *The Wexford Trilogy: A Handful of Stars;* Phoebe in *Goodnight Sweetheart* (three series, 1993-6, plus Christmas special, 1995); *The Lilac Bus; Casualty;* Viola in *Troubles;* Assumpta Fitzgerald in *Ballykissangel* (series, 1996).
Films: Thaddeus O'Sullivan in *December Bride.*
Address: c/o Barry Brown & Partner. Lives in south-east London.

KITCHEN, Gavin

Gavin Kitchen

Gavin Peter Kitchen. Actor. b. North Shields, 17 March 1964. Trained at the Arts Educational School.
TV: *Dickens of London* (1976, as a child); *Soldiers* (stage fighting); Baz in *The Paper Lads* (two series); Bryan in *A Visit to a Cousin;* Rick Seymour in *Mathspy;* Kevin Hedworth in *The Manageress* (series); Baxter in *Spender;* Dexter in *Byker Grove;* Danny Pearce in *Heartbeat;* Steve Marshall in *Emmerdale* (1993); Anthony Kerwin in *The Bill;* Billy Patterson in *Strike Force;* Police Inspector Davis in *Our Friends in the North.* Address: c/o JM Associates. Lives in Surrey. Single. Hobbies: Supporting Newcastle United, caving, mountain walking.

KITCHEN, Michael

Michael Kitchen

Michael Kitchen. Actor. b. Leicester, 31 October 1948. Member of the National Youth Theatre and assistant stage manager at the Belgrade Theatre, Coventry, before training at RADA (1967-9). Stage plays include *Romeo and Juliet, Richard II* and *Art of Success* (all RSC, 1986-7).
TV: *King Lear; The Brontës of Haworth; The Reporters* (Play for Today); *The Train; Country Matters; The Monkey's Paw; As Man and Wife; Affairs of Love; Lawrence and Frieda; Savages; Young Stephen Hind; Enemy; A Divorce; The Four Beauties; Churchill's People; Fall of Eagles; The Misanthrope; The Long and the Short and the Tall; School Play; The Guilty; Caught on a Train; A Room for the Winter; Maybury; Ladykillers; The Best of Everything; Freud; Staying Put; Love Story; The Browning Version; The Comedy of Errors; Brimstone and Treacle; No Man's Land; Bedroom Farce; Love Song; The Justice Game; Island Gardens; Minder; Home Run; Benefactors; Ball-Trap on the Côte Sauvage; The Pied Piper* (TVM); *Stay Lucky;* Roman in *Chancer;* James McCandlish in *The Advocates* (series); Russell Clark in *Inspector Morse: The Death of the Self;* Steven Vey in *The Guilty* (mini-series); Donald Blake in *Boon;* Graham Croxley in *The Good Guys; The Prodigal;* Roger Boshier in *Between the Lines;* The King in *To Play the King* (mini-series, 1993); Block in *The Trial* (Screen Two); Major Herbert Armstrong in *Dandelion Dead* (mini-series, 1994); Dudley Hooperman in *Pie in the Sky* (1994, 1995); Sir Helmsley Thwaite in *The Buccaneers* (series, 1995); Jeremy Swain in *Dirty Old Town* (Rik Mayall Presents); Townsend in *The Hanging Gale* (series, 1995); Jonathan Meyerbridge in *A Touch of Frost.*
Films: *Unman, Wittering and Zigo; Dracula Today; Breaking Glass; The Bunker; Breaking Glass; Towards the Morning; Out of Africa; Home Run; The Russia House; The Dive; Fools of Fortune; Hostage;* George Briggs in *Enchanted April.* Address: c/o ICM. Lives in Dorset. Partner: Dresser Rowena Miller; 1 s. Jack. Pets: One cat. Hobbies: Piano, guitar, flying, writing, tennis, riding.

KNOX, Barbara

Barbara Knox

Barbara Knox. Actress. b. Oldham, Lancashire, 1938. Previously acted as Barbara Mullaney. Left school at 15 to work as a Post Office telegraphist, then in offices, shops and factories. After amateur theatre, joined Oldham Rep. Acted on radio alongside comedians Ken Dodd, Jimmy Tarbuck, Ray Alan, Mike Yarwood, Les Dawson and Freddie Davies.
TV: *Emergency — Ward 10; Mrs Thursday; Never Mind the Quality, Feel the Width;* Sylvia in *Girls about Town; The Dustbinmen; A Family at War;* Rita Littlewood/Fairclough/Sullivan in *Coronation Street* (1972-).
Films: *Goodbye, Mr Chips.*
Radio: *Life with Lord Charles* (series, 1967); Daisy in *The Golden Parrot Club* (series, 1968); *Our Les* (series, 1973). **Records:** Album: *On the Street Where I Live* (1973). **Awards:** TV: *TVTimes* Best Actress award (1989). Address: c/o Saraband Associates/Granada Television. Lives in Worcestershire. m. 1954 1st Denis (dis 1977), 2nd John Knox (sep 1994); 1 d. Maxine (from 1st m.).

LACEY, Ingrid

Ingrid Lacey

Ingrid Lacey. Actress. Trained at the Bristol Old Vic Theatre School.
TV: Melanie in *Thunder Rock;* Eleanor Tilney in *Northanger Abbey* (Screen Two); Mary Widdowson in *Inspector Morse;* Inga in *The Endless Game* (pilot); Julia in *London's Burning;* Alice in *Saracen;* Helen Cooper in *Drop the Dead Donkey* (series); Sarah in *Never Come Back;* Diane in *She-Wolf of London;* Julie in *Dream Kitchen* (Video Fantasies); Veronica in *Strathblair;* Liora in *Sweating Bullets;* Billie Carleton in *White Girls on Dope;* Helen in *A Woman's Guide to Adultery* (mini-series, 1993); pushy public

relations executive Alison Dell in *The Chief* (series, 1994); Newspaper Reporter in *The Ruth Rendell Mysteries: Master of the Moor; Look at the State We're In!: Legal System;* Jane Grant in *The Bill;* Cynthia Hoskins in *Pie in the Sky.* Address: c/o Christina Shepherd.

LALLY, Teri

Teresa Lally. Actress. b. Coatbridge, Lanarkshire, 21 April 1961. Trained at Queen Margaret College Drama School. Qualified for her Equity actors' union card by forming a song-and-sketches group with college friends, playing at hotels and pubs in Edinburgh. Stage plays include *Don't Tell the Wife* (with Jimmy Logan) and *Never a Dull Moment.*
TV: Carol Wilson (née McKay) in *Take the High Road/High Road* (1983-); *The Video Show; Cameron on Camera; Ready or Not; Wheel of Fortune* (celebrity edition). TV commercials: Bank of Scotland; William Low's.
Films: *Restless Natives; Comfort and Joy.* Address: c/o Scottish Television. Lives in Glasgow. m. 1st Kenny Mackenzie (dis), 2nd journalist Scott Ferguson; 1 d. Lucy (b. Dec 1993, from 2nd m.).

Teri Lally

LANCASHIRE, Sarah

Sarah Lancashire. Actress. Daughter of TV scriptwriter Geoffrey Lancashire. Trained at the Guildhall School of Music and Drama. Stage productions include *Blood Brothers* (as Linda, Albery Theatre) and *Educating Rita* (title role, Queen's Theatre, Hornchurch).
TV: *Dramarama; Celebration; Watching; Bradley; My Secret Desire; About Face;* Wendy Farmer (1987) and Raquel Wolstenhulme/Watts (1990-6) in *Coronation Street; Exam Conditions; The Bill; Showstoppers* (1995, concert featuring West End and Broadway songs). Address: c/o Talent Artists. Lives in Oldham, Lancashire. m. music lecturer Gary Hargreaves; 2 s. Thomas, Matthew.

Sarah Lancashire

LANDEN, Dinsdale

Dinsdale Landen. Actor. b. Margate, Kent, 4 September 1932. Trained at the Florence Moore School of Theatre, Hove, East Sussex, before National Service in the RAF, where he formed a drama group.
TV: *She Stoops to Conquer; Easter; A Resounding Tinkle;* Pip in *Great Expectations; The Canterbury Tales; The Mask of Janus; The Spies; Mickey Dunne; London Assurance;* title role in *Devenish; Fathers and Families; The Glittering Prizes; Pig in the Middle; Events in a Museum; This Office Life; Arms and the Man; Fight against Slavery; Some Other Spring* (TVM); *The World of Peter Rabbit and Friends: The Tale of Tom Kitten and Jemima Puddle-Duck* (voice only); Jim Leonard in *Lovejoy;* Lord Brightlingsea in *The Buccaneers* (series, 1995).
Films: *The Valiant; We Joined the Navy; Mosquito Squadron; Every Home Should Have One; Digby — The Biggest Dog in the World;* Commander Matteson in *Morons from Outer Space.*
Address: c/o Michael Whitehall. m. actress Jennifer Daniel.

Dinsdale Landen

LANG, Belinda

Belinda Lucy Lange. Actress. b. London, 23 December 1955. Daughter of actor Jeremy Hawk and actress Joan Heal. Trained at the Central School of Speech and Drama. Stage plays include *Present Laughter* (Vaudeville Theatre), *Hobson's Choice* (Haymarket Theatre), *The Women, Tales from Hollywood* and *Antigone* (all National Theatre), *A Clandestine Marriage* (Albery Theatre), *Mrs Klein* (Apollo Theatre) and *Dead Funny* (Savoy Theatre and national tour).
TV: Beth in *To Serve Them All My Days;* Eileen in *A Brother's Tale;* Kate in *Dear John;* Sheila Walsh in *Bust;* Martha Brett in *The Bretts;* Lady Karen in *Stay Lucky;* Liza in *Second Thoughts* (five series, 1991-4); Bill in *2point4 Children* (five series, 1991-5, plus Christmas specials, 1994, 1995); Agatha Troy in *The Inspector Alleyn Mysteries* (series, 1993); Susanna Critchley in *Making News; The Inspector Alleyn Mysteries: Hand in Glove; The Inspector Alleyn Mysteries: Dead Water.*
Address: c/o Ken McReddie. Lives in London. m. actor Hugh Fraser; 1 d. Lily.

Belinda Lang

LANG, Robert

Robert Lang. Actor/Director. b. Bristol, 24 September 1934. Trained at Bristol Old Vic.
TV: *An Age of Kings; Emergency — Ward 10; That Was the Week That Was; Not So Much a Programme, More a Way of Life; For Maddy with Love; 1990; The Rivals of Sherlock Holmes; The Brack Report; Edward 'G' — Like the Film Star; Bristol 600; Semmelweiss; The Microbe Hunter; King Lear; On the Edge of the Sand; Lady Windermere's Fan; The Father; Antigone; D'Ardenelle* (mini-series); *The Birthday Party; Vanity Fair; The Contract; Parnell and the Englishwoman; To Each His Own* (TVM); Captain Broadbent in *The Darling Buds of May* (second series); Sir Roland White in *The Old Boy Network* (series); Geoffrey Jackson in *Boon;* General Halcut-Hackett in *The Inspector Alleyn Mysteries;* Lord Holloway in *Under the Hammer* (series, 1994); Police Chief in *Genghis Cohn* (Screen Two); David Lambert in *Anna Lee;* Robinson in *Ellington* (pilot); Lord Paltrey in *Bramwell.*
Films: *Savage Messiah; Night Watch.*
Address: c/o Julian Belfrage Associates. m. actress Ann Bell (qv); 1 d. Rebecca, 1 s. John.

Robert Lang

LANGRISHE, Caroline

Caroline Langrishe

Caroline Langrishe. Actress. b. London, 10 January 1958. Former member of the National Youth Theatre; showgirl at the Hilton Hotel, London.
TV: *The Glittering Prizes; The Brothers; Anna Karenina; Wuthering Heights;* Cosette in *Les Misérables* (TVM); *The Flipside of Dominick Hyde* (Play for Today); *Another Flip for Dominick* (Play for Today); Janet Holywell in *A Christmas Carol* (TVM, 1984); *Fortunes of War; Pulaski; Twelfth Night; The Return of Shelley; Boon; The Bill; Trainer; Exchange of Fire* (mini-series, 1993); Candice Costello in *Cluedo;* Dr Susan Lees in *Peak Practice;* Charlotte Cavendish in *Lovejoy* (two series, 1993-4); *Sharpe's Regiment.*
Films: *Eagle's Wing;* Carol in *Hawks.* Address: c/o Conway, van Gelder, Robinson. Lives in London. m. actor Patrick Drury; 2 d. Leonie, Rosalind.

LANSBURY, Angela

Angela Lansbury

Angela Brigid Lansbury. Actress. b. London, 16 October 1925. CBE, 1994. Trained at the Webber Douglas Academy, London, and Feagin Dramatic School, New York. Broadway stage plays include *Hotel Paradiso, A Taste of Honey, Anyone Can Whistle, Mame, Dear World, Gypsy, The King and I* and *Sweeney Todd.*
TV: *Sweeney Todd; Little Gloria – Happy at Last* (TVM); *Lace; The First Olympic Race; The Gift of Love: A Christmas Story* (TVM); *Rage of Angels: The Story Continues;* Jessica Fletcher in *Murder, She Wrote* (1984-); *A Talent for Murder* (TVM); *Shootdown* (TVM); *Wings of the Water; The Shell Seekers* (TVM); *The Love She Sought* (TVM); *Mrs 'Arris Goes to Paris* (TVM).
Films: *Gaslight; National Velvet; The Picture of Dorian Gray; Harvey Girls; Till the Clouds Roll By; The Hoodlum Saint; Tenth Avenue Angel; The Private Affairs of Bel Ami; If Winter Comes; State of the Union* (UK title *The World and His Wife*); *The Three Musketeers; The Red Danube; Samson and Delilah; Kind Lady; Mutiny; Remains to Be Seen; The Purple Mask; The Court Jester; The Key Man* (UK title *A Life at Stake*); *A Lawless Street; Please Murder Me; The Reluctant Debutante; The Long Hot Summer; A Breath of Scandal; The Dark at the Top of the Stairs; Summer of the 17th Doll; Blue Hawaii; All Fall Down; The Manchurian Candidate; The Four Horsemen of the Apocalypse* (voice only); *In the Cool of the Day; The World of Henry Orient; Dear Heart; Harlow; The Greatest Story Ever Told; The Amorous Adventures of Moll Flanders; Mister Buddwing* (UK title *Woman without a Face*); *Something for Everyone* (UK title *Black Flowers for the Bride*); *Bedknobs and Broomsticks; Death on the Nile; The Lady Vanishes; The Mirror Crack'd; The Last Unicorn* (voice only); *The Pirates of Penzance; The Company of Wolves; JFK.* Address: c/o William Morris Agency (US). m. 1st Richard Cromwell, 2nd film executive Peter Shaw; 1 s. Anthony, 1 d. Deidre, 1 step-s. David.

LARGE, Eddie

Eddie Large

Edward Hugh McGinnis. Comedian. b. Glasgow, 25 June 1941. Moved to Manchester at the age of nine and was an associate schoolboy footballer with Manchester City aged 15, but a road accident ended his hopes of turning professional. He met singer Cyril Mead (Syd Little, qv) in a local pub and the two teamed up, first as vocal duo Cyril Mead and Friend and then as comedians Little and Large.
TV: *Opportunity Knocks* (winners, 1971); *Crackerjack; Who Do You Do?; Now Who Do You Do?; The David Nixon Show; Seaside Special; The Wheeltappers and Shunters Social Club; The Little and Large Tellyshow; Little and Large; Disney Time; This Is Your Life* (subject); *The Children's Royal Variety Performance 1993.* Address: c/o Peter Prichard. Lives in Bristol. m. 2nd Patsy Ann; 2 d. Samantha, Aliston (both from 1st m.), 1 s. Ryan (from 2nd m.). Hobbies: Manchester City FC, golf.

LATHAM, Bernard

Bernard Latham

Bernard Latham. Actor. b. Manchester, 21 April 1951. Trained at Bristol Old Vic Theatre School.
TV: *The Practice; Carrott Del Sol; Tan Tro Nesa; The Danedyke Mystery; Crown Court; Fox; Coronation Street; Hard Times; Sally Ann; Flying Lady;* Policeman in *September Song;* PO Pomeroy in *I'll Be Watching You* (Ghosts); Rudy Warburton in *Chandler & Co;* Lucien Bex in *Agatha Christie's Poirot: Murder on the Links;* Sid Hope in *Dalziel and Pascoe.*
Films: *The Lovers; Boy Soldier.* Address: c/o Michelle Braidman Associates. m. Jane; 1 d. Emily.

LATHAM, Philip

Philip Latham

Philip Latham. Actor. b. Leigh-on-Sea, Essex, 17 January 1929. Trained at RADA. Stage plays include *The Gazebo* (Savoy Theatre), *Missing Persons, The Letter* and *The Winslow Boy* (all national tours).
TV: Willy Izzard in *Mogul; Maigret; When the Kissing Had to Stop; To Bury Caesar; Sergeant Cork; Poison Pen; The Campaign; A Month in the Country; Middlemarch; The Marquise; Justice;* Willy Izzard in *The Troubleshooters; Time-Lock; Whose Life Is It Anyway?; No Exit; Away from It All; The Caller; Is Nelly Dead?; Love Story; Good at Games;* Plantagenet Palliser in *The Pallisers; The Cedar Tree; Murder of a Moderate Man; The Killers; Lives of Our Own; Name for the Day; The Professionals; Hammer House of Horror; Nanny;* Wellington in *Number 10; Wellington; The Fourth Arm; Man from the Pru; Doctor Who; Jackanory Playhouse; Operation Democrat; Leaving; Tea in the Garden; From a Far Coun-*

try: Pope John Paul II (TVM). TV commercials: Midland Bank.
Films: The Dam Busters; The Wild and the Willing; Ring of Spies; Devil-Ship Pirates; The Secret of Blood Island; Dracula — Prince of Darkness; Doppelganger; The Last Grenade; Spy Story; Force 10 From Navarone. Address: c/o Bryan Drew. m. Eve; 1 d. Amanda, 1 s. Andrew. Hobbies: Golf, gardening.

Sam Lathem

LATHEM, SAM
Sam Lathem. Actor. b. London, 30 June 1966. Trained at the Webber Douglas Academy. Stage roles include Immigration Officer in A View from the Bridge (Strand Theatre and national tour).
TV: Billy Crewe and Jay Colkins in The Bill; Oscar in Exchange of Fire; Gary Parker in 2point4 Children; Eric in She's Out; PC Waterman in Class Act; Robbo in Our Friends in the North; DS Vaines in Bodyguards (pilot, 1996).
Films: Fred in The Mountain Road; Brian Reilly in Eye of the Storm.
Address: c/o Langford Associates. Lives in London. Single. Hobbies: Rugby, football.

LAURIE, Hugh
Hugh Laurie. Actor. Former member of the Cambridge Footlights revue. Stage productions include A Sense of Nonsense (revue, tour) and Gasping (Theatre Royal, Haymarket).
TV: The Crystal Cube; Alfresco; The Young Ones; Letters from a Bomber Pilot; Mrs Capper's Birthday; The Black Happy Families (series); South of Watford (presenter, LWT only); Saturday Live; George III in Blackadder III (series); A Bit of Fry and Laurie (four series); Friday Live; Les Girls; Blackadder's Christmas Carol; Morris Minor and the Majors; Blackadder Goes Forth; Bertie Wooster in Jeeves and Wooster (three series, 1990, 1992-3); The Laughing Prisoner; Leo in All or Nothing (mini-series, 1993); Fry and Laurie Host a Christmas Night with the Stars (1994); Look at the State We're In!: Local Government; Look at the State We're In!: The Status Quo; Unspeakable Verse (reader); The Adventures of Mole (voice only); The Snow Queen (voice only).
Films: Plenty; The Secret Policeman's Third Ball; Strapless; Peter's Friends; A Pin for the Butterfly; All or Nothing at All. **Books:** The Gun Seller. Address: c/o Hamilton Asper Management.

Hugh Laurie

LAWLEY, Sue
Sue Lawley. Presenter. b. Dudley, Worcestershire, 14 July 1946. Graduated from Bristol University. Journalist with Thomson Regional Newspapers (1967-70), before joining the BBC in Plymouth as a reporter, sub-editor and presenter.
TV: BBC Plymouth; Nationwide (1972-5, 1977-82); Tonight (1975-6); General Election and Budget coverage; BBC newsreader; Wogan with Sue Lawley; Sue Lawley (ITV interview programmes); Arena: Desert Island Discs (presenter, 1992); World in Action: The Granada 500 (1992); Biteback (monthly series, 1992-); News '44 (D-Day Remembered, 1994); Inside Track on Crime; Inside Track on Relationships; News 45: VE Day (1995); Hospital Watch; News 45: VJ Day (1995); Here and Now (two series, 1995-6). Address: c/o Noel Gay Artists. m. solicitor David Ashby (dis); 1 d. Harriet, 1 s. Tom.

Sue Lawley

LAWRANCE, Debra
Debra Lawrance. Actress. Trained at the National Institute of Dramatic Art, Australia.
TV: Glenview High; Ride on Stranger; Cop Shop; The Sullivans; Skyways; The Last Outlaw; guest role, then Daphne, in Prisoner (UK title Prisoner: Cell Block H); I Can Jump Puddles; Bellamy; Holiday Island; Carson's Law; A Country Practice; Waterloo Station; The Keepers; Sons and Daughters; Pat in Fast Lane; How the World Really Runs; The Bear; Living with the Law; Skirts; Pippa Fletcher/Ross in Home and Away (1990-).
Films: Before the Night Is Out; Flute Man; Silver City; Two Brothers Running; Evil Angels.
Address: c/o International Casting Service & Associates. m. actor Dennis Coard; 1 d. Grace.

Debra Lawrance

LAWRENCE, Josie
Wendy Lawrence. Actress/Entertainer. Member of Denise Black and the Kray Sisters, then appeared in the Comedy Store, London, which led to Whose Line Is It Anyway? on television.
TV: Rachel in Rachel and the Roarettes; Linda Prentice in Campaign; Friday Night Live; Agatha Christie's Poirot; Norbert Smith — A Life; Ryvita in Jackson Pace; Whose Line Is It Anyway?; Rory Bremner; Circe in Alas Smith and Jones; Janet Wilkins in Not with a Bang (series, 1990); I Love Keith Allen; Josie; Picture Box; 40 Minutes: Boobs in Toyland; Lucy in The Green Man (mini-series); Pass the Story; (bits of) Josie (compilation); Susie Farringdon-Cock in Queen of the Wild Frontier (The Comic Strip Presents...); Celebrity Mantelpiece (subject, 1993); Maggie Costello in Outside Edge (three series, 1994-6, Christmas special 1995); Sophie in Downwardly Mobile (series, 1994); voice of Pig-wig in Beatrix Potter: The World of Peter Rabit and Friends — The Tale of Pigling Bland; Cable TV Presenter in Absolutely Fabulous; Primrose in Sealed with a Loving Kiss (Paul Merton in Galton & Simpson's...).
Films: The American Way; Lottie Wilkins in Enchanted April.
Address: c/o The Richard Stone Partnership. Lives in East London.

Josie Lawrence

LAWSON, Charles

Charles Lawson

Quintin Charles Devenish. Actor. b. Enniskillen, 17 September 1959. Trained at Guildhall School of Music and Drama. Stage plays include *Murderers* (National Theatre), *Volpone, Julius Caesar, Henry VIII, Romeo and Juliet, Breaking the Ice, The Comedy of Errors, The Shepherd's Tale* (all RSC), *Henry IV, Parts 1* and *2*, and *Henry V* (all English Shakespeare Company).

TV: Seamus Duffryn in *Harry's Game;* Billy in *Four Days in July;* Dossie Wright in *Joyce in June;* Trigg in *The Firm; Crown Court; The Monocled Mutineer; Boon; The Bill;* Tommy Burns in *Upline;* Yizzel in *Bread; Valentine Falls;* Jim McDonald in *Coronation Street* (1989-).

Films: *Ascendancy; SS; I Cannot Answer That Question; Wilt.*

Address: c/o Barry Brown & Partner/Granada Television. m. Susie (sep 1994); 1 d. Laura-Kimberley. Partner: Make-up designer Lesley. Hobbies: Golf, horse-racing, riding.

LAWSON, Denis

Denis Lawson

Denis Lawson. Actor. b. 27 September 1947. Stage plays include *Pal Joey* (Albery Theatre), *The Lucky Chance* (Royal Court), *Lend Me a Tenor* (Globe Theatre), *The Importance of Being Earnest* (Royalty Theatre), *Lust* (Theatre Royal, Haymarket) and *Oleanna* (Duke of York's Theatre).

TV: Gobbo in *The Merchant of Venice; Beryl's Lot; Survivors; Anxious Anne; Slag Bag; Death of an Informer; The Girl Who Walked Quickly* (Armchair Theatre); *Fearless Frank; Diary of a Nobody; If Winter Comes; The Flipside of Dominick Hyde* (Play for Today); *Crown Court;* title role in *The Kit Curran Radio Show* (series, 1984) and *Kit Curran* (series, 1986); *Victoria Wood — As Seen on TV; Dead Head; That Uncertain Feeling; Love after Lunch* (TVM); *The Justice Game* (Series 2); *Boon; Bejewelled; One Way Out* (TVM); Malcolm in *El C.I.D.;* Towne in *Natural Lies* (mini-series); Victor Grace in *Born Kicking* (Screen One).

Films: *Dinosaur; Providence; The Man in the Iron Mask; Star Wars; The Empire Strikes Back; Return of the Jedi; The Steward Skeward; Local Hero; The Chain; The Zip.*

Address: c/o James Sharkey Associates.

LAWSON, Leigh

Leigh Lawson

Leigh Lawson. Actor. b. Atherstone, Warwickshire, 21 July 1943. Trained at the Mountview Theatre School and RADA. Stage plays include *The Merchant of Venice* (West End and Broadway).

TV: *Big Brother; Black Beauty; Trapped; Song of Songs; QB VII; William; Thriller; The Duchess of Duke Street; Disraeli; Why Didn't They Ask Evans?; Murder Is Easy; Black Carrion; Journey into the Shadows; Travelling Man; Lace; Queenie* (TVM); *Tears in the Rain* (TVM); *Voice of the Heart; I Accuse;* Neil Kinsey in *Kinsey* (two series).

Films: *Brother Sun, Sister Moon; Ghost Story; The God King; Percy's Progress; Love among the Ruins; Golden Rendezvous; The Devil's Advocate; Tess; Sword and Fire; The Captain's Doll; Sword of the Valiant; Deadline Madrid; Madame Sousatzka.* Address: c/o ICM. m. actress Twiggy Lawson (qv); 2 s. (including Ace from past relationship with actress Hayley Mills, qv), 1 d. Carly.

LAWSON, Twiggy

Twiggy Lawson

Leslie Hornby. Actress. b. London, 19 September 1949. Model before becoming a professional actress. Stage productions include *My One and Only* (Broadway).

TV: *Twiggs; Twiggy; The Frontiers of Science; Bring On the Girls; Roller Coaster; The Muppet Show; Pygmalion; Jukebox; The Sun Child; The Little Match Girl; The Great Diamond Robbery; Charlie the Kid; Young Charlie Chaplin; Betty;* Lady Janet Whitly in *Heartbeat* (Christmas special, 1994); *Sophie's World* (The Late Show, 1995).

Films: *The Boy Friend; W; Shadow of Evil; There Goes the Bride; The Blues Brothers; The Doctors and the Devils; Club Paradise; Madame Sousatzka; Istanbul.*

Records: Single: *Here I Go Again* (No 17, 1976). Albums: *The Boy Friend* (soundtrack); *Twiggy* (No 33, 1976); *Please Get My Name Right* (No 35, 1977). **Books:** *Twiggy* (autobiography); *Unlimited Twiggy.* Address: c/o ICM/Manager: Neville Shulman, 4 St George's House, 15 Hanover Square, London W1R 9AJ, tel 071-486 6363. Lives in London and Hollywood. m. 1st actor Michael Whitney (dec), 2nd actor Leigh Lawson (qv); 1 d. Carly (from 1st m.).

LAYTON, George

George Layton

George Michael William Layton. Actor/Writer/Director. b. Bradford, West Yorkshire, 2 March 1943. Trained at RADA. Stage roles include Fagin in *Oliver!* (Albery Theatre).

TV: *The Likely Lads;* Dr Paul Collier in *Doctor in the House, Doctor at Large, Doctor in Charge* and *Doctor at the Top;* Bombardier Solomons in *It Ain't Half Hot Mum; The Sweeney; Minder; Pigeon Street* (narrator); Vernon Potter in *Robin's Nest* (two series); PC Brian Booth in *My Brother's Keeper* (series); Voice in *All Night Long* (1994). As presenter: *That's Life!* (first series); *Pass the Buck.* As writer: *Doctor in the House; Doctor at Large; Doctor in Charge; Doctor at the Top; That's Life!; Robin's Nest; My Brother's Keeper* (with Jonathan Lynn); *Don't Wait Up* (creator, six series, 1983-90; winner, TRIC 1989

Best Comedy Series award); *Executive Stress* (creator, three series, 1986-8).
Films: Private Jacobs in *Stand Up Virgin Soldiers.* **Books:** *The Fib and Other Stories.*
Awards: Emile Littler Award. Address: c/o ICM. m. 2nd Moya; 2 s. Tristan, Daniel, 2 d. Claudie (all from 1st m.), Hannah (from 2nd m.). Pets: Chocolate labrador, tortoise. Hobbies: Tennis.

LE VAILLANT, Nigel

Nigel Le Vaillant. Actor. b. Karachi, Pakistan. Gained acting experience while studying at Oxford University. Stage plays include *All's Well That Ends Well, The Two Gentlemen of Verona, Titus Andronicus, A Midsummer Night's Dream, The Winter's Tale* (all RSC) and *Misery* (Criterion Theatre).
TV: *A Question of Guilt* (début, 1980); Edward in *Constance Kent;* Etonian in *Brideshead Revisited;* Valentine in *Jemima Shore Investigates;* Andy in *Minder;* Philip Courtauld in *Ladies in Charge;* Leitner in *Call Me Mister;* Gavin Freeman in *A Sort of Innocence;* David Herbert in *Poor Little Rich Girl;* Laurence Grainger in *Wish Me Luck;* Adam von Trott in *Christabel;* Hannay; Dr Julian Chapman in *Casualty* (series, 1990-3); Desmont Lee Wortley in *Agatha Christie's Poirot;* Petruchio in *Animated Shakespeare* (voice only); Simon in *Honey for Tea;* Paul Dangerfield in *Dangerfield* (two series,1995).
Films: Policeman in *The Jigsaw Man;* The Man in *Personal Services;* Reporter in *White Mischief;* Mayer in *Seven Minutes.* Address: c/o Christina Shepherd.

Nigel Le Vaillant

LE VELL, Michael

Michael Turner. Actor. b. Manchester, 15 December 1964. Trained at Oldham Theatre Workshop. Took his mother's maiden name and split it in two for his own professional name.
TV: *My Son, My Son; Fame Is the Spur, The Last Song; The Hard Word; A Brother's Tale; One by One;* Neil Grimshaw (1979), then Kevin Webster (1984-), in *Coronation Street, Royal Variety Performance* (with *Coronation Street* cast, 1989).
Address: c/o Noel Gay Artists/Granada Television. Lives in Saddleworth, West Yorkshire. m. actress Janette Beverley. Pets: Two German shepherd dogs, Goddess and Zak. Hobbies: Football, golf, squash.

Michael Le Vell

LEACH, Rosemary

Rosemary Anne Leach. Actress. b. Much Wenlock, Shropshire, 18 December 1935. Trained at RADA.
TV: *Z Cars; Armchair Theatre; The Power Game* (two series); *Germinal; Chariots of Fire; Roads to Freedom; On the Move; Jackanory; The Office Line; No That's Me over Here; The Wild Duck; Cider with Rosie; Birthday; Now Look Here; When the Wheel Turns; Don Quixote; Hands; Bermondsey; When Day Is Done; Prince of Denmark; Sadie It's Cold Outside; Tiptoe through the Tulips; Dad; Six Women; Hindle Wakes; Disraeli; Just between Ourselves; Life Begins at Forty; Hands; Tolstoy; The English in Love* (presenter); *Rumpole of the Bailey; All's Well That Ends Well; Othello; The Critic; The Jewel in the Crown; Swallows and Amazons; The Charmer; When We Are Married; Once in a Lifetime; Summer's Lease; Titmuss Regained;* Joan Craddock in *Growing Pains* (two series, 1992-3); Mavis Hunt in *An Ungentlemanly Act; The World of Peter Rabbit and Friends: The Tale of Tom Kitten and Jemima Puddle-Duck* (voice only); Mary in *Tender Loving Care* (Screen One); Lady Brightlingsea in *The Buccaneers* (series, 1995); Nan in *Blood and Peaches* (mini-series, 1995); Mrs Leslie in *Toby* (Chiller); *French and Saunders;* Mother in *Sealed with a Loving Kiss* (Paul Merton in Galton & Simpson's...).
Films: *Brief Encounter,* Mrs MacLaine in *That'll Be the Day, SOS Titanic; The Bride; Turtle Diary; A Room with a View; The Hawk.* **Awards:** Theatre: SWET Best Actress award (1982).
Address: c/o William Morris Agency (UK). m. Colin Starkey. Pets: A cat. Hobbies: Reading, embroidery.

Rosemary Leach

LEADER, Carol

Carol Leader. Actress. b. Colchester, Essex, 10 November.
TV: *Sally Ann; Play School; Play Away; Flambards; Chockablock; Honky Tonk Heroes; Young at Heart; Out of Step; Getting On; Studio; Late Starter; Information World; First and Last; Computing for the Terrified* (presenter, series, 1993); Mrs Crediton in *The Knock;* Carole Lennox in *The Bill;* Pam Milton in *Peak Practice;* Karen Mackie in *The Bill.* Address: c/o Lou Coulson. m. Michael Maynard; 1 s. Jonathan.

Carol Leader

LEADER, Howard

Howard Leader. Actor/Presenter. b. Romford, Essex, 13 August 1959. Uncle Stan Leader was a professional bass player with the Si Lorrie Jazz Band and toured with Glenn Miller during the Second World War. Trained in musical theatre at the Guildford School of Acting (1979-81). His passion for Victorian songs has brought him regular work in old tyme music-hall with the Globe Players and others.
TV: *Cockles; Pebble Mill at One* (musician); *The Day the Universe Changed; Can We Afford the Doctor?; Years Ahead;* General Von Schmelling in *'Allo, 'Allo* (1986-90); *Children in Need* (1987, 1988); *That's Life!* (1989-94); *Telethon '90; Blue Peter, Post Card from Malaysia.*
Videos: *Temptation* (Joan Armatrading promotional music video).
Address: c/o Edward Harris Personal Management, 26 Kiver Road, London N19, tel 0171-281 0445. Lives in Winchester, Hampshire. m. Carol Farley (sep). Partner: Yvette Austin. Hobbies: Golf.

Howard Leader

Stanley Lebor

LEBOR, Stanley

Stanley Harvey Lebor. Actor. b. East Ham, London, 24 September 1934. Trained at RADA. RSC productions include *Love's Labour's Lost, The Merchant of Venice* and *Timon of Athens*.
TV: Marcus Berlin in *Coronation Street; The Naked Civil Servant; Ready When You Are, Mr McGill; Holocaust; The Flaxborough Crab; Exiles; The Bass Player and the Blonde; Hunting Tower; Minder; All the World's a Stage; Beyond the Pale; The Dig; Shoestring; Visitor from the Other Side; The Acts of Peter and Paul; Enemies of the State; The Baker Street Boys; Under the Hammer; Reilly — Ace of Spies; Paradise Postponed; Secret Army; Ever Decreasing Circles; 'Allo, 'Allo; The Borrowers; The Bill*.
Films: *Oh! What a Lovely War; Nothing but the Night; Hennessy; A Bridge Too Far; The Medusa Touch; Flash Gordon; Gandhi; Superman IV: The Quest for Peace; Personal Services*. Address: c/o Joy Jameson. Lives in Canterbury, Kent. m. Jill Rodwell; 3 s. David, Thomas, Michael. Pets: Two cats.

Geoffrey Leesley

LEESLEY, Geoffrey

Geoffrey Leesley. Actor. b. Manchester, 1 June 1949. Trained at RADA (1970-2).
TV: *Hunter's Walk; General Hospital; Law Centre; Crown Court; Scorpion Tales; Coronation Street; Target; Emmerdale Farm; The Foundation; Armchair Thriller; Strangers; Fox; Let There Be Love; Minder; Hammer House of Horror; Ladykillers; The Cost of Loving; Nolan, with a Little Help; If You Go down in the Woods Today* (TVM); *The Common Lot; Rentaghost; Scene; Talisman; Harry's Game* (mini-series and TVM); *Another Flip for Dominick; Just Desserts; Space Station Milton Keynes; The Amazing Miss Stella Estelle; One by One; All Creatures Great and Small; Hi-de-Hi!; Only Fools and Horses; The Detective;* Det Con Terry Wilson in *Bergerac* (five series); Geoff Travis in *Albion Market* (1985-6); *The Two of Us; Floodtide; Mates; Who's Our Little Jenny Lind?;* Paramedic Keith Cotterill in *Casualty* (four series); Det Supt Frank Mathews in *Waterfront Beat* (two series); *This Is David Lander; Capstick's Law; Micromen; The Brothers McGregor; The Old Boy Network; Spooks; The Paul Merton Show; The Good Guys; As Time Goes By; Rides; The Darling Buds of May; The Frontline; Second Best;* John Harrison in *Brookside; Westbeach; The Bill; Michael Winner's True Crimes; Firm Friends; Medics; Six Sides of Steve Coogan;* DCI John Deane in *The Chief* (series, 1994); Gilbert Prestcote in *Cadfael;* Glynn in *Wycliffe;* Rex in *The Liver Birds*. Address: c/o Evans and Reiss. Lives in West Sussex. m. Bobbie Brown; 1 d. Anna, 1 s. Sam. Hobbies: Classical music, reading, watercolour painting.

Johnny Leeze

LEEZE, Johnny

John Glen. Actor. b. York, 31 December 1941. Former Army sergeant and tank recovery mechanic.
TV: *Strike; Strangers; Cupid Darts; Wrathdale; The Book Tower; Hallelujah;* Man in *Open All Hours; Last of the Summer Wine; England's Green and Pleasant Land; Intensive Care; Juliet Bravo;* Harry Clayton in *Coronation Street;* Lionel Brough in *All Creatures Great and Small;* Gamekeeper in *Stay Lucky;* Billy Hamilton in *Chimera;* Custody Sergeant in *Resnick;* Landlord in *Heartbeat; Harry;* Prison Officer in *Criminal; Cracker;* Hodges in *Seaforth;* Jack in *Common as Muck;* Ned Glover in *Emmerdale* (1994-).
Films: *Ladder of Swords*. Address: c/o ATS Casting/Emmerdale Production Centre. Lives in Cleethorpes. m. 29 March 1969 Carol (dis 1983); 2 d. Nicola, Holly. Partner: Fiancée Julie. Hobbies: Golf.

Ronald Leigh-Hunt

LEIGH-HUNT, Ronald

Ronald Leigh-Hunt. Actor. b. London, 5 October. Trained at the Italia Conti Stage Academy. West End stage plays include *Justice Is a Woman, Parents Day, The King and I, Underground* and *Funny Girl*.
TV: King Arthur in *The Adventures of Sir Lancelot* (series, 1956); *The Saint; Court Martial; The Lift; Rogue Herries; Freewheelers; The Brothers; The Dick Emery Show; The Avengers; Both Ends Meet; Crime of Passion; Warship; Crossroads; Blake's 7; Doctor Who* (two series); *On the Green; The Onedin Line; The Enigma Files; Diary of a Nobody; Hilary; Law of the Land; Emmerdale Farm; Airline; Minder; The Professionals; Citizen Smith; Strong Poison; Diamonds Are Forever; All in Good Faith; Slinger's Day; Remington Steele; Smart Money; The Bill;* Frankenstein: *The Real Story;* Roy in *One Foot in the Grave*.
Films: *The Paper Orchid; Sink the Bismarck!; The Story of Private Pooley; Khartoum; The Tiger Lily; Le Mans; Nelson's Touch; Never Take Yes for an Answer; Mohammed; The Omen*.
Address: c/o Ellison Combe Associates. Lives in Twickenham, Middlesex. m. Ann Pidgeon (dec); 1 d. Laura. Hobbies: Tennis, golf, motor racing, jazz.

Angus Lennie

LENNIE, Angus

Angus Wilson Lennie. Actor. b. Glasgow, 18 April 1930. Started career as a dancer at the age of 14 with Jimmy Logan's parents at the Metropole, Glasgow. Spotted by Vivian Van Damm while touring Scotland and subsequently appeared in *Revuedeville* at London's famous Windmill Theatre.
TV: *Knight Errant Limited; Virgil of the Secret Service; Sir Yellow; Bowler; Justice; The Onedin Line; Z Cars; Doctor Who; Clay, Smeddum and Greenden; Pack Up Your Troubles; HMS Paradise; The Borderers; The Dancing Princes; Kidnapped; Softly Softly; The Danny La Rue Show;* Shughie McFee in *Crossroads; Send in the Girls; The Bagthorpe Saga; The House with the Green Shutters;* Curtis in *The Taming of the Shrew; The Stanley Baxter Show;* Lawyer Petello in *Doon Castle; CBTV; Johnny Jour the*

Gibbet; The Mortimer Touch; Time Out for Peggy; The Hogmanay Show (Scottish Television); The Lion, the Witch and the Wardrobe; Mario; The Criminals; Roll on the Boat; A Piece of Ribbin; Davro's Sketch Pad; Hannay; The Les Dennis Laughter Show; Lovejoy; Rumpole of the Bailey; The Tales of Para Handy; In the Dark (pilot and series); All Night Long (series); ATV Night (1994, recreating role of Shughie McFee from Crossroads); The Upper Hand; The Smiths (Comedy First); Keeping Up Appearances.
Films: Piglet Ives in The Great Escape; 633 Squadron; Tunes of Glory; Oh! What a Lovely War; One of Our Dinosaurs Is Missing; Great; The Valiant; Petticoat Pirates.
Address: c/o MGA. Lives in London. Single. Hobbies: Travel.

LENSKA, Rula

Rula Lenska. Actress. b. St Neots, Huntingdonshire, 30 September 1947. Trained at the Webber Douglas Academy. Stage plays include Conversations with a Stranger (Old Vic).
TV: Dixon of Dock Green; The Doctors; The Brothers; Edward the Seventh; Special Branch; The Saint; The Seven Dials Mystery; Private Schultz; Take a Letter Mr Jones; To the Manor Born; Aubrey; Rock Follies; Minder; Boon; Design for Living; Eva in Family Pride; Roberta Rodgers in Casualty; Isabel Stevens in Stay Lucky (series, 1993); Living Dangerously (narrator, series, 1993); Duchess in The Detectives; Cheetahs — In the Land of the Lions (narrator); Brilliant Gardens (presenter, series, 1995).
Films: Soft Beds, Hard Battles; Alfie Darling; Royal Flash. Address: c/o Vernon Conway. m. 1st actor Brian Deacon (dis), 2nd actor Dennis Waterman; 1 d. Lara (from 1st m.).

Rula Lenska

LEWIS, Alun

Alun Bennett. Actor. Brother of actor Hywel Bennett (qv). Took his mother's maiden name as his professional name.
TV: Eddie in Van Der Valk; Rumpole of the Bailey; Alan in A Woman's Place; Jim Crankshaw in Eustace and Hilda; Charley in Charley's Aunt; Fisher in Crown Court; Gordon Harris in Angels; Frederick in The Strange Affair of Adelaide Harris; Kenrick in Fearless Frank; Bryn in New Girl in Town; Terry in Noah's Castle; Andrew in Lifelike; Robin in Rising Damp; The Professionals; Ray in Happy; Bob in Maybury; Jim in Minder; Athelstone in Findings on a Late Afternoon; Billy John in Ennal's Point; Hockey in The Falklands Factor (Play for Today); Peter in Giro City (TVM); Gareth in Jemima Shore Investigates; Matthew in Just Another Blues Song; Gifford in 92 Grosvenor Street; Bronco Billy in Boon; Lewis in The Choir, Bubby Boyle in Bowen (Series 3); Tony Barclay in Emmerdale Farm; Daryl in Birds of a Feather (six series, 1989-94, plus Christmas specials, 1993, 1994); Vic Windsor in Emmerdale (1993-).
Films: Smithfield; Experience Preferred but Not Essential.
Address: c/o Annette Stone Associates. m.

Alun Lewis

LEWIS, Howard Lew

Howard Lew Lewis. Actor. b. London, 21 August 1939. Radio operator and computer programmer before training at the Half Moon Theatre.
TV: Pulaski; Mr Pye; The Charmer; Corner House; The Two Ronnies; Byron in Open All Hours; Prospects; The Bill; F.L.I.P.; Elmo in Brush Strokes (six series, 1986-91); Jack and the Beanstalk; Rabies in Maid Marian and Her Merry Men (four series); Chelmsford 123 (two series); Minder; Artrageous; Harry's Mad.
Films: Brazil; Robin Hood: Prince of Thieves; Chaplin; Shadowlands. Address: c/o The Narrow Road Company. m. (dis). Hobbies: Steam railways, book collecting, music, photography.

Howard Lew Lewis

LEWIS, Martyn

Martyn Lewis. Newsreader/Presenter. b. Swansea, West Glamorgan, 7 April 1945.
TV: BBC Belfast reporter (1967-8); HTV Wales reporter/presenter (1968-70); ITN Northern correspondent, reporter and newscaster (1970-86); BBC TV News newscaster (1986-); Songs of Praise; Breakfast with Frost (stand-in presenter, 1993); Today's the Day (series, 1993-); Today's the Day Christmas Special (1994, 1995); Today's the Day Easter Special (1995). Documentaries: The Secret Hunters; MacGregor's Verdict; Fight Cancer; Crime Beat (series, 1996).
Videos: Battle for the Falklands (producer/writer, ITN).
Books: And Finally; Cats in the News; Dogs in the News; Today's the Day.
Address: c/o Roger Hancock/BBC TV. Lives in London. m. Lizzie; 2 d. Sylvie, Katie. Hobbies: Listening to jazz music, photography.

Martyn Lewis

LEWIS, Naomi

Naomi Lewis. Actress. b. Manchester, 24 March 1971. Trained at the Academy of Live and Recorded Arts. Stage roles include Maria-Elena and Mary Lou Sokoloff in Buddy (Victoria Palace, 1993), The Mistress in Evita (Prince Edward Theatre) and Sonia Walsk in They're Playing Our Song (Cockpit Theatre).
TV: Lost Empires; Elsa Feldmann in Emmerdale (1989-91, 1993, 1994).
Address: c/o Paul du Fer Associates. Lives in London. Single. Hobbies: Work, travelling.

Naomi Lewis

Stephen Lewis

LEWIS, Stephen

Stephen Lewis. Actor/Writer. Trained at Joan Littlewood's Theatre Workshop.
TV: *Always Ask for the Best* (as writer); *Wagger* (as writer); Inspector Blake ('Blakey')in *On the Buses; Don't Drink the Water, Rep; The Jugg Brothers; The McGuffin; Bodger and Badger;* Vince Bluett in *One Foot in the Grave;* Reggie in *The Paradise Club;* Van Helsing in *2point4 Children; TV's Greatest Hits;* Smiler in *Last of the Summer Wine;* Kid Blumenburg in *Look at It This Way;* 'Blakey' in *Alexei Sayle's Stuff;* Herbert in *The Great Kandinsky;* Harry Lambert in *Oh Doctor Beeching!* (pilot, 1995).
Films: *Sparrows Can't Sing* (also writer); *Staircase; On the Buses; Mutiny on the Buses; Holiday on the Buses;* Mr Dunkley in *Personal Services; The Krays.* **Awards:** Variety Club Silver Heart (1970). Address: c/o Frazer-Skemp Management. Lives in London.

Jennie Linden

LINDEN, Jennie

Jennie Linden. Actress. b. Worthing, West Sussex, 8 December 1939. Trained at the Central School of Speech and Drama. West End stage plays include *On Approval, Hedda Gabler* and *Killing Jessica.*
TV: *The Trouble with England; You Can't Win; For King and Country; Present Laughter; Return of Favours; Seasons of the Year; Lady Windermere's Fan; The Rivals; The Persuaders; Alive Alive O; His and Hers; Black Beauty; And No One Could Save Her* (TVM); *The Frighteners; My Last Duchess; Death of Sister Mary; The Visitors; Frame; His and Hers; The Sutt; Little Lord Fauntleroy; Lillie; Dick Turpin; The Breadwinner; Charlie Muffin; A Degree of Uncertainty* (Play for Today); *Jessie; Leap in the Dark; Our Mother's House; House on the Hill; Tales of the Unexpected; Low Key Lady on a High; Speed Train; Missing From Home; Pepys; Sharing Time; Lytton's Diary; The Practice; Home James!; Watching You, Watching Me; Menace Unseen; The Endless Game* (pilot); *Chancer; Lovejoy; Casualty.*
Films: Barbara in *Dr Who and the Daleks; Women in Love; Nightmare; A Severed Head; Vampira; A View from the Loft; Valentino; Charlie Bubbles; The Corsican Brothers; Hedda; The Little Matchgirl.* Address: c/o Creative Talent Management. m. Christopher Mann; 1 s. Rupert.

Richard Lindley

LINDLEY, Richard

Richard Lindley. Presenter. b. Winchester, Hampshire, 25 April 1936. Gained a BA (Hons) in English literature from Queen's College, Cambridge. Started career making commercials for an advertising agency.
TV: ITN reporter (1964-72), first on *Roving Report,* then on *News at Ten,* covering the Biafran War, Rhodesia's declaration of UDI, Sir Francis Chichester's lone voyage round Cape Horn and the Vietnam War; *Panorama* (presenter, 1972-88); recruited by the IBA to oversee the regulation of all national ITV news and current affairs programmes (1988); *This Week* (reporter, 1989); *ITN World News* (repeated as *ITN Morning News*) (1993-); *The Men Who Kept the Lights On* (documentary, 1994); ITN reporter. Address: c/o ITN. m.; 2 children.

Robert Lindsay

LINDSAY, Robert

Robert Lindsay. Actor. b. Ilkeston, Derbyshire, 13 December 1949. Trained at RADA. Began career as an ASM in Exeter. West End theatre roles include Jesus in *Godspell,* Bill Snibson in *Me and My Girl* (also on Broadway), Henry II in *Becket* and the title role in *Cyrano de Bergerac.*
TV: *Letter from a Soldier,* Jakey Smith in *Get Some In* (two series, 1975-6); Wolfie Smith in *Citizen Smith* (four series, 1977-80); *Seconds Out; All's Well That Ends Well; A Midsummer Night's Dream; Twelfth Night;* Edmund in *King Lear* (1984); *Give Us a Break;* Father Thomas in *Confessional* (TVM); Michael Murray in *G.B.H.* (series, 1991); Carter in *Nightingales* (series); *Prisoners of the Sun* (narrator, documentary series); *Mandela: From Prison to Premier* (narrator, documentary); Otto Schatz in *Genghis Cohn* (Screen Two); *The Natural World: Toadskin Spell* (narrator); Henry Farr in *The Wimbledon Poisoner* (mini-series, 1994); Jamie Diadoni in *Jake's Progress* (serial, 1995).
Films: *That'll Be the Day; Bert Rigby, You're a Fool; Strike It Rich* (also titled *Loser Takes All*).
Records: *Me and My Girl* (original soundtrack recording, 1986). **Awards:** SWET Laurence Olivier Award for *Me and My Girl* (1985); Tony, Antoinette Perry and Drama Desk awards as Best Actor in a Musical for *Me and My Girl* (Broadway, 1987). Address: c/o William Morris Agency (UK). Lives in West London. m. 1st 1974 actress Cheryl Hall (dis), partner actress Diana Weston (parted 1994), partner TV presenter Rosemarie Ford; 1 d. Sydney (from partnership with Diana Weston).

Shona Lindsay

LINDSAY, Shona

Shona Lindsay. Actress. b. Edinburgh, 4 December 1969. Made her professional début at the age of 11 in the title role of *Annie* (national tour). Trained at the Birmingham School of Speech and Drama. Former member of the National Youth Theatre. Other stage roles include Christine in *The Phantom of the Opera* (Her Majesty's Theatre). Plus *The Music of Andrew Lloyd Webber* (Prince Edward Theatre).
TV: Barbara Boyer in *The Secret Diary of Adrian Mole Aged 13¾* and *The Growing Pains of Adrian Mole; David Copperfield;* Young Lucy in *Lizzie's Pictures;* Lisa in *The Ritz;* Sara Briggs in *Crossroads* (1986-8); Sandra Potts in *Mother's Ruin.*
Records: Single: *Goodbye* (1988). Address: c/o Eric Glass. m. actor James Barron (qv) (dis).

LIPMAN, Maureen

Maureen Diane Lipman. Actress. b. Hull, East Yorkshire, 10 May 1946. D Litt, MA. Trained at LAMDA.

TV: *Doctor at Large; The Soft Touch; Don't Ask Us; The Lovers; Long Day's Journey into Night; File It Under Fear; Crown Court; Rooms; The Evacuees; Couples; Rogue Male; The Sweeney; Bobby Bluesocks; Jane Lucas in Agony; Smiley's People; Last Night; Another Dissident; Codename; Dangerous Davies – The Last Detective* (TVM); *The Knowledge; The Sporting Club Dinner; Jackanory Playhouse: The Witching Hour; Rolling Home;* Maggie in *Outside Edge; Love's Labour's Lost; See How They Run; On Your Way Riley; Absurd Person Singular; Absent Friends;* Julie in *Shift Work;* Sheila Haddon in *All at No 20; The Little Princess;* Tamara in *Exclusive Yarns; About Face* (two series); Enid Blyton in *Bookmark: Sunny Stories; Sister Wives* (narrator); *GI Brides* (narrator); *Holiday* (guest reporter); Joyce Grenfell in *Call Up the Stars* (VE Day concert, 1995); Jane Lucas in *Agony Again* (series, 1995); *Eskimo Day.*

Maureen Lipman

Films: *Up the Junction; Gumshoe; A Smashing Bird I Used to Know;* Trish in *Educating Rita; Water;* Lady in Bed in *National Lampoon's European Vacation;* Countess Esme in *Carry On Columbus.*

Books: *How Was It for You?; Something to Fall Back On; You Got an 'Ology?* (co-writer); *Thank You for Having Me; When's It Coming Out?*

Awards: TV: *TVTimes* Best Comedy Actress award for *All at No 20;* BAFTA Advertising Award as Best Actress for BT commercials. Address: c/o Hutton Management. Lives in North London. m.1973 playwright Jack Rosenthal; 1 d. Amy Sam Rachel, 1 s. Adam Philip. Pets: A cat called Pushkin. Hobbies: 'Thinking about almost writing something wonderful.'

LITTLE, Mark

Mark Little. Actor. Trained at the National Institute of Dramatic Art.

TV: *Skyways; Cop Shop; The Sullivans; Waterfront; The Keepers; Infinity Limited; Carson's Law; The Flying Doctors; Rafferty's Rules; The Dunera Boys; A Matter of Convenience; The Great TV Game Show; Comedy Company;* Joe Mangel in *Neighbours; Countdown Revolution; No Worries* (pilot); *The Big Breakfast* (presenter); *Time Out with… Mark Little* (Carlton only, 1994).

Mark Little

Films: *An Indecent Obsession; Short Changed; Starstruck; The Clinic; Once upon a Weekend; Smoko; Wills and Bourke, The Untold Story; Evil Angels; Golden Braid; Nirvana Street Murder; What's the Big Idea?* Address: c/o ICM.

LITTLE, Syd

Cyril John Mead. Comedian. b. Blackpool, 19 December 1942. Performed as guitarist and singer under real name while still working as a painter and decorator, before teaming up with Eddie Large (qv), first as vocal duo Cyril Mead and Friend, then as comedians Little and Large. *Opportunity Knocks* winners.

TV: *Opportunity Knocks* (1971); *Crackerjack; Who Do You Do?; Now Who Do You Do?; The David Nixon Show; Seaside Special; The Wheeltappers and Shunters Social Club; The Little and Large Tellyshow; Little and Large; Disney Time; This Is Your Life* (subject); *The Children's Royal Variety Performance 1993; Summer Sunday* (presenter, series, 1993).

Syd Little

Address: c/o Peter Prichard. Lives in Torquay, Devon. m. Sheree; 1 d. Donna (from 1st m.), 2 s. Paul, Dominic (from 2nd m.). Hobbies: Music, painting pottery, making model boats.

LLOYD, Kevin

Kevin Reardon Lloyd. Actor. b. Derby, 28 March 1949. Trained to be a solicitor and did amateur dramatics in his spare time before training at the East 15 Acting School (1970-3).

TV: *Z Cars; The Sweeney; Minder; Hazell; The Borgias; By the Sword Divided; Misfits; Shine on Harvey Moon; Bergerac; Dear John;* Don Watkins in *Coronation Street* (1983-4); *Young at Heart; Auf Wiedersehen Pet; The Last Company Car; Cockles; Up the Elephant and round the Castle; Dempsey and Makepeace; Talent; Midnite at the Starlite; All in Good Faith; Andy Capp; Boon;* Det Con 'Tosh' Lines in *The Bill; This Is Your Life* (subject).

Kevin Lloyd

Films: *Billy the Kid and the Green Baize Vampire; Link; Britannia Hospital; Trial by Combat.*

Address: c/o Saraband Associates. Lives in Duffield, Derbyshire. m. Lesley Marcelle; 4 s. Mark, James, Henry, Edward, 3 d. Sophie, Poppy, Chloe (dec), 1 adopted d. Elly (Eleanora). Pets: A dog called Queenie and 12 chickens. Hobbies: Football, cricket, rugby, tennis, travelling, reading.

LLOYD, Siân

Siân Mary Lloyd. Weather presenter. b. Maesteg, Mid Glamorgan, 3 July 1958. Began career with Cardiff independent radio station CBC as a presenter and trainee journalist, before entering television.

TV: *Wales Today* (researcher, BBC Wales, 1981-2); S4C (Welsh Fourth Channel, news and weather presenter, 1984-9); WTN special shooting executive (1989-90); *ITV National Weather* (presenter, 1990-); *LWT Weather* (1990-1); *Tomorrow's World* (1992); *See You Sunday* ('Lunch at Your Place' feature, 1992-3); *BAFTA Awards* (1993); *Eisteddfod* (S4C, 1993); *Get Going* (HTV, 1993).

Awards: Presenters Prize at International Weather Forecasters Festival (1993).

Address: c/o International Weather Producions/Dave Warwick. Lives in Cardiff and Bath.

Siân Lloyd

Sue Lloyd

LLOYD, Sue

Susan Margery Jeaffreson Lloyd. Actress. b. Aldeburgh, Suffolk.
TV: Cordelia Winfield in *The Baron* (series, 1966-7) and re-edited TVMs *Mystery Island* and *The Man in a Looking Glass; The Saint; Department S; Randall & Hopkirk (Deceased); His and Hers; Hadleigh; UFO; Justice; The Two Ronnies; The Sweeney; The Upchat Line; Barbara Brady/Hunter in Crossroads; Supergran; Eat the Rich; William Tell; The Trouble with Michael Caine; Bergerac; Agatha Christie's Miss Marple: A Caribbean Mystery; Red Nose for Courage* (The Comic Strip Presents...); *Keeping Up Appearances.*
Films: *The Ipcress File; Where's Jack?; Go for a Take; Corruption; Innocent Bystander; Percy; Spanish Fly; Revenge of the Pink Panther; The Stud; The Bitch; Lady Oscar; Eat the Rich; Bullet to Beijing.* Address: c/o Barry Burnett Organisation. Lives in London. m. actor Ronald Allen (dec 1991). Pets: Two cats.

Roger Lloyd Pack

LLOYD PACK, Roger

Roger Lloyd Pack. Actor. b. London, 8 February 1944. Son of actor Charles Lloyd Pack. Trained at RADA.
TV: *Softly Softly; Dixon of Dock Green; Survivors; Brassneck;* Liz in *The Naked Civil Servant;* Earl of Gloucester in *Shakespeare; The Professionals; Longshot; Henry VIII; Turtle's Progress; Private Schultz; The Crime of Captain Colthurst;* Trigger in *Only Fools and Horses; Making Good; Bouncing Back; I Thought You'd Gone; Video Stars; Miracles Take Longer; The Brief; Moving; In a Secret State; One for the Road; The McGuffin; Comrade Dad; The Deliberate Death of a Polish Priest; Inspector Morse; Alas Smith and Jones; The Blues; The Finding; Made in Spain; Room at the Bottom; The Contractor; Bad Boyes; What Is Truth — The Putney Debates; Prisoners of Childhood; The Stone Age; The Object of Beauty; Births, Marriages & Deaths; Byker Grove; Mr Bean; Zorro; The Chief;* David Irving in *Selling Hitler; The Gravy Train Goes East; Boon; Stay Lucky; The Bill; Archer's Goon; The Trial; The Krypton Factor; Trust Me* (Screen One); *Anna Lee — Headcase; Party Time; Citizen Locke; Lovejoy; The Clothes in the Wardrobe* (Screen Two); *2point4 Children;* Dr Rex Regis in *Health & Efficiency* (two series, 1993-5); *Dandelion Dead* (mini-series); *Without Walls: The Great Bore;* Owen Newitt in *The Vicar of Dibley* (series) ; *Blood and Peaches; The Perfect Match; Impasse* (Paul Merton in Galton & Simpson's...).
Films: *The Magus; The Virgin Soldiers; Secret Ceremony; The Go-Between; Hamlet; Fiddler on the Roof; Meetings with Remarkable Men; Cuba; Bloody Kids; '1984'; Prick Up Your Ears; The Cook The Thief His Wife & Her Lover; Wilt; American Friends; Princess Caraboo.* Address: c/o Kate Feast Management. Lives in London. m. 1st Sheila Mackie (dis), 2nd Jehane Markham; 1 d. actress Emily Lloyd (from 1st m.), 3 s. Spencer, Hartley, Louis (all from 2nd m.). Pets: A cat. Hobbies: Chess, tennis, gardening.

Philip Locke

LOCKE, Philip

Roy James Locke. Actor b. Marylebone, London, 29 March 1928. Trained at RADA.
TV: *Doctor Who; Mill on the Floss; Oliver Twist; Dick Turpin; The Omega Factor; Codename Icarus; Connie; Antony and Cleopatra; A Night Out; She Fell Among Thieves; Pennies from Heaven; Butterflies; Don't Count; Dead Man's Kit; The Disappearance of Harry; Box of Delights; The Young Delinquent; Trelawney of the 'Wells'; The Comic Strip Presents...; The Secret Garden* (TVM); *Bergerac; Jekyll & Hyde; Saracen; Virtuoso; Agatha Christie's Poirot; Inspector Morse; Jeeves and Wooster; The Ruth Rendell Mysteries: A Case of Coincidence* (mini-series, 1996).
Films: *Thunderball;* Vogel in *Escape to Athena; Porridge; Hitler: The Last Ten Days; Ivanhoe; And the Ship Sailed On; The Inquiry; Stealing Heaven.* Address: c/o Conway, van Gelder, Robinson.

David Lodge

LODGE, David

David William Frederick Lodge. Actor. b. Strood, Kent, 19 August 1921.
TV: *Emergency — Ward 10; Sunday Night at the Prince of Wales; After Hours; United!; Tottering Towers; Alexander the Great; The Reg Varney Revue; Carry On Laughing; Father Brown; Thriller; Barlow; Q6; Larry Grayson; Potter's Picture Palace; Q7; Lovely Couple; Q8; Murder at the Wedding; Q9; Beryl Reid and Friends; We the Accused; Worzel Gummidge; Spike Milligan; Superstars* (host); *Kelly Monteith; Minder; Names and Games; Britain's Strongest Man; Super Teams; Junior Superstars; Superstars; International Superstars; Look Who's Talking;* Crawley in *Lovejoy.*
Films: Selection (from 105): *Orders are Orders* (début, 1954, but unseen in final edited version); *Cockleshell Heroes; Private's Progress; Further up the Creek; I Only Arsked; Yesterday's Enemy; Jazzboat; Two Way Stretch; The League of Gentlemen; The Bulldog Breed; Dock Brief; Mrs Gibbon's Boys; On the Beat; Two Left Feet; A Shot in the Dark; Guns at Batasi; The Intelligence Men; San Ferry Ann; The Sandwich Man; Casino Royale; Oh! What a Lovely War; The Smashing Bird I Used to Know; The Red Bus; The Magic Christian; Eyewitness; The Railway Children; The Amazing Mr Blunden; Return of the Pink Panther; Revenge of the Pink Panther; Sahara; House of Death; Edge of Sanity.* Address: c/o CCA Management. Lives in Richmond-upon-Thames, Surrey. m. Lyn. Hobbies: Charity work.

Judy Loe

LOE, Judy

Judy Loe. Actress. b. Urmston, Manchester, 6 March 1947. Gained a BA in English and drama.
TV: *Ace of Wands; Man at the Top; General Hospital; Edward the Seventh; Woodstock; Man of Straw;*

Z Cars; Miss Jones and Son; The Upchat Line; Couples; Crown Court; Robin's Nest; Ripping Yarns; Heartland; Visitors for Andersons; When the Boat Comes In; The Home Front; Life after Death; Pam in Singles; Missing from Home; Yesterday's Dreams; Dr Elizabeth Stafford in The Chief; Eurocops; Sheila Massey in Peak Practice; Jessica Rattigan in Revelations (two series, 1994-6); Ros McGregor in Casualty. Address: c/o Peters Fraser & Dunlop. Lives in London. m. actor Richard Beckinsale (dec); 1 d. actress Kate Beckinsale. Partner: Film director Roy Battersby.

LOGAN, Phyllis

Phyllis Logan. Actress. b. Paisley, 11 January 1956. Trained at the Royal Scottish Academy of Music and Drama. Stage plays include Threads, On the Edge and The Hired Man.

TV: The White Bird Passes; The Goodtime Girls; Off-Peak; Time and the Conways; Lady Jane in Lovejoy; The McGuffin; Bust; Hemingway; Defrosting the Fridge; And a Nightingale Sang; And the Cow Jumped over the Moon; Effie's Burning; Nancy Muir in Guests of the Emperor; Lou Larson in Love and Reason (mini-series); Samantha Fisher in Kavanagh QC; Mrs Wilde in The Big One (Rik Mayall Presents); Anna Spalinsky in Here Comes the Mirror Man (Chiller); Det Supt Chalmers in Pie in the Sky.

Phyllis Logan

Films: Another Time, Another Place; Every Picture Tells a Story; The Chain; Janet Graham in The Kitchen Toto; Out of Time; The Enquiry; Angry Earth; Franz Kafka's It's a Wonderful Life (short, 1994).

Awards: Films: BAFTA Most Outstanding Newcomer award and London Standard Best Film Actress award, both for Another Time, Another Place.

Address: c/o CDA.

LOMBARD, Louise

Louise Lombard. Actress.

TV: Shakers; Private Practice (pilot); The Bill; Perfect Scoundrels; Clarissa Calder in Bergerac; Casualty; Jackanory; Lucy Gullmington in Catherine Cookson's The Black Velvet Gown; Anna in Chancer (Series 2); Lucy in Angels; Evangeline in The House of Eliott (three series, 1992-4); Evangeline Eliott in French and Saunders; Unspeakable Verse (reader); Liz Shaw in Bodyguards (pilot, 1996).

Louise Lombard

Films: Aids and Drug Abuse; Twice upon a Time. **Radio:** Twentieth Century Vampire.

Address: c/o Annette Stone Associates. Single. Partner: Actor Jeremy Gilley.

LONNEN, Ray

Ray Lonnen. Actor. b. Bournemouth, Dorset, 18 May 1940. Trained at the Hampshire School of Drama, Bournemouth, then became an ASM in Belfast.

TV: Emergency – Ward 10; The Power Game; Honey Lane; The Troubleshooters; Pathfinders; General Hospital; Melissa; Crown Court; Z Cars; Rooms; Jubilee; The Sandbaggers (three series); The Gentle Touch; Hammer House of Horror; Glamour Girls; title role in Harry's Game (mini-series, 1982); Tales of the Unexpected; The Brief; Murder Elite; Lovejoy; Yellowthread Street; Rich Tea & Sympathy; Singles; Cluedo; Rowley Carsons in Heartbeat; Editor in Harry; James Bowler in Johnny and the Dead (series).

Ray Lonnen

Films: Zeppelin; Lady Caroline Lamb; Murder Elite; Maneaters.

Address: c/o Langford Associatess. Lives in West London. m. 1st actress Lynn Dalby (dis), 2nd 1994 actress Tara Ward; 1 d. Amy, 2 s. Thomas, Rhys (all from 1st m.). Hobbies: Travel, playing tennis, cinema, listening to music.

LORD, Derek

Derek Lord. Actor. b. Belfast. Moved to Britain as a child, then emigrated to Australia. Trained at the Academy of Theatre Arts, Perth, Australia, and gained stage experience before returning to Britain.

TV: Billy; Davie Sneddon in Take the High Road (1984-); Nikola Stedul in The Yugoslav Hitman.

Films: Casey in The Hard Way; The Black Windmill; Cal.

Address: c/o Pat Lovett Agency. Lives near Largs, on the Clyde coast. m. actress Lana McDonnell; 1 s. Barry.

Derek Lord

LOTT, Barbara

Barbara Lott. Actress. b. Richmond-upon-Thames, Surrey, 15 May 1920. Trained at RADA.

TV: Nana; War and Peace; Six Days of Justice; Ballet Shoes; Spawn; Nightingale's Boys; The Survivors; The Duchess of Duke Street; Angels; Sexton Blake; Mrs Bennett in Rings on Their Fingers; Kids; Thomas and Sarah; Enemy at the Door; The Sandbaggers; Maybury; The Trial of Lady Chatterley; The All Electric Amusement Arcade; The Kit Curran Radio Show; Honeymoon; Mother in Sorry (series, 1981-8); Mrs Cravat in Tickle on the Tum; The Croydon Poisonings (In Suspicious Circumstances); Auntie Pearl in 2point4 Children; Woof!; Nanny in Law and Disorder; Mrs Carmichael in Daisies in December.

Films: The Party's Over; Unman, Wittering & Zigo; Electric Moon; The Pillow Book.

Radio: Lady Betty in Radio Channel (BBC Radio).

Address: c/o Marmont Management. Lives in South London. m. TV producer Stuart Latham (dec). Hobbies: Walking, gardening, tapestry, music.

Barbara Lott

William Lucas

LUCAS, William

William Thomas Clucas. Actor. b. Manchester, 14 April 1925. After Royal Navy, trained at Bradford Civic Theatre under Esmé Church and Rudolph Laban. Plays include *Run for Your Wife* (Duchess Theatre).
TV: *Portrait of Alison; The Paragon; The Infamous John Friend;* title role in *Rigoletto; A Flea off Pepe; Champion Road; Flower of Evil; Mogul; Warship;* Dr James Gordon in *The Adventures of Black Beauty* (series, 1972-4) and *The New Adventures of Black Beauty* (series, 1990); *Spoils of War; Doctor Who; The Two Ronnies;* Doublas in *On the Up* (Series 1); Stanley Webb in *Eldorado* (serial, 1992-3).
Films: *Calculated Risk; Payroll; Lost; Sons and Lovers; Crack in the Mirror; The Professionals; Bitter Harvest; Man at the Top.* Address: c/o Roger Carey Associates. Lives in Buckinghamshire. m. 1st (dis), 2nd Camilla; 2 s. Daniel, Thomas (both from 1st m.). Hobbies: Fishing, swimming, sailing.

Joanna Lumley

LUMLEY, Joanna

Joanna Lumley. Actress. b. Srinagar, Kashmir, India, 1 May 1946. Professional model for three years in London and on the Continent before turning to acting.
TV: Patient in *Emergency — Ward 10; Release; The Mark II Wife; Two Girls;* voice of Zaza the cat in *Hector's House;* Samantha Ryder-Ross in *It's Awfully Bad for Your Eyes, Darling...* (Comedy Playhouse and series); Elaine Perkins in *Coronation Street* (eight episodes, 1973); *The Protectors; General Hospital* (six episodes); *Steptoe and Son; Are You Being Served?; The Cuckoo Waltz; Up the Workers;* Purdey in *The New Avengers* (1976-7); *That Was Tory;* Sapphire in *Sapphire and Steel* (series, 1979-82); Kate in *The Weather in the Streets;* Lally Longbridge in *Mistral's Daughter* (mini-series); *Oxbridge Blues; The Glory Boys;* Sarawak in *Travels; Wogan* (stand-in chat-show host); Lady Drayton in *A Ghost in Monte Carlo* (TVM); *Women of Our Century: Dame Flora Robson* (presenter); *French and Saunders;* Victoria Cavero in *Lovejoy* (series, 1992); Loretta Stone in *A Perfect Hero; Trading Places* (guest); Patsy in *Absolutely Fabulous* (three series, 1992-5); Mrs Peacock in *Cluedo* (series); *QED: Art and Chips* (narrator); *Without Walls: Bad Ideas of the 20th Century — Germaine Greer on Youthism* (interviewer); *Wartime Romance and Epilogue* (The Love Weekend, presenter); Kate Swift in *Class Act* (two series, 1994-5); *Girl Friday* (documentary); Mrs Smiling in *Cold Comfort Farm; Jackanory: Who's a Clever Girl Then?* (storyteller); *Live for Peace — A Royal Gala* (VE Day 1995); *The Forgotten Toys* (voice only).
Films: *Some Girls Do;* English Girl in *On Her Majesty's Secret Service; The Breaking of Bumbo; Tam Lin* (UK title *The Devil's Widow*); Fanny Hill in *Games That Lovers Play; Don't Just Lie There, Say Something;* Jessica Van Helsing in *The Satanic Rites of Dracula; Lady Chatterley vs Fanny Hill;* Marie Jouvet in *Trail of the Pink Panther;* Countess Chandra in *Curse of the Pink Panther;* Marjorie in *Shirley Valentine.*
Records: Albums: Reader of *The One Hundred and One Dalmatians* (1984), named a notable children's recording by the American Library Association; reader of *Invitation to the Waltz* (1985).
Books: *Stare Back and Smile* (autobiography, 1989); *Forces Sweethearts* (1993); *Girl Friday* (1994). **Awards:** Emmy award for *Absolutely Fabulous* (1994). Address: c/o Caroline Renton. Lives in Canterbury, Kent. m. 1st writer Jeremy Lloyd (dis 1971), 2nd 1986 orchestra conductor Stephen Barlow; 1 s. James (b. 1967, from previous relationship with photographer Michael Claydon).

Michael Lumsden

LUMSDEN, Michael

Michael Lumsden. Actor.
TV: Henry in *Letters to Alice;* Vlad in *William Tell* (US title *Crossbow*); Young Wood in *The Adventures of Sherlock Holmes;* Aubrey in *Floodtide;* Goodall in *Wish Me Luck;* Jamie in *Victoria Wood;* Steve in *The Piglet Files;* Nicholas in *Watching;* Derek in *The Buddha of Suburbia;* Jack Martin in *Firm Friends;* Simon in *Health & Efficiency;* Brian in *My Good Friend* (series, 1995); Heslop in *Crocodile Shoes;* Ian Terson in *The Bill;* Robert in *For Valour;* Den Yorke in *Ghostbusters.*
Films: Tony in *No Pity* (National Film and Television School). Address: c/o The Narrow Road Company.

Cherie Lunghi

LUNGHI, Cherie

Cherie Lunghi. Actress. Trained at the Arts Educational School.
TV: Nancy in *Oliver Twist* (TVM,); *Sign of Four* (TVM); *Praying Mantis* (TVM); *Master of the Game; Tales of the Unexpected; Strangers and Brothers; Tales of the Klondyke; The Lady's Not for Burning; Harem* (TVM); *The Misanthrope; The Monocled Mutineer;* Gabriella in *The Manageress* (two series); *The Strauss Dynasty;* Adriana in *Intrigue* (TVM); *The Man Who Lived at the Ritz;* Audrey St John in *Guests of the Emperor* (mini-series); Mary Elizabeth in *Covington Cross* (pilot, 1992); Helen West in *A Question of Guilt;* Laura Testvalley in *The Buccaneers* (series, 1995).
Films: Guenevere in *Excalibur; King David; The Mission; To Kill a Priest; The Man Who Shot Christmas; Intrigue.* Address: c/o ICM. 1 d. Nathalie (from past relationship with film director Roland Joffe).

Jackie Lye

LYE, Jackie

Jacqueline Lye. Actress. b. Newcastle upon Tyne, 25 July 1959. Trained at the Central School of Speech and Drama (1978-81). West End theatre appearance as Michelle in *Strippers.*
TV: *Hell's Bells; Mog; Tripper's Day; Fresh Fields; Sink or Swim;* Sandra in *Brush Strokes* (six series);

Wanda the Human Anaconda in *Casualty*; Dot in *Tides of Laughter* (TV movie); *The Bill*; Mrs Holdsworth in *Harry's Mad* (two series). Address: c/o Janet Welch Personal Management. Lives in south-east London. Single. Pets: Cat. Hobbies: Working out in the gym, digging allotment, reading.

LYNAM, Desmond

Desmond Lynam. Sports presenter. b. Ennis, Co Clare, Ireland, 17 September 1942.

TV: *Grandstand; Sports Review of the Year; Sunday Grandstand*; Olympics and World Cup coverage; *Match of the Day; Match of the Day Live; Sportsnight; Holiday Outings; European Football Championship; Sports Review of the Year, Holiday* (guest reporter); *How Do They Do That?* (presenter, two series, 1994-5); *The Full Wax; Match of the Day — The Road to Wembley; European Cup Final; World Cup Grandstand* (1994); *The 3 Tenors in Concert* (1994); *Sunday Grandstand* (Wimbledon Championships, 1995); *World Athletics Championships*.

Radio: *Sport on 2; Sports Report; Today; Forces Chance; Treble Chance; Midweek.*
Address: c/o BBC TV Sport. m. (dis); 1 s. Patrick.

Desmond Lynam

LYNDHURST, Nicholas

Nicholas Lyndhurst. Actor. b. Emsworth, Hampshire, 21 April 1961. Trained at the Corona Stage Academy. West End stage plays include *The Foreigner* (Albery Theatre).

TV: *Our Show* (co-presenter, as a child); Davy in *Anne of Avonlea; Heidi*; Prince Edward/beggar boy Tom Canty in *The Prince and the Pauper; Peter Pan; Going Straight*; Adam in *Butterflies* (series, 1978-82); Rodney in *Only Fools and Horses* (series, 1981-); *Spearhead; To Serve Them All My Days*; Ashley in *The Two of Us* (four series, 1986-90), *Slimming Down*; Peter Chapman in *The Piglet Files* (two series, 1990-1); Chump Cosgrove (a PoW) in *Stalag Luft*; Gary Sparrow in *Goodnight Sweetheart* (three series, 1993, 1995, 1996, plus Christmas special, 1995).

Films: *Endless Night; Bequest to the Nation; Bullshot; Gun Bus.*
Address: c/o Chatto and Linnit. Lives in West Sussex.

Nicholas Lyndhurst

McALISTER, David

David McAlister. Actor/Presenter. b. Worthing, West Sussex, 2 April 1951. Son of variety artists Shaun McAlister and Judy Landale. Made his professional début at the age of 12 as Freidrich von Trapp in the original West End production of *The Sound of Music* (Palace Theatre). Other stage plays include *A Month in the Country* (Cambridge Theatre), *Oh Kay!* (Westminster Theatre), *The Mousetrap* (St Martin's Theatre), *Noel and Gertie* (King's Head Theatre) and *Peg* (Phoenix Theatre).

TV: *Brideshead Revisited; Princess Daisy; All at No 20; Farrington of the FO; Juliet Bravo; Brookside*; Raymond West in *Agatha Christie's Miss Marple: Sleeping Murder, Home James!; The Zero Option*; Commander Nichols in *A Taste for Death*; John Lynott in *Traffik*; Howard Allen in *Capital City*; Peter Burridge in *Freddie and Max*; Geoffrey Gooch in *Lovejoy*; Colin in *EastEnders*; Tobin in *Born Kicking*; Alec Bulson in *The Chief*; Inspector Glen in *Agatha Christie's Poirot*; Vicar in *Perfect Scoundrels*; Matthew Palmer in *Growing Pains* (two series, 1992-3); Brown in *Doomsday Gun*; Roy Plomley in *The Last Englishman* (Heroes & Villains); Neville in *BUGS*; Martyn Lewis in *Fatherland*.

Films: *The Music Lovers; Decline and Fall; Countdown to Danger; Who Dares Wins*. Address: c/o Hilary Gagan Associates. Lives in Guildford. m. 1 d. Amy, 1 s. Kieran. Hobbies: Gardening, tennis.

David McAlister

McANDREW, Deborah

Deborah Louise McAndrew. Actress/Singer. b. Huddersfield, West Yorkshire, 11 October 1967. Wrote musical *Nativity Inn* aged 14, then trained at Manchester University's drama department. Sang with 18-piece big band Force 10 for two years and jazz quartet Something Else for seven years.

TV: Angie Freeman in *Coronation Street* (1990-3); Liza Everett in *Heartbeat* (1994).
Address: c/o Barbara Pemberton Associates. Lives in Leeds. m. Tim. Hobbies: Choral singing, playing piano and guitar, painting, sewing.

Deborah McAndrew

McARDLE, John

John McArdle. Actor. b. Liverpool, 16 August 1949. Trained at the East 15 Acting School. Stage plays include *To* (Octagon Theatre, Bolton, and national tour).

TV: *Coronation Street* (two roles, including Det Con Meadows); *Charlie; Frankie and Johnny; How We Used to Live*; Billy Corkhill in *Brookside* (1985-90); *Underbelly*; Paul Garnet in *Gallowglass* (mini-series, 1993); Sam Harper in *Spender*; Harry in *Bambino Mio* (Screen One); DC Dave Corbyn in *The Chief*; Peter Cresswell in *Firm Friends* (series, 1994); Fred Spence in *Seaforth* (series, 1994); Louis Souter in *Finney* (series, 1994); Dilke in *Skallagrigg* (Screen Two); Tom Carter in *Cracker*; Phil Lane in *The Bill*; Keir in *Wycliffe*; Malcolm Freeman in *Rich Deceiver* (mini-series, 1995); Terry Tinniswood in *Heartbeat*; Simon Lloyd in *Kavanagh QC*; Charlie Woods in *And the Beat Goes On* (series, 1996).
Address: c/o Hope & Lyne. Lives near Burnley, Lancashire. m. 1st (dis), 2nd actress Kathy Jamieson (qv); 1 s. Justin (from 1st m.), 1 d. Katie.

John McArdle

Edith Macarthur

Gordon MacArthur

David McCallum

Eileen McCallum

Brian McCardie

MACARTHUR, Edith

Edith Macarthur. Actress. b. Ardrossan, Ayrshire, 8 March 1926. Began career with Wilson Barret Company at Royal Lyceum Theatre, Edinburgh (1948), followed by repertory theatre, RSC and West End productions.

TV: *The Borderers; Sunset Song; Weir of Hermiston; Dr Finlay's Casebook; Five Women; Love Story; Heartland; The Sandbaggers;* Judith Sutherland in *Sutherland's Law;* Elizabeth Cunningham in *Take the High Road* (1980-7); *Menace Unseen; French Fields;* Kitty in *The Long Roads* (Screen Two); Izabel Gant in *Doctor Finlay.* Address: c/o Larry Dalzell Associates. Hobbies: 'Music, reading, cat-watching.'

MacARTHUR, Gordon

Gordon MacArthur. Actor. b. Elgin, Morayshire, 7 November 1961. Trained at Guildhall School of Music and Drama. Stage plays with the Young Vic and Theatre of Comedy.

TV: *Boswell's London Journal; The Justice Game* (mini-series); Rev Michael Ross in *Take the High Road/High Road.* Address: c/o Ruth Tarko Agency. Single. Hobbies: Music, playing golf and the piano.

McCALLUM, David

David McCallum. Actor. b. Kelvinside, Glasgow, 19 September 1933. Father was leader of the Scottish Orchestra. Radio début in 1946. Trained at RADA (1949-51).

TV: Illya Kuryakin in *The Man from U.N.C.L.E.; Perry Mason; Teacher, Teacher* (TVM); *Hauser's Memory* (TVM); *She Waits* (TVM); *The Screaming Skull* (TVM); *Colditz; The File on Devlin; The Invisible Man* (TVM and series); Steel in *Sapphire and Steel;* Alan Breck in *Kidnapped;* Illya Kuryakin in *The Return of the Man from U.N.C.L.E.* (TVM); *OSS* (TVM); *Behind Enemy Lines* (TVM); *Alfred Hitchcock Presents...; The Wall of Tyranny* (US title *Freedom Fighter*)(TVM); *92 Grosvenor Street; The A-Team; Matlock; Hitchcock; The Return of Sam McCloud* (TVM); Alex Vesey in *Mother Love; Boon; The Man Who Lived at the Ritz; Murder, She Wrote; Father Dowling Investigates; Lucky Chances;* Prof Peter Plum in *Cluedo;* John Grey in *Trainer* (two series, 1991-2); *Library of Romance (Good Morning... with Anne & Nick,* storyteller); Cobb in *seaQuest DSV;* Cooper in *Heartbeat.* As director: *The Explorers: Charles Montague Doughty* (US title *Ten Who Dared*).

Films: *The Secret Place; Hell Drivers; Robbery under Arms; Violent Playground; A Night to Remember; The Long and the Short and the Tall; Carolina; Jungle Street; Billy Budd; Freud* (UK title *Freud — The Secret Passion*); *The Great Escape; To Trap a Spy; The Spy with My Face; Around the World under the Sea; The Greatest Story Ever Told; One Spy Too Many; The Spy in the Green Hat; Three Bites of the Apple; One of Our Spies Is Missing!; The Karate Killers; The Helicopter Spies; Sol Madrid* (UK title *The Heroin Gang*); *How to Steal the World; Mosquito Squadron; La Cattura (The Ravine); Frankenstein: The True Story; The Diamond Hunters* (US title *The Kingfisher Caper*); *Dogs; King Solomon's Treasure; The Watcher in the Woods; Critical List; Terminal Choice; The Wind; The Haunting of Morella; Fatal Inheritance;* Constable Abbott in *Hear My Song; The Dirty Weekend; Shattered Image; The Healer; Babylon V.* Address: c/o Hilary Gagan Associates. Lives in New York. m. 1st 1957 Jill Ireland (dis 1967), 2nd Katherine Carpenter; 1 d. Sophie, 4 s. Paul, Jason (dec), Valentine, Peter. Hobbies: Golf, computing.

McCALLUM, Eileen

Eileen McCallum. Actress. b. Glasgow, 2 December 1936. MBE, 1992. Daughter of teacher Gordon McCallum, who wrote the BBC radio *Children's Hour* series *Down at the Mains* and acted and sang on BBC Radio Scotland. Radio début on *Scottish Children's Hour* at the age of 12. Trained at the Royal Scottish Academy of Music and Drama (Gold Medal winner, 1959). S

TV: *Who Fought Alone?; Smeddum; Grey Granite; Sunset Song; Just Your Luck* (Play for Today); Jean Ross in *Garnock Way;* Isabel Blair/Mogan in *Take the High Road/High Road* (1980-); voice of Edwin Muir's wife in *The Vision of Edwin Muir; Just Another Saturday; Sweet Nothings; Baa Baa Black Sheep; The Scotched Earth Show; The Steamie; Taggart;* Elspeth Strickland in *Doctor Finlay;* Rev Jan McLardie in *Taggart: Secrets.* Address: c/o Young Casting Agency/Scottish Television. Lives in Edinburgh. m. Tom Fidelo; 3 s. Mark, Neal, Tim, 1 d. Sarah.

McCARDIE, Brian

Brian McCardie. Actor. b. Bellshill, Glasgow, 22 January 1965. Trained at Rose Bruford College of Speech and Drama.

TV: PC Ronnie Barker in *Waterfront Beat;* Bunny McKinnon in *Forget About Me* (originally titled *Snow Queen* and broadcast as a schools programme on Channel Four); Archie Henderson in *Doctor Finlay;* Vic Leigh in *Dirty Old Town* (Rik Mayall Presents). Address: c/o Conway, van Gelder, Robinson.

McCASKILL, Ian

Ian McCaskill. Weather presenter. b. Glasgow, 28 July 1938. Attended the Meteorological Office College before entering television.

TV: BBC TV weather forecaster (1978-); Central Television weather forecasts (1982-3); *Birds of a*

Feather (acting himself). Address: c/o BBC TV. Lives in Beaconsfield, Buckinghamshire. m. Lesley (dec April 1992); 2 d. Victoria, Kirsty. Hobbies: Collecting comic postcards, junk, swimming.

MacCORKINDALE, Simon

Simon MacCorkindale. Actor/Writer/Director. b. Isle of Ely, 12 February 1952. Trained at Studio '68.
TV: *The Pathfinders; Just William; The Skin Game; Jesus of Nazareth; I Claudius; Romeo and Juliet; Beasts; Three Weeks; Out of Battle; Quatermass; Quatermass Conclusion; Cabo Blanco; The Dukes of Hazzard; Wilfred Owen; The Mannions of America; Manimal; Falcon Crest* (also director); *Sincerely, Violet; Counterstrike* (also producer).
Films: *Death on the Nile; Riddle of the Sands; The Sword and the Sorcerer; Falcon's Gold; Jaws 3-D; Stealing Heaven* (producer); *That Summer of White Roses* (writer-producer).
Address: c/o James Sharkey Associates/Agency for the Performing Arts. m. 1st actress Fiona Fullerton (dis), 2nd actress Susan George.

Ian McCaskill

McCOWEN, Alec

Alexander Duncan McCowen. Actor. b. Tunbridge Wells, Kent, 26 May 1925. CBE. Trained at RADA. Many RSC and West End plays, plus Broadway productions of *Antony and Cleopatra, The Comedy of Errors, King Lear, The Misanthrope* and his one-man shows *St Mark's Gospel* and *Kipling*.
TV: *All for Love; Private Lives; Family Dance;* Malvolio in *Twelfth Night; The Young Visiters* (TVM); *Mr Palfrey of Westminster; The Secret Adversary; Storyboard;* David Hume in *Dialogue in the Dark;* Father McCarthy in *Maria's Child* (Screen Two); *Omnibus: A Day on the Mountain* (narrator).
Films: *A Midsummer Night's Dream* (short); *The Cruel Sea; The Divided Heart; The Deep Blue Sea; The Long Arm* (US title *The Third Key*); *Town on Trial!; The Good Companions; Time without Pity; The One That Got Away; The Silent Enemy; A Night to Remember; A Midsummer Night's Dream* (dubbed voice); *The Doctor's Dilemma; The Loneliness of the Long Distance Runner* (also titled *Rebel with a Cause*); *In the Cool of the Day; The Agony and the Ecstasy; The Witches* (US title *The Devil's Own*); *The Hawaiians* (UK title *Master of the Islands*); *Frenzy; Travels with My Aunt; Stevie; Hanover Street; Never Say Never Again; Forever Young; The Assam Garden; Cry Freedom; Personal Services; Henry V.*
Books: *Young Gemini* (autobiography, 1979); *Double Bill* (1980); *Personal Mark* (1984).
Awards: Theatre: Clarence Derwent Award for *As You Like It* (1960); Drama League of New York Best Actor award for *Hadrian VII* (1969); Variety Club and Drama League of New York Best Actor awards for *The Philanthropist* (1971). Address: c/o Conway, van Gelder, Robinson.

Simon MacCorkindale

McCOY, Sylvester

Sylvester McCoy. Actor. b. Dunoon, Argyll, 20 August 1943. Stage plays include *The Pied Piper* and *Twelfth Night* (both National Theatre), *Antony and Cleopatra, Can't Pay, Won't Pay, Abracadabra, The Pirates of Penzance* and *Temptation* (all West End).
TV: *Big Jim and the Figaro Club; Jigsaw; Tiswas; Dramarama; Starstrider; No 73; Eureka* (three series); *Hartbeat;* Birdie Bowers in *The Last Place on Earth;* title role in *Doctor Who* (1987-9, 12 stories, 42 episodes); *What's Your Story?* (presenter, two series); *Harum Scarum* (storyteller); *Pass-the-Story* (storyteller, 1992, 1993); *The Children's Royal Variety Performance 1992; Doctor Who: Dimensions in Time* (Children in Need, 1993); Angus in *Frank Stubbs;* Gash Senior in *Rab C Nesbitt.*
Films: *Dracula; Fireworks; The Secret Policeman's Ball; Three Kinds of Heat.*
Address: c/o Silvester Management. m. Agnes; 2 s. Sam, Joe.

Alec McCowen

McDONALD, Sheena

Sheena McDonald. Presenter. b. Dunfermline, Fife, 25 July 1954. Studied film at Bristol University and worked as a researcher with the Scottish Film Council before entering radio, then television.
TV: *Scotland Today; Scottish Assembly; Scottish Election Question Time; Scottish Books; Festival Focus; Between the Lines; Studio; Closer to Home; Freedom and...; Encore for the Arts; Into the Eighties; What's Your Problem?* (all for Scottish Television from 1981); *The Afternoon Show; Votes for Women; Scottish Eye; The World This Week; Right to Reply; The World This Week; Assignment: The United Nations — A New Resolution; Channel Four News: Midnight Special* (Election programmes, 1992); *Power and the People; Round IX; Dreams Among the Wreckage; Right to Reply Specials;* Liberal Democrats Live, Labour and Conservative party conference coverage (BBC, 1993, 1994); *God: For and Against; The Late Show; Serious Money* (series, 1994); *BAFTA Awards* (1994); *On the Record* (series, 1994); *Brave New World* (series, 1994); *The Diagnosis; After Dark Special; 100 Women* (series, 1994); *The Vision Thing* (two series, 1994-5); *The Great Pot Debate; And Finally: Bugger Bosnia; Lockerbie: The Maltese Double Cross; Lockerbie: The Debate; Power and the People; The Dying Rooms Debate; House to House* (series, 1996); *Scott of the Arms Antics.*
Radio: Reporter, presenter and producer for BBC Radio Scotland.
Address: c/o Curtis Brown. Lives in Edinburgh. Single.

Sylvester McCoy

Sheena McDonald

Trevor McDonald

McDONALD, Trevor

Trevor McDonald. Newscaster. b. Trinidad, West Indies, 16 August 1939. OBE, 1992. Worked in newspapers, radio and television in Trinidad before joining BBC radio in London as a producer for the Caribbean Service and the World Service, then moving to ITN.

TV: *Panorama; Dialogue* (both as interviewer, in Trinidad); ITN reporter (1973-8), sports correspondent (1978-80), diplomatic correspondent (1980-2) and *Channel Four News* diplomatic correspondent and newscaster (1982-7); *Channel Four News* diplomatic editor (1987-9), *News at 5.40* newscaster (1989-90) and *News at Ten* newscaster (1990-); *Wish You Were Here…?* (guest presenter, 1993); *Rugby World Cup 1995 Review; The Caballe Family Christmas with Cher* (1995); *Happy Birthday Ma'am.*

Books: *Clive Lloyd — A Biography; Vivian Richards — A Biography; Queen and Commonwealth; Fortunate Circumstances* (autobiography, 1993).

Awards: TRIC Newscaster of the Year (1993). Address: c/o The Jules Bennett Agency/ITN. m. 1st Josephine (dis), 2nd Sabrina; 2 s. Tim, Jamie, 1 d. Joanne.

McELWEE, Rob

Robert Ian McElwee. Weather presenter. b. Burton-upon-Trent, Staffordshire, 21 January 1961. Qualified as a weather forecaster with the Meteorological Office.

TV: BBC TV weather forecaster (1991-); *Gardeners' World* (guest expert); *EastEnders* (acting himself for background television forecasts).

Radio: BBC World Service, BBC Radios 3, 4 and 5 (1991-). Address: c/o BBC Weather Centre. Lives in London. m. 1993 TV announcer Rosanne Macmillan. Pets: Four cats. Hobbies: DIY (household and mechanical), driving anything (HGV licence), rally co-driving, travel, photography.

Rob McElwee

McENERY, Peter

Peter McEnery. Actor. b. Walsall, Staffordshire, 21 February 1940. RSC stage roles include Laertes, Clarence, Tybalt, Silvius and Johnny Hobnails in *Afore Night Come*, Patroclus and de Laubardamont in *The Devils*, Phillip of France in *Curtmantle*, Suffolk in *Henry VI*, Orlando in *As You Like It*, Lorenzaccio in *The Lorenzaccio Story*, Yescana in *Sons of Light* and Grandier in *The Devils*.

TV: *Lena, O My Lena* (Armchair Theatre, 1960); *Candida; Progress to the Park; Clayhanger; Romeo and Juliet* (US); *The Aphrodite Inheritance; The Jail Diary of Albie Sachs; Flicks; Pictures; Japanese Style; The Collectors; The Mistress; The Florence Nightingale Saga* (US series); *Safari* (US series); Jamie Matheson in *Witchcraft* (mini-series); *Boon; Berlin Break;* Fraser in *All Quiet on the Preston Front.*

Films: *Tunes of Glory; Victim; The Moonspinners; The Fighting Prince of Donegal; La Curée; J'ai tué Rasputin; Better a Widow…; Negatives; The Adventures of Gerard; Sleep Is Lovely; Entertaining Mr Sloane; Le Mur d'Atlantique (The Atlantic Wall); The Cat and the Canary; Wonderland.*

Address: c/o ICM. m. actress Stephanie Beacham (qv) (dis).

Peter McEnery

McEWAN, Geraldine

Geraldine McKeown. Actress. b. Old Windsor, Berkshire, 9 May 1932. ASM at Windsor Theatre Royal before becoming an actress in rep there. Stage plays include *Twelfth Night* (as Olivia), *Pericles* (as Marina), *Much Ado about Nothing* (as Hero) (all Shakespeare Memorial Theatre, Stratford-upon-Avon), *Much Ado about Nothing* (as Beatrice), *Hamlet* (as Ophelia) (both RSC, Stratford-upon-Avon), *Love for Love, Edward II, Armstrong's Last Goodnight, A Flea in Her Ear, Dance of Death, Home and Beauty, The Way of the World, The White Devil, Amphitryon 38, The Browning Version, Harlequinade, The Provok'd Wife, You Can't Take It with You* and *The Way of the World* (all National Theatre).

TV: *The Witch; Candida; Separate Tables; Pandora; Three Months Gone; The Magistrate; On Such a Night; We Are Strangers Here; Hopcraft into Europe; Dear Love; The Statue and the Rose; Fat* (Play for Today); title role in *The Prime of Miss Jean Brodie* (series, 1978); *Come into the Garden Maude; L'Élégance* (Aspects of Love); Mrs Proudie in *Barchester Chronicles;* Anne Dickens in *Tears before Bedtime* (series, 1983); Lucia in *Mapp and Lucia* (series, 1985-6); Mother in *Oranges Are Not the Only Fruit* (mini-series, 1990); Miss Farnaby in *Mulberry* (two series); *Continental Drift: Spring Lenin* (Screen-Play); voice of Auntie in *Not without My Handbag; Rory Bremner… Who Else?; French and Saunders.*

Films: *The Bawdy Adventures of Tom Jones; Escape from the Dark; Pit Ponies;* Lady Ammanford in *Foreign Body;* Alice in *Henry V;* Mortianna in *Robin Hood: Prince of Thieves;* Miriam in *Moses.*

Awards: TV: BAFTA Best Actress Award for *Oranges Are Not the Only Fruit.* Address: c/o Marmont Management. m. 17 May 1953 playwright-director Hugh Cruttwell; 1 s. Greg, 1 d. Claudia.

Geraldine McEwan

McFADDEN, Steve

Steve McFadden. Actor. Trained at RADA (winner, Derek Ware and Patrick Crane Awards).

TV: Billy in *The Firm; Minder; Hard Cases;* Staff Sgt Ballantine in *Vote for Them; The Bill; Ligmalion* (TVM); Nash in *Saracen;* Jones in *Bergerac; All Change;* Phil Mitchell in *EastEnders* (1990-).

Films: *Rossinanti; Buster.* Address: c/o Marina Martin Associates. m. (dis); 1 s. Matt. Hobbies: Boxing, karate, snooker, sailing, horse-riding, climbing, playing football.

Steve McFadden

MACFADYEN, Angus

Angus Macfadyen. Actor. Educated in France. Gained an MA (Hons) in French and English from the University of Edinburgh. Trained at the Central School of Speech and Drama. Writer of various plays, including *1905*, winner of the 1991 Questors Theatre Student Playwriting Award.

TV: *Two Golden Balls*; Philip in *The Lost Language of Cranes* (TVM); 2nd Lieutenant Pereira in *Soldier Soldier* (Series 2, 1992); *God of Happiness*; *Care*; *Destiny*; *Takin' Over the Asylum*.

Films: *Braveheart*; *Brylcreem Boys*. Address: c/o ICM.

Angus Macfadyen

McGANN, Joe

Joe McGann. Actor. b. Liverpool, 24 July 1958. Brother of actors Paul, Mark and Stephen McGann (all qv). Performed with the Liverpool Everyman Youth Theatre. Stage productions include *West Side Story* (Young People's Theatre tour), *Yakety Yak* (Half Moon and Astoria theatres), *Blood Brothers* (as Sammy, national tour), *Jack and the Beanstalk in the Wild West* (as the Giant, Young Vic), *Guys and Dolls* (as Sky Masterson, Haymarket Theatre, Leicester) and *The Long and the Short and the Tall* (as Private Bamforth, national tour).

TV: *Johnny Jarvis*; *The Gentle Touch*; *The Brothers MacGregor*; O'Dowd in *Rockliffe's Babies*; *Boon*; *Casualty*; *Norbert Smith — A Life*; *The Chronicles of Narnia*; Charlie Burrows in *The Upper Hand* (six series, 1990-5); *Harry Enfield's Television Programme*; Nat Briggs in *All Creatures Great and Small*; Sean Phelan in *The Hanging Gale* (series, 1995).

Films: *No Surrender*; *Kiss Cross*.

Address: c/o Marina Martin Associates. m. 1st art student Sarah (dis), 2nd actress Melissa Simmons (dis); 1 d. Charlotte (from 2nd m.).

Joe McGann

McGANN, Mark

Mark McGann. Actor. Brother of actors Joe, Paul and Stephen McGann (all qv). Stage productions include *Lennon* (title role, Everyman Theatre, Liverpool, and Astoria Theatre), *Old King Cole*, *Brown Bitter*, *Wet Nellies and Scouse*, *Blood Red Roses*, *1984*, *True Romance* (all Everyman Theatre, Liverpool), *Yakety Yak* (Half Moon and Astoria Theatres), *Blood Brothers* (as Mickey, national tour), *Up on the Roof* (Apollo Theatre), *Comedians* (Young Vic) and *Guys and Dolls* (as Sky Masterson, Haymarket Theatre, Leicester).

TV: *Moving on the Edge*; *Studio*; Mad Dog in *Scully*; Verezzi in *Zastrozzi*; *Les Girls*; title role in *John and Yoko: A Love Story* (TVM); Halliwell in *The Manageress*; *Yellowthread Street* (series); David Wright in *The Lady's Man — Archibald Hall* (Crime Story); Michael Dimmock in *The Last Word* (Comic Asides); *Murder Most Horrid II*; Conor Phelan in *The Hanging Gale* (series, 1995).

Films: *No Surrender*; *Business as Usual*; *Abducted*; *"Let Him Have It"*.

Address: c/o Jonathan Altaras Associates.

Mark McGann

McGANN, Paul

Paul McGann. Actor. b. Ireland. Brother of actors Joe, Mark and Stephen McGann (all qv). Stage productions include *Oi for England*, *The Genius*, *A Lie of the Mind* (all Royal Court), *Yakety Yak* (Half Moon and Astoria Theatres) and *Loot* (as Dennis, Ambassadors Theatre).

TV: Norman in *Whistling Wally*; *Russian Night*; title role in *Gaskin*; *Two Weeks in Winter*; *Give Us a Break*; Percy Toplis in *The Monocled Mutineer*; *The Importance of Being Earnest*; Cariani in *Cariani and the Courtesan*; *Open Space*; Colin in *Drowning in the Shallow End* (TVM); Joe Thompson in *Nice Town* (mini-series, 1992); *The Ancient Mariner* (English Time); Liam Phelan in *The Hanging Gale* (series, 1995); Chris Ryan in *The One That Got Away*.

Films: Barry in *Tree of Hands*; Raz in *Streets of Yesterday*; Anton Skrebensky in *The Rainbow*; Daniel Pascoe in *Dealers*; *Withnail & I*; Matthew Harris in *Paper Mask*; *Afraid of the Dark*; Golic in *Alien³*. Address: c/o Marina Martin Associates. Partner: Annie Milner; 1 s. Joe.

Paul McGann

McGANN, Stephen

Stephen Vincent McGann. Actor. b. Liverpool, 2 February 1963. Brother of actors Paul, Joe and Mark McGann (all qv). Acted with the Everyman Youth Theatre, Liverpool. Stage productions include *Yakety Yak* (Half Moon and Astoria Theatres), *Serjeant Musgrave's Dance* (Old Vic) and *Blood Brothers* (as Mickey, Albery Theatre).

TV: *Missing from Home*; *Juliet Bravo*; *Brookside*; Tex in *Help!*; Ivor Novello in *Stars in a Dark Night*; *Bergerac*; *Boon*; *Home Front*; Bob Street in *Streetwise*; Johann Strauss in *The Strauss Dynasty*; *Stay Lucky*; Andrei in *Grushko* (mini-series, 1994); Mark Cowley in *The Lifeboat*; Alexis Orlov in *Catherine the Great* (mini-series); Daniel Phelan in *The Hanging Gale* (series, 1995); Jimmy Dunn in *Where the Buffalo Roam* (pilot, 1995).

Films: *Business as Usual*.

Address: c/o Burdett-Coutts Associates. Lives in Saffron Walden, Essex. m. 1990 TV scriptwriter Heidi Thomas. Pets: Two cats called Maude and Edith. Hobbies: Football, genealogy, music.

Stephen McGann

Philip McGough

McGOUGH, Philip

Philip McGough. Actor. Stage plays include *Ducking Out* (West End), *Men's Beano*, *Once in a Lifetime*, *The Churchill Play*, *Antony and Cleopatra* and *The White Guard* (all RSC).

TV: In *Sickness and in Health; Hannay; Chancer; The Manageress; Only Fools and Horses; The Chief; Inspector Morse; French Fields;* Jim in *Forever Green;* Carey Hinde in *A Sense of Guilt;* Pryce in *The Eye of the Storm; Between the Lines;* Harold Roy in *Resnick: Rough Treatment* (mini-series, 1993); Sedley in *Justice for Gemma;* Bobby in *Sean's Show; The Magician;* Piers in *So Haunt Me;* Grkov in *Under the Hammer;* Leon in *The Big One* (Rik Mayall Presents...); Provost Marshall in *Sharpe's Gold; Casualty;* George Standish in *Hamish Macbeth;* Lennox in *BUGS;* Gerald Havergo in *Stick with Me, Kid.*
Films: *Give Us This Day; Tale of the City; Forever Young; The Fool; M. Butterfly.*
Address: c/o Barry Brown & Partner.

Tim McInnerny

McINNERNY, Tim

Tim McInnerny. Actor. b. Cheadle Hulme, Cheshire. Brother of actress Lizzy McInnerny.

TV: *The Black Adder; Edge of Darkness; Blackadder II; The Adventures of Sherlock Holmes; Great Writers: Thomas Mann;* Lord Topper in *Blackadder the Third; Anastasia: The Mystery of Anna* (TVM); *A Very British Coup; Shadow of the Noose;* Capt Darling in *Blackadder Goes Forth* (series); The Manager in *The Great Kandinsky;* Marty Deakin in *Casualty.*
Films: *Wetherby; Erik the Viking; August Saturday; Spaghetti Hoops.* Address: c/o ICM.

David McKail

McKAIL, David

David Frederick Mohr McKail. Actor. b. Glasgow, 13 March 1938. Trained at the Royal Scottish Academy of Music and Drama (1958-61). As Frederic (sic) Mohr, writes mainly solo plays.

TV: Title role in *Boswell for the Defence; Helen, A Woman of Today* (series); *Grange Hill; A Very British Coup* (series); *Take the High Road; Your Cheatin' Heart; Beatrix Potter; Goodbye and I Hope We Meet Again* (4-Play); Rod Lennox in *Advocates* (Series 1); *Van Der Valk; Lovejoy; At the End of Alex Cording;* Charles Conan-Doyle in *Encounters: The Other Side;* Gerald Ferguson in *Strathblair;* George Muir in *Doctor Finlay; Waiting for God; Heartbeat;* Dr McKenzie in *A Touch of Frost; Tell Tale Hearts;* Det Supt Coutts in *Michael Winner's True Crimes; Crimewatch UK; The Negotiator; Strike Command.*
Films: *Life at the Top; The Battle of Britain; The Four Feathers; Heavenly Pursuits; Silent Scream.*
Awards: Theatre: Two Edinburgh Festival Fringe Firsts, for *Bozzy* (1981, as actor-writer) and *The Admiral Jones* (1993, as writer). Address: c/o Chuck Julian Associates. Lives in London and Edinburgh. m. 1972 Nichola Ann. Pets: Two cats. Hobbies: Reading, writing, cooking.

McKAY, Glenda

Glenda Rose McKay. Actress. b. Leeds, 2 February 1971. Sister of actor Craig McKay. A-level in Theatre Studies. Played Pepper in *Annie*, aged 12 (Grand Theatre, Leeds, 1983).

TV: Rachel Hughes in *Emmerdale* (1988-); *Stargazers; The Krypton Factor Special.*
Films: Gudrun in *The Rainbow.* Address: c/o Emmerdale Production Centre. Lives in Leeds. Single. Hobbies: All sport, especially running and hill walking, painting, aromatherapy, going to the cinema and theatre, having a good time with friends.

Glenda McKay

McKEE, Gina

Georgina McKee. Actress. b. North East, 14 April 1964. Member of the National Youth Theatre (1979-82). Stage plays include *Mohicans* (national tour).

TV: *Quest of the Eagles* (serial); *Check It Out; Queen of Hearts; This Is History, Gran; Auf Wiedersehen Pet; Home Cooking; Floodtide; Inspector Morse; Rockliffe's Babies; The Ritz; Mohicans;* Julie in *The Lenny Henry Show; He's Asking for Me;* Koochi in *Talking Takes Two; The Paradise Club;* Lou in *Drop the Dead Donkey;* Dr Helen in *Medics;* Joanna in *Minder;* Paul Merton – The Series; Sue in *An Actor's Life for Me;* Katherine in *White Girls on Dope;* Evelyn Foster in In Suspicious Circumstances; Sarah Lightfoot in *Frontiers;* Ginnie Davies in *Casualty;* Mary Cox in *Our Friends in the North* (serial, 1996).
Films: *The Rachel Papers; Wilt;* Lucy Lisle in *Smack and Thistle;* Kim in *Naked.*
Address: c/o Roxane Vacca Management. Lives in London. m.

Gina McKee

McKELLEN, Ian

Ian Murray McKellen. Actor. b. Burnley, Lancashire, 25 May 1939. CBE, 1979; knighted 1991. Numerous awards for his stage roles, from Macbeth, Coriolanus, Othello and Richard III to Max in *Bent.*

TV: *Kipling* (1964); *Sunday out of Season; The Trial and Torture of Sir John Rampayne; David Copperfield; Hay Fever; So What if It's Just Green Cheese?; Edward II; Richard II; Ross; Keats; Hamlet; The Last Journey; Country Matters; Graceless Go I; The Recruiting Officer; Hedda Gabler; Macbeth; Every Good Boy Deserves Favour; Dying Day; The Scarlet Pimpernel; Walter* (TVM); *Walter and June* (TVM); *Loving Walter* (TVM, previous two re-edited); *Ian McKellen Acting Shakespeare; The South Bank Show: Ian McKellen's Diary; Suleyman the Magnificent* (narrator); Iago in *Othello; Countdown to War; D'Art* (pre-

senter); *Prisoners of Conscience* (presenter); The Chairman in *Sidney Sheldon's Windmills of the Gods* (mini-series); George Bernard Shaw in *Without Walls: Mister Shaw's Missing Millions; The Seven Ages of Radio* (Arena Radio Night, presenter); Bill Krawtz in *And the Band Played On* (TVM); *Playing the Dane* (Bard on the Box); Amos Starkadder in *Cold Comfort Farm; The Nation's Favourite Poems* (reader).
Films: *Alfred the Great; The Promise; A Touch of Love; Priest of Love; The Scarlet Pimpernel; The Keep; Zina; Plenty;* John Profumo in *Scandal; It's Only a Movie; The Ballad of Little Jo; I'll Do Anything; Last Action Hero; Six Degrees of Separation; The Shadow; Jack and Sarah.* **Awards:** TV: RTS Performer of the Year Award for *Walter* (1982). Address: c/o ICM. Lives in London. Single.

Ian McKellen

McKENZIE, Julia

Julia Kathleen McKenzie. Actress/Director. b. Enfield, Middlesex, 17 February 1942. Trained at Guildhall School of Music and Drama. West End and Broadway productions include *Mame, Side by Side by Sondheim, Guys and Dolls, Follies* and *Into the Woods*.
TV: Laurie Hamilton in *For Richer, for Poorer; The Two Ronnies;* Syvil Bryan in *Ike* (mini-series, 1978); *André Previn Meets Stephen Sondheim; Song by Song by Gershwin; The John Curry Show; The Stanley Baxter Show; Maggie and Her* (series); *That Beryl Marston...!; Fame Is the Spur; Sharing Time; Dear Box No; Guilt on the Gingerbread;* Hester Fields in *Fresh Fields;* Mrs Forthby in *Blott on the Landscape* (series); Mrs Herrick in *Those Glory, Glory Days* (TVM); *Absent Friends; Hotel du Lac* (TVM); *Julia and Company;* Hester Fields in *French Fields;* Mrs Poyser in *Adam Bede; Wish You Were Here...?* (guest reporter); Mrs Amberson in *Shadowy Third* (Ghosts); *The Snow Queen* (voice only).
Films: *The Wildcats of St Trinian's;* Gillian in *Shirley Valentine*.
Awards: TV: *TVTimes* Best Actress on TV award (1986) and Favourite Comedy Performance on TV award (1985, 1986, 1988). Address: c/o April Young. m. 1972 actor-director Jerry Harte.

Julia McKenzie

McKERN, Leo

Reginald McKern. Actor/Writer. b. Sydney, Australia, 16 March 1920. Awarded AO. Trained as an electrical engineer and worked as a commercial artist in Australia; came to Britain in 1946.
TV: *The Tea Party* (1965); Number Two in *The Prisoner; On the Eve of Publication; The Caucasian Chalk Circle; Churchill's People; Shades of Greene; The Sun Is God; 1999; The Adventures of Sherlock Holmes;* Horace Rumpole in *Rumpole of the Bailey* (Play for Today) and *Rumpole of the Bailey* series; *The Nativity* (TVM); *Country; The Lion, the Witch and the Wardrobe* (TVM, narrator); *Rumpole's Return; Country; Murder with Mirrors* (TVM); *Monsignor Quixote; The Master Builder;* Sir Arthur Quiller-Couch in *The Last Romantics* (Screen Two); Cyril in *A Foreign Field* (Screen One); *Unspeakable Verse* (reader).
Films: *Murder in the Cathedral; All for Mary; X the Unknown; Time without Pity; A Tale of Two Cities; Beyond This Place; The Mouse That Roared; Yesterday's Enemy; Jazzbout; Mikhali* (narrator); *Scent of Mystery* (UK title *Holiday in Spain*); *The Running, Jumping and Standing Still Film; The Day the Earth Caught Fire; Mr Topaze; The Inspector; The Horse without a Head; Doctor in Distress; A Jolly Bad Fellow; Hot Enough for June; King and Country; Help!; The Amorous Adventures of Moll Flanders; A Man for All Seasons; Assignment K; Nobody Runs Forever; The Shoes of the Fisherman; Decline and Fall... of a Birdwatcher!; Ryan's Daughter; Massacre in Rome; The Adventure of Sherlock Holmes' Smarter Brother; The Omen; Candleshoe; Damien — Omen II; The House on Garibaldi Street; The Last Tasmanian* (narrator); *The Blue Lagoon; The French Lieutenant's Woman; Ladyhawke; The Voyage of Bounty's Child* (narrator); *The Chain; Travelling North; A Foreign Field; On Our Selection.*
Address: c/o Richard Hatton. Lives in Bath. m. 1st (dis), 2nd actress Jane Holland; 1 d. actress Abigail (from 2nd m.), 1 adopted d. Harriet.

Leo McKern

MACKINTOSH, Andrew

Andrew Neil Mackintosh. Actor/Musician. b. Pennsylvania, USA, 9 August 1960. Grew up in Scotland and trained at Webber Douglas Academy. A musician who composes, plays clarinet, saxophones, guitars, keyboards and drums, and is a musical director.
TV: Music Teacher in *Every Breath You Take;* Paul Peters in *Coronation Street;* Undercover Agent in *Game, Set & Match;* *Agatha Christie's Poirot;* DS Alastair Greig in *The Bill.* Address: c/o Scott Marshall/The Bill. Lives in Stevenage, Hertfordshire. m. Lucy Abercrombie; 2 d. Melissa, Ottilie. Hobbies: Food, wine and conversation, cricket, table tennis.

Andrew Mackintosh

McLAUGHLIN, Lise-Ann

Actress. b. Dublin, Ireland, 24 June 1958. Began career acting at the Abbey Theatre, Dublin.
TV: *Miracles and Miss Langan; Passing Through; Teresa's Wedding; The Life of Sean O'Casey; A Life; Katie — The Year of the Child; Shadows on Our Skin; Easter 2016; Ties of Blood; Friends and Lovers; Invitation to a Party; Nobody's Property; We'll Meet Again; The Irish RM* (three series); *Dead Entry; Square Deal;* Arabella in *Haggard.*
Films: *Angel.* **Awards:** *TVTimes* Most Promising Newcomer to Television Award (1983). Address: c/o Christina Shepherd.

Lise Ann McLaughlin

Shelagh McLeod

McLEOD, Shelagh

Shelagh P V McLeod. Actress. b. Vancouver, Canada, 7 May. Trained at the Corona Stage Academy, London. Stage plays include *The Hitch-Hiker* (Royal Court) and *Joseph and the Amazing Technicolor Dreamcoat* (national tour).

TV: Young Jean in *Cream in My Coffee*; Bereknike in *The Cleopatras*; *QED* (US); Caro in *Shades*; *Charles & Diana: A Royal Love Story* (TVM); *Keats*; *Camille*; Clara Eyensford-Hill in *Pygmalion*; Leslie in *Loving Friends*; Carol Drayton in *The Winning Streak*; *The A-Team*; Lily in *Street Hawk*; Claudine de Valios in *Wish Me Luck*; Frances Blakley in *The King of the Olympics*; Jane in *Head Girl*; Sarah Carlisle in *Three of a Kind* (pilot, US); Grace Downs in *Rockliffe*; Marie Duro in *Charlie the Kid*; Alison Terry in *Dude*; *Loose Cannon*; *Max Munro*; Sue in *Shelley*; Hester McCulloch in *Boon*; Florence Carrington in *Agatha Christie's Poirot*; Lady Lavinia in *The Young Indiana Jones Chronicles*; Elizabeth in *Almost Grown*; Dr Jean Lowry in *Lovejoy*; Maria Romero in *The Chief*; Kate Webster in *Peak Practice* (Series 4, 1996).

Films: Joanna in *The Last Island*; Caroline in *Indian Summer*; Anna Krupp in *Success*; *The Gentle Touch*; Rosalie in *Lady Oscar*; Amanda in *Jack and Sarah*. Address: c/o Christina Shepherd. Lives in Cobham, Surrey, and Los Angeles. m. 1st James Carroll Jordan (dis), 2nd 1994 Marek Pilkington Miksa; 1 d. Katherine Elena (b. 6 June 1995, from 2nd m.). Pets: A cat called Pumpkin. Hobbies: Reading, travel.

MacLEOD, Tracey

Tracey MacLeod

Tracey MacLeod. Presenter/Writer. b. Ipswich, Suffolk, 30 October 1960. Gained a BA (Hons) in English from Durham University. Journalist for *Video Viewer, New Video Viewer, The Stage and Television Today* and *Films* magazine before entering TV. Arts correspondent for British Airways in-flight videos.

TV: *Wogan* (researcher); *Food and Drink* (researcher); *The Six o'Clock Show* (researcher); *Network 7* (reporter Series 1, producer-presenter Series 2); *The Late Show* (presenter and producer, 12 series, 1988-95); *New West* (co-producer, country music series); *Put It There* (Paul McCartney special); *Spike* (Elvis Costello *Late Show* special); Eurythmics special; *Edinburgh Nights* (Edinburgh Festival magazine programme, four series); *Rapido* (voice-over, four series); *A Stab in the Dark*; *The Booker Prize*; *London Kills Me*; *Juke Box Jury*; *Sean's Show*; *Wynton Marsalis* (interview with the jazz trumpeter, 1993); *The Booker Prize* (Late Show special, 1993 and 1995); *The Late Show French Week* (1994); *The Mercury Music Prize* (1994); *Late Again* (1994-5); *Late Jazz*.

Radio: GLR (BBC, London) weekly show (1991-).

Address: c/o PBJ Management. Lives in London. Single.

McNEILL, Gillian

Gillian McNeill

Gillian McNeill. Actress. b. Monifieth, Tay, 25 September 1965. Trained at the Royal Scottish Academy of Music and Drama.

TV: *The Houseman's Tale*; Lynne McNeil in *Take the High Road* (1987-94).

Address: c/o Ruth Tarko Agency. Lives in Glasgow. m. actor Richard Greenwood.

MacPHERSON, James

James MacPherson

James MacPherson. Actor. b. Hamilton. Started his working life as a lab technician in the neuropathology department of a Glasgow hospital for five years. At the age of 22, he joined an acting group in his home town of Hamilton and subsequently trained at the Royal Scottish Academy of Music and Drama. In 1986, after a stint with BBC radio, he landed the role of DS Jardine in *Taggart*.

TV: Det Sgt Mike Jardine in *Taggart* (1985-) and *Taggart — The Movie*; *The BAFTA Production Awards* (presenter, 1995).

Address: c/o Marina Martin Associates. Lives in Glasgow. m. Jacqueline, 1 s. Jamie, 1 d. Katie.

McROBERTS, Briony

Briony McRoberts. Actress. b. Welwyn Garden City, Hertfordshire, 10 February 1957. Stage productions include *Much Ado about Nothing, Hay Fever, The Browning Version, Peter Pan, And Then There Were None, The Curse of the Baskervilles, Betzi* and *Charley's Aunt*.

TV: *Bachelor Father*; *Peter Pan*; *The Crezz*; *True Patriot*; *Malice Aforethought*; *Butterflies*; *Diamonds*; *The Professionals*; *The Further Adventures of Lucky Jim*; *Sink or Swim*; *Strangers*; *Mr Palfrey of Westminster*; Receptionist in *Don't Wait Up*; *Brush Strokes*; *Fellow Traveller*; Carol in *EastEnders*; Sam Hagen in *Take the High Road* (1991-4).

Films: *Captain Nemo and the Underwater City*; *The Pink Panther Strikes Again*; *Edge of Sanity*. Address: c/o William Morris Agency (UK). m. actor David Robb (qv).

Briony McRoberts

McSHANE, Ian

Ian McShane. Actor. b. Blackburn, Lancashire, 29 September 1942. Acted on TV since 1962. Stage plays include *The Promise* (Broadway), *Inadmissible Evidence* and *Betrayal* (both Los Angeles).

TV: *A Sound from the Sea*; *You Can't Win* (series); *Wuthering Heights*; *What Would You Do?*; *Jesus of Nazareth*; *Roots*; *The Lives of Jenny Dolan* (TVM); *Code Name: Diamond Head* (TVM); *Disraeli*; *The*

Pirate (TVM); *Will Shakespeare; Dirty Money* (TVM); *The Letter* (TVM); *Marco Polo; Bare Essence; A.D.* (mini-series); *Evergreen* (mini-series); *Grace Kelly* (TVM); *War and Remembrance; Braker* (IVM); *The Murders in the Rue Morgue* (TVM); *Grand Larceny* (TVM); *The Great Escape; Minder; Charlie the Kid;* title role in *Lovejoy* (also co-producer, six series, 1986-94); *Columbo; Perry Mason: The Case of the Paris Paradox* (TVM); Andre Marchand in *Perry Mason: The Case of the Desperate Deception* (TVM); LeLand St John in *Rest in Peace, Mrs Columbo* (TVM); *Magnum;* Don Lockwood in *Dallas; Survival Special — The Nature of Russia* (narrator, trilogy); *Living Dangerously* (narrator, series, 1993); *The Natural World* (narrator); Ian Deegan in *White Goods;* Otis Cooke in *Soul Survivors* (mini-series, 1995); John Madson in *Madson* (series, 1996).

Films: *The Wild and the Willing; The Pleasure Girls; Sky West and Crooked* (UK title *Gipsy Girl*); *If It's Tuesday, This Must Be Belgium; Battle of Britain; Freelance; Pussycat, I Love You; Tam Lin* (UK title *The Devil's Widow*); *Villain; Sitting Target; The Left Hand of Gemini; The Last of Sheila; Ransom; Journey into Fear; Behind the Iron Mask* (UK title *The Fifth Musketeer*); *Yesterday's Hero; Cheaper to Keep Her; Exposed; Torch Light; Ordeal by Innocence; Too Scared to Scream; Torchlight.*

Records: Album: *From Both Sides Now* (1992). Address: c/o ICM. m. 1st 1965 actress Suzan Farmer (dis. 1968), 2nd Ruth Post, 3rd 1981 US actress Gwen Humble.

Ian McShane

MADELEY, Richard

Richard Madeley. Presenter. b. Romford, Essex, 13 May 1956. Reporter and news editor with Essex & East London Newspapers (1972-6) and producer and presenter with BBC Radio Carlisle (1976-8) before entering television.

TV: Border Television reporter, 1970-80; Yorkshire TV reporter and presenter (1980-2), including presenter of *Calendar, Calendar Goes Pop, Calendar at Your Service, Calendar Sport* and *Calendar Tuesday;* Granada TV reporter and presenter (1982-8), including presenter of *Granada Reports,* Election specials, *World in Action, Granada 500, Flying Start, Generations, AIDS, Quiz Night, Connections* and *Telethon; Runway* (quiz show, host); *This Morning* (co-presenter, 1988-); *Cluedo* (presenter, series, 1992); *Get a Life!* (series, 1995); *Champion Children Awards* (1996). Address: c/o Arlington Enterprises/Granada Television. m. co-presenter Judy Finnigan; 1 s. Jack, 1 d. Chloe, 2 step-s. Tom, Dan (twins).

Richard Madeley

MADOC, Philip

Philip Madoc. Actor. b. Merthyr Tydfil, 5 July 1934. Studied at the Universities of Wales and Vienna, then worked as a German and Italian interpreter for three years, before training at RADA. Acted with the RSC in *Measure for Measure* and *The Blue Angel.*

TV: *Manhunt; Last of the Mohicans; The Inheritors;* U-Boat Captain in *Dad's Army; Porridge; A Bouquet of Barbed Wire; Another Bouquet; Target; Doctor Who* (three roles); title role in *The Life and Times of David Lloyd George; If Tomorrow Comes* (TVM); *Monte Carlo* (TVM); *Fortunes of War; Court Case; A Very British Coup;* Lancing in *First Born* (mini-series, 1988); *Singles; Capital City;* Mike Burton in *Casualty;* Det Insp Noel Bain in *A Mind to Kill* (TVM, 1992) and series (1994-5); Paul Anderson (Beth and Mandy Jordache's barrister) in *Brookside* (1995).

Films: *Operation Crossbow; High Wind in Jamaica; The Spy Who Came in from the Cold; The Quiller Memorandum; Circus of Blood; Private I; Doppelganger; Hellboats; A Bequest to the Nation; Soft Beds and Hard Battles* (US title *Undercovers Hero*); *Operation Daybreak;* Trotsky in *Zina.* Address: c/o Peter Browne Management. Lives in Hertfordshire. m. 1st actress Ruth Madoc (qv, dis), 2nd Diane; 1 s. Rhys, 1 d. Lowri (from 1st m.). Pets: A dog. Hobbies: Trekking in the Himalayas and Andes.

Philip Madoc

MADOC, Ruth

Ruth Madoc. Actress. b. Norwich, Norfolk, 16 April 1943. ASM with Nottingham Rep before training at RADA. Stage plays include *Man from La Mancha* (Piccadilly Theatre).

TV: *Hunter's Walk; Leave It to Charlie; The Life and Times of David Lloyd George;* Gladys Pugh in *Hi-de-Hi!* (series, 1980-8); Mrs Evans in *Oliver's Travels.*

Films: *Under Milk Wood; Fiddler on the Roof; The Prince and the Pauper.* Address: c/o Saraband Associates. m. 1st actor Philip Madoc (qv) (dis), 2nd manager John Jackson; 1 d. Lowri, 1 s. Rhys (both from 1st m.).

Ruth Madoc

MAGILL, Ronald

Ronald Edmund Magill. Actor/Director/Writer. b. Hull, East Yorkshire, 21 April 1920. Toured with the *Stars in Battledress* concert party during the Second World War, then joined the Arena travelling theatre company. Actor, director and associate director at the Nottingham Playhouse for nine years. Wrote the book of a musical version of *A Christmas Carol,* adapted *Treasure Island,* Molière's *The Miser* and Goldoni's *The Servant of Two Masters* and *Mine Hostess* for the stage.

TV: *Special Branch; Parkin's Patch;* Amos Brearly in *Emmerdale* (regular 1972-92, on and off 1993-5).
Films: *Julius Caesar.*
Address: c/o Ken McReddie. Lives in South London. Single. Pets: A cat called Topper.

Ronald Magill

Magnus Magnusson

MAGNUSSON, Magnus

Magnus Magnusson. Broadcaster/Writer. b. Reykjavik, Iceland, 12 October 1929. Hon KBE. Family moved to Scotland when he was nine months old; reporter on the Scottish *Daily Express* and chief feature writer on *The Scotsman* before entering television.

TV: *Tonight; Chronicle; Cause for Concern; Unsolved Mysteries; Checkpoint; Mainly Magnus; Mastermind* (series, 1972-); *Living Legends; Vikings!; BC: The Archaeology of the Bible Lands.*

Books: *BC: Archaeology of the Bible Lands; Introducing Archaeology; Viking Expansion Westwards; Landlord or Tenant? — A View of Irish History; Magnus on the Move; Treasures of Scotland; Lindisfarne, The Cradle Island; Iceland Saga.* Address: c/o Rogers, Coleridge & White. m. journalist Mamie Baird; 3 d. Sally, Margaret, Anna, 1 s. Jon.

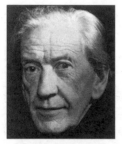

Leonard Maguire

MAGUIRE, Leonard

Leonard Maguire. Actor/Presenter/Writer. b. Manchester, 26 May 1924. Stage plays include *The Skin of Our Teeth, The Rivals, Crime and Punishment, Vivat! Vivat Regina!, Little Lies* (all West End) and *Coriolanus* (RSC). TV since 1949. More than 2,000 radio broadcasts (1950-63).

TV: *Perspective* (presenter, 1961-2); *Tempo* (presenter, 1962-3); *Dixon of Dock Green;* Robertson in *This Man Craig* (1963-4); Martin in *Candide;* 'Trash' in *Emmerdale Farm* (1972-3); Fletcher of Saltoun in *The Union of 1707;* Uncle in *EastEnders* (1986); Mr Grove in *Agatha Christie's Poirot;* Lord Chancellor in *The Law Lord;* Mr Watkins in *Memento Mori.*

Films: *The Day Christ Died; The Awakening;* Dr Humphreys, D Litt, in *The Honorary Consul;* Dr Moore in *The Lonely Passion of Judith Hearne;* Professor Broewer in *A Dry White Season;* Voice of the Books in *Prospero's Books; Occhio Pinocchio.*

Awards: Theatre: Edinburgh Festival Fringe Firsts for plays written and performed on the themes of Dunbar, Coleridge and Henrysoun (1976, 1977, 1978). Address: c/o Kerry Gardner Management. Lives in South of France. m. Frances; 3 children. Hobbies: Garden.

Sean Maguire

MAGUIRE, Sean

Sean Maguire. Actor/Singer/Presenter. b. London. Also a successful pop singer.

TV: *A Voyage round My Father* (début, aged five); *Grange Hill;* Aidan Brosnan in *EastEnders* (1993); Darren Hancock in *The Bill;* Simon in *Dodgem* (series, 1993); Jason Begley in *Growing Pains* (series, 1993); Marty Dangerfield in *Dangerfield* (two series, 1995); *Turning Points* (subject).

Films: *Monty Python's Life of Brian.*

Address: c/o Ian Allen, PO Box 136, Walsall WS3 4LJ. Lives in London. Single.

Patrick Malahide

MALAHIDE, Patrick

Patrick Malahide. Actor. b. Berkshire, 24 March 1945. Studied at Edinburgh University before becoming a stage manager in St Andrews, then turning to acting. Stage plays include *Map of the Heart* (Globe Theatre).

TV: *Snacker; The Standard; Dying Day;* Det Sgt Chisholm in *Minder* (five series, 1979-85); *Charlie; Dear Enemy; The Black Adder; Video Stars; The Pickwick Papers; Pity in History; The Russian Soldier; The December Rose; The Singing Detective; Miss Julie; After the War; The One Game; Our Geoff; The Franchise Affair; Lovejoy; Inspector Morse; Boon; Living with Dinosaurs; Children of the North; A Means of Evil;* Assistant Commissioner in *The Secret Agent* (mini-series); Dr Rank in *A Doll's House* (Performance); Robert Dangerfield in *The Blackheath Poisonings* (mini-series, 1992); *Force of Duty;* Chief Insp Roderick Alleyn in *The Inspector Alleyn Mysteries* (two series, 1993-4); Rev Edward Casaubon in *Middlemarch* (serial, 1994).

Films: *The Killing Fields; Comfort and Joy; A Month in the Country; December Bride; A Man of No Importance; Two Deaths; CutThroat Island; Till There Was You.*

Awards: Edinburgh Fringe Festival award for Best Solo Performance for *Judgement.*

Address: c/o Conway, van Gelder, Robinson. m. 1st 1970 Rosi Wright (dis), 2nd 1993 Jo Ryan; 1 s. Liam Duggan, 1 d. Mairi Duggan (both from 1st m.). Hobbies: Sailing, walking.

Tina Malone

MALONE, Tina

Tina Malone. Actress. Trained at Childwall Arts Theatre.

TV: Mrs P in *Harry Enfield's Television Programme;* Joyce in *Terraces;* Waitress in *Between the Lines;* Mo McGee in *Brookside;* Chrissie in *Sin Bin* (Screen Two); Moira in *Common as Muck.*

Films: Mrs Crane in *Blonde Fist;* Edna Clotworthy in *The Long Day Closes.*

Address: c/o Shane Collins Associates.

MALONEY, Nick

Nicholas J E Maloney. Actor. b. Liverpool, 4 June 1953. Trained at The Drama Centre. On stage, appeared in original London cast of Willy Russell's *Stags and Hens.*

TV: *The Saint; Square One; No Pasaran; Gaskin; Carrott's Lib; Terry and June; No Place like Home;*

Boys from the Blackstuff; David Copperfield Playhouse; C.A.T.S. Eyes; Filthy Rich and Catflap; Seekers; Colin's Sandwich; One Foot in the Grave; The Lenny Henry Show; Hale & Pace; Goggle Eyes; The Stanley Baxter Show; Mr Majeika; Why Lockerbie?; The Laughter Show; Very Big Very Soon; Trouble and Strife; Hardwicke House; Watching; The Brothers McGregor; Ties of Blood; Mr McGrath in Brookside and Damon & Debbie (mini-series); *The Marksman; About Face; This Is David Lander; Gentlemen and Players; Mr Hutchinson in Coronation Street; Harry Enfield's Television Programme; Men Behaving Badly; The Upper Hand; A Czech Drama; Prospects; Shelley; The Jim Davidson Show; Only Fools and Horses; Agatha Christie's Poirot; Marlene Marlowe;* Second PC in *Boon;* Psychiatrist in *The Detectives;* Det Sgt in *Birds of a Feather;* Sam in *Time After Time;* Laverick in *One Foot in the Grave;* Mr Hall in *The Bill;* Sergeant in *Twelve Angry Men* (Paul Merton in Galton & Simpson's ...); Piggy Pearson in *Outside Edge; Harry's Mad; Out of Tune.* As writer: Sketches for *Wysiwyg.*
Address: c/o The Narrow Road Company. Lives in Brighton, East Sussex. m. Carol; 2 d. Chloe, Laura, 1 s. Robert John Bosco. Pets: Retriever called Max.

Nick Maloney

MANTLE, Clive
Clive Mantle. Actor. b. Barnet, North London, 3 June 1957. Acted with the National Youth Theatre (1974-8). Trained at RADA (1978-80). Stage roles include Little John in *Robin Hood* (Young Vic), Lennie in *Of Mice and Men* (Mermaid Theatre), Achilles in *Troilus and Cressida* (RSC) and Dave Hershaw and Bottom in *Pocket Dream* (Albery Theatre).
TV: *Minder;* Sgt Smith in *Jane* (series); Little John in *Robin of Sherwood* (three series, 1984-6); Big Ben in *Dempsey and Makepeace;* Big Eddie Pilkington in *The Lenny Henry Show;* Edward in *Hard Travelling* (Screen One); Cuthbert in *Scoop; Hello Mum;* Sgt Schultz in *Air Base* (Play on One); Angel Gabriel in *Smith and Jones;* Baza in *Wyatt's Watchdogs;* Big Bad Bert in *Club X;* Vulcan in *Chelmsford 123;* Policeman in *Shelley;* Electricity Man in *One Foot in the Grave;* Sgt Ellis in *The Secret Life of Ian Fleming* (IVM); *F.L.I.P.;* Irate Husband in *Bottom; Boon;* Police Inspector in *Drop the Dead Donkey;* Philip in *Framed;* Chef in *Dogboy;* Globyool in *Wysiwyg;* Mike Barratt in *Casualty* (series, 1992-6); *A Bit of Fry and Laurie;* Messenger in *Jo Brand Through the Cakehole;* Sgt Major in *The Good Sex Guide; Alison* (BBC Schools); *Summer Holiday* (guest reporter).
Films: Ewan in *Orchard End Murder;* Bobby Sloane in *Party Party;* Thug on bus in *Foreign Body;* Thug in *Without a Clue;* Johnny Ladder in *Mack the Knife;* Hotel Manager in *White Hunter, Black Heart;* First Nuclear Man in *Superman IV – The Quest for Peace;* William in *Alien³.*
Awards: Theatre: Plays & Players Best Newcomer (1984).
Address: c/o Marjorie Abel. Lives in Bath. m. Zoë.

Clive Mantle

MARKS, Alfred
Alfred Marks. Actor. b. Holborn, London, 28 January 1921. OBE. Worked as an engineer and auctioneer before turning professional on the variety stage. Plays include *Where the Rainbow Ends, Spring and Port Wine, Don't Just Lie There, Say Something, The Entertainer, Twelfth Night* and *Fiddler on the Roof.*
TV: *Don't Look Now; Alfred Marks Time; Paris 1900; Albert and Victoria; The Good Old Days; Looks Familiar; Opinions Unlimited; Funny Man; Maybury; The Olympian Way; Theatre Quiz* (presenter); *Sunday Night at the London Palladium* (compère); Solomon Sr in *Lovejoy; The All New Alexei Sayle Show 2* (series, 1995).
Films: *Desert Mice; There Was a Crooked Man; Weekend with Lulu; Frightened City; She'll Have to Go; Scream and Scream Again.*
Address: c/o Barry Burnett Organisation. m. actress Paddie Neil; 1 d. Danielle, 1 s. Gareth.

Alfred Marks

MAROT, Irene
Irene Marot. Actress. b. Birkenhead, Cheshire. Stage productions include *John Paul George Ringo &... Bert, Last of the Red Hot Lovers, Who Killed Santa?, Dracula* (national tour) and *Top Girls.*
TV: *The Nation's Health; Widows; Boon; The Chronicles of Narnia; Here Is the News; Mother Love;* DD Dixon in *Brookside* (1990-4, 1995, 1996); Paula in *Cracker: Brotherly Love.*
Films: *The Little Drummer Girl; Intimate Strangers; Further and Particular; Getting It Right.*
Address: c/o Lou Coulson. Lives in London. Single.

Irene Marot

MARSDEN, Roy
Roy Marsden. Actor. b. London, 25 June 1941.
TV: *The Sandbaggers; Airline;* Chief Supt Adam Dalgleish in *Death of an Expert Witness; Goodbye, Mr Chips; Vanity Fair;* Det Chief Supt Adam Dalgleish in *Shroud for a Nightingale, Cover Her Face, The Black Tower, A Taste for Death* and *Devices and Desires; Inside Story;* Chief Supt Adam Dalgleish in *Unnatural Causes;* John Stockton in *Sherlock Holmes: The Last Vampyre;* Blick in *Frank Stubbs* (series, 1994); Col Mark Cook in *Against All Odds* (series, 1994); Commander Adam Dalgleish in *P D James' A Mind to Murder;* Sir William Boyd-Templeton in *Dangerous Lady.*
Address: c/o London Management. m. actress Polly Hemingway; 2 s. Joe, Bill.

Roy Marsden

Reginald Marsh

MARSH, Reginald

Reginald Marsh. Actor. b. London, 17 September 1926. RSC and National Theatre appearances. Also writer of the play *The Death Is Announced* (stage and TV) and *The Man Who Came to Die*.

TV: Dave Smith in *Coronation Street; The Planemakers; The Man Who Came to Die* (actor-writer, TV version of his stage play *The Death Is Announced*); *Gazette; The Power Game; The Ratcatchers; Barlow; My Name Is Harry Worth; Whodunnit?; Bless This House; The Sweeney; Crown Court;* Sir in *The Good Life; George and Mildred;* Sir Dennis Hodge in *Terry and June* (1979-87) and *Christmas with Terry and June* (1982); *Help!; Crossroads; Nye; Who Pays the Piper;* Chancy's Dad in *Searching* (series, 1995).

Films: *The Sicilians; Shadow of Fear; Jigsaw; Young Winston; The Day the Earth Caught Fire; Sky Pirates.* **Books:** *Much More Than Murder.* Address: c/o Plunket Greene. m. former actress Rosemary Murray; 3 d. Kate, Rebecca and Alison (twins), 3 s. John, Adam, Alexander.

Derek Martin

MARTIN, Derek

Derek William Rapp. Actor. b. Bow, East London, 11 April 1933. Corporal in RAF Police during National Service (1951-3). Worked as a meat porter at Smithfield Market, in motor racing, on building sites and as a rent collector before becoming a stuntman (1966-71), then a professional actor.

TV: *Paul Temple; Upstairs, Downstairs; Target; The Duchess of Duke Street; The Sweeney;* Det Insp Fred Pyle in *Law and Order* (1977); Det Chief Insp Berwick in *The Chinese Detective;* Ronald King in *King and Castle; The Bright Side; The Pickwick Papers; The Professionals; Hart to Hart; Minder; Dempsey and Makepeace; Only Fools and Horses* (Christmas special); Alex Morris in *Eldorado; The Cutter* (Short and Curlier); Kenny Stone in *The Bill;* Gary Marshall (deputy governor) in *The Governor* (two series, 1995-6); Dennis Pollock in *Ellington.*

Films: *The Long Day's Dying; Ragtime; Priest of Love.*

Radio: Jack Frost in *A Touch of Frost.* Address: c/o JLM. Lives in West London. m. 1st (dis), 2nd (dis); 2 s. David, Jonathan (twins). Hobbies: Golf, driving, cards.

Jessica Martin

MARTIN, Jessica

Jessica Cecelia Anna Maria Martin. Actress/Comedienne. b. Fulham, London, 25 August 1962. Daughter of jazz pianist Placido Martin. Gained a BA (Hons) degree in English and drama from London University. Trained at the Central School of Speech and Drama. Performed a stage act of singing and comedy impressions on the fringe cabaret circuit. Played Sally Smith in *Me and My Girl* (West End and national tour).

TV: *Copycats; Spitting Image* (voice impersonator); *Davro on the Box; Bobby Davro's TV Weekly; The Royal Variety Performance; Saturday Live; Paul Nicholas and Friends; Doctor Who* (acting role); *Michael Barrymore's Saturday Night Out; Tonight at 8.30* (acting role).

Films: *Bert Rigby, You're a Fool; The Garden.* Address: c/o Saraband Associates. Lives in London. Single. Hobbies: Collecting art deco and movie memorabilia.

Mel Martin

MARTIN, Mel

Mel Martin. Actress. Stage plays include *Rules of the Game, Heartbreak House* (both Haymarket Theatre), *Il Candelaio* (RSC) and *The Rehearsal* (Garrick Theatre).

TV: Violet Effingham in *The Pallisers; When We Are Married;* Dorelia MacNeil in *Journey into the Shadows;* Henrietta Musgrove in *Persuasion;* Adele in *Playing with Fire;* Stella in *Lytton's Diary;* title role in *Love for Lydia;* Mrs Otway in *Melba;* Vivien Leigh in *Darlings of the Gods;* Deborah Riscoe in *Cover Her Face;* Hazel in *Time and the Conways;* Fiona Samson in *Game, Set & Match;* Rosemary Henderson in *Inspector Morse;* Rosie in *Summer's Lease;* Persephone in *Orpheus and Eurydice;* Charlotte Davenheim in *Agatha Christie's Poirot;* Susan Lovejoy in *Lovejoy;* Jane Carlton in *The Men's Room;* Cicely in *Hancock;* Jessica Marston in *Boon;* Joanna in *The Big One;* Jennifer Creevey in *The Ruth Rendell Mysteries: Talking to Strange Men;* Deborah Riscoe in *Unnatural Causes;* Freda Battersby in *The Darling Buds of May: Climb the Greasy Pole;* Beverley in *Only Fools and Horses* (Christmas special, 1993); Beth Hudson in *Chandler & Co;* Mrs Jackson in *Casualty;* Sophie Cramer in *The Man Who Didn't Believe in Ghosts* (Chiller); Jane Fanshawe in *A Touch of Frost.*

Films: Lady Ann Howard in *The Adventures of a Lady;* Joan in *Business as Usual;* Mrs MacGregor in *White Hunter, Black Heart.* Address: c/o Markham & Froggatt.

Siân Martin

MARTIN, Siân

Siân Martin. Actress. b. Bromley, Kent, 28 October 1971. Graduated from Oxford University.

TV: Diane in *Pressing Engagement;* Angelina in *Who Stole the Soul;* Callie in *And Still I Rise;* Ginny in *Love All;* Gidea in *EastEnders.*

Films: Chrissy in *Welcome to the Terror Dome;* Mitra Trabrizian in *The Third Woman* (BFI production); Elle in *Young Soul Rebels;* BB in *The Body Beautiful* (BFI production, winner of New York Critics' Award and prizes at the Sydney, Ontario and Berlin Film Festivals). Address: c/o Langford Associates. Lives in London. Single. Pets: A cat called Mingus. Hobbies: Music, painting.

MATTHEWS, Francis

Francis Matthews. Actor/Director. b. York, 2 September 1930.

TV: *At Your Service Ltd; Triton; St Ives; My Friend Charles; A Little Big Business; Tim Fraser; My Man Joe; Dark Island; Last Man Out; Caroline; The Funambulists; Ever Since Paradise; The Talking Cat; The Last Enemy; O.S.S.; Dark Island; You Can't Win; Conflict in the Sun; Charlie's Place; My Man Joe; Hancock; A Cosy Arrangement; So Long Charlie; The Saint; A Little Big Business; The Avengers; The Yellow Pill; The Dolly Spike; Fade Out; No Hiding Place;* title role in *Paul Temple* (52 episodes, 1969-70); *The Morecambe and Wise Christmas Show* (1971, 1977); Eric in *Trinity Tales* (series); *Roof over My Head; Middlemen; Don't Forget to Write* (two series, 1977-8); Noël Coward in *Ike* (mini-series, re-edited as TVM *Ike: The War Years); The Marti Caine Show; The Ronnie Corbett Show; Follow Me* (70 episodes, 1978-9); *Crowther's Scrapbook; Crowther Collection* (series); *Moving* (pilot); *Tears before Bedtime* (series, 1983); QC in *Crown Court; The Gender Gap;* Alex Loding in *Brat Farrar* (serial); Silver Haired Gent in *The McGuffin* (Screen Two); Stephen in *May We Borrow Your Husband?;* Ambassador Matthews in *Roman Holiday* (TVM); *Taggart: Fatal Inheritance;* Duke of Connemara in *The Detectives.*

Films: *No Escape; Bhowani Junction; Woman Possessed; The Battleaxe; The Pursuers; Lamp in Assassin Mews; The Revenge of Frankenstein; Corridors of Blood; Small Hotel; Hell Fire Club; Treasure of Monte Cristo; Nine Hours to Rama; Bitter Harvest; Stitch in Time; Murder Ahoy;* Grant in *The Intelligence Men; Just like a Woman; Beauty Jungle; Rasputin; Dracula — Prince of Darkness; That Riviera Touch; Taste of Excitement;* Ruddock in *Crossplot;* Jason in *Champagne Rose Is Dead; Two Eyes of Crystal Water;* Harold Macmillan in *Moi, Général de Gaulle* (France).

Awards: TV: Italian Cinematographica Most Popular TV Actor award (1975).

Address: c/o Barry Burnett Organisation. Lives in Esher, Surrey. m. 1963 actress Angela Browne; 3 s. actors Paul (acts as Paul Rattigan), Dominic, Damien. Hobbies: Writing, tennis, gardening.

Francis Matthews

MATTHEWS, Sally Ann

Sally Ann Matthews. Actress. b. Oldham, Lancashire, 19 September 1970. Trained at Oldham Theatre Workshop. Stage roles include Deirdre Ollerenshaw in *Fur Coat and No Knickers* (national tour).

TV: Jenny Bradley in *Coronation Street;* Pat in *The Grove Family* (The Lime Grove Story); Nurse in *Stay Lucky; The Giant Nativity Festivity* (co-presenter, 1993); Lady Mullet/Wicked Niece in *Brill;* Tracey in *Missing Persons;* Paula in *Heartbeat;* Tracey in *Hetty Wainthropp Investigates.*

Address: c/o AIS Casting. Lives in West Yorkshire. Single. Pets: A cat called Fagiole, a horse called Marvel. Hobbies: Horse-riding, embroidery.

Sally Ann Matthews

MAUGHAN, Sharon

Sharon Mughan. Actress. b. Liverpool, 22 June.

TV: *Shabby Tiger; Dial M for Murder; The Main Chance; Huggy Bear; The Enigma Files; The Return of the Saint; The Flame Trees of Thika; Young Genius; Dombey and Son; By the Sword Divided; Inspector Morse; Hannay; Ticket to Ride; The Ruth Rendell Mysteries;* Penelope Cadwall in *Murder, She Wrote.* TV commercials; Nescafé Gold Blend.

Films: *Home before Midnight.* Address: c/o Lou Coulson. m. actor Trevor Eve; 1 d. Alice, 1 s. Jack.

Sharon Maughan

MAXWELL, Adam

Adam Maxwell. Actor. b. Glasgow, 28 January 1960.

TV: Sgt Stone in *Inspector Morse;* Firefighter Gray in *The Bill;* Chivers in *Sam Saturday;* Alex McGarry in *Eve Strikes Back;* Jack Jones in *Green and Pleasant Land;* Wax in *The Detectives;* Det Sgt Cartwright in *Casualty;* Brodie in *Roughnecks;* Ferguson in *Paparazzo; Sometime Never.*

Address: c/o Langford Associates. Lives in London. Single.

Adam Maxwell

MAXWELL, Lisa

Lisa Maxwell. Singer/Dancer/Actress/Presenter. b. Elephant and Castle, South London, 24 November 1963. Trained at the Italia Conti Stage Academy from the age of 11. Stage productions include *Annie* (Victoria Palace), *Russ Abbot's Madhouse Show* (national tour), *Russ Abbot's Palladium Madhouse* (London Palladium) and *Grease* (as Marty, Dominion Theatre).

TV: *The Many Wives of Patrick* (début, aged 11); *Ballet Shoes; A Place like Home* (BBC Schools); *Danger — Marmalade at Work; The Benny Hill Show; The Gender Trap; Radio; The Hello-Goodbye Man;* Zerlina in *Tripods; No Limits* (presenter); *The Bizz* (presenter); *Splash* (presenter); *Les Dennis's Laughter Show; The Joe Longthorne Show; Blankety Blank; Relative Strangers; The Satellite Show;* 'Janice', fan club secretary, in *The Noel Edmonds Saturday Roadshow; The Russ Abbot Show; The Lisa Maxwell Show* (series, 1991); *The Russ Abbot Christmas Show; Russ Abbot; Bottom; Noel's House Party; The ID Game* (pilot); Mojo in *Once in a Lifetime* (Comedy Playhouse); *Acapulco HEAT; Pardon My Spanish* (presenter, *This Morning*); *The Children's Royal Variety Performance 1994; Pardon My French* (presenter, *This Morning*).

Films: *The Dark Crystal;* Tracy in *Remembrance.* Address: c/o ICM/Lake-Griffin Smith Associates.

Lisa Maxwell

MAY, Jacquetta

Jacquetta May. Actress. b. Kent. Trained at Bristol University Drama Department.

TV: *The Bill;* Rachel Kominsky in *EastEnders* (1991-4); Edith Thompson in *One Little Hour* (In Suspicious Circumstances); Carla Wainwright in *Anna Lee* (pilot, 1994); Janice Hotchkiss in *Chandler & Co;* Rose Hall in *Crocodile Shoes* (series, 1994); Sister Julie Novac in *Cardiac Arrest* (Series 3, 1996).
Films: *The Naked Cell.* Address: c/o Stephen Hatton Management. Lives in East London.

Jacquetta May

MAYALL, Rik

Rik Mayall. Actor. b. Harlow, Essex.

TV: *A Kick Up the Eighties; The Young Ones; Mr Jolly Lives Next Door* (The Comic Strip Presents...); *More Bad News* (The Comic Strip Presents...); *The Lenny Henry Show; Blackadder II; Happy Families; Jackanory; Saturday Night Live; Hardwicke House; French and Saunders; Filthy Rich and Catflap; Northern Lights;* Alan B'Stard in *The New Statesman* (series); *Jake's Journey; Grimm's Tales; Blackadder Goes Forth;* Richie in *Bottom* (two series); *Love Hurts* (acting himself); *The Fwog Pwince the Twuth!* (storyteller); *Grimm Tales; Jackanory: George's Marvellous Medicine* (storyteller); *Rik Mayall Presents* (two series); *Horse Opera; A. B'Stard Exposed* (interviewed by Brian Walden); *Wham! Bam! Strawberry Jam!* (storyteller, series); *How to Be a Little S*d* (narrator, comedy series); *Jackanory: Jack and the Beanstalk* (storyteller); voice of Toad in *The Wind in the Willows* (1995); *The Snow Queen* (voice only).
Films: *The Eye of the Needle; Shock Treatment; Couples and Robbers;* Specialist Catering Commander in *Whoops Apocalypse; The Strike;* Drop Dead Fred in *Drop Dead Fred;* Sultan in *Carry On Columbus.* Address: c/o The Brunskill Management. m. make-up artist Barbara; 1 d. Rosie, 1 s. Sid.

Rik Mayall

MAYNARD, Bill

Walter Williams. Actor. b. Farnham, Surrey, 8 October 1928. Started in variety as Billy Williams and formed a double-act with Terry Scott but split up when Maynard wanted to switch to acting.

TV: *Great Scott — It's Maynard; Coronation Street; The Life of Riley; Paper Rose;* Harry in *Kisses at Fifty* (The Wednesday Play); title role in *Oh No It's Selwyn Froggitt* (single play, 1974, plus three series, 1976-8) and *Selwyn* (series, 1978); *Paradise Island; Bill Maynard in Person; The Gaffer* (three series, 1981-3); *Till Death Us Do Part; The Inheritors; Trinity Tales; Death of Glory; The Way of the World; Hunter's Walk; Father Brown; Tales of the Unexpected; Dangerous Davies — The Last Detective* (TVM); *Juno and the Paycock; Andy Robson; Spotlight; Worzel Gummidge; Minder; Dangerous Days; The Tale of Little Pig Robinson; Mike and Angelo;* George Trout in *Filipina Dreamgirls* (TVM); Claude Jeremiah Greengrass in *Heartbeat* (six series, 1992-7); *Maynard's Bill* (series, Yorkshire only, 1995).
Films: *Till Death Us Do Part; Hitler: My Part in His Downfall; Confessions of a Pop Performer; Carry On Abroad; Carry On Henry; Carry On at Your Convenience; Carry On Matron; Carry On Loving; Carry On Dick; Bless This House; Man about the House; Robin and Marian; It Shouldn't Happen to a Vet; All Things Bright and Beautiful; Oddball Hall; Hear My Song.* **Books:** *The Yo-Yo Man* (autobiography). Address: c/o The Richard Stone Partnership. m. Muriel; 1 d. Jane, 1 s. Martin (actor-singer Maynard Williams).

Bill Maynard

MAYNE, Ferdinand

Ferdinand Mayer-Börckel. Actor. b. Germany, 1916. Has also acted as Ferdi and Ferdy Mayne.

TV: *Aufderspur; The Ghost Sonata; The Levkas Man; Quest of Eagles; Call of Gold* (TVM); *The Pirate* (TVM); *Dynasty; Evita; The Greatest American Hero; Death of a Centerfold* (TVM); *Hart to Hart; The Optimist; Cagney and Lacey; The Winds of War; Sadat; Scarecrow & Mrs King; Frankenstein's Aunt; Dinner of Herbs.*
Films: Selection (from 110): *Old Mother Riley Overseas* (début, 1943); *Blue Murder at St Trinian's; Ben-Hur; Tommy the Toreador; Our Man in Havana; Those Magnificent Men in Their Flying Machines; Where Eagles Dare; The Magic Christian; The Vampire Lovers; When Eight Bells Toll; Les Grandes Vacances; Au Pair Girls; Barry Lyndon; Revenge of the Pink Panther; Fedora; Hawk the Slayer; The Secret Diary of Sigmund Freud; Yellowbeard; Conan the Destroyer; Night Train to Terror; Howling II: Your Sister Is a Werewolf; Habana Cabana; Frankenstein's Aunt; Pirates; Chief Zabù; The Choice; Magdalene; My Lovely Monster; Rier of Diamonds; Knight Moves; The Tigress.* Address: c/o Lou Coulson.

Ferdinand Mayne

MEAGHER, Ray

Ray Meagher. Actor. b. Australia. Formerly a professional rugby player.

TV: *Around Folk* (presenter); *Scientific Drama; Matlock; 1st Grade Rugby Union Match* (commentator); *Ben Hall; Frood & Friends; Dumble Adapter; Number 96; Rush; Pig in a Poke; Report from Gallipoli; Straight Enough; Women of the House; The Outsiders; Run from the Morning; The Restless Years; Horizon Five; Glenview High; The Oracle; Roadhouse; One Day Miller; Flip, Slide, Turn; Twin Towers; Arvo; Prisoner: Cell Block H* (two roles); *Cop Shop; Skyways; Secret Valley; Punishment; A Sporting Chance; Home Sweet Home; Holiday Island; Kingswood Country* (two roles); *Bellamy; Sound; A Country Practice* (two roles); *Noise Recycling; Waterloo Station; Keepers; Kings; Daily at Dawn; Five Mile Creek; Heads 'n' Tails; City West; Relatives* (TVM); *Mother and Son; Nationwide; A Fortunate Life; Colour in the Creek; Rafferty's*

Ray Meagher

Rules; Land of Hope; The Great Bookie Robbery; Five Times Dizzy; Vietnam; The Shiralee; Willing & Abel; True Believers; The Blue Lightning (TVM); Spit MacPhee; Alf Stewart in Home and Away (1988-).
Films: Mad Dog Morgan; The Chant of Jimmie Blacksmith; Money Movers; Do I Have to Kill My Child?; Newsfront; Because He's My Friend; Odd Angry Shot; The Journalist; 'Breaker' Morant; The Earthling; Music Room; Stress; Hoodwink; Mystery of Castle House; Dangermen; On the Run; Weekly's War; Fire in the Stone; The Chamberlain Report; Runaway Island; Mail Order Bride; Bootleg; Short Changed; The Blue Lightning; The Bee-Eater; Dark Age; Speed Graphic; Love Shed; On the Loose.
Address: c/o Lee Leslie Management/Channel 7. m. theatrical agent Lee Leslie.

MELIA, Michael
Michael Melia. Actor. b. 1945. National Theatre productions include Romeo and Juliet and Hamlet.
TV: There'll Almost Always Be an England; Village Hall; Kiss the Girls and Make Them Cry; Hazell; Fox; The Sweeney; Blake's 7; We the Accused; Diana; Doctor Who; Strangers; Maybury; The Chinese Detective; When the Boat Comes In; The Gentle Touch; A Christmas Present; Minder; Rumpole of the Bailey; Coronation Street; Collision Course; Travelling Man; Whoops Apocalypse; For 4 Tonight; The Hard Word; Dempsey and Makepeace; Big Deal; Bergerac; Campion; London's Burning; Inspector Morse; Reasonable Force; After Henry; The Bill; Room at the Bottom; Hollywood Sports; Here Is the News; Stay Lucky; Eddie Royle in EastEnders (1990-1); title role in Freddie Mills (In Suspicious Circumstances); Mick Brennan in Casualty; Brian Phillips in The Detectives; Peter Perry in The Bill.
Films: Juggernaut; The Hiding Place; Car Trouble; Girl in a Swing.
Address: c/o Silvester Management. m. actress Celia Foxe; 1 d. Charlotte, 1 s. Thomas.

Michael Melia

MELLINGER, Leonie
Leonie Mellinger. Actress. b. Berlin, Germany, 24 June. Trained at Central School of Speech and Drama.
TV: Sons and Lovers; Whale Music; Infidelities; Summer Lightning; Mr Palfrey of Westminster; Bergerac; Dead Head; Paradise Postponed; Small World; Hannay; The New Statesman; Frederick Forsyth Presents; Children Crossing; Stay Lucky; Maigret; Fireworks; Polly Innes in Wycliffe.
Films: Memoirs of a Survivor; Ghost Dance; Memed My Hawk; Zina; Partition; The Young Toscanini.
Address: c/o Peters Fraser & Dunlop. m. actor Robin Askwith (dis).

Leonie Mellinger

MERCER, Ian
Ian Mercer. Actor. b. Oldham, Lancashire. Originally trained as an engineer. Entered acting as an ASM at Oldham Coliseum (1979-81).
TV: Oi for England; Blue Money (TVM); The Monocled Mutineer; Brick Is Beautiful; Flowers in the Rain; Floodtide; Pete Jackson in Coronation Street; Shooting Stars (TVM); Love and Reason; The Riff Raff Element; The White House Farm Murders; The Wanderer – Rebirth (Sky Television); Criminal; DS Giggs in Cracker: The Mad Woman in the Attic and To Say I Love You; Peak Practice; Guy Simmons in Common as Muck (series, 1994); Gary Mallett in Coronation Street (1995-); The Treasure of Zavimbi (New Voices); Graham Glas in The Final Cut (mini-series, 1995); PC Craven in A Touch of Frost (series, 1996).
Films: Alex; The First Day. Address: c/o The Actors Group.

Ian Mercer

MERCIER, Sheila
Sheila Betty Rix. Actress. b. Hull, East Yorkshire, 1 January 1919. Sister of actor Brian Rix. Trained at the Stratford-upon-Avon College of Drama under Randle Ayrton. Toured with Donald Wolfit's Shakespeare Company at the outbreak of the Second World War. Appeared in many of Brian Rix's Whitehall Theatre farces (1956-69) and a Six of Rix tour (1972).
TV: Mrs Moss in Exercise Bowler (1946); one-off farces with the Whitehall theatre company; Dial Rix (series, 1962); Six of Rix (series, 1972); Annie Sugden in Emmerdale Farm (1972- , titled Emmerdale since 1989); Whose Baby?; This Is Your Life (subject, 1985); ITVTelethon '92.
Films: The Night We Dropped a Clanger; The Night We Got the Bird.
Books: Annie's Song: My Life & Emmerdale (autobiography, 1994). Address: c/o Spotlight/Yorkshire Television. Lives in Hawkhurst, Kent. m. 1951 actor Peter Mercier (dec 1993); 1 s. TV sound engineer and video editor Nigel David, 1 d. Monica Janet. Hobbies: Reading.

Sheila Mercier

MERTON, Zienia
Zienia Merton. Actress. b. Pegu, Burma, 11 December 1950. Trained at the Arts Educational School.
TV: Madigan: Lisbon Beat; Sandra Benes in Space 1999 (two series); The High Game; Dempsey and Makepeace; Beryl's Lot; The Floating Man; Wilde Alliance; The Brief; Capital City; Hijack to Mogadishu; Kipling; Casanova; Jackanory Playhouse; Ego Hugo; Leap into the Dark; Thank You Comrades; Contacts; Angels; Tenko; The History Man; Bergerac; Grange Hill; Lovejoy; Casualty; Prophecy (Chiller).
Films: Anna in The Six Wives of Henry VIII; Sunia in Masters of Venus; Ting Ling in The Most Dangerous Man in the World; Rosa Dax in The Adventurers; Lucy Ferner in Revolution; Aleya in Wenn du Bei Mir Bist. Address: c/o Langford Associates. Lives in London. Single. Hobbies: Reading, gardening.

Zienia Merton

MICHIE, John

John Michie

John Michie. Actor. Stage plays include *Number One* (Queen's Theatre), *Easy Virtue* (Garrick Theatre), *Prin* (West End), *Women Laughing* (Royal Court Upstairs) and *The Cherry Orchard* (national tour).
TV: *Albion Market; Rockliffe's Babies; Casualty; Agatha Christie's Poirot; Anything More Would Be Greedy; Taggart;* Trevor in *Moon and Son* (series); Jacob Armstrong in *Lovejoy;* Nick in *The Ruth Rendell Mysteries: Master of the Moor;* Cray in *BUGS;* Jeff Hopkinson in *The Vet;* Barry in *Bare Necessities;* Tim Morris in *London Bridge;* Mark Smith in *Brookside* (1996).
Films: *The Conquest of the South Pole; A Passage to India.* Address: c/o ICM.

MIDDLEMASS, Frank

Frank Middlemass

Frank Middlemass. Actor. b. Eaglescliffe, Co Durham, 28 May 1919. After nine years in the Army, entered acting with a repertory company in Penzance, Cornwall (1948). West End stage plays include *Little Boxes, Spitting Image, King Lear, Widowers' Houses, Rosmersholm, Heartbreak House, The Entertainer* and *You Never Can Tell.* Plus RSC productions of *Hamlet, Romeo and Juliet, A Midsummer Night's Dream* and *Love's Labour's Lost.*
TV: Staupitz in *Luther;* General Kutusov in *War and Peace; The Resistible Rise of Arturo Ui* (Play for Today); *Me! I'm Afraid of Virginia Woolf; The Edwardians; Caught in the Act; Last of the Summer Wine; Upstairs Downstairs; Who Killed Julia Wallace?;* Clayhanger; *The Sweeney; Poldark;* Basil Arkroyd in *Emmerdale Farm; Raffles; Crown Court; Anna Karenina; Measure for Measure; The Oresteia;* Soloman in *Kean; A Family Affair;* Marmaladov in *Crime and Punishment;* Freddy in *Two's Company;* Mr Bartlett Sr in *Adelaide Bartlett;* Algy Herries in *To Serve Them All My Days;* Dr Kirby in *Eden End;* title role in *The Boatman;* Sir William Guthrie in *Yes Minister;* title role in *Grandad;* Winchester in *Henry IV, Parts 1* and *2;* The Fool in *King Lear, Only When I Laugh;* title role in *Mr Dawe's Day;* Marvel in *The Invisible Man;* Brezhnev in *Squaring the Circle* (TVM); King Maajid in *Lace;* Henry Baker in *The Adventures of Sherlock Holmes;* Mr Brownlow in *Oliver Twist;* Gervase in *Knights of God;* Desmond in *All in Good Faith; The Bretts; A Bit of a Do; Close to Home; Alexei Sayle's Stuff;* Major Palgrave in *Agatha Christie's Miss Marple: A Caribbean Mystery;* Priestley in *Haunting Harmony;* Alex in *The Lost Language of Cranes* (TVM); Rocky in *As Time Goes By* (four series, 1992-5); Dr Alex Ferrenby in *Heartbeat* (four series, 1992-4); *KYTV;* Clive Parrott in *A Year in Provence;* Froelich in *The Memoirs of Sherlock Holmes; Doctor Finlay; A Better Life than Mine;* Professor Chalmers in *Doctor Finlay* (series, 1994).
Films: *Otley; Say Hello to Yesterday; Madame Sin; Barry Lyndon;* Windsor in *The Island; The River.*
Radio: Dan Archer in *The Archers* (last actor to play the role). Address: c/o Vernon Conway.

MIDDLEMISS, Philip

Philip Middlemiss

Philip Middlemiss. Actor. b. Hartlepool, 1963. Trained at LAMDA. Stage plays include *A Christmas Carol* (English Theatre Company), *Strippers* (national tour) and *Trackers* (National Theatre tour).
TV: *Ladies in Charge; Closing Ranks; Inspector Morse; Traffik; Christabel; Capital City;* Milton in *The Bill;* PC Barry Smith in *Waterfront Beat* (series); Des Barnes in *Coronation Street* (1990-).
Address: c/o Barry Brown & Partner/Granada Television. Lives in London and Manchester. Single. Hobbies: Collecting videotapes, watching Liverpool FC.

MILES, Annie

Annie Miles

Anne Miller. Actress. b. Tynemouth, Tyneside, 5 May 1958. Trained at the Webber Douglas Academy. Six seasons with the National Youth Theatre. Stage plays include *Stags and Hens* (as Linda, Young Vic), *The Rocky Horror Show* (tour of Germany and Italy), *Cabaret* (Strand Theatre) and *Soaplights* (as Cindy Balsheesh).
TV: *Sink or Swim; The Lonely Hearts Kid; Auf Wiedersehen Pet; The Optimist; Me & My Girl; All in Good Faith;* Sue Harper/Sullivan in *Brookside;* Mrs Dawson in *The Bill;* Sophie Milligan in *Harry;* Mrs Johnson in *Rumble;* Tracy in *Backup;* Sally Warrington in *Catherine Cookson's The Girl* (mini-series, 1996). Address: c/o Jane Lehrer Associates. Lives in London. Single. Hobbies: Keep-fit, piano.

MILES, Sarah

Sarah Miles

Sarah Miles. Actress. b. 1943. Trained at RADA.
TV: *James Michener's Dynasty; Great Expectations* (TVM in US, feature film in UK); *Walter* (TVM); *Walter and June* (TVM); *Loving Walter* (TVM, compilation of previous two); *Queenie* (TVM); *Harem;* Emilie in *A Ghost in Monte Carlo* (TVM); Katharine Armstrong in *Dandelion Dead* (mini-series, 1994).
Films: *Term of Trial; The Servant; The Six-Sided Triangle* (short); *The Ceremony; Those Magnificent Men in Their Flying Machines; I Was Happy Here* (US title *Time Lost and Time Remembered*); *Blow-Up; Ryan's Daughter; Lady Caroline Lamb; The Hireling; The Man Who Loved Cat Dancing; Great Expectations* (TVM only in US); *Pepita Jimenez* (also titled *Bride to Be*); *The Sailor Who Fell from Grace with the Sea; The Big Sleep; Priest of Love; Venom; Ordeal by Innocence; Steaming; Eat the Peach* (not seen in final edited version); *D'Ardanelle; Hope and Glory; White Mischief.*
Address: c/o Marina Martin Associates. m. screenwriter Robert Bolt (dis), Robert Bolt (remarried, dec).

MILLEA, Jim

James Millea. Actor. b. Leeds, 25 November 1958. Trained at the Rose Bruford College of Speech and Drama. National Theatre productions include *Six Characters in Search of an Author*, *Hey Luigi*, *Fathers and Sons* and *Ting Tang Mine*.
TV: Pete Whiteley in *Emmerdale*; Mr Fairbanks in *Families*; Jim Clayton in *Heartbeat* (1992); Photographer in *A Touch of Frost*; Mr Woods in *Children's Ward*; *Data Protection* (BBC Select TV); Shot Gun Robber in *Crimewatch UK*; Carl Armstrong in *Coronation Street* (two episodes, 1994); Van Driver in *3-7-11*; Stallholder in *Heartbeat*; Drunk in Hotel in *Criminal*; *Out of the Blue*.
Address: c/o Crouch Associates. Lives in London and Leeds. Single. Hobbies: Squash, football.

Jim Millea

MILLER, Mary

Mary Miller. Actress. b. Norfolk, 27 December 1933. Plays include *Il Candelaio*, *Melons* and *A Christmas Carol* (RSC) and *The Mysteries*, *Lark Rise*, *Candleford* and *The Recruiting Officer* (National Theatre).
TV: Marty (series, 1966-70); Frau Kemmerich in *All Quiet on the Western Front* (TVM); Bag Lady in *Seven Deadly Sins*; Wendy in *The Mosedale Horseshoe*; Anna in *Old Times*; Sally Rains in *Heart of the Country*; Mrs Pilkington in *After Pilkington*; Mrs Freeman in *The Inspector Alleyn Mysteries*; Joan Butcher in *EastEnders*; Hilary Kingston in *Casualty*; Richildis in *Cadfael*; Lady Probyn in *Kavanagh QC*.
Address: c/o Langford Associates. Lives in London. Single. Hobbies: Gardening.

Mary Miller

MILLER, Sam

Sam Gary Miller. Actor/Director. b. Saxmundham, Suffolk, 28 September 1962. Trained at the Arts Educational School (1984-7). Stage plays include *Richard II* and *Richard III* (both Phoenix Theatre).
TV: Brian in *Clowns*; *Fortunes of War*; *To See Ourselves*; Miles in *Wish Me Luck*; Billy in *This Happy Breed*; Brimble in *Campion*; Mark in *Boon*; Dumbo Dutton in *Piece of Cake*; Terry in *Casualty*; Jack the Ripper (mini-series and TVM); Ralph in *The Great Escape — The Final Chapter*, Christian in *Murder East, Murder West*; Frederick in *Van Der Valk*; Sgt John Maitland in *The Bill* (also directed two episodes).
Address: c/o Scott Marshall. Lives in London. Partner: Actress Janine Wood (qv). Hobbies: Guitar playing, cinema, chess, squash, golf, renovating old VW Beetles, watching gangster films.

Sam Miller

MILLIGAN, Spike

Terence Alan Milligan. Writer/Actor/Comedian. b. Ahmaddnagar, India, 16 April 1918.
TV: Paging You (1947); *Idiot's Weekly, Price 2d*; *A Show Called Fred*; *Son of Fred*; *Bookman*; *Monitor*; *Milligan at Large*; *Milligan's Wake*; *Muses with Milligan*; *The World of Beachcomber*; *Q5*; *Curry and Chips*; *The Other Spike*; *Oh in Colour*; *The Marty Feldman Comedy Machine*; *Milligan for All*; *The Last Turkey in the Shop Show*; *Q6*; *Melting Pot*; *Funniest TV Command in the World*; *Q7*; *Best of British*; *Q8*; *Survival*; *Q9*; *Pirates of Penzance*; *There's a Lot of It About*; *Just Like That!*; *Spike — Getting to Know a Goon*; *TV Heroes* (subject, 1993); *Q Milligan* (series, 1993, presenting sketches from his *Q* series); *Wolves, Witches and Giants* (narrator, children's series, 1995); *An Evening with Spike Milligan*; *Omnibus* (subject).
Films: Penny Points to Paradise; *London Entertains*; *Let's Go Crazy*; *Down among the Z-Men*; *Super Secret Service*; *The Case of the Mukkinese Battlehorn*; *The Running Jumping and Standing Still Film*; *Suspect*; *Watch Your Stern*; *What a Whopper!*; *Invasion Quartet*; *Spike Milligan Meets Joe Brown*; *Spike Milligan on Treasure Island, WC2*; *Postman's Knock*; *Fish and Milligan*; *The Bed Sitting Room*; *The Undertakers*; *The Magic Christian*; *The Magnificent Seven Deadly Sins*; *Rentadick*; *The Adventures of Barry McKenzie*; *Dot and the Kangaroo* (voice only); *Adolf Hitler — My Part in His Downfall*; *Alice's Adventures in Wonderland*; *Digby — The Biggest Dog in the World*; *The Three Musketeers: The Queen's Diamonds*; *The Cherry Picker*; *The Great McGonagall*; *Ghost in the Noonday Sun*; *Man about the House*; *Lost in the Wild*; *Barney*; *The Hound of the Baskervilles*; *The Last Remake of Beau Geste*; *The Prisoner of Zenda*; *Monty Python's Life of Brian*; *History of the World Part I*; *Yellowbeard*; *The Big Freeze*.
Radio: Opportunity Knocks; *Junior Crazy Gang*; *Those Crazy People, The Goons*; *The Goon Show*.
Address: c/o Norma Farnes. Lives near Rye, East Sussex. m. 1st June Marlowe (dis), 2nd singer Paddy (Patricia) Ridgway (dec 1978), 3rd former secretary Shelagh Sinclair; 3 d. Laura, Silé (from 1st m.), Jane (from 2nd m.), 1 s. Sean (from 1st m.). Plus 1 d. Romany (b. 1973, from relationship with Roberta Watt) and 1 s. James (b. 1976, from relationship with journalist Margaret Maughan).

Spike Milligan

MILLS, Adrian

Paul Adrian Mills. Presenter/Actor. b. Uppingham, Oakham, Rutland, 16 July 1956. Acted with the National Youth Theatre (1973-7). Trained at the Rose Bruford College of Speech and Drama (1974-7).
TV: Doctor Who; *Minder*; *Play for Today*; *Brookside*; *That's My Boy*; *Fairly Secret Army*; *Storybook International*; *That's Life!* (co-presenter); *Hi-de-Hi!*; *Breakfast Time* (1985-6); *South East News*; *Facing up to AIDS*; *Getaway*; *Lifeline*; *By Royal Appointment*; *People Today* (1990-2); Dave Preston in *Boon*; *That's Life! Summer Special*; *Biteback*; *Anything Goes* (Meridian only); *Good Fortune*; *Central Weekend* (Central Television only).
Address: c/o JGPM. Lives in West London. Partner: Emma. Hobbies: Cricket, tennis, cinema.

Adrian Mills

MILLS, Hayley

Hayley Mills

Hayley Catherine Rose Vivian Mills. Actress. b. London, 18 April 1946. Daughter of actor John Mills and actress Mary Hayley Bell. Trained at Elmhurst Ballet School.
TV: *Deadly Strangers; Only a Scream Away; Loveboat* (two specials); *The Flame Trees of Thika; Illusion of Life; Amazing Stories; Murder, She Wrote; Parent Trap II* (TVM); *Tales of the Unexpected; Good Morning Miss Bliss; Back Home; Parent Trap III* (TVM); *Parent Trap Hawaiian Honeymoon* (TVM); Joan Simmons in *Steven Spielberg's Amazing Stories: The Greibble.*
Films: *Tiger Bay* (acting début, 1959); *Pollyanna; Whistle down the Wind; The Parent Trap; In Search of the Castaways; Summer Magic; The Chalk Garden; The Moon-Spinners; The Truth about Spring; That Darn Cat; Sky West and Crooked; The Trouble with Angels; The Daydreamer* (voice only); *The Family Way; Pretty Polly; Africa — Texas Style!; Twisted Nerve; Take a Girl Like You; Mr Forbush and the Penguins; Endless Night; Deadly Strangers; What Changed Charley Farthing?; The Diamond Hunters; Appointment with Death; After Midnight; The Last Straw; Walk of Life.* **Books:** *My God* (1988). Address: c/o Chatto and Linnit. m. 1971 film director Roy Boulting (dis 1977); 2 s. Crispian (from m.), Jason Lawson (from subsequent relationship with actor Leigh Lawson, qv). Hobbies: Travel, reading, studying philosophy.

MILMOE, Caroline

Caroline Milmoe

Caroline Milmoe. Actress. b. Manchester, 11 January 1963. Attended Contact Youth Theatre, Manchester.
TV: Sandra Lord in *The Practice; Brick Is Beautiful;* Julie Jefferson in *Bread* (Series 1 and 2, 1986-7); *Valentine Park; Hot Metal; Celebration; The Bill;* Agatha Christie's *Poirot;* Sonia in *The Final Warning* (TVM); Lisa Horton/Duckworth in *Coronation Street* (1992-3); *Stuck on You* (Comedy Playhouse).
Films: *The Magic Toyshop; Without a Clue; The Fruit Machine.* Address: c/o Sharon Hamper.

MIRREN, Helen

Helen Mirren

Helen Lydia Mironoff. Actress. b. Hammersmith, West London, 1945. Born of a Russian father.
TV: *Behind the Scenes; Cousin Bette; Miss Julie; Coffin for the Bride; Jackanory; Little Minister; The Changeling; Bellamira; The Apple Cart; The Philanthropist; Mussolini and Claretta Petacci; The Collection; The Country Wife; As You Like It; Blue Remembered Hills; The Serpent Son; Quiz Kids; A Midsummer Night's Dream; Mrs Reinhart; After the Party; Cymbeline; Coming Through; Cause Célèbre* (TVM); *Red King, White Knight* (TVM); DCI/Det Supt Jane Tennison in *Prime Suspect* (mini-series), plus sequels *2* and *3* and *Prime Suspect* (three-part series, 1994); *French and Saunders.*
Films: *Herostratus; A Midsummer Night's Dream; Age of Consent; Savage Messiah; O Lucky Man!; Hamlet; Caligula; SOS Titanic; Hussy; The Long Good Friday; The Fiendish Plot of Dr Fu Manchu;* Morgana in *Excalibur; Cal; 2010; White Nights; Heavenly Pursuits; The Mosquito Coast; When the Whales Came; Pascali's Island; People of the Forest* (narrator); *The Cook The Thief His Wife & Her Lover; The Comfort of Strangers; Bethune: The Making of a Hero; Where Angels Fear to Tread; The Gift;* Annie Marsh in *The Hawk; The Madness of King George.* **Awards:** TV: BAFTA Best Actress on TV award (three times, for *Prime Suspect*, plus *2* and *3*). Address: c/o Ken McReddie. Partner: Taylor Hackford.

MITCHELL, Warren

Warren Mitchell

Warren Misell. Actor. b. Stoke Newington, London, 14 January 1926. Trained at RADA.
TV: Alf Garnett in *Till Death Us Do Part* and *In Sickness and in Health* (1985-92); *The Merchant of Venice; The Caretaker; Moss; Tickets for the Titanic;* Van Fox in *So You Think You've Got Troubles;* Uncle Jack in *Lovejoy; Wall of Silence* (Screen One); *Jackaroo; The Great Outdoors* (guest reporter).
Films: *The Passing Stranger; Manuela; Barnacle Bill; Girls at Sea; The Trollenberg Terror; Man with a Gun; Three Crooked Men; Tommy the Toreador; Hell Is a City; Surprise Package; Two-Way Stretch; The Pure Hell of St Trinian's; The Boy Who Stole a Million; The Curse of the Werewolf; Don't Bother to Knock!; The Silent Invasion; Postman's Knock; Village of Daughters; The Roman Spring of Mrs Stone; Incident at Midnight; The King's Breakfast; We Joined the Navy; The Main Attraction; Operation Snatch; The Small World of Sammy Lee; Calculated Risk; Unearthly Stranger; 70 Deadly Pills; Where Has Poor Mickey Gone?; The Sicilians; Carry On Cleo; The Intelligence Men; San Ferry Ann; The Spy Who Came in from the Cold; Help!; Promise Her Anything; The Night Caller; The Sandwich Man; The Jokers; Drop Dead Darling; Dance of the Vampires* (voice); *Diamonds for Breakfast; Till Death Us Do Part; The Assassination Bureau; The Best House in London; Moon Zero Two; All the Way Up; The Alf Garnett Saga; Innocent Bystanders; What Changed Charley Farthing?; Jabberwocky; Stand Up Virgin Soldiers; Norman Loves Rose; The Plague Dogs* (voice); *The Chain; Knights and Emeralds; Foreign Body; The Secret Policeman's Third Ball; Kokoda Crescent; Incident on the Line.* Address: c/o ICM. m. Constance Wake; 2 d. Rebecca, Anna, 1 s. Daniel.

MOCKFORD, Jeanne

Jeanne Mockford

Jeanne Mockford. Actress. b. London, 15 March 1931. Trained at RADA.
TV: *The Sea;* Senna the Soothsayer in *Up Pompeii;* Marjorie in *Hi-de-Hi!; Dear John;* Mrs B in *Last of the Summer Wine; Don't Wait Up; Keeping Up Appearances; The Bill; Julia Jekyll and Harriet Hyde.* Address: c/o Langford Associates. Lives in London. Single. Hobbies: Old films, crosswords.

MOLINA, Alfred

Alfred Molina. Actor. b. London, 24 May 1953.
TV: *Anyone for Denis?; Angels in the Annexe; C.A.T.S. Eyes; Blat; Casualty; Virtuoso; Apocalyptic Butterflies; The Accountant* (TVM); *Drowning in the Shallow End* (TVM); Det Sgt Blake in *El C.I.D.* (series, 1990); *Nativity Blues;* title role in *Hancock; The Trials of Oz* (Performance); *Angels* (single drama); Tadeusz Melnick in *A Very Polish Practice* (Screen One); *Trust Me* (Screen One); Tony Havens in *A Year in Provence; The Marshal;* title role in *When the Lies Run Out — Ian Spiro* (Crime Story); Titorelli in *The Trial* (Screen Two); Hamish in *Requiem Apache* (Alan Bleasdale Presents); *Nervous Energy* (Screen Two).
Films: *Ladyhawke; Number One; Raiders of the Lost Ark;* Sergei in *Letter to Brezhnev; Prick Up Your Ears; Manifesto; Not without My Daughter;* Oliver Syme in *American Friends;* Mellersh Wilkins in *Enchanted April.* Address: c/o Lou Coulson. m. actress Jill Gascoine (qv); 2 step-s. Sean, Adam.

Alfred Molina

MONCKTON, Patrick

Patrick Arnold. Actor. b. Budapest, 9 June 1945.
TV: *Brideshead Revisited; The Growing Pains of Adrian Mole; Crimeshow; The Secret Servant; William the Conqueror; Potter; Juliet Bravo; Head over Heels; The Gibraltar Trial Inquest; Minder; Professional Foul; Licking Hitler; Handles; Shadow of the Noose; Bergerac; Moon and Son; An Actor's Life for Me; The Brittas Empire; Screaming; Maid of Dunkirk; Riviera; Sherlock Holmes and the Leading Lady; Alfred Hitchcock Presents...: My Dear Watson; The Return of Sam McCloud* (TVM); *Woof!; The Bill* (two roles); *Dracula: The Series;* Michael Winner's True Crimes; *Agatha Christie's Poirot; The Upper Hand;* Asiz in *The Young Indiana Jones Chronicles; So Haunt Me; The Bill; Kung Fu: The Legend Continues.*
Films: Private Kirby in *The Victors;* Mr Penvale in *The First Kangaroos;* Cook in *Robinson Crusoe;* Miklos in *Hanna's War.* Address: c/o Langford Associates. m. Gail. Hobbies: Chess, travelling.

Patrick Monckton

MONKHOUSE, Bob

Robert Alan Monkhouse. Presenter/Comedian/Actor. b. Beckenham, Kent, 1 June 1928. OBE, 1993. Started career at the age of 15 by selling original jokes to variety comedians and cartoon strips to comics. Two years later, began performing as a stand-up comedian and trained as a cartoon film animator with Gaumont British before acting in RAF productions and radio (1947-9). Formed a scriptwriting team with Denis Goodwin and became the BBC's first contract comedian.
TV: *Garrison Theatre* (début, 1950); *The Bob Monkhouse Comedy Hour; My Pal Bob; For Love or Money; Candid Camera; What's My Line?; Mad Movies; Sunday Night at the London Palladium; The Golden Shot; Bonkers; Quick on the Draw; Looks Familiar; Celebrity Squares; I'm Bob — He's Dickie; Family Fortunes; The Bob Monkhouse Show; This Is Your Life* (subject, 1983); *Bob's Full House; Bob Says Opportunity Knocks; The $64,000 Question; Bob's Your Uncle; Celebrity Squares* (revived, three series, 1993-5); *Room 101; The Big Breakfast* (stand-in presenter, 1993); *An Audience with Bob Monkhouse; Gagtag* (two series); *Funny for Money; Monkhouse's Memory Masters;* (series, 1995); *The ITV Movie Awards* (presenter, 1995); *Bob Monkhouse on the Spot* (series, 1995). As actor: *Blackmail; The Informer; Friends in High Places; Take Three Girls;* Giles Lederman in *All or Nothing.*
Films: *Carry On Sergeant; Dentist in the Chair; The Bliss of Mrs Blossom; Weekend with Lulu; She'll Have to Go.* **Books:** *Crying with Laughter* (autobiography, 1993). Address: c/o Peter Prichard. Lives in Bedfordshire. m. 1st 1949 Elizabeth (dis 1972), 2nd 1973 Jacqueline; 1 d. Abigail, 2 s. Gary (dec 1992), Simon (all from 1st m.). Hobbies: Collecting vintage films.

Bob Monkhouse

MONTAGUE, Bruce

Bruce Montague. Actor/Writer. b. Deal, Kent, 24 March 1939. Trained at RADA. Entered TV in 1960.
TV: *Crane; Dimensions of Fear; The Saint; The Alpha Plan; The Linkman; Public Eye; The Thief of Baghdad; Special Branch; The Onedin Line; Lillie;* Leonard in *Butterflies; For Maddie with Love; Virginia Fly Is Drowning; The Concubine Cowboys; Kelly Monteith; Whoops Apocalypse!; Fairground; Sharon and Elsie; The Secret Army; Fresh Fields; District Nurse; The Trial of Klaus Barbie; The Vision; Agenda for Murder; Olympus Force; Agatha Christie's Poirot; 'Ex';* Michael Winner's True Crimes; *Taggart: Prayer for the Dead; Keeping Up Appearances.* Voice-overs: Quentin in *Chateauvallon* (French serial, English-language version).
Films: *George and Mildred.* Voice only: *A Christmas Carol; Treasure Island; A Connecticut Yankee in the Court of King Arthur* (all animated). Address: c/o Collis Management. Lives in Hove, East Sussex. m. 1962 Barbara Latham; 1 s. cinematographer Sam, 1 d. artist Kate. Pets: Cats. Hobbies: World travel.

Bruce Montague

MOORE, Brian

Brian Moore. Soccer commentator. b. Benenden, Kent, 28 February 1932. Journalist with *World Sports, Exchange Telegraph* and *The Times* before joining BBC Radio, then LWT in 1968.
TV: *The Big Match; On the Ball;* World Cup presenter and commentator; *The Big Match Live; The Match; The London Match; The European Match; The European Champions League Live; International Schoolboy Football; Over the Moon, Brian* (subject of documentary celebrating his 25 years as an ITV commentator);*The Sunday Match.* Address: c/o LWT. Lives in Kent. m. Betty; 2 s. Christopher, Simon.

Brian Moore

MOORE, Stephen

Stephen Moore

Stephen Moore. Actor b. Brixton, South London, 11 December 1937. Stage plays include *A Bedroom Farce* (West End and Broadway), *A Doll's House*, *Poppy*, *Peter Pan*, *Henry VIII*, *Twelfth Night*, *Penny for a Song* (all RSC), *The Hard Shoulder* (Aldwych Theatre), *Paris Match* (Garrick Theatre) and *Reflected Glory* (West End).

TV: *Dinner with the Family;* Jack in *Rock Follies;* *Just between Ourselves;* *Three Men in a Boat;* *Keep Smiling;* *Love on a Gunboat;* *Soldiers Talking Clearly;* *Happy Autumn Fields;* *Bedroom Farce;* Jasper in *Brideshead Revisited;* Wilson in *The Last Place on Earth;* *Solo;* George Mole in *The Secret Diary of Adrian Mole Aged 13¾* and *The Growing Pains of Adrian Mole;* *Small World;* Marvin in *The Hitch-Hiker's Guide to the Galaxy;* *Storyboard: Hunted Down;* *Clowns;* *Boon;* *Countdown to War;* Blore, MP; *Thacker;* Ray Morgan in *Lovejoy;* Hugh Marriner in *Love Hurts;* Hensen in *Van Der Valk;* Geoff Cole in *The Bill;* DS Billy Urquhart in *Between the Lines;* *Perfect Scoundrels;* *Tales from Hollywood;* Kevin in *Casualty;* Mayor Vincy in *Middlemarch* (series); Police Inspector in *Men of the World* (pilot); Quirk in *Love on a Branch Line* (series); Jeff in *Wake Up with...;* *Downwardly Mobile;* title role in *Paris;* *Message for Posterity* (Performance); *Just William;* *A Bit of Fry and Laurie;* Berkeley in *Sharpe's Sword;* *Dangerfield;* *The Thin Blue Line;* *Black Hearts in Battersea* (series); Nick in *And the Beat Goes On* (series).

Films: *The White Bus;* Major Steele in *A Bridge Too Far;* *The White Bird;* *Diversion;* *Laughterhouse* (retitled *Singleton's Pluck*); *Clockwise;* *Under Suspicion;* *The Hawk.* Address: c/o Markham & Froggatt.

MOORE, William

William Moore

William Moore. Actor. b. Birmingham, 19 April. Stage plays include *When We Are Married* (West End). Taught at Bristol Old Vic Theatre School.

TV: *Z Cars;* *Softly Softly;* *Middlemarch;* *Dombey and Son;* *Better than the Movies;* Station Master in *Dad's Army;* *The Dick Emery Show;* *Charles Bravo;* *Scott on...;* *Coronation Street;* *The Rivals of Sherlock Holmes;* *South Riding;* *The Brontës;* *Sam;* *Love Story;* *The Cedar Tree;* *The Fenn Street Gang;* *No Honestly;* *Dick Turpin;* *Sorry;* *My Husband and I.*

Address: c/o Joan Reddin. m. actress Mollie Sugden (qv); 2 s. Robert, Simon (twins).

MORAN, Tara

Tara Moran

Kathleen Tara Moran. Actress. b. Leeds, 1 June 1971. Started acting professionally while at school. Stage roles include Tessie and July in *Annie* (national tour, 1982-3), Molly in *The Fifteen Streets* (tour and West End) and Siân in *Barnaby and the Old Boys* (Vaudeville Theatre).

TV: Christine Carter in *Coronation Street;* Young Conservative in *The New Statesman;* Susan Brady and Alice Selby in *How We Used to Live;* Chelsea Richards in *Families;* *Cracker;* Mary Skillett in *Casualty* (series, 1993-4); Felicity Barnes in *EastEnders;* Julie in *Harry.* Address: c/o Susan Angel Associates. Lives in London. Partner: Medical editor Mark Cooney. Hobbies: Travelling, reading, exercise, socialising.

MORGAN, Garfield

Garfield Morgan

Garfield Morgan. Actor. b. Birmingham, 19 April 1931. Apprenticed as a dental mechanic before going to a Birmingham drama school. Director of productions, Marlowe Theatre, Canterbury (1957-8) and Library Theatre, Manchester (1959-60). Associate director, Northcott Theatre, Exeter (1976-8) and Nottingham Playhouse (1978-80). TV since 1955.

TV: *Softly Softly;* *Spindoe;* *Judge Dee;* *Randall & Hopkirk (Deceased);* *Department S;* *Hadleigh;* *Dear Mother... Love Albert;* *The Sweeney;* *Shelley;* *One by One;* *The 19th Hole;* Norman in *No Job for a Lady* (series); *Lovejoy;* William Curtley in *Born Kicking* (Screen One); Hilton in *Dangerfield.*

Films: *The Pumpkin Eater;* *The Story of Private Pooley;* *Perfect Friday.*

Address: c/o Michelle Braidman Associates. m. actress Dilys Laye (dis).

MORIARTY, Paul

Paul Moriarty

Paul Moriarty. Actor. b. London, 19 May 1946. Stage plays include *The Contractor* (West End), plus RSC and National Theatre productions.

TV: *Holly;* *Pelham;* *Coronation Street;* *Z Cars;* *Minder;* *The Sweeney;* *Jackanory;* *Love Story;* *Troilus and Cressida;* *The Gentle Touch;* *Casualty;* *Saracen;* *The Paradise Club;* *Troublemakers;* Sgt Rick in *Between the Lines* (two series, 1992-3); Sgt Bill Wells in *A Touch of Frost* (four series, 1992-6); Frank Hipwood in *The Bill;* Inspector Bonneau in *Maigret;* Abe Geach in *Wycliffe;* Samuel O'Rourke in *The Bill;* Sgt Dave Taylor in *Peak Practice;* Eric Short in *The Knock.*

Films: *Quest for Love;* *The Chain.*

Address: c/o Sharon Hamper Management. m. Teresa; 1 d. Jessica, 1 s. Matthew.

MORLEY, Donald

Donald Morley. Actor. b. Richmond-upon-Thames, Surrey, 9 June. Plays include *Make and Break* (as Peter Davis, Theatre Royal, Haymarket) and *Death of a Salesman* (as Willy Loman, Theatr Clwyd).

TV: *Destination Downing Street;* Walter Fletcher in *Coronation Street* (1961); Babbage in *Compact*

(one year); *The World of Wooster*; *The Gold Robbers*; *The Queen Street Gang*; *Freewheelers*; *Midnight Is a Place*; *A Raging Calm*; *Bless This House*; *The Dick Emery Show*; *Van Der Valk*; *Beryl's Lot*; Franklyn Prescott in *Emmerdale Farm*; Glossop in *Dad's Army*; *A Wilderness of Roses*; *Kill Two Birds*; *The Spy Killer*; *Big Boy Now*; *Westway*; *Cluff*; *The Mask of Janus*; *The Same Sky*; *The Dybbuk*; Randall QC in *The Duchess of Duke Street*; *A Land of Ice Cream*; *Waiting for Sheila*; *The Spy Within*; *Frontline Manager*; *Crown Court*; The Mayor in *Spooner's Patch*; *Arson Alert*; Lord Cross in *Disraeli*; *Fireworks for Elspeth*; *Going Straight*; *Open All Hours*; *Bergerac*; Stanley Baldwin in *Reilly — Ace of Spies*; *Strange but True*; *All for Love*; *Interest*; *A.D.*; *The Sweeney*; *No Place like Home*; Bank Manager in *All Creatures Great and Small*; *Poor Little Rich Girl*; *The Woman He Loved* (mini-series); Crawford in *Moon and Son*; Cecil Slocombe in *Grace and Favour*; Gerald in *The Brittas Empire*.
Films: *Mix Me a Person*; *Catch Us if You Can*; *System Four Computers*; *Revenge*; *Blowing Hot and Cold*; *Out of Sight*. Address: c/o Sandra Griffin Management. Lives in Richmond-upon-Thames, Surrey. m. Hobbies: Music, reading.

Donald Morley

MORLEY, Ken
Kenneth William Morley. Actor. b. Chorley, Lancashire, 17 January 1943. Abandoned a career as a teacher, took a degree in English and drama at Manchester University, then went into acting. Stage plays include *The Ragged Trousered Philanthropists*, *Valpone* (both Half Moon Theatre) and *The Beaux' Stratagem* (Cambridge Theatre).
TV: *Who Dares Wins*; *Quest*; *Bulman*; *The Return of the Antelope*; *All Passion Spent*; *Les Girls*; *The Management*; *Blind Justice*; *Chelmsford 123*; *Watching*; Flockenstuffen in *'Allo, 'Allo*; *You Rang, M'Lord?*; Reg Holdsworth in *Coronation Street* (1989-95).
Films: *Alfie Darling*; *Little Dorrit*. Address: c/o ICM. m. Sue; 1 s. Roger.

Ken Morley

MORRIS, Beth
Beth Morris. Actress. b. Goirseinon, West Glamorgan, 19 July 1949. Trained at the Cardiff College of Music and Drama. Plays include *Man and Superman*, *Banana Ridge* and *Travesties* (London and Broadway), *The Passion of Dracula* and *Mrs Grabofsky's Academy*.
TV: *Play of the Week*; *Play of the Month*; *Jude the Obscure*; *Minder*; *Z Cars*; *Softly Softly*; *I Claudius*; *David Copperfield*; *Ballroom*; *District Nurse* (two series); *Better Days*; *We Are Seven*; Rosie Douglas in *TellTale* (mini-series).
Address: c/o Ken McReddie. Hobbies: Reading, fishing.

Beth Morris

MORRIS, Jonathon
John Morris. Actor. b. Urmston, Manchester, 20 July 1960. As a child, acted in *Oliver* (title role) and *South Pacific* in amateur productions at Manchester Opera House. Trained at Bristol Old Vic Theatre School. Stage productions include *As You Like It*, *She Stoops to Conquer* (both Chichester Festival Theatre), *Wuthering Heights* (as Heathcliff, Cambridge Theatre Company), *Candida* (Yvonne Arnaud Theatre, Guildford), *Semi Monde* (Royalty Theatre), *Diary of a Somebody* (as Joe Orton, national tour), *La Cage aux Folles* (London Palladium), *Me and My Girl* (as Bill Snibson, Adelphi Theatre) and *The Rocky Horror Show* (Duke of York's Theatre).
TV: *Coronation Street*; *Crown Court*; *The Professionals*; *The Squad*; Phil in *That Beryl Marston...*; *The Agatha Christie Hour: In a Glass Darkly*; John Geste in *Beau Geste*; *Doctor Who*; *The Practice*; *Bingo*; *Hell's Bells*; Adrian Boswell in *Bread* (nine series, 1986-91); *The Consultant*; Rupert of Hentzau in *The Prisoner of Zenda*; Pete in *Ties of Blood*; *Jackanory*; *The Royal Variety Performance* (four times); *The Children's Royal Variety Performance*; *Pass the Story* (presenter); *The Movie Game* (host, three series, 1990-3); David in *Wild Oats* (Comedy Playhouse); *The Done Thing* (writer-presenter, *This Morning* series, 1993, 1994); *The Queen Mother's 90th Birthday Gala*.
Films: El Gallo in *The Fantasticks*.
Awards: Variety Club BBC Personality of the Year (1989); Best Dressed Man (1989). Address: c/o Knight Ayton Management. Lives in London. Single. Hobbies: All sports, dance, singing, reading.

Jonathon Morris

MORRISSEY, Neil
Neil Morrissey. Actor. b. Stafford, 4 July 1962. Trained at Guildhall School of Music and Drama. Stage productions include *The Bounty* (as Quintal, Tahiti and New Zealand tour) and *A Passionate Woman* (South of England tour and Comedy Theatre).
TV: *The Journal*; *Follow Through*; *A Fairly Secret Army*; *Juliet Bravo*; *Ellis Island* (mini-series); *Roll Over Beethoven*; *Travellers by Night*; *C.A.T.S. Eyes*; *Playing Away*; *Blood Runner*; *Pulaski*; *Gentlemen and Players*; Rocky in *Boon* (series); Tony in *Men Behaving Badly* (Series 2-4, 1992-5); Danny in *Stuck on You* (Comedy Playhouse); *Reeves and Mortimer*; *Trafford Tanzi*; David in *A Woman's Guide to Adultery* (mini-series); Paul Rochet in *Paris* (series, 1994); *The Morph Files* (narrator, series, 1996).
Films: *Bounty*; *Playing Away*; *Blood Runner*; *The Ballad of Kid Divine*.
Address: c/o ICM. m. actress Amanda Noar (sep 1991); 1 s. Sam. Partner: Actress Liz Carling.

Neil Morrissey

181

Bob Mortimer

MORTIMER, Bob

Robert Mortimer. Comedian/Writer. b. Middlesbrough, 23 May 1959. While practising as a solicitor, teamed up with Vic Reeves (qv) at the Albany Empire, Deptford, and developed their 'Big Night Out' act. **TV:** *Vic Reeves Big Night Out* (two series, 1990-1); *The Weekenders* (Bunch of Five); *The Smell of Reeves & Mortimer* (two series, 1993, 1995); *At Home with Vic and Bob; Dot on the Landscape* (series); *Reeves & Mortimer's Shooting Stars* (host, quiz show series); *Christmas Night with the Stars* (1994); *A Nose through Nature; Reeves and Mortimer – Xmas Shooting Stars* (1995).
Videos: *Vic Reeves Big Night Out.* **Records:** Single: *I'm a Believer* (with Vic Reeves and EMF, No 3, 1995).**Books:** *Big Night In* (with Vic Reeves, 1991).
Awards: BAFTA Originality award (with Vic Reeves, 1992); British Comedy Awards Best Live Performance award (with Vic Reeves, 1992). Address: c/o PBJ Management. Single.

Bruce Morton

MORTON, Bruce

Ian Bruce Morton. Comedian/Presenter. b. Paisley, 22 November 1959.
TV: *Halfway to Paradise; Club X; Open Air; The Shoe Fetishist's Guide to Bruce Morton; Saturday Night Clyde; Rab C Nesbitt; The Show; Blood Tied and Colour Blind; Paramount City; The Insiders; 45 Fever; Sin with Bruce Morton; Edinburgh Nights; The Late Show; Amsterdam by Night* (presenter, Pot Night); *Don't Give Up Your Day Job; TV6.*
Films: *Wheels.* **Awards:** Mayfest Comedy Award (1989); *Scotland on Sunday* Critics' Award (1992). Address: c/o Richard Bucknall Management. Lives in Glasgow. m. Pauline (dis).

Bryan Mosley

MOSLEY, Bryan

Bryan Mosley. Actor/Director. b. Leeds, 25 August 1931. Studied at Leeds College of Art (1944-6). Served with the RAF in air traffic control (1949-51) and, at the same time, started acting at the Byre Theatre, St Andrews. Trained at the Bradford Civic Theatre under Esmé Church (1952-4). Stunt fighter and arranger for theatre, films and TV, and founder-member of the Society of British Fight Directors.
TV: *Skyport; Little Doris; The Front Room; The High Game; The Rise and Fall of Nellie Brown; The Planemakers; The Saint; Z Cars; The Avengers; Adam Adamant; Bent; No Hiding Place;* Denis Rutledge in *Crossroads; The Villains; The Men from Room 13; Doctor Who; It's a Square World; The Arthur Haines Show; The Harry Worth Show; The Dick Emery Show; The Worker; The Clitheroe Kid; Queenie's Castle;* Alf Roberts in *Coronation Street* (1961 and 1968-); *Royal Variety Performance* (1989).
Films: *A Kind of Loving; Billy Liar; This Sporting Life; Rattle of a Simple Man; Up Jumped a Swagman; Where the Bullets Fly; Far from the Madding Crowd; Privilege; Diamonds for Breakfast; Charlie Bubbles; Death of Angels;* Cliff Brumby in *Get Carter.*
Awards: American TV and Radio Commercials Special Performance Citation (1969). Address: c/o Granada Television. Lives near Shipley, West Yorkshire, and Salford. m. 1956 Norma; 3 d. Jacqueline, Simone, Helen, 3 s. Jonathan, Bernard, Leonard. Pets: Cat called Lily. Hobbies: Photography, walking.

Peggy Mount

MOUNT, Peggy

Margaret Rose Mount. Actress. b. Leigh-on-Sea, Essex, 2 May 1918. Acted in amateur theatre while working as a secretary, acted in concert parties during the Second World War, then turned professional with the Harry Hanson Court Players. Many West End and RSC productions.
TV: Ada Larkin in *The Larkins* (series, 1958-63); Martha in *Winning Widows* (two series, 1961-2); Mrs Gabrielle Dragon in *George and the Dragon* (series, 1966-8); Virginia Browne in *John Browne's Body* (series, 1969); Maggie Robinson in *Lollipop Loves Mr Mole* (series, 1971) and *Lollipop* (series, 1972); Flora Petty in *You're Only Young Twice* (four series, 1977-81); *Those Wonderful TV Times; Spice Island Farewell; Just like Mum; The End of the Pier Show; It's Never Too Late* (pilot); Alice Jolie in *The Trial of Klaus Barbie;* The Judge in *Punishment without Crime; Doctor Who;* Aunt Fanny in *All Change* (Series 2, 1991); *Inspector Morse; Casualty; Virtual Murder* (TVM); *The Tomorrow People.*
Films: *The Embezzler; Sailor Beware!* (US title *Panic in the Parlor*); *Dry Rot; The Naked Truth* (US title *Your Past Is Showing*); *Inn for Trouble; Ladies Who Do; One Way Pendulum; Hotel Paradiso; Finders Keepers; Oliver!; The Chiffy Kids* (1976 serial); *The Princess and the Goblin* (voice only).
Address: c/o The Richard Stone Partnership. Lives in London. Single.

Patrick Mower

MOWER, Patrick

Patrick Archibald Mower. Actor. b. Pontypridd, 12 September 1940. Formerly an apprentice engineering draughtsman. Trained at RADA.
TV: *Front Page Story* (series, 1965); *Riviera Police; Dixon of Dock Green; Z Cars; The Avengers; Haunted; Curse of the Mummy's Tomb;* James Cross in *Callan* (series); *Czech Mate;* DCI Tom Haggerty in *Special Branch* (Series 3-4, 1973-4); Det Supt Steve Hackett in *Target* (two series, 1977-8); *The Flockton Flyer; The Sweeney; Bergerac;* title role in *Peer Gynt; Hammer House of Horror; Minder;* Edward in *King Lear; Dark Side of the Sun; Marco Polo.*
Films: *The Smashing Bird I Used to Know; Percy; Black Beauty; Catch Me a Spy; Gitano; The Devil*

Rides Out; Doctors Wear Scarlet; The Cry of the Banshee; One Away; The Devil's Advocate; Carry On England; Escape from El Diablo; Incense for the Damned.
Address: c/o Artists Management Group. Lives in Denham Village, Buckinghamshire. m. Audrey (dis), partner Anya Pope; 1 s. Simon, 1 d. Claudia. Pets: A cat. Hobbies: Writing, playing sport, gardening.

MUIR, Frank
Frank Muir. Scriptwriter/Performer. b. Broadstairs, Kent, 5 February 1920. CBE.
TV: And So to Bentley; Whack-O!; The Seven Faces of Jim (all as co-scriptwriter, with Denis Norden); Sound of Laughter; Call My Bluff; How to Be an Alien; We Have Ways of Making You Laugh; BBC assistant head of comedy (1964-7); LWT head of light entertainment (1968-9); TV Heaven (series, 1992); Notes & Queries with Clive Anderson (series).
Radio: Take It from Here; Bedtime with Braden (both as co-scriptwriter, with Denis Norden); My Word!; My Music. **Books:** Call My Bluff; You Can't Have Your Kayak and Heat It; Upon My Word!; Christmas Customs and Traditions; The Frank Muir Book; What-a-Mess; Take My Word for It; Frank Muir Goes Into...; What-a-Mess the Good; The Glums; The Second Frank Muir Goes Into...; Prince What-a-Mess; Super What-a-Mess; The Third Frank Muir Goes Into...; Frank Muir on Children; Oh My Word!; What-a-Mess and the Cat Next Door; The Fourth Frank Muir Goes Into...; The Big Dipper; A Book at Bathtime; What-a-Mess in Spring, What-a-Mess in Summer, What-a-Mess in Autumn, What-a-Mess in Winter; The Book of Comedy Sketches; What a Mess at the Seaside; The Complete and Utter My Word! Collection; What-a-Mess Goes to School; What-a-Mess Has Breakfast; What-a-Mess Has Lunch; What-a-Mess Has Tea; What-a-Mess Has Dinner; The Oxford Book of Humorous Prose. Address: c/o April Young. m. Polly, 1 d. Sally, 1 s. James. Hobbies: Collecting books, staring into space.

Frank Muir

MULLIN, Lawrence
Lawrence Mullin. Actor/Writer. b. Liverpool, 5 August 1953. Trained at Bristol Old Vic Theatre School.
TV: Rocky O'Rourke; Steve Fisher in Coronation Street; Doctor's Dilemma; Juliet Bravo; The Bill; Stoker; Sergeant in The Endless Game (pilot); Dear Roy, Love Gillian (Crime Story); Michael Winner's True Crimes; Crime Monthly; DS Gallagher in The Chief; Steve Mathews in Brookside (1993); Duty Sergeant in Between the Lines; Detective in Anna Lee; Carl Edwards in Degrees of Error (series, 1995).
Films: Travel Agent in Shirley Valentine. Address: c/o Shane Collins Associates. Lives in Walton-on-Thames, Surrey. m. actress Lynne Pearson; 1 d. Sadie, 1 s. Michael. Pets: A labrador called Ben. Hobbies: 'Walking, golf, swimming, snooker, a bit of an all-rounder.'

Lawrence Mullin

MULVILLE, Jimmy
Jimmy Mulville. Actor/Presenter/Producer. b. Liverpool. Former member of Cambridge Footlights revue and president of the Footlights Club. Runs Hat Trick Productions. Stage plays include Big in Brazil (Old Vic Theatre) and Who Dares Wins (national tour).
TV: The Steam Video Company; Who Dares Wins (also writer, four series); Aulus Paulinus in Chelmsford 123 (also co-writer, two series, 1988, 1990); Donald Redfern in That's Love (four series, 1988-92); Philip in G.B.H. (series, 1991); The Long Goodbye (talking about his father's suicide, 1995); Derek in Jake's Progress (serial, 1995). As presenter: Acropolis Now; The Hogmanay Show; Babylon 2; Just for Laughs (1990 Montreal Comedy Festival); Going Loco; Holiday '92; The Brain Drain (host, two series, 1992-3); Holiday Outings. As producer: The Big One (co-producer, series, 1992).
Films: Morons from Outer Space.
Radio: Radio Active (series, BBC Radio). Address: c/o Mayer & Eden. m. 1st (dis), 2nd Denise.

Jimmy Mulville

MURDEN, Karen
Karen Murden. Actress. b. Nottingham, 24 April 1970. Joined Central Junior Television Workshop aged 13.
TV: Your Mother Wouldn't Like It (two series); Hardwicke House; Beverley Grice in Crossroads (1986-8); Sheila in Tales of Sherwood Forest; Sarah Robbins in Jupiter Moon (BSB satellite channel serial, 1990); Irene Carter in EastEnders; Maxie in The Bill.
Address: c/o Sandra Boyce Management. Lives in North London. Partner: Dancer Nick Davion.

Karen Murden

MURNAGHAN, Dermot
Dermot Murnaghan. Journalist. Gained an MA in history from Sussex University and took a post-graduate course in journalism at City University, London. Former newspaper reporter.
TV: The Business Programme (researcher, then reporter, 1984-8); European Business Channel reporter and occasional presenter (1988-9); Business Daily and ITN World News (both Channel Four Daily, 1989-92); Porsche and Tears (documentary); A Whale of a Mess (documentary); Dispatches; Channel Four News; ITN Lunchtime News and weekend news programmes; The Big Story (series); The Big Story Special; Budget '93 (Nov 1993 Budget, City reporter); Budget '94 (co-presenter); Police Action Live (1995); The Budget – What Will It Mean to You? (1995).
Address: c/o ITN. Lives in Islington, North London. m. journalist Maria Keegan; 1 d. Kitty.

Dermot Murnaghan

MURPHY, Brian

Brian Murphy

Brian Trevor John Murphy. Actor. b. Ventnor, Isle of Wight, 25 September 1933. Trained at RADA. Was an original member of Joan Littlewood's Theatre Workshop (1955-72), at the Theatre Royal, Stratford East, appearing in *Oh What a Lovely War*, *The Hostage* and *Sparrers Can't Sing*. Other stage plays include *Sweeney Todd* (as The Demon Barber, Theatre Royal, Stratford East), *The Entertainer* (as Archie Rice), *Glorious Miles*, *On Your Way, Riley!*, *George and Mildred*, *Thark* (as Ralph Lynn, national tour), *The Merchant of Venice* (Young Vic and national tour), *Birthday Suite*, *Why Me?*, *The Government Inspector*, *Situation Comedy*, *When We Are Married* (Whitehall Theatre), *Peter Pan* (narrator, RSC at the Barbican) and *Run for Your Wife* (Criterion Theatre).
TV: Armchair Theatre; *Probation Officer; Callan; Z Cars;* George Roper in *Man about the House* and *George and Mildred; The Incredible Mr Tanner; L for Lester; Lame Ducks; All in Good Faith;* Buster in *Boon;* Stan in *Wizadora; Freddie Starr* (1993, 1994); George Manners in *Brookside;* Mr Foskett in *One Foot in the Grave* (Christmas special, 1994); Salesman in *Next of Kin* (1995).
Films: *Sparrows Can't Sing; The Devils; The Boy Friend; San Ferry Anne; Diary of a Nobody; Just like a Woman; Man about the House; George and Mildred.*
Radio: Ernest in *Citizens.* Address: c/o Saraband Associates. Lives in Bromley, Kent. m. 1st Carole Gibson (dis), 2nd Linda Regan; 2 s. Trevor, Kevin (both from 1st m.). Hobbies: Collecting films.

MURPHY, Cathy

Cathy Murphy

Catherine McKevih Maria Murphy. Actress. b. London, 7 August 1967.
TV: Laura the maid in *Andrew and Fergie: Behind the Palace Walls* (TVM); Shelly in *Screaming;* Lois in *Lucky Sunil;* Margaret in *That's Love;* Sandra in *The Bill;* Jonquil in *My Family and Other Animals;* Nurse O'Donnell in *Foreign Bodies;* Nurse Mary in *Amy;* Tilly in *The Effect of Gamma Rays on Man in the Moon Marigolds;* Sharon in *Sorry;* Carol in *Time Trouble;* Jane in *Your Place or Mine;* Gloria in *Nanny;* Housemaid in *Bleak House;* Paulette in *Stars of the Roller State Disco;* Val in *Tales out of School* (Made in Britain); Marion in *Agatha Christie's Poirot;* Miranda McDipper in *December Rose* (series); Sharon Elsworth in *May to December;* Mary in *She-Wolf of London;* Lorna in *EastEnders;* Wendy in *Stanley and the Women;* Vicky in *Minder;* Simone Foxall in *Streetwise* (series); *Pebble Mill;* Tilly Watkins in *The House of Eliott* (three series, 1992-4); Saleswoman in *Men Behaving Badly;* Mandy in *Crime Monthly;* Mandy Boxer in *The Bill;* Bryony in *Rumble* (series, 1995); Rita Baron in *Expert Witness; Karaoke.*
Films: Polly in *Moll Flanders; Captives;* Tubs in *Those Glory, Glory Days;* Linda in *A Love Child;* Esta in *The Phantom of the Opera;* Deborah in *Edge of Sanity;* Cornelia in *A.D.;* Beth in *UFO.*
Radio: *Noises On; Simon's Bug* (series); *Odds Against; The Cinderella Service.* Address: c/o Elaine Murphy Associates. Lives in Essex. Single. Pets: A toy poodle called Beaux Peep. Hobbies: Talking.

MURPHY, Glen

Glen Murphy

Glen Murphy. Actor.
TV: *Seconds Out; Harry Carpenter Never Said; The Jim Davidson Show; Scorpion; The Other 'Arf; Those Glory, Glory Days* (TVM); *Tucker's Luck; Luna; Murphy's Mob; Shine on Harvey Moon; Up the Elephant and round the Castle; Prospects; The Bill; Doctor Who; Rockliffe's Babies;* George Green in *London's Burning* (seven series).
Films: *Victor/Victoria; Empire State; Cry Freedom; Tank Malling.* Address: c/o Michael Whitehall.

MURRAY, Bryan

Bryan Murray

Bryan Murray. Actor. b. Dublin, Ireland, 13 July 1949. Trained at the Abbey Theatre School, Dublin. Joined the Abbey Theatre Company, where he played many leading parts and directed and co-wrote two musicals performed by the company. Later acted with the National Theatre Company and RSC.
TV: *Partners in Practice* (TV début, Irish soap); *Rifleman; Shepherd's Life; GBS;* George Bernard Shaw in *Oscar; Strumpet City; Bread or Blood; I'm a Dreamer, Montreal;* Flurry Knox in *The Irish RM* (two series, 1983-5); Ferdy O'Donnel in *The Year of the French; The Franchise Affair; Final Run;* Shifty in *Bread; Encore;* Harry Cassidy in *Perfect Scoundrels* (also co-creator, with Peter Bowles, two series, 1991-2); Trevor Jordache in *Brookside* (1993); *Hard Shoulder* (Funky Black Shorts).
Address: Peters Fraser & Dunlop. m. actress Angela Harding (sep); 1 d. Laura. Partner: Juliet; 1 s. Henry (b. 1992). Hobbies: Music and movies.

MURRAY, Cheryl

Cheryl Murray

Cheryl Frayling-Wright. Actress. b. Liverpool, 13 July 1952. Trained at the Elliot-Clarke School of Dance and Drama, Liverpool, from the age of eight, then at LAMDA. Stage plays include *Separate Tables* and *A Sting in the Tail* (both national tours).
TV: *Vienna 1900: Games with Love and Death; Microbes and Men; Dixon of Dock Green;* Julie in *Within These Walls;* Gillian in *Z Cars; Billy Liar; Crown Court* (four episodes); Suzie Birchall in *Coronation Street* (1977-83); *Supernatural; Hi-de-Hi!;* Jungle Jillian in *Sorry; Some You Win* (presenter);

Mother in *Zigger Zagger*; Arabella in *Our Young Mr Wignall*; *Eleventh Hour*; *Brookside*; Dot Dooley in *Midnight at the Starlight*; Maria in *Rich Deceiver* (mini-series, 1995); *Live at the Lilydrome*.
Address: c/o Nyland Management. Lives in Wilmslow, Cheshire. m. 1st (dis), 2nd (dis); 1 d. Louise. Pets: A cat. Hobbies: Cooking.

Jimmy Nail

NAIL, Jimmy
James Bradford. Actor/Singer. b. 1954. Ran his own construction company and sang in a rock band before turning to acting. Has since combined acting with singing and songwriting.
TV: Geordie in *Shoot for the Sun*; Oz in *Auf Wiedersehen Pet* (two series, 1983-4, 1986); Edwards in *Blott on the Landscape*; Nathan Loverridge in *Minder*; Wilmarch in *Wallenberg: A Hero's Story* (TVM); Metcalf in *Spyship*; Freddie Spender in *Spender* (also co-creator, with Ian La Frenais, three series, 1991-3; also writer of several episodes and producer); *Crocodile Shoes* (series, 1994, also writer, co-executive producer, director and composer); *The South Bank Show* (subject, 1995); *Jimmy Nail: Somewhere in Time… Somewhere on Tour* (in concert, 1995).
Films: Desmond Brock in *Morons from Outer Space*; Schmidt in *Master of the Game*; Tarik in *Robinson Crusoe*; Paul in *Dream Demon*; Boyle in *Just Ask for Diamond*; Rabbets in *Danny the Champion of the World*.
Records: Singles: *Love Don't Live Here Anymore* (No 3, 1985); *Ain't No Doubt* (No 1, 1992); *Laura* (No 58, 1992); *Crocodile Shoes*; *Big River*. Albums: *Crocodile Shoes*; *Big River*.
Address: c/o ICM. Lives in North London. m. social worker Miriam; 2 s. Tom, Freddie.

NALLON, Steve
Steve Nallon. Impressionist. b. Leeds, 8 December 1960. Gained a degree in English and drama from Birmingham University. Best known for his impersonation of Margaret Thatcher. Stage productions include *The Cloggies*, *Mrs Thatcher's Star Spangled Cabinet*, *Maggie and the Wolf*, *The Carnival of the Animals*, *Greenpeace Gala* (Royal Albert Hall), *A Cook's Tour* (Shaftesbury Theatre), *The Secret Policeman's Third Ball* (London Palladium), *Night of 100 Stars* (Adelphi Theatre) and *The Secret Policeman's Biggest Ball* (Cambridge Theatre).
TV: *Spitting Image* (voice impersonator and puppeteer, 1984-96); *World in Action*; *Bullseye Christmas Special*; *The New Statesman*; *Ten Glorious Years*; *Live from the Palladium*; *Face to Face*; *Frankie and Johnny* (TVM); *The James Whale Show*; *The South Bank Show*; *Arena*; *The Late Show*; *Staggering Stories*; *Rory Bremner… Who Else?* Also voice artist and puppeteer on more than 100 children's TV programmes, including *Cat's Eyes*, *The House of Gristle*, *Spooks of Bottle Bay* and *What's Up Doc?*
Radio: *The Afternoon Shift* (writer and feature maker).
Records: *Spit in Your Ear*; *Great Golden Gobs*; *No Clause 28*. Address; c/o Eric Glass.

Steve Nallon

NARASIMHAN, Meera
Meera Narasimhan. Actress. b. London, 28 September 1972. Originally acted under the name Meera Devon. Switched to her real name in January 1996. Trained at LAMDA and CSU, California.
TV: Flava in *Max Headroom*; Julie in *Head of the Class*; Indhira in *The Potting Shed*; Conceptia in *All at Sea*; Anna in *Exchange of Fire*; Kumari in *The Lodge* (series); Kalsoom in *Moving Story* (two series, 1994-5); Meera Choudri in *The Bill*; *Dangerfield*.
Films: Dr Leo in *The Admission*; Jenny in *The Prom*. Address: c/o Langford Associates. Lives in London and California. Single. Hobbies: Indian classical dance, yoga.

Meera Narasimhan

NEELY, Bill
Bill Neely. Journalist. Graduated in English and modern history from Queen's University, Belfast, and began his career with BBC radio in Northern Ireland (1981-4), starting at the height of the Republican hunger strikes, and after three years switched to television for the BBC there. Since moving to ITN, he has covered the fall of the Berlin Wall, the civil war in the southern Soviet Union (Armenia and Azerbaijan), the refugee crisis in Jordan, the plight of the hostages in Baghdad, the 1993 US presidential election and Bill Clinton's inauguration.
TV: BBC reporter in Northern Ireland (1984-7); *Breakfast Time* (1987-9); Sky News reporter (1989); ITN reporter (1989-), then Washington correspondent (1991-). Address: c/o ITN. m.

Bill Neely

NETTLES, John
John Nettles. Actor. b. St Austell, Cornwall, 1948. Took part in dramatic society productions while at Southampton University. A teacher before entering acting. RSC plays include *Antony and Cleopatra*.
TV: Paul in *The Liver Birds* (four series); Ian Mackenzie in *A Family at War*; *Black Beauty*; *Findings on a Late Night* (Play for Today); *The Merchant of Venice*; Sgt Jim Bergerac in *Bergerac* (series, 1981-91); Joe Green in *Boon*; Jim Bergerac in *The Detectives*.
Books: *John Nettles' Jersey*; *Nudity in a Public Place*. Address: c/o Saraband Associates. Lives in St Brelade, Jersey. m. Joyce (dis); 1 d. Emma. Hobbies: Swimming, scuba-diving, riding.

John Nettles

Nanette Newman

NEWMAN, Nanette

Nanette Newman. Actress/Presenter/Author. b. Northampton, 1934. Trained at the Italia Conti Stage Academy, then won the Leverhulme Scholarship to RADA. Writer of many cookery books.

TV: *Raiders of the Spanish Main* (feature film in US); *Journey into Darkness* (TVM); *Prometheus; The Fun Food Factory; London Scene; Stay with Me till Morning; Let There Be Love;* title role in *Jessie* (TVM); *Late Expectations; The Endless Game* (pilot).

Films: *Here We Come Gathering; Personal Affair; Triple Blackmail; Faces in the Dark; The League of Gentlemen; The Rebel; Pit of Darkness; House of Mystery; The Painted Smile; Twice round the Daffodils; The L-Shaped Room; The Wrong Arm of the Law; Seance on a Wet Afternoon; Of Human Bondage; The Whisperers; The Wrong Box; Deadfall; Captain Nemo and the Underwater City; Oh! What a Lovely War; The Madwoman of Chaillot; The Raging Moon; The Love Ban; Man at the Top; The Stepford Wives; International Velvet; Restless Natives.*

Awards: Films: Royal Variety Club Best Actress Award for *The Raging Moon;* London *Evening News* Best Actress Award for *International Velvet.* Address: Chatto and Linnit. Lives in Surrey. m. film director-screenwriter Bryan Forbes; 2 d. Sarah, TV presenter Emma (qv). Hobbies: Needlepoint.

NEWTON, Madelaine

Madelaine Newton. Actress. Stage plays include *And a Nightingale Sang* (national tour).

TV: *Squire; When the Boat Comes In* (three series, 1976-7, 1981); *One Summer News Day; Come In; Chance of a Lifetime; Spoils of War; Auf Wiedersehen Pet* (Series 2); *Geordie Racer; By George; Inspector Morse; Portrait of a Marriage; Blue Days, White Days; Justice for Gemma; Peak Pactice; Catherine Cookson's The Cinder Path* (mini-series); *Firm Friends; Boon; Grange Hill; The Detectives.* Address: c/o The Narrow Road Company. m. actor Kevin Whately (qv); 1 d. Catherine, 1 s. Kieran.

Madelaine Newton

NICHOLAS, Paul

Paul Nicholas. Actor/Singer. b. Peterborough, Cambridgeshire, 3 December 1945. Began career in 1964 as a rock 'n' roll piano player in The Savages, who backed cult hero Screaming Lord Sutch.

TV: *Z Cars; Early Struggles; Paul; Golden Sea Swallow of Knokke; Season of the Witch; Three Up, Two Down; CHiPS; Ladykillers; The Boys from Ipanema; A Little Rococo; Starburst;* Vince Pinner in *Just Good Friends* (series); *Doubting Thomas;* Neil Walsh in *Bust; Paul Nicholas and Friends;* James Shepherd in *Close to Home* (two series); *Playdays* (storyteller); *The Adventures of Spot* (narrator).

Films: *Cannabis; Blind Terror; Whatever Happened to Jack and Jill?; Stardust; Three for All;* Cousin Kevin in *Tommy; Lisztomania; Sergeant Pepper's Lonely Hearts Club Band; The World Is Full of Married Men; Yesterday's Hero; Alice; The Jazz Singer;* Mike McCann in *The Nutcracker; Invitation to a Wedding.*

Records: Singles: *Reggae like It Used to Be* (No 17, 1976); *Dancing with the Captain* (No 8, 1976); *Grandma's Party* (No 9, 1976); *Heaven on the 7th Floor* (UK No 40, 1977; US No 6, 1977). Albums: *Just Good Friends* (No 30, 1986). Address: c/o Paul Nicholas & David Ian Productions, Dominion Theatre, 4th Floor, 5 Bainbridge Street, London WC1A 1HP. Lives in Highgate, North London. m. 1st Susan (dec), 2nd Linzi; 1 d. Natasha, 1 s. Oscar (from 1st m.), 1 s. Alexander, 1 d. Carmen (from 2nd m.). Hobbies: Walking with children, snooker, swimming.

Paul Nicholas

NICHOLLS, Phoebe

Phoebe Nicholls. Actress. Stage plays include *Whose Life Is It Anyway?* (Mermaid Theatre), *Pravda* (National Theatre), *The Three Sisters* (Queen's Theatre), *An Inspector Calls* (National Theatre), *Hysteria* (Royal Court) and *Rutherford and Son* (National Theatre).

TV: *Secret Orchards; Brideshead Revisited; Blade on the Feather; Take Two; A Harmless Vanity; Waters of the Moon; All for Love; Bouncing Back; Poppyland; Hay Fever; Gentry; Drowning in the Shallow End* (Screen Two); *Tell Me More; Kavanagh QC;* Elizabeth Elliot in *Jane Austen's Persuasion.*

Films: *The Elephant Man; The Missionary; Ordeal by Innocence; Maurice; Heart of Darkness.* Address: c/o Jonathan Altaras Associates.

Phoebe Nicholls

NICHOLLS, Sue

The Hon Susan Frances Harmar-Nicholls. Actress. b. Walsall, Staffordshire, 23 November 1943, daughter of former Tory MP Lord Harmar-Nicholls. Trained at RADA. Stage plays include *London Assurance* (as Pert, RSC, Broadway), *Alfie, Don't Start without Me, How the Other Half Loves* (both national tours).

TV: Marilyn Gates in *Crossroads;* Brenda in *Not on Your Nellie;* Lydia in *Jangles;* Nadia Popov (the witch) in *Rentaghost;* Mrs Muddle in *Pipkin's; Tycoon; The Duchess of Duke Street; Solo; Wodehouse Playhouse; Doctor on the Go; Heartland; Village Hall; The Professionals;* Wanda Pickles in *Up the Elephant and round the Castle;* Joan Greengross in *The Fall and Rise of Reginald Perrin;* Audrey Roberts (née Potter) in *Coronation Street* (on and off 1979-85, regular 1985-); *Royal Variety Performance* (with *Coronation Street* cast, 1989).

Records: *Where Will You Be* (No 17, 1968); *All the Way to Heaven.* Address: c/o Barry Brown & Partner/Granada TV. Lives in London and Manchester. m. actor Mark Eden. Hobbies: 'Daydreaming.'

Sue Nicholls

NICHOLSON, Mavis

Mavis Nicholson. Presenter/Interviewer. b. Briton Ferry, 19 October 1930. Former advertising copywriter.
TV: *Mavis; Happy Returns; Mavis — Wanting to Know; Other People's Children; Volunteers; Medical Express; Good Afternoon; After Noon Plus; The Garden Party; Mavis Catches Up With...; Relatively Speaking; Third Wave with Mavis Nicholson; In with Mavis; Moments of Crisis* (series, 1993); *Faces of the Family* (series, 1994). **Books:** *Martha Jane and Me: A Girlhood in Wales* (1992).
Address: c/o Channel Four. m. journalist Geoffrey Nicholson; 3 s. Steve, Lewis, Harry.

Mavis Nicholson

NICHOLSON, Michael

Michael Thomas Nicholson. Journalist. b. Romford, Essex, 9 January 1937. OBE, 1991; Falklands Campaign Medal; Gulf Campaign Medal. Gained a BA (Hons) in politics from Leicester University. Political writer with D C Thomson (1962-3), then joined ITN in 1963 and has since covered more wars than any other British journalist, the Gulf War being his 15th.
TV: ITN reporter and war correspondent (1963-75), covering Vietnam, Biafra, Cambodia, Jordan, Indo-Pakistan, Laos, the Yom Kippur War, Beirut and Northern Ireland; ITN Southern Africa correspondent (1975-81), covering Rhodesia and Angola; ITN *News at 5.45* presenter (1982-5); *Return to Vietnam* (documentary); *The World This Week* (co-presenter); Washington presenter for ITN *World News* (*The Channel Four Daily*, 1989); ITN foreign affairs correspondent (1989-).
Awards: Three times winner of the RTS Journalist of the Year award (1978, 1982, 1992); RTS Reporter of the Year award (1979); BAFTA Richard Dimbleby Award (1982); RTS Journalist of the Year (1991). **Books:** *The Partridge Kite; Red Joker; December Ultimatum; Across the Limpopo; Pilgrim's Rest* (all fiction); *A Measure of Danger* (autobiography, 1991), *Natasha's Story* (1993).
Address: c/o ITN. Lives in Haslemere, Surrey. m. Diana; 2 s. Tom, William, 1 adopted d. Natasha. Pets: Koi carp, cats, dogs, doves, donkeys. Hobbies: Sailing.

Michael Nicholson

NIGHY, Bill

Bill Nighy. Actor. National Theatre plays include *Map of the World, Pravda, King Lear* and *Arcadia*.
TV: Vincent Fish in *Agony; Standing in for Henry; Fat, Fox; Soldiers Talking Cleanly;* Deasey in *Deasey's Desperate; Dreams of Leaving; Under the Skin* (Play for Today); *Easter 2016* (Play for Tomorrow); Meares in *The Last Place on Earth;* Goschen in *Reilly — Ace of Spies; Thirteen at Dinner* (TVM); *South of the Border; The Cat Brought It In; Making News; Antonia and Jane; The Men's Room;* Hugh Marriner in *Absolute Hell* (Performance); *Bergerac; The Eye of the Storm; Mistress of Suspense; Unnatural Causes; Peak Practice;* John Tracey in *Don't Leave Me This Way* (TVM); Roger Maitland in *The Maitlands* (Performance); David Cleeve in *Wycliffe* (series, 1994); Six Preachers in *God's Messengers*.
Films: Al in *The Little Drummer Girl;* Helmut in *Hitler's SS;* Barton in *Phantom of the Opera;* Tiger Brown in *The Threepenny Opera;* Julian in *Being Human;* John Tracy in *A Masculine Ending*.
Address: c/o Markham & Froggatt. Partner: Actress Diana Quick (qv).

Bill Nighy

NIMMO, Derek

Derek Nimmo. Actor. b. Liverpool, 19 September 1932. TV since 1958. Stage plays include *The Amorous Prawn, Duel of Angels, Charlie Girl, A Friend Indeed* and *See How They Run* (all West End).
TV: *All Gas and Gaiters; Oh, Brother!; If It's Saturday, It Must Be Nimmo; Oh Father!; My Hon Mrs; Sorry I'm Single; Life Begins at Forty; Third Time Lucky; Hell's Bells;* Lord Ledgerwood in *Neighbours;* Stephen Wolfe in *The Good Guys*.
Films: Fred In *Hot Enough for June; One of Our Dinosaurs Is Missing*.
Books: *Not in Front of the Servants; Oh, Come on All Ye Faithful: A Humorous Church Collection; As the Actress Said to the Bishop*. Address: c/o Michael Whitehall. m. Patricia Brown.

Derek Nimmo

NORDEN, Denis

Denis Norden. Broadcaster/Writer. b. Hackney, London, 6 February 1922. CBE. A theatre manager before writing for troop shows while in the RAF, then becoming a scriptwriter for variety shows and teaming up with Frank Muir (1947-64) to write for television and radio.
TV: As writer (with Frank Muir): *And So to Bentley; Whack-O!; The Seven Faces of Jim; Brothers-in-Law; The Glums*. As writer: *The Name's the Same; How to Be an Alien.* As writer-presenter: *Looks Familiar; It'll Be Alright on the Night; It'll Be Alright Late at Night; With Hilarious Consequences; 10 Years of Alright on the Night; 21 Years of Laughter; In on the Act; Pick of the Pilots; Denis Norden's Trailer Cinema* (B-movie trailers of the Fifties and Sixties, including Leonard Nimoy, Joan Collins and Sean Connery); *Denis Norden's Laughter File; Worst of Alright on the Night; The Second Worst of Alright on the Night; Laughter by Royal Command; A Tribute to Les Dawson* (1993); *The Utterly Worst of Alright on the Night; The Kids from Alright on the Night; 40 Years of ITV Laughter* (1995).
Films: As writer: *Buena Sera, Mrs Campbell; Every Home Should Have One; The Water Babies*.
Radio: As writer (with Frank Muir): *Take It from Here; Bedtime with Braden.* As writer-presenter: *My Word!; My Music.* Address: c/o April Young. m. Avril; 1 d. TV producer Maggie Norden, 1 s. Nick.

Denis Norden

NORMAN, Barry

Barry Norman

Barry Norman. Presenter/Writer. b. London, 21 August 1933. Son of film producer-director Leslie Norman. *Daily Mail* journalist who, after being made redundant, became a freelance film reviewer for TV. Invited to join the panel on BBC's *Late Night Line-Up* (1972) and subsequently to host the *Film* series.
TV: *Late Night Line-Up; Film* series (1972-); *Film* specials; *The Hollywood Greats* (1977-9); *Omnibus; The British Greats; Barry Norman in Chicago; Barry Norman's Hong Kong; Barry Norman on Broadway; Barry Norman's London Season; Barry Norman in Celebrity City; The Rank Charm School; Barry Norman at the Cannes Film Festival; Film '92 from LA with Barry Norman; Films of the Year with Barry Norman; Lenny Henry in Dreams; Film '93 Special — Robert Redford; Films of the Year with Barry Norman; The Oscars — The 66th Annual Academy Awards* (1994); *The Cannes Film Festival with Barry Norman* (1994); *Film 94 Summer Special with Barry Norman; Tom Cruise: A Film 95 Special* (1995); *The Oscars Ceremony* (live); *The Oscars* (highlights); *Woody Allen — A Film 95 Special* (1995); *Barry Norman at the Cannes Film Festival* (1995).
Books: *End Product; A Series of Defeats; To Nick a Good Body; The Hollywood Greats; The Movie Greats; Have a Nice Day; Sticky Wicket; The Film Greats; 100 Best Films of the Century.*
Awards: BAFTA Richard Dimbleby Award (1980); Award of the London Film Critics' Circle (1995). Address: c/o Curtis Brown. m. Diana; 2 d. TV presenter Samantha (qv), Emma. Hobbies: Cricket.

NORMAN, Samantha

Samantha Norman

Samantha Norman. Presenter. b. Stevenage, Hertfordshire. Daughter of TV presenter Barry Norman (qv) and journalist-novelist Diana Norman; granddaughter of film producer-director Leslie Norman. Features writer for the *Sunday Mirror Magazine*, the *Sunday Express*, *The Guardian* and *Radio Times* before entering television in 1989. Showbusiness columnist for the *Daily Mirror* (1993).
TV: *This Way Out* (arts programme, TVS only, 1989-90); *Dial Midnight; London Tonight* (features reporter, Carlton/LWT only); *The Weekend Show* (Anglia Television only); *Love Call* (Anglia Television only); VH-1 (satellite channel, 1994-), including *Into the Music; DesRes.*
Address: c/o The Roseman Organisation. Lives in London. m. Dr Piers Clifford; 1 s. Harry. Pets: Jack Russell called Finn, horse called Loner. Hobbies: Riding, watching boxing.

NUNN, Judy

Judy Nunn

Judy Nunn. Actress. Daughter of actress Nancy Nunn. Professional début at Perth Playhouse, aged 12. Moved to Sydney at the age of 19 and left for London three years later. Appeared on the West End stage in *Goodbye Charlie, The Hollow* and *Gaslight*, in *The Final Days* (Open Space Theatre) and *Guinness Book of Records* (revue), and worked in repertory theatre in Crewe, Worthing and Bournemouth. She also acted in BBC radio plays and on British Television. She returned to Australia in 1973.
TV: *The Onedin Line; Z Cars; The Befrienders* (all in UK); Irene Fisher in *Sons and Daughters; Beauty and the Beast* (panellist); *A Country Practice;* Vicki Stafford in *The Box; Skyways; Mother and Son; Prisoner* (UK title *Prisoner: Cell Block H*); *Bit Part; The Newman Shame* (TVM); *The Land We Love* (documentary, host); *Yes What;* Ailsa Hogan/Stewart in *Home and Away* (1988-). As writer: *Possession; Neighbours.*
Films: *Hostage; The Box; Song of Norway.* **Radio:** BBC drama and features in UK; *Brunswick Heads Revisited; Diaries of Lady Glenice; The California Birds; Moonlight over the Estuary.*
Books: Children's books; *The Glitter Game* (novel). Address: c/o James Laurie Management/Channel 7. m. actor Bruce Venables.

NUTKINS, Terry

Terry Nutkins

Terence Paul Nutkins. Presenter. b. London, 12 May 1946. Former Trusthouse Forte general manager with responsibility for the cetacean operation at four safari and leisure parks (1970-83). At the age of 11, helped author Gavin Maxwell to care for wild otters on the west coast of Scotland and the author subsequently became his legal guardian. Became a leading authority on marine mammals, and Johnny Morris invited him to present an item on dolphins in *Animal Magic*, of which he later became co-presenter. Has appeared in a TV studio with more wild creatures than any other presenter.
TV: BBC animal programmes (1977-80); *Animal Magic* (1981, and co-presenter 1981-3); *The Really Wild Show* (1987- , winner, BAFTA award for best children's factual programme); *What's Up Doc?; The Really Wild Roadshow; Growing Up Wild* (three series, 1993-5); *Pets Win Prizes* (co-presenter, two series, 1994-5). **Radio:** *Animal Corner* (1987- , BBC Radio 4).
Books: *Nutkins on Pets* (1989).Address: c/o John Miles Organisation. Lives in north-west Scotland. m. Jackie; 3 d. Jennifer, Suzi, Amanda, 3 s. Simon, David, Terry. Pets: Three dogs, three snakes, a tortoise, two cats, spiders. Hobbies: Diving.

OAKLEY, Robin

Robin Oakley

Robert Francis Leigh Oakley. Journalist. b. Kidderminster, 20 August 1941. Newspaper journalist, including assistant editor of the *Sunday Express, Now!* magazine and the *Daily Mail*, and political editor

of *The Times*, before joining BBC Television News as political editor.
TV: BBC Television News political editor.
Radio: *Week in Westminster; People and Politics* (BBC World Service).
Address: c/o BBC TV News & Current Affairs. Lives in Epsom, Surrey. m. June 1966 Carolyn Susan Germaine Rumball; 1 d. Annabel Louise Germaine (b. July 1971), 1 s. Alexander Guy Leigh (b. August 1973). Pets: A black labrador called Sorrel. Hobbies: Theatre, horse-racing.

OBERMAN, Claire
Claire Elizabeth Oberman. Actress. b. Holland, 21 February 1956. Brought up in New Zealand. Won a scholarship to the National Drama School, Wellington, at the age of 16.
TV: *Hunter's Gold* (series); *Moynihan; Joe and Koro; Mortimer's Patch* (all series in New Zealand); Kate Norris in *Tenko* (three series, 1981-4) and *Tenko Reunion* (1985); Daphne Fairbrother in *Hi-de-Hi!; Bottle Boys; The Two Ronnies;* Lonny Hope in *Paradise Postponed;* Jane Partridge in *Ladies Night;* Caroline Chetwyne in *Griffins;* Mortimer in *Fortunes of War;* Sandy Savage in *Gentlemen and Players;* Fiona in *Matlock;* Sarah in *To Be the Best* (mini-series); Alex Farrell in *Trainer* (Series 2, 1992).
Films: *Goodbye Pork Pie* (New Zealand, winner of Best Film Actress award); *Das Schöne Ende Dieser Welt* (*The Beautiful End of the World*) (Germany); Lady Holmes in *Patriot Games*.
Address: c/o Barry Burnett Organisation.

Claire Oberman

O'BRIEN, Peter
Peter O'Brien. Actor. b. Murray Bridge, Australia, 25 March 1960. Trained at St Martin Youth Theatre. After experience in amateur theatre in Adelaide, he sent a showreel tape to the Grundy Organisation, which secured him a role in the short-lived (17-week) series *Starting Out*. In 1985, after several other television appearances, he landed the part of Shane Ramsay in *Neighbours*. Now based in the UK.
TV: *Starting Out; Carson's Law; Prisoner* (UK title *Prisoner: Cell Block H*); *The Henderson Kids;* Shane Ramsay in *Neighbours* (1985-7); Dr Sam Patterson in *The Flying Doctors; The Trials of Oz* (Performance); Bill Hamilton in *Taggart: Death without Dishonour;* DC Coffee in *The Stonehouse Affair* (Crime Story); *The All New Alexei Sayle Show* (series, 1994); Cyril 'Scissors' Smedley in *Cardiac Arrest* (Series 2-3, 1995-6); *The All New Alexei Sayle Show 2* (series, 1995).
Films: *The Mortal Coil*.
Address: c/o Sharon Hamper Management. m. 24 December 1991 actress Joanna Riding (sep).

Peter O'Brien

O'BRIEN, Richard
Richard O'Brien. Actor. b. Cheltenham, Gloucestershire, 25 March 1942. Brought up in New Zealand. Creator and writer of the original stage production of *The Rocky Horror Show*.
TV: *A Hymn for Jim; Robin of Sherwood; The Crystal Maze* (four series, 1990-3); *Crystal Maze Kids' Special* (1992); *Rousseau* in *Full Stretch; The Brit Awards 1993; The Ink Thief* (series, 1994); Dr Phibes in *The Detectives*.
Films: *Carry On Cowboy; The Fighting Prince of Donegal; The Andromeda Strain; The Odd Job; The Rocky Horror Picture Show;* Fico in *Flash Gordon; Jubilee; Shock Treatment; Revolution*. Address: c/o Jonathan Altaras Associates. m. Jane Elizabeth Moss-O'Brien; 2 s. Linus, Joshua, 1 d. Amelia.

Richard O'Brien

O'BRIEN, Simon
Simon O'Brien. Actor/Presenter. b. Garston, Liverpool, 19 June 1965. Stage roles include Kav in Willy Russell's *Stags and Hens*.
TV: Damon Grant in *Brookside* (1982-7) and *Damon & Debbie* (mini-series, 1987); *Night Network; I Can Do That; Move It; Fraggle Rock* (all as presenter); *Power Club Plus* (presenter, BSB Now channel); *Young, Gifted and Broke; Standing Room Only* (presenter, two series, 1992-3); Vince in *Heartbeat; The Neighbourhood* (US sitcom, 1993); *Rough Guide to the World* (presenter, series, 1995).
Films: Kav in Willy Russell's *Dancin' thru the Dark* (film version of stage play *Stags and Hens*).
Address: c/o Annette Stone Associates. Single.

Simon O'Brien

O'CALLAGHAN, Tony
Tony O'Callaghan. Actor. b. North London, 16 June 1956. Trained at The Drama Centre. Stage roles include Rutilus in *Berenice* (Lyric Theatre, Hammersmith), Algernon in *The Importance of Being Earnest*, Peter in *Time and Time Again* and Raoul in *Phantom of the Opera* (all Century Theatre) and Tony in *Abigail's Party* (national tour).
TV: Bookie in *Jockey School; Murphy's Mob;* Brian in *Me & My Girl;* Chauffeur in *Terry and June; Dempsey and Makepeace;* Taxi Driver in *Three Up, Two Down;* Sharpe in *Hannay;* Danny Moran in *The Bill;* Geoff in *Castle of Adventure;* Paul Clarke in *The Upper Hand* (series); Det Sgt Lewis in *A Safe House* (Screen Two); Assassin in *Children of the North* (Screen One); Piggy in *About Face;* Sgt Matthew Boyden in *The Bill*. Address: c/o Scott Marshall/The Bill. Lives in North London. Single. Hobbies: Tennis, classic cars, antiques.

Tony O'Callaghan

Des O'Connor

O'CONNOR, Des

Des O'Connor. Entertainer/Presenter. b. Stepney, East London, 12 January 1932. Worked as a Butlin's Redcoat at Filey before turning professional, making his début at the Palace Theatre, Newcastle, in 1953. Variety engagements and summer seasons followed, plus performances at the Talk of the Town, the London Palladium and the Sydney Opera House.

TV: *Spot the Tune; Sunday Night at the London Palladium; For Love or Money; The Des O'Connor Show; Des O'Connor Now; Des O'Connor Tonight* (series and 1995 Christmas special); *Take Your Pick* (host, revived quiz show, two series); *Pot of Gold* (talent show, two series, 1993, 1995).

Records: Singles: *Careless Hands* (No 6, 1967); *I Pretend* (No 1, 1968); *1-2-3 O'Leary* (No 4, 1968); *Dick-a-Dum-Dum (King's Road)* (No 14, 1969); *Loneliness* (No 18, 1969); *I'll Go on Hoping* (No 30, 1970); *The Tips of My Fingers* (No 15, 1970); *The Skye Boat Song* (with Roger Whittaker) (No 10, 1986). Albums: *I Pretend* (No 8, 1968); *With Love* (No 40, 1970); *Sing a Favourite Song* (No 25, 1972); *Just for You* (No 17, 1980); *Des O'Connor Now* (No 24, 1984); *True Love Ways.*

Books: *Somebody Laughed* (autobiography).

Awards: *TVTimes* Favourite Male TV Personality (1969, 1970, 1971, 1972, 1973). Address: c/o IMG/Lake-Smith Griffin Associates. m. 1st Phyllis (dis), 2nd actress Gillian Vaughan, 3rd Jay; 4 d. Karen (from 1st m.), Tracey, Samantha (from 2nd m.), Kristina Eva (from 3rd m.). Hobbies: Golf.

Bill Oddie

ODDIE, Bill

William Oddie. Actor/Writer/Presenter. b. Rochdale, Lancashire, 7 July 1941. Former member of Cambridge Footlights revue.

TV: *That Was the Week That Was; Twice a Fortnight; Doctor in the House* and *Doctor at Large* (co-writer, with Graeme Garden); *Orson's Bag* (also writer); *Broaden Your Mind; We Have Ways of Making You Laugh; Galton & Simpson Playhouse; The Goodies* (also co-writer, seven BBC series); *The Goodies and the Beanstalk* (special); *The Goodies Rule: O.K.* (special); *The Saturday Banana* (presenter); *The Goodies* (ITV series, 1981); *Astronauts* (co-writer, with Graeme Garden); *From the Top; Fax; Oddie in Paradise; Titmuss Regained; The Travel Show; The Children's Royal Variety Performance 1993.; Bananaman* (voice only); *Bird in the Nest* (two series, 1994-5); Professor Rose in *The Detectives; London Wildlife Challenge.*

Records: Singles (all with The Goodies): *The In Betweenies/Father Christmas Do Not Touch Me* (No 7, 1974); *Funky Gibbon* (No 4, 1975); *Black Pudding Bertha* (No 19, 1975); *Nappy Love/Wild Thing* (No 21, 1975); *Make a Daft Noise for Christmas* (No 20, 1975).

Address: c/o London Management. m. 1st (dis), 2nd writer Laura Beaumont; 3 d. Kate (actress Kate Hardie, qv), Bonnie (both from 1st m.), Rosie (from 2nd m.).

Ian Ogilvy

OGILVY, Ian

Ian Ogilvy. Actor. b. Woking, Surrey, 30 September 1943. Worked backstage at the Royal Court Theatre before training at RADA. Stage plays include *The Waltz of the Toreadors* and *The Millionairess.*

TV: *The Liars; Upstairs, Downstairs; Affairs of the Heart; A Walk with Destiny;* Simon Templar in *Return of The Saint; Tom, Dick and Harriet; Design for Living; Horses; Anna Karenina; Menace Unseen; Maigret* (TVM); Peter Templeton in *Murder, She Wrote.*

Films: *Stranger in the House; The Sorcerers; Witchfinder General; The Invincible Six; Waterloo; Wuthering Heights; Fengriffin; No Sex, Please — We're British.;* Chagall in *Death Becomes Her.*

Awards: *TVTimes* Most Compulsive Character award (1978-9).

Address: c/o Michael Whitehall. m. former model Diane; 1 step-d. Emma, 1 s. Titus.

Rachel Ogilvy

OGILVY, Rachel

Rachel Ogilvy. Actress. b. Glasgow, 5 June 1965. Trained at the Royal Scottish Academy of Music and Drama. Stage roles include Hermia in *A Midsummer Night's Dream* (Scottish Chamber Orchestra).

TV: Swimmer in *Winners and Losers; Let's See: On the Beach* (presenter); Tamara in *City Lights;* Young Ann in *Misterioso;* Receptionist in *Ball on the Slates;* Bank Clerkess in *Britoil Fraud;* Tiffany Bowles in *High Road* (1994-). **Radio:** *Heart and Bone; After Icarus; Peggers and Creelers* (all BBC Radio Scotland). Address: c/o Pat Lovett Agency. Lives in London. Single.

April Olrich

OLRICH, April

Edith April Oelrichs. Actress. b. Zanzibar, 17 July 1941. Baby ballerina and soloist with Royal Ballet. Stage plays include *Wait a Minim* (Fortune Theatre and Broadway), *The Boys from Syracuse* (Theatre Royal, Drury Lane) and *Standing Room Only* (Chichester Festival Theatre).

TV: Arlette in *Maigret;* Stepdaughter in *Six Characters…; The Punch Revue;* Senna in *The Howerd Confessions;* Desiree in *Robert's Robots;* Pru in *Fresh Fields;* June in *Shaping Up;* The Stripper in *The Seven Deadly Sins;* Isadora in *She-Wolf of London;* Lucinda in *Teenage Health Freak;* Ivana Trump in *The Gallery.*

Films: *Room at the Top; The Skull;* Mme Petrovna in *The Intelligence Men; Macbeth;* Paula in *Rid-*

ing High; Battle of the River Plate; Seven Cities of Atlantis; Hussy; Princess Daisy; Oona in *Supergirl.*
Awards: Theatre: Whitbread Best Performance in a Musical award (Broadway, 1967).
Address: c/o Langford Associates. Lives in Kingston-upon-Thames, Surrey. m. 1st 1963 F D M Williams (dis 1967), 2nd actor Nigel Pegram. Pets: Foxes in the garden. Hobbies: Piano, clothes, swimming.

O'NEAL, Siri

Siri Willow Ceridwen Neal. Actress. b. Wales, 14 August 1972. Changed her professional name from Neal to the original family name of O'Neal in February 1996. (It was her grandmother's name, but her mother changed it to Neal.) Trained at LAMDA. Director of Bedrock Productions. Stage roles include Ivana Milosz in *Slip of the Tongue* (Shaftesbury Theatre) and Hilde Wangel in *The Master Builder* (Royal Lyceum Theatre, Edinburgh, Riverside Studios, London, and national tour). Has appeared with Czech theatre company Divadloo Na Provazku (Theatre on a String) in Czechoslavakia and worked on two concerts in the Czech Republic, including one of its largest music festivals, in Straznice, in 1994.

Siri O'Neal

TV: Charlotte in *Press Gang;* Linda in *Stay Lucky;* Lizzie Heart in *The Bill;* Christine Anderson in *Wycliffe; Jackanory;* Allegra in *Summer's Lease;* Sonia Gluck in *Artists in Crime;* Minty (Araminta Kane) in *Moondial;* Bethany Taffner in *The Cloning of Joanna May* (mini-series, 1992); Sandra Wilson in *Lovejoy;* Lizzie Hart in *The Bill;* Juanita in *Sharpe's Battle.*
Films: Suki in *The Rachel Papers;* Judith Wheater in *The Children;* Katie in *Jeopardy;* Helen Atkinson in *Waterland.* Address: c/o Susan Shaper Management. Lives in London. Partner: Actor Brian Cox (qv).

O'NEILL, Maggie

Maggie O'Neill. Actress. Stage plays include *A Month in the Country* (Cambridge Theatre Company) and *And Kai Dreamed a Dream* (Old Vic).
TV: *Killing Me Softly; Sean Devereux; He's Asking for It; Defrosting the Fridge;* Kathy in *Take Me Home* (mini-series, 1989); *Blore, MP; The Greek Myths: Theseus and the Minotaur; Window of Vulnerability; Made in Heaven; Boon;* Louise in *Friday on My Mind* (mini-series, 1992); Auntie Doris in *The Life and Times of Henry Pratt* (series, 1992); Aline Siward in *Cadfael* (series, 1994); Caroline Tanner in *The Dying of the Light* (drama-documentary); Emma Holman in *Number Six* (Chiller).

Maggie O'Neill

Films: Girl in Paradise Club in *Mona Lisa;* Kim in *Gorillas in the Mist;* Hazel in *Under Suspicion;* Berta in *Seven Minutes; The Artisans; Prime Suspect; When Pigs Fly.* Address: c/o ICM.

ONWUKWE, Ben

Ben Onwukwe. Actor. b. London, 21 August 1957. Gained a BA (Hons) in performing arts from Middlesex University. Stage plays include *Andromache* (Old Vic) and *The Emperor* (Royal Court).
TV: *Bandung File; Slinger's Day; Waiting for God; Splitting Up; The Bill; Inspector Morse; Bergerac; Hard Cases; Doctor at the Top; Growing Pains; Between the Lines; The Biz!;* Recall in *London's Burning* (five series).
Films: *American Roulette; The Chain.*

Ben Onwukwe

Address: c/o Barry Brown & Partner. Lives in North London. m. Patrice; 1 d. Maya, 1 s. Leo. Hobbies: 'Cinema, books, swimming, ruminating.'

ORCHARD, Nick

Nicholas Shaun Orchard. Actor. b. Bristol, 1 July 1957. Worked in stage management at Bristol Old Vic Theatre. Trained at Birmingham School of Drama. Stage plays include *Romeo and Juliet/Twelfth Night* (national tour and Westminster Theatre).
TV: *Out of the Past: Village of War; Maths Counts; The Brief; Look and Read: Badger Girl* (all BBC Schools); *In the Secret State; Timeless Tales;* Gavin in *EastEnders; Going to Work: Pressure of Work; Customer Care* (Channel Four Open College programme); *Beadle's About; Casualty; The Rita Rudner Show;* Gary Lipman in *Emmerdale;* Mr Thomas in *Coronation Street.*
Radio: *Outbreak of Fear; Ashley* (both BBC Radio Bristol).

Nick Orchard

Address; c/o Equity. Lives in London. m. Cuzz Scatlergood, 1 s. Oliver. Pets. A dog called Flim.

O'SHEA, Kevin

Kevin O'Shea. Actor. b. Enfield, Middlesex, 7 March 1952. Member of the National Youth Theatre (1968-71). Trained at the Bristol Old Vic Theatre School (1970-3). Stage plays include *Frozen Assets, The Bundle, A Midsummer Night's Dream* (all RSC) and *Equus* (National Theatre tour).
TV: Alienikoff in *Thank You Comrades;* Johnny in *We Think the World of You; Spearhead; The Professionals;* Det Sgt Pete Phillips in *The Gentle Touch* (22 episodes); Reginald Lee in *SOS Titanic* (TVM); Captain in *The Scarlet Pimpernel* (TVM); Calvin Turner in *Kelly Monteith; Johannes Huit in Shadow of the Noose; Secret Army;* The Pilot in *The Dirty Dozen: The Deadly Mission* (TVM); Max Hargreaves in *Grange Hill* (three series); *Double Dare; Crime Monthly;* Carl (Room Service Waiter) in *Second Thoughts.*
Films: *Black Joy; Woman on a Roof; Inseminoid.* Address; c/o CAM. Lives in London and Spain. m. 27 July 1990 Cristina Rodes. Pets: Gekkos. Hobbies: Flying (qualified glider pilot).

Kevin O'Shea

OSOBA, Tony

Tony Osoba

Anthony Osoba. Actor. b. Glasgow. Trained at the Royal Scottish Academy of Music and Drama.
TV: Hamish in *Charles Endell Esquire;* McLaren in *Porridge* (three series); Det Con Chas Jarvis in *Dempsey and Makepeace* (three series); Ahmed in *The Flame Trees of Thika; Snakes and Ladders; Reunion; The Professionals; Gruey; Return to Treasure Island; The Cleopatras; Churchill's People; Brookside; Bergerac; Minder; Doctor Who; Umbrella* (storyteller); Peter Ingram in *Coronation Street* (1990); *Making News; Scotch and Wry; The Cage; Resnick; Red Eagle; Between the Lines;* Xicotenga in *Golden Years;* Barrett in *The Bureaucracy of Love;* Det Supt Garrett in *The Bill;* Magistrate in *Crown Prosecutor.*
Films: *Game for Vultures; Who Dares Wins.*
Address: c/o Barry Brown & Partner. Lives in London. m. 7 July 1989 Sally Wignall. Hobbies: 'Classic cars (runs two old Jaguar E-Types), watching sport, playing pathetic games of golf and tennis, travel and history of countries visited, collecting old toys and books, more travel.'

O'SULLEVAN, Peter

Peter O'Sullevan

Peter John O'Sullevan. Horse-racing commentator/journalist. b. Kenmare, Ireland, 3 March 1918. CBE. Racing correspondent with the Press Association (1944-50) and *Daily Express* (1950-86).
TV: BBC TV horse-racing commentator (1946-), including races in Australia, South Africa, France, Italy and US. **Books:** *Calling the Horses* (autobiography, 1989).
Address: 37 Cranmer Court, London SW3. m. Patricia. Pets: Horses, one dog. Hobbies: Racehorses, travel, art, food and wine, plus (when invited) voice-overs.

O'SULLIVAN, Richard

Richard O'Sullivan

Richard O'Sullivan. Actor. b. Chiswick, West London, 7 May 1944. Started acting professionally as a child. Trained at the Corona Stage Academy. Stage plays include *Run for Your Wife* (Criterion Theatre).
TV: Title role in *Little Lord Fauntleroy* (aged 12); *Great Expectations;* Ronnie Hughes in *All Aboard; Thirty Minute Theatre; The Connoisseur* (Play of the Month); Dr Laurence Bingham in *Doctor at Large* (series, 1971) and *Doctor in Charge* (series, 1972-3); Keith in *Now Look Here…* (two series, 1971-3); Howard in *Father Dear Father* (series, 1972-3); Richard Gander in *Alcock and Gander* (series, 1972); Robin Tripp in *Man about the House* (six series, 1973-6) and *Robin's Nest* (five series, 1977-81, also writer of theme music); title role in *Dick Turpin* (series, 1978-80); Simon Harrap in *Me & My Girl* (six series, 1984-8); *The Giftie;* Adam Charlesworth in *Trouble in Mind* (series, 1991); *Holed; The Inside Track… on Parenting.*
Films: *Dance Little Lady; The Stranger's Hand; The Green Scarf; Make Me an Offer; The Dark Avenger* (UK title *The Warriors*); *The Secret; It's Great to Be Young; Raiders of the River* (serial); *Jacqueline; Dangerous Exile; The Nun's Story; Carry On Teacher; Witness in the Dark; And Women Shall Weep; A Story of David; Spare the Rod; The Young Ones; The Webster Boy; The Prince and the Pauper; Summer Holiday; Dr Syn — Alias the Scarecrow; Cleopatra; Wonderful Life; Every Day's a Holiday; A Dandy in Aspic; The Haunted House of Horror; Futtock's End; Au Pair Girls; Father Dear Father; Can You Keep It Up for a Week?; Man about the House; Dick Turpin* (TVM only in UK). **Radio:** Sam Benson in *Doctors* (two series, 1994-5, BBC Radio 4). Address: c/o Al Mitchell Associates. Lives in London. m. 1st model Diana Terry (dis), 2nd 16 April 1988 Christine Smart (granddaughter of Billy Smart); 1 s. James (from relationship with actress Tessa Wyatt in between two marriages). Hobbies: Golf, music.

OWEN, Bill

Bill Owen

William John Owen Rowbotham. Actor/Writer. b. Acton Green, West London, 14 March 1914. MBE. Originally acted as Bill Rowbotham. Started as stooge to a comic in 1938. Lyricist of songs for singers such as Sacha Distel, Matt Monroe, Pat Boone, Nana Mouskouri and Engelbert Humperdinck.
TV: *The Three Piece Suite; The Challengers; The Quiet Half-Hour; Seventeen Per Cent Said Push Off; Whatever Happened to the Likely Lads?; Taxi; Treasure Island; Coppers End; Coronation Street;* Compo in *Last of the Summer Wine* (Comedy Playhouse, 1973, and 18 series, 1973-95, plus Christmas specials); *Brideshead Revisited; Passing Through; Tales of the Unexpected; Uncle of the Bride* (TVM); *You and Me* (BBC Schools); Billy Rice in *The Entertainer* (Performance).
Films: Selection (from 46): *Song of the People* (début, short, 1945); *Holiday Camp; Once a Jolly Swagman; Hotel Sahara; The Story of Robin Hood and His Merrie Men; The Ship That Died of Shame ; Not So Dusty; Davy; Carve Her Name with Pride; Carry On Sergeant; Carry On Nurse; Carry On Regardless; Carry On Cabby; Georgy Girl; The Fighting Prince of Donegal; Headline Hunters; Kadoyng; O Lucky Man!; In Celebration; Smurfs and the Magic Flute* (voice only); *The Comeback;* Amos in *Laughterhouse* (retitled *Singleton's Pluck*). As writer: *Romance with a Double Bass.* Address: c/o The Richard Stone Partnership. m. 1st Edith Stevenson (dis), 2nd former actress Kathie; 1 s. Tom, 1 step-d. Kathie.

OWEN, Clive

Clive Owen

Clive Owen. Actor. Father Jess is a country & western singer who won the television talent show *New Faces* with his group, Jess and the Gingerbreads.
TV: Gideon Sam in *Precious Bane;* Stephen Crane in *Chancer* (two series, 1990-1); *Class of '61; The*

Magician; Nobody's Children; Doomsday Gun; DC George Byrne in The Magician; Bill in An Evening with Gary Lineker (TVM); Charlie MacFell in Catherine Cookson's The Cinder Path (mini-series, 1994); Nick Sharman in The Turnaround; Damon Wildeve in Return of the Native (Screen Two,).
Films: Vroom; Lorna Doone; Close My Eyes; Century.
Address: c/o ICM. Lives in London.

OWEN, Nicholas
Nicholas Owen. Newscaster. b. London, 10 February 1947. Newspaper journalist with the Surrey Mirror, Evening Standard, the Daily Telegraph and the Financial Times, and deputy business editor, then business editor of Now! magazine, before entering television in 1981. Left the BBC for ITN in 1984.

Nicholas Owen

TV: BBC TV reporter covering industrial stories in the North East; ITN Channel Four News business and economics correspondent, then presenter of news programmes on ITV and Channel Four, principally News at 12.30; The Parliament Programme; Midnight Special (ITN Gulf War news programme); ITN Lunchtime News presenter (1992-); Channel Four News: Midnight Special (Election programmes, 1992); Budget programmes; Budget '93 (both Budgets, co-presenter); Budget '94 (co-presenter); ITN royal correspondent (1994-).
Address: c/o ITN. Lives in Surrey. m. newspaper reporter Brenda; 1 d. Rebecca, 1 s. Anthony, 1 step-d. Justine, 1 step-s. Daniel. Hobbies: Reading, walking, sleeping.

OWEN, Nick
Nicholas Corbishley Owen. Presenter. b. Berkhamsted, Hertfordshire, 1 November 1947. Gained a BA (Hons) in classics from Leeds University. Journalist in newspapers (Doncaster Evening Post and Birmingham Post) and local radio (BBC Radio Birmingham) before entering television.

Nick Owen

TV: ATV/Central Television news and sports presenter, reporter and commentator (1978-83), including 1982 World Cup; TV-am sports presenter, then presenter of Good Morning Britain (1983-6); Midweek Sport Special (1986-92); World Athletics Championships 1987; Olympics '88; European and World Ice Skating Championships (1986-92); World Cup '90; Sporting Triangles (quiz show, host); royal film premières; Hitman; Thames Sport Special; Sportsworld Extra; Good Morning... with Anne & Nick (four series, 1992-6) and Good Morning (1995-6, individual shows without Anne Diamond); The Good Morning Advent Calendar with Anne & Nick; Wish You Were Here...? (guest presenter); A Summer Good Morning (highlights from Good Morning, series, 1993); Champions (series); UK Summer Special Olympics (1993); The Big Country Quest (presenter, series, 1994); Preston Front (acting himself).
Address: c/o Severn Management Services. Lives in Birmingham. m. 1977 Jill; 3 s. Andrew, Timothy, Christopher, 1 d. Jenny. Pets: A labrador called Suzi. Hobbies: Squash, football, cricket.

OWEN, Sid

Sid Owen

David John Sutton. Actor. b. Islington, North London, 12 January 1972. Trained at Anna Scher Theatre School. Made his film début at the age of nine as an extra in the TV movie Oliver Twist.
TV: Oliver Twist (as an extra); Metal Mickey; Shackleton; Bottle Boys; Mick in Jury; Everybody Here; No Adults Allowed; Timmy and Vicky; Give Us a Break; Winter Break; William Tell (US title Crossbow); Ricky Butcher in EastEnders (1988-).
Films: Younger Ned in Revolution (1985, playing Al Pacino's son).
Address: c/o Sandra Boyce Management. Lives in London. Single. Hobbies: Golf.

PACE, Norman
Norman Pace. Comedian. b. Dudley, Worcestershire, 17 February 1953. Worked as a teacher before forming a double-act with Gareth Hale and turning professional as an entertainer.
TV: Pushing Up Daisies; Coming Next; The Young Ones; Live from the Palladium; Saturday Live (host); Just for Laughs; The Saturday Gang; The Management; Hale & Pace (winner, Golden Rose of Montreux, 1989); Hale & Pace — The Business; Det Insp Peter Pascoe in A Pinch of Snuff (mini-series, 1994); Hale & Pace — The Tasty Morsels (compilation series); The Royal Variety Performance (1995).

Norman Pace

Books: Falsies; The Hale & Pace Book of Writes and Rons (both with Gareth Hale).
Records: Album: Hale & Pace Live in Concert (with Gareth Hale).
Address: c/o International Artistes. m. Beverley; 2 s. Liam, Charlie, 1 d. Holly.

PACKER, Suzanne
Suzanne Jackson. Actress. b. Cardiff, 1962. Sister of athlete Colin Jackson. Attended the National Youth Theatre of Wales and took a BA in theatre and drama at the University of Warwick. Trained at the Webber Douglas Academy.
TV: Bowen; Josie Johnson in Brookside (1990-1); Helen Mitchell in The Lifeboat.
Address: c/o Kerry Gardner Management. Lives in London. Single. Hobbies: Swimming, yoga, reading, watching sport.

Suzanne Packer

Nicola Pagett

PAGETT, Nicola

Nicola Mary Scott. Actress. b. Cairo, Egypt, 15 June 1945. Trained at RADA.

TV: *Flowering Cherry; Danger Man; Barlow at Large; The Persuaders!; Cock Hen and Courting Pit; Blood of Lamb; Dangerous Corner; Wicked Women;* Miss Elizabeth Bellamy in *Upstairs, Downstairs* (series); *The Rivals of Sherlock Holmes; Napoleon; The Sweeney; French without Tears;* title role in *Anna Karenina; War and Peace; Love Story; Scoop; Redundance — or the Wife's Revenge; Take the Stage; A Woman of Substance* (mini-series); *Aren't We All; Hand in Glove; Shadow of the Sun* (mini-series); Liz Rodenhurst in *A Bit of a Do* (two series); Sonia Drysdale in *Ain't Misbehavin'* (two series).

Films: *The Viking Queen;* Princess Mary in *Anne of the Thousand Days;* Clare in *There's a Girl in My Soup;* Anna in *Operation Daybreak; Frankenstein; Seven Men at Daybreak; Oliver's Story; Timeless Land; The Homecoming; Privates on Parade; All of You.* Address: c/o James Sharkey Associates. Lives in London. m. writer Graham Swannell; 1 d. Eve (b. 16 April 1979). Hobbies: Walking, gardening.

Michael Palin

PALIN, Michael

Michael Palin. Actor/Writer. b. Sheffield, South Yorkshire, 5 May 1943. Gained a degree in modern history from Oxford, where he wrote comedy material and acted in university productions.

TV: *The Marty Feldman Comedy Machine; The Frost Report; Do Not Adjust Your Set; Complete and Utter History of Britain; Monty Python's Flying Circus; How to Irritate People; Pythons in Deutschland; Secrets; Ripping Yarns; More Ripping Yarns; The Rutbles: All You Need Is Cash; Three Men in a Boat; Confessions of a Train Spotter; East of Ipswich* (TVM); *Number 27; Around the World In 80 Days;* Jim Nelson in *G.B.H.; Pole to Pole; Tracey Ullman: A Class Act; Great Railway Journeys: Derry to Kerry; Palin's Column; Oliver 2* (Comic Relief, 1995); *The Wind in the Willows* (voice only, 1995).

Films: *And Now for Something Completely Different; Monty Python and the Holy Grail; Pleasure at Her Majesty's; Jabberwocky; Monty Python's Life of Brian; The Secret Policeman's Ball; The Secret Policeman's Other Ball; Time Bandits* (also writer); *The Missionary* (also writer); *Monty Python Live at the Hollywood Bowl; Monty Python's The Meaning of Life* (also writer); *A Private Function; The Secret Policeman's Private Parts; Brazil; The Dress; A Fish Called Wanda; American Friends* (also writer). Address: c/o Mayday Management. Lives in London. m. 1966 Helen Gibbins; 1 d. Rachel, 2 s. Thomas, William.

Geoffrey Palmer

PALMER, Geoffrey

Geoffrey Palmer. Actor. b. London, 4 June 1927. Started as an unpaid trainee ASM at the Q Theatre.

TV: *The Avengers; Colditz; The Sweeney; Who Is Sylvia?; The Shopper; The Liberation of Eileen; Churchill's People; A Story to Frighten the Children; Maiden's Trip; The Scorpion Factor; Death of an Expert Witness; Games;* Jimmy in *The Fall and Rise of Reginald Perrin* (series, 1976-9); *The Houseboy; A Little Rococo;* Ben Parkinson in *Butterflies* (series, 1978-82); *Fawlty Towers; A Midsummer Night's Dream;* Leo Bannister in *The Last Song* (two series, 1981, 1983); Foreign Secretary in *Whoops Apocalypse!* (series, 1982); *Waters of the Moon; Absurd Person Singular; The Professionals; Cheap Day; Radio Pictures; Fairly Secret Army; Hot Metal; The Insurance Man; Season's Greetings; After the War; Christabel;* Donald Fairchild in *Executive Stress* (three series, 1986-8); *Bergerac; Blackadder Goes Forth; Smack and Thistle; A Question of Attribution* (TVM); *As Time Goes By* (five series, 1992-6); *Inspector Morse; The Real Thing* (narrator); *The Inspector Alleyn Mysteries: Hand in Glove; Stalag Luft; Magpie inthe Dock; Full Throttle* (Heroes & Villains); *Look at the State We're In!; Nanny Knows Best.*

Films: *O Lucky Man!; The Outsider; Retribution; The Honorary Consul; A Zed and Two Noughts; Clockwise;* Judge in *A Fish Called Wanda;* Saab Salesman in *Hawks;* Warren in *The Madness of King George.* Address: c/o Marmont Management. m. Sally; 1 s. Charles, 1 d. Harriet.

Toni Palmer

PALMER, Toni

Antonia Sarah Palmer. Actress. b. London, 17 September 1932. Trained as a dancer.

TV: *The Rag Trade* (series); *Within These Walls; Take My Wife; The Confederacy of Wives; Russ Abbot's Madhouse; King and Castle; West End Tales; Kelly Monteith; The Cuckoo Sister* (series); Blossom in *Only Fools and Horses; Mog!; Ellis Island* (mini-series); *Hi-de-Hi!; The Bill; London's Burning; Bergerac; Rumpole of the Bailey; Return of the Antelope; The Ghostbusters of East Finchley.*

Films: *The French Lieutenant's Woman; The Doctor and the Devils; Smashing Time; Ellis Island* (edited version of TV mini-series); *Personal Services; The Young Americans; Splitting Heirs; Sir Henry at Rawlinson End.* Address: c/o Barry Brown & Partner. Lives in Shepperton, Middlesex. m. 1st James Dark (dis), 2nd theatre writer-director Ken Hill (dec).

Judy Parfitt

PARFITT, Judy

Judy Parfitt. Actress. b. Sheffield, South Yorkshire, 7 November.

TV: *Girl in a Bird Cage; Jackson's Wharf; Bullseye; Sentimental Agent; Odd Man; Villette; Edith Nesbitt; The Suffragettes; Edward G; Daughters of the Late Colonel; The Edwardians; Malice Aforethought; Pride and Prejudice; Death of a Princess; Secret Orchards; Grand Duo; Redundant — or the Wife's Revenge; The Jewel in the Crown; Bon Voyage; The Charmer; The Charmings;* Lady Constance Lytton in

Shoulder to Shoulder; Guests of the Emperor; The Blackheath Poisonings (mini-series); *Medics; The Inspector Alleyn Mysteries; The Borrowers; The Lifeboat* (series); *P G Wodehouse's Heavy Weather*.
Films: *Hide and Seek; Hamlet; Galileo; Saturday, Sunday, Monday; Champions; Street Dreams; Mr Pyg; Maurice; Getting It Right; Diamond Skulls; King Ralph.* Address: c/o Conway, van Gelder, Robinson.

PARKIN, Simon
Simon Parkin. Presenter. b. Manchester, 11 April 1967. Entered radio in 1987 and TV a year later.
TV: *Children's BBC* (1988); *Now on Two; UP2U; Top of the Pops; The Ozone; CBBC2; But First This; Record Breakers; Going Live!; On the Waterfront; The 8.15 from Manchester; The Noel Edmonds Saturday Roadshow; Noel's House Party; Open Air; People Today; Jim'll Fix It; Children in Need; Hearts of Gold; The Ross King Show,* GMTV (1993-); *Go Getters; What's Up Doc?; Saturday Disney; Teen Win, Lose or Draw; The Word.* Address: c/o Dave Warwick. Single.

Simon Parkin

PARKINSON, Michael
Michael Parkinson. Presenter. b. Cudworth, South Yorkshire, 28 March 1935.
TV: *Scene* (Granada Television, producer-interviewer); *Granada in the North; World in Action; What the Papers Say; 24 Hours;* executive producer, LWT sports documentaries; *Cinema; Teabreak; Anatomy of Pop; Where in the World; Sports Arena; Movie Quiz; Parkinson* (BBC, then Channel 10, Australia); founder-member of TV-am (presenter of *Good Morning Britain*); *Give Us a Clue; All Star Secrets; Parkinson One to One; Parky; The Help Squad;* Presenter in *Ghostwatch; Bruce Forsyth — 50 Years in Showbusiness* (1992); *Les Dawson: The Entertainer* (1994); *Parkinson: The Interviews* (series); *Rumble in the Jungle* (narrator); *Going For a Song* (host, two series, 1995-6). Address: c/o IMG. Lives in Berkshire. m. TV presenter Mary Parkinson; 3 s. Andrew, Nicholas, Michael. Hobbies: Golf, cricket.

Michael Parkinson

PARRY, Ken
Ken Parry. Actor. b. Wigan, Lancashire, 20 June 1930.
TV: *Z Cars* (as 13 different villains); *The Sweeney; Crossroads; A Midsummer Night's Dream; The Merchant of Venice; Coronation Street; Home a' Plenty; Never Say Die; Hazell; The Big Sleep; Vice Versa; King's Royal; Filthy Rich and Catflap; The Young Ones; Kelly Monteith; Blott on the Landscape;* Jack Crossley in *Children's Ward* (six series); *Saracen;* Royston Bloat in *The House of Windsor.*
Films: *Just for Fun; The Bawdy Adventures of Tom Jones; The Liquidator; The Taming of the Shrew; Two Times Two; A Whole Lot of Trouble; Start the Revolution without Me; That's Your Funeral; The Adventure of Sherlock Holmes' Smarter Brother; The Adventures of Joseph Andrews; Spring and Port Wine; Come Play with Me; What's Up Nurse; Mistress Pamela; Benjamin Franklin; Life Force; D'Ardanelle; Lisztomania; The Rainbow Thief; The Miller's Tale.* Address: c/o PBR Management. Lives in London. Single. Hobbies: Good music, reading, vintage films, clairvoyance (is a spiritual medium).

Ken Parry

PARSONS, Nicholas
Christopher Nicholas Parsons. Actor/Presenter. b. Grantham, Lincolnshire, 10 October 1928.
TV: *The Eric Barker Half-Hour; The Arthur Haynes Show* (1956-66); *The Benny Hill Show* (1969-70); *Sale of the Century* (1971-84); *Alphabet Quiz; Mr Jolly Lives Next Door* (The Comic Strip Presents…); *Doctor Who; Laughlines* (BSB); *Cluedo* (series); *A Bit of Fry and Laurie; Just a Minute; Londoners.*
Films: *Master of Bankdam; To Dorothy a Son; Simon and Laura; An Alligator Named Daisy; Eyewitness; The Long Arm; Brothers in Law; Happy Is the Bride!; Too Many Crooks; Carleton-Browne of the FO; Upstairs and Downstairs; Doctor in Love; Let's Get Married; Carry On Regardless; Every Day's a Holiday; Murder Ahoy; The Wrong Box; The Ghost Goes Gear; Don't Raise the Bridge, Lower the River; Danger Point!; Mad Dogs and Cricketers* (also writer-director); *The Best of Benny Hill; Spy Story; Relatively Greek* (also director); *Mr Jolly Lives Next Door.* Address: c/o Susan Shaper. Lives in the Cotswolds and London. m. 1st 1954 actress Denise Bryer (dis 1984), 2nd 1995 Ann Reynolds; 1 d. Suzy, 1 s. Justin (both from 1st m.). Hobbies: Gardening, photography, repairing clocks and playing games (indoor and outdoor).

Nicholas Parsons

PASCO, Richard
Richard Pasco. Actor. b. Barnes, London, 18 July 1926. CBE, 1977. Trained at the Central School of Speech and Drama (Gold Medal winner). Acted with the RSC (1969-74, 1979-82).
TV: *Henry Irving; Dial M for Murder; Traveller without Luggage; Ivanov; The Three Musketeers; As You Like It; Julius Caesar; The Chief Mourner; The British in Love; Sweet Wine of Youth; The Poisoned Gift; Trouble with Gregory; Philby; Siegfried Idyll; The Emergency Channel; John Donne; Disraeli; Ghosts; Savages; The Houseboy; Timon of Athens; Let's Run Away to Africa; Pythons on the Mountain; Sorrell & Son; Arch of Triumph* (TVM); *Drummonds; Hannay; The Man from the Pru;* William Bryce-Morgan in *Inspector Morse: Dead on Time; Bird's-Eye View: Inis Fail/Isle of Destiny* (readings).
Films: *Sword of Sherwood Forest; Room at the Top; Yesterday's Enemy; The Gorgon; Rasputin; Hot Enough for June; The Watcher in the Woods; Wagner.* Address: c/o Michael Whitehall. m. 1st Greta Watson (dis), 2nd actress Barbara Leigh-Hunt; 1 s. William (from 1st m.).

Richard Pasco

Bill Paterson

Andrew Paul

Jeremy Paxman

Deena Payne

Daniel Peacock

PATERSON, Bill

William Tulloch Paterson. Actor. b. Glasgow, 3 June 1945. An apprentice quantity surveyor (1963-6) before training at the Royal Scottish Academy of Music and Drama (1966-9).
TV: *Licking Hitler; The Vanishing Army; The Lost Tribe; The Cherry Orchard; United Kingdom; Smiley's People;* Ally Fraser in *Auf Wiedersehen Pet* (Series 2); *The Cheviot; The Stag and the Black Black Oil* (Play for Today); Dr Gibon in *The Singing Detective; The Interrogation of John;* Jack Lithgow in *Traffik; Shrinks; Yellowbacks; Tell Tale Hearts* (mini-series); *Lenny Henry in Dreams; God on the Rocks* (TVM); *Artists for Bosnia* (performing *Death and the Maiden*); *Wall of Silence* (Screen One); *Yo Picasso; Hard Times; Jackanory* (storyteller); *The Turnaround* (pilot, 1995); *The Pen* (Tartan Shorts); Baxter in *Oliver's Travels* (series, 1995); *The Ghostbusters of East Finchley* (series, 1995); *First Light* (reading).
Films: *Friendship's Death; The Killing Fields; Comfort and Joy; Hidden City; A Private Function; Defence of the Realm; The Adventures of Baron Munchausen; Just Ask for Diamond; The Rachel Papers; The Witches; Chaplin; Truly Madly Deeply; Victory; Richard III.*
Address: c/o Marina Martin Associates. Lives in North London. m. stage and film designer Hildegard Bechtler; 1 s. Jack, 1 d. Anna. Pets: A hamster called Sammy. Hobbies: Cycling.

PAUL, Andrew

Paul Andrew Herman. Actor. b. London, 17 March 1961. Trained at the Anna Scher Theatre School from the age of 14. Stage productions include *Grease* (Astoria Theatre) and *Shout across the River* (RSC).
TV: Barry in *Help: The Setbacks; Tripper's Day;* Roger in *Barnet;* Timmy and Vicky; Tony in *Out of Tune;* Wayne in *Time of My Life; Out; Going Out; Mrs Capper's Birthday; Slinger's Day; The Bill; Gentlemen and Players; Sizzler; Vote for Hitler; After Image; Vote for Them; Inspector Morse; Missing Persons;* Paul in *Don't Wait Up;* PC Dave Quinnan in *The Bill.*
Films: *The Pirates of Penzance;* Betts in *Scum; Bellman and True.*
Address: c/o Scott Marshall. Lives in London. m. Laura; 2 s. Ben, Nicholas. Hobbies: Reading, cinema, music, golf, football, cricket (all sport).

PAXMAN, Jeremy

Jeremy Paxman. Presenter. b. Leeds, 11 May 1950.
TV: *Tonight; Panorama; London Plus; Six o'Clock News; Breakfast Time; Newsnight; The Bear Next Door; Did You See...?; France Decides: A Newsnight Special* (1992); *Election Call* (before European Parliament elections, 1994); *University Challenge* (questionmaster, two series, 1994-6); *Newsnight Special* (on French presidential electioins, 1995); *You Decide — with Paxman* (series, 1995).
Films: *Called to Account — How Roberto Calvi Died.*
Books: *A Higher Form of Killing; Through the Volcanoes; Friends in High Places.*
Awards: RTS International Current Affairs award (1984).
Address: c/o Simpson Fox Associates/BBC TV News & Current Affairs.

PAYNE, Deena

Diane Margaret Payne. Actress. b. Orpington, Kent, 29 August 1954. Trained in dance and drama at the Arts Educational School and under Nina Finburgh and Carlin Glynn. Singer with Alan Price and B A Robertson, and made albums with Eric Burdon, Alvin Lee, John Farnham and Alan Price. In original West End cast of *They're Playing Our Song.*
TV: *Oh Boy!; Top of the Pops; Superpop; Hogmanay; Get It Together; Gas Street; Pebble Mill at One; Rock Follies '77; The Bill;* Lorraine in *Tales of Sherwood Forest;* Viv Windsor in *Emmerdale* (1993-).
Films: *Valentino; Music Machine.* Address: c/o Elaine Murphy Associates. Lives in Hillingdon, Middlesex. m. percussionist Frank Ricotti (dis). Partner: Musician Steve Grant; 1 s. William Anthony Payne-Grant (b. 1992). Pets: A huge cat called Alfie. Hobbies: Cycling, sewing, cooking, reading, relaxing.

PEACOCK, Daniel

Daniel Peacock. Actor/Writer. b. London, 2 October 1958. Son of actor Trevor Peacock (qv); stepson of actress Tilly Tremayne. Trained at the Central School of Speech and Drama.
TV: *Shine on Harvey Moon; Radio; Long Distance Information; Little Armadillos;* Enoch Drain in *The Kenny Everett Show; Five Go Mad in Dorset* (The Comic Strip Presents...); *Five Go Mad on Mescalin* (The Comic Strip Presents...); *War; A Fistful of Travellers Cheques; The Beat Generation; Gino: Full Story and Pics* (The Comic Strip Presents...); *Assaulted Nuts; Just Good Friends;* Mental Mickey in *Only Fools and Horses; Robin of Sherwood; C.A.T.S. Eyes;* Denny in *The Lenny Henry Show; Girls on Top; Alas Smith and Jones; Supergran; From the Top; Valentine Park; Pulaski;* Nord in *Doctor Who; Mr Majeika; A Christmas Story; Hard Cases; Boon; Close to Home;* Jackson Pace (also writer); *Trainer; Diary of a Teenage Health Freak* (also writer, two series); Roger Morgan in *Cluedo;* Kazanzi in *One Foot in the Grave;* Gilby Watson in *Men of the World* (also deviser-writer, two series, 1994-5).
Films: *Scrooge; He Who Rides a Tiger; Quadrophenia;* Rudge in *Porridge; Red Saturday; Riding High; Electric Blue; Gandhi; Party Party* (also writer); Young Clouseau in *Trail of the Pink Panther; Jewel*

on the Nile; Supergrass; Whoops Apocalypse; Eat the Rich; The Strike; Blood Runner; Bull in Robin Hood: Prince of Thieves. Address: c/o Annette Stone Associates. Lives i Friern Barnet, North London. m. Ceri; 1 d. Carly (from previous relationship with Julia). Pets: Three cats. Hobbies: 'Watching Spurs.'

PEACOCK, Trevor

Trevor Peacock

Trevor Peacock. Actor/Writer. b. Tottenham, North London, 19 May 1931. Acted with RSC (1975-6).
TV: The Lads; The Old Curiosity Shop; Grandad; She Stoops to Conquer; A Choice of Evils (Play for Today); Soldiers Talking Clearly (Play for Today); Born and Bred; The Insurance Man; Twelfth Night; Pericles; Titus Andronicus; Henry VI; Oedipus at Colonus; The Lady's Not for Burning; Life of George Grosz; Wish Me Luck (Series 3); The Bill (two roles); Sweet Nothings (Screen One); Dodgem; Merlin of the Crystal Cave; Antonia and Jane; Shoot the Revolution; The Gravy Train; Last of the Summer Wine; Boon; Van Der Valk; Permanent Red; Dodgem; Spatz; Trainer; Minder; George Critchley in Growing Pains (series); Between the Lines; Maigret; A Very Polish Practice (Screen One); One Foot in the Grave; Chef!; Acky in The Riff Raff Element (two series, 1993-4); The Bill; Brighton Belles; Casualty; Harry; A Terrible Coldness — Graham Young (Crime Story); Love Hurts; The Smell of Reeves and Mortimer; Highlander; Mr Cadzow in Meat (Screen One); Jim Trott in The Vicar of Dibley (series, 1994); Mud; Stick with Me, Kid.
Films: Still Life; Gravedigger in Hamlet; Bejewelled; The Trial; Is Mr Death In? Address: c/o Scott Marshall. Lives in Richmond-upon-Thames, Surrey. m. 1st Iris (dis 1975), 2nd actress Tilly Tremayne; 1 s. actor-writer Daniel (qv), 1 d. Sally (both from 1st m.), 1 s. actor Harry, 1 d. Maudie (both from 2nd m.). Pets: Several cats, one dog. Hobbies: 'Music, leaping and rolling (down slopes).'

PEARSON, NEIL

Neil Pearson

Neil Pearson. Actor. b. Battersea, South London. West End stage roles include Hal in Loot.
TV: Morrie in Intimate Contact; Napper in Oi for England; John in Home Video; Cock Roach in Submariners; Bell Run; Nik Targett in Upline; The Adman in Les Girls; Jack Binge in Eskimos Do It; Mungo in Chelmsford 123 (two series); Dave in Drop the Dead Donkey (four series); Gary in That's Love; This Is David Lander; Tony Clark in Between the Lines (three series, 1992-4); The Travel Show (guest reporter, in Beirut); One Foot in the Past (guest reporter); Latin for a Dark Room (Tartan Shorts).
Films: Privates on Parade; The Secret Rapture. Address: c/o ICM. Lives in South London. Single.

PEASGOOD, Julie

Julie Peasgood

Julie Peasgood. Actress. Stage plays include Pericles, Baal, Nicholas Nickleby and Volpone (all RSC).
TV: Cherry Ripe and the Lugworm Digger (Seven Faces of Woman); A Journey to London; Five Red Herrings; Clayhanger; Survivors; This Year Next Year; The Beaux' Stratagem; The Law Centre; Whistling Wally; Dancers — Feel Free; The Optimist; Mountain Men; Imaginary Friends; Small World; Anne in First Born; Brush Strokes; Chains of Love; Alas Smith and Jones; Boon; Van Der Valk; Spender; Nellie in Perfect Scoundrels; 2point4 Children; Fran in Brookside; Roxy/Jenny in September Song (series, 1993); The 10%ers; Eden in Luv (two series); Taggart: Death without Dishonour; King of the Road (co-presenter, series); Newshound (co-presenter, series); Sandra in A Woman's Guide to Adultery (mini-series); Murder Most Horrid; Carmen Talbot in Chandler & Co (series); Good Morning... with Anne & Nick (TV critic); The Bill; BUGS; Men of the World; The Ruth Rendell Mysteries: Simisola.
Films: The Lake; Mary in The House of the Long Shadows. Address: c/o Peters Fraser & Dunlop.

PECK, Brian

Brian Peck

Brian Peck. Actor/Theatre director. b. Hull, East Yorkshire, 24 October 1930. Started career as a child actor in 1946, appearing in children's films. Trained at the Webber Douglas Academy (1951-2).
TV: Smike in Nicholas Nickleby (1957); Ride on the Donkeys; Walk on the Grass; The Exiles; Gracie; The Immortal Evan Harris; This Happy Breed; The Queen Came By; The Long Chase; Trial; The Dragon's Opponent; The Druid Circle; Dixon of Dock Green; The Brothers; Z Cars; Softly Softly; Six Days of Justice; Jackanory; Doomwatch; Coronation Street; Crossroads; Killers; An Englishman's Castle; Shadows; Culliford in Codename; Rising Damp; The Chief Mourner; Break in the Sun; Bly Jim and the Flguro Club; Hark at Barker; Say You Will; Strange but True; Minder; Murder Unproven; Open Season; Universe Downstairs; Barnet; Hells Bells; The Bill; Boon; Sorry!; Last of the Summer Wine; London's Burning; Soh
Films: Title role in The Voyage of Peter Joe. Address: c/o PBR Management. Lives in London and south-west France. m. 1959 actress Jennifer Wilson (qv); 1 d. actress-singer Melanie Peck.

PEERS, Kerry

Kerry Peers

Kerry Roberta Peers. Actress. b. Northophall, Mancot, Clwyd, 1 November 1964. Trained at the Central School of Speech and Drama (1985-8). Stage roles include Émile in Les Liaisons Dangereuses (RSC).
TV: Christine in Chimera (mini-series) and Chimera — The Movie (re-edited); We Are Seven; Jenny and WDC Suzi Croft in The Bill (1993-); The Touch, With Two Lumps of Ice; Nurse in September Song; Linda in The Marshal (pilot). Address: c/o Roxane Vacca Management. Lives in London. Partner: Keith. Pets: Two cats called Yoffi and Bruno. Hobbies: Swimming, cycling, reading, watching films.

Susan Penhaligon

PENHALIGON, Susan

Susan Penhaligon. Actress. b. Manila, Philippines. Trained at the Webber Douglas Academy.

TV: *Public Eye; Country Matters;* Prue in *A Bouquet of Barbed Wire* (series, 1976); Lucy Westenra in *Count Dracula; Fearless Frank; The Taming of the Shrew;* Helen in *A Fine Romance* (four series, 1981-4); *A Kind of Loving; Heather Ann; Remington Steele; A Kind of Living* (presenter); *Heart of the Country; Bergerac;* Julia Charlesworth in *Trouble in Mind* (series, 1991); *Casualty; Wycliffe.*

Films: *Say Hello to Yesterday; Private Road; Under Milk Wood; No Sex, Please – We're British; The Last Chapter* (short); *The Land That Time Forgot; Miracles Still Happen; House of Mortal Sin* (US title *The Confessional*); *Nasty Habits;* Janet in *The Uncanny; Leopard in the Snow; Patrick; Soldier of Orange* (also titled *Survival Run*). Address: c/o Marina Martin Associates. m. 1st Nicholas Loukes (dis), 2nd TV documentary director David Munro (dis 1983), 3rd actor Duncan Preston (dis 1993); 1 s. actor Truan Munro (from 2nd m.). Pets: A dachshund called JJ. Hobbies: Writing poetry, reading, holidays.

Tricia Penrose

PENROSE, Tricia

Patricia Penrose. Actress/Singer. b. Liverpool, 9 April 1970. Trained at the Elliott-Clarke School.

TV: Ruth (aged 14) and WPC Emma Reid in *Brookside; Help!; Albion Market; Boon;* Julie in *How to Be Cool; Split Ends; Katy's Story* (German TV); *Tydi Bywyd yn Boen! (Isn't Life a Pain!)* (TVM); *Shooting Stars* (TVM); *Medics; Coasting;* Louise in *Emmerdale; Terraces;* hotel receptionist in *Coronation Street;* Gina Ward in *Heartbeat* (Series 2-6, 1993-7); *Pardon My French* (co-presenter, *This Morning*).

Films: *Vroom; Cresta Run; Dancin' thru the Dark.* Address: c/o Joan Brown Associates. Lives in Liverpool. Single. Pets: A cat called Snowy. Hobbies: Listening to music, dancing, cinema and theatre.

Lynne Perrie

PERRIE, Lynne

Jean Dudley. Actress/Singer. b. Rotherham, South Yorkshire, 7 April 1931. Sister of actor-comedian Duggie Brown (qv). Formerly a singer-comedienne in clubs in UK, France, Germany, US and South Africa.

TV: *Slattery's Mounted Foot; Leeds United; Follyfoot; Mrs Petty; Queenie's Castle; The Intruder; Crown Court; It Was a Good Story, Don't Knock It;* Ivy Brennan (formerly Tilsley) in *Coronation Street* (1971-94); *Royal Variety Performance* (with *Street* cast, 1989); *Fight Cancer* (co-presenter).

Films: Mother in *Kes; Yanks.* Address: c/o Johnny Riscoe. Lives in Manchester. m. Derrick Barksby (sep); 1 s. Stephen. Hobbies: Horse and greyhound racing.

Bill Pertwee

PERTWEE, Bill

William Desmond Pertwee. Actor/Comedian. b. Amersham, Buckinghamshire, 21 July 1926. Nephew of playwright Roland; cousin of playwright Michael and actor Jon (qv).

TV: ARP Warden Hodges in *Dad's Army; Jackanory; Sykes; Billy Liar; Frost Weekly; The Larry Grayson Show; Pierrots;* Tom, Dick and Harriet; *Chance in a Million; Halls of Fame; Super Troupers; By Royal Command; Spytrap; Pob;* PC Wilson in *You Rang, M'Lord?; The Station Now Standing; Woof!*

Films: *The Seven Magnificent Deadly Sins; Psychomania; Carry On Loving; Dad's Army; Action; Confessions of a Pop Performer; What's Up Nurse; See How They Run.*

Radio: *Beyond Our Ken; Round the Horne.* Address: c/o The Richard Stone Partnership. Lives in Surrey. m. Marion; 1 s. actor James. Hobbies: Cricket, gardening, swimming.

Jon Pertwee

PERTWEE, Jon

John Devon Roland Pertwee. Actor. b. Chelsea, London, 7 July 1919. Son of playwright Roland; brother of playwright Michael; cousin of actor Bill (qv). Trained at RADA.

TV: *Toad of Toad Hall* (1946); *Round the Bend; 6.5 Special; Dangerous Cargo; Can Do; Sunday Night at the London Palladium* (compère); *Ivanhoe; Dick Whittington and His Cat; The Amazing Adventures of Commander Highprice; Evans Above; Glencannon; The Dickie Henderson Show; Five o'Clock Club; Jon Pertwee Show; The Good Old Days; Jackanory* (storyteller); *The Avengers; From Venus with Love; Three of a Kind; Beggar My Neighbour; The Rolf Harris Show;* title role in *Doctor Who* (third Doctor, 1970-4, 24 stories, 128 episodes); *The Three Doctors; The Final Chapter; Whodunnit?* (presenter, three series); *The Goodies;* title role in *Worzel Gummidge* (four series, 1979-82); *Worzel's Christmas Special: A Cup o' Tea an' a Slice o' Cake* (1981) and *Worzel Gummidge Down Under* (two series); *The Children's Royal Variety Performance* (1982, 1990); *Omnibus; The Five Doctors* (Doctor Who 20th-anniversary special, 1983); *SuperTed* (voice only); *The Little Green Man* (all voices); *The Curious Case of Santa Claus* (TVM); *Do You Know the Milky Way?; Virtual Murder* (TVM); *Doctor Who – Dimensions in Time; The Young Indiana Jones Chronicles; Doctor Who: Dimensions in Time* (Children in Need, 1993); *Harry Hills Fruit Corner.*

Films: Selection (from 47): *A Yank at Oxford* (début, 1937); *Knock on Wood* (Danny Kaye's stand-in); *Carry On Cleo; Carry On Cowboy; Carry On Screaming; A Funny Thing Happened on the Way to the Forum; Wombling Free* (voice only); *The Water Babies* (voice only); *The Boys in Blue; Have You Ever Heard of the Milky Way?; Carry On Columbus; Africana 2000.* Address: c/o Susan Shaper. Lives in Putney, London. m. 1st 1955 actress Jean Marsh (dis 1960), 2nd 1960 novelist Ingeborg Rhoesa; 1 d. actress Dariel, 1 s. actor Sean (qv) (both from 2nd m.). Hobbies: Water sports, art collecting.

PERTWEE, Sean

Sean Pertwee. Actor. b. London, 4 June 1964. Son of actor Jon Pertwee (qv); grandson of playwright Roland; nephew of playwright Michael. Trained at Bristol Old Vic Theatre School.

TV: *Hard Cases; Agatha Christie's Poirot; Casualty; Houseplant, Chancer, Lockerbie; The Chief; Harry Enfield's Television Programme; Speed; Christmas Cluedo; Clarissa; Virtual Murder* (TVM); *The Young Indiana Jones Chronicles; The Last Laugh; The Ruth Rendell Mysteries: Kissing the Gunner's Daughter; Boon; Peak Practice; The Changeling; Without Walls: For One Night Only — Errol Flynn; Cadfael; A Touch of Frost; Bodyguards.*

Films: *Prick Up Your Ears; Coping with Cupid* (BFI production); *London Kills Me; Swing Kids; Leon the Pig Farmer; Dirty Weekend; Shopping; I.D.* Address: c/o Jonathan Altaras. Lives in London. Single.

Sean Pertwee

PETTIFER, Julian

Julian Pettifer. Presenter. b. Malmesbury, Wiltshire, 21 July 1935.

TV: Southern TV reporter; *Tonight; 24 Hours; Panorama* (both as war correspondent); *90 South; War without End; Millionaire; Vietnam — The Other World; The Regiment; The Country Game; World about Us; The China Programme; The History of Civil Aviation; Nature Watch; Diamonds in the Sky; The Living Isles; World Safari; Only One Earth; Automania; Busman's Holiday; Africawatch; Missionaries; Safari UK; Biteback; See for Yourself — A Biteback Special; Defenders of the Wild; Ocean Challenge; The Little World of the Little Pony; Assignment; Murder in the Family* (narrator); *The Natural World* (narrator); *Frontline* (on Vietnam, 1993); *Ocean Challenge — One Year On; Sunday Brunch* (series, 1995); *Correspondent; Timewatch: The BBC in Vietnam; Right or Wrong* (series, 1995). Address: c/o Curtis Brown.

Julian Pettifer

PHILBIN, Maggie

Maggie Philbin. Presenter. b. Manchester, 23 June 1955. Gained a degree in English and drama.

TV: *Multi Coloured Swap Shop; The Show Me Show; Ticket to Ride; Tomorrow's World; The Saturday Picture Show; The Quest; Hospital Watch; Bodymatters Roadshow; Breast Cancer* (*This Morning*); *Primetime; Help Your Child with Reading.* Address: c/o Dave Winslett. m. Keith Chegwin (dis 1993); 1 d. Rose.

PHILLIPS, Leslie

Leslie Phillips. Actor. b. Tottenham, North London, 20 April 1924. Trained at Italia Conti Stage Academy.

TV: *Morning Departure* (1948); *My Wife Jacqueline; Voice in Vision; Heroes Don't Care; Carry On Admiral; Our Man at St Mark's; Impasse; Time and Motion Man; Mrs Moonlight; A Murder Has Been Arranged; The Reluctant Debutante; The Gong Game; Foreign Affairs; Blandings Castle; A Very Fine Line; The Suit; Father Dear Father; Culture Vultures; Casanova; Redundant — or the Wife's Revenge; You'll Never See Me Again; The Lion, the Witch and the Wardrobe; Mr Palfrey of Westminster; The South Bank Show; Monte Carlo; Rumpole of the Bailey; Summer's Lease; Chancer; GLC and Oxford* (both *The Comic Strip Presents…*); *Who Bombed Birmingham?; Life after Life; Thacker; The Trials of Oz; Boon; Lovejoy; Royal Celebration; The Changeling; Bermuda Grace* (TVM); *Honey for Tea; The House of Windsor; Love on a Branch Line; Two Golden Balls; The Ruth Rendell Mysteries: Vanity Dies Hard.*

Films: Selection (from 62): *A Lassie from Lancashire* (début, 1935); *Carry On Nurse; Carry On Teacher; The Navy Lark; Inn for Trouble; Carry On Constable; Doctor in Love; Crooks Anonymous; The Fast Lady; Doctor in Clover; Doctor in Trouble; Out of Africa; Scandal.* Address: c/o Conway, van Gelder, Robinson. m. 1st (dis), 2nd actress Angela Scoular; 2 d. Caroline, Claudia, 2 s. Andrew, Roger (all from 1st m.).

Maggie Philbin

PHILLIPS, Siân

Siân Phillips. Actress. b. Betws, Wales, 14 May 1934. Hon D Litt, University of Wales. Trained at RADA.

TV: BBC TV announcer and newsreader (aged 18); *The Quiet Man; A Game for Eskimos; Granite; The Garden of Loneliness; Treason; King's Daughter; Land of Song; Who's Next; Strangers in the Room; The Tortoise and the Hare; Don Juan in Hell; It Happened Like This; The Other Man; Eh Joe; Espionage; The Sex Game; City '68; Thief; Women Can Be Monsters; The Vessel of Wrath; The Beast in the Jungle; Story; Platanov; Sharing the Honours; Lady Windermere's Fan; The Man Outside; Shoulder to Shoulder; Jennie; Jackanory; The Shadow; How Green Was My Valley; I Claudius; The Achurch Letters; Heartbreak House; Boadicea; Off to Philadelphia in the Morning; The Oresteia; Crime and Punishment; Tinker, Tailor, Soldier, Spy; Winston Churchill — The Wilderness Years; Smiley's People; Barriors; Soan; The Carpathian Eagle; How Many Miles to Babylon; A Painful Case; Language and Landscape; George Borrow; The Two Mrs Grenvilles; Ewok 11; Out of Time; A Killing on the Exchange; Vanity Fair; I'd Like to Teach the World to Sing; The Show Spider; Shadow of the Noose; Perfect Scoundrels; Emlyn's Moon; Father Oleg/Mother Russia; Red Empire; Freddie and Max; The Borrowers; Fast Rewind: The RTS Lecture; Nearest and Dearest* (HTV); *A Mind to Kill; A Flick of the Switch; The Vacillations of Poppy Carew.*

Films: *Becket; Young Cassidy; Laughter in the Dark; Goodbye, Mr Chips; Murphy's War; Under Milk Wood; Beyond All Reason; Clash of the Titans; How Many Miles to Babylon; A Painful Case; Dune; Return to Endor; The Doctor and the Devils; Valmont; Dark River; Heidi; Age of Innocence.* Address: c/o Saraband. Lives in London. m. 1st D Roy (dis), 2nd 1959 actor Peter O'Toole (dis 1979), 3rd 1979 Robin Saks (dis 1992); 2 d. Kate, Pat (both from 2nd m.). Pets: Burmese cats. Hobbies: Gardening, drawing.

Leslie Phillips

Siân Phillips

Trevor Phillips

PHILLIPS, Trevor

Trevor Phillips. Presenter/Journalist. b. London, 31 December 1953.
TV: *Weekend World* (researcher); *The London Programme* (LWT, presenter and executive producer, 1987-); *Eyewitness; Nation* (presenter, series, 1993); *The London Programme Special* (one on race discrimination, one on children who rape, both 1994); *Rachel Nickell: The Untold Story* (*London Programme* special, 1994); *Westminster On-Line* (presenter, series, 1995); *The Radical Option — Reparations to Africa ; The Midnight Hour.* Address: c/o Jacque Evans Management. Lives in Muswell Hill, North London. m. 1981 Asha; 2 d. Sushila, Holly. Hobbies: Music.

PICKLES, Carolyn

Carolyn Pickles. Actress. b. Halifax, West Yorkshire, 8 February 1952. Daughter of Judge Pickles.
TV: *The Cost of Loving; Partisans; A Shepherd's Life; Bless Me, Father; Virginia Fly Is Drowning; Lace; The Gentle Touch; Willie's Last Stand; We'll Meet Again; Mr Right; Love Story; Whose Child; Letting the Birds Go Free; East Lynne; Miracles Take Longer; Juliet Bravo; Bulman; Bluebell; The Victoria Wood Show; The Enemy Within; Leaving Home; Blair;* Simone in *May to December* (six series, 1989-94); *Bread or Blood; Through the Dragon's Eye; Leopard; Chancer,* DCI Kim Reid in *The Bill; The Yellow Wallpaper,* Sarah Blake in *Boon;* Lady Ramsay in *The Tales of Para Handy* (two series 1994-5); Jane Rhodes in *Castles* (series, 1995); Geery Todd in *Casualty.*
Films: *Agatha; Tess; The Elephant Man; Brothers and Sisters; The Mirror Cracked; Champions.*
Address: c/o Conway, van Gelder, Robinson. Lives in London. m. artist Tark; 2 d., Lucy Jane, Hettie, 2 step-s. Tod, Theo. Pets: One cat. Hobbies: Four children and the occasional play, film, swim, sauna or doodle.

Carolyn Pickles

Ronald Pickup

PICKUP, Ronald

Ronald Alfred Pickup. Actor. b. Chester, 7 June 1940. Trained at RADA. TV since 1964.
TV: *Romeo and Juliet; Saint Joan; Roses of Eyam; Dragon's Opponent; All Good Men; Jennie; Long Day's Journey into Night; Mahler; Fight against Slavery; King Lear; Ghost Trio; Henry VIII; Memories; England's Green and Pleasant Land; Omnibus: The Life of Giuseppe Verdi; The Letter, Ivanhoe* (TVM); *Wagner; From a Far Country: Pope John Paul II* (TVM); *Einstein; Waters of the Moon; Orwell on Jura; Puccini; Fortunes of War; Bergerac; Chekhov in Yalta; Deathlock; The Hiding Place; Inspector Morse; Absolute Hell* (Performance); *John Le Carré's A Murder of Quality;* Andrew Powell in *A Time to Dance; The Golden Years* (TVM); *El C.I.D.;* Edwin Felt in *Lovejoy;* Roger Tundish in *The Riff Raff Element* (two series, 1993-4); Daniel Byrne in *The Rector's Wife* (series, 1994); *In the Cold Light of Day* (Screen Two); Sir Philip in *Dying Day* (Capital Lives, Carlton only, 1995); Douglas Beaumont in *Medics; Message for Posterity* (Performance); Jocelyn Fry in *Milner; Survival* (narrator); *The Nightmare Years* (mini-series); Brian Silcott in *A Very Open Prison* (Screen Two); *The Spirit of England* (presenter, series, 1995); title role in *King Henry IV* (Performance); Black Hearts in *Battersea* (series, 1996); Dr Richard Owen in *Silent Witness* (series, 1996); Moore in *The Ruth Rendell Mysteries: A Case of Coincidence.*
Films: *Three Sisters; The Day of the Jackal; Joseph Andrews; The Thirty-Nine Steps; Zulu Dawn; Nijinski; Never Say Never Again; Eleni; The Mission.* Address: c/o London Management. Lives in London. m. Lans Traverse; 1 s. Simon, 1 d. Rachel. Hobbies: Listening to music, walking, reading.

PIERCEY, Jennifer

Jennifer Piercey. Actress. Stage plays include *Saturday, Sunday, Monday, Equus, Joking Apart, Married Love, The Revenger's Comedies* (all West End) and *Golden Girls* (as the Doctor, RSC).
TV: *Bognor,* Martha in *Young Shoulders;* Beryl in *Man of Letters;* Sister Grant in *A Big Romping Boy,* Mrs Scott in *Grange Hill;* Giselle in *The Workshop;* Isa Mulvenny in *Portrait of Isa Mulvenny;* Mrs Campbell in *The Dunroamin' Rising;* Peggy Irvine in *Dialogue in the Dark;* Molly in *Home James!;* Mrs Jennings in *The Two of Us* (series); *Taggart;* WI Chairwoman in *Lovejoy;* Heather Lomax in *Advocates;* Chairwoman in *Rumpole of the Bailey;* Mrs Thompson in *Inspector Morse: Twilight of the Gods;* Lady Ailsa McKenzie in *Doctor Finlay;* Maureen Salmon in *The Chief* (Series 3, 1993); Antonia in *Absolutely Fabulous;* Mrs Pye in *Love on a Branch Line;* Eileen Wolstenhulme in *Coronation Street* (1995).
Films: Kirsty in *Another Time, Another Place;* Mrs Evers in *Friend or Foe* (BFI production).
Radio: Member of the BBC radio drama repertory company for two years. Address: c/o RKM.

Jennifer Piercey

Alexandra Pigg

PIGG, Alexandra

Sandra McKibbin. Actress. b. Liverpool. Stage roles include the stripper in *Metaphysics and Strip* (Everyman Theatre, Liverpool, and New End Theatre, Hampstead).
TV: Petra Taylor in *Brookside; Fast Eddie* in *Smart Money; Making Out; Murder East, Murder West.*
Films: Elaine in *Letter to Brezhnev, Strapless;* Bridget Baines in *A Chorus of Disapproval; Chicago Joe and the Showgirl.*
Awards: Films: *London Evening Standard* Outstanding Newcomer award for *Letter to Brezhnev* (1985). Address: c/o ICM.

PIGOTT-SMITH, Tim

Tim Pigott-Smith. Actor. b. Rugby, Warwickshire, 13 May 1946. Trained at the Bristol Old Vic Theatre School. Stage plays include *Bengal Lancer* and *Antony and Cleopatra*, plus RSC (1972-5).
TV: *Hamlet; Antony and Cleopatra; The Regiment; Doctor Who; The Glittering Prizes; North and South; Wings; Eustace and Hilda; Lost Boys; Measure for Measure; Henry IV, Part 1; No, Mama, No; 'Tis Pity She's a Whore; Hannah;* Hardy in *I Remember Nelson; Fame Is the Spur,* Brendan Bracken in *Winston Churchill — The Wilderness Years; The Hunchback of Notre Dame;* Ronald Merrick in *The Jewel in the Crown; State of Emergency; Dead Man's Folly; Challenge; The Secret Case of Sherlock;* Stafford in *The Chief* (Series 1 and 2); Francis Crick in *Horizon Special: Life Story;* Hubert in *The Bullion Boys* (Screen One); *Nomads of the Wind* (narrator, documentary series, 1994); Dr Evans/Mr Maradick in *Shadowy Third* (Ghosts).
Films: *Aces High; Romantic Rebellion; Joseph Andrews; Sweet William; The Day Christ Died; Clash of the Titans; Escape to Victory; Richard's Things; Lucky Village.*
Awards: TV: BAFTA, Broadcasting Press Guild and *TVTimes* Best Actor awards for *The Jewel in the Crown* (1984). Address: c/o Michael Whitehall. m. Pamela Miles; 1 s. Tom.

Tim Pigott–Smith

PILGER, John

John Richard Pilger. Journalist/Documentary film-maker. b. Sydney, Australia, 9 October 1939. D Litt, Staffordshire University, D Phil, Dublin City University. Trained with Australian Consolidated Press and worked on the Sydney *Daily Telegraph* and *Sunday Telegraph* (1958-62), as a sub-editor with Reuters in Britain and a journalist with the *Daily Mirror* (1963-85). Making TV documentaries since 1970.
TV: *World in Action* (two documentaries); *Midweek* (contributor), *Pilger* (four series); *Pilger in Australia; Personal Report — Pilger* (series); *The Selling of the Sea* (Westward TV only); *Do You Remember Vietnam?; Year Zero — The Silent Death of Cambodia* (winner of 15 international awards); *The Mexicans; Cambodia — Year One; Heroes; The Truth Game; The Last Day* (as playwright); *The Outsiders* (series); *Frontline: The Search for Truth in Wartime; Nicaragua; Burp! Pepsi v Coke in the Ice-Cold War; The Secret Country: The First Australians Fight Back; Japan: Behind the Mask; The Last Dream* (three-part series about Australia); *Cambodia — Year Ten; Cambodia — Year Ten Update; Cambodia — the Betrayal; War by Other Means; What the Papers Say; The Late Show* (interview with Noam Chomsky); *Return to Year Zero; Death of a Nation; Flying the Flag — Arming the World; Vietnam: The Last Battle.*
Books: *The Last Day; Aftermath: The Struggle of Cambodia & Vietnam* (with Anthony Barnett); *The Outsiders* (with Michael Coren); *Heroes; A Secret Country; Distant Voices.*
Awards: TV: BAFTA Richard Dimbleby Award (1991); Emmy Award (1991); International de Télévision Genève Award (1993). British Press Awards: Journalist of the Year (1967, 1979). Address: 57 Hambalt Road, London SW4 9EQ. m. journalist Scarth Flett (dis); 1 s. Sam (b. 1973, from m.), 1 d. Zoe (b. 1984, from subsequent relationship, now over, with journalist Yvonne Roberts). Partner: Jane Hill. Pets: Cat called Daisy. Hobbies: 'Sunning, swimming, mulling.'

John Pilger

PINDER, Steven

Steven Pinder. Actor. b. Whalley, Lancashire, 30 March 1960. Trained at The Drama Centre. Stage roles include Malcolm in *Watching* (national tour).
TV: Owen in *Foxy Lady* (two series); *Crown Court* (twice, as Paul Freeman and PC Charnley); Charlie in *Now and Then; Scotch and Wry;* Peter in *C.A.T.S. Eyes;* Roy Lambert in *Crossroads* (1985-8); Tony in *Hollywood Sports;* Max Farnham in *Brookside* (1991-).
Address: c/o Langford Associates/Mersey Television. Lives in London. m. Taj; 1 d. Pets: A dog called Westie. Hobbies: Militaria.

Steven Pinder

PIPER, Jacki

Jacki Crump. Actress. b. Birmingham, 3 August 1948. Trained at Birmingham Theatre School.
TV: Moneyfeather in *Kelly Monteith;* Jane in *The Rough with the Smooth;* Esther Pidgeon in *The Fall and Rise of Reginald Perrin;* Natasha in *Thriller;* Harriet in *Men of Affairs;* Avril in *Don't Dilly Dally;* Pearl in *Hogg's Back* (series); Ann Leston in *The Bill;* Margaret Talbot in *Dangerfield.*
Films: Sister Williams in *Carry On Matron;* Myrtle Plummer in *Carry On at Your Convenience;* Sally Martin in *Carry On Loving;* June in *Carry On up the Jungle;* Sue in *Doctor in Trouble;* Lyn Greer in *The Man Who Haunted Himself;* Carrie in *The Love Ban;* Ida in *Mr Love.*
Address: c/o Langford Associates. Lives in London. m. Douglas Barrell; 2 s. Nick, Tim. Pets: Two cats. Hobbies: Tennis, music-hall, reading, art (watercolours).

Jacki Piper

PIVARO, Nigel

Nigel Pivaro. Actor. b. Manchester, 11 December 1959. Trained at RADA. Stage plays include *Rich and Famous* (Community Theatre).
TV: Terry Duckworth in *Coronation Street;* Constable Pearce in *Hetty Wainthropp Investigates.*
Films: *The Revenge of the One-Armed Boxer; Meet Me Tonight in Dreamland.* Address: c/o Garricks.

Nigel Pivaro

PLANER, Nigel

Nigel Planer

Nigel Planer. Actor/Writer. b. London, 22 February 1953. Trained at LAMDA.
TV: *Not the Nine o'Clock News* (writer of sketches); Lou Lewis in *Shine on Harvey Moon* (1982-5, 1995); *The Young Ones* (two series); *Oxford* and *The Crying Game* (both The Comic Strip Presents...); *Roll Over Beethoven* (series); *King and Castle* (series); *Filthy Rich and Catflap; Number 27; Blackadder the Third; Blackeyes; Frankenstein's Baby; The Naked Actor; The Return of the Magic Roundabout* (presenter); *The Magic Roundabout* (narrator); *Bonjour la Classe* (series, 1993); *The Nicholas Craig Master Class; Jealousy* (The Comic Strip Presents...);*The Memoirs of Sherlock Holmes; Nicholas Craig's Interview Masterclass; Wake Up with...; Showstoppers.* As writer: Creator of Neil in *The Young Ones.*
Films: *Yellowbeard; Brazil; The Supergrass; Eat the Rich.* Address: c/o Peters Fraser & Dunlop.

PLATER, Alan

Alan Plater

Alan Frederick Plater. Writer. b. Jarrow-on-Tyne, Tyne & Wear, 15 April 1935. D Litt, Hull University.
TV: Original plays and series: *The Referees; A Smashing Day; So Long Charlie; See the Pretty Lights; Ted's Cathedral; Fred; The Villains; Three to a Cell; Six of the Best: Charlie's Place; The Incident; The Nutter; To See How Far It Is; Terry; Close the Coalhouse Door; Rest in Peace, Uncle Fred; Let There Be Light; Onion; Seventeen Per Cent Said Push Off; The Edwardians: The Reluctant Juggler; Tonight We Meet Arthur Pendelbury; Land of Green Ginger; Oranges and Lemons: Brotherly Love; Sporting Scene: The Needle Match; Bedtime Stories: Goldilocks and the Three Bears; Shoulder to Shoulder: Annie Kenney; The Loner; Trinity Tales; Masters and Servants: Practical Experience; Willow Cabins; Seven Days That Shook Young Jim; Fosdyke Saga; Oh No It's Selwyn Froggitt; For the Love of Albert; Short Back and Sides; Middlemen; By Christian Judges Condemned; Give Us a Kiss, Cristabel; The Party of the First Part; Curriculee Curricula; Night People; The Blacktoft Diaries; Reunion; Channel 4 and Five-Eighths; Get Lost!; Man Made the Slave; Orwell on Jura; Pride of Our Alley; The Family Rules; Thank You, Mrs Clinkscales; On Your Way, Riley!; The Beiderbecke Affair; On the Edge of the Sand; Coming Through; The Beiderbecke Tapes; Disarming Arguments; The Beiderbecke Connection; Tales of Sherwood Forest; Misterioso; Doggin' Around; Oliver's Travels.* Adaptations: *The Stars Look Down; Flambards; The Good Companions; The Black Pool* (unscreened); *Barchester Chronicles; The Clarion Van; Feet Foremost; Bewitched; The Intercessor; The Consultant; Agatha Christie's Miss Marple: A Murder Is Announced; Death Is Part of the Process; Fortunes of War; A Very British Coup; A Day in Summer; Selected Exits.* Episodic: *Z Cars; Crane; Front Page Story; Softly Softly; The First Lady; Cribb; Shades of Darkness; The Adventures of Sherlock Holmes; Campion; Spender; Maigret; Frank Stubbs.*
Films: *The Virgin and the Gypsy; Juggernaut; It Shouldn't Happen to a Vet; Priest of Love; The Inside Man.* Address: c/o Alexandra Cann Representation. Lives in London. m. 1st Shirley Johnson (dis), 2nd Shirley Rubinstein; 2 s. Stephen, David, 1 d. Janet (all from 1st m.), 3 step-s. Peter, John, Paul (all from 2nd m.). Hobbies: Jazz.

PLEASENCE, Angela

Angela Pleasence

Daphne Anne Angela Pleasence. Actress. b. Chapeltown, Sheffield, South Yorkshire. Daughter of actor Donald Pleasence and actress Miriam Raymond. Trained at RADA; studied clowning with Le Coq in Paris.
TV: *The Madam; The Erpingham Camp; The Chemistry of Love; The Whole Truth;* Monica Sutton in *Coronation Street* (1967); *Birthday; The Possessed; Joan — The Ladies; The Expert; The Last Train Through the Tunnel;* Catherine Howard in *The Six Wives of Henry VIII; Paul Temple; Marching Song; Churchill's People; Breath; The Demon Wood; A Legacy; Dixon of Dock Green; Saint Joan; Charlotte Brontë;* Fantine in *Les Misérables* (TVM); *Murder at the Wedding; The Walls of Jericho; The Hothouse; Barchester Chronicles; A Christmas Carol* (TVM); *Silas Marner: The Weaver of Raveloe; Mansfield Park; Somewhere to Run; Girls on Top; Anastasia; Stealing Heaven; Runaways; Casualty; The Bill.*
Films: *Here We Go round the Mulberry Bush; The Gaunt Woman; It's a Two-Feet-Six-Inches-Above-the-Ground World; Hitler — The Last Ten Days; Tales from beyond the Grave; Symptoms; The Godsend; Abelard and Héloïse; The Favour, the Watch and the Very Big Fish.* Address: c/o James Sharkey. m. actor Michael Cadman (dis); 1 s. Pascoe. Pets: German shepherd dogs. Hobbies: Reading, allotment.

POLLARD, Su

Su Pollard

Su Pollard. Actress. b. Nottingham, 7 November 1949. Started with the Co-operative Arts Theatre.
TV: *Summer Royal; The Comedians; A Silver Jubilee; Clock-on; Three Up, Two Down; We're Going Places; Get Set for Summer;* Peggy in *Hi-de-Hi!* (series); *You Rang, M'Lord?; The World of Peter Rabbit and Friends: The Tale of Tom Kitten and Jemima Puddle-Duck* (voice only); *The V Word;* Cicely Courtneidge in *Call Up the Stars* (VE Day concert, 1995); Ethel Schumann in *Oh Doctor Beeching!* (pilot).
Books: *Hearts & Showers.* Address: c/o Noel Gay Artists. m. teacher Peter Keogh.

POLYCARPOU, Peter

Peter Polycarpou

Peter Polycarpou. Actor. b. Brighton, East Sussex (of Greek Cypriot parents), 31 March 1957.
TV: *Hammer House of Horror; Dancers; The Last Days of Pompeii; The Professionals;* Diego Armado in

Jupiter Moon (BSB); *Capital City*; Chris Theodopoulopoulos in *Birds of a Feather* (six series, 1989-94, lus Christmas specials, 1993, 1994); *Rich Tea & Sympathy*; *Love Hurts* (singer of theme song).
Records: Single: *Love Hurts*. Address: c/o James Sharkey Associates. Lives in London. m. Sarah Lee (dis). Partner: Deborah Hodges. Hobbies: Model-making.

POPE, Eva
Eva Pope. Actress. Trained at the Webber Douglas Academy.
TV: Tanya Pooley in *Coronation Street* (1993-4); Becky in *Men of the World* (Series 2, 1995).
Films: *After the Wax* (London International Film School). Address: c/o London Management.

Eva Pope

PORRETT, Susan
Susan Jane Porrett. Actress. b. Potters Bar, Middlesex, 9 January. As a child, trained in ballet for 12 years. Started acting career as a student ASM in repertory theatre in Ayr (1967).
TV: *Bam! Pow! Zapp!* (The Wednesday Play, début, 1968); Alice in *Upstairs, Downstairs* (Series 1); *Doctor in Charge*; *The Duchess of Duke Street*; *Malice Aforethought*; *The Citadel*; Mrs Thomas in *Grange Hill* (1979-81); *Blott on the Landscape*; *Alphonso Bonzo*; *Billy Webb's Amazing Story*; *Agatha Christie's Poirot*; *Absolute Hell* (Performance); *Gallowglass*; *Precious Bane*; *The Bill*; *Middlemarch*; *Cold Lazarus*.
Films: *One of Our Dinosaurs Is Missing*; *Sir Henry at Rawlinson End*; Mrs Medcalf in *A Private Function*. Address: c/o Kate Feast Management. Lives in London. Single. Hobbies: Genealogy.

Susan Porrett

POSTLETHWAITE, Pete
Peter Postlethwaite. Actor. b. 1946. Has acted as Pete and Peter Postlethwaite. Worked as a teacher before going to drama school at the age of 24. RSC productions include *Bond's Lear*, *Richard III*, *Henry V*, *Cyrano de Bergerac*, *The Taming of the Shrew*, *King Lear*, *Macbeth*, *The Fair Maid of the West*, *A Midsummer Night's Dream* and *Every Man and His Humour*.
TV: *Thwum*; *A Day Out*; *The Muscle Market* (Play for Today); *Watching* (BBC production); *Coast to Coast* (Screen Two); *Blind Justice*; Major Knox in *Tumbledown* (TVM); Rick in *Tales of Sherwood Forest* (series); *No 27*; *They Never Slept*; *A Box of Swan* (Début on Two); *Poppylands* (Début on Two); *Needle*; *Zorro – The Marked Man*; *Boon*; *The Grass Arena* (TVM); Vince in *El C.I.D.* (series); *The Bill*; Chief Supt Neil Jameson in *Between the Lines*; *Lovejoy*; *Casualty*; *Sin Bin* (Screen Two); Obadiah Haeswell in *Sharpe's Company* and *Sharpe's Enemy*; Montague Tigg in *Martin Chuzzlewit* (series).
Films: *A Private Function*; *The Dressmaker*; *To Kill a Priest*; *Distant Voices, Still Lives*; *Treasure Island*; *Hamlet*; *A Child from the South*; *Split Second*; *Waterland*; *Alien³*; Captain Beams in *The Last of the Mohicans*; Guiseppe Conlon in *In the Name of the Father*; *A Pint o' Bitter* (retitled *On the Line*); *Suite 16*; *The Usual Suspects*; *When Saturday Comes*. Address: c/o Markham & Froggatt. Partner; 1 s.

Pete Postlethwaite

POWELL, Jenny
Jennifer Powell. Presenter. b. Ilford, Essex, 8 April 1968. Trained at the Italia Conti Stage Academy.
TV: *No Limits* (three series, 1986-8); *UP2U*; *Two by Two* (two series, 1988-90); *Top of the Pops* (1989); pilot for the Walt Disney Company; *Move It* (series, 1991-2); *Time Please* (scoreperson, Series 3); *Pick of the Week*; *Gimme 5* (four series, 1991-4); *Go Getters*; *Disney Club* (series, 1993-4, 1996); *Animal Crazy* (two series, 1994-5); *Cat's Eyes* (series); *Chroma Zone* (Nickelodeon satellite channel); *What's Up Doc* (series, 1994-); *Wheel of Fortune* (hostess, series, 1995); *Disney Parade* (series, 1995). Address: c/o Arlington Enterprises. Lives in Manchester. Single. Hobbies: Water-skiing.

Jenny Powell

POWELL, Robert
Robert Powell. Actor. b. Salford, Lancashire, 1 June 1944.
TV: *Doomwatch* (1970); *Bam, Pow, Zap*; title role in *Shelley* (BBC film); *Sentimental Education*; *Jude the Obscure*; *Mrs Warren's Profession*; *Mr Rolls & Mr Royce*, *The Caucasian Chalk Circle*; *Looking for Clancy*; title role in *Jesus of Nazareth*; *Pygmalion*; *Jane Austen in Manhattan* (TVM); *The Hunchback of Notre Dame* (TVM); *Canned Carrott* (series); *The First Circle* (Canadian series), *Frankenstein* (TVM), *Merlin of the Crystal Cave*; *Shaka Zulu* (mini-series and TVM); title role in *Hannay*; *Memories of 1970-91* (narrator); *The Golden Years* (TVM); DC Dave Briggs in *The Detectives* (four series, 1993-6); *The Legends of Treasure Island* (voice only); *Wish You Were Here…?* (guest reporter); *Great Crimes and Trials of the Twentieth Century* (narrator, series, 1994).
Films: *Robbery*; *Far from the Madding Crowd*; *Joanna*; *The Italian Job*; *Walk a Crooked Path*; *Secrets*; *Running Scared*; *Asylum*; *The Asphyx*; *Mahler*; *Tommy*; *Beyond Good and Evil*; *The Four Feathers*; *Cocktails for Three*; Richard Hannay in *The Thirty-Nine Steps*; *The Dilessi Affair*; *Harlequin*; *A Fair Way to Play* (short); *The Survivor*; *The Imperative*; *The Jigsaw Man*; *Secrets of the Phantom Caverns* (retitled *What Waits Below*); *D'Annunzio and I*; *Down There in the Jungle*; *Romeo-Juliet* (voice only); *Once on Chanuk Bair*. **Awards:** *TVTimes* Best Actor on TV award for *Jesus of Nazareth* (1978).
Address: c/o Jonathan Altaras Associates. m. former Pan's People dancer Babs (Barbara) Lord; 1 s. Barnaby, 1 d. Katherine. Hobbies: Cricket, tennis, golf.

Robert Powell

POWLEY, Mark

Mark Powley

Mark Chelmer Powley. Actor. b. Chelmsford, Essex, 4 October 1963. Brought up in Swindon, Wiltshire. Trained at LAMDA (1982-5). Stage roles include Angelo in *Piaf*.
TV: *Victoria Wood — As Seen on TV; Rockliffe's Babies; Bergerac;* PC Ken Melvin in *The Bill* (1987-92); Admiral Tudor in *Bluefields;* Neil Collins in *Casualty;* Ray Burnside in *Moon and Son;* Roger Ellis in *May to December;* Herr Kopfler in *Sherlock Holmes and the Leading Lady* (TVM); Darren Chambers in *Lovejoy; The Politician's Wife;* Tom in *Next of Kin* (two series, 1995-6, plus Christmas special 1995).
Films: *Time Warp Terror; Bloody New Year.* Address: c/o Scott Marshall. Lives in Shepherd's Bush, West London. m. 1989 ex-dancer Janis Jaffa. Hobbies: Golf, scuba-diving, cricket, snooker.

PRAED, Michael

Michael Praed

Michael Praed. Actor. b. Gloucestershire, 1 April 1960. Trained at the Guildhall School of Music and Drama. Stage productions include *The Pirates of Penzance* (West End), *Abbacadabra* (Lyric Theatre, Hammersmith) and *The Three Musketeers* (Broadway).
TV: *The Gentle Touch; The Professionals; Rothko; Video Entertainers;* title role in *Robin of Sherwood;* Prince Michael of Moldavia in *Dynasty;* Jake Lovell in *Jilly Cooper's Riders* (mini-series, 1993); *Without Walls: For One Night Only;* Marty James in *Crown Prosecutor* (series, 1995); *French and Saunders.* Address: c/o ICM. m. 1994 choreographer Karen Landau; 1 s. Gabriel.

PRESTON, Duncan

Duncan Preston

Duncan James Preston. Actor. b. Bradford, West Yorkshire, 11 August 1946. Trained at RADA. RSC productions include *Romeo and Juliet, Macbeth, Dingo, Pillar of the Community, Bingo* and *A Midsummer Night's Dream.* Other stage plays include *A Streetcar Named Desire, Of Mice and Men, Habeas Corpus* (all Mermaid Theatre) and *Hamlet* (national tour).
TV: *Hunter's Walk; Noble House; Buddy; Josie; Green Eyed Monster; Gentry; Sun Child; Victoria Wood — As Seen on TV* (series, 1985-6); Jonathan Haslam in *Surgical Spirit* (seven series, 1989-95); *The New Statesman; All Creatures Great and Small; Boon; Bergerac; Snakes and Ladders; The Bill; Victoria Wood's All Day Breakfast;* Pugmire in *Noble House;* Jim in *Happy since I Met You; The Good Sex Guide* (Series 2); Kevin's Dad in *Harry Enfield and Chums;* Geoffrey and Angela in *Six Sides of Coogan;* Jim in *Pat and Margaret* (Screen One); Slim Jim in *Holed.*
Films: *Press Gang; If Tomorrow Comes; Macbeth; Porridge; Scandalous; A Passage to India; Robin Hood; The Biggest Bank Robbery.* Address: c/o Barry Brown & Partner. Lives in London. m. actress Susan Penhaligon (qv) (dis). Hobbies: Golf, cricket, rugby.

PRINGLE, Bryan

Bryan Pringle

Bryan Pringle. Actor. b. Glascote, Staffordshire, 19 January 1935. Trained at RADA.
TV: *Portsmouth Defence; The Dustbinmen; On Giant's Shoulders; The Good Companions; The Bell; Love Story; Still Waters; Diary of a Nobody; Paradise Postponed; Radical Chambers; Auf Wiedersehen Pet; The Management;* Felix Norman in *Prime Suspect* (mini-series, 1991); Stan Mann in *Roots* (Performance); Barry in *Olly's Prison* (mini-series, 1993); Arnold in *So Haunt Me;* Mr Bebbington in *Once Upon a Time in the North* (series, 1994); Branwell in *Moving Story;* Pirbright in *P G Wodehouse's Heavy Weather;* Fatha in *The Detectives.*
Films: *Saturday Night and Sunday Morning; HMS Defiant; The Boy Friend; Bullshot; Brazil; Haunted Honeymoon; Consuming Passions;* Old Englishman in *3 Men and a Little Lady* (1990). Address: c/o Markham & Froggatt. m. actress Anne Jameson; 1 d. Kate, 1 s. Craster.

PROTHEROE, Brian

Brian Protheroe

Brian Protheroe. Actor. b. Salisbury, Wiltshire, 16 June 1944. Worked as a student technician in a pathological laboratory, then played in a folk group. Had hit records as a singer before becoming an actor. Stage plays include *Pump Boys and Dinettes* (Piccadilly Theatre) and *Lysistrata* (Wyndham's).
TV: *Two People; Strangers; Leave Him to Heaven; The Perfect House* (ITV Playhouse); *Cover; The Quiet Days of Mrs Stafford; Bavarian Nights;* Edward IV in *Henry VI* and *Richard III; Spider's Web;* Saturnius in *Titus Andronicus; Reilly — Ace of Spies; King and Castle; To Have and to Hold; Every Breath You Take;* Miles Beaufort in *Gentlemen and Players* (two series); James Brigsley in *Not a Penny More, Not a Penny Less;* Dr Leo Brompton in *Shrinks;* Matt in *Natural Lies* (mini-series, 1992); Philip in *Birds of a Feather;* Leonard Rosten in *Pie in the Sky;* Gordon in *Lovejoy.*
Films: *Superman; A Nightingale Sang in Berkeley Square* (also titled *The Big Scam* and *The Mayfair Bank Caper*). **Records:** Single: *Pinball* (No 22, 1974). Albums: *Pinball; Pickup; I/You.* Address: c/o Marmont Management. Lives in South London. Partner: Gilly; 1 s. Billy, 1 d. Rosie.

PRYCE, Jonathan

Jonathan Pryce. Actor. b. Holywell, Clwyd, 1 June 1947. Studied art for five years before winning a scholarship to train at RADA. Stage productions include *Comedians* (Old Vic, London, and New York),

Hamlet (title role, Royal Court), *The Taming of the Shrew*, *Antony and Cleopatra*, *Measure for Measure*, *Macbeth* (all RSC), *Uncle Vanya* (West End), *Accidental Death of an Anarchist* (Broadway), *Miss Saigon* (Theatre Royal, Drury Lane, and Broadway) and *Oliver!* (revival, London Palladium).

TV: *Daft as a Brush; Playthings; Bill Brand; Comedians; Partisans; Spasms; Glad Day; For Tea on Sunday; Timon of Athens; The Caretaker; Roger Doesn't Live Here Any More; School for Clowns; The Day Christ Died; Peter and Paul; Murder Is Easy* (also titled *Agatha Christie's Murder Is Easy*) (TVM); *Praying Mantis* (TVM); *Martin Luther – Heretic;* Wallace in *The Man from the Pru* (TVM); Gerd Heidemann in *Selling Hitler* (mini-series); John Wroe in *Mr Wroe's Virgins* (series, 1993); *Barbarians at the Gate* (TVM); Sam in *Thicker than Water* (mini-series, 1993); *The Royal Variety Performance* (with *Oliver!* cast, 1994).

Films: *Voyage of the Damned; The Day Christ Died; Peter and Paul; Breaking Glass; Loophole; Something Wicked This Way Comes; Two Weeks in Winter; The Ploughman's Lunch; Brazil; The Doctor and the Devils;* Charles in *Haunted Honeymoon; Jumpin' Jack Flash; Man on Fire; Hotel London; Consuming Passions; The Adventures of Baron Munchausen; The Rachel Papers; The Age of Innocence; Glengarry Glen Ross; A Business Affair; Shopping; Deadly Advice; Carrington;* Duncan Stewart in *Great Moments in Aviation*.

Awards: Films: Cannes Film Festival Best Actor for *Carrington* (1995). Theatre: Tony Award for *Comedians* (1977); SWET and Laurence Olivier Awards for *Hamlet* (1980); Laurence Oliver and Variety Club Awards for *Miss Saigon* (1989); Tony and Drama Desk awards for *Miss Saigon* (Broadway, 1990-1). Address: c/o James Sharkey Associates. Lives in London. Hobbies: Painting, drawing.

Jonathan Pryce

PUCKRIK, Katie

Katie Puckrik. Presenter. Began career as a singer in nightclubs (1986-90) and performed as a dancer.

TV: *The Word* (two series, 1991-3); film critic for *01- for London, First Night* and *Wide Angle; The Krypton Factor* (dramatic inserts, series, 1992); *Access All Areas* (host, series); *Press Gang; Fab FM: End of an Era; The Sunday Show* (two series, both 1995); *Pyjama Party* (series, 1996).

Videos: *Seriously Sexy; So You Wanna be a Model?*

Radio: *Fashion Icons* (host, series); *Mark Radcliffe Show* (contributor). Address: c/o ICM.

Katie Puckrik

PULESTON DAVIES, Ian

Ian Puleston Davies. Actor. Trained at the Guildhall School of Music and Drama.

TV: Stephen in *Brookside;* Reporter in *Forever Green;* Ben in *Boon;* Young Charlie in *The Old Devils;* John in *Grange Hill;* DC Barrett in *Between the Lines;* Frank Talbot in *The Bill;* TV Presenter in *The Politician's Wife;* Terry in *Hollyoaks*.

Films: Kevin in *Business as Usual*. Address: c/o The Narrow Road Company.

PUREFOY, James

James B M Purefoy. Actor. b. Taunton, Somerset, 3 June 1964. Trained at the Central School of Speech and Drama (1986-8). RSC productions include *The Man Who Came to Dinner, King Lear* (as Edgar), *The Tempest* (as Ferdinand), *Macbeth* (as Donalbain) and *The Constant Couple*.

TV: Mike Baker in *Coasting;* James McCarthy in *The Casebook of Sherlock Holmes; Eclipsed;* Mario Valetti in *The Cloning of Joanna May* (mini-series); *Boon;* Victor in *Angels* (single play, 1992); James Bennett in *Casualty;* Julian in *Rides* (Series 2, 1993); title role in *Darius Guppy* (Crime Story); Brian in *Calling the Shots* (mini-series); Nigel Miller in *The Prince;* Jimmy Turner in *Tears before Bedtime* (series, 1995), Spears in *Sharpe's Sword;* Nick Stuart In *Catherine Cookson's The Tide of Life* (mini-series).

Films: *Feast of July; Bye Bye Baby*. Address: c/o ICM. Lives in London. Single. Hobbies: Falconry.

Ian Puleston Davies

PURVES, Peter

Peter Purves. Presenter/Writer/Director/Producer/Actor. b. New Longton, nr Preston, Lancashire, 10 February 1939. Worked as an actor (1957-66).

TV: As actor. *Z Cars; Gideon's Way; The Girl in the Picture* (Armchair Theatre); *The Villains; Court Martial; Luther; The Girl in the Black Bikini;* Steven in *Doctor Who* (36 episodes); *EastEnders* (three episodes); *Doctor Who* special (BSkyB, 1992). As presenter: *Blue Peter* (860 episodes, 1967-78); *Record Breakers Christmas Special* (10 programmes, 1971-80); *Driver of the Year* (three series); *Sunday Live; Cruft's* (1976-); *Blue Peter Special Assignment* (1976-8); *The Acting Game* (host, four series, 1978-83); *Stopwatch* (five series); *We're Going Places* (three series); BBC darts presenter (1981-7), including seven World Championships and 15 Home Internationals; *Bullseye* (BBC Sport, five series); *Babble* (host, three series); *Crimewatch Midlands* (BBC Birmingham); *Inside Story* (BBC Birmingham); *Crimewatch Debate* (BBC Birmingham); *Ten Glorious Years; Superdogs* (three series); *TV Heroes* (subject); *Happy Families* (guest presenter); *Film Review* (guest reviewer).

Books: *Tess – The Story of a Guide Dog* (1981). Address: c/o Downes Presenters Agency. Lives in Northamptonshire. m. 1st writer Gilly Fraser (dis 1981), 2nd actress-singer Kathryn Evans; 1 s. Matthew, 1 adopted d. Lisa (both from 1st m.). Pets: Three dogs. Hobbies: Dogs, golf, theatre, cinema, reading.

James Purefoy

Peter Purves

Frederick Pyne

Anna Quayle

John Quayle

Diana Quick

Pauline Quirke

PYNE, Frederick

Frederick Pyne. Actor. b. London, 30 December 1936. Worked as a farmer in Cheshire and Cambridgeshire, then served in the RAF, before training at RADA. National Theatre at the Old Vic productions (1966-70) included *Love for Love, A Flea in Her Ear, Dance of Death, As You Like It, Rosencrantz and Guildenstern Are Dead, The Idiot, Tons of Money* and *The Collection.* Other stage plays include national tours of *Billy Liar, Hindle Wakes, Noises Off* and *Straight and Narrow.*

TV: *R3; Talking to a Stranger; The Three Princes; Macbeth; Crossroads; Dixon of Dock Green; An Affair of Honour; Justice;* Matt Skilbeck in *Emmerdale Farm.*

Address: c/o Paul du Fer Associates. Hobbies: Opera, ballet, theatre, charity work.

QUAYLE, Anna

Anna Quayle. Actress. b. Birmingham, 6 October 1937. Daughter of actor-producer Douglas Quayle. Toured in Douglas Quayle's Company. Trained at RADA. Stage plays include *The Case of the Oily Levantine* (Her Majesty's Theatre) and *The Boy Friend* (Old Vic and Albery Theatres).

TV: *Tempo International; The Avengers; Beauty Operators; Up the Chastity Belt; Grub Street; A Degree of Frost; What's My Line?; The Queen and the Robot; The Georgian House; Aquarius; James and the Giant Peach; In the Looking Glass; What a Performance; Arena; The Light Princess; Brideshead Revisited; Henry V; Sakharov; The People from the Forest; Father Charlie; Never the Twain; Marjorie and Men; Mapp and Lucia; Lytton's Diary;* Mrs Monroe in *Grange Hill.*

Films: *Drop Dead, Darling; Casino Royale; Smashing Time; Chitty Chitty Bang Bang; Mistress Pamela; Eskimo Nell; Three for All; The Seven-Per-Cent Solution; Adventures of a Private Eye; Never Take Yes for an Answer; Adventures of a Plumber's Mate; SOS Titanic; The Towers of Babel.*

Address: c/o CDA. m. Donald Baker; 1 d. Katy.

QUAYLE, John

John Quayle. Actor. b. Lincoln, 21 December 1938. Trained at RADA. Stage plays include *Habeas Corpus, When We Are Married, Watch on the Rhine, Noises Off, Life Begins at Forty* and *Run for Your Wife.*

TV: *Upstairs, Downstairs; Jumbo Spencer; The King's Dragon; Nanny; Pig in the Middle; Jane;* Mr Coles in *The Good Life; Charles & Diana: A Royal Love Story* (TVM); *Marjorie and Men;* Major Willoughby-Gore in *Farrington of the FO* (two series, 1986-7); *Terry and June; Tricky Business;* Woodley in *The 19th Hole* (series, 1989).

Films: *Privates on Parade.* Address: c/o Barry Burnett Organisation. Lives in London. m. Petronell. Pets: 'Pugs.' Hobbies: Shooting, riding.

QUICK, Diana

Diana Quick. Actress. b. Kent, 23 November 1946. Former member of the National Youth Theatre. Plays include *The Threepenny Opera, Billy* (both London West End), *Phaedra Britannica, Plunder, Troilus and Cressida, Tamburlaine* (all National Theatre), *The Women Pirates* and *The Changeling* (both RSC).

TV: *The Playground; Christ Recrucified; Complete and Utter History of Britain; Hamlet; Hopcraft into Europe; Napoleon and Love; Bedtime Story: The Sleeping Beauty; Mr Garrick and Mrs Woffington; Holding On; The Three Hostages; The Odd Job; Word for Word; At Last It's Friday;* Julia Flyte in *Brideshead Revisited; The Woman in White; It's My Pleasure; Dorothy Parker; Friday Night, Saturday Morning* (host, US); *Phantom of the Opera; Chekhov in Yalta; Cariani and the Courtesans; Kimberley Carlisle; Minder; Flesh and Blood; The Justice Game; Frederick Forsyth Presents; Smith and Jones; The Orchid House;* Lady Betty in *Clarissa;* Mrs Stevens in *Inspector Morse: Absolute Conviction;* Anaïs Nin in *Without Walls: The Art of Tripping, Part Two;* Lady Evelyn Carrados in *The Inspector Alleyn Mysteries;* Marion Glassford-Gale in *Dandelion Dead* (mini-series, 1994); Katherine Hillyard in *September Song* (Series 2-3, 1994-5); *Theatreland* (presenter, series, 1996).

Films: *Nicholas and Alexandra; A Private Enterprise; The Duellists;* Fiona Harris in *The Odd Job; The Big Sleep; Ordeal by Innocence; 19/19; Max Mon Amour; Vroom; Wilt.* Address: c/o Julian Belfrage Associates. Lives in Suffolk. m. actor Kenneth Cranham (qv) (dis). Partner: Actor Bill Nighy (qv).

QUIRKE, Pauline

Pauline Quirke. Actress. b. London, 8 July 1959. Acted since childhood. Trained at the Anna Scher Theatre School. Stage plays include *A Tale of Two Cities* (Royal Court).

TV: *Dixon of Dock Green* (aged eight); *Kids about Town; Days of Hope; You Must Be Joking; Eleanor; Jenny Can't Work Any Faster; General Hospital; Pauline's Quirkes; The Duchess of Duke Street; You Can't Be Serious; Lovely Couple; Pauline's People; Crown Court; The Further Adventures of Oliver Twist; Ain't Many Angels; A Name for the Day; Baby Talk; The Story of the Treasure Seekers; Life after Death; Angels;* Veronica in *Shine on Harvey Moon* (1982-5, 1995); *Girls on Top;* Sharon in *Birds of a Feather* (six series, 1989-95, plus Christmas specials, 1993, 1994); *Very Big Very Soon; Rockliffe's Babies; Casualty; The Good Sex Guide* (series, 1993); *Birthnight; Children in Need* (with

Linda Robson, 'singing Abba', 1993); *Jobs for the Girls* (presenter, documentary series, 1995, plus Christmas special, 1995); Doris Waters in *Call Up the Stars* (VE Day concert, 1995); Olive Martin in *The Sculptress* (serial, 1996).
Films: Dot in *Junket 89* (Children's Film Foundation production); *The Elephant Man; Getting It Right; The Return of the Soldier; QED; Little Dorrit; Still Lives.* **Videos:** *Stick It Out* (backing singer in Right Said Fred video, 1993). Address: c/o Artists Management Group. 1 d. Emily.

RAFFIELD, Paul

Paul Raffield. Actor. b. London, 19 June 1957. Gained an BA (Hons) in law from Cardiff University. Trained at The Drama Studio, London (1978-9). Stage plays include *The Taming of the Shrew* (national tour and Jordanian tour) and *Neville's Island* (as Angus, Apollo Theatre).
TV: Morgan in *The Gay Lord Quex;* Winston in *Hyperspace Hotel;* Tony in *Saracen;* Paul Williams in *Mathscope; Open University Training Video;* Doctor in *Canned Carrott;* Breakfast TV Man in *Press Gang;* Mr Powell in *Them and Us;* Angus in *Grange Hill;* Frank Simpson in *The Lodge;* Robert in *Joking Apart* (pilot 1991 in Comic Asides series, plus two series 1993-4); Adam in *2point4 Children;* Driver in *Karaoke.*
Films: Music Shop Manager in *Buddy's Song;* Customs Officer in *Springing Lenin.*
Radio: *Nicola Johnson* (Capital FM, London); Martin in *Date with Fate.*
Address: c/o Ken McReddie. Lives in London.

Paul Raffield

RAGGETT, Nick

Nick Raggett. Actor. b. London. Acted with the National Youth Theatre. Stage roles include Benjamin in *Joseph and the Amazing Technicolor Dreamcoat,* Slightly in *Peter Pan* (both national tours) and Jem in *To Kill a Mockingbird* (Mermaid Theatre).
TV: Barry in *The Fear;* Burgess in *The Bill;* Danny Holmes in *IT for the Terrified;* Gavin in *Arcadia;* Jake in *Streetwise;* Dennis in *The Darling Buds of May;* Johnny in *Minder;* Derek in *Lovejoy;* Simon Mathews in *Seconds Out;* Yates in *The Bill;* Freddie in *Get Back;* Henderson the Potato King in *Pie in the Sky* (three series, 1994-6). Address: c/o The Narrow Road Company. Lives in London.

Nick Raggett

RAMSAY, Louie

Louie Ramsay. Actress. National Theatre appearances in *Tyger, The National Health, The Good Natured Man, Jumpers, The Cherry Orchard, The Misanthrope, Macbeth, Equus* and *Eden End.* West End stage plays include *The First Fish* and *Fantastic Fairground,* plus the musicals *South Pacific* (understudying Mary Martin), *Twenty Minute South, Harmony Close, Meet Me in the Corner* and *For Adults Only.*
TV: *Five o'Clock Club* (presenter); *Stand-By* (presenter, advertising magazine); Comedy Playhouse; *Softly Softly; When the Boat Comes In;* Rita King in *Kings Royal* (two series); Lady Bentley in *Strike It Rich* (two series); Dora Wexford in *The Ruth Rendell Mysteries* (series) and *The Ruth Rendell Mysteries: Simisola* (mini-series, 1996). Address: c/o The Brunskill Management. Lives in London and Devizes, Wiltshire. m. 1st actor Ronan O'Casey (dis), 2nd actor George Baker (qv); 1 s.

Louie Ramsay

RANDLE, Mary Jo

Mary Jo Randle. Actress. RSC roles include Émilie in *Les Liaisons Dangereuses,* Cassandra in *Troilus and Cressida,* Tsvetayeva in *Philistines* and Audrey in *As You Like It.*
TV: Pilar in *The Flipside of Dominick Hyde* (Play for Today); Pauline in *Shine on Harvey Moon; Victoria Wood — As Seen on TV* (two series); Marion in *London's Burning;* Sister Rogers in *Act of Will* (miniseries); Sergeant Maitland in *Inspector Morse: Driven to Distraction;* Virginia in *EastEnders;* Vera in *Olly's Prison;* Jill in *'Ex'* (ScreenPlay); Miss Atkinson in *A Time to Dance* (mini-series); Jane in *Sister Wife;* Ella in *Van Der Valk;* Georgia Lang in *Casualty;* Renie Thompson in *The Ruth Rendell Mysteries: The Speaker of Mandarin;* Kate Norton in *Between the Lines;* DS Jo Morgan in *The Bill.*
Films: Winifred Turner in *Bad Behaviour.* Address: c/o Mayer & Eden.

Mary Jo Randle

RANTZEN, Esther

Esther Rantzen. Presenter. b. Berkhamsted, Hertfordshire, 22 June 1940. Gained an English degree from Oxford University, then joined the BBC in special effects, before moving into TV research. Joined *Man Alive* as production assistant, then *Braden's Week* as researcher-reporter (screen début, 1968).
TV: *Man Alive* (production assistant); *Braden's Week* (researcher-reporter); *That's Life!* (presenter-producer, 1973-94); *The Big Time* (reporter-producer); *That's Life — Having a Baby; Miss United Kingdom* (1978); *That's Family Life!; Children in Need; Drug Watch; Hearts of Gold* (eight series, 1992-6); *Childline; Talking to Myself; Children of Courage and Achievement; That's Life! Summer Special; That's Life: Talented Pets; The Family Show; To Russia with Love: That's Life! Special; Esther* (three series, 1994-6); *Never Too Late; The Best of Esther* (repeats); *Childwatch Plus Ten* (1996).
Address: c/o Noel Gay Artists. Lives in London and the New Forest. m. TV producer-writer Desmond Wilcox; 2 d. Emily, Rebecca, 1 s. Joshua.

Esther Rantzen

Andy Rashleigh

RASHLEIGH, Andy

Andy Rashleigh. Actor/Writer. b. East London, 23 January 1949. Trained at Bretton Hall College of Education. Taught drama and theatre in London and Jamaica for six years.
TV: Social Worker in *Life for Christine;* Uniformed Constable in *Brideshead Revisited;* Policeman in *Juliet Bravo;* Detective Sergeant in *Mitch;* Garage Man in *Dear Ladies;* Plain Clothes DS in *Strangers;* PC Woodhouse in *Coronation Street* (eight episodes); Fire Officer in *Crown Court;* Policeman in *The Adventures of Sherlock Holmes;* Trade Union Officer in *The Practice;* Pathologist in *The South Bank Show: Hawksmoor;* Colin Arnold in *Albion Market* (20 episodes); Motor Pool Expert in *The Bill;* Mr Johnson in *Dramarama;* Policeman in *Gems;* Chef in *Crossroads* (30 episodes); Mr Justice Scott in *Panorama;* Ted Sharp in *Emmerdale Farm* (20 episodes); Trev in *Making Out; Hale & Pace;* DS Pryde in *EastEnders* (1990); Eliot Creasy in *Jupiter Moon* (BSB serial, 1990); *Minder;* James Donald in *Seekers* (miniseries, 1993); Gerry Goold in *The Chief;* Chiropractor in *Massage* (Ghosts); Tony Bromley in *Out of the Blue* (series, 1995). As writer: *Crossroads.*
Films: *The Ploughman's Lunch; Acceptable Levels; Ends and Means.* **Radio:** *The Archers* (as writer). Address: c/o Michelle Braidman Associates. Lives in London. Partner: Maggie Wilkinson.

Jan Ravens

RAVENS, Jan

Jan Ravens. Actress. b. Bebington, Cheshire, 14 May 1958. Trained as a drama teacher at Cambridge University, where she was a member of Cambridge Footlights revue.
TV: *Just Amazing; Getting into Shape; Carrott's Lib; The Lenny Henry Show; The Kenny Everett Show; Friday People; Carrott Election Confidential; Farrington of the FO; All in Good Faith; Saturday Live; C.A.T.S. Eyes; Spitting Image* (voice impersonator); *No Frills; Whose Line Is It Anyway?; KYTV; Smith and Jones; Alexei Sayle's Stuff; An Actor's Life for Me; One Foot in the Grave;* Carol in *B&B;* Guinevere in *A Word in Your Era;* Martinique in *Luv* (two series, 1993-4); *Fireworks; Harry Enfield and Chums.*
Radio: *Just a Minute; Extra Dry Sherrin; Delve; Midweek; The Radio Programme; Loose Ends.*
Address: c/o Barry Burnett Organisation. m. composer-performer Steve Brown (sep 1993); 2 s. Alfie, Lenny.

Christopher Ravenscroft

RAVENSCROFT, Christopher

Christopher Ravenscroft. Actor. Trained at Bristol Old Vic Theatre School after gaining a law degree from Cambridge University. Many RSC roles, including Mountjoy in *Henry V* and Cassius in *Julius Caesar.*
TV: *John Halifax, Gentleman* (début, 1973); Orsino in *Twelfth Night;* Ephesian Gentleman in *Pericles;* Oberleutnant Kupper in *The Fourth Arm;* Mr Snobb/Young Cheeryble in *Nicholas Nickleby;* Stapleton in *The Hound of the Baskervilles;* Captain Lullier in *Gossip from the Forest; World in Action* (narrator); police sergeant in *Coronation Street* (1978); *Crown Court;* Det Insp Mike Burden in *The Ruth Rendell Mysteries* (stories re-edited as *The Ruth Rendell Mystery Movie*) (20 stories, 1987-92); Dr Baguley in *P D James' A Mind to Murder; The Ruth Rendell Mysteries: Simisola* (mini-series, 1996).
Films: Mountjoy in *Henry V.*
Address: c/o RKM. Lives in Manchester. m. theatre director Caroline; 1 s. Jack.

Jeff Rawle

RAWLE, Jeff

Jeff Rawle. Actor/Writer. b. Birmingham, 20 July 1951. Worked at Sheffield Playhouse before training at LAMDA. Stage plays include *Equus* (Albery Theatre), *Once a Catholic* (Wyndham's) and *Butley* (Fortune Theatre and national tour).
TV: Title role in *Billy Liar* (two series); *The Water Maiden; Death of a Young Man* (Play for Today); *Love on the Dole; Wilde Alliance; Singles; Juliet Bravo; Claire; Bergerac; Singles Weekend; Doctor Who; Country and Irish; Remington Steele; Call Me Mister;* Sgt Ridley in *Fortunes of War; Boon; Run for the Lifeboat; South of the Border;* Wilson in *Vote for Them; The Gift; Beyond the Pale; The Bill; A Perfect Hero; This Is David Lander;* George in *Drop the Dead Donkey* (series); AIDS Counsellor in *EastEnders;* Mark in *Moon and Son;* Ezra in *The Life and Times of Henry Pratt* (series, 1992); Jehovah's Witness in *Minder;* Stephen Lester in *The Chief; Blood and Peaches* (mini-series, 1995); *Look at the State We're In!; Legal System;* Paul in *Faith in the Future* (series, 1995); Derek in *Lord of Misrule* (Screen One).
Films: *Baal; A Hitch in Time; Correction, Please; Rating Notman; Duchamp; Crystal Gazing; Awayday; Laughterhouse* (retitled *Singleton's Pluck*); *The Doctor and the Devils.*
Address: c/o Annette Stone Associates.

Jacqueline Reddin

REDDIN, Jacqueline

Jacqueline Reddin. Actress. b. Dublin, Ireland, 1956. Moved to England at the age of two. Trained at Bristol Old Vic Theatre School. Stage productions include *Grease* (Astoria Theatre).
TV: *Brencham People* (Play for Today); *The Duchess of Duke Street; The Professionals; Return of The Saint;* Maggie in *Emmerdale Farm; Minder; Florence Nightingale; Tickle on the Tum; Hold Tight!; Hale & Pace;* Terry in *All Night Long* (series, 1994). Address: c/o Peter Macfarlane. Lives in Buckinghamshire. Partner: Singer Maynard Williams; 1 d. Jemma, 1 s. Luke.

REDDINGTON, Ian

Ian Reddington. Actor. b. Sheffield, South Yorkshire. Trained at RADA. RSC productions include *Piaf, Once in a Lifetime* and *The Taming of the Shrew.*
TV: Chairman in *The Bill;* Perez in *Yellowthread Street;* Rusty in *Hard Feelings* (Play for Today); Fire Inspector in *Sharon and Elsie;* Laker in *Boon;* Flash Leopard in *Three Up, Two Down;* Studio Director in *Making News;* Cliff Swales in *The Sharp End;* Chief Clown in *Doctor Who;* Vic Dancer in *Casualty;* Gregory Ponsford in *The Bill;* Oakley in *Inspector Morse;* Richard Cole in *EastEnders;* Peter Clemence in *Cadfael;* Stewart Hayes in *The Sculptress.*
Films: Bassett in *Highlander;* Thief in *Crime;* Ian in *The Last Laugh;* Spider in *Crimestrike;* Jack in *Who Needs a Heart.* **Records:** *Steel City (Move on Up); If It's Wednesday, It Must Be Wembley.* Address: c/o Ken McReddie. Lives in London. Single.

Ian Reddington

REDFERN, Michael

Michael Ian Redfern. Actor. b. Isleworth, Middlesex, 30 March 1943. Trained at the Corona Stage Academy. Best known on television as Dad in the Oxo commercials.
TV: Rufus Pargeter in *The Newcomers;* Chris Woods in *United!; Out; Muck and Brass; Hi-de-Hi!; Maybury; The Gentle Touch; The Young Ones; Carrott's Lib; Never the Twain; The Late, Late Breakfast Show* (regular member of 'The Hit Squad', 1982-3); *Up the Elephant and round the Castle; The Two Ronnies Christmas Show, Minder, Start Your Own Business* (Open University); *Cold Warrior, In the Secret State; Three Up, Two Down; The New Statesman; Terry and June; Comrade Dad; The Bill; Saturday Night Live; Sorry; Girls on Top; Checkpoint Chiswick; Relative Strangers; Filthy Rich and Catflap; Alas Smith and Jones;* Jock in *The 19th Hole;* Police Inspector in *Boon; Carrott Comprehensive;* Fitness Instructor in *I Charles de Gaulle;* Policeman in *In Sickness and in Health;* Air Traffic Controller in *London's Burning;* Mr Roberts in *Hope It Rains;* Chief Supt Fleming in *Michael Winner's True Crimes; The Golden Rule;* Mr Cooper in *Bottom,* Drill Sergeant in *Bye Bye Baby;* Det Chief Supt Brian Boyce In *Fool's Gold* (TVM); Lewis in *Library of Romance;* George in *Between the Lines;* PC Finch in *The Detectives;* Mr Warner in *Health and Efficiency;* Mr Warner in *Health and Efficiency;* Landlord in *The Bill.*
Films: Title role in *The Weaver's Tale* (Belgium); Commissionaire in *Hubcap* (Bournemouth Film School); George in *Square Eyed Junkie.* Address: c/o McIntosh Rae Management. Lives in Fetcham, Surrey. Partner: Carol; 1 s. Ashley. Pets: Four dogs, three cats. Hobbies: Golf, football, training.

Michael Redfern

REDING, Nick

Nick Reding. Actor. b. London, 31 August 1962. Began career as a stage hand.
TV: *Last Summer's Child; Stalky & Co; Henry IV, Pt 3; Richard III; The Remainder Man* (Play for Today); *Love and Marriage: Dearly Beloved;* Charlie Parker in *Oscar Wilde;* Harry Stokes in *Paradise Postponed; Chance in a Million;* Cruickshank in *The Monocled Mutineer;* Adam Ebram in *District Nurse;* George in *My Family and Other Animals;* Lawyer in *EastEnders;* PC Peter Ramsey in *The Bill;* Haki in *The Final Frame* (TVM); *Minder; The House of Eliott; The Count of Solar;* Sgt Mellor in *John Le Carré's A Murder of Quality;* Dave Giddings in *Frank Stubbs Promotes* (series, 1993); Parker in *A Touch of Frost;* Morasco in *BUGS.*
Films: *Real Life; Captive; Heroine.* Address: c/o William Morris Agency (UK). Lives in London. Hobbies: Travel, scuba-diving, parachuting, eating Japanese food.

Nick Reding

REDMOND, Siobhan

Siobhan Redmond. Actress. Gained an MA in English from St Andrews University, Fife.
TV: *Casualty; Bulman;* Janie Naismith in *The Advocates* (series, 1992); Sylvia Hannah in *The Bill;* Det Sgt Maureen 'Mo' Connell in *Between the Lines* (three series, 1992-4); *The High Life* (Comic Asides); *Rab C Nesbitt;* Shona Spurtle in *The High Life* (series, 1995); *Latin for a Dark Room* (Tartan Shorts); Joyce in *Nervous Energy* (Screen Two); Julie Cordova in *Sorry about Last Night.*
Address: c/o Conway, van Gelder, Robinson. Lives in London. Single.

Siobhan Redmond

REES, Norman

Norman Rees. Journalist. b. Cardiff, 2 March 1939. Seven years with the *Western Mail,* Cardiff, before entering television with TWW (now HTV). Later joined ITN as a reporter, covering the resignation of President Nixon, the Yom Kippur War, the signing of the Camp David Middle East peace agreement, the launch of the first US Space Shuttle, the election and inauguration of President Reagan and his attempted assassination. Deported from Uganda in 1982 for his reports of alleged atrocities against civilians by Milton Obote's troops. Spent three months in Argentina during the Falklands War, was in Tel Aviv when the Israelis invaded Lebanon and witnessed the PLO pull out of Beirut. After six years in management with ITN, he moved back to reporting in 1991, working on in-depth special reports for *News at Ten.*
TV: TWW reporter, scriptwriter, then news editor; ITN news editor (1968), Washington correspondent (1977), reporter (1981), assistant editor, chief assistant editor, then general reporter (1991-). Address: c/o ITN. m. Andrea, 1 d. Nicola, 1 s. Andrew.

Norman Rees

Roger Rees

Saskia Reeves

Vic Reeves

Brian Regan

Christopher Reich

REES, Roger

Roger Rees. Actor. b. Aberystwyth, Dyfed, 5 May 1944. Trained as an artist at Camberwell School of Art and Slade School of Fine Art in London, and painted sets at Wimbledon Rep before becoming a professional actor. Stage plays include *The Taming of the Shrew*, *Nicholas Nickleby* (both RSC, London and Broadway), *The Real Thing* (Strand Theatre), *Hamlet* (RSC) and *Hapgood* (London and Los Angeles). **TV:** *Place of Peace; Under Western Eyes; A Bouquet of Barbed Wire; Saigon – Year of the Cat* (TVM); *Imaginary Friends; Nicholas Nickleby;* Fred Holywell in a *Christmas Carol* (TVM, 1984); *The Comedy of Errors; Macbeth; The Voysey Inheritance; The Ebony Tower; Singles; Cheers.* **Films:** *Star 80; If Looks Could Kill;* Parnell in *Stop! Or My Mom Will Shoot.* **Awards:** Theatre: Tony Best Actor award for *The Taming of the Shrew;* Tony Best actor award for *Nicholas Nickleby.* Address: c/o ICM.

REEVES, Saskia

Saskia Reeves. Actress. RSC roles include Anne in *A Woman Killed by Kindness*, Annabella in *'Tis Pity She's a Whore*, Silvia in *The Two Gentlemen of Verona*, Miranda in *The Virtuoso.* **TV:** Greta in *Metamorphosis;* Rosie in *Children Crossing;* Antonia in *Antonia and Jane;* Philippa Monaghan in *In My Defence;* Helen in *Border Country;* Irene in *Summer's Day Dream;* Lady Mordaunt in *Citizen Locke; Blow Your Mind: One More Thing;* Lady Mordaunt in *Citizen Locke;* Irina Shestova in *Summer's Day Dream* (Performance); Bridget in *The Perfect Match.* **Films:** *December Bride; The Bridge; lose My Eyes; Traps.* Address: c/o Markham & Froggatt.

REEVES, Vic

James Moir. Comedian/Writer. b. Darlington, 24 January 1959. Teamed up with Bob Mortimer at the Albany Empire, Deptford, and developed their 'Big Night Out' act, subsequently taking it on a university tour. Jonathan Ross persuaded Channel Four chief executive Michael Grade to watch the show and the pair were given their own television series in 1990. **TV:** *Vic Reeves Big Night Out* (two series, 1990-1); *The Weekenders* (Bunch of Five pilot, 1992); *The Smell of Reeves & Mortimer* (two series, 1993, 1995); *At Home with Vic and Bob* (1993); *Dot on the Landscape* (series); *Reeves and Mortimer's Shooting Stars* (host, quiz show series, with Bob Mortimer); *Christmas Night with the Stars* (1994); *Shooting Stars* (host, with Bob Mortimer, quiz series, 1995); *A Nose through Nature; Reeves and Mortimer – Xmas Shooting Stars* (1995). **Videos:** *Vic Reeves Big Night Out.* **Records:** Singles: *Dizzy; I'm a Believer* (with Bob Mortimer and EMF, No 3, 1995). Album: *I Will Cure You.* **Books:** *Big Night In* (with Bob Mortimer, 1991). **Awards:** BAFTA Originality award (with Bob Mortimer, 1992); British Comedy Awards Best Live Performance award (with Bob Mortimer, 1992). Address: c/o PBJ Management. m.

REGAN, Brian

Brian Regan. Actor. b. Liverpool, 2 October 1957. Apprentice footballer with Liverpool football club. Assistant stage manager, then stage manager, at Liverpool Playhouse, before becoming a professional actor. Stage plays include *Stags and Hens, Hamlet* and *Blood on the Dole.* **TV:** Stevie King in *Murphy's Mob;* Terry Sullivan in *Brookside* (1982-); *Harry Enfield's Television Programme;* Chute in *Paparazzo* (pilot, 1995). Address: c/o Lou Coulson. m. Lisa; 1 d. Ashleigh.

REICH, Christopher

Christopher Reich. Actor. b. Manchester, 5 June. Trained at the Royal Manchester College of Drama. Stage roles include Milo in *Sleuth* (Garrick and Fortune Theatres). **TV:** *Anything but Murder* (NDF, Germany); Firente D'este in *The Borgias; Macbeth; Much Ado about Nothing; She;* Zihan in *Jesus of Nazareth; Dempsey and Makepeace; The Professionals; Bulman; A Walk in the Forest; Bonner; Bowen and Partner; Why Abertawe;* Heran in *The Glory Boys; Home to Roost; Fellow Feeling;* Box in *Dog's Ransom;* Rodney Melling in *Bergerac;* Dr David Samuels in *EastEnders;* Roberts in *Casualty.* As narrator: *The Natural World; Serpent's Embrace; Island in the Air.* **Films:** *Return of the Pink Panther* and *Revenge of the Pink Panther; Never Say Never Again; The Story; Selling Cannons; L'Autre Sherlock.* Address: c/o Langford Associates. Lives in London and Wales. m. actress Lisabeth Miles; 2 d. Lisa, Anna. Pets: A cat called Tom. Hobbies: Cooking, horse-racing.

REID, Anne

Anne Reid. Actress. Trained at RADA. Stage plays include *Wild Oats* (National Theatre). **TV:** Valerie Tatlock/Barlow in *Coronation Street; Crown Court; Strangers; Buggins Ermine* (Screenplay); *Matchfit* (Screenplay); *Heydays Hotel* (Screenplay); *My Father's House* (series); *Fathers and Families; The Mallens; Bleak House; Inappropriate Behaviour; Dawn and the Candidate* (4-Play); *Shine on Harvey Moon; Doctor Who; Victoria Wood – As Seen on TV; Victoria Wood: The Library; Victoria Wood: Men's Sana in Thingummy Doodah; About Face: Mrs Worthington's Daughter; Rich Tea & Sympathy; Very Big, Very Soon; A Bit of Fry and Laurie; The Upper Hand; Josie Smith; Boon; Casualty;*

Muriel McKay in *Gone Too Far – The Mystery of Mrs Muriel McKay* (Crime Story); *The Ruth Rendell Mysteries: Kissing the Gunner's Daughter, Victoria Wood: The Library; Micky Love* (Rik Mayall Presents); *The Bill; Heartbeat;* Rita Barrat in *Peak Practice;* Wendy Holmes in *Firm Friends; Medics; Seaforth;* Maeve in *Pat and Margaret* (Screen One); Pam in *Where the Buffalo Roam* (pilot); Renie in *Roughnecks* (series, 1995); *Hetty Wainthropp Investigates; Don't Dilly Dally on the Way* and *The Lift* (both Paul Merton in Galton & Simpson's...); voice of Wendolene in *A Close Shave: Wallace and Gromit; In Hitler's Shadow; Missing Persons.* Address: c/o Crouch Associates.

Anne Reid

REID, Beryl

Beryl Elizabeth Reid. Actress. b. Hereford, 17 June 1919. OBE, 1986. West End plays include *The Killing of Sister George* (also Broadway) and *Entertaining Mr Sloane.*
TV: *Mr Bowling Buys a Newspaper; The Girl Most Likely; Man o'Brass; The Hen House; Vic's Grill; Monitor; Show Time; Tonight; A-Z; The Beryl Reid Show; Comedy Playhouse; Not So Much a Programme, More a Way of Life; Wooster; Mrs Capper's Birthday; Beryl Reid; The Frog; Beryl Reid Says Good Evening; The Rivals; Father Dear Father; The Good Old Days; Alcock and Gander; Smike; The Goodies; Wink to Me Only; The Apple Cart; The Beryl Reid Special; When We Are Married; Flint;* Connie Sachs in *Tinker, Tailor, Soldier, Spy* and *Smiley's People; Worzel Gummidge; Does the Team Think?; Get Up and Go; Doctor Who;* Mrs Knox in *The Irish RM; The Secret Diary of Adrian Mole Aged 13¾* and *The Growing Pains of Adrian Mole; Minder; Late Starter; Alexei Sayle's Stuff; A Perfect Spy; The Beiderbecke Tapes; Didn't You Kill My Brother?* (The Comic Strip Presents...); *Duel of Hearts* (TVM); *Bergerac; Boon; Perfect Scoundrels; Shall We Gather at the River?; Cracker; The All New Alexei Sayle Show; Fine Time.*
Films: *Spare a Copper, The Belles of St Trinian's, The Extra Day, Two-Way Stretch, The Dock Brief* (US title *Trial and Error); Inspector Clouseau, The Assassination Bureau, Star!; The Killing of Sister George; Entertaining Mr Sloane; The Beast in the Cellar, Dr Phibes Rises Again; Father Dear Father, Psychomania; No Sex Please – We're British; Joseph Andrews; Rosie Dixon Night Nurse; Carry On Emmannuelle; Late Flowering Love* (short); *Yellowbeard; The Doctor and the Devils; High Spirits.*
Awards: TV: BAFTA Best Actress award for *Smiley's People* (1982).
Books: *So Much Love* (autobiography, 1984); *The Cat's Whiskers; Beryl, Food and Friends; The Kingfisher Jump.* Address: c/o James Sharkey Associates. m. 1st 1950 Bill Worsley (dis), 2nd 1954 musician Derek Franklin (dis). Pets: Nine cats. Hobbies: Feeding cats, cooking, gardening, RSPCA.

Beryl Reid

REID, Mike

Michael Reid. Actor/Comedian. b. London, 19 January 1940. Formerly a coalman and lorry driver.
TV: *The Saint; The Baron* (both as an extra); *The Comedians; Runaround* (presenter); Benny in *Yus My Dear* (two series, 1976); *Big Deal;* Frank Butcher in *EastEnders* (1987, 1988-94, 1995-6); Ronnie Richardson in *The Detectives; Wish You Were Here...?* (guest reporter).
Videos: *Mike Reid, Live and Uncensored* (1992); *Mike Reid, Live and Uncensored II* (1993); *Pussy in Boots* (1994). **Records:** Single: *The Ugly Duckling* (UK No 10, 1975). Album: *Mike Reid Sings...* (1993). Address: c/o Tony Lewis Entertainments. Lives in Essex. m. 2nd Shirley; 2 s. Mark (dec), Michael, 2 step-children. Hobbies: Golf.

Mike Reid

RHYS JONES, Griff

Griff Rhys Jones. Actor/Writer. b. Cardiff, 16 November 1953. Stage plays include *Charley's Aunt* (Aldwych Theatre) and *The Wind in the Willows* (National Theatre).
TV: *Not the Nine o'Clock News; Alas Smith and Jones;* Cornelius Carrington in *Porterhouse Blue; The Best of Smith and Jones; 'Ex'* (TVM); *Smith & Jones; QED: Knights of the Shining Piddock* (narrator); *Funnybones* (voice only, animated series, 1992); *The British Academy Awards* (presenter, 1993); *Total Relief: A Night of Comic Relief* (presenter, 1993); Ian Deasey in *Demob* (series, 1993); *The Secret Museum* (presenter); *Natural Neighbours* (narrator, series, 1994); *The Bookworm* (presenter, two series, 1994-5); *The Bookworm Special* (for Read and Write Together Week, presenter, 1995); *Davy in Sardines* (Comedy First); *Smith and Jones: Prime Cuts* (four compilations, 1995); *The Bookworm Summer Special* (presenter, 1995); *The Nation's Favourite Poems* (presenter, series, 1995).
Films: Graham in *Morons from Outer Space; Wilt; Shattered.* Address: c/o TalkBack

Griff Rhys Jones

RICE, Anneka

Annie Rice. Presenter. b. Cowbridge, South Glamorgan, 4 October 1958. Worked in Hong Kong (1979-82) in radio, and as a TV newscaster and producer (TVB), before returning to the UK.
TV: *CBTV; Treasure Hunt; Sporting Chance; Show Business; Family Trees; Wish You Were Here...?; Name and Games; Driving Force; World Circus Championships; Good Morning Britain; Challenge Anneka* (also co-deviser and executive producer, 1989-95); *The Other Side of Christmas; Holiday; Play It Safe!; Holiday Outings; 2point4 Children* (acting herself); *The Best of Challenge Anneka; Holiday of a Lifetime* (pilot); *Capital Woman* (Carlton only, 1993-5); *Passport* (pilot, 1992, and series, 1993); *Challenge Anneka Special.* Address: c/o BBC TV. m. theatre producer Nick Allott (sep); 2 d. Hobbies: Tennis.

Anneka Rice

Eric Richard

RICHARD, Eric

Eric Richard. Actor. b. Margate, Kent, 27 June 1940.
TV: *The Onedin Line; Shoestring; Mitch; Angels; Juliet Bravo; Home Sweet Home; Made in Britain; Games without Frontiers; Shogun; Open All Hours; Victoria Wood — As Seen on TV;* Sgt Bob Cryer in *The Bill; Wish You Were Here...?* (guest presenter). Address: c/o Peters Fraser & Dunlop. m. Christine; 1 s. Richard, 1 d. Frances. Hobbies: Motorcycling, music, sport.

RICHARD, Wendy

Wendy Richard

Wendy Richard. Actress. b. Middlesbrough, 20 July 1946. Trained at the Italia Conti Stage Academy. Showbusiness career started with her part on the No 1 single *Come Outside* with Mike Sarne (updated 25 years later with Mike Berry). Plays include *Are You Being Served?* (stage version of TV series).
TV: *Hugh and I; Harpers West One; The Arthur Haines Show; Dixon of Dock Green; Danger Man; No Hiding Place; Joe Nobody; The Making of Jericho; Z Cars;* Joyce Harker in *The Newcomers;* Doreen in *On the Buses; Please Sir!; The Fenn Street Gang; Up Pompeii!; Not On Your Nellie; Both Ends Meet; Spooner's Patch;* Edith Parish in *Dad's Army; West Country Tales;* Miss (Shirley) Brahms in *Are You Being Served?* (1973-84) and *Grace and Favour* (two series, 1992-3, screened in US as *Are You Being Served, Again?*); Pauline Fowler in *EastEnders* (1985-).
Films: *Doctor in Clover; No Blade of Grass; Bless This House; On the Buses; Carry On Matron; Gumshoe; Carry On Girls; Are You Being Served?*
Radio: *Trains Don't Stop Here Any More; Cat's Whiskers; Just a Minute;* reading of short stories for Holy Week; *It's My Future; Some of These Days; The Law Game; Listening Corner; Don't Talk to Me about Kids; Screenplay,* stood in for Ken Bruce on his BBC Radio 2 morning show.
Records: *Come Outside* (with Mike Sarne) (No 1, 1962).
Address: c/o MGA/BBC Elstree Centre. Lives in London. m. 1st Leonard Black (dis), 2nd Will Thorpe (dis 1984), 3rd 17 March 1990 Paul Glorney (sep 1994). Pets: Cairn terrier Shirley (Brahms) and cockateel Henry. Hobbies: Collecting frogs, clowns, condiment sets, tapestry work, plants.

RICHARDS, Stan

Stan Richards

Stanley Richardson. Actor. b. Barnsley, South Yorkshire, 8 December 1930. Worked as a Ministry of Labour clerk on leaving school, entered showbusiness as a dance-band pianist, formed comedy and musical quartet Melody Maniacs, then became a solo entertainer. Stage roles include Eddie Waters in *Comedians* (Theatre Royal, York).
TV: *The Price of Coal* (Play for Today); *Stepping Out* (Play of the Week); *Coronation Street; The Cuckoo Waltz; Crown Court; All Creatures Great and Small; Last of the Summer Wine;* Seth Armstrong in *Emmerdale* (1977-).
Films: *Yanks; Agatha.* Address: c/o Emmerdale Production Centre. Lives in Barnsley. m. February 1952 Susan (dec August 1994); 3 s. Alan, Keith, Irvin, 3 d. Joan, Dawn, June. Hobbies: 'Work. '

RICHARDSON, Ian

Ian Richardson

Ian Richardson. Actor. b. Edinburgh, 7 April 1934. CBE, 1989.
TV: *As You Like It; All's Well That Ends Well; The Canterbury Tales; Sorry...: Private View/Audience* (Play for Today); *A Voyage round My Father; Civilisation; Eyeless in Gaza; Danton's Death; Ike: The War Years; Churchill's Generals; Charlie Muffin; Private Schulz; Passing Through; A Cotswold Death; We Never Make Mistakes; The Woman in White; The Hound of the Baskervilles* (TVM); *The Sign of Four; The Master of Ballantrae;* Adrian Avigdor in *Mistral's Daughter* (mini-series); *Slimming Down; Mountbatten; Six Centuries of Verse; Monsignor Quixote; Star Quality; Blunt; Porterhouse Blue; The Devil's Disciple; Troubles; The Winslow Boy;* Cholet in *The Phantom of the Opera* (TVM); *The Gravy Train;* Francis Urquhart in *House of Cards* (mini-series, 1990), *To Play the King* (mini-series, 1993) and *The Final Cut* (mini-series, 1995); *The Gravy Train Goes East;* Governor Rex Hunt in *An Ungentlemanly Act;* Lee Mandeville in *Mistress of Suspense: Under a Dark Angel's Eye;* Niccolo Machiavelli in *Timewatch: Memo rom Machiavelli.*
Films: *The Marat/Sade; A Midsummer Night's Dream; Man of La Mancha; The Darwin Adventure; Brazil;* Sherlock Holmes in *The Sign of Four* and *The Hound of the Baskervilles;* Rear Admiral Bendish in *Whoops Apocalypse;* Sir Nigel Irvine in *The Fourth Protocol;* State Prosecutor in *Cry Freedom;* Father in *Burning Secret; Pursuit.* Address: c/o London Management.

RICHARDSON, Joely

Joely Richardson

Joely Richardson. Actress. b. London, 9 January 1965. Daughter of actress Vanessa Redgrave and director Tony Richardson; sister of actress Natasha Richardson (qv). Trained at RADA.
TV: *Body Contact; Behaving Badly; Heading Home; The Storyteller;* Lady Constance Chatterley in *Lady Chatterley* (series, 1993); *Anne Frank Remembered* (reading diary excerpts).
Films: *Wetherby;* 3rd Cissie Colpitts in *Drowning by Numbers; Rebecca's Daughters;* Princess Anna in *King Ralph;* Margrete in *Shining Through*). Address: c/o ICM. m. film producer Tim Bevan; 1 child.

RICHARDSON, Miranda

Miranda Richardson. Actress. b. Lancashire, 1958. Stage plays include *Moving* (Queen's Theatre).
TV: *The Hard Word; Sorell and Son; A Woman of Substance; Underworld; Death of the Heart; Blackadder II; After Pilkington;* Amy Hardwood in *Blackadder the Third; Smith and Jones;* Sarah Marriot in *Ball-Trap on the Côte Sauvage; Die Kinder (The Children);* Nurse Mary in *Blackadder Goes Forth; Redemption; The Storyteller; Old Times* (Performance); Sandra in *Mr Wakefield's Crusade* (series, 1992); Bettina in *Absolutely Fabulous; French and Saunders in... Space Virgins from Planet Sex; Broken Skin.*
Films: Ruth Ellis in *Dance with a Stranger; The Innocent; Underworld;* Mrs Victor in *Empire of the Sun; Dream of a Mad Monkey; The Fool;* Rose Arbuthnot in *Enchanted April; Damage; Tom and Viv;* Jude in *The Crying Game; Damage.* Address: c/o Kerry Gardner Management.

Miranda Richardson

RICHARDSON, Natasha

Natasha Jane Richardson. Actress. b. London, 11 May 1963. Daughter of actress Vanessa Redgrave and director Tony Richardson; sister of actress Joely Richardson (qv). Trained at the Central School of Speech and Drama. Stage plays include *A Midsummer Night's Dream* and *Hamlet* (both Young Vic).
TV: *In a Secret State; The Adventures of Sherlock Holmes: The Copper Beeches; Ghosts; The Barringtons;* Jill Morell in *Hostages* (drama-documentary, 1992); Catharine Holly in *Suddenly Last Summer* (Performance).
Films: *Every Picture Tells a Story; In the Secret State;* Mary Godwin in *Gothic; Patty; Fatman and Little Boy; A Month in the Country; Another Country;* Kate in *The Handmaid's Tale; The Comfort of Strangers.* Address: c/o Hutton Management.

Natasha Richardson

RICHIE, Shane

Shane Patrick Roache. Actor/Comedian/Presenter/Singer. b. North London, 11 March 1964. Joined the Young People's Theatre Group at the age of 15 and toured the UK in several productions. Became a Bluecoat entertainer for Pontin's. Starred on stage in *The New Adventures of Peter Pan* (Lewisham Theatre) and in *Grease* (Dominion Theatre, 1993-4).
TV: *Summertime Special* (1986); *Live from the Palladium; You Must Be Joking* (resident comedian, 1989); *Derek Jameson Tonight* (co-presenter, Sky One); *Up to Something* (sitcom series); *You Gotta Be Jokin'; Paramount City* (retitled *The London Underground* in US); *Caught in the Act* (presenter, Series 1, 1992); *Custard Pie Shoot-Out* (Children in Need, 1992); *Gone Live!* (Series 6); *The Children's Royal Variety Performance 1993; Win, Lose or Draw* (host, series); *Run the Risk* (co-host, two series); *Live and Kicking on Christmas Day* (*Run the Risk* special, 1993); *Win, Lose or Draw* (host, series, 1994); *The Children's Royal Variety Performance 1994; Lucky Numbers* (host, two series, 1995-6); *The Shane Richie Experience* (series, 1996).
Address: c/o International Artistes. Lives in Hillingdon, Middlesex. m. singer Coleen Nolan (of the Nolan Sisters); 2 s. Shane Jr, Jake. Pets: A dog called Harley. Hobbies: Go-karting.

Shane Richie

RIGG, Diana

Diana Rigg. Actress. b. Doncaster, South Yorkshire, 20 July 1938. CBE, 1987; Dame, 1994. Acted with the RSC (1962-4) and starred in the stage shows *Follies* and *Medea* (London and Broadway).
TV: *The Hothouse* (début, 1964); Emma Peel in *The Avengers* (two series, 1965, 1967); *Diana* (US); *In This House of Brede; Witness for the Prosecution; King Lear; Bleak House; Held in Trust* (documentary); *The Wicked Witch; A Hazard of Hearts* (TVM); *Mother Love; The Laurence Olivier Awards 1992* (host); *Mrs 'Arris Goes to Paris* (TVM); Frieda Von Stangel in *Genghis Cohn* (Screen Two); *Oliver 2* (Comic Relief, 1995); *Moll Flanders.*
Films: *A Midsummer Night's Dream; The Assassination Bureau; On Her Majesty's Secret Service; Hospital; Theatre of Blood; A Little Night Music; Evil under the Sun; Running Delilah.*
Address: c/o London Management. m. Archie Stirling.

Diana Rigg

RIGGANS, Mary

Mary Riggans. Actress. b. Glasgow, 19 July. Begun acting on BBC radio at the age of 10 in *Scottish Children's Hour* and made her TV début aged 16 in *A Nest of Singing Birds.* Continued working while studying for an MA at Glasgow University and acted with the university's drama society.
TV: *A Nest of Singing Birds; Dr Finlay's Casebook; Sunset Song; Weir of Hermiston; Just Your Luck* (Play for Today); *The Prime of Miss Jean Brodie; Annals of the Parish; Maggie; Benny Lynch; First among Equals;* schools programmes (presenter); Effie Macinnes/McDonald in *Take the High Road/High Road;* Rab C Nesbitt; *The Ship;* Mrs Adams in *Taggart: Double Exposure.*
Radio: *Scottish Children's Hour; Morning Story; Twelve Noon; Saturday Night Theatre.*
Awards: Radio: Radio Actress of the Year for *Till A' the Seas Gang Dry* (1983).
Address: c/o Scottish Television. Lives in Edinburgh. m. Malcolm; 1 d. research scientist Samantha. Hobbies: Watching rugby, tennis, knitting.

Mary Riggans

RINGHAM, John

John Ringham

John Henry Ringham. Actor. b. Cheltenham, Gloucestershire, 10 February 1928. Started as an ASM.
TV: Plays: *Hilda Lessways; Julius Caesar; Rainy Day Women; Daniel and Sinyavsky; To Encourage the Others; The Scottsboro' Case; Major Lavender; Rookery Nook; Galileo Galilei; Dr Faustus; The Caucasian Chalk Circle; Flat Bust; The Luddites; Death of Hitler; Shadowlands; The Cantor of St Thomas's; New World; After the Solo; Stargazy at Summerdown; Rogue Male.* Serials: *An Age of Kings; The Railway Children; Resurrection; Nana; Germina; The Forsyte Saga; Bleak House; David Copperfield; The Avenue; The River Flows East; The Donati Conspiracy; The Pallisers; A Tale of Two Cities; A Christmas Carol; Dickens of London; The First Churchills; Casanova; Man of Straw; Flambards; The Flaxton Boys; Taste for Death; Barchester Chronicles; Poldark; Pennies from Heaven.* Series: *Ghost Squad; Doctor Who; Dixon of Dock Green; Z Cars; Emergency — Ward 10; Fraud Squad; Softly Softly; Barlow at Large; Compact; The Newcomers; The Saint; The Baron; The Mind of Mr J G Reeder; The Avengers; Jury; Rosie; Angels; Crown Court; Just William; When the Boat Comes In; Orson Welles' Mysteries; New Scotland Yard; Hine; Catweazle; The Troubleshooters; Love Story; Spy Trap; Wilde Alliance; Crown Court; The Ghost of Motley Hall; Sherlock Holmes; All Creatures Great and Small; Warship; Raffles;* Captain Bailey in *Dad's Army; The Dick Emery Show; Up Pompeii; Bless Me, Father; The Charlie Drake Show; Moody and Pegg; Are You Being Served?; Yes Honestly; The Basil Brush Show; The Liver Birds; Black Beauty; Colditz; Terry and June; Some Mothers Do 'Ave 'Em; The New Statesman;* Mr Warrender in *Just Good Friends; Woof!;* Major Maxwell in *The Piglet Files; Casualty; The Bill; Hannay;* Chief Fire Officer in *London's Burning; Bergerac; Storytime; Birds of a Feather; The Darling Buds of May; The Governor.* Address: c/o Michael Ladkin Personal Management. Lives in London. m. Hedwig Felizitas; 2 d. Jessica Maria, Hannah Saskia, 2 s. Max John, Ben Franz. Pets: Three cats. Hobbies: Writing, playing the piano (Bach), allotment.

RINTOUL, David

David Rintoul

David Rintoul. Actor. b. Aberdeen, 29 November 1948. Trained at RADA.
TV: Archie Weir in *Weir of Hermiston; The Flight of the Heron; The Hunchback of Notre Dame; 1990; Crown Court; Warship; Lillie; Lord Peter Wimsey; Prince Regent; Henry VIII;* Dick Mallen in *The Mallens; One Chance in Four;* Mr Darcy in *Pride and Prejudice; A.D.; The Cherry Orchard; The Big Deal; The Dunroamin' Rising;* James Boswell in *Dialogue in the Dark; Taggart: Death Comes Softly; Kinsey; Agatha Christie's Poirot;* title role in *Doctor Finlay* (four series 1993-6); *The Inspector Alleyn Mysteries.*
Films: Title role in *Legend of the Werewolf.* **Radio:** David Balfour in *Kidnapped and Catriona;* Richard Hannay in *The Thirty Nine Steps.* Address: c/o Ken McReddie. Lives in London. Partner: Actress Vivien Heilbron (qv). Pets: Two tabby cats called Bill and Peter. Hobbies: Riding, sailing, music.

RIPPON, Angela

Angela Rippon

Angela Rippon. Presenter. b. Plymouth, Devon, 12 October 1944. Journalist on *The Independent,* Plymouth, before entering television.
TV: BBC Plymouth (reporter-presenter, 1966-9), including *Spotlight South West; Open House* (editor-presenter, Westward Television); *Westward Reports; Young Eyes; Generation Three* (all as producer, Westward Television); *The Silent Valley* (documentary, producer, winner of Silver Medal at the New York Film Festival); BBC TV News reporter and newsreader (1973-81); *News Extra; The Morecambe and Wise Christmas Show; The Eurovision Song Contest;* 1979 General Election (BBC); founder-member of TV-am (presenter of *Good Morning Britain); Live from London* (Channel 9, Australia); *The Don Lane Show* (Australia); *Angela Rippon Meets...; The Antiques Roadshow; People in Power; In the Country; Top Gear; The Rippon Reports; Come Dancing; Masterteam; What's My Line?;* Newsreader in *House of Cards; World of Dogs; Crufts '92; The Entertainers; An Invitation to Remember* (presenter); *Whatever Happened to...?* (presenter); *Day Out;* TV Presenter in *The Man Who Didn't Believe in Ghosts* (Chiller); *Schofield's Quest.*
Books: *Riding; Mark Phillips — The Man and His Horses; Angela Rippon's West Country; Victoria Plum; In the Country; Badminton — A Celebration.* **Awards:** TRIC Newsreader of the Year award (1976, 1977, 1978). Address: c/o IMG. Lives in London and Tavistock, Devon. m. Chris Dare (sep). Pets: A dog called Benson and a horse called Extra Time. Hobbies: Horse-riding, theatre.

RITCHIE, Kate

Kate Ritchie

Kate Ritchie. Actress. b. Sydney, Australia. Started dancing at the age of three and competed in many Eisteddfod competitions. Began appearing in TV commercials aged five.
TV: Molly in *Cyclone Tracy* (mini-series); Sally Keating in *Home and Away* (1988-).
Address: c/o James Laurie Management/Channel 7.

ROACH, Pat

Pat Roach

Pat Roach. Actor. b. Birmingham, 13 May. Also a professional wrestler.
TV: *The Sea Dragon; Minder; Bullseye; Three Wishes for Jamie; Hazell; Gangsters; Juliet Bravo; Tiswas;* Bomber in *Auf Wiedersehen Pet* (two series); *The Last Place on Earth; The Lenny and Jerry*

Show; We Love TV; The Saturday Show; The Jim Davidson Show; Harry's Kingdom; Coasting; Bergerac; The Detectives; Space Precinct; Reg Warren in *The Bill;* Mickey in *Ellington.*
Films: *Adventures of the Spaceman and King Arthur; A Clockwork Orange; Barry Lyndon; Rising Damp; Conan the Destroyer; Clash of the Titans; Raiders of the Lost Ark; Indiana Jones and the Temple of Doom; Never Say Never Again; Red Sonja; Willow; Indiana Jones and the Last Crusade; Return of the Musketeers; Superman III; Robin Hood: Prince of Thieves.* Address: c/o Peter Charlesworth.

Linus Roache

ROACHE, Linus
Linus William Roache. Actor. b. 1 February 1964. Son of actor William Roache (qv) and actress Anna Cropper (qv). Trained at the Central School of Speech and Drama. RSC stage roles include William in *Indigo,* Mark Antony in *Julius Caesar,* Aumerle in *Richard II,* Edgar in *King Lear* and Don Juan in *The Last Days of Don Juan.* Other stage roles include Clive in *Five Finger Exercise* (Cambridge Theatre company).
TV: Peter Barlow in *Coronation Street* (aged nine, five episodes); Peter Davison in *A Sort of Innocence;* Danny in *Saracen;* title role in *Omnibus: Vincent Van Gogh; Priest* (Screen Two); Tom in *Keeping Tom Nice;* DS Brian Tait in *Black and Blue* (Screen One); Bob Longman in *Seaforth* (series, 1994).
Films: *Mister God, This Is Anna; Priest.* Address: c/o Kate Feast Management. Lives in London. Single. Partner: Actress Rosalind Bennett (qv). Pets: A cat called Shakti. Hobbies: Travelling, picture framing.

ROACHE, William
William Patrick Roache. Actor. b. Ilkeston, Derbyshire, 25 April 1932. Entered acting after service in the Royal Welch Fusiliers (1951-6) in the West Indies and Germany, and as a captain in the Gulf.
TV: *Skyport; Knight Errant Limited; The Bulldog Breed; Biggles; Marking Time* (Play of the Week); Ken Barlow in *Coronation Street* (1960-); *Royal Variety Performance* (1989, with *Coronation Street* cast).
Films: *Behind the Mask; His and Hers; The Queen's Guards.* **Awards:** Pye Television Award joint winner, with Anne Kirkbride (qv) and Johnny Briggs (qv), for *Coronation Street* (1983).
Address: c/o Granada Television. Lives in Wilmslow, Cheshire. m. 1st actress Anna Cropper (qv) (dis 1974), 2nd 1977 actress Sara McEwan; 2 s. actor Linus William (qv) (b. 1964, from 1st m.), William James (b. 1986, from 2nd m.), 3 d. Vanya (from 1st m.), Verity Elizabeth (b. 1981), Edwina (b. 1982, dec 1984) (both from 2nd m.). Hobbies: Playing golf, horse-riding, tennis.

William Roache

ROBB, David
David Robb. Actor. b. London, 23 August 1947. Brought up in Edinburgh. Trained at the Central School of Speech and Drama.
TV: *Crown Court; The Glittering Prizes; I Claudius; French without Tears; The Winslow Boy; Wings; Wuthering Heights; Hess; Romeo and Juliet; The Caledonian Cascade; Hamlet; Hazell; Out; The Legend of King Arthur; The Flame Trees of Thika; Forgive Our Foolish Ways; Fanny by Gaslight; Ivanhoe* (TVM); *Charles & Diana: A Royal Love Story* (TVM); *Morte d'Arthur; The Last Days of Pompeii; Wallenberg: A Hero's Story* (TVM); *Off-Peak; First among Equals; Dreams Lost, Dreams Found* (TVM); *Wall of Tyranny* (TVM); *The Man Who Lived at the Ritz* (TVM); *Flight to Istanbul* (TVM); *Taggart; Parnell and the Englishwoman; To Be the Best* (mini-series); *Up the Garden Path; Some Other Spring* (TVM); Andrew Menzies in *Strathblair* (two series, 1992-3); Brutus in *Julius Caesar* (Shakespeare: The Animated Tales); Henry Reeve-Jones in *Casualty* (series, 1995-6); *Half the Picture* (Screen Two).
Films: *Conduct Unbecoming; The Four Feathers; The Deceivers.*
Address: c/o William Morris Agency (UK). m. actress Briony McRoberts (qv).

David Robb

ROBBIE, Sue
Susan Jennifer Robinson. Presenter. b. London, 5 July 1949. BA (Hons) degree in psychology and English from Keele University. Taught English in a comprehensive school for four years and worked as an air stewardess with British Airways for a further four years before entering television in 1982.
TV: Granada Television continuity announcer; *First Post; Hold Tight!; Sneak Preview; Weekend; Children's ITV; Cartoon Crackers; Connections; Names and Games; TX; Ark Royal – The Rock Show; Video Active; The Dodo Club; Breakfast Time; Showreel 87; The Dodo Christmas Club; ITV Telethon; 01- for London; Pick of the Week; Emergency (This Morning); Consumer File (TSW, 1989-92); Streetwise (The Channel Four Daily); Business South West* (TSW); *Sixth Sense* (Anglia TV); *Project I.T.; The Magic and Mystery Show* (Anglia TV); *Fair's Fair* (series, HTV and Westcountry Television only). Voice-overs: *Your Living Body; The Micro at Work; Chemistry in Action; World in Action; Network First.* Address: c/o Arlington Enterprises. Lives in Cheshire. Single. Hobbies: Walking, yoga, films, metaphysics/spirituality.

Sue Robbie

ROBERTS, Ben
Ben Roberts. Actor. b. Bangor, Clwyd, 1 July 1950.
TV: *Tales of Sherwood Forest;* Chief Insp/Acting Supt/Chief Insp Derek Conway in *The Bill* (1989-).
Address: Spotlight/The Bill. Lives in Nottingham. m. Helen; 1 s. Joe. Pets: An old cat called Henry. Hobbies: Doing up old cars.

Ben Roberts

ROBERTS, Ivor

Ivor Roberts

Ivor Roberts. Actor. b. Nottingham, 19 July 1925. Returned to theatre after war service in the Navy.
TV: *Doctor Who; Secret Army; Bergerac; Sam; Born and Bred; Dombey and Son; The Sailor's Return; Yes Minister; Minder; Sorry; The New Statesman; Coronation Street; The Bretts; Shadow of the Noose; Snow; Better Days; We Are Seven; The 19th Hole;* Thomas Jenner in *The Bill;* Barnes in *You Rang, M'Lord?;* Arnold in *Oh Doctor Beeching!* (pilot, 1995);
Films: *Hopscotch; Sweet William; Another Country; Portrait of Evil; Personal Services; We Think the World of You.* Address: c/o Howes and Prior. m. Iris; 1 d. Melanie.

ROBINSON, Anne

Anne Robinson

Anne Robinson. Presenter/Journalist. b. Crosby, Liverpool, 26 September. Current affairs reporter on *The Sunday Times* for 10 years, woman's editor, then deputy editor and columnist on the *Daily Mirror.* As assistant editor at the *Daily Mirror,* she was the first woman in the history of Fleet Street to edit a national paper, before moving to *Today* as a columnist in 1993, when she also left her show on BBC Radio 2 to present *Watchdog* on television. Left *Today* when it closed in 1995.
TV: *Breakfast Time* (TV critic); *Points of View; Just Questions; Anne Robinson at the GHI* (*This Morning,* 1992); *Watchdog* (presenter, series, 1993-5); *Watchdog Holiday Special* (Easter Monday, 1994); *Bardbrain* (Bard on the Box, 1994); *Watchdog Special* (on British beaches, 1995).
Address: c/o BBC TV. m. journalist John Penrose (sep); 1 d. Emma.

ROBINSON, Robert

Robert Robinson

Robert Robinson. Presenter. b. Liverpool, 17 December 1927. Gained a degree in English language and literature from Exeter College, Oxford. Trained as a journalist after National Service.
TV: *Picture Parade; Points of View; Ask the Family; All Our Yesterdays; Call My Bluff; The Fifties; Brain of Britain; Robinson's Travels; The Book Programme; Word for Word; The Book Game; Robinson Country; Behind the Headlines; Robinson Cruising; B Traven.* **Radio:** *Today* (1971–4); *Stop the Week; Brain of Britain.* **Books:** *Conspiracy; Landscape with Dead Dons; Inside Robert Robinson; The Dog Chairman; Everyman Book of Light Verse; Bad Dreams* (novel); *Prescriptions of a Pox Doctor's Clerk.* Address: c/o BBC TV. m. Josephine; 2 d. Lucy, Suzy, 1 s. Nicholas.

ROBINSON, Tony

Tony Robinson

Anthony Robinson. Actor/Writer. b. London, 15 August 1946. Stage début at the age of 12 in the original production of *Oliver!* Trained at the Central School of Speech and Drama.
TV: Ernie Roberts in *Horizon: Joey; Points of View* (presenter); *Who Dares Wins;* Baldrick in *The Black Adder, Blackadder II, Blackadder the Third* and *Blackadder Goes Forth; Bergerac;* Sheriff of Nottingham in *Maid Marian and Her Merry Men* (also writer, four series); *Stay Tooned* (presenter); *House of Payne; Teenage Health Freak; Blood and Honey* (storyteller and writer, series); *Time Team; Great Journeys; Blue Heaven* (series); *The Good Sex Guide* (series); *The Good Book Guide* (presenter, series); *The Good Sex Guide* (series, 1993); *Total Relief: A Night of Comic Relief* (reporting on AIDS in Uganda, 1993); Marcus in *A Woman's Guide to Adultery; Time Team* (presenter, two series, 1994-5); Willie in *Minder;* Chris Pringle in *Law and Disorder; The Red Nose Awards 94* (co-host, 1994); *The Story of Snow White* (*Stay Tooned!* special, 1994); *Great Journeys: The Caribbean with Tony Robinson; Sunday Brunch; The Natural World: Parrots – Look Who's Talking* (presenter); *Wrestling with the Big One* (writer-presenter, Sunday Brunch series, 1995); *Wild About Essex* (presenter, series, 1995); *Hospital Watch.* As writer only: *Fat Tulip's Garden* (series); *Odysseus – The Greatest Hero of Them All* (series).
Films: *NeverEnding Story III.* **Books:** *Maid Marian* comic books, plus children's books.
Address: c/o Kate Feast Management. Lives in Bristol. Single. Partner: Teri Bramah; 1 d. Laura Shepherd Robinson, 1 s. Luke Shepherd Robinson.

ROBSON, Linda

Linda Robson

Linda Robson. Actress. Trained at the Anna Scher Theatre School.
TV: *Jackanory Playhouse* (aged 12, 1970); *Pauline's Quirkes* (aged 17); *Within These Walls; General Hospital; Pauline's People* (1981); *Mary's Wife; Ain't Many Angels; The Good Neighbour; If Only; Cribb; Going Out; Agony; The Other 'Arf; The Case of the Middle Aged Wife; Chains;* Maggie Moon/Lewis in *Shine on Harvey Moon* (series, 1982-5, 1995); *Harry's Game* (mini-series and TVM); *L for Lester; Up the Elephant and round the Castle; Lizzie's Pictures; Elphida; Bad Boys; Thin Air; South of the Border; The Bill; Undergrounds;* Tracey in *Birds of a Feather* (six series, 1989-94, plus Christmas specials, 1993, 1994); *The Good Sex Guide* (series, 1993); *Children in Need* (with Pauline Quirke, 'singing Abba', 1993); *Jobs for the Girls* (presenter, documentary series, 1995, plus Christmas special 1995); Elsie Waters in *Call Up the Stars* (VE Day concert, 1995).
Films: Daisy in *Junket 89* (Children's Film Foundation production); *Absolution.*
Videos: *Stick It Out* (backing singer in Right Said Fred video, 1993). Address: c/o Artists Management Group. m. 16 Sep 1990 Mark; 1 d. Lauren (from previous relationship), 1 s. Louis (from m.).

RODERICK, Sue

Sue Roderick. Actress. Bilingual in Welsh and English.
TV: June in *Shelley; End of Season; A Penny for Your Dreams; The Max Boyce Show;* Joyce in *To Each His Own;* Sara in *The Committee;* Megan Morgan in *Coronation Street; Lazarus* (series); *The Bill;* Joyce in *Dinas; Licyris Olsorts; Pobol-y-Cwm; The Life of Eliza;* Lyn Thomas in *Selected Exits;* Bronwen Pugh in *The Lifeboat* (series, 1994); *Casualty;* Norma Moody in *Oliver's Travels* (series, 1995); *Trip Trap.*
Films: Gwen in *The Angry Earth;* Lizzie Roberts in *Hedd Wyn; Rebecca's Daughters;* Ruby in *Morphine and Dolly Mixtures.* Address: c/o Scott Marshall.

Sue Roderick

RODGERS, Anton

Anton Rodgers. Actor/Director. b. Wisbech, Cambridgeshire, 10 January 1933. Trained at the Italia Conti Stage Academy and acted as a child on stage. Subsequently trained at LAMDA.
TV: *Ukridge; The Elusive Pimpernel; The Organisation; Zodiac; Rumpole of the Bailey; Lillie; The Flaxborough Chronicles; Fresh Fields; Comeback; Talking Takes Two; Murder by Mirrors* (TVM); *Pictures; Sharing Time; French Fields; After the War, Goodbye and I Hope We Meet Again* (4-Play); Alec Callender in *May to December* (six series, 1989-94); David Scott-Fowler in *After the Dance* (Performance); *Travel UK* (guest presenter); *Old Bear Stories* (narrator, series, 1994).
Films: *Carry On Jack; Rotten to the Core; The Man Who Haunted Himself; Scrooge; The Fourth Protocol.* Address: c/o Michael Whitehall. m. 1st Morna, 2nd actress Elizabeth Garvie; 1 d. publisher Thalia, 4 s. film cameraman Adam (both from 1st m.), Barnaby, Dominic, Luke (all from 2nd m.).

Anton Rodgers

RODRIGUES, Tania

Tania Maria Rodrigues. Actress. b. Hong Kong (Indian), 10 September 1965. Gained a BA (Hons) in English and drama. Trained at The Drama Studio. Speaks English, Cantonese and French.
TV: Kamla Verma in *The Real Eddy English;* Katie in *Oranges Are Not the Only Fruit;* Khadia in *Lovejoy;* Joanne Khan in *Coronation Street* (12 episodes); *A Nice Arrangement* (Short and Curlies).
Films: The Bride in *Before the Wedding; Dancin' thru the Dark.* **Radio:** *Dora.* Address: c/o Actorum. Lives in London. m. Matthew Marsh. Hobbies: Aromatherapy, swimming, having fun.

Tania Rodrigues

RODSKA, Christian

Christian Rodskjaer. Actor. b. Cullercoats, 5 September 1945. Began career as a student at Salisbury Rep, earning £3 10s (£3.50) a week. Stage plays include *And a Nightingale Sang* (Queen's Theatre).
TV: Ron Strycker in *Follyfoot* (series, 1971-3); *The Exercise* (Play for Today); *Night People* (Play for Today); Duncan in *Tenko Reunion;* Esca in *The Eagle of the Ninth; Oliver Twist* (serial); Bernard in *Bergerac; The Galactic Garden; The Diary of Anne Frank;* Arthur Barras in *The Stars Look Down;* Tant in *This Year, Next Year; Coronation Street; Hallelujah;* Tom Nesbitt in *The Nesbitts Are Coming* (series, 1980); Beaverbrook in *Number 10; In Loving Memory; The World Cup – A Captain's Tale;* Father Bailey in *The Fifteen Streets;* Alexander Dewar in *Taggart;* Felix in *Wish Me Luck; Battalion; Dramarama: Snakes and Loofahs;* Dr O'Rourke in *Brookside* (10 episodes); *Campion;* Hedley in *The Bill; Spooks;* Neil Kinnock in *Thatcher: The Final Days; Casualty;* Sgt Moers in *Maigret;* Supt George Ellis in *Spender;* Dr Reiss in *Michael Winner's True Crimes; Medics;* Larry's Landlord (Leonard Davidson) in *Chandler & Co;* Hawthorne in *Licensed to Live;* Colin in *Casualty;* Giles Rawle in *Wycliffe;* Crake in *Sharpe's Mission.*
Films: *Les Misérables; The Reckoning; Penny Gold; The Likely Lads; Separate Rooms.*
Radio: Roger Ditchley in *The Fosdyke Saga* (1983-5); *Winston* (five series, 1989-94); more than 600 plays for BBC Radio. Address: c/o Evans and Reiss. Lives in Bath. m. Jacqueline; 1 s. pilot Ben (played Oliver in BBC TV's *Oliver Twist*), 1 d. student Camille. Pets: A cat. Hobbies: Sailing, skiing.

Christian Rodska

ROEVES, Maurice

Maurice Roëves. Actor/Director/Writer. b. Sunderland, Tyne & Wear, 19 March 1937. Trained at the Royal College of Drama, Glasgow. Stage plays include *Tunes of Glory* (world première).
TV: Scobie in *Sept and Scobieman; The Gambler; On the Line; The Sweeney; Moses* (TVM); *Target; Oil Strike North; Danger UXB; Twelfth Night; SOS Titanic* (TVM); *Inside the Third Reich; Heather Ann; Magnum PI; Remington Steele; The Quest; Lytton's Diary; Doctor Who; Bergerac; Big Deal; The Chinese Detective; The Journals of Brigitte Hitler;* Vince in *Tutti Frutti; Unreported Incident; Bookie* (mini-series); *North and South Book II; Movie of the Month; Days of Our Lives; Father, Son 'n' Holy Terror* (as writer); *Codename; Hunter; Jake and the Fat Man; Hunter; Middle for Diddle* (as writer); *El C.I.D.; Rumpole of the Bailey;* Mal Balmer in *Spender;* Young Young McGurn in *Rab C Nesbitt* (series); *Murder, She Wrote; 919 Fifth Avenue;* Eddie Gemonill in *The Negotiator.*
Films: *The Fighting Prince of Donegal; Ulysses; Oh! What a Lovely War; A Day at the Beach; When Eight Bells Toll; Young Winston; Transfusion; The Eagle Has Landed; Escape to Victory; The Final Option;* Major Steele in *Who Dares Wins; The Big Man; Hidden Agenda; Last of the Mohicans; The Negotiator; Judge Dredd.* Address: c/o ICM. Lives in Los Angeles, USA, and Ealing, West London. m. 1st (dis), 2nd (dis); 1 d. Sarah.

Maurice Roëves

Jean Rogers

ROGERS, Jean

Jean Rogers. Actress. b. Perivale, Middlesex, 2 February 1942. Trained at the Guildhall School of Music and Drama. Stage plays include *Perchance to Dream* (national tour). More than 1,500 radio broadcasts. **TV:** Nurse Rogers in *Emergency — Ward 10;* Julie Shepherd in *Crossroads; Here's Harry; Charge; Comedy Playhouse; Callan; George and Mildred; General Hospital; Watch* (presenter); *Calendar* (presenter, Yorkshire Television regional news magazine); Dolly Arcaster/Skilbeck in *Emmerdale* (1980-91); Mrs Dart in *Law and Disorder.*
Address: c/o David Daly Associates. m. 1st Terry Moakes (dis), 2nd TV assistant director Philip Hartley; 1 d. Justine, 1 s. Jeremy, four step-d. Pam, Zoe, Lucy, Jody. Hobbies: Cooking, wine-making, gardening, badminton, yoga.

ROGERS, Katharine

Katharine Rogers

Katharine Rogers. Actress. b. London, 21 December 1960. Performed with Anna Scher's Children's Theatre (aged 15). Trained at RADA. RSC productions include *A Midsummer Night's Dream, Romeo and Juliet, Camille, The Party, Today, Golden Girls, Red Noses, The Castle* and *Crimes in Hot Countries.*
TV: *Bloody Kids; The Magnificent One; Johnny Jarvis; Only Yesterday;* Firewoman Josie Ingham in *London's Burning.*
Films: *Quadrophenia.* Address: c/o Hope & Lyne. Lives in North London. Single.

ROPER, David

David Roper

David Anthony Roper. Actor. b. Bradford, West Yorkshire, 20 June 1944. Worked as an accountant (1961-9). Trained at the Bristol Old Vic Theatre School (1969-71).
TV: *Country Tales; Churchill's People; Crown Court;* PC Sadler in *Coronation Street* (1974); *My Brother's Keeper;* Chris Hawthorne in *The Cuckoo Waltz* (three series, 1975-7); *Joe and Mary;* Charlie Fisher in *Leave It to Charlie* (three series, 1978-80); *The Oresteia; On the Razzle; No Problem; What Mad Pursuit; Wally; A Bit of a Do; Capstick's Law; The Gift; Maxwell's House; Families;* DCI 'Nick' Nichols in *Harry* (series, 1993); *Stanley's Dragon;* Sam Bishop in *Brookside;* Dobey in *Ain't Misbehavin'* (series, 1994); Geoff Barnes in *EastEnders* (1994-5); Sam Archibald in *Taggart: Prayer for the Dead; Eleven Men against Eleven.*
Address: c/o Susan Angel Associates. Lives in France. m. 1st Margaret Jean Hammond (dis), 2nd Jacqueline Anne Edwards (dis), 3rd Andrea Lynne Ashdown; 3 s. George Antony (b. 1971, from 1st m.), Harry, Jack (twins, from 3rd m.). Hobbies: Writing, squash.

ROSE, Clifford

Clifford Rose

Clifford Rose. Actor. b. Hamnish, Herefordshire, 24 October 1929. Began career with the Elizabethan Theatre Company. RSC productions include *All's Well That Ends Well, A Dream of People* and *Moscow Gold.*
TV: *The Roads to Freedom;* Snell in *Callan; Elizabeth R; The Lady from the Sea;* Charles Burton in *Buccaneer; Strife; The Pallisers; How Green Was My Valley; Devil's Crown;* Richard II; Kessler in *Secret Army;* title role in *Kessler; The Cold Room; A Married Man; Strangers and Brothers; Reilly — Ace of Spies; Oxbridge Blues; Love's Labour's Lost; One by One; The Mozart Inquest; Oedipus the King; Fortunes of War; Gentlemen and Players; Inspector Morse; Agatha Christie's Poirot; The Gibraltar Inquest; War and Remembrance; G.B.H.;* Jolivet in *Maigret.*
Films: *The Marat/Sade; Callan; Work Is a Four-Letter Word; The Wall; Terry on the Fence; The Good Father.* Address: c/o Markham & Froggatt. Lives in London. m. actress Celia Ryder; 1 d. Alison, 1 s. Jonathan. Hobbies: Travel, gardening, music, languages.

ROSEANNE

Roseanne Barr. Actress/Writer. b. Salt Lake City, Utah, USA, 3 November 1952.
TV: *Fast Copy* (1985); *Funny; Rodney Dangerfield — It's Not Easy Bein' Me; The Tonight Show Starring Johnny Carson 24th Anniversary Special* (1986); *On Location: The Roseanne Barr Show* (also writer, 1987); *Lifetime Salutes Mom; The Comedy Store 15th Year Class Reunion* (1988); *Like Mother, Like Daughter;* Roseanne Conner in *Roseanne* (also co-creator and creative consultant, series, 1988-); *Just for Laughs: The 1991 Montreal International Comedy Festival* (1992); *Little Rosey* (voice only).
Films: Ruth Patchett in *She-Devil.*
Books: *Roseanne — My Life as a Woman* (autobiography, 1989).
Awards: ACE Funniest Female Performer in a Television Special, Funniest Female in a Comedy and Best Comedy Special for On Location: the *Roseanne Barr Show* (all 1987). Address: c/o William Morris Agency (US). m. 1st 1974 Bill Pentland (dis), 2nd 1990 Tom Arnold (dis), 3rd 1995 Ben Thomas; 2 d. Jessica, Jennifer, 2 s. Jake (all from 1st m.), Buck (b. 1996, from 3rd m.).

ROSLIN, Gaby

Roseanne

Gaby Roslin. Presenter. b. London, 10 July 1962. Trained at the Guildford School of Acting.
TV: *Hippo* (Superchannel); *ITV Telethon '90; Motormouth; Pick of the Week; Only Fools and Turkeys;*

The Big Breakfast (1992-5); *The Real Holiday Show* (three series, 1995-6); *Predators* (series, 1995); *Children in Need* (1995); *The Gaby Roslin Show* (series, 1996).
Address: c/o Arlington Enterprises. Lives in London. m. 1995 actor-musician Colin Peel.

ROSS, Jonathan

Jonathan Ross. Presenter. b. London, 17 November 1960. Former researcher for TV game shows.
TV: *Have Words; George Michael; The Last Resort; The Incredibly Strange Film Show; One Hour with Jonathan Ross; Tonight with Jonathan Ross; British Comedy Awards* (host, 1991-5); *Viva Elvis!; Americana* (series); *Saturday Zoo* (series); *Game for a Game!* (*Total Relief: A Night of Comic Relief*, 1993); *Fantastic Facts!* (presenter, series, 1993, special, 1994); *Jonathan Ross Presents* (series, 1994); *The 10%ers* (acting himself); *The Movie Awards* (host, 1994); *Gagtag* (host, comedy quiz series, 1994); *Jonathan Ross Presents: David Copperfield; How to Win the Lottery; The Ultimate Playboy – Jonathan Ross Meets Hugh Hefner; Prince Cinders* (voice only, 1995); *Late and Languid with Jonathan Ross* (*Comic Relief*, 1995); *It's Marty Resurrected: Some of the Best of Marty Feldman; The Travel Show* (guest reporter); *Mondo Rosso* (series, 1995); *In Search of James Bond with Jonathan Ross; The Brits Are Coming.* **Radio:** *Drug Alert.* Address: c/o Gary Farrow, Jonathan Ross Enterprises, Suite 3, 15 Clanricarde Gardens, London W2 4JJ, tel 071-727 6251. Lives in North London. m. Jane; 1 d. Betty Kitten.

Gaby Roslin

ROSS, Nick

Nicholas David Ross. Presenter. b. London, 7 August 1947. Entered broadcasting as a reporter-presenter for BBC radio in Northern Ireland (1971-2) before moving to TV. Still a frequent radio broadcaster.
TV: *In Question; Scene around Six* (both BBC Northern Ireland); *Man Alive* (reporter-director, 1976-83); *Man Alive Report; Out of Court* (presenter-director); *The Editors; Play for Today; Portrait of a 'Terrorist'; Fair Comment; Did You See...?; Breakfast Time; Out of Court* (1982-4); *Sixty Minutes* (1983-4); *Newsnight; Horizon; Crimewatch UK* (1984-); *Watchdog* (1985-6); *On the Record; A Week in Politics* (1986-8); *Crimestoppers; Drugwatch; Family Show; Crime Limited* (three series, 1992-4); *Crimewatch File; The Inside Track... on Parenting; Crime Limited Special: Hostage; The Family Show; The Family Call: On Men; Star Memories; Westminster with Nick Ross* (series, 1994-5); *Conference Live '95* (political party conferences, 1995). As producer: *The Fix; The Cure; Man Alive: The Biggest Epidemic of Our Times.* Address: c/o Jules Bennett Agency. m. Sarah Caplin (*Watchdog* editor); 3 s. Adam, Sam, Jack.

Jonathan Ross

ROSSINGTON, Norman

Norman Arthur Rossington. Actor. b. Liverpool, 24 December 1928. Trained at Bristol Old Vic.
TV: *Peace and Quiet* (1957); *The Tommy Cooper Show; Tracy and Me; The Army Game* (1957-9); *Our House; A Resounding Tinkle; A Tune on the Old Tax Fiddle; The Fall of Mendel Crick; A Little Bit of Gold Said Jump; Pig in the Middle; Prisoner and Escort; Tea at the Ritz; The Close Prisoner; The Big Noise; Here's Harry; The Incident; The Paraffin Season; Into the Dark; Hold My Hand Soldier; The Seasonal Swing; Search for the Nile; Not Only... but Also; O Gosh!; Red Handed; Lily Jumps and Jim Loses; Man of Our Times; Spanner in the Works; The Big Flame; The Ticket; Travelling Where; Wally Wenpole; Diddled; Curry and Chips; The Borderers; The Long Distance Piano Player; Lenin; Hamlet; His and Hers; Sealed with a Loving Kiss; As Good Cooks Go; The Misfit; Comedy Playhouse; Rhubarb; Armchair Theatre; Village Hall; Roads to Freedom; Search for the Nile; Casanova; Amelia Quint; Budgie; The Changeling; When the Boys Come to Play; Crime of Passion; Vinegar Trip; Crown Court; Hunter's Walk; Carry On Christmas; Follow That Dog; Six of Cilla; Captain Brassbound's Conversion; Z Cars; Crown Court; No More Monkey Business; On the Move; Jumbo; Bobby Bluesocks; The Venturers; I Claudius; Mr Big; Target; Big Jim and the Figaro Club; The Beryl Reid Show; Wembley Conference; Masada; In Sickness and in Health; The 19th Hole; The Bill; Tonight at 8.30; Brookside; Last of the Summer Wine; Sharpe's Regiment.*
Films: Selection (from 48): *Keep It Clean* (début, 1955); *I Only Arsked!; Carry On Sergeant; Carry On Nurse; The League of Gentlemen; Doctor in Love; Saturday Night and Sunday Morning; Carry On Regardless; Lawrence of Arabia; The Longest Day; Crooks Anonymous; The Krays; "Let Him Have It".* Address: c/o Collis Management. Lives in London and Cheshire. m. (dis). Hobbies: Carpentry.

Nick Ross

Norman Rossington

ROTHWELL, Alan

Alan Rothwell. Actor/Presenter/Writer. b. Oldham, Lancashire, 9 February 1937. Trained at RADA.
TV: David Barlow in *Coronation Street* (1960-8); *Top Secret; Z Cars; Hickory House* (presenter); *Daisy, Daisy* (presenter); *Picture Box* (presenter-writer-producer); *The Nightbear* (writer-producer); Johnson in *The Lie; Crown Court*; Nicholas Black in *Brookside; Angel Voices; All Creatures Great and Small; Children's Ward; How We Used to Live; Conspiracy of Cells; The Fool of the World and the Flying Ship* (voice-over); *Sherlock Holmes: The Master Blackmailer*; Examiner in *Medics; Mother's Ruin; Crime Limited*; President in *Into the Fire; Missing Persons*; Vicar in *Heartbeat; Hetty Wainthropp Investigates.*
Films: *Two Living, One Dead; Phil in Linda; Nothing but the Best*; Brantner in *Zeppelin.*
Radio: Jimmy Grange in *The Archers.* Address: c/o Laine Management. Lives in Stockport, Cheshire. m. 2nd Maureen; 2 s. Toby, Ben (both from 2nd m.). Hobbies: Music, walking, reading.

Alan Rothwell

ROUTLEDGE, Patricia

Patricia Routledge

Patricia Routledge. Actress. b. Birkenhead, Cheshire, 17 February. OBE, 1993. Trained at the Bristol Old Vic Theatre School. Stage plays include *Richard III* and *Henry V* (both RSC).
TV: *Hobson's Choice; Victoria Regina; Z Cars; Samson and Delilah; Sense and Sensibility; Tartuffe; David Copperfield; Nicholas Nickleby; Steptoe and Son; Jubilee; Plain Jane* (Jubilee); *Jackanory; The Cost of Loving; Crown Court; The Imitation Game; A Visit from Miss Protheroe; Green Forms; The Years Between; Doris and Doreen;* Miss Schofield in *A Woman of No Importance* (Alan Bennett monologue, 1982); *The Beggar's Opera; The Two Ronnies; Victoria Wood – As Seen on TV; Home Video;* Marjorie in *Marjorie and Men; When We Are Married; Cleo Laine and Friends; Tales of the Unexpected; Sophia and Constance;* Miss Ruddock in *Talking Heads: A Lady of Letters; Five to Eleven; Let's Face the Music;* Ivy in *First and Last;* Hetty Wainthropp in *Missing Persons;* Hyacinth Bucket in *Keeping Up Appearances* (five series, 1990-5); *Bookmark: Miss Pym's Day Out; Lizzie Dripping and the Witch* (storyteller); *Omnibus: Hildegarde of Bingen* (narrator); title role in *Hetty Wainthropp Investigates* (series, 1996).
Films: *To Sir with Love; Pretty Polly; The Bliss of Mrs Blossom; 30 Is a Dangerous Age, Cynthia; Don't Raise the Bridge, Lower the River; If It's Tuesday, This Must be Belgium; Lock Up Your Daughters; Girl Stroke Boy; Keep off the Grass.* **Records:** Album: *Presenting Patricia Routledge.*
Address: c/o Marmont Management. Lives in Kensington, West London. Single.

ROWLANDS, Patsy

Patsy Rowlands

Patsy Rowlands. Actress. b. London, 19 January 1934. Trained at Guildhall School of Music and Drama.
TV: *The Gamblers; In Loving Memory; Public Eye; Pinky; Arthur through the Looking Glass; Père Goriot; Inside George Webley; Imperial Palace; Kate; Bless This House; Follow That Dog; The Squirrels; Kinvig; Ladies; The History of Mr Polly; Juliet Bravo; Hallelujah; George and Mildred; Robin's Nest; Carry On Laughing; Mooncat and Company; The Little Princess; Charlie the Kid; Crimestrike; Rainbow; My Son, My Son; One by One; When We Are Married; Imaginary Friends; Femme Fatale* (Screen Two); *The Bill.*
Films: *A Kind of Loving; The Bawdy Adventures of Tom Jones; Deadline for Diamonds; Carry On Again Doctor; Carry On Loving; Alice's Adventures in Wonderland; Carry On at Your Convenience; Carry On Matron; Bless This House; Please Sir!; Carry On Girls; Joseph Andrews; Tess; Little Lord Fauntleroy.*
Address: c/o Saraband Associates. m. Malcolm Sircom (dis); 1 s. Alan.

ROYLE, Carol

Carol Royle

Carol Buchanan Royle. Actress. b. Blackpool, Lancashire, 10 February 1954. Daughter of actor Derek Royle and film make-up artist Jane Royle; sister of actress Amanda Royle. Trained at the Central School of Speech and Drama (1973-6). RSC roles include Ophelia in *Hamlet*, Cressida in *Troilus and Cressida*, Princess of France in *Loves Labour's Lost* and Mrs Arbuthnot in *A Woman of No Importance.*
TV: *The Cedar Tree* (three series); *Blake's 7; The Professionals; Waxwork* (TVM); *Heartland; Girl Talk; The Racing Game; Possibilities* (Play of the Week); *Shades of Darkness: Feet Foremost; The Outsider* (series); *Judgement Day* (Storyboard); *Bergerac; When the Walls Come Tumbling Down; Oxbridge Blues; A Still Small Shout; Ladies in Charge* (Storyboard and series); *Hedgehog Wedding* (TVM); *Life without George* (three series); *The London Embassy; Blackeyes; Casualty.*
Films: *Tuxedo Warrior; Deadline.* Address; c/o Christina Shepherd. m. Julian Spear; 1 s. Taran, 1 d. Talitha (b. 1995). Pets: Three dogs. Hobbies: Tapestry, painting, reading.

RUSHTON, William

William Rushton

William Rushton. Actor/Writer/Comedian. b. Chelsea, London, 18 August 1937.
TV: *That Was the Week That Was* (1963); *Not So Much a Programme, More a Way of Life; Don't Just Sit There; Up Sunday; Jackanory; Grubstreet; When Santa Rode the Prairie* (also writer); *Celebrity Squares; Dawson and Friends; You Can Make It; Those Wonderful TV Times; Ask a Silly Answer; Open House; Star Turn Challenge; Blankety Blank; I'm Sorry I Haven't a Clue; Wake Up Wizzy; The Day of the Grocer,* Dr Watson in *Comedy Playhouse; Does the Team Think?; The Cobblers of Umbridge; Ultra Quiz* (co-presenter); *The Kenny Everett Show; Through the Keyhole; Noel's Telly Addicts; This Is Your Life* (subject); *Rich Pickings* (*This Morning*, 1994-5); *Rory Bremner... Who Else?* (illustrator only).
Films: *Nothing but the Best; Those Magnificent Men in Their Flying Machines; The Bliss of Mrs Blossom; Adventures of a Private Eye; Monte Carlo or Bust; Flight of the Doves.* Address: c/o Roger Hancock. m. actress Arlene Dorgan; 1 s. Toby (Tobias), 2 step-s. Matthew, Sam.

RUSSELL, Jenna

Jenna Russell

Jenna Russell. Actress. West End stage plays include *Girlfriends, Follies* and *Les Misérables.*
TV: *Coming Out; QPR Askey Is Dead; Broken Homes; Your Place or Mine; Sacred Hearts; P'Tang Yang Kipperbang* (TVM); *Sister Catherine; The Party; The Fear; Saracen; The Bill; Better Class of Person; Purple People Eater; Missing Persons; Home to Roost;* Maggie in *On the Up* (three series, 1990-92); Susan Dobson in *The Bill.* **Records:** Single: *Red Dwarf* (theme song). Albums: *An Evening with Alan Jay Lerner; Save the Children; Les Misérables.* Address: c/o London Management.

RUTTER, Barrie

Barrie Rutter. Actor. b. Hull, E Yorkshire, 12 December 1946. Former National Youth Theatre member.
TV: *Apprentices; The Saint; Queenie's Castle; Our Kid; Bavarian Nights; Astronauts; The Oresteia; The Big H; Way Up Stream; The South Bank Show: Great Writers; Countdown to War;* Mr Maskell in *Heartbeat;* Barry Ryan in *Crown Prosecutor.* Address: c/o Michelle Braidman Associates. m. author and university lecturer Dr Carol Rutter; 2 d. Briony, Rowan.

Barrie Rutter

RYALL, David

David Ryall. Actor. b. Shoreham-by-Sea, West Sussex, 5 January 1935. Trained at RADA (1962-4).
TV: *Love for Lydia; The Knowledge; The Singing Detective; The River; The Paradise Club; Woman in Black;* Inspector Teal in *The Saint* (series, 1989-90); *1992; Perfect Scoundrels; Boon; Inspector Morse: Driven to Distraction; Jack the Ripper* (mini-series); *TECX; Birmingham Six; The Men's Room; The Chief; Shelley; For the Greater Good; Anglo-Saxon Attitudes; Witchcraft; The Woman in Black; Secret Agent; Prime Suspect; The Borrowers; Running Late; Diana: Her True Story; The Gingerbread Man; Prime Suspect 2; Goodnight Sweetheart; Prime Suspect 3;* Sir Bruce Bullerby in *To Play the King* and *The Final Cut;* Tom Harley in *Casualty* (series, 1993-4); *The Entertainer* (Performance); *Law and Disorder; Moving Story; Milner; The Bill; Lovejoy; The Woman in Black; Prime Suspect: The Scent of Darkness; Hamish Macbeth; Mrs Hartley and the Growth Centre* (Screen Two); *Jake's Progress; A Touch of Frost; Pie in the Sky.*
Films: *The Russia House; The Elephant Man; Empire of the Sun; Wilt;* George in *Truly Madly Deeply; The Story of Mary Lindell; Revolver; Justice; Where the Wolves Howl; Black Beauty; Carrington; Restoration.* Address: c/o Scott Marshall. Lives in London. m. 1st Gillian Eddison (dis 1985), 2nd Cathy Buchwald; 1 s. Jonathan, 2 d. Imogen (both from 1st m.), Charlotte (from 2nd m.).

David Ryall

RYAN, Helen

Helen Ryan. Actress. b. Liverpool, 16 June 1938. Trained at RADA.
TV: *Edward the Seventh; Hannah; My Father's House; C.A.T.S. Eyes;* Lady Jenvey in *Harry;* Princess of Wales in *The Memoirs of Sherlock Holmes;* Aunt Phoebe in *Just William* (1995).
Films: *The Elephant Man; The Hawk.* **Radio:** *A Room with a View.*
Address: c/o Representation Joyce Edwards. m. Guy Slater (dis); 1 s. Daniel, 1 d. Rebecca.

Helen Ryan

SACHS, Andrew

Andrew Sachs. Actor/Writer/Narrator. b. Berlin, Germany, 7 April 1930.
TV: Manuel in *Fawlty Towers* (two series); *James and the Giant Peach; Krek Bristle; Took & Co; Crown Court; Rising Damp; The Tommy Cooper Show; The Dawson Watch; Lovely Couple; The Tempest; The History of Mr Polly; This Is Your Life* (subject); *Dead Ernest* (series); *It's Your Move; Play It Again; The Discovery of Animal Behaviour; Rainbow Safari* (writer-presenter); *It'll All Be Over in Half an Hour; There Comes a Time...* (series); *The Galactic Garden* (also co-writer); *Points of View; You Gotta Have Heart; When in Spain* (presenter/co-writer); *Assert Yourself* (presenter/co-writer); *Berliners* (presenter/co-writer); *Bergerac; Mixing It; Woof!; QED: Whatever Happened to the Leisure Age?* (presenter-actor); *The Mushroom Picker; Every Silver Lining* (series); *Pirates* (two series); *Watch Art; Horizon: Einstein; Minder.* Voice only: *Survival; The World about Us; Horizon; Timewatch; Chronicle; The Natural World; QED; Equinox; Everyman; Heart of the Matter; Open University; The Foul Smell of Success; Flight of the Condor; Architecture at the Crossroads; Supersense; The Encircled Sea; Kingdom of the Sun/Deep/Plains; The Nobel Century; Life Sense; The Price; Jurassic Park — The Real Story; William's Wish Wellingtons; Children's Hospital; Eyewitness; The Night after Christmas; Gambling for Gorillas; The Forgotten Toys.*
Films: *Hitler: The Last Ten Days;* Friar Tuck in *Robin Hood Junior; Romance with a Double Bass; Are You Being Served?; Revenge of the Pink Panther;* Gerard in *History of the World Part 1; Taxandria; The Mystery of Edwin Drood.* Plus training films for Video Arts (1973-90), including *How Not to Exhibit Yourself.* Address: c/o The Richard Stone Partnership. Lives in London. m. actress Melody Lang; 1 d. Kate, 2 s. Bill (William), TV and radio presenter John. Pets: Two Cavalier King Charles.

Andrew Sachs

ST CLEMENT, Pam

Pamela St Clement. Actress. b. Harrow-on-the-Hill, 12 May 1942. Trained at Rose Bruford College.
TV: *Thinkabout; High Pavement Blues; The Tripods; Indelible Evidence: Gaslight; His and Hers; Orson Welles' Great Mysteries; Thomas and Sarah; Way of the World; The Onedin Line; The Fenn Street Gang; Van Der Valk; Follyfoot; All Our Saturdays; One of the Boys; Shoulder to Shoulder; Within These Walls; Enemy at the Door; Matilda's England; Shall I See You Now?; A Horseman Riding By; Bottle Boys; Can We Get On Now, Please?;* Mrs Eckersley in *Emmerdale Farm; C.A.T.S. Eyes; Minder; Shoestring; Private Schultz;* Noreen Mullin in *Together; Not for the Likes of Us; The Nation's Health; Angels; Dangerous Davies — The Last Detective* (TVM); *We'll Meet Again; Ladykillers; The Chinese Detective; The Clergyman's Daughter; Maths Counts; Struggle; King;* Pat Butcher (née Wicks) in *EastEnders.*
Films: *Our Cissie; The Hunchback of Notre Dame; Doomwatch; Hedda; SS; The Bunker; Scrubbers; Biggles; Czechmate.* Address: c/o Saraband Associates. m. Andrew Gordon (dis).

Pam St Clement

Pamela Salem

SALEM, Pamela

Pamela Fortunée Salem. Actress/Producer. b. Bombay, India, 22 January. Educated in India and Britain, and at Heidelberg University, Germany. Trained at the Central School of Speech and Drama.
TV: *Jason King; The Onedin Line; Doctor Who; Blake's 7; Carnforth Practice* (series); *Sons and Daughters of Tomorrow; Into the Labyrinth; Seagull Island; Succubus;* Monica Burton in *Buccaneer* (series); *The Consultant; Tripods* (series); *Magnum PI; The Professionals; General Hospital; Crown Court; Strangers; All Creatures Great and Small; Lytton's Diary; Night Train to Murder* (TVM); *Boon; Ever Decreasing Circles; Doctor Who* (two series); *Thirteen at Dinner* (TVM); Joanne in *EastEnders; Howards' Way;* Chantal Moriac in *French Fields* (three series); *The Chain; El C.I.D.; Fish in the Sky* (producer, documentary); *The Paradise Club; Perfect Scoundrels; Trainer; As Churchill Said to Me; Don't Leave Me This Way* (TVM).
Films: *The Bitch; The First Great Train Robbery;* Miss Moneypenny in *Never Say Never Again; After Darkness;* Herodias in *Salome; God's Outlaw.* Address: c/o Burdett-Coutts Associates. Lives in London. m. actor-producer Michael O'Hagan. Pets: Battersea Dobermut dog called Dolly, tropical fish. Hobbies: Reading, swimming, walking, collecting shells, scuba-diving.

Peter Sallis

SALLIS, Peter

Peter Sallis. Actor. b. Twickenham, Middlesex, 1 February 1921. Trained at RADA.
TV: *Into the Dark; How to Murder Your Wife; The Big Eat; Public Eye; Spider's Web; The Moonstone; The Diary of Samuel Pepys; Barlow; The Pallisers; Softly Softly; The Flaxborough Chronicles; Yanks Go Home; A Crowded Room; Leave It to Charlie; Daedalus Equations;* Cleggy in *Last of the Summer Wine* (Comedy Playhouse, 1973, and series, 1973-); *Murder Most English; Raffles; The Obelisk; Across a Crowded Room; You're Not Watching Me Mummy; She Loves Me; Tales of the Unexpected; Ladykillers; The Kamikaze Ground Staff's Reunion Dinner; Strangers and Brothers; Mountain Men; Lucy Walker; Witness for the Prosecution* (TVM); *Uncle of the Bride* (TVM); *The Bretts; The New Statesman; Come Home Charlie and Face Them;* Henry Tong in *Rumpole of the Bailey.*
Films: *Child's Play; Anastasia; Julie; The Scapegoat; The Doctor's Dilemma; A Night to Remember; Saturday Night and Sunday Morning; Doctor in Love; No Love for Johnnie; Curse of the Werewolf; I Thank a Fool; Clash by Night; The VIPs; Mouse on the Moon; The Third Secret; Rapture; Charlie Bubbles; Inadmissible Evidence; Scream and Scream Again; My Lover, My Son; The Reckoning; Taste the Blood of Dracula; Wuthering Heights; The Night Digger; Frankenstein: The True Story; Full Circle; The Incredible Sarah; Too Many Chefs; Dracula;* voice of Wallace in *A Grand Day Out, The Wrong Trousers* and *A Close Shave* (shorts). Address: c/o Jonathan Altaras. m. actress Elaine Usher (dis and remarried); 1 s. Crispian.

John Salthouse

SALTHOUSE, John

John W Salthouse. Actor/Writer. b. London, 16 June 1951. Son of boxer Johnny Lewis. Turned to acting after career as professional footballer with Crystal Palace was ended by a leg injury. Trained at LAMDA.
TV: *Man above Men; Love on a Gunboat; Back Page; Enemy at the Door; Maiden's Trip; A Christmas Carol; Not Quite Cricket; Abigail's Party; Jemima Shore Investigates; Those Glory, Glory Days* (TVM); *Big Deal; Glamour Night;* Det Insp Galloway in *The Bill* (three series); *Making Out; Boon; Thinkabout Science; The Ruth Rendell Mysteries: From Doon with Death;* Mike Monroe in *EastEnders; Taggart: The Hit Man; Maigret; Casualty; One Last Lie; The Turnaround; An Independent Man; Rich Deceiver.*
Films: *The Spy Who Loved Me; A Bridge Too Far; An American Werewolf in London; Give My Regards to Broad Street; Prick Up Your Ears.*
Address: c/o Roxane Vacca Management. Lives in London. m. actress Heather Tobias; 1 s. William. Pets: Two cats. Hobbies: Coaching children at soccer and cricket, watching sport.

Jennifer Saunders

SAUNDERS, Jennifer

Jennifer Saunders. Actress/Comedienne. b. Sleaford, Lincolnshire, 12 July 1958. Trained at the Central School of Speech and Drama, where she met and teamed up with Dawn French.
TV: *Five Go Mad in Dorset; Five Go Mad on Mescalin; Slags; Summer School; Private Enterprise; Consuela; Mr Jolly Lives Next Door; Bad News Tour; South Atlantic Raiders; G.L.C.; Oxford; Spaghetti Hoops; Le Kiss; Wild Turkey; Demonella; Jealousy* (all The Comic Strip Presents...); *Girls on Top; Happy Families; French and Saunders* (three series, 1987-95); *The Storyteller: Sapsorrow;* Edina Monsoon in *Absolutely Fabulous* (also writer, three series, 1992-5); *The Full Wax; Dusty; French and Saunders in... Space Virgins from Planet Sex; French and Saunders Christmas Special* (1994); *Prince Cinders* (voice only); *Queen of the East* (Heroes & Villains); *French & Saunders Go to the Movies* (compilation).
Films: *The Supergrass; The Strike.* **Books:** *A Feast of French & Saunders; Absolutely Fabulous.*
Address: c/o Peters Fraser & Dunlop. Lives in Richmond-upon-Thames, Surrey, and Devon. m. 1985 actor Adrian Edmondson (qv); 3 d. Ella, Beattie, Freya.

Jimmy Savile

SAVILE, Jimmy

Jimmy Savile. Presenter. b. Leeds, 31 October 1926. OBE, 1970; knighted, 1990.
TV: *Top of the Pops; Jim'll Fix It* (1971-94); *The Obituary Show; 20 Years of Jim'll Fix It* (1995).

Radio: Radio Luxembourg (1958-67); BBC Radio 1 (1968-), including *Savile's Travels*.
Books: *As It Happens* (autobiography); *Love Is an Uphill Thing; God'll Fix It*.
Address: c/o BBC TV/National Spinal Injuries Centre, Stoke Mandeville Hospital, Mandeville Road, Aylesbury, Buckinghamshire HP21 8AL. Lives in Leeds. Single. Hobbies: Cycling, running, walking.

SAWALHA, Julia
Julia Sawalha. Actress. b. London. Trained at the Italia Conti Stage Academy.
TV: *Casualty; El C.I.D.;* Lynda in *Press Gang* (three series); *How Others See Us; The Outing; Inspector Morse; Spatz; The Keeper; Ghost Train* (guest presenter); Hannah in *Second Thoughts* (five series); Saffron in *Absolutely Fabulous* (three series); *Lovejoy;* Mercy 'Merry' Pecksniff in *Martin Chuzzlewit* (serial); Lydia Bennet in *Pride and Prejudice* (serial, 1995); Hannah in *Faith in the Future* (series).
Films: Chrissy in *Buddy's Song.* Address: c/o A.I.M.

Julia Sawalha

SAYLE, Alexei
Alexei Sayle. Actor/Comedian/Writer. b. Liverpool, 7 August 1952.
TV: *OTT; The Young Ones* (also writer); *Those Glory, Glory Days* (TVM); *Whoops Apocalypse!; Give Us a Break; Upline; Doctor Who; The Caucasian Chalk Circle; Les Girls; City Tails; Didn't You Kill My Brother?* (The Comic Strip Presents…, also writer); *Love Child; Comic Roots* (also writer); *Alexei Sayle's Stuff* (also writer); *Spaghetti Hoops* (The Comic Strip Presents…); *Le Kiss* (The Comic Strip Presents…); *Night Voice* (ScreenPlay); *Selling Hitler; Small World; Itch* (also writer); *Lovejoy; The Gravy Train Goes East; Golden Palace; Queen of the Wild Frontier* (The Comic Strip Presents…); *The Big Three-O* (presenter); *Sex Drugs and Dinner* (presenter); *The All New Alexei Sayle Show* (also writer); *Rubbish, King of the Jumble* (voice only); *Drive* (presenter); *BBC Design Awards* 1994 (presenter); *QED; Jackanory;* Alain Degout in *Paris; The All New Alexei Sayle Show 2; One for the Road; Sorry about Last Night.* As writer-presenter: *Arena: The History of the Ford Cortina; Great Bus Journeys of the World; Great Railway Journeys.*
Films: *Repeater; The Secret Policeman's Other Ball;* Golodkin in *Gorky Park; The Bride; The Supergrass; Whoops Apocalypse; Solar Warriors; The Love Child; The Strike; Siesta; Mr Corbett's Ghost; Indiana Jones and the Last Crusade; Reckless Kelly; Carry On Columbus; A Circling of Sharks.* Address: c/o Mayer & Eden. Lives in London. m. Linda. Pets: Cat called Tiger. Hobbies: Walking, cycling.

Alexei Sayle

SCALES, Prunella
Prunella Margaret Rumney Illingworth. Actress/Director. b. Sutton Abinger, Surrey, 22 June 1932. Daughter of actress Catherine Scales. Trained at Old Vic Theatre School and Herbert Berghof Studio, New York.
TV: *Coronation Street; Marriage Lines; Fawlty Towers; The Merry Wives of Windsor; A Wife like the Moon; Outside Edge; Grand Duo; Target; Doris and Doreen; Bergerac; Jackanory; An Evening with Queen Victoria; Never the Twain; Wagner; Absurd Person Singular; Slimming Down; Mapp & Lucia; When We Are Married; What the Butler Saw; The Index Has Gone Fishing; Natural Causes; Beyond the Pale; After Henry; Queen Victoria: Evening at Osborne; Kennet and Avon* (presenter); *A Question of Attribution; The Rector's Wife; The World of Peter Rabbit and Friends; Fair Game; Signs and Wonders; The World of Lee Evans; Look at the State We're In!; Nanny Knows Best; Searching; Dalziel and Pascoe; Lord of Misrule.*
Films: *Laxdale Hall; Hobson's Choice; What Every Woman Wants; The Crowded Day; Room at the Top; Waltz of the Toreadors; Escape from the Dark; The Hound of the Baskervilles; The Boys from Brazil; The Wicked Lady; Consuming Passions; The Lonely Passion of Judith Hearne; A Chorus of Disapproval; Freddie as F.R.O.7* (voice only); *My Friend Walter; Second Best; Wolf; An Awfully Big Adventure.* Address: c/o Conway, van Gelder, Robinson. Lives in Wandsworth, South London. m. 1963 actor Timothy West (qv); 2 s. actor Samuel Alexander, Joseph John Lancaster. Pets: A black cat called Coleman. Hobbies: 'Listening to music, sewing, growing things.'

Prunella Scales

SCANNELL, Tony
Tony Scannell. Actor. b. Kinsale, County Cork, Eire, 14 August 1945. After leaving the RAF, trained at the East 15 Acting School and Joan Littlewood's Theatre Workshop.
TV: *The Gentle Touch; Sergeant Cribb; All the Fun of the Fair; Little Lord Fauntleroy; Up the Elephant and round the Castle; Blue Money; Flying Lady;* Det Sgt Ted Roach in *The Bill* (1984-93).
Films: *Flash Gordon; Cheap Perfume.*
Address: c/o Sharon Hamper Management/Manager: Mike Smith. Lives in London and Kent. m. 1970 Melanie (dis); 1 s. Sean. Hobbies: Golf, music, cycling.

Tony Scannell

SCHATZBERGER, Simon
Simon Schatzberger. Actor. b. Nottingham, 28 March 1968.
TV: *Your Mother Wouldn't Like It; Luna; Because I Say So; Press Gang; The Two of Us; Trouble in Mind; The Return of Neville Dedd; Marlene Marlowe Investigates; Jackanory.*
Address: c/o Frazer-Skemp Management.

Simon Schatzberger

David Schneider

SCHNEIDER, David

David Amos Schneider. Actor/comedian. b. London, 22 May 1963. Grandparents were in Yiddish theatre in Europe and London. Member of the award-winning team who wrote and starred on TV in *The Day Today* and on radio in *Knowing Me, Knowing You* and *On the Hour*. Stage plays include *Peer Gynt*, *The Good Person of Szechuan*, *Ghetto* and *Fuente Ovejuna* for the National Theatre.

TV: *Up to Something; Up Yer News!* (writer and performer, Sky TV); *The Phil Cool Show; London Underground; F.L.I.P.; Hangar 17* (three series); *Space Vets* (two series); *Heading Home* (Screen Two); *On the Hour* (writer and performer, pilot); *The Day Today* (writer and performer, series); *The Full Monty; Mr Bean; The Glam Metal Detectives* (The Comic Strip Presents...); *Paris; The Saturday Night Armistace* (series, 1995); Bradley in *The Peter Principle* (pilot, 1995).

Radio: *On the Hour* (writer and performer, two series); *Knowing Me Knowing You... with Alan Partridge* (writer and performer, series). Address: c/o London Management. Lives in London. Partner: Actress Sandy McDade.

Phillip Schofield

SCHOFIELD, Phillip

Phillip Bryan Schofield. Presenter. b. Oldham, Lancashire, 1 April 1962. Emigrated to New Zealand with his parents, where he entered television, before returning to Britain. Stage productions include *Joseph and the Amazing Technicolor Dreamcoat* (title role, West End, 1992-3).

TV: *Shazam; Music Awards* (both in New Zealand); Children's BBC; *Saturday Superstore; Take Two; Newsround; Royal Variety Performance; Going Live!; Schofield's Europe; Children in Need Report; Television's Greatest Hits; The SOS Awards; Gordon T Gopher; Television's Greatest Christmas Hits; Gone Live!; The Children's Royal Variety Performance 1993; Schofield's Christmas TV Gold* (1993); *Talking Telephone Numbers* (three series, 1994-6); *Schofield's Quest* (pilot, 1994, two series, 1994-5); *Schofield's TV Gold* (1994, 1995); *Tenball* (series, 1995); *Schofield in Hawaii; One in a Million*.

Radio: Capital Radio; BBC Radio 1. Address: c/o James Grant Management.

Brough Scott

SCOTT, Brough

Brough Scott. Racing presenter. b. London, 12 December 1942. Graduated in history from Radley College, Oxford. An amateur, then professional, National Hunt jockey (1962-71), riding exactly 100 winners, before giving up through injury. Had started journalism and broadcasting during previous injury spells. Joined ITV racing commentary team in 1977, subsequently providing coverage for Channel Four. Became *Sunday Times* racing correspondent in 1974, then joined *Racing Post*.

TV: BBC racing commentaries (1970); ITV racing and *Channel 4 Racing* presenter (1977-); *Something to Brighten the Morning* (biography of Mill Reef); *The Derby Stakes* (writer-presenter); *The Challenge of the Sexes* (Southern Television); *Sporting Chance* (Tyne Tees Television); *George Stubbs the Painter; Breeders Cup* (NBC).

Radio: *The Thoroughbred*. **Books:** *The World of Flat Racing; On and off the Rails*.

Awards: Racing Journalist of the Year (1977); Sports Council Award (1983); Sports Journalist of the Year (1983). Address: c/o LWT/*Racing Post*, 120 Coombe Lane, Raynes Park, London SW20 0BA. m. former British skier Susie McInnes; 2 d. Sophie, Tessa, 2 s. Charlie, Jamie.

Kristin Scott Thomas

SCOTT THOMAS, Kristin

Kristin Scott Thomas. Actress. Sister of actress Serena Scott Thomas (qv). Educated at Cheltenham Ladies' College. Trained at the Central School of Speech and Drama and École Nationale des Arts et Technique de Théâtre, Paris. Speaks fluent French.

TV: *Sentimental Journey* (German TV); *Chameleon/La Tricheuse* (Australian TV); *Mistral's Daughter; Blockhaus* (German TV); *L'Ami d'Engance de Maigret* (French TV); *Titmuss Regained; The Endless Game* (pilot); *Precious* (TVM); *The Secret Life of Ian Fleming* (TVM); Kate in *Framed* (TVM); Victoria Rolfe in *Look at It This Way* (mini-series, 1992); Sister Gabriel/Anna Gibson in *Body & Soul* (series, 1993); *Belle Epoque* (French mini-series).

Films: *Djamel et Juliette; L'Agent Troubel; La Méridienne; Under the Cherry Moon; Force Majeur; Bille Em Tête;* Lady Brenda in *A Handful of Dust; Dr Grassler* (Italy); *Aux Yeux du Monde; Bitter Moon; Angels & Insects; Four Weddings and a Funeral; La Salade; Richard III*. **Awards:** Films: *Evening Standard* Most Promising Newcomer award (1989). Address: c/o ICM. Lives in Paris. m.; 2 children.

Serena Scott Thomas

SCOTT THOMAS, Serena

Serena Scott Thomas. Actress. Sister of actress Kristin Scott Thomas (qv). Formerly a model.

TV: *Agatha Christie's Poirot; She-Wolf of London; The Green Man;* Mandy in *The Guilty* (mini-series, 1992); *The Inspector Alleyn Mysteries; Headhunters;* Princess of Wales in *Diana: Her True Story* (mini-series); Hebe in *Harnessing Peacocks;* Kathy in *Bermuda Grace* (TVM); *After All; Sherwood's Travels;* Clair in *Clair de Lune* (Rik Mayall Presents); *The Road to Dusty Death* (US pilot). TV commercials: Fiat Uno.

Films: *"Let Him Have It"*. Address: c/o ICM.

SEAGROVE, Jenny

Jennifer Ann Seagrove. Actress. b. Malaysia, 4 July. Trained at the Bristol Old Vic Theatre School.
TV: *The Brack Report; Soldier Soldier* (Granada Television production); *Lucy Walker; The Woman in White; Diana* (serial); *Crown Court; Three Men in a Boat; Killer; In like Flynn;* Emma in *A Woman of Substance* (mini-series); *Mask of the Devil; Hold the Dream; The Sign of Four; Mountain Men; The Betrothed; Magic Moments; Some Other Spring* (TVM); *The Eye of the Beholder; Incident at Victoria Falls* (also titled *Sherlock Holmes and the Incident at Victoria Falls*) (TVM); *Deadly Games.*
Films: *Local Hero; Nate and Hayes* (UK title *Savage Islands*); *A Shocking Accident; Moonlighting; To Hell and Back in Time for Breakfast; Tattoo; Appointment with Death; A Chorus of Disapproval; The Guardian; Bullseye!; Incident at Victoria Falls* (also titled *Sherlock Holmes and the Incident at Victoria Falls*) (re-edited version of TVM); *Miss Beatty's Children.* Address: c/o Marmont Management. Lives in London m. M Sharma (dis). Pets: A dog, Tasha. Hobbies: Sports, walking in the country, antique fairs.

Jenny Seagrove

SECOMBE, Harry

Harry Secombe. Presenter/Comedian. b. Swansea, West Glamorgan, 8 September 1921. CBE, 1963; knighted, 1981. Clerk in a steel mill, then entertained in Forces shows during the Second World War while serving as a lance bombardier in the Royal Artillery (1936-46). First found fame on radio with The Goons (1949-60). Eleven Royal Command Performances.
TV: *The Harry Secombe Show; Secombe and Friends; Sing a Song of Secombe; Fall in the Stars; Have a Harry Christmas; Have a Harry Birthday; Harry Secombe's World of Music; Easter Story; Captain Beaky and His Band; Secombe with Music; Highway* (1983-93); *Sunday Morning with Secombe* (series, 1994); *D-Day Commemoration with Sir Harry Secombe; Live for Peace – A Royal Gala* (VE Day 1995).
Films: *Hocus Pocus; Helter Skelter, Fake's Progress* (narrator only); *London Entertains; Penny Points to Paradise; Down among the Z Men; Forces' Sweetheart; Svengali; Davy; Jet Storm; Mr Bumble* in *Oliver!; The Bed Sitting Room; Song of Norway; Rhubarb; Doctor in Trouble; The Magnificent Seven Deadly Sins; Sunstruck; A Fair Way to Play* (short). **Radio:** *Variety Bandbox; Welsh Rarebit; Junior Crazy Gang; Those Crazy People, The Goons; The Goon Show; Educating Archie.*
Books: *Goon Abroad* (1982); *The Harry Secombe Diet Book* (1983); *Arias and Raspberries* (autobiography); *Harry Secombe's Highway* (1984); *The Highway Companion* (1987); plus two novels, various children's books and short stories. Address: c/o Willinghurst Ltd, 46 St James's Place, London SW1A 1NS. Lives in Surrey. m. 1948 Myra Atherton; 2 d. Jennifer, Katy, 2 s. actor Andrew, David. Pets: A black cat called Vince. Hobbies: Photography, golf, sketching, cricket, travel, literature.

Harry Secombe

SEED, Graham

Graham Seed. Actor. b. London, 12 July 1950. Trained at RADA. Stage productions include *Toad of Toad Hall* (as Mole), *Me and My Girl* (as Gerald) and *Tons of Money* (national tour).
TV: *I Claudius; Who's Who; Brideshead Revisited; Bergerac; Edward the Seventh; CAB; Good and Bad at Games;* Charlie Mycroft in *Crossroads;The Upper Hand; Prime Suspect; Madson.* **Radio:** Nigel Pargetter in *The Archers.* Address: c/o Michelle Braidman Associates. m. Clare Colvin; 1 d. Nicola, 1 s. Toby.

Graham Seed

SELBY, Tony

Actor. b. Lambeth, London, 26 February 1938. Trained at the Italia Conti Stage Academy.
TV: *The Changeling; A Tap on the Shoulder; Three Clear Sundays; Up the Junction; Silent Song; Another Day, Another Dollar; A Night Out; Comedy Playhouse; The Devil a Monk Would Be; The Hard Word; The Gentleman Caller; The Inquisitors; Present Laughter; The Informer; The Break; Ace of Wands; A Touch of the Tiny Hackets;* Cpl Percy Marsh in *Get Some In* (1975-8); *Cockles; Antigone; Hideaway;* Glitz in *Doctor Who; The Good Life; The Sweeney; Minder; The Lady Is a Tramp; C.A.T.S. Eyes; Bergerac; Casualty; The 19th Hole; Lovejoy;* Max Taplow in *Love Hurts* (series); Bert Finch in *Mulberry* (series); *Law and Disorder; The Detectives; Casualty; The World of Lee Evans.*
Films: *The Queen's Guards; Press for Time; Witchfinder General; Alfie; Villain; Before Winter Comes; Adolf Hitler – My Part in His Downfall; Nobody Ordered Love.*
Address: c/o A.I.M. m. 1st (dis), 2nd Gina Sellers; 1 d. Samantha, 1 s. Matthew (both from 1st m.).

Tony Solby

SERLE, Chris

Chris Serle. Presenter. b. Bristol, 13 July 1943. Studied modern languages at Trinity College, Dublin. Spent four years as an actor, starting his career at Bristol Old Vic Theatre. Joined the BBC as a radio producer in 1969 and later moved to television.
TV: *Parkinson* (as producer); *That's Life!* (1980-); *In at the Deep End* (three series, 1981-7); *Medical Express; Sixty Minutes* (reporter); *Windmill* (three series); *People; Wordpower; People and Places; The Computer Programme; Greek Language and People; Friday Now* (LWT only); *Health Circuit* (BSB); *Now Listen* (BSB); *Lingo! How to Learn a Language; Shoot the Video; Never Too Late; Sailaway; UK Today* (syndicated worldwide); *Runway.* Address: c/o Curtis Brown. Lives in West London. m. Anna; 2 s. Harry, Jack. Hobbies: Sailing, rowing, vintage cars.

Chris Serle

John Sessions

Carolyn Seymour

Jane Seymour

Patricia Shakesby

Paul Shane

SESSIONS, John

John Marshall. Actor. b. Largs, Ayrshire, 11 January 1953. Studied English at Bangor University, where he performed his first one-man show, *Last Tango in Bangor*, then completed a PhD at Macmaster University, Toronto, before training at RADA. Stage plays include *The Orton Diaries* (as Joe Orton).

TV: Solo work: *Saturday Review; A History of Psychiatry; Saturday Night Live; John Sessions' New Year Show; On the Spot; Some Enchanted Evening; Tall Tales; Likely Stories.* Drama: *Educating Marmalade; Tender Is the Night; The Madness Museum; Boon; Happy Families; Girls on Top;* Zipser in *Porterhouse Blue; Gramsci; Menace Unseen;* Croser in *A Day in Summer;* Dickens in *Ackroyd's Dickens;* Lord Pennistone in *The New Statesman;* McMurdo in *Jute City; Life with Eliza* (series); Boswell in *Tour of the Western Isles;* John Locke in *Citizen Locke; Without Walls: The Art of Tripping, Part Two* (voice only). Variety: *Spitting Image; Whose Line Is It Anyway?; The Lenny Henry Show; Around Midnight; Laugh, I Nearly Paid My Licence Fee; A Clip round the Year; After Midnight; The Cellar Show.*

Films: *The Sender; The Bounty; Gunbus; Whoops Apocalypse; Castaway; Henry V; Sweet Revenge; The Pope Must Die* (US title *The Pope Must Diet*). Address: c/o Markham & Froggatt. Lives in London. Single.

SEYMOUR, Carolyn

Carolyn Von Benckendorff. Actress. b. Aylesbury, Buckinghamshire, 6 November. Trained at the Central School of Speech and Drama.

TV: Jenny in *Take Three Girls* (Series 2); *Justice;* Abby Grant in *The Survivors; Return of The Saint; Jack's Place; Over My Dead Body; Masquerade; Twilight Zone; Hart to Hart; Remington Steele; Civil Wars; Alfred Hithcock Presents; Class of '96; The Trials of Rosie O'Neill; Magnum PI; Matlock; Cagney and Lacey; Family Ties; LA Law; Murder, She Wrote; Star Trek: The Next Generation; Quantum Leap; Reform School Girls* (TVM).

Films: *Steptoe and Son; Gumshoe; The Odd Job; The Bitch; Midnight Cabaret; Zorro, The Gay Blade; Unman, Wittering & Zigo; Destination Unknown; Mr Mom; The Ruling Class; Congo.*

Address: c/o Langford Associates. Lives in Los Angeles. m. film director Peter Medak (dis); 1 s. Joshua Paul, 1 d. Daisy. Pets: 'Several — rescues any stray!' Hobbies: Cooking, travel.

SEYMOUR, Jane

Joyce Frankenberg. Actress. b. Hillingdon, Middlesex, 15 February 1951. Former dancer with the London Festival Ballet (aged 13). Stage plays include *Amadeus* (Broadway).

TV: *The Strauss Family; The Pathfinders; The Onedin Line; The Double Deckers; The Leather Funnel; The Hanged Man* (TVM); *Our Mutual Friend; King David; Captains and Kings; Benny and Barney: Las Vegas Undercover* (TVM); *Seventh Avenue; Killer on Board* (TVM); *Seventh Avenue; The Four Feathers; The Awakening Land; Dallas Cowboy Cheerleaders* (TVM); *Love's Dark Ride* (TVM); *The Pirate* (TVM); *East of Eden* (TVM); *Phantom of the Opera* (TVM); *Jamaica Inn* (TVM); *The Haunting Passion* (TVM); *The Scarlet Pimpernel* (TVM); *Dark Mirror* (TVM); *Obsessed with a Married Woman* (TVM); *The Sun Also Rises* (TVM); *Crossings* (mini-series); *War and Remembrance;* Mrs Simpson in *The Woman He Loved* (mini-series and TVM); *Onassis;* Emma Prentice in *Jack the Ripper* (mini-series); *The French Revolution; Discovering Britain; Angel of Death* (TVM); Dr Michaela Quinn in *Dr Quinn: Medicine Woman.*

Films: *Oh! What a Lovely War; Oktober-Dage* (UK title *The Only Way*); *The Best Pair of Legs in the Business; Young Winston; Frankenstein — The True Story* (TVM only in US); Solitaire in *Live and Let Die; Sinbad and the Eye of the Tiger;* Serina in *Battlestar Galactica* (TVM only in US); *The Four Feathers* (TVM only in US); *Matilda; Oh Heavenly Dog; Somewhere in Time; Lassiter; Head Office; The Tunnel; Keys to Freedom; The French Revolution; Matters of the Heart.*

Books: *Jane Seymour's Guide to Romantic Living.* Address: c/o London Management. Lives in Bath and Los Angeles. m. 1st (dis), 2nd (dis), 3rd David Flynn (dis); 2 children (both from 3rd m.).

SHAKESBY, Patricia

Patricia Shakesby. Actress. b. Cottingham, East Yorkshire, 6 November 1942. West End stage plays include *The Real Inspector Hound, Night of the Iguana* and *Suddenly at Home.* Acted in RSC productions of *Romeo and Juliet, Hamlet, Troilus and Cressida, Love Girl and the Innocent* and *La Ronde.*

TV: Susan Cunningham in *Coronation Street; Z Cars; Saturday while Sunday; War and Peace; Crime and Punishment; Late Starter; Sapphire and Steel; Yes Minister; The Pity of It All; Flowering Cherry;* Polly Urquhart in *Howards' Way.* Address: c/o Roger Carey Associates. m. (dis).

SHANE, Paul

Paul Shane. Actor. b. Rotherham, South Yorkshire, 19 June 1940. An amateur stand-up comic in Northern clubs while working as a miner, before turning professional. Switched to acting in 1974. Stage productions include *Hi-de-Hi!* and *Fur Coat and No Knickers* (national tour).

TV: *A Day Out* (Play for Today); *Keep an Eye on Albert* (Play for Today); *Summer Season* (Play for Today); *Coronation Street; Vampires; Buses; Sounding Brass; The Old Crowd; Turtle's Progress; Muck and Brass; Life for Christine; The Generation Game;* Ted Bovis in *Hi-de-Hi!* (series, 1980-8); Syd Scouse in *Supergran; This Is Your Life* (subject); Alf Stokes in *You Rang, M'Lord?* (pilot, 1988; four series, 1990-3); Harry James in *Very Big Very Soon* (series, 1991); Honest Norman in *Woof!; The Right Result;* Perry Champagne in *Chucklevision;* Ernie Potts in *Mother's Ruin;* Jack Skinner in *Oh Doctor Beeching!* (pilot, 1995). Address: c/o ATS Casting. m. Dory; 3 d. Janice, Andrea, Gillian.

SHANNON, Johnny
John Shannon. Actor. b. Lambeth, South London, 29 July 1932. Began acting career after meeting James Fox, who recommended him for the role of gangster boss Harry Flowers in the film *Performance.*
TV: *The Gold Robbers; Dixon of Dock Green; Z Cars; Budgie, Six Faces of a Man; The Operation* (Play for Today); *Go for Gold; The Donati Conspiracy; The Dick Emery Show; Never Mind the Quality, Feel the Width; Beryl's Lot; The XYY Man; The Sweeney; Old Dog with New Tricks; Pursuit; The Other One; The Losers; Hazell and the Greasy Gunners; Fawlty Towers; The Enigma File; Minder; Secret Army; Tales of the Unexpected: Man at the Top; The Morecambe and Wise Show; Angels; The Chinese Detective; The Professionals; The Kenny Everett Show; Union Castle; The Boy Who Won the Pools; Watch All Night; Give Us a Break; Keep It in the Family; Billy Bunyan in Big Deal; Supergran; The Bright Side; Keeping Score; Queenie* (mini-series); *Coast to Coast* (TVM); *Bust; High Street Blues;* Alfie Phillips in *EastEnders.*
Films: *Performance; Villain; That'll Be the Day; Flame; Sweeney; The Great Rock and Roll Swindle; Runners; Absolute Beginners; Scandal.*
Address: c/o Chatto and Linnit. Lives in Bexleyheath, Kent. m. Rose; 1 s. Gary, 1 d. Terry. Hobbies: Boxing, horse-racing.

Johnny Shannon

SHARPE, Lesley-Anne
Lesley-Anne Maria Sharpe. Actress. b. Liverpool, 28 December 1964. Trained at Liverpool Theatre School and the Arts Educational School. Plays include *Annie* (Victoria Palace) and *Watching* (tour).
TV: *Boys from the Blackstuff;* Dawn Finney in *Brookside;* Carol in *Coronation Street; Albion Market;* Harriet Mills in *What Now?;* Debbie Yates in *Boon* (second series); *Harry Enfield's Television Programme;* Joey's girlfriend in *Bread; The Bill;* Marie Jenson in *EastEnders.*
Address: c/o Elaine Murphy Associates. Lives in Tottenham, North London. Single. Hobbies: Watching Everton FC, football in general, British motorbikes, going to ballet.

Lesley-Anne Sharpe

SHARROCK, Ian
Ian William Sharrock. Actor. b. Darley, near Harrogate, North Yorkshire, 20 December 1959. Trained at the Corona Stage Academy from the age of 11. Stage roles include Mole in *The Wind in the Willows* (National Theatre, Old Vic).
TV: Title role in *Smike* (aged 13); John Darling in *Peter Pan;* Rhodes in *Scum; Games* (Play for Love); Jackie Merrick in *Emmerdale Farm* (1980-9); *She-Wolf of London; Heartbeat; Ain't Misbehavin'; Agent Z & the Penguin from Mars.*
Films: *The Mackintosh Man; A Warm December; Candleshoe.* **Radio:** Alan in *Equus.* Address: c/o Susan Angel Associates. Lives in Chelmsford, Essex. m. 1985 Pamela; 1 d. Natalie Clare, 1 s. William Ian. Pets: Labrador cross called Barney, two cats called Tom and Billy, one goldfish. Hobbies: 'Bad golf, sleeping.'

Ian Sharrock

SHAW, Martin
Martin Shaw. Actor. b. Birmingham, 21 January 1945. Worked as a sales clerk before training at LAMDA. Stage productions include *Look Back In Anger* (Royal Court and Criterion Theatre), *They're Playing Our Song* (Shaftesbury Theatre), *Are You Lonesome Tonight?* (Phoenix Theatre and Australia) and *An Ideal Husband* (Theatre Royal, Haymarket).
TV: *Travelling Light; Doctor at Large; Villains; Hamlet; Achilles Heel; Helen – A Woman of Today; Love's Labour's Lost; The Explorers; Electra; Spice Island Farewell; Z Cars; Sutherland's Law; Beasts; Buddyboy; The Duchess of Duke Street; Our Kid; Exiles; The New Avengers;* Doyle in *The Professionals;* Jack Butcher in *Cream In My Coffee, Face Lift; East Lynne;* Sir Henry Baskerville in *The Hound of the Baskervilles* (TVM); Captain Scott in *The Last Place on Earth; The Most Dangerous Man in the World; Who Bombed Birmingham?;* Chief Supt Mike Barclay in *Black and Blue* (Screen One); Dep Chief Commissione/Chief Constable Alan Cade in *The Chief* (series).
Films: *Macbeth; The Golden Voyage of Sinbad; Operation Daybreak; Ladder of Swords.*
Records: Single: *Cross My Heart and Hope to Die.*
Address: c/o Hutton Management. m. Maggie; 2 s. Luke, Joe, 2 d. Sophie, Kate.

Martin Shaw

SHELLEY, Cindy
Cindy Shelley. Actress. b. Barnet, Hertfordshire, 23 March 1960. Trained at the New School of Speech and Drama. Stage plays include a national tour with the Polka Children's Theatre.
TV: *Going to Work; Cockles; Long Live the Babe; Tenko; Tenko Reunion;* Abby Howard in *Howards' Way;* Kate in *Bottom.* Address: c/o Silvester Management. m. Philip; 1 d. Hannah.

Cindy Sholloy

Jack Shepherd

SHEPHERD, Jack

Jack Shepherd. Actor/Director/Writer. b. Leeds, 29 October 1940. Trained at The Drama Centre.
TV: *Full House; The Ballad of Ben Baggot; All Good Men; Pigeon – Hawk or Dove?; Occupations; The Actual Woman* (writer); *Girls of Slender Means; Bill Brand; Through the Night; Ready When You Are Mr McGill; Ten Days That Shook the Branch; Count Dracula; Mr and Ms Bureaucrat; The Devil's Crown; The Killing; Nina; Underdog* (writer); *The Unborn; Sons and Lovers; Clapperclaw* (writer); *A Room for the Winter; The Mysteries; Hard Travelling; The Holy City; Escape From Sobibor; Scoop* (TVM); *The Party; The Hospice; Cracking Up; Omnibus: Vincent Van Gogh; Body Contact; Blind Justice; A Day in Summer* (TVM); *The Murderers Are among Us; The Act; Nobody Here but Us Chickens; Ball-Trap on the Côte Sauvage* (TVM); *Misterioso; Shoot to Kill; Woman at War; Trust Me; Tales from Hollywood; Lovejoy; Det Supt Charles Wycliffe in Wycliffe; Between the Lines; Calling the Shot; Hope in the Year Two; Over Here.*
Films: *The Virgin Soldiers; The Bed Sitting Room; Luces y Sombras; Twenty-One; The Big Man; Object of Beauty; Angry Earth; Black Permanent; Blue Ice.*
Address: c/o Markham & Froggatt. m. 1st Judy Harland (dis), 2nd Ann Scott; 1 d. Jan, 1 s. Jake (from 1st m.), 2 twin d. Victoria, Catherine, 1 s. Ben (all from 2nd m.).

Simon Shepherd

SHEPHERD, Simon

Simon Shepherd. Actor. b. Bristol, 20 August 1956. Trained at the Bristol Old Vic Theatre School.
TV: *This Lightning Only Strikes Twice; My Father's House; Sorrel and Son; Lord Alfred Douglas in Lillie; The House on Garibaldi Street* (TVM); *The Jewel in the Crown; Stalky and Co; Sweet Wine of Youth; Aubrey Beardsley; The Blue Dress; A Murder Is Announced; Time and the Conways; Company & Co; A Man Called Intrepid; May We Borrow Your Husband; The Dark Angel; Chancer; Cleudo; Agatha Christie's Poirot;* Dr Will Preston in *Peak Practice* (four series, 1993-6); *Beyond Reason; Bliss* (pilot).
Films: *The Insatiable Mrs Kirsch;* Edgar in *Wuthering Heights;* Dr Harding in *The Doctor and the Devils; Lords of Discipline; Deadline; Fire, Ice and Dynamite; Henry V.*
Address: c/o ICM. Lives in the West Country. m. designer Alexandra Byrne; 2 s., 2 d.

Dinah Sheridan

SHERIDAN, Dinah

Dinah Mec. Actress. b. North London, 17 September 1920. Trained at the Italia Conti Stage Academy.
TV: *Picture Page* (first regular BBC TV broadcast, October 1936); *Gallows Glorious; Winning Streak;* Angela Latimer in *Don't Wait Up* (series); one of 'Couple' in *Keeping Up Appearances; All Night Long.*
Films: *Give My Heart; Irish and Proud of It; Landslide; Father Steps Out; Behind Your Back; Merely Mr Hawkins; Full Speed Ahead; Salute John Citizen; Get Cracking; 29 Acadia Avenue; For You Alone; Murder in Reverse; Hills of Donegal; Calling Paul Temple; The Story of Shirley Yorke; The Huggetts Abroad; Dark Secret; No Trace; Paul Temple's Triumph; Where No Vultures Fly; The Sound Barrier; Appointment in London; The Story of Gilbert and Sullivan; Genevieve; The Railway Children; The Mirror Crack'd.* Address: c/o ICM. m. 1st actor Jimmy Hanley (dis), 2nd film producer-director John Davis (dis), 3rd John Merivale (dec); 1 d. actress-TV presenter Jenny Hanley (from 1st m.).

Cathy Shipton

SHIPTON, Cathy

Catherine Ellen Shipton. Actress/Writer. b. Forest Hill, South London, 27 March 1957. Trained at the Rose Bruford College of Speech and Drama (1977-80).
TV: *Hold the Back Page; Out on the Floor; Oedipus;* Lisa 'Duffy' Duffin in *Casualty* (1986-93); *One Foot in the Grave* (Christmas special); *Taggart: Devil's Advocate; Agent Z & the Penguin from Mars.*
Films: Dulcie in *Little Sir Nicolas.* **Books:** *Marathon Running* (1996).
Address: c/o Scott Marshall. Lives in London. Partner: Actor Christopher Guard (qv). Pets: Two dogs called Bess and Pip, two fish called Jasper and James. Hobbies: Running, walking, dancing, cooking.

SILVERA, Carmen

Carmen Blanche Silvera. Actress. b. Toronto, Canada, 2 June. Trained at LAMDA.
TV: *Z Cars;* Camilla Hope in *Compact; Beggar My Neighbour; New Scotland Yard; Sergeant Cork; Doctor Who;* Mrs Gray in *Dad's Army; Two Women; Within These Walls; The Gentle Touch; Before Water Lilies; Lillie; Whoops Apocalypse!; Maggie and Her; Tales of the Unexpected; The Generation Game; Little and Large; The Paul Daniels Show;* Edith Artois in *'Allo, 'Allo* (nine series, 1984-92); *The Best of 'Allo 'Allo* (presenter, 1994). Address: c/o Barry Burnett Organisation. Lives in London. m. J P Cunliffe (dis). Hobbies: Playing cards, crosswords, reading, golf, painting, cooking.

Carmen Silvera

SIMONS, William

Clifford William Cumberbatch Simons. Actor. b. Mumbles, 17 November 1940.
TV: *Mr Rose;* Harry Bates and Jim Cawley in *Coronation Street; Little Sunbeam; Paper Roses; A Family at War; Sam; Crown Court* (1974-83); *The Last Party;* Will Croft in *Emmerdale Farm; Snacker; Yanks Go Home; Beryl's Lot; Parables; Doctor Who; The Sweeney; Enemy at the Door; Losing Her; Julius Caesar; Blacktoft Diaries; Even Soloman; Cribb; The Bell; Number 10; Beatrix Potter; Being Norman; Give Us a*

Break; Pope John Paul II (TVM); *The Wedding; Cockles; Minder; A Month in the Country; Late Starter; Dempsey and Makepeace; Blott on the Landscape; The Bird Fancier; Too Young to Fight; Auf Wiedersehen Pet; Boon; Time for Murder; Juliet Bravo; Death Is Part of the Process; The Refuge; Rumpole of the Bailey; Surveillance; Bergerac; The New Statesman; A Bit of a Do; Wish Me Luck; The Bill; The Ruth Rendell Mysteries: A Sleeping Life; Haggard; Stay Lucky; Love Hurts; The Darling Buds of May; Tales of Mystery and Imagination; Lovejoy;* PC Ventress in *Heartbeat* (six series 1992-7); *The Inspector Alleyn Mysteries; The Woman in Black.* Address: c/o Saraband Associates. Lives in London. m. Jennifer Jane Royle Lowther.

William Simons

SIMS, Joan
Irene Joan Sims. Actress. b. Laindon, Essex, 9 May 1930. Trained at RADA after winning a scholarship.
TV: *Vegetable Village; The Stanley Baxter Show; Carry On Christmas; Till Death Us Do Part; The Way of the World; The Dick Emery Show; Carry On Laughing; Sykes; Seven of One; The Howerd Confessions; The Two Ronnies; Love among the Ruins; Lord Tramp; East Lynne; Your Move; Born and Bred; Worzel Gummidge; In Loving Memory; Ladykillers;Virginia Fly Is Drowning; Waters of the Moon; Crown Court; Poor Little Rich Girls; Cockles; Agatha Christie's Miss Marple: A Murder Is Announced; Hay Fever; Deceptions; Farrington of the FO; And There's More; Tickle on the Tum; Simon and the Witch; Only Fools and Horses; Victoria Wood; Living Life Lately; On the Up; Fumed Oak* (Tonight at 8.30); *Boys from the Bush; Tender Loving Care; One Foot in the Algarve; Smokescreen; As Time Goes By; My Good Friend; Just William.*
Films: Selection (from 71): *Will Any Gentleman...?* (début, 1953); *Trouble in Store; Doctor in the House; The Belles of St Trinian's; Doctor at Sea; Dry Rot; Carry On Admiral; Carry On Nurse; Life in Emergency Ward 10; Carry On Teacher; Carry On Constable; Doctor in Love; Carry On Regardless; Nurse on Wheels; Carry On Cloo; Carry On Cowboy; Doctor in Clover; Carry On Screaming; Don't Lose Your Head; Follow That Camel; Carry On Doctor; Carry On Up the Khyber; Carry On Camping; Carry On Again, Doctor; Carry On Up the Jungle; Doctor in Trouble; Carry On Loving; Carry On Henry; The Magnificent Seven Deadly Sins; Carry On at Your Convenience; Carry On Matron; The Alf Garnett Saga; Carry On Abroad; Not Now Darling; Carry On Girls; Don't Just Lie There, Say Something; Carry On Dick; Carry On Behind; One of Our Dinosaurs Is Missing; Carry On England; Carry On Emmannuelle; The Fool.* Address: c/o MGA.

Joan Sims

SINCLAIR, Suzanne
Suzanne Sinclair. Actress. b. London, 12 January 1960. West End stage plays include *Killing Jessica.*
TV: *Newsfile; Saturday Stayback; Fool of Me; The Lenny Henry Show; There's a Lot of It About; Victoria Wood — As Seen on TV; Grange Hill; The Dressing Room;* WPC Debbie Mulvaney and Angela Thorpe in *The Bill.* For FR3, France: *Le Loufiat; L'Escale; Le Bal D'Irène;* Sophie in *Ne M'Appelez Plus Gloria.*
Films: *Hard Facts;* Mona in *Quadrophenia;* Andie in *Bellona;* Thorn in *White Angel.* Address: c/o Langford Associates. Lives in London. Single. Hobbies: Marathon runner, karate (black belt).

Suzanne Sinclair

SINDEN, Donald
Donald Sinden. Actor. b. Plymouth, Devon, 9 October 1923. CBE. Brother of actor Leon Sinden (qv). Trained at the Webber Douglas Academy.
TV: *Bullet in the Ballet; Our Man from St Mark's; The Prisoner; The Organisation; Two's Company; Discovering English Churches; All's Well That Ends Well; Present Laughter; Never the Twain; The Rivals.*
Films: *Portrait from Life; The Cruel Sea; A Day to Remember; Mogambo; You Know What Sailors Are; The Beachcomber; Doctor in the House; Mad about Men; Simba; Above Us the Waves; Josephine and Men; An Alligator Named Daisy;Tiger in the Smoke; Eyewitness; The Black Tent; Doctor at Large; The Captain's Table; Rockets Galore; Operation Bullshine; Your Money or Your Wife; The Siege of Sydney Street; Twice round the Daffodils; Mix Me a Person; Decline and Fall... of a Birdwatcher; Villain; Rentadick; Father Dear Father; The Day of the Jackal; The National Health; The Island at the Top of the World; That Lucky Touch; Helicopter; The Children.* Address: c/o ICM. m. Diana Mahony; 2 s. Jeremy (qv), Marc (qv).

Donald Sinden

SINDEN, Jeremy
Jeremy Mahony Sinden. Actor. b. London, 14 June 1950. Son of actor Donald Sinden (qv); brother of actor Marc Sinden (qv); nephew of actor Leon Sinden (qv). Trained at LAMDA (winner, Forsyth Award).
TV: *The Expert; The Sweeney; Crossroads; The Bass Player and the Blonde; Danger UXB; Soldiers Talking Cleanly; School Play; For Maddie with Love; Fothergill; Have I Got You Where You Want Me?; Brideshead Revisited; Holding the Fort; Never the Twain; Squadron; Number 10; The Far Pavilions; Chance in a Million; Fairly Secret Army; Lytton's Diary; Mountbatten — The Last Viceroy; Three Up, Two Down; Robin of Sherwood; All at No 20; If Tomorrow Comes; Harem; Bergerac; Have His Carcase; Fortunes of War; The Management; After the War; Square Deal; Virtuoso; Don't Wait Up; Blackheart the Pirate; Scarfe on Paradise; Early Travellers in North America; Trainer; Middlemarch; The Famous Five; As Time Goes By; The House of Windsor; The Detectives.*
Films: *Star Wars; Rosie Dixon Night Nurse; Chariots of Fire; Ascendancy; The Innocent;* Woodford in *Madame Sousatzka; The Object of Beauty; "Let Him Have It".*
Address: c/o ICM. Lives in London. m. actress Delia Lindsay; 2 d. Kezia, Harriet.

Jeremy Sinden

Leon Sinden

Marc Sinden

Guy Siner

Valerie Singleton

Peter Sissons

SINDEN, Leon

Leon Fuller Sinden. Actor. b. Ditchling, East Sussex, 20 July 1927. Brother of actor Donald Sinden (qv); uncle of actors Jeremy (qv) and Marc Sinden (qv). Began career in MESA, a Brighton-based ENSA group, in 1941. Turned professional in 1948. Stage plays include *Ross* (Haymarket Theatre), *Semi-Detached* and *London Assurance* (both Broadway).
TV: Uncle Roderick in *Scoop; Rebecca; Assassination Run; Taggart;* Mr Carradine in *Take the High Road.* Address: Young Casting Agency. Lives in London and Perth. Single. Pets: Three-legged cat. Hobbies: Auctions, holidays, music.

SINDEN, Marc

Marcus Sinden. Actor/Artistic Director. b. London, 9 May 1954. Son of actor Donald Sinden (qv); brother of actor Jeremy Sinden (qv); nephew of actor Leon Sinden (qv). Trained at Bristol Old Vic Theatre School. Currently artistic director, Mermaid Theatre. West End plays include *Enjoy, Her Royal Highness, Underground, School for Scandal, Two into One, Ross* and *Over My Dead Body.*
TV: *Fiddlers Green; Dick Turpin; If You Go down in the Woods Today* (TVM); *Strange but True; Crossroads; Home Front; Magnum PI; Never the Twain; Rumpole of the Bailey; Bergerac; All at No 20; Wolf to the Slaughter; Oratory; The Country Boy Century Falls; Emmerdale;* Major Drake in *Against All Odds* (series, 1994).
Films: *Manges d'Hommes; Clash of Loyalties; White Nights; The Wicked Lady; Carry On Columbus; The Mystery of Edwin Drood; Decadence; Princess.*
Radio: *The Spy Who Came in from the Cold; The Frog Prince.*
Address: c/o Christina Shepherd. Lives in London. m. Joanne; 1 s. Henry (b. 1980), 1 d. Bridie (b. 1990). Hobbies: Theatre history, history of stunt-work, motor-racing, cricket.

SINER, Guy

Guy Siner. Actor. b. New York City, USA, 16 October 1947. Trained at the Webber Douglas Academy. West End plays include *The Biograph Girl, Toad of Toad Hall, Don't Dress for Dinner* and *'Allo, 'Allo.*
TV: Pylades in *I Claudius;* Francis Simard in *Life at Stake* (series); Heinrich in *Secret Army;* David Stevens in *Softly Softly;* Arthur Naylor in *Z Cars;* Ravon in *Doctor Who;* Lt Gruber in *'Allo, 'Allo* (nine series); Noël Coward in *You Rang, M'Lord?;* Philip Silverman in *The Brittas Empire.*
Films: Thomas in *Great Harry and Jane.*
Radio: *When in Germany* (presenter). **Awards:** Rodney Millington Award (1971).
Address: c/o Barry Burnett Organisation/Don Buchwald & Associates. Lives in Los Angeles. Single.

SINGLETON, Valerie

Valerie Singleton. Presenter/Writer. b. Hitchin, Hertfordshire, 9 April 1937. OBE. Won a scholarship to RADA, acted in rep and worked on TV advertising magazines before joining the BBC as an announcer.
TV: *The Arnold Doodle Show* (advertising magazine); BBC Television announcer (1962-4); *Blue Peter* (1962-72); *Blue Peter Royal Safari; Blue Peter Special Assignments* (four series); *Val Meets the VIPs; Nationwide;* Interviewer in *Citizen Smith; Tonight; Tonight in Town; Migrant Workers in Europe; Echoes of Germany; The Money Programme* (1980-8); *Travel UK* (series); *Next* (presenter, series, 1994-5); *Backdate* (host, quiz show, series, 1996).
Radio: *PM* (1981-93); *Maxwell – The Last Days* (narrator). Address: c/o Arlington Enterprises. Lives in London. Single. Pets: A cat called Daisy. Hobbies: Museums, London and its history, sailing, photography, travelling, exploring new places, antique browsing.

SISSONS, Peter

Peter Sissons. Newsreader. b. Liverpool, 17 July 1942. Joined ITN as a trainee in 1964 and became a reporter three years later, covering the Middle East War. Wounded during the Nigerian civil war (1968).
TV: ITN (1964-89) as trainee, general reporter, foreign correspondent, news editor, industrial editor (1974-8), presenter of *News at One* (1978-82) and presenter and associate editor of *Channel Four News;* BBC TV as presenter of *The Six o'Clock News* and *Question Time* (four series, 1990-93) concurrently, then *The Nine o'Clock News; The BBC Banned Audition Tapes* (*Total Relief: A Night of Comic Relief,* 1993). Address: c/o BBC TV. Lives in Kent. m. Sylvia; 1 d. Kate, 2 s. Jonathan, Michael.

SLATTERY, Tony

Tony Slattery. Presenter/Actor/Comedian. b. London. Member of Cambridge Footlights revue while studying at university.
TV: *Saturday Stayback; TX; Behind the Bike Sheds* (as writer); *Boon; Whose Line Is It Anyway?; Saturday Night at the Movies; This Is David Harper; Drowning in the Shallow End; S & M; The Magic Hare* (storyteller); Tristan in *That's Love* (series); *The Music Game* (presenter, series); *The Krypton Factor* (series); *Ps and Qs* (host, quiz show); Queen Boadicea in *A Word in Your Era;* Nick Brim in *Just a Gigo-*

Io (series, 1993); *The Full Wax; Just a Minute; Going For a Song* (team captain, antiques panel game, two series, 1995-6).
Films: *Peter's Friends.* Address: c/o ICM. Lives in Stockwell, South London.

SMILLIE, Carol
Carol Smillie. Presenter/Actress/Model. Formerly one of Scotland's top fashion models and fashion editor of the *Sunday Scot.*
TV: *Wheel of Fortune* (hostess, six series); *The Justice Game; Open Air; Children in Need; A Word in Your Ear; The Main Event; That's History; Celebrity Squares; Monarchs of the Glen; ITV Telethon; Win, Lose or Draw; The Travel Show; Travel Spot (Good Morning... with Anne & Nick,* 1992-); *The Travel Show Guides* (series); *TV Weekly; The Big Breakfast* (guest presenter, 1994); *The Boat Show* (1994); *Summer Holiday* (series); *Good Fortune (1994); Holiday* (series); *Hearts of Gold* (co-presenter, Series 7-8, 1995-6). Regional only: *Scotland Today* (fashion presenter, Scottish Television); *The Art Sutter Show* (Grampian Television); *The Talking Loud Show* (Scottish Television); *Wemyss Bay* (Scottish Television); *Scottish Women* (Scottish Television); *Late and Live* (Tyne Tees Television).
Address: c/o Dave Warwick. m. Alex; 1 child.

Tony Slattery

SMITH, David
David Smith. News correspondent. b. London, 5 March 1952. Gained an MA in English literature from Oxford University and speaks Spanish, Italian and Arabic. Joined Reuters as a correspondent, in Spain and Italy (1974-8), before moving into television with ITN (1979).
TV: ITN Africa correspondent (1979-81), Europe and Middle East correspondent (1981-3), Middle East correspondent (1984-6); lecturer on Middle East affairs at University of Michigan (1986-7); ITN *Channel Four News* foreign affairs correspondent (1987), Moscow, then Washington correspondent.
Books: *Mugabe – A Biography* (1981); *Prisoners of God – The Conflict of Arab and Jew* (1987).
Awards: RTS International Reporting Award (1983) for coverage of an attack on British troops in Beirut. Address: c/o ITN. m. Pamela Reading; 2 children.

Carol Smillie

SMITH, Liz
Betty Smith. Actress. b. Scunthorpe, 11 December 1925. Began career in weekly rep at the Gateway Theatre, Westbourne Grove, London. After seven years, she left showbusiness to bring up her two children but returned to join The Stage, Charles Marowitz's company, then worked for a while in Butlin's holiday camps for the Forbes Russell Company before being spotted by director Mike Leigh.
TV: *Bootsie and Snudge; No Honestly; I Didn't Know You Cared; The Dick Emery Show; The Sweeney; Crown Court; Emmerdale Farm; The All Electric Amusement Arcade; The Fortune Hunters; Nicholas Nickleby; The Hunchback of Notre Dame; Spend Spend Spend; Murder Rap; Russ Abbot's Madhouse; In Loving Memory; Mr Right; Russian Night 1941; Now and Then; Partners in Crime; Separate Tables; The Life and Loves of a She-Devil; Little Dorrit; Welcome to the Times; King and Castle; Valentine Park; Imaginary Friends; Road; Bust; The Prodigal Mother; Christmas Is Coming; All in Good Faith; Young Charlie; Tinniswood's North Country; Words of Love; Singles; Dunrulin; Nona; El C.I.D.; The Bill; Making Out; Bottom; Underbelly;* Bette/Belle in *2point4 Children* (series); *Lovejoy; Cluedo; Good Parenting Guide; Making Waves; The Young Indiana Jones Chronicles; Without Walls: For One Night Only; Wise Children; Bad Voodoo; Pirates; The Mask; Blow Your Mind: Wise Children; Takin' Over the Asylum; Doggin' Around* (Screen One); Letitia Cropley in *The Vicar of Dibley* (series, 1994); *Karaoke.*
Films: *Agatha; The Pink Panther; All Things Bright and Beautiful; Duellist; Mud; The Monster Club; Dracula; Sir Henry at Rawlinson End; The French Lieutenant's Woman; A Private Function; Whoops Apocalypse; D'Ardanelle; We Think the World of You; High Spirits; Jake's Progress; Apartment Zero; Bert Rigby, You're a Fool; Little Dorrit; The Cook The Thief His Wife & Her Lover; Dakota Road; Princess.*
Awards: Films: BAFTA Best Supporting Actress for *A Private Function* (1984).
Address: c/o Conway, van Gelder, Robinson. m.; 2 children.

David Smith

SMITH, Mel
Mel Smith. Actor/Director. b. London, 3 December 1952. Studied experimental psychology at Oxford University, but left before completing the course to become an assistant director at the Royal Court Theatre, then moved to the Bristol Old Vic, the Young Vic, followed by the Crucible Theatre, Sheffield, as associate director. Became a writer for the BBC2 comedy series *Not the Nine o'Clock News.* Stage plays include *Not in Front of the Audience* (also directed, Theatre Royal, Drury Lane).
TV: *Not the Nine o'Clock News; Alas Smith and Jones; Minder; Muck and Brass; Smith and Goody; Colin's Sandwich; The Best of Smith and Jones; The British Academy Awards* (presenter, 1993); Stephen Milner in *Milner; Smith and Jones: Prime Cuts* (four compilations, 1995).
Films: *Slayground; Babylon; Bullshot; Number One; Restless Natives; National Lampoon's European Vacation; Morons from Outer Space; The Princess Bride; The Wolves of Willoughby Chase; The Tall Guy* (also director); *Wilt; Father Christmas* (voice only); *Lame Ducks; Brain Donors.* Address: c/o TalkBack.

Liz Smith

Mel Smith

Mike Smith

SMITH, Mike

Mike Smith. Presenter. b. Hornchurch, Essex, 23 April 1955. Began career in hospital radio (1974), before joining BBC Radio 1 as a researcher and standby presenter. Moved to Capital Radio (London) in 1978, presenting the Sunday afternoon chart programme within a year and occasionally appearing on television. Returned to Radio 1 in 1982 and left radio for TV two years later.

TV: *Greatest Hits; CBTV; Breakfast Time; Family Tree; The Late, Late Breakfast Show; Speak Out; Live Aid; The Royal Tournament; Motor Fair; Airport 86 — Live; Secret's Out; The Montreux Rock Festival; First AIDS; Driving Force; Wogan* (guest presenter); *Transit; Family; Trick or Treat; That's Showbusiness; No Kidding* (series); Phone-In Presenter in *Ghostwatch; Hearts of Gold* (series); *That's Showbusiness New Year's Eve Show; Young Driver of the Year* (series, 1993); *That's Showbusiness! Special* (Children in Need, 1993); *Tunnel Vision: Le Walk; Body Heat* (series, 1994); *That's Showbusiness Christmas Special* (1994); *That's EastEnders* (1995); *The Exchange Preview; The Exchange* (series, 1995); *Body Heat* (series, 1995); *That's Showbusiness — Movies Special.*

Radio: Radio 1 researcher and standby presenter; Capital Radio presenter; Radio 1 presenter.

Awards: Radio: Sony Awards DJ of the Year (1986, 1987), Variety Club Radio Personality of the Year (1987). Address: c/o Jonathan Altaras Associates. m. TV presenter Sarah Greene.

Jon Snow

SNOW, Jon

Jonathan Snow. Newscaster. b. Ardingly, Sussex, 28 September 1947. Cousin of news presenter Peter Snow (qv). Began career as a radio reporter for LBC/IRN (1973-6). Moved to ITN in 1976 and reported from around the world, including Iran, Iraq, Afghanistan and the Falklands, as well as following Pope John Paul II on a historic trip back to his native Poland. *Channel Four News* presenter since 1989.

TV: ITN as reporter (1976-83), Washington correspondent (1984-6), diplomatic editor (1986-9) and presenter of *News at One* (1988) and ITN weekend programmes, then *Channel Four News* presenter (1989-); *Election '92* (main presenter, 1992 General Election, ITV); *Back to Basics.*

Awards: Monte Carlo Television Festival Golden Nymph (1979); RTS Journalist of the Year (1980); RTS International News award (1981, 1982); Valiant for Truth Media Award (1981); RTS Home News award (1989) for *Channel Four News* coverage of Kegworth air disaster.

Address: c/o ITN. Lives in London. Partner: Madeleine Colvin; 2 d. Leila, Freila. Pets: Two cats, two rabbits. Hobbies: Cape Cod, France, playing the piano, painting.

Peter Snow

SNOW, Peter

Peter John Snow. News presenter. b. Dublin, 20 April 1938. Cousin of newscaster Jon Snow (qv). Read classics at Balliol College, Oxford, did part-time work, including teaching and guiding tourists around London, then returned to teaching, before joining ITN.

TV: ITN (1962-79) sub-editor, reporter, newscaster and (1966-79) diplomatic correspondent; *Newsnight* (presenter/reporter, 1980-); *World Chess Championship* (1993); *Eurovision 94 — Tips for Le Top; Europe Decides* (1994); *Poll on Kohl* (1994); *The Big Picture; Local Elections '95* (1995).

Books: *Leila's Hijack War* (co-author); *Hussein* (biography, 1972).

Address: c/o BBC TV News. Lives in London. m. 1st 1964 Alison Carter (dis 1975), 2nd 1976 Canadian TV journalist Ann Macmillan; 2 s. Shane (from 1st m.), Daniel (from 2nd m.), 3 d. Shuna (from 1st m.), Rebecca, Katherine (both from 2nd m.). Hobbies: Sailing, skiing.

Jane Snowden

SNOWDEN, Jane

Jane Snowden. Actress. b. York, 31 January 1965. Former member of the National Youth Theatre, starring as Juliet in *Romeo and Juliet.*

TV: *All Passion Spent; A Very Peculiar Practice; The Pyrates; Gaudy Night;* Emily in *Wish Me Luck;* Maureen Dyson in *Inspector Morse: The Death of the Self.*

Films: Jenny in *The Frog Prince* (acting début).

Address: c/o ICM. Lives in London. m. actor James Simmons.

SOMERVILLE, Geraldine

Geraldine Somerville. Actress.

TV: *Agatha Christie's Poirot; Casualty;* Biddy Millican in *Catherine Cookson's The Black Velvet Gown;* Marie Cousins in *The Bill;* DS Jane Penhaligon in *Cracker* (three series, 1993-5); Ann Welch in *The Deep Blue Sea* (Performance); title role in *After Miss Julie* (Performance).

Address: c/o Ken McReddie. Lives in South London.

Geraldine Somerville

SOMERVILLE, Julia

Julia Somerville. Newscaster. After graduating from Sussex University, worked on *Homes and Gardens* and *Woman's Journal,* then joined the PR section of *Woman's Own* and became editor of a computer group's house magazine for two years before joining the BBC (1973).

TV: BBC sub-editor, chief sub-editor, reporter, labour affairs correspondent (1981-4) and *Nine o'Clock*

News newsreader (1984-7); ITN newscaster (1987-), including *News at One, News at 12.30, News at Ten* and *Lunchtime News; 3D* (current affairs series).
Address: c/o ITN. m. 1st (dis), 2nd (sep).

SPALL, Timothy

Timothy Spall. Actor. b. London, 27 February 1957. Trained at RADA (Bancroft Gold Medal winner). RSC productions include *The Merry Wives of Windsor, Nicholas Nickleby, Knight of the Burning Pestle, Baal.*
TV: Barry in *Auf Wiedersehen Pet; Brylcreem Boys; Cotswold Death; Home Sweet Home; Three Sisters; The Cherry Orchard; Remembrance; Vanishing Army; Body Contact; Broke; The Tale of Little Pig Robinson;* Chico in *Nona* (Performance); *Boon; Murder Most Horrid;* Jimmy Beales in *Roots* (Performance); *Rab C Nesbitt; Red Dwarf; Tracey Ullman: A Class Act;* Robert Cunningham in *Spender;* title role in *Frank Stubbs Promotes* (series, 1993) and *Frank Stubbs* (series, 1994); Margaret Rutherford in *Without Walls: For One Night Only ;* Kevin Costello in *Outside Edge* (three series, 1994-6, plus Christmas special, 1995); Phil in *Nice Day at the Office* (series, 1994); *Oliver 2 (Comic Relief, 1995).*
Films: *Quadrophenia; Raise the Titanic!; The Missionary; The Bride; The Sinking of the Titanic; Predator; To Kill a Priest; Life Is Sweet; Dream Demon; Gothic; The Sheltering Sky; White Hunter, Black Heart.*
Address: c/o Markham & Froggatt. Lives in South London. m. Shane; 2 d. Pascale, Mercedes, 1 s. Rafe.

SPENDLOVE, Rob

Rob Spendlove. Actor. b. London, 1 May 1953. Studied drama at Middlesex Polytechnic, then worked as a teacher, before setting up his own theatre company, touring London schools. Stage productions include *Godspell* (as Judas, national tour) and *Jesus Christ Superstar* (Palace Theatre).
TV: *Strangers;* Roger Huntington in *Brookside* (1982-3); *Lizzie's Pictures; Winds of War; Queenie;* Rick Sneaden in *Closing Ranks; That's Love; Hard Cases;* Det Chris Tierney in *TECX;* DI Shand in *Lovejoy;* John in *El C.I.D.;* Malcolm in *Natural Lies* (mini-series, 1992); Coles in *Fool's Gold* (TVM); CSM Michael Stubbs in *Soldier Soldier* (Series 3-5, 1993-5); Dave Davis in *Class Act; Casualty.*
Films: *Tai-Pan.*
Address: c/o Conway, van Gelder, Robinson. Lives in North London. m. actress Sandy Hendrickse.

SPIRO, Alyson

Alyson Spiro. Actress. Stage roles include Andrea in *The Genius* (Royal Court).
TV: Naomi in *Flat Bust;* Liz in *The Enigma Files* (series); Mary Divine in *King's Royal* (series); Kath Borrow in *Fell Tiger* (series); Alison Gregory in *Brookside;* Cheryl Stacey in *Sam Saturday;* Julie Hart in *The Bill;* WPC Bryant in *Casualty;* Mary Ramis in *If You See God, Tell Him;* Margaret Speel in *Prime Suspect 3;* Mrs Hill in *The Bill;* Sarah Sugden in *Emmerdale* (1994-).
Films: *Birth of the Beatles; She'll Be Wearing Pink Pyjamas; The Amnesty Files; Northern Crescent.*
Address: c/o Mayer & Eden. Lives in London. m.; 3 d. Ella, twins Cara and Georgia.

SPRIGGS, Elizabeth

Elizabeth Jean Williams. Actress. b. Buxton, Derbyshire, 18 September 1929. Trained for opera at the Royal School of Music, then switched to straight acting. RSC productions include *Hamlet, Henry IV, Romeo and Juliet, The Merry Wives of Windsor, A Delicate Balance, Women Beware Women, The Winter's Tale* and *London Assurance* (also West End and Broadway).
TV: *Black and Blue; Prometheus; Village Hall; The Glittering Prizes; Love Letters on Blue Paper; The Expert; Victorian Scandals; Abel's Will* (Play of the Week); Calpurnia in *Julius Caesar; A Quiet Life;* Maud Lowther in *Wings of a Dove; The Dybbuk; The Enigma;* Connie Fox in *Fox; Tales of the Unexpected* (twice); *The Cause; We, the Accused; His Masterful Servant;* title role in *The Kindness of Mrs Radcliffe; Cribb; Bognor Heroes; Crown Court;* Mother Radcliffe in *Frost in May; The Haunting of Cassie Palmer; Our Winnie;* Nan in *Shine on Harvey Moon* (series, 1982-5, 1995); *Intensive Care; A Spider's Web;* Mistress Quickly in *The Merry Wives of Windsor;* Lady Muriel Royce in *Strangers and Brothers; Mistress in Those Glory, Glory Days* (TVM); *Jackanory; Bergerac; The Devil's Disciple; Doctor Who; A Kind of Living;* Witch in *Simon and the Witch* (two series); *Young Charlie Chaplin; Gentlemen and Players; Singles;* Aunt Peggy in *Watching* (three series); Mae in *Oranges Are Not the Only Fruit; Survival of the Fittest; Soldier Soldier; Boon; The Old Devils;* Inge Middleton in *Anglo-Saxon Attitudes; The Young Indiana Jones Chronicles; Heartbeat;* Eva Peterle in *The Ruth Rendell Mysteries;* Mrs Mason in *Sherlock Holmes: The Last Vampyre; The Mouse in the Corner;* Daphne Shotley in *Lovejoy;* Aunt Agatha in *Jeeves and Wooster; Pinch of Snuff; The Inspector Alleyn Mysteries; Middlemarch; Taking Over the Asylum; Making Waves; Class Act; The Tomorrow People;* Sairey Gamp in *Martin Chuzzlewit; Henry IV.*
Films: *Work Is a Four-Letter Word; Richard's Things; Lady Chatterley's Lover; An Unsuitable Job for a Woman; The Cold Room; Sakharov; Parker; Yellow Pages; The Hour of the Pig; Impromptu; Sense and Sensibility; The Secret Agent.*
Address: c/o Harbour & Coffey. m. 1st Kenneth Spriggs (dis), 2nd Michael Jones (dis), 3rd musician Murray Manson; 1 d. make-up artist Wendy (from 1st m.). Pets: Cats. Hobbies: Reading, gardening.

Julia Somerville

Timothy Spall

Rob Spendlove

Alyson Spiro

Elizabeth Spriggs

STABLEFORD, Howard

Howard Stableford. Presenter/Reporter. b. Poynton, Cheshire, 12 April 1959. Worked for BBC Radio Lancashire and Northampton, before moving into TV.

TV: *Jigsaw; Puzzle Trail; Beat the Teacher; Newsround; Tomorrow's World* (1985-); *Tomorrow's World in Seville; Tomorrow's World in Tokyo* (1993); *Tomorrow's World in Los Angeles* (1994); *Beachwater* (series, 1994); *The 11th Hour* (series, 1995-6); *Tomorrow's World in Bombay* (1996). Address: c/o Dave Winslett Entertainments. Lives in Kingston-upon-Thames, Surrey. m. Lizanne. Pets: Two cats, Preston and KC ('After our home towns — KC being short for Kansas City'). Hobbies: Running, motorbikes, squash, scuba-diving.

Howard Stableford

STACY, Neil

Neil Stacy. Actor. b. Stowupland, Suffolk, 15 May 1941. Performed with the Oxford University Dramatic Society. Stage plays include *The Second Mrs Tanqueray* (National Theatre), *Holiday Snap* (Theatre of Comedy) and *Sometimes Sing* (Albery Theatre).

TV: *War and Peace; Man Outside; Dead of Night; Colditz; Barlow at Large; The Pallisers; Mr Garrick and Mrs Woffington; The Way of the World; Law Centre; Return of The Saint; Crown Court; The Standard; Strangers; Quatermass; To Serve Them All My Days; Nanny; Shackleton; The Fourth Arm; Strangers and Brothers; Duty Free; Cold Warrior; Three Up, Two Down; Rumpole of the Bailey; Haggard;* Major Hinchcliff-Jones in *Lovejoy;* Sir Nicholas Foulsham in *The House of Windsor* (series, 1994). Address: c/o Michael Whitehall. Hobbies: Medieval history.

Neil Stacy

STAFF, Kathy

Kathy Staff. Actress. b. Dukinfield, Cheshire, 12 July 1928. Began career with a touring theatre company in Scotland. Stage plays include *Two into One* and *When We Are Married* (both Theatre of Comedy) and *The Rivals* (national tour).

TV: *Castlehaven; Within These Walls; Hadleigh; Coronation Street; Sez Les; Separate Tables; The Benny Hill Show;* Winnie Purvis in *Emmerdale Farm;* Doris Luke in *Crossroads;* Mrs Blewett in *Open All Hours* (series); Nora Batty in *Last of the Summer Wine* (Comedy Playhouse, 1973, plus 18 series, 1973-93, and Christmas specials); *Freddie Starr; The Lenny Henry Christmas Show* (1995).

Films: *A Kind of Loving; The Dresser; The Family Way; Camille; Little Dorrit.* Address: c/o London Management. m. John; 2 d. Katherine, Susan. Hobbies: Choral singing, church work.

Kathy Staff

STANDING, John

Sir John Leon (fourth baronet). Actor. b. London, 16 August 1934. Son of actress Kay Hammond (née Dorothy Katherine Standing). Studied at art school, before becoming a professional actor. Stage plays include *Titus Andronicus* (RSC) and *Plunder, The Philanderer* and *Tonight at 8.30* (all National Theatre).

TV: *Arms and the Man; The First Churchills; Charley's Aunt; Love Story; Tartuffe; The Dirtiest Soldier; Rogue Male; The Sinking of HMS Victoria; Home and Beauty; Ms or Jill and Jack; Nanny's Boy; The Relapse; The Other 'Arf; All the World's a Stage;* Sam Collins in *Tinker, Tailor, Soldier, Spy; The Young Visiters* (TVM); *Waterloo; Hart to Hart;* Colonel Pickering in *Pygmalion;* Duke of Windsor in *To Catch a King* (TVM); Edward Wigate in *Lime Street* (series, 1985-6); *Visitors; Hotel; Murder, She Wrote; Our Planet Tonight; Hunter;* Sir George in *Sidney Sheldon's Windmills of the Gods; LA Law; Chameleons; The Endless Game; Spooks;* Peter Duckham in *The Old Boy Network* (series, 1992); Alan Stacey in *Night of the Fox* (mini-series); Malise Gordon in *Jilly Cooper's Riders* (mini-series, 1993); Bishop Robert Young in *The Choir* (series, 1995).

Films: *A Pair of Briefs; The Iron Maiden* (US title *The Swingin' Maiden*); *The Wild and the Willing* (US title *Young and Willing*); *Hot Enough for June; King Rat; All the Right Noises; The Psychopath; Walk, Don't Run; Torture Garden; Thank You All Very Much* (US title *A Touch of Love*); *The Millstone; Zee and Co* (US title *X, Y, and Zee*); *All the Right Noises; Rogue Male; The Eagle Has Landed; The Class of Miss MacMichael; The Legacy* (also titled *The Legacy of Maggie Walsh*); *The Elephant Man; The Sea Wolves; Privates on Parade; Captain Stirrick; Invitation to the Wedding; Nightflyers.* Address: c/o Jonathan Altaras Associates. m. 1st actress Jill Melford (dis 1972), 2nd 7 April 1984 writer Sarah Kate Forbes; 2 s. Alexander (from 1st m.), Archie, 2 d. India, Octavia.

John Standing

STAPLETON, John

John Martin Stapleton. Presenter. b. Oldham, Lancashire, 24 February 1946. Began his career as a journalist on the Oldham *Evening Chronicle* and later worked for the now-defunct *Daily Sketch* in Fleet Street. Joined Thames Television in 1970 to work on *This Is Your Life* and moved on to present the regional magazine programme *Today* before switching to the BBC, then returning to ITV in 1993.

TV: *Today* (regional news magazine, Thames Television, 1971-5); *Nationwide* (1975-80); *Medical Express; Miss United Kingdom; Miss England; Time to Talk* (chat show, BBC North West); *This Week Special: The Confait Case; Panorama* (1980-1); *Newsnight;* Budget programmes (co-presenter, BBC); *Good Morning Britain* (TV-am); *Credo; Nightline* (Sky News); *Watchdog; Watchdog Special; London*

John Stapleton

Plus (BBC South East only); *South Today* (BBC South only); *BBC Breakfast News;* 3D (discussion on juiling young offenders, 1993); *The Time The Place* (series, 1993-).
Address: c/o Arlington Enterprises. Lives in Middlesex. m. TV presenter Lynn Faulds Wood; 1 s. Nicholas. Hobbies: Cricket, swimming, watching Manchester City FC.

STARKE, Michael
Michael Starke. Actor. b. Liverpool, 13 November 1957. Worked as a dustbinman, then fronted a comedy showband that toured Liverpool, Newcastle and Scotland. Stage plays include *Blood Brothers* (as Sammy), *One for the Road, Hamlet, The Winter's Tale* and *Be-Bop-a-Lula* (national tour).
TV: Gasman in *Boys from the Blackstuff;* Black-Guard in *Tripods;* Sinbad (né Thomas Sweeney) in *Brookside;* Forester in *Watching.*
Films: Member of Rock Band in *No Surrender; Distant Voices, Still Lives.*
Address: c/o Tobias Management/Mersey Television.

Michael Starke

STAUNTON, Imelda
Imelda Staunton. Actress. Stage plays include *A Chorus of Disapproval* (National Theatre), *Fair Maid of the West* (RSC), *They Shoot Horses Don't They?* (RSC), *The Corn Is Green* (Old Vic), *The Wizard of Oz* (as Dorothy, RSC), *Uncle Vanya* (Vaudeville Theatre) and *Into the Woods* (Phoenix Theatre).
TV: *Easy Money;* Nurse White in *The Singing Detective;* Edith in *Ladies in Charge; The Heat of the Day; The Ruth Rendell Mysteries: Sleeping Life;* Cheryl in *Yellowbacks;* Stephanie Saunders in *An Englishman's Wife;* Dwarfish in *They Never Slept;* Izzy Comyn in *Up the Garden Path* (three series, 1990-93); *A Masculine Ending* (TVM); *Don't Leave Me This Way* (TVM); *June in Antonia & June;* Muriel Spry in *If You See God, Tell Him* (series, 1993); Jenny Beales in *Roots* (Performance); *It's a Girl* (host); Susan in *Frank Stubbs; Mole's Christmas* (voice only); *Jackanory: Delilah and the Dishwater Dogs* (storyteller); *A Bit of Fry and Laurie; Look at the State We're In: Local Government;* Stella in *Is It Legal?* (series, 1995); *The Snow Queen* (voice only).
Films: *Comrades;* Mary in *Peter's Friends;* Margaret in *Much Ado about Nothing; Deadly Advice; Sense and Sensibility.* **Awards:** Theatre: Olivier Award as Best Supporting Actress for *A Chorus of Disapproval* and *The Corn Is Green* (1985); Olivier Award as Best Actress in a Musical for *Into the Woods* (1991). Address: c/o Kerry Gardner Management. Lives in North London. m. actor Jim Carter.

Imelda Staunton

STEADMAN, Alison
Alison Steadman. Actress. b. Liverpool, 26 August 1946. Acted with Joan Littlewood's Theatre Workshop from the age of 19.
TV: *Hard Labour* (The Wednesday Play, 1973); Candice Marie in *Nuts in May; Through the Night; Our Flesh and Blood;* Beverly in *Abigail's Party; Pasmore; P'tang Yang Kipperbang* (TVM); *The Muscle Market; Tartuffe; Nature in Focus; Coming Through; The Caucasian Chalk Circle;* Mrs Marlow in *The Singing Detective; The Finding; Virtuoso; A Small Mourning;* Jackie Johns in *Newshounds; 1000 Nights;* Lauren in *Gone to the Dogs* (series, 1991); *Selling Hitler;* Hilda Plant in *Gone to Seed* (series, 1992); *Without Walls: Degas and Pissarro Fall Out;* Elinor Farr in *The Wimbledon Poisoner* (mini-series, 1994); Eve Kendall in *Kavanagh QC;* Mrs Bennet in *Pride and Prejudice* (serial, 1995); *Coogan's Run; No Bananas.*
Films: *Champions; Number One; A Private Function; Clockwise; Stormy Monday; The Adventures of Baron Munchausen; The Short and Curlies;* Jane in *Shirley Valentine; Wilt; Life Is Sweet; Blame It on the Bellboy.* Address: c/o Peters Fraser & Dunlop. m. writer-director Mike Leigh; 2 s. Leo, Toby.

Alison Steadman

STEED, Maggie
Margaret Baker. Actress. b. Plymouth, Devon, 11 December 1946. Trained at Bristol Old Vic Theatre School. RSC productions include *The Comedy of Errors* and *Hamlet.*
TV: *Fox; The History Man; Clapper; Claw;* Rita Moon in *Shine on Harvey Moon* (series, 1982-5, 1995); *Charlie* (TVM); Maria Tromp in *Van Der Valk; Little Richard Wrecked My Marriage;* Janine in *The Ruth Rendell Mysteries: The Speaker of Mandarin;* Mrs Pettigrew in *So Haunt Me;* Aunt Vickie in *Lipstick on Your Collar* (series, 1993); Mrs Raffald in *The Clothes in the Wardrobe* (Screen Two, 1993); Ellen in *Olly's Prison* (mini-series, 1993); Margaret Crabbe in *Pie in the Sky* (three series, 1994-6); *Martin Chuzzlewit.*
Films: *Babylon; Intimate Contact.* Address: c/o Richard Stone Partnership. Lives in London. Single.

Maggie Steed

STEEL, John Kay
John Kay Steel. Actor. b. Glasgow, 18 January 1966. Trained at the Royal Scottish Academy of Music and Drama. Stage roles include Boyet/Dumain in *Love's Labour's Lost* (Amsterdam tour).
TV: Eric Lundy in *The Bill;* Richard Hayman in *Taggart;* Hacker in *Surgical Spirit;* Finn in *The Romans;* Brodie in *Strathblair* (five episodes); Johnstone in *Roughnecks;* Ian Hinton in *Take the High Road.*
Films: Sam Silvio in *Laws of Mortal Danger;* Jesus Christ in *The Revolutionary.*
Address: c/o Langford Associates. Lives in London. Single. Hobbies: Photography, travel.

John Kay Steel

Shirley Stelfox

STELFOX, Shirley

Shirley Stelfox. Actress. b. 11 April 1941. Stage roles include Sue Lawson in *Not Now, Darling* (Strand Theatre) and Phoebe in *Toad of Toad Hall* (Duke of York's Theatre).
TV: *Hobson's Choice; A Pin to See the Peepshow; Owen MD; General Hospital; Between the Wars; Wicked Women; The Liars; Crown Court; Coronation Street* (two roles); *Strangers; Monica Swaine; S.W.A.L.K.; Bootle Saddles* (series); *Knights of God* (serial); Madge Richmond in *Brookside; Radical Chambers; Bergerac; King and Castle;* Carol May in *Making Out* (three series); *Stay Lucky; Voice;* Rose in *Keeping Up Appearances* (Series 1); Mrs Parkin in *Heartbeat;* Helen in *Civvies* (series, 1992); Lucy in *Get Back* (series, 1992); Mrs Larch in *The Bill;* Jean in *Common as Muck* (series, 1994); Vera in *Pat and Margaret* (Screen One); Gill Gibson in *The Bill*.
Films: Prostitute in *'1984';* Shirley in *Personal Services.* Address: c/o A.I.M. Lives in Stratford-upon-Avon. m. 2nd actor Don Henderson (qv), 1 d. Helena (from 1st m.), 1 step-d. Louise, 1 step-s. Ian.

Denise Stephenson

STEPHENSON, Denise

Denise Stephenson. Actress. Stage plays include many in America and *Savage in Limbo* (Gate Theatre).
TV: *Gauguin the Savage; Nobody's Perfect; Winners and Losers;* Alicia in *Ticket to Ride; The Piglet Files; Saracen;* Mrs Henderson in *Waterfront Beat; Berlin Break;* Zelda Bishop in *Pie in the Sky;* Katie in *Second Thoughts;* Lorraine Drinkall in *Next of Kin;* Val Douglas in *Thief Takers;* Cathy Priest in *Peak Practice.*
Films: *An American Werewolf in London; Made in Heaven; Gotham.*
Address: c/o Sharon Hamper Management.

Nicola Stephenson

STEPHENSON, Nicola

Nicola Stephenson. Actress. b. Oldham, Lancashire, 5 July 1971. Trained at the Oldham Theatre Workshop from the age of 12. On leaving school, she and friends co-founded The Old School Stage Society, performing at Oldham Coliseum, The Green Room, Manchester, the Edinburgh Festival and the National Students' Drama Festival.
TV: *Jossy's Giants; The Rainbow; Children's Ward; Family Tree; Medics; The Final Frame* (TVM); Margaret Clemence in *Brookside* (1990-4); Lizzie in *Nice Day at the Office* (series, 1994); *Go Back Out the Way You Came.* Address: c/o Lou Coulson.

Pamela Stephenson

STEPHENSON, Pamela

Pamela Stephenson. Actress/Comedienne. b. Auckland, New Zealand, 4 December. Grew up in Australia. Trained at the National Institute of Dramatic Art, Australia. Moved to Britain in 1976. Stage shows include *Small but Perfectly Formed, Naughty Night Nurses without Panties Down Under No 2* and *Shocking Behaviour.*
TV: *Within These Walls; Space 1999; The New Avengers; Target; Hazell; The Professionals; Funny Man; Man from the South; Behind the Scenes with…; Mike Yarwood Christmas Show; Not the Nine o'Clock News* (series); *Move Over Darling; Lost Empires; Saturday Night Live.*
Films: *Stand Up Virgin Soldiers; The Comeback; History of the World Part I; The Secret Policeman's Other Ball;* Lorelei Ambrosia in *Superman III; Scandalous; Bloodbath at the House of Death; Finders Keepers.* Address: c/o John Reid Enterprises. m. 1st actor Nicholas Ball (dis), 2nd comedian Billy Connolly (qv); 3 d. Daisy, Amy, Scarlett Layla.

Juliet Stevenson

STEVENSON, Juliet

Juliet Stevenson. Actress. Trained at RADA (Gold Bancroft Medal winner). RSC stage roles include Titania and Hippolyta in *A Midsummer Night's Dream,* Isabella in *Measure for Measure,* Cressida in *Troilus and Cressida,* Rosalind in *As You Like It* and Mme de Tourvel in *Les Liaisons Dangereuses.* Plus Fanny in *On the Verge* (Sadler's Wells Theatre) and title role in *Hedda Gabler* (National Theatre).
TV: Joanna Langton in *Maybury;* Barbara Mallen in *The Mallens;* Fliss in *Bazaar and Rummage;* Elizabeth von Reitburg in *Freud;* title role in *Antigone;* Antigone in *Oedipus at Colonus;* Rosalind in *Life Story;* Hilda Spencer in *Stanley;* Ruth in *Out of Love;* Vicky in *Living with Dinosaurs;* Lucy Sadler in *Amy;* rape victim in *Omnibus: Rape;* Claire in *The March;* Nina in *Cello;* Margaret in *In the Border Country* (4-Play); Nora Helmer in *A Doll's House* (Performance); *Prisoners of Conscience* (presenter, 1992); Rosalind Franklin in *Horizon Special: Life Story; Living with Dinosaurs; Artists for Bosnia* (performing *Death and the Maiden,* 1993); Fraulein Burstner in *The Trial* (Screen Two); *Who Dealt?* (1993, David Bailey's directorial début); Lucy in *Aimee* (Screen Two, 1994); *Great Journeys: Morocco with Juliet Stevenson* (presenter, 1994); Flora Matlock in *The Politician's Wife* (mini-series, 1995);
Films: *Drowning by Numbers; Ladder of Swords; Truly Madly Deeply; The Trial; Secret Rapture.*
Awards: TV: ACE cable TV network Best Supporting Actress award for *Life Story.* Films: London Evening Standard Film Awards Best Actress 1991 for *Truly Madly Deeply.* Theatre: *Drama* magazine Best Actress award for *Measure for Measure; Time Out* Best Actress award for *Death and the Maiden;* nominated for Laurence Olivier Best Actress award three times, for *Measure for Measure, Troilus and Cressida* and *Yerma.* Address: c/o Markham & Froggatt.

STEWART, Alastair

Alastair James Stewart. Newscaster. b. Emsworth, Hampshire, 22 June 1952. Studied economics, politics and sociology at Bristol University. Entered TV with Southern Television.

TV: Southern Television reporter, industrial correspondent, presenter and documentary-maker (1976-80); ITN industrial correspondent (1980-4), then co-presenter of *Channel Four News* (1984-6) and presenter of *News at 5.40* (1986-9), Washington correspondent (1990) and presenter of *News at Ten* (1989 and 1991-2); co-presenter of *Election '87* and *Election '92*; presenter of five ITV Budget programmes (1988-92); *The Parliament Programme*; Gulf War Service of Thanksgiving; *London Tonight* (LNN for Carlton and LWT, 1993-); *Missing* (pilot, 1992, series, 1993-); *Golden Arrows: The British Television Advertising Awards*; *Local Elections Special* (Carlton only, 1994); *Police Stop!; The Sunday Programme* (GMTV, 1994-); *Police Camera Action!* (1994-); *The Carlton Forum for the Future of London* (Carlton only); *The Victory Parade* (VE Day 1995); *Healthwatch Live; Missing at Christmas* (1995). Address: c/o LNN/GMTV. Lives in Hampshire. m. 1978 former TV production assistant Sally-Ann Jung; 2 s. Alexander, Freddie, 1 d. Clemmie (Clementine). Pets: Horse, dog , cat, rabbit, bantams, frogs, toads, newts. Hobbies: Work, antiques, eating out, wide range of music.

Alastair Stewart

STEWART, Jeff

Jeffrey James Stewart. Actor. b. Aberdeen, Grampian, 28 October 1955. Trained at The Drama Centre.
TV: *The Nightmare Man;* Harry Fellows in *Crossroads; Minder; Doctor Who; Angels; Hi-de-Hi!; Reilly – Ace of Spies; Roots;* PC Reg Hollis in *The Bill.*
Videos: Pop promotional video: Sam Brown's boyfriend in *Can I Get a Witness?*
Address: c/o McIntosh Rae Management/The Bill. Lives in London. Single. Hobbies. Food, music, theatre, lying on beaches, long-distance running (London Marathon twice and Moscow Marathon once).

Jeff Stewart

STOURTON, Edward

Edward John Ivo Stourton. Presenter. b. Lagos, Nigeria, 24 November 1957. Gained an MA from Trinity College, Cambridge, where he was president of the student union. Joined ITN as a trainee in 1979.
TV: ITN trainee (1979), *Channel Four News* scriptwriter, item producer, home news editor and chief sub-editor (1983), *Channel Four News* reporter (1985, specialist areas included Lebanon and Northern Ireland), *Channel Four News* Washington correspondent (1986-8) (and presented special programmes on the Iran-Contra hearings for Channel Four); BBC TV News Paris correspondent (1988-90), providing reports for BBC TV News, *Newsnight* and *The Late Show;* ITN diplomatic editor (1990-3), also working as Conservative campaign correspondent during the 1992 General Election and presenting ITN news programmes; BBC TV News (1993-), including presenter of *One o'Clock News.* Documentaries: *Assignment: Shot by a Kid; Assignment: The Drug War – RIP.*
Radio: *The Violence Files; Asia Gold* (both BBC Radio 4); special programmes for BBC Radio 4 during the 1995 Conservative leadership election. Address: c/o BBC TV News. Lives in London. m. 1980 Margaret McEwen; 2 s. Ivo, Thomas, 1 d. Eleanor. Pets: A spaniel called Jazz. Hobbies: Reading, tennis.

Edward Stourton

STRACHAN, Michaela

Michaela Strachan. Presenter. b. Ewell, Surrey, 7 April 1966. Trained at the Arts Education School in dance, drama and singing. Began career in musicals, playing Liza in *Seven Brides for Seven Brothers* on a national tour, then at the Old Vic, the Alexandra Theatre, Toronto, and the Prince of Wales Theatre.
TV: *Wide Awake Club; Wacaday; Wac 90; Wac Extra; Hey Hey It's Saturday; Michaela* (all TV-am); *The Hit Man and Her; Owl TV; Cool Cube* (BSkyB); *But Can You Do It on TV?* (two series); *Boogie Box* (Music Box cable TV); *Freetime; Go Getters* (two series); *Beetle Drive; Naruhodo – The World; The Children's Royal Variety Performance* (host 1991, guest star 1992); *The Really Wild Show* (co-presenter, four series, 1993-6); *Electric String Vest* (Children's Channel); *Ratkan II* (Children's Channel); *Michaela's Map* (Children's Channel); *The Summer Crunch* (Children's Channel); *The Cape to Cape Challenge; Really Wild Guide to Britain; Science Zone* (BBC Schools); *Disneytime; The Enemy Within: Michaela Strachan on Anorexia; The Really Wild Guide to Britain* (series, 1995); *The Web.*
Radio: *Take 5* (BBC Radio 5). **Records:** Singles: *Happy Radio; Take Good Care of My Heart.* Album: *Grease.* Address: c/o Michael Ladkin Personal Management. Lives in Bristol. Single. Hobbies: Water-skiing, horse-riding, swimming, tennis.

Michaela Strachan

STRAKER, Mark

Mark Williams. actor. b. London, 9 March 1956.
TV: *Number 73; Henry's Leg; Radio Phoenix; The Bill; They Came from Somewhere Else; For Valour; Kindred Spirits;* Carter in *Doctor Who;* Hanham, NCO in *Chips with Everything; Absent Friends;* PC Sharp in *Casualty;* Nigel Parnaby in *Birds of a Feather;* Dinsdale in *Lovejoy;* Dinsdale in *Boot Street Band;* James Jefferson in *EastEnders; Punt and Dennis;* Perez in *Down to Earth;* Colin Buxton in *Casualty.*
Films: *The Idiot;* Peter in *Sick Call;* Matthew in *End of the Real;* Petrie in *Exchange of Fire.*
Address: c/o Langford Associates. Lives in London. Single.

Mark Straker

Christopher Strauli

John Stride

Nick Stringer

Gwyneth Strong

Imogen Stubbs

STRAULI, Christopher

Christopher Strauli. Actor. b. Harpenden, Hertfordshire, 13 April 1946. Trained at RADA (Spotlight Award and William Poel Prize winner). West End plays include *Season's Greetings*.

TV: *A Family at War; Owen MD; Harriet's Back in Town; Angels; Warship;* Churchill in *Edward the Seventh; For Tea on Sunday;* Bunny in *Raffles;* Eustace in *Eustace and Hilda Trilogy;* Norman in *Only When I Laugh* (four series); *Gentle Folk; Romeo and Juliet; Measure for Measure; Aubrey Beardsley; Strangers and Brothers; Parlez Franglais; A Crack in the Ice; Dempsey and Makepeace; Lytton's Diary; Full House* (three series); *Names and Games; Victoria Wood — As Seen on TV; Fortunes of War; Bergerac.*
Films: *SOS Titanic; Rising Damp.*
Address: c/o Bryan Drew. m. Lesley; 2 d. Belinda, Hanneli, 2 s. Barnaby, Dominic.

STRIDE, John

John Stride. Actor. b. London, 11 July 1936. Trained at RADA. Made his professional début at Liverpool rep (1957) before joining the Army. On demob, joined the Old Vic Theatre.

TV: *Scarlet and Black; Knock on Any Door; Love Story; The Bonus; Detective; The Main Chance; The Heiress; Force of Circumstance; Papillons; Visit from a Stranger; Photograph; Wilde Alliance; Love among the Artists; Hess; The Ice House; Henry VII; Diamonds; Lloyd George; Conversations with a Stranger; Thirteen at Dinner* (TVM); *Lytton's Diary; Imaginary Friends; The Trial of Klaus Barbie; Jumping the Queue; Chelworth; Agatha Christie's Poirot;* Alun in *The Old Devils;* Sir Bernard Bellamy in *Growing Rich;* Sir Derek O'Callaghan in *The Inspector Alleyn Mysteries;* Dr Roberts in *Brighton Belles.*
Films: *Bitter Harvest; Macbeth; Something to Hide; Juggernaut; Brannigan; The Omen; A Bridge Too Far; Macho; Innocent Heroes.* Address: c/o Richard Hatton. m. 1st actress Virginia Stride (dis), 2nd actress April Wilding; 3 d. Philippa, Lindsay, Eleanor.

STRINGER, Nick

Nick Stringer. Actor. b. Torquay, Devon, 10 August 1948.

TV: *Pickersgill People; Devil's Crown; Playhouse: The Affront; The Sweeney; Minder; Butterflies; Shoestring; Squadron; The Professionals; Come to Mecca; Crown Court; Johnny Jarvis; Open All Hours; Lucky Jim; One By One; Dempsey and Makepeace; Auf Wiedersehen Pet; The Collectors; C.A.T.S. Eyes;* Jumbo Mills in *Only Fools and Horses; A Sort of Innocence; Blind Justice; About Face; Bergerac; Boon; Press Gang; The New Statesman; Black and Blue Lamp; Home Front; Shadow on the Sun; This Is David Lander;* PC Ron Smollett in *The Bill.*
Films: *The Shout; The Long Good Friday; Clockwise; Personal Services;* Terence Davies trilogy.
Address: c/o Kerry Gardner Management. Lives in Kenilworth, Warwickshire. m.; 1 d. Pets: Two Welsh border collies. Hobbies: Drinking good wine.

STRONG, Gwyneth

Gwyneth Strong. Actress. b. London, 2 February 1959. Professional début at the age of 11 in *Live Like Pigs* (Royal Court). Other stage plays include *Shout across the River* (RSC).

TV: *Shadows;* Princess Dagmar in *Edward the Seventh; Jubilee: Age of Hypocrisy; The Story of Ruth; Breakaway Girls; The Ladies; Early Struggles; The Factory; Radio; Love Story: Mr Right;* Linda in *Rainy Day Women; It's a Lovely Day Tomorrow; Inside Out; From a Far Country: Pope John Paul II* (TVM); Tina Fawcett in *Paradise Postponed; King of the Ghetto; Living with Dinosaurs;* Cassandra in *Only Fools and Horses;* Linda Thompson in *Nice Town* (mini-series); Mary Shelley in *Writing on the Line;* Cynthia in *The Clothes in the Wardrobe* (Screen Two); Charlotte in *99-1* (series); *Casualty;* Mary Painter in *The Bill;* Joyce in *Don't Dilly Dally on the Way* (Paul Merton in Galton & Simpson's …); Patricia Denning in *Silent Witness.*
Films: *Cry Freedom;* Mary Valley in *Nothing but the Night; Bloody Kids; Dark Water; Horrid Intermission; Afraid of the Dark; Crimetime.*
Address: c/o William Morris Agency (UK). Lives in London. Single; 1 s. Oscar, 1 d. Lottie.

STUBBS, Imogen

Imogen Stubbs. Actress. b. Rothbury, Northumberland, 20 February 1961. West End plays include *Saint Joan* (title role, Strand Theatre).

TV: *The Browning Version;* Ursula Brangwen in *The Rainbow; Othello; Relatively Speaking;* Helen Banner in *After the Dance* (Performance); title role in *Anna Lee — Headcase* (pilot, 1993) and *Anna Lee* (series, 1994); *The Enemy Within: Imogen Stubbs on Panic Attacks.*
Films: *Nanou; A Summer Story; Fellow Traveller; Erik the Viking; True Colours; A Pin for a Butterfly.*
Address: c/o ICM. Lives in West London. Partner: Theatre director Trevor Nunn; 1 child.

STUBBS, Una

Una Stubbs. Actress. b. London, 1 May 1937. Trained as a dancer at La Roche Dancing School, Slough.
TV: *Cool for Cats;* Rita in *Till Death Us Do Part; Star Pieces; Piano Short;* Inge in *Penny Gold; Rainbow* (storyteller); *What's It All About;* Jo Ransley in *Them and Us* (Comedy Playhouse); *The Good Old Days;*

Second House; Twelve Noon; Give Us a Clue; Aunt Sally in Worzel Gummidge (four series, 1979-82), Worzel's Christmas Special: A Cup o' Tea an' a Slice o' Cake (1981) and Worzel Gummidge Down Under (two series, 1987, 1989); Fawlty Towers; Victoria and Maria; A Christmas Lantern; The Morecambe and Wise Show; Educating Marmalade; Time of Your Life; Home Rules; Afternoon Club; Cannon and Ball; Child's Play; Square Pegs; The Heritage Game; Happy Families; Rita in In Sickness and in Health; Good Morning Britain (TV-am, presenter, 1987); Morris Minors Marvellous Motors; Tricky Business; Victoria Wood: We'd Quite Like to Apologise; Woolcraft (This Morning); Off the Cuff (This Morning); Threads (This Morning); Room for Improvement (This Morning); Cluedo; It's Nearly Saturday; Heartbeat; Deltawaves.

Films: Sandy in Summer Holiday; Barbara in Wonderful Life; Rita in Till Death Us Do Part.
Books: In Stitches (1984); A Stitch in Time (1985); Cinderella (1987).
Address: c/o The Richard Stone Partnership. Lives in London. m. 1st actor Peter Gilmore (dis), 2nd 1969 actor Nicky Henson (qv) (dis 1975); 3 s. Jason (from 1st m.), Christian, Joe (both from 2nd m.). Hobbies: Going to the theatre, cinema and galleries, sewing, walking.

Una Stubbs

SUCHET, David
David Suchet. Actor. b. Paddington, London, 2 May 1946. Brother of newscaster John Suchet (qv). Trained at LAMDA. RSC productions include Othello, Richard II, The Tempest and Measure for Measure.
TV: Edward Teller in Oppenheimer (mini-series); Reilly — Ace of Spies; The Last Day; Being Normal; title role in The Life of Freud; title role in Blott on the Landscape; Colin in Oxbridge Blues; Playing Shakespeare; King and Castle; Time to Die; Jackanory; Murrow (TVM); Glougauer in Once in a Lifetime; Leopold Bloom in Ulysses; Judge O'Connor in Cause Célèbre; Shakespeare in Bingo; Nobody Here but Us Chickens; The Last Innocent Man (TVM); title role in Agatha Christie's Poirot (three series, plus two specials); Tom Kempinski in Separation; title role in Timon of Athens; Science Fiction: Hair Soup; Adolf Verloc in The Secret Agent (mini-series); Days of Majesty (narrator); More Than a Touch of Zen.
Films: A Tale of Two Cities; The Hunchback of Notre Dame; The Trenchcoat; Master of the Game; Red Monarch; Little Drummer Girl; The Falcon and the Snowman; Gulag; Song for Europe; Mussolini; Thirteen at Dinner; Iron Eagle; Harry and the Hendersons; To Kill a Priest; Why the Whales Came; A World Apart; The Lucona Affair; The Last Innocent Man. **Awards:** TV: RTS Best Actor for Song for Europe, The Life of Freud and Blott on the Landscape (1986); ACE Best Supporting Actor for The Last Innocent Man (1987). Films: Marseilles Film Festival Best Actor award for Red Monarch (1983); BAFTA Best Supporting Actor in a Film (1989). Address: c/o ICM. Lives in Harrow, Middlesex. m. actress Sheila Ferris; 1 s. Robert, 1 d. Katherine. Hobbies: Music, photography, ornithology.

David Suchet

SUCHET, John
John Suchet. Newscaster. b. London, 29 March 1944. Brother of actor David Suchet (qv). Gained an MA (Hons) in political science and philosophy. Joined Reuters news agency (1967) as a graduate trainee and worked in the Paris bureau, covering the 1968 student riots, before moving into TV.
TV: BBC TV News sub-editor (1971-2); ITN sub-editor (1972-3), chief sub-editor (1973-6), reporter (1976-81), Washington correspondent (1981-3), presenter of News at One, News at 12.30, News at 5.40 and News at Ten; original presenter of ITN World News (Superchannel, 1987-9); News at 12.30 presenter (1989-92); News at 5.40 presenter (1992-); Election '92 (co-presenter); plus News at Ten and Budget programmes; Diana — The End of a Fairytale? (presenter); Annus Horribilis (presenter); The Nation Remembers (round-up of VE Day events, 1995).
Books: TV News: The Inside Story (1987). **Awards:** RTS Journalist of the Year award for coverage of Philippine elections (1986). Address: c/o ITN. Lives in London. m. 1st Moya (dis), 2nd Bonnie; 3 s. Damian, Kieran, Rory (from 1st m.). Hobbies: Classical music, photography.

John Suchet

SUGDEN, Mollie
Mollie Sugden. Actress. b. Keighley, West Yorkshire, 21 July 1922. Trained at Guildhall School of Music and Drama.
TV: Hugh and I; Please Sir!; Doctor in the House; For the Love of Ada; Mrs Hutchinson (Sandra's mother) in The Liver Birds; Mrs Slocombe in Are You Being Served? (1973-85) and Grace and Favour (two series, 1992-3); Nellie Harvey in Coronation Street; Whodunnit?; Come Back Mrs Noah; Tea Ladies; That's My Boy; My Husband and I; Mrs White in Cluedo; Mrs Robson in Oliver's Travels.
Films: The BFG (voice). Address: c/o Joan Reddin. m. actor William Moore; 2 s. Robin, Simon (twins).

Mollie Sugden

SULLIVAN, Dean
Dean Sullivan. Actor/Director. b. Liverpool, 7 June 1955. Teacher before turning pro as an actor.
TV: Jimmy Corkhill in Brookside (1986-); All I Want for Christmas (presenter).
Radio: Sam Jackson in The Merseysiders (BBC Radio Merseyside serial, 1988-90).
Address: c/o Mersey Television. Lives in Liverpool. Single. Hobbies: The theatre, reading, writing, collecting modern paintings and ceramics.

Dean Sullivan

Dudley Sutton

SUTTON, Dudley

Dudley Sutton. Actor. b. 1933. Stage plays include *The Hostage* (Wyndham's) and *Macbeth* (Old Vic).
TV: *Armchair Theatre; Madam Sin* (TVM); Urwin in *Porridge; Bergerac; Juno and the Paycock; Smiley's People; Radio; Shine on Harvey Moon; The House* (TVM); *Widows; The Beiderbecke Affair; Noble House;* 1996: *Sir Harry Streeter; Blackheart the Pirate;* Tinker in *Lovejoy* (1986-94).
Films: *Go to Blazes; The Boys; The Leather Boys; Rotten to the Core; Crossplot; The Walking Stick; One More Time; A Town Called Bastard; The Devils; Mr Forbush and the Penguins; Diamonds on Wheels; Paganini Strikes Again; The Stud; Cry Terror; Great Expectations; The Pink Panther Strikes Again; One Hour to Zero; Come Una Rosa al Naso; Fellini's Casanova; Valentino; The Prince and the Pauper; No 1 of the Secret Service; The Big Sleep; The Playbirds; The London Connection; George and Mildred; The Island; Brimstone and Treacle; Those Glory, Glory Days; Lamb; Chain Reaction; The Rainbow; Caravaggio; Edward II; Orlando.* Address: c/o Annette Stone Associates.

Janet Suzman

SUZMAN, Janet

Janet Suzman. Actress. b. Johannesburg, South Africa, 9 February 1939. Hon D Litt, Leicester and Warwick Universities. Trained at LAMDA. Many RSC roles.
TV: *Family Reunion;* Masha in *The Three Sisters;* Joan in *Saint Joan;* Lacy Macbeth in *Macbeth;* title role in *Charlotte Brontë;* title role in *Hedda Gabler;* Cleopatra in *Antony and Cleopatra;* Florence Nightingale in *Miss Nightingale;* Viola in *Twelfth Night; Shakespeare or Bust; Clayhanger; The Greeks; Escape — Banned;* Edwina Mountbatten in *Mountbatten — The Last Viceroy; Bright Smiler; The Singing Detective; The Miser;* Chester in *The Secret Agent* (mini-series); *Inspector Morse: Deadly Slumber; Omnibus; The ABC of Democracy* (co-presenter); *The Windsors* (narrator, series); *Not as Bad as They Seem.*
Films: *A Day in the Death of Joe Egg; Nicholas and Alexandra; The Black Windmill; The Voyage of the Damned; The House on Garibaldi Street; Nijinsky; Priest of Love; The Draughtsman's Contract; And the Ship Sails On; The Zany Adventures of Robin Hood; Nuns on the Run; A Dry White Season; Leon the Pig Farmer.* **Awards:** Theatre: Winner, *Evening Standard* Best Actress award twice (1973, 1976). Address: c/o William Morris Agency (UK). m. theatre director Trevor Nunn (dis); 1 s. Joshua.

Geoffrey Swann

SWANN, Geoffrey

Geoffrey Swann. Actor/Director. b. Leicester, 8 June 1951. Trained at the Royal Scottish Academy of Music and Drama. Artistic director of Brighton Actors' Theatre since 1991.
TV: Title role in *Lord Peter Wimsey* (ZDF, Germany); Julian Knighton in *The Ruth Rendell Mysteries: Speaker of Mandarin;* Baines in *Agatha Christie's Poirot;* Duncan Cousins in *Second Thoughts* (series); Robert Clarke in *Harry.* Address: c/o Noel Gay Artists. Lives in Brighton, East Sussex. Partner: Sally. Pets: Three black cats. Hobbies: Travel, modern art.

Clive Swift

SWIFT, Clive

Clive Swift. Actor. b. Liverpool, 9 February 1936. Gained experience in drama societies at Cambridge University. Co-founder of The Actors' Centre. Many RSC roles (1960-8).
TV: *Compact; Dombey and Son; Dig This Rhubarb!; Birthday; Love Story; Mad Jack; Roll on Four o'Clock;* Inspector Waugh in *Waugh on Crime; South Riding; The Sailor's Return* (TVM); Albert Benbow in *Clayhanger; All's Well That Ends Well; The Brothers; The Liver Birds; Chronicle; Home Movies; Goodbye America; Romeo and Juliet; Henry IV; Dr Jekyll and Mr Hyde; The Potsdam Quartet; Winston Churchill — The Wilderness Years; Tales of the Unexpected: Stranger in Town; The Further Adventures of Lucky Jim; Bless Me, Father; The Gentle Touch;* Bishop Proudie in *Barchester Chronicles; Pericles; Doctor Who; The Pickwick Papers; First among Equals; Martin Luther — Heretic; All Together Now!;* Inspector Morse; Cause Célèbre; Journey's End; Minder; Shelley; Double First; Laura and Disorder; Othello; A Very Peculiar Practice;* Richard Bucket in *Keeping Up Appearances* (five series, 1990-5); L P Hartley in *Bare Heaven; Inspector Morse; A Ghost Story for Christmas: A Warning to the Curious; Boon; Heartbeat.*
Films: *Catch Us if You Can; Frenzy; The National Health; Excalibur; A Passage to India; Pack of Lies.* Address: c/o Roxane Vacca Management. Lives in London. m. author 1960 Margaret Drabble (dis 1975); 1 d., 2 s. Hobbies: Playing and listening to music, watching sport, reading.

Eric Sykes

SYKES, Eric

Eric Sykes. Actor/Comedian/Writer. b. Oldham, Lancashire, 4 May 1923. OBE, 1986.
TV: *Sykes* (1960-80); *Sykes versus ITV; Curry and Chips; The Eric Sykes Spectacular; Charley's Aunt; Summer in Blackpool; The Plank; If You Go down in the Woods Today* (also producer-director, TVM); *Sykes of Sebastopol Terrace; Mr H Is Late* (also writer-director, TVM); *The 19th Hole* (series).
Films: *Orders Are Orders; Charley Moon; Tommy the Toreador; Watch Your Stern; Very Important Person; Invasion Quartet; Village of Daughters; Kill or Cure; Heavens Above!; One Way Pendulum; The Bargee; Those Magnificent Men in Their Flying Machines; Rotten to the Core; The Liquidator; The Spy with a Cold Nose; The Plank* (also writer-director, short); *Shalako; Monte Carlo or Bust!; Rhubarb; The Alf Garnett Saga; Theatre of Blood; It's Your Move* (also writer-director, short); *The Boys in Blue;*

Gabrielle and the Doodleman; Absolute Beginners; The Big Freeze.
Radio: *Educating Archie; Variety Bandbox* (both as writer).
Address: c/o Norma Farnes. m. Edith Milbrandt; 3 d. Catherine, Susan, Julie, 1 s. David.

SYLVESTRE, Cleo
Cleopatra Mary Sylvestre. Actress/Presenter. b. Hitchin, Hertfordshire, 19 April 1945.
TV: Melanie in *Crossroads* (1970-2); *Coronation Street; Till Death Us Do Part; You and Me; Merry-Go-Round; Play School; Minder; Catherine; The Gemini Factor; Rockliffe's Babies; Black and White in Colour; Happy Families;* Ms Jonson in *Grange Hill; The Bill; If You See God, Tell Him; Trevor and Caroline.*
Films: *The Attendant.* Address: c/o Elaine Murphy Associates. Lives in Hackney, East London. m. 1977 Ian Palmer (dec 1995); 2 d. Zoe, Lucy, 1 s. Rupert. Pets: Two cats called Leo and Sinbad, many frogs and toads. Hobbies: Music, theatre, cooking (including making jam, pickles, chutneys, wine and bread).

Cleo Sylvestre

SYMS, Sylvia
Sylvia May Laura Syms. Actress/Director. b. London, 6 January 1934. Trained at RADA.
TV: *The Romantic Young Lady; The Devil's Disciple; The Powder Magazine; Climbing for Glory; Terminus; Bat out of Hell; Love Story; The Trap; The Saint; Danger Man; Something to Declare; The Human Jungle; The Avengers; Armchair Theatre; The Baron; Friends and Romans; The Chief Whip Sends His Compliments; The Bridesmaid; Clutterbuck; The Adventurer; The Mike and Bernie Music Show; My Good Woman* (two series); *The Movie Quiz; Murder Will Out; The Truth about Verity; Love and Marriage; I'm Bob, He's Dickie; Tell Us Another; Nancy Astor; Your Move; Crown Court; Nancy Astor; Sorry Darling;* Mrs Easterbrook in *Agatha Christie's Miss Marple: A Murder Is Announced; Murder at Lynch Cross; Intimate Contact; Countdown; The Ruth Rendell Mysteries; Doctor Who; Rockliffe's Follies; May to December; The Laughter of God;* Margaret Thatcher in *Thatcher: The Final Days; Natural Lies; Mulberry;* Isabel de Gines in *Peak Practice* (three series); *An Invitation to Remember; Catherine Cookson's The Glass Virgin; The Chemistry Lesson* (Ghosts); Lady Thatcher in *Half the Picture* (Screen Two); *Blood and Fire; Kavanagh QC.*
Films: *My Teenage Daughter; The Birthday Present; No Time for Tears; Woman in a Dressing Gown; Bachelor of Hearts; The Moonraker; Ice Cold in Alex; No Trees in the Street; Ferry to Hong Kong; Expresso Bongo; Conspiracy of Hearts; Les Vierges de Rom; The World of Suzie Wong; Flame in the Streets; Victim; The Quare Fellow; The Punch and Judy Man; The World Ten Times Over; East of Sudan; Operation Crossbow; The Big Job; Danger Route; Hostile Witness; The Image Makers; Run Wild, Run Free; The Desperados; Asylum; The Tamarind Seed; Give Us Tomorrow; There Goes the Bride; It's Your Move; Absolute Beginners; Intimate Contact; A Chorus of Disapproval; Shirley Valentine; Shining Through; Dirty Weekend; Staggered.* Address: c/o Barry Brown & Partner. Lives in London. m. 1956 Alan Edney (dis 1989); 1 s. Benjamin, 1 d. Beatrice (actress Beatie Edney). Pets: A dog called Molly. Hobbies: Gardening.

Sylvia Syms

TAMM, Mary
Mary Tamm. Actress. b. Dewsbury, West Yorkshire, 22 March 1950. Trained at RADA.
TV: Julie in *Raging Calm; The Scarlet Woman; Whodunnit?; Hunter's Walk; Warship; Return of The Saint;* Pauline Ogden in *Coronation Street;* Romana in *Doctor Who* (26 episodes); Jill Frazer in *The Assassination Run; The Treachery Game;* Selina in *Girls of Slender Means; The Donati Conspiracy; The Inheritors; Only When I Laugh; Quest for Love; Not the Nine o'Clock News;* Blanche Ingram in *Jane Eyre; Bergerac; The Hello-Goodbye Man; Worlds Beyond; Three Kinds of Heat* (TVM); *Agatha Christie's Poirot; Perfect Scoundrels; The Bill; Casualty;* Penny Crosbie in *Brookside* (1993-5); *The Darkening.*
Films: Sigi in *The Odessa File; Witness Madness; The Likely Lads; The Doubt; Rampage; Pressing Engagement.* Address: c/o Langford Associates. Lives in London. m. Marcus Ringrose; 1 d. Lauren Zoe. Pets: One dog, three cats, two rabbits. Hobbies: Riding, computer Scrabble, painting, reading.

Mary Tamm

TANDY, Mark
Mark Napper O'Connor Tandy. Actor. b. Westmeath, Athlone, Ireland, 8 February 1957. Read drama at Bristol University. Trained at the Webber Douglas Academy.
TV: *Aubrey Beardsley; The Jewel in the Crown; Nicholas Nickleby; Gems; Murder Not Proven; Bookmark; Call Me Mister; Hedgehog Wedding; Catherine; Pulaski; Hannay; Inspector Morse; Vote for Hitler; Saracen; Gibraltar Inquest; Tygo Road; Portrait of a Marriage; Prince* (TVM); *Scarfe on Art; Duel of Hearts* (TVM); *The Chess Sultan; A Small World; Prince; A Time to Dance* (mini-series); *Eye of the Storm; As Time Goes By; So Haunt Me; Absolutely Fabulous; Agatha Christie's Poirot; The Buccaneers.*
Films: *Defence of the Realm; Captive;* Lord Risley in *Maurice; Wings of Fame; Loser Takes All;* Manus in *The Railway Station Man; Howards End.* Address: c/o Conway, van Gelder, Robinson. Lives in Notting Hill, West London. m. Amanda Marmot; 2 s. Napper, Patrick.

Mark Tandy

TAPLEY, William
William Tapley. Actor. Grew up in South Australia. Trained at RADA.
TV: *Under the Hammer; Thank You Mr Atkins; A Breed of Heroes* (Screen One); *Buccaneers;* Phineas North in *High Road; Which Way to the War; Back Up.* Address: c/o Scott Marshall. Lives in London.

William Tapley

TARBUCK, Jimmy

Jimmy Tarbuck

James Tarbuck. Comedian/Entertainer/Quizmaster. b. Liverpool, 6 February 1940. OBE, 1994. Worked as a garage mechanic and milkman after leaving school. Aged 18, became compère with a touring rock 'n' roll show, then a Butlin's Redcoat. Aged 22, he was spotted by impresario Val Parnell.
TV: *Comedy Bandbox* (début, 1963); *Sunday Night at the London Palladium* (guest, then resident compère); *The Jimmy Tarbuck Show; Tarbuck's Back; It's Tarbuck; Tarbuck's Luck; Winner Takes All* (quizmaster, 1975-87); *The Bob Hope Classic Cabaret; Royal Variety Performance* (1981); *A National Salute to the Falklands Task Force* (1982); *Live from Her Majesty's; This Is Your Life* (subject, 1983); *Tarby and Friends; Bring Me Sunshine; Live from the Piccadilly; Live from the Palladium; The Frame Game; Tarby after Ten; Wish You Were Here…?* (guest presenter, 1992); Johnny McKenna in *The Detectives; Tarbuck Late* (presenter, talk show, two series, 1994-5); *An Audience with Jimmy Tarbuck.*
Books: *Tarbuck on Golf; Tarbuck on Showbusiness.*
Awards: Variety Club Showbusiness Personality of the Year award (1986).
Address: c/o Peter Prichard. Lives in Surrey. m. Pauline; 2 d. actress Liza (qv), Cheryl, 1 s. James. Hobbies: Golf, supporting Liverpool Football Club.

TARBUCK, Liza

Liza Tarbuck

Liza Ann Tarbuck. Actress/Presenter. b. Liverpool, 21 November 1964. Spent three years with the National Youth Theatre. Trained at RADA. Stage roles include Katrina in *Bazaar and Rummage* (tour).
TV: Angie in *Tumbledown;* Facility in *Mr Majeika;* Pamela Wilson/Lynch in *Watching* (seven series, 1987-93); Dana in *Victoria Wood: Men's Sana in Thingummy Doodah; Chimera; The Weekend Show* (presenter, series, 1995).
Radio: *The Comedy Quiz.* Address: c/o The Richard Stone Partnership. Lives in London. Single. Pets: Dog, two goldfish. Hobbies: Sport of all kinds, darts, music, gardening, DIY, Internet, computers.

TARMEY, William

William Tarmey

William Cleworth Piddington. Actor. b. Manchester, 4 April 1941. Worked in the building trade, singing in clubs by night, before entering TV as an extra. Landed the role of Jack Duckworth in *Coronation Street* after several bit-parts in the serial. Performs as a singer with the group Take Ten and does solo club work in cabaret. He conducted the Hallé Orchestra in 1989.
TV: *Strangers; Crown Court; The Ghosts of Motley Hall; The Glamour Girls; Thicker than Water* (Play for Today); *Rising Star* (sang with own group, Take Ten); *King Lear;* Jack Duckworth in *Coronation Street* (on and off 1979-83, regular 1983-); *Royal Variety Performance* (with *Coronation Street* cast, 1989).
Records: Single: *I'll Be with You Soon* (with Elizabeth Dawn (qv), 1989). Album: *The Other Side of Me* (1992). Address: c/o Granada Television. Lives in Manchester. m. Alma; 1 s. Carl, 1 d. Sara.

TARRANT, Chris

Chris Tarrant

Christopher John Tarrant. Presenter. b. Reading, Berkshire, 10 October 1946. Gained a BA (Hons) in English literature. Worked as a night guard for Securicor in the West Midlands, studied for the Central Office of Information, then taught English in a South London comprehensive school for 10 months, before taking an ACTT director's course.
TV: *ATV Today* (reporter, ATV); *Tiswas; OTT; Saturday Stayback; The Six o'Clock Show* (LWT); *Prove It; PSI; Everybody's Equal; The Disney Christmas Special; Tarrant on TV; Crazy Comparisons; A Carlton New Year* (Carlton only, 1993); *Tarrant's 10 Years on TV* (1993, plus series, 1995); *The Main Event* (series, 1993); *Lose a Million* (game show series, 1993); *Tarrant on TV Special* (1993); *Pop Quiz* (series, 1994); *The Opposite Sex* (series, 1994); *Man o'Man* (series, 1996).
Radio: Breakfast show on Capital Radio, then Capital FM (1986-). **Awards:** Variety Club Personality of the Year (1992). Radio: Sony Radio Personality of the Year (1991). **Books:** *Ken's Furry Friends; Fishfriars Hall.* Address: c/o PVA Management. Lives in Surrey and Warwickshire. m. 1st Sheila (dis 1981), 2nd 1991 Ingrid; 3 d. Helen, Jennifer (both from 1st m.), Samantha (from 2nd m.), 1 s. Toby (from 2nd m.). Pets: Golden labrador called Bimbo. Hobbies: Fishing, cricket.

TARRANT, Colin

Colin Tarrant

Colin Tarrant. Actor. b. Shirebrook, Nottinghamshire, 14 June. Gained a BA in English and Drama from Exeter University and a Cert Ed from Clifton College of Education, Nottingham. RSC productions include *The Winter's Tale, Titus Andronicus, The Two Gentlemen of Verona, Henry IV, Pts 1* and *2.*
TV: Will Brangwen in *The Rainbow;* Inspector Monroe in *The Bill* (1989-). Address: c/o CAM. Lives in London. m. (dis); 1 s. Juma Kwasi Woodhouse. Hobbies: Football, reading, theatre, cinema.

TAYLFORTH, Gillian

Gillian Taylforth. Actress. b. London, 14 August 1955. Trained at the Anna Scher Theatre School.
TV: *Eleanor* (Play for Today); *Zigger Zagger; The One and Only Phyllis Dixey; The Rag Trade; Thunder*

Cloud; Little Girls Don't; Watch This Space; Hi-de-Hi!; Big Jim and the Figaro Club; Sink or Swim; On Safari; The Gentle Touch; Minder; Fast Hand; Kathy Beale in EastEnders (1985-).
Films: The Long Good Friday.
Books: Kathy and Me (autobiography, 1995).
Address: c/o Saraband Associates/BBC Elstree Centre. Lives in Highbury, North London. Partner: Geoff Knights. Hobbies: Dancing, keeping fit, reading, music, swimming, cooking, any sport.

TAYLOR, Benedict

Benedict Sean Taylor. Actor. b. London, 18 April 1960. Joined the RSC, aged nine, acting in The Winter's Tale, The Man of Mode, Macbeth and King John. Later in Peter Pan (London Coliseum).
TV: The Other Woman (Play for Today); Union Castle; Mitch; The Gentle Touch; Barriers; Beau Geste; A Flame to the Phoenix; Jackanory; The Far Pavilions (mini-series); The Facts of Life; Bergerac; The Dirty Dozen; Video Stars (Play of the Week); The Last Days of Pompeii (TVM); The First Modern Olympics (TVM); The Corsican Brothers; My Brother Jonathan; Black Arrow (TVM); Thirteen at Dinner; 92 Grosvenor Street; Love Is Ever Young; Drums along Balmoral Drive; The South Bank Show; A Perfect Spy; Vanity Fair; Tales of the Unexpected; A Duel of Hearts (TVM); An Actor's Life for Me; Pieter in The Darling Buds of May (second series); The Three Musketeers (Family Channel); The Royal Family; Dead Men's Tales; Julian Whitfield in Danielle Steel's Jewels (mini-series); Atin in The 10%ers (series, 1994); Sixtus in The Young Indiana Jones Chronicles.
Films: The Innocents (as a child); Say Hello to Yesterday (as a child); The Watcher in the Woods; Black Arrow; Every Time We Say Goodbye.
Address: c/o Sharon Hamper Management. Lives in London. m. Hobbies: Travelling, reading, music, films, theatre, galleries, skiing, climbing, swimming, cycling, riding, scuba-diving.

TAYLOR, Gwen

Gwendoline Allsop. Actress. b. Derby, 19 February 1939. Worked as a bank clerk for eight years before training at the East 15 Acting School (1965-8). Stage plays include Harvest (Ambassadors), Top Girls (Royal Court and New York), Trumpets and Raspberries (Phoenix), The Maintenance Men (Comedy Theatre), Time of My Life (Vaudeville) and Hamlet (national tour and Gielgud Theatre).
TV: The Land of Green Ginger (Play for Today); John Halifax, Gentleman; The Common (Play of the Month); Rutland Weekend Television (series, 1976); Pickersgill People; Return Fare (Play of the Week); Ripping Yarns; Sounding Brass (series); Only When I Laugh; Skirmishes (Playhouse); The Link Game; Forever Young; Billy 3: A Coming to Terms for Billy; Billy 4: Lorna; Antigone; Amy Pearce in Duty Free (three series, 1984-6, plus 1986 Christmas special); Ties of Blood; Slip Up; Yes, Prime Minister; Colin's Sandwich; Liz in Sob Sisters (series, 1989); Rita Simcock in A Bit of a Do (two series, 1989); Sauce for the Goose; Happy Christmas, I Love You; Keeping Tom Nice; Celia Forrest in The Sharp End (series, 1991); Inspector Morse: Happy Families; Murder Most Horrid; Annie in Screaming (series, 1992); Gen Masefield in Conjugal Rites (two series, 1993-4); Came, Out, It Rained, Went Back in Again (ScreenPlay Firsts); Annie in The Detectives; title role in Barbara (Comedy First); Nesta in Moving Story; Some Kind of Life; Virginia Gilmore in Class Act.
Films: Monty Python's Life of Brian; Richard's Things; Some Kind of Life. Address: c/o James Sharkey Associates. Lives in North London. m. 1963 Frederick Blount (dis 1967). Partner: Playwright Graham Reid; 3 step-children.

TAYLOR, Shirin

Shirin Taylor. Actress. Trained at Bristol Old Vic Theatre School. Stage plays include Educating Rita (title role, Piccadilly Theatre) and Three Birds Alighting on a Field (as Julia, Royal Court Theatre).
TV: Cleopatra; Shine on Harvey Moon; Cockles; One by One; Boon; Ties of Blood; Sue Kirk in Crossroads; Love with a Perfect Stranger; Harold and Hiram; Give Us a Break (series); Rosa in I Woke Up One Morning (two series); Doctor Who; T-Bag Strikes Again; Soft Soap (pilot); Sally in Bust (series); Storyteller in Mersey Stories; Brenda in Private Practice (pilot); The Ruth Rendell Mysteries. The Best Man to Die; Jackie Ingram in Coronation Street (1990-1, 1992); The Bill (four roles); Casualty (two roles); Helen Cartwright in A Touch of Frost. Address: c/o RKM. Lives in London. Single.

TEALE, Owen

Nigel Teale. Actor. b. Swansea, West Glamorgan, 20 May 1961. Trained at the Guildford School of Acting. Stage plays include Run for Your Wife (West End) and The Comedy of Errors (Bristol Old Vic).
TV: The Mimosa Boys; Maldak in Doctor Who; Dai in Knights of God; Ham Peggoty in David Copperfield; One by One; The Bureaucracy of Love; Nic in Way out of Order; Strife; John O'Brien in The Fifteen Streets; Det Sgt Mike McCarthy in Waterfront Beat; Bentley Drummle in Great Expectations; Bob North in The Ruth Rendell Mysteries: The Secret House of Death (mini-series, 1996).
Films: The Unknown Soldier in War Requiem. Address: c/o Markham & Froggatt. m. actress Dilys Watling (dis); 1 s. Ion-Rhys. Hobbies: Golf, tennis, water sports.

Gillian Taylforth

Benedict Taylor

Gwen Taylor

Shirin Taylor

Owen Teale

TEWSON, Josephine

Josephine Tewson

Josephine Tewson. Actress. b. Hampstead, North London, 26 February. Trained at RADA. Has been a foil for comedians such as Ronnie Barker, Ronnie Corbett, Dick Emery, Jimmy Tarbuck, Bruce Forsyth, Les Dawson, Frankie Howerd, Charlie Drake, Larry Grayson and Bernie Winters. Stage plays include *Noises Off* (Savoy Theatre) and *Woman in Mind* (Vaudeville Theatre).

TV: *Hark at Barker; Wodehouse Playhouse;* Bates in *His Lordship Entertains; Son of the Bride; It's Tarbuck; Casanova 73; The Dick Emery Show; The Les Dawson Show; The Larry Grayson Show; The Two Ronnies; No Appointment Necessary; Odd Man Out; Shelley; Terry and June; The Caucasian Chalk Circle; Rude Health; Clarence;* Elizabeth in *Keeping Up Appearances* (five series, 1990-5); *Coronation Street.*
Films: *The Hound of the Baskervilles; Wilt.*
Address: c/o International Artistes. m. 1st 27 September 1958 actor Leonard Rossiter (dis 1963), 2nd 12 June 1972 dental surgeon Henry Newman (dec). Hobbies: Watching cricket, music.

THAW, John

John Thaw

John Thaw. Actor. b. Manchester, 3 January 1942. Son of a lorry driver. Left school with one O-level and worked in a bakery. Trained at RADA. Stage plays include *Night and Day* (West End), *Serjeant Musgrave's Dance* (National Theatre) and *Henry VIII* (RSC, Stratford-upon-Avon).
TV: *Francis Durbridge Presents; Z Cars;* Sergeant John Mann in *Redcap* (series); *The Younger Generation; Thick as Thieves* (series); Jack Regan in *Regan* (Armchair Cinema, 1974) and *The Sweeney* (series, 1974-8); *Drake's Venture; Killer Waiting; Mitch; Home to Roost* (series); title role in *Inspector Morse* (series, 1987-92); Sir Arthur Harris in *Bomber Harris; The Mystery of Morse* (documentary, 1993); *Stanley and the Women* (series); Peter Mayle in *A Year in Provence* (series, 1993); James Kavanagh QC in *Kavanagh QC* (two series, 1995-6); Rt Hon George Jones MP in *The Absence of War* (Screen Two); *Inspector Morse: The Way Through the Woods.*
Films: *The Bofors Gun; The Last Grenade; Sweeney!; Sweeney 2; The Grass Is Singing; Cry Freedom; Business as Usual.* Address: c/o John Redway Associates. Lives in Chiswick, West London. m. 1st Sally Alexander (dis), 2nd actress Sheila Hancock; 2 d. actress Abigail (from 1st m.), Joanna, 1 step-d. actress Melanie Thaw (qv) (both from 2nd m.).

THAW, Melanie

Melanie Thaw

Melanie Ross. Actress. Daughter of actress Sheila Hancock (qv) and step-daughter of actor John Thaw (qv). Trained at RADA. Stage plays include *The Man Who Came to Dinner* (as June), *The Constant Couple, The Tempest* (as Miranda), *Restoration* (as Hardacre) (all RSC), *Pride and Prejudice* (as Elizabeth Bennet, national tour) and *The Cabinet Minister* (as Imogen Twombley, Albery Theatre).
TV: *Bergerac* (début); *Van Der Valk; Wedded; Great Expectations;* Sue Lawrence in *Trainer* (Series 2, 1992); *The Bill;* Sandy in *Peak Practice; Fever;* Claire Bicknall in *Pie in the Sky.* Address: c/o ICM.

THOMAS, Gareth

Gareth Thomas

Gareth Thomas. Actor. Trained at RADA. Stage experience with the RSC.
TV: *Z Cars; Coronation Street; Parkin's Patch; Stocker's Copper; Sutherland's Law; Topper's Copper; Country Matters; How Green Was My Valley; Children of the Stones; Fathers and Families; Gotcha; Who Pays the Ferryman?; Blake's 7; Hammer House of Horror; The Bell; The Citadel; Love and Marriage; The Adventures of Sherlock Holmes; Dog Food Dan and the Carmarthen Cowboy; By the Sword Divided; Morgan's Boy; Better Days;* Bulstrode in *London's Burning; Chelworth; To Each His Own* (TVM); George Robinson MP in *Medics;* Harry Thomson in *Crown Prosecutor* (series, 1995).
Address: c/o Noel Gay Artists.

THOMPSON, Derek

Derek Thompson

Derek Thompson. Actor. b. Belfast. Began career as half of a singing duo with his sister Elaine, then joined various rock groups, before acting in repertory theatre. Stage plays include *Strawberry Fields* (Young Vic), *WC/PC* (Half Moon Theatre), *The Bells of Hell* (Garrick Theatre), *The Garden of England* (Shaw Theatre) and *Serjeant Musgrave's Dance* (Old Vic).
TV: *Softly Softly* (début); Harry Moon in *Rock Follies of '77;* (series); Det Sgt Jimmy Fenton in *The Gentle Touch;* Spooner in *Me! I'm Afraid of Virginia Woolf; The Danedyke Mystery;* Jonathan in *Hard to Get; The Photograph;* Billy Downes in *Harry's Game* (mini-series and TVM); *Bergerac;* Will Thurley in *Brookside;* Frank in *The Price;* Bruce Curran in *Fighting Back;* Charlie Fairhead in *Casualty* (1986-).
Films: Ken in *Yanks;* Jeff in *The Long Good Friday;* Andy in *Breaking Glass;* Hourigan in *Wild Geese II.* Address: c/o Jonathan Altaras Associates. Lives in Bristol. m. theatre director-turned-writer Christine (dis), partner: actress Dee Sadler; 2 s. Jack, Charlie.

THOMPSON, Emma

Emma Thompson. Actress. b. London, 15 April 1959. Daughter of actor Eric Thompson.
TV: *Tutti Frutti; Fortunes of War; Thompson* (series); *The Winslow Boy; Knuckle; Look Back in Anger*

(Thames Television only); Marie Bonner in *The Blue Boy*.

Films: Kate Lemon in *The Tall Guy*; *Henry V*; *Howards End*; *Impromptu*; Grace/Margaret Strauss in *Dead Again*; *Peter's Friends*; Beatrice in *Much Ado about Nothing*; *My Father the Hero*; *The Remains of the Day*; *In the Name of the Father*; *Carrington*; *Sense and Sensibility* (also screenwriter).

Awards: Best Actress Oscar and Golden Globe for *Howards End* (1993); Best Screenwriter Oscar for *Sense and Sensibility* (1994).

Address: c/o Hamilton Asper Management. m. 1989 actor-director Kenneth Branagh (qv) (sep).

Emma Thompson

THOMPSON, Ian

Ian Thompson. Actor. b. Chester, 11 August 1939. Stage roles include Lance in *Suez* (national tour).

TV: *A Family at War* (series); *The Persuaders!*; *That's Your Funeral*; *Dear Mother – Love Albert*; *Spytrap*; *Hunter's Walk*; *General Hospital* (series); *Prowling Offensive*; *Oh No It's Selwyn Froggitt*; *Crown Court* (two roles); *Richard in Sam* (series); *Softly Softly*; *The Sweeney*; *Couples*; *The Dummy*; *Sutherland's Law*; *Ruggles Gates* in *Married Love*; Ed Saunders in *Headmaster* (series); Sir Francis Sykes in *Disraeli*; *Why Can't I Go Home?*; *Angels*; *Holding the Fort*; *Private Schultz*; Derek in *County Hall* (series); *On the Line*; *Mitch*; *Jackanory Playhouse*; *Freud*; *Walrus*; *The Gentle Touch*; *Oscar*; *Dempsey and Makepeace*; Alfred Jackson in *Bluebell*; Jim Fowler in *Inside Story*; *Bergerac*; *Boon*; The Vicar in *Andy Capp*; *A Perfect Spy*; *Sitting Targets*; Meadows in *The Mountain and the Molehill*; *63 Highmere Park*; *All Creatures Great and Small*; *The Maguire Family*; *The Bill* (three roles); Andrew Prior in *Medics*; *EastEnders*; *Gone to the Dogs*; *Moon and Son*; *Tales from Hollywood*; *Between the Lines*; *Westbeach*; *Crime Monthly*; *Crime Limited*; *Health & Efficiency*; Ronnie Woods in *Emmerdale* (1995); *Our Friends in the North*; Parkor in *The Bill*; Mr Finch in *A Village Affair*; Dr Arnison in *Catherine Cookson's The Girl* (mini-series, 1996); Det Insp Ulph in *The Ruth Rendell Mysteries: The Secret House of Death* (mini-series, 1996); Willie Noolan in *Dalziel and Pascoe*.

Films: Dr Fisher in *Baxter*; Derek in *A Touch of Class*; Sergeant Bradshaw in *Madhouse*; Jim Bowden in *The Class of Miss MacMichael*. Address: c/o Scott Marshall.

Ian Thompson

THORN, Barbara

Barbara Thorn. Actress. Stage plays include *The Taming of the Shrew* (Theatre Royal, Stratford East), *Happy as a Sandbag* (Ambassadors Theatre) and *Lottes Electric Opera Film* (New London Theatre).

TV: Doris in *Game, Set & Match*; *Grange Hill*; *Tripods*; *Love and Marriage: Lucifer*; *Elizabeth Alone*; Inspector Frazer in *The Bill*; *TECX*; Mrs Pope in *Law and Disorder*; Judith Ingleby in *Pie in the Sky*.

Films: Sheila Doel in *84 Charing Cross Road*. Address: c/o Silvester Management.

THORNE, Angela

Angela Thorne. Actress. b. Karachi, Pakistan, 25 January 1939. Trained at Guildhall School of Music and Drama. Best known for her impersonation of Margaret Thatcher, such as in *Anyone for Denis?* (Whitehall Theatre and TV). Other stage plays include *You Never Can Tell* (Haymarket Theatre).

TV: *Take a Sapphire*; *The Canterville Ghost*; *That Was the Week That Was*; *Ballet Shoes*; *Horizon*; *To the Manor Born*; Maggie in *Anyone for Denis?*; *Three Up, Two Down*; *Paying Guests*; *Farrington of the FO*; Emma in *The Good Guys*.

Films: *Oh! What a Lovely War*; *Yellow Dog*; *The BFG* (voice only).

Address: c/o Michael Whitehall. m. Peter; 2 s. Rupert, Laurence.

Barbara Thorn

THORNTON, Frank

Frank Thornton Ball. Actor. b. London, 15 January 1921. Trained at the London School of Dramatic Art. West End stage plays include *Me and My Girl* (Adelphi Theatre), *Much Ado about Nothing* (Strand Theatre) and *It Runs in the Family* (Playhouse Theatre).

TV: *The Taming of the Shrew*; *It's a Square World*; *The World of Beachcomber*; *Steptoe and Son*; *Hancock's Half Hour*; *HMS Paradise*; *The Apple Cart*; *Time and the Conways*; *Love Thy Neighbour*; *The Tommy Cooper Show*; Captain Peacock in *Are You Being Served* (series, 1973-84) and *Grace and Favour* (two series, 1992-3); *The Taming of the Shrew* (TVM); Reverend in *The Upper Hand*.

Films: *Radio Cab Murder*; *Cloak without Dagger*; *Johnny You're Wanted*; *Portrait of Alison*; *Stock Car*; *Tarnished Heroes*; *It's Trad Dad*; *The Dock Brief*; *Doomsday at Eleven*; *The Tomb of Ligeia*; *The Wild Affair*; *The Murder Game*; *Gonks Go Beat*; *The Early Bird*; *Carry On Screaming*; *A Funny Thing Happened on the Way to the Forum*; *Danny the Dragon*; *30 Is a Dangerous Age, Cynthia*; *A Flea in Her Ear*; *The Assassination Bureau*; *The Bliss of Mrs Blossom*; *Crooks and Coronets*; *The Bed Sitting Room*; *The Magic Christian*; *Till Death Us Do Part*; *Some Will, Some Won't*; *The Private Life of Sherlock Holmes*; *All the Way Up*; *The Rise and Rise of Michael Rimmer*; *Up the Chastity Belt*; *Our Miss Fred*; *Bless This House*; *That's Your Funeral*; *No Sex Please – We're British*; *Digby the Biggest Dog in the World*; *Steptoe and Son Ride Again*; *Keep It Up, Jack!*; *The Three Musketeers: The Queen's Diamonds*; *Vampira*; *Spanish Fly*; *Side by Side*; *The Bawdy Adventures of Tom Jones*; *Are You Being Served?* Address: c/o David Daly Associates. Lives in London. m. 1945 Beryl Evans; 1 d. stage manager Jane Thornton (b. 1966).

Angela Thorne

Frank Thornton

Richard Thorp

THORP, Richard

Richard Thorp. Actor. b. Purley, Surrey, 2 January 1932. Started his working life in his father's shoe business but performed in amateur dramatics. Trained at the Guildhall School of Music and Drama.
TV: Dr John Rennie in *Emergency — Ward 10; Oxbridge 2000; Honey Lane; Public Eye; Maupassant; A Family at War; The Cedar Tree; To the Manor Born; Strangers; The Benny Hill Show; Here's Harry;* Alan Turner in *Emmerdale* (1982-).
Films: *The Dam Busters; The Barretts of Wimpole Street; The Good Companions.*
Address: c/o David Daly Associates/Yorkshire Television. Lives in Calderdale, West Yorkshire. m. 1st (dis), 2nd (dis), 3rd TV floor manager Noola; 1 d. Emma (from 3rd m.), 1 step-d. Sarah (from 3rd m.), 3 children from previous marriages.

David Threlfall

THRELFALL, David

David Threlfall. Actor. b. Manchester, 12 October 1953. Trained at Manchester Polytechnic School of Theatre. RSC roles include Mike in *Shout across the River*, Slender in *The Merry Wives of Windsor*, Victor in *The Suicide*, Antony in *Julius Caesar* and Smike in *Nicholas Nickleby* (London and Broadway).
TV: *On the Good Ship Yaki Hicki Doola; I Want to Be like You; The Kiss of Death* (Play for Today); *Scum* (Play for Today); *Rolling Home; The Life and Adventures of Nicholas Nickleby; The Brylcreem Boys; Arena;* Edgar in *King Lear; The Gathering Seed; Dog Ends* (Play for Today); *The Daughter-in-Law;* Leslie Titmuss in *Paradise Postponed* (series, 1986); Hugh Warner in *Jumping the Queue* (mini-series); Andy in *Person to Person; Seeking in the Dark; The Marksman; Murderers among Us; Casualty of War;* Stanley Rode in *John Le Carré's A Murder of Quality;* Bell in *Nightingales* (two series, 1990, 1992-3); Leslie Titmuss in *Titmuss Regained;* Prince of Wales in *Diana: Her True Story* (mini-series); Alan in *A Statement of Affairs* (mini-series, 1993); Martyn Day in *Fighting for Gemma;* Syl in *The Clothes in the Wardrobe* (Screen Two); Lenny Smart in *Men of the World* (two series, 1994-5).
Films: *Red Monarch; When the Whales Came; The Russia House;* Highland in *Patriot Games.*
Radio: Tom in *The Fosdyke Saga* (BBC radio, 1983-5). Address: c/o James Sharkey Associates.

Debbie Thrower

THROWER, Debbie

Deborah Thrower. Presenter/Journalist. b. Nairobi, Kenya, 17 November 1957. BA (Hons) in French from King's College, London. Reporter on *South London Guardian, Lynn News and Advertiser* (King's Lynn), then BBC Radio Leicester reporter and BBC Radio Solent news producer before entering TV.
TV: *South Today* (BBC South, reporter-presenter); *Hospitalwatch* (reporter-presenter); reporter and newsreader with BBC TV News (*Six o'Clock News, One o'Clock News, Nine o'Clock News*); *Out of Court; Lifeline; The Thrower Report; Coast to Coast* (TVS news magazine); *Songs of Praise; Fifteen Minutes from Now* (BSB); *Along the Pilgrims Way; Meridian Tonight* (Meridian); *That's Gardening* (Meridian); *Meridian Audit* (Meridian); *Meridian Business Awards* (Meridian); *Spotlight* (Meridian); *Local Heroes* (Meridian); *The Health Report* (Meridian); *First Light* (series, 1995-6).
Radio: Guest presenter for BBC Radio 2 shows (standing in for Gloria Hunniford, John Dunn and Derek Jameson); *You and Yours; Nation of Shopkeepers; Soundtrack; Animal Hospital; Sunday; The Odd Couple; Call Debbie Thrower; Debbie Thrower Show* (BBC Radio 2, 1995-).
Address: c/o Downes Presenters Agency. Lives in Hampshire. m. 1983 Peter Thompson; 1 d. Bryony, 1 s. Samuel. Pets: A black labrador. Hobbies: Swimming, food, collecting junk.

Malcolm Tierney

TIERNEY, Malcolm

Malcolm Tierney. Actor. Stage plays include *Othello, Love for Love, Hobson's Choice* (all National Theatre), *Measure for Measure, Macbeth* (both RSC), *Richard II* and *Richard III* (both Phoenix Theatre).
TV: *Love on the Dole; The Love School; Where Adam Stood; Family Life; The Main Chance; Collision Course; Poldark; Crime and Punishment;* Richard Warrington in *Spoils of War; Crown Court;* title role in *L S Lowry — A Private View* (drama-documentary); Garfield in *The Home Front; All the World's a Stage; Pope John Paul II; The Barretts of Wimpole Street; Spyship; The Gentle Touch; Bergerac; C.A.T.S. Eyes;* Tommy McArdle in *Brookside;* Charlie Gimbert in *Lovejoy* (series); *Room at the Bottom; Doctor Who; Hannay;* Geoffrey Ellsworth-Smyth in *A Bit of a Do;* Patrick Woolton in *House of Cards* (mini-series, 1990); Ivan Zoffany in *Put on by Cunning.*
Films: *Family Life; All Neat in Black Stockings; The Eagle Has Landed; Escape to Athena; The Medusa Touch; Star Wars; McVicar; Little Dorrit.* Address: c/o Marmont Management.

Paula Tilbrook

TILBROOK, Paula

Paula Tilbrook. Actress. Stage plays include *Effie's Burning* (title role, National Theatre).
TV: *Pit Strike; Tales of the Unexpected;* Hilda in *All Day on the Sands; Thicker than Water* (Play for Today); *Stay with Me Till Morning; The Reason for Things;* Mrs Tattersall in *Open All Hours;* Mrs Enright in *Last of the Summer Wine; Walter* (TVM); Mrs Tibbett in *Sharon and Elsie* (two series); Vera in *Cockles; Glorious Day;* Mrs Walmsley in *The New Statesman;* Betty Hunt in *Brookside;* Mrs Midgeley in *South of the Border;* Paula in *In Sickness and in Health; The Oldest Goose in the Business;* Aunt Flo in

Andy Capp; title role in *Effie's Burning; The Final Frame* (TVM); Mrs (Vivienne) Barford in *Coronation Street;* Violet Rokeby in *Lovejoy;* Speaker in *To Play the King* (mini-series, 1993); *So Haunt Me;* Olive in *Once Upon a Time in the North;* Mrs Cullen in *Moving Story;* Betty Eagleton in *Emmerdale* (1994-);
Films: *Wetherby; A Private Function; Yanks; Resurrected.* Address: c/o Tobias Management.

TILBURY, Peter

Peter Tilbury

Peter Tilbury. Actor/Writer. b. Redruth, Cornwall, 20 October 1945. Began as an ASM and actor at Chelmsford Rep. Acted with the RSC and National Theatre Company.
TV: *The Expert; Perils of Pendragon; Dixon of Dock Green; My Son Reuben; Diamond Cracked Diamond; Whodunnit?; Butterflies; C.A.T.S. Eyes;* Lionel Peel in *Agatha Christie's Miss Marple: Nemesis; Fortunes of War;* Chris Knott in *First Born* (mini-series); *Casualty; It Takes a Worried Man; This Is David Lander; The Bill;* Restaurant Manager in *Chef!* (series); Ken in *Get Back.* As writer: *Sprout; Shelley; Sorry, I'm a Stranger Here Myself; It Takes a Worried Man.*
Films: *Our Day Out; Breaking Glass; Those Glory, Glory Days.* Address: c/o Jill Foster.

TIMOTHY, Christopher

Christopher Timothy

Christopher Timothy. Actor. b. Bala, Gwynedd, 14 October 1940. Trained at the Central School of Speech and Drama. Stage plays include *Chips with Everything* (New York) and *Macbeth* (Young Vic).
TV: *Fly on the Wall; Kate; The Three Sisters; Twelfth Night; Julius Caesar; Lord Peter Wimsey; Murder Must Advertise; The Kitchen; The Moon Shines Bright on Charlie Chaplin; Take Three Girls; The Flaxborough Chronicles: Murder Most English; All the World's a Stage; Much Ado about Nothing;* Roy in *Some Mothers Do 'Ave 'Em;* James Herriot in *All Creatures Great and Small* (series, 1978-90); *Take Three Women; The Royal Variety Performance* (1982); *A History and Its Heritage; A Family and Its Fortune.*
Films: *Othello; Here We Go round the Mulberry Bush; Alfred the Great; The Virgin Soldiers; The Mind of Mr Soames; Spring and Port Wine; Some Sunday; Up the Chastity Belt.*
Books: *Vet behind the Ears.* Address: c/o Markham & Froggatt. m. Annie Veronica Swatton (dis); 2 d. Tabitha, Kate, 4 s. Simon, Nicholas, Robin, David.

TITCHMARSH, Alan

Alan Titchmarsh

Alan Fred Titchmarsh. Presenter/Interviewer. b. Ilkley, West Yorkshire, 2 May 1949. Began his working life as a gardener, training at the Royal Botanic Gardens.
TV: *Nationwide* (1980-3); *Breakfast Time* (1983-6); *The Chelsea Flower Show* (1983-95); *That's Gardening; Let's Go!; Open Air* (1986-7); *Daytime Live* (1987-92); *Songs of Praise* (1989-93); *The Growbiz Quiz; More than Meets the Eye; Scene Today; Pebble Mill* (1991-); *Titchmarsh's Travels; Titchmarsh on Song; Lifeline* (appeal); *Gardeners' World; Sweet Inspiration; Pebble Mill Encore; Secret Gardens; Pebble Mill Special.*
Books: *Supergardener; Alan Titchmarsh's Avant Gardening; The English River.*
Awards: Gardening Writer of the Year (1980, 1983). Address: c/o Arlington Enterprises. Lives in Hampshire. m. 1975 Alison; 2 d. Polly, Camilla. Pets: Two dogs. Hobbies: Boating, riding, theatre.

TOBIN, Anny

Anny Tobin

Anny Tobin. Actress. b. Clonmel, County Tipperary, Ireland, 30 March 1945. Brought up in Sevenoaks, Kent. While working for the United Nations Environment Programme in Nairobi, Kenya, she started acting with the Donovan Maule Theatre repertory company. Returned to Britain as a professional actress in 1977. Stage roles include Kate in *Dancing at Lughnasa* (Garrick Theatre and national tour).
TV: Susan in *Lifelike* (Play of the Week); Sister Duffy in *Angels; The Life of Michael Faraday* (US); Mrs Favell in *Shadow of the Noose;* Diane Ellison in *Brookside;* Mary Ellen O'Brien in *The Fifteen Streets* (mini-series); *Soldier Soldier;* Lizzie Cook in *Milner;* Mrs Bonetti in *Wycliffe.* Address: c/o Sally Hope Associates. Lives in South London. m. actor Peter Harding. Pets: Yorkshire terrier called Oliver.

TOMELTY, Frances

Frances Tomelty

Frances Tomelty. Actress. RSC roles include Titania in *A Midsummer Night's Dream,* Queen Elizabeth in *Richard III,* Portia in *The Merchant of Venice* and Mrs Darling in *Peter Pan* (all RSC).
TV: *Catchpenny Twist* (Play for Today); Theresa in *Blue Money; Strangers;* Sister Milroy in *Testament of Youth;* Juno in *Juno and the Paycock; Lytton's Diary; Iris in the Traffic, Ruby in the Rain;* Polly in *Under the Skin* (Play for Today); *Bazaar and Rummage;* Sheila Hatch in *The File on Jill Hatch; Radio Pictures; A Perfect Spy;* Grace Craven in *Inspector Morse: Last Seen Wearing; Boon;* Lorraine Hope in *Spender; Perfect Scoundrels; Work* (4 Play); *A Celebration of Irish Culture: Bright through the Tears;* title role in *Stella;* Julie Lang in *Cracker;* Danielle Farge in *Nobody's Children;* Annie McGann in *Casualty;* Commander Stone in *99-1* (Series 2, 1995); Eva Mount Stephens in *Murder of a Memsahib* (In Suspicious Circumstances); *The Nation's Favourite Poems* (reader); Gina Lomax in *Kavanagh QC.*
Films: *Bellman and True; Bullshot; Lamb; The Field; Lamb; High Boot Benny; Half a Shave.* Address: c/o Mayer & Eden. Lives in North London. m. musician-actor Sting (dis); 1 d. Katherine.

TOMPKINSON, Stephen

Stephen Tompkinson. Actor. b. Blackpool, Lancashire. Trained at the Central School of Speech and Drama. Stage roles include Paul in *No One Sees the Video* (Royal Court).
TV: Kevin in *Tales of Sherwood Forest;* Jim Wilson in *The Manageress;* Marcus Worton in *Chancer;* PC Clark in *Minder;* Julian in *After Henry;* Woody in *Made in Heaven;* Tony Mitten in *Casualty;* Eric in *And a Nightingale Sang;* Damien Day in *Drop the Dead Donkey* (four series); Spock in *All Quiet on the Preston Front;* Mark in *Downwardly Mobile* (series, 1994); Philip Welch in *The Deep Blue Sea* (Performance); Jeremy Craig in *A Very Open Prison* (Screen Two); Father Peter Clifford in *Ballykissangel* (series, 1996).
Films: *Brassed Off; Treacle.* **Awards:** TV: Top Television Comedy Actor (1994). Radio: Carleton Hobbs Award (1987). Address: c/o Barry Brown & Partner. Lives in London. Hobbies: Cricket, cinema.

Stephen Tompkinson

TRANTER, Penny

Penelope Elspeth Barr. Weather presenter. b. Kilwinning, Ayrshire, 17 June 1961. Gained an environmental sciences degree from the University of East Anglia, then was trained by the Meteorological Office before joining the BBC.
TV: Weather forecasts for BBC1, BBC2, BBC Worldwide, BBC Prime, SSVC.
Radio: Weather forecasts for BBC Radios 3, 4 and 5. Address: c/o BBC Weather Centre. Lives near Bath. m. Dr Martyn Tranter; 1 s. Ievan (b. July 1994). Hobbies: Sailing, squash, tennis, walking, music.

Penny Tranter

TREACHER, Bill

William Charles Treacher. Actor. b. London, 4 June 1937. After National Service became a steward with the P&O Line for four years, mainly in the Far East, so that he could earn enough money to get through drama school. Trained at the Webber Douglas Academy. West End stage plays include *Shout for Your Life* (Vaudeville Theatre), *Uproar in the House, Stand by Your Bedouin, Let Sleeping Lives Lie* (all with the Brian Rix Theatre of Laughter Company at the Garrick Theatre and on a national tour, 1967-9) and *Murder at the Vicarage* (Fortune Theatre).
TV: *Z Cars; Dixon of Dock Green; The Dick Emery Show; Dad's Army; Black Tulip; Softly Softly; Bless This House; The Professionals; Angels; Maggie and Her; Grange Hill; Fanny by Gaslight; Sweet Sixteen; The Agatha Christie Hour; Bergerac; The Lady Is a Tramp;* Chadwick in *The Bright Side* (series, 1985); *Who Sir? Me Sir?;* Arthur Fowler in *EastEnders* (1985-95).
Films: *Pop Pirates.* **Radio:** Sidney, the milkman, in *The Dales* (1965-9).
Address: c/o Glyn Management, The Old School House, Brettenham, Ipswich IP7 7QP. Lives in Suffolk. m. actress Kate Kessey; 1 s. Jamie, 1 d. Sophie. Pets: A dog called Toto. Hobbies: Gardening, sailing.

Bill Treacher

TREVES, Frederick

Frederick William Treves. Actor. b. Cliftonville, Margate, Kent, 29 March 1925. Trained at RADA. Stage plays include *Map of the Heart* (Globe Theatre).
TV: *Crown Court; The Main Chance; The Hanged Man; Churchill's People; Z Cars; The Two Ronnies; The Brothers; The Naked Civil Servant; Willow Cabins; Doran's Box; Softly Softly; Goodbye America; The Sinking of HMS Victoria; When the Boat Comes In; Forgotten Love Songs; The Devil's Brood; Life at Stake; The House of Caradus; Suez; All Creatures Great and Small; Destiny; An Englishman's Castle; Gentle Folk; Doctor Who; Bognor; The Cherry Orchard; Country Strangers; Stalky & Co; PQ 17;* Colonel Leyton in *The Jewel in the Crown; A Flame to the Phoenix; Strangers and Brothers; The Invisible Man; The Magic Mirror; Antigone; Wynne and Penkovsky; My Brother Jonathan; Mountbatten, The Last Viceroy* (TVM); *Silas Marner: The Weaver of Raveloe; Brat Farrar; Yes, Prime Minister; The Good Dr Bodkin Adam; Miss Marple; Hedgehog Wedding; The Maneaters of Kumaon; Inspector Morse; After the War; Game, Set & Match; Rumpole of the Bailey; Death of a Son; Bomber Harris; Summer's Lease; The Return of Black Beauty; Bergerac; For the Greater Good; Agatha Christie's Poirot; Parnell and the Englishwoman; The Black Candle; God on the Rocks; Downtown Lagos; Lovejoy; Jeeves and Wooster;* Lord Quillington in *To Play the King;* Lord Saltery in *Under the Hammer; The Inspector Alleyn Mysteries: Scales of Justice; Between the Lines; The Politician's Wife; The Chief; Casualty; The Vet.*
Films: *Agatha; The Sweeney; Charlie Muffin; The Elephant Man; Hawks; Devices and Desires; Defence of the Realm; The Fool; Afraid of the Dark; The Young Indiana Jones Chronicles; Underbelly; Paper Mask.* Address: c/o April Young. Lives in London. m. Margaret; 2 s. Frederick, Patrick, 1 d. Jennet. Hobbies: Gardening, walking, reading.

Frederick Treves

TROUGHTON, David

David Troughton. Actor. b. Hampstead, North London, 9 June 1950. Son of actor Patrick Troughton; brother of actor Michael Troughton (qv). Stage plays include *A Midsummer Night's Dream* (RSC).
TV: *The Regiment; Armchair Theatre; Wings; Man of Destiny; Molière; The Norman Conquests; Our Mutual Friend; Chips with Everything; David Copperfield; Wessex Tales; Backs to the Land; Crime and Punishment; Tales of Sherwood Forest;* Mr Pritchard in *Hi-de-Hi!;* Bob Buzzard in *A Very Peculiar Practice* (series); *The Trials of Oz* (Performance); Terry Carpenter in *Boon;* Barton Russell in *Agatha*

David Troughton

Christie's Poirot; Eric Sweety in *Bonjour la Classe* (series, 1993); Wellesley in *Sharpe's Eagle;* Ron Rust in *A Few Short Journeys* (Stages).
Films: *Dance with a Stranger; The Chain.*
Address: c/o Markham & Froggatt. m. actress Alison Groves; 3 s. Sam, Jim, William.

TROUGHTON, Michael

Michael Troughton. Actor. b. Hampstead, North London, 2 March 1955. Son of actor Patrick Troughton; brother of actor David Troughton (qv). Began career as an ASM and actor at the Unicorn children's theatre, then ASM at Watford. Stage plays include *The Taming of the Shrew* (RSC tour).
TV: *Backs to the Land; The Mill on the Floss; Love Story; A Moment in Time;* Victor in *Testament of Youth; The Fatal Spring; Bless Me, Father; The Member for Chelsea; The Grudge Fight; Nancy Astor; Sorrell and Son; A Crack in the Ice; Minder; C.A.T.S. Eyes; Boon;* Piers Fletcher-Dervish in *The New Statesman* (series); *2point4 Children; The Gingerbread Girl; Timebusters* (fantasy adventure game series); Marquess of Tipperary in *The Detectives; The Bill; Crown Prosecutor; Goodnight Sweetheart;* Allen Symonds in *Silent Witness.* Address: c/o JM Associates. m. Caroline Rake; 1 s. Matthew, 1 d. Sally.

Michael Troughton

TULLY, Susan

Susan Tully. Actress. b. Highgate, North London, 20 October 1967. Trained at the Anna Scher Theatre School from the age of seven. Two years later, she was one of the presenters of the LWT Saturday morning children's programme *Our Show* and later co-presented *The Saturday Banana* with Bill Oddie.
TV: *Our Show; The Saturday Banana* (both as co-presenter, as a child); *Why Can't I Go Home?; Never Never Land;* Suzanne in *Grange Hill;* Michelle Fowler in *EastEnders* (1985-95).
Films: *Second to the Right and on Till Morning.* Address: c/o Saraband Associates.

Susan Tully

TURNER, Stephanie

Stephanie Ann Turner. Actress/Director. b. Bradford, West Yorkshire, 25 May 1944. Gained a BA (Hons) in drama from Manchester University. West End stage plays include *Say Goodnight to Grandma, Absurd Person Singular, Just between Ourselves* and *One Flew over the Cuckoo's Nest.*
TV: Girls' pipe band member in *Coronation Street* (1967); *Z Cars* (semi-regular, 1972-6); *Sam; The Sweeney* (series); *Play for Today; Play of the Month;* Inspector Jean Darblay in *Juliet Bravo* (three series, 1980-2); *Lady Windermere's Fan; Boon; Small Zones; Van Der Valk;* Dinah Reynolds in *Casualty;* Marcia Thompson in *The Bill; Scene: The Blood That's in You* (BBC Schools); Doreen Rawlings in *Peak Practice;* Mrs Jarvis in *A Touch of Frost.* **Awards:** Variety Club Personality of the Year (1981). Address: c/o Michael Ladkin Personal Management. Hobbies: Gardening, yoga, reading.

Stephanie Turner

ULLMAN, Tracey

Tracey Ullman. Actress/Comedienne. b. Hackbridge, Buckinghamshire, 30 December 1959.
TV: *Three of a Kind; The Young Visiters* (TVM); *Girls on Top; The Tracey Ullman Show* (winner, two Emmy awards); *Tracey Ullman: A Class Act* (series, 1993); *Tracey Ullman Takes on New York; The Out of Towner; Love and War; Holiday* (guest reporter, 1995); *Tracey Ullman Takes On...* (series, 1996).
Films: Sandra in *Give My Regards to Broad Street;* Alice Park in *Plenty;* Fiona in *Jumpin' Jack Flash;* Rosalie Boca in *I Love You to Death; Death Becomes Her* (not seen in final, edited version); *I'll Do Anything.* Address: c/o ICM. m. TV executive Allan McKeown; 1 d. Mabel Ellen, 1 s. John.

Tracey Ullman

USTINOV, Peter

Peter Alexander Ustinov. Actor/Writer/Director/Producer. b. London, 16 April 1921. CBE, 1975; knighted, 1990. Trained at the London Theatre Studio.
TV: *Omnibus: The Life of Samuel Johnson; Storm in Summer; Barefoot in Athens* (all US); *The Mighty Continent* (narrator); *Gideon; The Hermitage* (narrator); *Storm in Summer* (TVM); *Einstein's Universe; The Ballerinas; The Well Tempered Bach; World Challenge; Peter Ustinov's Russia; Peter Ustinov in China; Thirteen at Dinner* (TVM); *Dead Man's Folly* (TVM); *Three Act Tragedy* (TVM); *Around the World in 80 Days; The French Revolution; Glasnost and Glamour; The Mozart Mystique; Ustinov on the Orient Express; Ustinov Meets Pavarotti; In Private with sir Peter Ustinov; The Old Curiosity Shop, Huydn Gulu, Inside the Vatican; An Evening with Sir Peter Ustinov; Russia Now; Paths of the Gods.*
Films: Selection (from 58): *Hullo Fame!* (début, 1940; *One of Our Aircraft Is Missing; School for Secrets* (writer-director); *Vice Versa* (writer-director); *Private Angelo* (also writer-director); *Odette; Hotel Sahara; Quo Vadis?; The Sundowners; Romanoff and Juliet* (also director); *Billy Budd; One of Our Dinosaurs Is Missing; Logan's Run; The Last Remake of Beau Geste; Death on the Nile; Tarka the Otter* (narrator only); *Evil under the Sun; Memed My Hawk* (also director); *Appointment with Death; Grandpa* (voice only). Address: c/o William Morris Agency (UK). Lives in Bursins, Switzerland. m. 1st 1944 Isolde Denham (dis 1951), 2nd 1954 French Canadian actress Suzanne Cloutier (dis 1971), 3rd 1972 Hélène du Lau d'Allemans; 3 d. Tamara (from 1st m.), Pavla, Andrea, 1 s. Igor (all from 2nd m.). Pets: Russian breed of dog. Hobbies: Tennis, collecting classical records and old prints.

Peter Ustinov

Anthony Valentine

VALENTINE, Anthony

Anthony Valentine. Actor. b. Blackburn, Lancashire, 17 August 1939. Began as a child actor. Trained at the Valerie Glynn Stage School. Stage plays include *No Sex, Please We're British* (Strand Theatre).
TV: *Whirligig* (aged 11); *Vice Versa; Billy Bunter; Rex Milligan; Children of the New Forest* (all as a child); *A for Andromeda; The Scarf; John Gabriel Borkman; An Age of Kings; Armchair Theatre; The Avengers; Codename;* Toby Meres in *Callan; The Donati Conspiracy;* Major Mohn in *Colditz; Justice; Sunset Song; Love Me to Death; Space 1999;* title role in *Raffles; Minder; The Dancing Years; Masada; Hammer House of Horror; Tales of the Unexpected; The Carpathian Eagle; Murder Is Easy; Airline; The Second Holmes; I Have Been Here Before; Dangerous Corner; Bergerac; Robin of Sherwood* (two series); *Lovejoy, Lime Street; The Fear; Pulaski; A Father's Revenge* (TVM); *After the War; Hannay; The Price of Fame; The Dirty Dozen; The Winds of Change; Boon; The Return of Sherlock Holmes; Van Der Valk; Trainer; The House of Eliott; The Fifth Corner; Stay Lucky; Moon and Son; The Age of Treason; Covington Cross; Body & Soul;* Col Carter in *Jilly Cooper's Riders; The Detectives; The Knock.*
Films: *No Way Back* (aged 10); *Girl on the Pier; The Damned; West 11; Performance; To the Devil a Daughter; Escape to Athena; The Monster Club; Identikill; Fatal Mission.* Address: c/o ICM. Lives in Surrey. m. actress Susan Skipper. Pets: Two cats. Hobbies: Walking, gardening.

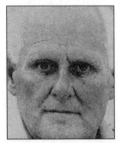

Peter Vaughan

VAUGHAN, Peter

Peter Ewart Ohm. Actor. b. Wem, Shropshire, 4 April 1924. Started as an ASM in repertory theatre.
TV: *Deadline Midnight; The Gold Robbers; A Chance of Thunder; I Thank a Fool; When the Kissing Had to Stop; Stalingrad; The Saint Steps In; My Wildest Dream; A Most Curious Crime; Madigan: The Lisbon Beat* (TVM); *The Eyes Have It; The Case of the Mirror of Portugal; Affair of the Avalanche Bicycle & Tyre Company Ltd; The Pallisers;* Harry Grout in *Porridge;* Philby, *Burgess and MacLean; Treasure Island; Oliver Twist; Great Expectations; Winston Churchill – The Wilderness Years; Citizen Smith; Fox; Henry VIII; Coming Out of the Ice; Jamaica Inn* (TVM); *Under the Hammer; Czech Mate; Forbidden; Bleak House; Haunted Honeymoon; Sins; Coast to Coast; Monte Carlo; When We Are Married; Harry's Kingdom; Strife; The Bourne Identity* (TVM); *Codename: Kyril; War and Remembrance; Our Geoff; Game, Set & Match; The Boscombe Valley Mystery; Countdown to War; Under a Dark Angel's Eye; Chancer; The Return of Sherlock Holmes; Prisoner of Honor* (TVM); *The Prague Sun; Murder Most Horrid; A Ghost Story for Christmas: A Warning to the Curious;* Winston Greeves in *Mistress of Suspense: Under a Dark Angel's Eye;* Marek in *Lovejoy; Nightingales* (series); *Circle of Deceit; The Spot FX Man; Heart of Darkness; The Fatherland; Dandelion Dead; Murder Most Horrid II; Omnibus; Rab C Nesbitt; The Choir;* Delaney in *Oliver's Travels* (series, 1995); Felix Hutchinson in *Our Friends in the North* (serial, 1996).
Films: Selection (from 44): *Sapphire* (début, 1959); *Village of the Damned; The Punch and Judy Man; Straw Dogs; Porridge; Zulu Dawn; The French Lieutenant's Woman; The Remains of the Day.* Address: c/o ICM. m. 1st 1952 actress Billie Whitelaw (dis 1964), 2nd 1966 actress Lillias Walker; 1 s. David (from 2nd m.), 2 step-d. Victoria, Alexandra (from 2nd m.). Pets: Two dogs, one cat..

Richard Vernon

VERNON, Richard

Richard E Vernon. Actor. b. Reading, Berkshire, 7 March 1925. Trained at the Central School of Speech and Drama. Stage productions include *Peter Pan, Hay Fever* and *Saturday, Sunday, Monday.*
TV: *A Friend Indeed; The Man in Room 17; Sextet; Sarah; Upstairs, Downstairs; Edward the Seventh; The Duchess of Duke Street; Aren't We All?; The Sandbaggers; Ripping Yarns; Suez; The Hitch-Hiker's Guide to the Galaxy; Something in Disguise; Nanny; Waters of the Moon; Roll Over Beethoven; Paradise Postponed; The Return of the Antelope; Yes, Prime Minister; A Gentleman's Club;* Lionel Leering in *Rumpole of the Bailey, The Camomile Lawn;* Sir Lionel in *Bonjour la Classe; You Rang, M'Lord?; Rides;* Sir Horace Mainwaring in *Class Act* (two series, 1994-5); Lord Dunstable in *Frank Stubbs; Lovejoy.*
Films: Selection (from 34): *Conquest of the Air* (début, 1936); *The Servant; The Yellow Rolls Royce; Goldfinger; A Hard Day's Night; The Intelligence Men; The Satanic Rites of Dracula; The Pink Panther Strikes Again; Evil under the Sun; Gandhi; Lady Jane; A Month in the Country; A Masculine Ending.* Address: c/o Julian Belfrage Associates. m. actress Benedicta Leigh; 1 d. Sarah, 1 s. Tom.

Lesley Vickerage

VICKERAGE, Lesley

Lesley Vickerage. Actress. Trained at The Drama Studio.
TV: Police Constable in *Inspector Morse: Dead on Time;* WPC Jenny Dean in *Between the Lines* (Series 1, 1992); Second Lieutenant/Capt Kate Butler in *Soldier Soldier* (Series 2-4, 1992-4); Trisha Simmons in *The Bill; The Chamber* (pilot, 1995); Vornholt in *BUGS* (Series 2, 1996). Address: c/o Hamilton Asper Management.

James Villiers

VILLIERS, James

James Michael Lyle Villiers. Actor. b. London, 29 September 1933. Trained at RADA.
TV: *The First Churchills; Lady Windermere's Fan; The Millionairess;* Professor Higgins in *Pygmalion; The Double Kill* (TVM); *The Other 'Arf;* Sir Geoffrey Cyon in *Spectre* (TVM); *Unity; Mrs Silly; The Scarlet*

Pimpernel; The Good Doctor Bodkin Adams; The Dirty Dozen; Fortunes of War; Radical Chambers; Hemingway; Anything More Would Be Greedy; Chelworth; Charles Collingridge in House of Cards; The Gravy Train Goes East; A Perfect Hero; Lionel Beckwith in Lovejoy; The Memoirs of Sherlock Holmes.
Films: Selection (from 44): Late Night Final (début, 1954); Carry On Sergeant; The Entertainer; Girl in the Headlines; King and Country; Daylight Robbery; The Alphabet Murders; The Wrong Box; Half a Sixpence; Otley; A Nice Girl like Me; Some Girls Do; Blood from the Mummy's Tomb; The Ruling Class; The Amazing Mr Blunden; Joseph Andrews; For Your Eyes Only; Under the Volcano; Honour, Profit and Pleasure; Scandal; Mountains of the Moon; King Ralph; "Let Him Have It"; $E=MC^2$. Address: c/o ICM. Lives in Arundel, West Sussex. m. (dis). Hobbies: Collecting antiques, watching sport.

David Vine

VINE, David
David Martin Vine. Sports presenter. b. Newton Abbot, Devon, 3 January 1935.
TV: Westward Television news and sports reporter (1962-6); BBC TV sports presenter and commentator (1966-), including Olympic Games, Commonwealth Games, Horse of the Year Show, World Ski Cup, Wimbledon Tennis Championships, bowls and all snooker championships; Miss World; Eurovision Song Contest; Jeux Sans Frontières; A Question of Sport (first nine years); Ski Sunday (17 years); The Superstars. **Books:** The Superstars. Address: c/o BBC TV Sport. Lives in Oxfordshire. m. Mandy; 2 s., 2 d. Pets: Bichon Frise called Big Louis. Hobbies: Food, wine, gardening, home.

VINE, John
John Leslie Vine. Actor. b. Banbury, Oxfordshire, 20 February 1951. Trained at the Rose Bruford College of Speech and Drama. Began career with Ian McKellen's Actors Company.
TV: Knights of God; Bust; The Moneymen; The Seven Dials Mystery; King's Royal; Kate the Good Neighbour; DI John Massingham in Death of an Expert Witness, Shroud for a Nightingale and Cover Her Face; Murder Not Proven; QED; Not a Penny More; The Franchise Affair; Rockliffe's Folly; Boon; The Ruth Rendell Mysteries: The Best Man to Die; Rides; Red Fox; Van Der Valk; Casualty (two roles); A Touch of Frost; The Bill (two roles); Diana: Her True Story; Westbeach; All in the Game; Cracker; 99-1; The Chief; The Knock.
Films: Sweeney II; Richard's Things; Gandhi; Eureka; The Keep.
Address: c/o Conway, van Gelder, Robinson. Lives in Eastbourne, East Sussex. m. Alex; 2 s. Tom, Oliver. Pets: Cross collie dog called Blossom. Hobbies: All sports, travel, the beach, after-dinner speaking.

John Vine

VORDERMAN, Carol
Carol Jean Vorderman. Presenter. b. Bedford, 24 December 1960. Engineering MA from Cambridge.
TV: Countdown (resident statistician, 1982-); The Game; Sounds Good (two series); Kid's Kafe; Ask No Questions (co-presenter); So We Bought a Computer; Power Base; Circuit Training; Take Nobody's Word for It; Micro Mindstretchers; Ask Carol (Wide Awake Club); Countdown Masters (Channel Four Daily, 1989-91); The Software Show; Book Tower: Science Books; A Search Out Science Special; Carol's Fab Lab (WAC '90); Inset (Teaching Science in the Primary School); The Vorderman Report (Calendar, Yorkshire Television only); How 2 (six series, 1990-5); Sum Chance; A Way with Numbers; Car Wise (This Morning); Parent Power (This Morning); Video Class Times Tables (This Morning); Postcards from Down Under; Pick of the Week; Music on ITV (HTV); Chips with Everything (This Morning); Seeing Stars; The Andrew Norton Hypnotic Experience; Experiment!; GMTV education and technology correspondent; Notes & Queries with Clive Anderson; World Chess Championship; Breaking Glass; Tomorrow's World (1994-5); On Your Marks (Yorkshire Television only); Entertainment Today (series, 1996).
Address: c/o John Miles Organisation. Lives in Maidenhead, Berkshire. m. Patrick King; 1 d. Katie.

Carol Vorderman

VOSBURGH, Tilly
Tilly Vosburgh. Actress. b. London, 17 December 1960.
TV: Two People; Starting Out; Maria Martin; Minder; The Victoria Wood Show; Hold the Back Page; Treatment; File on Jill Hatch; Tears before Bedtime; Meantime; You'll Never See Me Again; Raspberry; The Function Room; Strong Poison; Debbie in Will You Love Me Tomorrow (TVM); The Bill (two roles); A Perfect Spy; Radical Chambers; Agatha Christie's Poirot; Morning Sarge; This Is David Lander; The House of Payne; Irene Saunders in Inspector Morse; Delia in The Men's Room; Jackie Greenwood in The Good Guys; Moira in Perfect Scoundrels; Jools Legge in Full Stretch (series); Peak Practice; Frank Stubbs; Black Hearts in Battersea; A Touch of Frost; Impasse (Paul Merton in Galton & Simpson's...).
Films: The Pirates of Penzance; The Missionary; Un in Erik the Viking; Tight Trousers.
Address: c/o Annette Stone Associates.

Tilly Vosburgh

VOSS, Philip
Philip James Voss. Actor. b. Leicester, 20 August 1936. Trained at RADA.
TV: Det Sgt Stewart in Bad Company; Cunningham in Catherine Cookson's The Dwelling Place; Richard Jordan in A Village Affair; Sir Duncan in Indian Summer.
Address: c/o Kate Feast Management. Lives in Bushey, Hertfordshire. Single

Philip Voss

Bill Waddington

WADDINGTON, Bill

William J Waddington. Actor/Comedian. b. Oldham, Lancashire, 10 June 1916. First radio broadcast 1940, followed by numerous variety shows. First TV programme 1946, from Radio Olympia. Toured as principal comedian with US singing stars Frankie Laine, Dorothy Lamour, Lena Horne and Billy Daniels. Appeared in two Royal Variety Performances (1955, 1989).
TV: *A Family at War; Dear Enemy; Talent; Fallen Hero; The Mating Season; Cousin Phyllis; Second Chance*; Percy Sugden in *Coronation Street* (1983- , after four bit-parts in the serial); *Royal Variety Performance* (with cast of *Coronation Street*, 1989).
Radio: More than 800 comedy and variety broadcasts, starting with *Ack, Ack, Beer, Beer* (1940).
Books: *The Importance of Being Percy* (autobiography, 1992); *Percy's War* (1994).
Address: c/o Granada Television. Lives in High Lane, Cheshire. m. 1st Evelyn (dis), 2nd (dis), 3rd actress-singer Lillian Day (dec); 2 d. Denise, actress Barbara.

Lou Wakefield

WAKEFIELD, Lou

Anne-Louise Wakefield. Actress/Writer/Director. b. Leicester, 20 April 1951. Stage plays as actress include *Top Girls* (Royal Court and Broadway).
TV: As actress: *Shoulder to Shoulder; An Imaginative Woman; The Linden Tree* (Play of the Month); *Girls of Slender Means; The Sweeney; Joggers; Inside Out* (series); *Happy Families*; Dee Dee in *The Refuge; Casualty; The Bill; This Is David Lander; TECX; Inspector Morse: Deadly Slumber; Growing Pains*. As writer: *Battleaxes; Never Say Die* (two series); *Happy Ever After; Private Eyes; Westbeach; Firm Friends* (two series); *Not Cricket* (serial) As director: *Sense of Place: Tuebrook Tanzi; A Sense of Place: Somewhere More Central; Revolting Women* (series); *Never Say Die* (series); *Desmond's* (six episodes).
Radio: Jackie Woodstock in *The Archers; Tartuffe*. **Awards:** TV: RTS award as writer of *Firm Friends*. Address: c/o Mayer & Eden. Lives in London. Single. Hobbies: Playing cricket.

Gary Waldhorn

WALDHORN, Gary

Gary Waldhorn. Actor. b. London, 3 July 1943. Trained at Yale University Drama School, US.
TV: *Outside Edge; All for Love; Love and Marriage; The Prisoner of Zenda; Drummonds; Mrs Capper's Birthday; All at No 20; Moving; Brush Strokes; After Pilkington; Minder; Mr Palfrey of Westminster; Campaign; Missing Persons; Rumpole of the Bailey; The Chief; Titmuss Regained; Gallowglass* (mini-series); *Cut and Run* (Comedy Playhouse); *Lovejoy*; David Horton in *The Vicar of Dibley* (series); *Twelve Angry Men* and *Doctor in the Lift* (both Paul Merton in Galton & Simpson's ...); *French and Saunders*.
Films: *Zeppelin; The Chain; Escape to Victory; Sir Henry at Rawlinson End; Chinese Whispers.*
Address: c/o Jonathan Altaras Associates. m. (dis); 1 s. Joshua.

Anna Walker

WALKER, Anna

Anna Walker. Presenter. b. Sheffield, South Yorkshire, 4 December 1964. Gained a BSc (Hons) in zoology from Bristol University, before taking a Writing for TV News course and Court Reporting course with ITN.
TV: Assistant producer, BBC science and features department (1985-7), including *Tomorrow's World, Bodymatters* and a *QED* special on AIDS; *Farming Outlook* (Tyne Tees only, 1987); *Tomorrow's World* (six months, 1988); *Calendar* (presenter-reporter, Yorkshire TV, 1988-90); *Sportsdesk* (BSB Sportschannel, 1990-1); *On the Line; Grandstand* (Grand National, London Marathon, Triathlon, Grand Prix); *Wish You Were Here...?* (reporter, five series, 1991-6); *Sportsnight* (Winter Olympics and sporting trophies report); *Ski Sunday; Winter Olympics* (reporter in Albertville, BBC Sport); *Summer Olympics* (reporter in Barcelona, BBC Sport); *Women's Soccer; The London International Boatshow; Heart of the Country; BBC Breakfast News* (sports bulletins); *Sunrise* (newscaster, BSkyB); *Goals on Sunday* (BSkyB); *Sky Sports Centre* (BSkyB); *King of the Road; King of the Road Revisited; Live at Five* (newscaster, BSkyB); *Car of the Year '95*. Drama appearances: Newsreader in *Underbelly;* Reporter in *TECX;* Sports Reporter in *Frank Stubbs Promotes*. Address: c/o Jane Hughes Management. m. 30 September 1995 William Herrington. Hobbies: Watching and playing sports, especially skiing, tennis and golf.

Roger Walker

WALKER, Roger

Roger Walker. Actor. b. Bristol, 22 December 1944. Brought up in Derbyshire. Trained at the Rose Bruford School of Speech and Drama. Stage roles include Boniface in *The Beaux' Stratagem* (RSC tour).
TV: *Rainbow* (musician and performer, 350 episodes, and writer of 75 songs in four years); *Crossroads; Emmerdale; Shoestring; Sink or Swim; Playhouse; County Hall; Squadron; Goodbye Mr Kent; CBTV; Bodger and Badger; The Sooty Show; Expert Witness; Where the Buffalo Roam; Troubles and Strife; Bread; Terry and June; Prospects; Brookside; Gentlemen and Players; Big Deal; Pulaski; Hale & Pace; Sam Saturday; Waterfront Beat; Blackeyes; Circle of Deceit; Oranges Are Not the Only Fruit* (mini-series); *The Bill; The Darling Buds of May;* Frank Carruthers in *A Time to Dance* (mini-series); Bunny in *Eldorado* (1992-3); *Paul Merton — The Series;* Mr Colegate in *Over the Rainbow* (series); *Woof!; Casualty, Heartbeat; The Upper Hand; The Detectives; Where the Buffalo Roam* (pilot); *Thief Takers.*
Films: *A View to a Kill; Morons from Outer Space; The Worp Reaction; The Morticians' Tea Party; A*

Secret Weapon. Address: c/o Evans and Reiss. Lives in Teddington, Middlesex. m. 1st (dis), 2nd actress-turned-agent Ann Curthoys; 2 d. Anna, Sarah (both from 1st m.), 1 step-d. Emma, 1 step-s. actor Huw Higginson (qv). Pets: A cat called Horace, a rabbit called Robert. Hobbies: Sailing (Transatlantic in 1988).

WALKER, Rudolph

Rudolph Walker. Actor. Plays include *The Tempest* (Mermaid Theatre and Old Vic).
TV: *Hadleigh; Bill* in *Love Thy Neighbour; Another Day; The Chinese Detective; hank God for UDI; Playboy of the West Indies; Maybury; The Hope and the Glory; Black Silk; The Lenny Henry Show; Boon; The Thief; Wole The Bandung File; Rules of Engagement; The Book Liberator* (4-Play); *Mr Bean; Toussaint l'Overture; The Bill* (three roles); *Escape from Kampala* (ScreenPlay); *For the Greater Good; Dizzy Heights; Badger and Bodger; Bitter Harvest; Between the Lines; Lovejoy; Scene* (BBC Schools); *Brighton Boy; Hypotheticals* (voice-over); *The English Programme* (narrator); *The Pirate Prince; Resort to Murder; The All New Alexei Sayle Show* (series); *That's English; Get Me to the Crematorium on Time; Casualty; Scarlett; The All New Alexei Sayle Show 2* (series); PC Gladstone in *The Thin Blue Line*.
Films: *Universal Soldier; Love Thy Neighbour; The Last Giraffe; The Spaghetti House Siege; Death of a Black; The President; Lebenslinien; Big George Is Dead; Elphida; Smack and Thistle; King Ralph; "Let Him Have It"; Bhaji on the Beach*. Address: c/o Mayer & Eden. m. Lorna; 2 children.

Rudolph Walker

WALLACE, Julie T

Julie Therese Wallace. Actress. b. Wimbledon, South London, 28 May 1961. Trained at LAMDA.
TV: Ruth in *The Life and Loves of a She-Devil* (mini-series, 1986); *Morning Sarge; Selling Hitler; Stay Lucky; Timo Riders;* Miss Candy in *The Life and Times of Henry Prull, Lovejoy;* Fiona Carrington-Cock In *Queen of the Wild Frontier* (The Comic Strip Presents...); *Heartbeat;* PC Sandy Taylor in *The Detectives*.
Films: *The Living Daylights; he Threepenny Opera; Hawks; The Lunatic*. Address: c/o Annette Stone.

Julie T Wallace

WALLER, Kenneth

Kenneth Waller. Actor. b. Huddersfield, West Yorkshire, 5 November 1927.
TV: *Are You Being Served?; All Creatures Great and Small; Doctor Who; Big Deal; Coronation Street; Down to Earth; Juliet Bravo;* Old Mr Grace in *Are You Being Served?* (series, 1981); Ferret in *Big Deal* (series, 1984-6); *Boon;* Grandad in *Bread* (series, 1986-91); Skipper in *Down to Earth*.
Films: *Room at the Top; Scrooge; Chitty Chitty Bang Bang; Fiddler on the Roof*.
Awards: Variety Club BBC TV Personality of the Year (1988). Address: c/o Shane Collins Associates. Lives in North London. Single. Hobbies: Playing the piano and bridge, going to the opera.

WALTER, Harriet

Harriet Mary Walter. Actress. b. London, 24 September. Trained at LAMDA. Niece of actor Christopher Lee. Many RSC stage plays, including *All's Well That Ends Well* (also Broadway).
TV: *The Imitation Game* (Play for Today); Varya in *The Cherry Orchard* (Play of the Month); Amy Johnson in *Amy; The Price; Girls on Top; Dorothy L Sayers Mysteries; The Good Father* (TVM); *Omnibus* (about Caryl Churchill); *Margaret Paston; Benefactors; They Never Slept, The Men's Room* (series); *Ashenden; Inspector Morse: The Day of the Devil; The Maitlands* (Performance); *Bookmark: The Most Beautiful Dress in the World; A Man You Don't Meet Every Day* (Without Walls special); *Hard Times*.
Films: *Reflections;* Harriet in *Turtle Diary; Milou en Mai; La Nuit Miraculeuse;* Amelia Cleverly in *They Never Slept;* Jeannine in *The Hour of the Pig; Sense and Sensibility*.
Awards: Theatre: Laurence Olivier Best Actress Award (1988).
Address: c/o Conway, van Gelder, Robinson. Lives in Fulham, West London. Single.

Kenneth Waller

WALTERS, Julie

Julie Walters. Actress. b. Birmingham, 22 February 1950. Started training as a nurse but left to study for a teacher's certificate in English and drama at Manchester Polytechnic School of Theatre.
TV: *Talent; Good Fun; Nearly a Happy Ending; Living Together; Happy since I Met You; Say Something Happened; Intensive Care; Boys from the Blackstuff; Monologue* (one-woman show of Billy Bennett monologues); *Wood and Walters; Unfair Exchanges; The Secret Diary of Adrian Mole Aged 13¾, Victoria Wood — As Seen on TV; The Birthday Party; The Victoria Wood Show; Talking Heads; Victoria Wood* (series); *Julie Walters & Friends; G.B.H.; Victoria Wood's All Day Breakfast; The Clothes in the Wardrobe* (Screen Two); *Getaway; Wide Eyed and Legless* (Screen One); *Bambino Mio* (Screen One); *Sister, My Sister; Holiday* (guest reporter); *Pat and Margaret* (Screen One); *Requiem Apache* (Alan Bleasdale Presents); Julie Diadoni in *Jake's Progress* (serial, 1995); *Roald Dahl's Little Red Riding Hood*.
Films: *Occupy!; Educating Rita; Unfair Exchanges; She'll Be Wearing Pink Pyjamas; Car Trouble; DreamChild* (voice only); *Personal Services; Prick Up Your Ears; Buster; Mack the Knife; Killing Dad; Stepping Out; Just Like a Woman*. **Awards:** Films: BAFTA Best Film Actress, Golden Globe and Variety Club Best Film Actress awards for *Educating Rita* (1983). Address: c/o ICM. Lives in Sussex. Partner: Grant Roffey; 1 d. Pets: Cats, doves. Hobbies, Reading, travel.

Harriet Walter

Julie Walters

Zoë Wanamaker

WANAMAKER, Zoë

Zoë Wanamaker. Actress. b. New York, USA, 13 May 1949. Hon D Litt, South Bank University. Daughter of actor-director Sam Wanamaker. Trained at the Central School of Speech and Drama. Stage plays include *Dead Funny* (RSC), *Piaf* (London and New York) and *Loot* (Broadway).
TV: *The Silver Mark; Village Hall; The Beaux' Stratagem; The Devil's Crown; Baal; Strike; All the World's a Stage; Richard III;* Clementine in *Edge of Darkness* (mini-series); *Paradise Postponed; Poor Little Rich Girl; Ball-Trap on the Côte Sauvage; The Dog It Was That Died; Othello;* Emma Pickford in *Inspector Morse; Prime Suspect;* Tessa Piggott in *Love Hurts* (three series); *The Real Thing* (narrator); Charlotte Collard in *The Blackheath Poisonings* (mini-series); *The Countess Alice* (TVM); *Total Relief: A Night of Comic Relief* (reporting from Ethiopia, 1993); *The Long Goodbye* (talking about death of her father); Lizzie in *The Widowing of Mrs Holroyd* (Performance); *Peak Performance* (narrator).
Films: *Hitler: The Last Ten Days; Inside the Third Reich; The Hunger; The Raggedy Rawney.*
Awards: TV: BAFTA award. Theatre: Laurence Olivie and Tony awards.
Address: c/o Conway, van Gelder, Robinson. m. actor Gawn Grainger.

Simon Ward

WARD, Simon

Simon Ward. Actor. b. Beckenham, Kent, 19 October 1941. West End plays include *Rear Column.*
TV: *Carried by Storm; Bloomsday; French Cricket; Flowering Cricket; The World of Wooster; The Flying Swan; Smith as Killer; Calf Love; The Son; The Dark Number; Accolade; Jackanory; Spoiled; Chips with Everything; The Misfit; The Black Tulip; The Roads to Freedom; The Breakthrough; The Leather Funnel; The Rear Column; Valley Forge* (TVM); *Diamonds* (series); *An Inspector Calls; 'Allo Beatrice; Philip Japp Special; Treats; The Corsican Brothers* (TVM); *Around the World in 80 Days; A Taste for Death; Lovejoy; The South Bank Show: Anthony Hopkins;* Stringer (Margaret Rutherford's husband) in *Without Walls: For One Night Only;* Will Harvey in *The Ruth Rendell Mysteries: The Strawberry Tree* (mini-series).
Films: *If…; Frankenstein Must Be Destroyed; I Start Counting; Quest for Love; Young Winston; Hitler: The Last Ten Days; The Three Musketeers: The Queen's Diamonds; Dracula; All Creatures Great and Small; Deadly Strangers; The Four Musketeers: The Revenge of Milady; Aces High; Die Standarte (Battle Flag); Holocaust 2000; Children of Rage; The Four Feathers; Dominique; Raising Daisy Rothschild; Zulu Dawn; The Sabina; The Monster Club; The Bomber; Supergirl; L'Étincelle; Leave All Fair; Double X; Ghost Writers.* Address: c/o ICM. m. Alexandra Malcolm; 3 d. actress Sophie (qv), Claudia, Kitty.

Sophie Ward

WARD, Sophie

Sophie Ward. Actress. Daughter of actor Simon Ward (qv).
TV: *The Other Window; Chester Mystery Cycle Plays; Buensham People; The Wild Duck; Ibsen; Frost in May (Antonia White Quartet); Too Young to Fight, Too Old to Die; Casanova; A Time of Indifference; The Shell Seekers;* Molly Kendal in *Agatha Christie's Miss Marple: A Caribbean Mystery; Events at Drimagheen; The Class of '61; MacGyver,* Eden HIllyard in *A Dark Adapted Eye* (mini-series, 1994); *Taking Liberty; Prophecy* (Chiller); Alice Jordan in *A Village Affair;* Alison in *Nelson's Column.*
Films: *The Copter Kids; Full Circle; Half Way Round the Circle; A Shocking Accident; Return to Oz; Young Sherlock Holmes; Little Dorrit; A Summer Story; Aria; Young Toscanini; Benvenuto Cellini; The Monk; The Strauss Dynasty; Wuthering Heights; Crime and Punishment.* Address: c/o London Management. Lives in Gloucestershire. m.vet Paul Hobson; 2 s. Nathaniel, Joshua.

Derek Waring

WARING, Derek

Derek Waring. Actor. b. London, 26 April 1930. Brother of scriptwriter Richard Waring. Trained at RADA.
TV: *The Killers; Public Eye; The Informer; Not in Front of the Children; The Gold Watch Club; Sherlock Holmes; Callan; The Doctors; Z Cars; Marked Personal; The Avengers; Carrington VC; Moody and Pegg; Forget Me Not; She; And Mother Makes Three; Crown Court; An Unofficial Rose; Forget Me Not; Killers; The New Avengers; Two's Company; Miss Jones and Son; The Flaxborough Chronicles; Hi-Summer; Wings; George and Mildred; Thundercloud; Doctor Who; The Professionals; Partners; Don't Rock the Boat;* Albert Harrison in *Law and Disorder;* Mr Cooper-Bassett in *Keeping Up Appearances.*
Films: *Dunkirk; I Accuse; Battle of Britain; Hitler: The Last Ten Days.*
Address: c/o Barry Burnett Organisation. m. actress Dorothy Tutin; 1 d. Amanda, 1 s. Nicholas.

George Waring

WARING, George

George Edward Waring. Actor/Director. b. Eccles, Manchester, 20 February 1927.
TV: *Strife* (Play for Today); *Z Cars;* Joe Lever in *Mrs Thursday; Doctor Who; Softly Softly;* Tom Meek in *Castlehaven; Crown Court; Armchair Thriller; Tightrope;* Clerk in *Six Days of Justice; The Adventures of Black Beauty;* Pit Manager in *Sam; The Investigation; Sergeant Cork; The Train Now Standing;* Arnold Swain in *Coronation Street;* Wilf Padgett in *Emmerdale Farm; Squaring the Circle* (TVM); *Andy Capp; Mixed Blessings; No Place like Home; After the War; The Bill; Forever Green; Agatha Christie's Poirot.*
Films: *God's Outlaw.* Address: c/o Janet Welch Personal Management. m. 1st Gerty Lave (dis), 2nd actress Geraldine Gwyther; 1 s. Geoffrey Larard, 1 d. Georgina Hannay (both from 2nd m.).

WARK, Kirsty

Kirsteen Wark. Presenter. b. Dumfries, 3 February 1955. Gained a degree in Scottish Studies from Edinburgh University. Joined BBC Radio as a researcher in 1976. Moved to television as a producer, then presenter. Formed Wark, Clements and Company with producer Alan Clements in 1990.

TV: *Agenda; Current Account* (both as assistant producer); *Reporting Scotland* (producer); *Seven Days* (producer-presenter). As presenter: *Reporting Scotland; Left Right and Centre;* 1992 and 1995 General Elections; *Up Front; Breakfast Time* (two years); *Words Apart; The Late Show; Edinburgh Nights; Nelson Mandela Concert; Special Olympics; One Foot in the Past* (four series); *Newsnight* (1993-); *Late Again Italian Special; Sex; Election Special; Newsnight: Ceasefire Special; In Search of Power* (series).
Address: c/o Wark, Clements and Company, The Production Centre, The Tollgate, Marine Crescent, Glasgow G51. m. producer Alan Clements; 1 d. Caitlin, 1 s. James.

Kirsty Wark

WARREN, Marcia

Marcia Warren. Actress. b. Watford, Hertfordshire. Trained at the Guildhall School of Music and Drama (first Gold Medal winner, Comedy Prize winner).

TV: *Kids; London Belongs to Me; The Rivals of Sherlock Holmes; Public Eye; Rainbow; Tolpuddle Inheritance; Crown Court; Follies; The History of Mr Polly; The World of J B Priestley; Crossroads; Bradley;* Vera Botting in *No Place like Home* (four series); *Leaving* (two series); *I Woke Up One Morning* (two series); *Now and Then* (two series); *Behaving Badly* (series); *We'll Think of Something* (series); *South by South East; Boon; Bookmark; Miss Pym's Day Out; Virtual Murder* (TVM); *Casualty; Keeping Up Appearances; Psychotherapy; The Bill; The All New Alexei Sayle Show; September Song; Searching; Just William.*
Films: *Mr Love, Spoilers; Don't Start Me Up Again.* **Awards:** Theatre: Laurence Olivier Award for Outstanding Comedy Performance for *Stepping Out* (1984).
Address: c/o Scott Marshall. Lives in Richmond-upon-Thames, Surrey. Single. Hobbies: Food, flowers.

Marcia Warren

WARWICK, James

James Warwick. Actor. b. Broxbourne, Hertfordshire, 17 November 1947. Trained at the Central School of Speech and Drama (Spotlight Award winner). West End stage plays include *The Family Dance, On the Spot, Pride and Prejudice, The Secret Lives of Cartoons* and *And Then There Were None.*

TV: *Late Night Line-Up* (TV début, as an ostrich); *The Onedin Line; Terracotta Horse; Rock Follies; Edward the Seventh; Turtle's Progress; Doctor Who; Telford's Change;* Suggie de Bathe in *Lillie; Why Didn't They Ask Evans?; The Seven Dials Mystery; The Secret Adversary; Follow the Yellow Brick Road; Nightmare Man; The Bell; Tales of the Unexpected: The Sound Machine;* Tommy in *Partners in Crime; Virtual Realities; Kathmandi — The Fragile Valley* (narrator-presenter, Discovery satellite channel); *Scarecrow & Mrs King; Dead Head; Howards' Way; Bergerac; Blore MP; Don't Wait Up; Perfect Scoundrels;* Charles Tremain in *Love Hurts; Hart to Hart; Profiles; Civil Wars; The George Carlin Show; Murder, She Wrote; Babylon 5; Iron Man* (animated); *Camelot* (animated). Address: c/o Ken McReddie. Lives in London and Los Angeles. Single. Hobbies: Travel, music, keeping fit.

James Warwick

WARWICK, Richard

Richard Warwick. Actor. b. Dartford, Kent, 24 April 1945. Trained at RADA.
TV: *The Vortex; Please Sir!; The Last of the Mohicans; Warship; Brensham People; School Play; A Fine Romance; It's My Pleasure;* Frank in *The Lost Language of Cranes* (TVM).
Films: *Romeo and Juliet; If...; The Bed Sitting Room; First Love; The Breaking of Bumbo; Alice's Adventures in Wonderland; Sebastiane; The Tempest.* Address: c/o Peter Charlesworth.

Richard Warwick

WATERMAN, Dennis

Dennis Waterman. Actor. b. London, 24 February 1948. Trained at the Corona Stage Academy.
TV: Title role in *Just William* (aged 16); *Fair Exchange* (US series, as a child); *Cry Baby Bunting; Terry; Journey into the Unknown; The Right Attitude;* Carter in *Regan* (Armchair Cinema, 1974) and *The Sweeney* (series, 1974-8); Terry McCann in *Minder; The World Cup — A Captain's Tale* (also co-producer); *Mr H Is Late; Minder on the Orient Express* (TVM); *Sextet; The First Kangaroos* (TVM); Bobbo in *The Life and Loves of a She Devil;* Thomas Gynn in *Stay Lucky* (four series, 1989-93); Tony Carpenter in *On the Up* (three series); John Neil in *Circle of Deceit* (1993); *Match of the Seventies* (presenter, series, 1995); Eddy Saxe in *Class Act;* John Neil in *Circles of Deceit* (1996).
Films: *Night Train for Inverness* (aged 11); *Ali and the Camel* (serial, voice only); *Snowball; The Pirates of Blood River; Go Kart Go!; Up the Junction; The Smashing Bird I Used to Know; A Promise of Bed; I Can't... I Can't* (UK title *Wedding Night*); *My Lover, My Son; The Scars of Dracula; Fright; Man in the Wilderness; Alice's Adventures in Wonderland; The Belstone Fox; Fright; Sweeney!; Sweeney 2; A Dog's Day Out* (short); *Cold Justice; Father Jim.* **Records:** Singles: *I Could Be So Good for You* (No 3, 1980); *What Are We Gonna Get 'Er Indoors* (with George Cole (qv), No 21, 1983). Albums: *Down Wind with Angels; Waterman.* Address: c/o ICM. m. 1st Penny (dis), 2nd actress Patricia Maynard (dis), 3rd actress Rula Lenska (qv); 2 d. Hannah, Julia (both from 2nd m.).

Dennis Waterman

Jack Watson

WATSON, Jack

Jack Watson. Actor. b. London, 15 May 1921. Started career as stooge Hubert to his father, comedian Nosmo King, and worked in variety for 15 years before becoming a straight actor after a part in *Z Cars*.
TV: Bill Gregory in *Coronation Street; Z Cars; The Troubleshooters; Arthur of the Britons; Upstairs, Downstairs; The Hanged Man; The Charges; Sky; The Georgian House; The Onedin Line; Killers; Goodbye America; Warship; Rob Roy;* George in *Some Mothers Do 'Ave 'Em; Who Pays the Ferryman?; Treasure Island; All Creatures Great and Small; The Cost of Loving; Kidnapped; A Horseman Riding By; The Camerons; Square Mile of Murder; Masada* (TVM); *Juliet Bravo; Into the Labyrinth; Kings Royal; Journeys of Marco Polo; Heather Ann; The Talisman; Diana Magnox;* James Godbolt in *Edge of Darkness* (mini-series, 1985); *Agatha Christie's Miss Marple; Death Wish; New World; Little Sir Nicholas; Casualty;* Arthur Milne in *Love and Reason;* Hammer in *Minder;* Vernon in *Common as Muck.*
Films: *The Man Who Was Nobody; Peeping Tom; The Queen's Guards; Konga; Time to Remember; Fate Takes a Hand; Out of the Fog; This Sporting Life; Five to One; Master Spy; The Gorgon; The Hill; The Night Caller; The Idol; Grand Prix; Tobruk; The Strange Affair; The Devil's Brigade; Decline and Fall... of a Birdwatcher!; Midas Run; Every Home Should Have One; The Mackenzie Break; Kidnapped; Tower of Evil; From Beyond the Grave; The Four Musketeers: The Revenge of Milady; Juggernaut; 11 Harrowhouse; Brannigan; Treasure Island; The Wild Geese; Schizo; North Sea Hijack; The Sea Wolves; The Antagonists* (abridged version of TVM *Masada*). Address: c/o Sarah Crouch, 11 Southwick Mews, W2 1JG, tel 0171-436 4626. Livs in Bath. m. Betsy; 2 d. Penelope, Fiona, 1 s. Alastair.

Ken Watson

WATSON, Ken

Kenneth Watson. Actor/Writer. b. London. Trained at RADA.
TV: *Diamond Run; The Undoing; King and Country; The Barretts of Wimpole Street; The Brothers; Emergency — Ward 10;* Ralph Lancaster in *Coronation Street; Crown Court; Emmerdale Farm; Darwin;* Brian Blair in *Take the High Road; Roll on Four o'Clock; Losing Her; Too Close to the Edge; Singles; Airline;* Carter in *Wycliffe.* As writer or script editor: *From Inner Space; The Westerners; Fancy That; The Bill.*
Films: *Dr Who and the Daleks; Great White Hope; The Belstone Fox.* Address: c/o Silvester Management. m. TV make-up artist Joan Watson; 1 d. Kate, 1 s. Jamie. Hobbies: DIY, collecting books.

Moray Watson

WATSON, Moray

Moray Watson. Actor. b. Sunningdale, Berkshire, 25 June 1928. Trained at the Webber Douglas Academy. West End stage plays include *Small Hotel, Plaintiff in a Pretty Hat, A River Breeze, The Bad Soldier, Smith, The Grass Is Greener* (also in the film version), *The Doctor's Dilemma, You Never Can Tell, The Rivals, On Approval, Hay Fever, Two into One, Don't Just Lie There, Say Something, Married Love, Lettice and Lovage* and *Body and Soul.* Also on Broadway in *The Public Eye and the Private Ear.*
TV: Richard in *Compact; The Borderers; On Approval; Quiller; Upstairs, Downstairs; A Place in the Sun; The Pallisers; Murder Most English; Rumpole of the Bailey; Company and Co; Pride and Prejudice; Winston Churchill — The Wilderness Years; Doctor Who; Tales of the Unexpected; Nobody's Perfect; Union Castle; Yes Minister; Minder; Rude Health; Agatha Christie's Miss Marple: The Body in the Library; Star Cops; Flying Lady; Seal Morning; Campion; Norbert Smith — A Life; The House of Eliott;* Brigadier in *The Darling Buds of May; Don't Wait Up;* Sykes in *Stay Lucky;* Davincourt in *Berenice; Tales of Mystery and Imagination;* Brigadier John Harris in *Dangerfield;* Henry Huxley in *Crown Prosecutor; Medics.*
Films: *The Grass Is Greener; Every Home Should Have One; The Valiant; Operation Crossbow; The Sea Wolves; Crazy like a Fox.* Address: c/o Michael Whitehall. Lives in London. m. 1955 actress Pam Marmont; 1 d. Emma, 1 s. Robin. Pets: Golden retriever bitch called Dancer. Hobbies: Gardening.

Tom Watt

WATT, Tom

Thomas Erickson Watt. Actor. b. Wanstead, East London, 14 February 1956. Gained a BA (Hons) in drama from Manchester University. Stage plays include *The Foreigner, The Cherry Orchard* and *An Evening with Gary Lineker* (all West End).
TV: *The Old Firm;* Wally in *A Kind of Loving; My Father's House;* Duane in *Never the Twain; Family Man;* Lofty Holloway in *EastEnders; Night Network* (co-presenter); *South of the Border; The Last Laugh; And a Nightingale Sang; Boon; Arena* (presenter); *The Channel Four Daily* (presenter); Gordon in *Stuck on You* (Comedy Playhouse); *In the Club; Dads* (pilot); *Rookies.*
Films: *Patriot Games.* **Books:** *The End* (1993); *A Passion for the Game* (1995). Address: c/o ICM. Lives in London. m. Ann.

Ruby Wax

WAX, Ruby

Ruby Wax. Actress/Comedienne/Writer. b. Chicago, Illinois, USA, 19 April 1953. Trained at the Royal Scottish Academy of Music and Drama. Spent five years with the RSC.
TV: *Not the Nine o'Clock News* (writer only); *Girls on Top* (also as writer); *Don't Miss Wax; Miami Memoirs; East Meets Wax; Wax on Wheels.* (chat-show); *Miami Beach; The Full Wax* (four series); *AIDS Update '92* (presenter); *Wild Turkey* (The Comic Strip Presents...); *Wax after Birth* (Birthnight,

presenter); *Ruby's Hit and Run* (series); *Wax Cracks Hollywood; Mama's Back!* (writer only); *Wax Uncut* (uncut version of interview with Billy Crystal in *The Full Wax*); *Wax Meets Madonna;* Candy in *Absolutely Fabulous; Wax Cracks Cannes; Ruby's Health Quest* (series, 1995); *Ruby Wax Meets...* (series, 1996). Address: c/o Peters Fraser & Dunlop. Lives in Holland Park, West London. m. 3rd TV producer Ed Bye; 1 s. Max, 2 d. Madeleine, Marina.

WEBB, Danny

Danny Webb. Actor. Stage plays include *Carnival Wars* (Royal Court), *Serious Money* (Royal Court and Broadway), *Death and the Maiden* (Duke of York's) and *Dead Funny* (Vaudeville Theatre).

TV: *Twelfth Night; Jackanory Playhouse; The Racing Game; The Imitation Game; Mackenzie; We'll Meet Again; Passmore; The Other 'Arf; Star Struck; Whatever Happened to the Heroes?;* Gavin Taylor in *Brookside* (1982-3); *Video Stars; Tucker's Luck; More Lives than One; Do You Know the Milky Way?; Slip-Up; Intimate Contact; Bergerac; Tales of Sherwood Forest; Hard Cases; Capital City; Agatha Christie's Poirot; Boon; The Saint; Confusions of a Modern Man; Made in Heaven;* Bernie Weston in *The Jazz Detective* (series, 1992); *Clubland; The Young Indiana Jones Chronicles; Head Hunters;* Brian Duffield in *Comics* (mini-series, 1993); Ray in *A Woman's Guide to Adultery* (mini-series, 1993); Gerry McCarthy in *99-1* (two series, 1994-5); Roger Garrison in *Headhunters;* Mr Simon Betancourt in *Cardiac Arrest* (series, 1994); Steven Petit in *The Bill;* Mrs Hartley and the Growth Centre (Screen Two); *A Touch of Frost; Our Friends in the North; Mrs Hartley and the Growth Centre; Murder Most Horrid.*

Films: *No Exit; The Unapproachable; The Year of the Quiet Sun; Billy the Kid and the Green Baize Vampire; Defence of the Realm; Henry V;* Much the Miller in *Robin Hood; Alien³.* Address: c/o ICM.

Danny Webb

WEBSTER, Gary

Gary Webster. Actor. b. Whitechapel, East London, 3 February 1964. Former member of the National Youth Theatre Worked as stage-door keeper and odd-job man at the Shaw Theatre, London, before training at LAMDA.

TV: *The Bill;* Colin in *Inspector Morse: The Dead of Jericho; London's Burning;* Graham in *EastEnders;* Paul in *Boon;* DS Tilling in *Taggart: Evil Eye; Life after Life;* Ray Daley in *Minder.*

Films: Paul's Man in *Empire State;* Anthony in *Out of Order.* Address: c/o Hope & Lyne. Single.

Gary Webster

WELLAND, Colin

Colin Williams. Actor/Writer. b. Leigh, Lancashire, 4 July 1934. Worked as an art teacher before joining the Library Theatre, Manchester.

TV: As presenter: *North at Six.* As actor: *The Verdict Is Yours;* PC Graham in *Z Cars* (1964-7); *United Kingdom; Man at the Top; Left; Passage to England; The Cost of Loving; Blue Remembered Hills; Jack Point; Cowboys; How to Stay Alive* (presenter). As writer-actor: *Banglestein's Boys; Slattery's Mounted Foot; Say Goodnight to Grandma; Roll on Four o'Clock;* Harty in *Femme Fatale* (Screen Two). As writer: *Catherine Wheel; The Hallelujah Handshake; A Room Full of Holes; Leeds United; Kisses at Fifty; The Wild West Show; Your Man from Six Counties.*

Films: *Kes; Villain; The Straw Dogs; Sweeney!;* Bransky's Manager in *Dancin' thru the Dark.* As writer: *Yanks; Chariots of Fire; Chaplin; The Yellow Jersey; Twice in a Lifetime; A Dry White Season.*

Awards: Best Original Screenplay Oscar for *Chariots of Fire.* Address: c/o Peter Charlesworth. m. former teacher Pat; 3 d. Genevieve, Catherine, Caroline, 1 s. Christie.

Colin Welland

WELLING, Albert

Albert Welling. Actor. b. London, 29 February 1952. Gained a BA (Hons) in drama from Manchester University. Stage plays include *Made It Ma* (Royal Court) and *Thursday's Ladies* (as Victor, West End).

TV: *Telford's Change; Sergeant Cribb; Rumpole's Return; A Voyage round My Father; Crown Court; Auf Wiedersehen Pet; Out of Step; The Consultant; The Clarion Van; The Gathering Seed; Shine on Harvey Moon; Paradise Postponed; Lovejoy; EastEnders; Howards' Way; Tales of the Unexpected; Bulman; Wish Me Luck; Inspector Morse; Boon; Casualty; Titmuss Regained; Stay Lucky; Sam Saturday; Moon and Son; The Bill* (two roles); *A Touch of Frost: Nothing to Hide;* Chief Supt Richards in *Pie in the Sky; The Day Today; Between the Lines; Moving Story; Kavanagh QC; Drop the Dead Donkey; The Biz!; BUGS.*

Films: *Backbeat.* Address: c/o Barry Brown & Partner. Lives in Bedford. m. 1982 actress Judy Riley; 2 s. Benedict, Kaspar. Pets: A black labrador called Ella, a cat called Tabby. Hobbies: Reading, travel.

Albert Welling

WENBAN, Amanda

Amanda R Wenban. Actress. b. Sydney, Australia, 24 May 1955. Attended the Royal Ballet School; danced with the London Festival Ballet (1974-84). Trained at the Central School of Speech and Drama.

TV: *A Bit of a Do* (second series); *Families* (1991-3); *The Piglet Files;* Angharad McAllister in *Emmerdale* (1993-5); *Home and Away; Echo Point; Revelations.* TV commercials: Gold Blend coffee.

Films: *The Fool; Nijinsky.* Address: c/o The Narrow Road Company. Lives in Australia. m. actor Michael Duggan; 1 d. Bridget.

Amanda Wenban

Timothy West

Danniella Westbrook

Karen Westwood

Kevin Whately

John Wheatley

WEST, Timothy

Timothy Lancaster West. Actor. b. Bradford, West Yorkshire, 20 October 1934. CBE, 1984. Hon D Litt. Son of actor Lockwood West. Became an ASM at Wimbledon Theatre (1956), then a professional actor.
TV: *Randall & Hopkirk (Deceased); Big Breadwinner Hog;* Bolingbroke in *Richard II;* Mortimer in *Edward II; The Boswell and Johnson Show; Joy; Hine;* Horatio Bottomley in *The Edwardians;* title role in *Edward the Seventh; Villains; The After Dinner Game; Cottage to Let;* Bounderby in *Hard Times;* Wolsey in *Henry VIII; Crime and Punishment;* title role in *Churchill and the Generals* (TVM); *Tales of the Unexpected;* Emperor Vespasian in *Masada* (TVM); *Murder Is Easy* (TVM); *Oliver Twist* (TVM); Bradley Hardacre in *Brass* (two series, 1983, 1990); Winston Churchill in *The Last Bastion* (TVM); *The Nightingale Saga* (TVM); *Tender Is the Night* (TVM); *Agatha Christie's Miss Marple: A Pocketful of Rye; The Monocled Mutineer; A Very Peculiar Practice;* title role in *The Good Doctor Bodkin Adams; A Roller Next Year; What the Butler Saw;* Harry King in *Harry's Kingdom; The Sealed Train; When We Are Married; The Garden of Evelyn;* Gorbachev in *Breakthrough at Reykjavik; Strife; A Shadow on the Sun; The Contractor; Campion; After Henry;* Derek Blore in *Blore, MP; Kennet and Avon* (presenter); Thomas Beecham in *Beecham; Survival of the Fittest; Why Lockerbie?;* DCI Jimmy McKinnes in *Framed* (miniseries); *Hiroshima;* Lord Reith in *Without Walls: Reith to the Nation* (drama-doc); *Smokescreen; Muder Most Horrid II; Eleven Men against Eleven; Cuts; The Place of the Dead; Over Here* (narrator).
Films: *Twisted Nerve; The Looking Glass War; Nicholas and Alexandra; Hitler: The Last Ten Days; The Day of the Jackal; Soft Beds and Hard Battles; Hedda; Operation Daybreak; Joseph Andrews; The Devil's Advocate; Agatha; News From Nowhere; The Thirty-Nine Steps; Rough Cut; The Antagonists* (abridged version of TVM *Masada*); *Oliver Twist;* Capt de Wit in *Cry Freedom; Consuming Passions.*
Awards: TV: *TVTimes* Best Actor on TV award (1975); RTS Best Actor on TV award (1979). Address: c/o James Sharkey Associates. m. 1st Jacqueline Boyer (dis), 2nd 1963 actress Prunella Scales (qv); 1 d. Juliet Miranda (from 1st m.), 2 s. actor Samuel Alexander, Joseph John Lancaster (both from 2nd m.). Pets: A cat called Coleman, four goldfish. Hobbies: Boating, travel, listening to music.

WESTBROOK, Danniella

Danniella Westbrook. Actress. b. 5 November 1973. Trained at the Sylvia Young Theatre School. Stage productions include *Joseph and the Amazing Technicolor Dreamcoat* (Royalty Theatre).
TV: *To Have and to Hold; Grange Hill; Bad Boyes; Alfonso Bonzo; Agatha Christie's Miss Marple; The London Programme;* Sam Mitchell/Butcher in *EastEnders;* Dawn in *Frank Stubbs Promotes* (series, 1993) and *Frank Stubbs* (series, 1994). Address: c/o Sylvia Young Management.

WESTWOOD, Karen

Karen Smith. Actress. b. Dumfries, 26 November 1964. Trained at Mountview Theatre School.
TV: *You Rang, M'Lord?; Taggart; The Ruth Rendell Mysteries: An Unkindness of Ravens; Lovejoy; The Good Guys;* Rebecca Bannerman in *Families* (two series); *The Inspector Alleyn Mysteries: Dead Water; The Bill; The Tales of Para Handy;* Jane Browning in *Annie's Bar;* Amber Martin in *The Sculptress.*
Films: Fanny Godwin in *Rowing with the Wind;* Rosaline in *The New Look;* Emma in *Isabella Knightley.* Address: c/o Elaine Murphy Associates. Lives in North London. m. (dis). Pets: A miniature schnauzer called Louis. Hobbies: Avid reader, gardening.

WHATELY, Kevin

Kevin Whately. Actor. b. Tyneside, 6 February 1951. Trained at Central School of Speech and Drama.
TV: *Coronation Street; The Dig;* Neville in *Auf Wiedersehen Pet;* Sgt Fletcher in *Agatha Christie's Miss Marple: A Murder Is Announced;* Det Sgt Lewis in *Inspector Morse* (series, 1987-92); *Night Voice* (ScreenPlay); Steve in *B&B; The Mystery of Morse* (documentary); Dr Jack Kerruish in *Peak Practice* (three series, 1993-5); *Jackanory* (storyteller); *Inspector Morse: The Way Through the Woods* (1995); Ian Armstrong in *Trip Trap* (Screen One).
Films: *The English Patient;* Hopkins in *Skallagrigg.*
Address: c/o CDA. m. actress Madelaine Newton (qv); 1 d. Catherine, 1 s. Kieran.

WHEATLEY, John

Martyn John Wheatley. Actor. b. Leeds.
TV: *Maybury; Nanny; Attachments; The Thirteenth Day of Christmas; A Very Peculiar Practice; Vote for Them; Shackleton;* Julian McKenzie in *Game, Set & Match; The Light That Shines;* Martin Hopkins in *Fallen Hero; Kiss of Death;* Joe Broughton in *Coronation Street;* Bob in *Do the Right Thing;* Peter Temple in *Crown Prosecutor; The Bill* (two roles); Jack Edwards in *Casualty;* Dale in *Kavanagh QC; BUGS.*
Address: c/o Barry Brown & Partner. London. Single. Pets: Two cats.

WHICKER, Alan

Alan Donald Whicker. TV broadcaster/Writer. b. Cairo, Egypt, 2 August 1925. Director with Army Film and Photo Section, then a war correspondent in Korea, foreign correspondent, novelist, writer and radio

broadcaster before switching to television (BBC 1957-68, ITV 1968-82, BBC 1982-92, ITV 1992-).
TV: *Tonight* (reporter, 1957-64); *Whicker's World* (1959-); *Whicker Down Under; Whicker on Top of the World!; Whicker in Sweden; Whicker in the Heart of Texas; Whicker down Mexico Way; The Alan Whicker Report; The Solitary Billionaire; Whicker's New World; Whicker in Europe; Whicker's Walkabout; Broken Hill — Walled City; Gairy's Grenada; World of Whicker; Whicker's Orient; Whicker within a Woman's World; Whicker's South Seas; Whicker Way Out West; Whicker's World — Down Under;* Peter Sellers memorial programme; *Whicker's World Aboard the Orient Express; Around Whicker's World in 25 Years* (1982); *Whicker's World: The First Million Miles* (1982); *Whicker's World: A Fast Boat to China; Whicker!* (series of talk shows); *Whicker's World: Living with Uncle Sam; Whicker's World Down Under: Living with Waltzing Matilda; Whicker's World: Hong Kong; Whicker Way Out West; Whicker's World: Spain; Around Whicker's World: The Ultimate Package; Whicker's World: The Absolute Monarch; Whicker's Miss World; Whicker's World: The Sun King; South-East Asia: Whicker's World Aboard the Real Oriental Express; Whicker — The Mahathir Interview; Whicker's World: Pavarotti in Paradise.*

Alan Whicker

Films: *The Angry Silence.* **Books:** *Away — with Alan Whicker; Within Whicker's World; Whicker's New World; Whicker's World Down Under.* **Awards:** BAFTA Richard Dimbleby Award (1978). Address: Le Gallais Chambers, St Helier, Jersey. Partner: Valerie Kleeman.

WHITBY, Martyn
Martyn Whitby. Actor. b. Nottingham. Trained at the Guildhall School of Music and Drama.
TV: *The District Nurse; Shine on Harvey Moon;* Policeman in *Magnum PI;* Mal Evans in *John and Yoko; Dempsey and Makepeace; Bust;* David Hughes in *Emmerdale Farm;* Mr Hebdon in *The World of Eddie Weary;* Roger in *Jobs for the Boys, Harry Enfield's Television Programme;* Davey in *Soldier Soldier; The Bill* (four roles); Desk Sergeant in *EastEnders; This Boy's Story* (TVM); *Van Der Valk; Sam Saturday;* Custody Sergeant in *Love Hurts; Zig Zag: Roman Britain; Casualty; White Goods; Goodnight Sweetheart; In the Cold Light of Day* (Screen Two); DI Franks in *Harry, Minder;* Insp Phillips in *Wycliffe.*

Martyn Whitby

Films: Mikhail in *Sakharov; Success Is the Best Revenge.* Address: c/o Walmsley Horne Associates.

WHITE, Frances
Frances Victoria Christine White. Actress. b. near Leeds, 1 November 1938. Daughter of film production designer Frank White. Trained at the Central School of Speech and Drama.
TV: *The Victorian Chaise Longue; Blue and White* (Armchair Theatre); title role in *Omnibus: Dusky Ruth; Lord Raingo;* Andrea Warner in *Raging Calm* (series); *Summer and Winter; Justice; The Secret Agent; The Stick Insect;* Christine Jarvis in *Hunter's Walk;* Linda Clark in *A Little Bit of Wisdom* (series); *They Don't Make Summers...; The New Men; Hero with a Past;* Julia in *I Claudius;* Queen Charlotte in *Prince Regent; Wednesday's Child* (documentary); Kate Hamilton in *Crossroads; Frances and Richard; Looking for Vicky; Nobody's Perfect; Rumpole of the Bailey; I Woke Up One Morning* (two series); *Paradise Postponed;* Dorothy in *A Very Peculiar Practice* (two series); *A Perfect Spy; Chelworth;* Miss Vera Flood/Mrs Vera Tipple in *May to December* (six series, 1989-94); *Cluedo; Casualty; Harry's Mad.*

Frances White

Films: Dinah in *The Pumpkin Eater;* Liz Bartlett in *Press for Time;* Mary Fleming in *Mary Queen of Scots.* Address: c/o Langford Associates. m. Anthony Hone (dis); 1 d. university lecturer Kate. Pets: A cat called Clio. Hobbies: Gardening, reading, listening to music.

WHITE, Julianne
Julianne White. Actress. b. Sydney, Australia. Stage shows include *Tommy Steele Show* (singer-dancer), *Danny La Rue Show* (singer-dancer) and *The Best Little Whorehouse in Texas* (Theatre Royal, Drury Lane).
TV: In Australia: Diana Field in *Prime Time* (six months); Number 36 in *Zero Zero* (Mike Batt video musical); *A Country Practice;* Stacey Daniels in *Waterloo Station* (six months); Diana Trent in *The Young Doctors.* In UK: *The Young Ones; Minder;* Donna Nightingale in *The New Statesman;* Jasper Carrot show; *Little and Large;* lawyer Sarah Townes in *Brookside* (1989); Dame Edna Everage Christmas special; *Shelley; Tropical Heat; Pirates;* Raelene Adams in *Backup.*

Julianne White

Address: c/o Scott Marshall. Lives in London. m. musician Mike Batt; 1 s. Luke.

WHITE, Sheila
Sheila White. Actress/Singer/Dancer. b. Highgate, North London, 18 October 1950. Started career with Terry's Juveniles at the age of 12, before training at the Corona Stage Academy. West End productions include *The Sound of Music, Dames at Sea, The Biograph Girl* and *Little Me.*
TV: *Alice in Wonderland; Z Cars; Emergency — Ward 10; Oranges and Lemons; Dear Mother... Love Albert; Poldark; Love School; The Songwriters;* Messalina in *I Claudius; Ladies of Ridgemead; The Pickwick Papers; Tiptoes; Jazz Age; Don't Rock the Boat* (series); *Gone to Seed; Framed; The Bill; Casualty.*

Sheila White

Films: *Here We Go round the Mulberry Bush; Ghost Goes Gear; Stranger in the House; Oliver!; Confessions of a Window Cleaner; Confessions of a Pop Star; Confessions of a Driving Instructor; Mrs Brown You've Got a Lovely Daughter; The Spaceman and King Arthur; The Silver Dream Racer; Biograph Girl; They're Playing Our Song.* Address: c/o Barry Burnett Organisation. m. Richard Mills.

WHITEHEAD, Amanda

Amanda Whitehead. Actress. b. Oldham, Lancashire, 12 March 1965. Attended Oldham Theatre Workshop and trained at the Royal Scottish Academy of Music and Drama.
TV: Extra in *Tutti Frutti;* Emma Aitken in *Take the High Road* (1989-94); Sandra in *Out of the Blue*.
Address: c/o Harbour & Coffey. Lives in Oldham, Lancashire. Single. Pets: Two black dogs called Harry and Sammy. Hobbies: 'Travelling (have been to Africa, India, Nepal, Thailand, Australia, New Zealand, Borneo and Malaysia, Fiji, America and Canada, courtesy of *High Road*), sign language, walking.'

Amanda Whitehead

WHITEHEAD, Geoffrey

Geoffrey Whitehead. Actor. b. Sheffield, South Yorkshire, 1 October 1939. Trained at RADA.
TV: *The Bulldog Breed; Z Cars; The Avengers; Jane Eyre; The Sweeney; Some Mothers Do 'Ave 'Em; Affairs of the Heart; Upstairs, Downstairs; Crown Court; Hadleigh; Last of the Best Men; Robin's Nest; The Foundation;* title role in *The Rivals of Sherlock Holmes; Inside the Third Reich; The Kit Curran Radio Show; Who Dares Wins; Reilly — Ace of Spies; The Cleopatras; The Consultant; Alas Smith and Jones; Pinkerton's Progress; The Doll; Chelmsford 123; Scarecrow & Mrs King; Peter the Great; The Fourth Floor; War and Remembrance; A Strike out of Time* (TVM); *The Strauss Dynasty; Executive Stress;* Richard in *Second Thoughts* (series); *The House of Eliott; Between the Lines; Just a Gigolo; A Very Open Prison* (Screen Two); *Twelve Angry Men, Impasse* and *The Lift* (all Paul Merton in Galton & Simpson's...).
Films: *The Rocking Horse Winner*.
Address: c/o Bryan Drew. m. actress Mary Hanefey; 1 d. Clare, 1 s. Jonty.

Geoffrey Whitehead

WHITELAW, Billie

Billie Honor Whitelaw. Actress. b. Coventry, Warwickshire, 6 June 1932. CBE, 1991. Began her career in children's radio serials. Stage plays include *Othello, Hobson's Choice, Tales of Hollywood* (all National Theatre), *After Haggerty, The Greeks* and *Passion Play* (all RSC).
TV: *Lena, O My Lena* (Armchair Theatre, 1960); *No Trams to Lime Street; The Fifty Pound Note; Beyond the Horizon; Resurrection; The Poet Game; You and Me; The Strange Case of Dr Jekyll and Mr Hyde* (TVM); *Anna Christie; Wessex Tales; Beckett; Ghost Trio; Not I; Happy Days; Jamaica Inn; Committee; Private Schultz; The Secret Garden; The Picnic; Imaginary Friends; A Tale of Two Cities* (TVM); *Camille* (TVM); *The Secret Garden* (TVM); *The Fifteen Streets; John Le Carré's A Murder of Quality* (TVM); *Lorna Doone; Joyriders; The Cloning of Joanna May* (mini-series); Rose Gutteridge in *Firm Friends* (two series); Phoebe Rice in *The Entertainer* (Performance); *Rory Bremner, Apparently*.
Films: *The Fake; Companions in Crime; The Sleeping Tiger; Room in the House; Small Hotel; Miracle in Soho; Gideon's Day; Carve Her Name with Pride; Bobbikins; The Flesh and the Fiends; Hell Is a City; Make Mine Mink; No Love for Johnnie; Mr Topaz; Payroll; The Devil's Agent; The Comedy Man; Becket; Charlie Bubbles; Twisted Nerve; The Adding Machine; Start the Revolution without Me; Leo the Last; Eagle in a Cage; Gumshoe; Frenzy; Night Watch; The Omen; Leopard in the Snow; The Water Babies; An Unsuitable Job for a Woman; The Dark Crystal* (voice); *Tangier; Slayground; The Chain; Shadey; Murder Elite; Maurice; The Dressmaker; Joyriders; The Krays; Freddie as F.R.O.7* (voice only); *Deadly Advice*.
Awards: TV: TV Actress of the Year (1960); Best TV Actress (1972). Films: BFA Best Film Actress award for *Charlie Bubbles* (1968) and *Sextet* (1972). Radio: Best Radio Actress (1987).
Address: c/o ICM. Lives in London and Suffolk. m. 1st 1952 actor Peter Vaughan (dis 1965), 2nd writer Robert Muller; 1 s. opera company stage manager Matthew Norreys (b. 1967).

Billie Whitelaw

WHITELEY, Arkie

Arkie Whiteley. Actress. Trained at the Central School of Speech and Drama (1985-8).
TV: Donna Mason in *Prisoner* (UK title *Prisoner: Cell Block H*); *A Town like Alice; Slippery Slide; A Family Man* (all in Australia); *Drowning in the Shallow End* (Screen Two); *People like Us but Beautiful* (4-Play); *The Secret Life of Ian Fleming* (TVM); *Perfect Scoundrels; Van Der Valk; Love Hurts;* Jo Scott in *Natural Lies* (mini-series); *Bullets;* Nina in *Gallowglass* (mini-series); Helen Ames in *Kavanagh QC*.
Films: *Killing of Angel Street;* Lusty Girl in *Mad Max 2; Razorback; Scandal;* Betty in *Princess Caraboo*. **Awards:** TV: Australian Film & TV Best Supporting Actress award for *A Town like Alice*.
Address: c/o Jonathan Altaras Associates.

Arkie Whiteley

WHITFIELD, June

June Rosemary Whitfield. Actress. b. London, 11 November 1927. OBE, 1985. Trained at RADA.
TV: *Beggar My Neighbour; The Best Things in Life; Hancock's Half Hour; Scott on...;* June in *Happy Ever After* (five series) and *Terry and June* (ten series) (1974-87); *It Doesn't Have to Hurt* (presenter); *Terry and Julian;* Edina's mother in *Absolutely Fabulous* (three series).
Films: *Carry On Abroad; Carry On Girls; Bless This House; The Spy with the Cold Nose;* Janet Rimmington in *Not Now, Comrade; Carry On Columbus*.
Radio: *Take It from Here;* Eth in *The Glums; The News Huddlines*. Address: c/o April Young. Lives in London. m. Tim Aitchison; 1 d. actress Suzy Aitchison (qv). Pets: A dog named Rabbit.

June Whitfield

WHITROW, Benjamin
Benjamin Whitrow. Actor. b. Oxford, 17 February 1937.
TV: *The Brontës of Haworth; Fathers and Families; The Merchant of Venice; The Kidnapping of James Cross; Abel's Will; Tales of the Unexpected; By George; Franklin and Jessica; King Lear; All for Love; A Moment in Time; Nanny; Minor Complications; Suez; Minutes and Men; On Approval; The Factory; Harry's Game; Hay Fever; Paying Guests; Bergerac; A Bit of Fry and Laurie; Ffizz; Chancer;* Paddy O'Rourke in *The New Statesman;* A Diplomat in Japan (drama-documentary); Dr Laurence Reeve in *Peak Practice;* Mr Mallet in *Moving Story; The Bill;* Mr Bennet in *Pride and Prejudice* (serial, 1995).
Films: *A Man for all Seasons; Quadrophenia; Brimstone and Treacle; A Shocking Accident; Clockwise; Personal Services; On the Black Hill; Hawks.* Address: c/o Lou Coulson.

Benjamin Whitrow

WHITTAKER, Sally
Sally Whittaker. Actress. b. Middleton, Lancashire, 3 May 1963. Trained at Oldham Theatre Workshop and the Mountview Theatre School. Appeared as a dancer in *The Metal Mickey Road Show*, then toured Britain and America with the Abbadaba Theatre Company, including old-time music-hall, and appeared in the pantomime *Beauty and the Beast* (Oldham Coliseum). Subsequent stage plays include *A Taste of Honey* (Octagon Theatre, Bolton).
TV: Wendy in *Juliet Bravo; The Practice; Hold Tight!;* Sally Webster (née Seddon) in *Coronation Street* (1986-); *Royal Variety Performance* (with *Coronation Street* cast, 1989). Address: c/o Barry Brown & Partner/Granada Television. Lives in Bowdon, Cheshire, and North London. m. TV scriptwriter Tim Dynevor; 1 d. Phoebe (b. April 1995). Hobbies: Horse-riding, keep-fit, walking.

Sally Whittaker

WILBY, James
James Wilby. Actor. b. Rangoon, Burma, 20 February 1958. Attended public school in Britain before graduating from Durham University and training at RADA. Stage plays include *Another Country*.
TV: *The Adventures of Sherlock Holmes; The Crooked Man; The Bill; Dutch Girls; The Storyteller: Sapsorrow;* Sydney Carton in *A Tale of Two Cities* (TVM); *Mother Love; Adam Bede;* Charlie in *You Me and It* (mini-series, 1993); Sir Clifford Chatterley in *Lady Chatterley* (series, 1993); Ade Lynn in *Crocodile Shoes* (series, 1994).
Films: *Privileged; DreamChild; A Room with a View; Maurice; A Handful of Dust; A Summer Story; Howards End; Conspiracy; Immaculate Conception.*
Address: c/o ICM. Lives in London. m. Shana; 1 s. Barnaby.

James Wilby

WILCOX, Paula
Paula Wilcox. Actress. b. Manchester, 13 December 1949. While acting with the National Youth Theatre, was asked to star in *The Lovers* TV series. Stage plays include *Bedroom Farce* (Prince of Wales Theatre), Eliza Doolittle in *Pygmalion* (Shaw Theatre), *Hedda Gabler* (as Thea Elvsted, Cambridge Theatre), *Shirley Valentine* (title role, Duke of York's) and *The Queen & I* (as the Queen, Vaudeville Theatre).
TV: *The Dustbinmen; On the House* (series, 1970); Beryl in *The Lovers* (two series, 1970-1); Janice Langton in *Coronation Street; Kate; Hadleigh; The Liver Birds; On Her Majesty's Pleasure;* Chrissy in *Man about the House* (three series, 1973-4); Elizabeth Jones in *Miss Jones and Son* (two series, 1977-8); *The Cost of Loving; Remember the Lambeth Walk?; Noel Gay;* Cynthia Bright in *The Bright Side* (series, 1985); *Boon;* Angela Heery in *Brookside;* Ros Fiddler in *Fiddlers Three* (series, 1991); *Crazy Comparisons* (team captain); Rosalind Paynter in *Casualty;* Sara Bean in *Smokescreen* (series, 1994); Ivy in *Blue Heaven* (series, 1994); *Present Spirits; The Queen's Nose.*
Films: *The Lovers; Man about the House; The Higher Mortals.*
Address: c/o William Morris Agency (UK). m. 1st actor-director Derek Seaton (dec 1979), 2nd 1991 businessman Nelson Riddle Jr. Hobbies: Swimming, fashion, football, reading.

Paula Wilcox

WILLCOX, Toyah
Toyah Willcox. Actress/Presenter/Singer/Writer/Producer. b. Birmingham. Trained as an actress at the Old Rep Drama School, Birmingham. After being cast in director Derek Jarman's film *Jubilee*, formed her own rock band and performed as Toyah. Found success as both an actress and singer. Stage plays include *Cabaret* (as Sally Bowles, West End), *Three Men and a Horse* (National Theatre, West End), *Peter Pan* (national tour) and *A Midsummer Night's Dream* (as Puck, Open Air Theatre, Regent's Park).
TV: *Dr Jekyll and Mr Hyde; Old Grey Whistle Test Christmas Special* (1981 New Year's Eve concert from the Theatre Royal, Drury Lane); *The Ebony Tower; Anything Goes* (presenter, Meridian only); *Time Off* (presenter, Meridian only); *Magic and Mystery Show* (presenter, Anglia Television only); Gigi in *Maigret; The Ink Thief* (children's series, 1994); *Brum* (narrator, children's series, 1994); *Tomorrow Calling* (Short and Curlies); Deborah Drake in *Kavanagh QC; Discovering Eve* (presenter, series, 1995).
Films: Mad in *Jubilee;* Monkey in *Quadrophenia;* Miranda in *The Tempest; American Days; Thérèse Raquin.* Address: c/o The Roseman Organisation. m. Robert Fripp. Pets: A white rabbit called Beaton. Hobbies: Roller-blading, para-gliding.

Toyah Willcox

Michael Williams

WILLIAMS, Michael

Michael Williams. Actor. b. Manchester, 9 July 1935. Trained at RADA. Stage plays include *Celebration* (Duchess Theatre), *Two into One* (Theatre of Comedy), *The Comedy of Errors*, *The Taming of the Shrew*, *The Merchant of Venice*, *As You Like It*, *Troilus and Cressida*, *London Assurance*, *The Winter's Tale* and *King Lear* (all RSC), *Twists* (revue, Arts Theatre), *Mr and Mrs Nobody* and *Pack of Lies*.
TV: *Elizabeth R; Shadow on the Sun; A Raging Calm; The Hanged Man; The Comedy of Errors; My Son, My Son; Love in a Cold Climate; Ice Age; Turtle's Progress; Quest of Eagles;* Mike in *A Fine Romance* (three series, 1980-82); *Amnesty; Shakespeare Master Class; Behaving Badly; Blunt;* N V Standish in *Double First; Angel Voices; Happy Christmas, I Love You; A Hell of a Road;* Billy Balsana in *September Song* (three series, 1993-5); Barry Masefield in *Conjugal Rites* (two series, 1993-4); DCI Knowland in *Kavanagh QC.*
Films: *Marat/Sade; Eagle in a Cage; Dead Cert; Alexander the Great; Enigma; Educating Rita; Henry V.* Address: c/o Julian Belfrage Associates. m. actress Judi Dench (qv); 1 d. actress Finty Williams.

WILLIAMS, Natasha

Natasha Williams

Roselyn Agatha Williams. Actress. b. Trelawny, Jamaica, 18 July 1961. Trained at the Webber Douglas Academy. Stage plays include *Ambulance, Royal Borough* (both Royal Court).
TV: *The Roughest Way; Three Kinds of Heat; Out of Order; Brookside; Fighting Back; South of the Border; The Ruth Rendell Mysteries: No Crying He Makes; London's Burning;* WPC Delia French in *The Bill.*
Films: *Nuns on the Run; A Connecticut Yankee in King Arthur's Court.*
Address: Barry Brown & Partner. Lives in Brixton, South London. Single. Hobbies: Gardening.

WILLIAMS, Simon

Simon Williams. b. Windsor, Berkshire, 16 June 1946.
TV: *The Regiment;* Captain James Bellamy in *Upstairs, Downstairs; Up School; Man in a Suitcase; Squash; Floreat Nilho; Romance; Wodehouse Playhouse; Mr Big; Liza; Agony; Company and Co; Strangers; The Return of the Man from U.N.C.L.E.; Kinvig; Artists in Crime; The Mixer; Crazy Comparisons* (team captain); Dr Charles Cartwright in *Don't Wait Up* (six series, 1983-90); Insp Roderick Alleyn in *The Inspector Alleyn Mysteries* (pilot); Geoffrey in *The Upper Hand;* Lord St Simon in *Sherlock Holmes: The Eligible Bachelor,* Ken Hawkes in *Demob;* Gerald Triggs in *Law and Disorder* (series, 1994); Laurence in *Agony Again* (series, 1995).
Films: *Katcho; Blue Haze; Breaking of Bumbo; Pace Good-bye; Joanna; The Touchables; Demon's Delight; The Incredible Sarah; Jabberwocky; No Longer Alone;* Michael in *The Uncanny;* Tony in *The Odd Job; The Prisoner of Zenda; The Fiendish Plot of Dr Fu Manchu.* **Books:** *Kill the Lights* (novel).
Address: c/o Jonathan Altaras Associates. Lives in Oxfordshire. m. 1st actress Belinda Carroll, 2nd Lucy Fleming; 1 s. Tamlyn, 1 d. Amy.

Simon Williams

WILMOT, Gary

Gary Owen Wilmot. Actor. b. Kennington, London, 8 May 1954. Son of Harold Wilmot, lead singer with Fifties group The Southlanders. Formed double act Gary Wilmot and Judy in 1976, touring theatres and clubs, and making TV début on *New Faces* (won three times). Went solo in 1979. West End stage productions include *Me and My Girl, Carmen Jones* and *Copacabana.*
TV: *New Faces; Royal Variety Performance; Children's Royal Variety Performance; Royal Night of 100 Stars; Saturday Gang; Cue Gary; This Is Your Life* (subject); *Showstoppers* (presenter, one-off and series, 1995); *Call Up the Stars* (VE Day concert, 1995).
Awards: Variety Club Silver Heart Award for Most Promising Artiste (1986). Address: c/o Dee O'Reilly Management. Lives in London. m. Carol Clark (sep); 2 d. Katie, Georgia. Hobbies: Sport, DIY.

Gary Wilmot

WILSHERE, Barbara

Barbara Edith Eileen Wilshere. Actress. b. South Africa, 7 December 1959. Moved to UK at the age of five and was brought up near Manchester. Trained at the Bristol Old Vic Theatre School. London stage plays include *The Deep Blue Sea* (as Ann Welch, Haymarket Theatre), *Heaven* and *Flarepath.*
TV: *Tripods; A Woman of Substance* (mini-series); Jane Gladwyn in *Moving* (series, 1985); *The Adventures of Sherlock Holmes: The Solitary Cyclist;* Carol Broadbent in *Albion Market* (serial, 1985-6); Paula in *Deadhead; Ending Up; The Paradise Club* (series); *The Bill* (two roles); *Gone to Seed; Casualty; Michael Winner's True Crimes;* Kate Roberts in *Between the Lines* (two series, 1993-4); *Pie in the Sky; Do the Right Thing.* Address: c/o Scott Marshall. Lives in Chiswick, West London. m. Paul Ridley; 2 s. Jack, Hugo. Pets: A cat called Totty. Hobbies: Cooking, Badminton.

WILSON, Francis

Barbara Wilshere

Francis Wilson. Weather presenter. b. Irvine, Ayrshire, 27 February 1949. Gained BSc from Imperial College, London University, then trained at RAF Farnborough with the Met Research Flight for three

years. Entered TV with Thames Television, before moving to the BBC, then Sky.
TV: *Thames at Six* (Thames Television); *Thames News* (Thames Television); *Breakfast Time; BBC Breakfast News; QED; The Parent Programme; Sporting Chance; Sky News* (BSkyB).
Books: *Spotter's Guide to Weather; Guide to Weather Forecasting; Weather Pop-Up Book; Great British Obsession.*
Address: c/o Sky TV. m. Eva; 2 s. Joshua, James. Pets: A bloodhound dog and cats. Hobbies: Spain.

Francis Wilson

WILSON, Jennifer
Jennifer Wenda Lohr. Actress. b. London, 25 April 1935. Originally intended to be a dress designer and trained in art at Sibford School, South East Technical College, but switched to acting when she won a scholarship to RADA. West End plays include *Lend Me Five Shillings* (Vaudeville), *Peter Pan* (Coliseum) and *Spring and Port Wine* (Apollo).
TV: *Romeo and Juliet* (US); Kate Nickleby in *Nicholas Nickleby* (serial, 1957); *You Never Can Tell; Antigone; A Doll's House;* title role in *The Widowing of Mrs Holroyd;* Kay in *Time and the Conways; Collect Your Handbaggage; The Second Mrs Tanqueray; This Happy Breed; Hobson's Choice; Dixon of Dock Green; Z Cars; Softly Softly; No Hiding Place; A Man of Our Times;* Jenny Hammond (née Jennifer Kingsley) in *The Brothers* (series, 1970-7); *The Befrienders; Cavalcade; You and Me.*
Films: Mrs Pooley in *Private Pooley; Sammy Going South; The Yellow Rolls Royce.* Address: c/o PBR Management. Lives in London and south-west France. m. 1st artist Stanley Swain (dis), 2nd 1959 actor Brian Peck; 1 d. actress-singer Melanie Peck (from 1st m.). Pets: A dog called Ki-Ki and two cats called Muppe and Compo. Hobbies: Cooking, collecting paintings and antiques, travel.

Jennifer Wilson

WILSON, Richard
Iain Colquhoun Wilson. Actor/Director. b. Greenock, Renfrewshire, 9 July 1936. OBE, 1994. Worked as a research scientist before training at RADA.
TV: *Dr Finlay's Casebook; The Revenue Men; My Good Woman; Crown Court; Big Boy Now; Cilla's World of Comedy; Pickersgill People;* Jeremy Parsons in *A Sharp Intake of Breath* (two series); *Through the Night; Some Mothers Do 'Ave 'Em; In Loving Memory; Chalk and Cheese;* Dr Gordon Thorpe in *Only When I Laugh* (three series, 1979-81); *Virginia Fly Is Drowning; Victorian Scandals; The Sweeney; Poppyland; The Adventures of Sherlock Holmes; Walking the Plank; Murder by the Book; The Holy City; Emmerdale Farm;* Richard Lipton in *Hot Metal* (Series 2, 1988); Eddie Clockerty in *Tutti Frutti* (series, 1987); *Room at the Bottom; High and Dry; Normal Service;* Victor Meldrew in *One Foot in the Grave* (five series, plus Christmas specials, 1994, 1995, and special for *Total Relief: A Night of Comic Relief,* 1993); *The Woman He Loved* (mini-series); *Fatherland; Selling Hitler;* Rev Jonathan Green in *Cluedo; Inspector Morse: Absolute Conviction; The Other Side of Paradise; Unnatural Pursuits; The Life and Times of Henry Pratt; The Trouble with Mr Bean; The Full Wax; One Foot in the Algarve; Richard Wilson: A Life beyond the Grave* (presenter); James Forth in *The Vision Thing* (ScreenPlay); *One Foot in the Algarve* (*One Foot in the Grave* Christmas special, 1993); Ben Glazier in *Under the Hammer* (series, 1994); *Gulliver's Travels;* Bill Webster in *Lord of Misrule* (Screen One). As director: *Commitments; Remainder Man; Under the Hammer* (all Play for Today); *A Wholly Healthy Glasgow; Changing Step.*
Films: *John Goldfarb, Please Come Home; The Trouble with 2 B; Those Glory Glory Days; Passage to India; Foreign Body; Whoops Apocalypse; Prick Up Your Ears; How to Get Ahead in Advertising; A Dry White Season; Fellow Traveller; Kremlin Farewell; Carry On Columbus; Soft Top, Hard Shoulder;.*
Awards: British Comedy Awards Top Television Comedy Actor award (1991); BAFTA Best Actor, Light Entertainment, twice (1991, 1993); BAFTA Scotland Best TV Actor (1993). Address: c/o Conway, van Gelder, Robinson. Lives in London. Single. Pets: A horse. Hobbies: Squash, eating.

Richard Wilson

WILSON, Sean
Sean Wilson. Actor. b. Crumpsall, Manchester, 4 April 1965. Trained at Oldham Theatre Workshop, then teamed up with a friend to perform in cabaret.
TV: *Crown Court; Travelling Man;* title role in *Mozart's Unfinished* (Channel Four film); Martin Platt in *Coronation Street* (1985-). Address: c/o Julia MacDermot/Granada Television. Lives in Oldham. Single. Pets: Goldfish, tropical fish, a budgie called Bill.

Sean Wilson

WILTON, Penelope
Penelope Wilton. Actress. b. Scarborough, North Yorkshire, 3 June 1946. Trained at The Drama Centre.
TV: *King Lear; The Widowing of Mrs Holroyd; The Norman Conquests;* Virginia in *Country; Ever Decreasing Circles; Madly in Love; The Monocled Mutineer; The Sullen Sisters;* Anne in *Ever Decreasing Circles* (series); Beatrice in *Screaming* (series); Homily in *The Borrowers* (two series, 1992-3); Hester Collyer in *The Deep Blue Sea* (Performance); *Landscape* (Performance).
Films: *Joseph Andrews; The French Lieutenant's Woman; Laughterhouse* (retitled *Singleton's Pluck*); *Cry Freedom; Clockwise.*
Address: c/o Julian Belfrage Associates. m. actor Daniel Massey (sep); 1 d. Alice

Penelope Wilton

Victor Winding

WINDING, Victor

Victor Winding. Actor. b. London, 30 January 1929. Trained as a draughtsman, acted in amateur dramatics and taught drama at night school before becoming a professional actor. Stage plays include *Run for Your Wife* (Duchess Theatre).

TV: Dr Fairfax in *Emergency – Ward 10; Probation Officer; No Hiding Place; The Informer; The Saint; Doctor Who;* Inspector Fleming in *The Expert; The Flaxton Boys; Menace; Warship; Thriller; Sporting Tales; The Judas Goat; Z Cars; Open House; Fall of Eagles; Crown Court;* Tad Ryland in *Emmerdale Farm; Private Diaries; Literary Profiles;* Victor Lee in *Crossroads; Turtle's Progress; Bognor; It Takes a Worried Man; Jemima Shore Investigates; Shelley; Country Tales; Angels; Little and Large; Winter Harvest; Strike It Rich; Yes, Prime Minister; Menace Unseen; The Bill;* Kenneth Pigot in *Deadly Obsession* (Crime Story); *Casualty; Falling through Blue; Guilty; EastEnders.*

Films: *Frightmare; The Confessional; Schizo; The System; The Medusa Touch.*

Address: c/o The Richard Stone Partnership. m. Rosalind Allen (dis); 3 d. Celia, Kay, Jane, 1 s. Julian. Hobbies: Reading, travelling, gardening.

Frank Windsor

WINDSOR, Frank

Frank Windsor. Actor. b. Walsall, Staffordshire, 12 July 1927. Stage plays include *Travesties* (as Lenin, RSC), *Every Good Boy Deserves Favour* (as The Psychiatrist, Mermaid Theatre), *Mr Fothergill's Murder* (Duke of York's), *Pack of Lies* (Lyric Theatre) and *The Woman in Black* (Fortune Theatre.

TV: *A for Andromeda;* Det Sgt/Det Chief Supt John Watt in *Z Cars, Softly Softly* and *Softly, Softly: Task Force; An Age of Kings; Whodunnit?; Jack the Ripper; Headmaster; Crown Court; Kidnapped; The Union; Into the Labyrinth; Dangerous Davies – The Last Detective* (TVM); *Oedipus at Colonus; Middle Men; All Creatures Great and Small; First among Equals;* Harry Bradley in *Flying Lady* (two series); title role in *The Real Eddy English* (series); *Chancer; The Fifteen Streets; Doctor Who* (two roles); *Boon; Casualty; Chancer;* Supt 2 and Chief Supt in *The Detectives;* Ken Alton in *Peak Practice; Lovejoy; Finding Sarah; Jealousy* (Capital Lives, Carlton only); Cyril Wendage in *September Song* (series, 1995); Simon Armstrong in *Trip Trap* (Screen One).

Films: *This Sporting Life; Spring and Port Wine; Sunday, Bloody Sunday; The Drop Out; Assassin; Too Many Chefs/Someone Is Killing the Great Chefs of Europe; Coming out of the Ice; The London Connection; The Shooting Party;* General Washington in *Revolution.* **Radio:** Bomber Harris in *Bomber* (series, BBC Radio). Address: c/o Scott Marshall. m. former dancer Mary Corbett; 1 d. Amanda, 1 s. David.

Anna Wing

WING, Anna

Anna Eva Lydia Catherine Wing. Actress. b. Hackney, London, 30 October 1914. Trained at the Croydon School of Acting. Stage plays include *It Runs in the Family* (Playhouse Theatre).

TV: *Sons and Lovers; The Crucible; Smiley's People; The Woman in White; Skirmishes; Sink or Swim; Making Good; The Chinese Detective; Sorry; Father's Day; The Old Men at the Zoo; Give Us a Break; Crown Court; The Witches of Grinnygog; The Invisible Man; Flying Lady; Picture Friend* (Play for Today); *Comrade Dad;* Lou Beale in *EastEnders;* Aunt Wilhelmina in *Dowie and His Mates* (Comedy Playhouse); Gran in *I Like It Here;* Grandma in *Collision Course;* Gran in *The Grove Family* (The Lime Grove Story); Lou in *Spatz;* Watt on Earth; Mrs Tutt in *Bonjour la Classe; The Late Show; French and Saunders;* Chairwoman in *Jake's Progress; Men of the World;* Jo's Mum in *Jo Brand Through the Cakehole.*

Films: *Full Circle; Providence; Xtro; Runners; The Ploughman's Lunch; Darkest England; Meet Me Tonight in Dreamland; Last Rites* (National Film School); *Chez Moi* (Denmark); *101 Dalmations.*

Address: c/o McIntosh Rae Management. Lives in London and Brighton. m. actor Peter Davey (dis after two years), partner poet Philip O'Connor (sep after seven years); 2 s. actor-director Mark Wing Davey (from m.), writer Jon Wing O'Connor (from partnership). Hobbies: Painting, writing, people.

Mark Wingett

WINGETT, Mark

Mark Wingett. Actor. b. Melton Mowbray, Leicestershire, 1 January 1961.

TV: *C.A.T.S. Eyes; The Professionals; Fords on Water; Private Schultz; Take Three Women; 1984; Fox; The Ravelled Thread; Grudge Fight;* PC Jim Carver in *Woodentop* (Storyboard, *The Bill* pilot, 1983) and PC/DC Carver in *The Bill* (1984-).

Films: *Quadrophenia.* Address: c/o London Management. Lives in London's East End. m. Sharon; 1 d. Jamila. Hobbies: Scuba-diving (qualified instructor), underwater photography.

Ray Winstone

WINSTONE, Ray

Ray Winstone. Actor. b. London. Former schoolboy international footballer. Stage roles include Sweeney in *Dealer's Choice* (National Theatre and Vaudeville Theatre).

TV: School Bully in *Sunshine over Brixton;* Carlin in *Scum; Mr Right; Death Angel; Minder;* Kenny in *Fox* (series); *The Lonely Hearts Kid; Fairly Secret Army; Bergerac;* Will Scarlet in *Robin of Sherwood* (three series); *Ever Decreasing Circles; C.A.T.S. Eyes; Father Matthew's Daughter; Boon;* Chief Det Ford in *Pulaski; Home to Roost; Blore, MP; Playing for Time* (pilot); title role in *Palmes;* Weaver in *Mr*

Thomas; *Absolute Hell* (Performance); *Paint; Underbelly; Birds of a Feather;* Charlie Brett-Smith in *Black and Blue* (Screen One); Sgt Godley in *Between the Lines;* Martin Sweet in *Get Back* (two series, 1992-3); Ed in *Nice Town; Murder Most Horrid;* Jack Swan in *The Negotiator; Casualty; Space Precinct; The Bill;* Thane in *The Ghostbusters of East Finchley* (series, 1995); CPO Jack Evans in *Kavanagh QC.*
Films: Billy in *That Summer;* Carlin in *Scum;* Kevin in *Quadrophenia;* Billy in *All Washed Up; Number One;* title role in *Tank Malling;* Peters in *Ladybird Ladybird.* Address: c/o CAM.

WINTER, Gordon
James Gordon Winter. Actor. b. London, 14 February 1956. Performed as a rock singer in the independent groups English Subtitles, Gorp and Kill Ugly Pop (1978-85), releasing seven albums.
TV: *Burning Ambition; Best Friends; The Bill* (two roles); *Young, Gifted and Broke;* Blind Michael Dunne in *The Paradise Club; Blag!;* Christopher in *Boon;* 'Griefstricken' in *Birds of a Feather;* Detective Ray Boyle in *South by South East; Moon and Son; Fantastic Facts; Sean's Show;* Lenny in *Minder;* Ron Rumsby in *Frank Stubbs Promotes* (series, 1993) and *Frank Stubbs* (series, 1994); PC Dodds in *The Plant;* Stuart in *Casualty; Samson Superslug.*
Films: *Caravaggio; Aria; The Painters; Mickey Finn; The Candy Show* (National Film and Television School); *Split Second;* Dr Xavier in *Invisible Woman; Untitled.*
Address: c/o The Narrow Road Company. Lives in London. Single. Hobbies: Motorcycling, Asian travel.

Gordon Winter

WITCHELL, Nicholas
Nicholas Witchell. Journalist. b. Cosford, Shropshire, 23 September 1953. Joined the BBC on its news training scheme in 1976.
TV: BBC Northern Ireland reporter (1978-82); BBC TV News reporter (1982-3) and correspondent in Ireland (1984), Beirut and the Falklands; *Six o'Clock News* (newsreader, 1984-9); *BBC Breakfast News* (newsreader, 1989-94); *Breakfast with Frost* (stand-in presenter, 1993); *Panorama* correspondent (1994-5); BBC TV News diplomatic correspondent (1995-). **Books:** *The Loch Ness Story.* Address: c/o BBC TV News. Lives in London. Partner: Carolyn Stephenson; 1 d. Arabella (b. 6 July 1994).

Nicholas Witchell

WOGAN, Terry
Terry Wogan. Presenter. b. Limerick, Ireland, 3 August 1938. Worked as a clerk for the Royal Bank of Ireland for five years before joining RTE radio as a newsreader/announcer.
TV: *Lunchtime with Wogan; Come Dancing; Miss World; Eurovision Song Contest; A Song for Europe; Variety Club Awards; Carl-Allen Awards; Disco; Startown; Blankety Blank; What's on Wogan; You Must Be Joking; Wogan* (Saturday evenings 1982-4, three weekday evenings, 1985-92); *Auntie's Bloomers; The Health Show* (series); *Terry Wogan's Friday Night* (chat-show series, 1992-3); *Children in Need; More Auntie's Bloomers; Stoppit and Tidyup* (narrator); *I Said No* (narrator, cartoon); *Wogan Meets... Billy Crystal; The Full Wax; The BBC Banned Audition Tapes* (Total Relief: A Night of Comic Relief, 1993); *Do the Right Thing* (two series 1994-5); *Eurovision 94 – Tips for Le Top* (1994); *Les Dawson: Entertainer* (1994); *Auntie's New Bloomers* (1994, 1995); *The Best of Auntie's Bloomers; Auntie's Sporting Bloomers* (one-off and series 1995); *Wogan's Island* (series, 1995); *Auntie's Brand New Bloomers* (1995); *The Great British Song Contest – The Final* (1996).
Radio: RTE (newsreader/announcer); *Late Night Extra; Terry Wogan* (Radio 2, afternoon show, then breakfast show). **Books:** *Wogan on Wogan* (autobiography).
Awards: TV: *TVTimes* Most Popular TV Personality award for 10 consecutive years.
Address: c/o JGPM. Lives in Berkshire. m. former model Helen Joyce; 1 d. Katherine, 2 s. Alan, Mark.

Terry Wogan

WOLF, Rita
Rita Wolf. Actress. b. Calcutta, India, 25 February 1960. Brought up in Camden Town, London, and trained at the Royal Court Youth Theatre.
TV: *Arena* (profile of Joint Stock Theatre Company); *Romance, Romance;* Meena in *Albion Market;* Asha in *Tandoori Nights* (two series); *Mohammed's Daughter; Rockliffe's Babies; One by One;* Princess Rania in *Saracen; Shelley;* Felicity Khan in *Coronation Street* (1990); *Kingdom Come* (Début on 2); *The Conversion of St Paul* (Début on 2); *Eyo Contact; Out: Khush;* Atima in *Calling the Shots.*
Films: *Majdhar; The Chain;* Tania in *My Beautiful Laundrette; Slipstream.*
Address: c/o Sandra Boyce Management. Lives in London.

Rita Wolf

WOLFENDEN, Stuart
Stuart Wolfenden. Actor. b. Rochdale, Lancashire, 7 February 1970. Trained at Oldham Theatre Workshop.
TV: Hall in *Jossy's Giants; The Adventures of Sherlock Holmes;* paper boy Craig Russell and mechanic Mark Casey in *Coronation Street;* Craig in *Making Out;* Billy Shaw in *My Kingdom for a Horse;* Jimmie in *A Time to Dance* (mini-series); Pete in *Heartbeat;* Chuck in *Emmerdale.*
Address: c/o Laine Management. Lives in Oldham., Lancashire. Single.

Stuart Wolfenden

WOOD, Janine

Janine Wood. Actress. b. Bournemouth, Dorset, 30 December 1963. Trained at The Drama Centre. Stage plays include *Romeo and Juliet, A Midsummer Night's Dream, The Kiss, The Hired Man, Black Coffee, Habeas Corpus, Mrs Warren's Profession* and *Dealing with Clair*.
TV: Clare in *After Henry* (series, 1988-92); *Davro's Sketch Pad*.
Address: c/o Jane Lehrer Associates. Lives in London. Partner: Actor Sam Miller (qv).

Janine Wood

WOOD, Victoria

Victoria Wood. Comedienne/Writer. b. Prestwich, Lancashire, 19 May 1953. D Litt, Lancaster and Sunderland Universities. Acted with Rochdale Youth Theatre Workshop. Gained a degree in drama from Birmingham University and worked on regional TV and radio, singing her own songs, while still a student. Won ITV talent show *New Faces* (1975) and gained a regular spot on *That's Life!* (1976).
TV: *New Faces* (winner); *That's Life!*; *Talent* (Screenplay, writer); *Nearly a Happy Ending; Wood and Walters: 'Two Creatures Great and Small'; Happy since I Met You* (Screenplay); *Wood and Walters* (series, 1982); *Victoria Wood — As Seen on TV* (two series, 1985-6, special, 1987); *Victoria Wood Now; Take the Stage; Cabbages and Kings; Jackanory; The Victoria Wood Show; Victoria Wood* (series, 1989); *Victoria Wood: Mens Sana in Thingummy Doodah; Victoria Wood's All Day Breakfast* (Christmas special, 1992); *An Audience with Victoria Wood; Victoria Wood — Sold Out;* Margaret in *Pat and Margaret* (Screen One, also writer); *Victoria Wood: Live in Your Own Room* (Christmas special, 1994); *Victoria Wood's Dirty Weekend — A 'Comic Relief' Presentation* (1995); *Great Railway Journeys*.
Awards: TV: Pye Colour Television Most Promising New Writer award for *Talent* (1979); British Comedy Award as Top Female Comedy Performer (1995). Address: c/o The Richard Stone Partnership. Lives in London. m. magician Geoffrey Durham; 1 d. Grace, 1 s. Henry.

Victoria Wood

WOODVINE, John

John Woodvine. Actor. b. Tyne Dock, Durham, 21 July 1929. Stage plays include *Dancing at Lughnasa* (Garrick Theatre) and *Nicholas Nickleby* (as Ralph Nickleby, RSC, London and Broadway).
TV: Det Insp Witty in *Z Cars* (series); Det Chief Supt John Kingdom in *New Scotland Yard* (1972-4); *Murder with Mirrors* (TVM); *Squaring the Circle* (TVM); *Edge of Darkness; The Browning Version; All Creatures Great and Small; William Danby; A Month in the Country; Knights of God; Room at the Bottom; All in Good Faith; Les Girls; The New Statesman; The Black and Blue Lamp; The Dog It Was That Died; A Tale of Two Cities; Blue Smoke, Red Moon; Who Bombed Birmingham?;* title role in *Pontius Pilate; The Pirate Prince; Runaway Bay* (three series); *An Actor's Life for Me; Medics; Spender; Civvies; Tell Tale Hearts;* The Dean in *Medics; The Trial* (Screen Two); *A Pinch of Snuff; Romeo and Juliet; Faith;* Bobo Simpson Sr in *Finney* (series); *Harry;* Judge Mellor in *Crown Prosecutor;* Admiral Croft in *Jane Austen's Persuasion* (Screen Two); *Oliver's Travels; Heartbeat; The Merchant of Venice; Doctor Finlay*.
Films: *An American Werewolf in London; Deceptions; Vote for Hitler; A Nightingale Sang; Danny the Champion of the World; Countdown to War; Wuthering Heights; The Trial; Dragonworld; Fatherland; Leon the Pig Farmer*. Address: c/o Scott Marshall.

John Woodvine

WOODWARD, Edward

Edward Woodward. Actor. b. Croydon, Surrey, 1 June 1930. OBE. Trained at RADA.
TV: *Sword of Honour;* title role in *Callan* (1967-73); *Au Pair Swedish Style; Entertaining Mr Sloane; Murders in the Rue Morgue; Night of Talavera; Julius Caesar; The Listener; A Dream Divided; Scott Fitzgerald; Bit of a Holiday; Evelyn; The Bass Player and the Blonde; Saturday, Sunday, Monday; Cleo; Rod of Iron; The Trial of Lady Chatterley; Nice Work; Blunt Instrument;* Callan in *Wet Job; Winston Churchill — The Wilderness Years; Spice of Life; Arthur the King* (TVM); *Love Is Forever* (TVM); *A Christmas Carol* (TVM); Robert McCall in *The Equalizer* (series, 1985-90); *Codename: Kyril; Uncle Tom's Cabin* (TVM); *The Man in the Brown Suit* (TVM); *Sherlock Holmes; Over My Dead Body; World War 2; In Suspicious Circumstances* (storyteller, three series, 1992-4); Nev in *Common as Muck* (series, 1994).
Films: *Where There's a Will; Inn for Trouble; Becket; The File of the Golden Goose; Incense for the Damned; Young Winston; Hunted; Sitting Target; The Wicker Man; Callan; Three for All; Stand Up Virgin Soldiers; 'Breaker' Morant; The Appointment; Who Dares Wins; Comeback; Champions; King David; Mister Johnson; The Man in the Brown Suit; Merlin and the Sword; Hands of a Murderer; Deadly Advice*. **Records:** Singles: *The Way You Look Tonight* (No 42, 1971). Albums: *Grains of Sand; This Man Alone* (No 53, 1970); *Love Is the Key; The Edward Woodward Album* (No 20, 1972).
Address: c/o Peters Fraser & Dunlop. m. 1st actress Venetia Barratt (dis), 2nd actress Michele Dotrice; 2 d. Sarah (from 1st m.), Emily Beth (from 2nd m.), 2 s. actor Tim (qv), Peter (both from 1st m.).

Edward Woodward

WOODWARD, Tim

Tim Woodward. Actor. b. London, 24 April 1953. Son of actor Edward Woodward (qv). Trained at RADA but left to tour with Glasgow Citizens' Theatre. Stage plays include *The Taming of the Shrew*.
TV: *Chips with Everything; Balzac; Within These Walls; French Without Tears; Wings; The Cost of Lov-*

Tim Woodward

ing; *Journals of Brigid Hitler*; *Cousin Phyllis*; *Tales of the Unexpected*; *Antonia White Quartet*; *Guests of the Nation*; *East Lynne*; *The Irish RM*; *The Affair of the Pink Pearl*; *The File on Jill Hatch*; *All the World's a Stage*; *The Case of the Frightened Lady*; *Pope John Paul II* (TVM); *Lady Windermere's Fan*; *A Killing on the Exchange*; Squadron Leader Rex in *Piece of Cake*; *Dark Angel*; *Iphigenia at Aulis*; *Greek Trilogy*; *Traitors*; John Thompson in *Families*; *Absolutely Fabulous*; *The Good Guys*; Keith in *Closing Numbers* (TVM); Det Con Ken Shipley in *Pie in the Sky*; *Go Back Out the Way You Came*; *The Governor*.
Films: *Galileo*; *The Europeans*; *Reds*; *King David*; *Salome*; *Personal Services*; *The Murder of Sir Harry Oakes*. Address: c/o Larry Dalzell Associates. Lives in London. Single. Hobbies: Motorbikes.

WOODYATT, Adam
Adam Woodyatt. Actor. b. Wanstead, Essex, 28 June 1968. Trained part-time at the Sylvia Young Theatre School. Stage productions include *Oliver!* (West End), as a child, and *On the Razzle* (as Ragamuffin, National Theatre).
TV: Shiner in *The Baker Street Boys*; Dave Firkettle in *The Witches of Grinnygog*; Ian Beale in *EastEnders* (1985-). Address: c/o Johnson's. Lives in Borehamwood, Hertfordshire. Single. Hobbies: Golf, football, cricket, computers.

Adam Woodyatt

WOOLDRIDGE, Susan
Susan Wooldridge. Actress. b. London. Daughter of composer and conductor John De Lacy Wooldridge and actress Margaretta Scott. Started as an ASM at the Crucible Theatre, Sheffield. Stage plays include *Look Back in Anger* (as Alison Porter, Young Vic).
TV: *The Naked Civil Servant*; *John McNab*; *The Racing Game*; Ann Biddle in *A Fine Romance*; Daphne Manners in *The Jewel in the Crown*; *Frankenstein*; Amanda Brewis in *Agatha Christie's Dead Man's Folly* (also titled *Dead Man's Folly*) (TVM); *Fifteen Years*; Kathleen Scott in *The Last Place on Earth*; *Hay Fever*; *Time and the Conways*; *Frankenstein*; *Night Mother*; *Dead Man's Folly*; *The Devil's Disciple*; *The Dark Room*; *Pastoral Care*; *The Small Assassin*; *Ticket to Ride*; *Changing Step* (TVM); *The Pied Piper* (TVM); *Crime Strike* (TVM); *Bergerac*; *Broke* (She-Play); Maggie in *Medics*; *The Ruth Rendell Mysteries: An Unwanted Woman*; *The Hummingbird Tree* (Screen One); *A Class Act*; Rosamund Grant in *The Inspector Alleyn Mysteries*; Ann Whelan in *Bad Company* (mini-series, 1993); Sarah Napier in *Under the Hammer*; Jeanetta in *All Quiet on the Preston Front* (series); Patricia Cleeve in *Wycliffe* (series, 1994); Jeanetta in *Preston Front* (series); *Without Walls Special: The Writing Game*.
Films: *Butley*; Harriet in *The Shout*; Lily Sutton in *Loyalties*; Molly in *Hope and Glory*; Monica in *How to Get Ahead in Advertising*; Lady Wilson in *Bye Bye Blues*; *Just Like a Woman*.
Awards: TV: BAFTA Best Actress and Alva Best Actress for *The Jewel in the Crown* (1984). Films: BAFTA Best Supporting Actress for *Hope and Glory* (1987). Address: c/o Jonathan Altaras Associates.

Susan Wooldridge

WORTH, Helen
Cathryn Helen Wigglesworth. Actress. b. Leeds, 7 January 1951. Grew up in Morecambe, Lancashire. Trained as a dancer at the Corona Stage Academy. Appeared in *The Sound of Music* (West End, aged 12).
TV: *Scene at 6.30* (Granada Television news magazine, aged 10); *Z Cars* (aged 10); *Doctor Who*; *The Doctors*; Gail Potter/Tilsley/Platt in *Coronation Street* (1974-); *Royal Variety Performance* (with *Coronation Street* cast, 1989).
Films: *Oliver!*; *The Prime of Miss Jean Brodie*.
Radio: Two years in BBC radio repertory company. Address: c/o Granada Television. Lives in London and Cheshire. m. actor Michael Angelis. Hobbies: Gardening, cooking, eating.

Helen Worth

WRAY, Emma
Jill Wray. Actress. b. Birkenhead, Cheshire, 22 March 1965. Trained at the Rose Bruford College of Speech and Drama, then sang with three-part harmony group the Blooming Tulips.
TV: Brenda Wilson in *Watching* (seven series); Tracy in *Minder*; Pandora in *Boon*; Minty Goodenough in *Defrosting the Fridge*; Pippa in *Stay Lucky* (tour series, 1989-93); Julie in *The Big Game*; Donna in *True Love*. Address: c/o Burdett-Coutts Associates. Lives in London.

Emma Wray

WRIGHT, Steve
Steve Wright. Presenter. b. Greenwich, London, August 1954. Ran a radio station at Eastwood High School, Essex, then worked as an insurance broker, electronics engineer and backstage in the theatre, also running his own jingles business and working in hospital radio in his spare time. Joined the BBC as a researcher, later worked in the record library, then in record promotion, before entering radio.
TV: *Pauline's Quirkes*; *Home Truths* (host, quiz show series, 1994); *Steve Wright's People Show* (two series, 1994-5); DJ in *Sorry About Last Night*.
Radio: Radio Atlantis (Belgium); LBC (London); Thames Valley Radio (Reading); *The Read and Wright Show* (with Mike Read on Thames Valley Radio); Radio Luxembourg (1979); BBC Radio 1 (1980-95); BBC Radio 2 (1996-). Address: c/o JGPM. Lives in Oxfordshire. m. Cindi; 1 s. Tom, 1 d. Lucy.

Steve Wright

Stephen Yardley

Marjorie Yates

Paula Yates

Pauline Yates

David Yip

YARDLEY, Stephen

Stephen Yardley. Actor. b. Ferrensby, North Yorkshire, 24 March 1942. Trained at RADA (1960-3).
TV: *Dr Finlay's Casebook;* Martin Barrett in *Coronation Street; The XYY Man; Widows; Z Cars; Secret Army; War and Peace; Roads to Freedom; Harriet's Back in Town; Napoleon and Love; Remington Steele; Blood Money; Tom Gratton's War; Germinal; Nana; A Tale of Two Cities; Fanny by Gaslight;* Ken Masters in *Howards' Way; Virtual Murder* (TVM); Gilbert in *Brighton Belles;* John Mason in *Law and Disorder.*
Films: *Doctor and the Devils; The Shooting Party; Adolf Hitler — My Part in His Downfall.* Address: c/o Hilda Physick Agency. m. (sep); 1 d. Rebecca, 1 s. Joshua. Hobbies: Squash, sailing, painting.

YATES, Marjorie

Marjorie Yates. Actress. b. Birmingham, 13 April 1941. Trained at Guildhall School of Music and Drama.
TV: *Couples;* Audrey in *Kisses at Fifty* (The Wednesday Play, 1973); *Connie; All Day on the Sands; Change in Time; Morgan's Boy; Lovely Day Tomorrow; Marya; Couples; The Sweeney; A Very British Coup; June; The Bill* (two roles); *Boon; Villains;* Hilda Avory in *The Ruth Rendell Mysteries: The Speaker of Mandarin;* Mrs Hope in *Fighting for Gemma* (drama-doc); Jean Fairlie in *Annie's Bar* (serial, 1996).
Films: *The Black Panther; The Optimists; Legend of the Werewolf; Stardust; Priest of Love* (1981); *Wetherby;* Mother in *The Long Day Closes.* Address: c/o Kate Feast Management. Lives near Stratford-upon-Avon. m. university administrator and councillor Michael Freeman (dis 1994); 1 d. Polly, 1 s. Carl. Pets: Newt, frogs. Hobbies: Wildlife, conservation.

YATES, Paula

Paula Yates. Presenter. b. Colwyn Bay, 24 April 1960. Daughter of TV presenter, producer, director, writer and designer Jess Yates and novelist Heller Toren (née Elaine Smith).
TV: *The Tube; 01- for London; Baby, Baby; Sex with Paula* (1986, unscreened in the UK until 1995); *Entertainment UK; 01; Cue Paula,* then *The Big Breakfast* (including *Paula's Boudoir, Baby Talk, Beauty Talk, The Plant Doctor, Singing Lessons, Camera Talk*); *The Wednesday Weepie* (series); *Late Licence; The Legend of the Tube* (presenter, 1995); *Best of The Tube* (presenter, series, 1995).
Books: *Rock Stars in Their Underpants; A Tale of Two Kitties* (children's story); *Blondes; Sex with Paula.* Address: c/o Channel Four. Lives in London. m. 1986 rock musician Bob Geldof (sep); 3 d.

YATES, Pauline

Pauline Yates. Actress. b. St Helens, Lancashire, 16 June. Joined Oldham Rep straight from school.
TV: *Hancock; Cruise; Go On, It'll Do You Good; The Second Interview; Emma's Time; The Bridesmaid; Louise; Sentimental Education; A Room in Town; Bachelor Father; The Doctors; Crime of Passion; Home and Away* (Granada TV production); *Harriet's Back in Town; Bootsie and Snudge; Nightingale's Boys; Going, Going, Gone; Free; Savages; My Honourable Mrs;* Elizabeth Perrin in *The Fall and Rise of Reginald Perrin* (series); *England's Green and Pleasant Land; The Emperor's New Hat; Rainbow; Rooms; Keep It in the Family* (series); *Hold the Dream; Touch of Danger; A Small Mourning; So Haunt Me.*
Films: *The Four Feathers; She'll Be Wearing Pink Pyjamas.* Address: c/o Kate Feast Management. m. actor-writer Donald Churchill (dec 1991); 2 d. Jemma, Polly. Hobbies: Reading, swimming, tapestry.

YIP, David

David Nicholas Yip. Actor. b. Liverpool, 4 June 1951. Trained at the East 15 Acting School (1970-3).
TV: *It Ain't Half Hot Mum; Savages; Whodunnit?; Spies; Quatermass; Readabout* (storyteller); *The Cuckoo Waltz; 3-2-1; The Chelsea Murders; Going to Work; Treehouse* (storyteller); *Doctor Who; Mystery of the Disappearing Schoolgirls; Play School* (storyteller); *The Professionals; Adventure Game; Jackanory* (storyteller); *So You Think You Can Believe Your Eyes;* John Ho in *The Chinese Detective* (two series); *The Caucasian Chalk Circle; King and Castle; Making Out; Murder on the Moon* (TVM); Dr Michael Choi in *Brookside; Wail of the Banshee; Rear Window: White Girls on Dope;* Leonard in *Every Silver Lining* (series, 1993); *Wild Justice* (TVM); *Rich Deceiver; Thief Takers; BUGS.* Narrations/voice-overs: *Here and Now: Liverpool Chinese* (writer-presenter); *Cockney John Chinaman; History of Shipping; East End; Young Thai Boxer; The Thai Boxer; Scene: Young Vietnam; Knock, Knock; The Late Show: Moving the Mountain; Votes for Wong; Only One Earth: China; The Late Show: The China Video; Bicycles.*
Films: *Indiana Jones and the Temple of Doom; A View to a Kill; Ping Pong; Empire of the Sun; Highlander; Out of Order; Hawks; Destiny San Francisco; Chinese Method; Goodbye Hong Kong; As Long as There Is Sky and Earth.* Address: c/o Mayer & Eden. m. 1st Liz Bagley (dis), 2nd actress Lynn Farleigh (qv). Hobbies: Tennis, swimming.

YORK, Michael

Michael Hugh York-Johnson. Actor. b. Fulmer, Buckinghamshire, 27 March 1942.
TV: *Rebel in the Grave; The Forsyte Saga; Jesus of Nazareth; True Patriot; Much Ado about Nothing; A Man Called Intrepid* (TVM); *The White Lions; Vendredi* (France); *The Phantom of the Opera; For Those I Loved; Twilight Theatre; The Weather in the Streets; The Master of Ballantrae* (TVM); *Space; Actors on Acting; Dark Mansions; The Far Country; British Rock: The First Wave* (narrator); *Are You My Mother?;*

Ponce de Leon (Tall Tales); *Sword of Gideon* (TVM); *Knots Landing; The Four Minute Mile; The Heat of the Day; Sophocles' Theban Plays* (host); *The Lady and the Highwayman* (TVM); *The Hunt for Stolen War Treasure; Till We Meet Again; The Story of Anglicanism; Night of the Fox; Duel of Hearts* (TVM); *The Road to Avonlea; River of Gold* (narrator); *Secret of the Sahara; Gardens of the World* (narrator); *The Out of Towner; Teklab; The Magic Flute* (narrator); *Fall from Grace* (TVM); *Nicolas Slonimski: A Touch of Genius* (narrator); *CBS Reports: Hitler and Stalin* (narrator); *September; A Young Connecticut Yankee in King Arthur's Court; Not of This Earth; seaQuest DSV; Danielle Steel's The Ring;* .

Michael York

Films: *The Mind Benders; The Taming of the Shrew; Smashing Time; Confessions of a Loving Couple; Accident; Red and Blue; The Guru; Romeo and Juliet; The Strange Affair; Justine; Alfred the Great; Black Flowers for the Bride; Zeppelin; La Poudre d'Escampette; Cabaret; England Made Me; Lost Horizon; The Three Musketeers: The Queen's Diamonds; Murder on the Orient Express; The Four Musketeers: The Revenge of Milady; Great Expectations; Conduct Unbecoming; Touch and Go; Seven Nights in Japan; Logan's Run; The Island of Dr Moreau; The Last Remake of Beau Geste; Death on the Nile; The Riddle of the Sands; Fedora; Final Assignment; The White Lions; For Those I Loved; Le Sang des Autres; Success Is the Best Revenge; L'Aube; Dark Mansions; Joker; Phantom of Death; City Blue; A Proposito di Quelle Strana Ragazza; The Return of the Musketeers; Midnight Cop; The Wanderer; The Long Shadow; Wide Sargasso Sea; Rochade; The Magic Paintbrush; Eline Vere; Discretion Assured; The Shadow of a Kiss; David Copperfield's Christmas; Timeless India* (narrator); *Gospa.* Address: c/o London Management. Lives in Los Angeles. m. 1968 US writer and photographer Patricia Frances McCallum. Hobbies: Travel, art.

YORK, Susannah
Susannah Yolande-Fletcher. Actress. b. London, 9 January 1942. Trained at RADA. TV since 1959.
TV: *Armchair Theatre* (début); *The Crucible; The Creditors; La Grande Breteche; The Rebel and the Soldier; The First Gentleman; The Richest Man in the World; Fallen Angels; Prince Regent; Second Chance; he Golden Gate Murders* (TVM); *We'll Meet Again; The Other Side of Me; Agnes of God; Star Quality; The Two Ronnies; The Man from the Pru; The Haunting of New; Devices and Desires; Trainer.*

Susannah York

Films: *Tunes of Glory; There Was a Crooked Man; The Greengage Summer; Freud — The Secret Passion; Tom Jones; The Seventh Dawn; Scene Nun, Take One* (short); *Scruggs* (short); *Sands of the Kalahari; Kaleidoscope; A Man for All Seasons; Sebastian; Duffy; The Killing of Sister George; They Shoot Horses, Don't They?; Lock Up Your Daughters!; Oh! What a Lovely War; Battle of Britain; Country Dance; Jane Eyre; Zee and Co; Happy Birthday, Wanda June; Images; Gold; The Maids; Conduct Unbecoming; Sky Riders; That Lucky Touch; Eliza Fraser; The Shout; Long Shot; The Silent Partner; Superman; Falling in Love Again; The Awakening; Alice; Loophole; Late Flowering Love* (short); *Superman II; Yellowbeard; 99 Women; A Christmas Carol; Pretty Kill; Memories; Bluebeard, Bluebeard; The Apple Tree; Superman IV: The Quest for Peace* (voice only); *Just Ask for Diamond; A Summer Story; American Roulette; Melancholia; A Handful of Time; The Higher Mortals.* **Books:** *In Search of Unicorns; Lark's Castle.* Address: c/o Jonathan Altaras Associates. m. actor-writer Michael Wells (dis); 1 d. Sasha, 1 s. Orlando.

Barbara Young

YOUNG, Barbara
Barbara Young. Actress. b. Brighouse, West Yorkshire, 9 February 1936. Trained at Bradford Civic Theatre.
TV: *Pardon the Expression;* Doreen Cropper in *How's Your Father* (two series, 1974-5); *The Reporters; Looking for Clancy; I Claudius; Hazell* (series); *Out of Town Boys; On Giant's Shoulders; Crime and Punishment; The Good Companions; Bless Me, Father; Praying Mantis* (TVM); *Coronation Street; The Gentle Touch; The Bill; The Dorothy L Sayers Mysteries; A Perfect Spy; Witness; The Roughest Way; Sleepers; Have His Carcase; Dempsey and Makepeace; Buggins Ermine; Split Ends; All Good Things; Sleepers; Virtual Murder* (TVM); *The Memoirs of Sherlock Holmes; Lovejoy; Cracker; The Vacillations of Poppy Carew.*
Films: *White City; Hidden City.* Address: c/o John Grantham. m. playwright Jack Pulman.

YOUNG, Helen
Helen Elizabeth Young. Weather presenter. b. Crawley, Sussex, 10 June 1969. Qualified as a weather forecaster with the Meteorological Office in 1990 after gaining a BSc (Hons) in geography.
TV: HTV weather presenter; BBC *News West* weather presenter; BBC TV national weather presenter; *Sunny Spells; Women in Science* (Open University). Address: c/o BBC TV Weather Centre. Lives in London. Single. Hobbies: Squash, skiing, running (ran the 1992 London Marathon), playing the clarinet.

Helen Young

YOUNG, Paul
Paul Young. Actor. b. Edinburgh, 3 July 1944. Son of actor John Young and theatrical agent Winifred Young. Trained at the Royal Scottish Academy of Music and Drama.
TV: *Sunset Song; Homework;* Mr Parker in *Take the High Road* (1987-90); *Holy City; Something Got to Give; Doom Castle; Taggart; Brond; House on the Hill; Brigadista; Extras; Leaving; The Justice Game* (mini-series); Ken Miller in *No Job for a Lady; Hooked on Scotland; Agatha Christie's Poirot; The Bill;* Andrew Campbell in *The Tales of Para Handy* (two series, 1994-5); Patrick Liddell in *Taggart: Legends.*
Films: *Geordie; Submarine X-1; SOS Titanic; Another Time, Another Place; Chato's Land; The Girl in the Picture.* Address: c/o Christina Shepherd. m. Radio Clyde journalist Sheila Duffy; 2 d. Hannah, Katie.

Paul Young

Agent Addresses

A&B Personal Management
5th Floor
Plaza Suite
114 Jermyn Street
London SW1Y 6HJ
Tel: 0171-839 4433/4

A.D.A. Enterprises
78 St Margaret's Road
St Margaret's
Twickenham
Middlesex TW1 2LP
Tel: 0181-892 1716

A.I.M.
5 Denmark Street
London WC2H 8LP
Tel: 0171-836 2001

A&J Management
551 Green Lanes
Palmers Green
London N13 4DR
Tel: 0181-882 7716

ATS Casting
26 St Michael's Road
Headingley
Leeds LS6 3AW
Tel: 0113-230 4300/4334

Marjorie Abel
50 Maddox Street
London W1R 9PA
Tel: 0171-499 1343

The Actors' Agency
197 Roden Street
West Melbourne
Victoria 3003
Australia
Tel: (0061) 3 329 2488

Actors Alliance
Bon Marché Building
444 Brixton Road
London SW9 8EJ
Tel: 0171-326 0070

The Actor's Group
4 Newton Street
Piccadilly
Manchester M1 2AW
Tel: 0161-228 0771/2

Actors Network Agency
55 Lambeth Walk
London SE11 6DX
Tel: 0171-735 0999

Actorum
3rd Floor
21 Foley Street
London W1P 7LH
Tel: 0171-636 6978

Jonathan Altaras Associates
27 Floral Street
London WC2E 9DP
Tel:0171-836 8722

Alvarez Management
86 Muswell Road
Muswell Hill
London N10 2BE
Tel: 0181-883 2206

Amor Reeves Management
80 Crawthew Grove
London SE22 9AB
Tel: 0181-693 7733

Susan Angel Associates
1st Floor
12 D'Arblay Street
London W1V 3FP
Tel: 0171-439 3086

Arlington Enterprises
1/3 Charlotte Street
London W1P 1HD
Tel: 0171-580 0702

D&J Arlon Enterprises
Pinewood Studios
Pinewood Road
Iver
Buckinghamshire SL0 0NH
Tel: (01753) 650808

Artists Management Group
11/13 Broad Court
Covent Garden
London WC2B 5QN
Tel: 0171-240 5052

Australian Creative Management
Second Floor
169 Phillip Street
Sydney
NSW 2000
Australia
Tel: (0061) 2 232 4900

Aza Artistes
652 Finchley Road
London NW11 7NT
Tel: 0181-458 7288/0181-891 0087

BSA
Trinity Lodge
25 Trinity Crescent
London SW17 7AG
Tel: 0181-672 0136

Bagenal Harvey Organisation
141/143 Drury Lane
London WC2B 5TB
Tel: 0171-379 4625

George Bartram Associates
Creative House
5 Commercial Street
Birmingham B1 1RS
Tel: 0121-643 9346

Julian Belfrage Associates
68 St James's Street
London SW1A 1PH
Tel: 0171-491 4400

The Jules Bennett Agency
19 Lainson Street
Southfields
London SW18 5RS
Tel: 0181-265 5491

Blackburn Sachs Associates
37 Barnes High Street
London SW13 9LN
Tel: 0181-878 3077

Rebecca Blond Associates
52 Shaftesbury Avenue
London W1V 7DE
Tel: 0171-434 2010

Sheila Bourne Management
2-2-6 Greenwich Business Centre
49 Greenwich High Road
London SE10 8JL
Tel: 0181-469 2726/0181-694 8646

Sandra Boyce Management
1 Kingsway House
Albion Road
London N16 0TA
Tel: 0171-923 0606

Ruth Boyle Management
Willow Dene
New Lane
Nun Monkton
York YO5 8EP
Tel: (01423) 331199

Michelle Braidman Associates
10/11 Lower John Street
London W1R 3PE
Tel: 0171-437 0817

Barry Brown & Partner
47 West Square
London SE11 4SP
Tol: 0171-928 1229

Joan Brown Associates
3 Earl Road
London SW14 7JH
Tel: 0181-876 9448

Peter Browne Management
Pebro House
13 St Martins Road
London SW9 0SP
Tel: 0171-737 3444

The Brunskill Management
Suite 8a
169 Queen's Gate
London SW7 5HE
Tel: 0171-581 3388/0171-584 8060

Richard Bucknall Management
Garden Studios
11/15 Betterton Street
London WC2H 9BP
Tel: 0171-379 0344

Burdett-Coutts Associates
Riverside Studios
Crisp Road
London W6 9RL
Tel: 0181-563 1040

Barry Burnett Organisation
Suite 42-43
Grafton House
2-3 Golden Square
London W1R 3AD
Tel: 0171-437 7048/9

Burton Management
Canalot Studios
222 Kensal Road
London W10 5BN
Tel: 0181-964 5077

CAM
19 Denmark Street
London WC2H 8NA
Tel: 0171-497 0448

CCA Management
4 Court Lodge
48 Sloane Square
London SW1W 8AT
Tel: 0171-730 8857

CDA
Apartment 9
47 Courtfield Road
London SW7 4DB
Tel: 0171-370 0700

CSM (Artistes)
St Dunstan's Hall
East Acton Lane
London W3 7EG
Tel: 0181-743 9982

Sara Cameron Management
40 Redbourne Avenue
Finchley
London N3 2BS
Tel: 0181-343 0433

Alexandra Cann Representation
337 Fulham Road
London SW10 9TW
Tel: 0171-352 6266

June Cann Management
6/1 Ridge Street
North Sydney
NSW 2060
Australia
Tel: (0061) 2 922 3066

Roger Carey Associates
64 Thornton Avenue
Chiswick
London W4 1QQ
Tel: 0181-995 4477

Peter Charlesworth
Second Floor
68 Old Brompton Road
London SW7 3LQ
Tel: 0171-581 2478

Chatto and Linnit
Prince of Wales Theatre
Coventry Street
London W1V 7FE
Tel: 0171-930 6677

Chiltern Casting
2a Eaton Road
West Derby
Liverpool L12 7JJ
Tel: 0151-254 1686

Stiven Christie Management
80a Dean Street
London W1V 5AD
Tel: 0171-434 4430

Jean Clarke Management
Camco House
Bear Street
Leicester Square
London WC2H 7AS
Tel: 0171-930 6996

Shane Collins Associates
24 Wardour Street
London W1V 3HD
Tel: 0171-439 1976

Collis Management
182 Trevelyan Road
London SW17 9LW
Tel: 0181-767 0196

Conway, van Gelder, Robinson
3rd Floor
18-21 Jermyn Street
London SW1Y 6HP
Tel: 0171-287 0077

Vernon Conway
5 Spring Street
London W2 3RA
Tel: 0171-262 5506/7

Clive Corner Associates
73 Gloucester Road
Hampton
Middlesex TW12 2UQ
Tel: 0181-941 8653

Lou Coulson
37 Berwick Street
London W1V 3RF
Tel: 0171-734 9633

Crawfords
2 Conduit Street
London W1R 9TG
Tel: 0171-629 6464

Creative Talent Management
The Basement
93 Hereford Road
London W2 5BB
Tel: 0171-792 3411

Crouch Associates
9/15 Neal Street
Covent Garden
London WC2H 9PF
Tel: 0171-379 1684

Curtis Brown
Haymarket House
28-29 Haymarket
London SW1Y 4SP
Tel: 0171-396 6600

David Daly Associates
68 Old Brompton Road
London SW7 3LQ
Tel: 0171-581 0121

Larry Dalzell Associates
Suite 12
17 Broad Court
London WC2B 5QN
Tel: 0171-379 0875

Hazel de Leon
Pine Trees
Pine Trees Drive
The Drive
Ickenham
Middlesex UB10 8AE
Tel: (01895) 274077

Felix De Wolfe
Manfield House
376/378 Strand
London WC2R 0LR
Tel: 0171-379 5767

Direct Line Personal Management
CHEL
Room 35
26 Roundhay Road
Leeds LS7
Tel: 0113-244 4991

Downes Presenters Agency
96 Broadway
Bexleyheath
Kent DA6 7DE
Tel: 0181-304 0541

Bryan Drew
Mezzanine
Quadrant House
80/82 Regent Street
London W1R 6AU
Tel: 0171-437 2293

Paul du Fer Associates
12 Alfred Road
London W3 6LH
Tel: 0181-896 0393

**Kenneth Earle
Personal Management**
214 Brixton Road
London SW9 6AP
Tel: 0171-274 1219

Ellison Combe Associates
16 Evelyn Gardens
Richmond-upon-Thames
Surrey TW9 2PL
Tel: 0181-940 7863

Equity
Guild House
Upper St Martins Lane
London WC2H 9EG
Tel: 0171-379 6000

Essanay
2 Conduit Street
London W1R 9TG
Tel: 0171-409 3526

Evans and Reiss
221 New Kings Road
London SW6 4XE
Tel: 0171-384 1843

Jacque Evans Management
11a St John's Wood High Street
London NW8 7NG
Tel: 0171-722 4700

Norma Farnes
9 Orme Court
London W2 4RL
Tel: 0171-727 1544

Kate Feast Management
10 Primrose Hill Studios
Fitzroy Road
London NW1 8TR
Tel: 0171-586 5502/3/4

Alan Field
11 Arden Road
Finchley
London N3 2AB
Tel: 0181-346 7861

Mike Fisher Management
26 Elizabeth Court
Cororans
Pilgrims Hatch
Brentwood
Essex CM15 9PL
Tel: (01277) 230683

Jill Foster
3 Lonsdale Road
London SW13 9ED
Tel: 0181-741 9410

Fox Artists Management
Concorde House
101 Shepherd's Bush Road
London W6 7LP
Tel: 0171-602 8822

Frazer-Skemp Management
34 Bramerton Street
Chelsea
London SW3 5LA
Tel: 0171-352 2922/3771

French's
26 Binney Street
London W1Y 1YN
Tel: 0171-629 4159

GMM
15 Wardour Mews
D'Arblay Street
London W1V 3FF
Tel: 0171-734 0033

Hilary Gagan Associates
3 New Burlington Street
London W1X 1FE
Tel: 0171-439 1371

Barbara Gange Management
40 Elizabeth Street
North Richmond
Victoria 3121
Australia
Tel: (0061) 3 429 2650

Robyn Gardiner Management
Suite 5
30 Clarke Street
South Melbourne
3205 Victoria
Australia
Tel: (0061) 3 696 2826

Kerry Gardner Management
15 Kensington High Street
London W8 5NP
Tel: 0171-937 3142

Garricks
7 Garrick Street
London WC2 9AR
Tel: 0171-240 0660

Noel Gay Artists
6th Floor
76 Oxford Street
London W1N 0AT
Tel: 0171-836 3941

The Gersh Agency
232 North Canon Drive
Beverly Hills
CA 90210
USA
Tel: (001) 213 274 6611

Eric Glass
28 Berkeley Square
London W1X 6HD
Tel: 0171-629 7162

Goodwin Associates
12 Rabbit Row
Kensington Church Street
London W8 4DX
Tel: 0171-221 9364

Gores/Fields Talent Agency
10100 Santa Monica Boulevard
Suite 700
Los Angeles
California 90067
USA
Tel: (001) 213 277 4400

J Carter Gibson Agency
9000 Sunset Boulevard
Suite 801
Los Angeles
CA 90069
USA
Tel: (001) 213 274 8813

James Grant Management
The Courtyard
42 Colwith Road
Hammersmith
London W6 9EY
Tel: 0181-741 4484

John Grantham
4 Paddington Street
London W1M 3LA
Tel: 0171-224 4434

Joan Gray Personal Management
29 Sunbury Court Island
Sunbury-on-Thames
Middlesex TW16 5PP
Tel. (01932) 788544

Green and Underwood
2 Conduit Street
London W1R 9TG
Tel: 0171-493 0308

Sandra Griffin Management
6 Ryde Place
Richmond Road
East Twickenham
Surrey TW1 2EH
Tel: 0181-891 5676

Hamilton Asper Management
6th Floor
76 Oxford Street
London W1N 0AT
Tel: 0171-836 3941

Sue Hammer
Personal Management
Otterbourne House
Chobham Road
Ottershaw
Chertsey
Surrey KT16 0QF
Tel: (01932) 874111/2

Sharon Hamper Management
4 Great Queen Street
London WC2B 5DG
Tel: 0171-734 1827/0171-404 5255

Roger Hancock
4 Water Lane
London NW1 8NZ
Tel: 0171-267 4418

Harbour & Coffey
9 Blenheim Street
New Bond Street
London W1Y 9LE
Tel: 0171-499 5548

Harris & Goldberg Talent Agency
2121 Avenue of the Stars
Suite 950
Los Angeles
CA 90067
USA
Tel: (001) 213 553 5200

Richard Hatton
29 Roehampton Gate
London SW15 5JR
Tel: 0181-876 6699

George Heathcote Management
10 St Martin's Court
London WC2N 4AJ
Tel: 0171-379 1081

Stephen Hatton Management
The Basement
142a New North Road
London N1 7BH
Tel: 0171-359 3593

George Heathcote Management
10 St Martin's Court
London WC2N 4AJ
Tel: 0171-379 1081

Dee Hindin Associates
44 Royal Crescent
Holland Park Avenue
London W11 4SN
Tel: 0171-603 3129

Hindworth Management
235/241 Regent Street
London W1V 3AU
Tel: 0171-434 3944

Hobson's Personal Management
Burlington House
64 Chiswick High Road
London W4 1SY
Tel: 0181-747 8474

Sally Hope Associates
108 Leonard Street
London EC2A 4RH
Tel: 0171-613 5353

Howes and Prior
66 Berkeley House
Hay Hill
London W1X 7LH
Tel: 0171-493 7570

Jane Hughes Management
Ashworth House
PO Box 123
Knutsford
Cheshire WA16 9HX
Tel: (01565) 650202

Mike Hughes Entertainments
Prince of Wales Theatre
Coventry Street
London W1V 7FE
Tel: 0171-930 9161

Bernard Hunter Associates
13 Spencer Gardens
London SW14 7AH
Tel: 0181-878 6308

Hutton Management
200 Fulham Road
London SW10 9PN
Tel: 0171-352 4825

ICM
Oxford House
76 Oxford Street
London W1N 0AX
Tel: 0171-636 6565

IMG
Media House
3 Burlington Lane
London W4 2TH
Tel: 0181-742 6208/6267/9977

Inter-City Casting
383 Corn Exchange
Manchester M4 3DH
Tel: 0161-832 8848

International Artistes
Mezzanine Floor
235 Regent Street
London W1R 8AX
Tel: 0171-439 8401/2/3/4/5

**International Casting
Service & Associates**
Fourth Floor, Cornelius Court
147a King Street
Sydney
NSW 2000
Australia
Tel: (0061) 2 232 6955

**International Creative
Management**
8899 Beverly Boulevard
Los Angeles
CA 90048
USA
Tel: (001) 213 550 4000

JGM
15 Lexham Mews
London W8 6JW
Tel: 0171-224 3414

JGPM
2 New Kings Road
London SW6 4SA
Tel: 0171-736 7828

JLM
242 Acton Lane
London W4 5DL
Tel: 0181-747 8223

JM Associates
77 Beak Street
London W1R 3LF
Tel: 0171-434 0602

JSE
York House
18 The Parade
Claygate
Surrey KT10 0QZ
Tel: (01372) 471120

JY Publicity
100 Ebury Street
London SW1W 9QD
Tel: 0171-730 9009

Carole James Management
2 Water Lane House
Water Lane
Richmond-upon-Thames
Surrey TW9 1TJ
Tel: 0181-940 8154

**Susan James
Personal Management**
22 Westbere Road
London NW2 3SR
Tel: 0171-794 8545

Joy Jameson
2.19 The Plaza
535 Kings Road
London SW10 0SZ
Tel: 0171-351 3971

Johnson's
8 Archates Avenue
Chafford Hundred
Grays
Essex RM16 6QS
Tel: (01375) 394845

Chuck Julian Associates
Suite 51
26 Charing Cross Road
London WC2H 0DH
Tel: 0171-437 4248/0171-240 1301

Kean & Garrick
Rayleigh House
2 Richmond Hill
Richmond-upon-Thames
Surrey TW10 6QX
Tel: 0181-940 5559

Keane Management
1246 Pittwater Road
Narrabeen 2101
Australia
Tel: (0061) 2 970 6311

Knight Ayton Management
10 Argyll Street
London W1V 1AB
Tel: 0171-287 4405

LWA
52 Wardour Street
London W1V 3HL
Tel: 0171-434 3944

**Michael Ladkin
Personal Management**
11 Southwick Mews
London W2 1JG
Tel: 0171-402 6644

Laine Management
Matrix House
301/303 Chapel Street
Salford M3 5JG
Tel: 0161-835 2122

Lake-Smith Griffin Associates
15 Maiden Lane
Covent Garden
London WC2E 7NA
Tel: 0171-836 1020

Langford Associates
17 Westfields Avenue
London SW13 0AT
Tel: 0181-878 7148

James Laurie Management
39 Waterloo Street
Surry Hills
NSW 2010
Australia
Tel: (0061) 2 690 1266

Barbara Leane & Associates
261 Miller Street
North Sydney
NSW 2060
Australia
Tel: (0061) 2 957 1847

Bernard Lee Management
Moorcroft Lodge
Farleigh Common
Warlingham
Surrey CR3 0PE
Tel: (01883) 625667

Jane Lehrer Associates
26 Danbury Street
London N1 8JU
Tel: 0171-226 2404

Leigh Management
14 St David's Drive
Edgware
Middlesex HA8 6JH
Tel: 0181-951 4449

Lemon, Unna and Durbridge
24/32 Pottery Lane
London W11 4LZ
Tel: 0171-727 1346/0171-229 9216

**L'Epine Smith &
Carney Associates**
10 Wyndham Place
London W1H 1AS
Tel: 0171-724 0739

Lee Leslie Management
72 Glebe Point Road
Glebe
NSW 2037
Australia
Tel: (0061) 2 660 4777

Tony Lewis Entertainments
Regent House
235/241 Regent Street
London W1R 8TL
Tel: 0171-734 2285/6/7

Limelight Management
9 Coptic Street
London WC1A 1NH
Tel: 0171-436 6949

Lindsay Casting
22 Druids Cross Road
Liverpool L18 3EB
Tel: 0151-722 5091

London Management
2/4 Noel Street
London W1V 3RB
Tel: 0171-287 9000

Pat Lovett Agency
Suite 5
Greenside House
Greenside Place
Edinburgh EH1 3AA
Tel: 0131-557 5565

Robert Luff
294 Earls Court Road
Kensington
London SW5 9BB
Tel: 0171-373 7003/1070

Dennis Lyne Agency
108 Leonard Street
London EC2A 4RH
Tel: 0171-739 6200

MGA
Concorde House
18 Margaret Street
Brighton BN2 1TS
Tel. (01273) 685970

MPC Entertainment
MPC House
15/16 Maple Mews
Maida Vale
London NW6 5UZ
Tel: 0171-624 1184

McCartt-Oreck-Barrett
10390 Santa Monica Boulevard
Suite 310
Los Angeles
CA 90025
USA
Tel: (001) 213 553 2600

MacFarlane Chard Associates
7/8 Little Turnstile
London WC1V 7DX
Tel: 0171-404 2332

McIntosh Rae Management
Thornton House
Thornton Road
London SW19 4NG
Tel: 0181-944 6688

McIntyre Management
15 Riversway
Navigation Way
Preston PR2 2YP
Tel: (01772) 720205

Ken McReddie
91 Regent Street
London W1R 7TB
Tel: 0171-439 1456

Jennifer Maffini
32 Stafford Mansions
Stafford Place
London SW1E 6NL
Tel: 0171 828 4595

Magnolia Management
136 Hicks Avenue
Greenford
Middlesex UB6 8HB
Tel: 0181-578 2899

Hazel Malone Associates
26 Wellesley Road
Chiswick
London W4 4BN
Tel: 0181-994 1619

**Andrew Manson
Personal Management**
288 Munster Road
London SW6 6BQ
Tel: 0171-386 9358

Markham & Froggatt
4 Windmill Street
London W1P 1HF
Tel: 0171-636 4412

John Markham Associates
6 Dale Park Road
London SE19 3TY
Tel: 0181-653 4994/2507

Marmont Management
Langham House
308 Regent Street
London W1R 5AL
Tel: 0171-637 3183

Billy Marsh Associates
19 Denmark Street
London WC2H 8NA
Tel: 0171-379 4004

Scott Marshall
44 Perryn Road
London W3 7NA
Tel: 081-749 7692

**Carol Martin
Personal Management**
19 Highate West Hill
London N6 6NP
Tel: 0181-348 0847

Marina Martin Associates
6a Danbury Street
London N1 8JU
Tel: 0171-359 3646

**Nigel Martin-Smith
Personal Management**
Half Moon Chambers
Chapel Walks
Manchester M2 1HN
Tel: 0161-832 8259

Mayday Management
68a Delancey Street
London NW1 7RY
Tel: 0171-284 0242

Mayer & Eden
34 Kingly Court
London W1R 5LE
Tel: 0171-434 1242

Melbourne Artists Management
643 St Kilda Road
Melbourne
Victoria 3004
Australia
Tel: (0061) 3 515228

John Miles Organisation
Cadbury Camp Lane
Clapton-in-Gordano
Bristol BS20 9SB
Tel: 0117-985 4675/6770

Miller Management
82 Broom Park
Teddington
Middlesex TW11 9RR
Tel: 0181-943 1292

Al Mitchell Associates
5 Anglers Lane
Kentish Town Road
London NW5 3DG
Tel: 0171-482 5113

Morgan and Goodman
1 Old Compton Street
London W1V 5PH
Tel: 0171-437 1383/5293

William Morris Agency (UK)
31-32 Soho Square
London W1V 6HH
Tel: 0171-434 2191

William Morris Agency (US)
151 El Camino Drive
Beverly Hills
CA 90212
USA
Tel: (001) 213 274 7451

Elaine Murphy Associates
1 Aberdeen Lane
Highbury
London N5 2EJ
Tel: 0171-704 9913

Norman Murray & Anne Chudleigh
243/245 Regent Street
London W1R 5DD
Tel: 0171-629 4817

The Narrow Road Company
21-22 Poland Street
London W1V 3DD
Tel: 0171-434 0406

Nyland Management
2 Abney Road
Heaton Chapel
Stockport SK4 4QW
Tel: 0161-442 2224

**Mervyn O'Horan
Personal Management**
140 Beckett Road
Doncaster
South Yorkshire DN2 4BA
Tel: (01302) 321233

Dee O'Reilly Management
112 Gunnersbury Avenue
Ealing
London W5 4HV
Tel: 0181-993 7441

Otto Personal Management
Regency House
75/77 St Mary's Road
Sheffield S2 4AN
Tel: 0114-275 2592

PBJ Management
5 Soho Square
London W1V 5DE
Tel: 0171-287 1112

PBR Management
138 Putney Bridge Road
London SW15 2NQ
Tel: 0181-871 4139

PVA Management
Hallow Park
Hallow
Worcestershire WR2 6PG
Tel: (01905) 640663

Pelham Associates
Brighton Media Centre
Jew Street
Brighton BN1 1UT
Tel: (01273) 323010

Barbara Pemberton Associates
I-MEX House
40 Princess Street
Manchester M1 6DE
Tel: 0161-228 6616

Peters Fraser & Dunlop
503/4 The Chambers
Chelsea Harbour
Lots Road
London SW10 0XF
Tel: 0171-344 1000

Hilda Physick Agency
78 Temple Sheen Road
London SW14 7RR
0181-876 0073/5561

Piccadilly Management
Unit 123
23 New Mount Street
Manchester M4 4DE
Tel: 0161-953 4057

Plunket Greene
4 Ovington Gardens
London SW3 1LS
Tel: 0171-584 0688

Peter Prichard
Mezzanine Floor
235 Regent Street
London W1R 8AX
Tel: 0171-352 6417/8/9

Principal Artistes
4 Paddington Street
London W1M 3LA
Tel: 0171-224 3414

Nina Quick Associates
Second Floor
12 Abingdon Road
London W8 6AF
Tel: 0171-937 2116/7

RKM
121 Gloucester Place
London W1H 3PJ
Tel: 0171-224 4493

Razzamatazz Management
Crofters
East Park Lane
Newchapel
Nr Lingfield
Surrey RM7 6HS
Tel: (01342) 835359

Joan Reddin
Hazel Cottage
Wheeler End Common
Lane End
Buckinghamshire HP14 3NL
Tel: (01494) 882729

John Redway Associates
5 Denmark Street
London WC2H 8LP
Tel: 0171-836 2001

John Reid Enterprises
32 Galena Road
London W6 0CT
Tel: 0181-741 9933

Caroline Renton
23 Crescent Lane
London SW4 9PT
Tel: 0171-498 7217

Representation Joyce Edwards
275 Kennington Road
London SE1 6BY
Tel: 0171-735 5736

Stella Richards Management
42 Hazlebury Road
London SW6 2ND
Tel: 0171-736 7786

Rigal Management
109 Albert Bridge Road
London SW11 4PP
Tel: 0171-228 8689

Rogers, Coleridge & White
20 Powis Mews
London W11 1JN
Tel: 0171-221 3717

The Roseman Organisation
46 Sutton Court Road
London W4 4NL
Tel: 0181-742 0552

Rossmore Associates
1a Rossmore Road
Marylebone
London NW1 6NJ
Tel: 0171-258 1953

Royce Management
34a Sinclair Road
London W14 0NH
0171-602 4992

STE Representation
9301 Wilshire Boulevard
Suite 312
Beverly Hills
CA 90210
USA
Tel: (001) 213 550 3982

St James's Management
Meadow Cottage
Steels Lane
Oxshott
Surrey KT22 0QQ
Tel: (01372) 843761

Saraband Associates
265 Liverpool Road
Islington
London N1 1LX
Tel: 0171-609 5313/4

Anna Scher Theatre Management
70/72 Barnsbury Road
London N1 0ES
Tel: 0171-278 2101

Judy Schoen & Associates
606 North Larchmont Boulevard
Suite 309
Los Angeles
CA 90004
USA
Tel: (001) 213 962 1950

Tim Scott Personal Management
Studio 57
South Bank Commercial Centre
140 Battersea Park Road
London SW11 4NB
Tel: 0171-978 1352/1358

Severn Management Services
36 Chadbrook Crest
Richmond Hill Road
Edgbaston
Birmingham B15 3RL
Tel: 0121-454 6905

Susan Shaper Management
174/178 North Gower Street
London NW1 2NB
Tel: 0171-388 6996

David Shapira & Associates
15301 Ventura Boulevard
Suite 345
Sharman Oaks
CA 91403
USA
Tel: (001) 818 906 0322

James Sharkey Associates
21 Golden Square
London W1R 3PA
Tel: 0171-434 3801

Vincent Shaw Associates
20 Jay Mews
Kensington Gore
London SW7 2EP
Tel: 0171-581 8215

Christina Shepherd
84 Claverton Street
London SW1 3AX
Tel: 0171-630 9191

Silvester Management
122 Wardour Street
London W1V 3LA
Tel: 0171-734 7232

Simpson Fox Associates
52 Shaftesbury Avenue
London W1V 7DE
Tel: 0171-434 9167

Spotlight
7 Leicester Place
London WC2H 7BP
Tel: 0171-437 7631

Annette Stone Associates
9 Newburgh Street
London W1V 1LH
Tel: 0171-734 0626

The Richard Stone Partnership
25 Whitehall
London SW1A 2BS
Tel: 0171-839 6421

Michael Summerton Management
336 Fulham Road
London SW10 9UG
Tel: 0171-351 7777

Sutton, Barth & Vennari
145 South Fairfax Avenue
Suite 310
Los Angeles
CA 90036
USA
Tel: (001) 213 938 6000

Sydney Talent Co
60 Kalimna Drive
Baulkham Hills
NSW 2153
Australia
Tel: (0061) 2 624 6055

Talent Artists
4 Mews House
Princes Lane
London N10 3LU
Tel: 0181-444 4088

TalkBack
33 Percy Street
London W1P 9FG
Tel: 0171-631 3940

Ruth Tarko Agency
50/52 Cecil Street
Hillhead
Glasgow G12 8RJ
Tel: 0141-339 8037/0141-334 0555

Stacey Testro Management
Second Floor
153 Park Street
South Melbourne
Victoria 3205
Australia
Tel: (0061) 3 690 7116/3991

Thomas & Benda Associates
361 Edgware Road
London W2 1BS
Tel: 0171-723 5509/0083

Nick Thomas Enterprises
Event House
Queen Margaret's Road
Scarborough YO11 2SA
Tel: (01723) 500038

Jim Thompson
1 Northdown Road
Belmont
Surrey SM2 6DY
Tel: 0181-770 3511/2

Tobias Management
Regency Court
62/66 Deansgate
Manchester M3 2EN
Tel: 0161-832 5128

Triad Artists
10100 Santa Monica Boulevard
16th Floor
Los Angeles
California 90067
USA
Tel: (001) 213 556 2727

Gary Trolan Management
30 Burrard Road
London NW6 1DB
Tel: 0171-431 4367/0171-794 4429

Twentieth Century Artists
Suite 303
3800 Barham Boulevard
Los Angeles
California 90068
USA
Tel: (001) 213 850 5516

United Talent Agency
9560 Wilshire Boulevard
Beverly Hills
California 90212
USA
Tel: (001) 213 273 6700

United Talent & Literary Agency
5 Stratford Place
London W1N 9AE
Tel: 0171-409 1310

Roxane Vacca Management
8 Silver Place
London W1R 3LJ
Tel: 0171-734 8085

Thelma Wade
Personal Management
54 Harley Street
London W1N 1AD
Tel: 0171-580 9860/0171-637 8022

Walmsley Horne Associates
36 Aybrook Street
London W1M 3JL
Tel: 0171-487 3534

Dave Warwick
649 Knutsford Road
Latchford
Warrington WA4 1JJ
Tel: (01925) 632496

Janet Welch
Personal Management
32 Hill Street
Richmond-upon-Thames
Surrey TW9 1TW
Tel: 0181-332 6544

Tony West Entertainments
PO Box 25
Formby
Merseyside L38 0DA
Tel: 0151-931 2717/
2318/0151-924 7697

Michael Whitehall
125 Gloucester Road
London SW7 4TE
Tel: 0171-244 8466

David Wilkinson Associates
115 Hazlebury Road
London SW6 2LX
Tel: 0171-371 5188

Dave Winslett Entertainments
4 Cliff End
Purley
Surrey CR8 1BN
Tel: 0181-668 0531

Witzend Management
Old Avenue
Weybridge
Surrey KT13 0QB
Middlesex TW1 2PF
Tel: (01932) 821010

Writers & Artists Agency
11726 San Vicente Boulevard
Suite 300
Los Angeles
CA 90049
USA
Tel: (001) 213 820 2240

April Young
11 Woodlands Road
Barnes
London SW13 0JZ
Tel: 0181-876 7030

Young Casting Agency
7 Beaumont Gate
Glasgow G12 9EE
Tel: 0141-334 2646/0141-339 5180

Sylvia Young Management
Rossmore Road
Marylebone
London NW1 6NJ
Tel: 0171-723 0037/8543

Television Company Addresses

Anglia Television
Anglia House
Norwich NR1 3JG
Tel: (01603) 615151

BBC TV
Television Centre
Wood Lane
London W12 7RJ
Tel: 0181-743 8000

BBC TV News & Current Affairs
As above

BBC TV Weather Centre
As above

BBC TV Sport
As above

BBC Bristol
BBC Broadcasting House
Whiteladies Road
Clifton
Bristol BS8 2LR
Tel: 0117-973 2211

BBC Elstree Centre
Clarendon Road
Borehamwood
Hertfordshire WD6 1JF
Tel: 0181-953 6100

The Bill
63 Windsor Avenue
Merton Abbey
London SW19 2SN
Tel: 0181-540 0600

Border Television
The Television Centre
Durranhill
Carlisle CA1 3NT
Tel: (01228) 25101

Carlton Television
101 St Martin's Lane
London WC2N 4AZ
Tel: 0171-240 4000

Central Broadcasting
Central House
Broad Street
Birmingham B1 2JP
Tel: 0121-643 9898

Channel Four Television Corporation
124 Horseferry Road
London SW1P 2TX
Tel: 0171-396 4444

Channel 7
Television Centre
Epping
NSW 2121
Australia
Tel: (0061) 2 877 7777

Channel Television
Television Centre
St Helier
Jersey JE2 3ZD
Channel Islands
Tel: (01534) 689999

Emmerdale Production Centre
Sunny Bank Mills
Town Street
Farsley
Pudsey
West Yorkshire LS28 5XX
Tel: 0113-255 6608

GMTV
The London Television Centre
Upper Ground
London SE1 9LT
Tel: 0171-827 7000

Grampian Television
Queen's Cross
Aberdeen AB9 2XJ
Tel: (01224) 646464

Granada Television
Granada Television Centre
Quay Street
Manchester M60 9EA
Tel: 0161-832 7211

Grundy Television
27 Church Street
Richmond
Victoria 3121
Australia
Tel: (0061) 3 429 2533

HTV Wales
The Television Centre
Culverhouse Cross
Cardiff CF5 6XJ
Tel: (01222) 590590

HTV West
The Television Centre
Bath Road
Bristol BS4 3HG
Tel: 0117-977 8366

ITN
200 Gray's Inn Road
London WC1X 8XZ
Tel: 0171-833 3000

ITV Network Centre
200 Gray's Inn Road
London WC1X 8HF
Tel: 0171-843 800

International Weather Productions
London Television Centre
Upper Ground
London SE1 9LT
Tel: 0171-827 7645

LNN
The London Television Centre
Upper Ground
London SE1 9LT
Tel: 0171-827 7700

LWT
The London Television Centre
Upper Ground
London SE1 9LT
Tel: 0171-620 1620

Meridian Broadcasting
Television Centre
Southampton SO14 0PZ
Tel: (01703) 222555

Mersey Television
Campus Manor
Childwall Abbey Road
Childwall
Liverpool L16 0JP
Tel: 0151-722 9122

Scottish Television
Cowcaddens
Glasgow G2 3PR
Tel: 0141-332 9999

Sky Television (BSkyB)
6 Centaurs Business Park
Grant Way
Isleworth
Middlesex TW7 5QD
Tel: 0171-705 3000

Thames Television
Teddington Studios
Broom Road
Teddington Lock
Teddington
Middlesex TW11 9NT
Tel: 0181-614 2800

Tyne Tees Television
The Television Centre
City Road
Newcastle upon Tyne NE1 2AL
Tel: 0191-261 0181

Ulster Television
Havelock House
Ormeau Road
Belfast BT7 1EB
Tel: (01232) 328122

Westcountry Television
Langage Science Park
Plymouth PL7 5BG
Tel: (01752) 333333

Yorkshire Television
The Television Centre
Leeds LS3 1JS
Tel: 0113-243 8283